AF225981

An
Exposition
Of
John

An
Exposition
Of
John

George Hutcheson

Sovereign Grace Publishers, Inc.
P.O. Box 4998
Lafayette, IN 47903

Printed In the United States of America
By Lightning Source, Inc.

TO

THE RIGHT HONOURABLE AND NOBLE LADIES,

THE LADY MARGARET LESLY,

LATE COUNTESS OF BUCCLEUCH, NOW COUNTESS OF WEEMS, LADY ELCHO, ETC.

AND

THE LADY MARY SCOT,

COUNTESS OF BUCCLEUCH, LADY SCOT OF WHITCHESTER, ETC., HER HOPEFUL DAUGHTER,

Grace, mercy, and peace, through Jesus Christ, be multiplied.

RIGHT HONOURABLE,

IT hath been of old foreprophesied that in the perilous latter times there should be many murmurers and complainers, (Jude, ver. 16,) who are seldom, if at all, satisfied with their lot and with the dispensations of God towards them, and that because (as is there added) they walk after their own lusts, and so cannot but quarrel what doth cross them in that woful course, and complain of their best and most useful enjoyments if they find not that satisfaction which they lust after in them; and we, in our times, have but too many sad experiences of distempers of this kind, evidencing the corrupt frame of our hearts, and our great distance from God occasioning these distempers. But right discerners will judge otherwise of the Lord's dealing; they will submit unto, and acknowledge mercy in, what is profitable, though it be not pleasant, but grievous; they will read and acknowledge mercy in what they feel and suffer, when they consider how much more they deserve; and they will admire the mercies which are remembered and continued with them in the midst of wrath. Humility, as it is a safe grace, and layeth a man low, beneath the violent blasts which shake the lofty cedars, so it is free of that unthankfulness wherewith pride is attended and plagued, 2 Tim. iii. 2; and in particular, true grace and humility will teach men to covet earnestly after the best things, and to prize them, and bless themselves in the enjoyment thereof, though otherwise their condition be sad and grievous; and indeed, if men under affliction ought to inquire after and esteem of God because he hath endowed them with reasonable souls, and teacheth them more than the beasts of the earth, and maketh them wiser than the fowls of heaven, Job, xxxv. 9—11, how much more ought they to prize the more special mercies of God continued with them; and especially, that in the holy scriptures he affords unto them the means of knowing themselves, and an offer of Christ, with all the consolations flowing from him, and an interest in him, and directions how to apply and improve the same in all cases. Though this be the great and choice mercy afforded to the world, Psa. cxlvii. 19, 20, and to be esteemed of above thousands of gold and silver, Psa. cxix. 72, as being able to make us wise unto salvation, and containing matter of songs in the house of our pilgrimage, yet it is not the simple enjoyment of this mercy, nor any pretence of an estimation thereof, that can prove a people blessed, unless in practice they labour to improve the mercy, and do make use thereof as a glass wherein to behold and know themselves what they are, and be invited thereby to embrace and close with Christ revealed therein, upon his own terms, and do study daily to testify their subjection to God speaking in his word, by setting it before them as the rule of their conversation, and to rejoice in the consolations thereof over all their sorrows, blessing the Lord daily for the continuance thereof with them, though he strip them of other things. And here there is but too just cause of regret that though our day be short, our journey long, and our way clear, yet the generality of the visible church and professors are either idle or out of their way, and in their greatest throng [tumult] are but labouring in the very fire for vanity. If we look upon the most part of these, we shall find that being ignorant of their true good, or not giving credit to what is revealed in the word concerning it, they do spend their strength in seeking after any good, yea, or any show of it, that hereby they may deceive and lull themselves asleep, and take the best course they can to skin over those wounds, grievances, and discontents which do attend miserable and fallen man, the perfect cure whereof is only to be found in Jesus Christ; and that, by seeking more than is to be expected in and from the creature, they do not only miss of their aim, but deprive themselves of that good they might find in the right use of the good creatures of God, all the days of their life. But it may further be regretted that the abuse of this mercy is more universal than that only such should be charged with it. Sad experience doth testify how truly the apostle did give warning that in the last days vilest abominations should mask themselves under a form of godliness, denying the power thereof, 2 Tim. iii. 1—5; and since the profession of religion hath been in any reputation among us, how frequently do we find men make use of a pretence of piety to render their vilest errors plausible, yea, to carry on their selfish and carnal designs; whence it has come to pass that innocent and lovely holiness suffers for their sake, and the name of God is blasphemed, and holiness so generally stumbled at through them. Beside, if we look upon those who fear God indeed, how sadly may it be lamented that they are idle, and turned off from their great work to needless diversions and distractions; and among those who are most busy, how few are to be found who follow a right method in their walking. Many do covet more after what is adorning than after what is saving; some do earnestly desire after satisfaction to their sense in the ways of God, without acquainting themselves with the solid way of living by faith; some do habituate themselves to a trade of discouragements, under which, after they have wrestled awhile with anxieties and bitterness, they fall faster asleep in security than if they had a Dalilah in their bosom; and generally that summary description of a gospel way held out by the apostle, Phil. iii. 3, is but the practice of very few. Men do not worship God in the spirit, because they learn not to rejoice in Christ Jesus; and this they study not, because they are not put from all confidence in the flesh, or in anything beside Christ. And if they would begin at having no confidence in the flesh, and look upon their being emptied of all things as a call, not only to close with, but to rejoice in Christ and his imputed righteousness, they would find virtue flowing from him daily, to enable them to worship God in a lively and spiritual way, and to order their conversation as becometh the gospel.

As these considerations serve exceedingly to commend the patience and long-suffering of God, who hath not removed his candlestick from us, notwithstanding our not walking in the light, and our abuse of corrections which have been sent to chasten us for not entertaining the offer of salvation, and to quicken us in our Christian course; and as they ought to excite all, in their stations, to mourn before the Lord, and to stand in the gap to make up the breach; and ministers in particular, to be instant in season and out of season, if so be there may yet be a returning to him who smiteth, and we may become an afflicted and poor people, trusting in the name of the Lord, and he may delight in us, and call us Hephzi-bah, and our land Beulah; so it also hath prevailed with me to contribute my mite in this public way, (beside my ordinary weak travels in my charge,) and to make offer of this Exposition on that rich treasure of the gospel written by John—a subject (though handled by me briefly, and in much weakness) full of the substance and marrow of religion, tending (as John himself giveth an account of his scope in it, chap. xx. 31) to point out Christ the true remedy for sin, in his person and offices, and to direct us how to attain salvation through faith in him—which being to come to public view, I have made bold to present it to the world under your honourable names, and to join you together in this dedication whom God hath conjoined in the strict bond of nature, which is daily confirmed by that mutual respect, tenderness, and affection, which you bear one towards the other.

It is not much my way, and I know your honours do not expect it, that I should stuff this application with large commendations of you, or with acknowledgments of your respects to myself, and your kindnesses towards others of my relations; my great scope in it is, as to encourage you in the good way wherein both your honours are engaged in your several measures, so to excite and engage you yet more to improve your eminency (as you are or may be capable of this service) for the advancement of Christ's interests in this backsliding and degenerate time; not that Christ needeth any such help, who by weak things can confound the mighty, and by things that are not bring to nought things that are, but that it is your own true honour and interest not to be among those nobles of Tekoa who put not their necks to the work of the Lord, but to subject yourselves unto him, and lay out yourselves, in your stations, for promoving his kingdom and the advancement of piety and the work of the gospel.

As for your honour my Lady Weems, all the lovers of Christ in Scotland do with thankfulness remember their obligations to your late father, the right honourable Earl of Rothes, of precious memory, whom the Lord raised up to be a prime instrument in the late Reformation, and who spent himself, till his last breath, in that public service. And those who know your ladyship best will bear witness that you have endeavoured, in your sphere, to trace his steps, not only in your private and secret practice, but in your open countenancing and encouraging of godliness and honest ministers of the gospel at all occasions; wherein I trust you shall be helped to persevere and abound unto the end. Your honour hath received many favours from the Lord, particularly that he hath made you a joyful mother of children, who are (the Lord continuing their life, for which I pray) to succeed in several honourable families of the land, beside those of them who are, or may be, placed in other families by marriage, which, I doubt not, you look upon as a strong obligation to lay forth yourself that they may prove friends to truth and piety in their station and generation; in subserviency whereunto I have presented this piece to your ladyship, as containing a brief hint at many of those precious truths which are necessary to salvation, and useful to be inculcated upon those who mind the way to heaven.

And for your honour my Lady Buccleuch, albeit, by reason of your young and tender years, many of those truths here presented may transcend your capacity for present, yet as your grave, prudent, and sweet disposition and behaviour, your opposition to profanity, and respect to the sabbath-day, and your careful observance of such duties of religion as your tender age is capable of, do much refresh those who are concerned in you and converse with you, (as being things not usual in so tender an age, especially in one who wants not sufficient baits of worldly advantages and contentments to divert you,) and do give good ground of hope that, if the Lord continue you, you shall prove an ornament to your dignity and station; so it hath engaged me to prefix your name also to this piece, as an incitement to you to proceed in that good course, and that your ladyship may have a help ready at hand, from whence, as you grow up, you may drink in that sound doctrine which is according to godliness.

Now that the Lord himself may bless you both, in all your relations and concernments, may continue you long together, may make you a blessing to each other, and may bless this and the like means unto you, for your furtherance in faith and godliness, till you come to your eternal rest, is the hearty prayer of

Your honours' obliged servant in the gospel,

GEORGE HUTCHESON.

TO THE READER.

CHRISTIAN READER,

THAT I do again appear in print floweth from no other cause but my desire to do service to the church of Christ in my generation, and to contribute my endeavours for promoving that public design of making the holy scriptures yet more clear unto the Lord's people. Some while ago I received such an intimation of my mortality as did excite me to improve my time the best I could; and accordingly I made haste to perfect this Exposition, which formerly I had begun to cast in this mould out of some notes of sermons I had preached on this gospel; and now, through the good hand of God upon me, thou hast it here presented complete unto thee. I shall not say much to what is mine in it; but this may commend it unto thee, that the subject-matter is indeed divine, and as full of that marrow of the Christian religion as any other parcel of holy writing. Here the profoundest mysteries of religion are opened up by a beloved disciple; Christ is lively pointed out, in his person and offices, and in his heart and affection, to his people; we are here directed in the way of closing with him by faith; and the sure grounds of lost sinners' confidence are clearly demonstrated. And albeit this Exposition be swelled up to a great bulk upon my hand, yet such are the riches of this treasure, that whoso would search into it will find that I have only gathered some gleanings, and for what I have hinted at I could with much less trouble have given it more at large than contracted it in these bounds. I need say nothing to the mould of it, being the same with that I made use of in the pieces formerly published; only, if any do think that the sum of each chapter is given too briefly, especially towards the beginning of the book, they will find (for satisfaction) that to save myself and them a labour, I have, in going through the several parts of the chapter, supplied that defect, and given a sum of every part as I came to it. If any shall conceive that upon several places, to which they may turn, the notes are not so many nor so full as might be expected, they may be pleased to consider that (beside my too true apology of my inability to satisfy the expectation of the judicious and learned, for whom this work is not chiefly intended) my scope is not, in this, to proceed after the way of a sermon on a select place, upon which occasion many things might be brought in, but, commenting upon an entire book of scripture, I satisfied myself with the most obvious things upon every particular verse; and beside, some purposes frequently occurring, I resolved to be more brief upon these afterward of which I had once, and it may be again, spoken before. And whoso will he pleased to read the whole, or to compare the notes on those passages which frequently occur, in all the places where they are observed, will, I hope, find more satisfaction than if they look only on some one place. If the reader find many repetitions, not only of the same doctrines, but it may be also of the same cautions or reasons couched in and subjoined to the doctrines, he should consider, beside other reasons, that in a work of such bulk, wherein there are so many doctrines, it was almost impossible to get all in my view at once, that so I might have corrected needless repetitions. And as the doctrines are, I hope, the genuine doctrines of every place, and are inculcated by Christ in his frequent repetitions of them, so I conceived it not fit to omit them, especially seeing I could almost as briefly, and, I suppose, to better purpose, repeat them, than refer the reader to the place where they had been formerly observed. I shall add no further apology in behalf of this undertaking, but whatever my failings have been in it, (and I believe judicious readers will find more escapes than I could myself observe,) yet I hope thou wilt find the Exposition sound, and the observations pertinent and orthodox, and such as may, through the Lord's blessing, contribute to thy edification in the faith which is in Jesus Christ. To his grace thou art commended by

Thy servant in the work of the gospel,

GEORGE HUTCHESON.

EXPOSITION

OF THE

GOSPEL ACCORDING TO JOHN.

OHN the son of Zebedee, being called from the fisher-trade to be an apostle, Matt. iv. 21, 22, was in a special way favoured of Christ during the time of his abode in the world, being admitted to be one of the witnesses of some of his special miracles, Mark, v. 37, of his transfiguration, Matt. xvii. 12, and of his agony in the garden, Matt. xxvi. 37. He was likewise entrusted by Christ, upon the cross, with the care of his mother, John, xix. 26, 27, and, which is above all, he was one specially beloved of Christ, and very intimate with him, John, xiii. 23; xxi. 20, 24. After Christ's ascension, and the pouring out of the Spirit, he is employed with the rest in proclaiming the glad tidings of salvation, and was joined with Peter in healing of the cripple, and enduring of the trials which followed thereupon, Acts, iii. and iv. After that, we find him sent with Peter to Samaria, Acts, viii. 14, &c. Afterward, as histories record, he went to Asia the Lesser, where he did propagate the kingdom of Christ, not only by preaching unto them, but by writing, at the direction of the Holy Ghost, to the edification of the whole church, as appeareth by his epistles, the Revelation, and this gospel, whereof he declareth he was the penman, John, xxi. 20, 24.

His scope in this narration of the history of Christ is to prove that Christ-man is also the very Son of God, and to clear up the way of salvation through faith in his name, as he declareth, chap. xx. 31. And more particularly, the time and occasion of his writing of it, as is recorded in ecclesiastical history, was, that during the time of his exile in Patmos, where he wrote the Revelation, the churches in Asia were infested with many seducers, publishing their pernicious errors, as may be gathered also from his epistles to the seven churches there (Revelation, ii. and iii.), and namely with Ebion and Cerin-thus, who denied the divinity of Christ; therefore, after his return, and so long after all the rest of the apostles were dead, he is set on work by Christ to write this gospel, and add this witness to the other three, to make up a most perfect narration for the use of the church in all ages, wherein he doth, in a very sublime way, describe and assert the person, natures, and offices of Jesus Christ, against all the errors of that time, or which might afterward trouble the church; and, as the beloved disciple that had lien in his Master's bosom, he soareth very high in speaking of the great mystery of godliness. In his narration he doth not insist to repeat what had been sufficiently recorded by the other evangelists, but pitcheth chiefly upon some noted and special actions of Christ, adding thereto divers of his excellent sermons upon the chief points of Christian religion, together with his solemn prayer before his passion, which, in the Lord's holy and wise providence, had been reserved for such a time and such a penman, and wherein the deepest mysteries of faith, and the rich treasures of the godly's comfort, are clearly and satisfactorily pointed out.

The parts of this history are—1. A description of Christ to ver. 37 of chap. i. 2. A narration of the execution of his offices, in his doctrine and actions, during the time of his life and ministry, to chap. xviii. 3. The history of his death and sufferings, chap. xviii. and xix. 4. The history of his resurrection, with some passages confirming the same, chap. xx. and xxi.

CHAPTER I.

IN this chapter—first, John describeth Christ, the subject of the gospel, pointing out his divinity, and his manifestation of himself to the world before, and by, his incarnation, to ver. 15. Next, he confirmeth this doctrine from sundry testimonies of John the Baptist concerning Christ to ver. 37. Lastly, he relateth the calling of five disciples, to the end of the chapter.

Ver. 1. *In the beginning was the Word, and the Word was with God, and the Word was God.*

In the first part of the chapter John asserteth the divinity of Christ, ver. 1, 2, and confirmeth his assertion, and proveth his subsistence and manifestation of himself to the world before his incarnation, ver. 3, 4, 5. Then, to make way for the doctrine of his manifestation in the flesh, he begins with the sending of John the Baptist, his forerunner, ver. 6, 7, by occasion of whom he describeth yet more of Christ, his excellency and dignity in his manifestations and offices, to ver. 14. And, in the last place, he describeth his incarnation, and proveth that he became God and man in one person, ver. 14.

In this verse the godhead of Christ is asserted and confirmed from his eternity, from his co-existence and society with the Father, and by express assertion declaring him to be true God, one in essence with the Father and the Holy Ghost.

DOCTRINES.

1. Christ is called "the Word" both here and verse 14, and 1 John, i. 1, v. 7, Revelation, xix. 13, and elsewhere; not only because he is the chief subject of the written word or scripture,—being the great promise made and often repeated in the Old Testament, He in whom all the promises are yea and amen, the substance and truth of all the law-types and shadows, the end of the law and kernel of the gospel,—but further, because as a word is a mean of revealing a man's mind to others, so Christ hath revealed the Father in his own person, being "the brightness of his glory, and the express image of his person," (Heb. i. 3 ;) so that God is to be taken up, and is savingly known only as he hath revealed himself in Christ ; and in his office, as he is the wisdom of the Father, (Prov. viii. 12, 22, 23,) and knoweth all the Father's secrets, so he is "the Word" of the Father, as declaring him, his mind and will, to the church in all ages. (Matt. xi. 27 ; John, i. 18.)

2. As Christ, in his person, natures, and offices, is the great theme of the gospel, and ought to be the matter of our study, so particularly it is needful that believers do know and take him up as God ; not only that they may avoid errors concerning his person, but that they may see how little need he had of the sons of men, whom yet he came to seek and save for their own good ; not to receive from them, but to give unto them ; that their faith may be led through the vail of his flesh to this rock of his godhead, where it will get sure footing, in his essence and attributes, against all assaults ; that the ignominy of his cross may not obscure his glory, but they may have high and honourable thoughts of their humbled Lord in his lowest estate ; that they may see the infinite worth that is in his sufferings to satisfy justice, and to expiate sin, considering the dignity of his person ; and that this may teach them rightly to receive his doctrine, and not to be ashamed of his truth and the profession of his name, or to suffer for him who is so excellent a Lord. For these, among other reasons, doth John begin this gospel with so sublime a description of the godhead of Christ.

3. The godhead of Christ doth appear in his being eternal, and that he had his proper and perfect subsistence, not only before his incarnation, but before the first point of time wherein God began to create all things ; for "In the beginning was the Word." He doth not say, as Moses, (Gen. i. 1,) whom he imitates in this beginning of his gospel, In the beginning God created the Word ; but, "In the beginning"—when all things created got a beginning—"the Word was," and did actually subsist. He thus describeth his eternity, that he was in the beginning, because there is nothing before the first period of times beginning but eternity, and because our shallow conceptions can follow eternity no further, but only over the border of time.

4. Christ as God is a person distinct from the Father, yet undivided and unseparable from the Father in his essence, with whom he eternally co-exists ; and this is another evidence of his godhead ; for "the Word was with God ;" where the word, in the original rendered God, with the article, is taken personally for the Father, (as is also cleared 1 John, i. 2,) signifying that he is one person and the Father another, with whom he was ; as also, that notwithstanding the distinction of the persons yet he is inseparably with the Father, in the same essence and nature, being in, as well as with, the Father, and the Father in him, (John, xiv. 10, 11,) and eternally with him, so that the Father is never without him. (John, xvii. 5.)

5. However men may take liberty to carp at these proofs of Christ's godhead, alleging from his incarnation that he was but man, or that, there being but one God, the simplicity of the divine essence cannot admit of plurality of persons, or that Christ, in the exercise of the mediatory office, declareth that his Father is greater than he ; or whatsoever else unstable and deluded men may pretend ; yet the Holy Ghost puts the godhead of Christ, his equality and unity in essence with the Father, out of all controversy, and would have it out of doubt in the hearts of believers, and all their reasonings in this supernatural mystery subjected to the revealed word, which saith, "And the Word was God ;" where the Greek word signifying God, without the article, is taken essentially for the divine nature, signifying that as the Son is a distinct person from the Father, so he is one God with him, in the same indivisible nature and essence, communicate unto him from the Father, and with him to the Holy Spirit, so that their name, nature, properties, glory, and working, are one.

Ver. 2. *The same was in the beginning with God.*

John doth here repeat and conjoin the two first assertions concerning the eternity and co-existence of the Son with the Father ; which is no idle repetition, but teacheth—

1. How little able we are to comprehend this great mystery, which we can but take in by little and little, and must put that together as children do letters, syllables, and words, till we attain a more full understanding thereof for our comfort

and salvation; therefore doth John repeat and conjoin these two parts of the description.

2. The knowledge of Christ as God is a truth to be much and often inculcated upon believers, and which they ought to study again and again, and dwell upon, as having more in it than will be seen at first view; and when they have found most in it, yet there is infinitely more to be found in that inexhaustible fountain; for so much also doth this repetition teach.

3. It is but a robbing of Christ of his glory to attribute unto him the name of God under any notion, or acknowledge any glory to belong unto him, unless his subsistence from all eternity, and his eternal godhead, one in essence with, and a distinct person from, the Father, be acknowledged, for John repeats and conjoins his eternity with the other—" The same was in the beginning with God"—to shew that this assertion of his eternity is to be joined with all the rest; and that from all eternity he was God with the Father, one in essence, and a distinct person.

4. Christ, " who is God over all, blessed for ever, Amen," was in himself perfectly blessed, and infinitely happy and glorious, from all eternity with his Father before the world was made; which he needed not to make, but only it pleased him so to do, that he might let his glory shine therein, and communicate of his fulness thereunto, and especially to the children of men; for so much also doth this assertion, that he " was in the beginning with God," before he made all things, (ver. 3,) import, as is also expounded, Prov. viii. 22—32.

5. The eternity of the Son of God is a subject worthy of serious meditation to believers, that so they may read all that tender-heartedness, these bowels of compassion, that mercifulness and sympathy which is in him, to be not a man's only, and in our kinsman, but in him who is also the eternal God, whose thoughts and purposes are eternal and immutable like himself; so much also may this repeated assertion teach us—" The same was in the beginning," by repeating whereof he puts us in mind to study it often, that we may reap more and more of the comforts thereof.

6. The Son's coexistence with the Father is also a matter seriously to be considered by believers, wherein they may see the deep wisdom and rich love of God, who hath found a way of reconciliation of lost man by the same in nature and essence who is the party offended, and that the unity of the divine essence and the distinction of persons should contribute to make the redemption and reconciliation of lost man effectual by him; wherein also believers, who have fled to Christ for refuge, may not only find him to be true God, able to supply all wants, and to save to the uttermost, but may also find the Father in the Mediator, as being one in essence with him, 2 Cor. v. 19; and so, what he willeth the Father also willeth. This also the repetition of his being " with God" may teach us, and that we should study it till we draw these or the like encouragements from it.

VER. 3. All things were made by him; and without him was not any thing made that was made.

John having asserted the godhead of Christ as coeternal and coessential with the Father, he proceeds to prove the same yet further by effects of his divine attributes manifested in time, whereby he proves his subsistence before his incarnation from several steps of his manifestation of himself to the world from the beginning thereof. The first step of this manifestation and proof of his godhead was in the creation of all things at the beginning, which is so universally ascribed unto Christ, as nothing created is excepted from being his handiwork.

DOCTRINES.

1. The world and all things therein are not eternal, but had a beginning, and were made by God; for this truth, which is undeniable to right reason, is here made clear by revelation, " All things were made."

2. Creation is an act of divine power; and it is a proof of Christ's godhead that he is the Creator of all things, visible and invisible, and that all the creatures owe their very being to Christ the Son of God; for " all things were made by him." (Col. i. 16; Heb. i. 2.) They " were made by him" as working from the Father; the Father creating " by him," the order of working following the order of subsistence of the divine persons.

3. Christ is clearly excluded from being of the number of creatures, in that he is not an instrument, but a co-worker with the Father and Spirit in the work of creation, and that not of some creatures only, but of all things that have a being by creation; so much doth John's amplification inculcate—" and without him was nothing made that was made," where " without him," as a Creator, doth not seclude the rest of the persons who are with him in their order of operation in that work, but clearly secludeth him from being a creature, or anything that was made.

4. It is useful and profitable for believers to read the godhead of Christ as shining in the creation of all things by his omnipotent power, wherein they may read a ground of interest to go to him as his own creatures, when other relations are obscured, as Psalm cxix. 73. They may see omnipotent power able to produce what they need of very nothing, Rom. iv. 17, and able to make a new work of creation in their regeneration, 2 Cor. iv. 6; Ephes. ii. 10; and they may see all creatures at His command who made them, and that they who are his servants, and under his protection, need not fear any creatures, Isaiah, li. 12, 13. For these among other causes doth John point forth the divinity of Christ; as, shining in this glass and mirror, " all things were made by him," &c.

VER. 4. In him was life; and the life was the light of men.

A further manifestation of Christ, and proof of his godhead and subsistence before his incarnation, appeared in his communicating of further excellency to some creatures than their bare being, as life to all living creatures, which was derived from him and preserved by him. And unto man, with his natural life, the light of reason and understanding also, together with holiness, and the image of God, which was implanted in him at first.

DOCTRINES.

1. It doth set forth the glory of Christ, and is a proof of his godhead, that all creatures that live have and hold their life of him, not as an instrument, but as the fountain from whence their life floweth and is preserved, for " in him was life." Not only hath he life in himself essentially from the Father, John, v. 26, but the life of all living creatures was " in him" as in the fountain cause, as the stream is in the fountain, and the rays of light in the sun; and "in him" still as the preserver when it is given, as the fountain constantly feeds the stream, that it dry not up, for " in him we live," (Acts, xvii. 28;) and " he upholdeth all things." (Heb. i. 3.)

2. Believers ought to study the godhead of Christ their head as shining in his giving life to all living creatures, and their having their life still in him; that when they shall observe such variety of living things, from the least to the greatest, fed by that fountain, they may come confidently to him for life and quickening, as to him who can create life, can restore a soul, and quicken a dead piece of clay ; that they may not be discouraged by their baseness when they come to him who disdains not to communicate life to the basest worm and smallest midge; that they may hold their spiritual life of him, and by abiding in him in whom life still is even when they get it ; and that they may not fear the decay of their life when they dwell in him in whom the inexhaustible fountain of life is, who preserveth and continueth the life of all creatures. So much doth this proof of Christ's godhead teach. " In him was life."

3. In the creation man was exalted not only above lifeless creatures by having life, but above all creatures, except angels, by being endowed with a reasonable soul, and a faculty of understanding, and with the image of God, consisting in the lightsome and sweet estate of clear knowledge in the understanding of holiness and righteousness in the will, and of peace, joy, and comfort in the affections, for "the life was" not only the life, though man have life, but " the light of men ;" he was endowed with a life of light.

4. The reasonable soul of man, and the image of God wherein he was at first created, was Christ's gift, not as Mediator (which office he did enter upon but after the fall), but as the Son of God, working with and from the Father, by which work his godhead is proven, the rays of his glory shining so brightly in the making of man, that little world, and especially of his most noble part, the soul, that none can consider themselves rightly but they will see a finger of God in that work. For this is another proof of his divinity : " The life"—or the Son of God, the fountain and preserver of life in living creatures—"was the light of men," or their life of light was from him as the fountain and preserver, as was before said of life.

5. Christ the Son of God, by creating man after his own image, and enduing him with a reasonable soul, hath not only laid obligations upon him not to employ these noble endowments against his Maker, but he hath also given an especial pledge of his own respect to mankind, and a proof of his power, as Mediator, to restore that image of God which he at first implanted in him ; as also of his infinite and perfect knowledge of all things for his people's good; and of that life of light and felicity which he enjoyeth in himself with the Father and Holy Spirit, to the sight and fruition whereof he will at last bring believers, in such a measure as finite man can be capable of ; for therefore is this proof of his divinity held forth by John, for the instruction and comfort of believers.

VER. 5. And the light shineth in darkness; and the darkness comprehended it not.

A further proof of Christ's godhead, and of his subsistence and manifestation of himself before his incarnation, is taken from his dealing with man after the fall. He who is light in himself, and the fountain of light in man, did by divers means shine in man's understanding, and before man, now darkened by his fall, but was not entertained nor taken up as becometh. This is chiefly to be understood of the sparkles of the light of nature shining in the darkened mind of man, Rom. ii. 15, and of Christ's shining in the view of all men in the works of creation, holding forth his eternal power and godhead with the Father, Rom. i. 20; though nature's light could not by these means take him up nor acknowledge him; not secluding also (as is cleared from ver. 10, 11, where this subject is enlarged,) his shining in the church in all ages, after the fall of man, to his incarnation, as well as after it, as God and Mediator, by divine revelation, types, and shadows, and other means; in which respect, though some did acknowledge him as God and Mediator, yet no man was able so to do, as at no time else, by the strength or light of nature, and very few did acknowledge him at all, considering their natural darkness, in the predictions and types pointing him out.

DOCTRINES.

1. Man is fallen from that life of light and comfort whereinto he was created, and is become a dark mass of sin and misery, darkened in his mind with ignorance and abominable errors and mistakes, and in his will and affections with vices and lusts, and liable to a dark estate of discomfort and sorrow ; for so is supposed here that he is not only dark, but " darkness," being wholly deprived of that light of the image of God, and overclouded with thick darkness.

2. The Son of God did not cease in all ages, by sundry rays and beams, and means and instruments, to communicate himself to fallen man, but did manifest himself unto all mankind by the light of nature, holding out some sparkles of light concerning a Deity, and some principles of justice and moral virtue, and by the works of creation and providence ; and to his church, by divine revelation did hold forth his person and office ;—all which do prove him to be God subsisting before his incarnation, and do manifest his self-sufficiency that doth communicate himself to man now fallen from him ; as also his love and pity to his own that would thus follow them,

and do prove that he exercised his office of Mediator before his incarnation ; for it is a proof of Christ's godhead, and manifestation to the world in former ages, that "the light"—or Christ, the enlightener of mankind—"shineth in darkness ;" and he saith " shineth" in the present time, because Christ's manifestation of himself doth not cease in all ages and times, though the way of it to his church be changed by his incarnation ; and because his manifestations under the gospel are but the same continued thing that was formerly, though in a different way.

3. Whatever light men have by nature, or may gather from the book of creation, yet such is the power of darkness in man's nature that all who are left to these means do not receive that light so as to let it shine through them to direct their actions, but do captivate it in unrighteousness, Rom. i. 18 ; nor do they take up that light which they have and use to be from God, but become proud of it as if it were their own ; nor do they take up God as manifesting himself in the works of creation, but become vain in their imaginations, and darken their own foolish heart more and more ; far less do they discern the Son of God equal with the Father, nor can they discern him as the true remedy of sin thereby ; for " the darkness comprehended not the light that shineth in darkness."

4. No man, at any time, by the light and strength of nature, can take up or savingly embrace Christ as God and Mediator, whatever outward means he have ; and particularly before his incarnation, many to whom he was revealed in promises and types did not look so far as to him who was to be incarnate, but did rest upon these shadows as if they had been the mean appointed for remedy of their misery ; which fault is not to be attributed to his dimness who was clearly revealed, though under a veil, but to men's own darkness ; for of these also it was true " the light shineth in darkness, and the darkness comprehendeth it not." And the point is of general verity in all ages where this " light shineth" at any time, though the order of the narration (it being spoken before the sending of John the Baptist) lead us to understand it of the church before his incarnation.

Ver. 6. There was a man sent from God, whose name was John.

7. The same came for a witness, to bear witness of the Light, that all men through him might believe.

In the next branch of the first part of the chapter, John having spoken of the manifestation of Christ before his incarnation, and how it did not suffice, he cometh to his more clear manifestation under the gospel, and beginneth (as the rest of the evangelists, and because of that prophecy, Mal. iv. 5,) at John the Baptist, his forerunner, and by occasion of him speaks yet more of Christ. Concerning this forerunner, we have here held out his calling, his name, and the ends of his calling and office, which were to point out and bear testimony concerning Christ, that men might be drawn to faith in him.

1. A special mean and way whereby Christ shineth to the world, and helpeth the world to know him, is the ministry of men, whereby he condescendeth to our weakness, who could not endure more glorious instruments ; he trieth our obedience and acknowledgment of his authority in the weak messengers ; and he maketh manifest that the excellency of the power whereby they do so great things is of him. Therefore doth he bring in John's ministry as a particular mean whereby he shined.

2. Ministers of Christ must not run unsent, but ought to have a calling from God, either extraordinary (in extraordinary times and cases) or ordinary, as being that which will afford them matter of courage in undertaking their work, of comfort under difficulties, and of hope of success ; for so John " was a man sent from God"—to wit, in an extraordinary way, as Christ's forerunner.

3. Albeit an unregenerate man may be a lawful minister, yet they will, in a most lively way, proclaim that grace of God bringing salvation who have themselves obtained grace and favour by it. And it is a sweet thing when men prove answerable to these names and titles which scripture giveth them, because of their Christian profession ; for this forerunner's "name was John"—a name given by the angel, without the consent of friends, (Luke, i. 13, 59, 60, &c.,) which in the Hebrew signifieth one that had obtained grace and favour, or, one to whom the Lord had been gracious, that he might actively proclaim the same to others, and a name to which John's carriage was answerable. He was one, in giving of whom the Lord shewed himself gracious to his parents, Luke, i. 13 ; one to whom the Lord was gracious, in sanctifying of him from his mother's womb, and in making of him faithful and successful in his ministry, Luke, i. 15, 16, 17, 77, 78.

4. The chief and special end of a ministry is—to point out Christ in his excellences and usefulness to lost men, to declare him in his person, offices, and benefits ; how he should be believed in, served, or suffered for. John, " came to bear witness of the Light,"or of Christ in his glorious excellency, and as he is the light of dark man in his comforts and directions.

5. Faithful ministers are to preach Christ, as his witnesses, with plainness, with fidelity, in not adding or diminishing, with boldness and constancy, and as men by whom Christ (who needs not any testimony from men) doth temper and fit his light to our capacity, and who will be witnesses one day against them who do not receive their doctrine ; for " the same came for a witness, to bear witness of the Light."

6. The end and scope of a minister's witnessing and preaching is, and should be, to bring self-condemned sinners to believe in Christ. His preaching of the law and wrath is in order to that, and to bring men to see their need of Christ, and should be joined with the doctrine of the gospel. His preaching of the doctrine of sanctification and holiness should be joined with the doctrine of faith in Christ, from whom

virtue floweth for that end. And faithful ministers should not be content that their excellent gifts lead men to esteem of themselves, but it should be their endeavour to lead men unto Christ; for, albeit John did threaten sharply, and call them a generation of vipers, and did press repentance and renovation hard, yet "the same came for a witness, that men through him" (or by his ministry, and his leading them not to rest or doat upon himself) "might believe."

7. No man is secluded from being allowed to believe in Christ, who hath the offer, but every one, of whatsoever condition or quality, how heareth the gospel, is bound to make this use of it, following the due order appointed for sinners to come to Christ. And particularly, under the gospel, Christ is to be held forth as the common refuge of all his people, of whatsoever kindred or nation; for John "came for a witness, that all men might believe," not that all, even of Judea, heard John, but that all who heard were thus obliged, and all indifferently of any nation were now allowed, to come to Christ.

> Ver. 8. He was not that Light, but was sent to bear witness of that Light.
>
> 9. That was the true Light, which lighteth every man that cometh into the world.

The particular testimonies of this witness are intermitted till verse 15, &c. And before John comes to speak of Christ's further shining and manifesting himself by taking on our nature, he takes occasion, from what hath been said of John the Baptist, to speak some more of Christ's excellency, his manifestations and offices; first, with relation to John the Baptist, ver. 8, 9; next, in reference to his ill entertainment in the world and visible church, ver. 10, 11; thirdly, in relation to those who did receive and embrace him, ver. 12, 13.

In these verses, because many doated on John the Baptist, and some were suspicious that he might be the Messiah, Luke, iii. 15; therefore John holds forth Christ's excellency as far above John the Baptist in his manifestations of himself, he being that true original light who enlightens all mankind with the light of reason and understanding, and who is the author of gracious illumination in every one who obtain that mercy, and John being but a witness to point out that light.

DOCTRINES.

1. It is a weakness incident to men to doat, and to have overweening thoughts of excellent instruments, and to give them more than is their due, which would be prevented and corrected; for there is need to clear that John "was not that Light," or the Messiah the fountain of light, though he was "a burning and shining light," being enlightened by him. (John, v. 35.)

2. The highest honour of a minister is to be appointed a proclaimer of Christ's excellency, and an instrument to hold forth Christ's light, and administer the outward ordinance, leaving the blessing to be conferred by Christ. And this honour is no more to be denied to them, than what is Christ's due is to be ascribed to them; for John "was sent to bear witness of that light."

3. Christ is light by nature and of himself, not by participation only, as creatures are; and whatsoever is said of him as a light is truly and really in him, and whatsoever is borrowed from the creatures to set out his excellency is in him really and truly, and they are but shadows compared with him; for "that was the true Light," saith he. Not that John was a false light; but He was light by nature—John, a star and candle, borrowing light, and lighted from him. What is said of the light of truth in him, against error, of comfort against trouble, of remission, of reconciliation, &c., is really and truly to be found in him, and in him only; and all the excellency we find in light for the good of creatures is far more eminently and truly to be found in him for the good of souls.

4. The efficacy and virtue of Christ—the Light of his people—is such as he can not only shine on them and make them discernible, as the sun doth on inferior creatures, but he can shine through them, and make them to be enlightened themselves. This sun shining can give an eye to what he shineth on, for "the true Light lighteth," &c.

5. All the light that men have is borrowed from Christ. All the light of reason and nature that every one hath, and all the light of arts, sciences, and inventions, are from him; and any light of saving grace, sound knowledge, or true comfort that any have, it is from him only; for in all these respects he "lighteth every man that cometh into the world." He giveth to all the faculty of reason and understanding; and though every man be not enlightened with grace, nor yet with special gifts and sciences that others have, yet it holds still good, that no man is so enlightened but he who hath it from him. As when it is said, Psalm cxlv. 14, "The Lord upholdeth all that fall, and raiseth up all that be bowed down," the meaning is, not that none who fall and are bowed down are let to lie so, but all raised up, but that none of these are raised up or upholden but by him only.

> Ver. 10. He was in the world, and the world was made by him, and the world knew him not.
>
> 11. He came unto his own, and his own received him not.

The manifestations and shining of this true light are here spoken of—to aggravate the sin of the world and visible church giving him ill entertainment—as a clearer commentary of what was said, ver. 5. As for the world, albeit Christ had made the world, and was still present in it by his power and providence, yet the men of the world did not know him nor take him up. As for the visible church of Israel, albeit, beside his common manifestations in the world, he came yet nearer to them, yet the body of them did not receive nor embrace him. This challenge holds true of the world and of the visible church in all ages, to whom he draweth near by his word and ordinances, though here it be spoken especially with relation to the time before his incarnation, if not also to his coming in person to the church of Israel. (Luke, xx. 13—15.)

DOCTRINES.

1. Christ, from the creation to his incarnation, was ever in the world as God, (as he also still is,) in his essence filling heaven and earth, and in his providence preserving and upholding all things, and manifesting himself in variety of dispensations; so universal is the providence of the believer's Head, for " He was in the world."

2. As Christ's creating of the world is a manifestation of his glory to be seriously studied, (and therefore is here again repeated,) so his creating of it is sufficient to prove his constant presence in it, it being impossible for the creatures made by him to subsist without him; therefore it is subjoined to the former, " He was in the world, and the world was made by him," as a proof that he behoved to be in it, because he made it.

3. It is the sin of the world not to know or take notice of Christ in his manifestations; and particularly it is the sin of men without the church that they do not acknowledge nor glorify God when he manifests his glory to them in the works of creation and providence, for "the world knew him not."

4. God may justly make use of very common favours and means as sufficient to aggravate the sin of such as do not acknowledge him; for, saith he, " He was in the world, and the world was made by him, and the world knew him not," which imports that his making of the world, and his presence in it, was such a manifestation as might have led them to know, acknowledge, and glorify him as God, and that they were without excuse who, having these means, did it not, (Rom. i. 20;) and that the common favour of men's being, and God's providence about them, doth heighten their sin who do not acknowledge their Maker. (Isa. i. 3.)

5. Besides Christ's common interest in all mankind as their Creator, and his special interest in his own elect and converted people, he hath also an interest in a visible church, and they in him, which no other people have, and that by virtue of a visible covenant and election to the external privileges of the church, for in this respect the body of Israel are his own, or his peculiar people. This interest may give self-condemned sinners a liberty to go to him, as born in his own house, when other privileges are obscured from them.

6. Christ even before his incarnation was present in the church of Israel, and beside his common and general presence, he drew nearer unto them in his word, and ordinances, and types, pointing him out as Mediator, till at last he came to them in person, for even then " He came unto his own." (See Acts, vii. 38; 1 Cor. x. 9.)

7. All the favour and kindness that is betwixt Christ and his people begins at him, and he is at the pains to seek and come to them first, though he stand in no need of them, for " He came unto his own."

8. Common relations betwixt Christ and a visible church are so far from proving a people's good condition as to the particular state of their soul, that such may, and oftentimes do, refuse to make Christ and his offer welcome, for "his own received him not."

9. The nearer the relation be betwixt Christ and his people, and the greater his offer be, the sin of not making use of it is the greater in itself, and he will take the refusal the worst at their hand, as being a despising of his love, for whereas "the world knew him not," (ver. 10,) their sin was greater that they " received him not" when they knew him, and so sinned of contempt. And Christ takes this ill, and accounts it a great aggravation of this sin that they did it who were " his own," and they to whom " he came."

10. As the great sin without the church is ignorance, and not acknowledging and glorifying of God, so the great sin within the church is contempt of Christ, and not embracing of him nor his offer, for " the world knew him not," but " his own received him not."

> Ver. 12. But as many as received him, to them gave he power to become the sons of God, even to them that believe on his name:
> 13. Which were born, not of blood, nor of the will of the flesh, nor of the will of man, but of God.

Christ's excellency and manifestation of himself are here spoken of with relation to those who at any time do embrace his offer made in the church. His excellency herein appeareth, 1. In prevailing with some to make him and his offer welcome, though many reject it. 2. In advancing them to the dignity of adoption and sonship who thus embrace him; and he further clears how it is that men do receive Christ—to wit, by faith, and whence it is that any come to believe, and so attain to the dignity of sons, even from a principle of regeneration, which is wrought by no power of the creature, but by God only

DOCTRINES.

1. Howsoever many within the visible church do reject Christ, yet there will still be some to make him welcome. As he never lighteth a candle but where he hath some lost groat to seek, so he hath excellency, even when many despise him, to allure hearts and virtue, not to take a refusal, but to draw his own till they be made willing, for there are who receive him.

2. Such as make the offer of grace rightly welcome do first welcome and receive Christ himself, not contenting themselves with his common gifts, nor yet seeking first after his saving graces, but after himself, that he may work these in them, for they receive him.

3. Christ is received and made welcome by faith; and all they who, hearing of the offer made to the church on Christ's part, do, out of the sense of their need, embrace, and consent, and roll themselves upon Christ thus offered, these have made up an union with him, and are believers, though as yet they have not attained to particular assurance, which is the fruit of the Spirit of adoption, (Ephes. i. 13, 14,) for they who receive him are even they that believe.

4. Such as rightly believe in Christ ought not to take him up as in their presumption, security, fear, or discouragement, they may imagine, but they ought to cleave close to the word revealing him, and bring all their thoughts of him to the

touchstone thereof, correcting them thereby, and submitting thereunto, for they " believe on his name," or as he hath revealed himself.

5. As all spiritual privileges are in Christ's hand and disposing, so, albeit we be by nature children of wrath; yet he offers reconciliation to such, and whosoever they be that by faith receive him, he conferreth upon them the privilege to become heirs and co-heirs with himself, and children unto God, with allowance to call him Father; and instead of a slavish and worldly spirit, and a spirit of fear and bondage, he giveth them the spirit of enlargement, and of sons, and a disposition suitable to their dignity and high calling in every condition; for " as many" (of whatsoever rank or condition) " as received him, to them he gave power" (or right, privilege, and dignity) " to become the sons of God."

6. As it is by faith that we come to the privilege of adoption, by closing with Christ, the only begotten Son, so when we have believed, adoption is still his gift, it being still of grace that he exalts us to that dignity; and when we have done all, the comfort of that dignity must be his work, by sending the spirit of sons into our hearts, to loose our bands and elevate our hearts, for " he gave power to become the sons of God."

7. Every one who is adopted to be a son of God must have a new birth and spiritual being in Christ by a change of disposition, and qualities of the soul going along with that privilege, to prove the truth of it, for these sons of God are born—to wit, again. By this change they will be led to esteem highly of this dignity, (1 John, iii. 1,) to study conformity with Christ their elder brother, (Rom. viii. 29,) and to perform obedience, whatever they can attain to, with children's dispositions, out of fear to offend their Father, (1 Pet. i. 14,) which are the kindly evidences of adoption.

8. Faith and receiving of Christ is so much the gift of God, as first by regeneration Christ must make an inward offer, and join himself to us, and give us this hand to grip, before we can by faith actively receive him or set about the work of sanctification by faith, for all who " believe on his name were born again."

9. The change of man out of nature into grace is a kind of new birth of the man, in producing whereof there will be some travailing in pain; by it there is brought forth a proportionable new man of grace, spreading itself (though weakly, as in the natural man) through the whole man; also a new life and likeness to the Father, an appetite after food suitable to that life, and a being sensible of hurt from what is contrary to this life, for so is imported in that they are " born."

10. Regeneration cometh not by natural generation, or by the dignity of men's race and descent from pious progenitors, for they " were born, not of blood," or of bloods—that is, by descent from their ancestors of many generations, of which the Jews boasted.

11. Men's free will, or natural power, is quite dead in the matter of regeneration; its utmost endeavours can contribute nothing to this work, for they " were born, not of the will," or the strongest inclinations " of the flesh."

12. Whatever singular endowments of learning, wisdom, or valour men have, yet none of these do prove regeneration, nor can they contribute anything to such a work, for they " were born, not of the will of man," or of famous and virtuous men, as the word in the original often signifieth.

13. Regeneration is God's own work, who employeth his word as the seed, (1 Pet. i. 23,) sendeth his ministers as instruments to sow this seed, (Gal. iv. 19,) and who quickeneth this seed by the Spirit, who is the immediate worker of regeneration in order of operation, (John, iii. 6, 8 ;) and so, whatever excellency regenerate men may have, they are still bound to acknowledge that grace prevented them and made them to differ from others, for they " were born," not of anything, " but of God."

VER. 14. And the Word was made flesh, and dwelt among us, (and we beheld his glory, the glory as of the only begotten of the Father,) full of grace and truth.

John cometh here to speak of Christ's humanity, his incarnation and manifestation in the flesh, whereby he became God and man in one person; and declareth, further, how he abode in our nature on earth for a season; how the glory of his divinity shined forth even in that abasement in the view of his disciples and followers; and what the benefits were he was filled with for sinners' good, to whom he came, and among whom he abode, even grace and truth, in opposition chiefly to the curse and shadows of the law, as appeareth from ver. 17.

DOCTRINES.

1. The sinfulness and ingratitude of the world and visible church will not make void Christ's love to his own, nor will hinder him to draw so near unto them (and to others for their sake) as is needful for their redemption and salvation, and may yet further convince others of their ingratitude, for, notwithstanding that ingratitude, (ver. 10, 11,) he drew nearer yet, and " was made flesh."

2. So great was the difficulty of restoring the image of God in lost man, and of restoring him to God's favour and the dignity of sonship, that no less could do it than the natural Son of God becoming the Son of man to suffer in our nature; and so great was God's and Christ's love as to lay a foundation of reconciliation betwixt God and man in the personal union of the divine and human nature in Christ; so much is imported in that " the Word was made flesh."

3. The person of the godhead that was incarnate was neither the Father nor the Holy Ghost, but the Son, the second person, for " the Word was made flesh." There being a real distinction of the persons, that one of them is not another, and each of them having their proper manner of subsistence, the one of them might be incarnate and not the other; and it is the godhead—not simply considered, but the person of the Son subsisting in that godhead—that was incarnate; and it was very convenient that the second, or middle person (in order of subsistence) of the blessed Trinity should be the reconciler of God and man, and that He by whom all things were made should be the restorer and maker of the new world, and

that He who was the express image of the Father should be the repairer of the image of God in us.

4. The Son of God became true man, and did take on our nature, with all the essential properties thereof, and all the common infirmities thereof, yet without sin ; for so much is imported in that he " was made flesh," by which name is not signified that he assumed only a body, his divinity supplying the place of a soul ; for as the soul is sometime taken for the whole man, Acts, xxvii. 47, so also is flesh, Psalm cxlv. 21 ; and the scripture speaks expressly of Christ's soul, Matt. vi. 38 ; of his will, Matt. xxvi. 39 ; and knowledge, or wisdom, as man, Luke, ii. 52. Nor doth it signify that he took on our nature, as it is corrupted with sin by the fall, as flesh is sometimes taken, for he was separate from sinners, Hebrews, vii. 26. But the designation serveth to point out the reality of his human nature, that he was true man, having a real body, with all the properties thereof ; and it points out his abasing of himself, that he united not only our soul to himself, but even our flesh and body, wherein we agree with beasts ; and that he took on the sinless infirmities and frailties of man, as flesh oftentimes signifieth, Isaiah, xl. 6 ; Psalm lxxviii. 39, that so he might sympathize with us as a merciful and faithful high-priest.

5. Albeit Christ did assume both a soul and a body, yet these did not make up another person in Christ, distinct from the person of the Son of God, but the personal subsistence of his humanity was prevented in his conception, by its being assumed into a personal union with his godhead, and that without any change on the godhead's part, and without mixture or confusion of the natures and properties flowing from the same ; for so are we taught in that "the Word was made (or became) flesh"—that is, being God from all eternity, and remaining so still, he became also man, in respect of the unity of the person ; and yet the Word and flesh remain distinct still in their own natures and properties, though the properties of either nature be ascribed to the whole person with relation to that nature to which they do belong, and both concur in the operations required in execution of the office of Mediator. And by reason of this union he is a fit Mediator betwixt God and man ; his sufferings are of infinite worth, being the sufferings of one who is God, Acts, xx. 28 ; and is able not only to suffer, but to carry through the work, to apply his own purchase, and repair all our losses.

6. As the ingratitude of the world did not hinder the Son of God to come into the world, and to take on our nature, so it pleased him in our nature to live in the world for a space, that so he might prove the truth of his humanity to those who conversed with him ; that he might sanctify the earth by his residence upon it, as a place of his people's pilgrimage ; that He might in his own person who was greater than Moses abrogate the ceremonies of Moses, and that he might perfect the work of man's redemption appointed to him of the Father ; wherein his great love appeared, that no provocation, no contradiction of sinners, did prevail with him to leave the earth till he had perfected his work, for " the Word

was made flesh, and dwelt among us," saith John, in name of all the apostles.

7. The Son of God, his incarnation and dwelling in our nature, is the substance of the type of the ancient tabernacle in the church of Israel ; his human nature and flesh is that true tabernacle wherein he dwelt. (Heb. viii. 2 ; ix. 11.) The glory of his godhead did fill this tabernacle and shine forth in view of his disciples (as after followeth) as the glory of the Lord filled that tabernacle, Exodus, xl. 34, 35. And the Son of God thus incarnate is the trysting place wherein sinners may draw near unto, and meet with God, as of old they sought him in the tabernacle. Therefore it is said in the original, He, or the Word, dwelt as in a tent, or tabernacle, among us.

8. Christ our Lord, during his abode in the world, was content to submit to a mean and pilgrim's life, that through his poverty many might become rich ; that he might sanctify a poor condition of life to his followers ; and that he might assure us of his being a fellow-feeling high-priest, having been in his own person partaker of our miseries ; for so much also is imported in that he dwelt as in a tent, or tabernacle (which is the habitation of pilgrims), among us. And to this also doth the type of the ancient tabernacle agree, which was ambulatory, and fitted to their wandering condition, though Christ also be the substance of the type of the fixed temple. (John, ii. 21.)

9. Christ also came into the world, and dwelt in it, to undertake a warfare, and did undertake devils, men, death, and all that had anything to say against his people, and did overcome them, that so his people might have to do with vanquished enemies, and might go to him in need, as to one who had experience of hard conflicts and exercise in his own person ; for so much further doth his dwelling as in a tent (which is a military habitation) import.

10. Christ in his abasement and sufferings did not cease to be the same glorious and excellent Lord still, and this his glorious excellency and godhead did shine through the veil of his flesh, and in his low condition, and was seen by all them who got anointed eyes, and seriously considered it ; for, saith John, in name of the apostles and believers, we saw (or did contemplate, and seriously view, till we discerned) his glory ; his star appearing while he was lying in a manger ; the angels proclaiming his birth to the shepherds ; his disputing with the doctors when he was young ; the glorious appearances at his baptism and transfiguration ; yea, the whole course of his doctrine, miracles, and sufferings, ascension, and pouring out of the Holy Ghost afterward, did abundantly evince this. And by this we are taught not to judge of him nor of his members according to outward appearance.

11. Christ as God comes of the Father by way of inexpressible generation proper to himself only, as being an eternal generation, by communication of the same essence and properties, and a generation wherein the Father is not before the Son, but both alike eternal. And this his glory did shine forth in his lowest condition, for his glory was " the glory as of the only begotten of the Father"—that is, such glory as was suitable

and becoming God's only begotten Son ; for "as" here is not a note of similitude or likeness, as when we say of a beggar, he goeth as (or like) a king, but a note of suitableness, as when we say of a king, he goeth as (or as becometh) a king. And by this Christ is commended to his people as he who should be only and chief in their hearts.

12. Albeit Christ conversed in the world in a poor and mean condition, yet his furniture for the world's behoof was rich ; and particularly there was in him grace, or the free favour of God, as a remedy for that wrath which the law revealeth because of sin, and the gifts of grace to cure and remove sin. In him did the fulness of the godhead dwell bodily, and on him as man was the Spirit poured forth above measure; and he had fulness of this grace to supply all his people's wants, to make up the greatness of their misery, and to overcome even their abuse of grace ; for he "dwelt among us full of grace," as the construction in the original conjoineth them.

13. Christ also came into the world fraught with truth, and fulness of truth, being as God truth itself, and as man, full of truth by virtue of the personal union, having treasures of knowledge for all our ignorance and errors, the truth of all the shadows of the law, and what was foretold of him by word or signs being found in him, and all that is in him and said of him being true and solid, and such as will not disappoint us, whereas other things without him prove but shadows ; for he "dwelt among us full of truth."

VER. 15. *John bare witness of him, and cried, saying, This was he of whom I spake, He that cometh after me is preferred before me: for he was before me.*

In the second part of the chapter John confirmeth this his doctrine concerning Christ from four testimonies of John the Baptist, given after the baptism of Christ, to ver. 37. The first, from this verse to ver. 19; the second, from ver. 19 to ver. 29; the third, from ver. 29 to ver. 35; the fourth, ver. 35, 36.

In the first testimony he holds forth the excellency of Christ, first, as being above himself in dignity, ver. 15; next, as being above all believers in the point of fulness and sufficiency for the supply of lost sinners, ver. 16 ; thirdly, as being preferred to Moses, the minister of the law, ver. 17; fourthly, as being preferred to all men in the point of knowing and revealing of God, ver. 18.

In the first branch of this commendation—Christ being now immediately gone from John after his baptism to be tempted in the wilderness (and therefore he saith, "This was he," (speaking of one who had been with him, but was now gone)—John doth repeat his former testimonies, and apply them to this individual person who had been with him, wherein he had declared, and yet again doth declare, that howsoever Christ did come after him in time of nativity, and in time of manifestation and execution of his office; yea, and after him for a time in place, as coming to be baptized by him, and as yet more obscure than he; yet he was truly before him in dignity of person and office, as being the eternal God.

DOCTRINES.

1. It is a commendable and sweet thing when ministers prove faithful in their trust, and mind the work about which they are sent; for John was sent " to bear witness of the Light," ver. 7, and accordingly his practice is, "John bare witness of him."

2. The testimony of faithful ministers doth not evanish with the publication thereof, nor dieth with themselves, but continueth as a constant witness to all those to whom the knowledge thereof cometh ; and particularly it is so with the doctrine of extraordinary messengers, whose doctrine being recorded standeth as a constant witness; for in the original it is, " John beareth witness of him," in the present time, though John was long since dead.

3. Faithful ministers having to do with hearers at a great distance from God, who are deaf, and distracted with the noise of tumultuous lusts, had need to be earnest and instant in their doctrine, and should in plain terms, (not going about the bush,) with boldness and fearlessness, and with fervency, and not for the fashion only, publish what they have in commission ; for in these respects "John bare witness of him, and cried." Beside that John, entering to his ministry in a year of jubilee, as is supposed, did thus become the trumpeter to proclaim " the acceptable year of the Lord."

4. Christ needeth not visible manifestations of himself to invite such as know him from the word to commend him, and esteem highly of him; for John, before Christ came unto him, or he saw him, had given ample testimonies concerning him—" This was he of whom I spake"—even all those testimonies before Christ's baptism recorded by the other evangelists.

5. As faithful ministers ought to be preparing people for Christ's manifestations of himself, so when he doth manifest himself, a minister is yet needful to expound these manifestations to be the thing promised, that so they may not be mistaken nor stumbled at; therefore John, having spoken of Christ before he manifested himself, finds it needful to apply that doctrine to that person, that they might not stumble at his low condition. " This was he of whom I spake." And we are ready to fall in the like mistake of his promised comforts and outgates when they come.

6. Christ's real excellency and worth is such, that commenders of him according to his word will never have cause to change their note, but when he manifests himself they will see all true that was said of him, and when again he obscureth himself, there is no cause to change our thoughts; for here, when Christ comes to John, he points him out as making good all he had said, and when now he is gone to the wilderness, to be hungry, and to be tempted of the devil, John saith the same things of him, " This was he of whom I spake," &c.

7. As Christ is still above, and preferred before, the choicest of ministers, however he abased himself in the days of his flesh, and subjected himself to fulfil all righteousness, so it is the duty, and will be the practice, of faithful ministers and honest Christians, to abase themselves that Christ may be exalted, and to guard against any respect

that may encroach upon his honour; for thus did John preach of him, first and last, " He that cometh after me is preferred before me."

8. The dignity and eternity of Christ's person as God sets him up above all creatures, how excellent soever; for albeit as man he was for a time made a little lower than the angels, yet by virtue of the personal union he is, even as man, made head of angels; and as God, there is no comparison betwixt him and the creatures: so much doth John's reason teach us, he " is preferred before me: for he was before me."

VER. 16. And of his fulness have all we received, and grace for grace.

In the next branch of this commendation John preferreth Christ to all believers, as being he in whom all fulness dwelleth, and from whose fulness all graces and gifts that ever any had, or hath, do flow, in all the steps and degrees thereof.

DOCTRINES.

1. All men, and even the choicest of Christ's servants, are by nature, and of themselves, empty of anything that is good; for so much is implied in that we must receive of his fulness.

2. All fulness of grace and goodness for supply of believers' wants is treasured up in Christ. He hath an increated fulness as God, and as man, a created fulness—a fulness of dignities and prerogatives—a fulness of divine perfections, gifts, and graces, answerable to these dignities; the fulness of the godhead dwelleth in him bodily, and the Spirit without measure is poured out upon him; for this is also supposed, that he hath " his fulness."

3. The fulness that is in Christ is for the supply. of all believers' wants, as their treasure and storehouse. Those who come to him he needs them not to receive from them, but to give unto them; he needs not their fulness, but their emptiness, that his fulness may overflow to the supply thereof. And this may invite sinners to come to him as they need; for " of his fulness" we receive.

4. God hath, in great mercy, so ordered the way of his people's salvation as not to entrust their own stock of grace into their own hands, as he did to Adam before the fall, but to put them and their allowance in Christ's hand, that He might keep it for them who can contain infinitely more than they could receive, and they may come and draw it daily out of him as they need; for so is it ordered here, that he hath the fulness, and we receive " of his fulness."

5. There is no man of any rank, quality, or degree, that hath any gift or grace but he hath it of Christ. The most eminent ought to look humbly on what he hath as Christ's gift, and the meanest ought to adore and acknowledge His wisdom and love who lets out such a measure to every member as he pleaseth; for " of his fulness have all we"—prophets, apostles, believers, &c.— " received."

6. Whatever believers get from Christ, yet he remaineth still full. As the sea diminisheth not by rivers coming from it, and as the sun doth not wear nor lose light by giving light to all, so

Christ is still the same for fulness, notwithstanding what he communicateth; for it is " of his fulness" we all receive, it is still fulness when all receive of it.

7. Whatever any receive of Christ it comes of grace, and not of merit; and the free favour of God and the gracious effects thereof are the chief fruits flowing from Christ's fulness; for in both these respects, it is said, all we receive, and (or even) grace.

8. Whosoever do receive true grace from Christ, they will be receiving grace after grace; and as they do not receive grace all at once, but by degrees, and so should not sit up on any measure received, so Christ's giving of grace unto them is an argument why he will give them yet more grace; for " we have received grace for grace"—that is, grace upon grace, grace after grace, and more grace, because he hath already given grace.

9. Not only what the elect do receive at their first conversion, but even what they receive after grace given, comes not of merit, but from the first to the last is grace still; for it is " grace for grace," and so still grace, and grace for grace's sake. (Rom. xii. 6; Ephes. iii. 7.)

10. This grace received by us " for grace," or " answering to grace," as the original will bear, may relate to grace in Christ and coming by Christ; and so it may teach further—

1. Christ is not only the storehouse from whose fulness grace floweth to believers, but the procuring cause thereof also, grace being given to them because of his redemption and righteousness made theirs of free grace, and because his gracious acceptance with the Father as Mediator takes in all his people in and with him. Thus do we receive " grace for (or because of) grace" in him, and flowing from him. (See Rom. v. 15, 17; Ephes. i. 6.)

2. As every believer is a member of Jesus Christ's mystical body, so do they in their own measure, as members, receive grace answering to the grace poured out on him as Head, being made sons and co-heirs answering to his dignity in their measure, and getting proportionable holiness, that there may be a conformity betwixt Head and members; for so we do receive " grace for grace," or " answering to grace "—to wit, in him.

VER. 17. For the law was given by Moses, but grace and truth came by Jesus Christ.

In the third branch of this commendation (which cleareth also the former, of his fulness to communicate " grace for grace," and therefore is joined with it by the particle *for*,) John preferreth Christ not only to himself, but to Moses also, on whom the Jews doated so much, and that both in respect of the doctrine and benefits brought by either of them to the world, Moses being the minister of the law which reveals wrath, and pointeth out Christ in dark types, and sanctification under ceremonial washings, and Christ bringing grace and truth with him, to relieve such as groaned under these legal administrations; and in respect of their persons and way of conveying these benefits, Moses being but an instrument and messenger carrying that doctrine which he delivered, and Christ being the author and procurer of those benefits which he revealed to the world.

DOCTRINES.

1. The faithful servants of Christ will not only be afraid to meddle with his glory themselves, but will cry down all glory that is given to any other, to Christ's prejudice, and will study to exalt him above the most excellent of men, considered in their best things; therefore John preferreth Christ unto Moses, as well as to himself, and that in those things wherein Moses was most eminent, as his going up to the mount to God, and his receiving of the law from him.

2. Albeit the doctrine of free grace was revealed in Moses' time and by him, (and renewing grace, and grace as a remedy against the rigour of the law was then known,) yet it was but very obscurely revealed, and sparingly set forth, in comparison of the times of the gospel; and in his ministry the pedagogy of the law was much insisted on, pressing the moral law of duties under the pain of the curse, and holding out Christ under dark shadows. In this respect it is said "the law was given by Moses," in opposition to "grace and truth" brought "by Jesus Christ."

3. The legal pedagogy, as it is contradistinguished from the grace offered in the gospel, is a very hard and unsupportable yoke; for in that respect the moral law requireth complete and personal obedience, under the pain of God's curse, and yet giveth no strength to perform anything; it beareth in our duty upon us with rigour and terror, discovereth our misery without shewing a remedy, bringeth on a spirit of bondage without any hope of release, irritates and provokes nature to sin yet more, &c.; and the ceremonial law contained but a shadow of good things to come, was a veil cast over Moses' face, and was a toilsome yoke: for these causes the law by Moses is postponed to what Christ bringeth.

4. In Christ there is an ease and relief to believers against all the burdensomeness of the law; and particularly by the gospel he hath published the free grace and favour of God, accepting the self-condemned sinner in him, and freely justifying the ungodly through his imputed righteousness, conferring grace freely to sanctify and cure the perverseness of men's nature, and so fitting them for glory. He hath also taken off the veil of Moses' face, being himself the substance of all the shadows, and having given the performance of all the promises; for "grace and truth came by Jesus Christ."

5. Albeit Christ hath abolished the ceremonial law, and hath abolished the moral law to believers, in its condemning, cursing, and irritating power, yet none get good of grace through Christ but such as are sent by the law, as self-condemned, to him for a remedy, and such as continue under the law as a rule of life, being enabled to the obedience thereof by Christ; for not only doth Christ bring "truth" of sanctification, answering to all their legal purifications under the law, but "grace" also, which presupposeth a work of the law discovering sin and wrath, and grace enabling such as come to him to endeavour obedience thereunto; and thus Christ established the law, not only by fulfilling the same in his own person as our surety, but by making his members also to walk in some measure according to it, which the law of itself could not do.

6. Christ is above Moses, not only in respect of the benefits or doctrine he publisheth, but, in respect of his efficiency about these benefits, he is above him and all other messengers, who are but instruments and messengers publishing the doctrine which they receive, and the benefits held out therein; whereas Christ is the author and procurer, as well as the publisher, of the spiritual benefits of the gospel; for "the law was given by Moses,"—as a messenger, receiving the same from God to deliver it to the people,—"but grace and truth came (or was made, or brought to pass) by Jesus Christ."

Ver. 18. No man hath seen God at any time; the only begotten Son, which is in the bosom of the Father, he hath declared him.

In the last branch of this commendation Christ is preferred to all men in the point of seeing and knowing of God, and in particular to Moses, of whom it is said that he saw God, and God talked face to face with him. (Deut. xxxiv. 10; Num. xii. 8.) It is here declared that God is invisible and incomprehensible by any, save by his Son Jesus Christ, who being one in essence with the Father, and upon all his councils, doth perfectly know him, and doth reveal unto mankind all that they know of him.

DOCTRINES.

1. God, as being a Spirit, is invisible to the bodily eyes of any, though some rays of his glorious majesty have at some times been seen; nor can any creature take up the infinitely glorious essence of God with the eyes of their mind, but very angels cover their faces before him. Nor is there any knowledge of God at all attainable by men of themselves, and what they see and know by revelation is but as nothing in comparison of what Christ hath. All this is imported in that "No man hath seen God at any time"— to wit, with bodily eyes, or fully, as Christ doth, or without him.

2. Albeit God be invisible and incomprehensible by any of themselves, yet there is a declaration and manifestation of him to sinful man, and a knowledge and sight of him attainable, in so far as is necessary to salvation; for so are we taught here that God is "declared."

3. As Christ perfectly seeth, and knoweth and comprehendeth the Father, so the declaration and manifestation of God to man, and especially that which is saving and sanctifying, is by Christ, who from the beginning of the world was the only revealer of God to the church; and especially at his incarnation he hath revealed the Father in himself, and the knowledge of him and his will unto salvation by his doctrine; for the Son, "he hath declared him."

4. Albeit God have many sons by creation (as angels, Job, i. 6; and Adam, Luke, iii. 38) and by adoption, yet he hath only one natural Son

begotten of his substance, by eternal and incomprehensible generation, who as he perfectly comprehendeth the Father, so he cannot but infallibly declare him, being the express image of his person; for Christ is "the only begotten Son," and this is one ground of his declaring the Father.

5. Christ is one in essence with the Father, coexisting with him from eternity, and is one with him in regard of familiarity and delight, and was and is upon all the Father's counsels; and this doth yet further assure the church of the certainty of what he declareth of God, and doth set out their happiness who have Him for their friend and surety who is so intimate with the Father; for this is another ground of his declaring the Father, that he "is in the bosom of the Father," which imports oneness, intimacy, and delight, that he hath a near sight and intimate acquaintance with the Father. (See Prov. viii. 30.)

Ver. 19. And this is the record of John, when the Jews sent priests and Levites from Jerusalem to ask him, Who art thou?

20. And he confessed, and denied not; but confessed, I am not the Christ.

21. And they asked him, What then? Art thou Elias? And he saith, I am not. Art thou that prophet? And he answered, No.

John's second testimony after the baptism of Christ was given upon occasion of commissioners sent unto him from the council at Jerusalem, and expressed in way of conference betwixt them and him, wherein, being posed concerning his person and authority, he declares negatively that he was neither the Messiah nor Elijah in proper person, nor that great prophet they expected, ver. 19—21. Next, being further posed, he declareth positively that he was Christ's forerunner, of whom Isaiah had fore-prophesied, ver. 22, 23. Thirdly, being further interrogated concerning his office and administration of baptism, he cleareth them in that, ver. 24—27. Lastly, the apostle John subjoineth the circumstance of place where this testimony was given, ver. 28.

From these verses, wherein he declareth what he was not, learn—

1. Church judicatories for managing of Christ's matters, and for trial of new doctrines and opinions, are an approved ordinance of God; and such as are entrusted with that power ought to go very gravely and tenderly to work when Providence puts them upon the trial of any such emergent; for these in Jerusalem, from whom these commissioners came, were their great council, appointed of old by God, for these matters; and their carriage in not condemning John untried and unheard, and their using of him respectively, in sending grave men for descent, office, (and of their most eminent sect also, as appears, ver. 24,) to him, are rules of prudence in such procedure worthy of imitation.

2. In a corrupt and declining time of the church, ordinarily the teachers are furthest out of course, and are not with the first to inquire after Christ, but behind many; for notwithstanding all John's doctrine before Christ's baptism, yet it is after that, ere the council of Jerusalem inquire after him or it, and but to little purpose then either, as the sequel sheweth.

3. Whatever be the purposes of corrupt men in inquiring after, or debating about truth; yet God can make use thereof to bring out more of his truth, and give occasion to his servants to publish it yet more; for though these came rather to quarrel and jangle than to be edified, yet it drew out a record of John, which is of use to the church in all ages.

4. It is not only requisite that new doctrines be tried and examined, but the authority of men who publish the same, not upon an ordinary call, nor in an ordinary way, is subject to trial also, and that in the first place; for their first question (which John holds himself bound to answer) is, "Who art thou?" intimating that if he were not an authorized person he was bound to cease.

5. It is the duty of truly godly men to walk respectively towards church judicatories appointed of God, even when such as bear sway in them are corrupt; nor ought they deny a testimony to the truth when they are called to it, and so long as there is any hope or appearance of doing good by it; for John, though he was an extraordinary man, yet is content to give an account to the commissioners of that corrupt council, seeing they sat in Moses' chair; and by this means he doth confirm the truth for the good of others.

6. Visible churches and councils, even such as have most peculiar privileges, may err, and have erred, and that particularly, when they look more to tradition than to scripture; for these instructions do clear the council of Jerusalem to have erred, in that they suppose the Messiah could be come (as John's answer to their first question understands them) without a forerunner; in that they dreamed (following tradition) that Elijah was to come in proper person; (for in that sense only John denieth that he was Elijah, though otherwise he was he, as coming in the spirit and power of Elijah, Matt. xi. 14; Luke, i. 17;) and in that they dreamed, from Deut. xviii. 15, 18, of any singular prophet to be raised up after the succession of prophets in the Old Testament, in the time of the Messiah, beside the Messiah himself, to whom that passage is applied, Acts, iii. 22, and so John denieth that also, though otherwise he was a "prophet of the Highest." (Luke, i. 76.)

7. As God's servants, in all their testimonies, ought to be plain, bold, affectionate, ingenuous, and constant, so, in particular, they ought to be ingenuous and fervent in renouncing the honour due to their Master, not fleeing from it for the fashion only, that it may follow them the faster. Therefore "he confessed, and denied not; but confessed, I am not the Christ;" not standing on what they might do to him not finding him to be so.

8. Such as come not to the Word to be edified, but to jangle and catch advantage, it is righteous with God to leave them lying in their errors and mistakes, without clearings. Therefore doth John not clear their mistakes concerning Elias or the prophet; nor clear in what sense he was Elias, but nakedly answers their questions according to their apprehensions of things.

Ver. 22. Then said they unto him, Who art thou? that we may give an answer to them that sent us. What sayest thou of thyself?

23. He said, I am the voice of one crying in the wilderness, Make straight the way of the Lord, as said the prophet Esaias.

John being further posed concerning his person and calling, declareth that he had authority and commission to be Christ's forerunner, and to prepare his way, as was fore-prophesied by Isaiah. Whence learn—

1. The reason which these commissioners give for their so earnest questioning of him may teach every man to be faithful in what is committed to his trust, especially in matters of public concernment relating to the church of God; for, say they, "Who art thou? that we may give an answer to them that sent us. What sayest thou of thyself?"

2. As faithful ministers ought not to encroach upon their Master's honour, so they ought not to pass from that authority that is due to them, but assert it as need requireth; for so doth John here declare what his commision and place was.

3. Every one who undertakes the work of the ministry ought to be clear of his calling, and have a warrant for it, either ordinary or extraordinary, according as the calling he claims to is, as being that whereon a minister's courage, comfort, and success, doth much depend; therefore John sheweth his warrant for his extraordinary calling out of the prophet—"as said the prophet Isaiah," to wit, chap. xl. 3; for whatever use these words had to comfort the captives in Babylon with the hope of a speedy return, and of heralds to publish it, and ushers to prepare their way, and of removing of all impediments, yet in the substance it pointed at the manifestation of Christ and his forerunner, as this text maketh clear.

4. Christ's coming into the world was stately and kingly, however in appearance it seemed base; and wherever he is received he will be received as a king. Therefore came he with an usher and forerunner, crying to prepare his way when he manifested himself, which is the prerogative of kings, whereas private persons will come in with less noise and at narrower passages. "I am," saith he, "the voice of one crying, Make straight," &c.

5. Men have hearts naturally unprepared for Christ to come into, which must be cured before he come; they are naturally averse from the purity of true religion, full of mountains of vanity, pride, and ambition, valleys of dejection, discouragement, unbelief, and hollow-hearted hypocrisy, crookedness and deceitfulness in their hearts and ways, whereby men deceive themselves and others, and hide the need of Christ from themselves; roughness of their passions, humours, and lusts, ready to reject all warnings and offers; and all these make men's hearts an unstraight way for Christ's chariot to march in; therefore, cried John, "Make straight the way of the Lord," under this including the making low of mountains, the exalting of valleys, &c., of which, Luke, iii. 5, from Isaiah, xl. 4; and

turning the heart of the children to the fathers, &c., of which, Luke, i. 16, 17, from Mal. iv. 5, 6.

6. As all men in all places are naturally unfit for receiving of Christ, so ordinarily the offer of him is worse entertained in places of eminency than in more obscure corners; therefore is this proclamation made, not in Jerusalem, but "in the wilderness," (or hill country of Judea, where the inhabitants and cities were fewer, Josh. xv. 61,) a place where he would more readily be received than in Jerusalem.

7. Albeit that Christ commands us to prepare his way, that he may shew us our duty, and make use of exhortations, as a mean whereby he works upon his own. Yet this work of preparation is not in our power, but must be His work whose reward is with him, and his work before him. And unto such as he convinceth of their own inability he will first come with a work of conversion unto faith and repentance, that this may make way for his coming with consolation and sensible manifestation; therefore is this command sweetened with a promise, Isaiah, xl. 3, 4, &c.; Luke, iii. 4, 5.

Ver. 24. And they which were sent were of the Pharisees.

25. And they asked him, and said unto him, Why baptizest thou then, if thou be not that Christ, nor Elias, neither that prophet?

26. John answered them, saying, I baptize with water: but there standeth one among you, whom ye know not;

27. He it is, who coming after me is preferred before me, whose shoe's latchet I am not worthy to unloose.

These commissioners, seeking advantage, as being no friends to the gospel, do question John further concerning his office and administration of baptism, seeing he was neither the Messiah nor any of these extraordinary men; to which he answers that he pretended to no more than the administration of the outward ordinance, the efficacy whereof depended on Christ, and that he did this much because he was the forerunner of Christ, who was already come, though yet unknown to them; and that Christ in his person and dignity was so far above him as he was not worthy to do him the meanest service.

DOCTRINES.

1. It is an evidence of a sick and corrupt church when corrupt men are entrusted with most grave and weighty employments in it, for so was it with the church of the Jews when they which were sent were of the Pharisees—a precise sect, abounding in error, superstition, and hypocrisy, as the history of the gospel maketh manifest.

2. Corrupt men are more ready to jangle and lie at wait for advantages than to embrace the truth of God delivered by his servants; for these Pharisees take no notice of what he had said from Isaiah, nor seek to be further cleared in it, but think they have an advantage of him that he

should to presume to baptize, "Why baptizest thou then, if thou be not that Christ?" &c.

3. It was an uncontroverted truth, both among friends and foes in the Jewish church, that at the coming of the Messiah there should be some changes in the way of religion, and an institution of new ordinances; for the Pharisees have nothing to say against his baptism, if he were Christ, or Elias, or the prophet; their only objection is, "Why baptizest thou then, if thou be not that Christ, nor Elias, neither that prophet?" And John's answer, "I baptize, but there standeth one among you," &c., importeth that he being Christ's forerunner, who was now come into the world, it was lawful for him to administer this sacrament.

4. Ministers ought to arrogate no more unto themselves than to be ministers and dispensers of the external means of word and sacraments, leaving the glory of the efficacy thereof unto Christ entirely; and people ought so to be affected in coming to these ordinances; therefore, saith John, "I baptize with water," not denying that Christ also baptized with water, nor yet denying that baptism administered by him was accompanied with grace and the Spirit of God, but he only compareth his person and office with Christ's, and sheweth that whatever grace came by the sacrament administered by him, yet he was not the giver of it, but Christ only, who had appointed him to dispense the outward seal.

5. Christ may be among a people, and yet they who reckon themselves very high in the church neither see him nor know him; for, saith John, "there standeth one among you,"—not that he was present then at that time, for he came but the next day to him from the wilderness, ver. 29; but that he was come into the world, and conversant with the Jews,—"whom ye know not."

6. It is the duty of ministers, and will be the care of such as are faithful and zealous, to exalt and commend Christ at all occasions, that men may fall in love with him; therefore doth John again repeat his doctrine, "He it is, who coming after me is preferred before me, whose shoe's latchet I am not worthy to unloose."

7. The more high employment and the more eminent gifts men have, and the more ready men are to esteem of them, the more will they abase themselves if they be truly gracious, and be affected with the excellency of Christ; for it is John, the greatest among them that are born of women, and so much esteemed among the Jews, and the forerunner of Christ, who thus abaseth himself, "He is preferred before me, whose shoe's latchet I am not worthy to unloose."

8. Albeit Christ, of free grace, do honour men with eminent employments under him, and particularly ministers of the gospel, yet such as know Christ and themselves well will not only see that they are unworthy of the high employments they have, but even to do the basest service to him; for John saith not, I am unworthy to be his forerunner, though employed in that service, but "whose shoe's latchet I am not worthy to unloose," which was a mean and base office.

VER. 28. These things were done in Bethabara beyond Jordan, where John was baptizing.

Unto this testimony the apostle John subjoineth the place where it was given; it was, as the name signifieth, an ordinary place of passage over Jordan. This is remarked, not only to confirm the truth of the testimony by recording the circumstances, but,

1. To shew that as this place where John baptized and preached was an ordinary entry to the land of Canaan, so Christ, whom he preached, is the author, and the sacrament he administered a mean of entry into the heavenly Canaan.

2. To shew that faithful ministers ought to omit no opportunities, but to take advantage of all occasions for setting forth of Christ and gaining of souls to him; therefore doth John make use of Bethabara, to preach and baptize in, because of the daily concourse that was there.

VER. 29. The next day John seeth Jesus coming unto him, and saith, Behold the Lamb of God, which taketh away the sin of the world.

This is John's third testimony concerning Christ after his baptism, given in Christ's own presence, when he returned to John after his temptations in the wilderness; wherein, first, he points out Christ as the true sacrifice for expiating of sin, ver. 29; next, he again applieth his former doctrine concerning the Messiah to this person, ver. 30; thirdly, he sheweth how he came to know him, and thus to testify of him, which was not upon any acquaintance by eyesight, but when he got commission for his ministry it was revealed to him that the Messiah was in the world, and to be manifested by him, ver. 31; and that he got a sign from God whereby to discern the Messiah, which was accomplished in this person, ver. 32, 33, upon the sight whereof he was encouraged to proclaim Christ to be the "Son of God," ver. 34.

In this verse, John, who had hitherto set forth Christ in the dignity and excellency of his office, doth now declare how he was to execute his office, and to bring about these benefits, which was by suffering; and therefore he points out Christ as the substance of the passover and daily sacrifices, who by the merit and virtue of his death takes away the sin of his own, both Jews and gentiles,

DOCTRINES.

1. Faithful ministers and such as know Christ will diminish nothing of his commendation for any outward dispensations he may meet with; for the occasion of this testimony declareth that when John was publishing the former testimonies, Christ was absent, and particularly under his temptations in the wilderness, (as the harmony maketh clear,) and yet in the meantime he had been commending him.

2. Such as faithfully point out and commend Christ, he will give them occasion to do it yet more by becoming more familiar with them, that so they may make him better known; for whereas John had preached Christ faithfully, "the next day John seeth Jesus coming unto

him," and so will he do still, though he come not any more in person.

3. As faithful ministers get more clear and renewed sights of Christ, so they ought to improve those dispensations by making him known yet more to others; for when Christ cometh to John, he publisheth a new testimony, and points out yet more of him.

4. It is no small part of Christ's excellency in the eyes of lost sinners, that he was pleased to condescend to be a suffering and crucified Lord, whereby he purchaseth unto them so great a good, and gave such a demonstration of his love, in that he would buy their well-being at so dear a rate, and lay his own exaltation in pledge of it; therefore, however carnal Jews stumbled at a crucified Messiah, yet John holds him out as excellent, in that he was " the Lamb of God," or a sacrifice for sin.

5. The world without Christ is lying in wickedness under sin, and under all that followeth upon it; under the guilt of Adam's sin, and the corruption of nature, under the dominion and power of actual sin, and under the curse and wrath of God for it; and the sense of this it is which will make thoughts of a crucified Christ sweet; for so is supposed here, in these words, " the sin of the world."

6. Man's misery through sin and wrath for sin is such as he can only be relieved from it by Christ, the true sacrifice for sin; for he is " the Lamb of God who taketh away sin," and only he, since the beginning of the world. (Rev. xiii. 8.)

7. The legal sacrifices and the paschal lamb were but types of Christ, the true sacrifice for sin, and the substance of all they shadowed out is only to be found in Him who was without spot and blemish; who is separated from sinners, as the paschal lamb was set apart on the tenth day of the month; who expiates sin by his death, which theirs did but typically; whose blood applied doth quiet the conscience and turn away the curse, as upon sprinkling the blood of the passover the destroying angel passed over; who was content to be killed and roasted in the wrath of God (as the passover was in the fire) that we might live, and that he might be food for us; and who was content to undergo all this meekly and patiently for our cause; therefore is he called " the Lamb," with relation specially to the passover and the lambs employed for daily sacrifice, and with relation to the properties of these beasts pointing out the way of his suffering, as Isa. liii. 7.

8. Albeit the paschal lamb and lambs for sacrifice were God's creatures, and appointed and enjoined by God in the general for these typical uses, yet the choosing out and setting apart of such as were most fit, according to God's direction, was man's work, and his judgment was interposed in it. But Christ, the true sacrifice, was singled out exclusively by God, who, out of his infinite love to lost man, did design him for that work in his eternal counsel and the covenant of redemption, when man had no way to help himself; who separated him from sinners by spotless sanctification, to be a perfect sacrifice, and who sent him out of his own bosom to accomplish the work of redemption : for these causes is he called " the Lamb of God," as his peculiar privilege above these types.

9. Christ is the true Saviour, who taketh the burden of sin from off his people, and bears it himself, and by bearing of it doth destroy and abolish it. This he did by his death in transferring the guilt of their sin upon himself, and bearing the punishment and wrath due to it, by which he hath merited the taking of sin away out of God's sight, and obtained a dominion over it; and this is made forthcoming to his people, partly by justification, wherein the merit of Christ's death is applied for taking away the guilt and punishment due to sin, so as it shall not be inflicted ; partly by sanctification, wherein the power of his death is applied for subduing and purging the filth of sin, till the believer be presented spotless; he is '" the Lamb of God which taketh away sin ;" or, taketh it off them, beareth it himself, and taketh it quite away ; for the word will import all these.

10. The virtue and efficacy of Christ's death doth expiate and take away the sin of the universality of his elect throughout all the world, and is not restricted to Jews only, as these typical sacrifices were, but extended to all his elect among the gentiles also; for he " taketh away the sin of the world," which is not to be understood of all and every man (for their sins are not taken away), but of his own scattered through the world, and in all ages of it, and particularly as taking in gentiles as well as Jews, as the word " world" is taken, 1 John, ii. 2. Beside, they may also be called " the world," as being many in themselves, as being in his estimation as good as all the world, and they who will one day be set apart from the rest of the world, and make up a peculiar world of themselves.

11. Christ, coming into the world for the redemption of lost man, ought to be looked on as wonderful in his incarnation, sufferings, and in the love from whence this floweth; and as rare and matchless, there being no Immanuel but one, no love, no actions like his, and therefore much to be admired and esteemed of; and all who would reap benefit by him ought to turn their eyes off all other things, expecting no such benefit from them, in whole or in part, and fix them only on him. All these are imported in this duty to which John inviteth his hearers to " behold (or see, and fix our eyes upon) the Lamb of God !"

VER. 30. This is he of whom I said, After me cometh a man which is preferred before me : for he was before me.

John here applieth his former doctrine concerning the Messiah (which he had preached both before Christ's coming to him and since he went to the wilderness, ver. 15, 27) to Jesus Christ now present. Whence learn—

1. Ministers can never enough be careful in setting out Christ's excellency, notwithstanding any outward condition wherein he is; nor in putting away any honour due to Christ, when it seemeth to be given to them; nor in studying his eternal godhead, and commending his excellency above all, because of that; for this is the sum of that doctrine which here again he incul-

cates—"After me cometh a man which is preferred before me : for he was before me."

2. God doth approve in his servants, not fits and flashes, but fixedness and constancy in their discerning Christ and his glory in his lowest estate, and they will find no cause to repent, or eat in any honourable thoughts they have had of him; therefore doth John, as no reed shaken with the wind, adhere unto, and again publish, his former doctrine.

3. The same things spoken over and over again of Christ will not be tasteless to such as know his excellency; and truths often inculcated are the truths which we come oftenest short in taking up, and yet should study most. So much also doth John's frequent repetition of this doctrine teach.

4. The dignity and excellency of Christ as God becometh comfortable to the church, being found in our nature, by his becoming man and her kinsman, that he may do the duty of a kinsman and Redeemer to her; therefore doth John point him out under the name of a man—"After me cometh a man," &c.

5. Faithful preaching and commending of Christ is a mean, making way for a more full sight of him both to the preachers and faithful receivers of what is taught; for John at last gets him now present to point out whom he had so often commended unseen.—"This is he of whom I said," &c. And all faithful preachers and receivers of their testimony may expect the day when they shall see Him whom they commended and believed in, face to face.

VER. 31. And I knew him not : but that he should be made manifest to Israel, therefore am I come baptizing with water.

Lest any should question how John knew this person to be the Messiah whom he had preached, he declareth how he came to know him and got ground for this testimony. And first, he declareth that when he entered upon his calling he knew not Christ by face, or at least that he had not had any converse with him to know him to be the Messiah; only he knew by revelation his offices, and that he was in the world, shortly to be manifested; and therefore he was sent, by the immediate call of God, to preach his approach and being at hand, and by his doctrine and baptism to hold out the benefits to be had by him, having assurance, also, that in the time of his ministry he should have occasion to point out his person to Israel as being his forerunner.

DOCTRINES.

1. It is an unjust calumny and prejudice against the ministers of the gospel, that what they say of Christ is done but for by-respects; and particularly there was no cause to suspect these extraordinary messengers sent to point out Christ, now come into the world, of any collusion with him, or double-dealing; therefore God so ordered it, that, to prevent this, John, though a kinsman of Christ's according to the flesh, should not know him, either not seeing him by face or having no converse with him.

2. A bodily sight of Christ, or acquaintance with him outwardly, is not simply needful for enabling a minister to point him out savingly to the world, albeit all the apostles behoved to have been such as had seen and had conversed with him in the flesh, Acts, i. 21, 22. And therefore Paul was ravished to the third heaven to supply the want of seeing him in the flesh, 2 Cor. xii. 2; 1 Cor. xv. 8. Yet, even in the days of his flesh, called men were able to preach him upon spiritual acquaintance by faith, though they had not seen or known him in the flesh; for John was sent to manifest him to Israel when yet he " knew him not."

3. Men called of God to the work of the ministry must not stand back because of the conscience of much inability, but ought to hazard on the call, expecting that their furniture shall grow upon their hands as they need it; for John is sent not only to preach Christ, but to point him out when yet he " knew him not," but had a promise that he should know him, as afterward he did.

4. The chief end of the ministry of the word and sacraments is, to point out and to make an unknown Christ known to the world and the church; for " that he should be made manifest to Israel, therefore am I come baptizing with water." John had, indeed, a peculiar end in his ministry, to preach that the kingdom of God was at hand, that Christ was come in the flesh, and to point him out in person; but the general end of the ministry, in which he also joined, is to point him out to faith, in his merit, virtue, and efficacy.

5. Baptism with water is an ordinance of God, wherein Christ is also held forth as the pardoner and purger of his people, the washer and renewer of their person and nature; and this was the end of John's baptism also, for, saith he, I am come to baptize with water, " that he should be made manifest."

6. The Lord, who is sovereign Lord of the world, and may reveal Christ to whom he will, was pleased to make Israel his peculiar people, and to give unto them the first offer of Christ and of all the privileges of the gospel, that he might keep his promise made to their fathers, Rom. xv. 8, and that he might leave a pledge of his fidelity, that no affection to the rest of his sheep could make him break what he had said; for John was sent, that he might " be made manifest to Israel."

VER. 32. And John bare record, saying, I saw the Spirit descending from heaven like a dove, and it abode upon him.

33. And I knew him not : but he that sent me to baptize with water, the same said unto me, Upon whom thou shalt see the Spirit descending, and remaining on him, the same is he which baptizeth with the Holy Ghost.

34. And I saw, and bare record that this is the Son of God.

John declareth further, that he got a sign from God whereby he might know the true Messiah and the baptizer with the Holy Ghost, which being accomplished on Christ at his baptism, Matt. iii. 16, did confirm John, and encourage him to proclaim Christ to be the Son of God. Whereas John saith, ver. 33, that he knew not Christ, it is not to be understood as if he knew him not at all before the accomplishment of that sign,—for it is clear, from Matt. iii. 13, 14, he knew him when he came to be baptized,—but the meaning is, that when John entered to his ministry, and got the promise of this sign, he knew not Christ by face, though afterward, about the time of his baptism, he knew him first by revelation, and was yet more confirmed by the accomplishment of the promised sign.

DOCTRINES.

1. The glorious evidences of Christ's excellency and godhead, when he came into the world, are not cunningly devised fables, but most certain and infallible truths; for "John bare record, saying, I saw," &c. He giveth a solemn testimony of it.

2. Christ, in his solemn entry to his offices, was sealed from heaven, and stated in them, that so the church may learn to embrace him with all respect. Therefore doth the Spirit descend upon him in this visible glorious way, and the Father bare witness to him, as it is, Matt. iii., all the persons of the Trinity manifesting themselves on Jordan's bank.

3. Christ is endowed with the Spirit from on high for executing of his offices, and it is made manifest that the Spirit is to be found on him, and sought from him; for " I saw the Spirit descending from heaven upon him," where the Spirit, who filleth heaven and earth, is said to descend in respect of that visible manifestation and sign of his presence.

4. The Spirit's descending " like a dove"—a meek, harmless, and affectionate creature—pointed out what Christ is in his own nature to them that come to him, even meek, harmless, loving, and not dreadful; what he is in the execution of his office, even he in whom the Father is well pleased and pacified, and he who bringeth the good news of assuaging the deluge of wrath, as Noah's dove of the drying up of the flood; and what he is in the operations of his Spirit upon his people, that they are made meek, harmless, and lowly, as doves, not like birds of prey.

5. Albeit all Christ's members do receive of the Spirit in their measure, yet it is Christ's prerogative to have the Spirit resting on him; not only as God is the Spirit of one essence with him, proceeding from the Father and him, and so is ever present with him, but even as man, by virtue of the personal union, the Spirit floweth and resteth on Christ, and efficaciously worketh in him all divine graces and virtues without measure, and immutably, so that none can come wrong to him at any time for receiving of his Spirit. Therefore it is said, " it abode upon him." (See Isa. xi. 2, 3.)

6. Christ, in taking on our nature, did so cover his glory with the veil of our flesh and common infirmities, that he could not be known by bodily sight from another man, without divine revelation and evidences from God; for without this, John saith, "I knew him not." (See Matt. xvi. 17.)

7. The Lord is very tender and careful of his servants, to encourage and confirm them in their calling and message, and will not fail to perform what he hath promised for that effect when he sendeth them out, for John saith he saw this sign in a peculiar way, as being to him an accomplishment of that promise given to him: for God had said to him, "Upon whom thou shalt see the Spirit descending," &c., and now it was accomplished.

8. The Spirit resteth upon Christ, and was manifested to be on him by a visible sign, not only for himself, and to point out his excellency, but for the churches' good, and to certify them that he received the Spirit to communicate unto them, either extraordinarily, when need required, or ordinarily, to work that inwardly by his Spirit which baptism sealeth and signifieth; for this sign served to point out that Christ is " he which baptizeth with the Holy Ghost," which is spoken partly with relation to the extraordinary pouring out of his Spirit after his ascension, as appeareth from Acts, i. 5; partly with relation to the external ordinance of baptism administered by John and others, whereof he only can give the substance when by his Spirit he sanctifieth and cleanseth the believer.

9. Albeit that extraordinary signs and wonders be not now needful to confirm the doctrine so oft confirmed already, yet every minister would be sure grounded in what they testify to be the mind of God, and what they know of Christ's excellency, they would not hide nor conceal it; so much may be learned from John's way, who " saw, and bare record."

10. This truth, that Jesus the Son of Mary is also the Son of God in the same person, was confirmed by infallible evidences, and by eye and ear witnesses; for " I saw, and bare record that this is the Son of God." (See 2 Pet. i. 16; 1 John, i. 1.)

11. It is not enough to receive Christ as excellently endowed for the discharge of his offices, but to receive and believe in him as the Son of God by eternal generation, as being the groundstone of our salvation, of our comfort, peace, and strength; therefore doth John hold him out, not only as the baptizer with the Holy Ghost, but as " the Son of God." (See 1 John, v. 5.)

VER. 35. Again the next day after John stood, and two of his disciples;

    36. And looking upon Jesus as he walked, he saith, Behold the Lamb of God!

This is John's fourth testimony, upon which followed the conversion of some disciples, and so it leadeth us to the last part of the chapter. The occasion and sum of the testimony is, that John being the next day left alone with two of his disciples, (or such as had embraced his doctrine, and were more than common hearers,) and Christ coming by, he again points him out as the true sacrifice for sin. Whence learn—

1. As Christ doth not fail to cast opportunities of well-doing in his servant's way, so they ought to neglect no occasion of doing good and of leading men to Christ; for Christ, " the next day

after" the former testimony, walketh by them, going now away, as appeareth from ver. 38, 39. And John will preach and point him out, though but to two disciples.

2. Christ's faithful servants will make conscience to exalt him, and to lead people to him, and not to themselves; and that not only in public, where many may observe, but even in their most private converse it will be their care that such as respect them most may be led from them to Christ; therefore John, even in private with two disciples, is so careful to point out Christ.

3. A sight of Christ is not only an occasion, but a notable help, to enable ministers to preach and point him out to others; for as John, "looking upon Jesus as he walked," is encouraged to commend him, so a sight and enjoyment of his spiritual presence will notably furnish men to speak of him.

4. It is the duty of faithful ministers to be much in preaching of Christ crucified, and pointing him out as the only propitiatory sacrifice for sin, as being a chief point of Christian knowledge, and a powerful mean of conversion; therefore doth John again point him out as such, "Behold the Lamb of God!"

VER. 37. And the two disciples heard him speak, and they followed Jesus.

38. Then Jesus turned, and saw them following, and saith unto them, What seek ye? They said unto him, Rabbi, (which is to say, being interpreted, Master,) where dwellest thou?

39. He saith unto them, Come and see. They came and saw where he dwelt, and abode with him that day: for it was about the tenth hour.

From this to the end of the chapter we have the calling of five disciples, not to the apostleship,—for that was afterward, nor yet simply by conversion, at least all of them, for some of them were John's disciples, and believed in the Messiah to come; and Nathanael was a sincere man,—but to the acknowledgment and embracing of the person of Jesus Christ as the promised Messiah.

The first two wrought upon by John's last testimony are Andrew, as appeareth from ver. 40, and (belike) John, because he marketh the circumstances so punctually. They hearing John's doctrine, are taken with it, and follow Christ; and Christ inquiring their errand, they declare they sought him as their teacher, and to have more acquaintance with him, upon which they are warmly invited, and stay with him all night, learning excellent things, as appeareth from the effects.

DOCTRINES.

1. Small ordinances and few words may do much good when Christ is pleased to breathe, and that which hath no effect at one time may yet be blessed at another; for John's short testimony doth now work on all that were his hearers at that time, though we read of no effect the same doctrine more amply enlarged had the day

before. "The two disciples heard him speak;" they so heard now as their hearts were touched and drawn to believe.

2. As the doctrine of Christ, as a sacrifice for sin, is sweet to such as are trained in the school of repentance, as John's disciples were, so this doctrine is the chief instrument of conversion; whatever other divine doctrine men receive it will but turn them moralists, unless they also receive and embrace the doctrine of Christ crucified, and himself so held out in it to make them Christians indeed; for "Behold the Lamb of God!" was the doctrine they "heard him speak," which wrought upon them.

3. Such as do rightly hear Christ preached will never get rest till they attain to some more acquaintance with himself; the heart touched by the Word is set on work to follow after and seek communion with him, and for this end will miss and follow after him, never resting till they get him. So much are we taught by these disciples' practice; they "heard him speak, and they followed Jesus."

4. Christ taketh notice and knoweth well enough who they are that follow him, although his back seem to be towards them; for his turning and seeing them follow importeth that he knew they were behind him.

5. Albeit Christ seem to go away from those who follow him and let them follow awhile, that so he may stir them up and exercise and discover their faith the more, yet ere all be done he will turn and manifest himself unto them. So much are we taught by this practice, "Jesus turned, and saw them following."

6. Such as follow Christ would very seriously try and inquire their end in so doing, whether it be ease and outward things or spiritual ends, whether himself or his gifts, and what estimation they have of him if they be seeking himself; and before they do this and be single in their aim they will not find Christ's sweet entertainment. Therefore Christ at first propoundeth this question, "What seek ye?" as needful to be answered, and till then he keeps a distance.

7. One right end of seeking Christ is, out of the sense of our ignorance and errors, to employ Him to be our soul's master and teacher who can infallibly and effectually instruct. So much may be gathered from that title they give him—They say unto him, "Rabbi, (which is to say, being interpreted, Master,)" or Teacher.

8. Such as have any sound knowledge of Christ will use means to be more acquainted with him; and such as come to him for right ends will not have soon done their errands with him nor get enough of him. So much is imported in their answer, "Where dwellest thou?" as minding to have more familiar acquaintance with him than to get a little information by the way only.

9. Such as seek Christ for himself will get warm invitations and entertainment from him at last, and as they are not willing to have soon done with Christ, so he will find means to hold them on with him; for "he saith unto them, Come and see;" he doth not tell them that they might come when they liked, but draweth them along with him. And if we take it up spiritually, it

imports that his sincere followers will be made to know by experience the place where his honour dwelleth by tasting of the blessing of public ordinances till they come to dwell with him for ever; and that they can better take up these things by seeing and experience than by any report.

10. When Christ giveth invitations it is wisdom in his people to embrace the offer, and not to sit their time when either the Word or the lively operation of the Spirit with it is calling and alluring their hearts; for upon his call "they came and saw where he dwelt."

11. Such as follow Christ's call may not only get what good they expect, but his providence may cast unexpected benefits in their way; for they "abode with him that day; for it was about the tenth hour;" or (according to the Jews' calculation, who divided every day into twelve hours, which therefore were longer in summer and shorter in winter) two hours before night. They came only to know the place of his abode, but Providence ordered that they got a night's lodging with him, that they might learn more of him.

VER. 40. One of the two which heard John speak, and followed him, was Andrew, Simon Peter's brother.

41. He first findeth his own brother Simon, and saith unto him, We have found the Messias, which is, being interpreted, the Christ.

42. And he brought him to Jesus. And when Jesus beheld him, he said, Thou art Simon the son of Jona: thou shalt be called Cephas, which is by interpretation, A stone.

The next that is called is Peter, whom his brother Andrew (one of the former two) finding, he declareth how he had found the Messiah, and bringeth him to him; and Christ promiseth to make him of a mean man, a prime believer and instrument in his work, and giveth him a name answerable.

DOCTRINES.

1. Such as have gotten any knowledge of Christ, and are brought in to him, ought to be careful to invite others unto him. And albeit such as are unrenewed may be instruments of conversion to others, (otherwise we should hear none in faith of a blessing to that ordinance, since we cannot be infallibly certain of the conversion of any,) yet such as are converted will be most zealous that way, and ordinarily are most successful; therefore doth Andrew, being now called, seek Simon, and bring him to Christ.

2. True grace sanctifieth natural affection, and maketh a man express it, by seeking their spiritual good to whom he is bound by nature; therefore Andrew seeketh "his own brother Simon."

3. God may, by a weak instrument, call a man to Christ, who will prove a more excellent and notable instrument than himself. He may make mean ones instruments of good to very eminent ones; for Peter, the great apostle, is called by Andrew.

4. Kindness begins on Christ's side, and his grace doth prevent the sinner; for Andrew, the instrument of Peter's good, "first findeth his own brother," which importeth he was seeking him, and did find him before he dreamed of so good news.

5. Jesus of Nazareth is the Messiah promised in the Old Testament, whom the prophets and the godly looked for; so doth Andrew reckon. "We have found the Messias," implied also that he and his brother had been of those who looked for him.

6. The finding of Jesus Christ, the promised Messiah, is good news indeed, and the most excellent of purchases, as making the finder eternally happy; for these are the good news that went among them—"We have found the Messias."

7. It is the will of God that his mind in scripture be not hid up in a dark language, but that it be made plain and intelligible to all who seek the way of salvation therein; therefore is the Hebrew word "Messias" interpreted "the Christ," in Greek, in which the New Testament was written, for the use both of gentiles and Jews, as being then a common language; so also ver. 38, 42.

8. The titles and styles given to Christ in scripture are not to be lightly passed over, but pondered what may be held out in them for our edification and comfort; and particularly, that he hath taken to himself the title of being the anointed one by the Spirit without measure, for the discharge of all his offices for the churches' good; therefore also is his name, "the Messias," which signifieth "the Anointed," interpreted in Greek, "the Christ," signifying the same.

9. Whatever is wanting in the light of instruments pointing out Christ, will be made up if the hearer go to Christ himself; and faithful preachers will not be at ease till they draw hearers to Christ; and hearers should be tractable when means are offered, and not rest upon any man's word, but go to Christ themselves; for Andrew, having little more to say, draws him to Christ, and Peter goeth with him; "he brought him to Jesus."

10. Christ doth perfectly know all that come to him, and what concerns them, and this he discovereth, that they may be encouraged to employ him in all exigents, and may walk before him as a heart-searching God; therefore, "when Jesus beheld him, he said, Thou art Simon," &c. At first view he lets him see he knew him.

11. Christ will welcome those that come to him, whoever were the instruments of their conversion, nor will he despise them for their outward mean condition; for he welcometh Peter, though called by the private instruction of Andrew, as well as those who were called by John, and that albeit he was poor "Simon, the son of [fisher] Jona."

12. Such as come to Christ he giveth them a new nature, and admits them into his family as children; for his giving him a new name imports he was now a born child in his family, and he his Father.

13. Whatever dignity and excellency Christ

confer upon his converts, yet he would not have them not forgetting what they are of themselves, that this may still keep them humble, and command Christ's grace the more; therefore, with the promise he puts him in mind that he is "Simon, the son of Jona."

14. As constancy and firmness in the truth, and profession thereof, in variety of times and trials, is a commendable excellency, so the dispensation of the measures of faith, whereby professors are stronger or weaker, are in Christ's own hand; and it is not only believers' duty to be firm, but Christ's promise also, who undertakes to make them such, so far as he seeth it meet; for the thing signified by this name, "Cephas," or "a stone," is constancy, as Peter's excellency, and Christ, by giving him this name, undertaketh to make him so.

15. The Lord doth not measure nor judge of his servants by their fits of weakness, but by the constant tenour of their way; and in great mercy he giveth confirmations to his own, whom he is to try, that when their weakness appeareth they may not lose hope; for Christ calleth Simon, "Cephas," or, a fixed believer, notwithstanding his slips that followed, and by this name would forearm him against discouragement therefrom.

Ver. 43. The day following Jesus would go forth into Galilee, and findeth Philip, and saith unto him, Follow me.

44. Now Philip was of Bethsaida, the city of Andrew and Peter.

The fourth disciple, whom Christ himself sought out and called, is Philip, and to this is subjoined the place of Philip's habitation, being the same with Andrew and Peter's also. Whence learn—

1. As Christ was constant and diligent about his Father's work, so he will not fail to go wherever he hath an errand, or any to bring in, and wherever he cometh he hath some to find; for "the day following," without loss of a day, "Jesus would go forth," from the place where he stayed after he passed by John, "into Galilee," because he had Philip to seek.

2. Such as Christ hath a purpose of love unto, he will not only prevent them, but will find them out and gain them; for "he findeth Philip."

3. Christ hath divers ways of calling and bringing men to him, so that none are to carve out a way to themselves, as if there were none else, nor are any to suspect their being accepted by Christ, when they come to him, though they have not been dealt with in all things as others; for here we have some called by John, some by private instruction, and Philip called by Christ's own mouth, and yet all alike welcome.

4. Such as would prove the truth of their conversion ought to renounce all things in affection and practice, in so far as they hinder from Christ, ought not to presume to go before Christ, in prescribing their way to him, nor to follow their own wit, will, or lusts, but to follow him as a teacher and guide, and as a pattern of obedience to the moral law, and suffering for righteousness,

and to do this constantly. So much is imported in this invitation, "Follow me," which Philip obeyed, as the sequel declareth.

5. The work of the gospel and kingdom of Christ may begin in very obscure places, and among mean persons, that so none may despise a day of small things; for here he begins the gathering of his kingdom (which afterward overspread the world) in obscure Galilee, and among men of an obscure town—Bethsaida.

6. The wickedness of a place will not seclude Christ's favour from particular persons, who are his own in it; for Bethsaida was a wicked place, as appeareth from Christ's woes denounced against it, Matt. xi. 20, 21, yet from thence he calleth three eminent instruments.

Ver. 45. Philip findeth Nathanael, and saith unto him, We have found him, of whom Moses in the law, and the prophets, did write, Jesus of Nazareth, the son of Joseph.

46. And Nathanael said unto him, Can there any good thing come out of Nazareth? Philip saith unto him, Come and see.

The last who is called here to embrace Christ for the Messiah is Nathanael, who is wrought upon, partly by Philip, ver. 45, 46, partly by Christ himself, ver. 47—49. And upon his believing, he is commended, and promises of greater things given for his encouragement, ver. 50, 51.

As for Philip, the instrument's part, he, finding Nathanael, declareth how they had found the promised Messiah, and when he stumbled at Christ, because of the place of his residence or birth, as was supposed, Philip inviteth him to come to Christ for clearing of that doubt.

DOCTRINES.

1. As Christ by one word can draw a soul to him, so conversion is best proved by effects, and particularly by zeal in seeking to promote the kingdom of Christ and the good of our neighbour's soul in our station, it being an inseparable companion of the new nature to seek to multiply the kind; for Philip was gained by one word, and proveth it by "finding Nathanael," and seeking to gain him.

2. Private conference and mutual edification is a notable means for advancing the kingdom of Christ in ourselves or others; for by these means Christ gathereth his disciples here.

3. The Messiah was spoken of and foretold both in the law and in the prophets; and the godly, before his coming, waited for him by studying these scriptures. And Jesus is the true Messiah, in whom all things that were foretold are accomplished, the finding of whom is the best of news; for these are Philip's news to Nathanael, "We have found him of whom Moses in the law, and the prophets, did write," importing that Moses and the prophets did write of him, as is clear from Gen. iii. 15, and xlix. 10, Deut. xviii. 18, and frequently through the prophets; importing also, that Philip, Nathanael, and other godly men were versed in the scriptures, pointing him out, and fed upon him as held forth in

the word, and that the finding of him now in person was joyful news unto them.

4. Such as are true converts, and love Christ, may yet be very weak in knowledge, yea, and err also, especially when anything of Christ is learned from tradition or vulgar report, and not from the scripture; for so doth Philip mistake in calling him "Jesus of Nazareth," if it be taken for the place of his birth, and not of his education, (Matt. ii. 23,) and "the son of Joseph," as the common report was.

5. Men are naturally ready to stumble at something of Christ, yea, even good men may have prejudices to mar their own growth and progress; for Nathanael stumbleth at the place—"Can there any good thing come out of Nazareth?"—not so much because Christ must be born at Bethlehem, as because of the baseness of the place, the inhabitants of Galilee where Nazareth was being a blockish and gross people, so that it was generally conceived no prophet could arise from thence. (John, vii. 52.) And this good man is overtaken with that evil of the generation; whereas there is no place so base or bad, but God, when he pleaseth, can raise eminent instruments out of it, or otherwise do it good.

6. No prejudices should hinder men to come to Christ, and albeit others cannot solve their doubts, yet a blink of him will easily dispel them; for Philip answereth his doubt with "Come and see;" intimating his own weakness to satisfy all his doubts, that it was his duty to come to Christ notwithstanding, and that Christ could clear him.

> VER. 47. Jesus saw Nathanael coming to him, and saith of him, Behold an Israelite indeed, in whom is no guile!
>
> 48. Nathanael saith unto him, Whence knowest thou me? Jesus answered and said unto him, Before that Philip called thee, when thou wast under the fig tree, I saw thee.
>
> 49. Nathanael answered and saith unto him, Rabbi, thou art the Son of God; thou art the King of Israel.

Nathanael being persuaded to come to Christ by Philip, Christ, by commending the sincerity of his heart, and (when Nathanael wonders at Christ for knowing that) by declaring unto him where he had been, doth discover his godhead unto him, which so worketh as to draw Nathanael to a confession of his godhead and office. Whence learn—

1. Christ will in mercy pass over the faults, prejudices, and mistakes of those who do not persist in them, but come to him; for Christ welcometh and receiveth Nathanael even while he is coming, and taketh notice of him when he minded it not, and speaks of him and not to him.

2. Christ is an exact discerner of men, both their inside and outside, and the knowledge of this should draw men to him; for Christ gains ground on Nathanael by discovering how exactly he knew him.

3. Albeit all who came of Jacob after the flesh were Israelites in the external court, yet all that were so by visible covenant were not such inwardly and in the inward court of God; and Christ is a discerner both of the one and the other, who cannot be deceived; therefore saith he of Nathanael, "Behold an Israelite indeed," or "truly," importing that many were not truly such, or in the spirit.

4. The true mark of a true Israelite in the spirit is, not perfection or sinlessness, but sincerity, whereby men having gotten grace, and closed with Christ, and applied the virtue of his blood, are enabled to serve God from right principles and for right ends, and are in so far purged from hypocrisy and dissimulation that it doth not reign in them, but they love truth and hate guile; they labour to be in reality and in secret what they seem to others to be; they are jealous of the unsoundness of their own hearts, and daily vexed with it; they set against all by-ends in religion, and aim at perfection in it. Thus was Nathanael "an Israelite indeed, in whom is no guile!"—to wit, reigning or approven.

5. Albeit Christ be the author of every grace men have, yet he will not spare to commend it in them; and particularly he is a notable commender of sincerity where he findeth it, and that so much the more as men are sincere in a corrupt time; for he commends Nathanael, a sincere man in that time. "Behold an Israelite indeed, in whom is no guile!" Men need not seek themselves, for such as are sincere Christ will commend them.

6. The practical knowledge of Christ, and particularly that he is a searcher of hearts, is such as will strike those who attain unto it with admiration and wonder; for, saith Nathanael, surprised with this encounter, "Whence knowest thou me?" as little dreaming how Christ could know him, and especially his heart and inside, seeing he had never seen him before.

7. Confused and surprising thoughts concerning Christ out not to be rested on, but the knowledge of him ought to be dived further into till we get distinct satisfaction; for Nathanael doth not rest here, but dives into the matter—"Whence knowest thou me?"—that he might know whence this knowledge came, and how he should be affected with it; and Christ answereth him, to give proof of his willingness to satisfy modest inquiries.

8. Christ's omniscience and perfect knowledge of all things, particularly those things that concern his people, is such as when he hath discovered so much as may make men wonder, he hath yet more to discover if he please; for Christ tells Nathanael how he knew yet more of him, "Before that Philip called thee," &c. A sight of this did overcome David, Psalm cxxxix. 1—6.

9. Christ hath an eye upon his people before that any instrument deal with them, to draw them unto him; from whence it is that instruments fall upon them and are successful; for Christ condescends particularly on this to Nathanael—"Before that Philip called thee, I saw thee."

10. Christ's omniscience as God, and his providence about all things, particularly about his people, doth condescend to very meanest things, even postures of the body, circumstances of time

and place, and by this he would assure them of his taking notice of greater things that may concern them; for, saith he, "Before that Philip called thee, when thou wast under the fig tree, I saw thee."

11. As a sincere heart, through God's blessing, will easily receive satisfaction concerning Christ, and be gained to him, so the kindly fruit of such a work is to beget a high estimation of Christ; for Nathanael is satisfied, and his satisfaction brings out a fair confession and commendation of Christ.

12. The more a soul knows of Christ, it will not only esteem him, but think and speak the more reverently of him and to him; therefore doth Nathanael call him "Rabbi," which he did not before.

13. Christ's all-seeing eye is an infallible proof of his godhead, whereby he knoweth all things of himself, which every one would study who embrace and close with him; for whereas Philip had called him "the son of Joseph," ver. 45, Nathanael is convinced of more from what he heard; "Thou art the Son of God," and as such an one closeth with him.

14. That which maketh Christ's godhead comfortable to his people is, that as Mediator, and by virtue of his offices, they have a peculiar interest in him; and particularly that he is a king unto them who will employ his divine power to subject them to his government, and to protect and defend them; therefore Nathanael subjoineth, "Thou art the King of Israel." We need not inquire whether by "Israel" he understood the nation of Israel only, being yet ignorant of the extent of Christ's kingdom, or all the "Israel" of God also, seeing the truth in that point is elsewhere sufficiently clear to us.

VER. 50. Jesus answered and said unto him, Because I said unto thee, I saw thee under the fig tree, believest thou? thou shalt see greater things than these.

51. And he saith unto him, Verily, verily, I say unto you, Hereafter ye shall see heaven open, and the angels of God ascending and descending upon the Son of man.

In the last place, we have Christ's entertaining of this convert, in commending his believing on so easy terms, and promising further grounds of confirmation; and particularly he promiseth unto him, and all of them, a sight of heaven opened, and of angels ascending and descending on him. This promise may indeed have an allusion to Jacob's vision of the ladder, Gen. xxviii., as accomplished in Christ, who is the opener of heaven, and the way to it; who reacheth to heaven in his divine original, and to earth in his manhood, and whom angels serve. But it seemeth more safe to take it literally, for some signs of his glory manifested to some, that by their ministry it might be published to all; and as before this heaven had been opened at his baptism, Matt. iii., and angels ascended and descended, as he had service for them, and particularly at the publication of his birth, and in the time of his temptation in the wilderness, so afterward heaven was in a sort opened at

his transfiguration and ascension, and angels ministered to him in his agony, resurrection, and ascension. We may also safely conceive that this might have been yet more literally accomplished, according to the promise, though the accomplishment be not recorded, as many other particulars were not, John, xx. 30, 31.

1. Christ is really well-pleased with the faith and conversion of any, and would have them to look on it as no common benefit; and he is the better pleased the more easy terms we believe upon, when we believe though we see not, or against sense; or close with him, notwithstanding manifold difficulties; for, saith Christ, admiring and commending his own grace in him, "Because I said unto thee, I saw thee under the fig tree, believest thou?"

2. As Christ hath still more and more proofs of himself to give for confirmation of our faith as we need, so they who are willing to believe on less apparent grounds shall be more and more confirmed, and see still greater cause of believing; for this is Christ's promise to Nathanael, "Thou shalt see greater things than these."

3. The encouragements allowed by Christ to particular believers are intended and recorded for the comfort of all believers in the like need and following the same way, for so is this promise given, "He said unto him, I say unto you"—that is, to all then present. Even particular extraordinary promises, made to particular persons, do allow general comfort to all believers in an ordinary way, though they are not to expect what is extraordinary. So much appeareth from Joshua, i. 5, compared with Heb. xiii. 5.

4. Christ's promises would be looked on as sure and infallible, being not only promised by Him who cannot lie, but most gravely asserted for our confirmation; and we ought to be humbled for our infidelity, which so readily mistrusts him, and to admire his indulgent condescendency to satisfy our weakness; therefore Christ prefixeth to this promise, "Verily, verily, I say unto you"— a grave and vehement asseveration, putting the matter beyond all doubt and controversy. Not that this maketh the promise any surer on his part, but that our weakness and unbelief needeth it, and he condescends unto it; and having given this assurance expects absolute and entire credit to what he saith.

5. The sight of Christ's glory is the great encouragement and ground of believers' confirmation, as being all for them and their good, and letting them see what excellency there is in him to be relied upon; therefore is there a promise of Nathanael's confirmation by seeing more of Christ's glory.

6. Christ our Mediator is approved from heaven, and he by whom heaven, formerly shut against sinners, is opened; for it is a part of Christ's glory that "heaven is open" with relation to him, testifying an approbation of him, and his acceptance for him and his.

7. It doth also illustrate Christ's glory, and further confirm believers' faith, that Christ is Lord of angels even in his state of humiliation, and hath them ready at his call, as he or his people

shall need their service; for it is also promised they shall "see the angels of God ascending and descending upon the Son of man," or moving from earth to heaven and from heaven to earth as he required.

8. All this glory of Christ is further comfortable when he is found dwelling in our nature with it; yea, and delighting in this his condescendence, and to be our kinsman; for it is promised they should see all this "upon the Son of man," shewing that the Son of God was also the Son of man, and that he delighted to be so, and therefore doth so often take this title to himself.

CHAPTER II.

In this chapter we have—first, a miracle wrought by Christ in Cana of Galilee in turning water into wine, the occasion, working, and manifestation whereof, with John's observation upon it, are recorded, to ver. 12; next, Christ's removal to Capernaum, and his short abode there, ver. 12; thirdly, his going to Jerusalem, with his purging of the temple there, and his disciples' observation upon it, to ver. 18; his conference with the contentious Jews, whereby also his disciples did profit afterward, to ver. 28; and his carriage towards some who pretended to believe, to the end of the chapter.

Ver. 1. And the third day there was a marriage in Cana of Galilee; and the mother of Jesus was there:

2. And both Jesus was called, and his disciples, to the marriage.

In recording this first miracle of Christ John begins with three occasions thereof. The first and remotest is, a marriage feast, which is described from the place Cana, a village of Galilee, lying at least within a day's journey to Capernaum, as appeareth, John, iv. 46, 50, 52; called "of Galilee," to distinguish it from another Cana, or Kanah, in the tribe of Asher, Josh. xix. 24, 28, which lay farther off from Capernaum, being near Zidon. It is also described from the time of it, which was the third day,—to wit, after the former conferences mentioned, chap. i., or after his coming into Galilee, of which, chap. i. 43. The second and nearer occasion is, that Christ's mother was there, (being, as appeareth, a friend to some of the parties, in that it is not said she was invited, and she is solicitous for the want of wine, ver. 3, and hath some power with the servants, ver. 5,) and that Christ and his disciples were invited to it.

DOCTRINES.

1. Christ's practice, being now to enter on his public ministry, teacheth us not to pass away time, but to be frequently about the employments of our calling, for he lets few days pass but he is manifesting himself openly by word and work.

2. In Christ's account marriage is an honourable ordinance, to which he will not deny his presence and countenance, for he is at this marriage, and honoureth it with his first miracle.

3. Feasting, and better fare than ordinary, and calling of friends together at marriage, are lawful, providing the rules of sobriety, prescribed in the word to such feasts, be observed; and it is not against Christian sobriety in any person to countenance their kindred or friends in marriage-feasts, for "there was a marriage"—or marriage-feast, as the word importeth, wherein they had wine, ver. 3;—"and the mother of Jesus was there. And both Jesus was called, and his disciples," and they came.

4. Albeit men cannot now have a like occasion of inviting Christ, yet this practice may mind us, 1. That married persons do need and should seek Christ's presence to their marriage. 2. Men in marriage-feasting ought so to carry themselves in the use of their liberty as they might invite Christ to it, and not to take such profane liberty as may provoke him not to countenance them. 3. Such as would be kind to Christ, and welcome him, ought to prove it by their kindness to his disciples also. 4. Christ's working a miracle upon this occasion teacheth that in our most cheerful and free times we would be still mindful of doing all to God's glory and not omit any occasion of honouring him.

Ver. 3. And when they wanted wine, the mother of Jesus saith unto him, They have no wine.

4. Jesus saith unto her, Woman, what have I to do with thee? mine hour is not yet come.

The third and nearest occasion of this miracle is the want of wine, occasioned, as would appear, rather through their poverty, and that some of their guests (and belike Christ and his disciples, newly come to the country) had not been expected, than through any excess. Unto this is subjoined the miracle itself, in recording whereof John sets down what passed betwixt several parties in the preparations to it and manifestation of it; and first we have, by way of preparation, Mary's part with Christ, and his answer. She being sensible of the want, and respecting (as should seem) her kinsfolks' credit, and having known many things of her son, partly by the angel's intimation at his conception, partly by what Simon, and Anna, and John the Baptist had said of him, if not also by his own private information during his private life, that he was shortly to manifest himself by doctrine and miracles,—she, I say, knowing this, doth represent the matter unto him for remedy; but he, judging of her discourse by her secret thoughts, doth sharply reprove her for thinking to usurp power over him in the works proper to his godhead, and belonging to his office, and for prescribing of times to him wherein to work, though he were otherwise willing to do the thing.

DOCTRINES.

1. Such is Christ's tenderness that he doth not discover wants that he may leave men in misery, but that he may take occasion to let the riches

of his power, providence, mercy, and help, be seen; for their wanting wine, whatever cause it flowed from, was the occasion of this miracle.

2. Very lawful suits and requests to Christ may be ill-managed and propounded; and there may be greater ill in saints' ways than they are aware of, or do see; for it was a very lawful course to go with needs to Christ, and yet he findeth matter of reproof in her so doing; and albeit Mary seems to deal very submissively in telling the need, " They have no wine," without prescribing, yet Christ, who understood the secret thoughts of her heart, findeth great presumption in it; so Peter little dreamed that Satan should borrow his tongue in wishing well to his Master till himself told it, Matt. xvi. 22, 23.

3. Such is Christ's vigilancy, and zeal, and tenderness, that as he discovereth so he will not bear with faults in those that are dearest to him; for he faileth not to reprove his own mother.

4. Albeit Mary was blessed among women in being the mother of Christ, yet was she not free of sin, not only original but even of actual out-breakings; for seeing Christ, who could not err, reproveth her, she is not faultless. And this is registrate in scripture to prevent men's conceiting of that blessed woman above what is meet.

5. It is an affront offered to Christ's glory to think that Mary's motherhood gave her any power over him to direct him in works wrought by his divine nature, or in works of his office of Mediator, or to employ her for that end; for his reproof taxeth this secret presumption in herself, while as he who was subject to her as man during his private life as to a mother, Luke, ii. 51, doth now say unto her, " Woman,"—not mother, as accounting her to have no motherly authority in the matter of his office; and, " What have I to do with thee?" thou hast nothing to do to meddle by any motherly power (for as a supplicant she might) with what I do now in my public office, not so much as to obtain a miracle of me.

6. Christ's saddest reproofs of his people for their miscarriages in coming to him ought not to put them out of hope that he will respect their real necessities in due time, as he seeth meet; for though Christ thus reprove, yet the last part of it, " mine hour is not yet come," importeth that it would come, yea, and that he had been waiting for it, and thinking on the matter before she spake.

7. Even when Christ is about to manifest himself, yet our time wherein we would have him work and his time wherein he will work are often very different; we are hasty, and would be through straits without any humbling exercise and trial of graces, but Christ looks on these fruits as better than simple outgate, [merely getting out,] and our presuming to prescribe to him is matter of reproof; for " mine hour is not yet come," saith he, reproving Mary, who would have had an outgate already.

8. Whatever our desires be under wants, yet Christ will not manifest his help when it would please us best, but when his glory in working may be best seen, and particularly when our emptiness without his help is most sensibly seen; for when wine began to be scant, as the words will bear, and was sparingly distributed, was the fittest time in Mary's account for keeping the bridegroom's credit, and hiding the want; but Christ's hour was " not come" till the want was better known and felt, and by his so doing he looks more to the setting forth of his own glory than to saving the credit of a creature.

VER. 5. His mother saith unto the servants, Whatsoever he saith unto you, do it.

Secondly. By way of preparation to the miracle Mary's part with the servants is recorded; she taking with the reproof, and being humbled, and yet gathering hope from what he said, directeth the servants to give simple and absolute obedience to Christ's directions, that so they might not fall in her fault, and he might do the work. Whence learn—

1. As we are not to think of Mary above what is meet, so we are not to run on another extremity, in not thinking reverently of her, and as becometh; for John, notwithstanding Christ's sharp word, calleth her Christ's mother still.

2. It is an evidence of a truly gracious heart, and of one that sinneth of ignorance or infirmity, and not of pride or obstinacy, that it taketh with a reproof from Christ, and humbly submitteth to it; for so doth Mary in not answering again, though sharply reproved.

3. As Christ, by reproving his people's faults, taketh not away ground of hope that he will do them good, so it is the mark of one who taketh kindly with a reproof that their humility hindereth them not to take advantage and grip to anything that may give hope, whereas proud discouragement is ready, under a pretence of humility, to cast away all ground of hope when it is reproved; for humbled Mary's speech to the servants importeth that she gathered from Christ's word some ground of hope, which she laid hold on.

4. Such do take rightly with a reproof, and do prove that they are bettered by it, who do labour to prevent the ill they have fallen in in others as well as in themselves; for so doth Mary's direction to the servants teach, that she would have them humble and submissive, and not to prescribe.

5. Christ's commands ought to be the rule of our actions, to which we ought to give simple, implicit, and absolute obedience, without questioning or murmuring; and the best way to come speed at Christ's hands is to give him all his will by submission, especially in things outward, and in the time, manner, and measure of giving spiritual things also; providing that in things outward we do not pretend to submission only out of design to get our will; and in things spiritual, that our submission flow not from careless security, and produce not negligence in the use of means, but that it be a fruit of faith and humility, and a guard to keep the heart from fretting when it hath done duty. This subjection and submission is held forth in Mary's direction, " Whatsoever he saith unto you, do it."

VER. 6. And there were set there six water-pots of stone, after the manner of the purifying of the Jews, containing two or three firkins apiece.

7. Jesus saith unto them, Fill the waterpots with water. And they filled them up to the brim.

8. And he saith unto them, Draw out now, and bear unto the governor of the feast. And they bare it.

Thirdly. John recordeth Christ's part with the servants, which is contained in two directions given by Christ, and their obedience. The first is, to fill up some great vessels (used by them for holding of water for purifying themselves) with water, which they did; and this was by way of preparation to the miracle. The second is, to draw out and carry this wine to the governor of the feast, whose skill was best, and his senses most entire, which they also obey; and this direction pre-supposeth the miracle wrought by his secret power, and their obedience maketh way to the manifesting of it.

DOCTRINES.

1. This manner of the purifying of the Jews, for which they had the water-pots, to have water still in readiness, whether it be understood of purifications enjoined by the law, or of the multiplied washings brought in among them by tradition, Mark, vii. 3, 4, &c., doth teach that apostates and such as have lost the life of religion may yet be unwilling to quit all show of religion, but may hold up external ceremonies, yea, may be ready then to multiply them most, as quieting anything of a natural conscience that is left, and as being very easy and craving no inward exercise of the heart; for so was the manner of the Jews in their declining times.

2. It is not in vain to wait for anything Christ giveth hope of by his word, for he will make it good in due time; as here the want of wine is supplied by miracle, of which he gave some hope by his speech to his mother.

3. Christ doth not deceive people in the good turns he doth for them, but they are all real, and every circumstance of them being marked doth confirm the same and set out his glory; therefore are the circumstances so narrowly marked to set out his glory in proving that there was no deceit in the miracle; " the waterpots" (and not hogsheads, where wine-dregs might have given some relish to water) do prove there was no jugglery; their matter being " of stone," not capable of the scent of former liquor, confirmeth the same; their great capacity prevented suspicion of stealing in of wine, which might have been suspected of lesser vessels; his employing of the servants and not his disciples takes off any suspicion of collusion; his sending it to the ruler or orderer of the feast without so much as tasting it himself shewed how certain he was of the thing.

4. Wherever Christ cometh, he is worthy of his own room, and doth liberally recompense any entertainment he or his receive from any; for whether his presence and his disciples' (being beyond the number of guests expected) occasioned the want or not, yet he payed his dinner well

with abundance of wine, in " six waterpots, containing two or three firkins apiece."

5. Miracles wrought by Christ for confirming his doctrine were such works as were useful and profitable to men, such as this, whereby he would condemn such as boast of idle and useless miracles, serving for no profit, which savour not of Christ, nor of power from him, nor of his doctrine, to be confirmed by them. And by this also he would prove himself to be the merciful Saviour of sinners, in that he manifests himself to be God by these works and the like, when he might have proved it by sad judgments on sinners.

6. It is no difficulty for Christ to work the greatest work he pleaseth, and to make a change from worse to better; for this miracle is wrought immediately by his godhead, without so much as a word; only he bids them fill water and draw wine.

7. Christ in his deepest humiliation and abasement is full of majesty, and he knoweth how to get instruments to do him service when he pleaseth; yea, he can bow their hearts who in appearance know nothing of him to be foot and hand for his work; for being in the form of a servant, yet these servants (who knew him not, as would seem) obey all his directions, how useless soever they seemed to be.

Ver. 9. When the ruler of the feast had tasted the water that was made wine, and knew not whence it was : (but the servants which drew the water knew ;) the governor of the feast called the bridegroom,

10. And saith unto him, Every man at the beginning doth set forth good wine; and when men have well drunk, then that which is worse : but thou hast kept the good wine until now.

Fourthly. John recordeth the ruler of the feast's part, whereby the miracle was manifested, He wondering at the goodness of the wine, and not knowing whence it was, calleth for the bridegroom, and ascribeth this provision to his prudence, (rather, as may be conceived, than to his parsimony,) which was not ordinary at such occasions; with which we are to conceive that the servants who knew the matter, as is said here, did make the miracle manifest, as appeareth from ver. 11. What the ruler saith of giving of wine to men who have well drunk is to be understood, not of excess, but of drinking to satisfaction. However, it is but a simple narration without an approbation on Christ or his penman's part. Nor did Christ, by affording so much good wine to them who had already drunk so much, give any evidence of his allowance of intemperance, for he had another end in it, ver. 11; and besides, all the creatures which men daily consume by excess are his gift by common providence, to which men's excess and abuse cannot be imputed. But it is a man's duty to look on Christ's liberality as a trial to his sobriety.

DOCTRINES.

1. Christ's works, when they are rightly considered, will be found worthy of commendation,

and albeit the worker were not known, yet they will commend themselves; for the ruler commendeth the wine, when he " knew not whence it was."

2. In a miraculous transubstantiation, or change of one substance into another, sense will be judge and bear witness to it; for the ruler having " tasted the water that was made wine," findeth by his taste that it is wine.

3. Ignorance of Christ's hand in a work makes men to ascribe it to others, and so take Christ's glory from him; for " the ruler called the bridegroom," and ascribed it to him.

4. In the comparison which the governor of the feast maketh betwixt other men's way and the bridegroom's, which was indeed Christ's work, we have a fit resemblance betwixt the fashion of the world and Satan, and Christ's way; they set out their best commodities first, but worse come after, but Christ in his dealing may begin more harshly, but he is still the longer the better.

VER. 11. This beginning of miracles did Jesus in Cana of Galilee, and manifested forth his glory; and his disciples believed on him.

This history is closed with John's observation upon the miracle, that for order, it was the first, that the place was " Cana of Galilee," that the fruit of it was the setting forth of the glory of his godhead, and confirming his disciples in their faith in him. Whence learn—

1. Christ did begin to work miracles, not in his infancy, nor in the time of his private life, but when he entered to his ministry, and to publish his doctrine, which his miracles were to confirm; for John saith, not only this was the first miracle he did in Cana, though that was true, but, " This beginning of miracles did Jesus," as being simply the first.

2. Christ doth not choose persons or places for manifesting himself in or to them, as men or carnal reason would judge, nor will he stand to manifest his glory in an obscure place, and by so doing make it famous; therefore it is again marked that he did this in " Cana of Galilee," now made famous, of an obscure village, by his working.

3. Christ's glory is his supreme end in all his working, to which all other ends and effects must be subordinate; for he did this, " and manifested forth his glory."

4. The end of Christ's miracles was to set forth his own proper glory of his godhead, as principal agent of them, though his manhood sometime concurred as a minister in the work; for he " manifested forth his glory," as doing this by his own power, whereas prophets and apostles were but instruments in what was done by them.

5. It is a part of God's glory that he only can work a true miracle, and neither Satan nor any instrument by their own power; for in this miracle he manifested his glory proper to him as God.

6. One work and miracle of Christ doth set forth his glory much, being well considered; for by this one he " manifested forth his glory;" for in it shined the glory of his omnipotency, and of his liberality; by it he declared that he is a supplier of wants wherever he cometh; that he can bring excellent things out of that which is naughty; that he can make things more comfortable than they are in their own nature; that it is he who turns water into wine, and sorrow into joy; that he made that change betwixt water and wine in a moment which nature doth but in a year, by making water to fructify the vine.

7. Such as have believing in Christ will be needing daily confirmation of faith, and will get it; and such as have got good by his word, and believed it, shall also find confirmation from his working; for " his disciples," who were already called (chap. i.), get new confirmation, and ' believed on him."

8. A right sight of Christ in his glory and properties is a notable help to faith, and calleth for it at our hands, whereas narrow thoughts of him feeds unbelief; for he " manifested forth his glory; and his disciples believed."

9. Beside the common use of Christ's works and benefits, which the world gets, it is the privilege of disciples to get spiritual advantage thereby also; for when the banqueters got wine by this miracle the disciples got more faith also.

VER. 12. After this he went down to Capernaum, he, and his mother, and his brethren, and his disciples : and they continued there not many days.

Here, in the second part of the chapter, we have Christ's departure from Cana to Capernaum, with his company in going thither, and his short abode there, occasioned, as appeareth from ver. 13, by the near approach of the passover. It is not needful to inquire what his errand was there, and upon what occasion his mother and brethren went with him; whether because Joseph was now dead, and so he took care of his mother, or because they would convey him on his way, or because his brethren were to go up to Jerusalem with him; only this voyage was before that, Matt. iv. 13, when he came to dwell in Capernaum, for then John was cast into prison, Matt. iv. 12, but now he was not, as appeareth from John, iii. 24.

DOCTRINES.

1. Christ was content to submit himself to the wanting of a certain abode and settled dwelling in the world, that he might sanctify our pilgrimage and tossed condition to us, and to invite his followers willingly to be removed or tossed from place to place, as he hath service for them. So much are we taught by this his removal.

2. Christ hath errands in eminent places as well as obscure, and will not despise eminent persons or places for their eminency more than the base for their baseness; and he can make the work of his kingdom in a land advance from obscure beginnings and places to be more eminent and conspicuous. So much may we gather from Christ's going out of obscure Cana to Capernaum, a chief city in Galilee.

3. As it is wisdom in Christ's own to go still in his company, so others also may be with him so long as his way and theirs lieth together, or

when he is working gloriously, and his gospel hath credit; for after this miracle we find not only "his mother, and disciples," but "his brethren," or kinsfolk, with him, who yet believed not in him, John, vii. 5.

4. Christ may stay longer or shorter while, and do little or much, in a place as he pleaseth; and particularly, he stayeth or removeth according as may contribute to advance the great work of his glory and of sinners' salvation; for he "continued there not many days," as having more to do at this time in Jerusalem.

Ver. 13. And the Jews' passover was at hand, and Jesus went up to Jerusalem,

14. And found in the temple those that sold oxen and sheep and doves, and the changers of money sitting:

15. And when he had made a scourge of small cords, he drove them all out of the temple, and the sheep, and the oxen; and poured out the changers' money, and overthrew the tables;

16. And said unto them that sold doves, Take these things hence; make not my Father's house an house of merchandise.

Followeth, Christ's going up to Jerusalem at the passover, and (which is the first branch of this part of the chapter) his purging of the temple, wherein he fulfilled that prophecy, Mal. iii. 1—3, in the beginning of the solemn execution of his office, and declared his glory as much as in the former, or any miracle, having not a lifeless creature in its obediential subjection to work upon, but Satan, acting in malicious men to oppose him. The pretext of this abuse, which he reforms, was taken partly from the law, Deut. xiv. 23—26, requiring that those who dwelt far off should bring money, and buy their sacrifices at Jerusalem; partly from the condition and other ordinances of the Jews—as of old, the males, from twenty years old and upward, did pay half a shekel to the Lord, according to the law, Exod. xxx. 12—15. So we find that practice continued, 2 Kings, xii. 4; 2 Chron. xxiv. 9; beside other voluntary oblations of all sort of persons, which are frequently mentioned in the Old Testament; all which did occasion the necessity of changing greater coin into lesser, as the word in the original signifieth. Others of them, living in divers countries, needed to have their strange coin changed into current money to buy sacrifices. Now the covetousness of the rulers brought these things into the outer court of the temple, under a pretext of having them near at hand to the people, and that the cattle that were there had been already overseen by the priests to be perfect; if not also, that they were more acceptable which were bought there. These corruptions Christ reformeth, partly by terror and force, driving the men and their cattle out with a scourge made (belike) of the cords wherewith they led and tied the cattle, and overthrowing the tables with the money; and partly by his word, commanding some to take away their commodities, and forbidding all to profane the temple with

their merchandise. What is here said concerning the temple is not to be applied to places set apart for public worship under the gospel,—for however it be a fault to apply such places to common and profane uses, especially to the impeding of public worship, except in the case of necessity, yet they are not typically holy, as the temple was,—but to the church of Christ.

DOCTRINES.

1. The observation of Easter, and such like days, is a Jewish rite, proper to them, and not belonging to the Christian church; for John, who wrote last, knew it for no other than the Jews' passover, or a feast of theirs.

2. Christ our Lord went up to Jerusalem at the passover, in obedience to the ceremonial law yet in force, Exod. xxxiv. 23, and that he might take occasion, in the concourse from all places in this public time, to publish his office and doctrine; by the first, to teach us condescendence and reverence to all the ordinances of God; and by the second, that we should neglect no occasion of promoving the honour of God in our stations.

3. Great abuses may creep into the visible church, and corruption may get far in; for so was it here; he "found in the temple those that sold oxen and sheep," &c. This one was the fruit of many more.

4. The covetousness of churchmen is the great breeder and entertainer of abuses and corruptions in the house of God, whatever be the pretences they are cloaked with; for this was the rise of the abuses here.

5. There is no hope of reforming abuses in the church till Christ come and take order with them; and when such as should see to it will not, Christ will find a way for it, though he will not approve of men's following any unlawful course, or to which they have not a calling to promove this; for here Christ cometh to purge, and when the civil magistrate was heathen, and cared not for religion, and the ordinary church rulers had a hand in the transgression; yet Christ doth it by his absolute authority, as Lord of the house.

6. When other means fail, Christ can use violent remedies, and by plagues put sinners from their courses; yea, when he cometh to reform, he may see it just to smite the very creatures for sinners' cause. So are we here taught, in that by force "he drove them all out of the temple, and the sheep, and the oxen."

7. Our Lord's face is very terrible when he is angry, even in his abasement; and a weak mean of reformation in his hand, and assisted with his power and terror, will serve the turn; for "when he had made a scourge of small cords," (more fit in appearance for affrighting children than for this work,) "he drove them all out," and none durst resist him.

8. It is the duty of all such as are employed in a work of reformation to testify their zeal and integrity by not minding or seeking their own things under pretext thereof; so much doth Christ's practice teach, who "poured out the changers' money, and overthrew the tables," but put none of it up.

9. There ought to be no trifling nor composition in the matter of corruptions in the house of God; no less must satisfy than putting them out at doors, as here Christ doth.

10. Corruptions, even after they have been cast out by Christ's own hand, may yet creep in again into the house of God, in which case, Christ will deal more severely; for Christ, having purged the temple in this first year of his ministry, hath it again to purge of the same evils, Matt. xxi. 12, 13, in the last year, where, instead of "an house of merchandise," he chargeth them with making it "a den of thieves."

11. Reformation will not be thorough when only force and violent remedies are applied to purge, unless instruction be joined with it, to take out the roots of corruptions out of men's minds, and to make them willing to concur and reform themselves; for Christ joineth his word here, bidding some " Take these things hence," and warning all not to abuse his house.

12. As Christ is Lord and heir of his Father's house, the church, Heb. iii. 6, and therefore careth for it, so all who have relation to God as their Father, their hearts will rise in his quarrel, when his honour, house, or service are wronged; nor can they endure the presence of what defileth his house, " Make not," saith he, " my Father's house an house of merchandise."

13. Albeit men would pass over faults done to God's house, and bear with them, yet Christ will not, but in due time will see to the redressing of them; as here we see in this instance.

14. Things lawful, being done in a wrong time and place, become sin; as it is also unlawful to spend what is dedicated to God in common or profane uses; both which are reproved in this, " Make not my Father's house," dedicated to him, " an house of merchandise," though merchandise be lawful in its own time and place.

Ver. 17. And his disciples remembered that it was written, The zeal of thine house hath eaten me up.

Unto this is subjoined the observation and use the disciples got of it. The Spirit suggested to them that passage, Psalm lxix. 9, at that time, or afterward, and let them see it was then accomplished in Christ, though it had its own verity in David, the type. Whence learn—

1. It is the property of disciples to construct well of Christ's working, and get a right sight thereof, how rude and tumultuous soever it seem to others; for so do the disciples here.

2. Christ's working will be well constructed, and tend to edification, when his word and working are compared together, as the disciples are led to do.

3. Such as are faithful disciples and conscientious hearers have the promise of a sanctified memory, by the Spirit's bringing scriptures to their remembrance as they need; for thus it was that " his disciples remembered that it was written," &c. Yet we ought in this to guard against neglect of searching scripture, expecting somewhat to be suggested; against leaning to the suggesting of it, as the reason why we fasten faith on it, rather than if we found it by search, agreeing with our need, which were to make it no divine scripture to us, but when it is suggested; and against Satan's delusions, who may suggest scriptures unto souls taken with this way, under false glosses.

4. Much is spoken of Christ in the Old Testament under types, and it should be our care in reading it to understand these types well, and see Christ the truth in them; for so do the disciples see a prophecy of Christ held forth in the profession and practice of David the type.

5. Zeal, providing it be according to knowledge, Rom. x. 2, is a commendable grace, when men are employed about right things, not negligently and for the fashion, but affectionately, as herein Christ hath given us a pattern, who excelled in all graces, and particularly that of zeal.

6. As God's house and the matter of his kingdom and ordinances are the chief object of zeal, which should be balanced with meekness in our own matters, so true zeal is the only right and acceptable principle of reformation, and men will go no further in the study of reformation than there is zeal or indignation against what dishonoureth God, and love to that which honoureth him; for upon this principle did Christ reform, and he was affected with the zeal of God's house.

7. Albeit true zeal do trust God with caring for his own affairs, and so is neither diffident nor hasty, yet the nature of it is to be a spending grace, and it will affect the person with pain till what is amiss in God's house be rectified; and it will incline a man, having God's call, to stoop to meanest employments, and to fear no hazards in carrying on God's work; for " The zeal of thine house hath eaten me up;" and Christ evidenced how much his zeal affected both body and mind, by abasing himself to this mean employment of scourging out beasts and men, and by exposing himself to their fury, if he had not been armed with divine terror.

8. Albeit that zealous instruments were removed, and love and zeal among men should decay, and they neglect and become careless of the matters of God, yet Christ never wanteth zeal to resent and redress the wrongs done to God's house; for of him it is still true, " The zeal of thine house hath eaten me up."

Ver. 18. Then answered the Jews and said unto him, What sign shewest thou unto us, seeing that thou doest these things?

19. Jesus answered and said unto them, Destroy this temple, and in three days I will raise it up.

Followeth in the second branch of this part of the chapter Christ's conference with the contentious Jews, even those, it seems, who were driven out, who being put to the door, and he drawing back his terror, they (in these verses) begin to question his authority to do as he had done; for seeing those that were in power did tolerate these things, they reckon that it was boldness in him to undertake it, unless he had an extraordinary calling, or were the Messiah, and if so he were, they desire a proof of his commission by some sign. Christ, in answering, remits them (but in dark terms) to his death—which he foresaw, and would permit them to put him to—and to his resurrection, to prove that he was the true Messiah, and Saviour of sinners.

DOCTRINES.

1. A work of reformation of God's house will never want opposition from corrupt men, even when Christ and his terror is eminently seen in it; for Christ met with opposition thus far, that we should not stumble when we meet with more.

2. Obstinate wicked men, and especially polluters of the house of God, will hardly be reformed, however they be convinced; for these Jews answer again, or except against what he did, now when terror had driven them out, and they had nothing to say.

3. Whatever pretences men may have, wherewith they think to palliate their corruptions in God's service, and make them plausible, yet when Christ cometh, he will make their greatest patrons speechless in that cause; for they are put to the door with silence, and when they would carp most they dare say nothing in defence of the corruptions themselves, only they question his authority to purge them out.

4. When men's hearts are once hardened in ill courses, even a shake with the terror of God will not gain them, but so soon as the fit is over, they will not fear impudently to speak against Christ, for so do they when he draweth back his terror.

5. When enemies of reformation cannot justify their own faults, they will rather quarrel the calling of reformers than yield to the convincing truth held out by them; for their question importeth their questioning of his calling to do this, since he had given no sign for it.

6. Enemies of reformation and unbelievers are not content with warrants from the word, nor with such confirmations as God prescribeth, unless they get signs of their own carving; for it was not their fault simply to seek a sign, seeing Christ was to confirm his authority and doctrine by signs, but that (beside that they had no intention to believe however) they were nothing at all wrought upon by the words foretelling this, nor are they content and convinced by the sign Christ had even now wrought upon themselves, in that one man had chased them all, being overcome with the conscience of the filthiness of their fact, and the sense of his majesty.

7. No man ought to undertake a work of reformation but he who hath a calling thereto, and can instruct it by evidences suitable to the nature of the calling he claimeth to; for this question doth import that if Christ could not prove his authority he had done unwarrantably, though the action were good in itself.

8. Christ did foreknow all his own sufferings, and would not hinder, but willingly permitted them to come on, and underwent them; for "Destroy this temple," is not a command of Christ, but a prediction foretelling their malice, and a permission to them to do their uttermost.

9. The malice of superstitious and greedy enemies of truth and reformation will be satisfied with no less than the lives of reformers; and as God permitted Christ to be killed, so he may permit the lives of notable reformers to be taken by enemies, that so they may be made conform to their Head, and that their sufferings may be a seal and testimony to their doctrine; for " Destroy this temple," doth import that he knew no signs would satisfy them, but to have him killed, hereby also teaching all his followers what to expect in doing the like work.

10. Christ foreknew that he would not succumb in his sufferings, but would overcome death, and all the malice of his enemies, by giving them their will, and then rising again the third day by his own power, as it accordingly came to pass; for, saith he, " Destroy this temple, and in three days I will raise it up."

11. Christ's death and resurrection from the dead is an infallible sign that he is the Messiah and true Redeemer of sinners, having authority to order abuses in his own house; for herein he did the works of the Redeemer of sinners, and triumphed over death, and proved himself to be God, Rom. i. 4; therefore doth he remit them to this sign, to prove his authority.

Ver. 20. Then said the Jews, Forty and six years was this temple in building, and wilt thou rear it up in three days?

21. But he spake of the temple of his body.

These Jews, mistaking Christ's speech, do again carp, supposing he had meant of the material temple. But John cleareth Christ's meaning, whereas they, as would appear, were left to their mistakes. Whence learn—

1. It is God's judgment on haters of truth that Christ speaketh in parables to them; and that they are given up to mistake and carp at him, and are left in their mistakes; for so fared it with these Jews, to whom Christ spake of his body under the name of the " temple."

2. As it is no new thing to see men wrest Christ's speeches, so a main cause of men's mistakes in religion is when they understand figurative speeches as if they were proper; for the Jews err in taking what Christ spake of his body under the name of the temple, the type thereof, as if it had been spoken of the type itself.

3. A work of reformation is a work of great difficulty, and may encounter with much opposition and many delays before it be perfected; for so much doth the Jews' exception against Christ's words, taken in their own sense, import. " Forty and six years was this temple in building," reckoning all the time betwixt Cyrus's edict, or their laying the foundation, and the sixth year of Darius, wherein it was finished, after many delays, Ezek. vi. 15. Or, however their supputation hold, yet it was certainly long in building.

4. Men do mistake Christ (take his words as they will) when they measure his power by their carnal reason; for take them even in their own sense, it was not impossible for him to rear up the temple in three days, since he was God, and did undertake a greater work, even to raise up his own body from the dead.

5. Scripture doth expound itself, and what is dark in one place is cleared in another; for John doth here clear Christ's meaning, " He spake of the temple of his body."

6. Christ's body is the truth of that type of the temple; for as God did declare the temple to be his dwelling place, so in him dwelleth the fulness of the godhead bodily. As the temple was the trysting [appointed] place, where sinners found God in the mercy seat, and where he gave out his oracles, so in Christ incarnate God is to be found reconciled with sinners, and he is to be heard, revealing the Father and his mind ; and as the temple was a magnificent stately palace, yet more glorious within than in outward show, so also was Christ's body and human nature, framed by the finger of the Holy Ghost, without original corruption, and filled with excellent endowments, and the inhabitation of the godhead ; therefore is his body spoken of under the name of the type, and called " the temple of his body."

VER. 22. When therefore he was risen from the dead, his disciples remembered that he had said this unto them ; and they believed the scripture, and the word which Jesus had said.

John recordeth the use the disciples got of this conference, not presently, but after the resurrection of Christ—namely, that then this passage is brought to their remembrance, and they were confirmed in the faith of this and other scriptures, which spake of his resurrection. Whence learn—

1. Even true disciples may be such babes in knowledge that for a long time they will little understand what Christ saith ; for it was long before the disciples took up the meaning of this passage.

2. It is a mark of true disciples, that however they be ignorant, yet they will not carp at what they understand not, as enemies do, but will in silence reverence all that Christ saith ; for when the Jews quarrelled, ver. 20, we find them silent.

3. Disciples may hear that at one time, the understanding and benefit whereof may be reserved to be gotten by them at another time, and that, it may be, long thereafter ; for " When therefore he was risen from the dead, his disciples remembered that he had said this unto them," &c.

4. The doctrine of the cross, and of victory and deliverance from the same, even when it seemeth to prevail most over the sufferer, is a doctrine which disciples are slowest to learn and believe of any, because of their carnal conceptions of Christ and his kingdom, and of their discouragement when these are disappointed ; for it was " when he was risen from the dead," that the disciples remembered, and understood, and believed this doctrine as they ought. (See Luke, xxiv. 45, 46.) And thus also is the lot of his members ofttimes judged of.

5. As Christ will accomplish in due time what he hath spoken, so the event of matters, being compared with the scripture, will clear many mistakes, and be a notable confirmation to faith, and an exposition of many scriptures ; for " When he was risen," they then " remembered" and " believed" this and other scriptures.

6. The doctrine of Christ was agreeable to the scriptures, and both alike sure, it being all one to have his mind in scripture, and to have himself speaking immediately, seeing he is the author of both ; for " they believed the scripture, and the word which Jesus had said," as being both alike sure and to one purpose.

VER. 23. Now when he was in Jerusalem at the passover, in the feast day, many believed in his name, when they saw the miracles which he did.

24. But Jesus did not commit himself unto them, because he knew all men,

25. And needed not that any should testify of man : for he knew what was in man.

Lastly. In this part of the chapter John recordeth some further of Christ's proceedings at this feast, that he wrought such miracles as drew divers to profess faith in him, whose profession he would not trust, as knowing well what they were, as he doth all men, even what is most inward and secret in them, and that of himself, without any information from others. Whence learn—

1. Albeit Christ will not satisfy the curiosity or tempting humours of men, yet he will not deny to work whatsoever may be needful for the confirmation of the faith of his own ; for though he would grant no present sign to the contentious Jews, ver. 18, yet he did miracles " in Jerusalem at the passover, in the feast day," though it be not recorded in particular what they were, hereby also giving us to understand that when Christ cometh to work a work of reformation, as here, he may sometimes second it, not with miracles now, but with notable and wonderful works of providence, to gain credit to his work, and faithful instruments about it, and, it may be, to quash the fury of malicious opposites.

2. It is not unusual for some natural men to be so far affected with Christ and his working as to be convinced in their judgment of some excellency in him, and be drawn to profess some sort of embracing of him, and yet they remain still in nature and unconverted ; for " many believed in his name," or professed to do so, who yet were unsound, as the sequel cleareth.

3. It is a clear evidence of unsoundness when Christ's works are the chief thing drawing men to profess faith, and not his word, revealing his nature and properties ; for such was their faith, they believed because " they saw the miracles which he did." Such converts are not affected with their own misery and Christ's mercy, and so have not a right principle ; and Christ's works will not be always alike glorious, and so their affection bottomed on that will ebb and flow, and at last evanish.

4. As Christ no sooner begins to reform but Satan, in enemies, will be raising storms and laying snares for him, in which unsound converts will not prove trusty nor back him, but be ready to turn enemies, so it is wisdom in trying times to be wary whom we trust, even of professors ; for " Jesus did not commit himself unto them"— that is, seeing hazard appearing, he would not familiarly converse with them as men to be con-

fided in; for he kept but one Judas of such, and he betrayed him.

5. Albeit we cannot infallibly discern of professors before they discover themselves, yet Christ knoweth hypocrites before they discover themselves to men; for " he knew all men," and them among the rest, so as not to trust them.

6. Christ's discovering of one or more hypocrites is a document [admonition] to all to take heed to themselves, as being seen and known of him; therefore is his knowing them expressed in general, " He knew all men."

7. Christ's knowledge of men is not conjectural or by report, but certain, as being by and from himself as God; for " he needed not that any should testify of man."

8. Christ doth infallibly know what is inmost or most secret and hidden in man, the thought whereof should excite all to self-examination, and be an encouragement to the sincere. So much is imported in this reason, " for he knew what was in man."

CHAPTER III.

THIS chapter containeth, first, Christ's conference with Nicodemus concerning regeneration and faith in him for attaining salvation, to ver. 22; next, John's last testimony concerning Christ, some occasions whereof are recorded, to ver. 27, and the testimony itself from thence to the end.

VER. 1. There was a man of the Pharisees, named Nicodemus, a ruler of the Jews:

2. The same came to Jesus by night, and said unto him, Rabbi, we know that thou art a teacher come from God: for no man can do these miracles that thou doest, except God be with him.

The occasion of this conference and sermon of Christ is Nicodemus, a Pharisee, and not one of the common sort, but a ruler and member of the council, his coming to Christ by night, and in his discourse giving him reverent titles, and testifying that he and the rest of the Pharisees were convinced by Christ's miracles that he was a teacher sent of God, however their malice drove them over the belly of their light. Whence learn—

1. So great is the excellency of Christ, and the riches and efficacy of his grace, as he can not only convince, but will even, when he pleaseth, convert and draw in greatest enemies to him; for Nicodemus, a Pharisee and " ruler of the Jews," came to Christ, and albeit the beginnings were but small, yet they came to further maturity afterward.

2. Even persecutors and haters of Christ may be so far convinced of his excellency in his ministry as in cold blood they will be forced to see God shining in it; for saith Nicodemus, in name of his associates, the Pharisees and rulers, " Rabbi, we know that thou art a teacher come from God;" and the like thoughts may men be forced to have of his working and presence in and with good ministers, who yet have not found enough evidences of grace for all that.

3. There may be alike conviction and light in men's minds which yet doth not work alike on their will and affections; but many, who know as much as others, being left to the natural corruption of their hearts do yet sit still when these others by the power of grace are drawn to Christ; for saith Nicodemus, " we know," &c., and yet only he came to Jesus.

4. Great places, and honour, and credit, prove ofttimes great snares to men to hold them from Christ, or from such an open avowing of him as becometh; for Nicodemus " came to Jesus by night," as fearing to lose his place and reputation with the rest, or to sustain some damage, or being unwilling to be found ignorant, and one that needed come to be taught. So great cause have men to be content with their mean estate, which hideth them from many snares, and to pity and have charity to others who have greater temptations.

5. Men may seem to have very high thoughts of Christ who yet come far short of that estimation that is due to him; for all he saith is " Rabbi, thou art a teacher come from God," or an extraordinary teacher, whereas he was God over all.

6. Christ's miracles were known, even to enemies, to be done by no jugglery, and to be such as could be wrought only by divine power, and to be a proof of his authority; for it was acknowledged " no man can do these miracles that thou doest," (of which see chap. ii. 23,) " except God be with him."

VER. 3. Jesus answered and said unto him, Verily, verily, I say unto thee, Except a man be born again, he cannot see the kingdom of God.

Followeth the conference itself, and Christ's instructing of this Pharisee, wherein, first, he presseth the necessity of regeneration, ver. 3; secondly, meeting with an ignorant scholar, he repeats and explains the way of this birth, ver. 4—8; thirdly, Nicodemus, continuing yet ignorant, is rebuked for the same, and for the unbelief common to him with the rest of the Pharisees, ver. 9—12; fourthly, he leads Nicodemus up to the knowledge of himself as the only revealer of spiritual mysteries, and author of salvation through faith in him, ver. 13—15; fifthly, this way of salvation and the certainty thereof is confirmed and commended from the love of God in sending Christ for that end, ver. 16, 17; unto which is subjoined the condemnation of such as shall, by unbelief and delight in their sinful ways, reject this remedy, ver. 18, 19; proving that it is their evil deeds which makes them so to do, ver. 20, 21.

In this verse Christ begins with this Pharisee at the first principles of religion, and by a grave asseveration teacheth the necessity that all men have of a change by regeneration if they would expect to enjoy a part either in the kingdom of grace or glory, for so this " kingdom of God" may be extended to signify. It is said, Christ answered and said this to him, either because Nicodemus had moved a question concerning this matter unto him whom he had called " a teacher," ver. 2, though it be not recorded, or because Christ saw his need, and answered to it by applying fit remedies, and seeking to cure all his ills at the root.

DOCTRINES.

1. Christ is very meek to such as come to him, though with many weaknesses, and will not fail to take pains upon them to bring them further up; for though Nicodemus failed, in acknowledging him only for a teacher, and stealing to him by night, yet Christ passeth over all this, and, considering his need, doth teach him.

2. The great business of men, especially professing themselves scholars at Christ's school, should be, to know the way of salvation, and how to be in a state of grace, and in the way to glory; for so much doth Christ's grave and doubled asseveration—in pressing this point as most necessary, and his propounding the want of a part in this kingdom as a certification sad enough, whatever a man have else—teach us.

3. Every man by nature, be he in appearance better or worse, is out of the state of grace and unmeet for glory till a change be wrought. So much doth Christ gravely assert—" Verily, verily, I say unto thee, Except a man" (be who he will, an epicure, or civilian, or painted Pharisee, a gross sinner, or under the power of original and heart corruption only) " be born again, he cannot see" (or enjoy, or partake of, or, as it is ver. 5, " enter into") " the kingdom of God." And by this doctrine Christ puts this Pharisee from all conceit of himself, by discovering his danger of perishing, that so he may become teachable.

4. For working of this change in man, man's nature is not in such a condition as needs some reparation only, but is wholly corrupt; nor will a bare acknowledgment of Christ, nor a moral reformation of carriage and principles, nor common gifts and graces, serve a man's turn unless there be a change of the whole man from the state of corruption to the state of holiness, and a restoration and renovation, in some measure, of that image of God wherein he was created; for a man must be " born again," or " the second time," as Nicodemus expresseth it ver. 4, before he be right. The word rendered " again," signifieth also to be born all of new, as a man, going to build his house better, razeth it to the very bottom to lay a new foundation, and as a man beginning to declare a matter from the very original and first rise of it; and so Luke useth the word, Luke, i. 3.

5. This change and renovation is called a birth, with allusion to a man's being born of his mother, because of many resemblances betwixt the one and the other. As, 1. As a child is not born without some pain, so every true convert finds some pain, in less or more degree, in working this change; and they who find least at first may meet with more afterwards. 2. As in a birth a new creature is brought forth, so in regeneration there is (not a new substance of soul and body, but) a new nature communicated, in the renovation of the faculties of the soul and of our nature, and not a patching up of the old. 3. As in a birth there is a perfect creature brought forth in respect of parts, so regeneration goeth through the whole man, and worketh a change upon it. 4. As it is not a birth, when there is never so much pain, and yet there is nothing brought forth, so convictions, terrors, challenges of conscience, and a spirit of bondage, will not prove a man regenerate, unless the beginnings contribute to, and be followed with, the bringing forth of this new creature. 5. As in a birth the creature is brought forth living, endued with properties, inclinations, and dispositions, agreeable to the nature that begat it, so by regeneration there cometh a principle of new life, whence flow new actions, desires, comforts, and contentments, in some measure of resemblance and conformity with God. 6. As a babe new born is sensible of what is contrary to that life it hath, and is desirous of the means that may preserve that life, so every regenerate person will feel hurt from what is contrary unto grace, and will long after the means appointed for feeding of it. 7. As every born child hath an inclination to love those who are begotten of the same parents, and hath a natural inclination to multiply its kind, so regeneration leads men to love all those who bear the image of God, and to desire an enlargement and increase of Christ's family. 8. As upon the birth there ariseth a visible relation betwixt the child born and its parents, so in regeneration, beside the change of disposition, wherein progress is made by sanctification, there is a relative change of a man's state and person being ingrafted in Christ the stock, by Christ's application of himself unto him, and his apprehending of Christ by faith, whereby he becometh a Son of God through Christ.

6. This change by regeneration, as it is of the whole man, so it cannot be wrought by any power in man, but must come from above. At first man is passive, and Christ must apply himself to him before he can do anything; and what he doth afterward for carrying on this work he must do it by strength drawn from Christ apprehended by faith, after that faith is wrought in him; for so the original also beareth, " Except a man be born from above."

7. A regenerate man is not only enabled to see and discern the things of God, but is translated into the state of grace and made sure of glory, the state of grace being the porch of heaven, and grace, glory in the bud; for from Christ's assertion we may clearly gather, that a man who is " born again" shall " see the kingdom of God."

8. Such as are regenerate, and brought into the state of grace, come under a peculiar dominion of God, being not only under the external ordinances and government of his kingdom, but having a throne erected to God in their hearts, righteousness and grace reigning over the law and the curse, the love of Christ set up as a commander in them, and they abiding under the shadow of his wings and protection; and at the end of their course they enter into glory, the felicity whereof can be no better expressed to our capacity than under the similitude of a kingdom, which is the

greatest outward glory and happiness imaginable here. For these causes is the felicity of a regenerate man held forth under the name of enjoying a part in " the kingdom of God," whereby not only the state of glory is to be understood, as Acts, xiv. 22, and frequently but the external administration of the gospel, as is frequent in the gospels, (see Matt. xxi. 43,) and the state of men regenerate by the gospel, as Rom. xiv. 17, and elsewhere.

VER. 4. Nicodemus saith unto him, How can a man be born when he is old? can he enter the second time into his mother's womb, and be born?

Nicodemus, taking up Christ carnally, as if he had been speaking of a natural birth, objects against his doctrine as prescribing that which was impossible.

DOCTRINES.

1. Christ's doctrine is then rightly heard when every hearer maketh application thereof to himself, and trieth what conformity there is betwixt their way or condition and it; for so doth Nicodemus question the possibility of this doctrine in his person, " How can a man be born when he is old?" as he was.

2. Nature is so far from grace, that not only it hath it not, but is even ignorant of it, and the way of its working; for so was Nicodemus here.

3. Men may know many things in religion and yet be ignorant of the matter of soul changes, wherein common illumination, as well as nature, faileth men; for Nicodemus, a doctor, is ignorant of the matter of regeneration.

4. It is a great part of the corruption of men's judgment and cause of their ignorance, that they cast spiritual things in a carnal mould, and will not believe that for which they see not probabilities in reason; so doth Nicodemus take up regeneration, and therefore judgeth it impossible: " Can he enter the second time into his mother's womb, and be born?"

5. It ought (and to a sensible soul will) to be matter of sad affliction when men find themselves in a condition giving little or no hope of salvation; for Nicodemus's question imports a great perplexity in him, when his ignorance made him look on that as impossible which Christ told him was the only way to heaven and happiness.

6. Whatever perplexity or ignorance men have it is good to bring it out to Christ as the only remedy and way to help it; for Nicodemus goeth not away, but layeth out his case to Christ.

VER. 5. Jesus answered, Verily, verily, I say unto thee, Except a man be born of water and of the Spirit, he cannot enter into the kingdom of God.

Christ, in his answer, repeateth what he had said of the necessity of regeneration, and withal cleareth the way of it for Nicodemus's information, shewing that this birth was not natural, but spiritual, wrought by the Spirit, whose working is like unto water cleansing filth. To under-

stand this water of baptism will not agree with this place, for this water doth certainly regenerate, but every one that is baptized is not certainly regenerate, as witness Simon Magus, Acts, viii. 13, 23, and others. Further: this water is pressed as absolutely necessary to salvation, whereas men may go to heaven without baptism if it be not contemned; as of old, the elect seed of Abraham, who died in the wilderness without circumcision, were saved; so the thief on the cross was saved without baptism; therefore, as Matt. iii. 11, " the Holy Ghost and fire" signify one thing, or the Spirit working like fire in purging dross, so the " water and Spirit" signifieth the Spirit working like water. Hence it is that, ver. 6, he repeats only " the Spirit," as including all that is here signified by the " water and Spirit;" and this expressing of the Spirit's working, under the name of water, is no unusual expression in the Old Testament, Isa. xliv. 3; Ezek. xxxvi. 25.

DOCTRINES.

1. No apprehension of impossibility in the matter of regeneration doth warrant men to shift the thoughts of the necessity of it, or to think that any less than regeneration will avail them to salvation; for Christ, notwithstanding Nicodemus's doubt, presseth it as necessary, and gravely interposeth his authority (whom Nicodemus acknowledged for a teacher come from God) to persuade him of it: " Verily, verily, I say unto thee, Except a man be born of water and of the Spirit, he cannot enter into the kingdom of God."

2. As Christ is meek and tender unto such as bring their doubts and ignorance unto him, (and therefore informeth Nicodemus,) so men's questioning of truth, and their propounding of doubts against it, is an occasion that Christ makes use of for clearing of truth yet more, for he taketh occasion of Nicodemus's doubt to clear the doctrine of regeneration.

3. Regeneration is wrought neither by the power of nature, nor by outward ordinances only and alone, but by the efficacy of the Holy Spirit, who doth prevent the sinner, and bless outward means to him, before he can be changed; for a man is " born of the Spirit."

4. The Spirit, in working this change of regeneration, worketh like water; for as water cleanseth what is filthy, and makes it bright, so the Spirit doth apply the blood of Christ for cleansing polluted nature, and renewing of it in true holiness; as water cooleth and refresheth the thirsty and faint-hearted, so the benefits purchased by Christ being applied by the Spirit, do refresh the fainting souls of sinners in the perplexities and pangs of the new birth, or afterward, Ps. xlii. 1; and as water fructifieth the barren ground, so the Spirit maketh the regenerate man fruitful in every good word and work; therefore is this birth described to be a man's being " born of water and of the Spirit."

VER. 6. That which is born of the flesh is flesh; and that which is born of the Spirit is spirit.

Christ subjoineth a reason of the necessity of regeneration for attaining salvation, and the certainty of the regenerate man's salvation; because men by nature are corrupt and opposite unto that kingdom, and a renewed nature is made suitable to it. Whence learn—

1. The corruption of men's nature, being well seen, would soon discover the necessity of a change by regeneration, and none will slight this but they who are ignorant of the former; therefore doth Christ, upon this ground, press the necessity of a new birth.

2. Men by nature, or by their natural birth, are altogether corrupt and fleshly creatures, in all the powers and faculties of soul and body, for he "that is born of the flesh is flesh," or one lump of corruption, "flesh" being taken here for corrupt nature, and so including not outward and fleshly sins only, but even the corruption of the mind also, as Gal. v. 19—21.

3. The corruption of men's nature is transmitted by generation and propagation from their parents, and so is the seed of actual transgressions before they break forth; and (however children of church members be born federally holy and in visible covenant, 1 Cor. vii. 14, yet) every one who cometh of Adam in the ordinary way of generation is infected with it, for "that which is born of the flesh," or of corrupt man, "is flesh."

4. Whatever dignity men may be born to, yet all that we can claim by our natural birth is, that by it we are secluded from heaven, for our condition by nature is held forth as a reason why we must be regenerate before we enter into the kingdom of God.

5. The corruption by our natural birth, and our unfitness for heaven thereby, is, to the Lord's own, cured and made up by the spirit of regeneration, for therefore is it subjoined, "That which is born of the Spirit is spirit."

6. A true evidence of regeneration, and of men's being fitted for heaven by it, is when men become spiritual in disposition, senses, and discerning, motions and inclinations, and in actions, leaving a stamp of their dispositions even upon their common actions; and when they labour not only to have habits of grace, but to have the spirit of these graces, or the daily influences of the Spirit, to make them lively, fresh, and active; for "that which is born of the Spirit is spirit," not by a change of substance, but as is before explained.

VER. 7. Marvel not that I said unto thee, Ye must be born again.

8. The wind bloweth where it listeth, and thou hearest the sound thereof, but canst not tell whence it cometh, and whither it goeth: so is every one that is born of the Spirit.

Christ seeing Nicodemus at a stand, and marvelling at that which he was saying of this new birth as at a thing impossible, he forbids him to marvel; and by a similitude taken from the wind he cleareth the matter yet more, and sheweth that it is nothing the less true that he could not comprehend the way of it; for as the wind bloweth freely, and at the command of no creature, and as the sound and effects thereof prove that it is, and yet men's reason cannot reach to know from whence it ariseth and whither it goeth, or

from how far it cometh and how far it goeth, seeing at the same time there are contrary winds in several places of the earth, so in this spiritual birth and change, wherein the Spirit worketh freely and efficaciously, it may be sensibly found by effects, although the manner and way how it is wrought be incomprehensible.

DOCTRINES.

1. Albeit God's works, and particularly in regeneration, be glorious and excellent, at which faith may far more wonder than at a man's conception in the womb, Ps. cxxxix. 14, yet Christ condemneth that wondering as sinful which floweth from unbelief, and from men's counting that impossible which they cannot comprehend; therefore Christ forbids such wondering—"Marvel not that I said unto thee," &c., when yet he holds out the thing as incomprehensible. So excellent is the nature of faith, that it maketh that to be a commendable duty which were sinful if coming from unbelief.

2. Albeit all men, even the greatest doctors, lie under a necessity of being regenerated if they would be saved, yet Christ is excluded from that number, being sanctified in his conception by the Holy Ghost, and born without sin; therefore he secludeth himself here, and includeth Nicodemus and all others when he saith, "Ye must be born again."

3. By the fall of Adam, man's understanding falleth short even in comprehending natural things, and there are depths in nature, and even in things most obvious to sense, wherein natural light doth fail; so it is said here of the wind—thou "canst not tell whence it cometh, and whither it goeth." And by many questions about such things is Job put to a nonplus, Job, xxxviii. and xxxix.

4. Good use may be made of common and obvious things to further spiritual-mindedness and to help to satisfy us and quiet our reasonings in spiritual things; for Christ by this similitude casteth a copy to all, to be led by thoughts of the wind to think on regeneration, and silenceth his wondering by making his common sense and reason about the wind subservient to quiet his faith about this mystery; and by the consideration of such things as these God bringeth Job to dust and ashes before him.

5. The Spirit's working is compared to wind, not only here, and in that extraordinary pouring out of the Spirit, Acts, ii. 1, 2, but Cant. iv. 16; not only because the Spirit and wind have one name in the original languages of the scriptures, but because of many things wherein the one resembleth the other; and in the text (to go no further) we have these: 1. As the wind bloweth through the world freely, not staying for the command, nor caring for the prohibition, of any creature, so the Spirit, in his working, is a free agent, working where, on whom, when, and in what measure he pleaseth, and will be hindered by none—"the wind bloweth where it listeth." 2. As there is somewhat in the wind which is sensible, and felt, or heard, proving that it is, "thou hearest the sound thereof," so is the working of the Spirit discernible in the effects by them that have it; only as the wind is not always

alike loud, nor sensible, so the working of the Spirit is not always, nor in all alike discernible; and as they who hear the wind must have the sense of hearing clear, so men who desire to feel the effects of the Spirit would not overcloud their own discerning with jealousies and misrepresentations; and withal it would be considered that the Spirit is one gift, and discerning of him and his working is another gift, (1 Cor. ii. 12,) to be sought of him, or else we may mistake. Likewise this discerning faculty may sometime be kept up where the true work is, either for trial, that we may not build ourselves on what is within us, but on Christ; or for chastisement, because we have grieved the Spirit. There may also be some babes in Christ who cannot for a time discern their own members, though they really have them. 3. As there is somewhat in the wind incomprehensible to natural reason—" thou canst not tell whence it cometh," &c.—so in the Spirit's working there is somewhat not only beyond the reach of natural reason, 1 Cor. ii. 14, but even above sanctified reason, as to know how he insinuates himself with the Word upon us, and frameth that hidden man of grace. There are mysteries here to be adored, and calling for praise that he should work so admirably in us, rather than to be pried into. In all these respects is this comparison of the wind applied—" So is every one that is born of the Spirit."

VER. 9. Nicodemus answered and said unto him, How can these things be?

10. Jesus answered and said unto him, Art thou a master of Israel, and knowest not these things?

Nicodemus continuing in his ignorance, notwithstanding all this pains, is reproved for it by Christ, as being a shame for a man of his calling to be ignorant of such truths, which were so necessary and clear. Whence learn—

1. When divine truths are told in plainest terms, and as fitted as can be to vulgar capacities, yet they will be still obscure to a natural mind; for Nicodemus is yet ignorant, when Christ hath illustrated the matter; much more may men be ignorant when others teach.

2. The great cause of men's ignorance of divine things is, their carnal reason, which (especially in able men) keeps them from simple believing and resting on what is revealed, till they see a reason for everything; for this is Nicodemus's constant objection, " How can these things be?"

3. This carnal reason is not easily beat down, nor will any external means or speaking (though even by Christ) do it, till some more powerful means be added; for after all this pains to solve that doubt when it was first propounded, ver. 4, it sticks to him yet.

4. Where Christ hath taken pains in teaching, and men do not profit, there he will sharply rebuke this, being one mean to stir up men to make progress in his school; therefore doth he thus reprehend Nicodemus, though more mildly than he dealt with other Pharisees.

5. A special mean of humbling men (especially such as have parts) and making them more capable of Christ's instruction, is to convince them of their gross ignorance; for knowledge is that whereby men differ from beasts, and therefore to see the want of that will lay their pride, Ps. lxxiii. 22; and conceit of knowledge doth puff up men, till they be discovered what they are, 1 Cor. viii. 1, 2; therefore doth Christ discover to Nicodemus, whose carnal reason and parts made him stand out, that he is an ignorant, and knoweth not. (See Prov. xxx. 2, 3.)

6. Every man, as he hath a calling and station in church or commonwealth, ought to be answerable unto it, and have endowments suitable; for Christ from his place argueth that he ought to have been been better acquainted with these things.

7. Men may have great learning, and be teachers of the church, and yet be ignorant of the sound principles of religion and regeneration, not only in an experimental, but even in a contemplative way, when a church is fallen in apostasy, and the matter of trying such is neglected, and especially where superstitious observances come in the room of the sound exercises of religion; for in this declining church, where traditions and superstitious rites prevailed, a master of Israel " knoweth not these things "

8. It is a great sin and shame of teachers to be found ignorant, who should have knowledge to instruct others, especially in the sound principles of religion; for, saith he, " Art thou a master of Israel, and knowest not these things?"

9. The more clearly truths be revealed, and the more weighty they be in themselves, men's ignorance is the more blameworthy; for, saith he, " Knowest thou not these things ?"—the very principles and fundamentals of religion, and which were revealed to Israel, among whom thou art a master. That they were of old revealed, appeareth from Deut. xxx. 6 ; Ps. li. 10; Jer. xxxi. 33 ; Ezek. xi. 19 ; xxxvi. 25, 26, and elsewhere.

VER. 11. Verily, verily, I say unto thee, We speak that we do know, and testify that we have seen; and ye receive not our witness.

In the next place, Christ reproveth his unbelief accompanying his ignorance, which was common to him with the rest of the Jews, especially the Pharisees. This he doth upon two grounds, whereof the first (in this verse) is taken from the assurance he had of the certainty of his doctrine, it being perfectly known as by eyesight. This way of certainty, by seeing, is attributed to Christ, ver. 32, as proper to him who was in the bosom of the Father; and taking it thus strictly, while Christ saith, " We have seen," it may be understood of the whole Trinity bearing witness with him, John, viii. 16, 29 ; 1 John, v. 7. But taking this seeing more largely, the expression seemeth rather to take in John the Baptist, who was the present public witness with Christ at that time, and who, as others, prophets and apostles, had the certainty of what he preached in his own measure, from Christ's illumination, and did indeed preach what was most certain, and what Christ revealed out of the bosom of the Father, though few did believe and embrace either Christ's testimony or his.

DOCTRINES.

1. Where Christ hath men to reprove for ignorance, there will be also unbelief found that is blameworthy; for not only cannot ignorant men believe, but in many things men are bound to embrace truth by faith, though they cannot comprehend them by natural reason, and so unbelief is the cause of not closing with these high mysteries; therefore doth Christ challenge Nicodemus for not receiving the witness, or not embracing this truth by faith, resting on the authority of God the Revealer.

2. Ill scholars that come to Christ may be led back to see more of their misery, common to them with others, that so they may not rest on anything they think peculiar in themselves, but be stirred up effectually to study to profit; therefore doth Christ shew Nicodemus that he was lying yet in the common sin of others—" Ye receive not," &c.

3. Whatever mistakes men have about spiritual truths, yet they are infallibly certain in themselves, and infallibly known to Christ, who revealed them out of the bosom of the Father, as the sure ground of our faith, and that he cannot mislead such as he teacheth; therefore doth Christ so gravely assert and inculcate this principle—" Verily, verily, I say unto thee, we speak that we do know, and testify that we have seen." The latter word explains the former, that he is as certain of it as of a thing seen, though not with bodily eyes.

4. Such is Christ's condescendence, as to take in sinful men with him in the same yoke of bearing witness to the truth, and of partaking in their measure in the same honour with him, the chief Shepherd, and of holding out the same infallible truth with him from the word, though their persuasion and certainty of it be from his gift, and inferior to his; therefore, saith he, " We speak," &c., John being a conjunct witness, speaking the same sure truth, and knowing it certainly in his measure, though Christ knew it in a higher way, both as God of himself, and as man by virtue of the personal union.

5. As it is no strange thing to see men (however they may hear, yet) not liking, embracing, nor believing most certain and saving truths, even when spoken by Christ himself, so the certainty of divine doctrine will aggreage [aggravate] the sin of unbelief; for, saith he, " We speak that we do know, &c., and ye receive not our witness." His doctrine is called a testifying and witness, as being both certain in itself, such as solemn depositions of faithful men are, and a standing testimony against them who believe it not.

VER. 12. If I have told you earthly things, and ye believe not, how shall ye believe, if I tell you of heavenly things?

The second ground upon which Christ reproveth and aggreageth [aggravateth] his unbelief is, the plainness of his doctrine. Christ had spoken of heavenly things in a plain way, under a similitude taken from earthly things, as ver. 8, and if he did not comprehend and believe them so, what would he do if they had been spoken of as heavenly things, in a style suitable to their own nature.

DOCTRINES.

1. It is the will of Christ that teachers of souls do not affect high and lofty styles, and quaintness of expression, but that in doctrine they descend as low as may be, and accommodate themselves to the capacity of people; for herein Christ commends his own love in drawing the copy—" I have told you earthly things."

2. Even spiritual things, when they are spoken of under earthly similitudes, are but earthly things in comparison of what they would be, being spoken of in their own language and terms; therefore he calleth them, being so expressed, " earthly things," in comparison of " heavenly things," expressed in a suitable style. There is an eminency in these things above what any similitude can express, and when we come to know as we are known, we will find it so.

3. When all is done that can be to bring down spiritual things to a people's capacity, yet there is no power in men of themselves to understand or close with them; for Christ found it so—" I have told you earthly things, and ye believe not;" and ministers need not think it strange if their doctrine be no better entertained than Christ's was.

4. The plainness of doctrine doth aggreage [aggravate] the sin of ignorance and unbelief, and make it more inexcusable; for it is a challenge—" I have told you earthly things, and ye believe not," &c.

5. Such as are rightly convinced of their dullness in taking up spiritual things, when plainly expressed, will much more see their inability to take up these things in their own nature; and, however, this will stand as a witness how far men are from knowledge or closing with spiritual things; for so doth Christ hold out—" If I have told you earthly things, and ye believe not, how shall ye believe, if I tell you of heavenly things?"

VER. 13. And no man hath ascended up to heaven, but he that came down from heaven, even the Son of man which is in heaven.

If we understand these words properly, of ascending to heaven and enjoying eternal felicity, it doth indeed hold good that only Christ entereth there by his own virtue, and all others only through and by him; and so the scope of this verse will be the same with ver. 14, 15, of which in its own place. But the dependence on the former purpose, and the expression of this in the by-past time, whereas Christ was not yet ascended in his human nature, leads us rather to understand this ascending to heaven figuratively, of comprehending heavenly mysteries, and entering on God's council concerning the way of salvation, as it seemeth to be understood, Romans, x. 6, 8, with Deut. xxx. 11, 12, 14. And so the meaning is, that no man of himself can know or take up these things, that being Christ's prerogative, who manifested himself from the bosom of the Father, in our nature, and yet as God is still in heaven; and thus Christ, having reproved Nicodemus for his ignorance, doth yet shew the remedy thereof in himself. Whence learn—

1. Christ's sharp word is not his last word to his own, but when he hath challenged most sharply for any fault, he is willing to offer himself, the only remedy, to cure it; for so doth he deal with Nicodemus's ignorance.

2. It is alike impossible for men, by their own parts and natural endowments, to take up and comprehend spiritual mysteries, as to climb up to heaven and enter upon God's council; therefore is it called an ascending up to heaven.

3. In so far as sinners come to a true and saving knowledge of heavenly mysteries, they are in a sort transported up to heaven from off the earth, as knowing the counsels of God, and being ravished with what they know; therefore also is it called an ascending to heaven. If Capernaum were exalted to heaven, Matt. xi. 23, because of the offer of these things, what are they who in some measure comprehend and embrace them?

4. It is proper to Christ the Mediator only, in some sense, to ascend to heaven, and comprehend spiritual mysteries, both for the measure and degree of knowledge in these things, which, as God, is infinite, and as man, is large as the human nature is capable of, and for the kind and manner of knowledge, which, as God, is of himself, and as man, by virtue of the personal union, whereas all others who have any knowledge they have it from him; for "no man hath ascended up to heaven," (or comprehended these things fully, or of themselves,) "but he that came down from heaven."

5. The Son of God in the bosom of the Father was pleased to condescend so far as to manifest himself unto the world in our nature, that so he might in our nature understand heavenly mysteries, and communicate the knowledge thereof to his people; therefore it is marked as the ground of his ascending to heaven, or comprehending of these things for his people's use, that he "came down from heaven, the Son of man," hereby shewing that his abasing of himself did exalt him as Mediator, God-man, to that dignity, to be the storehouse of wisdom and knowledge to his people; and that his love in stooping so low to bring and communicate knowledge to us is remarkable;—in all which we are not to understand that Christ, as God, did change place by his incarnation, but only did stoop and demit himself to assume the human nature in a personal union.

6. Christ, by his incarnation and becoming man, did not cease to be God, but continueth still the same, filling heaven and earth; for he that descended down from heaven, is in heaven, and so is upon the counsel of God still, to teach us infallibly.

7. The Son of God hath assumed the human nature into so strict a personal union, that what is proper to either nature is ascribed unto the person under whatsoever name; for, saith he, "the Son of man which is in heaven," which is not to be understood, as if either his human nature came from heaven (for he is speaking of what still is there) or that his human nature were in every place, but that the same person who is the Son of man according to our nature is in heaven according to his divine nature, and yet but one person still. And hereby Christ sheweth his love to our nature, that under that name he ascribeth what is proper to his godhead, to himself.

Ver. 14. And as Moses lifted up the serpent in the wilderness, even so must the Son of man be lifted up:

15. That whosoever believeth in him should not perish, but have eternal life.

Christ here pointeth out himself as the Saviour of sinners, having sufficient virtue to cure the sinfulness and misery of such as flee to him by faith, and to keep them from perishing, and save them; this he doth under the type of the brazen serpent lifted up in the wilderness at God's command, for curing of the Israelites bitten with the fiery serpents, Numbers, xxi. 6—9. Christ, by subjoining this to the doctrine of regeneration, doth partly teach Nicodemus the way of attaining regeneration, which is by the Spirit's applying of the merit and virtue of Christ's death in the first act thereof, and by the regenerate man's applying the same by faith, for carrying on that work, to cure themselves perfectly; and partly he teacheth him that regenerate men are not to rest on anything in them, but must be led out of themselves to Christ for attaining salvation.

DOCTRINES.

1. Truly regenerate men, and such as are minding that work in earnest, will see great cause and need to make much use of Christ; for so much doth this doctrine and the dependence thereof teach.

2. Christ, and the use to be made of him, was pointed out to believers under the Old Testament by types and figures, which, as it should sweeten unto us the reading of these things, so it should point out our mercy, that we have not such dark and long prospects through which only they could look to him, but we may see him more clearly; for Christ sheweth here that he was typified by the lifted-up serpent.

3. It is our duty to dip in the application of this and the like types, till we find the agreement that is betwixt the truth and the type; for so doth Christ cast us a copy in the explication of this type, wherein we may see — first, they agree in the original occasion; as Israel's deadly misery occasioned the setting up of the serpent, so the occasion of Christ's sending into the world was man's sin and misery, man being so bitten with that old serpent that the venom is gone through him all, and he become liable to intolerable pain, if his conscience were not lulled asleep. Secondly, they agree in the impulsive cause; that as the serpent was a remedy of God's own prescribing, out of his great mercy, so is this remedy for lost sinners. Thirdly, they agree in their present condition when they were made use of; for as the serpent was like that which bit them, so was Christ true man, the second Adam, answering to him by whom sin came into the world; as

this serpent was without venom, so was he without sin; as the serpent was made of brass, and not of gold, so appeared he not in glorious state, nor majesty; and as the serpent was a very unlikely mean in itself, so they needed clear eyes who would see salvation coming by a suffering Lord, by a worm and not a man. Fourthly, they agree in the use to be made of them, and in the fruits that follow thereupon; and so—1. As the serpent was " lifted up" on a pole at God's command, that the offer of this remedy might be made conspicuous unto all Israel, so Christ, in regard of God's decree and sentence against sin, and in regard of predictions concerning him, " must be lifted up" on the cross, and be broken there, that this ointment might be let out for our cure; and he is made conspicuous to the church on the pole of the gospel, that faith may get footing on the offer made of him. 2. As the way of cure by the serpent was a look, so it is believing in him, and laying hold on him by faith, that only bringeth cure of the guilt of sin, of the pain of conscience through sin, and of the dominion of sin. 3. As it was ground enough for any bitten Israelite to look to this serpent, that he had need and thirsted for cure by this appointed mean, so a felt sense of sin is a warrant sufficient for sinners to lay hold on Christ, the offered remedy. 4. As a simple look, though at a great distance, and in some with weaker eyes, brought cure to them who were bitten, whatever they were, so a weak act of true faith, and at a great distance, will cure the bitten sinner without exception : " Whosoever believeth," and though his faith were never so weak, if it be faith. 5. As this look healed the bitten Israelite, and kept him from death, so though all men are in a state of perishing, and secluded from heaven without Christ, yet by faith in him sinners are freed from death, and made heirs of life; they shall " not perish, but have eternal life," and this includeth remission, reconciliation, perseverance, and all the means leading to these ends, and is a benefit far beyond what an Israelite got by looking to the serpent.

VER. 16. For God so loved the world, that he gave his only begotten Son, that whosoever believeth in him should not perish, but have everlasting life.

Christ insisteth to point out himself to Nicodemus as the author of eternal life, and to confirm and illustrate the former doctrine, as the particle " for" importeth. And here the benefit of giving him unto the world is commended from the free love of God contriving such a way of the salvation of lost sinners; and the certainty of sinner's salvation through faith in him is confirmed from this—that it is God's very end in sending him, that believers should not perish. Whence learn—

1. The world of itself is liable to perdition, and under sinfulness and misery, from which there is no deliverance but by Christ the Son of God only, for so it is here implied.

2. This way of man's deliverance is not to be ascribed to anything in man procuring the same, for God might justly have damned all, but to the free love of God only; for so are we here taught.

3. Love to lost man is not to be looked upon as shining in Christ only, who willingly gave himself to redeem him, but in the Father also, who, loving lost man, sent his Son to suffer and do the office of a Mediator, that through his mediation he might, not begin to love them, but communicate the effects of his love in a way agreeable to his justice; for " God loved the world," and that antecedently to his giving Christ, and as a cause of it.

4. This love, being rightly studied, will be found matchless and inexpressible, and so will all think of it who are sensible of an interest in it, and of the fruits of it. " God so loved the world." (See 1 John, iii. 1.)

5. The matchlessness of this love may appear if we consider—1. The person who loveth, even God, who was provoked by man, and who standeth in no need of man, or of anything, to add to his infinite happiness : " God loved." 2. The object loved, which is, " the world," whereby we are not to understand all and every man, (for that were to make God be disappointed of his will, and of what he intends towards man out of his love, seeing all get not good of Christ, and to have him giving Christ for them for whom he will not sanctify himself nor intercede, John, xvii. 9, 19,) but only his own in the world among lost mankind, who are not only gathered from among all nations and conditions of men in the world, and not of the Jews only, (as " the world" is taken, 1 John, ii. 2 ; See John, xi. 51, 52 ; Rom. iii. 29 ;) and who (as there is a community or world of the reprobates as distinguished from the elect, John, xvii. 9, so they) make up a world or community of themselves, 2 Cor. v. 19 ; John, vi. 33 ; but they are by nature the same that others of the world are, of the same race of cursed mankind, and not only living in the world, but after the fashions of the world; and herein shineth the matchless love of God, that he would not so far abandon lost mankind but he would have a new and holy community to himself from among them, and would love those who had nothing loveworthy in themselves more than they who were left in their miserable estate. 3. This matchless love appeareth in the effects or gift bestowed by it, even the Father's only Son, by eternal generation and communication of the same essence, to be a ransom and Mediator for sinners : " God so loved the world, that he gave his only begotten Son." This gift and an interest in it speaketh more love than any other benefit a man can receive, 1 John, iv. 9, and assureth of all other things in so far as they tend to the man's good, Rom. viii. 32.

6. The way whereby benefit is reaped and gotten from this gifted Saviour is only by faith, whereby a man, being put out of himself and seeing himself in the same condition with the lost world, doth flee to Christ, the only remedy, and roll himself upon him as a sufficient Saviour; for it is " he that believeth in him" that " shall not perish." Albeit a self-condemned sinner have not a particular assurance of an interest in Christ, yet he believeth when he casteth himself upon him on all hazards; and albeit he miss

many other qualifications, yet he is not to stand back, but to come to Christ to get what he wanteth.

7. Albeit Christ be given only to the elect, yet unto the visible church the offer is held out generally upon condition of faith, whereby reprobates are left inexcusable through their voluntary rejecting this mercy, and the elect, through God's blessing on these offers and exhortations, are brought in in a way agreeable to their nature as rational creatures; therefore is this gift and offer spoken of indefinitely, " that whosoever believeth should not perish;" otherwise, to say that this indefinite offer is the sum of God's purpose and will revealed in scripture concerning sinners' salvation, is not only repugnant to scripture, speaking of particular election and of the giving of some to Christ, and of working faith in them, but is injurious to God's perfection, in ascribing such confused and indistinct thoughts to him as a general decree, which may consist with the saving of all or of none.

8. Such as come to Christ, the Lord maketh no exception of what they have been, nor of the degrees of their faith, if it be true; for " whosoever believeth shall not perish."

9. Every believer in Christ is not only delivered from perishing by Christ's underlying wrath for him, but is stated in a right unto eternal felicity, which he shall certainly attain; for he shall " not perish, but have everlasting life"—to wit, here, in the pledge and bud, and hereafter, in full enjoyment.

10. The felicity purchased by Christ to believers is such as only deserveth the name of life, all other life being but as death in comparison of it, and it will be eternally and without end such; therefore it is called " everlasting life."

Ver. 17. For God sent not his Son into the world to condemn the world; but that the world through him might be saved.

To confirm the certainty of believers' salvation, Christ insisteth yet upon the end of God's sending him in the flesh, which was not to condemn the world, but for the salvation of the world through him. If we understand this of God's intention in sending Christ into the world, then " the world," in the last two sentences, must be understood only of the elect of Jew and gentiles, as ver. 16, and 1 John, iv. 14, for whose salvation and deliverance from condemnation Christ came into the world; but if we look to the nature of the work which Christ was sent to do, it may be taken more largely for men in the world indefinitely; for not only Christ in his first coming came not to judge and sentence any, but to hold out the way of life as a meek Saviour and Mediator, as Luke, ix. 55, 56; John, xii. 47, but nothing he did then was to procure condemnation to any, but, on the contrary, to make offer of salvation to lost man, though accidentally, by reason of man's corruption, and not making use of him, his coming did heighten men's condemnation, as ver. 18, 19.

1. It is a lesson we are negligent in taking up, yet a lesson wherein Christ would have us well versed and rooted, to know the sure and happy condition of those who believe in him, that we may be stirred up to study to partake thereof; therefore doth he so much inculcate the certain advantage to be had thereby.

2. In the matter of man's redemption, the Son of God was pleased to demit himself in our nature to be the Father's servant and ambassador, that we may be assured of the Father's being well pleased with what he doth; for so much are we taught in that " God sent his Son." (See Matt. iii. 17.)

3. It pleased the Son of God, at the Father's appointment, to cast a veil upon his glory, by appearing on earth in our nature, and to converse among men, and endure all their contradiction and enmity, that he might finish the work given him to do; for he was sent "into the world," which is to be understood here of the habitable world and of men in it, and savouring of it; and this commendeth his love, that at his Father's appointment he came willingly among such.

4. It is as certain that believers shall be saved as it is certain God cannot be frustrated of his end in sending his Son into the world; therefore it is subjoined, as a reason of that, ver. 16, believers shall not perish, &c., " for God sent not his Son into the world to condemn the world," &c.; yea, his not sending his Son to condemn, as he might have done, is a clear evidence of his willingness to save believers.

5. Such as are Christ's own, of Jew and gentile, through the habitable world, who fly to him by faith, whatever they be, or whatever they meet with, yet may be sure of salvation, and not to be condemned, having a Saviour sent to them to free them from wrath and work out their salvation by his merit and efficacy; and in this they may glory over all difficulties, and say, " God sent not his Son to condemn the world," &c.

6. Albeit Christ may be eventually for the falling of many, and his coming will afford sad matter of ditray [condemnation] against them, yet all the blame of this lieth upon themselves, who stumble at the rock they should build themselves upon, who reject their own mercy by offer, and by opposition thereunto do harden and blind themselves. So much also do these words teach, being understood of the nature of his work and carriage, as is above explained.

Ver. 18. He that believeth on him is not condemned: but he that believeth not is condemned already, because he hath not believed in the name of the only begotten Son of God.

Christ goeth on to clear and illustrate the certainty of the salvation of believers in him, by shewing, on the contrary, the condemnation on unbelievers, whom he declareth to be under a double condemnation, one by the law and another by the gospel; every unbeliever is condemned already by the sentence of the law, which they lie still under, and have it confirmed by the gospel, since they do not by faith lay hold on the offered and only remedy for their liberation. Whence learn—

1. Albeit Christ came into the world to save his own, yet he actually saveth none but such as he giveth faith unto, whereby they renounce themselves, and close first with him, and then with all the promises in him; and this is the method wherein he deals with all his elect; for it is " he that believeth on him" that " is not condemned."

2. However believers in Christ deserve condemnation of themselves, as having many things condemnable in them, and however the law may accuse and trouble them, yet they are freed from actual condemnation; for " he that believeth on him is not condemned."

3. Believers are not only freed from condemnation in the life to come, but immediately upon the exercise of faith a sentence absolvitory is passed, which standeth firm till the last day, wherein it shall be solemnly declared; for " he that believeth is not condemned" in the present time.

4. Albeit such as flee to Christ, and expect not to be condemned, ought to study holiness, without which no man will see God; yet the condition required for reversing the sentence and absolving the self-condemned sinner is only faith put in exercise, as laying hold on Christ's righteousness, which alone can answer the law, and endureth constantly, whereas our holiness is imperfect and variable, like the moon; therefore it is " he that believeth on him," or hath faith in exercise, not in the habit only, that " is not condemned."

5. Every unbeliever (such as all by nature are) hath the sentence of condemnation already passed against him by the law, under which he lieth, having only the thread of his life betwixt him and full execution of it; therefore it is said, " he that believeth not is condemned already." The sentence of the law standeth, since he hath not come to Christ to get it repealed. (See Rom. ii. 9; Gal. iii. 10.)

6. Albeit the sentence of the law be sufficient to condemn mankind, and will condemn all them who have not heard of Christ, yet, under the gospel, unbelief and not receiving of Christ is the great condemning sin; for as no sin will condemn the man who fleeth to Christ, the remedy, so when the remedy is not embraced, the sentence of the law is ratified in the gospel and court of mercy; for " he that believeth not is condemned, because he hath not believed." The sentence is declared just, and confirmed by a new sentence, since he will not take help, and thus unbelief is the great unpardonable sin, Mark, xvi. 16; whereas other sins (that against the Holy Ghost excepted, because it is joined with final impenitency) would be pardoned if men would believe.

7. It aggreageth [aggravateth] the sin of unbelief that the sinner rejecteth so excellent a one as Christ, whose excellency proveth him an all-sufficient Saviour, and who is so clearly manifested to be so; or if he pretend to believe, yet he doth not take up Christ as he is revealed in the word, nor groundeth his faith on the word, nor followeth the order prescribed therein, but taketh up a Christ according to his fancy, and taketh a dream for faith; for " he hath not believed in the only begotten Son of God," nor in his name, whereby he is clearly revealed, nor according to it.

VER. 19. And this is the condemnation, that light is come into the world, and men loved darkness rather than light, because their deeds were evil.

Christ insisteth on the second cause of sinners' condemnation, which is, their slighting of the offer of mercy in the gospel. And beside what was intimated in the former verse, of the ratifying of the law's sentence upon their not embracing the remedy, he addeth the heavy condemnation that it brings on men, while they not only embrace not, but do contemn, the remedy of misery, and delight rather in their own ways; and withal he sheweth the reasons of this, which are, men's evil deeds.

DOCTRINES.

1. The world without Christ lieth in darkness, void of spiritual light, and full of errors and of the works of darkness; God is withdrawn from the creatures, and they wander and stumble (as in the dark) upon Satan's snares; their case is void of true peace and comfort, as men in a dark pit; their way tends to utter darkness; and yet, as men in the dark, their case and misery is not discerned in its own colours; for, in opposition to all this, it is said " that light is come into the world" by Christ's being manifested in the gospel.

2. Christ offered in the gospel hath brought a remedy for all sin and misery, bringing light to discover men's case in its true colours, light to dispel the darkness of errors and the vileness of sinful lusts, light for direction, and light of comfort to make things pleasant and comfortable, upon solid grounds of reconciliation; for " light is come into the world."

3. Where Christ manifesteth himself, men will not so easily be drawn from their woful condition but their old darkness will be suiting their hearts to hold the grip it hath, as well as the light suiteth for entrance; for their loving the one more than the other supposeth that both come in competition to their choice.

4. Such is the perversity of men's nature as not only not to embrace Christ, offering himself, but to love their woful condition far beyond the offered remedy; to like to abide in darkness rather than to see their misery or need of him, and to like their own deluded peace better than to follow after his true comforts; for " men loved darkness rather than light."

5. Where Christ, offering himself in the gospel, is not received in love, but contemned, it bringeth sadder condemnation than the breaking of the law, as being a sinning against the remedy, and that with a high hand, an undervaluing of him, and doing of what they can to make void his pains; for " this is the condemnation, that light is come into the world," &c.

6. Men's living in ill works is an evidence of their rejecting Christ, it being evil deeds that makes light hateful to men; for " men loved darkness rather than light, because their deeds were evil;" their love to their evil ways maketh

them hate this light, as it is discovering, and so they go no further, nor attain to the refreshing light of it, and maketh them that they cannot quit their lusts and come under Christ's yoke.

VER. 20. For every one that doeth evil hateth the light, neither cometh to the light, lest his deeds should be reproved.

21. But he that doeth truth cometh to the light, that his deeds may be made manifest, that they are wrought in God.

Christ proveth that it is men's ill deeds which causeth them to hate the light, from two general positions; the first whereof (being a proverbial sentence, and holding true both in natural and spiritual light) sheweth, that evil doers hate the light lest it should discover them; and the second, that the godly, on the contrary, delight to have their ways tried and made manifest by this light. Whence learn—

1. Whoever is yet in nature, and on whom Christ hath not shined with the renewing light of the gospel, is an evil-doer, not only in a legal sense, (as all have sinned, and the godly do sin daily,) but habitually; it is his course, study, and endeavour to do that which displeaseth God, and this study of doing evil is the air he breathes in: such is he who "doeth evil."

2. The gospel hath not only a refreshing light to comfort sinners in the due order, but a reproving and discovering light, which (however men will stand as long as they are able in the defence of their own righteousness, yet) will convince and discover them to themselves; for this is the light here spoken of, which reproveth or discovereth, or (as the word is) argueth and convinceth men to be what they are; and, albeit nature will discover some gross sins, yet men's self-righteousness, the emptiness of moral civility, &c., must be of the word's discovering; and albeit the law, which is spiritual, discover these also, yet it is ascribed to the gospel in this challenge, because it aggravateth these sins so much the more that the gospel discovereth them, with the offer of a remedy.

3. The great plea betwixt Christ and sinners in the gospel is about this reproving light's getting place, and about men's being discovered to themselves, as being the first lesson where the most part of men stick, and so get no more; for they hate the light and come not to it.

4. As in the matter of natural light evil doers wait for the dark, Job, xxiv. 15, so it is a mark of evil-doers that they hate the spiritual light, and shun all means of searching and knowing themselves, as wishing such things were not sin, not desiring to know them to be so, and wishing there were not a God to punish them; for " every one that doeth evil hateth the light."

5. All those who do not (out of jealousy over themselves) come to the word with a desire to be discovered to themselves, but desire to hear what may flatter them in sin, and to whom it is not only their tentation at some times, but their habitual frame, to take ill with reproof; all these, I say, do prove themselves evil-doers and haters of the light, whatever respect they pretend to

have to it; therefore doth he explain who are haters, "neither cometh to the light, lest his deeds should be reproved."

6. A mark of a man who hath embraced Christ in the gospel is (not sinlessness, but) a study and endeavour to do what is commanded in the word of truth, and to do it in truth and sincerity; for he "doeth truth."

7. As the godly man must have been at the light before he can do the truth, so this light maketh him jealous and suspicious of himself, as knowing that Satan and a deceitful heart may outwit him, and therefore he loveth self-searching and examination well, whereby he may know himself; for this is his character, "He cometh to the light, that his deeds may be made manifest," not so much to others as to himself.

8. The godly man's jealousy of himself will not be satisfied in comparing himself with others, or the fashions of the world, or with the external duties required in the law, or in judging of himself as self-love would prescribe, but it bringeth him to God's balance and the light of the word as his judge, for " he cometh to the light," &c.

9. The matter wherein a godly man puts himself to trial are his particular actions, and that daily, and not now and then only, for he cometh "that his deeds may be made manifest."

10. That which the sincere man trieth in his ways, and which only quieteth his conscience about them, is when he findeth them agreeable to God's direction (whatever others think of them) and tending to his glory; when he findeth they are done by him whose person is in God by reconciliation, and who hath his strength in God by dwelling in him by faith; for he trieth his works, that "they are wrought in God"—that is, at the direction of God, and by a person dwelling in God by reconciliation, so empty in himself, that he not only now and then employeth God, but dwelleth in them for strength; so " to live and walk in the Spirit," is to be understood Gal. v. 16, 18, 25.

VER. 22. After these things came Jesus and his disciples into the land of Judea; and there he tarried with them, and baptized.

23. And John also was baptizing in Ænon near to Salim, because there was much water there: and they came, and were baptized.

24. For John was not yet cast into prison.

Followeth in the second part of the chapter John's last testimony given to Christ before his imprisonment, three occasions whereof to ver. 27. The first and more remote occasion is, that Christ, leaving the city, Jerusalem, came to the territory of Judea, and baptized there by the ministry of his disciples, and that John (being yet at liberty) was busy baptizing also at the same time, and having left Bethabara, on the other side of Jordan, was come to Ænon, (supposed to be in Manasseh, or Galilee, where Herod, who beheaded him, had power,) and baptizing there. Their baptizing both at one time occasioned that emulation (ver. 25, 26) which drew out the testimony.

DOCTRINES.

1. Christ was pleased to submit unto a tossed life, and went from place to place according as he had ado, or sinners to convert; for " after these things Jesus came" (from Jerusalem, where he was ordinarily ill-welcomed) " into the land of Judea," where he got work, and had occasion to do good.

2. It is the duty of Christ's disciples to follow him whithersoever he goeth ; and however Christ may get many fleeces of followers, yet it is only disciples that follow him in weal and woe, for therefore (and not only because it was their particular calling) is it marked, that Jesus came with "his disciples into the land of Judea."

3. Christ's own bodily presence, being filled with the Spirit without measure for his people's good, did not take away the use of external ordinances of word and sacraments, as being the means in and by which he conveys himself and his grace and fulness to his people ; for " he tarried with them, and baptized"—to wit, by the ministry of his disciples, John, iv. 2 ; he used the same means that he appointed John to use, that he might bind all to ordinances.

4. The ordinances of Christ are as truly his ordinances in the hands of weak men appointed thereunto, as if he did administrate the same himself; for so is here said of baptism in particular : " He tarried and baptized," when his disciples did administrate it. The virtue of ordinances doth not depend on the excellency of the instruments.

5. It is the duty of ministers to continue their diligence, whatever other means Christ use to further his own work ; and God's raising up of clearer lights should not discourage faithful ministers to go on in their duty, for albeit Christ was now getting the name, yet " John was also baptizing."

6. Whatever circumstantial difference there was betwixt Christ's and John's baptism, yet in substance they were the same, pointing out and sealing up the same thing; therefore they baptize together at one time, and people go to both of them as to the same ordinance.

7. Under the gospel the administration of ordinances are not confined to any one place, for John baptizeth in Ænon as well as in Bethabara, with other water as well as Jordan, and Christ is baptizing in another place.

8. Ministers who are free ought to choose such places for to exercise their calling in, where, in wisdom, they find maniest [most] circumstances concur for furtherance of the work of God; for he baptized in Ænon " because there was much water there" to baptize withal. This doth not by any consequence give us to infer that John did not sprinkle or pour water on those he baptized, but that he dipped them ; for in these hot countries— water being so scarce that ofttimes it occasioned contention to get it for necessary uses, as appeareth Gen. xxvi., Exod. ii., and elsewhere—it needeth not seem strange that John was not permitted to make use of wells, even for sprinkling the multitudes that came to him, but behoved to go to rivers and brooks, where the water was copious and common.

9. Where God employeth his servants he will give them success in some measure ; and albeit God raise up more shining lights, yet the work of God, in the hands of any faithful ministers, will not wear out of request among believers; for when Christ is baptizing, yet " they came, and were baptized by John."

10. The most faithful of God's servants may expect hard measure from the world for their pains, and that they will do what they can to impede them in their work, for it is here supposed that John was cast into prison, though not yet.

11. The servants of God are not, upon fear of danger, to lie by of their own accord, but while they have liberty and opportunity of doing good they ought to use it well, that it may further their account in a day of trial; for it is a reason why John still baptized, for " he was not yet cast into prison."

Ver. 25. Then there arose a question between some of John's disciples and the Jews about purifying.

26. And they came unto John, and said unto him, Rabbi, he that was with thee beyond Jordan, to whom thou barest witness, behold, the same baptizeth, and all men come to him.

The second and nearer occasion of this testimony is a debate betwixt some Jews and some of John's disciples whether his baptism or their washings were best for purging of sin ; and the Jews, it seemeth, having nothing to object against John or his baptism, will yet depress it what they can by casting up Christ and his baptism as now outshining John ; whereupon his disciples, out of carnal emulation, come to him with a regrate, that Christ, who was brought in credit by his testimony, did now gather disciples of himself, and carry all the praise from him ; and this is the third and nearest occasion of the testimony. Whence learn—

1. Truth will always be liable to contest so long as men are carnal, and especially times of reformation will readily breed debates and questions; for " there arose a question" at this time.

2. None are more bold and ready to fall on debates than those who are weakest in religion, having much rash zeal, being conceited of the little light they have, and ignorant of their own inability, and of the subtlety of errors and heretics; for it was " some of John's disciples," who were weak, very ignorant and emulous of Christ, who enter on this question.

3. Adversaries of the truth are so deeply rooted in their superstitious customs as they will be as ready and bold to dispute for them as others are for truth, especially when they meet with a weak party ; for the Jews question with John's disciples about purifying.

4. It is an old policy of adversaries of the truth, when they can do no better, to put Christ's friends by the ears among themselves ; for so it is supposed the Jews did here, by casting up Christ's baptism to disparage John.

5. Such disciples as are weak, and rash, and

foolishly forward in debates, get more hurt than good by them one way or other; for John's disciples are sent away poisoned with carnal emulation and envy against Christ.

6. In so far as men know Christ, he will grow in their estimation, and men will come down and get only their own room; for it is supposed that Christ's train was greatest: he "baptizeth, and all men come to him."

7. Carnal emulation is an old and great sin in the church, and even among professors, it being the foul fruit of a carnal temper to look on the success and applause of one man's gifts as the debasing of another's who is faithful; to count the thriving of the work of God in one minister's hand the disgracing of another who is not so flocked unto; to be sorry that any praise should go by ourselves, or those we esteem of; or to be taken up, not so much with what concerneth the gospel and the glory of God, as with the reputation of men employed about it; for in all these they failed; they think Christ wrongeth John, that his rising disgraceth him, (and therefore they give him honourable titles, and debase Christ as one that had been with him, and brought in credit by him) and the thriving of the work in Christ's hand angereth them, since it brought (as they judged) their master out of request: "Rabbi, he that was with thee beyond Jordan," &c. (See 1 Cor. iii. 4.)

8. It is a great injury done to Christ when his voluntary humiliation abaseth him in men's hearts, when men think he is obliged to any for giving him due respect, or that he wrongeth any when he is in greatest repute in his church; for herein they wrong him, in casting up that "he was with John beyond Jordan," as one of his hearers, in alleging ingratitude upon him in baptizing to John's prejudice, who had borne witness to him and brought him in credit, and in quarrelling that "all men come to him."

Ver. 27. John answered and said, A man can receive nothing, except it be given him from heaven.

Followeth the testimony itself, wherein John represseth their emulation, partly by shewing that the dispensations of God to every man are to be acquiesced in, ver. 27; and by remitting them to his former doctrine, wherein he had asserted the difference betwixt Christ and him, ver. 28; and partly by an ample commendation of Christ's excellency, wherein he points out the differences, not only betwixt Christ and himself, in his peculiar office of being a forerunner, but betwixt Christ and all men; and namely, that Christ is the bridegroom, he and others but servants and friends, ver. 29; that Christ's glory was on the growing hand, and his splendour decreasing, ver. 30; that Christ is as far above men as heaven is above earth, ver. 31; that he is far above all in his knowledge of divine things, which he reveals, ver. 32, (though his doctrine be but ill entertained, ver. 32;) and so men deprive themselves of the dignity of setting their seal to the truth of God, ver. 33, which yet is undoubtedly spoken by Christ as having the Spirit without measure for that as for other ends, ver. 34; that he is the beloved Son, having the

charge of the elect, and a sovereignty over all things for their good, ver. 35; and that salvation is to be attained only by faith in him, without which men will perish, ver. 36.

In this verse, John, in a general assertion, sheweth that the difference betwixt Christ and him (as betwixt men and men) for dignity of calling, gifts, efficacy, and success, flowed from a divine dispensation, which could not nor should be quarrelled, unless men would bark against heaven. Whence learn—

1. Faithful ministers will be far from emulation themselves and from fostering it in others; and where grace is lively, it will resist temptations, which would kindle the fire of emulation; for when they blow at his corruption, zeal to Christ's honour doth not only quench that fire, but sets him on work to quench it in them.

2. Every excellency and lawful calling men have is from God, who dispenseth variously for eminency in calling, gifts, and success, as he pleaseth; for so is here imported, that God giveth from heaven what men have in their several measures.

3. Men are to submit to dispensations of Divine Providence in what they enjoy of any of these, and upon that ground ought to cure carnal emulation, it being neither lawful nor to any purpose to do otherwise; for John keepeth down his own, and curbeth their emulation with this: "A man can receive (or take to himself) nothing, except it be given him from heaven;" from which these grounds of curing this disease may be gathered: 1. Any calling or gift, and any success men have in the exercise of their calling and gifts, is from God, which they ought rather to acknowledge, than quarrel what they want. 2. The variety of dispensations which men are ready to quarrel is chiefly in gifts and excellences given for the use of others, and which are adorning rather than saving; for of these the text is speaking, and men have the less cause to quarrel for a less measure of these, if they have the truth of saving graces necessary unto life. 3. There can be no envying of any who excel us in these, without reflecting on God who hath so dispensed his own gifts; for it is "from heaven" that the difference is. 4. As no man can lawfully usurp any calling which he hath not from God, (as they would have had John above Christ,) so it will be to no purpose to aspire higher in calling or gifts than God hath set men, nor will it prosper. No man can receive (or take to himself) but what is given from heaven; he can neither lawfully usurp a calling nor think to be blessed in it if he usurp it; nor can he prosper in stretching himself beyond his gifts and abilities, or in hunting after eminency and reputation by them.

Ver. 28. Ye yourselves bear me witness, that I said, I am not the Christ, but that I am sent before him.

He remits them to his former doctrine, chap. i. 20, and attests their own consciences if he had not clearly told them that he was not the Messias, but his forerunner. And this is the first and a great difference betwixt Christ and him. Whence learn—

1. Faithful ministers, and especially such as have eminent gifts, ought so to carry themselves in doctrine and practice as to give no occasion to people to esteem more of them than is meet, or to have emulation and envy; for so had John put marches betwixt Christ and himself.

2. Let ministers walk never so circumspectly and wisely, yet people are ready to debord [mistake] and run on such extremities; for so had John's disciples done, though clearly warned.

3. Negligent hearing, or forgetting of doctrine preached, is the ground of much mischief which might be prevented; for they miscarried through not heeding what John had said, as judging that he had spoken but modestly of himself; or they could not think of a greater, considering his gifts; or they had forgotten this in their fit.

4. However people may miscarry with fleshly emulation, yet the testimony of ministers' sincerity, in walking circumspectly and labouring to prevent such exorbitancies, will give ground of peace and comfort; for, saith he, " Ye yourselves bear me witness, that I said, I am not the Christ."

5. Christ is so far above all ministers that it becometh them to put marches betwixt him and themselves. And he is so great a king, and there is so much need of preparation to receive and entertain him, that it is the highest honour of ministers to be ushers to prepare his way; and it is their duty to prepare the way for him by stirring up people to receive him, and not to stop the way by obscuring of him, or keeping people hanging on them; for this was John's office and high honour—" I am not the Christ, but am sent before him."

VER. 29. He that hath the bride is the bridegroom: but the friend of the bridegroom, which standeth and heareth him, rejoiceth greatly because of the bridegroom's voice: this my joy therefore is fulfilled.

John proceedeth to a second difference betwixt Christ and himself—namely, that Christ is " the bridegroom" to whom the church is to be married, and it is a great enough honour to him, or any minister, to be employed betwixt him and his people, to invite them to him, and to see Christ enjoy his own people's affection, and them brought to enjoy fellowship with him by their ministry; and this made him, instead of envying, to rejoice at the success Christ the bridegroom had. This difference and employment, though it was peculiar to John in some respects, yet may take in all faithful ministers.

DOCTRINES.

1. The relation betwixt Christ and his people is a relation of marriage, wherein the supreme and all-sufficient Lord condescendeth to take lost sinners to himself in a sure bond, not to be broken for every fault; doth make them one with himself; deigneth them with communication of estates, he taking part in their wants, and sharing with them in his fulness, and alloweth them dignities and entertainment suitable to their state and relation; and, on the other hand, his people are bound to embrace this offer, to acquiesce in him, to be subject unto him, and give him alone their heart and affections, not prostituting themselves to any other, nor ought any other to usurp a headship over them, nor urge for that respect and room that is due to him alone; for the relation is expressed under these terms of " bride" and " bridegroom," who hath the bride, and enjoyeth her.

2. The relation betwixt Christ and his people is expressed as espousals, and under the name of " bride" and " bridegroom," rather than under the notion of a complete marriage, not only because it is begun here, and to be consummated in heaven, but because, however Christ's affection respects rather his people's profit than their humours, yet it is still fresh and tender towards them, as of persons new married, or in terms of it.

3. Albeit ministers do not usurp Christ's place, yet their office, being faithful in their duty, affordeth them abundant honour, under the name of " the friends of the bridegroom," an office which was usual in those times in the solemnities of marriage, wherein are held forth—1. It is their great honour to be accounted and be friends to Christ. 2. It is also their honour to be friends, especially to further the marriage, and that Christ will be honoured by their attendance, and commending, and appearing for him, and by their inviting the bride to embrace him, and being instrumental to bring them together; such were the friends of the bridegroom, his most especial and intimate friends. 3. It is also their duty to do him honour, by waiting on him as servants, to receive his directions, and get commissions to deliver from him, and it is their dignity to stand in so near a relation, though of servants, for so is imported in that he " standeth," as servant and friend, near the bridegroom. Such service of him is great honour. 4. It is also their dignity to bring the bride to hear the bridegroom, and it will be matter of their great joy to see the church brought to acquaintance with Christ by their ministry; for " he standeth and heareth him, and rejoiceth greatly because of the bridegroom's voice," as the friend of the bridegroom standing in the bride's chamber, and seeing the parties brought together by his means, and himself admitted to be a witness of the fruit of his pains. This dignity faithful ministers may attain in their own measure, though John had it in a peculiar way, even in that which his disciples quarrelled—to wit, his seeing so many of his followers embrace the Messiah in person, whom he had pointed out unto them.

4. Faithful ministers, blessed of God and denying themselves, have more complete matter of joy in the church's thriving, though with their own abasement, than any they could have by their own advancement, or usurping what is not due to them; therefore saith John, " this my joy is fulfilled," by seeing people flock to Christ. What is an eyesore to envy will be matter of joy to sincerity.

VER. 30. He must increase, but I must decrease.

A third difference betwixt Christ and John is, that John, shining as the morning-star before him, the Sun of Righteousness, was to be obscured more and more by Christ's appearing, and his extraordinary office of preparing the way to Christ was to give place to the full manifestation of him and the gospel, which was to shine more and more brightly. This is not to be understood of any real decay in John, but of his decreasing in the estimation of men, and appearing to be but what he was when Christ was seen. Whence learn—

1. When Christ is not known he will be but little thought of, and not duly acknowledged; and then others may be too much esteemed; for so John insinuates that Christ was not fully manifested nor esteemed of as became, and that himself was but too much esteemed by many, yea, by some to be the Messiah, through ignorance of Christ.

2. Where Christ manifesteth himself, and is truly known, men's estimation of him will be upon the growing hand, as the light shineth more and more unto the perfect day; there being such excellency in him as cannot at once be comprehended, and the more he is seen the more will he be esteemed and accounted excellent; and his kingdom and glory will still increase; for "he must increase," not in himself, but in manifestation and estimation.

3. As the shining of Christ in his glory will obscure the excellency of other things, so particularly of ministers, not in respect of what they are appointed for of Christ, (for so they will come more in request,) but in respect of men's overweening conceits. Their light and glory will be seen to be borrowed from him, as the day-star doth borrow light from the sun; his splendour and light will obscure and swallow up their borrowed light as the rising sun doth the day-star; their light and shining will be looked on as subservient to lead men to Christ, and not to be doated or rested on; for this (beside what was singular in John's calling, which therefore was to cease) is imported in this—" He must increase, but I must decrease."

4. Carnal envy and emulation will be so far from getting satisfaction, that men who give way to it may expect to find more and more occasions of it, and more and more temptations to it, in God's holy providence; therefore John tells his envious disciples that they should see him yet less esteemed and Christ more—" he must increase, but I must decrease."

5. Faithful servants of Christ, whose scope in their ministry is to commend and set him out, will be content to be abased and obscured, providing he be exalted and come in request, and to see the Master more esteemed than themselves, the servants; therefore John speaks of this as a dispensation he was content with.

Ver. 31. He that cometh from above is above all: he that is of the earth is earthly, and speaketh of the earth: he that cometh from heaven is above all.

A fourth difference, wherein Christ is not only above John but all men, is taken from the excellency of his person. In respect of the divine original of his person, he is above all men and all creatures; and men whose original is of the earth do resemble it, and savour of it in their speech, whereas he, not only in his person, but in that also, is above all, as is cleared in the next verse.

DOCTRINES.

1. Christ did not begin to be when he manifested himself on earth, but had his perfect and glorious being before; for " he cometh from above," and consequently was there before.

2. It is Christ's prerogative to be matchless and singular above all creatures in glory, excellency, efficacy of operation, and every perfection. He is above angels, above principalities and powers, above pastors in the visible church, above all the members in the mystical body; and all things in the world are under his feet; for he is "above all."

3. It is not possible for created conceptions to take up Christ's excellency as it is in itself, but must point it out, by setting it above all created excellency, further than which they cannot follow it; therefore doth John say no more to it, but he " is above all."

4. Whatever may be the perverse or blinded judgments of men, yet, in due time, that which is most eminent before God will carry the preeminence even before men, above what they otherways doated on; for so much doth this verse, with the former, teach: " He must increase," for he is indeed "above all."

5. Christ's excellency is indeed founded upon real worth, being above all, because his original is divine, and from heaven. Not only is he incomparable in his descent as God, but in his humanity, his conception, and sanctification of his nature, and the union thereof with the person of the Son of God are from above; for " he cometh from above," or "from heaven," (as it is in the end of the verse,) who " is above all."

6. It pleased this excellent and matchless Lord to stoop so low as to commend his love to sinners by coming unto them, to seek and purchase them and their affection; for " he cometh from above."

7. Albeit Christ, by coming on earth, did put a veil upon his glory, yet his stooping did derogate nothing from his sovereignty and highness; for " he that cometh from above is above all."

8. Man's original is so low and base, and men do so much resemble it, that it is high presumption to enter in any comparison to Christ; for, in opposition to what was said of Christ, that " he cometh from above, and is above all," it is added, " he that is of the earth is earthly," or, " of the earth." Not only is man " of the earth," in respect of the original of his body, and the union of the soul with it, and so infinitely inferior to him who is also God over all, and but dust and ashes before him, Gen. xviii. 27, but every man is " of the earth," in regard of the corrupt qualities he hath by ordinary generation, of which he savoureth, save in so far as he is renewed by Christ; and yet that is but imperfect here, and far beneath the divine condition and state of Christ, even as man; and thus to be " earthly," or " of the earth," or "world," is to be understood of men's corrupt estate and condition,

John, viii. 23; James, iii. 15. (See 1 Cor. xv·
47—49.)

9. As man in his person is inferior to Christ,
so also in his office and doctrine; his way of it,
and his authority in it, is far beneath Christ's;
for "he that is of the earth speaketh of the
earth;" whereby we are not to understand that
their doctrine according to the word is earthly,
or indited by the wisdom of the flesh, though indeed they be subject to error, nor yet that their
calling and authority to preach it is from the
earth, or men,—for in both these respects John's
baptism and ministry was from heaven,—but,
1, in respect of men's natural condition, they
savour and can speak only of things of the earth,
and what they can do beside that is by gift.
2. Those who are enabled and endowed with
authority to speak the things of God; yea, suppose they be regenerate also; yet their renovation and gifts are so imperfect that their way of
preaching savoureth of their original, and putteth
them far beneath Christ; and therefore the best
have need of touched lips daily, Isaiah, vi. 5—7.
3. Their authority in preaching is from Christ,
and as far inferior to his as the earth, or the foot-
stool from off which (as the word signifieth)
they speak, is to heaven, or the throne from
which he speaketh; and thus the comparison
seemeth to be instituted, Heb. xii. 25.

10. It is our part to dwell much on the
thoughts of the excellency and sovereignty of
Christ, and to see it shining in every step of his
dispensations towards us; therefore it is repeated, "he that cometh from heaven is above
all," partly to inculcate this point, and partly to
point him out as excellent in doctrine above
man, who "speaketh of the earth," which is
further insisted on in the next verse. For albeit
he stooped to our weakness in speaking heavenly
things under earthly similitudes, ver. 12, yet his
way and authority even in that was altogether
heavenly, John, vii. 46.

VER. 32. And what he hath seen and heard,
that he testifieth; and no man receiveth his
testimony.

A fifth difference betwixt Christ and all men
is taken from his knowledge, and the manner of
it. All men of themselves do but speak and
savour of the earth, ver. 31, and what they have
above this is of free gift; but Christ in this also
is above all, having the knowledge of that doctrine which he delivereth by seeing and hearing
—that is, by a clear, full, certain, and immediate
comprehension of it, as being in the bosom of
the Father and upon all his council, whereof
men's being eye and ear witnesses of what they
speak is but a shadow; and yet for all this,
John regretteth that so few embrace his doctrine,
of which, see ver. 11. Whence learn—

1. It is Christ's prerogative to have the knowledge of divine truths of himself from the
Father, and to have all others who know anything beholden to his bounty and illumination;
for his doctrine is, "what he hath seen and
heard" in a way peculiar to him.

2. It sets out the bounty of Christ that he
doth not keep up this knowledge, but discovereth
it, that so sinners may have a sure guide and
teacher, and the solemn testimony of an eye and
ear witness, on which they may lean; for "what
he hath seen and heard, that he testifieth." It is
called a testifying, both in respect of the certainty of the matter, and in respect of Christ's
earnest persuading of men to embrace it, as testifying seemeth to import, Acts, xviii. 5.

3. Christ's gracious condescendence in revealing the counsel of God concerning man's salvation gets but ill entertainment in the world, the
most part of men either not hearkening to him,
or not embracing his offer with respect, affection,
or faith; for "no man" (that is, very few, or none
in comparison of them who do otherwise, though
some there are, ver. 33,) "receiveth his testimony." Let them hear it as they will, yet they
do not receive nor embrace it as becometh; and
therefore also it is called a testimony, as witnessing against them that they receive not so certain
a truth.

4. It ought and will be matter of regret to all
the friends and servants of Christ that his doctrine is so ill received in the world; for whereas
John's disciples complained, ver. 26, that "all
men" came to Christ, he seeth rather cause to
complain that "no man receiveth his testimony."

VER. 33. He that hath received his testimony
hath set to his seal that God is true.

The receiving of the doctrine of the gospel
being the great business as to promoving of the
salvation of sinners, therefore John insisteth on
it, and aggreageth the sin of unbelievers, from
the great dignity which is put upon believers, in
that they are honoured by their faith solemnly
to ratify and bear witness unto the truth of God.
Whence learn—

1. How many soever do reject Christ and his
doctrine, yet he will still prevail with some; for
it is here imported that there are who receive
"his testimony."

2. Whosoever do receive Christ and his doctrine will find that they have to do with a true
God, who cannot lie nor will disappoint them;
for so is imported "that God is true," and will
prove so to such.

3. Faith embracing the doctrine of Christ
doth also glorify God by subscribing to the truth
of his word, and doth, so far as believers can,
ratify the truth of the word, that others may
embrace it; and so the believer is also honoured
of God in that his testimony is taken in so great
a matter; for "he that hath received his testimony hath set to his seal that God is true," (see
Rom. iv. 20;) whereas, on the contrary, unbelievers (beside their own prejudice thereby) do
speak blasphemy against God, 1 John, v. 10.

VER. 34. For he whom God hath sent speaketh
the words of God: for God giveth not the
Spirit by measure unto him.

That receivers of Christ's doctrine do seal the
veracity of God is confirmed from this reason,
that he is the sent angel of the covenant, and
therefore speaketh the mind and truth of God.

This is again confirmed from another ground, that Christ hath the Spirit without measure, as for other ends (of which in the next verse) so also to reveal the Father and his mind infallibly; and this also sets forth his excellency above all others. Whence learn—

1. It is believers' duty to study much and be persuaded that what is revealed in the word is the mind of God, and that it is his truth which is sealed by believing; for so much doth this confirmation of the former assertion teach, that they seal " that God is true," because what Christ propoundeth to be believed is his word.

2. As they who are sent of God ought to speak only what they have in commission, so sending by God and speaking of God's mind for inviting sinners to believe must go together; for they are conjoined even in Christ. (See Heb. v. 4, 5.)

3. Christ is a messenger sent of the Father in a way peculiar to himself, not only in his coming to the earth, but in the exercise of a public calling thereupon, being the great angel and mediator of the covenant, and the chief prophet of his church; for it is " he whom God hath sent" in a singular way.

4. As Christ's sending so also his speaking of the mind of God is in a way peculiar to himself; not only is the matter which he speaketh infallibly the words of God,—so that it is all one to have his mind, and to be upon the Father's counsel, 1 Cor. ii. 16,—but though others may speak God's word for matter, and be infallibly guided in doctrine also, yet he hath this privilege of himself—and his authority in speaking is singular—not only from God, but being God who speaketh, and the man Christ having a more divine way of uttering the mind of God than any mere man. So much is imported in that he " speaketh the words of God."

5. Christ as Mediator is endued with the Spirit for discharge of his office, and particularly for revealing the mind of God, whereby he teacheth all who are sent on such an employment to have much need and make much use of such furniture. So much doth this reason of speaking the words of God import, " for God giveth the Spirit unto him."

6. Albeit Christ as man have not an infinite measure of the Spirit, (though indeed in that person the fulness of the godhead dwells, as being God also, for that were to be no more man but God) yet the gifts and graces of the Spirit are poured out upon the man Christ in a measure far above all creatures; for though every believer be " complete in him," (Col. ii. 10,) yet as for what is inherent in them they have but diversity of gifts of the Spirit, 1 Cor. xii. 4, &c.; Ephes. iv. 7; but he hath all sorts of gifts, Isa. xi. 2; they, as members of the body, have but gifts for some and fewer uses, Rom. xii. 3, 4, he for all uses, Isaiah, lxi. 1—3; they have a measure of gifts which are capable of increase, he above measure, so much as the human nature is capable of, which, though it be finite in itself, yet it cannot be measured nor comprehended by us. So much is imported in that " God giveth not the Spirit by measure unto him," being understood of his manhood; so Psalm xlv. 7; though (as was said) if we speak of his person, he hath the Spirit infinitely and without measure, Col. i. 19; ii. 9. This fulness became Christ as man, that he might be a fit temple of the godhead, and as Mediator, that he might be the universal head of his church and storehouse of his people.

VER. 35. The Father loveth the Son, and hath given all things into his hand.

A sixth difference is, that Christ as the beloved Son is the Mediator of his people, who hath them and all things for their use and good, and a sovereignty over all things concredited to him as Mediator. Whence learn—

1. The excellency of Christ above all other ambassadors is, that he is the Son and they are but servants; so are we here taught.

2. Christ is the object of the Father's love in a peculiar way: as a Son, and not a servant, in respect of his person; and as Mediator, he is pointed out as the beloved Son, in whom God will be found well pleased, Matt. iii. 17, as he who is beloved, and hath purchased love to others because of his death, John, x. 17; so willing was the Father to be reconciled, as he whose being beloved answereth our being unworthy of love, and is a pledge of the Father's love to us, John, xvii. 23. So much is imported in that " the Father loveth the Son."

3. In carrying on the redemption of sinners, as the matter is accorded betwixt the Father and the Son, so the redeemed are not left to themselves, but are put on Christ's hand to purchase and be forthcoming for them, and all things are concredited to him that may tend to their good; for " the Father loveth the Son" in the quality of Mediator, " and hath given all things into his hand," under which "all things" we are to comprehend the elect themselves, who are instead of all things to him, together with all the gifts and graces of the Spirit (of which ver. 34) needful for their conversion and salvation, which are not entrusted to ourselves, but to Him who can keep us and them and let them out as we need; and a dominion over all things that may contribute to help or hinder his people's happiness, that he may order them so as may be for their good. And this power he hath as God with the Father, and as man and Mediator by donation and gift from the Father, Matt. xi. 27; xxviii. 18; and thus the believers' happiness is firm, being transacted betwixt such parties, the Father being satisfied in the Mediator, and they entrusted to Him whose dear purchase they are; and therefore he will not lose them who hath capacity to receive their furniture far above what they could hold, power to maintain, wisdom to guide and dispense their allowance, dominion to curb all enemies and opposition, and a commission and charge to be answerable for them; all which may invite us to be content that we be nothing, and that we and all our furniture be in his hand.

VER. 36. He that believeth on the Son hath everlasting life: and he that believeth not the Son shall not see life; but the wrath of God abideth on him.

The last difference, and the use to be made of all the excellency of Christ formerly mentioned, is, that he is to be believed in for attaining of eternal life, and that without this we perish. Whence learn—

1. It is the prerogative of Christ above all others, even the choicest messengers of God, that he is the object of saving faith, as being the Son of God, equal with the Father; for so are we taught here, and by this John would quench all carnal emulation in his followers.

2. The excellency of Christ is never rightly studied nor acknowledged till it draw men out of themselves, and discover fulness and worth in him to be closed with by faith; therefore doth John sum up all this doctrine concerning Christ in this use—that the Son should be believed on.

3. Such as close with Christ by faith are not only sure of eternal life at the close of their days, but they have it here, partly in the word of promise, partly in Christ who is the fountain of it, and in whose hands it is given, and partly in the bud of begun communion with Christ, which is a heaven on earth; for " he that believeth on the Son hath everlasting life," where faith only is held out as the hand to receive this benefit.

4. How excellent soever Christ be yet there are still many who will not close with him nor see any worth in him wherefore they should renounce themselves and flee to him; for it is imported there are who " believe not the Son."

5. Unbelievers do lie under the dreadful hazard of the loss of salvation, which only deserveth the name of a life, other living being but a death without it. While they do not believe, they have no right to it nor bud of it, and continuing therein, they are eternally secluded from it, without so much as a sight thereof, save so much at the last day as shall add to their torment in hell; for " he that believeth not the Son shall not see life."

6. Unbelievers are not only secluded from heaven, but are under wrath, which is sad and insupportable, as being the wrath of God; this wrath, under which the unbeliever is by nature, by reason of the sentence of the law, resteth upon him in the state of infidelity till he hath filled up his measure and be ripened for hell, and then he lieth eternally under wrath; for he " shall not see life; but the wrath of God abideth on him;" and by all these considerations would John press his hearers to flee from the danger by believing.

CHAPTER IV.

In this chapter we have, first, Christ's removal from Judea into Galilee, to ver. 4; next, what occurred by the way at Sychar, to ver. 43; lastly, his entertainment, and what he did in Galilee, to the end.

VER. 1. When therefore the Lord knew how the Pharisees had heard that Jesus made and baptized more disciples than John,

2. (Though Jesus himself baptized not, but his disciples,)

3. He left Judea, and departed again into Galilee.

The occasion of Christ's removal was, that the Pharisees began to take notice of his gathering and baptizing more disciples than ever John did, (though, indeed, he baptized none but by his disciples,) and Christ knowing of this, and what they were hatching upon it, did decline their fury, and went again into Galilee, where he had been before, chap. i. 2. Whence learn—

1. The messengers of the gospel, getting success, may look to meet with envy and malice from Satan and his instruments, and especially from corrupt churchmen, for the Pharisees heard how " Jesus made and baptized disciples;" they heard it with a hostile mind, and with a purpose to do him hurt, which therefore made Christ to withdraw.

2. The more that men study to bear down truth, and the work of the gospel, the Lord can make it to flourish the more; and though one instrument be laid aside, yet he can raise up another, in whose hands it will prosper yet more; for they who did bear down the work in John's hand (who, as some think, was now in prison) find it rising more in Christ's; he " made and baptized more disciples than John," which seemeth to relate to that, chap. iii. 26.

3. As it is an evidence of a wicked disposition to have hatred against Christ and his ministry upon the very report of it, so it is a judgment on those who will not themselves come to hear and see that his way and his servants be so represented to them by others as may stir up their corruptions and set them on edge to persecute; for the Pharisees but heard all this, that set them on edge, and that (as appeareth) by no friends to Christ.

4. Albeit the people of God may be in a very secure condition when persecution cometh, (and God may send persecution of purpose to stir them up,) yet persecution is an evidence of so much fruit and success of a ministry as is Satan's eyesore; for here persecution is raised against Christ in Judea, because he " made and baptized more disciples than John."

5. Christ observeth and knoweth how every one is affected, and be men's machinations what they will, yet none will steal a dint [momentary opportunity] on him, but he will know their projects beforehand, to avoid them if he please; for " the Lord knew how the Pharisees had heard" these things, as he might easily do by his omniscience.

6. Christ's disrespect from men diminisheth nothing of his true excellency and worth, nor ought it to obscure it in his people's hearts; for when the Jews are about this, John calleth him the Lord, which is a name of majesty and dominion.

7. The preaching of the gospel is the great and principal work of the ministry, whereof administration of sacraments is an accessory; and Christ would not have men to judge of the efficacy of baptism as depending on the minister, and would have all to put a difference betwixt

the outward seal, which any instrument authorized thereto may administrate, and the thing signified, for which he alone must be depended upon; for these reasons, and to teach this, it was that "Jesus himself baptized not, but his disciples," which is added by way of correction to the report: he betook himself to preaching as the great work, 1 Cor. i. 17. He taught his followers to look on baptism administrated by his disciples in his name to be as sufficient as if he had administrated it himself, and by baptizing none at all he kept that distance clear betwixt the ministers and his part in that ordinance.

8. It is lawful for ministers to withdraw themselves from the plots of persecutors, when their calling is cleared so to do by the general rules of the word relating to such a case and practice; for upon this ground Christ "left Judea, and departed again into Galilee," or a more obscure place, and more remote from the Pharisees' power.

9. No pretence of confidence ought to slacken men's diligence in the use of lawful means for their own preservation; for albeit Christ knew his hour was not yet come, yet he used means, and withdrew.

10. Albeit Christ might either have prevented or repressed his enemies' fury by his omnipotency, yet he choosed rather to let it break forth, and used this mean of his own preservation, that he might fight with the weapons of his weak followers, and in his own person sanctify these means, of retiring and fleeing in hard times unto them; therefore he who might have stayed in Judea, and driven the Pharisees out, chooseth rather to leave Judea, and depart into Galilee.

VER. 4. And he must needs go through Samaria.

5. Then cometh he to a city of Samaria, which is called Sychar, near to the parcel of ground that Jacob gave to his son Joseph.

6. Now Jacob's well was there. Jesus therefore, being wearied with his journey, sat thus on the well: and it was about the sixth hour.

In the second part of the chapter John recordeth what was Christ's carriage and success in his way to Galilee, in bringing in some first-fruits of the gentiles, and of those without the Jewish church; and, first, he recordeth his conference with the woman of Samaria in his disciples' absence, to ver. 27; next, their return, her going to the city to bring out the people, and his conference with the disciples in her absence, to ver. 39; thirdly, the conversion of some more of that city, to ver. 43.

Unto this conference with the woman some occasions are permitted. As, 1. That his straight way from Judea to Galilee lay through (not the city, but) the country of Samaria, and therefore he came there, ver. 4. 2. That coming unto Sychar, a city of the territory of Samaria, where Jacob's well was, he was so wearied with his journey, and the heat at noon, (which was their sixth hour,) that he rested upon, or beside, the well, while his disciples provided meat, ver. 5, 6,

and so Providence set the tryst [appointment] with her who was coming. This Sychar is the same with that place of Jacob's abode, Gen. xxxiii. 18, 19, called there Shechem, and this description of it here mentioned relates to that, Gen. xlviii. 22, the interpretation whereof I remit to its proper place.

DOCTRINES.

1. When persecutors have done their worst, neither Christ nor his followers will want work or success so long as the Lord pleaseth; for Christ, driven from Judea, finds both in Samaria.

2. As persecution and exile should not put Christ's servants from minding their calling, and as they should employ the very time of their journey in seeking to do good, so a very short time, through God's blessing, may produce great effects; for so doth Christ's practice and success, while he is on his journey, teach us.

3. In every step of men's way they should study to have a clear calling, especially for doing those things whereat others are apt to stumble and take offence; therefore Christ, however his love put a necessity upon him to visit these wandering sheep, (and he did not stand to go to a hateful place to seek them,) yet, being the minister of circumcision, Rom. xv. 8, and having forbidden his disciples to go to the Samaritans, Matthew, x. 5, he will have his journey thither freed of obloquy by the necessity of his going that way from Judea to Galilee; "he must needs go through Samaria," as being his straight way, as appeareth, Luke, ix. 51, 52, and xvii. 11, and is clear to them who know the situation of that country.

4. A lawful and necessary calling maketh converse lawful with those with whom otherwise it were not justifiable, for therefore he went "through Samaria," and that warrantably, since it was the straight way to Galilee.

5. Piety and faith in God have a sweet savour and smell above any excellency that men can hunt after beside; therefore is this place so eminent, even in 'Christ's time, by reason of Jacob's abode, who worshipped God there, Genesis, xxxiii. 19, 20; and because of his faith in giving that land to his children when they were sojourners in Egypt.

6. Christ took on, not only our nature, but the common infirmities thereof, and he is to be as seriously eyed as emptied in his humanity, as in the glory of his godhead, for the comfort of sensible sinners who come to such an high priest; therefore it is recorded that he was "wearied with his journey" ere half the day was spent, and that, through weariness, he "sat thus on (or beside) the well"—that is, even as the seat offered, or as wearied men use to sit.

VER. 7. There cometh a woman of Samaria to draw water: Jesus saith unto her, Give me to drink.

8. (For his disciples were gone away unto the city to buy meat.)

9. Then saith the woman of Samaria unto him, How is it that thou, being a Jew, askest drink of me, which am a woman of Samaria?

for the Jews have no dealings with the Samaritans.

The third and nearest occasion of this conference is, that while he was sitting there a woman of Samaria (originally of that country, it seems of the town of Sychar) cometh to draw water, upon which followeth the conference, wherein he leads her from one thing to another till she come to know him to be the Messiah.

It may be summed up in this order:—1. Christ seeking a drink in his disciples' absence, ver. 7, 8, gets a tart answer, ver. 9. 2. He, discovering how much she mistook him, and that he had better water to give her than she would offer him, ver. 10, she reasons against this his offer, ver. 11, 12. 3. Christ, pointing out yet further the excellency of what he offered, ver. 13, 14, doth beget but a natural desire in her after it, ver. 15. 4. Christ, not prevailing by his offers, doth discover her misery to her, and that he knew her lewdness, ver. 16—18. 5. The woman, upon this, taking him to be a prophet, ver. 19, propounded the controversy betwixt the Jews and the Samaritans concerning the place of public worship, ver. 20, and gets a full resolution to it, ver. 21—24. 6. The woman, upon this discourse, bringing to remembrance the Messiah who was to come, is brought to know that Christ was he, ver. 25, 26.

In the first discourse betwixt them, (in these verses,) Christ seeking drink, both to quench his thirst and that thereby he might take occasion to confer with her, she casts up the dissensions betwixt the Samaritans and Jews, tartly checking him that in his need he would now make use of her. Here John inserts that the disciples (who, it seems, were not so many as afterward) were gone to buy provision, as a reason why she found Christ alone, and why he employed her and not them to get drink. As for this great distance betwixt the Jews and the Samaritans, it began first at the defection of the ten tribes from the temple at Jerusalem and from the house of David, and did increase, partly, when heathen nations, with some few Israelites, did possess that land which had been given to Israel, the brethren of the Jews, and did invent a mongrel way of religion, (2 Kings, xvii.,) partly by reason of many injuries done to the Jews by these Samaritans, who, however they boasted to be descended of Jacob when the Jews were in any good condition, (as appeareth in part from ver. 12,) yet they were their bitter enemies in their adversity, as appeareth from Ezra, Nehemiah, and the histories of those times; and, chiefly, this difference was heightened when the Samaritans, with some apostate Jews, built a temple in Mount Gerizim, in opposition to that at Jerusalem, and so that country became a shelter of all apostate Jews.

DOCTRINES.

1. Providence may be intending much mercy to those who are unworthy of it and are little minding it; for this "woman of Samaria," who was a vile woman, ver. 18, "cometh to draw water," and mindeth no other thing, and yet Providence made her to tryst [meet] with the Saviour of sinners, and with him when he was actually under the feeling of our infirmities, being weary and thirsty, and so a meet Lord to deal with such an insensible woman.

2. It is no strange thing to see Christ and his followers much straitened in outward things; to see them need a drink of water, and have scarce any willing to supply them; and to have their dinner to seek at dinner-time; for this hath our humbled Lord sanctified to his followers in his own person, and by this his want he hath recovered their right to outward benefits, which was forfeited in Adam.

3. Albeit Christ humbled himself, and became poor, that through his poverty we might become rich, yet hath he also left an example to his meanest followers of studying an honest way of living and providing for their subsistence, and not by scandalous beggary, or being burdensome; for he sent his disciples " to buy meat."

4. There may be somewhat betwixt Christ and those he will do good unto that it were not meet that even disciples should know of it; therefore, among other causes, " the disciples were gone away unto the city," that they might not be witnesses to Christ's ripping up of her shameful fault in this conference, nor to her miscarriages in her discourses with him.

5. It is a commendable practice in men to be constant in their habit and fashions, and not affect novelty in these; for herein Christ hath cast a copy, being known at first to be a Jew by his habit and language.

6. It need not seem strange if Christ or his people not only want and get no supply, but be mocked and insulted over in their necessities by those who may help them; for Christ, being thirsty, gets a taunt instead of a drink. (See John, xix. 28, 29, with Ps. lxix. 21.)

7. Contentions about religion are ordinarily very hot, and draw not only to alienation of affections, but even to the breaking the bonds of civil society and converse; for so was it here, " the Jews had no dealings with the Samaritans."

8. It is an evidence of a malicious heart to insult over the miseries of any, and to take advantage of the misery of those they hate, to do them all the spite they can; for so much doth her taunt import, " How is it that thou, being a Jew, askest drink of me, which am a woman of Samaria? for the Jews have no dealings with the Samaritans." As if she had said, Ye regard us not at other times, but now, when ye need, ye seek us, and therefore I will not answer you.

9. Self-love is so deeply rooted in every one that even the basest cannot endure to be despised; for the ground of her quarrel is, that they were contemned by the Jews—" the Jews have no dealings with the Samaritans."

10. Christ is a Lord who will not stand on any impediment, but will come over them all, to reconcile sinners to himself; for he keeps no such distance with Samaritans, nor with a lewd woman among them, and counts it his glory to take so wild a creature.

VER. 10. Jesus answered and said unto her, If thou knewest the gift of God, and who it is that saith to thee, Give me to drink; thou wouldest have asked of him, and he would have given thee living water.

In Christ's second speech to her he lets her see how much she mistook her own mercy; for if she had known him, she would not only not have refused his request, but would have turned a supplicant to him, and he would have given her better and living water; whereby we are to understand the Spirit of God, and the graces of the Spirit acted by him, as chap. vii. 38, 39.

DOCTRINES.

1. Christ's meekness passeth over much frowardness, which he findeth in his own in the time of their conversion, and by his goodness he overcometh their ill; for so much doth this reply to the woman teach.

2. Ignorance of Christ, and what he hath and is ready to give, is a great ground of sinners' miscarriage towards him; for Christ findeth this want here—" If thou knewest," &c.

3. Christ is then known rightly and savingly when he and all that he hath are looked on as freely gifted to the world by the Father, (as well as by himself,) and made theirs by offer to be embraced in the due order; for therefore is he named " the gift of God," as is expounded in the following words.

4. Christ being rightly known, it will add to his commendation in a sensible heart that he is at the pains to come unto them, and prevent them with offers of himself, and especially that he stooped so low as to take on their infirmities; therefore also it is added, as a ravishing consideration, " If thou knewest who it is that saith unto thee, Give me to drink," or that the Messiah, compassed with infirmities, should be at her hand.

5. When Christ is rightly known, as offered to the world for the salvation of lost man, it will beget a thirst after him, and put souls to seek the supply thereof by prayer, and that they cannot stay away from him; and they will see him seeking sinners, rather to give to them than to receive of them; for " if thou knewest, thou wouldest have asked of him," rather than have refused him a drink of water.

6. Christ hath better things to give sinners than anything he can ask of them, or they can offer him, and particularly the well of life is in Christ's hand to dispense it as he will; for, instead of her water, he hath " living water" to give her.

7. Christ, who makes offer of grace before we seek it, will not refuse it to them who ask it, nor will former sins hinder their acceptance who come to seek grace; for even to this wicked woman he saith, " Thou wouldest have asked, and he would have given thee living water."

8. The grace of Christ, communicated by the Spirit, is compared to " water," not only that he might allude to her water, but to point out its cleansing and fructifying virtue, and that it will quench the thirst of a burnt-up soul; and it is compared to " living water," &c., springing, as Gen. xxvi. 19, because it hath an enlivening, quickening virtue, and because of its constant endurance unto eternal life, as it is, ver. 14.

Ver. 11. The woman saith unto him, Sir, thou hast nothing to draw with, and the well is deep: from whence then hast thou that living water?

12. Art thou greater than our father Jacob, which gave us the well, and drank thereof himself, and his children, and his cattle?

The woman, in her reply, reasons against Christ's offer, alleging that this water was either to be given out of that well, (and that could not be, seeing the well was deep, and he had nothing to draw with,) or out of a better well, and that was, to prefer himself to Jacob, who himself and all his family was content with the water of this well, and left it to them. Whence learn—

1. It is the property of natural men to take up spiritual things in a carnal way, and they are not able to discern grace till they have it; for so doth this woman understand Christ as if he were speaking of elementary water. " Sir, (saith she, in civil courtesy,) whence hast thou that water?"

2. We are also naturally enemies to our own good, and prone to dispute against our own happiness, that we may deceive ourselves; so far are we from preparations in ourselves to conversion; for she reasons against this living water, as in her judgment impossible to be had or given.

3. We are also naturally so addicted to our own carnal sense that we will believe nothing revealed by Christ further than we can see a reason or outward appearance for it; for she judged it impossible he could have living water, seeing he could not draw it out of that well, nor could shew a better.

4. A chief deceiving principle, making men enemies unto, and careless of, truth and grace, is their pretence of antiquity and succession unto it, and their descent from religious progenitors; for she boasted Jacob was their father, who gave the well, and therefore slighted the offer of a better, as being well enough in her own conceit.

5. None are so ready to boast of antiquity, and of interest in pious progenitors, as they who have least cause so to do; for, saith she, " our father Jacob gave us the well, and drank thereof himself," &c., and yet they were but heathens, who had come in the room of Jacob's children, who had forfeited their right; and however, they were far from Jacob's spirit, who would satisfy their soul with that which only supplied his bodily necessity, and served his cattle as well as him.

6. It is a notable injury done unto Christ to plead any antiquity or succession to it in prejudice of him or his truth, or to cry up any above him; for it was her fault to cry up Jacob, and her interest in him, that she might slight him and his offer—" Art thou greater than our father Jacob?" &c.

7. Sobriety and a simple way of living, albeit it may be found among pagans, yet it is a notable ornament to grace in the godly; when nature, which is content with little, is not overcharged with creatures, to the dishonour of God, abuse of the creatures, and prejudice of men's better estate;

and when men by their carriage declare that their bodies and flesh is not their best -part, which they care most for. So much doth Jacob's practice, contenting himself to drink of this well, with " his children and cattle," teach us.

VER. 13. Jesus answered and said unto her, Whosoever drinketh of this water shall thirst again :

14. But whosoever drinketh of the water that I shall give him shall never thirst ; but the water that I shall give him shall be in him a well of water springing up into everlasting life.

Christ, in his third speech to this woman, doth not carp at her contradicting and carnal humour, but points out the excellency of his offer above what she gloried in, from the effects of both. The water she spake so much of (as all other outward contentments) could not give any abiding satisfaction even to the body, but his living water should have enduring and lively effects and satisfaction, till it were completed in glory. Whence learn—

1. A great cause of men's despising of spiritual things is their ignorance of them, and of their excellency and worth; therefore Christ taketh so much pains to clear this.

2. A special mean helping to point out the worth of spiritual things is to compare them with earthly things, and take up the super-excellent worth that is in the one above the other; for thus doth Christ commend this living water.

3. Whatever pains men take to follow after, or drink up, outward contentments, yet they will find no abiding satisfaction therein, and will sooner drink them dry than quench their own thirst; for what is said of this water is true of all things of the same kind.

4. The Lord hath so ordered it, that men's outward necessities should recur often upon them after the use of means, that so they may be humbled, and made to depend constantly on Providence, and to seek better things, yet with the thankful use of what they have; and in particular, God hath put men to much trouble to uphold a cottage of clay, and hath framed it so as to need constant new supplies, that we may mind our mortality daily. So much doth this dispensation of Providence point out: " Whosoever drinketh of this water shall thirst again."

5. The water of life, albeit Christ did purchase it, yet it must be his free gift to us, who cannot buy it; and his offer includeth a promise of giving it to every one who will receive it in the due order, and that indifferently, without respect of persons; for so much is imported in that he calleth it " the water that I shall give him ;" he saith not, I can give, but " I shall give him"—to wit, if he will receive my offer, and that indefinitely, " whosoever" he be.

6. Whoso partakes of the true grace of God, it will so refresh and satisfy him as to quench his thirst after vanity and earthly delights, and make them tasteless, and to give him contentment in the want of all things. So much is imported, in part, in this promise : " Whosoever drinks of this water shall never thirst."

7. Albeit such as enjoy the grace of God in part will still need and desire more of it, and feed in part on hunger and thirst, while they are within time, 1 Pet. ii. 2, 3 ; Matt. v. 6, yet they shall never fall again under a deadly thirst of total want of this water, a seed still remaining in them; and their mouth being still at the well, they are rather quenching thirst than thirsty, and when they have gotten their full draught at the end of their race, they are satisfied, and never thirst any more; for so much also is included in this promise, " he shall never thirst."

8. Whosoever receive the true grace of Christ in any measure, get also the Spirit of Christ, as the fountain, to make grace thus enduring in itself and its effects; for " the water shall be in him a well of water."

9. The Spirit and grace of Christ in believers is not a stream or a pond, that may run dry, but " a well," and a " springing" well, of inexhaustible fulness, virtue, and refreshment; nor is it such a well which may rot and make water ill tasted, but it is a springing well, still fresh; and where the Spirit is entertained formality will be a stranger; nor is it only a spring to abide within its banks, but a well of water " springing up," or leaping up, and watering all about. The Spirit and grace of Christ floweth out in all the carriage of men who receive the same, making them fruitful, and never to have done with duties, (but the more they do, still the more before their hand,) and active and vigorous in them, as a well boiling up. It floweth out also upon others, unto their good and edification, according to the station and vocation wherein God hath placed them.

10. As the truly godly have no term-day of religion but eternity, and their desire is to keep fresh till the end, so where the Spirit of Christ is, he will still be venting of his virtue and riches from day to day, and letting out more and more to the sinner till eternity come, wherein all the banks of incapacity, sin, distance, ignorance, mortality, &c., being broken down, and the windows of heaven being opened, this stream and well becometh an ocean, and grace, smothered here under corruption and infirmity, gets leave to expatiate itself in glory; for it shall be " a well of water springing up into everlasting life."

VER. 15. The woman saith unto him, Sir, give me this water, that I thirst not, neither come hither to draw.

The woman, in her reply, expresseth a desire to have this water for her own ends. Whence learn—

1. The bars of ignorance and naughtiness even in the elect, hindering them from Christ, are not easily broken; for so much appeareth in this woman's answer. Whether we understand her to speak by way of derision, or rather that Christ's spiritual preaching did discover some excellency in these things to her, (as it may fall out even in natural minds,) yet she took them up but in a natural way ; and accordingly her desire is but carnal.

2. Even nature may have a loathing at these outward infirmities that follow sin, and yet will not be affected with spiritual wants without renovation; and such may have a desire to be happy and free of these troubles when yet they seek this happiness under the sun, and ofttimes in that which proveth their greatest misery; for she desires to be rid of thirst, and of pains in seeking water.

3. It is the great fault of many, that they would be content of as much of Christ as may serve their base ends, and no more; and particularly, it is but a natural and carnal desire after spiritual things when they are sought for supply of natural imperfections and wants, and for the accomplishment of natural imagined happiness; for such was her desire—"Give me this water, that I thirst not, neither come hither to draw."

VER. 16. Jesus saith unto her, Go, call thy husband, and come hither.

17. The woman answered and said, I have no husband. Jesus said unto her, Thou hast well said, I have no husband:

18. For thou hast had five husbands; and he whom thou now hast is not thy husband: in that saidst thou truly.

At this fourth speech we may begin the second part of the conference, wherein Christ having prevailed so little by his offer and commendation of free grace, doth now discover her misery unto her, whereby she is at length and by degrees brought to know him. Therefore he bids her go call her husband, and bring him with her, and she denying she had any, he commends her ingenuity, and lets her see that he knew her lewdness. Whence learn—

1. As grace is little known or esteemed of so long as we know not our misery, so where the offer of mercy doth not persuade, Christ will discover their misery to his own, to make them either come quickly to him or else resolve on hell; for therefore, after the former offers had no success, doth he rip up her bosom.

2. Christ is very meek and tender even in discovering of misery to men so long as they are not incorrigible, and is willing that they should judge and accuse themselves, that he may deal tenderly with them; therefore doth he so mildly bid her "Go, call thy husband," that he might draw a confession out of her own mouth.

3. It is not every sin whereof natural men are guilty for which they can at first be capable of conviction; for every sin will not be odious to every one in every condition, but there are some sins which only grace, and much grace, and grace in exercise, will see to be sinful; therefore, though she was guilty of many other sins, yet Christ pitcheth only on this sin of gross filthiness, as that which would be seen best by her.

4. It is not every sight of sin that will convince the sinner, but Christ must put it home upon the conscience, and discover sin to be marked by his all-searching eye before it work upon him; for she knew her own condition, (and therefore saith, " I have no husband," as shifting the matter whereof she supposed him to be ignorant,)

but without any sense, till he rip up her bosom, and let her see he knew her.

5. Christ will commend a small good under much dross; and particularly he accounts of a true acknowledgment, even of a heinous crime, as a commendable duty; therefore doth he make so much of her confession, " Thou hast well said; thou saidst truly."

6. Christ hath particular knowledge of what sins men are lying in, how hid soever, and particularly he hath an eye upon secret uncleanness; and how loath soever sinners be to be discovered by Christ, yet where he pleaseth and hath a purpose of mercy no shiftings will hide them. So much doth this large discovery after her shifting confession teach : " Thou hast had five husbands, and he whom thou now hast is not thy husband."

7. Such is the pollution of our nature, that lust will be insatiable unless grace curb it. So much appeareth in this woman, who after so many marriages doth live in uncleanness.

VER. 19. The woman saith unto him, Sir, I perceive that thou art a prophet.

20. Our fathers worshipped in this mountain ; and ye say, that in Jerusalem is the place where men ought to worship.

The effect of this discovery is, that the woman is brought to acknowledge him for a prophet, and thereupon propounds to him the great question concerning the place of public worship betwixt the Samaritans and the Jews, the one pretending that Mount Gerizim was the place where Sanballat, by permission of Alexander the Great, had built a temple for Manasseh, his son-in-law, who for that marriage with his daughter was put from the priesthood at Jerusalem, and the other pleading for Jerusalem as the place. As all Israel were enjoined to worship in the place which God should choose for them, Deut. xii. 5, 6, so the Jews had particular and clear warrant that, after the rejection of Shiloh, Jerusalem was the place, 1 Kings, viii. 29 ; xiv. 21 ; 2 Kings, xxi. 4 ; Psalm lxxviii. 67—69 ; cxxxii. 13, 14. But the Samaritans, who rejected all scripture but Moses' writings, regarded not this, and alleged that the place they worshipped on was the mountain of blessing, Deut. xi. 29, and that their progenitors had worshipped there of old, Gen. xxxiii. 18, 20, for it was near to Shechem.

DOCTRINES.

1. Christ's discovering of sin, and making the sinner to be touched with it, breeds more respect and estimation of him ; for now she thinks more of him than formerly.

2. The work of illumination in the elect may have weak beginnings at the first, and very apparent high thoughts of Christ may come far short of his worth ; for her to perceive in him a prophet was very much, yet far beneath what he was, and what she knew him after to be; for however Christ was indeed a prophet in a super-excellent manner, yet she as yet saw nothing in him above ordinary prophets.

3. The Lord may see it fit to awaken and con-

vert a great sinner very gently at first, that so he may shew his abundant tender mercy, that they may not be deterred from closing with him, and particularly that such as live at a great distance from ordinances and the society of God's people may not be overcharged with difficulties which they cannot there alone get through. So much appeareth in his dealing with this woman of Samaria, a stranger.

4. The Lord in his holy providence hath so ordered as there will be controversies about the way of truth and his worship, that the godly may be stirred up to study and embrace the truth more affectionately, and that he may have a ready plague of strong delusions and lies for them who receive not the truth in love. So much may we gather from this controversy betwixt the Jews and the Samaritans.

5. It is a necessary and commendable duty in such as profess the true God not to be ignorant of the matters of religion, nor of the controversies that fall out about it; for even this profane Samaritan had knowledge of this controversy, and of the grounds they had for it, yea, she knew the Messiah was to come, ver. 25.

6. A wakened conscience will be careful to lay the groundwork of religion sure, and men being serious about getting of heaven, they will be diligent to know the right way, and for this end will omit no occasion of getting light. So much may be gathered from her practice, that, taking him for a prophet, she propounds that grand question unto him, to get resolution rather than to think she started that national difference to shift any discourse about her own vileness.

7. A wakened conscience is always so jealous of itself, and its way in matters of controversy, as to omit no mean of information; and such as embrace superstition and a false way of religion can never be established nor have sound peace, as they will find when the conscience is put to it; therefore the first scruple that presents itself is this question concerning their way of worship.

8. It is no new thing to see antiquity opposed to Christ's own express ordinances; and antiquity and the practice of some is a crooked rule to follow when it contradicts the current of the scriptures, yea, and of the practice of such as are commended therein: such were the Samaritans' pretences, "Our fathers worshipped in this mountain," &c., when yet God had appointed another place, and the godly in their times frequented it.

VER. 21. *Jesus saith unto her, Woman, believe me, the hour cometh, when ye shall neither in this mountain, nor yet at Jerusalem, worship the Father.*

Christ, in discussing of this question, answereth in two assertions: first, that both these ways of worship were to give place to a better; for the time was approaching, (at his death, and the honourable burial of the ceremonies,) that the public and lawful worship of God should not be astricted to any certain place, and so the Samaritan worship, because unlawful, and the Jewish way, because temporary, should be abolished, and that partition wall be broken down. Whence learn—

1. It is great wisdom, in discovering of errors and false ways, so to point them out as those who are misled be brought from them, not to another way not much better, but to the right way indeed; therefore Christ takes pains, in the first place, not only to draw her off Samaritanism, but from the Jewish way also, which was to be abolished, to Christianity.

2. There was a time wherein it was lawful and ordained that the public worship of God should be at one certain place— to wit, at Jerusalem, and that under shadows they should find out Christ; for while he saith, "the hour cometh," wherein it shall not be so, he implieth that before it was so, and that lawfully.

3. God may lawfully change the way of his worship when he pleaseth, seeing anything is therefore worship and lawful in it, only because he appointeth it; therefore doth Christ foretel the Lord's changing of the Jewish way of worship.

4. After Christ's coming and death, the public worship of God is no more ascribed to any certain place or nation, nor to be performed in types and shadows. So much doth this assertion teach us: "The hour cometh, when ye shall neither in this mountain, nor yet at Jerusalem, worship," compared with ver. 23. (See 1 Tim. ii. 8.) Otherwise it was lawful to have gospel worship at Jerusalem, as the apostles had, but not there more than in another place; and many Jews were Christians, and worshippers of God, though not they and their proselytes only. This partition-wall began to be abolished by Christ's doctrine in his ministry, and was quite abolished of right by his death, though the Jews had an indulgence for their way, till the honourable burial of the ceremonies in the destruction of the temple, which was the public place where the most of these ceremonies, and the most solemn of them, were acted and gone about, and were thereunto astricted by divine institution.

5. True worship, as it must have God's command, so it must be performed to him as a Father, apprehended to be so through Christ, and must flow from a filial affection; therefore it is called a worshipping "the Father," importing that interest and affection which worshippers do at least pretend unto.

6. Such is the power of Christ accompanying gospel dispensations, as will not only discover the ill of contrary ways, but actually make them give place thereunto; for so much are we taught, in that Christ assures not only that we should not, but shall not, so worship; and thus have we seen it accomplished.

7. Men are ordinarily so rooted in their opinions and errors which they have drunk in, that it is very hard to drive them from them; therefore must Christ press this—" Woman, believe me."

8. As the way of salvation must be taken up by faith, and not by sense or reason, so Christ is worthy to be believed, and his word is a warrant sufficient for faith, how little soever he be credited; for, saith he—" Woman, believe me."

9. Christ not only revealeth ground sufficient for our faith, but such is his tenderness and respect to our weal, that he will even entreat for credence at our hands, and be our supplicant that we would discharge our duty for our own good; therefore doth he entreat—" Woman, believe me."

VER. 22. Ye worship ye know not what: we know what we worship: for salvation is of the Jews.

In the second assertion Christ speaks to her question more distinctly; and lest, from what he had said of the abolishing of both for the time to come and of their giving place to that spiritual worship, she should gather that they were both in themselves at least equal; therefore he here speaks of both these ways, being compared each with other, and in respect of their use till that fulness of time should come; and in this respect he condemns the Samaritan worship as being an ignorant way, and wanting warrant of the word, and preferreth the Jews, as having clear ground for their worship, and it being pointed out in the scriptures as the way to heaven and salvation; the Saviour also being to come of them, and the doctrine of salvation which was among them being to go out from them into all the world, according to the prophecy, Isa. ii. 3. Whence learn—

1. No good intentions, no zeal or pretence whatsoever, can justify anything in God's worship which hath not sure warrant of the word, and is not gone about in the knowledge and faith thereof. So much is included in this reproof of the Samaritans and commendation of the Jews: "Ye worship ye know not what; we know what we worship." To transgress this rule, and to take in any device of men in God's worship, doth in so far make the true God an idol as to imagine him to be such an one as will accept of such false worship.

2. Christ, as he took on the form of a servant, is content to rank himself with the true church as a member, to teach all to esteem highly of such a society—" We (saith he) know what we worship."

3. Not only is worship devised by men not warrantable, but it is not the way to heaven, seeing there can be no salvation but in God's institute way; and the case of those who follow devised worship is so much the more dangerous if they want also the doctrine of salvation in matters of faith and manners. Both these are included in this reason, "for salvation is of the Jews;" that salvation was to be found in that church, their way of worship being appointed and approven of God, and the saving doctrine and oracles of God concerning faith, worship, and manners, being also committed to them, and among them.

4. It was the special privilege of the Jews, and a testimony of God's approving of them as his church, that the Saviour of sinners was to come of them, and the doctrine of salvation, pointing him out, to sound from among them in all the earth: so much also doth this reasoning import, as hath been explained.

VER. 23. But the hour cometh, and now is, when the true worshippers shall worship the Father in spirit and in truth: for the Father seeketh such to worship him.

24. God is a Spirit: and they that worship him must worship him in spirit and in truth.

Christ returneth to enlarge and explain his first assertion, and sheweth what is to come in place of the Jewish worship to be abolished—to wit, that the time was even at hand wherein not only there should be no distinction of place or nations in the matter of worship, but in place of carnal and typical worship, performed by the Jews in one place, all true worshippers, in every place, should worship "in spirit and in truth;" for which he giveth two reasons: first, that God requireth such worship; secondly, that this is most agreeable and pleasing to his spiritual nature. As for these two properties of worship—"in spirit and in truth," they must be taken in opposition to the properties of the former worship, and so they come to one in substance, that instead of external ceremonies, which are called carnal, Hebrews, vii. 16; ix. 10; and shadows, Heb. x. 1; the Lord would have a spiritual worship, and the truth of what was represented by these shadows, as Rom. xii. 1; Heb. xiii. 15, 16. And this agreeth well with the reasons subjoined; for however the Lord did require and was pleased with these external forms, in the infancy of the church, yet he never did accept of them, save in so far as they led to this, which is so agreeable to his nature, and were not rested on by the worshipper. But we may further extend these properties, not only to the matter of worship, but to the manner of it also, that the Lord, who is a Spirit, doth require that lawful worship should be performed "in spirit"—as opposite to a formal way of worship—"and in truth," as opposite to hypocrisy; not that God did approve of the want of these before, but that by the removal of these external rites, wherewith worshippers were much taken up, and which the best saw not clearly enough through, he was to discover this way more fully, and make them more free to attend it; and by pouring out of his spirit he was to work it more generally.

DOCTRINES.

1. The correction and reformation of the worship of God was reserved for the days of the gospel, and to be brought about by Christ; therefore, saith he, "the hour cometh, and now is," when this change shall be. He saith " now is," either because it was instantly approaching at his death, or because he was even now beginning this reformation by his ministry.

2. They who profess themselves worshippers of the true God ought to perform it with humble and affectionate reverence, and with subjection and submission to him, considering his majesty and their own vileness; for so much doth the word rendered "worshippers" import, being a similitude taken from dogs fawning and casting themselves down at their master's feet.

3. Albeit all who profess the true God, and are not avowed atheists, will have some sort of worship, yet all of them will not be found true and approven worshippers, either for matter or manner; therefore are some called " true worshippers" by way of distinction from others.

4. The true worship of God under the gospel doth not consist in the external pomp of ceremonies and observations, but is spiritual, simple, and substantial; for they shall " worship the Father in spirit and in truth," not in carnal shadows, which, if being God's own ordinance, yet did take up worshippers so (through their own weakness) as ofttimes to keep them from minding this spiritual worship, how much more may it be expected that the more external pomp there be of men's devising there will be the less spiritual truth?

5. It is not sufficient to make an approven worshipper that they do not multiply rites and ceremonies, but their worship must be chiefly inward, flowing from grace engaging the heart in God's service, and from the breathing and influence of the Spirit; not resting on an external form of lawful worship, or any bodily exercise about it. So much also are we taught from this, that worship must be " spirit," or spiritual, for the manner of performance as well as for its nature in itself.

6. God requires also in a worshipper that with avoiding of formality, which is but a deceitful, hypocritical show of worship, he studies sincerity and straightness of heart, not dealing negligently, or for by-ends in God's service; for worship must be " in truth."

7. It is the Lord's will and appointment alone that can give a being to true worship, and to this must all our reasonings about this matter be subject. And therefore his enjoining of spiritual, substantial, and sincere worship should commend it to his people. So much doth the subjoining of this reason—" for the Father seeketh such to worship him"—teach.

8. All the true worship that God gets is of his own seeking and procuring, and having wrought it he takes pleasure in it. So much also may his seeking such import, that he sent Christ to make a conquest of spiritual worshippers, and seeketh such as being those he delighteth in.

9. God in his nature is a most pure and simple substance, free of all mixture and composition, and infinite in perfections; and he is to be conceived of spiritually, avoiding all carnal and gross conceptions; for so much are we taught— " God is a Spirit," infinite above angels or spirits of men, who yet are the most simple, pure, and perfect of creatures.

10. The right way of worshipping of God is when men study to do that which is most agreeable to his nature, which is most pleasing unto him; and men who know him cannot but see that it is not carnal and outward performances that please him, but that which is performed in inward sincerity and real substance; for so much doth this second reason, confirming the former, teach—" God is a Spirit, and they that worship him must worship him in spirit and in truth."

Ver. 25. The woman saith unto him, I know that Messias cometh, which is called Christ: when he is come, he will tell us all things.

26. Jesus saith unto her, I that speak unto thee am he.

By this discourse concerning the change of religion the woman is brought to remember of the Messiah's coming, for the full clearing of all doubts, to whom, as appeareth, she remits the controversy; and Christ doth assure her that he is the same person. Whence learn—

1. Some knowledge of the mysteries of religion may be found among those who otherwise are very far off, whereby the Lord would condemn all those who, being in a nearer relation, do yet remain grossly ignorant, and all those who content themselves with notional knowledge; for this woman—a Samaritan, not only knew the Messiah was promised, but was expecting him as near at hand, in regard that things fore-prophesied before his coming were accomplished, and especially that the sceptre was removed from Judah: " I know that the Messiah cometh," saith she.

2. It is the will of God that the scriptures and truths of God should be made plain to the capacity of all, and that men should not please themselves with forms of words in the matter of knowledge, but should be acquainted with the thing itself; therefore is the name " Messiah" expounded "which is called Christ," (not by the woman, who understood that name well enough, but by John,) for the use of all readers, that they might know what was signified by that name.

3. Resolution in a controversy of religion is only to be had and sought from Christ, who is the infallible resolver of all who come to his light; therefore doth she remit the matter to him.

4. As the will of God concerning religion and the way of salvation was not fully revealed till Christ came from the bosom of the Father, so Christ came to be a teacher of his church, and hath fully revealed the counsel of God concerning his service and man's salvation, so as there is no place for adding or diminishing. So much is imported in her expectation, " When he is come, he will tell us all things"—to wit, which relate to this subject in hand.

5. Christ is not far off from any who have a high estimation of him, and a desire after him, how great soever the distance seem to be to themselves; for to this woman, so affected, he is at hand : " I am he."

6. It doth commend Christ's great condescendence, that he not only came into the world, but was pleased to converse with the vilest of sinners to do them good; for saith he, " I am he that speaketh unto thee," a lewd woman, and a scoffer.

7. It commendeth also his great compassion towards needy sinners that his secret is with them, and that he will reveal himself unto them when he lets others lie in darkness; for though upon wise grounds he forbade his disciples to make him known, and would not himself answer many captious and tempting questions of the Jews to this purpose, yet he will not conceal

himself from this Samaritan, now convinced of her need of him.

8. None can know or take up Christ, though present with them, and speaking to them, unless he reveal himself; therefore doth this woman need this declaration.

Ver. 27. And upon this came his disciples, and marvelled that he talked with the woman: yet no man said, What seekest thou? or, Why talkest thou with her?

28. The woman then left her waterpot, and went her way into the city, and saith to the men,

29. Come, see a man, which told me all things that ever I did: is not this the Christ?

30. Then they went out of the city, and came unto him.

In the next branch of this part of the chapter is recorded, first (in these verses), that the conference being broken up by the disciples' return, (who wondered at their Master's carriage, and yet would not challenge it,) she proveth how she was affected with it, by forgetting her own errand, and going to invite those of the city to come to him, wherein she had success. Whence learn—

1. Poor sinners may meet with so sweet a time in Christ's company that the company even of disciples would be an interruption to it; for she had so sweet a time with Christ that the disciples' coming puts an end to it. They had been sent " to buy meat," ver. 8, and now they returning, the conference breaks up, or at least shortly after.

2. Providence doth wisely and graciously order dispensations towards his people, so as they are not prejudged thereby, but they tend to good; therefore doth not the disciples come till she knew him to be the Messiah, and till the breaking up of the conference tended to a greater good in sending her to bring in more.

3. Christ will demit himself, and stoop so low to a poor sinner, as is marvellous to flesh and blood; and there is more kindness, meekness, and humility in him alone than in all his followers; for " his disciples marvelled that he talked with the woman," or that he should take notice of such an one; and it seems he was upon the close of his discourse, and had not yet ended when they came. He is so compassionate as he needs no intercessors.

4. It is no strange thing to see Christ's followers soon forget themselves, and being advanced by grace, to become so proud as to despise others; for they who were even now chosen out of the dust " marvelled that he talked with the woman."

5. Such reverence is due to Christ in his working as when we can see no reason for what he doth, yet we are bound not to quarrel, but to suppress our own thoughts; for so did they: " yet no man said, What seekest thou? or, Why talkest thou with her?"

6. When a soul hath tasted of Christ and his excellency, other things will be little regarded, which before were in great esteem; for so was it with this woman; she came to draw water for her thirst, and thought much of that water, but now she forgot her errand, " and left her waterpot, and went her way."

7. True grace is communicative of itself, and knowledge of Christ will make a person diligent to spread his name, and particularly to those they have greatest interest in; for " she goeth to the city," where she dwelt, " and saith to the men, Come," &c.

8. Such as are kindly inviters of others to Christ, from any saving knowledge of him, they will not be content that men rest on their report, but would have them taste and see themselves; nor will they be content to send others, but will go to share themselves: " Come (not go), and see a man," saith she.

9. As Christ knoweth all that men do, so his searching and discovering word is a special mean of conversion, and a sanctified sight of one sin, discovered by Christ, will open men's eyes to see more; therefore, albeit Christ spake many good words to her, yet this was the hook that catched her; he " told me all things that ever I did;" she saith, " all things," either because that in one instance he gave proof of his ability so to do, or because that discovery represented other things to her as seen by him.

10. Christ's doctrine is then effectual, and prevaileth, when himself is seen in and by it; therefore subjoineth she, " Is not this the Christ?" not as doubting of it herself, seeing he had told her, but as pointing it home to them, that they may consider of such an opportunity.

11. Weak instruments, and such as have but small knowledge and weak faith, yea, even women in their stations, labouring in the gospel, shall not want their own success, but may have powerful effects; for upon this weak woman's invitation " they went out of the city, and came unto him."

Ver. 31. In the mean while his disciples prayed him, saying, Master, eat.

32. But he said unto them, I have meat to eat that ye know not of.

33. Therefore said the disciples one to another, Hath any man brought him ought to eat?

34. Jesus saith unto them, My meat is to do the will of him that sent me, and to finish his work.

Secondly, we have recorded Christ's conference with the disciples in absence of the woman, and before the Samaritans came to him, tending to commend the work of the ministry in bringing in of souls. And first, in his own practice he declareth that his delight in that work entrusted him by the Father took his mind off bodily refreshment, even when he had need of it, and was more refreshful to him than meat or drink could be. Whence learn—

1. Christ is not only meek towards lost sinners, but most indefatigable, yea, and refreshed, in seeking their good, even to the forgetting of his own necessities; for in this also his disciples

come short of him, who would have him now eating of what they had bought, whereas he not only needs to be put in mind of his necessary food, though he had been weary and faint, ver. 6, but tells them, " I have meat to eat," and that delight in his calling allayed the sense of outward necessities.

2. It is also Christ's prerogative to be the chief improver of time, and entertainer of spiritual purposes, whereas others that are often and much in his company may be, and too often are, very carnal; for albeit it was necessary that Christ and his disciples should have bodily refreshment, yet the disciples in this bewray their own disposition, which was yet rude, in that when others are not with Christ, to keep up and draw out spiritual purposes from him, they mind only meat: " In the mean while (when the woman was away) his disciples prayed him, saying, Master, eat;" wherein Christ reproves their temper, by setting on foot a spiritual purpose necessary for them, and improves that short while of the woman's absence well.

3. When the Lord offers an occasion of doing good to souls, (especially which will not so readily occur at another time,) it should be followed, so far as health will permit, with the neglect of anything of lesser consequence; for so doth Christ reckon of this occasion of doing good to the Samaritans : " I have meat to eat;" it made him forget meat, and was as meat to him.

4. The refreshments that are found in God's service and doing of his work are but known to very few ; yea, even disciples may be much ignorant thereof for a time, and do always come short of that delight that Christ found therein; for saith he, " I have meat to eat that ye know not of." They were but yet rude, and knew not this, at least under these terms of meat, (as Thomas knew not Christ under the name of a " way," John, xiv. 5,) nor did they know it yet in experience, nor could they reach that height of delight Christ found in it.

5. As a carnal disposition and temper is not soon cured, even in disciples, so this is a great impediment to them in taking up Christ's mind, while they judge carnally of what he saith; for so much doth their discourse, till Christ cleared them, import : " Therefore said the disciples one to another, Hath any man brought him ought to eat?"

6. Christ is so careful in helping his people, that their very necessities are an invitation to him, though they fail in not employing him; therefore, although they do but discourse among themselves, and (out of modesty, or otherwise) do not inquire at him, yet he cleareth them.

7. The saving of lost sinners is a special point of God's will, which he will have accomplished; for Christ calleth this work he is about " the will of him that sent me," that men might neither look on God as averse from sinners' salvation, nor on that work as uncertain what the issue of it will be.

8. Christ is entrusted by the Father with the work of saving sinners, and sent into the world with a commission for that effect; therefore doth Christ speak of himself as sent of God, to perform this his will.

9. Christ is entrusted not only to undertake the work of sinners' salvation, but to bring it to perfection, as accordingly he did, for he was sent " to finish his work," or the work enjoined by the Father; and as he perfected the work of redemption on the cross, John, xix. 30, and did faithfully preach these glad tidings, and convert souls in his generation, so he stands still engaged to see that whole work perfected.

10. Christ undertook this work entrusted to him, not of necessity, but willingly, and went about it with more delight than a hungry man hath in meat, that so he might commend his love to us, that he might teach ministers to be delighted in this work, 1 Thess. ii. 19, 20 ; iii. 8 ; Acts, xx. 24, and that he might teach all to go about God's service in their stations as their delight and recreation, for saith he, " My meat is to do the will of him that sent me," &c.

VER. 35. Say not ye, There are yet four months, and then cometh harvest? behold, I say unto you, Lift up your eyes, and look on the fields; for they are white already to harvest.

In the next place, Christ stirs them up to the like affection and diligence in their calling, which he presseth on them from several reasons : the first is taken from the ripeness of people, and their willingness to hear (whereof there was a present instance in the Samaritans that were coming forth), which therefore was to be improved. Whence learn—

1. As people may be sometimes ripe for a ministry as corn is for reaping, (as when people flock to ordinances when they are offered, after they have lain long in ignorance, or under a dead ministry,) so such an opportunity should not be neglected by ministers, as that which will not be easily recovered ; therefore compareth he the condition of people to fields " white already to harvest," which is a season that cannot be neglected without much damage and loss of the grain.

2. Men's diligence in their worldly affairs, foreseeing and preparing for the opportunities of them, should be a spur to ministers to set their heart upon their work, to mark the case of their people, to long for a disposition in them for embracing the gospel, and to improve it when they find it in any measure. So much doth this comparison import : " Say not ye, there are yet four months, and then cometh harvest? behold, I say unto you, Lift up your eyes, and look on the fields," &c. He saith " four months," either because it was so much to the harvest, and they had been speaking of it by the way, or because, generally, men mind it a long time before, and much more ought they to take notice of the present ripeness of people for the ministry.

VER. 36. And he that reapeth receiveth wages, and gathereth fruit unto life eternal : that both he that soweth and he that reapeth may rejoice together.

A second reason pressing this duty is taken from the profit following on this work, which is both a free reward in their own persons and the reward of being instrumental to save others, as 1 Tim. iv. 16, the effect of both which is the joint joy of the prophets as sowers, and of them as reapers, as is after explained, wherein there is an allusion to the joy of reapers in harvest, and their feasts after it was gathered in, Isa. ix. 3. Whence learn—

1. Albeit faithful ministers deserve nothing at God's hand, and albeit they lie under much contempt in the world, yet, beside what reward of honourable maintenance is due for their encouragement, they shall not want an eternal reward from God, for " he that reapeth receiveth wages."

2. Albeit such as are brought in to Christ by the ministry may seem many times to be called to encounter many storms, yet when they are ripe for God's barn they shall be brought unto eternal life, where they will be at quiet, for the fruit is gathered " unto life eternal."

3. The service of God, and his blessing upon it, is reward enough of itself; and, particularly, faithful ministers have a promise that they shall be blessed with fruit in their labours, and it is reward enough that they are honoured to be instrumental in the salvation of any; for it is a promise and a part of the wages, he " gathereth fruit unto eternal life."

4. As there is joy in heaven at the conversion of a sinner, and there will be unspeakable joy at the perfecting of the congregation of the first-born, so faithful ministers have allowance of joy in the bringing in of souls, which will be completed in the day of Christ ; for here the end of their labour is to " rejoice."

5. God's allowance of joy is so free that none who labour faithfully are secluded from it, whatever their success be, and so full that all may share in it, without envy at one another's happiness and success, for " both he that soweth and he that reapeth rejoice together."

VER. 37. And herein is that saying true, One soweth, and another reapeth.

38. I sent you to reap that whereon ye bestowed no labour: other men laboured, and ye are entered into their labours.

A third reason (illustrated by a similitude) is taken from the easy task wherein the apostles were now employed, in comparison of Moses and the prophets before them; they had much pains, as in ploughing and sowing, with little seen fruit, but by this they had made the work more ripe for the apostles, having, by their preaching and writing to the church, laid a ground for the apostles' speedy success.   For clearing this purpose, we are to consider, 1. This comparison doth not chiefly hold in respect of the gentiles, where the apostles are said to plant, 1 Cor. iii. 6, and to lay a foundation, Rom. xv. 20; see also 2 Cor. x. 15, 16, (though in this also they had the advantage of the prophet's doctrine, delivered to the Jews, to confirm what they said by it ;) but the comparison holds in respect of the church of Israel, where the prophets had laboured, and to which the apostles' first commission was, Matt. x. 6.   Consider, 2. This comparison is not to be taken as if the apostles took no pains at all, but it is to be understood comparatively, that the prophets' great pains made them come better speed with less pains. Nor is it to be understood as if the prophets reaped or converted none, but that their fruit was small, considering their pains in comparison of the apostles', who, under the dispensation of the gospel, reaped the fruit of their pains.

DOCTRINES.

1. A spiritual mind will make good use of common proverbs, even in spiritual purposes, as Christ doth here.

2. The Lord seeth it fit, in his deep wisdom, not to let all his servants have alike difficulties in their calling, nor alike success, but may let some be at great pains in preparing for Christ, and sowing the precious seed, who yet will be out of the world before any remarkable fruit of it appear ; and may let others see very rich fruits of their labours in their own time ; for so were the prophets sowers and the apostles reapers ; the one laboured with little visible success, the other brought in many, sometimes even with one sermon.

3. Such as labour faithfully in the Lord's work, albeit they have not much visible success, yet they are neither disapproved nor useless, but are doing useful service in their generation, and working to the hand of others, under whom the fruit of their labours will appear; for so the prophets were sowers, and the apostles " entered into their labours," and reaped the fruit of their sowing.

4. The more easy the Lord makes a minister's work, by sending him, not to pagans, but to a visible church, prepared aforehand by the faithful labours of others, the more delight should he have in going about it.   So much doth the force of the reason import : " I sent you to reap that whereon you bestowed no labour," &c., therefore ye should be affected with your work.

5. This also layeth an obligation on those who have long enjoyed ordinances to give proof of their profiting under former ministers, by being fitted to receive the word more fruitfully from those who follow after.   So much, also, doth this similitude teach, that the church of Israel was like a ripe field to the apostles, as having been prepared thereto, as a manured and sown field ; and such is the duty of others.

VER. 39. And many of the Samaritans of that city believed on him for the saying of the woman, which testified, He told me all that ever I did.

40. So when the Samaritans were come unto him, they besought him that he would tarry with them : and he abode there two days.

41. And many more believed because of his own word ;

42. And said unto the woman, Now we believe, not because of thy saying : for we have heard him ourselves, and know that

this is indeed the Christ, the Saviour of the world.

In the last branch of this part of the chapter John proceedeth to record the conversion of more of the Samaritans of Sychar, and for that end he returns to prosecute that narration, ver. 29, 30, setting down, first, the cause which drew (at least) many of them to go out, which was, their giving credit to the woman's testimony, ver. 39 ; next, their request to Christ when they came to him, and his granting thereof, ver. 40 ; thirdly, the effect of his doctrine among them, which is, the conversion of many more, who belike, out of curiosity or otherwise, had gone out with the rest, ver. 41 ; the effect of which conversion is their declaration to the woman that their faith did not depend on her testimony, but on the sure ground of his own instruction, ver. 42, which may also be safely understood of them who get some measure of faith by her information, and were confirmed by his own doctrine, but chiefly of those who were drawn out to see him, though as yet they believed not.

From ver. 39, learn—1. Very weak instruments may be very richly blessed when they employ themselves for Christ ; for this woman prevaileth, not only to bring them out, but " many of the Samaritans believed on him for the saying of the woman," &c.

2. When one can say but little of Christ, yet if it be spoken from experience and feeling, it may be more persuasive to invite men to believe than much more which is spoken from notional knowledge ; for such was this woman's testimony of him which was so successful : " He told me all that ever I did."

3. As it is a commendation to be easily persuaded to believe, so when a people are ripe, a very weak mean, through God's blessing, will draw them in ; for these Samaritans are persuaded by less than many incorrigible Jews had daily.

4. As true faith may be wrought by degrees, so Christ hath a great estimation even of the smallest beginnings of it ; therefore he giveth it the name of believing.

From ver. 40, learn—1. It is a good preparation, where men are thus far prevailed with as to draw near where Christ is to be found, and take a trial of him ; for the Samaritans (belike more than believed) came to him, and this drew on more.

2. Christ, being rightly taken up, his company will be more desired, and especially the weakest degree of faith will breathe out desires after its own confirmation, by enjoying more of him ; therefore " they besought him that he would tarry with them."

3. Christ is very tender and willing to grant the desires of those who long for his company ; therefore, albeit he had forbidden his disciples to go in the way of the Samaritans, Matt. x. 5, and albeit the time of spreading his glory to the world was not yet come, yet for a prelude of the calling of the gentiles, and out of respect to their need, " he abode there."

4. As Christ measures the time of his sensible presence according to his own purpose and his children's necessity, so a very short while of his company is a great blessing ; therefore " he abode there two days" only, as being the minister of circumcision and of the Jews, and yet that is marked as a mercy to them, whereas many now think little that his sun stands still in one horizon.

From verse 41, learn—1. Such as are not wrought upon by instruments are not yet desperate if Christ take them in hand ; for " more believed" than would give credit to the woman.

2. Christ being found speaking in and by his word, will have such clearness in discovering himself, and such efficacy in persuading, that it will prevail with those that otherwise stand out ; for " his own word," spoken by him, prevailed with them.

3. A short time in Christ's company may do much good through his blessing ; for in two days " many more believed."

From verse 42, learn—1. Albeit that instruments speaking may be a mean to draw people to hearken or give some assent to truth, yet it is Christ himself who must work a persuasion, and faith is never established till it get rooting on Christ's speaking and sealing the word by the Spirit ; and then anything men can say cometh short of what they find in him, and they will undervalue men's authority when it comes in competition with his. All this is imported in that they " said unto the woman, Now we believe, not because of thy saying ; for we have heard him ourselves," &c. ; where they do not despise her as an instrument, but declare that their faith is bottomed on a surer ground than her word.

2. The right knowledge of Christ in his person and offices, and particularly that he is the Saviour of sinners offered to all nations, is a notable mean to draw souls to rest on him and embrace him ; for this doctrine Christ taught to convert them, and this their faith rests upon ; we " know that this is indeed the Christ, the Saviour of the world," and not of the Jews only

VER. 43. Now after two days he departed thence, and went into Galilee.

44. For Jesus himself testified, that a prophet hath no honour in his own country.

45. Then when he was come into Galilee, the Galileans received him, having seen all the things that he did at Jerusalem at the feast : for they also went unto the feast.

Followeth in the third part of the chapter Christ's coming into Galilee, with his entertainment and working of another miracle there. This history, being interrupted from ver. 3, by the narration of what occurred by the way, is now prosecuted ; and in these verses John relates his coming thither after his removal from Sychar, ver. 43 ; that expecting (according to the common proverb) no respect in his own city, Nazareth, therefore he went not thither, or stayed not there, ver. 44, (but went to Cana, as it is, ver. 46,) and that as he travelled through Galilee towards Cana he was entertained and welcomed by them who had been at Jerusalem, at the feast, and had seen his miracles there, verse 45.

From verse 43, learn—It is the duty of the Lord's servants closely to follow their calling from him, even though it should seem they might do more good elsewhere; therefore, notwithstanding his success in Samaria, yet " after two days he departed thence, and went into Galilee," being a part of his charge as minister of the circumcision.

From verse 44, learn—1. Christ is a prophet among and above others, and whatever charge he lay on others to teach his people, yet he remains still the chief teacher himself; for the proverb importeth that he was " a prophet."

2. The prophets, or messengers carrying the word of God, should have honour and a due estimation of the dignity of their calling and gifts, testified by reverence to their persons, obedience to their doctrine, and honourable maintenance; for so much doth the proverb import, that a " prophet" should have " honour," and honour includeth all those; their being spiritual parents, rulers, and Christ's ambassadors, calleth for this.

3. It is an usual and ordinary fault that the servants of God are most disrespected among their own; for such is men's naughtiness by nature that things that come from afar like them best, and that acquaintance with men's persons, parents, &c., breeds contempt. Therefore Christ met with this, and " testified" it as ordinarily true, that " a prophet hath no honour in his own country." (See Luke, iv. 22—29.)

4. Since Christ's doctrine cannot be in request where the messengers carrying the same are not in estimation, therefore such as ingrately contemn ministers are justly deprived of the benefit of the ministry; therefore is this set down as a reason why he went not to, or stayed not in, Nazareth, but went to Cana.

5. It is the duty of the servants of God to arm and guard themselves against contempt and disrespect, that it stumble them not, especially after they have enjoyed better times; therefore not only doth Christ resolve on it, but " testified" concerning it when he came to Galilee, that his disciples, who had seen him better esteemed of among the Samaritans, might not mistake.

From verse 45, learn—1. Distance of place and necessity of pains should not hinder men from frequenting of ordinances, and it is commendable where it is so; for the Galileans " also went unto the feast." Their great pains may condemn them that are lazy, and yet have fewer difficulties.

2. Albeit Christ get no respect nor welcome in one place, yet he will get it elsewhere; and those who have observed his dealing best will respect him most; for " the Galileans received him, having seen all that he did at Jerusalem," &c.

3. Every work of Christ whereof we see not present success is not therefore lost, but may have rich fruit ready to appear in due time; for the fruits of Christ's miracles at Jerusalem (which, chap. ii. 23, are marked only in general to have produced some sort of faith) appear more clearly in Galilee.

4. Albeit fairest shows of good, founded only on the sight of Christ's works, will prove but unsound, yet in so far are Christ's miracles rightly made use of as they tend either to confirm doctrine or induce men to receive and hear it, and to welcome the messengers thereof for that end; for so was it here : they " received him," (or made his person welcome, and admitted him as a teacher among them,) " having seen all the things that he did," &c.

Ver. 46. So Jesus came again into Cana of Galilee, where he made the water wine. And there was a certain nobleman, whose son was sick at Capernaum.

47. When he heard that Jesus was come out of Judea into Galilee, he went unto him, and besought him that he would come down, and heal his son : for he was at the point of death.

Followeth the miracle wrought upon the son of a nobleman, unto which is premitted [explained] some antecedents and occasions—as namely, (in these verses,) the place where it was wrought; the person on whom—a nobleman or courtier's son ; and that his father, hearing of Christ's coming into Galilee, goeth unto him, entreating for his son in his extremity.   Whence learn—

1. Where Christ hath manifested his glory and done good to any, there will be need of confirmations, and Christ will not be wanting therein, but will count it a homely place to come to again where he hath done a good work before ; therefore it is marked that he " came again into Cana of Galilee, where he made the water wine."

2. The grace of God is free, and the Lord hath his elect and precious ones, even of all ranks; for here he gains " a certain nobleman," or courtier, belonging, as appeareth, to Herod, to whom Galilee belonged, Luke, xxiii. 7, and it may be, was that Chuza, of whom, Luke, viii. 3.

3. Men's greatness and nobility doth not exempt them or theirs from common calamities and crosses, for his " son was sick at Capernaum ;" and it maketh the cross heavier the more they have to give them.

4. Many of God's elect never come to Christ till they be driven by a cross, and particularly sickness of children is one special mean whereby Christ draweth his own to make acquaintance with him; for his going to Christ upon this occasion imports not only that it was his duty thus to respect his child, but that Christ took occasion of this distemper to draw him in to himself.

5. Many who come to Christ in trouble do not give him that glory by faith that they ought, but are ready to limit him to a certain way of working, beyond which their faith can see no probability of help; for albeit he conceived Christ could heal his son, yet he ties his virtue to his bodily presence; he " besought that he would come down, and heal his son."

6. As great and pressing need should stir us up to do our duty, so it is an argument meet to

prevail with Christ by; therefore it is subjoined, " for he was at the point of death," as the reason of the parent's diligence, and as the argument propounded to Christ.

VER. 48. Then said Jesus unto him, Except ye see signs and wonders, ye will not believe.

Christ will not at first grant this request and work the miracle, but first studies to cure a more dangerous soul-sickness in this man and others, that nothing but outward miracles did at [satisfied] them, or affected them; for this was all the man's errand to Christ, and it seems to have been the common temper of those in Galilee who received him, ver. 45, and of those in Cana, ver. 46, and therefore he deals first about it; and this is another antecedent of the miracle. Whence learn—

1. It is a dangerous and general disease of men not to affect Christ so much for spiritual benefits as for his outward workings, and not to ground their estimation of, and confidence in him, upon his word, but on his works; for such was the disease here—" Except ye see signs and wonders, ye will not believe."

2. Albeit it be our fault to be more affected with bodily than spiritual wants, and we do come to Christ more for the one than for the other, yet spiritual and soul ills are the greatest, though less felt, and require speediest help; for so much is imported in Christ's method of curing the one before the other, whatever need of haste there seemed to be that he should cure his son first.

3. The more common an ill be it needs the greater haste in curing of it; therefore Christ falls on this with the nobleman, as being the disease not only proper to him, but common to those where he was—" ye will not believe."

4. As it is good to come to Christ, even with outward straits and troubles, so Christ may see it fit to suspend intended help that he may do our souls good; and wherever Christ giveth an outward favour in mercy he doth also some good to the soul with it, as here, in this example, is to be seen.

VER. 49. The nobleman saith unto him, Sir, come down ere my child die.

50. Jesus saith unto him, Go thy way; thy son liveth. And the man believed the word that Jesus had spoken unto him, and he went his way.

The nobleman is so pressed with the present trouble that he little heeds what Christ said, and therefore repeats and reneweth his suit with more haste and diffidence than before, (and this is yet another occasion and antecedent of the miracle,) yet Christ granteth his request, intimating that the miracle was already wrought, though not in his way, yet in a better; and withal he cureth his unbelief, making him to go his way at his command, leaning to his word. Whence learn—

1. Such is man's weakness and frailty that distractions with grief or fear will draw his mind from heeding instructions from Christ, and out-ward vexations will draw the mind from the thoughts he should have about spiritual and better things; for he is so taken up with his child's case that he took little notice of what Christ said, only he is so far humbled and pressed with need as not to startle at a rough answer.

2. Where there is pressing need and any spark of faith it maketh a supplicant importunate, and that he will not give over meet with what he will; therefore doth he renew and press his suit again: " Sir, come down," &c.

3. Weakness in faith expresseth itself in much haste under pressing needs. So much doth his supplication import: " Sir, come down ere my child die."

4. Unbelief or weakness of faith hath more base thoughts of Christ than are seen at first, and the more it be exercised it will appear the more, for in his second request he not only astricts Christ's virtue to his bodily presence, but limits his power further, as if he could do nothing, though present, if his son were once dead— " Sir, (saith he,) come down (and that) ere my son die"—both of which were a fault, either to limit him to a way of working or to limit his power, as if anything were too hard for him.

5. Such is Christ's tenderness and mercy that when he hath reproved our faults, and we have come ill speed in amending them, yet he will not leave us so, but will respect great need and weak faith more than much unbelief and ill-deserving. So much appeareth in his granting this man's suit.

6. As Christ may be answering the main of his people's desire when they get not satisfaction in every particular circumstance, and as Christ will not be prescribed unto or limited in the way of his working, so his refusal to satisfy his people in their way is in mercy, and because he purposeth to do better. So appeareth here: the best this man could devise was, that at Christ's coming to Capernaum his son should recover; but Christ doth better than so, and sheweth it is done already: " Go thy way; thy son liveth," or, is well.

7. Christ hath absolute power of sickness and health, of life and death, and with one word can chase away a deadly disease at never so great a distance. So much doth he teach this nobleman here, that being at Cana he could chase away sickness at Capernaum: " Thy son liveth."

8. Christ can do a weak believer a good turn, and with that amend his faults also, and make his former reproofs to work; for now this man " believed the word that Jesus had spoken unto him, and (at his command) went his way," not doubting but all would be well.

VER. 51. And as he was now going down, his servants met him, and told him, saying, Thy son liveth.

52. Then inquired he of them the hour when he began to amend. And they said unto him, Yesterday at the seventh hour the fever left him.

53. So the Father knew that it was at the same hour, in the which Jesus said unto him, Thy son liveth : and himself believed, and his whole house.

Followeth the manifestation of this miracle, which is declared to be wrought in the former verse, and the effects of it. The servants meeting this nobleman with the good news of his son's recovery, he finds, after diligent inquiry, that the time of it trysted [agreed] with the time that Christ spake to him, whereby he is confirmed in faith, and his family drawn in to God with him. Whence learn—

1. It is the duty of servants not only to be faithful in their master's affairs but to be affected with them, and to sympathize with their condition, whether it be sad or joyful. So much appeareth in the practice of these servants, who " met" their master with the good news.

2. Good news will, sooner or later, meet the man who believeth and resteth on God's word ; for so much doth this nobleman find in experience.

3. As a believer is bound to observe all the circumstances of Christ's working that may confirm faith, so experience and observation will prove the truth of what he believeth, and will speak in the same terms with the promise ; for this man finds not only that true which Christ had said, but, trying it to the uttermost, he finds the miracle to have been wrought that same time that Christ spake.

4. Much advantage may be reaped by men's communicating their knowledge, experience, and observations one with another, whereby they may help each other to a more full acknowledgment of Christ ; for the servants knew the child's recovery, and the time of it ; the master knew the word Christ had spoken, and the time of it ; and these being put together they mutually draw other to know Christ and his power and goodwill.

5. Temporal favours are then indeed blessed when the experience of God's goodness in them advanceth our soul's good, and is a mean either to beget or advance our faith in Christ ; for so is it here, " he believed," or was confirmed in what was begun before.

6. As Christ bringeth salvation to the house he cometh unto, and may do good to the souls of many by one work, so where a master of a family is brought to Christ it giveth good ground of hope that others of the family will do well ; and however, what experience any one of a family getteth of Christ all the family are bound to make use of it : all this may be gathered from this, that " himself believed, and all his house."

VER. 54. This is again the second miracle that Jesus did, when he was come out of Judea into Galilee.

John concludeth this history with a remark that this miracle was the second which he wrought in Galilee, (the first being done in the same place, chap. ii.,) and that he did it after he came from Judea thither. Whence learn—

1. Christ's works, and particularly his more special manifestations of himself, ought to be marked and kept in memory ; as here John's practice, after so many years, and his recommending that observation to the church in all ages, teacheth.

2. Christ's present works and manifestations ought not only to affect us themselves, but should bring his former works to remembrance, that they may be considered and commended also ; so doth this miracle call the former to remembrance.

3. However men may study to bear down Christ in the world, yet it will be to no purpose, for in one place or other he will be still reaping fruit and manifesting his glory ; therefore it is marked that he did this miracle (as also the former) " when he was come out of Judea into Galilee," to shew that their driving him from thence by their malicious plottings did not hinder him to shew forth his glory elsewhere, nor hinder sinners to believe in him.

CHAPTER V.

In this chapter, first, we have another miracle of Christ's working, in curing an infirm man in Jerusalem, at the feast, and on the sabbath day, to ver. 10 ; next, we have the Jews quarrelling with the healed man as a sabbath-breaker, and their plotting of Christ's death, when they knew him to be the author of that work, to ver. 17 ; thirdly, Christ's apology for what he had done, ver. 17, and for asserting his equality with the Father in maintaining his deed ; which he further proves by many reasons, to ver. 31, and by many witnesses, which were so clear and convincing as gave him just cause to reprove them for their wilful unbelief, from ver. 31 to the end.

VER. 1. After this there was a feast of the Jews; and Jesus went up to Jerusalem.

Several circumstances are premitted [explained] unto the history of this miracle, to ver. 8, whereof the first is a general description of the time and place of it : it was done at Jerusalem, at a feast, to which " Christ went up." As this history doth not follow immediately upon the former, though in general it be said it was " after this," but several things intervened, (which John omitteth, as being employed not so much to confirm the same doctrine by repeating it, as to record what the rest had omitted,) so this is the cause why we cannot certainly determine what this feast was at which " Christ went up ;" nor is it much material for our use. Only we may gather from this—

1. The solemn feasts observed by the Jews at God's appointment were peculiar and proper to themselves, and not obliging nor belonging to the Christian church ; for therefore is this called " a feast of the Jews."

2. Christ was pleased to subject himself unto the law, not only the moral, to free his people from the condemnation thereof, but to the ceremonial law also, that he might free his church from the yoke thereof; therefore "Jesus went up to Jerusalem," in obedience to the law requiring this appearance, Exod. xxxiv. 23.

3. Opportunities of advancing the kingdom of Christ, and of doing good in our station, ought not to be omitted, but taken hold of, though it seem to tend to our own trouble or hazard that we do so; therefore also "Christ went up to Jerusalem," at the feast, though he met with trouble there, because he had occasion of setting out his glory by healing the man, and by preaching in that solemn assembly.

VER. 2. Now there is at Jerusalem by the sheep market a pool, which is called in the Hebrew tongue Bethesda, having five porches.

3. In these lay a great multitude of impotent folk, of blind, halt, withered, waiting for the moving of the water.

4. For an angel went down at a certain season into the pool, and troubled the water: whosoever then first after the troubling of the water stepped in was made whole of whatsoever disease he had.

The next thing premitted [explained] is, a more particular description of the place of this miracle. It was wrought at the sheep gate, (as the word may be read,) of which Neh. iii. 1, so called, because, being near the temple, the sacrifices were brought into the city at that gate; or at "the sheep market," (as we translate the word,) a place near that gate, where, according to the liberty granted by the law, Deut. xiv. 24—26, men might provide themselves of sacrifices; though now the corruption of men had brought these commodities into the temple, John, ii. 14. More particularly, this miracle was wrought at a "pool," which, whatever use it had of old, (it may be, among others, for washing the beasts before they were presented,) was now honoured with the Lord's presence manifested there in curing the diseases of all such as went into it, after an angel's troubling the waters, and therefore was frequented with a number of sick persons who attended that sign, and were accommodated in "five porches" built about the pool. The name of this pool, "Bethesda," may either signify "the place of pouring out"—to wit, of water, either into the pool by conduits, (being possibly that of Hezekiah, 2 Kings, xx. 20,) or out of it by pipes, for several uses, or it may signify "the house of mercy," because of the proofs of God's mercy manifested to the sick there. As for the time of the beginning or ceasing of this miracle it is needless to search into it, seeing scripture elsewhere is silent about it, only it seemeth to have begun but of late among them.

DOCTRINES.

1. The place where these persons lay being a place of great concourse, and from whence they went into the temple to worship, doth teach us that it is a necessary meditation for men to have frequent and serious thoughts of their own frailty, that they may be humbled, and may be stirred up to press more earnestly after God, in whom all is made up. This did the Lord preach by presenting these sad spectacles to men's view, in that public place, as they went to the temple.

2. Hospitality and compassion towards the afflicted is a commendable duty, and the pains that a declining people put themselves to in that kind may stand up as a witness against others; for though the Jews were now declined, yet the pool had "five porches," either built for the sick, or now converted to that use.

3. Where Christ cometh to any place he will be sure to give a special visit to the desolate and afflicted, and be at pains to come to them who are not able to come to him; for so is it to be supposed here, (as is afterward cleared,) that Christ, coming to Jerusalem, cometh to the pool where the sick lay.

4. From this miraculous manifestation of God in the church of the Jews we may learn—1. Where God continueth a church, although the people be wicked, yet he will not fail to give some tokens of his presence, specially for the good and behoof of his elect among them; therefore when the Jews had now long wanted public prophets, and were under deep distress, the Lord giveth this miraculous proof of his presence, to confirm them, and especially the elect, that he did not forget them; to establish them in the love of their own religion, when idolaters did prevail over them, and to stir them up to expect the Messiah. 2. Incurable diseases and infirmities are not therefore desperate and hopeless; for God from heaven can help that which no means on earth can do good to; and it is his ordinary way to interpose and appear when matters are incurable and remediless otherwise. So much are we taught here, in that the "blind, halt, withered," and the disease whatsoever it was, was cured, and by these cures on the body the Lord giveth proof what he can do to souls and inward conditions, or other outward lots. 3. Means of God's appointment, how improbable like soever, should not be contemned, everything being therefore useful because God appoints and blesseth it; therefore made he use of the water of this common pool, and that when it was "troubled," (which, it seems, should make it more hurtful,) to be stepped into; though, it seems, there was no virtue put into the water, but only the troubling of it was a sign of God's presence there. 4. Whatever good the Lord do by any mean, yet we are to see that all the virtue and blessing cometh down from heaven; for "an angel went down and troubled the water," before that men got any good by stepping into it. 5. It is the duty of all such as are sensible of wants or infirmities to flock to appointed means, and take up their abode there, as being the Lord's trysting place; for so doth the practice of these sick persons teach, who abode and lay in the porches of the pool. 6. Much sense of need will make men assiduous and constant in their waiting on and in the use of lawful means, not giving over for delays and disappointments; for albeit the angel went down but "at a certain

season," and albeit he only who stepped first in was healed at that time, and many being there, would be disappointed and prevented by others, yet they lay still waiting.

VER. 5. And a certain man was there, which had an infirmity thirty and eight years.

6. When Jesus saw him lie, and knew that he had been now a long time in that case, he saith unto him, Wilt thou be made whole?

7. The impotent man answered him, Sir, I have no man, when the water is troubled, to put me into the pool: but while I am coming, another steppeth down before me.

The third thing premitted is a description of the man on whom the miracle was wrought. It is not declared who he was, (for those whom Christ cures are best known by their misery and his mercy,) nor yet what his particular disease was, though it seemeth it hath been sore, and kept him lying, ver. 6; only it is declared he had been long under it. Unto this is further added a previous conference betwixt Christ and him, wherein Christ, being sensible of his case, stirreth up his desire of cure by propounding a question about it, ver. 6, in answer to which the man proveth his desire by his waiting on the means, notwithstanding he was helpless and oft disappointed.

DOCTRINES.

1. Not only are men subject to bodily infirmities, but it may please the Lord, for wise ends, to let some spend a lifetime, or a large part of it, in sickness and weakness, as if they had been born for no other end but to bear such a cross; for "this man had an infirmity thirty and eight years." (See Psalm lxxxix. 47.)

2. As it is the duty of the afflicted to wait on means, so long as God appoints any for their help, so when Christ cometh they will be first regarded who have been longest and sorest troubled; for as this "man was there," so "Jesus saw him lie," and took notice of him before all the rest.

3. Such as have been kept long, and longer than others, under trouble, may be but reserved for Christ's own hand, and for his manifesting his glory in doing of them good; for so much did this man find in experience.

4. Christ needs no information to acquaint him with the afflicted's case; he taketh notice of the measure of their trouble, and knoweth its continuance; for he "saw him lie," through sickness and heartlessness, having been so often disappointed, "and knew that he had been now a long time in that case."

5. When Christ is willing to manifest himself for the afflicted, yet he would have our desires after his help stirred up, and not blunted by any delay; therefore saith he unto the man, "Wilt thou be made whole?" not as doubting of it, (for his desire had drawn him thither, and kept him there,) but to quicken it up as a preparative to the receiving of the mercy, and to give pledge to all that continued desires, notwithstanding all delays, will be satisfied, ere Christ give over the afflicted.

6. It is a real proof of our desire of help under distresses when we are sensible of our misery thereby, when we give not over to wait on, in the use of means, and when we are afflicted with disappointments in using them; for thus doth the man prove his desire in answer to Christ's question.

7. One may be in a very abject-like condition, and seem to be neglected both of God and men, whom yet the Lord purposeth to do much good unto; and one may meet with many disappointments in the use of means who yet will get deliverance in a better and more comfortable way; for so was it with this man, and so did he find.

8. It may be the lot of the afflicted, not only to be sick and unable to help themselves, but to be left destitute, without any to help them, which sheweth what mercy they enjoy who have if it be but one to attend them in sickness; for this man had no man to put him "into the pool."

9. It is a token that sickness, helplessness, and disappointments are blessed, when these make us more meek and humble; for his moan is such; meekly doth he speak of the inhumanity of those about him, and of others' (who possibly came there after him) getting in, while he is disappointed.

10. It is the duty and commendation of those in distress never to quit hope, nor weary to wait on, so long as there is any possibility of any deliverance by any lawful means, albeit they were ever so long delayed or disappointed; for so did this man, notwithstanding all he met with.

11. It is our great weakness that our hope and expectation of help and relief goeth no further than we see outward means, nor can we conceive what Christ's power and goodness is ready to do for us till he reveal it himself; for this man hath only his eye upon that known help, and by his regreet to Christ insinuates a desire that he would shew that kindness to him which others had neglected; but little doth he dream of that which was in Christ's heart.

VER. 8. Jesus saith unto him, Rise, take up thy bed, and walk.

9. And immediately the man was made whole, and took up his bed, and walked: and on the same day was the sabbath.

Followeth the miracle itself, wrought by Christ's power, and at his command, making the sick man arise, and carry his own bed, and walk. To this is added a more particular description of the time of this miracle, that it was on the sabbath, which occasioned the following controversy and debate.

DOCTRINES.

1. Such is Christ's goodness and pity towards his afflicted people as to prevent their hopes and prayers, with doing great things for them in their need; for Christ cureth the man who neither asked it from him nor dreamed he would do it. (See Eph. iii. 20.)

2. All Christ's dealing with his own, in distress, endeth in healing of them at last, how little soever it seem to promise; for so doth his conference with this man.

3. Christ is not tied to means, ordinary or extraordinary, but can work without both when he pleaseth, and by his word of command can do greatest things, and cure most desperate diseases, and not only command, but work that which he commands, and by his word convey virtue and efficacy, and give strength to obey; for he doth not take the man to the pool, but by his word cureth him.

4. Albeit in trouble all means and probability should fail us, yet their case is never desperate who have Christ to go unto. So much also doth this instance teach us; yea, singular afflictions, and disappointments under them, may end in a more eminent and singular way of deliverance, as this man found; and long delay in waiting on, in the use of means, may be made up with a speedy completing of the delivery when Christ begins; for in an instant the man is made whole.

5. Christ's miracles and wonderful works upon and for the afflicted are so real and thorough as will make them speak for themselves, and they should be observed by all; for this command—"Rise, take up thy bed, and walk," which he obeyed—importeth that this cure was a thorough cure, and that he would have the man satisfied about it, and all to remark it.

6. As Christ doth his great works that his glory may be manifested and not buried, so a work appointed by him for setting forth of his glory may and should be set about, and that without any violation of the sabbath; therefore he not only commands him, "Take up thy bed, and walk," that the miracle might be published, but alloweth it to be done on the sabbath, not only because he was Lord of the sabbath, and so might dispense with the observation of it, but because this was no servile work enjoined for a worldly end and commodity, but a mean appointed by himself for setting out his glory, and so was subservient to the great end of the sabbath.

7. Such things within the compass of our calling as tend to the setting forth of Christ's glory, are to be set about with a single eye and heart, albeit we know others would stumble and carp; for so did Christ in his station; he stood not on the Jews' stumbling in commending this to be done on the sabbath, as minding hereby to hold out his own glory in the miracle, and in the following dispute.

VER. 10. The Jews therefore said unto him that was cured, It is the sabbath day: it is not lawful for thee to carry thy bed.

11. He answered them, He that made me whole, the same said unto me, Take up thy bed, and walk.

12. Then asked they him, What man is that which said unto thee, Take up thy bed, and walk?

13. And he that was healed wist not who it was: for Jesus had conveyed himself away a multitude being in that place.

Followeth the second part of the chapter, wherein is recorded the Jews' opposition to the man before they knew the author of the miracle, ver. 10—13, and their malice against Christ when he is known to be the author of it, ver. 14—16.

In these verses, they, challenging the man for breach of sabbath, ver. 10, he defends himself by the warrant he had gotten from Christ, ver. 11; and when they desire to know the author of that warrant, ver. 12, he is not able to resolve them, for Christ had withdrawn himself in the press immediately after the miracle was wrought, ver. 13. Whence learn—

1. When Christ is doing greatest works there will still be some who get no good of them, but will rather suck poison and gall out of them, for this glorious work meets with opposition and persecution.

2. It is the duty of all the members of the visible church, in their stations, and especially of magistrates and ministers, to see to the observation of the sabbath day, even by others as well as by themselves; for these Jews' (who seem to have been of the Pharisees and rulers) quarrelling about a breach of sabbath, was a commendable duty in itself, if the charge had been true. (See Exod. xx. 10; Neh. xiii. 15.)

3. Hypocritical and superstitious persons may pretend to much zeal for God's glory when they are but naught; for, say they, "It is the sabbath day; it is not lawful for thee to carry thy bed," as pretending to be zealous for the law, Jer. xvii. 21, 22, when yet they were but a naughty crew; yea, albeit it may be alleged that at first they knew not what was wrought on the man, and so might be excused in part, yet it is not to be justified that they condemn so rashly before they examine the matter; as it is usual that hypocritical zeal is still rash and censorious.

4. Divine warrant is sufficient to guard the conscience against any challenges of sin, and may justify that which otherwise were condemnable; for such is the man's apology: "He that made me whole, the same said unto me, Take up thy bed, and walk." And albeit he knew not Christ particularly, ver. 13, yet he saw so much of his glory in that miracle, such power in his word, and such virtue flowing from him, as warranted him to look on Christ as having sufficient authority to command him and warrant his obedience, seeing Joshua, only an extraordinary man, was warranted to command all Israel to march about Jericho, if not, also, to take it, on the sabbath day.

5. Where Christ bestoweth a favour, or sendeth relief to the troubled, in mercy, it will leave a stamp of subjection to his command behind it, and incline the receiver to obedience; for so is imported in this man's apology: "He that made me whole, said to me, Take up thy bed," and how can I decline a command, coming from such an one?

6. Albeit occasion be offered to obdured men to see Christ's glory in his working, yet they care not for the knowledge of it, but will rather

slight it, and study to bear him and it both down. So much doth their second question, ver. 12, teach. Albeit the man had told them of the cure, yet they heed not that, but only his saying, " Take up thy bed, and walk," that they might traduce him as a sabbath-breaker; and albeit it be probable they knew who was the author of such a work, yet they will not let it appear, but with contempt inquire, " What man is that which said unto thee, Take up thy bed?" &c., that they might brand him as a presumptuous man, who durst, as they judged, oppose his commands to God's law; whereas a due estimation of the miracle might have led them to judge otherwise of his person and commands.

7. Christ's works and undertakings will then only be rightly constructed and judged of when he is taken up in his person as God, and not man only; for this will discover him to be above the law, and that he can effectuate that which no man could. So much may we gather from their ground of calumny, in that they take him up only as a man : " What man is that?" &c.

8. Christ may be doing some good to them who have no distinct and clear knowledge of him, it being one thing to do the work, and another to manifest himself to be the worker of it; for the man " wist not who it was," albeit he " was healed" by him, and had some respect to him.

9. Christ's withdrawing of himself, which he might easily do in the throng, and which is subjoined as a reason of the man's ignorance, serveth not only to clear the man that his ignorance was not through his neglect, but further may teach— 1. No prejudice at Christ or his outward condition should obscure the glory of his working; therefore he withdrew, that the outward baseness of his person might not cause them to undervalue his working. 2. By this he teacheth how hateful the seeking after vainglory is in his eyes, for by withdrawing he shunned the present applause of the multitude. 3. By this practice he hath sanctified such a lot to his people, as when they are doing good to be necessitated to withdraw themselves because of it; and he teacheth all, as not to flee trials when called to them, so not to thrust themselves rashly on them, but to wait for God's calling; therefore he withdrew, to decline, for a time, these his enemies, who might be enraged, and to shun their fury till afterward that he is called out to defend his own work.

Ver. 14. Afterward Jesus findeth him in the temple, and said unto him, Behold, thou art made whole : sin no more, lest a worse thing come unto thee.

15. The man departed, and told the Jews that it was Jesus, which had made him whole.

16. And therefore did the Jews persecute Jesus, and sought to slay him, because he had done these things on the sabbath day.

Here we have the Jews persecuting of Christ when it was made known he was the author of the miracle. The way of the revealing of it was, that Christ finding the man, doth give him wholesome directions how to make use of his deliverance, ver. 14, and he doth thankfully publish Christ to be the author of his cure, ver. 15; upon which the Jews do persecute him, by traducing him as a profaner of the sabbath, and by plotting how to take away his life, ver. 16.

From ver. 14, learn—1. It is a sweet fruit of trouble when we study thankfulness to God for deliverance from it, by frequenting his house and public worship without neglect of private; for therefore was he in the temple, giving thanks to God, as acknowledging that though he knew not who Christ was, yet he had been God's instrument to him; yea, Christ's own practice, in being there, is a pattern for our reverencing of ordinances.

2. It is not only our duty, but our great happiness also, to be frequenting public ordinances, as being the trysting [appointed] place of Christ's presence; for here Jesus found him in the temple, which was a benefit he little expected.

3. Where Christ giveth outward favours and deliverances in special love, he will give also spiritual mercies and benefits with them; and such as are thankful for what they have received Christ will come and give them more; for this man, with the cure, gets direction for his soul's estate, and that in the temple, where he came to bless God.

4. Such as have gotten great mercy and deliverance from Christ have need of direction how to guide it that they do not miscarry under it; and even when they have some good beginnings they need yet further upstirring; therefore doth Christ, by his exhortation, prescribe a diet for this cured man; and albeit he was at pains to come to the temple to offer thanks, yet Christ finds it needful to give him this warning.

5. When men have gotten deliverance from outward trouble they ought to take heed of resting on it, neglecting God, their duty, and souls' good. So much doth this exhortation import, that, being made whole, he should not think he had no more to do with God, nor needed any other thing, but should mind his duty, otherwise God could reach him,

6. Bodily health, and the curing of infirmities which deprive us of it, is a mercy to be seriously considered, and which layeth on a special obligation to duty, especially if we have been long under the infirmity, if it hath been sad and heavy, and if our deliverance from it hath been remarkable; therefore doth Christ begin his direction with this—" Behold, thou art made whole," that finding now by experience the reality and benefit of his health, so miraculously wrought after his long and sad disease, he should be so affected with it as to take with the following direction.

7. It is a special help for getting a right use of our condition, to see trouble and sickness flowing from sin as the sluice to let it in; to see that Christ knoweth men well enough, and what they are, though they take but little notice of him; and this is to be remembered when the trouble procured by sin is over; for while Christ directs him to sin no more, it importeth that sin had drawn on his former sickness, that Christ would not have him forgetting this when the smart of the rod was gone, and that albeit he knew not

Christ, yet Christ knew him, and what he had been. Whether this man had drawn on this sickness by some gross provocation, I will not determine, but it is certain that sickness and trouble entered in by sin, and that every one hath so much sin as to deserve sharpest plagues here and hereafter.

8. It is not sufficient that men being delivered do profess their thankfulness, or see their former guilt, unless the sense thereof, and of its bitter fruits, and of their deliverance, restrain their after sinning, and stir them up to prevent it for the future, and so be reformed by God's dealing; at least (since they cannot be sinless) they would watch diligently over it, and not let it reign in them. So much is imported in this direction— " Sin no more."

9. Sin is not easily avoided or shaken off, but when men have smarted for sin, and have been graciously delivered, and tasted of God's mercy, they may yet be tempted, and are ready to sin yet more, and need caution to prevent it. So much, also, doth this direction and warning, given to the man, teach us: " Sin no more."

10. The best preservative against affliction and trouble is, not to run every course which flesh and blood may suggest for avoiding it, but to beware of sin, which, if it hold not off trouble, yet may assure us that God doth correct us in love, and not in anger. So much doth the reason of this direction import: " Sin no more, lest a worse thing come unto thee."

11. As all trouble is in itself an evil, whatever good God may bring out of it and by it, so whatever any have lain under God can easily send worse ; for while he threatens him with a " worse thing," it imports that other trouble is evil, though not all in a like degree, and that God could send a worse condition than thirty-eight years' sickness. He can add to outward trouble, Lev. xxvi. 18, 21, 24, 28, and to spiritual plagues, Matt. xii. 45 ; 2 Pet. ii. 20 ; he can send them both together in their extremity, Lam. ii. 22 ; and can send eternal punishments instead of temporal.

12. Such as continue in a course of sinning after they have been afflicted, and have been delivered, and tasted of God's favour to soul or body, do hereby take a way to kindle divine displeasures and increase trouble ; for so much is held forth here, " Sin no more, lest a worse thing come unto thee ;" which calleth for much jealousy over what good things we seem to have under affliction, for much wariness, that we rest not upon outward deliverance, and for much abiding in Christ and keeping of grace in exercise.

From ver. 15, 16, learn—1. It is the duty and commendable practice in those who have gotten experience of Christ's power and pity to proclaim it, for setting forth of his glory and invitation of others to come and partake ; therefore " the man departed, and told the Jews that it was Jesus, which had made him whole." And this he did out of gratitude towards Christ, (whom he knew either from himself or others about him,) and to invite the Jews to make use of Christ, if they had any such employment for him.

2. Sound doctrine meets ofttimes with corrupt hearers, who are more enraged thereby ; and honest-minded men, following their duty in singleness, may occasion persecution, and yet be blameless, as having done but their duty, and given no just occasion, and so are free of what followeth ; for upon this man's publishing Christ to be the author of his cure, the persecution ariseth, but without any fault in him.

3. The rising and spreading of Christ's glory is an eye-sore to corrupt teachers and people, who are thereby discovered to be what indeed they are, and their seeming glory obscured ; and persecution is the ordinary entertainment that Christ, manifesting his glory, may look for at the hands of such ; for " therefore," upon the report, " did the Jews persecute Jesus," by their reproachful tongues, and devising how to take his life, either in a tumult or judicially.

4. Such is the cruelty of persecutors, that, if they had their will, nothing but the death of those they oppose would satisfy them ; and such as are persecutors with the tongue, and spare not men's names, will also be ready to take their lives, if opportunity offer, and they can get a pretext for it ; for they " sought to slay him," upon pretence of the law of sabbath-breaking, Num. xv. 32, 33, &c. And this is marked as their disposition who had spoken contemptibly of him, ver. 12, and continued to do so still, since they could go no further.

5. Great cruelty against Christ may be masked with fairest pretexts, even of zeal for God and his commands ; and sufferers are not to expect but that they shall be loaden with calumnies under their sufferings ; for they " sought to slay him, because he had done these things on the sabbath day." As persecutors will think shame to publish their malice and the causes of it, so this way of procedure maketh persecution most sharp, John, xvi. 1—3.

6. Whatever be the malice, desire, or endeavours of wicked men, yet the life of Christ and his followers is not in their hand, but the Lord may make their malice their own plagues, and preserve his people while he hath any service for them ; for though they " sought to slay him," yet all their endeavours at that time tended only to their own trouble.

Ver. 17. But Jesus answered them, My Father worketh hitherto, and I work.

In the third part of the chapter we have Christ's apology for his working this cure on the sabbath, in answer either to their thoughts or to somewhat they expressed to him, ver. 17, and his prosecution thereof, upon the increase of their rage, ver. 18, 19, &c.

At other times, upon the like occasion, we find him making apology for himself or his followers, by way of retortion, as Matt. xv. 1—3, which, though it could not justify an unlawful act, yet it might stop their mouths who maliciously quarrelled with others, and yet were more guilty themselves ; sometimes by pleading necessity, as Luke, vi. 2, 3 ; xiv. 3—5, in which case the sabbath is made for man, Mark, ii. 27 ; and Christ commends his love, that when he gets a distressed sinner, even on the sabbath day, he will not delay his help till the morrow ; sometimes by pleading that works of piety and charity do not violate the sabbath, Matt. xii. 5, 7; Luke, vi. 9; but here Christ justifieth himself from a more sublime reason, that he may take occasion to set out the glory of his godhead. And whereas the weight of their challenge was grounded on the fourth command, wherein God had not only commanded us to rest on the sabbath, but had by his own example, in resting from all his works on that day, pressed it, therefore Christ removeth the mistake, shewing that the Father, ever since the creation, hath continued working without any intermission, and this without any violation of the sabbath; and that himself, as he is one in essence with the Father, so he is undivided in working from him, the Father's work and his being one, and therefore his working on the sabbath could not be challenged, and he being God might command the man to carry his bed when he pleased, and when it contributed to set forth his glory. Whence learn—

Albeit the Lord, after the creation of all things in six days, did cease from the creating of new kinds of creatures, Gen. ii. 2, yet he is still, without intermission, (even on the sabbath,) working, by preserving and upholding all the creatures he hath made—without which they could not subsist a moment—and by governing and overruling of all things, how small, contingent, or casual soever they be; for " My Father worketh hitherto," which speech doth not exclude the time following, but sheweth that there is no intermission in that work. (See Acts, xvii. 28; Matt. vi. 26, 30, x. 29, 30; Exod. xxi. 13.)

2. Christ the Son of God is joined with and undivided from the Father in working, and that not in one work alone, or at some time only, but in all works, and without intermission. As the Father created all things by him, so with and from the Father he preserveth and governeth all things; for " My Father worketh hitherto, and I work," even the same works which he worketh. (See Heb. i. 2, 3.)

3. God, and Christ as God, is above all law which he hath prescribed to the creature; he works on the sabbath, and doth not violate it; he may do what he pleaseth, without quarrelling; and may command what he pleaseth, and make it service; for so doth the scope of the apology teach, that Christ, being undivided from the Father in working, was God, and so not subject to the law of the sabbath, and might command the man to carry his bed, and warrant him in so doing.

VER. 18. Therefore the Jews sought the more to kill him, because he not only had broken the sabbath, but said also that God was his Father, making himself equal with God.

The fruit of this apology among the Jews is, that their rage of persecution is increased the more by it, and they thirst the more for his life; and that because he not only had broken the sabbath, as they alleged, but had asserted that God was his Father in so peculiar a way as made him equal with God. Whence learn—

1. Clear declaration of truth will not satisfy wicked and malicious men, but the more Christ and the light is held out to such, it is hated the more; for after his apology, " therefore the Jews sought the more to kill him."

2. No vindication nor defence of lawful practices will wipe off the misconstructions of prejudged men, but they will stick by their prejudices, and maliciously fasten them upon the innocent; for let him say what he will, yet " he had broken the sabbath," not in deed, but as they alleged.

3. Albeit God have many sons by creation and adoption, yet Christ is his Son in a peculiar and proper way, by eternal generation, and communication of the same essence; for so doth the Jews understand him: he said, " God was his Father," or his Father in a proper and peculiar way, otherwise they could not have quarrelled with him; and Christ doth not refute this.

4. Christ's conjunction with his Father in working doth prove his equality with the Father, and that he is of the same essence, and doth partake of the same omnipotency; for so much do they soundly gather from his apology, ver. 17, that he made " himself equal with God;" neither doth Christ call them calumniators, nor clear any mistake in it, as in other cases he doth, John, xxi. 23, but clears and confirms what they challenged, (though they gathered a vicious consequence, that he should be killed as a blasphemer;) and what they collect is asserted by the apostle, Phil. ii. 6.

5. Such may be the corruption of a visible church as very truth may be accounted blasphemy and a ground of putting men to death; for albeit it be horrid blasphemy for any creature to equal itself with God, yet they were far wrong when they would slay Christ for asserting the comfortable and supernatural truth of his godhead.

VER. 19. Then answered Jesus and said unto them, Verily, verily, I say unto you, The Son can do nothing of himself, but what he seeth the Father do: for what things soever he doeth, these also doeth the Son likewise.

Christ insisteth in his apology to the end of the chapter, and cleareth and confirmeth that which offended them in his discourse, of his equality and conjunction with the Father, which doth infer the justifying of his work on the sabbath. For this end he produceth many instances and arguments of his equality, to ver. 31, and then produceth many witnesses testifying concerning him, whereof he maketh use, in the rest of the chapter. What Christ here speaks of himself is to be understood of his godhead, or divine nature, though he mention his commission to come into the world, ver. 23, and his becoming man, ver. 27, to shew that as he is man and Mediator, that the majesty of his godhead might not deter sinners from coming to him, so his condescendence did take away none of his glory, nor his equality with the Father as God.

In proving this equality—1. He insists, in general, to prove his conjunction in operation with the Father, which he had asserted, ver. 17, promising further and greater manifestations of it, ver. 19, 20. 2. He produceth particular instances of this conjunction and equality, to ver.

31 ; and namely, that he is equal with the Father in quickening the dead, ver. 21 ; in the matter of judgment and authority, ver. 22 ; in being the object of divine honour, ver. 23 ; in giving eternal life to believers on his word, ver. 24 ; in quickening dead souls by his word, ver. 25 ; in having a fountain of life, ver. 26, (which may be cleared by his authority as Mediator also, ver. 27 ;) and in his power, to be shewed in the resurrection and general judgment, ver. 28, 29 ;—all which is summed up, by way of conclusion, ver. 30.

In this verse, after a grave asseveration, we have two assertions ; in the first (which is negative) is declared that what the Son doth he doth it from the Father, and doth nothing separate or divided from him, and so sheweth that he doth only what the Father doth, though there be a distinction and order of his working from the Father. In the second (which is positive, and a confirmation of the former) is declared, that the Son doth all that the Father doth, and the Father doth nothing without him ; and withal, that there is an unity and equality of the working of the Father and Son, both in matter and manner. Whence learn—

1. As truth is not to be quit and forsaken because of opposition, so truth will lose nothing by opposition, but Christ will take occasion thereby to clear it more, and make it shine the brighter ; for notwithstanding their rage, he insists to inculcate and clear this truth the more.

2. The mysteries of religion, especially concerning God, and Christ as God, and plurality of persons in the unity of essence, ought to be spoken of, heard, and thought upon, with much gravity, reverence, and sobriety ; therefore doth he begin this doctrine with a grave asseveration, " Verily, verily."

3. Christ's equality and unity with the Father is a truth hardly received or believed by the hearts of men, as being a mystery above the reach of natural reason, and yet it is worthy to be received, for setting forth of his greatness, and the dignity of his person ; for grounding our faith in him, and for assuring us of the certain success of his undertakings ; therefore also it is inculcated with a " Verily, verily."

4. In taking up divine and supernatural mysteries, we are to submit unto and acquiesce in divine revelation, whatever carnal reason suggest to the contrary. So much also doth his confirming this truth, and obviating all objections, with his asseveration, teach us.

5. As the Father and Son are one in nature and essence, so are they undivided and inseparable in operation and working, and the Son worketh only what the Father worketh ; for " the Son can do nothing of himself" (or separate from the Father) but what the Father doth ; and that he cannot work otherwise but in conjunction with the Father, doth not argue any impotency in him, but his strait union with the Father.

6. Albeit the Father and Son be one in essence and operation, yet are they distinct persons ; and there is an order of subsistence and operation to be observed betwixt the Father and the Son. So much are we taught, in that the one is " the Son," the other " the Father," and so distinct each from other, and in that " the Son doth nothing of himself," which doth not seclude Christ's own proper power as God, but holds out (beside his conjunction with the Father) that in order of working he worketh from the Father ; and it is yet further confirmed, in that he doth " what he seeth the Father do," which seeing, (as that shewing also, ver. 20,) though it be an expression fitted to our capacity, and borrowed from among men, who shew their children their skill by acting and practising thereof before them, that they may imitate it, yet it is not to be understood as if Christ's work were posterior to the Father's work, and done in imitation of his, as is after cleared, but it points out that unspeakable communication, whereby the Father communicates unto the Son his nature, will, wisdom, and power ; and so the Son in order of subsistence is from the Father, and points out also that the Son knoweth the Father's working, because he works the same work with him, and from him.

7. The Son is not only joint with his Father in working, or execution of his purposes, but is upon all his counsels also, and perfectly understandeth all his purposes. So much also may be gathered from his " seeing what the Father doth," and the Father's shewing, ver. 20, importing that he is conscious to all his Father's counsel and working, as having the same wisdom communicated from the Father to him.

8. Christ's works are not only like unto the Father's but the same in substance, as flowing from one and the same essence and power ; " for what he doeth, these things also doeth the Son."

9. Christ, in working with the Father, acts not as an instrument subordinate, but, as there is an unity in the work, so also in the manner of it, by the same power, wisdom, liberty, authority, &c., the order of operation being observed ; for " these things also doeth the Son likewise," or, in like manner.

10. Christ is joint with the Father, not in one or some only of his works, but in all that he doeth, for " whatsoever things he doeth, these doeth the Son likewise."

11. It is comfortable to the church to be much in studying Christ's excellency, to look on his working as the work of God, who can effectuate what he will, and that the works which he works they are the works of the Father also, and to see him on all the Father's counsels and undertakings, whereby believers may see nothing contrived from all eternity, or acted within time, but what he, who is their Head and Mediator also, hath a hand in. So much may be gathered from this doctrine, whereby he sets out his own glory for our use.

VER. 20. For the Father loveth the Son, and sheweth him all things that himself doeth : and he will shew him greater works than these, that ye may marvel.

This unity and equality in operation betwixt the Father and the Son is again repeated, confirmed, and amplified, from several considerations. 1. That this unity floweth from and is conjoined with the Father's special love to the

Son. 2. That this communication of counsel and power in operation is universal, as he communicates his whole essence; and, 3. He promiseth more ample proofs of this equality than they had seen in the late cure, though they should make but little good use of it. This promise of more ample proofs of his equality with the Father, though it be verified in all the following instances, to which this is a transition, yet as to them, it is to be understood specially of his great miracles wrought afterward, of opening the eyes of the blind, raising the dead, &c. Whence learn—

1. There is true love betwixt the Father and the Son accompanying their communion in essence and operation; and Christ is beloved of the Father in a special manner, not only as Mediator and man, by virtue of the personal union, but as God he is the object of his eternal love, as being the substantial image of himself and the splendour and brightness of his glory; "for the Father loveth the Son, and sheweth him," &c. (See Prov. viii. 30.) And it teacheth us to tryst [accord] with the Father's love by coming to the Son to be assured of it in him; and as Christ is beloved, and therefore gets the Father's counsels, so by studying to be beloved of God we are sure to get his mind and secrets, in so far as is for our good, John, xv. 15.

2. As the Father and the Son are all-sufficiently blessed in themselves with the Holy Spirit, loving and delighting in one another without needing of the creature, so it commends God's love to sinners that he would send the beloved Son of his bosom to them, and Christ's love, who would come out of the Father's bosom, who would have his delights among the sons of men also, and would purchase to himself love and an object of love from among them; and it should teach all to love him who is the Father's beloved, and in whom others are beloved. So much further may be gathered from this: "the Father loveth the Son."

3. God's love is communicative and will manifest itself in effects according to the capacity of the party beloved. So much appeareth in that unspeakable love of the Father to the Son, "the Father loveth the Son, and sheweth him all things," &c., or communicateth his nature, wisdom, and power for operation with him; which is expressed in terms taken from among men, because of our weakness, and ought to be spiritually taken up and not carnally conceived of; and therefore also these terms of the Father's shewing and the Son's seeing are made use of to prevent all carnal and gross conceptions of this inexpressible communication from the Father, and participation by the Son.

4. Christ, as he is and knoweth and worketh from the Father, so he is not posterior but co-eternal with him in his nature and attributes, and worketh in the same time with him; for he "sheweth him," not what he hath done, but what he "doeth," as being joint with him in counsel and working, and at all times, and consequently in his being also.

5. It is a point to be much and often studied, that the glory, not only of the Father, but of Christ, as God, shineth in all the Father's works, that so we may adore the infinite glory of our Head, and may see him in all that is done in the world; therefore is it again inculcated that "the Father sheweth him all things that himself doeth."

6. Christ's omnipotency, working from the Father, is infinite, and when great things are done by him it cometh far short of what omnipotency can do, and will do as need requires; for "he will shew him"—or communicate with him in, and he, from the Father, will work before your eyes—" greater things than these."

7. Albeit Christ's works do speak his praise, and his own will get good of them and glorify him for them, yet most part of men, and especially hardened enemies, will reap no saving benefit by them; Christ may convince them of his glory in his works, may dash their unbelief, and make them wonder, but they go no further than stupid astonishment; for " he will shew him greater works, that ye may marvel." He speaks of their wondering at the Father's end, and his, in these works, as to them, because it is indeed his glory to convince them so far and put them to silence; and withal it is his righteous judgment to give them up, to reap no more fruit by his working.

VER. 21. For as the Father raiseth up the dead, and quickeneth them; even so the Son quickeneth whom he will.

Christ produceth several instances and proofs of his conjunction and equality with the Father, which are greater than that of the cure wrought on the man; whereof the first is the quickening of the dead and raising them up, wherein he worketh as the Father worketh; not that he quickeneth some and the Father others, but that he is joint with the Father in these works, and equal with him in doing them, working even so as the Father worketh them; not as an instrument, but " whom he will"—that is, as a principal agent, by the same authority and absolute freedom of will with the Father. This quickening and raising may very safely be understood both of quickening those who are dead in sin and of raising up of all at the last day, of both which he speaks more distinctly, ver. 25, 28, not excluding also his miraculous quickening and raising up of particular persons, such as Lazarus, &c., as a proof of what he had foretold to the Jews, ver. 20. Nor is this conjunction of the Father and Son in this work to be understood as excluding the Holy Ghost, who works from the Father and the Son in this operation, Rom. viii. 11; 1 Cor. xii. 10, 11. But Christ here speaks to the present point in controversy, which the Jews denied.

DOCTRINES.

1. Quickening and raising of the dead, whether bodily or spiritually, is an act of omnipotency, and proper to God only; therefore doth Christ set it out as his Father's prerogative, and his as equal with him, to raise up the dead and quicken them. (See Deut. xxxii. 39; 1 Samuel, ii. 6; Psalm lxviii. 20.)

2. As Christ's power to quicken the dead is a

proof of his equality with the Father, and sheweth the infiniteness of the power communicated from the Father to him, so this proof of his godhead, and of the Father's also, doth give to them who come to God through him sufficient ground of confidence in lesser difficulties, may establish their hearts when nothing but omnipotency can effectuate what they need, and is promised to them, and may give those who have found his quickening virtue confidence in coming to him to recover their decayed spiritual condition. So much may faith gather from this: "As the Father raiseth up the dead, and quickeneth them; so the Son quickeneth." (See Rom. iv. 17.)

3. Christ in his working is absolute, sovereign, and independent, as the Father is; for he "quickeneth whom he will," and hath the dispensation of his power absolutely in his own hand; which as it is verified in spiritual renovation, and in miraculous raising up of some, so in all his actions to deny him absolute sovereignty to work as he pleaseth is to deny him to be God, Psalm cxv. 3. Though his people have this comfort, that what is his will is their weal.

VER. 22. For the Father judgeth no man, but hath committed all judgment unto the Son:

A second instance of this equality (which is also a proof of the Son's absolute power and sovereignty in quickening the dead, "whom he will," ver. 21,) is the judging of all things communicated to him from the Father, who judges none without him, but by him. By "judgment" we are to understand an absolute dominion and sovereignty over men and all the creatures. In the first part of the verse, indeed, it is restricted to men, and holds out God's dominion and divine authority in absolving or condemning them, in adjudging them to live or die, as a confirmation of what was said, ver. 21; but in the second part of the verse it is to be taken more largely, for the government and administration of all things in heaven and earth, and so it is a confirmation of the former part, importing that the Father doth not any particular act of government without the Son, because he hath committed the administration of all acts of government to the Son, by whom, as God, he executeth them; beside that he hath given to him dominion over all things as Mediator, for the church's behoof, of which elsewhere, Matt. xi. 27; xxviii. 18. And while he saith, "the Father judgeth no man," it is spoken according to the Jews' conception, who did separate him from the Father, and the meaning is, not that the Father hath so given up the government of all to the Son as to divest himself of it, for that is contrary to ver. 17, 19—21, and multitudes of scriptures, but that he doth not judge any alone or separate from the Son, but in and by him; and so the Son also doth not judge his alone, ver. 30, for the Father doth so communicate all to the Son as yet he hath all.

DOCTRINES.

1. There is a dominion and sovereignty exercised in the world, and over men and all creatures therein, whereby they are not left to their own arbitriments, or to uncertain contingency, but are under the government of a Supreme Providence; for so is imported that there is a judging of men, and "all judgment."

2. It is the prerogative of God only to be sovereign Judge and Governor of the world, who having created men and all things, may dispose of them at his pleasure; who is everywhere present in heaven and earth to govern all things; whose omniscience taketh up all things, even the secrets of hearts; whose providence extendeth to all; and whose power is infinite, to execute the pleasure of his will; for so is here held out, as a proof of Christ's equality with the Father, that he hath "all judgment" from the Father.

3. Christ as God hath the government of the world communicated to him from the Father; he hath power of life and death, of absolution and condemnation, and the administration of all things in his hand; so that we are to look on nothing in the world as done by the Father alone, or separate from the Son, but that all is done by him who is also the church's Head; for so much are we taught, in that "the Father judgeth no man, but hath committed (or given) all judgment unto the Son," as is before explained, which giving, on the Father's part, and receiving by Christ, is not out of his indigency, or to supply his defects, (which is an imperfection, Acts, xx. 35,) but it is given and received by communication and participation of the same essence.

VER. 23. That all men should honour the Son, even as they honour the Father. He that honoureth not the Son honoureth not the Father which hath sent him.

The end of this communication with the Son (and a third proof of his equality with the Father) is, Christ's participation in divine honour with the Father, which whosoever deny to him, they deny it also to the Father. Whence learn—

1. There is an honour due to God only, and not to be given to any other, consisting in the admiring and publishing of his infinite excellency and perfection, in subjecting ourselves to him with absolute submission, and in offering up religious worship and homage to him; therefore doth Christ prove his equality with the Father, by partaking of the same "honour" with him.

2. God's glory, and the manifesting thereof, is his supreme end in all his works in the world, which we should set before us in all our ways, and submit in every dispensation whereby he is glorified; for he "judgeth," and "committeth judgment to the Son; that all men should honour the Son," &c. (See Prov. xvi. 4; John, xii. 28.)

3. The glory of the excellency of wisdom, sovereignty, all-sufficiency, power, and every other attribute, is due to God from men, in his administration of the world; and men ought rather to study matter of his praise than of complaining and quarrelling therein; for it is the very end of his administration of all, by his Son, "that all men should honour the Son." &c.

4. Christ is equal with the Father in participating of divine honour; as he hath the same throne and power of administration with him, so no less glory is due to him than is due to the Father, for "all men should honour the Son, even as they honour the Father." (See John, xvii. 5.) He is to have the same glory of believing in him, John, xiv. 1, of love, fear, invocation, bowing of the knee, &c., with the Father.

5. As no man hath, or enjoyeth, or acknowledgeth the Father but he who acknowledgeth the Son, and the Father in and through him, 1 John, ii. 23, so, however men do pretend to acknowledge one true God, yet they cannot withdraw honour from the Son, but they deny it to the Father, who will not be honoured but in and through the honouring of the Son; for "he that honoureth not the Son honoureth not the Father."

6. Christ, as he is true God, equal with the Father, so he sustains the relation also of being the Father's ambassador, sent into the world for the redemption of lost man, by the exercise of his Mediatory office; for so is imported here, that "the Father hath sent him." And this he takes delight to speak of in the midst of his divine glory, that the Jews might not stumble at that condescendence wherein he delighted so much.

7. Christ's condescendence to come into the world as Mediator of sinners diminisheth nothing of his divine glory, but in the same person he remains true God, to be equally honoured with the Father; for though he be "sent," yet he is to be honoured "even as the Father." He is not an ambassador, whose honour ceaseth by the presence of the king, but remaineth equal with the Father, though in respect of that voluntary dispensation, as God-man, he is inferior.

8. As the Father is honoured in and through the honour given to the Son, as God equal with him, so also is he honoured in his authority, by men's acknowledging of Christ as sent of him into the world; and whoever despise Christ, they offer injury unto God, in both these respects. So much also may we gather in that "he that honoureth not the Son honoureth not the Father which hath sent him."

Ver. 24. Verily, verily, I say unto you, He that heareth my word, and believeth on him that sent me, hath everlasting life, and shall not come into condemnation; but is passed from death unto life.

The fourth instance of Christ's godhead and equality with the Father is held out in several particulars relating to man's salvation—namely, that the doctrine of the gospel is his word; that it requireth absolute faith and closing with God through him, and that he gives perseverance and eternal life to such as believe in the Father through him, according to the word. Whence learn—

1. It is the great and undeniable evidence of men's giving due honour unto Jesus Christ, the Son of God, when his word is acknowledged and received as becometh; and when by making use thereof we do promove our own eternal happiness. So much may be gathered from the dependence from this verse on the former; he is then honoured when his word is heard. For in this work the glory of his godhead shineth brightly, and his love to his people is such as to account himself especially honoured in that which promoveth their happiness.

2. Christ would have men very serious in the matter of esteeming his word, and of their own salvation, and would have them taking him up, as very serious about it, and very real in what he saith concerning their well-being; therefore doth he begin with an asseveration—" Verily verily, I say unto you," to shew that the way of sinners' salvation was no small matter in his mind, and that he was worthy to be credited concerning it, and to invite them to seriousness.

3. The doctrine of the scripture is Christ's voice, who as God, equal with the Father, is the prescriber of men's duty, and of the way of their salvation, an authorizer of a rule of faith and manners to bind the conscience, and who, as Mediator, is the purchaser of the good news of the gospel for lost sinners; for saith he, it is "my word," not as a messenger carrying it only, as Paul saith of himself, that the gospel was his, Rom. ii. 16; nor yet only as the purchaser of good tidings, (though both these be true,) but as principal author, with the Father, of that doctrine, and particularly of the gospel, whether published by himself or by his ambassadors, Luke, x. 16.

4. Christ's doctrine is to be reverently attended and hearkened unto, and absolute obedience is due to what he saith, without exception. And for this end He is to be heard in every message who is God over all, and who speaketh from heaven, and who in his voice of the gospel hath not that dreadful sound which accompanied the law, Heb. xii. 19, &c., attending it; for it is their duty that they hear "my word," saith he, "hearing" importing obedience thereunto, and attention as previous to that, and all this because it is his "word." (See Deut. xviii. 15.)

5. The doctrine of Christ, and especially of the gospel, is then rightly heard when we bring faith, and not our reason and corrupt sense, to judge of it, and when it puts a sinner out of himself to flee by faith to a refuge; for so is added, "He that heareth my word, and believeth." Christ's doctrine may be a stumbling-block and foolishness, if we bring not faith, 1 Cor. i. 18, 23, and whatever change the gospel work on men, yet it works not savingly till it drive men out of themselves to live by faith.

6. Faith, whereby the doctrine of Christ is embraced to salvation, is not our own, but God's gift, and wrought by means of hearing the word; for so much is imported in the order—"He that heareth, and believeth." (See Rom. x. 17.)

7. Saving faith, begotten by the word, doth lay hold on God through Christ the Mediator, and resteth on God as the proper object; for he "believeth on him that sent me," where Christ doth not seclude himself from being the object of faith, as God, (which elsewhere he so clearly asserteth, John, i. 12; iii. 16; xiv. 1,) more than he denieth the Father to be the author of his

doctrine when he calleth it "my word." But he speaks thus, partly with reference to the Jews' conception, who thought that he and his doctrine had nothing to do with God; therefore he sheweth that as he was one with the Father, so his doctrine tended to, and was a means of begetting faith in him; and partly to shew the order of saving faith, that as it dare not fix on God immediately, but in and by the Mediator, so it cannot rest till ultimately it rest on God in Christ his Son, equal, and the same essentially with him. (See Acts, xx. 21; 2 Cor. iii. 4; 1 Pet. i. 21.)

8. Albeit all men by nature be lying dead in sins and trespasses, and be liable to bodily death and mortality, even albeit they come to Christ, yet such as, by hearing the word, are drawn to believe on God through him, get spiritual life, and not only shall they have, but they already have, eternal life by covenant-right, in the bud and earnest of it, Eph. i. 13, 14; 1 John, v. 11, and in their head Christ, Ephes. ii. 5, 6; for of such Christ saith, "he hath everlasting life," as John, iii. 16, and he "is passed from death unto life," or, translated from under the state and sentence of death by a sentence of life passed in his favour in justification, and put in a living condition by sanctification; and this is the reason why the believer "hath everlasting life." (See the like form of speech, 1 John, iii. 14.)

9. The believer in Christ hath eternal life on so sure terms that he is out of peril of perishing, and is gifted with perseverance till full fruition come; for he "hath everlasting life, and shall not come into condemnation; but is passed from death unto life."

10. The sentence passed in the believers' conscience, according to the word, shall stand firm, and be ratified by God, in his judging of men; for he that "hath everlasting life," by believing, "shall not come into condemnation," &c., importeth this also. (See 1 John, iii. 21.)

11. Albeit Christ, being God over all, blessed for ever, doth not stand in need of man, nor any of his creatures, yet such is his all-sufficiency and bounty as he delights to give proofs of his godhead in saving his people, and making them happy; therefore doth he bring this proof to confirm his assertion, from his being able and willing to save them who believe in God through him.

<hr>

Ver. 25. Verily, verily, I say unto you, The hour is coming, and now is, when the dead shall hear the voice of the Son of God: and they that hear shall live.

The fifth instance of his godhead and equality with the Father doth amplify the former in ver. 24, for whereas there he proved his godhead by being the author of eternal life to believers, here he promiseth to give faith to his own, by causing them to hear his voice who are of themselves dead, and making them, by hearing and believing, to live a life of grace here, till it be perfected in glory.

DOCTRINES.

1. However Christ may propound the doctrine of eternal life conditionally to the visible church, yet the promises are absolute in his intention towards the elect, and he is the undertaker for performing all the conditions which he requireth of them, when they are humble and flee to him. So much is held out, in that Christ undertakes to give faith, and cause the dead to hear, which was required as a condition in the former verse.

2. We have much need to be oft stirred up to be grave and serious in studying Christ's glory, and about the matters of our salvation, and to be stirred up to give credit to what he saith and undertaketh for lost sinners; therefore doth Christ again inculcate this doctrine with "Verily, verily, I say unto you."

3. The great manifestation of the power of Christ's word and spirit was reserved for the days of the gospel; for Christ saith, "the hour" (or acceptable season, to be well improven, and therefore measured by an hour) "is coming," (after my resurrection, and pouring out of the Spirit,) "and now is," (in some measure by my ministry and John's) "when the dead shall hear," &c. Not that he gave not proof of this before his incarnation, but it was now to be in greater measure, and with greater efficacy.

4. Whatever remainders of the image of God, and whatever excellency natural men may have, yet they are spiritually dead till Christ come unto them, being destitute of spiritual life, and of the favour and peace of God, being dead by a sentence of the law passed against them, and being under this insensible, and unable to help themselves; for here they are called "the dead."

5. Such is the power of the gospel, as being the voice of the Son of God, that not only will it speak to them who have ears, but it will raise dead souls to life by conversion, and give them an ear to hear, and make them to believe; for "the dead shall hear the voice of the Son of God."

6. Such as are regenerate and raised from the dead by the word of the gospel, and who do close with it, and Christ in it, by faith, their begotten life shall be cherished and entertained and carried on by enjoyment of begun conformity and communion with Christ, till it be perfected with glory; for "they that hear (or, being regenerate, are made so to hear as to believe) shall live."

<hr>

Ver. 26. For as the Father hath life in himself; so hath he given to the Son to have life in himself;

What Christ hath said in the two former verses is here confirmed, that he can give everlasting life to believers, and quicken those who are spiritually dead, because Christ, as God, hath a fountain of life equal with the Father, communicated to him from the Father by eternal generation. And this is the sixth instance and proof of his equality with the Father. Whence learn—

1. The power and efficacy of the gospel for quickening and keeping in the life of believers, will never be rightly seen nor believed till we

see that inexhaustible fulness that is in Christ for that effect, who hath all fulness of life in himself, as God, to be forthcoming to his own, as a cause of life in them, and when that is seen, difficulties will easily be removed; therefore doth he prove the truth of the former doctrine by this reason: they " shall live," because he " hath life in himself" equally with the Father.

2. No less is able to beget, and keep in and cherish life in the elect, and to revive it when it is decaying and ready to die, than that infinite and independent fountain of life which is God's own prerogative. So much also doth this dependence teach; no less can assure that the dead shall hear, and that the quickened shall persevere in life, than such a fountain employed for that end. So many invincible impediments are there in the way of our quickening, and so many blasting storms doth our life meet with.

3. It is the property of God to be a living God; that independent inexpressible life is his own essence and nature, and he is the fountain of all life in the creatures; for it is God's prerogative, and a proof of Christ's equality with him, that he " hath life in himself."

4. This property of life is common to each person of the blessed Trinity, to the Father and to the Son; yet the Father is first in order in having of it, and doth communicate it to the Son; for of both it is said, he " hath life in himself," and that the Father " hath given" it to the Son, which is to be understood of his communicating it, in communicating his nature with him, by eternal generation; and as for the human nature, this is only gifted to it, in this respect, that by the grace of the personal union the human nature is assumed into the unity of person with him, who hath this life by eternal generation.

5. The Father's communicating of life to the Son argues no inequality nor inferiority in the Son, but he hath the same life, infinitely, independently, and equally with the Father; for "as" the Father hath it, " so" hath the Son; and he hath it " in himself," as the Father hath. Such a fountain and storehouse have believers to trust to.

VER. 27. And hath given him authority to execute judgment also, because he is the Son of man.

To confirm the former reasons, and because they might be ready to stumble at what Christ said of himself, when they looked on him in his human nature, therefore he declareth that not only as God he hath a fountain of life equally with the Father, but that he " hath authority given him" from the Father " to execute (or do) judgment, (even) because he is the Son of man." By executing or doing of judgment, (of which, ver. 22,) we are to understand a dominion and government over all things, and particularly the power of life and death, to condemn or absolve, which will be especially verified in the judgment of the last day, of which he speaketh, ver. 28, 29. And Christ saith, authority is given him to do this, " because he is the Son of man," or, " as he is the Son of man," whereby we are not to understand his human nature, simply considered, but his office and his human nature as united in one person with the godhead; that because he is God-man, the Mediator of sinners, and took on our nature for that end, therefore he hath all power committed to him as Mediator, for the good of the church, the exercise whereof he fully entered upon after his resurrection, Matt. xxviii. 18; Rom. xiv. 9; Rev. i. 18; Philip. ii. 8—11; and that in his human nature, though he be not advanced to the participation of divine properties, yet he is advanced to that lordship over all the creatures that he is capable of, Rom. xiv. 9; Phil. ii. 9, 10, and gifted with that dignity and authority to be in the unity of person, one with him, who is sovereign lord over all; and he is the visible actor and judge in these administrations, which could be done by none but him who is God also, and particularly in the last day, wherein he shall be judge in visible shape, Acts, x. 42; xvii. 31; according to the prophecy of him under the same name, Dan. vii. 13.

DOCTRINES.

1. The eternal Son of God, equal with the Father, did in the fulness of time become true man in one person with his godhead; for " the Son of God," ver. 25, is also " the Son of man."

2. Man's nature is highly exalted in our head Christ, his human nature being not only advanced to that dignity above all creatures that it can be capable of, in itself, but being in the unity of person the same with him who is Lord over all, and the visible actor of the works of the godhead, for " the Son of man hath authority given him," &c.

3. As Christ hath from the Father a native dominion as God, by eternal generation, so he hath also a donative kingdom, as Mediator, God-man, for the good of his church, whereby he not only ruleth over his church, but hath all power in heaven and earth, and all things in his hand, which may either hinder or promote her happiness; for the Father " hath given him authority to execute judgment, because he is the Son of man." And this is to be looked on as better and surer in Christ's hand, who is our head, than in our own.

4. The redemption of lost sinners is so acceptable to the Father that he will not only accept a ransom, but will honour the Redeemer, and confer dignity upon him, for effectuating that work; for " because he is the Son of man" and Mediator, the Father " hath given him authority to execute judgment." (See Philip. ii. 8—10; John, x. 17.)

5. Christ hath undertaken to work the work of redemption of sinners, and so hath engaged himself to carry it through, and the Father, according to his covenant with him, hath invested him with what was requisite for perfecting that work; for " he is the Son of man" for that end, and therefore the Father " hath given him authority," &c.

6. Christ in the work of redemption, and administration of all things for the elects' behoof, is the Father's commissioner, and clothed with a delegated authority, for which he is accountable to the Father for all those whom he hath given

him, and all their allowances and lots, and for the administration of all things in order to them. Not a lot they meet with but he will give an account of it, as beseeming his dominion and trust, and tending to their welfare; for as " the Son of man" and Mediator, this " authority is given him" as to a delegate.

7. The dignity of Christ's human nature being united with the godhead, and his dignity as Mediator, as it shines in many particular acts and administrations, so particularly in that he' will be the visible judge of quick and dead, in his human nature, at the last day; wherein Christ, despised in the world because of his outward baseness, will be glorious, and contemners of his offer of mercy will find his Lamb's face terrible, and wherein believers will find their advocate their judge; for his executing of judgment, " because he is the Son of man," doth point at this ultimately.

Ver. 28. Marvel not at this : for the hour is coming, in the which all that are in the graves shall hear his voice,

29. And shall come forth; they that have done good, unto the resurrection of life; and they that have done evil, unto the resurrection of damnation.

Hitherto Christ hath given divers proofs of his godhead and equality with the Father, and amongst the rest, one from his quickening of those who are spiritually dead; and hath declared his supreme authority to absolve and condemn, and to govern and judge all, as God incarnate. Now finding the Jews but amazed and astonished at this doctrine, he labours to put them from that by producing a new proof of his power and godhead, to be shewed in the resurrection, by quickening the dead, raising them up, bringing them to judgment, and sentencing them according to their works. And by this instance he confirmeth what he said of his power to quicken dead souls, by a proof which they would think more marvellous, and holds out a particular evidence of that authority, ver. 27, wherein in his human nature he should so be visible judge as yet his procedure should prove him to be true God also.

DOCTRINES.

1. Christ's glory hath but little room and place in our narrow hearts when it is set before us; and in his humanity and state of humiliation hardly will men give unto him the glory of his godhead; for they but marvelled at these things, as that which their hearts could not receive.

2. As it is commendable for men, when Christ manifests himself and his glory in the word, to close with it by faith and believing, to admire and wonder at that infinite depth of excellency in him which cannot be comprehended, so to misbelieve and wonder, and be astonished at what Christ saith, because we cannot comprehend it by sense or reason, is the great and ordinary sin of too many hearers; for such was the fruit of the Jews' hearing, reproved by Christ: " Marvel not at this."

3. Christ's power for quickening and converting sinners, and his having authority to execute judgment, should not be thought strange of, considering what he is, and that wonders are ordinary with him : " Marvel not at this," saith he, Christ hath still more and more proofs of his godhead to let forth, if need be, and the proof of his godhead and power in the general resurrection may stay our hearts from distrustful wondering at what he declareth of himself; for Christ refutes their wondering at what he had said by this new proof; not that the resurrection of the body is a greater proof of power in itself than the quickening of a dead soul,—wherein all the powers and faculties of man are prone to resist God's operation, whereas men's dead bodies have an obediential subjection to his power,—but this proof of his power is more visible and obvious to men's senses than the other, and more difficulty appears in the work, to carnal reason, which takes not up the power of spiritual death, and thinks it easier to work on a man having a reasonable soul and bodily ear, than on dead bodies having no sense nor understanding to hear his voice; and therefore Christ proveth the one by the other.

4. How impossible soever it seem to carnal reason, yet it is clear from the word that there will be a resurrection of the dead, that both godly and wicked may receive a full recompence according to their ways, and that for this end there shall be a reuniting of the soul to the body in the grave to make them living persons again; for they " that are in the graves shall hear his voice," which presupposeth that their souls shall be united to their bodies in their graves.

5. Albeit the time of the resurrection and general judgment be unknown to any, save to God only, Matt. xxiv. 36, yet it is certainly coming, and all are bound to mind that it is so; for " the hour is coming, in the which they shall hear his voice," &c. (See James, v. 9.)

6. This resurrection will be universal, of all, whether dead sooner or later; none of the godly will be lost, but will meet in that general assembly; nor shall any of the wicked shift this day of compearance, [trial] for " all that are in the graves shall hear his voice," &c.; whereby we are not to seclude those who shall " be changed," 1 Cor. xv. 51, as if no notice should be taken of them in that day, though they need not a resurrection; nor yet are we to seclude others who never got a grave, but were torn, drowned, burnt, or devoured by wild beasts and monsters; for all will be " delivered up," Rev. xx. 13. Only under this, as the most usual course taken with dead bodies, all the dead are comprehended ; and by this evidence of power on them who are rotten and resolved to dust in their graves, proof is given how easy it is for him to raise up all.

7. This universal resurrection will be of the same bodies that lived on earth and were laid in the grave, which as his omnipotency can effectuate, so his justice, purchase, and promise, requires that the same body should receive the reward of its ways, and that he should not lose his purchase; for they " that are in the graves," or the same body that lived and was laid there, being dead, " shall hear his voice." (See John, xix. 25—27.)

8. The mean employed in the resurrection is

the voice of Jesus Christ, who shall descend "with a shout," 1 Thess. iv. 16, and with the "sound of a trumpet," sounded by angels, and backed with his authority, Matt. xxiv. 31, which not only those who remain and are alive, but those who are dead shall hear, all the world over, (their souls having now re-entered into their bodies,) and shall call them out, to the terror of the wicked and comfort of the godly; for "all that are in the graves shall hear his voice."

9. The souls of men being united to their bodies, and their bodies endowed with qualities suitable to the estate for which they are appointed, shall, at the call of Christ, rise out of their graves, and be brought before the judgment-seat of Christ, the godly rejoicing to go meet their bridegroom, and the wicked forced to appear, who could wish that hills and mountains would cover them; for they "shall hear his voice, and shall come forth."

10. In the day of the resurrection and general judgment there will be only two sorts of persons —good or evil; and all the godly will be reckoned to have "done good," how small soever the degree of their goodness hath been, and how many faults soever they have had, if their course and way hath aimed at good; yea, the evil deeds of such as sincerely close with Christ, if it were but at their death, shall be forgotten; and, on the other hand, all the wicked shall be accounted evil-doers, how many soever moral virtues they have had, or albeit they have been painted hypocrites, and that because they have not made their peace through Jesus Christ; for there shall be only then "they that have done good, and they that have done evil."

11. Albeit there may be many mistakes in this world, and the godly may be misconstructed and slandered, and the wicked and hypocrites may be cried up and seem to be very good, yet in the day of judgment men's ways will appear in their true colours, and their actions and ways shall be clearly known to the Judge, who will distinguish and rank them accordingly on his right and left hand, for then it will be clear who "have done good," and who "have done evil."

12. According as men live in this world, and die and go out of it, accordingly will they be found in the resurrection and judgment, without any change; for in that day men are reckoned according as they "have done good or evil"—to wit, in this life.

13. Albeit Christ will not reward men for their good works as he punisheth them for their wickedness in the general judgment, yet he will proceed in that day according as their works shall evidence their state, that they have been believers in Christ, or living in the bond of iniquity, to punish them for the one, and to reward them of free grace according to the other; therefore will it be taken notice of in that day, who "have done good" and who "have done evil." (See Matt. xxv. 34—45.)

14. Albeit the Lord see it fit, for wise reasons, to let common lots befal the wicked and the godly within time, and albeit the wicked may prosper in the world, when the godly, holding fast their integrity, are in deep distress, yet, in the resurrection and general judgment, God will give a full and final recompence to men according to their ways; for the godly shall be raised up and brought to judgment, that they may be entered into the possession of a blessed and eternal life, wherein they shall enjoy God and Christ, and the company of saints and angels, and sing hallelujahs for ever; and the wicked to get the sentence of condemnation passed by the law and gospel executed upon them, and to be in the pit, tormented with the devil and his angels for ever; and they shall be raised by virtue of that sentence, and by the power of the Judge, to have it executed, and not by virtue of Christ's life and resurrection as their Head, 1 Cor. xv. 23; for they "shall come forth; they that have done good, unto the resurrection of life; and they that have done evil, unto the resurrection of damnation."

VER. 30. I can of mine own self do nothing: as I hear, I judge: and my judgment is just; because I seek not mine own will, but the will of the Father which hath sent me.

This verse is a conclusion of this part of Christ's apology, for his curing of the man, and commanding him to carry his bed on the sabbath day, and for his asserting his unity and equality with the Father; wherein, from the former purpose, he sums up these conclusions:— 1. That he is inseparable from the Father in operation, as ver. 19, having no private power of his own, (as they conceived of him as a mere man,) but the same in essence, power, and operation with him. 2. That he is on all the Father's counsels, and hath the power of administration of all things communicated to him from the Father, which is pointed out under the name of hearing, as it is ver. 19 by seeing, to hold forth the spirituality of the way of communicating, and his infinite comprehension of all that is communicated, as hearing and seeing all. 3. That his government and administration is most just, as seeking no satisfaction to any will of his own contrary to, or diverse from, the Father's, as he is God; and that he doth this not only as God simply, but as God now incarnate also, being the same still with the Father, and acting in all things according to the will of God. And though as man he hath a will distinct from his will as God, and so diverse from the Father's will, yet that did act in subordination to the will of God, Matt. xxvi. 39. Whence learn—

1. The divinity of Christ is a truth that may no ways be quarrelled, and doth call for our second and serious thoughts; therefore doth he recapitulate his apology that this truth may be inculcated.

2. Such is the strict conjunction and perfect unity of the Father and the Son that the Son neither doth nor can do anything without the fellowship of the Father, so that in all his working the Father is to be seen and taken up; for "I can of mine own self do nothing," saith he.

3. Christ, in the administration of all things, and executing of his purposes in this life, and at the day of judgment, is upon the Father's counsel acting from him; and all Christ's administrations are upon counsel and conclusion taken betwixt the Father and the Son; for saith he, "As I hear, I judge."

4. Christ's administrations and sentences are all just and right, doing injury and violence to no man, nor ought they to be stumbled at by any, for " my judgment is just," saith he.

5. The reason of the justice of Christ's judgment is, because it is agreeable to the will of the Father, with whom he is one, and whose will is the rule of justice, as being supreme and absolute Lord; which will Christ, being incarnate and God-man, did conform himself unto in all things; for "my judgment is just, because I seek not mine own will," (nor have any will contrary to or diverse from his, as hath been explained,) " but the will of the Father which hath sent me."

VER. 31. If I bear witness of myself, my witness is not true.

Followeth to the end of the chapter the second part of Christ's apology, wherein, having by many instances proven his unity and equality with the Father, he proceedeth to produce witnesses, testifying concerning him, which were so clear as gave him just cause to season them with challenges for their wilful unbelief and rejecting of him, and to threaten them with being judged and condemned before God. And, 1. Waving an ordinary exception, which might be moved against his testimony of himself, ver. 31, he cleareth that the Father had by many witnesses testified concerning him, ver. 32,—namely, by the testimony of John the Baptist, ver. 33, (a witness, whom though he produced, not because he needed it, but for their good, ver. 34, yet one who was truly eminent, and whose eminency might condemn their inconstancy, ver. 35;) by the works he did, ver. 36; by his immediate testimony from heaven, of whom they were ignorant, and looked nothing like his manifestations to them, ver. 37, 38; by the testimony of the scriptures, verse 39. 2. Unto these he subjoins challenges for several faults—namely, for their wilful unbelief in not coming to him, ver. 40, 42, (though he sought them not for any need he had of them, ver. 41;) for want of the love of God, ver. 42; for not embracing him, whereas they would receive a seducer, ver. 43; and for their pride and vainglory, which causes their unbelief, verse 44. 3. Because of these evils, he warneth them of being accused and judged before the tribunal of God, assuring them that even Moses would be against them, ver. 45; seeing they could not believe Moses, who wrote of him, since they believed not him, ver. 46; and it was no wonder they slighted him since they believed not Moses, ver. 47.

In this verse we have a transition, wherein Christ obviates an ordinary objection against the former part of this apology—to wit, that his testimony of himself could not be authentic, of which also John, viii. 13. Christ, by this sentence, doth not grant this as true, (for the contrary is asserted, John, viii. 14,) but only, by way of preterition, passeth it to make way for the following testimonies confirming his testimony of himself, that he might let them see he had witnesses beside to convince them, though he were silent. Whence learn—

1. In reading of holy scripture great care is to be had for finding out the true sense thereof, and that we be not drawn away, by what it seems to say at first view, to take up a sense contrary to truth, and other clear scriptures; and particularly words spoken by way of objection or preterition, and giving, and not granting, are to be distinguished from affirmations; for so is this to be understood: " If I bear witness of myself, my witness is not true;" to expound it otherwise were to contradict truth.

2. Albeit that men may lawfully speak that which is true of themselves when they have God's call unto it, yet ordinarily, such is the frailty of any who is a mere man, that he is but a bad witness in his own cause, being but a liar, and so subject to err, being readily poisoned with self-love in what concerneth himself, and being ready, in what is true, to seek himself; for upon this truth is this objection grounded, which had some colour if Christ had been only a man.

3. Albeit Christ be of himself " the Amen, the faithful and true witness," (Rev. iii. 14,) to all that know him, yet, for further confirmation of his people, and for conviction of wilful opposers, he is content to deny himself, and produce witnesses to testify for him. So much doth this preterition and proceeding to the testimonies teach us.

VER. 32. There is another that beareth witness of me; and I know that the witness which he witnesseth of me is true.

Albeit this verse may be understood of John, (of whom, ver. 33,) who, as he testified of Christ, so Christ commends and alloweth of his testimony, yet it seems rather to be understood of the Father, who is the other witness with himself, John, viii. 18; and it doth point, not so much at any particular testimony, of which ver. 37, as in general sheweth that all these ensuing testimonies had authority from him; concerning this testimony, Christ declareth his persuasion of the truth and certainty thereof. Whence learn—

1. Albeit that Christ, the true and faithful witness, be ofttimes accounted so infamous in the world as not to be believed, yet, as he is above all proof to his own, so he wants not witnesses to testify for him. So much doth his producing them in this apology teach.

2. As Christ came into the world in obedience to the Father, and to bear witness of him, so was he assured to be avowed and owned of him, and accordingly found so; and as he honoured the Father, so did the Father honour and bear witness of him; for " there is another that beareth witness of me."

3. Christ, as he is one in nature and essence with the Father, so is he a distinct person from him; for he " is another that beareth witness."

4. God's testimony concerning Christ is undoubtedly true, and to be rested on, and all other testimonies are therefore true, because God's authority is interposed in them; for " the witness which he witnesseth of me is true," and the rest of the testimonies have weight, because they are his testimonies.

5. It is not enough for our comfort that we have God's testimony approving us, but we should

know that it is so, and ought to study the certainty and sure ground that is in such a testimony, that it may bear us up against all opposition, and enable us to avow it, and having believed, to speak as we stand in need; therefore Christ, having asserted that the Father beareth witness of him, doth subjoin, " and I know that the witness which he witnesseth of me is true," as resting upon the truth and reality that is in such a testimony.

Ver. 33. Ye sent unto John, and he bare witness unto the truth.

The first particular witness produced here, whereby the Father testifieth concerning him, is John the Baptist, who, without any partial respect to Christ, did simply bear witness to the truth concerning him; and this testimony he presseth from their own practice, who seemed so much to respect him as to send honourable commissioners to him, chap. i. 19; and to be willing to stand to his testimony concerning the Messiah, yea, and to offer that honour to him, if he would have accepted it; and therefore they were bound to esteem of his testimony, especially when they found him so self-denied as not to seek his own honour. Whence learn—

1. It is the duty and commendation of Christ's messengers to be witness-bearers for him, and with zeal and fidelity to publish his excellency upon any hazard; and they ought to assume no more to themselves, but to be heralds of his praise, that sinners may be drawn to him; for John " bare witness unto the truth" concerning Christ. (See chap. i. 7.)

2. Faithfulness is the great ornament and duty of Christ's witnesses, that, without any by-respect, they publish only what is truth, and that nothing which is truth (be it of less or more importance) want a testimony from them, as they are called to it; for " he bare witness unto the truth" was his commendation in this testimony, and it is a pattern to all others; and Christ thus describes his testimony concerning himself, that none might except that there is such a difference betwixt the matter of John's testimony and what may be their trial as to make them shrink if there be a divine truth in it.

3. The doctrine and faithful testimonies of Christ's servants will live to their commendation, and be of use when themselves are gone; for Christ repeats John's testimony to his commendation, and for the use of the Jews, when now John was in appearance dead; for he speaks of him as one that was, ver. 35.

4. The respect that men have seemed at least to carry to faithful ministers, and the excellent graces of God that they might have observed in them, will be a witness against them if they do not respect and credit their doctrine; for so doth Christ urge from their practice and John's fidelity and self-denial: " Ye sent unto John, and he bare witness unto the truth," and renounced that honour which they would have conferred on him.

Ver. 34. But I receive not testimony from man: but these things I say, that ye might be saved.

Unto this testimony of John, Christ subjoins two things: first, by way of correction, that he needed not man's testimony, nor did produce it for anything it could add to him, but only for their good and salvation, if so be that testimony of John, whom they seemed to respect, might draw them to come to him and be saved. Whence learn—

1. Christ doth so condescend and stoop for the good of his people as yet he will not have his greatness and majesty forgotten or slighted; therefore doth he add this correction, lest they should mistake his condescendence.

2. Christ doth then get his own room in men's estimation when he is seen to be such an one as needs nothing without himself, and needs nothing to commend him but himself, and when they are brought to see and acknowledge that he is nothing the greater or better when all are for him, nor the worse though all were against him; that his truth and doctrine needs no man's testimony for confirmation of it, being sufficiently confirmed by his own authority; and that men's commending of him adds nothing to him, though it be their own and others' advantage that they do so; therefore saith he, " I receive not testimony from man."

3. Albeit Christ need nothing of himself, but is all-sufficient and infinitely glorious, yet he condescends much to man's weakness and for his good; for albeit he " receive not testimony from man," yet, saith he, " these things I say"—I borrow a testimony from John for your cause— " that ye might be saved."

4. The nature of Christ's ministry tends to the salvation of sinners, how cross-like soever it seem to work to such an end; and in his ministry he intends the salvation of his own, whom his love doth follow when they are among the crowd of enemies; for " these things I say"—not only in producing this testimony, but even in the harshest of this apology—" that ye might be saved;" not that he intended the salvation of all these, but that the nature of his work tended to that end, and he intended the salvation of his own among them.

5. Albeit the salvation of men be their great and eternal happiness, yet they are ready to lay many obstructions in the way thereof, which it is Christ's great love and condescendence to pass over; for so much also is imported in his saying these things, that they " might be saved." They obstructed the way of their own salvation, and Christ condescended to take the stumbling-blocks out of the way.

Ver. 35. He was a burning and a shining light: and ye were willing for a season to rejoice in his light.

The second thing subjoined to this testimony is a qualification added to his depressing of John's testimony, lest any should think that by what he had said he had vilified John and his testimony; therefore he guards it with a commendation of him, as being an eminent man for clearness of doctrine and vigour of zeal, and effectual in his doctrine, even among those corrupt Jews, both Pharisees and others, who went out to him, Matt.

iii. 5, 7, wherein also he checks them for their inconstancy, who so soon wearied of what they seemed to be so much affected with.

DOCTRINES.

1. Albeit ministers be nothing in comparison of Christ, nor are they to think that they can add anything to him, yet they will not want their own due commendation; for so doth Christ's commending of John, after what he had said, ver. 34, teach us.

2. Without the knowledge of God and a lively ministry holding out the same from the word, the world lieth in the darkness of ignorance and error, wandering in the unfruitful works of darkness and under the disconsolate estate of misery, without any comfortable sight of God's favour; for ministers being a " light," (which serveth to enlighten what is dark,) importeth so much.

3. Faithful ministers are appointed of Christ for remedying this darkness; and it is their duty and commendation not only to shine in their conversation, (as all Christians are bound to do, Phil. ii. 15, 16,) but by purity and clearness of doctrine to point out the way of salvation and remedy of all grievances to sinners; for " he was a shining light." The word is, a "lamp," or "lantern," not only pointing at this, that such a light should not be put under a bushel, Matt. v. 15, but that his light was not native and from himself, but lighted from that bright Sun, and that the light of the ministry serves for our use in this dark night of time, (and therefore they are also called stars,) but will cease in the other life, as John's shining candle was put out when Christ the Sun of Righteousness was manifested.

4. It is also the duty of a faithful minister, not only by clearness of doctrine to shine round about him, but also to have his light seasoned with much zeal and love, that so it may affect his own heart and burn up his own corruptions, may warm and stir up others, may make him move upward, as fire doth, in his motions, and may make him active and vigorous in his calling, though with the wasting of himself; for " he was a burning and a shining light."

5. Qualifications and gifts are not bestowed upon all ministers in a like measure and degree, but Christ dispenseth them variously, that he may shew forth his absolute freedom in bestowing, and that the glory of success may not be ascribed to men's gifts when he shall effectuate great things by weakest instruments; and he doth bestow gifts on men according to their employments in several times or places; for this commendation of John imports that he was gifted above others, even honest instruments, being more than a prophet, Matthew, xi. 9—11. (See 1 Cor. xii. 15—17.)

6. The brightest and most zealous lights of the church have but their time of it in the world, and men will have the offer and benefit of them but for a season. They are subject, as well as others, to the common condition of mortality, and ofttimes they spend themselves speedily with burning and shining to others, yea, and are hastened out of the world by persecution; beside, the Lord by removing of them doth put an end to their toil, and call them to enjoy the fruit of their labours, doth chastise the ingratitude of the world, and exercise his own in it, and doth make way for setting forth the riches of his glory in raising up and creating new stars in their place; for here it is said of John, " he was a burning and a shining light," but now is put out and gone.

7. When Christ's faithful servants are dead and gone, yet their commendation liveth in his estimation; therefore doth he commend John when now he is gone by death, or at least is in prison.

8. A sound and powerful, a clear and lively ministry, may have strange effects, even among unrenewed people; the excellency of their doctrine, when it shines among a people who have long lain under the darkness of ignorance and superstitious traditions, the countenance of ministers from great men, (as John had from Herod,) the excellency of their gifts, together with a common work of the Spirit upon hearers, may produce strange effects in them who have no true grace nor faith; for saith he, " ye were willing to rejoice in his light;" there was none but John in their account, and they were much taken up with him.

9. Men's affections may be much aloft, and they may have great fits of joy and delight through the novelty and excellency of doctrine, and through some apprehension of that at a distance, which the word speaks of, who yet have no sound grace, as never having been humbled for sin, nor laid hold on Christ, on whom alone sound joy is founded, Phil. iii. 3; for these temporaries " were willing to rejoice," or, delighted to rejoice. (See Matt. xiii. 20, 21; Mark, vi. 20; Heb. vi. 4, 5.)

10. It is also an evidence of men's unsoundness when they are more taken with men, and with their gifts, as their own, than they are affected with God as the author of these gifts, or do find his power accompanying the exercise of them in effects upon their hearts; for they rejoiced " in his light," or, in that light as his, not seeing nor feeling God in it.

11. Temporary motions wrought in men by a lively ministry are not to be leaned to by themselves, nor are ministers to look much to the respect that comes from such, for it will be but momentary. Their unsoundness will not bear out, and when ministers meet with discountenance from great men and with the cross, and do touch their darling sins, they will give over; for they " were willing to rejoice," but " for a season," or an hour; and particularly they rejected him when Herod turned his enemy, and when he did testify concerning Christ, whom they liked not.

12. Men's temporary fits will be a witness against them after they have made apostasy, and their respect to a minister will witness against their not receiving his message; for their former carriage is now a check to them for their apostasy; and they are declared to be perverse who, when they could upon no pretence reprove John, but must admire him, yet they would not credit his testimony of Christ.

Ver. 36. But I have greater witness than that of John: for the works which the Father hath given me to finish, the same works that I do, bear witness of me, that the Father hath sent me.

The second particular testimony produced by Christ, whereby also the Father witnesseth concerning him, is that of his works, in doing miracles, and the work of redemption, which he declareth to be a greater witness than that of John, and that they prove abundantly that he is sent of the Father, as the Messiah and Saviour of the world. Whence learn—

1. Albeit our hearts be naturally jealous and suspicious of divine truth and of what Christ saith of himself, yet he hath abundance of witnesses for curing of this disease and putting us beyond all cause of suspicion; for beside John he hath more and " greater" witnesses, that in their mouths every word may be established, 2 Cor. xiii. 1.

2. Christ is willing and ready to give proof of his excellency, not only by his own or others' words, but by his working really to prove it to their sense and satisfaction; for he hath a witness of his " works."

3. Christ's workings are not dumb works, but are speaking testimonies of his glory, and we never take them up rightly till we see that in them; for his works do bear witness that the Father hath sent him, as his own Son, to be the Saviour of the world, and that he is not contrary to the Father in his working, as they alleged.

4. Albeit the testimony of the meanest instrument concerning Christ, being according to the word, is as true as any other witness, yet, if we respect degrees of convincing evidence, the testimony of Christ's own works is a clearer confirmation of his godhead, office, and doctrine, than the best of men's testimonies; for not only is this testimony more intrinsical than the commendation of another, but his doing these things that were fore-prophesied of the Messiah is an undeniable proof, and therefore he remits John to it, Matt. xi. 3—5, and his doing of them in his own name proveth that he did them of himself from the Father; therefore saith he that his works are a " greater witness than that of John," proving that the Father hath sent him; for he could not have done what he did, not only by way of confirmation of the doctrine of the scriptures, (which seducers by their miracles do not, Deut. xiii. 5,) but so agreeable to predictions of scripture concerning the Messiah, if he had not been God and sent of the Father, and if he had called himself what he was not. And albeit prophets and apostles wrought great miracles, who were not the Messiah, yet this infringeth not the clearness of this testimony; for these miracles did only confirm their calling, authority, and doctrine, and that they were what they called themselves, (which was not that they were the Messiah,) and so do Christ's miracles confirm his doctrine and what he said of himself; next, they were but instruments, and that not of the miracle, but of the word and sign by which it was done, and they expressly declared that it was not in their own name or power any such thing was done, Acts, iii. 12, 16, but Christ was principal agent, and wrought them in his own name;

and in this respect he did " the works which none other man did," John, xv. 24.

5. All the works that Christ did were entrusted him from the Father, not only to undertake but to finish and perfect them; as God the Father did communicate his nature and operation with him, and as Mediator, he had a commission by the common counsel of the blessed Trinity; for they were the works which the Father gave him to finish.

6. Christ is faithful in his trust, and what is committed to him he doth; for saith he, " the works which the Father hath given me to finish, (are) the same works that I do."

7. As Christ's works do prove his excellency in himself, so also do they commend him to his people as being sent out of the Father's love for their good, an all-sufficient and omnipotent Mediator, able to effectuate all his purposes, and worthy to be rested on by them; for saith he, they " bear witness of me, that the Father hath sent me."

Ver. 37. And the Father himself which hath sent me, hath borne witness of me. Ye have neither heard his voice at any time, nor seen his shape.

38. And ye have not his word abiding in you: for whom he hath sent, him ye believe not.

The third particular testimony is that of the Father, which is neither to be understood of that in the scriptures, of which ver. 39, nor yet of any internal revelation of Christ, as Matt. xvi. 17, but of his immediate testimony to Christ, that as he had described him of old to be such an one as he was found, Isa. xlii. 1, 2, &c.; liii.; Zech. ix. 9, &c., and elsewhere; so he had given him an immediate testimony at his baptism, Matthew, iii. 17, as afterward in his transfiguration, Matt. xvii. 5, of which 2 Peter, i. 17: that which is subjoined in the end of ver. 37 may be looked on as pointing at the unusualness of such a manifestation of God, they never having heard a voice from heaven in their time, nor seen any visible sign, (not to represent God's essence, but to assure them of his presence,) but when God owned Christ by a voice from heaven, and when the likeness of a dove was the sign of the Spirit's coming on him; and therefore this testimony was the more to be regarded. But the following verse, and Christ's way of subjoining reproofs to his testimonies, leads us rather to understand it as a reproof of their ignorance of he Father, of whom they glorified so much; for whereas they were much puffed up, and might readily oppose this unto that immediate testimony given unto Christ, that they were the people whose fathers had heard the voice of God, Exod. xx. 18, 19, 22; Deut. iv. 12; and with whose prophet, Moses, God had spoken familiarly, and given him a very near manifestation of himself, Num. xii. 8, (not in a bodily way, Deut. iv. 12, but spiritual and intellectual, of his back parts, Exod. xxxiv. 6.) Christ sheweth them that all this was nothing to them; they neither had nor looked like any such manifestations, but were deaf and blind to them, ver. 37.

And whereas they might object that though such manifestations were gone, yet they had the word, which was delivered by the ministry of Moses to their fathers, and in them to their successors and children; Christ answers that it had not its due place with them, since they believed not in him, ver. 38.

DOCTRINES.

1. God is so faithful to them whom he employs in his work that they shall not want his testimony and approbation to bear them out against all opposition and contradiction of men; of this his carriage towards his Son is a special instance, and a pledge to his own of what they may expect in their own measure; "the Father which hath sent me hath borne witness of me."

2. The Father's immediate testimony of Christ is especially to be taken notice of as being a witness above all doubt, 1 John, v. 9, 10, and shewing that Christ is famous and excellent in heaven, whatever esteem men have of him on earth; therefore that the Father himself hath borne witness of him is superadded as greater than the testimony of his works, which yet was a " greater witness than that of John," ver. 36. And indeed the presence of the glorious Trinity made that witness most solemn, and the opening of heaven shewed that through him heaven was propitious to sinners on earth.

3. Men may be ready to delude themselves, because of great things of God manifested to the church and nation whereof they are, and to their progenitors, who yet themselves come far short, and are nothing like these things; for so did the Jews upon what Moses and their fathers had found, when yet saith he, " Ye have neither heard his voice at any time, nor seen his shape"— that is, not only had they none of these extraordinary manifestations, which are not usual in declining times, but they had not knowledge of God like to that which may be attained, which is, a clear, solid, and satisfactory knowledge of God, as of one whom we know by seeing and hearing. This they wanted, and so proved that they were not Moses' disciples, nor looked like that people whose progenitors had seen so much of God.

4. The word of God is sufficiently able to compense and make up the want of any extraordinary manifestation; for so is implied here in that which Christ meets with, that they had the word from their progenitors, to make up the want of those manifestations; which Christ doth not refute, seeing the word is the ordinary and sure way for attaining the knowledge of God. (See 2 Pet. i. 17—19.)

5. It is not enough to prove men to be in a good estate, that they have the word, unless by faith it get access into the heart, and it be fastened and kept there, as a treasure, and as seed to bring forth fruit; and this may be wanting in them who pretend to much estimation of the word; for so saith Christ unto the Jews, " ye have not his word abiding in you;" it must be an engrafted word, where it doth any good, James, i. 21.

6. Where Christ is not believed in and received as sent of the Father, there the word is not rooted, nor is there any saving knowledge of it; and particularly the Jews (who did not, or yet do not, receive Christ, now exhibited under the New Testament, nor are led by the Old Testament to him) have not one word savingly of it; for this is the reason of the former challenge— " for whom he hath sent, him ye believe not."

VER. 39. *Search the scriptures; for in them ye think ye have eternal life: and they are they which testify of me.*

The fourth particular witness is that of the scriptures, which (by occasion of the former challenge) he exhorts them to search into, as being high in their estimation, and that deservedly, and as bearing witness unto him. Whence learn—

1. The Lord, in deep wisdom and love, hath prevented all occasion of delusion, and hath made his people's way clear and sure, by setting down his mind in holy writ, which is his infallible word, and the rule for finding out truth, and deciding all controversies in religion; therefore doth Christ remit them to the scriptures, or written word, as to God's rule in this controversy.

2. The way of salvation, and all things needful for attaining thereof, are fully revealed in scripture, and was held forth even in the Old Testament, much more now both in Old and New; for saith he, " in them ye think ye have eternal life," which was a true thought, as to the scriptures pointing out of the way, though they might be deluded in their application as to themselves, or thinking to be saved by the having or reading of it. (See 2 Tim. iii. 16, 17.)

3. Albeit the scriptures be plain and clear in all things necessary to salvation, and the entrance thereof give light, Psalm cxix. 130, yet they are a depth not soon comprehended, or by superficial search, but are a treasure in a mine, to be found out by digging and painful pondering of every word and sentence, (none whereof are expressed in vain, or at random, but all divine,) by considering of the scope and dependence, and comparing scripture with scripture, and humble and single dependence upon God; for he recommends the scriptures to be searched.

4. This treasure will be found out by the painful searcher, and it is the common duty of all the visible church to read and search into the scriptures, that they may find it; therefore doth he enjoin this search as a thing possible, and enjoineth it to the Jews in common, who were his hearers at this time. (See Acts, xvii. 11.)

5. As men, yea, and a visible church, may be very corrupt, and yet pretend to estimation of the scriptures, and allow people the use thereof, and may be opposing Christ, and yet dream of salvation by the scriptures,—for both these are true of the Jews here,—so men who profess hope of salvation that way ought to prove the reality of it by their being much in the study of the scripture, that they be not deluded in their hope, and may feed on it and find the comfort of what they solidly gather from it; for Christ makes use

of their granted principle to press this search—
" Search the scriptures, for in them ye think ye
have eternal life."

6. The scope of the scriptures, and particularly of the Old Testament, is to point out and
bear witness of Jesus Christ, of his person, natures, and offices, of his birth, life, death, sufferings, and the glory that should follow, and of the
benefits that come through him; and it should
be our aim in searching of the scriptures to find
out Christ in them, and what they witness of
him; without which our study is to little purpose; " Search the scriptures, (saith he,) and
they are they which testify of me." (See Acts,
iii. 22—24.)

VER. 40. And ye will not come to me, that ye
might have life.

Unto these testimonies Christ subjoineth very
sad challenges and reproofs of this people; and
first, he challengeth them for their wilful unbelief; and that albeit John, his works, the Father, and the scriptures which they pretended to
esteem of, did prove what he was, and point
him out as the author of that life which they
professed to seek, verse 39, yet such was their
obstinacy, as they would not come to him nor believe in him. Whence learn—

1. That which God offers in Christ to lost
sinners is that which only deserveth the name
of life, in grace here and glory hereafter, as
being the true remedy of our spiritual death,
and without which our life on earth is scarce
worthy the name; therefore it is called "life."

2. Men may be so far deluded as to conceit
they will get life, when yet they neglect the
means of life; for these Jews thought to " have
eternal life," ver. 39, and yet they take not the
right way to it.

3. The life of lost sinners is only to be found
in Christ, who is the purchaser, storehouse,
keeper, and dispenser thereof, the Mediator of the
covenant, and the mid-man betwixt God and
sinners; for so is here held out; they must
" come to me," saith he, ere they live.

4. The way how sinners come to partake of
this life is by their coming to Christ by faith;
and whoever they are that have a pressing need
of Christ, and, whatever discouragements they
find, cannot abide away from him, and who,
whatever distance they are at, yet are moving
towards him, though with a slow progress, and
are still seeking more enjoyment, whatever they
have, —these are true believers, and will not
miss of life, but their soul shall be kept in life till
they come to live with him for ever; for the
condition required is, to come to Christ, which is
in effect to believe, as is expounded, chap. vi. 35,
and upon this it is imported that they shall " have
life."

5. Albeit life be to be found only in Christ,
yet few make use of him for that end; but most
part, being ignorant of themselves and of him,
conceiting of their own well-being, or to get life
some other way, being taken up with earthly
things, given up to judicial obduration, or not
pleasing the terms of getting life by renouncing their own righteousness and pleasures,—
most part, I say, being thus prejudged, do neglect this offered salvation; for so is challenged
—" ye will not come to me."

6. The great obstruction of faith and aggravation of unbelief is men's wilfulness in not coming
to Christ. Some will not come and believe in
him out of their malice and obstinacy, (as many
of these Jews would not come to him, though he
proved never so clearly what he was;) others
are plagued with brutish sensuality; and they
who think they would come, but apprehend reasons why they dare not, will find that " will not"
is the great impediment, and that they do not
believe because they are not willing to be stript
of themselves, as faith in Christ requireth they
should be, Rom. x. 3. Otherwise, there is no impediment lieth in the comer's way but love removeth it; he will welcome them who have
refused many invitations, have wandered far,
fallen into gross sins, played the harlot with
many lovers, &c., provided they will come to
him, to seek grace to repent for and amend them;
yea, the dead may come to him to get life, if
they resolve not that they will not; and they
who have some weak desire may come to him to
get willingness, therefore the challenge is—" ye
will not come," which in many of them was
obstinacy upon grounds of malice, and brutish
stupidity; and most part of unbelievers are
guilty of it, in some degree, upon other grounds.
(See Psalm lxxxi. 11; Rev. xxii. 17.)

7. Christ will challenge men's not embracing his
offer and invitation, to come and get life, especially when there is much of will in it. The
contempt of his offer is a great indignity, and
will condemn men; his people's unbelief is a sin,
to be avoided at his command, under pain of his
displeasure; his love will make a quarrel of it,
that we should be straitened in our own bowels,
when there are bowels of affection in him to be
let forth; and he is really offended at that pride
(though masked with a show of humility) which
makes that the self-condemned sinner will not
embrace him upon gospel terms; for it is a
challenge here—" ye will not come," &c., so
that it is our great advantage to be mourning for
the unbelief we find in us, and when our unbelief
is our burden.

VER. 41. I receive not honour from men.

Lest they should think that in commending
himself and challenging them he was hunting
after vainglory, as false teachers do, Christ obviates that mistake, and sheweth that he was
seeking no such thing, nor was capable of any
addition of honour from the creature. Whence
learn—

1. Christ is so omniscient that he knoweth
and marketh the thoughts of every one that he
dealeth with. So much doth his obviating their
thoughts teach.

2. It is the usual fault of men that they have
but low and base thoughts of Christ, and that
they measure and judge of him and his followers
by themselves; for this suspicion of Christ imported that they looked on him as a mere man,

and as they were themselves ambitious, ver. 44, so did they judge of him, and so are his servants judged of.

3. Christ was no hunter after vainglory, nor is he capable of any addition of honour by men's acknowledging of him, nor ought men to think that he seeks them because he hath any need of them, or that they add anything to him, when he makes them somewhat; for albeit men are bound to manifest and declare his superexcellent glory, and men by sin do what they can to dishonour him, as who would cast dirt or spit against the sun? yet his infinite glory is neither capable of addition nor diminution from the creature; for "I receive not honour from men."

VER. 42. But I know you, that ye have not the love of God in you.

A second fault (and a cause of the former, ver 40,) for which he challengeth them, is their want of the love of God, and so he sheweth that he challenged them, not because they respected not him, but that he might convince them of this want, and take from them that great pretence of love to God and zeal to the sabbath commanded by God, upon which they pretended they opposed him, and his working of that miracle. Whence learn—

1. It is the woeful case of men to be void of the love of God, love being the fountain of desiring and fruit of enjoying communion (in part) with him; being the true root of all sound obedience and the sum of the commandments, and that which is the evidence of being beloved of him, and will make obedience to be active, constant, and pleasant; therefore Christ summeth up their woeful case in this: "ye have not the love of God in you."

2. True love to God doth not consist in outward pretences and shows, but must have a sure root of affection within, breaking forth in deed and in truth; and men may pretend zeal to God's glory and for his ordinances who yet have no true love to God; for they pretended that all their opposition to Christ flowed from zeal for the sabbath and God's glory; and yet saith he, "ye have not the love of God in you."

3. Christ doth perfectly and exactly know men, and what is in them, let them mask themselves as they will, and he will in due time decipher and detect the unsound; therefore saith he, "I know you, that ye have not the love of God in you."

VER. 43. I am come in my Father's name, and ye receive me not: if another shall come in his own name, him ye will receive.

The third fault challenged is their not embracing him who is come in his Father's name, whereas they would receive a seducer coming in his own name; wherein their great perversity and injustice towards him, and God's judgment on them, appeared. Whence learn—

1. Albeit Christ be God over all, equal with the Father, and Lord over his own house, and so acts in his own name, yet it pleased him to condescend as Mediator, not only to purchase life to them that come to him, but to be at pains, and come into the world clothed with a commission and authority from the Father, to make offer of this purchased life, that by his condescendence he might commend his love to his people, and teach them humility, and not to run on a calling unsent, and that we might look on him as approven of the Father, and that such as come to him, the Father will accept them; for saith he, "I am come in my Father's name." (See Philippians, ii. 5—7, &c.; Matthew, iii. 17; Hebrews, v. 4, 5.)

2. Christ thus coming is to be received, his doctrine to be heard, himself to be acknowledged for such in his person, offices, commission, and benefits, as he declareth himself to be; to be rested on and embraced, to be employed and submitted to as such; for so is imported in that they should "receive him."

3. Albeit Christ be the great ambassador of the Father, not a servant, but the Son, Matt. xxi. 37; and albeit he was singular in his administration of his office, and all tending to the good of sinners; yet such is the perverseness of the world, as not to make him welcome; for it is the peculiar privilege of the elect to be drawn to him, and [as to] others, they neither see his excellency nor feel their need of him; therefore saith he, "I am come in my Father's name, and ye receive me not."

4. Such as reject Christ and receive him not are destitute of the love of God, nor have they any evidence of respect to him, since Christ is the clearest image of the Father, and cometh in his name, and the Father will not be acknowledged but in and through him; therefore by this doth he prove that challenge, ver. 42.

5. When Christ manifests himself to the world, it is usual with Satan to hound out seducers and false teachers, to study to bear him down, to seduce souls, and by their courses to make the way of truth odious; for so is imported that another shall come, pretending either to be the Christ, or to hold him out to others. (See Matt. xxiv. 5, 24; Acts, v. 36, 37.)

6. Albeit false teachers pretend to come in God and Christ's name, Matt. xxiv. 5, yet they do but come in their own name, as having no commission when they run, as making themselves, their reputation and advantage, their chief aim in their undertaking, and as speaking the imaginations of their own heart and brain, without any warrant from God; for "another shall come in his own name."

7. Such as love not God nor embrace Christ or his sent servants, may take worse in their room, and will easily receive and embrace false teachers and seducers. Men's nature is propense to evil courses, and is readiest to be affected with what is wrong; and seducers are more ready to serve men's humours than faithful ministers may be; and withal it is God's just judgment on the world to give them up to such, since they will not receive the love of the truth, 2 Thess. ii. 10—12; therefore saith he, "if another come in his own name, him ye will receive." This is the heinous sin of men, to affront Christ, to respect Satan in his messengers before God in his

Son, and to prefer lies to truth; and it is their dreadful punishment to be given up to such delusions, because they will not see the light, or do receive it only as it may serve their turn, or weary of the light, and walk not answerable to it. And men should be ashamed of their errors, as being their plague, and a proclamation that they have not received the love of the truth.

VER. 44. How can ye believe, which receive honour one of another, and seek not the honour that cometh from God only?

The fourth challenge (and the chief cause of their unbelief, and not embracing Christ) is for their pride and vainglory, which they hunted after among men, not contenting themselves to be approven and respected of God, by embracing his Son by faith. (See chap. xii. 43.)

DOCTRINES.

1. True believers and receivers of Christ are all one: they do indeed believe in Christ who, out of affection and sense of need, do close with and embrace Christ offering himself in the gospel, albeit they have not attained to lively assurance, and without this, historical assent will not prove saving faith; therefore receiving, ver. 43, and believing, in this verse, do mutually explain one another; so also John, i. 12.

2. Albeit faith be the gift of God, and it be impossible for any natural man to believe of himself, yet men, by continuance in sinful ways, and entertaining particular reigning sins, may add to this impotency, may lay more impediments in the way of God's working faith, and may be convinced that their case is inconsistent with true faith; for "How can ye believe?" saith he, intimating that they had superadded impediments of believing to their condition by nature,—as a crooked twig, by growing, becometh more difficult to be made straight,—and that themselves might see that their temper was inconsistent with faith.

3. As faith, which supposeth a man regenerate and subdued to Christ and his yoke, and which purifieth the heart, is inconsistent with the dominion of any one lust or corrupt affection, so, in particular, it cannot consist with the dominion of ambition, and affectation of vainglory; for albeit we be bound to honour all men, and magistrates in particular, 1 Peter, ii. 17, and are bound in honour to prefer one another, Rom. xii. 10; and albeit believers ought so to carry themselves as the way of God may be honoured in and because of them, Rom. ii. 24; yea, albeit they cannot hinder, nor is it their sin, if undue honour be offered unto them, provided they mourn for it, and receive it not, yet when men hunt after respect from men, and do receive it with lustful delight, and rest on it as the chief scope of their actions, it is an evidence of no faith, or that what they pretend to is unsound; therefore, albeit some such be said to believe, where it prevailed but in part, John, xii. 42, yet where it bears full sway, and it only is sought after, he saith, "How can ye believe, which receive honour one of another?" And indeed, such do evidence that they have not closed with Christ on his own terms of self-denial and being convinced of their worthlessness; that they will take most pains on their outside, to be seen of men, and so cannot but neglect sincerity; and that their ambition and love of respect from men will draw them to apostasy and prove their unsoundness when they are called to undergo an ignominious cross.

4. God alloweth and conferreth much honour upon true believers; they have an honour of state and privileges, in being sons and friends to God; they have the honour of his approbation in their conscience, yea, and sometimes his respects to them are made conspicuous to the world, and they are allowed to wait for the honour of eternal exaltation; for there is " the honour that cometh from God" to such.

5. As this true honour comes from God alone, whose approbation only may be rested on, and who can advance those whom he approveth, and make them honourable, so sincere believers must seek after this, which is so necessary, by studying humble sincerity in his sight, following those duties that are in least respect in the world, and not resting on so much only as may gain them honour from men; and as they must seek after it, not contenting themselves with less, so they must be content with this, and be loosed from the love of honour from men, not regarding how they be looked on by the world because they embrace Christ; therefore it is imported, they should " seek the honour that cometh from God only." (See Rom. ii. 29; 2 Cor. x. 18.)

6. Whatever may be men's duty in seeking to approve themselves even to the consciences of men, and not to neglect just disrespect in the world, under pretext of approving themselves to God, yet such as ambitiously hunt after vainglory, and respect from men, do prove themselves to be careless of God's approbation, since hunting after the one and seeking the other cannot consist together; for here they are opposed: " Ye receive honour one of another, and seek not the honour that cometh from God only."

VER. 45. Do not think that I will accuse you to the Father: there is one that accuseth you, even Moses, in whom ye trust.

To make the former challenges have place, Christ warns them of being judged and accused before the tribunal of God; and that he might prevent the thoughts of their hearts, (who leaned to Moses as their great teacher, John, ix. 28, 29, and believed to be absolved and saved by following the law given by him, and so regarded not Christ's challenges,) he declareth that not only he, but Moses' law, would accuse and condemn them, and so leads a special scripture witness for himself, even Moses' law. While Christ saith he will not accuse them, it is not a simple denial, (for his doctrine and offer of salvation will be the sad condemnation of sinners,) but it is spoken according to their opinion who regarded little his opposition; and therefore he declares that even Moses, their great friend, would be their party, not in respect of his person, but his writings.

DOCTRINES.

1. Sinners continuing obstinate after abundance of conviction may look for appearing before God's tribunal to have the matter discussed, and ministers ought to set this before them; therefore doth Christ here put them in mind of being accused " to the Father."

2. Sin unrepented of, and the sinners' not fleeing to Christ for pardon and purging of it, will draw on sharp and sad accusations before the tribunal of God; both law and gospel, God's justice, men's own consciences, the Spirit resisted by them in his moral suasions, Acts, vii. 51, yea, all the pains taken on them, will contribute to this work; for it is supposed they will be accused " to the Father."

3. Such as reject Christ, and do neglect challenges for this, it is because they have some false confidence beside, which bolsters them up in their opposition, for so had the Jews; " Moses, in whom ye trust," saith he; they gloried of being his disciples who spake with God, and thought to be safe by looking to his law.

4. Whatever be the confidence which seemeth to uphold men in their misregarding of Christ, it will not only fail them, but turn an accuser to make up their ditty, [condemnation;] for " even Moses, in whom ye trust, will accuse you to the Father."

5. Whatever men may think of Christ's being an adversary, yet not only is it sad when the Saviour of sinners turns the sinners' accuser, but he will find many witnesses to prosecute his sentence and challenge against the despisers; godly men, whom such glory of in opposition to him, will be ready to be their greatest enemies, and the word of God in the ministry of his servants, extraordinary or ordinary, will bear witness against them, whatever respect they seem to carry thereunto; for saith he, " Think not that I will accuse you to the Father," (or, albeit ye think light of that, though too sad for you to bear, yet) " there is one that accuseth you, even Moses, in whom ye trust," not only because the sentence of the law stood against them, but all his writing and doctrine should accuse them, as is after cleared.

VER. 46. For had ye believed Moses, ye would have believed me: for he wrote of me.

Christ confirmeth this assertion by this reason: Moses could not but be a witness against them who believed not his doctrine; now, none could believe his doctrine who believed not in Christ, since he wrote so clearly of him. Whence learn—

1. Eminent instruments in God's house are never rightly entertained but when their doctrine is received and entertained by faith; for whatever they boasted of Moses, yet Christ imports that they believed not his doctrine: "had ye believed Moses."

2. Men may pretend to trust God's servants and their message who yet have no true faith—and namely, when their trust goeth contrary to the meaning and scope of the word. Such was their trust in Moses, rejecting Christ, ver. 45, which yet was no believing.

3. There can be no true believing of the doctrine of the word but where it leads men to the acknowledgment and embracing of Christ; " For had ye believed Moses, ye would have believed me."

4. Such as did indeed believe scripture prophecies concerning the Messiah did also acknowledge the accomplishment in Christ's person when he came; and he who acknowledgeth not the one did not truly believe the other; " For had ye believed Moses, who wrote of me, ye would have believed me," when ye see the accomplishment.

5. Moses, in his doctrine, did write and testify of Christ; not only did he hold him out in express prophecies, Gen. iii. 15; xxii. 18; xlix. 10; Deut. xviii. 18, and elsewhere; and did point him out under the shadows and types of the ceremonial law, and of the brazen serpent, the manna, the rock that followed them, &c., but the scope and drift of all his writing tended to him, Rom. x. 4; Gal. iii. 24; and the way and conveyance of the legal administrations pointed at somewhat beyond them; for in the very entry it was shewed him that these were but shadows of better things in heaven, Exod. xxv. 40, with Heb. v. 5; his unveiling of his face, when he went to God, Exod. xxxiv. 34, shewed that such as were familiar with God saw some other thing than they could see through the veil; the consciences of such as were apprehensive of sin and wrath would easily discover that these could not quiet them; their frequent repetition pointed out their insufficiency, Heb. x. 11; yea, God himself declareth how far they mistook themselves or the law who looked on it as a covenant of works to get life by it, Deut. v. 27—29. Upon all these grounds it is said, " he wrote of me."

VER. 47. But if ye believe not his writings, how shall ye believe my words?

Christ closeth this challenge with an amplification taken from that which is more in their esteem to that which they accounted less of, shewing, that if they did not believe Moses' writings, who himself was so high in their esteem, and whose writings they acknowledged to be divine scripture, it was no wonder they gave Him no credit of whom they had no such account, though indeed he was infinitely above him. Whence learn—

1. Christ our Lord was content to undergo contempt and disrespect, and to be looked on as inferior to his very servants, that so he might make his people truly honourable, and might sanctify contempt to them, and particularly that his servants might not be discouraged when they are slighted, considering that none contemn them but they contemn those whom they profess to esteem more of. Therefore Christ speaks of himself here as inferior to Moses in their eyes, and acquiesceth in this, that they contemned Moses, whom they boasted of as well as him.

2. The writings of Moses, as of other penmen of scripture, are worthy to be believed, even all and every part of them; for it is a challenge, " ye believe not his writings."

3. Such as will not believe the scriptures would

not believe Christ, nor esteem of him, if he were in the world speaking to them; for "if ye believe not his writings, how shall ye believe my words?" (See Luke, xvi. 29—31.)

CHAPTER VI.

IN this chapter we have recorded, first, a miracle, of Christ's feeding a great multitude with a few loaves and fishes, to ver. 16; next, his miraculous walking on the sea, to come to his disciples in their need, to ver. 22; thirdly, Christ's sermon, or conference with those who followed him, concerning the bread of life, with the effects and consequents of the conference, to the end of the chapter.

VER. 1. *After these things Jesus went over the sea of Galilee, which is the sea of Tiberias.*

This history of the miracle of the loaves is the same with that which is recorded, Matt. xiv. 13, &c.; Mark, vi..32; Luke, ix. 10, &c.; and here are mentioned some antecedents, occasions, and circumstances of the miracle, to ver. 5; some preparations to it, to ver. 11; the form of the miracle, ver. 11; and some consequents following upon it, to ver. 16.

In this first verse we have a general connexion and transition from what had been formerly said to what now followeth, with a general designation of the time and place of this miracle. As for the time of it, it is said to be " after these things," which is not to be understood as if this followed immediately upon what is spoken of, chap. v.; for then Christ was in Jerusalem, now he is in Galilee; but John doth pass over many things that are marked by the other evangelists, and doth only pitch upon the history of these miracles, though marked by others, because they gave occasion to the following sermon, which the rest had omitted. And in particular, the other evangelists do clear that this followed upon the beheading of John the Baptist, Matt. xiv. 10—13, &c., which trysted [agreed] also with his disciples' return after he had sent them out to preach, Mark, vi. 29—32, &c.; and with Herod's hearing of his fame and desiring to see him, Luke, ix. 7—10, &c. As for the place, it is said he "went over the sea of Galilee," &c. This lake in Galilee, through which Jordan runs, gets several names in scripture from several places upon the banks of it, as here it is called "the sea of Tiberias," from a town built there by Herod the tetrarch, and named from Tiberius the Roman emperor. We need not conceive that Christ went over the lake to the opposite shore, for Tiberias and Bethsaida (to the bounds whereof he went, Luke, ix. 10) were both on one side of that lake, and the people followed him on foot, ver. 2, with Mark, vi. 33; but he passed over some creek or bay of that lake, that so he might more speedily retire himself into a desert place, as the rest call it, and might ease his wearied disciples, who had been toiled with travel, and be rid of the press of the multitude, at least for a time. From these words, as they are clear, we may learn—

1. Christ's practice and lot teacheth that his servants ought to be very busy in their stations, and may expect, and should submit unto, a tossed, unsettled life; for he is whiles [sometimes] in Judea, and whiles in Galilee, about his calling, and is here driven to new wandering.

2. Christ's and his servant's entertainment in the world is ordinarily such as most desert and barren places will be more sweet and comfortable than any other; therefore Christ leaveth the cities and retires to a desert, shunning Herod's fury. (See Heb. xi. 37, 38.)

3. As it is no right way to keep Christ among a people to wrong his servants, (for he removes when John is slain,) so it is lawful for ministers to withdraw themselves from the dangers wherewith they are threatened, providing the trial be personal, and they may do it without wronging their cause and calling; for so hath Christ taught us, who " went over the sea of Galilee," &c., to shun the rage of Herod, who, being engaged in persecution, would be at more of it.

4. As Christ's servants may have much toil, and should spend themselves willingly in his work, so he will be solicitous for them who serve him, and careful to give them needful refreshments and breathings; for such is his care of his disciples here, who return wearied unto him.

VER. 2. *And a great multitude followed him, because they saw his miracles which he did on them that were diseased.*

This verse contains a remote occasion of the miracle and a consequent of Christ's removal, which is, that many did follow him, considering the miracles he had done; and their following him till they were hungry occasioned the miracle in feeding of them.

DOCTRINES.

1. Persecution and trouble will not make Christ have a thin back, when he sees it meet to honour himself by having many followers, for here " a great multitude followed him," though Herod be seeking him, and he go but to a desert place, where they could be but ill accommodated; and this speaks sadly against the laziness of many in times of greater quiet.

2. Such as have an errand to Christ, or any estimation of him, will be at pains to follow him; for so did they here, yea, " and outwent them," Mark, vi. 33, though they were not, at least all of them, well principled.

3. It is not enough that multitudes pretend great respect to Christ, and follow him for outward considerations and advantages, unless their principles and their motives be yet more spiritual; for herein they fell short in that they followed him " because they saw his miracles," not taking up the true excellency of his person thereby, nor being affected with his doctrine or seeking their own spiritual good; but the great wheel in all this was their being affected with his works as a novelty, and the outward benefit they had thereby;

and therefore, however now they follow him on all hazards, yet afterward, when he lets them see their error, and presseth spiritual things upon them, they voluntarily forsake him, ver. 66. It is better to feel one miracle wrought upon the heart in changing of it, than to be affected with many outward miracles.

4. Christ doth perfectly know and take notice who they are that do follow him, and what their principles and motives are; for here an account of it is given and registered; and afterward he lets them know it more clearly.

5. Christ makes himself known by these miracles on the diseased, not only to fulfil the prophecies that went before him, Matt. xi. 5, with Isa. xxxv. 6, but to shew that he came by his miracles to do good, Acts, x. 38, and not to satisfy curiosity, and to teach that his company and dispensations are very alluring to invite men to come to him, for they will find many diseases and wants among his followers, and him taking notice of them all, and curing them, even miraculously.

VER. 3. *And Jesus went up into a mountain, and there he sat with his disciples.*

Followeth another antecedent of the miracle, shewing, that however the people do follow and interrupt him, yet he went up for awhile into a retired mountain with his disciples, to refresh them with his company. This mountain was not the place where the miracle was wrought; but after he had rested awhile here he came down to the plain to the multitude, as may be gathered from ver. 15. Whence learn—

1. Refreshment, after labour and travel in God's service, is so necessary and so lawful that Christ will have a care to afford it to his servants, even in greatest throng of business; therefore, albeit the people do follow and interrupt him, yet he "went up into a mountain" for this end.

2. It is the sweet refreshment of Christ's followers, when they have not only vacation for a time from their laborious toil, but when they enjoy some familiar hours of fellowship with himself, being free from the noise of distractions in the world; for thus were they refreshed, "there he sat with his disciples," where no doubt he refreshed their bodies with rest and food, as may be gathered from Mark, vi. 31, but chiefly their souls with divine conferences.

3. Christ is the wise dispenser of his servants' refreshments and breathing times, who doth let out their allowances as they may be most useful, and not prejudicial unto them; for he doth not bring them, after their toil, to a place of delights, but to a desert and " a mountain," to rest them in, and allows it but for "awhile," or " a little," as it is, Mark, vi. 31, and presently they are at work again. If Christ did not deal thus they would find rest and excess of delights waste them more than toil itself.

VER. 4. *And the passover, a feast of the Jews, was nigh.*

In this verse, the circumstance of the time of this miracle, which was but generally spoken of, ver. 1, is now more expressly declared, that it was about the time of the passover; and so if that feast, chap. v. 1, were the passover, this should be the third since his baptism, for the first is spoken of, chap. ii. 13. This circumstance is marked, not only to confirm the truth of the history, or to put us in mind that these anniversary feasts were peculiar to the Jews, or to shew how seasonably Christ did preach of eating the spiritual food of their souls about that time the passover was to be eaten; but further, it would appear that Christ went not up to this feast, for it is here marked, that a little before that time he is in the desert places of Galilee, and nothing is marked of his going up afterward to it by the rest of the evangelists; and John, vii. 1, seems to point out his continued resolution, after this sermon, to stay in Galilee; and, John, vii. 3, 4, his brethren do challenge him for lurking; and, John, vii. 21, he seems to point at that work at the pool of Bethesda (of which, chap. v.) as the work which he had last done among them, and which stuck much in their minds at Jerusalem. As for the multitude that followed him, it is not needful to inquire whether they went up after this to the feast or not; but for his part, it teacheth—

1. Corrupt churchmen are as dangerous, and as much to be avoided, as any persecutors; for as he withdrew for a time from Herod, though he went afterward to Capernaum, ver. 59, belike, because Herod was gone to the feast, as he used sometimes to do, Luke, xxiii. 7, or, because he would not alway lurk, so he kept himself without the reach of the scribes and Pharisees.

2. It is no strange thing to see Christ and his servants secluded from the public and solemn meetings of the church because of dangers and snares laid for them; and in such a case it is their affliction, not their sin, to stay away; for so much doth Christ's practice and lot teach. Though it be remarkable how prudently he carrieth it, that he will not give offence by staying in the cities at such a time, but retireth himself till the importunity of the people bring him back again.

3. Christ would have his people expecting preservation in the use of all ordinary lawful means; and for this end he who could by his omnipotency restrain the fury of men, doth sanctify that way in his own practice which his people are to walk in; for he doth stay away though he could have gone there, and have preserved himself even when he was among their hands.

VER. 5. *When Jesus then lifted up his eyes, and saw a great company come unto him, he saith unto Philip, Whence shall we buy bread, that these may eat?*

6. And this he said to prove him: for he himself knew what he would do.

7. Philip answered him, Two hundred pennyworth of bread is not sufficient for them, that every one of them may take a little.

Followeth the introduction and preparations to the miracle, wherein is recorded what passed betwixt Christ and some, or all, of his disciples, and betwixt them and the people, before the miracle was wrought. In these verses is recorded that Christ, taking notice of the multitude, doth pose Philip, how they might be provided, ver. 5; which he doth, not out of ignorance or irresolution, but to try him, ver. 6. Philip gives such an answer as bewrays his weakness in the matter, by shewing that much money (and possibly more than they could command) would not buy a mouthful, far less full refreshment, to every one of such a multitude, ver. 7. We are to consider that this was not the first thing Christ did with them; but after he had pitied the multitude, and preached unto them, and healed their sick, and after he had refused to send them away in the evening fasting, at the disciples' desire, (all which are recorded by the other evangelists,) he at last falls upon this, and other questions recorded by the rest, for the further trial and discovery of the disciples.

From verse 5, learn—1. There is no trouble, nor distraction, nor desire of ease, will hinder Christ from taking notice of them who come to him, even albeit they have many defects in their coming; therefore albeit Christ had withdrawn to refresh himself and his disciples, and it was much indiscretion in them to interrupt him, yet he takes notice of them, and pitying them, doth preach unto them, and cure their sick, as is recorded by the rest. And this may teach Christ's servants not to take it in evil part though they be kept so busy in their calling as to want sometimes that kindly rest that is allowed upon [to] them. (See 2 Cor. xi. 27, 28.)

2. As an ardent affection after Christ's company will make men ofttimes forget their own outward necessities so they may enjoy him, (as here we find the multitude follow him to a desert place, without any provision,) so Christ will not fail to take notice of all the necessities, even bodily, of those that follow him; for here he is careful of what they had neglected.

3. Christ will put his followers, who have been long in his company, and have seen much of him, to give a proof of their proficiency thereby, before he let them see new proofs of his power; for such was his scope in this question, " Whence shall we buy bread, that these may eat?" He would first try what was in the thoughts of his disciples, who heretofore had seen many of his miracles. And the question seems to be put to Philip, not so much because he had been the mouth of the disciples in desiring Christ to send the multitude away, as because now he was an old scholar, and among the first of his followers, John, i. 43, (as Andrew also was, John, i. 40,) and yet long after this he is but rude and ignorant, John, xiv. 8, 9.

From verse 6, learn—1. Christ's words (as also his dispensations) will very readily be mistaken and misconstructed unless himself explain what is his scope in them; therefore it is necessary that he clear it here.

2. Christ's scope in his words (as also in his dealing) is ofttimes only to try them with whom he hath to do; and when he hath so done he can let them find that his trying word, or dispensation, is not all, but he hath more to say and do; for " this he said to prove him," and yet after that he did the work. (See Deut. viii. 15, 16.)

3. Christ will even have the weakness of his own followers tried, partly that what is known to him, and yet lurking, may be discovered to them, and so they may not conceit of more than they have, and the evil which before lurked and was unseen, may be cured when it is discovered; and partly that He may be exalted who is all-sufficient to do what he pleaseth, when their weakness layeth them by; for these causes did he prove Philip, and belike the rest also, as appears afterward in Andrew.

4. Christ needs not consult with any nor the help of any man's wit in the greatest extremities; nor is he ignorant, or uncertain and irresolute what to do, whatever his way of carrying on his work seem to say; therefore it is added, for confirmation, " for he himself knew what he would do."

From verse 7, learn—1. When Christ puts even his most eminent followers to trial, they will prove weak, if they be left to themselves; for so appears here in one and more of them, though they had seen many proofs of him.

2. When men judge by sense or reason, and do look to likelihoods and probabilities, and not to Christ's power, they will soon be at their wits' end in extremities, and unable to answer doubtful cases; for so much doth his answer teach, " Two hundred pennyworth of bread is not sufficient for them, that every one of them may take a little." It is not needful to determine how much this sum was according to our coin, but it is sufficient to know that it was a great sum to them, and would have bought more than he made use of to feed the people with.

3. It is Christ's way ofttimes to do that for his people whereof there is no probability or likelihood, that so his glory may shine the more brightly in it; for so it appears in his working this miracle, and feeding the multitude, when there was no appearance how it should be done. And this should warn men, as not to tempt God in an ordinary calling, by neglecting ordinary means, so also not to be discouraged with improbabilities when they are in need and have to do with Christ.

Ver. 8. One of his disciples, Andrew, Simon Peter's brother, saith unto him,

9. There is a lad here, which hath five barley loaves, and two small fishes: but what are they among so many?

Followeth a further preparation to the miracle, in Andrew's giving an account of their provision, though with as little faith and expectation of what Christ was to do as Philip had shewed. It seems that after Christ had bid them try what they had, Mark, vi. 38, Andrew gave him an account that a little boy had so many loaves and fishes, (which belike were carried about for the disciples' use, Matt. xiv. 17; Mark, vi. 38; Luke, ix. 13;) but all that was nothing for feeding so many.

DOCTRINES.

1. Weakness and shortsightedness is not the temper of one only, but of all Christ's followers if they be put to it, and every disciple will be ready to discover his own weakness faster than another's in a day of trial; for Andrew acquits himself no better than Philip here, though he was one of the first disciples.

2. As Christ did not neglect to provide such outward things as were necessary for himself and his followers, so his provision is such as may teach sobriety and contentment with a mean condition unto all; for he hath only " five barley loaves and two small fishes."

3. Such as would imitate Christ ought to be tender and ready to communicate to the necessities of others were their own portion never so small; for not only Christ but his disciples are willing to bestow their small provision upon the multitude, though they judge it could serve them in no stead.

4. It is worthy of serious and frequent observation to consider how weak sense and reason will prove in God's matters, how much Christ will lay by the hope and expectation of creatures before he appear in his glorious working, and how he will work that for a needy people that is little expected by any; therefore also is Andrew's weakness marked, " What are they among so many?" as well as Philip's, that it might contribute to set out Christ's glory in this miracle.

VER. 10. And Jesus said, Make the men sit down. Now there was much grass in the place. So the men sat down, in number about five thousand.

Followeth a nearer preparation to the miracle, wherein Christ having laid by the expectation of his disciples, commands that they bid the people sit down upon the grass, (which was rank in that country and climate at that season,) whereunto the people, who were a great many, give obedience, and so Christ proceeds to feed them.

DOCTRINES.

1. Christ takes no advantage of his people's weakness and dulness to hinder him to do good when it is needed; for notwithstanding their slowness of heart to give him glory, yet he goeth to the miracle for their good and the people's.

2. It is Christ's way, ofttimes, to refute the doubts of his people by his working, and by real proofs of his power and love; for he stayeth not to debate with his disciples about their doubts, but refutes them by the following work.

3. Christ may see fit to engage his own in strange-like service, and to impose commands upon them that seem absurd to sense and reason, and yet give a good account of all in his time; for such was this command to make the men sit down upon the grass, to a bare table, and yet he fed them all.

4. It is the commendation of Christ's followers when, how weak soever their faith be, yet they subject themselves to his commands and yield obedience without any reasoning; for such was both the disciples' and the people's practice here; they being commanded by Christ do " make the men sit down," and the " men sat down," though none of them saw well what Christ was about to do.

5. Every circumstance of Christ's work which sets out his glory ought to be marked, and he will order his working so that these may be seen; therefore it is marked as setting out Christ's glory, that they were " in number about five thousand" whom he fed, which is to be understood of the men only, besides women and children, Matt. xiv. 21. And this is marked in this place because Christ commanded that they should be so set down in ranks and companies, Mark, vi. 39, 40; Luke, ix. 14; as the disciples might easily mark the number of them.

VER. 11. And Jesus took the loaves; and when he had given thanks, he distributed to the disciples, and the disciples to them that were set down; and likewise of the fishes as much as they would.

In this verse we have the miracle itself, and the manner of it, that Christ, having given thanks, did distribute to the disciples, and they to the people, and that it grew among all their hands, so that every one got as much as they would. Whence learn—

1. Christ's undertaking to do great things for his people will not prove evanishing flourishes, but real works; for he who bid [bade] them do several things in order to this work, doth now work it gloriously.

2. This thanksgiving and blessing premitted to [preceding] the miracle teacheth—1. That all our refreshments should be sanctified and gone about with prayer and praise, Deut. viii. 10, considering that they are great mercies, though ordinary; that it is his word and blessing which maketh them feed us; that this is a mean to draw down a blessing upon them, as Christ here doth on the loaves and fishes; that hereby they are sanctified to us, 1 Tim. iv. 4, 5; and that it is a mean to sweeten common mercies to us when we acknowledge them to come down from heaven as proofs of love, and do so take them out of his hand. 2. That cheerfulness and thankfulness to God is to be made conscience of by them who have sober and coarse fare as well as if they had choicest dainties; for so doth Christ's practice teach when he had but barley loaves and fishes. 3. That God alone must have the glory of all the wonderful works he doth for his people. Therefore doth Christ give thanks and bless, as Mediator, to testify that it was by the power of God that he, being one with the Father, did the work.

3. This miracle itself, and the distribution by the disciples to the people, and the increase of the loaves, teacheth—1. As by curing the sick and diseased Christ proved himself to be a physician for all their plagues and sores, so by this he proves himself to be the true spiritual food of souls, as he cleareth in the following sermon. 2. It is not abundance that is necessary for

the maintenance of the life of man, but God's blessing upon what a man enjoys, be it less or more ; for so doth this miracle teach.

3. It is Christ that sends every man his portion and allowance, through whose hands soever it comes; for though the disciples give immediately to the people, yet it is Christ, who by them doth distribute.

4. Christ allows much benefit upon his servants, and minds it in his employing them betwixt him and his people; for he employeth them to distribute unto the people, not so much that they might get wherewith to refresh themselves and satisfy their hunger, but especially that their faith might be confirmed by being so near witnesses of the glory of this miracle.

5. Obedience to a command and making use of what we have is a mean to make it increase and grow as there is need; for in distributing that small portion at Christ's command it grows.

6. Christ's servants may expect to have their endeavours blessed when they get their furniture out of his hand and employ themselves as his instruments in dispensing thereof; for the disciples' getting their provision out of Christ's hand, and so distributing it, to feed his people, it grows among their hands.

7. Christ's allowance is very large; he can make coarse fare of barley bread and fish satisfy men, with his blessing; he can make little of it suffice never so many, and let every one have no scant ; for they got all " as much as they would."

VER. 12. When they were filled, he said unto his disciples, Gather up the fragments that remain, that nothing be lost.

13. Therefore they gathered them together, and filled twelve baskets with the fragments of the five barley loaves, which remained over and above unto them that had eaten.

Followeth some effects and consequents of this miracle; and first, the people being satisfied, Christ commands the fragments to be gathered up, whereby the truth of the miracle is confirmed, not only that the people are filled, but there is more left than they laid down at first. Whence learn—

1. Christ's miracles are such as sense will bear witness unto, and he will make his people's sensible satisfaction bear witness for him how really good he is unto them ; for so is this miracle confirmed from the effect—" they were filled."

2. As the Lord's people should not be doubtful or anxious in wants, so when he giveth greatest plenty they should be frugal and thrifty, and should beware of abusing greatest abundance ; for though he had now fed them miraculously, yet saith he, " Gather up the fragments that remain, that nothing be lost."

3. Such as at Christ's command lay out what he hath given them for supplying the necessities of others may expect to be no losers, but rather gainers ; for the disciples who gave out their provision find it returned with advantage,

and instead of five loaves and two fishes, they " filled twelve baskets with the fragments," &c.

VER. 14. Then those men, when they had seen the miracle that Jesus did, said, This is of a truth that prophet that should come into the world.

A second effect and consequent of this miracle is, that hereby they are led to acknowledge him to be that great prophet whom the Jews expected, according to the prediction, Deut. xviii., which was indeed true of him, however they did not take him up, as became, in his person, offices, and benefits, beside that they went far wrong in the following purpose. Whence learn—

1. This knowledge of the scriptures and of the Messiah which continued among the Jews in these corrupt and declining times, may witness sadly against the ignorance of men in the days of the gospel when yet light is far clearer.

2. Christ's working should discover unto people somewhat concerning himself; and the use of his miracles is to discover unto us what his offices are, and to confirm us in the faith thereof; for " those men, when they had seen the miracle that Jesus did, said, This is that prophet." Though it be remarkable that this affects them more than many miracles, as contributing to feed their belly, and being generally beneficial to all, whereas healing of diseases was but only for the good of a few ; and beside, they took occasion to dream of an easy life under this Messiah.

3. Christ should be taken up and expected in the word of promise, that so his manifestations of himself may be more sweet when they come ; for this heightens their estimation of him, that he is the " prophet that should come into the world," who had been promised unto them, and whom they had so long expected. (See Isaiah, xxv. 9.)

4. Points of truth, especially concerning Christ, should not be superficially and slightly closed with, but men should be persuaded of the truth of them, that so they may boldly confess and profess them as they are called to it; for say they, " This is of a truth that prophet."

5. Among other offices of the Messiah he is also the prophet of his people, and the great teacher of the church, from whom all other teachers have their commission; who teacheth his people infallibly and effectually, and who was to exercise this office at his incarnation and coming into the world; for so much doth their designation of him, according to scripture prophecy, teach : " This is that prophet;" for that prediction of Moses, Deut. xviii. 18, did ultimately and chiefly point at him, Acts, iii. 22.

VER. 15. When Jesus therefore perceived that they would come and take him by force, to make him a king, he departed again into a mountain himself alone.

A third effect and consequent of the miracle is, that the people, out of blind and furious zeal, would have set him up to be their king, if he, foreseeing it, had not departed again into the mountain, (where he and the disciples had been, ver. 3,) and that alone, having commanded his disciples to go to sea, as the other evangelists do record. And so this is a transition to the following miracle.

DOCTRINES.

1. There is no point of divine truth received by natural men but their hearts are ready to detain the same in unrighteousness, and to leaven it with their own corrupt principles; for they who acknowledge him to be the prophet, according to the scripture, and who had warrant also to receive the Messiah as a king, do yet pervert all this with their corrupt conceptions of his kingdom.

2. Christ is ordinarily much mistaken even by those who acknowledge him, and particularly his kingdom is ofttimes conceived of amiss; for so do they here. Though they knew him to be the promised Messiah, yet they leave that, and take themselves only to his kingly office, not to submit themselves to his spiritual yoke and government, but expecting carnal liberty and a prosperous condition under their promised king; and for begetting of these conceptions there concurred—1. Their mistake and carnal conceptions of scriptures pointing at Christ's kingdom, wherein they were fostered by the corrupt glosses of their teachers, who pointed out the Messiah as a worldly monarch, coming to subdue all nations under his and their feet. 2. Their own carnal disposition, which minded no other want but that of their belly, and therefore could conceive of no other remedy and advantage by him but that they should live at ease and with much liberty under him, and he give them their meat without toil, as he had done in the late miracle. 3. They were more sensible of the yoke of oppression wreathed about their necks by the Romans, and of their slavery that way, than they were of sin and soul slavery, and therefore they could not take up Christ rightly, nor make right use of him, but dreamed only of deliverance from their outward slavery by him. All these evils would be guarded against by them who would conceive aright of Christ; and, in a word, men would beware of dreaming of great things under the sun in Christ's company, and when they engage themselves in the ways of godliness.

3. Men may have fits of zeal, pretending more to honour Christ, and be more furious and violent in the expressions thereof, than those who have spiritual and pure zeal, and yet all of it be but fleshly and sinful; for such is their blind zeal here; all they pretend to in it is to honour Christ and exalt him as a king, and they will do it violently and " by force," never minding the danger wherein they involved themselves thereby; and yet there was nothing but flesh in it. Carnal zeal, whatever it pretend, yet it sails both with wind and tide, and therefore such impetuous, furious motions are to be suspected.

4. Rash and carnal blind zeal for Christ and his kingdom is one of Satan's great engines, whereby he labours to bring real prejudice to Christ and his kingdom; for by this attempt of theirs, not only were all thoughts of his spiritual kingdom banished and swallowed up in the thoughts of a carnal monarchy, but this was the ready way to raise a scandal on him, as guilty of treason, and to draw the Romans on him and them, and all his followers, to cut them off.

5. Christ is omniscient, and knoweth what is rolling in every man's mind, and he will not be surprised nor overreached by any design of men; for " Jesus therefore perceived that they would come and take him by force," &c.

6. Christ will not approve of any honour offered to him which he hath not prescribed and enjoined, were it cloaked with never so much of apparent zeal; for he refuseth and declineth all this honour, as not required by himself.

7. Albeit Christ be a true king over his church, and do exercise a spiritual kingdom in it, and have also a spiritual government established for keeping his subjects in order, yet he came not into the world to be a worldly king, nor to administrate a kingdom which is of this world; nor is his kingdom prejudicial to the thrones and civil government of men, but the best pillar they have, if they will suffer him to rule among them. Therefore doth Christ refuse all this offer, as not competent to him; and this teacheth his followers to beware of usurping lordly dominion under pretext of administering the things of his kingdom.

8. As Christ's followers should shun popular applause and worldly pomp, (as their Master's example here doth teach,) so true zeal against these should be very fervent and real, and not for the fashion only; therefore Christ not only prevents their motion before it break forth, but withdraws himself alone, having sent his disciples away, that they may not find him; and this he did, not only to avoid all occasion of suspicion, or prudently to break their fit of zeal, (which could not have been diverted by his staying and reasoning with them,) but also to testify how really he abhorred their course, and so gave a pattern to all his followers not to put away applause so as they would have it follow them, but really to detest it.

9. Such as do not make right use of Christ and his company, but do only expect carnal things of him, are justly punished with the want of his company, as here he deals with this people.

10. That Christ, when he withdrew, went to prayer, (as is remarked, Matt. xiv. 22, 23; Mark, vi. 46;) it may teach—1. Christ hath sanctified to his people the exercise of prayer in all their needs, and he is the great Intercessor for them, under all their miseries and distresses. So much doth his practice teach; for albeit he was true God, and so needed not pray, yet as he was a man under the law, he would pay this homage and fulfil all righteousness, and by making use thereof in his need, Heb. v. 7; Matt. xxvi. 39, he hath sanctified this exercise to all his needy people. And by this practice he teacheth, that as Mediator his intercession is always ready in a strait, and he delights in that exercise, as here he had this people's folly to pray about, and his disciples' following trial to hold up to the Father. 2. Prayer is a special mean of entertaining communion with God, and a mean of converse with him, wherein they who are most holy will be

most frequent; as Christ's practice doth teach, who at all occasions did converse with his Father in the practice of this duty. 3. Private prayer doth require as much privacy and retiredness as may conveniently be had, that men's spirits may settle and be composed for that duty. So much also doth this practice of Christ teach, (in going alone to the mountain to pray,) as it is a pattern to us, though he himself was not pestered with any sinful distractions. 4. When men get much applause in the world it is their duty not only to shun it, but then to be much in converse with God, partly to guard their hearts from being blown over at unawares, and partly to make sure that all is right betwixt God and them. So much also may Christ's practice of prayer at this time, as it is a pattern to us, teach.

Ver. 16. And when even was now come, his disciples went down unto the sea,

17. And entered into a ship, and went over the sea toward Capernaum. And it was now dark, and Jesus was not come to them.

18. And the sea arose by reason of a great wind that blew.

Followeth to ver. 22, the second part of the chapter, containing a second miracle, of Christ's walking on the sea to come to the disciples in their need, with the antecedents and consequents thereof; the antecedents thereof are recorded ver. 16—18; the miracle itself, ver. 19; and the consequents of it, ver. 19—21.

In these verses we have the antecedents of this miracle, that the disciples, at his command, go to sea without him, and being at sea in the night-time, they are tossed with a violent tempest and contrary wind, as is observed, Matt. xiv. 24. It is here said they went "toward Capernaum," where the succeeding sermon was preached, ver. 59, yet, Matt. xiv. 34, "they came into the land of Gennesaret," and, Mark, vi. 45, they are commanded to go unto Bethsaida. But this is easily reconciled; for their way was toward and by Bethsaida, and Gennesaret was the name of the country where Capernaum stood, and though he landed not at the city yet he stayed not till he came to it.

DOCTRINES.

1. It is not unusual that upon the back of sweetest refreshments and manifestations of Christ the people of God meet with a stormy and sharp exercise. Such was the lot of the disciples after this miracle; for—1. A constant gale of sweetness is not easily borne while we are within time, but we must be exercised with changes. 2. It is meet that he take proof of our proficiency by former manifestations, as being given, not only for present delight, but for a future use; as here he tries how the disciples' faith was strengthened by the former miracle, and so is marked, Mark, vi. 51, 52. 3. It is by these changes that men get new proofs of their own weakness, and new proofs of his goodness, for the confirmation of their faith; all which they would want if they had not renewed exercise.

2. As men should be clear of a calling from God to anything they undertake, that this may support them in what they may meet with, (as the disciples were constrained to this journey by Christ, Matt. xiv. 22,) so they ought not to judge of the rightness of a way by what they meet with in it, seeing sharpest trials may meet men in God's own way, and in the way of their duty; for when they are going "over the sea toward Capernaum," at Christ's command, the storm ariseth.

3. The Lord's people may expect that their trials will be measured out according to their growth, and according to the time which they have had wherein to make proficiency; for whereas before this the disciples had a tempest, Matt. viii. 23, 24, &c., yet this is now a sharper trial. Then, Christ was with them, though asleep; now, he is away. Here it is dark night, which we read not of there; here they have not only a storm of wind, as there, Mark, iv. 37, but a contrary wind, Mark, vi. 48. They are also not near the shore, but in the midst of the sea, ver. 19; Matt. xiv. 24; and it is long ere Christ come to them, Matt. xiv. 25, with which they are not tried in the other storm.

4. In the trials of the Lord's people they may expect that all circumstances will concur that may sharpen the trial and make the exercise deep; and trials may be completely dreadful, wherein yet the Lord will give a good issue; for so was this trial ordered in every afflicting circumstance before marked. (See Lam. ii. 22.)

5. It is a sad addition to the trials of the Lord's people that ordinarily they are attended with much confusion, darkness, and perplexing irresolution, so that they cannot see through their troubles, nor what to do under them. So much may be gathered by analogy from this circumstance, that " it was now dark" when the storm arose, so that they could not know where they were. And frequently trouble gets the name of " darkness" as the saddest ingredient in it.

6. It is God's way so to order his dealing with his people as easy and successful-like beginnings may have a very hard procedure before the way and work be ended; for here they entered at " even," and it is still fair till dark night, and that they are far in. By this, Christ, on the one hand, doth train on and engage his people in his way, and, on the other hand, he tries them, being engaged, and warns them to be humble and sober when all things inwardly or outwardly succeed well with them.

7. It is also a great addition to trouble when Christ is absent, or hides or withdraws himself. The want of him may raise a storm in the greatest calm, and his presence can make a calm in a storm, and therefore it must be sad when both they are in trouble and miss him. So much may be gathered from this circumstance, " and Jesus was not come to them." It is true the text speaks of his bodily presence, which did not always hold off a storm, Matt. iii. 23, 24. But if the want of that was sad to them, how much more must it be sad when his spiritual presence by faith is wanting in trouble? Yet as he is not always absent when he is not seen, so it is needful sometimes to be exercised with that in

trouble, because, otherwise, trials would not be trials.

8. They who through abundance of enjoyments are but little sensible of their own mercy, or tender of the need of others, are justly put to essay the case of such in their own experience, that they may know the hearts of strangers ; for the disciples, who, through constant enjoying of Christ's company, were ofttimes little sensible of the case of poor ones, who got but now and then an opportunity to meet with him, and who even at the last miracle would have had the people sent away, Mark, vi. 35, 36, are now put to know what it was to want his company in a time of need, that they might love it the better, and pity others the more.

9. When a people are in a very desolate and low condition in their own eyes, it may be they are yet so far from issue that harder and sadder trials are yet to come ; for when they are disconsolate by reason of the dark night and Christ's absence, and that before the storm came, (as appears from the order of the narration,) Christ, instead of coming, sends a sad storm to add to their bitter condition by the trysting [appointment] of all these together : " and the sea arose," &c. (See Jer. xiv. 19.)

10. The Lord's people may expect, in troubles, that though they will not be drowned nor swallowed, yet they will have sad and fearful tossings before they see an outgate ; for "the sea arose," whence the ship was "tossed with waves," Matt. xiv. 24. And this is a fit emblem of the condition of the church, and the Lord's people in it ; for — 1. As mariners are often tempest-beaten, by reason of the unsettledness of the element wherein they travel, so this world is so uncertain and unsettled, and there are so many raging lusts of wicked men in it, that it is a wonder if the church get but one hour for breathing in it. 2. Tempests do so toss mariners that they stagger, and are put to their wits' end, Psalm cvii. 27 ; and so are the church and godly, in their afflictions, ofttimes staggering and like to fall, tossed, and put from all their resolutions, Psalm cix. 23 ; Isaiah, liv. 11 ; 2 Cor. vii. 5. 3. Tempests are dreadful in this, that present death is before men, and but very little betwixt them and it, even a poor thin vessel, and it much beaten ; and so also may afflictions pursue the Lord's people, as there will be little betwixt them and death in their own account, and they may have deliverance to seek betwixt the jaw-bones of death, Psalm ix. 13 ; yet in all this it is sweet that it is the Lord who raiseth the storm, and hath the winds in his fists.

11. It is yet a sad addition unto trouble, when the Lord's people are not only afflicted under their present lot, but there is a strong course and stream of-providence meeting them in the teeth, and crushing, and making ineffectual, all their endeavours to help themselves ; for so much may be gathered from this : that there was "a great wind that blew," which not only caused the sea to arise, but was contrary to them in their course, Matt. xiv. 24, as if heaven were opposing any course they should essay in this extremity. (See Psalm lxxx. 4.)

VER. 19. So when they had rowed about five and twenty or thirty furlongs, they see Jesus walking on the sea, and drawing nigh unto the ship : and they were afraid.

20. But he saith unto them, It is I ; be not afraid.

Followeth the miracle itself, or Christ's coming unto them in a miraculous way, for their comfort in this distress, which they mistaking, are more affrighted, ver. 19, till he by his speaking unto them do comfort and assure them, ver. 20. And these are some of the consequents of his miraculous appearance.

From ver. 19, learn—1. As it is a mercy in a strait to have any known duty wherein to employ ourselves, so no difficulty should deter nor discourage us from duty, but the faster difficulties do grow we should be the more busy, even albeit it should be to small purpose so to do ; for so is imported here, that they rowed forward, and they were toiling with it, Mark, vi. 48. Albeit they could promove little thereby, by reason of the storm and contrary wind, yet, since Christ had commanded they should make forward, they hold at the duty.

2. Whatever be the pressing need of Christ's followers in troubles, and their constant cleaving to duty for all that ; and whatever be Christ's purpose of love towards them, yet he seeth it fit ofttimes not to come to them at first, but will let the trial go on till it come to a height, and be a trial indeed, and put them seriously to it ; for before he came he lets them row " about five and twenty or thirty furlongs," (the last of which make near four miles, eight furlongs going to a mile,) and, Mark, vi. 48, he came not till the fourth watch of the night, which is the morning watch. We are indeed very sparing of ourselves in trouble, and do soon begin to think that we are low and tried enough, and therefore would be delivered ; but our wise Lord seeth that we need more.

3. Whatever be Christ's delaying to help his people in trouble, and whatever may be their fears and apprehensions, upon the extremity of their troubles, yet deliverance, in his due time, will certainly come unto them, and when their difficulties are at the height his help will be nearest, for here, after all their toil, he cometh.

4. Christ needs not our diligence to move him to help us in trouble, but his own knowledge and observation of our case will plead for pity and help when the trial is perfected ; for he cometh unto them when there is no mention of their crying to him, because (as it is, Mark, vi. 48,) " he saw them toiling in rowing." Albeit it be our duty to call on him in trouble, yet his affection and sympathy will read supplications from our necessity.

5. Christ is not only a careful observer and tender sympathizer in his people's trouble, but he is ready to come over all impediments, and to make up the distance betwixt them and him, that he may help them ; for when it was impossible for them to come to him, he is at the pains, and " walks on the sea, and draws nigh."

6. Christ is omnipotent to bring deliverance unto his people, and to remove impediments out of the way of their help; and nothing will impede him to come to them in their need, but he who is Lord of all will make a way through greatest difficulties; for he "walks on the sea, and draws nigh;" whereby he proves himself greater than Moses, who went only through a divided sea, whereas he walks on the sea itself, and proveth that a deep sea and a great storm lying betwixt him and his people will not withhold his company. We are not here to conceive any change wrought in Christ's body, as if it were denied of its natural properties that so he might thus walk; for we find Peter walking also on the sea, Matt. xiv. 29; but herein appeared the power of his godhead, carrying his manhead upon the sea, and any change that was, was wrought on the sea, which his omnipotency did turn into a pavement to walk on.

7. It is a sweet sight of our difficulties to consider that what doth most affright and trouble us, yet Christ is secure of it, and hath it under his feet; for this was the first dawning of their deliverance, that Christ treads upon that sea, and makes a walk and way of that which threatened to devour them, and so he proved himself Lord of it, though they were not yet delivered from it.

8. As Christ's followers do meet with more trials than others, so shall they be made witnesses of more proofs of his power and love than others; for beside the former miracle, whereof they and the multitude were witnesses, this new trial brings them the sight of a new miracle.

9. Christ, even when he comes to deliver his people in a remarkable way, may be mistaken, and even mercies may be matter of fear and terror to them; for when he thus cometh, "they were afraid," supposing it to be a spirit, and not dreaming of him, as is marked by the rest. This need not seem strange, if we consider—1. That natural infirmity in sinful man is apt to be affrighted with strange apparitions, as they conceived this to be. 2. It is natural to men to misconstruct of the Lord's dealing, and to misapprehend his best dispensations, and to create groundless fears unto themselves; and when it is otherwise, it is his special gift and mercy to them. 3. Crushing of spirit with many troubles will make anything take a deep and readily a wrong impression on men; as they, being now much broken with their former tossing and cross dispensations, look upon this through the same perspective. Minds broken and crushed with many troubles are but ill judges of God's dealing. 4. The conscience of guilt, when it is awaked in a storm, will readily judge of dispensations rather according to men's deservings than according to what Christ may intend in them. 5. Christ's method and way in bringing about deliverance is ofttimes so strange, and the means and ways of it so unlikely and contrary in appearance, and so like himself and his power and wisdom, that it is no wonder our shallow conceptions do not take him up at first; for such was his way here. 6. Men's want of faith in trouble, and their limiting of Christ to their way and means, not leaving him a latitude, may occasion many mistakes when he appears; for it appears they were not believing that help would come from him, far less that he would walk upon the sea, and therefore they mistake. All these, being considered, may afford us many necessary cautions, and may teach us that it is our own apprehensions and mistakes that puts an edge on many of our trials, and not his dealing, if it were rightly understood. (See Isaiah, xl. 27, 28.)

10. When Christ hath appeared to deliver his people he may see it fit to put them yet to deeper exercise and fear before they come to the comfortable issue. He may let trouble be augmented when he comes to remove it, and may let out the sharpest pang and darkest hour when delivery and daylight are nearest; for whatever was their weakness in this mistake and fear, yet Christ not only "drew nigh," but in his providence ordered that it should be so, and for this end "he would have passed by them," Mark, vi. 48, that so he might make his appearance conspicuous, and might try them, as Luke, xxiv. 28. This way of dealing contributes to humble his people yet more, to fit them for deliverance, and to make it sweet when it cometh.

From ver. 20, learn — 1. Albeit Christ may sometimes delay to appear for his people, and to manifest himself unto them in trouble, yet when the trial is come to an extremity and height he will not fail speedily to appear and speak warmly to them; for now, when they are not only afflicted, but in extremity of fear, he will not have them tortured with it, but "saith unto them, It is I."

2. Christ must not only appear, but must discover himself before we can discern him, or be free of mistakes concerning him; for though he was in their view, yet that did not avail till he said, "It is I."

3. Christ's speaking and word is the infallible and sure mean whereby he discovers himself unto his people, without which his dealing will be readily mistaken; and it is from his word that they must get the first comfortable sight of their condition, and their begun deliverance must be laid hold on there; for it was his silence made his dealing to be mistaken, and therefore he begins their deliverance and comfort by his word, which will loose many doubts: "but he saith unto them, It is I."

4. Faithless, discouraging fear is that which the Lord's people most readily are inclined to under trouble, as being but the expression of the dross of their hearts, and that which is more easily attained than humility or any other good use. Such was their condition here: "they were afraid."

5. It is acceptable service to God to oppose faithless fears in trial, and to be wrestling against them when they most violently assault us; for there is a command of Christ for so doing: "be not afraid."

6. It is the great victory of the Lord's people, and a sufficient deliverance unto them, if, when they are in greatest extremities, they be delivered from slavish fear; for such is Christ's antidote and issue allowed on his disciples, when they are in great danger and perplexity: "be not afraid."

7. The sovereign remedy against fear in troubles, and the only right sight of troubles, is to see Christ in them, whose presence and manifesting of himself takes away all cause of slavish fear, and who being seen to have the chief hand in his people's trials, it doth warrant them to expect no hurt by them; for this is the sovereign remedy of fear—"It is I; be not afraid."

8. When Christ hath propounded most ample ground of encouragement, yet our endeavours thereupon will not remove our fears, nor rectify our dispositions, till he interpose also, and apply the encouragement by his word of command; for Christ counts it not sufficient to propound that comfortable doctrine, "It is I," leaving the use thereof to be gathered by themselves, but he enforces the inference with his command: "It is I; be not afraid."

VER. 21. Then they willingly received him into the ship: and immediately the ship was at the land whither they went.

In this verse we have the warm entertainment given by the disciples unto Christ, after they knew him, and so were delivered from their late fear, together with the issue of their whole trial, in that they get to land, and that immediately. And these are the rest of the consequents of this his miraculous coming unto them. Whence learn—

1. As Christ's company should always be sweet and welcome to his own, so trials ought to make their estimation thereof to grow, and a known Christ will be found sweet company in trouble; for "then they willingly received him into the ship."

2. Love to Christ, even among disciples, may grow so cold and remiss, that there will be need of trials and separation for a time, to quicken it again; for this was one chief cause of all this distance and trial, that they who were (so to say) cloyed with his company, and therefore thought but little of their condition who came to him upon occasion, might, after this separation and storm, make him more welcome, and willingly receive him. Thus doth the Lord cure drowsiness and security, by withdrawing, and making even desertions bring about much good. (See Cant. v. 1—5, &c.)

3. Whatever be the tossings and perils wherewith Christ's followers may be exercised, yet they will not perish, but will certainly come safe to land, one way or other, either sooner or later, here or hereafter; for so much may be gathered from this instance, that the tossed ship and disciples came to land.

4. Christ's presence being manifested to his afflicted people will produce sweet changes and heaps of mercies and wonders to them and for them; for beside his coming to them in a miraculous way, now there are two wonders more—one, that the storm is calmed, as it is, Matt. xiv. 32; and another, that they were "immediately at land."

5. Whatever be the tossings of the Lord's people, yet none of his purposes towards them shall be made void, and their following of commanded duty shall have a good and desired issue; for it is not their mercy only that they get to land anywhere, (which yet is a mercy to tempest-beaten men, who may be driven far from their course,) nor doth the contrary wind drive them back to the land from whence they came, but "the ship was at the land whither they went," and so their voyage held good.

6. Christ will let his people lose none of their toil, wherein they spend themselves (as would appear) to little purpose, but he will make it all up with his presence; and, when he cometh, he will further them as much as trouble hath hindered them; for they who were toiled in rowing against a contrary wind, are, upon his coming, "immediately at the land," &c.

VER. 22. The day following, when the people which stood on the other side of the sea saw that there was none other boat there, save that one whereinto his disciples were entered, and that Jesus went not with his disciples into the boat, but that his disciples were gone away alone;

23. (Howbeit there came other boats from Tiberias nigh unto the place where they did eat bread, after that the Lord had given thanks:)

24. When the people therefore saw that Jesus was not there, neither his disciples, they also took shipping, and came to Capernaum, seeking for Jesus.

25. And when they had found him on the other side of the sea, they said unto him, Rabbi, when camest thou hither?

Followeth unto the end of the chapter Christ's excellent sermon, or conference with his followers, some occasions whereof are recorded, ver. 22—25, and the sermon itself, with the effects and consequents that followed thereupon, in the rest of the chapter.

In these verses we have the occasions of this sermon (which also are a further effect of the miracle of the loaves,) the first whereof is more remote, that the multitude, who had been miraculously fed, knowing that Christ had not gone with his disciples, and that there was no other boat there, did the next day expect that possibly they would find him there still, on the mountain to which he went; but finding him gone, as well as the disciples, they (being provided of other boats, as is marked, ver. 23) do follow and seek him. The other occasion of the conference (ver. 25) is more near, that having found him, they enter into familiar discourse with him, and inquire concerning his getting to that place. It is not needful to determine whether they suspected anything of his miraculous passage, though it be not improbable that they were taught, as well as the disciples, thereby; and one work of Christ in feeding men miraculously may discover more of him, and that he can pass over a sea without a boat; and they who were on land, free of a storm, may have a better sight of

Christ's power than disciples in their perplexity, whose judgments and discerning were confounded with tentation and trouble; yea, their narrow marking of circumstances—that there was no other boat there, may import they suspected it, by their following him when they found him not there; and, indeed, narrow consideration will discover more of him than slight observers do ordinarily remark. But that which is certainly clear is, that they, not finding him there, do seek him where his disciples were, and Providence furnisheth them with boats for their passage.

From verses 22, 23, 24, learn—1. The hot moods and fits of temporaries will not always cool at the first, but they may continue very earnest for awhile; for so did it prove in this people, who, it seems, stayed all night in the desert place watching for him, and are eagerly seeking him "the day following." They are said to stand "on the other side of the sea," (though the desert near to Bethsaida was on the same side with Capernaum, where Christ now was,) because the nearest way to it was by sea, and the disciples had gone that way.

2. Such as follow Christ but for a wrong end, he will soon be weary of their company, and they will lose it; for so did it fare with these: "Jesus was not there," but had slipped from among them ere they were aware.

3. When Christ is away it is the duty of such as respect him to resolve to follow him on any terms; and even temporaries will not be put away with every repulse, but may seem for a time to follow the faster; for such is their practice here, they will go after and seek him, though they should leave their families and interests.

4. It is great folly and blindness in men to doat upon places wherein Christ hath gloriously manifested himself, when he is removed thence in the ordinary signs of his presence; for so much doth their practice teach; they would not stay in that place (though famous for a miracle and Christ's presence) when he is away, but do follow him.

5. When Christ is withdrawn, men will be at a loss where to find him, and to know whither he is gone, if they consult with reason; for so much do they find: he is not there, and yet they cannot (when they have considered all circumstances) discern how or whither he is gone. (See Cant. v. 6.)

6. Albeit Christ be not always visibly seen in the company of his disciples, yet it is safest seeking him where they are, for so do they with good success. They saw him not go with his disciples, yet they "came to Capernaum, seeking for Jesus," not only because that was the place of his education, but because the disciples went thitherward, as it is like they knew when they went away. (See Cant. i. 7, 8.)

7. Such as have their heart and eye on Christ, resolving to follow him, his providence will serve them with means that they may follow him; for they who resolve to follow, and had no boats, are within a while provided, as verse 23. And if he do so to hollow-hearted men, how much more to others?

8. In mentioning the place of the miracle John takes notice that they did eat bread, "after that the Lord had given thanks," to shew—

1. That spiritual minds are much taken up with observation of spiritual things, even when greatest outward wonders are a working; for he passeth the miracle in a word, but speaks more fully of that refreshing and edifying thanksgiving. 2. Christ's way of speaking to his Father, in prayer and praise, was very ravishing, and did take deep impression upon spiritual observers who were witnesses of it; therefore is it now so warmly remembered by John. 3. It is one great lesson in Christ's school to learn that the blessing of all enjoyments are in God's hand, and to fall in love with prayer and praise as the mean of drawing out that blessing as it is needed; therefore, also, John remembers the thanksgiving, or blessing, especially as the mean of drawing down the blessing on these few loaves. 4. Such as are due observers of Christ's wonderful works will have high and reverend thoughts of him; therefore John doth on this occasion name him "the Lord."

9. Such as are but temporaries and hollow-hearted may get through, without difficulties, where Christ's peculiar followers will meet with storms, he having more proofs of love to let out on them and to them; for they get through the sea easily where the disciples were tempest-beaten.

From ver. 25, learn—1. Christ may condescend to be found even of hollow-hearted men who follow him, that so he may witness that their perdition is of themselves, and that he is willing to reclaim them, and that he may give a public testimony how willing he is to receive sincere seekers when he is so condescending to such as these; for they "found him on the other side of the sea"—to wit, at Capernaum, as appeareth, ver. 24 with 59; for albeit Christ landed in the country beside, where he wrought some cures, (as is recorded in the parallel places, Matt. xiv. 34, &c.; Mark, vi. 53, &c.,) yet he was entered the city before these men met with him.

2. Temporaries may have as much show and outside as those who are sincere; so that none are to be tried thereby, but men must distinguish betwixt true piety and familiarity with Christ and a show or estimation of it; for they make a great noise and fair show when they come to Christ.

3. Temporaries may give Christ very fair language and titles, if that will suffice him, and will not fail so to do so long as he doth not cross their idols and designs; for their compellation is, "Rabbi."

4. Temporaries also may pretend to very great familiarity with Christ, and may think themselves very great in his court, and homely with him. So much doth this familiar question about his coming there import. They judged that the great work he had done for them had made them of worth before him, and great men in his account.

5. Whatever be the flourish and pretences of hollow hearts, or their pains in following Christ, yet this doth witness their unsoundness, that they make no right use of him when they have the opportunity, but do curiously and idly pass away their time; for all they have to say is, "Rabbi, when camest thou hither?" which seemeth to re-

late not only to the time, but to the manner also of his coming; and albeit it give some hint that they suspected he came in a miraculous way, yet they were but curious and idle in propounding the questions, as the sequel more fully cleareth.

VER. 26. Jesus answered them and said, Verily, verily, I say unto you, Ye seek me, not because ye saw the miracles, but because ye did eat of the loaves, and were filled.

Followeth the sermon itself, preached in the synagogue of Capernaum, ver. 59, wherein Christ points out the true bread of life unto them, and the excellency and way of partaking thereof, with several other passages, upon which several effects and consequents do follow. This doctrine is held out by way of conference, because he is oft interrupted by their questions to him, or their grudgings and debates among themselves, upon which more of the doctrine is brought forth.

I shall take up the parts thereof in this order: 1. Christ discovers and reproves their corrupt ends in the pains they took, ver. 26, and directs them to labour and take pains for better and more spiritual food, ver. 27. 2. They seek direction how to labour, and he points out faith in himself as the way for attaining this spiritual food, ver. 28, 29. 3. They require a sign before they will believe in him as a new teacher, seeing Moses (whose scholars they profess to be) had given them manna in a miraculous way, ver. 30, 31; and Christ, upon occasion of this, sets out the excellency of the bread offered by him above manna, ver. 32, 33. 4. They professing a great desire after this bread so commended, ver. 34, he describes it more plainly to them, ver. 35, discovers their hypocrisy in their desires, ver. 36, and sheweth that his elect would not deal so with him, and should, accordingly, be well entertained and cared for, ver. 37—40. 5. They carp at his doctrine, and that He should so commend himself whose base original they supposed they knew, ver. 41, 42; and he cleareth whence their not believing in him did flow, ver. 43—46, and commends himself to be the object of saving faith, and the bread of life, ver. 47, 48, far more excellent than manna, ver. 49—51, shewing, also, in what respect he is this bread, even in his flesh, or by reason of his incarnation and suffering, ver. 51. 6. They understanding the last part of his doctrine carnally, ver. 52, he doth more seriously inculcate the necessity and advantage of eating his flesh, or closing with him as God incarnate and crucified, commending yet again this food above manna, ver. 53—58; unto which is subjoined a designation of the place where he preached these things unto them, ver. 59. 7. Some events and consequents are recorded which followed on this doctrine and conference—namely, that many of his disciples do yet carp at this doctrine, ver. 60, and he reprehends their stumbling, ver. 61, clears and vindicates his doctrine, ver. 62, 63, and points out the true cause of their mistakes, ver. 64, 65, and that many of them made apostasy and defection from him, ver. 66, upon occasion whereof he confirms his twelve apostles, ver. 67—69, and warns them of the unsoundness of one among themselves, ver. 70, 71.

In the first place, Christ, in this verse, discovers them unto themselves, shewing, that notwithstanding all their pains and insinuations with him, yet they were not straight in their ends, nor were they so much as affected with his glory shining in that miracle they had seen; but it was only the filling of their own bellies that made them so earnest. Whence learn—

1. Christ is neither taken nor will be deceived with fairest shows of pains and much respect to him, but will see and discover unsoundness when yet there is much outward appearance to the contrary; therefore, notwithstanding their pains in following him, and their insinuations ver. 24, he knoweth, and, without being affected with what they did, declareth what they were; and his verdict is to be submitted unto.

2. Christ is so tender, even of hypocrites, that he will not abruptly put them away, but will deal with them; and as their case must be told them before they can know it, so he will discover them unto themselves, and take pains upon them, so long as they will stay with him and hear; therefore he doth not abandon them, though carnal, but "answered them," and in great compassion discovers their case, that they may not deceive themselves.

3. Albeit it be a most needful thing that men of double hearts be discovered to themselves, that so way may be made for a cure, yet it is a very hard task to convince hypocrites and make them sensible of their condition, considering that men are naturally blind, that their outward pains may make them appear somewhat in their own eyes, and that most of such go on till they be judicially blinded and given up to conceit; therefore is this doctrine begun with a double asseveration, "Verily, verily, I say unto you," as pointing out the necessity of this doctrine, and withal, how difficult it is for such doctrine to have place.

4. Albeit painfulness be commendable, yet the true difference betwixt time-servers and sincere professors is not always to be taken from their outward diligence; but they may be exceeding diligent who yet are not welcome to Christ, but have a false heart lurking under it; and there may be so much unsoundness under seeming forwardness as casts it all down; for here it is granted to them: "Ye seek me," and that with as much forwardness, once and again, as could be, and yet they are but naught. (See Ps. lxxviii. 34—37; Isa. lviii. 1, 2.)

5. Albeit Christ be displeased with the faults of hypocrites seeking of him, yet he is so tender that he will approve even of their pains and endeavours, in so far as they are materially good in themselves, though they go about them sinfully; therefore he acknowledgeth, "Ye seek me;" and doth not condemn, but yields to that as good in itself if they had done it rightly.

6. Christ, in trying of men, looks not only to their diligence, that for matter it be agreeable to his will, but chiefly to the ends and principles of men, and their manner of doing that which is right; for he trieth them thus here, by pointing out wherefore, and for what cause, they seek him.

7. As it is a rare thing to see men who are naturally filled with self-love free of by-ends in seeking Christ, so to seek him because of outward advantages, which sometimes accompany him and his way, is the basest and lowest of by-ends, and a practice which he exceedingly abhors; for this is their bias here: " Ye seek me, not because ye saw the miracles, (of which ver. 2 and 14,) but because ye did eat of the loaves, and were filled."   To follow him only because of miracles, neglecting his doctrine, were bad enough, but this is yet worse, when only their own belly drew them, and they did not take up his scope in this miracle, which was, to hold forth that he was the true food of souls.

8. Men's hearts are so deceitful that when they seem to be most taken up with Christ's glory in his working, yet they may in reality be only affected with attaining or expecting their own ends; for though they seemed to be much taken up with the miracle, ver. 14, 15, yet Christ declares that they sought him, not because they saw the miracles, but because they did eat of the loaves.   Albeit Christ condescended to confer bodily benefits upon them by his miracles, yet it was their fault not to see the glory of his godhead shining in them, nor to look on them as signs confirming his doctrine, that they might believe it, but that in the height of their applause they should only mind their own belly.

Ver. 27. Labour not for the meat which perisheth, but for that meat which endureth unto everlasting life, which the Son of man shall give unto you: for him hath God the Father sealed.

In the next place, Christ, having thus reproved them, doth also direct them how to amend their fault, by employing their pains and care chiefly about the spiritual good of their souls, and not about these perishing things.   And this he presseth upon them, partly from the consideration of the one and the other food, and partly from his promise to give that spiritual food unto them if they seek it sincerely; which he confirmeth further from his being authorized, furnished, and manifested to be the Messiah, the Saviour and helper of lost sinners. Whence learn—

1. Christ doth not reprove the faults of men out of malicious spleen, but he is so ready to cherish desires of seeking himself, that even when men are unsound in seeking him he reproves them, not to put them away, but to cure them, and make them sound; therefore doth he subjoin this direction and warm encouragement to the former reproof.

2. As unsoundness in seeking Christ is a disease that must be cured, otherwise it will draw on perdition, so even that is a disease which Christ is ready to cure, and hath medicine for. So much appeareth in this pains taken on these seekers.

3. Men will never employ themselves rightly in seeking Christ till first their hearts be weaned from earthly things, and fall most in love with what concerns their souls' eternal welfare, and till the things of the world cease to be their principal labour and end, and they cease to follow Christ and religion for worldly ends and advantages; for so much is imported in this direction: " Labour not for the meat which perisheth, but for that meat," &c.; which prohibition is not to be understood absolutely, as if it were simply unlawful to labour or take pains about the things of the world, (for that is contrary to scripture rules, Gen. iii. 19; 2 Thess. iii. 10; 1 Tim. v. 8; and if the world were kept in its own room it would prove no enemy to grace,) but it is to be taken comparatively, (as in the like phrase, Matt. ix. 13,) that they should not only, or chiefly, be taken up with the world, neglecting what is better, as all mankind is since Adam fell from God to the creature, and that they should not make the world their aim in seeking him, as they did.

4. Albeit men can merit no more by their works than the beggar's craving merits the alms, yet men are not to expect that they will come to the enjoyment of spiritual things with idleness or wishes only, but they must be at pains for them, and such pains as flesh and blood will find it hard labour; for saith he, " Labour not— but for that meat," &c., where he diverts their affections and eagerness from off these earthly things, and sets them upon the right object.

5. It may help to wean our hearts from the world when we consider that however natural hearts feed upon the things of the world, and their souls imagine satisfaction in them, yet if they had the world at their will, they will get no more of it but their bit of meat, which the poorest may attain unto; therefore doth he comprehend all earthly things under the name of " meat," not only because it was their meat they were now most taken up with, but to point out what was the most they might expect of the things of time, let them have what dreams they please, and to suggest an argument why they should not toil so much for that which could afford them so little. (See Eccles. v. 11.)

6. It may also cool our affections to the world when we consider that however men want not enough of toil when they embrace the world for a portion, (for they labour for this meat,) yet all they labour for is but of a perishing nature, and perisheth in the using, Matt. xv. 17.   It serves but to uphold a perishing life, and cannot prevent its perishing at last, 1 Cor. vi. 13.   And where souls get no better, and men do only and mainly labour for it, it will cause them to perish eternally; for this is another ground of dissuasion; it is " the meat which perisheth."

7. Christ doth here commend himself and his spiritual graces to be laboured for under the name of " meat." 1. Because now they were earnestly seeking for meat, therefore he points out himself as excellent and better meat: thus to the woman of Samaria, coming for water, he points out himself as " living water," chap. iv. 10.   And so it teacheth that whatsoever men seek in the creature they will find it more eminently and excellently in Christ, if they will come to him. 2. To shew the necessity sinners have of Christ, and his usefulness to them; for as meat is the mean of preserving life, so not only unrenewed sinners continue dead without

him, but the souls of those who have any life will be in peril of starving without him; and if they feed upon him their souls shall live and be refreshed by him. 3. To shew His love who, as meat is prepared for eating by fire, so he was content to be roasted in the fire of God's displeasure that he might be fit food for starving and pining souls. 4. To shew the near conjunction that must be betwixt Christ and them who reap spiritual benefit by him; for as food must be eaten, and digested, and turned into our substance, before it can nourish, so must we apply Christ, and have him dwelling in us, before we draw forth of his refreshing virtue.

8. It doth commend Christ, and may quicken our appetite and desire after him, that he is food which neither perisheth in using nor diminisheth, how many soever partake of it, and maketh them who partake thereof to endure and be happy for ever, and therefore ought to be esteemed of above other food as much as our souls are better than our bodies, and our eternal welfare to be preferred to our temporal life; for it is another argument pressing this labour, he is " that meat which endureth unto everlasting life," both in himself and in his effects in believers.

9. Albeit ofttimes such as labour most for earthly things may starve and want for all their pains, yet it may encourage men to seek Christ that none shall do it in vain, but however he may see it fit to sharpen their appetite with delay, yet he will at last satisfy them; therefore doth he quicken them yet more with a promise that what they labour for shall be given.

10. Christ is so liberal and faithful in rewarding them who seek him, that even carnal hypocrites will not be refused if they quit their unsoundness, and put him in the room of the idol they are seeking; for on these terms the promise is made, even to those whom he had reproved— " unto you."

11. Whatever pains men are bound to take, or do take, in seeking Christ, yet all the reward they receive is of free gift, and sincere seekers will see it to be so; for he " shall give it unto you," saith he.

12. As Christ is the true food of souls, so is he the giver thereof, and all of it must come through his hand; for " the Son of man shall give" it, not only by giving himself to death, that he might purchase life, and become fit food, but by the actual application of himself and his purchased benefits to every hungry sinner.

13. Christ's affinity to us, and his being our kinsman and of the same nature with us, is a pledge to them that seek him that he will tenderly and faithfully supply their necessities; therefore doth he take the name of the " Son of man" in this promise, to shew that he whose delight was among the sons of men, Prov. viii. 31, and delighted to design himself often by this name, and he who took on our nature, and stooped to subject himself to our sinless infirmities, will be tender of them who come to him and need him.

14. Christ is to be acknowledged to be he whom the Father hath authorized and furnished to be the Saviour and Redeemer of lost sinners, and the storehouse from whence they are to expect their spiritual good; and the Father hath made it undeniably manifest that he is the true Messiah who was to be expected; for so is imported in this — " him hath God the Father sealed;" whereby we are to understand, partly, that as kings give sealed warrants and commissions to their ministers of state, who are sent out or employed in great affairs, 1 Kings, xxi. 8; Esther, iii. 12; viii. 8; so Christ is the Father's great ambassador, authorized and sent out by him to this work; partly, that as a seal represents on wax that which is engraven on it, so the Father hath communicated to him his divine essence and properties, and stamped and filled him with all divine perfections for carrying on that work, having the fulness of the godhead dwelling in him; all knowledge, to reveal his Father's will and direct his people; affection, to come down from heaven for sinners' good, and to love them who abhorred him; the spirit without measure to refresh, power to sustain them, &c.; and partly, that as a seal annexed to a commission is a public evidence of the person's authority, so Christ's endowments are visible marks whereby to know him; and the miracles wrought by him, and that voice from heaven, Matt. iii. 17; xvii. 5; with the accomplishment of all the prophecies in him, were clear evidences that he was the true Messiah, and of the Father's installing him in that office.

15. Christ's being thus sealed by the Father is a sure pledge that seekers of him will obtain spiritual food from him; therefore it is subjoined, as a reason of his giving this meat, " for him hath the Father sealed;" for we may assuredly gather that the Father would not seal a commission but to one who could be answerable. His fulness, being God, and sealed by God, doth assure us of great abundance and liberality in him; and he who is the Son will be faithful in his trust, since Moses, the servant, was so, Heb. iii. 2—6.

VER. 28. Then said they unto him, What shall we do, that we might work the works of God?

29. Jesus answered and said unto them, This is the work of God, that ye believe on him whom he hath sent.

This exhortation of Christ draws out a new question from the hearers, in answer to which Christ points out the right way of attaining this spiritual food which he hath held out unto them. We are not necessarily to conceive that they propound this question in a taunting manner, as if they would declare to Christ that Moses had commanded them to do works which are acceptable to God, and they did them, and therefore would know what new law he would prescribe unto them, (though this be not unsuitable to their disposition, which they bring forth, ver. 30, 31, and afterward; and it is very true that none are worse to deal with than they who are sitten down upon outward performances, everything they do putting them so far out of Christ's reverence in their own account;) but we are rather to conceive, that not being as yet hopeless but Christ will satisfy their carnal desires, therefore they keep fair with him; and hearing him speak of "labour," which he understood chiefly of faith, and of other works as fruits of faith, they understand it only of works according to the doctrine of their teachers, and therefore desire to be directed what to work which might be acceptable to God. Christ answers their question, and leads them to that one work of believing on Him who is sent of the Father. Whence learn—

1. Men may endure many rubs from Christ, and seem to come a great length in terms of agreement with him, who yet are unsound, and will never close with him; for here these carnal hearers do quietly digest that reproof, ver. 26, and seem to be so taken with his offer as they want only information what to set about.

2. Such as resolve to seek Christ and things spiritual will need much of Christ's own direction how to labour and employ themselves for attaining thereof; for so much doth their question import.

3. Men by nature cannot take up the right way of justification and salvation, as being a mystery; and particularly men by nature do retain such a deep impression of the first covenant of works, and are so ignorant of the perfection of the law and of their own impotency, that they know no way of acceptance before God but the way of works, and doubt no more of themselves; but if Christ tell them their duty they will do it; for such is their principle and bold undertaking here: " What shall we do that we might work ?" —that is, tell us, and we shall do it. (See Deut. v. 27; Mic. vi. 6, 7; Rom. ix. 31, 32; x. 3.)

4. Men, in following the way of happiness, must not make it their only aim to please themselves in what they do, but must submit to follow that which pleaseth God, and which he shall enjoin; for so much do they insinuate while they are desiring to " work the works of God;" whereby we are not to understand the good works, which are not only commanded, but wrought by God in his people; for they dream of no need of his working anything in them; but it is a Hebrew phrase, which signifieth works commanded, and acceptable, and pleasing to God.

5. Whatever be men's conceit of their own works, yet it is only by faith that sinners come to reconciliation with God, and to enjoy Christ to be souls' food unto them; for, in opposition to all their works, he leads them to this one " work," that they believe. And his calling it a " work" doth not import that faith as a work doth justify,—for it is only the hand to receive Christ who is our Righteousness,—but he gives it this name, speaking in their own terms who doated on works; and so the doctrine of faith is called a " law," Rom. iii. 27, because the Jews boasted so much of the law. And though other duties be required also of his people, yet he names this only, because it only embraceth Christ for righteousness and life; it is the only remedy for a soul lying under the conscience of guilt or any difficulties; and it is through faith that we can do any good works, and that they are accepted, and the imperfections thereof covered.

6. No faith will serve men's turn for justification and life but that which closeth with and embraceth Christ the Mediator, as sent of the Father, by his incarnation and manifestation in the flesh, and by his authorizing of him to exercise that office ; for so is here required, " that ye believe on him whom he hath sent;" whereby he warns men not to rest on general assents to every divine truth as a faith sufficient for salvation, unless they close with Christ; and teacheth, that it is no saving faith to acknowledge and believe in God where Christ is not acknowledged; that it is not enough to profess faith in a Messiah (as the Jews did) unless Christ be taken up and acknowledged to be that Messiah already manifested, (so 1 John, iv. 2, 3;) and that faith must first close with Christ the Mediator, by whom it finds access to God, and comfortable resting on him. (See 1 Peter, i. 21.)

7. Such as do upon right terms close with Christ as sent of the Father, and do not only in the general assent that he is the true Messiah come in the flesh, but do heartily close with him as such, and give him the glory of his person and offices, and do employ him accordingly, are about a work acceptable and well pleasing to God ; therefore it is called " the work of God," not so much because he works it in his people, (though that be true, Eph. ii. 8; and it is not by our works, but his work about us and in us, that we are saved,) as in their own terms, ver. 28, that it is acceptable to him, being commanded by himself, 1 John, iii. 23 ; and therefore lost sinners need not be afraid to make use of it.

Ver. 30. They said therefore unto him, What sign shewest thou then, that we may see, and believe thee ? what dost thou work ?

31. Our fathers did eat manna in the desert ; as it is written, He gave them bread from heaven to eat.

This answer produceth a new question from them, wherein they bewray more of their carnal minding of their own belly ; for whereas Christ hath taken them off their error of leaning to the works of the law and Moses, and hath directed them to faith in himself for attaining life and salvation, they (finding that he was not like to satisfy their carnal expectations) do object that they cannot take his word to renounce Moses and the works of the law given by him, in the point of justification and acceptance with God, and to believe in him as a new doctor, till he shew greater signs for confirmation of that doctrine than hitherto he had done, seeing Moses had done the like, or greater works, than yet he had shewed them. He had indeed fed many of them miraculously, but it was only with coarse barley loaves and for one time ; but Moses had fed all their fathers, and that for the space of forty years, and with excellent manna from heaven, for which they cite scripture ; and thus they resolve that either he shall satisfy their desires, in feeding them and filling their bellies, or they shall have some plausible pretext for forsaking him, as not being such an one as Moses was in their father's days.

From verse 30, learn—1. Albeit it behoved

Christ to confirm his doctrine, at the first promulgation thereof, by miracles and signs, yet men did sin many ways in seeking of them, as these do here; and namely, 1. When men only tempt him in seeking them, not purposing to believe, how gloriously soever he work, as the Pharisees did, Matt. xvi. 1, and here they are rather seeking a quarrel than edification. 2. When men do not first believe the word, and then seek these as helps to confirm their faith, but require signs to induce them to believe, and would have sense satisfied before they will act faith; for they will have a " sign," that they " may see, and believe." 3. When men ungratefully forget and slight Christ's former working, unless he work more as they desire; for they undervalue all he hath done unless he do more. 4. When men limit Christ, and are not content with any works but what they prescribe and carve out to him to do; for though they saw many miracles, ver. 2, yet their instancing in what Moses had done, in the next verse, sheweth that they would be pleased with nothing but with filling their bellies in a miraculous way, without their pains. Now albeit signs are not now to be expected, Christ's doctrine being already sufficiently confirmed, yet this is a clear emblem of the carriage of misbelievers, who do not magnify the word, nor are willing to close with Christ, but take pleasure in quarrelling his dealing, and do prescribe to him and limit him in his dealings, and seek to have their sense first satisfied, otherwise they will not believe.

2. Faith in Christ is not only a way whereof we are ignorant by nature, but a course we are very averse from when we know it, and a course that naturally we incline not to follow unless we see signs and wonders; for when he hath directed them in this way of believing, ver. 29, they shew their disaffection to it, and that nothing but signs will persuade them to it: " What sign shewest thou then, that we may see, and believe thee?" &c.

3. Let unsound men flatter Christ never so much for a time, yet their unsoundness will end in cavillations and quarrellings at last; for albeit they were much affected with Christ's work, ver. 14, and seem even now to give up themselves to be his scholars, yet now, the meat being out of their belly, and finding that they are not like to come speed in what they accounted their main errand, they fall a quarrelling.

4. Such as cannot endure the sharp edge of the word, nor are profited by it, will soon undervalue Christ's working, and forget any impression it made upon them; for they who cannot endure this his doctrine do now make light account of the miracle they lately so much esteemed of.

5. Such as are taken up with earthly things and their own belly will not only lightly esteem of Christ's works if they contribute not to their ends, but things spiritual and eternal will have little bulk in their eyes in comparison of these; for notwithstanding all they had seen, and that Christ even now had promised to do a greater work, in giving them the bread of life, yet say they, " What dost thou work?" as thinking little of all that, since they get not their bellies filled.

From verse 31, learn—1. God hath extraordinary and miraculous ways of supplying the wants of his own, when ordinary means fail; and the distress of his people tends but to render his providence and care about them the more remarkable; for so much is pointed out in the history of the manna, and in that testimony (which they summarily cite from Psalm lxxviii. 23—25) wherein it is recorded.

2. However hypocrites may mask themselves, and carry themselves plausibly for a time, yet they will not always lurk, but at last will bewray themselves and their carnal dispositions and desires; for while they insist only on this miracle in Moses' time, neglecting other great works done by his ministry, they declare that that challenge, ver. 26, was true, and that it was only meat and the loaves they were seeking, however they even now pretended to more.

3. As men may have much knowledge of the scripture who are never a whit the nearer to close with Christ, so they who make not a right use of knowledge are justly given up to abuse it to their own destruction; for here they have such knowledge, not only of the history, but of other scriptures speaking of the manna, as is a clear proof of their parents' instructing them according to the law, Deut. vi. 6, 7, and may shame the ignorance of men in times of greatest light; and yet they will not discern nor embrace the spiritual things of Christ; yea, they employ their knowledge as a weapon to fight against him.

4. Christ, in the offer of his gospel, hath not only to do with men who are so gross and absurd that on no terms they will close with him, but with the strong holds and reasonings of witty men, who will dare to rub affronts on him, and pretend much reason, yea, and scripture, for not embracing him; for such are these here; they will not refuse to believe on him, but upon some show of reason and scripture, and if they leave him, they will so carry it as if he should bear the blame, and not they, as being (in their account) inferior to Moses.

5. It is a great sin of men, and a great injury done to any of the faithful servants of God, when they are cried up, to obscure [darken] and bear down Christ and his truth: and this is all the end for which wicked men do, at any time, commend any of them; for such was their scope here, in commending Moses and what was done in his time, though unjustly, seeing it was not needful to feed them miraculously now when they were in a fruitful land, and not in a barren wilderness. (So also John, iv. 12.)

6. It is one fruit of the perverse and lustful dispositions of men that they are never satisfied with things that are present, and will be ready to cry up a formerly despised mercy that they may undervalue a present offer; for this manna was much loathed by their fathers when they had it, though now their children esteem of it when it is gone, that so they may undervalue Christ's present offer.

VER. 32. Then Jesus said unto him, Verily, verily, I say unto you, Moses gave you not that bread from heaven; but my Father giveth you the true bread from heaven.

Christ, in answering to this question, doth not meddle with their asking of a sign, but, as before he cleared the way of attaining this spiritual food, so here he takes occasion to set forth the excellency thereof by comparing it with, and preferring it unto, the manna whereof they boasted so much. The comparison is propounded in this verse, which may be diversely understood,—as, 1. That it was not Moses (of whom they gloried in opposition to him) who gave them even that manna; for it was the Father that gave it, upon Moses' petition, who also doth now offer this true bread, and that of free grace, without any previous desire of theirs. This is a truth in itself, and sheweth how Christ will debase them whom men do unjustly cry up to the prejudice of truth; but it doth not reach Christ's full scope here. 2. That the manna was not given from heaven—that is, from the celestial heaven, but only from the air and clouds, which frequently in the Old Testament is called heaven; but Christ, this spiritual food, is given from the heaven of glory; yet neither doth this exhaust the scope. Therefore, 3. I take the comparison to be instituted betwixt the nature and effects of manna, which was given by the ministry of Moses, and this food given by the Father; that, however manna was a sacrament and type of Christ, and in that respect was called "spiritual meat," 1 Cor. x. 3, yet it was not bread from heaven, or true spiritual food, in effect and of itself, but only bodily food; but this is "true bread from heaven"—that is, real spiritual food, and the substance and truth of all these types pointing it out.

DOCTRINES.

1. It is not to any purpose to follow a contentious and quarrelling people in their endless debates with Christ and about his doctrine, but the best way of dealing with them is constantly to hold out unto them their need of Christ, and that singular excellency that is in him; therefore Christ stands not to debate with them about signs, but goeth on to point the excellency of this food, and how needful it was for them if they looked for life.

2. Unbelief is a disease ill to be cured, and it is no easy matter to draw men from doating on the external privileges they have enjoyed, that they may learn to prize and esteem of what is spiritual and more excellent; therefore Christ, in pressing this doctrine, must use double asseverations—"Verily, verily," because they would account but little of his bare word in this matter.

3. There is no outward privilege enjoyed of old, and which the church wants under the gospel, but it is all made up in Christ with advantage; for here better bread is daily offered than that of manna was.

4. Christ is the truth and substance of all the types in the Old Testament; and particularly the type of manna is fulfilled in him, in his incarnation and coming into the world. In his original he comes from a better heaven than that whence manna came; he is but little, small, and despised in the eyes of men, and yet is white and spotless, as manna was, and of a sweeter taste to right discerners, and feeds and entertains a better life than manna did; he is all-sufficient

to feed all his people, (as manna furnished all Israel,) and is laid freely forth, to be gathered and received by all of them, as manna fell daily round about the camp; and the weakest believer shall not come behind with the strongest, in sharing in him according as the manna was equally divided; therefore is he called "the true bread from heaven," with relation to manna as the type.

5. The holiest of ministers do not confer the thing signified in a sacrament, nor is the outward element of the sacrament the thing signified by it, which feeds the soul; but God hath the giving of that in his own hand, and if he be not employed, men will get but the earthly part of the sacrament; therefore, albeit Moses was a minister in giving them manna, which was the type and outward element, yet saith he, " Moses gave you not that bread from heaven, (or the thing signified,) but my Father giveth," &c. And thus he not only debaseth manna in comparison of himself, but speaks the more meanly of it, in respect they looked not so much to the spiritual signification thereof, but only propounded it as an instance to invite Christ to give the like carnal satisfaction to their bellies.

6. Such as stand in need of true spiritual food have both the Father and the Son ready and engaged to give it unto them; for whereas he had said, "the Son of man shall give it unto you," ver. 27, now saith he, "my Father giveth the true bread;" wherein he doth not only, as Mediator, give the glory of all to his Father, but sheweth that the Father concurreth with him in this, and giveth it by his hand.

7. Even such as are, at present, but carnal and unsound, are not secluded from the offer of Christ, but, upon right terms, may expect that he will be gifted to them; therefore, saith he, even to those hearers, "but my Father giveth you," &c.—that is, by me maketh offer of it, to be embraced upon right terms, and in the due order.

VER. 33. For the bread of God is he which cometh down from heaven, and giveth life unto the world.

In this verse the assertion concerning this true bread given by the Father is repeated, and cleared and enlarged in a description thereof, which agreeth not to manna; wherein, 1. It is declared that this is the true bread of God which comes down from heaven, to give life to lost and dead men, which manna could not do. 2. This benefit is enlarged, that whereas any benefit that manna brought was peculiar to Israel only, this is appointed to give life to all sorts of persons as well as the Jews. Whence learn—

1. Albeit not only manna, but even our ordinary refreshments, are of God, and from him, yet Christ is the bread of God by way of excellency, as being indeed divine food, and food for our better part, and food wherein God manifests his riches and fulness as God, and wherein he ought to be clearly seen; therefore, saith he, "the bread of God is he," &c., or, he is divine bread, and bread which comes from God in a singular way. And he speaks of this bread as a

person having action; "he cometh down," &c.; because it is Christ's person and benefits accompanying him, which, being applied, do give life.

2. Benefits of God ought to be in esteem with us, according as they have much of God shining clearly in them, and in giving of them, which will commend spiritual benefits before temporal, and lesser benefits, coming more immediately and sensibly from his hand, before greater favours, wherein that is not so visible; for this is an argument to commend him as the true bread—"for he is the bread of God."

3. All mankind by nature is in a lost condition, lying spiritually dead, and being obnoxious to eternal death without Christ; for this is the case of "the world," that they need "life."

4. Man's lost and dead condition is irremediable by himself, or any other mean under heaven; for this life must "come down from heaven."

5. Christ is the true bread and food, that not only preserves life and keeps from eternal death, but doth put life and quickening even in the dead; and such as do partake of Christ will live, and become lively in their motions and actions, for this "bread of God giveth life."

6. Christ (that he might become fit food to quicken dead souls, and might stoop to them who could not ascend to him) hath been pleased to come down from heaven to earth unto sinners, not in regard of his godhead's changing of place, seeing he fills heaven and earth, but in regard of state, in that he stooped to be incarnate, and did assume our nature on earth by a personal union to himself; nor yet that his human nature was from heaven, but that the sanctification, manner of conception, and personal union thereof unto the godhead, was divine and from heaven, and wrought by the virtue and power of the Holy Ghost. In these respects is this bread of God commended, that "he cometh down from heaven, and giveth life."

7. The spiritual benefits and refreshments of Christ are not proper to Israel only, but common to all nations; and as the offer is made indifferently to all sorts of persons where the gospel cometh, so he is applied to his own elect, of all nations and ranks of persons, for he "giveth life unto the world," not to Israel only, but to his own, of all sorts and conditions throughout the world, who in themselves differ nothing from the rest of the world till grace prevent them, and therefore they get the common name of "the world."

VER. 34. Then said they unto him, Lord, evermore give us this bread.

Christ's commending of this bread produceth a vehement desire and earnest petition for it; albeit they had wickedness enough to propound this desire by way of taunt, desiring him who made such fair offers to give some real proofs of it, yet it seems rather to flow from their ignorant and carnal disposition, who, hearing of such bread, and conceiving of it but carnally, desire to partake of it constantly, as Israel did of the manna. Whence learn—

1. The commendation of spiritual things may produce strange motions and desires and affections in men, who yet are but carnal; while as they have but carnal conceptions of things spiritual, and their desires are neither serious, nor constant, nor laborious; for here the former commendation produceth very vehement desires, and strong insinuations with Christ, calling him "Lord," that they may have their will, and yet the issue proves them to be but naught in all this.

2. As all men by nature are carnal, so their conceptions of things spiritual are but carnal, and their desires are agreeable to their dispositions; for such was their conception and desire here; they are far from Christ's purpose, and dream of nothing but bodily refreshment in all this.

3. As men's lustful hearts are vehement and ardent upon their desired objects, so sudden changes; and when people on a sudden become vehement in desiring spiritual things, it gives just ground of suspicion that, at best, there is much of flesh in these desires, seeing (whatever grace can do, yet) such desires are not attained without much wrestling and much sense of former negligence, and are, for the most part, carried on against strong tides of opposition; for their very instancy on a sudden is a strong evidence that they conceived but carnally of the matter.

VER. 35. And Jesus said unto them, I am the bread of life: he that cometh to me shall never hunger; and he that believeth on me shall never thirst.

Christ returns an answer to this desire to ver. 41, wherein, 1. He describes more plainly what and who this bread is, ver. 35. 2. He discovers their hypocrisy, and checks them for not being that in reality which here they pretend to in their desires, ver. 36. 3. He sheweth that his own elect would not deal so with him, and should be well dealt with, according as was given him in commission, ver. 37—40.

In this verse, 1. Christ, upon occasion of their desire, doth declare what and who this bread of life is; he had told before the excellency thereof, and that he and his Father would give it to them who seek it sincerely; now he brings out more of his mind, declaring that he is "the bread of life." 2. He doth again repeat and inculcate the way of partaking of this bread, which is, by believing and coming to him, (of which, see chap. v. 40.) 3. He confirms that he is "the bread of life," and points out the excellency thereof from an effect, which is, that the partakers of him shall find complete refreshment in him, for the preserving and perpetuating of their spiritual life. Whence learn—

1. Christ is so tender of any desires after himself that he will labour and take pains to make the best that can be, even of natural and carnal desires, and not cast them away at first, but labour to make them better, and set them right; therefore doth he answer this carnal crew, and propound an object to elevate their desires.

2. A right sight of Christ, and his commending of himself to sinners, is a special mean to

make desires spiritual, and elevate them towards him; for he points out and commends himself here for that end.

3. Christ is not only the giver of that food which begets and entertains spiritual life, and which is most necessary, and should be most sweet to sinners, but he himself is the food of our souls also, who gave himself to death, that he might be prepared meat for us, who by his merit doth purchase life, and by his efficacy being applied doth dispense and entertain that life; for saith he, " I am the bread of life"—that is, who hath life in himself, and who merits, begets, maintains, and perfects life in them who embrace and apply him. And he speaks of himself under the notion of " bread," because it was bread which that carnal people was seeking.

4. The right way of feeding on Christ for the entertainment of spiritual life, and of finding him the bread of life, is, by faith to embrace and close with him, his person, offices, and offers, and exercise our faith on him daily; for he is the bread of life to him " that believeth."

5. To come to Christ and to believe in him are all one; and he that is made sensible of his distance from Christ, and of the excellency and fulness that is in him, and doth turn his course and eye towards him, and is still moving on towards him, is a believer, whatever he enjoy; for " he that cometh to me:" is explained by this: " he that believeth on me."

6. Christ's offers unto all and every one that cometh unto him are not fair compliments, but produce real satisfaction; as this promise subjoined doth teach.

7. As all they who come not to Christ will eternally pine away under the want of all satisfaction, so they who embrace him shall find all-sufficiency in him for all wants, and that eternally; for this bread satisfieth both hunger and thirst, as, in scripture phrase, " bread" is put for all bodily refreshment; and it is promised, he shall " never hunger," and " never thirst;" whereby we are to understand—1. That they who embrace him, though they will long after more of him, yet they shall never again hunger after the husks of sin, nor after satisfaction thereby to the lusts of the flesh. 2. Albeit there will be lustings and longings after these, even in them who have embraced Christ, yet in so far as they have come to Christ, and are renewed, they will be rid of them. 3. They shall not any more pine under the destroying hunger of total want, though they will still have a hunger of wholesome appetite to prepare them for feeding, and have food at hand to supply and satisfy it. 4. This promise of being delivered from hunger and thirst is but begun to be accomplished here, and daily going on, and shall be perfected hereafter, when believers shall enjoy complete and total satisfaction throughout all eternity.

Ver. 36. But I said unto you, That ye also have seen me, and believe not.

In this verse Christ doth sadly regrate [exhibit] and discover their hypocrisy, and that notwithstanding all their fair pretences, ver. 34, yet they were but wilful despisers of him, in that, however they had not only seen him, but were convinced what he was, ver. 14, yet they would not believe; and this he declares to be the more odious, that he had told them of it before, and yet they had not amended it.   Whence learn—

1. When Christ is manifesting himself by his word or working unto a people, then his eye is upon them, marking how they profit: so much doth he intimate unto them here. (See Ezek. xxxiii. 31.)

2. Christ will not be deceived with fair shows in a people, but can discover a rotten and perverse heart under plausible pretences and professions; for whereas they seemed to be so earnest, ver. 34, that there needed no more but to discover and offer that bread unto them and they would embrace it, he sheweth that it was far otherwise, and that it was not ignorance, or want of opportunity, but perverseness, that kept them back.

3. It is no wonder that Christ be much grieved with, and have many sad complaints of, unfruitful and hypocritical hearers, considering their deceitful hypocrisy, the great injury they do to him by slighting of him, and that they deprive themselves of so sweet advantages by him; therefore doth he, who knew them well enough, and what a sweet offer of life they slighted, break out in this sad rebuke, the manner whereof sheweth that it came from a grieved spirit.

4. As men may come a great length in conviction and knowledge who yet do not believe, so whatever they attain by hearing, Christ will account it all nothing if they come not to close with him by faith, without which neither is he honoured nor do they reap profit; for Christ grants they had " seen" him, and yet that avails not, since they " believe not."

5. The more conviction and light men have in the matters of Christ and the gospel, their unbelief is the more odious; for thus doth he aggreage [aggravate] their sin, " ye also have seen me, and believe not." (See John, xii. 37; xv. 22, 24.

6. It doth also aggravate the sin of unbelief, and prove the unsoundness of men, that they have been often told of their fault, and yet do not amend it; for this adds unto the challenge, that he had told them of it before : " But I said unto you," &c. And albeit we find it not directly mentioned before, yet we are not to doubt of it, since he asserts that he had said it, and we find it insinuated, ver. 26, where he tells them they followed him for carnal ends, even after conviction, ver. 14.

7. So long as sinners are not ashamed to continue in their courses of unbelief and slighting of Christ, ministers should not weary to tell them of it over and over again; for so much doth Christ's example teach, who having reproved this fault doth not fail to inculcate it again.

Ver. 37. All thát the Father giveth me shall come to me; and him that cometh to me I will in no wise cast out.

Christ, having thus pointed out their obstinacy in unbelief, doth (to ver. 41) comfort himself and strengthen the weak, who might stumble at the unbelief of so many, by ascending up to the fountain of faith and conversion, assuring himself that the elect would come unto him; and promising all tender usage and welcome to them; which he confirms by reading over his commission unto them. And by this means also he layeth before them their sad case, and that their practice said much to it, that they did not belong unto him; yet so as he doth not terrify, but warmly invite any who had a mind to come to him. In this verse—1. He comforts himself that, misbelieve who would, yet undoubtedly all those that were given unto him would come unto him. 2. He assureth all those who come of tender and warm acceptance. Whence learn—

1. Albeit many who slight Christ's call may yet be elect, and at last embrace him; and albeit we cannot certainly conclude the reprobation of any in this life by any mark in them, if it be not found that they have sinned unto death, yet to reject Christ after conviction is an evidence of a reprobate condition, and such as continue in it have sad cause of fear lest they be indeed reprobates; and whatever be Christ's purpose towards any, yet it is a special mean to terrify sinners from their refusing of Christ, to affright them with reprobation; for so doth Christ here deal with these unbelievers, pointing out unto them what their way might portend of them.

2. However Christ and his servants have ofttimes cause to complain of the small fruit of their labours, yet this is matter of comfort—that all the elect will, in due time, be brought in; for so doth Christ comfort himself here. (See Rom. xi. 7.)

3. Albeit the offer of the gospel be made generally to all who hear it, yet the special purpose of God for good is towards some only, and not others; for there are who are given by "the Father," and not others.

4. It is the great dignity and happiness of the elect that they are from eternity given to Christ in the covenant of redemption, as the reward of his sufferings, to come to him in due time; and that they are given to him in trust, to be accountable and forthcoming for them; for so is here declared, that there are whom "the Father giveth" him; wherein is imported that they were the Father's first, not only by virtue of his general right in all creatures, Psalm xxiv. 1, but by particular election, and that, being the Father's, they are given to Christ both from eternity, to be redeemed by him, and as the reward of his sufferings, and in time, to be drawn to him, and therefore both "the Father giveth" them in the present time, and "hath given" them before, ver. 39. (See John, xvii. 6; Isa. liii. 10; Psalm xxii. 30.)

5. As those who are thus given unto Christ are many, how many soever reject him, so they are high in his esteem, and as much as if all were given unto him; therefore are they called, "All that the Father giveth," not only to shew their number, but the word in the original is more emphatic, and importeth as much as "all things," to shew that indeed they are his "all,"

and that he accounts of them as much as, and above, all things beside. And thus the expression is more clearly, Eph. i. 10.

6. The elect, and such as are given to Christ, may for a time be, and really by nature are, as far away and estranged from him as any other; for they are given and yet are to come to him. This may make them thankful, humble, and charitable, when they are converted.

7. Such as are elected and given to Christ will certainly in due time come to him; their being given from eternity produceth their being given and coming in time; for God is faithful, who will not frustrate Christ of what he hath purchased, and the power that draweth them is invincible and irresistible; therefore saith he, "All that the Father giveth me shall come to me."

8. Conversion and coming unto Christ is not a cause, nor is the foresight thereof antecedent to election, but it is only a fruit following thereupon; for such is the order here, they are given by "the Father," and upon that their coming necessarily followeth. (See Acts, xiii. 48.)

9. It is not men's moral changes, nor their following external ordinances, that prove them given to Christ, but their coming to him, and closing with and embracing of himself as Mediator; for so are we taught here: They who are given "come to me," saith he.

10. Such as really come to Christ and embrace him have not only the present comfort of communion with him, but are warranted from this to gather their eternal election, and that they have been given over to Christ, and committed to his charge and care; therefore is their coming put as an effect and evidence of their being given.

11. Such as are come to Christ have warrant to expect welcome and warm entertainment, whatever they have been before; for so much doth the promise subjoined teach, which is made to all, without exception. (See Jer. iii. 1.) And particular notice and care is taken of every one, as if there were no more; and therefore, albeit the former speech was general—"All that the Father giveth," yet the promise is more particular, "him that cometh," &c.

12. Such as come to Christ are put into a state of much familiarity and comfort, and may expect more from him than can be well conceived or expressed; for albeit this promise be expressed only in a negative, "I will not cast him out," yet it imports much more of his warm entertainment; and namely, that they are taken into his family, are brought near him by reconciliation and friendship, have all their conditions respected by him, enjoy much of his presence, have him to be accountable for them, and to make all their lots by his gracious providence tend to their good. All things shall be theirs, (and not they slaves to their idols,) and Christ to the advantage; nothing shall discommend their person to him; their condition shall plead rather for pity than wrath; wants shall not render them unacceptable, but rather a conceit of fulness; under afflictions, and in performing duties, he shall be undertaker, to work all their works in them and for them; and all of them shall find the door kept open till they be entered into glory.

without the reach of all their enemies, where they shall feed on the light of his countenance, shall follow and enjoy him, and be made like unto him. All this, and much more, is imported in this promise.

13. It is the great comfort of such as come unto Christ that as their allowances are rich, so their state is safe and secure; and whatever their fears, mistakes, or quarrellings may be, yet they shall never be again deprived of that happy condition; for so much is expressed in this promise, " I will not cast him out"—that is, they are taken into that sweet estate not to be cast out or rejected again. Saints do indeed ofttimes complain of casting off, but they are the words of sense and not of faith; they may seem to be cast off when really it is not so; they may lose degrees of fellowship for a time, but cannot be deprived of it totally, and for ever; they cannot be secluded from his favour and love, and an interest in him, though sometimes they may be deprived of some effects and manifestations and fruits thereof; they may be deprived for a time of what contributes to their well-being, but not of what is necessary for their being in grace; yea, he will not permit them to cast out themselves, Jer. xxxii. 40.

14. Christ's promises to those who come to him are very sure, and such as (whatever doubts or jealousies they may have, yet) he would have them on no terms to question, especially in what concerns his purpose, nor to reject them finally or totally; therefore doth he so vehemently assert this : " I will in no wise cast him out," where the doubled negatives in the original serve to make the assertion strong, and to carry their faith over all their doubts and fears.

VER. 38. For I came down from heaven, not to do mine own will, but the will of him that sent me.

39. And this is the Father's will which hath sent me, that of all which he hath given me I should lose nothing, but should raise it up again at the last day.

40. And this is the will of him that sent me, that every one which seeth the Son, and believeth on him, may have everlasting life : and I will raise him up at the last day.

Christ confirms this promise—of entertaining them who come to him, by shewing the end of his incarnation and coming into the world, and by rehearsing a part of his commission unto them. He declareth in general, ver. 38, that his errand into the world is to do his Father's will who sent him, and not his own, which is not to be understood that, as God, he hath a different and contrary will to the Father's, (though as man, he hath a distinct and subordinate will to his,) but the meaning is, he came not to do his own will only (as the Jews alleged of him), but the Father's also, and that in this work he was the Father's commissioner, sent to do what he had entrusted to him, and not, as the Jews gave out, one who did that for which he had no

warrant. Next, he declareth more particularly, ver. 39, for confirmation of the promise, what this will of the Father's is which he came to do—to wit, that those that are given him should be preserved from perishing, and be raised up at the last day: this is again repeated, ver. 40, not only for further certainty and comfort, but in the repetition it is explained who they are that are given to him, even such as see and believe in him; and what is the benefit they shall reap at the resurrection, even everlasting life.

From ver. 38, learn—1. Christ, in entertaining them that come to him, is not only led thereunto by his own mercy and bounty and love towards them as the reward of all his sufferings, but doth also stand obliged thereunto by virtue of a commission and trust laid upon him by the Father, and accepted and undertaken by him; therefore doth he mention " the will of him that sent me" as a reason of his fidelity in this matter.

2. Christ hath given an ample proof of his love and pledge of his fidelity in his trust in his stooping to take on our nature, and assuming it in a personal union to himself on earth; for saith he, " I came down from heaven," of which see ver. 33. And this he mentions here, not only to shew how much it cost him to exalt us, but to be a confirmation and pledge of his tenderness and fidelity in welcoming sinners who come to him; for who can suspect him who made himself like his brethren (yet without sin), that he might be a fit high priest? and to assure us that as he stooped to our low condition, and to be humbled with us, so he would have us exalted with him. What assurance may it afford us that he would come down from heaven to dwell with us? that the beloved Son would make himself the butt of all the wrath due to our sins? that the sovereign Lord of the creatures would endure their opposition and enmity, that they might be friends to us? and that he took on the form and condition of a servant, and continued so till he had perfected what concerned us?

3. Such as are employed in any station by God ought to have a constant look to the will of God and the end set before them in that station, that so they may aim at it; for so doth Christ's example teach, who looked to " the will of him that sent him," that he might do it.

4. It is as sure that Christ will warmly cherish them that come to him as it is certain he is faithful in his trust; for such is the force of the confirmation, " I will in no wise cast him out, for I came, not to do mine own will, but the will of him that sent me." If he do his Father's will, as he still doth, then such shall not be cast out.

5. The Father's will and good pleasure is the last and ultimate ground that faith can seek to settle itself upon; and particularly, it is sufficient to answer all our reasonings against Christ's rich offers, that it is the Father's will such mercies should be conferred; for so is also imported here, that they have not only Christ's fidelity engaged to make them welcome, but it is the Father's will they should be accepted so, and that may silence all doubtings.

From verse 39, learn—1. It doth commend the gospel to us, that it contains an extract of the deep counsels of God, and of the eternal transactions betwixt the Father and the Son concerning lost man, in so far as is for our good; for he brings out and reads in the gospel his very commission, and some articles of the covenant passed betwixt the Father and him.

2. The first fountain and rise of the salvation of any of lost mankind is in the absolute and sovereign will and pleasure of God; for here he mentions " the will of him that sent him" as the first original of all, from whence their giving to Christ, their coming, and safety, do flow.

3. Those whose salvation the Father willeth are given over to Christ in his eternal purpose, to be brought to him in due time; for so is here held out.

4. Such as are given to Christ by the Father, and do in time come to him, are put in his keeping, and he hath a charge of them, not to lose any the least of them; for " this is the will of him that sent me, that of all he hath given me I should lose nothing;" wherein the Father doth so commit the trust unto him as he still keeps them in his own hand also, John, x. 28, 29.

5. Christ's charge and care of those that are given to him extends even to the very day of their resurrection, that there he may make a good account of them, when all perils and hazards are now over, and that he may not so much as lose their dust, but gather it together again, and raise it up in glory, to be a proof of his fidelity; for saith he, " I should lose nothing, but should raise it up again at the last day," and so death and dissolution prove no loss.

From verse 40, learn—1. It is a truth that needs much and often to be inculcated upon us, that all spiritual advantages and benefits come to us, and are to be had only in Christ, and that in him they are all very sure; therefore doth he again repeat this doctrine concerning what is to be had in him, and that they will surely get it who come to him. About this truth we have naturally many doubts, and are averse from submitting to it; and when we close with it, it begets love, it moderates all our cares and fears, and strengtheneth us to endure all hardships.

2. However such as flee to Christ in the sense of their misery are prone to doubt of God's will to accept them, rather than of anything else, yet it is out of all controversy that his will is to do good to such; therefore it is again repeated, " This is the will of him that sent me," &c., to remove all doubts and fears.

3. Such as are given to Christ, to be under his charge and participate of his benefits, are drawn to believe on him, and it is the Father's will, and a part of the transaction betwixt him and the Son, that faith be the way to partake of these benefits, and not the fulfilling of the impossible condition of the works of the law; for they who are " given" to Christ are expounded to be they who believe on him, and it is the Father's will that such partake of these benefits here mentioned, as of the rest of his purchase. Albeit mortification, holiness, &c., do prepare for the possession of these benefits, and do evidence a right thereunto, and the begun possession thereof, yet it is only faith in Christ that giveth the right and title, that so it may be of grace.

4. A special mean of begetting faith in Christ in men, is to see and know him spiritually, to have him revealed unto them, and to get open eyes, that they may see and contemplate him, till they see beauty in him which may allure them to renounce themselves and flee to him, and till they see fulness and all-sufficiency to answer all their doubts; for they see (or contemplate) the Son, who believe on him.

5. It is covenanted betwixt the Father and the Son that believers shall (beside his tender dealing and care within time) be made partakers of everlasting life; for it is explained that not to " lose" them, verse 39, is that they " may have everlasting life."

6. For the further assuring of believers of their eternal happiness it is also covenanted that they shall have this life in present possession, in the earnest and first fruits thereof; for they " have everlasting life" even here, and before their raising up.

7. Christ, having given an earnest penny of salvation, will not suffer it to be lost by any difficulty or impediment in the way, but will carry believers through all difficulties, till he destroy death and the grave, and raise up their very dust, that in body and soul they may partake of that bliss, and that he may make it manifest that death and rotting in the grave doth not make void his interest, nor cause his affection to cease; therefore it is added, " and I will raise him up at the last day."

8. Albeit believers are not all of one growth or size, but some are weak and some strong; some little children, some young men, and some fathers; yet all of them, without exception, have right to the benefits conferred by Christ, and the weak as well as the strong are under his care and charge, yea, and may expect the more tender usage from him who carrieth the lambs in his bosom, &c., Isa. xl. 11; therefore is the charge and promise universal, that " every one which believeth on him may have everlasting life."

Ver. 41. The Jews then murmured at him, because he said, I am the bread which came down from heaven.

42. And they said, Is not this Jesus, the son of Joseph, whose father and mother we know? how is it then that he saith, I came down from heaven?

Followeth their bad use of this sweet doctrine. The clearer Christ speaks, they discover the more of their disposition, and testify their discontent of spirit by murmuring. They pass over all that Christ had said beside, and do carp only at what he had said in direct answer to their desire, ver. 34, wherein he asserts himself to be that bread of life, ver. 35, which he had said did come down from heaven, ver. 33. This they carp at, that he, whom they supposed they knew to be but the son of Joseph and Mary, should speak so great things of himself; wherein they not only bewray their ignorance of his divine nature and miraculous conception, but their gross error, in alleging that he was the son of Joseph.

From verse 41, learn—1. Men may pretend to much affection and estimation of Christ who yet will prove but inconstant, seeing they proceed not on solid grounds ; for they who cried him up, ver. 14, 15, do now vilipend [vilify] him, and carp that he should commend himself.

2. Such as do not get good of Christ and the gospel, nor do embrace him when he is offered, will certainly grow worse ; the powerful gospel will bring out their heart, and their unsoundness will draw on more unstreightness; for so fared it with them who sought and heard Christ for a wrong end; the longer and the more they hear, they grow the worse.

3. It is no strange thing to see corrupt men not only not embrace saving doctrine, but that they murmur and fret against it, and spit out their gall against the messengers thereof, either secretly or openly ; for such is the entertainment Christ and his doctrine gets: " The Jews (as they were who followed and heard him) murmured at him," or secretly muttered against what he said.

4. Such as turn carpers and secret grudgers at the doctrine of Christ do not only prove their present unsoundness, but are on the way to further and more horrid apostasy; for so doth the sequel prove in these; this was the beginning of a breach betwixt him and them, which came at length to a greater height. The highest degrees of apostasy would not be digested at first by many, but murmurings, grudgings, and mistakes, do by little and little habituate them unto it.

5. Such as carp at Christ's doctrine, and deny unto him the glory of his excellency in his person and offices, do not only wrong him, but ingrately despise their own great mercy ; for this point which they murmured at, that he is " the bread which came down from heaven," doth not only set forth his glory, but was most sweet and comfortable to lost sinners, as holding out his rich offer, and his gracious condescendence and love, that he would stoop and come down to give life and refreshment to them.

6. Though Christ had spoken much more than this, and that which concerned them very nearly, yet they take notice of no more but this one word. We may conceive the reasons to be— 1. This having displeased them, it casts down all the rest; as ofttimes one word, crossing carnal hearts, will irritate their corruptions, to reject all they hear, were it never so useful and inoffensive, Jer. xxvi. 3, 6, with 9. 2. It may be conceived, that however they understood and did resent the hard news that were insinuated against them, ver. 37, yet they will not quarrel upon that, but upon a more plausible ground; to shew how subtle unfriends to Christ are, that can mask their discontent with fairest colours, and not discover the bottom of their hearts. Or, 3. It may be conceived that not only passion because of what Christ said, but their own conceit of themselves, hindered them from taking up that sentence indirectly hinted at, and therefore Christ doth inculcate it again, ver. 44, 45, And so it teacheth that men who are puffed up with a conceit of themselves will not readily take with a reproof or discovery

of their condition, especially if it be done but indirectly, and not held forth in express terms.

7. When inquiry is made, it will be found that it is not Christ's doctrine, but men's own corruptions and mistakes, that cause them to stumble; for if they understood his meaning to be that his very body descended from heaven, (as their following reasoning doth import they did,) this was but their own fancy, for he speaks of his godhead and of the manner of his conception; and to deny his divinity and miraculous conception was but their own ignorance of the scriptures, Isa. vii. 14 ; ix. 6.

From verse 42, learn—1. Sins of progenitors may bring posterity very low, and put even the posterity of kings into a mean condition; for Joseph, the supposed father of Christ, and his -mother, were both of the blood royal of the kings of Judah, and yet they lived in a poor condition, which occasioneth this mentioning of them with contempt.

2. It pleased our Lord not only to stoop and become man, but to be born of base and mean parentage, that so he might accomplish prophecies, Isaiah, xi. 1 ; liii. 1 ; that he might shew that his kingdom is not of this world, might sanctify a mean condition to his own, and by his poverty make many rich, 2 Cor. viii. 9 ; and that, in God's righteous judgment, reprobates might stumble at him; for so was it with him here; his supposed father and his mother were in no great account at this time.

3. It is the disposition and plague of hypocrites and belly-gods that they stumble at Christ's outward base estate, and do not see his true and spiritual glory shining through that veil; for such were they who see not the mystery of his incarnation, nor the glory of his godhead, but do stumble on this: " Is not this Jesus, the son of Joseph, whose father and mother we know?"

4. It is a great engine of Satan to oppose Christ and his truth, by raising and spreading untruths, to bear him and it down ; for this was a grand cause of their stumbling—that they falsely supposed him to be " the son of Joseph," which did obscure the glory of his miraculous conception and birth. Thus also did Satan labour to bear him down by a general reproach cast upon his country, John, i. 46 ; vii. 52. Thus did he endeavour to obscure his resurrection, Matt. xxviii. 13—15. And it is no wonder to see Christ and his truth suffer prejudice by hereditary misreports and calumnies in all ages.

5. Much outward familiarity with Christ and his servants will readily breed contempt of him in carnal hearts; for their knowing of him, his mother, and supposed father, makes them slight him, notwithstanding his miracles : " Is not this Jesus, whose father and mother we know ?"

6. Corrupt and blinded reason in men is a great enemy to God and their own souls, while it musters up things partly false and partly true in their own kind, to oppose against supernatural truth, and to drive men from embracing of Christ; for they please themselves in their reasonings against Christ's assertions, partly alleging false principles, that he was " the son of Joseph," and nothing but a mere man, and partly measuring his miraculous conception by their prin-

ciples of reason, whence they reason it to be absurd that he should say, " I came down from heaven." Men had need to subject their reasonings to divine revelation in the things of God, lest they wrong him and themselves both.

VER. 43. Jesus therefore answered and said unto them, Murmur not among yourselves.

44. No man can come to me, except the Father which hath sent me draw him : and I will raise him up at the last day.

Christ, in his reply, doth not (as was also marked on ver. 32) enter into debate with them, or refute their ignorant sophistry; but—1. He sheweth that the root and true cause of their unbelief was not in his doctrine, nor from any just ground of exception they had against it, but from somewhat in themselves, to ver. 47. 2. He repeats and inculcates the former doctrine, that life is to be had only through faith in him, and that he is the true " bread of life," and cleareth yet more distinctly in what respect he is the true bread and spiritual food, to ver. 52.

In these verses—1. Christ sheweth that he took notice of their murmuring, and doth dissuade them from it, as having given no just cause thereof by his doctrine, ver. 43. 2. He confirmeth this by pointing at the root of their unbelief and murmuring, even their natural impotency and averseness from him, which also is the condition of all men till such time as divine power be interposed to draw them, and then all who are drawn come, and Christ undertakes to be accountable for such. And by this way of preaching Christ would draw them from their idle debates, and would terrify them by letting them see that their unbelief proved they were lying still in nature, and that God had yet wrought no change upon them, but had left them to themselves; and withal he would let them see their loss who, by not embracing him, were secluded from his care.

From ver. 43, learn —

1. Christ knows and takes notice of most secret murmurings and mutterings and repinings against God, his word, or servants, were they never so closely or handsomely con veyed ; for albeit it seems they spake not out these things, but whispered them among themselves, as the text hath it, and the word in the original imports, yet Christ knoweth it and tells them of it.

2. Murmurings and repining against God and divine truth, upon whatsoever pretence, are displeasing to Christ, as being a causeless distemper, reflecting injuriously upon God; therefore doth he prohibit it as a thing displeasing to him : " Murmur not among yourselves."

From ver. 44, learn—1. Whatever be the pretences of murmurers against Christ and his truth, yet the true cause thereof is in themselves, and not in him nor in it; therefore doth he lead them from that carping at his doctrine to see their own natural disposition, which bred such a distemper.

2. Men by rejecting Christ and murmuring at his offers do bewray so much of their own corrupt dispositions, and that they are so far left to themselves by God, as might be matter of horror

unto them if their eyes were open ; for this is the scope of this doctrine here, to let them see, not only that they are corrupt, but that God hath not wrought on them as he doth on those who are his elect, as ver. 37, that so he may let them see what sad things their condition spake to them. And Christ doth often recur to this with these contentious Jews, not to make them sit down upon this as an excuse (which it is not), but partly to shew that, however the Lord's purposes concerning men be hid and secret, yet by their own carriage they may bring out strange evidences of it, and (however the reprobation of any particular person cannot be certainly known by any mere man, so long as the person is within time, yet) men's perverse carriage doth prove a reprobate disposition for present, and being persevered in, is a black mark of their deplorable state; and partly, to shew that Christ will not take an affront at the hand of any ; but as they who love him shall find that they were first beloved of him, so they who reject him, and persevere in it, will find (to their eternal confusion) that he did give them up to their own hearts, to walk in these ways, in punishing whereof he will manifest the glory of his justice.

3. Albeit it be the duty of all who hear the gospel to embrace Christ, and albeit it be justly commanded to discover our inability, and as a mean which God maketh use of to work thereby upon his own, yet no man hath naturally any liberty or power to receive Christ, or come in faith to him; but every man by nature (whatever his inclination, education, or moral virtues be) hath lost all power to do any spiritual good by Adam's fall, and remains dead in sin; for " no man can come to me," saith he—to wit, of himself, as is after cleared.

4. This natural impotency in man cannot be cured by mere moral suasion or holding out of the offer of Christ in the gospel; but with this there must be a powerful and effectual work of God in changing and renewing of men's nature, infusing of the habits of grace and faith, quickening them from their deadness, and exciting of those graces which he infuseth, and effectually inclining their heart and mind to embrace Christ, and close with him, and adhere to him; for this is the only remedy of man's impotency, that " the Father draw him." To ascribe unto God no more but moral suasion in this work is to allow him no more hand in good than Satan hath in evil, and consequently to ascribe unto man as much praise of doing good as he is reprovable for evil. And it ascribes unto man the glory of making himself to differ from another who had the same offer with him, but would not be persuaded. (See 1 Cor. iv. 7.)

5. Divine power, in curing and recovering of lost man, hath not only to do with impotency, but with averseness, with a corrupt will, strongly inclined to evil, and with corruptions which will resist and oppose him in his working; for so much doth this drawing import.

6. The powerful grace of God is invincible, and will effectuate his purpose over all impediments. He will not only bear down the resistance and opposition that corruptions make, but he who is Lord of the will, will sweetly incline

and powerfully allure it, and make the man most willing to come to Christ; for if none " can come, except the Father draw him," then certainly they whom he draweth do come, and so Christ's promise subjoined and the following verse do clear.

7. This drawing is ascribed to " the Father which hath sent Christ," not secluding the rest of the persons, seeing every work of God which relateth to the creatures is common to the whole blessed Trinity, and Christ hath a hand in this same work, ver. 46, with Matt. xi. 27. (See John, xii. 32.) Nor yet is this expression only used to shew that the Father is first in order of working this work, as he is first in order of subsistence, but it points out further—1. That the Father, who entered in a covenant with the Son, and sent him into the world to obey his will and perform those duties he had voluntarily undertaken, is in a special manner obliged, by virtue of that paction, to bring unto his Son the promised seed and reward of his sufferings. 2. It serveth to shew that, however he be a righteous God, and will have justice satisfied for the sins committed even by his elect, yet as the Son did voluntarily submit to that dispensation, to pay the price, though he was also the party offended, so the Father doth also so love them as he draws them to Christ, that his justice may be satisfied in him, and that his love towards them may let forth itself in comfortable and sensible effects. And this will teach us so to magnify the tenderness of the Mediator as not to entertain wrong thoughts of the Father.

8. The great misery of those who are not wrought upon to come to Christ is clearly to be seen and read in the warm usage they meet with who embrace him; therefore doth Christ hold out his undertaking for them who are brought to him, that he may let these murmurers see their great loss.

9. Time will certainly come to an end, and all perfection and contentment which men imagine in the things of it will have a period; for days do at last come to " the last day."

10. Whatever believers find in Christ within time, yet their eyes are chiefly fixed upon eternity and upon the expectation of settled happiness there; therefore do they need to have a promise concerning " the last day" so often repeated unto them.

11. Such as are brought to Christ by the Father he will never abandon them till he have raised them up at the last day, and presented them blameless and complete before the Father, that they may for ever be with him; for saith he, " and I will raise him up at the last day."

Ver. 45. It is written in the prophets, And they shall be all taught of God. Every man therefore that hath heard, and hath learned of the Father, cometh unto me.

Christ doth confirm his assertion concerning the Father's drawing from the prophecies of the Old Testament which speak of the days of the gospel, wherein it is foretold that all the elect and confederates in the Spirit shall be taught of God to embrace Christ offered in the gospel, Isa. liv. 13; Jer. xxxi. 33, 34; whence he inferreth that every one who is thus taught doth come and embrace him. This teaching is not to be understood as secluding a teaching ministry under the gospel; for the very text includes hearing and learning; and this interpretation should not only rub an imputation upon Christ and his apostles' practice,—who in these very times of the gospel did preach and appoint a ministry, and ordained ministers, and who did continue teaching and exhorting when yet they acknowledge this promise to be accomplished, 1 John, ii. 20, 21, 27, 28; 1 Thess. iv. 9, 10,—but it should strike also against all private mutual edification as well as public teaching, which yet the decriers of a ministry will not allow; yea, they intrude themselves as preachers that they may cry down preaching and a ministry; but the meaning is, that God, in and by the means, should teach them that however means be necessary, yet it is not they, but the Spirit's teaching that prevails with them, and that under the gospel this teaching should be more general and conspicuous.

DOCTRINES.

1. It is by the scriptures that all controversies and debates in matters of religion must be decided; therefore doth he remit the proof of his assertion to what " is written in the prophets."

2. Not only Christ's outward condition and practice, but his doctrine, are in all things agreeable to the doctrine and predictions of the Old Testament concerning the Messiah and what should be fulfilled in his days; therefore doth he cite " the prophets" as foretelling the same things of the days of the Messiah which he now asserts. And he who was truth itself doth condescend to confirm his doctrine thus.

3. God's way of drawing in sinners to Christ, as it consists not in bare moral suasion, so neither is it a working upon men as insensible stocks or irrational creatures, but he deals with them in a rational way, and by his efficacious teaching doth cure the blindness of their mind, and open and incline their hearts; for his drawing, ver. 44, is by this teaching, " they shall be taught of God"— to wit, in the use of means, yet so as they find God in them, as is before explained.

4. It is the privilege of all the elect that in their own measure they are taught by God; and how small soever their knowledge be, yet they are taught what is necessary for bringing them to Christ, and made wise unto salvation; for the promise is universal as to them: " they shall be all taught of God." (See 1 John, ii. 13.) And Christ doth cite it with the copulative " and," whereby it is joined in the prophets with the other promised mercies, to lead us to the study of the rich and many mercies that do accompany it and are given with it.

5. Such as are taught by God in the use of means will not only get an ear to hear, but will not rest on that till they get a heart to understand and learn by their hearing; for they who are taught of God are " every man that hath heard, and hath learned of the Father."

6. God's teaching of his people doth not only illuminate the mind, or give the power of believ-

ing, but doth also give the act and exercise of faith, and certainly bring them to Christ, for every man that hath heard and learned "cometh unto me."

7. No light nor illumination of the mind, nor any other change, will prove a man taught of God unless he be convinced of his own misery and of Christ's mercy, and brought to close with him, and daily to come unto him, and practise this lesson of coming; for this is the evidence of a man that hath heard and learned—he "cometh unto me."

VER. 46. Not that any man hath seen the Father, save he which is of God, he hath seen the Father.

In this verse Christ clears the former testimony, and inference from it, by shewing that God's teaching doth not import that men must first see God and be taught of the Father apart and without him; for not only is the Father invisible to the eye of our body, (which is also true of the Son and Spirit, save in so far as the Son of God was incarnate, and made manifest in the flesh,) but there is also no immediate sight of the mind, or knowledge of the Father, in his essence, will, or ways about saving of sinners, but what Christ the Son hath; and therefore all others must be taught, not immediately by the Father, but mediately in and by him; and Christ's scope in this is not only to clear the mistake that might arise, but to make way for returning to his former doctrine, by leading them to himself, in whom, and by whom alone, they could expect anything the Father promiseth.

DOCTRINES.

1. Men, in hearing and studying sublime and divine truths, have need of much caution and wariness that their carnal and shallow conceptions and imaginations do not beget mistakes and errors about them, and withdraw them from the simplicity of what is revealed; therefore doth Christ find it needful to prevent mistakes about this mystery.

2. God's condescending to stoop to sinners should be entertained with due reverence, and should not hide from us that distance that is betwixt his majesty and our baseness, nor hinder us to keep at due distance with him; therefore, having spoken of his condescending to teach us, he guards that by exalting the Father, and shewing that there is no immediate seeing or knowing of him. Hence it is that even that sweet name, "the Lord thy God," is declared to be a "glorious and fearful name," Deut. xxviii. 58.

3. Not only is the Father invisible, but he doth not reveal himself, or his will concerning the salvation of sinners, immediately unto men, or as Christ seeth and knoweth him and it, but is an incomprehensible God—a light which no man can approach unto, 1 Tim. vi. 16; for saith he, "Not that any man hath seen the Father"—to wit, immediately, or without Christ, and as Christ seeth him, as is after cleared; for albeit he did familiarly converse with, and reveal himself more immediately to some in respect of others, and particularly to Moses, Ex. xxxiii. 11, Num. xii. 8; yet any bodily sight he got was but of his back parts, Exod. xxxiii. 23, and but "the similitude of the Lord," Num. xii. 8, or some external sign of his glorious presence with him, and not a sight of his essence, which only Christ doth immediately see and comprehend. And what he got revealed of God, by his speaking with him mouth to mouth and face to face, it was only through and by Christ, (who is the revealer of the Father,) and far short of that knowledge and sight, and of the way of it, which Christ hath. (See on John, i. 18.)

4. Christ is of the Father another way than either angels, or men, or saints—to wit, neither by creation, nor regeneration or adoption, but by unspeakable generation proper to himself; therefore it is ascribed to him in a singular way that he "is of God."

5. This way of being of the Father makes it Christ's privilege to be singularly and immediately acquainted with him, and to be the teacher and revealer of the Father to all that know him; for "he which is of God, he hath seen the Father;" and this clears that it is by him men are "taught of God," ver. 45. (See Matt. xi. 27.)

VER. 47. Verily, verily, I say unto you, He that believeth on me hath everlasting life.

Christ having digressed thus far (being interrupted with their murmuring) to shew the cause of their distemper, returns now to inculcate and press the former doctrine, taking occasion from the former verse, wherein he hath spoken of his immediate knowledge and seeing of the Father. And, first, he gravely asserts and seals the truth of that doctrine which points out salvation to believers in him. Whence learn—

1. Christ's immediate acquaintance with the Father is forthcoming for believers' good; therefore unto that doctrine, ver. 46, is this subjoined for their comfort.

2. Such as do know and take up Christ rightly will see great cause of trusting him and closing with him. So much, also, doth the dependence of this on the former verse import, that they who take him up to be one who immediately seeth the Father, will find ground to credit this doctrine, whatever they thought of it before.

3. This repetition, and pressing this doctrine, doth hold out how necessary these truths are. 1. That men be taken up with their own salvation, and the way of attaining it, as being the mean to drive away many idle and needless janglings; therefore doth he waive the answer to their sophistry, and direct them how they may attain "everlasting life." 2. It is necessary that men study much that eternal life is to be had only in and by Christ, and will certainly be attained so: this he again repeats here. 3. It is necessary that all false ways to heaven be cried down, and that men look on faith as the only and sure way of taking hold of Christ, and of getting life in him; for to such is the promise again repeated. 4. Men should also study that this offer of life is indefinite, and it will be undoubtedly granted to all who shall or will believe;

for it is indefinite; "he that believeth," be he what he will, or be they never so many. 5. It is also to be seriously studied, that believers have eternal life, in some respects, even here—to wit, in Christ, and by faith in the earnest penny and first fruits; for "he that believeth hath everlasting life."

4. The confirmation of this doctrine, by a double asseveration, teacheth—1. Men are by nature so addicted to the covenant of works, and so loath to be stripped of their own worth and righteousness, that they are hardly persuaded that faith in Christ is the way to life, and very unwilling to embrace and rest in it; for this asseveration imports that there is a controversy in this matter. 2. Corrupt reason will never end this controversy, but we must take us to Christ's word alone to satisfy us; therefore he useth no dispute, but asserteth it on his truth and word. 3. This truth (however controverted) is most certain, and without all controversy, for it is "Verily, verily" true. 4. It is most needful and profitable that sinners believe and close with this truth, and make use of it; therefore doth he inculcate and assert it. 5. Christ alloweth such as believe in him to be very confident and persuaded of his accepting of them, and of their eternal happiness; therefore doth he strongly assert, that " Verily, verily," they have " everlasting life."

Ver. 48. I am that bread of life.

Next, Christ repeats his former doctrine, and confirms the former assertion, by shewing that he is the bread of life. (See ver. 35.)

DOCTRINES.

1. Men by nature are soul-starved, pining away under the want of souls' food; and not only so, but they are so dead that they know nor feel it not; for that he is "the bread of life," imports not only this their pining condition, but their being dead under it. Otherwise, if they truly felt it, it were a sign of a good condition to be sensible of their worst estate.

2. Christ is unto the needy soul all that it can need. He is, by way of excellency, the food of souls, which quickens them when they are dead, and refresheth them, and preserveth the life which he giveth; for saith he, " I am that bread of life."

3. This excellent virtue in Christ to give and preserve life is ground of confidence to a believer, that by closing with him he shall have everlasting life; therefore is this subjoined as a confirmation of the former assertion in ver. 47.

Ver. 49. Your fathers did eat manna in the wilderness, and are dead.

50. This is the bread which cometh down from heaven, that a man may eat thereof, and not die.

Thirdly, Christ illustrates this quickening virtue of this bread by comparing it again with manna, which was but weak, and could not preserve their fathers from death, ver. 49; whereas this bread, which came down from heaven, doth deliver and preserve them from death who eat of it, ver. 50. This that is said of manna, that the fathers who ate thereof are dead, may be understood two ways, and in both respects the opposition will stand firm betwixt it and this bread:—1. That though manna was excellent and pure food, yet it could not so much as save their fathers from bodily death; but this saves the soul from spiritual death; is a remedy against bodily death, and a preservative both of soul and body against everlasting death. 2. That though their fathers did eat manna, as it was spiritual meat, 1 Cor. x. 3, and a sacrament pointing out Christ, yet many of them perished eternally; but the partaker of this bread is sure of everlasting life.

DOCTRINES.

1. A special way to find out the excellency of Christ is to compare him with what seems to have any excellency in it, and then see how far he outshines it; for to this end is he again compared with manna. (See Phil. iii. 7.)

2. Whatever it be that would come in competition with Christ, in the matter of worth, is not only infinitely inferior to him, but should be abased as a thing of naught; therefore, albeit manna in itself was an excellent gift of God, yet when they doated so much upon it, Christ finds it necessary to vilify it thus.

3. It may lessen our estimation of any outward thing, when we consider that it cannot so much as perpetuate itself with us, or us with it; and far more, that it cannot prove a remedy against perdition; for thus doth he abase manna: " Your fathers did eat manna in the wilderness, and are dead."

4. Unbelievers do partake only of the outward part of the sacraments, and that is so far from saving them, that their abuse thereof tends to their perdition; for thus also did they " eat manna," as it was a sacrament, " and are dead."

5. It doth set forth the excellency of our true spiritual food, that it cometh down from heaven, far above the clouds whence manna came; and so is divine food, proclaiming God's love and condescendence to lost man; for " This is the bread which cometh down from heaven."

6. Christ's coming down from heaven, and offering himself in the gospel, is a sufficient invitation and ground for hungry sinners to come and feed upon him; for it " cometh down from heaven, that a man may eat thereof."

7. Christ is such spiritual food as will prove a remedy and preservative against death, both spiritual and eternal, and so swalloweth up any bitterness that is in bodily death; for this bread cometh from heaven, " that a man may eat thereof, and not die."

Ver. 51. I am the living bread which came down from heaven: if any man eat of this bread, he shall live for ever: and the bread that I will give is my flesh, which I will give for the life of the world.

In this verse—1. Christ goeth on to shew the excellency of this bread which he had commended above manna. And speaking of himself in the first person, (whereas in ver. 50

he had spoken of himself, under the name of bread, in the third person,) he declareth that he is that living bread, the partaker whereof shall live eternally in bliss with him. 2. He brings out yet more of his mind concerning this true food, by shewing in what respect he is this food—to wit, by reason of his incarnation, and taking on our flesh, or nature, and by his giving of this a ransom for sin, whence flows the purchase and application of life to his own of all nations ; so that the sense of this is, not that his flesh, eaten in a carnal way, by the mouth of the body, is this living bread, nor yet that his humanity separate from his godhead gives life, (for both these conceits are afterward refuted ;) but the meaning is, that Christ's incarnation and taking on our nature as our kinsman is a channel and conduit, through which the quickening virtue that is in his godhead is communicated unto us ; and his offering up himself in that nature, by his eternal Spirit, doth purchase and merit that this quickening virtue be actually applied and communicated ; and his suffering is, as it were, the preparing of him to be fit meat to us.

From the first part of the verse, learn—1. It is a point to be much and often studied that only Christ is the fountain and feeder of our spiritual life, lest our hearts turn aside to other confidences ; therefore, having spoken of this bread in the third person, he finds it necessary again to assert—" I am the living bread, which came down from heaven."

2. It may confirm our faith that Christ can give and preserve spiritual life, when we consider that he is not a dead creature, as manna was, but himself a living Christ, and fountain of life ; for saith he, " I am the living bread," &c.

3. Christ is not only a remedy against death which came by sin, but he giveth to his own a life of happiness, which lasts eternally ; for so is here declared, he that eats " shall live for ever," —to wit, in glory ; for otherwise reprobates shall live for ever in hell.

4. Christ must be applied by faith, of all those who would find his virtue ; for this bread must be eaten, and then the eater " shall live."

5. As Christ is that, and much better, to the soul that food is to the body, so faith in applying him hath some affinity with eating, as here it is expressed ; for it is as needful to the soul as eating is to the body ; it must be the work of empty and longing souls, as eating is the work of hungry men. Christ must be received and united to us by faith, as meat is let down to be turned into our substance, by eating ; being thus received, he will refresh and strengthen the soul, as meat doth a hungry man ; and faith must be daily exercised, out of new sense of want, as eating is daily renewed by reason of new appetite.

From the latter part of the verse, learn— 1. The whole world, without Christ, is dead in their dispositions, and lying under the sentence of death pronounced in the law ; for so is here imported, in that he must come and give life.

2. The only remedy of this evil, and ransom of lost sinners, is, the incarnation of Christ, and the giving of his human nature to suffer death ; for the bread is my flesh, given " for the life of the world ;" or, to purchase life to sinners dead in sin. In all ages of the world, even before his incarnation, he obtained life to sinners, because of the covenant, wherein he had bound himself to take on our nature, and in it to satisfy justice, which now he hath performed. And albeit Christ in his whole person be Mediator, and the party engaged to satisfy justice, yet it was in his human nature that he underwent the punishment ; and his human nature was supported therein, and his sufferings had worth and merit, because of the union of the human nature with the godhead in one person.

3. Christ is not only the ransom of lost sinners, but the giver thereof also ; he not only willingly offered himself to suffer, but was priest as well as sacrifice—yea, and altar also ; for saith he, " I will give my flesh."

4. Christ came into the world to give, and now hath given, his life for the world—that is, for his own in it, in all ages and nations, who are in themselves as bad as any in the world, and many of them, of all ranks. In these respects it is said—I give my flesh " for the life of the world."

5. That same flesh and human nature of Christ that is offered up a ransom to justice is also the bread of life for souls to feed upon ; for the bread " is my flesh, which I will give for the life of the world." It is Christ's suffering and death from whence our life floweth, and Christ crucified is the carcass on which souls feed. And it is ascribed to his flesh, or human nature, (as his paying the ransom is also ascribed to it,) because, however the quickening virtue and efficacy flow from the godhead to which his flesh is united, yet it is by his incarnation and suffering that this becomes food to us.

6. As Christ must not only be given a ransom for our sins, but also given and applied to us, to quicken and feed our souls, so Christ is the giver of himself both ways ; he gave himself to the Father to purchase life to his own, when many of them were not in being, far less believers, and he doth apply himself unto them for life when they believe ; for both these are expressed here : " The bread that I will give (to wit, by way of application,) is my flesh, which I will give (by way of ransom) for the life of the world."

VER. 52. The Jews therefore strove among themselves, saying, How can this man give us his flesh to eat?

This new point of light which Christ brings forth to clear the way of this spiritual feeding, occasions a further discovery of his hearers, who, understanding his words carnally, did stumble at them, and strive among themselves about them—that is, they did in a fighting, tumultuous way, express their stumbling one to another ; or, it seems that some understood him aright, or gave him charity, others took him up carnally, and stumbled, and so they fell to strive. Whence learn—

1. Carnal men and misbelievers will grow still the longer the worse, when pains are taken upon them, and they do not profit ; for after misbe-

lieving and murmuring, they fall a brawling and contending, they "strove," or fought. All, or most part of them were in a rage at what he had said.

2. Division, and strife, and tumult, may follow upon the doctrine of the best preachers, and yet the doctrine is not to blame, but only men's corruptions; for upon Christ's preaching—"the Jews strove among themselves."

3. Carnal misbelievers do put a carnal sense upon Christ's spiritual words, and so do occasion their own stumbling; for this they stumble at—"How can this man give us his flesh to eat?" They understand it of bodily eating, and this they cannot endure, because it is inhuman to eat man's flesh, and his own body could not be food that way to all the world, far less could it give life. But Christ meant no such thing; they stumble on their own mistakes; and they who assert such a bodily eating of Christ's flesh, and yet do not stumble at it, are more brutish than these Capernaites.

4. The right way to be satisfied about any point of truth or doctrine is to come to Christ himself in his own appointed means; and they who neglect this are justly left to stumble in darkness; for herein they failed: they "strove among themselves" about it; but come not to him for resolution.

VER. 53. Then Jesus said unto them, Verily, verily, I say unto you, Except ye eat the flesh of the Son of man, and drink his blood, ye have no life in you.

Followeth Christ's answer to this, wherein he doth not alter his words, but presseth more and more the necessity of believing on him and closing with him as crucified, under the terms of eating his flesh and drinking his blood. And, 1. He presseth it from their danger if they do it not, ver. 53. 2. He encourageth to it, by shewing the advantage thereof, ver. 54. 3. He proves the real advantage of feeding on him, ver. 55—57. 4. He concludes this sermon with a recapitulation of somewhat said before, concerning the excellency and usefulness of this bread, ver. 58, unto which the evangelist subjoins a designation of the place where Christ preached these things, ver. 59.

In this verse he presseth the necessity of feeding on him, from the consideration of their danger who neglect it, which is, that wanting this souls' food they can have no spiritual life in them, but are dead in their sins. Whence learn—

1. Ministers must not change nor alter their doctrine because of men's humours, but, let people quarrel as they will, they must press it the more that it is opposed; for Christ repeats the same doctrine in the same terms, notwithstanding their discontent.

2. Christ is not ashamed of his stooping to take on our infirmities for our good; therefore doth he design himself the Son of man, not only to clear that his incarnation was the way to make himself ours, and that we may expect good from him who is of our own nature, but to shew

that he thought no shame of it, however they in disdain called him "this man," or "this one," ver. 52.

3. There is a daily spiritual feeding upon Christ by faith, necessary to salvation, as men must eat daily for preservation of life; for this is it which Christ presseth here in this chapter, and not (as some dream) a sacramental eating of his body, far less an eating of his flesh in a corporal manner in the sacrament; for—1. The sacramental eating was not yet instituted and appointed, and therefore could not be here inculcated. 2. This eating is so necessary to salvation and life, as none can have life without it, and all live who get it, ver. 54; but neither of these can be said of sacramental eating; for before it was instituted, they who were saved went to heaven without it—yea, and after it was instituted many (and particularly children) have gone, and go to heaven, without it; and all are not saved who partake of it.

4. Men will never feed on Christ for salvation in earnest, unless they look upon it as a matter of life and death; therefore doth Christ so press it upon them, and that with a "Verily, verily."

5. It is the application of whole Christ, as incarnate, and in his sufferings, that brings life; and Christ being applied will prove complete nourishment; therefore, having spoken before only of his flesh, now he adds his blood; they must eat his flesh "and drink his blood," to shew that they must apply him wholly, and that he will be complete nourishment.

6. Such as do not make spiritual application of nor feed upon Christ crucified have no spiritual life or communion with God, but continue dead in their sins, and shall not partake of eternal life; for "Except ye eat the flesh of the Son of man, and drink his blood, ye have no life in you;" they are already dead, irrecoverably, unless they make use of this remedy.

VER. 54. Whoso eateth my flesh, and drinketh my blood, hath eternal life; and I will raise him up at the last day.

Christ, having thus terrified them, doth now allure them to feed on him by shewing the advantage of doing it—to wit, that they shall have eternal life in the bud, and shall be raised up at the last day fully to enjoy it. Whence learn—

1. When Christ sheweth himself terrible, and threatens us with danger, it is but to fit us for the promise, and stir us up to make his offers welcome; therefore doth he subjoin this sweet encouragement to the former sad certification.

2. The sincere application of Christ brings life, and though such as apply him do yet find a body of death in themselves, yet they are passed from death to life, and do enjoy a begun sight of God and heaven in part; for "Whoso eateth my flesh, and drinketh my blood, hath eternal life" even here.

3. Such as do partake of this begun life will not be satisfied with anything they find within time till they come to full fruition; and Christ will raise them up to enjoy the perfection of it

at the last day; therefore it is added, "and I will raise him up at the last day."

4. Such as close with Christ he will not only perform the promises which they are actually believing and expecting, but will do great things for them when they are not sensible, nor able to co-operate. So much is imported in that he "will raise him up," when his dust is little sensible; nor can be active in that matter.

VER. 55. For my flesh is meat indeed, and my blood is drink indeed.

To confirm the certainty of this encouragement he subjoins several arguments which both prove the assertion and are so many motives to excite them to feed upon him; and, 1. He brings a proof that feeders on him have life from the excellency of this food, that it is not counterfeit but real food, able to confer and maintain life. Whence learn—

1. Albeit men do need bodily refreshments, and (when they do not feed on Christ) will not want their own contentment, yet all these, in comparison of Christ, are but vain and empty; they are but deceitful meat, meat that perisheth; the best of them are but husks, and afford but shadows of that sweetness, refreshment, strength, and life, which he gives. So much doth this expression, "meat indeed," &c., import, that albeit, besides bodily refreshments and the lawful contentment men may have in their outward enjoyments, they will also be putting other things in Christ's room; yet all these are not indeed what they seem to be when compared with him.

2. Whatever shadow of excellency or contentment men find in the creatures, the reality thereof is to be found in Christ, and him only; for whatever they thought of meat and drink, all that, and much better, is to be found here: "My flesh is meat indeed, and my blood is drink indeed."

3. This sweetness and excellency in Christ should allure needy souls to feed upon him; and Christ's commending himself for that end sheweth how well they are allowed so to do; therefore doth he bring in this commendation as a reason and an encouragement to them to come, and an assurance that they shall find life; "for my flesh is meat indeed," &c.

VER. 56. He that eateth my flesh, and drinketh my blood, dwelleth in me, and I in him.

A second motive to feed on him, and reason to prove that feeders have life, is taken from the union that is betwixt Christ and feeders on him; that as meat is turned into the eater's substance, so they and Christ become one; and upon feeding there followeth a mutual inhabitation. Whence learn—

1. Union with Christ doth produce in souls a life begun in grace here and to be perfected in glory; for Christ brings this indwelling as an argument to prove that feeders have life.

2. Albeit such as do but taste of Christ and his goodness may spit out again what they have tasted, yet true feeders will abide in him by constant dependence, and unite themselves to him, that they may have life, and feeding will make up this union; for "he that eateth my flesh, and drinketh my blood, dwelleth in me;" feeding draweth him to abide more and more in Christ, and it makes up this union on the feeder's part.

3. As the true feeder is united to Christ and abides in him, so Christ also doth abide in him by constant influence and quickening virtue, to make him live, and so the inhabitation is mutual, for he "dwelleth in me, and I in him."

VER. 57. As the living Father hath sent me, and I live by the Father: so he that eateth me, even he shall live by me.

A third reason proving that feeders have life, and that life flows from union with Christ, is taken from Christ's union with his Father, and his being sent by him to do the office of a Mediator; wherein he declareth that as the Father hath sent him to be a Mediator and soul-feeder to believers, and as the Father who sent him liveth of himself, and he (the second person) liveth by the Father, so they who feed on him shall live by him. Of this doctrine see, in part, on chap. v. 26.

DOCTRINES.

1. It is a truth to be much pressed, and wherein we have need to be well rooted, that life and spiritual well-being is to be had only in Christ embraced by faith, both as purchaser and applier; therefore is this again inculcated: he that eateth me shall live by me.

2. Christ is such a fountain of virtue and life that even the dead may expect life by closing with him; for life, or to live by him, is promised to feeders.

3. Such is a believer's interest in Christ that whatever Christ hath shall be forthcoming for him, as he needs it; for so doth the argument run, that as he liveth so they shall live. (See John, xiv. 19.)

4. The Father's sending of Christ into the world to be the Redeemer and Saviour of his people is a sure pledge that feeders on him shall live; seeing he will not frustrate the Father's end, but will do the work he is sent about; therefore is this used as an argument—the Father hath sent me, &c.

5. As the Father hath a fountain of life in himself, and the Son hath the same life communicated to him, with his essence, from the Father, and this dwelleth in the man Christ by the personal union, so this life of the Father and Christ is a pledge that believers shall live; for "as the living Father hath sent me, and I live by the Father; so he that eateth me, even he shall live by me." Believers' lives must be sure for which there is such a pledge, and that fulness of the godhead and life that dwells in the man Christ cannot but put life and preserve life in all that close with him; yea, Christ's living by the Father is not only a pledge of our life, but our life holds also some proportion or similitude to his; for as he hath life communicated by eternal generation, so by regeneration we are made par-

takers of the divine nature, 2 Pet. i. 4—to wit, in respect of qualities, as he subsists in his life, as man, by virtue of the personal union with the godhead, so do we live by virtue of the mystical inhabitation or union with God by his Spirit; and as he, as man, had a created life here, and now lives gloriously at the Father's right hand, so by the gracious operation of God's Spirit we shall be made to conform to Christ, and partake of the same life for kind.

6. Albeit in our application of Christ we must begin at his cross and death, yet his whole person is forthcoming to make believers live; therefore, in place of his flesh and blood, he speaks generally, " he shall live by me," pointing at his whole person.

VER. 58. This is that bread which came down from heaven: not as your fathers did eat manna, and are dead : he that eateth of this bread shall live for ever.

59. These things said he in the synagogue, as he taught in Capernaum.

In the conclusion of this discourse, 1. Christ repeateth his former doctrine, pointing out his excellency as bread of life from his divine original, his excellency above manna, and the effects of feeding on him. 2. John designs the place where Christ preached this sermon, which was their synagogue at Capernaum, or the place where they of that city did assemble (as the word signifieth) for reading the law, and ordinary moral worship. This erecting of synagogues in the several places of the land hath been of old appointed by God for the people's edification, albeit they behoved to perform ceremonial worship in the temple at Jerusalem. (See Acts, xv. 21, with Psalm lxxiv. 8.) And the designation of the place is recorded here, to shew that at this Christ closed his sermon, and that what is after recorded was only occasional, and upon their removal, or after they were gone thence.

From ver. 58, learn—1. The blind and corrupt hearts of men are not easily brought to close with saving truths, but either they do reject them or do soon forget and let them slip : so much doth this inculcating of the commendation of this heavenly bread import.

2. It is absolutely necessary that men do not halt nor hesitate in the matter of closing with Christ and feeding upon him, but that over all impediments they take up their need of him, and make use of him accordingly; therefore it is so much borne upon them again and again.

3. Ministers must not be weary to press ill learned truths, but their inculcating them is one mean to make them be received; for therefore doth Christ tell the same things over again.

4. One main impediment unto the success of truth is men's natural inclination to their old errors and principles, and their unwillingness to quit them; for so is here imported, that Moses and the manna which came from heaven did so stick with them that they could dream of nothing so excellent, and therefore he takes pains to refute this.

5. Christ being known in his true excellency and worth, both in respect of his original and the benefits which are conferred by him, will be found far above anything men doat on, and richly able to make them happy; therefore is he held out here as come down from heaven, and making men to live for ever, neither of which could be said of manna, as hath already been cleared.

From ver. 59, learn—1. When the Lord brings a nation into visible covenant with himself, it is his will that care be had to keep up his worship, and to spread the knowledge of his name in all the corners of the land; for to this end did their many synagogues tend.

2. It is the duty of Christ's servants to take hold of all occasions within the compass of their calling to publish truth and work upon souls; for therefore did Christ teach in the synagogue of Capernaum, that he might take occasion to speak to many when they convened there.

3. However men disrelish Christ's doctrine, yet it is truth, and so innocent and harmless that it needs not seek a corner, but may be avowed; therefore he went publicly to " the synagogue" with it. (See Matt. xxvi. 55; John, xviii. 20.)

4. Christ takes notice of places where he hath preached, and what means he sends to such and such places; that as hereby he testifieth his respects, so their conviction may be greater if they bring not forth answerable fruits; therefore is it recorded that this was done " in Capernaum," where he often taught, but with small fruit, Matt. xi. 23.

VER. 60. Many therefore of his disciples, when they had heard this, said, This is an hard saying; who can hear it?

Unto the end of the chapter we have the events and consequents that followed on this sermon; and the first is, that they carp at his doctrine, and cannot digest it, ver. 60; and he doth vindicate and clear what he had said, ver. 61—65.

In this verse their hard censure of this doctrine of Christ's is recorded; they declare it to be intolerable, blasphemous, and so absurd that none could hear it. And this is recorded to be the practice even of many of his disciples, whereby we are not to understand the twelve apostles, who yet stay with him, ver. 67, nor yet is it to be understood of those seventy disciples who were all teachers, Luke, x. 1; but it was such as had given up their names to him, to follow him and learn of him. And so this sermon stumbled not only the common multitude at Capernaum, or those who followed him over the sea for loaves, but even many of his ordinary followers mistook it.

DOCTRINES.

1. When Christ hath taken most pains to inculcate and clear saving and necessary truths, yet ordinarily the most part will never make them welcome; for they were " many" who stumbled —to wit, in comparison of those to whom his doctrine was savoury.

2. Professions of visible interest in Christ will not always prove sound to the end, but the most

part of such professors will, sooner or later, when their trial and tentation comes, stumble at him, his way and truth; for " many of his disciples" did here miscarry.

3. Carnal hearts, as they do not understand, so they cannot digest the spiritual truths of Christ; and their corrupt disposition disrelishing the word, is a main stumbling block unto them; for this was the cause of their miscarriage here—They said, " This is an hard saying," or, intolerable. It was not so indeed, but as they understood and took it carnally; and the blame was not in the doctrine, but in their corrupt taste, which made what was sweet bitter to them.

4. Carnal men, and such as get no good of hearing, are in peril to grow still the longer the worse, and at last impatient of hearing at all; for they who murmured and strave before, come now to this: " who can hear it?"

5. Corrupt men do measure all others by themselves, and their pride and self-love makes them imagine that Christ and his truth can relish no better with any than it doth with them; therefore say they, " who can hear it?" thinking none could like it more than they, wherein they were far mistaken, ver. 68.

VER. 61. When Jesus knew in himself that his disciples murmured at it, he said unto them, Doth this offend you?

Followeth Christ's answer to their murmuring, which seems to have been spoken after they were now come out of the synagogue. In it he reprehends their stumbling, ver. 61, clears his doctrine, ver. 62, 63, and points out the true cause of all their mistakes, ver. 64, 65. In this verse it is recorded that Christ perfectly knew and took notice of their murmuring, and doth challenge and reprove their unjust and causeless stumbling. Whence learn—

1. It is Christ's prerogative to know most secret things in himself, neither needing sight nor information, nor yet any divine revelation extrinsical to his person, such as the prophets had; but by virtue of the union of his human nature to the godhead, his human nature by revelation from the godhead is made to know what is needful, though it be not made omniscient of itself; for " Jesus knew in himself," when they had gone aside, and discoursed upon this matter apart from him.

2. Christ makes use of this his knowledge to take notice what his followers are doing, and what fruits follow upon his doctrine and preaching to them, as here we see.

3. Christ doth take notice of, and is offended with, the corrupt affections of men, and the secret outbreakings thereof, how secretly soever they be conveyed; therefore doth he reprove that which he " knew in himself" they were guilty of.

4. Stumbling, and being offended at Christ's doctrine and dispensations, whether by the weak or malicious, is a great impediment to the success of the gospel, and a great fault in men; therefore doth he reprove that they were offended, or scandalized, and stumbled.

5. Murmuring and repining, or quarrelling, at that which Christ saith or doth, is a sad evidence of stumbling, and of hazard of falling; therefore from their murmuring he gathers their being offended.

6. When Christ's followers and disciples do stumble and take offence, the fault is the greater; therefore saith he to his disciples, " Doth this offend you?" God hath taken most pains on them, they have professed the contrary, and their stumbling giveth more offence, and therefore is the more odious.

7. Albeit many stumble at the doctrine of Christ; some at the doctrine of the cross, others at the depth of his decrees; some at the strict doctrine of holiness and renouncing our own righteousness, and some at the simplicity of the doctrine of the gospel; yet there is no just ground of offence in any of these: and in particular, it is a causeless and sinful stumbling when men offend at the sweet doctrine of closing with and feeding upon Christ; therefore saith he, with indignation, " Doth this offend you?"—to wit, my doctrine, and in particular, this sweet and easy doctrine, formerly taught.

VER. 62. What and if ye shall see the Son of man ascend up where he was before?

In this and the following verse Christ doth clear his doctrine, at which they stumbled so much. And first, whereas they stumbled that he who appeared so much in outward baseness should say he came down from heaven, verse 41, 42; he declareth that his ascension into heaven should prove the truth of that to their conviction and shame. And this also helps to clear their mistake about eating of his flesh. It doth not necessarily infer that they should be witnesses of his ascension, but that he should indeed ascend, and that the truth and certainty of this should shame them for their base thoughts of him. Likewise, while it is said he shall " ascend up where he was before," it is not to be understood as if his godhead did change place, and leave heaven at his incarnation; for however he stooped, in respect of state, to appear on earth in our nature, yet he is still in heaven, John, iii. 13. Nor is it the meaning that his human nature did descend from heaven, seeing in respect of that he ascended; but the meaning is, that the ascension of his human nature, by local change of place, should clearly prove that he came from heaven in respect of his divine nature's stooping to be clothed with our flesh; and both these two are spoken of the whole person in respect of the personal union, though they be verified but in the one or other nature. Further it is to be marked that Christ's ascension doth prove his godhead, and that he came down from heaven; to wit, not simply, for Enoch and Elijah did ascend to heaven, who yet were not there before, but in regard that he did arise and ascend by his own power, John, ii. 19; x. 18; Psalm lxviii. 18; John, xx. 17.

DOCTRINES.

1. Albeit men will not at present believe the excellency and glory of Christ, yet it will be discovered, and they may see it to their convic-

tion and shame, either in mercy or in judgment; for so doth he intimate, that they should see their folly when they "see the Son of man ascend up." (See John, viii. 28; Luke, xii. 22, 67, 69.)

2. Christ's ascending into heaven is a clear proof of his godhead, and that he descended from heaven in his incarnation; therefore doth he confirm the one by the other. (See Rom. i. 4; Eph. iv. 8, 9.)

3. Christ's ascension into heaven in his human nature is a sufficient refutation of all carnal conceptions of partaking of Christ, or of eating his flesh; therefore also doth he bring in this, when they stumbled at eating of his flesh, to shew that his ascension into heaven might refute all such conceits.

VER. 63. It is the spirit that quickeneth; the flesh profiteth nothing : the words that I speak unto you, they are spirit, and they are life.

In the next place, Christ clears that which chiefly offended them, concerning his flesh and the quickening power, and the eating thereof. This he clears in two assertions: 1. "It is the spirit that quickeneth; the flesh profiteth nothing." This may be understood as a clearing of what he said concerning the eating of his flesh, that it was not a carnal, fleshly eating of him that could profit anything, but it is a spiritual eating of him by faith, that bringeth that quickening and life of which he hath spoken. But it seemeth rather to clear what he had said concerning the quickening power of his flesh and human nature, and by " spirit" and " flesh" we are to understand here his divine and human nature, as Rom. i. 3, 4; 1 Pet. iii. 18. And so the meaning is, that however much had been spoken of life to be given by partaking of his flesh, yet this is not to be understood of his flesh considered by itself, and without his godhead, as they conceived him to be a mere man; but all the quickening virtue that is ascribed to his flesh, or human nature, doth flow from his godhead, to which it is united. And this also doth condemn their conceit of bodily eating his flesh, seeing a spirit, without which the flesh profiteth nothing, cannot be eaten. 2. The second assertion is, " the words that I speak unto you, they are spirit, and they are life," wherein Christ directly refutes their stumbling at what he spake of eating his flesh, which they understood in a carnal sense, of eating with the mouth of the body. He declares that these words are not to be taken in a carnal, gross sense, but in a spiritual way, and being so taken, and Christ spiritually laid hold upon, the doctrine will not be found hard, but very refreshful, and to contain that which brings life to the weary soul. And so the spirit is taken for what is spiritual, John, iii. 16.

DOCTRINES.

1. Albeit Christ's flesh and human nature was quickened in itself, and have quickening virtue to merit, communicate, and preserve life in believers, yet the godhead is the fountain from which all this floweth, and that which giveth

merit and efficacy to all his sufferings and obedience; for " it is the spirit that quickeneth."

2. Such as do not look on Christ's flesh as the flesh and blood of the Son of God, nor do lay hold on him by faith as God incarnate, that they may attain life, but do look on him as mere man, or as one whose flesh is to be eaten in a bodily manner, will never find that quickening virtue in and from him which he declares to be in himself; for " the flesh profiteth nothing"—to wit, in this respect. It is true, as God incarnate, his flesh is the very price of life, the first receptacle of our spiritual life, and (being laid hold on by faith) the conduit to convey life to us; but being considered as a mere man, and his flesh to be eaten bodily (as the Capernaites did), in that respect it profiteth nothing; for no mere man can give life, nor merit it, to lost sinners; and outward bodily feeding cannot be refreshment nor food to souls.

3. Scripture is the best commentary to itself, in regard what is spoken more darkly in one place is cleared in another; for so doth Christ expound the words he spake.

4. What Christ hath formerly spoken of eating his flesh is to be understood spiritually, of eating by faith, and not of bodily eating; for so doth Christ declare : " The words that I speak unto you, they are spirit."

5. None but they who understand Christ's words spiritually will find them lively in operation; for being " spirit," or taken spiritually, then " they are life," and then only.

6. The doctrine of the gospel, pointing out salvation by faith in Christ crucified for sinners, is both spirit and life. It is a doctrine of a spiritual nature, the instrument and mean whereby the Spirit worketh and communicates himself, Gal. iii. 2, and tends to make us spiritual; and by it is life revealed, offered, conferred, and carried on to perfection by the Spirit; for thus it is commended: his words, "they are spirit, and they are life." (See Rom. viii. 2; 2 Cor. iii. 6.)

VER. 64. But there are some of you that believe not. For Jesus knew from the beginning who they were that believed not, and who should betray him.

65. And he said, Therefore said I unto you, that no man can come unto me, except it were given unto him of my Father.

Christ, having cleared his doctrine, doth point out the true cause of their ignorance and mistakes, and of their stumblings at his doctrine— to wit, their unbelief, (which, because it was a peremptory censure, therefore John brings the ground of it from the depth of Christ's divine foreknowledge,) ver. 64; and withal he brings to their remembrance what he had said, ver. 44, intimating he had spoken it with an eye to their corrupt dispositions, and to let them see that it was nothing in him, but want of grace in them, that made this distance and stumbling.

From ver. 64, learn—1. Whoever they be that stumble at Christ's word as unsavoury, the true cause thereof is in themselves, whatever they pretend; therefore doth Christ retort that imputation cast upon his word, ver. 60, as flowing from the distemper of their own heart.

2. Such as do not understand Christ's doctrine spiritually, nor do find it spirit and life in operation, have their own unbelief to blame for it; therefore doth he assign that as the cause of all their distemper: "there are some of you that believe not." This darkens the understanding, and deadens the heart also. (See Heb. iv. 2, 3.)

3. Christ would have his servants very tender and careful that in discovering of faults among hearers they do not discourage any who are innocent, nor any who have a desire to be healed. So much doth his own practice teach, in that, though they were many who were wrong here, yet he propounds the reproof very gently: "there are some of you," &c., not only to intimate that some were free, but to guard against the deterring of all by a general rebuke.

4. Christ's reproofs and admonitions from his word should be looked upon as flowing from good grounds and certain knowledge beyond any that the creature hath, or can attain unto; therefore doth John vindicate this seeming hard censure of Christ's from the imputation of rashness, by shewing that "Jesus knew from the beginning," &c.

5. As all unbelievers are in a dangerous condition, so traitors and enemies to Christ and his doctrine, under pretence of friendship, are among the first and worst of unbelievers; therefore albeit Judas was an unbeliever also, yet he is set alone here; Jesus knew "who they were that believed not, and who should betray him."

6. As there are many of those who do hear the gospel who neither do nor will believe on Christ, and some who will turn treacherous enemies, so Christ is not surprised thereby, but doth perfectly foreknow what men will prove; for he "knew from the beginning" all this, as being God, to whom all things are known from everlasting.

7. As there may be, and ofttimes are, very corrupt men in Christ's company and among the visible societies of his people, so it is his will that men be admitted to continue therein so long as they profess external subjection, without making inquiry into their spiritual estate; therefore Christ, when he judgeth these men, giveth a reason of it from his divine knowledge, to warn all mere creatures that they presume not to pry into these secrets; and albeit he knew them well enough, yet he never rejected them till first they bewrayed themselves.

From ver. 65, learn—1. Christ hath very grave and important reasons for what he saith, though we ofttimes do not see them. So much doth he make known concerning his former doctrine, though they had little considered it: "He said, Therefore said I unto you," &c.

2. Albeit hearers be ofttimes so stupid and blinded with self-love that they never lay doctrine to heart unless it be said, Thou art the man, (as we see even in David,) yet it is the duty of all so to hear as they make particular application of what is heard; for so much doth Christ point at while he tells that what he spake in general was with an eye to them.

3. It is a truth, to be much and frequently studied, that men are naturally impotent of themselves to come to Christ, and that they have rather cause to mourn under the sense of this, when they close not with Christ's doctrine, than to quarrel him; therefore doth Christ repeat this doctrine over again.

4. Such as do not flee to Christ, and embrace him in the sense of their misery, are a ready prey for all evil courses; therefore doth Christ lead them up to this as the cause of all their distempers.

5. Such as get power and strength to come to Christ do not receive it according to any merit in them, but by free gift; therefore is that drawing, ver. 44, explained from the cause thereof—"except it were given unto him of my Father;" wherein is held out that both power to come and their very actual coming is God's free gift. (See Eph. ii. 8; Phil. i. 29, ii. 13; Rom. vii. 18, 19.)

VER. 66. From that time many of his disciples went back, and walked no more with him.

Followeth another and worse event, that followed upon this sermon, even the open apostasy of many of his followers, ver. 66, with Christ's confirmation of his apostles, and warning them of the unsoundness of some of themselves, to the end of the chapter. In this verse it is declared that even these disciples (of whom, ver. 60) are so far from being taken with Christ's doctrine, or from listening to his vindication thereof when they murmured at it, that they are the more irritated, and do make open apostasy. Whence learn—

1. As there are times of visible flocking unto Christ, so there are times of trial, wherein there will be as great scattering and apostasy from professions; for so are we here taught, that many "went back," and (as it should seem, comparing ver. 67) all that were present, but the twelve.

2. Christ's doctrine is a touchstone of true profession, and such as do not profit by his preaching, nor grow better by his reproofs or discoveries of their evils, and the remedies thereof, will still grow worse till they make open apostasy; for it was "from that time" they "went back"—that is, after he had preached himself unto them, and had discovered that the true cause of their murmuring was only in themselves, and that this could be remedied only by God.

3. Albeit such as have in sincerity given up their names to Christ will neither totally nor finally fall away, yet not only may they make a foul defection for a time and in part, but visible professors may totally fall away; for "many of his disciples went back," &c.,—that is, many unsound professors did altogether renounce him, and albeit, it may be, some did again recover their feet, yet no mention is made of it here.

4. Men's former professions and engagements to Christ and his truth will aggravate their apostasy, and add to the sin thereof; therefore also it is marked that they were disciples who "went back." (See Gal. iii. 3; iv. 15.)

5. Albeit unsound professors seem to cast the world and their old fashions behind their back for awhile, yet their heart is not really weaned from them, nor are they really cast out; and when temptation cometh, and they find not that in Christ which they expected, they will turn back to their old vomit again; therefore it is said they " went back," or to the things behind them. So dangerous is it for professors to have Satan gone out, and not cast out, Luke. xi. 24; to have anything wherein to delight beside Christ, when they close with him; or to have these things which they seemed formerly to slight bearing bulk again in their eyes, however they may seem to palliate it with becoming more wise and prudent than at first they were.

6. As it is the duty of all professors to hold communion with Christ, and converse with him, and publicly to own him in the midst of a perverse generation, (without which greatest pretences of secret friendship is of no avail, John, xii. 42, 43,) so when men do quit this practice, and do not wait upon the ordinances as they were wont, it is an undeniable sign of woeful apostasy, whatever they pretend to; for it is the proof of their apostasy, " they walked no more with him," nor did publicly own him, nor wait upon his ministry.

VER. 67. Then said Jesus unto the twelve, Will ye also go away?

Upon this sad event and defection of many, Christ confirms his twelve apostles, and yet warns them that all who were unsound had not gone away at this defection. The way of confirming them is by a question, posing them concerning their resolution, which draws out an ample confession and testimony of Peter, in name of the rest.

From Christ's question in this verse, learn—
1. Christ is not much troubled, though never so many of the rotten crowd do desert him; therefore he never speaks a word to them, but only to the twelve.

2. When many are making defection it may so shake even the soundest that they will need warning and confirmation; therefore doth he put them to it, if they " also" would " go away?" Even the godly have seeds of the same evils which draw others away; evil example is very forcible, especially when it is general; and sin is very infectious, especially when it is carried on with plausible pretexts; and therefore it is no wonder if men be in hazard in such a case; and backsliders are (beside their own defection) guilty of weakening the hands of others.

3. Albeit Christ stand not in need of any followers, nor needs he be anxious though all should forsake him, yet he will take pains to confirm and keep such as are his own; therefore doth he deal with " the twelve."

4. The nearer Christ's relations be to any, and the more proofs of love they have received, he will take it the worse to be forsaken by them, and this should be a mean to keep such from defection; therefore saith he, " Will ye also go away?" intimating that their departure would touch him more than what all the rest had done, and therefore they should guard against it.

5. Whatever respect Christ have to any of his people, yet he will detain none against their will, but will have them a willing people who follow him; for this cause it is that he puts it to themselves, Will ye go away? to intimate that he will not accept of them (though no more were left) except they be willing; which yet is not to be understood as if he left it simply arbitrary to them to do as they listed in it, but his speech insinuates a reproof of them that went away, and therefore warns them to take heed they do not follow them. It is also a mean which he sanctifieth unto them, and ties them faster, while he seems to cast the reins loose, and withal he who requires willing service doth give to his own to be willing.

VER. 68. Then Simon Peter answered him, Lord, to whom shall we go? thou hast the words of eternal life.

69. And we believe and are sure that thou art that Christ, the Son of the living God.

Followeth the apostle's answer to this question, given by Peter in the name of the rest; wherein, 1. By a contrary question he professeth their constancy, and that they knew none beside to whom they could or would go, and therefore would adhere to him. 2. He gives reasons for this his assertion, taken from Christ's sweet and precious doctrine, ver. 68, and from their faith and assurance concerning his offices and person, that he is the true Messiah, the Son of God, ver. 69.

From ver. 68, learn—1. Were they never so many who make defection from Christ, and think little of his company, yet there will still some be found of another stamp, as here we see in Peter.

2. Men may be of a more forward and ready spirit in some outward actings for Christ than others, who yet are as honest as they; therefore Peter appears with the first, not because he was the eldest professor, (for Andrew was called before him,) nor yet because he had more faith and love to Christ than the rest; for we may conceive that (at least) the beloved disciple came not behind with him; but it flowed from his forward spirit and temper, which as sometimes it made him foremost in good, so at other times it drove him as far wrong, that he might be humbled.

3. As hypocrites may lurk for a time undiscerned by others, even in shaking times, so true grace makes men charitable of others, so long as they bewray not their unsoundness by visible effects; and it is a sweet companion of gracious forwardness and zeal, to be charitable, and not when men are rigid censurers of others; therefore forward Peter answers in name of all, (we,) not secluding Judas. And however his charity was mistaken, yet he could judge no otherwise of him, seeing he stayed still when the rest went away. (See 1 Cor. xiii. 7.)

4. Man since the fall is so empty and poor a creature that he must have somewhat without him to delight and rest in for happiness; and if

he do not choose Christ he will put some other thing in his place; for Peter's question imports that if they went away from Christ they behoved to go to some other: " to whom shall we go?"

5. Such as have a mind to quit Christ had need to consider first where they will get a better master, and that, change when they will, they will surely change for the worse; for " to whom shall we go?" saith he, as never looking for such entertainment anywhere as they had with him.

6. True disciples, and such as know Christ's singular excellency, will not endure to hear of any separation from him; (for this question imports his abhorrence of going away from such a Lord to any other;) and all they who would close and walk with him sincerely should study and learn to know him to be the chief and most excellent of choices.

7. Such as would stand fast in times of defection should have frequent thoughts of eternity, and of the life that is laid up there for such as are sincere; therefore Peter fixes his eye on " eternal life," and where that may be found which leads to it when he is about the choice of a master.

8. The doctrine of Christ and of the gospel is the only doctrine of eternal life; it not only manifests and brings to light that there is an eternal life, and makes offer of it, but it points out the only right purchase of it and way to it; it is the mean of regeneration and begetting of faith, and being embraced, doth give a right unto eternal life, and the first-fruits of it, till they come to full possession; therefore is his doctrine called " the words of eternal life." And in all these respects it is preferred above the doctrine of all the philosophers, and in most of them not only above the corrupt doctrine of those times wherein Christ lived, but even above the law of Moses, as it is considered in opposition to him or without him.

9. Whatever be the verdict that corrupt men give of Christ's doctrine, yet sincere disciples will judge of it according as it is, and as he accounts of it; for what others accounted " an hard saying," ver. 60, Peter reckons to be " words of eternal life," according to Christ's own verdict, ver. 63.

10. Such as are seriously minding eternal life will cleave to the true doctrine that leads to it, and will not abandon it, nor the messengers thereof, no, not in times of greatest defection; for it is one reason why they will not leave him, not only because he is the Messiah, but he hath " the words of eternal life."

11. It is Christ's special prerogative, and the reason of sincere professors' cleaving to him, that he hath the words of eternal life in a peculiar manner, being not only the dispenser and minister thereof in the days of his flesh, and that in a way of authority, sweetness, and efficacy proper to himself, but being also the purchaser of these glad tidings, and being he who gives commission to all that preach them, and he who gives efficacy thereunto, to make them the power of God to salvation; for Peter, in all their names, professeth that they do cleave to him

as he who, in all these respects, hath " the words of eternal life."

From verse 69, learn—1. It is the duty of sincere professors as to cleave to all truth, so in particular to avow all the truths controverted in the time, of what importance soever they be; therefore doth Peter, beside the excellency of Christ's doctrine, confess him also in his person and office, which were the truths then opposed, and though they be fundamental truths, yet were accounted but little by the opposers thereof.

2. The more men know of Christ, they will find the more bands to tie them to him, and the more preservatives against defection from him; and particularly, the true knowledge of his office and person may invite men to cleave to him, forsake him who will; therefore Peter subjoins this as a new argument.

3. It is not bare and naked knowledge of what Christ is that will tie men's hearts to him unless they embrace what they know by faith; therefore Peter gives it as a reason of his constancy, " we believe that thou art that Christ;" and albeit this seem to be nothing but an historical assent to what the devils do confess, yet as it is joined with Peter's resolution, " to whom shall we go?" as the ground of it, it is an act of saving faith; for a firm faith of the person and office of Christ, with adherence unto him and recumbency on him, is the exercise of saving faith.

4. It is not reason that can take up the mysteries concerning Christ's person, incarnation, and offices, but faith must close with them upon divine revelation; therefore saith he, " we believe" this.

5. As true faith and saving knowledge go together, so the knowledge which is gathered by experience and observation of events according to the word is a great help to faith; for saith he, we believe, and have known, as it is in the original. As there is a seeing, or knowledge, that goeth before and with faith, ver. 40, (for albeit many things revealed be in themselves mysteries and above the reach of our capacity as to the nature, reason, and manner of them, yet faith knoweth that these things are, and so closeth with them,) so this is an experimental knowledge following on faith, wherein, by considering the accomplishment of prophecies concerning the Messiah, in his person, they were experimentally confirmed in what they believed.

6. It ought and will endear Christ to all true disciples and make them cleave to him, that he is the only true Messiah promised to the fathers, who is appointed by the Father to exercise the office of a king, priest, and prophet, to his church, and who is anointed with the Spirit above measure for that end, from whom his people may expect the fruits of all these offices, the participation of his fulness and communion with him in his dignity; for this is a reason of Peter's resolution: " thou art that Christ," that promised Messiah and anointed one.

7. It doth further heighten the estimation of Christ in the hearts of believers, and is a strong bar against defection from him, that he is the Son of the living God by eternal generation and communication of the same essence; and so he is the only excellent choice, is able for all his

offices, and to give worth unto his sufferings; and as he hath a fountain of life communicated from the Father, so he is able to beget and preserve life in his people. All this is imported in that other reason, thou art " the Son of the living God."

> VER. 70. Jesus answered them, Have not I chosen you twelve, and one of you is a devil?
>
> 71. He spake of Judas Iscariot the son of Simon: for he it was that should betray him, being one of the twelve.

Christ having drawn out this confession, doth correct Peter's charity, and warn them of a yet sadder defection of one of those twelve whom he had chosen to be apostles; unto which John subjoins a declaration, shewing who it was that Christ spake of. Whence learn—

1. In times wherein men appear very forward and resolute, when others are turning away, Christ alloweth them not to be secure, but would have them warned and sensible of the hazard of more and worse defection; therefore, when a few of many have now stood, Christ seeth fit to tell them they were not all sound.

2. Albeit Christ do approve of men's charitable judgment of others, yet that judgment is not still according to verity, nor to be built upon by hypocrites; therefore, albeit Christ do not reprove Peter's charity, yet he sheweth that it is mistaken of one in the number.

3. Very general apostasies, reducing sincere professors to a small number, will not always separate all the chaff from the wheat; but when multitudes make defection, and only a very few do stand, there may be yet hypocrites and traitors even among these; for Judas went not yet away with the stream of this defection, because he kept the bag yet, and his tentation was not yet come.

4. As there is no society in the earth so holy but it is possible some of them may be wicked, yea, and they may have an eminent spiritual calling and office in the church who yet are but wicked hypocrites, and will totally and finally fall away and betray Christ, so the eminency of men's office and employment renders their defection the more odious; and particularly, apostasy is very odious in ministers; therefore saith he, " Have not I chosen you twelve, and one of you is a devil?" whereby, partly, he insinuates that their election to an office was no ground to build upon that they were all sound; and partly he aggravates his defection from this, and therefore puts it to be considered by them, by this question. It is not needful to inquire why Christ made choice only of twelve, and would have that number filled up when Judas went to his place, Acts, i. 21, 22, &c.; it sufficeth us, that as Israel, according to the flesh, sprang from twelve patriarchs, so he would have his Israel in the spirit collected and brought to him by twelve apostles.

5. Such as, being entrusted by Christ, do not only make apostasy but turn persecutors and traitors to him, are not only adversaries to him, as Satan is, but do resemble the devil (who is a liar and murderer) in cruelty, under pretext of friendship, are acted and possessed by him, and are odious unto God, as he is; therefore the traitor gets this name, " one of you is a devil," because he " should betray him," which is far different from what he said to Peter when he called him Satan, Matt. xvi. 23; for it was only a fit of tentation in him, wherein Satan abused his corruption and tongue for the time; but Satan had a dwelling and dominion in Judas.

6. How closely soever hypocrites and traitors carry themselves among God's people yet they will not deceive Christ, but he knoweth them well enough, though all should give them charity; for so much doth he declare here.

7. Albeit Christ, when he warns the societies of his people, would have all to try and watch over themselves, yet such as are sincere should have no thoughts that he is suspicious of them or doth not approve of them; for both these appear here; he warns them in general of the unsoundness of one, not naming him, not only because he would let him discover himself and would not hinder that work wherein he was to be an instrument, but that they might all search themselves; and yet John names him particularly, and for what cause Christ spake so of him; and this he did, not only to free another apostle called Judas also, Luke, vi. 16, (and therefore he describes the traitor from his parentage and from his country, Iscariot, or a man of that city Kerioth, Josh. xv. 25, or, as some take it to be, a Syriac word, and render it a purse-bearer, and so it is a designation of him from his particular employment in Christ's company, John, xii. 6; xiii. 29,) but also to shew that this general doctrine did reflect upon none of the rest of the apostles' integrity.

CHAPTER VII.

IN this chapter, John continueth his narration of Christ's life and doctrine, recording first, that to avoid the fury of those in Judea he continued still in Galilee, after the former sermon, till the feast of tabernacles, ver. 1; secondly, that he refused to go up with his friends to that feast, ver. 2—9; thirdly, that at last he went up, ver. 10, with what he did, and what occurred concerning him at that feast; and namely, 1. The people's carriage and speeches about him before he shewed himself, ver. 11—13. 2. His preaching in the mid-days of the feast, and his conferences and debates with the people and inhabitants of Jerusalem, and his hazard from the Pharisees thereupon, ver. 14—36. 3. His sweet sermon on the last day of the feast, with the effects thereof, and the confusion that arose in the council of the rulers about him, from ver. 37, to the end.

> VER. 1. After these things Jesus walked in Galilee: for he would not walk in Jewry, because the Jews sought to kill him.

In this verse it is shewed that after these things, which are mentioned in the former chapter, Christ abode still " in Galilee," avoiding the fury of those in Judea, who sought to slay him because of that work he had long since done, in curing the impotent man on the sabbath day, chap. v., as appears from ver. 19 and 23 of this chapter. So the verse sheweth the connexion of the history that Christ stayed away from that passover mentioned chap. vi. 4, and continued in Galilee till the feast of tabernacles, of which, ver. 2; and it contains also a brief transition of what occurred betwixt the former sermon and that feast, wherein John briefly passeth over many things which are recorded at length by other evangelists, that he may dwell on those things which they had omitted.

DOCTRINES.

1. Christ is not bound to any place, were it never so eminent, but he may abandon it, and betake himself to another, according as he seeth cause; for he forsakes eminent Jewry, and betakes himself to base Galilee; and the reason why he stayed there when he left Jewry was because he was the minister of the circumcision, and therefore behoved to be still in some of the places where Israel dwelt, such as Galilee was.

2. Whatever may be the suspicions of men concerning Christ's proceedings, yet he hath wise reasons which may, and will, justify them all; for whereas it should seem that he should rather have conversed where the learned rabbis were than among the simple Galileans, and his remaining in corners might give men occasion to suspect the candour of his proceedings, yet the reason he giveth being considered, doth sufficiently evince that he had just cause for what he did.

3. A violent death is the least that Christ and his faithful servants may expect for their good offices to a wicked world, if it were not prevented; for " the Jews" (or men of Judea, and especially their rulers) " sought to kill him."

4. The rancour and malice of wicked men against Christ is so inveterate that no length of time will mitigate or allay their fury; for although that work was long since done, yet they still " sought to kill him."

5. Albeit Christ will not take away his presence and ordinances from a people, because of every sin, but doth rather offer himself to sinners as a physician to the diseased, yet cruelty and persecution is a just cause and forerunner of his departure; and faithful ministers may for a time withdraw themselves, being threatened with personal hazard, if they may conveniently get it done. Both these are imported in this resolution: " He would not walk in Jewry, because the Jews sought to kill him."

6. Albeit Christ's servants may warrantably, in some cases, withdraw from personal danger, yet they should beware of dishonouring God by doing it out of slavish fear, or in a timorous way, but should use that mean of self-preservation as a duty commanded; for so much doth his own practice teach, of whom it is not said—He durst not; but " He would not walk in Jewry," because he was commanded to preserve himself till his hour came.

7. Albeit Christ knew that his hour was not come, and so needed not fear them, though he were in the midst of them; yea, being God, he could restrain them, or rid himself out of all their hands, as ofttimes he did; yet it pleased him to use this mean of retirement and withdrawing of himself for his own preservation, not only that, as sometime, he proved himself God by miraculous preserving of himself, so he might also temper these manifestations, that they might not be kept back from doing that which he came into the world to suffer; but further, also, that he might give proof of his deep humiliation and abasement for our sake; that he might, in his own person, sanctify such a lot to his people; and that he might teach them to expect God's providence about them, for their preservation, in the use of lawful means.

8. As Christ and his servants will not want employment in some places of the world, however they be entreated in others, so albeit they may be secluded from many places and parts of their calling, yet they have no warrant to be idle, but ought still to be doing good, as they may; therefore, albeit he stayed in Galilee, yet he did not lurk there, but " walked in Galilee," or went about from place to place, preaching and working miracles, as was his way, Acts, x. 38.

9. Christ is not only tender to such as come to him, but will also be at pains to seek them who have need of him, to do them good; for he " walked in Galilee;" he stayed not in one place, that any who had need might come to him, but he walked about to seek them.

Ver. 2. Now the Jews' feast of tabernacles was at hand.

3. His brethren therefore said unto him, Depart hence, and go into Judea, that thy disciples also may see the works that thou doest.

4. For there is no man that doeth any thing in secret, and he himself seeketh to be known openly. If thou do these things, shew thyself to the world.

5. For neither did his brethren believe in him.

Followeth the second part of the chapter, wherein Christ refuseth to go up in his brethren's company to the feast of tabernacles. Their desire is contained in these verses, to which Christ returns his answer in the following purpose.

In these verses, consider—1. The occasion which induced them to make this proposition, (which also points at the time of his continuance in Galilee,) ver. 2; namely, that the feast of tabernacles was now approaching, which was one of their three yearly solemnities, Leviticus, xxiii. 34, wherein (beside other performances common to it with other feasts) they went out of their houses and dwelt in booths made of boughs of trees, not only to be a type of Christ's incarnation and dwelling in our flesh, but to keep them in remembrance of their preservation in tents in the wilderness, before they came to the promised land.

2. Their desire that he would depart hence, and go up to Judea, and shew himself to the world, the meaning whereof is, not that they would be rid of him, or cast him in his enemies' hands, but they could not endure that their kinsman should lurk in so base a place, and not go to Judea, where he might get more credit, and wherein they thought to share; and therefore they desire that he would go up with them to this solemn feast, and so Christ himself expounds their desire, ver. 8, and so was the custom that kinsmen went up together to these feasts, Luke, ii. 44.

3. The motives they use to induce him to hearken to their desire are two: in one of them, ver. 3, they pretend respect to the disciples which he had gathered in Judea, (chap. iii. 22, 26; iv. 1,) who, as they insinuated and pretend, were slighted and exposed to temptations, through his long absence, and those miracles he wrought in corners might contribute much to strengthen them. In the other, ver. 4, they discover more of their ambitious intentions; they think it unhandsome for a man of so eminent gifts to lurk in corners, nor can they understand what could be his aim, if it were not to rise and become eminent by his gifts; and therefore would have him casting himself where he might get best opportunity of being taken notice of.

4. John records the true ground of this carnal motion in them, ver. 5. They were but yet in nature, and did conceive carnally of him, and sought only to make advantage by their relation to him, and to advance their own carnal ends and designs; and this makes it clear that (as his brethren were not any other children borne by Mary, but his kinsmen, called brethren, after the manner of the Hebrews, so) they who made this motion were not any of his kinsmen whom he called to be apostles, for they were already converted and chosen, chapter vi. 70, but some others.

From ver. 2, learn—1. The hard and uncertain lots of God's people will, in due time, have a good issue and matter of praise; for so is held out in their keeping the "feast of tabernacles," in remembrance of the issue of their wandering. And it is a lively emblem of the sweet issue that shall be of the godly's wandering, when they shall enter out of the wilderness of this world into their heavenly Canaan.

2. Albeit we are ready to forget our troubles and the mercies wherewith they have been sweetened, when they are past and over, yet it is God's will they should be remembered with thankfulness and sobriety, and with readiness to follow God whenever he calls to new troubles. So much also is imported in their yearly observation of this feast, wherein they were not only thankfully to remember the mercy, but by their going out of their houses and dwelling in booths, and that at the time of gathering in their fruits, and when their barns were full, (for that was the time of this feast, Exod. xxiii. 16; Deut. xvi. 13,) they were to testify that present mercies had not made them forget former trials; that they would use them soberly, and were ready yet to leave all at his call who had guided them so well in former trials.

3. Albeit praises be due to God, in all ages, in thankful remembrance of his mercies, yet the way of testifying thereof by solemn feasts is Jewish, and not to be continued under the gospel; therefore is it called, as formerly, "the Jews' feast."

From ver. 3, 4, learn—1. Carnal men, when they have the occasion of spiritual, public solemnities and ordinances, do not mind the right end or God's honour in going about them, nor do they make conscience of spiritual preparation, that they may profit by them, but all their care is how to attain their own carnal ends, particularly of vainglory, in and by them; for when this feast "was at hand," ver. 2, all the preparation of these men for it was to get Christ with them, that they might come to credit by him at it.

2. Christ's carnal friends and followers do follow him only for their own ends, and in expectation of carnal respect and glory by him; for such was their scope in this desire.

3. It is high presumption in creatures to presume to prescribe to Christ what to do, or when to do it, and particularly to employ him so to order his matters as may most advance their carnal ends, and bring them in esteem; for it was not simply a fault to wish him in Judea, for he went afterward, ver. 10; nor yet to desire he should be known to the world, seeing it was his end in coming to shine as the light of the world; but it was their fault to carve out and prescribe to him when to depart, and to be so impudent as to desire that his manifestations might be made subservient to their vainglorious and carnal designs.

4. Men, when they are prosecuting their carnal and ambitious ends, will not want spiritual and plausible pretexts wherewith to mask them; for so much appears in their first reason, " go into Judea, that thy disciples also may see the works that thou doest," wherein they seem to be so taken up with thoughts of the public good of his followers, as they dare indirectly challenge him for slighting them so long. It is indeed a truth, that Christ will have a care of such as give up their names to him, wherever they are, that they faint not for want of necessary encouragement; but they failed in propounding this, in that they made it but a mask to their carnal ends, (as, indeed, God looks not only to desires, but to the end and scope of the desirers;) that they could think to learn him how to respect his people, or guide them better than he did; that they tied his encouraging of his followers to his bodily presence and miracles, whereas he was God, to support them in his bodily absence; and that they think it a fault he should withdraw his visible presence, even from his disciples, when he is called of God to shun imminent dangers.

5. Carnal and unrenewed men do make it their only aim to become great by any gifts and endowments they have received; and they are so

ignorant of another way, that they measure even the most godly by their own dispositions, and do count them but silly who do not thirst after glory and respect; therefore, say they, for no man "doeth any thing in secret, and he himself seeketh to be known openly;" whereby they do not mean so much that he rubbed up himself by lurking in corners as a deceiver, and not coming to view as an honest man should do, but their carnal disposition thought it impossible that a man could be gifted as he was and not thirst after reputation in the world; and therefore, supposing that this was Christ's aim also, they wonder he was so silly, and did not prosecute his ends more vigorously.

6. Men of eminent gifts are exposed to very great danger if they want sincerity, having (beside their own hearts, that can tell them too well what they are,) many carnal friends, who may be Satan's instruments, to suggest unto them temptations, to be puffed up with conceit, and to carnal courses and aims; for here Christ was tried with it, though the prince of the world found nothing in him.

7. Such as are carnal and ambitious hunters after vainglory do care nothing what they are or do in secret, but all their thought is about what is open and public, and how to frequent public conventions, and make shows, that they may be taken notice of; for so much appears in their counsel: "If thou do (or since thou doest) these things, shew thyself to the world."

From ver. 5, learn—1. The grace of God doth not go by blood or natural acquaintance, but by free gift; for they are "his brethren," and yet that proves not their grace, "neither did his brethren believe in him" more than the Capernaites, and therefore they are in as little account with him. And herein Christ's example is ground of comfort to them who have and are ofttimes put to trials by graceless friends, though afterward we find a change, Acts, i. 14.

2. The truth of the grace of God in men will appear, especially, in their taking up Christ by faith as he hath revealed himself, and in their closing with and embracing of him, out of the sense of their great need; for this is the evidence of their want of grace: they did not believe in him—that is, they did not take up what he was, nor close with him.

3. When men are ambitious, and hunt after vainglory, and when they dare presume to teach Christ his duty, it is an evidence of a graceless condition, at least in so far; therefore it is given as a reason of their former presumption and ambition, "for neither did his brethren believe in him."

Ver. 6. Then Jesus said unto them, My time is not yet come: but your time is alway ready.

7. The world cannot hate you; but me it hateth, because I testify of it, that the works thereof are evil.

8. Go ye up unto this feast: I go not up yet unto this feast; for my time is not yet full come.

9. When he had said these words unto them, he abode still in Galilee.

In these verses we have Christ's answer and refusal returned to their desire, both by word and practice, wherein—1. Christ sheweth that there was a great difference betwixt him and them, ver. 6. His time was not yet come, whereas theirs was alway ready; which, however it be true in general, that natural men, though by right they have not allowance to do what they list at any time, yet in effect and practice they walk as they list, and take any time they please; whereas he behoved to choose times, and walk according to his Father's direction; yet it seems here rather to shew what difference there was betwixt him and them in this going up. He who was maligned and hated behoved to wait for a fit time and season lest he should cast himself on a snare and tempt God, but they could come no time wrong, being in no such peril. This difference (2.) he confirms from a reason, ver. 7. They might go up at any time, seeing the world could not hate them who were but yet children of this world; but he behoved to choose his fit time, being hated of the world because of his plain and free doctrine. 3. From this he inferreth, ver. 8, that they might go when they list, but he would not go till his full time came. 4. His practice is recorded, ver. 9, as agreeing with his resolution.

From ver. 6, learn—1. Meekness doth beseem Christ and his followers, and that they meet the impertinences of carnal men without heat or passion; therefore doth Christ so meekly answer their carnal desire.

2. The Lord hath appointed times and seasons for every course and lawful action which prudent and godly men are bound to observe; for so doth Christ observe that his "time is not yet come" to go to that feast.

3. Times of trouble and danger to the godly should make them very tender, to wait on God's direction for every step of their walking, that they neither cast themselves needlessly on trouble nor yet do sinfully labour to avoid it; for so much doth Christ's practice teach, who, being in danger, found that his "time is not yet come" to go up, albeit the feast was near, because he was to go up privately; and as he knew his time by the Spirit of the Lord resting on him, so he used this caution, that he might profess his voluntary humiliation, even to sinless fear, for his people's good,-and that he might leave a pattern to them.

4. Such is the ordinary temper of this world that Christ and his followers must ofttimes lurk, when carnal men may appear in it without hazard; therefore saith he, "but your time is alway ready."

From ver. 7, learn—1. Unrenewed men, whatever their privileges be, are but of the same stamp and in the same condition with the rest of the world; they do savour of it, and, continuing in that condition, will get their portion in it; therefore are the Jews and the rulers, from whom Christ's hazard was at this time, called "the world," albeit they judged far otherwise of themselves, considering their privileges.

2. Albeit the Lord, in his righteous judgment,

do sometimes make the men of the world plagues and scourges one to another, yet as there can be no communion kept with the world unless men will share in their wickedness, so it is most usual that worldlings agree well enough together; therefore saith he, " The world cannot hate you," being such as themselves are.

3. Such as the men of the world are, such are their actions and fruits; for the works of the world are evil. Not only have they gross, vicious actions, but even such actions as are in themselves good or indifferent are in them evil.

4. Unrenewed men will not readily be troubled or vexed about their actions, but would sleep securely if others did not vex them with telling them of their way; for this is the world's trouble here, that he testified that their works are evil.

5. Whatever be the hazard, yet Christ's servants are bound, in their stations, to bear witness against the evil courses of the world; for so doth Christ's practice teach.

6. Such as would be faithful in their generation, in witnessing against the courses of the world, must lay their accompt to be hated for their pains; for such was Christ's lot; " but me it hateth, because I testify of it," &c.; and this he did encounter with, not only to expiate our love to the world, and our sinful communion with it, but to cast us a copy of what we are to expect.

7. Such is the perversity of the corrupt world, that no evidence of affection, in dealing with them for their good, will gain them, but rather incense them; for albeit he but testified of their works, by his innocent life and doctrine, to reclaim them from them, yet the world hated him.

8. Whatever pretences of zeal persecutors of Christ and his followers may have, yet the true cause of their spleen is the opposition that is made to their wickedness and hypocrisy; for albeit they pretended to hate him, because he had profaned the sabbath, as they alleged, yet Christ sheweth the true cause of this hatred, " because I testify of it, that the works thereof are evil."

From verse 8, learn—1. Christ approveth that ordinances be reverenced; and albeit men be corrupt who administer them, and they but carnal who go unto them, yet he allows not that they neglect or give over the use of the lawful ordinances as his appointed means; therefore saith he, " Go ye up unto this feast," which, however in some respects it imports only a permission, and giving up of them to themselves who were so carnal, (as is to be after cleared,) yet, simply considered, it imports an approbation of that ordinance, and that it was their duty to frequent it.

2. Such as seek Christ's company only for carnal and ambitious ends may expect to want it, even in going about sacred ordinances; for in so far did Christ give them up, as to want his company in this journey, where they expected only carnal advantages by him: " Go ye up: I go not up yet to this feast."

3. Tender walkers, especially in times of trouble and hazard, will be very accurate in the least circumstances. So much appeareth in Christ, who goeth not up yet, because, albeit the time in general was come, yet it was " not yet full come," and therefore he would not yet stir.

From verse 9, learn—1. It is not enough, especially in times of trial, that men have clear light and good principles, unless they have also honesty and resolution to follow their light; for herein Christ hath given us example, who, upon these grounds, " abode still in Galilee."

2. Christ is not changeable, and one thing in his expressions and another in his doings and actions, but is uniform, and still the same in his doings and sayings, as here we see.

3. When the Lord giveth clear light to any to know their duty, they must not be shaken from it upon any terms, whatever pretences might militate to the contrary to brangle their resolution; therefore, albeit Christ knew that men would take advantage to carp at him because of his lurking in Galilee, and this refusal might savour of contempt of his kinsmen, yet, knowing that his time was not yet full come, " he abode still in Galilee."

VER. 10. But when his brethren were gone up, then went he also up unto the feast, not openly, but as it were in secret.

Followeth the third part of the chapter, wherein is recorded Christ's going up to the feast, with what followed thereupon. In this verse is shewed that at his own appointed time he went up, yet in a private way, not in the company of his kinsmen and friends, but with his disciples and some few followers, possibly (among other reasons) that they might not intercept him by the way, and that he might try their thoughts of him before he appeared, as afterward it fell forth. And here John passeth over some things that occurred in his journey, (which are recorded by some of the rest,) that so he may hasten to the following history.

DOCTRINES.

1. Such as have not embraced nor closed with Christ, but remain still in their natural condition, may yet be very careful to observe outward ordinances; for " his brethren were gone up."

2. Albeit the Lord's servants may for a time, in some cases, withdraw themselves from danger, yet when God calls them to appear, they should do it without shrinking, though the danger continue; for when his time was full come " he also went up unto the feast," though the malice of the Jews was not yet abated.

3. The cruelty and ingratitude of a people will not hold Christ away where he hath any good to do; for he went up again to Jerusalem, however they stood affected to him.

4. Courage in following of a calling should not be looked on as inconsistent with prudence, and with the carriage of ourselves in a secret or open way, as may most contribute for the great work of our calling; therefore Christ went up, " not openly, but as it were in secret," whereby he not only sheweth that he subjected himself to this wary way, that he might purchase unto us boldness before God, but, as in the former purpose, we are taught how he sanctified flight and retirement in his own person, and as afterward he leaveth us a pattern of undoubted boldness,

so here, by carrying himself privately till he come up, and till the people be convened, and his enemies somewhat settled, after they miss him at the beginning of the feast, he would teach them that as faint-heartedness is none of his lessons, so neither is temerity and rashness approven by him; and that great circumspection should be used in our engaging in trial, and then it should be resolutely managed.

VER. 11. Then the Jews sought him at the feast, and said, Where is he?

12. And there was much murmuring among the people concerning him: for some said, He is a good man; others said, Nay; but he deceiveth the people.

13. Howbeit no man spake openly of him for fear of the Jews.

In these verses we have the first thing that occurred at the feast concerning him—to wit, the carriage and speeches of the Jews and people, either before he came, or before he shewed himself. And, 1. It is said, ver. 1, that they made inquisition for him, which may be taken as the multitude's fact who had heard of him, or had heard him preach and seen his miracles, who now miss him at the feast,—as indeed, when Christ's doctrine and works are notable and famous, many may talk of him and desire to see him, who yet make but little use of him or them either,—but it seems rather to be meant of the wicked Jews and their rulers, who sought to slay him; and this appears, not only from their contemptible designation of him, " Where is he?" but from their names—" the Jews," (the men of Judea, and chiefly the rulers, called often by that name, not only because they were of Judea, but because the guilt of their cruelty lay upon many of the nation, who joined too much with them in it, as well as themselves,) who are said to seek his life, ver. 1, and who are distinguished here from " the people," or multitude, ver. 12, and are cause of terror to the people, ver. 13. 2. The people express their different thoughts of him, some allowing him the charity of being a good man, and others traducing him as a seducer, ver. 12. 3. The manner of the conference is secret, by way of muttering, and that for fear of the Jews, ver. 13, which is to be understood chiefly of the better sort, that they durst not speak openly of him; yet it may be conceived also, that they would have all to let it alone, that so the matter might be buried.

From verse 11, learn—1. It is one part of Christ's and his followers' trial and hard lot that their persecutors do labour to bear them down, by putting contempts and affronts upon them before the world; for so do they speak of him, " Where is he?" with contempt and disdain.

2. Albeit enemies seem to think very contemptibly of Christ and his followers, and of what they can do against them, yet for all that they will not get the terror of him put out of their hearts; for albeit they seem to despise him, yet they " sought him," to take him out of the way.

3. Albeit Christ and his followers should carry themselves never so modestly, yet persecutors will not let them alone; and while they cease to be, they will still be an eye-sore to the world; for albeit he had now stayed long away, and had not troubled them, and there was no appearance of his coming, or being come, as yet, more than at the last passover, yet they are not at ease, but " sought him."

4. Even public solemnities of sacred worship will not mollify nor direct persecutors from their bloody designs; for " then the Jews sought him at the feast."

From verse 12, learn—1. Men by their violence and cruelty thinking to suppress Christ and his truth, may readily thereby awaken people to think and say more of him; for upon the back of their search it is subjoined, " And there was much murmuring" (or secret whisperings, the cause whereof is shewed, ver. 13,) " among the people concerning him," pointing out (as would appear) that their narrow search for him put him in the people's minds and mouths. And so not only Christ is spoken of when they were dumb, and would have others silent, but, beyond their intentions, they occasion this themselves.

2. This people's making Christ the subject of their conference, even behind his back, when yet all of them had little or no knowledge of him, and many of them no love at all to him, may shame them who should know more, and who profess more love unto him, and yet entertain but few thoughts of him, and little conference concerning him.

3. Christ and his truth are ofttimes the subject of great contradiction in the world, and do encounter with variety of tempers among men; for so was it here; some are bitter, and others are more charitable.

4. Not only open enemies do great wrong to Christ, but even some seeming well-wishers, by their indifferent way of pleading for him, and their shallow conceptions of him, do prove themselves to be but small friends unto him; for such were these here, who pleaded only, " He is a good man."

5. As it is a very great iniquity in men, when they not only err themselves from the truth, but turn seducers of others, (for here they object it as a justly odious crime, " he deceiveth the people,") so it is no strange thing to see men brand Christ and his friends with this infamous title of being deceivers, and under this pretext to cry down all that can be alleged in their defence; for " others said, Nay; (he is no good man;) but he deceiveth the people." (See 2 Cor. vi. 8.)

From verse 13, learn—1. It is the sad case, and too often the condition of the visible church, to be so corrupt as truth dare not be avowed in it; and the teachers thereof become a terror to all who would maintain sound doctrine; for so was it here: " Howbeit, (whatever they whispered, yet) no man spake openly of him, for fear of the Jews."

2. Faithless and slavish fear in men will easily bear down their affection to Christ if it be but coldriffe [mere profession] and ill principled; for so did it with these here, who had but little to plead for him.

3. When Satan cannot prevail by violence, he may sometimes essay to weary Christ and his followers out by burying all debates and controversies, that in process of time truth may wear out and be buried; for, as was hinted in the exposition, so may it be taken here also; they would have none to speak at all concerning him on any side, that so thoughts of him may wear out in time, he having been so long absent. However it be, yet this is a course that ofttimes prevaileth much, (though men never gain their point by it,) and it should warn us to look on being let alone many time as a trial.

VER. 14. Now about the midst of the feast Jesus went up into the temple, and taught.

Followeth the second thing which occurred at this feast, containing Christ's preaching in the mid-days of the feast, with the consequents that followed thereupon, to ver. 37. In this verse is recorded that Christ went publicly into the temple and taught, whereby he supplied the defect of the dumb and corrupt priests, who at such solemnities were bound to teach the people out of the law. Whence learn—

1. Christ's not appearing till "the midst of the feast," sheweth that albeit he subjected himself to fulfil all righteousness, yet his great errand was not the feast, but the gaining of souls at it. And it teacheth that the gaining of souls to Christ is the great work and end, to which the use of all ordinances should be directed.

2. While they are about sacrifices in the temple, Christ goeth up and teacheth there, no doubt (as appeareth from the following sermon, ver. 37) inviting them to himself, as the substance of all these shadows; and it teacheth that when people are taken up with the practice of external ordinances, they have much need of Christ's teaching, that they rest not on these, but press after the marrow and substance of them. This was the great sin of that time, that they rested on these rites, and had few or none to bid them go forward. And albeit the true religion be a living way, wherein men may still continue fresh and lively, even to old age, Psalm xcii. 13, 14, yet formality is a very frequent disease, and they who labour hard till they attain to somewhat may be ready to sit down when they have attained it.

3. In that Christ, who before lurked and kept himself secret, doth now appear openly in the temple, it teacheth that whatever caution Christ's servants should use, yet, when their calling presseth them, they should without fear cast themselves, if it were in the midst of bodily dangers, as their Master did before them.

4. Albeit John record many sermons which the rest omit, yet he doth not express what Christ preached at this time, only it appears from the following verse that his doctrine was admirable. This the Lord hath in deep wisdom ordered, to teach that as we are bound to know what Christ revealeth, so we should be sober, and set bounds to our curiosity, when he is pleased to keep up anything; and as Christ hath revealed all that is necessary for salvation, so by his wrapping up some things in silence he would sharpen our appetite, and increase our desire after that day wherein we shall know as we are known.

VER. 15. And the Jews marvelled, saying, How knoweth this man letters, having never learned?

Followeth, to ver. 37, the effects of this public appearing of Christ, which may be taken up in this order:—1. There is a conference with the Jews, who marvelled at his doctrine, ver. 15, wherein he vindicates his doctrine, ver. 16—18, and the miracle he had wrought before, in which debates the multitude have some hand, ver. 19—24. 2. They of Jerusalem barking against him, ver. 25—27, he returns them an answer, ver. 28, 29, which hath some effects, ver. 30, 31. 3. The rulers sending to take him, ver. 32, he preacheth yet more, ver. 33, 34, and is carped at by the hearers, ver. 35, 36.

In this verse it is recorded that they hearing Christ preach so well and learnedly, though he was never brought up at their public schools, do marvel at it, instead of seeing God in it. This is ascribed to " the Jews," which may be either understood generally of the multitude there convened, who were of that nation, or it may be, his malicious enemies did begin this debate and conference, though afterwards the multitude, who knew not their plots, ver. 20, do interpose in it; and it is not unlike that by this wondering they would bring Christ in suspicion, as not having his skill by good means, seeing he was no scholar.

DOCTRINES.

1. Christ's knowledge and insight in the things of God is admirable, even his enemies being judges; for " the Jews marvelled," &c.; they admired both the measure of his knowledge and the way of attaining it without means; though this, being extraordinary in him, is not to be drawn into ordinary imitation.

2. Whatever be the seeming great effects of Christ's doctrine among a people, yet so long as they want faith it will be all to no purpose; for albeit it was much that they should marvel, yet, since they believed not, it was, in the best of them, nothing else but stupidity. The least degree of saving faith is beyond all admiration without it.

3. The corrupt heart of man is ready to retort even the most undeniable and convincing arguments pleading for Christ, and to make use of them to their own hardening; for albeit Christ's knowing of " letters, having never learned," was an undeniable evidence that he was taught of God, and filled with the Spirit, according to the prophecy, Isaiah, xi. 2, 3, yet they use it as a ground of exception.

4. Such is the perversity of corrupt men by nature in opposing of Christ, that nothing can be done or said but they will bend their wits to cavil at it; for if Christ had preached but in an ordinary way they would have thought nothing of him; and if he preach to admiration, then they will strive to render that suspicious.

VER. 16. Jesus answered them, and said, My doctrine is not mine, but his that sent me.

Followeth Christ's reply, wherein he vindicates his doctrine, and then justifieth his old practice; and, first, he declareth that he had not his doctrine from Satan, nor by any human art or industry, but from his Father, whose ambassador he was, and that he spake not his own mind only, but the Father's. While he saith it is not his, but the Father's, the meaning is, not to seclude him simply, but to shew that he devised it not of himself as man, (as they conceived only of him,) and without the Father, but as he was God, equal with the Father, and so naturally knew all his mysteries, and as man had knowledge thereof by communication from his godhead, so all this was communicated to him from the Father, who sent him to the world to reveal his counsel; and this might appear in his divine furniture without all human industry. Whence learn—

1. As Christ fully knows the Father's mind and counsel, so he is the faithful revealer thereof; for his doctrine is the Father's who sent him; it is from the Father, and he publisheth it.

2. It may commend the doctrine of the gospel, that not only it is of God, but that he sent his Son into the world to publish it; for so doth Christ commend his doctrine here.

3. It is the duty of faithful ministers, not only to wait for a calling from God, but to see that they bring nothing forth but what they have from God; for herein Christ is a pattern, who was sent, and whose doctrine was not his own, but his that sent him.

4. No doctrine or preacher, how admirable and ravishing soever, are to be heard in the church but they who are sent and bring their message from God; therefore, albeit they "marvelled" at him, ver. 15, yet he thinks not that enough unless they be persuaded that he and his doctrine are of God.

5. It is the duty of faithful ministers to lead people from themselves to God, and to ascribe what is excellent in them to him, that he alone may have the glory; therefore Christ, when he is "marvelled" at, draweth their eyes to God, who sent and furnished him.

Ver. 17. If any man will do his will, he shall know of the doctrine, whether it be of God, or whether I speak of myself.

18. He that speaketh of himself seeketh his own glory: but he that seeketh his glory that sent him, the same is true, and no unrighteousness is in him.

Next, because they would not readily credit him in asserting his doctrine to be of God, therefore he subjoins two rules and helps whereby they might be enabled to try doctrine and teachers, the first whereof is required in the person who would try doctrine, ver. 17—to wit, that he be a pious man, and one who, according to light received, walks in God's ways; such an one hath the promise that he shall be made able to discern whether his doctrine be divine or devised by himself. The second rule and help in trial, ver. 18, relates to the person and doctrine to be tried, wherein he asserts that a man who runs unsent, and preacheth his own inventions, doth in his carriage and by his doctrine but seek to exalt himself; whereas he who, being sent of God, makes it his scope in his carriage to exalt God only, and the nature of his doctrine tends to that, doth prove that he is a preacher of truth, and that there is no unrighteousness nor fraud in his doctrine. For understanding of this we are to consider—That Christ, in giving these rules of trial, doth not seclude other rules and proofs of the truth of his doctrine already given, chap. v., and particularly that of scripture,—for Christ in scripture makes it elsewhere clear that good men, in some cases, may be misled with error, and unrenewed men may know and embrace truth, though not savingly; and, on the other hand, erroneous teachers and doctrines may pretend to be much for God, and may cry out on truth as denying to God his glory,—but Christ's meaning is, to shew that his doctrine being undeniably true and according to scripture, it was odious in them to contradict it by wicked rebellion, and to evidence by their opposition that they were not tender walkers; and that this is so much the more heinous, that they saw his whole carriage and the nature and scope of his doctrine tend only to glorify his Father, and not to advance his own private glory.

DOCTRINES.

1. It is the duty of the Lord's people not to receive doctrine or teachers upon trust, but to try and discern who are sent of God, and who not, and who speaks true or false doctrine; for it is here imported that they should know who are sent, and whether their doctrine be " of God," or of themselves.

2. Every man is not a fit discerner of Christ's doctrine, but many, through their own default, are left destitute of such a mercy; for so doth the requiring of qualifications in those who try import.

3. Such as truly fear God, and make conscience of known truth in their conversation, have his promise for ability and discerning to try doctrine; for so doth the promise expressly hold out: " If any man will do his will, he shall know of the doctrine, whether it be of God," &c.; which we may branch out in these:—1. Such have indeed the promise of discerning, whereas ungodliness and loose practices provoke God to withhold discerning light. 2. Albeit the godly may, and many times do err, and are misled, yet ordinarily that is but the fruit of some former defection in practice. 3. Men's fleshly humours and passions, in debating and seeking out of truth, while yet their practice is not subjected to the rule, is not the right way to come speed. 4. Such as have no use for truth nor end in searching it out, but only to inform their judgment or satisfy their curiosity, may readily get leave to go wrong. 5. Such as make conscience of known light in their practice are in God's way for attaining further light in dubious controversies. 6. Such as come to hear with a purpose to examine doctrine by carnal reason, and to like or dislike of it, according as it shall relish or be displeasing to their lusts, will readily reject sound doctrine; but he that cometh with a subjected mind and fixed

resolution to receive and obey what shall be found to be the will of God, shall get a discerning spirit, unless God have him to humble for some former guilt of which he hath not yet repented.

4. The great scope of preachers and of their doctrine should be, to deny and abase themselves, and to exalt and seek God's honour; for so doth Christ teach, ver. 18, that a teacher should seek "his glory that sent him," and so himself did in carriage and doctrine.

5. Such as do run unsent, and do broach their own inventions and errors, certainly affect the praise of men and hunt after vainglory, let them pretend to what modesty and humility they will; for "he that speaketh of himself seeketh his own glory," the scope of his carriage tendeth to that. And albeit self-seekers may be for the truth, and may make use of it for their own ends, yet they are fitted to go wrong if they have a tentation, and they will go wrong before they be not respected, yea, and God is provoked to give them up to go wrong.

6. As true doctrine doth tend to set forth God's glory and to exalt him, so corrupt doctrine, devised by men, doth not aim at God's glory indeed, whatever it seem to do; for in this respect also, "he that speaketh of himself seeketh his own glory;" the nature of his doctrine riseth no higher than his own or another creature's glory; whereas he that is true, or sound in doctrine, "seeketh his glory that sent him." That this may appear, consider—1. Many corrupt and erroneous doctrines do eminently exalt the creature in its merit, free-will, liberty to dispose of its actions, &c., to the manifest depriving of God of the glory of grace, dominion, and sovereignty, to the abasing of Christ and his sufferings, the denial of providence, &c. 2. Many opinions and practices in religion, though they pretend to and seem to speak much self-denial in those who profess and practise them, yet they never ascend to give glory to God, but to exalt another creature in his room,—such as that voluntary humility in worshipping of angels, Col. ii. 18. 3. Though some erroneous opinions get place in the world, and are cried up as exalting God and Christ, yet he will have no such honour, and it is but a real dishonouring of him to think that he needs a lie to set out his glory, and to maintain error under a pretext that otherwise he will want his glory. (See John, xiii. 7—9.) 4. As no erroneous opinion doth tend to God's glory, so no erroneous person doth really mind it in maintaining that error, but would exalt himself under a pretext of humility, and seeks to be accounted and reputed of as somewhat, because of his new opinions.

7. To preach sound doctrine is great faithfulness to God and to the souls of people who are taught; whereas the unsound teacher commits the greatest and most cruel of frauds, as being false to God and to the souls of people; therefore it is said of the teacher of sound doctrine, "the same is true, and no unrighteousness is in him;" not that they are perfect, (though Christ was so, being truth and righteousness itself,) but that being true, he deals righteously in not having any fraud in his doctrine.

VER. 19. Did not Moses give you the law, and yet none of you keepeth the law? Why go ye about to kill me?

Christ having vindicated his doctrine, proceeds now to vindicate his practice in healing the impotent man, chap. v., which had so long stuck in their minds as an odious practice. This he doth upon two grounds, whereof the first (in this verse) is by way of retortion upon themselves, that they should seek to slay him for a supposed breach of the law, when yet none of themselves, to whom the law was given by Moses, did keep it. For clearing this reason—1. We must remember that Christ hath already justified this deed (chap. v.) upon convincing grounds, and therefore now he useth only such defences as might pinch them a little nearer. 2. As this comparison of his deed with their transgressions doth noways argue that he was guilty as they were, so neither is it Christ's scope to teach men to think their own faults the less that others are guilty also. 3. Nor is it Christ's scope that men should repine because they are reproved by others that are guilty, nor yet that men's own guilt should altogether close their mouths from reproving of others; for neither was he guilty, nor is he teaching men how to defend themselves in ill courses. But Christ is reasoning here, not so much to the matter as to the persons of those that persecuted him, and sheweth that they were not meet challengers of him who were so gross violators of the law in their own practice, and that, however they pretended great zeal to the sabbath in persecuting him, yet their own carriage testified how little they respected the law, being guilty of horrid transgressions, and many of them making the law void by their traditions.

DOCTRINES.

1. Faithful ministers ought not only to be able to hold forth sound doctrine, and to give a reason of it, but also to stop their mouths who, by unjust aspersions cast upon their persons, labour to frustrate and make void their ministry; therefore Christ, having defended his doctrine, doth now vindicate his practice.

2. As Christ knoweth the secret intentions of his enemies, so he is always ready to remove all scruples against him, and to clear that he is unjustly hated and persecuted; for he knew their present intentions (of which, ver. 25), though the people were ignorant of it, ver. 20, and puts them to it, "Why go ye about to kill me?"

3. As the law of God doth oblige men to obedience by reason of His authority who enjoineth it, so it adds to the obligation when a people consider how eminently God hath been seen in enjoining of it, and what privileges they enjoy by having it; therefore, when he is about to urge their obligation to obedience from the law, he presseth them to consider—"Did not Moses" (whom not only ye honour, but who was trenchman [a companion], and conversed familiarly with God when he appeared in glory upon the mount) "give you the law?" and not to other nations, Ps. cxlvii. 19. He speaks to them who were successors to those who received it, as if they had been then present.

4. Albeit the law hold forth and oblige men to duty, yet not only are there some who grossly transgress against it, but there are none who can make it appear that they keep it perfectly; for saith he, " yet none of you keepeth the law," and not some only. And albeit there were many better than they who sincerely endeavoured to observe it, yet even these did not attain to perfection.

5. Albeit men may, and should, in their stations, reprove and censure others who are guilty, even though themselves be compassed with infirmities and failings, yet not only it is sad when gross transgressors of the law have power in their hands which they employ against the innocent as if they were guilty, (as here they did with Christ,) but it concerns every one who hath a calling to reprove and censure—1. To labour, so far as may be, to be blameless themselves, otherwise they do undergo much shame, and do frustrate the end of their dealing with others, Matt. xxiii. 4. 2. To be more taken up with their own failings than with the failings of others, Matt. vii. 3—5. And upon this, 3. To deal compassionately with others in their failings, as being conscious to themselves of their own infirmities. All this is imported in Christ's challenge of them, (as it is before explained,) that they should deal so violently with him for a supposed breach of the law, when yet they were little affected with their own real miscarriages.

6. The Lord reckons it to be but hypocrisy and fury when men pretend zeal for God against others, and in some matters and failings, and yet do allow themselves in as bad or worse courses; for so much also doth Christ's reasoning import, that however they pretended it was zeal for the law and sabbath made them so hot in pursuing him, yet if it had been so they would have made more conscience of it in their own practice; and indeed many may pretend the honour of God in somewhat they do, who, when their other works are seen, do give their profession the lie.

VER. 20. The people answered and said, Thou hast a devil : who goeth about to kill thee ?

Christ is interrupted in his apology by the multitude, who, being ignorant of the rulers' plots, (which others knew better, ver. 25,) and seeing him get liberty to preach, and none molesting him, cry out that he was mad and possessed that should apprehend any such thing. Whence learn—

1. Albeit persecutors have many on their side to be enemies to Christ, yet there are but few of them who are made privy to their plots and cruel projects ; as here we see " the people," or multitude, ignorant of all this, " who goeth about to kill thee ?" Many who are on persecutors' side [among persecutors] are to be pitied, and not to be suspected as accessory to all the machinations of their leaders.

2. It is great want of charity when men do not only tax a particular fact which they suppose to be wrong, but do also reflect upon the person who doth it, and pass hard censures upon the principles from which it floweth ; for albeit his apprehension had been false, (as it was not, and

men are bound to trust Christ's verdict rather than their own sense and reason,) yet it was hard measure because of this to assert, " Thou hast a devil." This was a very frequent designation among them of one that was distracted and erred dangerously ; for whereas they could acknowledge God's fatherly hand in moderate chastisements, they looked upon grosser distempers as an evidence that a man was delivered over to the executioner's hand, which, however it be not still true, and is very sad when it is true, yet a saint may be exercised with a messenger of Satan, 2 Cor. xii. 7, and yet be in his Father's hand still ; only it is to be marked, that they are affected with what they think to be a visible possession who yet were little troubled with a spiritual possession, under which many of them were kept in bondage.

3. It is the lot of Christ and his followers to lie buried under the most horrid of calumnies, even to be looked on as acted, guided, and directed by an evil spirit ; and Christ himself submitted to this, that he might sanctify such a lot to his followers, as here we see, and frequently elsewhere in the evangelists.

VER. 21. Jesus answered and said unto them, I have done one work, and ye all marvel.

22. Moses therefore gave unto you circumcision ; (not because it is of Moses, but of the fathers ;) and ye on the sabbath day circumcise a man.

23. If a man on the sabbath day receive circumcision, that the law of Moses should not be broken ; are ye angry at me, because I have made a man every whit whole on the sabbath day ?

Christ passeth over this calumny without a reply, and goeth on with his discourse, wherein he cleareth the multitude what the quarrel was the Jews had against him, and subjoineth a second reason for vindication thereof taken from a parallel act approven by themselves. The sum is, that however they marvelled at his deed, yet they had like practices among themselves justified by the law ; for Moses did give them a law, received from the fathers, that circumcision should be administered on the eighth day, and they did circumcise on the sabbath day, if it fell to be the eighth, without any scruple or violation of the law, yea, in obedience to the law ; and therefore they had no cause to be angry at him because he had healed a man both in soul and body on the sabbath. The parallel here is not so much betwixt the person of Christ and Moses as betwixt the ordinance enjoined by Moses and practised by them, and Christ's deed ; for clearing whereof, consider—1. The equality, or parallel, consists in this : that as circumcision was a work of piety, as being a sacrament and seal of the covenant, so also it was a work of necessity in respect of the precept that the law of Moses might not be broken ; and on the same grounds was Christ's work to be justified, being a work of piety to heal a man's soul, and a work of charity and necessity to help a man who had been so long in distress. We need not insist to inquire why the Lord would have circumcision precisely on the eighth day; whether because he would have the seventh day (which physicians account a critical day) over before this painful sacrament were administered, but would have it delayed no longer, or upon some other typical reason: it sufficeth us that God's will is a sufficient reason for his command. 2. There may also some disparity be found betwixt these two, which pleads yet more strongly for Christ's practice—as, 1. In administering of circumcision there was more pains and labour on the sabbath than in what he did, having with a word made the man whole. 2. Circumcision, though an ordinance of God, yet was painful, and for awhile hurtful to the body; he, on the contrary, healed him who had been long pained. 3. Albeit circumcision was a work of piety, because it was a seal of the righteousness which is by faith, yet many who received it did not get their hearts circumcised; and therefore his deed was much more a work of piety, having not only healed the man's body, but his soul also; for so the parallel runs, and so these words are to be understood, " I have made a man every whit whole," or, the whole man whole, and so appears in part from his adhering to Christ's directions, when they are quarrelled, chap. v. 10, 11.

DOCTRINES.

1. Christ's followers ought to be deaf men to reproaches, and to carry themselves modestly when they meet with personal injuries and affronts; as here Christ by his practice doth teach, who never so much as owned their bitter reflection, ver. 20.

2. Men who are most wicked and lewd may yet so far delude themselves, or seek to deceive others, as they cannot look upon some supposed ills but with wonder and astonishment; for these vile men did " all marvel" at this work of Christ, pretending to detest it as a horrid profanation, when yet they were nothing affected with their own gross abuses and violation of the law.

3. It is great injustice and want of charity to stumble at one failing of a man (suppose it to be real) who makes not a habit of it, but otherwise is blameless; therefore saith he, " I have done one work, and ye all marvel;" wherein he not only opposeth his own work to their frequent circumcising on the sabbath, but sheweth that it was a great testimony of his innocency that they could object but that one work to him, and that it was great injustice to tax him so hardly, (though it had not been right,) seeing he had no custom of such transgressions.

4. The Lord in his deep wisdom hath so contrived his law that albeit divers precepts concurring at one time may seem to cross one another, yet no man that is not under the power of an erring conscience (who, whatever way he turn him, doth either sin materially against the law, or interpretatively against God, in going over the light of his conscience) will ever want a lawful outgate, but may follow one command without violation of another; for so doth Christ's arguing teach: his instance of circumcision with-

out profanation of the sabbath, and his arguing from thence to justify his own practice, sheweth that these particular instances are grounded on a general rule, that in the concurrence of many seeming contrary precepts it is the will of God that one of them should give place to the other for that time, and that without sin in him who doth so; which may be branched out thus:—1. A general command gives way to a special precept when both cannot be observed at one time; as here the general command of sanctifying the sabbath gives place to the command of circumcision on the eighth day, when that day fell to be the sabbath. 2. The moral duties of the first table take place of duties of the second table when they come in competition; though a man be bound to provide for his family, to love his friends, wife, and children, yet all these must give place to his love to God and his truth, and he must forsake all these, yea, and (in some respect) hate them, when they would hinder him in his duty to God. 3. Ceremonial duties and external performances of the first table do give place to moral duties of the second table; and therefore Christ frequently justifieth his own and his disciples' practices on the sabbath, by shewing that God required mercy and not sacrifice.

5. Albeit it be the will of God that his people do sanctify the sabbath by ceasing from their ordinary employments, yet several works may be done thereupon without violation thereof; for Christ's instancing of circumcision on the sabbath, without breaking of the law of Moses, and of his own fact [case], sheweth that these instances are grounded on this general rule, that the doing of every work upon the sabbath is not a violation thereof; and particularly—1. Works of piety are the very sanctifying of the sabbath; as here, to administrate a sacrament and do good to a man's soul; and the priests were blameless in killing and washing sacrifices on that day, Matt. xii. 5; and we, under the gospel, should go about our work with more delight on that day, in regard it is more spiritual and easy than formerly. 2. Some works, albeit they be not works of piety, yet are lawful, in so far as they are necessary means of, and have a tendency unto, works of piety; so were they allowed a sabbath day's journey to go to their solemn meetings and worship; and the pains that men take in needful apparelling and refreshing of their bodies, and going to the public places of worship, are no violation of the sabbath if they be done with a sabbath day's heart. 3. Works of mercy and charity are also lawful on the sabbath, as here it was lawful to relieve a miserable man, (so also Luke, xiv. 5,) providing they be such works, indeed, not only in the intention of the worker, but such as in their own nature are necessarily required for performance of mercy and charity. 4. Works of necessity may lawfully be done on the sabbath, though they were servile employments; as here circumcision was, in respect of the command, and his healing of the man. (See Luke, xiii. 15.) Yet, that we abuse not this, and violate the sabbath under a pretext of necessity, we ought—1. To distinguish betwixt a necessity that is inevitable, into which Providence casts us, and a necessity that is only contracted through our own former negligence;

the first doth warrant us to work what we are necessitated to do, but the other doth involve us in guilt, whatever may be done upon it. 2. We are to distinguish betwixt a necessity that is only imminent or possible, and feared that it may come, and a necessity that is incumbent and present; the former cannot warrant a man to work on the sabbath, but the latter doth. A man must not gather in his corn upon the sabbath because he fears it may rain the next day, or a flood may come and carry it away, but a man may recover and preserve his corn on the sabbath from being carried away with a present inundation. 3. We are to distinguish betwixt the ceasing of gain, by the intermission of a lawful calling on the sabbath, and an emergent damage, by reason of some providential dispensations; the former doth not warrant working on the sabbath day, but the latter doth. Albeit it be necessary that a man improve his means in a lawful calling for the maintenance of his family, yet it is not lawful for him to continue his trade and calling on the sabbath, upon pretence that he will be a loser by the intermission thereof; but a man may lawfully recover his means from fire, water, or other accidents, on that day.

6. Men who are possessed with self-love and with prejudice against others will readily count that a fault in their neighbours which yet is no fault, and will allow that in themselves which they condemn in others; for so doth Christ's reasoning from their practice to his deed import, that they did these things as approven service, as they were, and yet when he did the like, they were angry at him; and so doth he elsewhere plead from the example of David, and of their priests, Matt. xii. 3—5.

7. Whatever persecutors of Christ and his people do pretend, yet the rising glory of Christ and of his truth is the true cause of their spleen; therefore, albeit they made a noise about the man's carrying of his bed on the sabbath, chap. v. 10, yet he tells them the true cause is, " I have made a man every whit whole on the sabbath day," and so am glorified.

8. Christ's pleading for this as a work of piety, as the parallel beareth, and hath been shewed in the exposition, doth import that Christ did heal this man's soul as well as his body; and so it teacheth—1. As men have soul diseases as well as bodily, whereof they should be chiefly sensible, and which, till they be cured, men are never completely whole, so it may be an encouragement to go to Christ with outward troubles, that in seeking help to these, men may get that and spiritual mercies also; for so dealt he with this poor man, whose great care was only to be healed of his long infirmity. 2. It is a very dangerous condition to be sent to Christ with outward trouble, and yet not get some spiritual and saving benefit from him, with their deliverance, before they come away; for it was Christ's way when persons were brought to him with outward troubles, to cure their souls before they came away. It saith much to the incurableness of men's spiritual condition when they are afflicted, and make some fashion of coming to Christ with it, yea, and are delivered, and yet continue unrenewed.

9. His pleading this as a work of charity and necessity teacheth that mercy and compassion in Christ will omit no occasion of shewing itself comfortable to the miserable and them that are in necessity; for he will not intermit to help them when he seeth them, even albeit it be the sabbath. And this will yet further appear if we consider that one might object that there was no such necessity, but the man who had endured that infirmity thirty-eight years might endure it yet one day; whereas circumcision, in respect of the command, could not be omitted. But the answer is easy, that not only the duty of charity requireth that the miserable be presently helped, but, however the man might have endured it, yet Christ's love and pity laid on the necessity, and could not forbear. And albeit the man might be hardened in his trouble by reason of long continuance, yet Christ's pity is as tender towards him as if it had been the first day; yea, so much the more, as he had endured it so long, albeit in deep wisdom he reserved the cure for his own hand. This may help to correct the jealous thoughts of God's people, who complain that they are forgotten under their long-continued trials.

10. In declaring that Moses gave them circumcision Christ adds a correction, "not because it is of Moses, but of the fathers," (as, indeed, it was given to Abraham long before, Gen. xvii. 10,) whereby—1. He would put them in mind that there was a covenant and promise made, and seals annexed to it, long before the giving of the law by Moses, that so they might gather that the law, which came after, could not make the promise void, as it is argued, Gal. iii. 17. 2. Because they doated so much upon Moses, yea, and eyed him more than God, in the ordinances they received by his ministry, therefore Christ puts him in his own room, and sheweth, that precious ordinances were given to others as well as to him. It teacheth, that when eminent instruments are too much doated on and idolized by men, it provokes the Lord to debase them, and to let it be seen that they are but his instruments, as here he doth with Moses.

VER. 24. Judge not according to the appearance, but judge righteous judgment.

Unto this argument Christ subjoins an inference or conclusion, that it was their duty to judge righteously of his work, and not to be led by appearances, such as looking, on the one part, to Moses' authority, and on the other, to his baseness, and so to condemn him, but should compare the one fact with the other, and see how they agreed, and rather see a divine power shining in his works, setting forth his glory and justifying them, than stumble at his works by judging him, according to outward appearance, to be a mere man.

DOCTRINES.

1. Christ and the friends of truth desire nothing but righteous judgment, and will not be afraid to go to the bar with their enemies if they can get justice and equity; for he desires that they "judge righteous judgment." He had al-

ready examined his own way, and found it to be right, and therefore feared no trial; and so should his people sit upon their own assize.

2. Men are ofttimes so blinded with visible appearances and masks, with passions, interests, and prejudices, that they see not through causes as they are in truth, but do judge of them according as they are represented in a false mirror, either judging of a cause as it is masked with pretences, or loaded with prejudices, or according as they esteem of the person that owns it; therefore it is requisite they be warned that they "judge not according to the appearance," or according to external appearance, or the outward view they take of persons.

3. Whosoever do condemn what is right, because of their prejudice against persons, or out of respect to persons, do justify what is wrong; and whoso do rashly judge of things, without considering all circumstances, do deal unrighteously before God; for so much is here condemned by Christ: "Judge not according to the appearance, but judge righteous judgment." (See Deut. i. 16, 17.)

Ver. 25. Then said some of them of Jerusalem, Is not this he, whom they seek to kill?

26. But, lo, he speaketh boldly, and they say nothing unto him. Do the rulers know indeed that this is the very Christ?

27. Howbeit we know this man whence he is: but when Christ cometh, no man knoweth whence he is.

Christ having thus debated with the Jews and multitude about his doctrine and practice, he (in the second place) is assaulted by the inhabitants of Jerusalem, who knew the rulers' plots better than others. And, 1. They cry out upon their rulers, wondering what is become of their zeal and forwardness who were seeking him to kill him, and yet now, when he preaches so boldly, they meddle not with him. 2. They allege, in derision, that the rulers were so moderate, possibly, because they believed him to be the Messiah; but as for them, they think they have strong reasons wherefore they could not join with them in that opinion; for they know whence this man is, whereas no man will know whence the Messiah is when he cometh. As for the first part of their reason, it cometh more fitly to be considered in Christ's answer, but in the second part, they assert a manifest untruth; for albeit Christ, in respect of his godhead, was prefigured by Melchizedek, who in that state is brought in scripture, without father and mother, without descent, having neither beginning of days, nor end of life, Heb. vii. 3, and it is said of Christ, in that respect, Who shall declare his generation? Isa. liii. 8, yet it is as clear that, in respect of his humanity, the scripture clearly points out what tribe he should come of, his descent, family, and lineage, and the place of his birth.

DOCTRINES.

1. When wicked men are put to silence in debates, yet will they not be gained, but this will irritate their corruptions to start new questions about truth, and new prejudices against the maintainers thereof; for their not replying to his reasonings makes it clear they were convinced; and yet this availeth not, but they are irritated and embittered that the Pharisees are not more violent, and run to new debates.

2. Ordinarily they who enjoy most advantages in a visible church do in a declining time prove worst of any; for they of Jerusalem, the chief city, and the place of solemn public worship for all the nation, are more upon the persecutors' plots, and more enraged than any.

3. God can preserve his own in the faithful discharge of their duty in ill times in an admirable way, so that even their enemies themselves may wonder at it; for say they, "Is not this he whom they seek to kill?" and yet "he speaketh boldly, and they say nothing to him." They wonder that, considering his boldness and the ruler's resolutions, he was not despatched, seeing they might easily do it when he cast himself among their hands. But hereby they do also hold out (though they considered it not) that there was an admirable providence of God about him, restraining them till his hour came. And indeed it is no less than a wonder to see God's people carried through amidst the many secret and cruel plots of men, Psalm cxxiv. 1; and it would be admired yet more by saints if they were privy to all the sore hearts enemies have for their miscarried designs.

4. It will never be men's honesty and courage in an evil time that will hasten trouble upon them, before God see it meet to try them; but their fainting doth rather provoke God to send upon them what they fear, and would decline; for of this Christ's experience is an ample proof. He was in the midst of enraged persecutors; he spake boldly, and yet say they, "Lo, they say nothing to him;" they give him not so much as an ill word for his pains.

5. Wicked rulers and persecutors when they are worst will never want instigators to encourage them in it, yea, and to carp at them that they are not violent enough; for such did those of Jerusalem prove to the Pharisees.

6. Free preaching is that which the world cannot endure, nor hear, without being enraged; for that "he speaketh boldly" is their eyesore.

7. A visible church may grow so corrupt that it will be accounted the greatest crime and reproach that may be to receive or profess the most necessary and fundamental truths; for they account it a great indignity in Jerusalem to "know indeed that this is the very Christ." They have reason to acknowledge God's mercy who live in times wherein it is their glory, and not their reproach, to avow this; and the godly, even in a visible church, should be looking that their trial may come to that height in declining times.

8. Such as are in power, and do not rule for God, are justly contemptible, and slaves, in a sort, to them who follow them in wickedness; for the rulers must take a taunt from their persecuting associates and followers.

9. It is undeniably gross and abominable wickedness for men to profess they know and

acknowledge Christ, and yet to persecute him and his truth; for so much do these men grant, that if the rulers knew he were the Christ, it was sufficient to turn them from their resolutions of killing him.

10. It is commendable that men, in matters of religion, do not pin their faith upon the sleeve of any, how eminent soever they be, and though they were never so much esteemed by themselves, but that they have a reason of their hope in themselves; for albeit these men erred dangerously in the particular, yet their principle is good in the general, that though the rulers should believe him to be the Christ, yet they could not go along with them so long as they thought they had reason to the contrary.

11. Error is very dangerous and ensnaring; and albeit many may seem to be led away by others into error, yet experience will readily prove that error doth so bewitch them as the tentation that drew them on will not bring them off again; for albeit they were drawn on chiefly by their leaders' example to oppose Christ, yet they profess that though their rulers would come off yet they will not.

12. Erroneous persons and despisers of Christ are much fostered in their way by their conceit of their own knowledge, and even by a pretence that they know and respect Christ more than any beside; therefore they make great boast of their knowledge, and particularly of the Messiah, whom they expected, and yet are opposing him when he appeareth.

13. The not comparing of scripture with scripture, but taking any single sentence that seems to plead for what we would be at, is a very great nursery and cause of error; for such is their reasoning here: they catch at one thing, speaking of the Messiah's divinity, and take no notice of other places with which that should have been compared.

14. The right way to read the scriptures concerning Christ is to take up both those scriptures which speak of his humanity and voluntary humiliation, and those which point out his divinity and glory, and see them all accomplished in him, yet distinctly, so as we are not to expect that to be verified of his manhood which is proper to his godhead, nor yet that his godhead in itself suffered any change by the personal union; for herein also they failed in their reasoning, urging that what was said of the Messiah's godhead should be verified of him according to his human nature.

15. If any think it strange how these understanding men should so far mistake, seeing nothing was more clear and frequent in scripture than whence the Messiah is, as man, and that in respect of all circumstances, his mother, place, and time of his birth, parentage, &c., they should consider that (beside what may be spoken to afterward, of their sinning against light) this people were so taken up with and fostered by their traditions in a dream of Christ's outward glory and pomp, that they could not heed nor understand anything concerning his humiliation, how clearly soever it was revealed; and of this we have a clear instance in the disciples themselves, who, being taken up with the same dream, could not understand Christ when he spake most clearly of his sufferings, Mark, ix. 31, 32; Luke, ix. 44, 45; xviii. 31—34. And it teacheth how dangerous a frenzy vain imaginations and delusions are, which will so possess men's minds that clearest sunbeams of truth will not be discerned by them unless God in mercy recover them out of the snare of the devil.

VER. 28. Then cried Jesus in the temple as he taught, saying, Ye both know me, and ye know whence I am : and I am not come of myself, but he that sent me is true, whom ye know not.

29. But I know him : for I am from him, and he hath sent me.

Christ, being grieved at this impudent cavil, doth reply unto it with much boldness and zeal. And, 1. He declareth that however they knew him, and whence he came, yet their carriage proved that they knew not the Father that sent him. 2. He subjoins that he was comforted in this—that whatever they thought of him, yet he knew that he was sent from the Father who is true, and however they knew not the Father, yet he knew him, as being from him, and sent by him into the world. For clearing this a little, consider—1. The great difficulty here is, how to understand these words, " Ye both know me, and whence I am," being compared with what follows, that they knew not the Father; for they are taken up diversely—as, (1.) By way of irony and holy derision; as if Christ had said, Ye think ye know me well enough, but ye know me not at all as ye should, since ye know not the Father who sent me, and that I am come from him. And this indeed holds true in general, that conceit is a great prop unto mistakes and errors, and a hindrance unto closing with Christ; that men's not closing with Christ by faith doth flow from ignorance of the Father; and that conceit of knowledge is very hateful to Christ, seeing he doth, in a holy manner, mock it. (2.) The words may be taken as declaring them to know Christ, and yet to be ignorant of him, but in diverse respects. They knew him and whence he was, as man, (though even in that they erred if they supposed him to be the carpenter's son,) yet they knew not the Father nor him, as God, proceeding from the Father, and sent by him; and indeed, they have need to be quicksighted who know Christ as he is in truth, and they who do know much will perceive, when they get opened eyes, that they are ignorant of far more of him. These interpretations have indeed these truths in them, and do agree well with the temper of the body of the Jews, who were very ignorant. But Christ's zeal and indignation in this discourse, (testified by crying,) with the consideration of those he speaks unto, may lead us to look yet more narrowly into the words. Therefore (3), when we consider that Christ is not now dealing with the multitude, but with the companions of the rulers, who knew all their plots, ver. 25; with those who even now had been convinced in the matter of Christ's healing the man on the sabbath, and had therefore, in great rage, started this new quarrel; and with those who would have taken him, though they had no warrant from the rulers, ver. 30,—when, I say, we consider these things, the words may run very well thus: That Christ chargeth upon them that they knew him well enough, and yet against their light would not acknowledge him, but delighted to cavil; and this is not strange, for it was the great sin of the rulers that they sinned against their light in opposing of Christ, and so might also their associates. (See John, iii. 2; Matthew, xxii. 16.) The only difficulty against this interpretation is, that it seems not to agree with what is afterward said, that they "knew not him that sent him." But so is also said of the rulers, who sinned against their light, that they knew not the Father nor Christ, John, xviii. 2, 3, because, however they knew as much as to make them guilty of sinning against light, yet they knew him not savingly, and their carnal conceptions concerning the Messiah made them maliciously reject all the convincing arguments that this was he, since they saw no satisfaction to their desires in him. Consider—2. As for these proofs of Christ's knowing the Father, verse 29, the last of them is clear of itself, that Christ, being sent ambassador from the Father, behoved to know him who sent him, and to have ample instructions and knowledge of his mind. As for the other proof, "I am from him," however it may be taken generally that he came from the Father, and not only so, (for one may come from another, and yet know little of him or his mind either,) but came clothed with a commission and furnished with instructions, as his sending imports; or it may point out that he did voluntarily come, as well as the Father sent him; yet it seemeth clearer to understand it of his eternal generation, and being from the Father as God, and so it points out a higher proof of his knowing the Father beside his being an ambassador.

DOCTRINES.

1. Such is the perversity of men in opposing Christ and the gospel, that it is hard for them who have any zeal of God to get it endured. So much did Christ testify by his vehemency in speaking to these: he "cried in the temple as he taught."

2. The violent, malicious, and affronted opposition of men should not blunt nor dash zeal, but rather set an edge upon it in all those who would approve themselves to have antipathy against sin; therefore Christ cries as he taught. To be calm so long as our particular case is not touched, however God be dishonoured, is stupidity and not meekness, and an evidence of the want of the zeal of God.

3. Among other trials and exercises that Christ and his followers do meet with in the world, from the ignorance of men and their infirmities, this is one of the chief, that they will have to do with men who directly against their light do oppose him and his truth, (for such did Christ meet with here;) and it may warn men to take heed how they slight and go over their light in ordinary walking, lest, in process of time, they maliciously contradict their light; and to beware of engaging against truth, lest they be left to themselves to run to hell before they stop.

4. Men's opposing of truth and Christ against their light is not only a sad trial to the zealous, but a horrid iniquity in itself, and will be a witness for the friends of truth in the bosom of opposers; therefore Christ not only cries against this, but bears their knowledge upon them, as a witness for him, and an aggravation of their sin: "Ye both know me, and ye know whence I am."

5. Whatever light malicious opposers of Christ have, which will aggreage [aggravate] their own guilt, yet their opposition proves that they have no saving knowledge of God nor of him; therefore saith Christ to them, Him that sent me ye know not. Whatever light and knowledge of God men have, yet they know nothing indeed, and savingly, but what their heart submits unto and embraces, and what the Son reveals of him, Matt. xi. 27, and what tends to eternal life, John, xvii. 3.

6. Such as are approven of God ought not to be shaken by the misconstructions and malicious oppositions and cavillations of men; therefore doth Christ set forth his own grounds of comfort and assurance to testify that he would not be moved by all their opposition nor needed a testimony from them.

7. Albeit the gaining and conversion of one soul be of more worth than a whole world, yet it is one good end of a ministry to convince malicious men, and not leave them without a witness; therefore also doth Christ assert his calling and commission before these malicious men, that they might know there was not only a prophet, but the Messiah among them. (See Ezek. ii. 5.)

8. It is a sweet encouragement under trial when men know they have a calling from God to what they are opposed in, and that they do not undertake it of themselves; for when Christ saith, " I am not come of myself," &c., it not only imports that he was indeed sent by the Father, but holds out his ground of encouragement from his calling; and if men knew what it was to bear the burthen and consequence of any course they undertake, it would make them afraid to run without a call.

9. Such as would reap comfort by any call from God should study much his fidelity and truth, and that, whoever despise them, yet he will not misregard them who employeth them; therefore doth Christ subjoin, " he that sent me is true"—to wit, in his promises and covenant made with him, the Mediator, when he sent him into the world, and therefore will accordingly own him in his going through his state of humiliation. And this also is of general use and comfort to all who are called of God, 1 Thess. v. 24. And as men would not quit the comfort and clearness of their calling, so they would take heed that atheism do not brangle the truth of those promises made to them in following that calling.

10. Such as would savingly know Christ, especially in his state of humiliation, and would not maliciously oppose and contradict any light they have, should labour to know the Father that sent him, that so they may see better what

Christ is and what the hazard is of rejecting him; for so much also is insinuated in this challenge, " he that sent me is true, whom ye know not." Had they seen the Father more in Christ they had not maliciously stumbled at his baseness, nor durst they have hazarded to oppose him.

11. Men who would cleave to and be encouraged in God in times of opposition should not take up truths concerning him by guess, but should be certain of them by faith; therefore doth Christ assert, " I know him."

12. Whoever be ignorant of God, yet Christ knoweth him and his will perfectly, and is sufficiently able to reveal him to others who desire to learn at him; for saith he, " But I know him."

13. Christ's perfect knowledge of the Father appeareth from his eternal godhead, that he is from the Father, and the same in essence with him, and so communicates with him in his eternal knowledge of himself, and in his counsels, and from his commission from the Father, which imports that he came with full instructions from him; for these are here given as reasons of his knowledge: " for I am from him, and he hath sent me." And this not only serves to put us out of all doubt that Christ doth reveal the Father infallibly, but being held out as the ground of that challenge, and as that which supported him under their malicious opposition, it teacheth men that however they cannot attain to this measure of clear and near knowledge, yet if they would be borne out in times of opposition they must study to know God and his truth by that measure of communion with him which he allows upon sinful men.

Ver. 30. Then they sought to take him: but no man laid hands on him, because his hour was not yet come.

Before John proceed to the third effect that followed on this first appearing of Christ in the mid-days of the feast, he inserts two consequents that followed on the former debate. The first is, that these enraged men, being galled with Christ's former discourse, would have taken him by violence, but Providence did restrain them, because his time to suffer was not yet come. Whence learn—

1. The more that malicious men are dealt with and convinced, the further will they be from any good, and the more exasperated; as here we see in these men, who raged before, and now are quite mad in their fury.

2. Violence and persecution against the persons of faithful teachers is an evidence of men that maliciously oppose truth, and the lot which is to be expected from such; for they (whom Christ asserts to have sinned against their light, ver. 28, 29,) " sought to take him," that they might kill him,) or deliver him up to their rulers.

3. It is the prerogative of God that to him belong the issues from death, and that he can preserve his servants in the midst of their enemies, even when they are in the height of their rage; for " no man laid hands on him."

4. God needs no means to preserve his servants, but can secure them as well by an invisible hand of providence as if they had all visible helps in the world; for so did he give proof to his Son here.

5. Many a good turn are men made to do, and to omit many an evil, for which they will never be rewarded as service, as being not done or omitted from any principle of grace, but from a hand of providence restraining them; therefore it is marked that " no man laid hands on him," not from any remorse or honesty in them, but from God's providence about Christ, " because his hour was not yet come."

6. Albeit Christ's followers may expect that at last the Lord, for wise reasons, will not let the malice of men cease till they be brought to suffering, yet the time thereof is in God's hand, and not in the power of bloody men; and they may boldly go on in their lawful calling, believing that enemies will not anticipate his time; for this reason of not taking him, " because his hour was not yet come," imports that he was indeed to suffer; that God had the timing of that in his own hand, and that till his time came all their malice could not avail.

Ver. 31. And many of the people believed on him, and said, When Christ cometh, will he do more miracles than these which this man hath done?

The second consequent of the former debate (which also is a transition and introduction to the third general effect of his public preaching) is, that however the great ones were angered, yet many of the common people did believe on him, as concluding that whoever expected another Messiah, yet they were sure there would none come who could work greater miracles than he had done, and so it was folly to expect another. John doth not declare what these miracles in particular were that affected them, only it seemeth they were not present miracles, but those he had done in former times; therefore they say, he " hath done" them. And as for this ground of their faith, that he wrought singular miracles, albeit the scope and end of his miracles was to confirm his doctrine, and that he was the Messiah; and if thereby they were led not only to acknowledge him, but to reap benefit by his word and offices, they were certainly in the right way; but if they were only led and affected with his miracles, and rested there, it was very defective; and though the power and glory of Christ shining in his works did affect them, yet, wanting a root, it could not but soon fade; as many may think they have attained to some perfection when yet they are indeed but to begin. They who are pricked in their hearts are yet commanded to begin repentance, Acts, ii. 37, 38; yet it is to be observed that this and the like changes are called believing on him, partly because they were good in themselves, and a beginning of good, and to shew that Christ would not have good beginnings despised by the godly when they find them in themselves, even albeit hypocrites may have them, who yet fall back again; for their fault was, not that they had these, but that they had not more, and made not progress; and partly to shew that Christ himself is a very large commender and esteemer of grace, who will give such fair titles to small beginnings. But leaving to determine what the change wrought on them was, we may from the verse learn—

1. Christ, when he pleaseth, can make his work to prosper, even in the midst of his enemies; and when they are maliciously opposing and using their utmost endeavour against him, he can pluck some, yea many, out of their hand; for even at this time many believed on him.

2. Albeit grace be insured to no sort of people more than another, yet it is ordinarily the meaner sort with whom it prevails most; for they are of the people, or multitude, who believed, when the rulers and their followers in Jerusalem are persecuting. Men who live at ease and in pleasure ordinarily see little need of anything beside; they see no need of prayer or dependence on God, having all things at hand; yea, it is a wonder if they be not persecutors.

3. Let men expect what they will beside Christ for happiness, yet he is singular, and none can expect a better than he; so much do they acknowledge, that let men dream what they will of another Messiah, yet "when Christ cometh, will he do more miracles than these which this man hath done;" he will indeed be found the chief of ten thousand.

4. Albeit Christ's servants may take much pains whereof they see no present effects, yet God may bless these same labours with success afterward; for the miracles which Christ "hath done" before do now take effect with some.

VER. 32. The Pharisees heard that the people murmured such things concerning him; and the Pharisees and the chief priests sent officers to take him.

Followeth the third thing that followed on his public appearing in the mid-days of the feast, wherein is recorded the violence of the Pharisees and rulers, ver. 32, and Christ's sermon upon occasion of that, ver 33, 34, with the Jews' carping at his expressions, ver. 35, 36. In this verse is related that the mutterings of the people in favour of Christ coming to the Pharisees' ears, they, with the chief priests, send some officers to apprehend him; albeit there was by right but one high-priest at once, yet here are mentioned more chief priests; belike they were the heads of those twenty-four courses, or orders of priests, of which we read, 1 Chron. xxiv., or the high-priest and his deputy, who acted many things under him, and did officiate for him when he was legally unclean.

DOCTRINES.

1. Some may attain to a measure of respect to Christ who yet have not attained to a competency of courage to avow it publicly in times of hazard; for the people did but murmur "such things concerning him."

2. Even in societies where many countenance the gospel, and where they carry themselves most cautiously, there may still some be found who are but spies and observers in behalf of persecutors; for here, where many believed and did but murmur these things, the matter is brought to the Pharisees' ears, who were the most strict sect, and most rigid against Christ.

3. Christ's rising glory, and his success in the gospel, will enrage enemies and draw on trouble; for they who were taxed of slackness before, ver. 25, 26, when they hear of his success, and that men begin to commend him, could bear it no longer; though indeed they came too late to quench that fire, seeing trouble will never separate Christ and them that truly believe. It is true, indeed, that God will sometimes give a flourishing church some breathings of tranquillity, Acts, ix. 31, and will send persecution to rouse up his people from security; but ordinarily, it is little apparent success of the gospel, and little prejudice done to Satan's kingdom that makes him and his instruments quiet.

4. Bloody and violent persecution is the last refuge of hypocrites, and that which may be expected from them when they are vexed; for they use no other arguments, but "sent officers to take him," that they might bring him before their judicatory, whereof yet they retained some name and shadow. When Satan and his instruments come to this, it is an evidence that they are indeed vexed, and at their last gasp.

5. Christ is the great butt of persecutors' malice, who, as he let his followers get few or no blasts while he was in the world, so he stands still on the head of them who fight under his banner, and will reckon with persecutors as they who would pour out all the hatred they let out on his people on him only, if he were within their reach; for here we see their disposition who sent to take him only, not troubling the professors.

VER. 33. Then said Jesus unto them, Yet a little while am I with you, and then I go unto him that sent me.

34 Ye shall seek me, and shall not find me . and where I am, thither ye cannot come.

Followeth Christ's sermon on this occasion, spoken in audience of all the people, as appeareth, ver. 35, and of the officers also, as may be gathered from ver. 46. The sum of it is, that however they thought him a thorn in their side, and that they would never be well till he were gone, yet he would continue the time appointed him, and then he would return to the Father. But they needed not be so earnest, for they would want him but too soon, and should not find him, though they would gladly have him. So that this doctrine contains not only a consolation, which Christ takes unto himself, that he would be preserved from their fury till his hour was come, and then would return unto his Father, where he would be without their reach, but a threatening also against the persecutors; for albeit the same be also said to his disciples, chap. xiii. 33, yet in different senses; for though the outward separation was the same, yet his heart was diversely affected towards them; the separation of the one was but for a time, and in part only; but the others, perpetual and total, as is to be cleared in its own place. Here the meaning is, that they would want him but too soon, and he being gone, in their ensuing calamities they should miss their promised Messiah, but find none, since they sought another than him; and though they would be glad of him, yet they should not be able to find or come to him in heaven, seeing they understood not spiritual seeking, and wanted faith whereby to obtain access.

DOCTRINES.

1. It beseemeth Christ's followers not to be moved with dangers, but rather to be affected with pity towards persecutors, and to warn them of their danger; for so doth Christ here; he is not daunted with the coming of these officers, but preaches out his own encouragements and their hazard to them. (See Acts, xx. 23, 24; Jer. xxvi. 14, 15.)

2. It is but folly for persecutors to think to gain their point by violence, or to put away Christ and his truth, for they will not be rid of him till he have done his work, but so long as he pleaseth he will stay, and vex them more who are already angry enough; therefore saith he, notwithstanding their great haste, Yet awhile am I with you. (See Luke, xiii. 31—33.)

3. Men have little cause to be weary of Christ, nor need they seek to put him away by violence and persecution; for their contempt and malice against him, and their not making use of him, will cause him to go away but too soon; therefore saith he to them, it is but "Yet a little while am I with you," being now near the end of his ministry, and so he tells them they would have him but too short while.

4. When persecutors are doing their utmost, yet it is but a little while that Christ and his followers will be troubled with them, for death will put an end to the worst of it. So much also is imported in this, "Yet a little while am I with you, and then I go," &c.

5. While Christ expresseth his violent death and sufferings in these terms, "I go," &c., he not only imports that he voluntarily underwent that death, otherwise none of them had power over his life, John, x. 18, but also teacheth his followers not to be strangers unto death, nor to look even upon a violent death for truth in those colours wherein sense would present it, but to be so familiar with death, and dwelling on thoughts of mortality, that they may willingly close with it when they get a call, and say, "I go."

6. It may sweeten the godlys' thoughts of death, even a violent one, to consider that here they are strangers, then they go home; here they are unknown and persecuted, there they will be owned and respected by God; for so doth our Forerunner cast us the copy: "I go unto him that sent me," where I will be at home with my Father. (See 2 Cor. v. 1—4, 6; Phil. i. 23.)

7. Albeit it be sufficient matter of comfort to the godly that God can, and when he pleaseth will, preserve them in the midst of dangers, yet it adds to their comfort that the day cometh wherein they will be visibly above the reach of all their enemies, and be made to triumph over them; for so much also is held out here in Christ's encouragement, that when he is gone he would be above their fury, and they should not reach him though they would. (See 1 Cor. xv. 54, 55.)

8. Greatest despisers of Christ may be made to miss and desire him when he is gone; for saith he, "Ye shall seek me." Not only shall many of them desire to have him to persecute, but to no purpose, (as is said before;) but in the ensuing calamities they would earnestly long for and desire their Messiah, to be a comfort unto them.

9. There are many who may earnestly seek after Christ, who yet, in God's judgment, shall never find him; for "Ye shall seek me, and shall not find me." (See Amos, v. 11, 12.) For not only was their desire too late, now when he is gone, (and seldom is such a desire sincere,) but, 1. They failed in seeking their Messiah in general, continuing to despise him and persecute him in his members; and so many pretend to love piety when it is spoken of in a general notion, and yet do persecute it when they see particular effects of it in any. 2. They failed in desiring a Messiah bodily present with them when now he is gone to heaven; and herein they reap the just fruit of their despising him when they had him among them, and of their carnal dispositions, that could not ascend by faith to him, if they had acknowledged him to be the Messiah. 3. They failed in their end in desiring the Messiah, not that he might expiate their sin and bring in everlasting righteousness, but only that he might deliver them from trouble and make them prosper under him in the world. And therefore it is just that such seekers come no speed, how earnest soever they seem to be.

10. Such as desire not Christ's company where they are in this life are justly secluded from coming to be where he is; for therefore saith he to those who would persecute him from among them, "Where I am, thither ye cannot come." Not only shall they be denied access in their seeking, but shall be secluded for ever from his and his people's blessed society.

Ver. 35. Then said the Jews among themselves, Whither will he go, that we shall not find him? will he go unto the dispersed among the Gentiles, and teach the Gentiles?

36. What manner of saying is this that he said, Ye shall seek me, and shall not find me: and where I am, thither ye cannot come?

This sad and grave doctrine gets but bad entertainment among these wicked hearers, who, instead of making use of this sad message and admonition, do carp at his expressions, wondering what he meant by them, or if his meaning was to leave them and go to the Jews dispersed among the gentiles; for otherwise they could make no sense of them. It seems they carp thus, not out of ignorance,—for they might easily have understood what he spake so plainly, ver. 33, of going to him that sent him,—but they evidence their perversity and malice in that they never trouble themselves to keep him, nor propound anything to him for information, but do only agitate the matter captiously among themselves.

DOCTRINES.

1. Such is the perversity of malicious men that they will not only not regard admonitions and threatenings, but will openly scorn them, and wilfully mistake, and force obscurity upon the doctrine of faithful teachers, that they may deride them; for so did they here with Christ and his doctrine.

2. Men do bewray their own corrupt dispositions, pretend what they will, when they dare carp and cavil at doctrine as dark and unclear, and yet never come to Christ or the means he hath appointed for resolution; for albeit they once and again repeat his words, and descant upon them, and carp at them, yet they said it but "among themselves," and so prove that they desired not satisfaction, but were glad of somewhat to quarrel.

3. It is also a black mark upon men (be their pretences what they will) when they are little careful to keep Christ with them, or to make use of him while they have him; for whatever they pretend of obscurity in his doctrine, yet they avow it clearly enough that they understood he was to leave them, and yet are not affected with it.

4. It is the ordinary sin of a privileged people that they will not be sensible of any hazard of Christ's forsaking and leaving them; for while they inquire "Whither will he go?" they insinuate that if he were the true Messiah he could get no such people as them to go to, and if he went to the "dispersed among the Gentiles," (or Greeks, as the gentiles are ofttimes called in the New Testament, because the Greeks, under Alexander and his successors, had been lately of greatest note among the nations,) "and teach the Gentiles," it would rub more on him, as not being the true Messiah who left them, than upon them. And yet not only did what they apprehend come upon them, (for he left them, and sent his disciples to the gentiles and those scattered Jews to whom Peter and James wrote their epistles,) but even what they say was a refutation of their presumption; for the condition of their dispersed brethren was a witness and evidence of what they all deserved, and how much pains God had taken to drive them from that carnal conceit of their singular privileges and prerogatives.

Ver. 37. In the last day, that great day of the feast, Jesus stood and cried, saying, If any man thirst, let him come unto me, and drink.

From this unto the end of the chapter John recordeth Christ's sweet sermon upon the last day of the feast, ver. 37—39, with some effects of it among the people, ver. 40—44, and the confusions that arise in the council of the Pharisees about him, ver. 45—53.

In this verse is recorded, that this being the last and great day of the feast, wherein the people were again solemnly convened to public worship, being to depart on the morrow, Christ takes hold of this opportunity with fervency and boldness to make offer of his refreshing grace to all those who, being thirsty, do come to him. It is not needful to determine that on this day they had a custom of drawing water out of the pool of Siloam, with an eye to that scripture, Isà. xii. 3, but it is certain, that in this Christ doth repeat that proclamation of the free mercate [offer] of his grace which we have, Isaiah, lv. 1; and albeit by thirsting we are chiefly to understand a spiritual langour and desire after spiritual things, yet it doth not seclude but such as thirst even after other things should come to Him who alone is able to answer their expectations, as Isa. lv. 2.

DOCTRINES.

1. While as Christ returns no answer to their malicious carping, ver. 35, 36, but makes this large offer to all of them, or at least to such as would be convinced and come, it teacheth, partly, that meek Christ will follow even despisers with his gracious offers, and will digest all their effronted debordings, [affronts and misconduct,] if at last they will embrace him; and partly, that he is so earnest and so busy, when there is an opportunity to offer and do good to any, that he will not care to give his enemies the last word of him, and will say to them, as Joab said in another case to the man, 2 Sam. xviii. 14, I may not tarry thus with thee?

2. Opportunity may seem strangely to slip away and be lost, as to getting any good done, even when not only faithful men, but Christ himself, is about the managing of the work of the gospel; for now it is come to "the last day, that great day of the feast," (as both the first and last were holy convocations, Lev. xxiii. 34—36,) and the people, after eight days' attendance, are ready to go away before they close with his offer.

3. Opportunities should be the more carefully managed, that they are shortly like to pass over; therefore doth Christ bestir himself on this "last day."

4. When people are ready to retire themselves from solemn exercises and assemblies, to their ordinary employments and vocations, they have need to have their hearts seasoned and guarded with useful instructions; therefore doth Christ publish this needful doctrine on that day, that it might bear them company home.

5. Albeit Christ be always rich and good unto his people, yet it is his ordinary way to bless eminent and solemn times of his people's worship with much of him; therefore also doth he make "that great day of the feast" yet greater by his sweet sermon and offer of himself upon it.

6. The truth of God and riches of Christ ought to be proclaimed with such courage, fervency, and zeal, as becomes such a message, and as may invite hearers to take notice of it; therefore "Jesus stood (whereas the use then was to sit and teach) and cried," not only that he might be seen and heard in that great crowd, but to

testify his courage when they sent to kill him, and his fervent zeal to have this doctrine believed and embraced.

7. Man is a barren and all-needy creature, burnt up with wants and necessities, and not able to supply them of himself; for so much doth their thirsting import, that they are burnt up, and must have somewhat without them to cool and refresh them.

8. There is no satisfaction for empty man in any course he takes till he come to Christ, and embrace and close with him. Neither will the world and things therein satisfy their expectation who lust after these things; nor will external performances satisfy them who have any true thirst; for this is the only remedy, " Let him come unto me." (See Matt. xi. 28 ; Isa. lv. 2.)

9. As men are bound to have spiritual thirst after Christ that they may be satisfied, and as Christ will satisfy and refresh such, so he doth allow and invite all those who have essayed many courses, but in vain, to come to him and find what they want; for both are comprehended here : " If any man thirst, let him come unto me and drink." For clearing and enlarging whereof, consider—1. Christ is so condescending that he will not refuse even those who have wandered far, seeking contentment, before they would come to him, but will take up a man after he hath been refused at all other doors, and him who hath spent his strength for that which is not bread, and drunk many a puddle dry, and yet is not satisfied, Hos. ii. 6, 7. 2. It is no matter what a man hath been before, so now he be driven to Christ, having essayed the vanity of all things beside : " If any man thirst, let him come ;" and albeit the thirst of many after other things hath been sinful and dishonourable to Christ, yet he will accept of them if they come ; yea, albeit they want many things that are required in such as come, yet he will make them welcome if they come to get these things. 3. Albeit spiritual thirst and indigency, when it is discovered, be a very humbling condition ; yet it should be looked on as Christ's forerunner, and as an invitation, call, and warrant, put in the thirstiest hand, that he may come ; for " If any man thirst," it saith from Christ, " let him come unto me." 4. Albeit thirst be nothing else but a discovery, and a making of us sensible of our necessity, yet it is Christ's way to take no other advantage of his people's necessity than to let out of his fulness to them, and let them see that it is indeed their fulness, and (in some respect) matter of their encouragement to dwell in the sense of emptiness ; for he giveth " thirst," that he may give " drink ;" and therefore his keeping of his people under ought not to be stumbled at. 5. The propounding of this condition, " If any man thirst," is not to be understood as if we must first beget sense of need in ourselves and then come 'to Christ ; nor doth it warrant any souls who would be at Christ to seclude themselves because they think they are not thirsty ; for albeit it do point out what is our duty, yet it is his work to beget it who sends his work before him, that he may bring his reward with him, Isa. xl. 10, and who by offering of grace as a mean doth ofttimes beget

it ; but the scope is rather to invite men to come upon this ground, that if they come indeed, they do, by their coming, prove they have thirst, whatever they think of themselves, and that any who are come this length, that they would come if they had thirst, they may come with what they have, and get more thirst by coming to him ; therefore are all these conditional offers summed up in this : " Whosoever will, let him take of the water of life freely," Rev. xxii. 17. 6. It is Christ's will that thirsty souls should not only come to him by humble dependence, but that they should enlarge themselves and partake of their privileges and his refreshments, that so they may be satisfied and acquiesce in him, may confirm themselves in their choice of him, and forsake other delights, and may refute their own tentations and unbelief by tasting how good he is; for it is his will they come to him and drink, or partake largely of his refreshments. (See Cant. v. 1 ; Psalm lxxxi. 10.)

VER. 38. He that believeth on me, as the scripture hath said, out of his belly shall flow rivers of living water.

Christ insists upon this promise, and enlargeth it ; and, 1. He shews that the way of thirsty souls coming to him is by believing. 2. He explains this drinking, that it shall not be a petty refreshment for a season, but the believer shall get Christ himself, and the graces of his Spirit, to dwell in him as a full fountain, and to flow forth for refreshing of himself and others. 3. This is further confirmed from the promises in scripture ratifying this offer of Christ's. He points at no particular place of scripture, but comprehends all which speak of the graces of the Spirit under the name of waters, refreshing and watering barren ground, of which see Isa. xliv. 3, lviii. 11, and elsewhere.

DOCTRINES.

1. The right way of a thirsty soul's coming to Christ for refreshment is by believing ; for so is it explained, " He that believeth on me." And albeit many other exercises and duties be required, yet this is only named—1. Because it must be the root from which the rest must spring. 2. Because nothing we have can be right or acceptable without faith laying hold on Christ and his righteousness. Humility without it will prove but discouragement, a study of holiness and conformity to the law but a stumbling at his righteousness, Rom. ix. 31, 32, and diligence will but tend to security. 3. Because albeit a needy soul should be stripped of all things beside, yet that will be no warrant to cast away confidence, but they must cherish it so much the more.

2. As we are to rest upon no consolation as sure but what is recorded and grounded in scripture, so it may encourage men to believe in Christ, that in him and by him we are sure to find the accomplishment of all that the scripture promiseth ; for he maketh here a promise that it shall be with believers " as the scripture hath said."

3. He doth not name the particular scripture, not only because there are many of them, (as

hath been said,) and he would have his people study and search them all out, that they may see the fulness of the promise, but further, by this he would teach that he would have his people well acquainted with scripture, that they may know where the promises are to be found; therefore doth he only name the scripture in general, here and elsewhere, only Acts, xiii. 33, we find 'the psalm quoted.

4. It may encourage us to study much acquaintance with scripture, that the substance of the gospel and of Christ's riches are treasured up and held forth even in the writings of the Old Testament; therefore, also, when Christ maketh his richest offers he needs say no more but that he will do "as the scripture hath said." The sum of all religion is comprehended in the writings of Moses, and therefore Christ doth prove even the resurrection out of them, Matt. xxii. 31, 32. The prophets are God's own commentary upon these, and the application of the doctrine thereof unto several conditions of men in several times; and the New Testament is a clear unveiling of Moses' face, and holds out the accomplishment of what he fore-shadowed.

5. Such as out of sense of need come to Christ will not only fi'.d some particular refreshment, or for awhile only, but they will get a fountain to be in them; for it is not a drink only to cool them in this or that particular thirst, but a river put in them to flow out; they get a seed of God to abide in them.

6. Christ's Spirit, and the refreshments thereof, are so communicated unto believers as they take deep root in them; for they are in their belly, or their heart, or very inward parts, where meat is swallowed down to be digested into our substance; and this doth difference it, not only from prophetic illumination, which came upon men from without, and which a Balaam may have, but from the motions that came upon rotten-hearted sinners, who, for all they get, yet continue dark in themselves, like the moon.

7. The Lord's allowance to his people is very liberal and bountiful, and abundantly sufficient to satisfy them; for albeit the great ocean of refreshment abide still in himself, yet he lets out unto them no less than a river, yea, and rivers, every grace flowing out like a river, as is said of peace. Isa. xlviii. 18; see Ps. xxxvi. 8.

8. The Spirit of Christ doth remain and abide perpetually in believers, to whom he is given; for these are "rivers of living water," not only because they are still fresh and make lively, but because they are a spring, which doth perpetually flow out and run, and therefore is called living (Gen. xxvi. 19) in the original. (See Zech. xiv. 8.) And this doth difference it from the wicked's puddle, which doth run dry, and from what the temporary receiveth. And albeit the regenerate man finds many intermissions of the refreshments of this spring through his own pride, unbelief, and idleness, yet the fountain remaineth still, 1 John, iii. 9.

9. Where the Spirit and the graces thereof are received by a believer and entertained by faith, the sweet influences thereof will flow forth for the refreshing of themselves and others in their stations, and that with much refreshment and life; for the rivers of living waters shall flow, and that out of his belly, which is the seat of delight, John, xx. 15. As a spring sends forth streams to water the ground about it, and as the heart of man sendeth forth life and refreshment to every faculty and member, and as a general in an army sends out reserves to reinforce his parties, so the graces of the Spirit in believers will flow forth into their behaviour and carriage, to make their heart be strong, to make their tongue drop what is savoury, to make their feet like hinds' feet, &c., and to refresh and gain ground upon others.

VER. 39. (But this spake he of the Spirit, which they that believe on him should receive: for the Holy Ghost was not yet given; because that Jesus was not yet glorified.)

Here we have John's commentary upon this last promise, who, belike, not understanding this himself (as they were ignorant of many things) till Christ was risen from the dead, doth now take pains to clear others who might be in the like condition. He declareth that by this living water is meant the spirit and graces thereof which believers were afterward to receive, the giving whereof was suspended till the glorification of Christ, the head of believers. This began in that solemn day, Acts, ii., and doth continue still throughout all ages of the church.

DOCTRINES.

1. As the doctrine of Christ in scripture doth ofttimes need to be interpreted because of our shallow capacity, so the best commentary upon scripture is itself, and the comparing of one scripture with another; for John by this exposition doth not only express his sympathy with those who might possibly be in the same condition that some time he was, but doth point out the safe way of expounding scripture, and sheweth that it doth explain itself.

2. Whatsoever virtue is in water for cleansing of filth, for cooling and refreshing the thirsty, and fructifying of barren ground, and whatever is promised in scripture under the metaphor of waters, is all to be found in a spiritual way, in receiving of the spirit and graces thereof by faith; for so is here explained, " But this spake he of the Spirit," &c. (Compare chap. iv. 10, 13, 14, Zech. xiv. 8.)

3. While he saith, believers should receive the Spirit, and the Spirit was not yet given, or, was not yet, (not in respect of his personal subsistence, but in respect of the measure of his gifts and graces to be poured out upon believers,) it doth relate partly to the times of the law, and teacheth—that albeit believers under the law did partake of the Spirit in some measure, yet all that is nothing in comparison of that measure which is poured out under the gospel; in that respect " the Holy Ghost was not yet given," which may shame them who make not use of their ample allowance, but do, under the gospel, come far short of many who lived under the pedagogy of the law. Partly it relates to the

present condition of the disciples and his followers, who were not yet endued with power from on high, and therefore were but weak and ignorant in many things; and it teacheth—that were men even in Christ's company, yet they will not profit much without the Spirit.

4. It pleased our blessed and glorious Lord to abase himself by undergoing a state of humiliation till he perfected the work of man's redemption; for so is here imported, and in this respect the Lord of glory " was not yet glorified," but continued under the veil of his state of humiliation.

5. The pouring out of the Spirit in ample measure is, in the wisdom of God, reserved till the glorification of Christ as Mediator, that so the proportion might be kept betwixt the head and the members; for " the Holy Ghost was not yet given (to believers); because that Christ was not yet glorified." And as our blessed Lord did once abase himself so far as believers must be kept back from their allowance till he, who was a worm and not a man, be glorified, so we may expect that he will not rest till we come up to share with him, now that he is exalted; and we should be content to stoop and share with him in the sad sufferings of his cause and interests, expecting that when he exalts himself in it he will respect the desolate, Psalm cii. 16, 17. And we having now to do with an exalted Lord, should expect much from him, Psalm lxviii. 18; Acts, ii. 23; v. 31.

6. While as under this promise is comprehended all that pouring out of the Spirit which followed upon the glorification of Christ, (and these gifts in the primitive times, among the rest, as a peculiar instance) the meaning is, not to put the saving graces of the Spirit, conferred upon believers, in the same rank with those extraordinary gifts that were conferred upon some temporary believers then; nor yet is it the meaning that believers now should expect the same fruits of the Spirit for kind that were conferred on some believers then; but it tends to shew, that the saving graces of the Spirit are as excellent (and more) than many gifts that had a greater lustre, and the promise is richly fulfilled when men get these, albeit they want the other; that albeit all believers do not work the like visible wonders with the apostles, yet by the receiving of the Spirit, as great wonders are wrought upon themselves in a spiritual way, for thereby the dead are quickened, the deaf made to hear, the blind to see, the lame to leap, the withered made fresh, and they get new tongues to speak the language of Canaan, which they understood not before; and that their way of carriage and deportment who received the Holy Ghost in these primitive times should be a pattern to all those who would prove that they do now partake of the Spirit.

Ver. 40. Many of the people therefore, when they heard this saying, said, Of a truth this is the prophet.

41. Others said, This is the Christ. But some said, Shall Christ come out of Galilee?

42. Hath not the scripture said, That Christ cometh of the seed of David, and out of the town of Bethlehem, where David was?

43. So there was a division among the people because of him.

44. And some of them would have taken him; but no man laid hands on him.

In these verses we have the effects of this sermon among the hearers; some are so affected with it that they acknowledge him to be that great prophet promised to Israel, Deut. xviii. 18, whom they understood to be another than the Messiah; others do confess him to be the Christ, but others oppose against that, that he (as they supposed) came out of Galilee, whereas, according to the scriptures, the Messiah was to come out of Bethlehem; and upon this diversity of opinions there ariseth a schism and division among them; but there are some so violent that they will dispute none but with their hands, and yet are impeded.

DOCTRINES.

1. Christ's doctrine will not want effects among hearers, but will either gain ground upon them, or put them to disquiet, debate, and vexation, as here we see.

2. Schism and division is an ordinary consequent that follows upon the preaching of the gospel, not through the gospel's fault, but by reason of the diverse tempers of men, unto whom it is preached; for " there was a division among the people because of him."

3. Diversity of opinions in matters of religion is a mean and occasion of divisions and rentings among a people; for it was upon their different apprehensions concerning him that this division arose " among the people."

4. Men's ignorance, or not right understanding, or taking up of the truth, and one of another, may breed division, whereas otherwise there would be an agreement; for they who said " Of a truth this is the prophet," and they who said " This is the Christ," did in effect agree; for he is a prophet, and that is one of his offices as Messiah, to be that great prophet of whom Moses spake, Deut. xviii.; and yet their own mistakes in conceiving that these two were different bred a division betwixt them.

5. Men may be much affected with Christ and his excellency who yet come far short of the truth of what is in him, and who do not come to him as a Saviour; for when they are affected with him as a prophet, yet they come far short, and do not see him to be the Christ.

6. As for those who acknowledged him to be the Christ, we may either conceive that they did but see him to be so, but yet made no use of him, (as indeed the conviction of many doth produce but small or no effects,) or that they were indeed sincere, and yet no more mention is made of them; for the Lord seeth it fitting ofttimes to bury the memory of many of his dear children in silence, who yet are no less honest than those who are more famous. Thus albeit the Lord did choose Matthias, Acts, i. 23, 26, and that rather

than Joseph, whom it seems the apostles preferred to him, and therefore mention him first, yet it pleased him never to registrate a word more of him. And by this he would teach, that to be famous, and in an account in the world, or noted among professors, is not the great business in religion, nor that which the truly sincere will make much account of.

7. Mistakes and ignorance are a great impediment to the success of the gospel. This appears, not only in them who mistook the prediction concerning the prophet, as if he were to be another than the Messiah, but in those also (either the same or other persons) who, being indeed acquainted with the scriptures, which make mention of Christ's lineage and the place of his birth, are yet ignorant of the truth about Christ's nativity, supposing that he was of Galilee, because he was educated and resided most there: "Shall Christ come out of Galilee? Hath not the scripture said that Christ cometh of the seed of David, and out of the town of Bethlehem, where David was?" which indeed was true in itself, and true of Christ, Matt. ii. 1, though they were ignorant and mistook him.

8. Men are ofttimes exceeding guilty in the matter of their own ignorance, because they do so affect it, and do not search for knowledge, but rather delight to have somewhat to cavil at; for such was their way here; as they knew from scripture where Christ should be born, so they might easily have been cleared of their doubt, if they had inquired at himself, his mother, or disciples; but they desire to cavil and shew their wit against him.

9. There are some men so brutish in their violence against Christ, that his fairest offers and his respect among others do but set them on edge against him; for after this sweet preaching, and after that some were affected, "some of them would have taken him."

10. The Lord in his wise providence doth so order that many who are very eager to wrong Christ and his followers shall yet want power to do it; for "no man laid hands on him," which followed, not from any natural conscience or reverence in them towards him, but from the over-ruling and restraining power of God.

VER. 45. Then came the officers to the chief priests and Pharisees; and they said unto them, Why have ye not brought him?

46. The officers answered, Never man spake like this man.

Followeth the confusions that arose in the council of the rulers about Christ, occasioned partly by the return of the officers without him, to ver. 50, and partly by some divisions among themselves, ver. 50—53. Albeit this was a solemn day, yet it seems they stay not at the public service, but are convened in council against him, being earnest to have him taken before the feast were ended, that so they might prevent his withdrawing of himself among the multitude. And albeit they had sent out the officers before, ver. 32, (and belike they did so from day to day,)

that they might watch all occasions for apprehending of him, yet it seemeth they had received strict injunctions to bring him this day, lest the occasion should be lost. And in these verses we have their return without their errand, and when they are posed why they did so, they give a better account of the preaching than of their commission, declaring that he preached so singularly that they could not meddle with him. Whence learn—

1. Albeit it be both lawful and necessary that seducers be restrained by civil power, yet it is a mark of a decayed and persecuting church when ecclesiastic rulers lay aside all use of their spiritual weapons, and do only arm themselves with force and power; for so was it here; their instruments to do their affairs for them were officers, and therefore no wonder they employ them against Christ, to bring him before them by force.

2. The Lord's providence is all-sufficient when he pleaseth, to disappoint his fiercest enemies, and to make them miss their errands and purposes; for the messengers return without success.

3. As it is a great evidence of men's pride when they think nothing should stand in their way, and they do rage when they are disappointed, so the Lord seeth it meet to vex persecutors, and to make their own confident creatures grieve them; for by reason of their disappointment they are in a rage, and do pour it out upon their own servants, who did not serve their ends well enough—"Why have ye not brought him?"

4. It is righteous with God that they whose great work is to oppose Christ's doctrine, and who shut all doors that themselves be not troubled with it, should be forced to hear their own creatures preach his praise, little to their contentment; for these rulers would not hear Christ, and their care was to hinder any from hearing him, and now they are made to hear their own officers preach of him in their own defence

5. As Christ's doctrine is singular, far above the law, so also was he singular, in his way of it, for authority, humility, grace, power, and evidence; for so do the officers confess of him—"Never man spake like this man;" they never heard a scribe preach in that manner. (See Psalm xlv. 2; Luke, iv. 22; Matt. vii. 28, 29.)

6. Such is the power of Christ's doctrine that even such as come unto it with a prejudice, and with a purpose to persecute the messengers thereof, may be taken by it themselves, and if not converted, yet bridled and restrained; for this is the reason why they brought him not—"Never man spake like this man," and therefore they were bound up, and had no power to meddle with him; and albeit there be no great evidence of their conversion, (for many may like preaching, and it have strange effects on them, who yet are far from God; and belike, if they had been indeed converted, they would hardly have returned with any account,) yet Christ can and hath converted even such; and it doth speak his praise, that by the means of spiritual preaching he can restrain men's fury when yet they are not really converted, nor their heart changed.

Ver. 47. Then answered them the Pharisees, Are ye also deceived?

48. Have any of the rulers or of the Pharisees believed on him?

49. But this people who knoweth not the law are cursed.

The Pharisees, who were ill pleased with their returning without their errand, are more nettled with their reason, and do upbraid them that they should suffer themselves to be deceived who were their own attenders, when yet none of the grandees or learned rabbis had closed with Christ; only an accursed crew (as they esteem them) of ignorant people doated on him. Whence learn—

1. It is an old but unjust imputation to account such as embrace Christ and his truth deluded; for so do they reckon here—" Are ye deceived?"

2. Christ, when he pleaseth, can add to the vexation of persecutors by bringing the knowledge of the truth, which they persecute in others, in among their own confident creatures, and making them respect it whom they would least suspect of any; for they are now put to it, to apprehend that Christ is coming in among their own followers, and that they are " also deceived."

3. When corrupt men are never so much convinced, yet all that will but contribute to increase their rage and their opposition to truth; for albeit it might have pleaded much for Christ among them that their very creatures are affected with his doctrine; yet all that followeth thereupon is their greater eagerness to bear him down.

4. Such as express any respect to Christ and his truth in evil times may expect much allurement and insinuation from Satan to draw them back, and that enraged persecutors will cover their fury with enchantments, to see if they can prevail; for these words, "Are ye also deceived?" although spoken in anger, yet do not tend expressly to cry them down who had said somewhat on Christ's behalf, but to insinuate with them that they should quit that course, alleging, not only that they were " deceived," but that however the multitude went wrong, yet they expected better things of them who were their ordinary followers.

5. Such as will not stoop to Christ nor respect the honour of being his servants are justly left to stoop to their own servants, to entreat for their countenance in their wrong course; therefore these eminent rulers must thus insinuate and flatter their base officers, that they may not want a back in their course.

6. It is nothing strange to see eminent men for authority and parts so puffed up with their own grandeur, and with a conceit of their own learning and knowledge, that they will not stoop to Christ nor embrace him; for they confess that not " any of the rulers (or governors of the Jews) or of the Pharisees, (their eminent sect, though not all of them rulers) have believed on him."

7. It is an old engine of Satan to keep men from Christ by reason of the opposition made unto him by eminent and able churchmen; for this is the reason whereby they think to dissuade them—" Have any of the rulers or of the Pharisees believed on him?" But this will prove a weak argument to them who have learned to call no man rabbi.

8. To live ignorant of God, especially in a visible church, is, in effect, a cursed condition; for this is a general truth—the " people who knoweth not the law, are cursed," though it be ill applied here.

9. It is an ordinary device of Satan to deter men from embracing the truth by branding them with odious and unjust imputations who do follow it; for this they urge as another strong argument: " But this people who knoweth not the law are cursed," speaking contemptibly of them as a base, ignorant, and cursed crew; whereas not only is it high presumption in church rulers thus to undervalue God's heritage in respect of themselves,—but if all this had been true, yet it was unjust for them to lay all the blame upon the people, when themselves were they who kept the people in ignorance,—but it was most unjust thus to traduce the followers of Christ, who by seeking to the fountain of blessedness, and embracing the promised Messiah, did prove their knowledge and blessedness; whereas they themselves were in effect blind (many of them by malicious shutting of their eyes) and cursed.

Ver. 50. Nicodemus saith unto them, (he that came to Jesus by night, being one of them,)

51. Doth our law judge any man, before it hear him, and know what he doeth?

While they are thinking to reclaim their officers, a new confusion ariseth among them, and they are refuted in their proud brag concerning the unanimity of their rulers, by God's stirring up of Nicodemus, who, though he do not yet openly avow Christ, yet pleads that he might have fair justice, and that they who tax the people of ignorance of the law would not manifest their own ignorance in condemning him unheard, and before they examined narrowly what he had done. Whence learn—

1. Christ, when he pleaseth, can give persecutors more work than they can overtake, and raise up so many witnesses for himself that they will hardly know how to refute them all; for before they have done with the officers Nicodemus gives a new testimony.

2. God can turn persecutors loose even where they think they are surest, and raise difference of judgment even where they bless themselves in their unity; for they use it as a strong argument to their followers, ver. 48, that the rulers are all against Christ, and now they are refuted by Nicodemus, a ruler.

3. Such as are but infirm and weak may yet get courage in a time of need to speak for Christ; and albeit true faith may lie long lurking, when it is beset with the tentation of a great place, yet Christ can draw it out when he needs it; for " Nicodemus, who came to Jesus by night," chap. iii. 1, 2, dare now say somewhat in coun-

cil for him; and albeit yet he do not openly avow him, but only pleads for that which is due to the greatest malefactor, yet it is taken by them as a testimony to Christ, and afterward we will find him appear better. Christ will not want witnesses so long as there is a timorous Nicodemus, a politic Gamaliel, yea, or an ethnic Pilate, to employ.

4. Albeit the hazard of ill company be but too discernible in many who converse with them; and albeit where the Lord gives a calling, the overcoming of that one difficulty of departing from respect and accommodations would prevent many tentations that follow on staying; yet it is not the will of God that men abandon a lawful station because of the corruptness of those who are employed with them in it; nor yet that they should quit their station in a church judicatory so long as that church hath not received a bill of divorce, and the judicatory is in itself God's ordinance, and the members such officers as are warranted by the word to be there, and not of men's devising, however they be corrupt; therefore it is marked of Nicodemus, without any blemish, that he was "one of them," and now in council with them; for this council was God's ancient ordinance, and the church of the Jews was yet a true church, and the rulers, how corrupt soever, were men in lawful ecclesiastical office; and elsewhere, it is not believing rulers' fault that they were rulers, but that they wronged Christ by their silence in their station. (See John, xii. 42.)

5. It is the lot of Christ and his followers to meet with much partiality and foul play in the world, so that they will not be allowed the fair justice that is not denied even to malefactors; for so doth Nicodemus's apology import, that they would judge him before they hear him, and know what he doth, which is not only contrary to the word, but to all equity, in any procedure, which requireth that judges should hear parties, and be clearly satisfied in matter of fact, before they proceed to sentence. (See Exod. xxiii. 1; Lev. xix. 15; Deut. xvii. 4.)

6. Men may very readily fall in that fault which they will soon discern in others; and they who tax others of ignorance may give proof of much ignorance themselves, especially when they are blinded with passion; for whereas they condemned the people as ignorant, verse 49, Nicodemus findeth their practice less agreeable to the law: "Doth our law (given to us the Jews, and of the knowledge whereof we, the rulers, do glory) judge any man before it hear him," &c.

Ver. 52. They answered and said unto him, Art thou also of Galilee? Search, and look: for out of Galilee ariseth no prophet.

53. And every man went unto his own house.

Followeth their reply to Nicodemus, with the conclusion of their whole consultation. Albeit Nicodemus spake but very little, and that which might have been said for any delinquent, yet he meeteth with as hard a rub as if he had said more. They do upbraid him with Galilee, and do assert that they are so sure that Christ, who came (as they supposed) out of Galilee, is not so much as a prophet; that if he were "also of Galilee" they would respect him the less; and therefore they bid, "Search, and look," not so much if Nicodemus were a Galilean, as if he could produce any record testifying that ever a prophet had risen out of Galilee; yet it is remarkable that however they were thus more and more enraged, yet they scatter without any conclusion against Christ. Whence learn—

1. Persecutors are so furious that if a man speak but mildly and equitably in Christ's cause, and do not oppose him as furiously as themselves, they will be sure to account him an enemy; for so do they deal with Nicodemus, who spake nothing but what justice requireth, even though the party pleaded for deserved to be condemned.

2. It is a token of fury in men, and of their rage against Christ, that when any plead for him they are not answered in reason, but their persons are reflected on; for so do they answer Nicodemus's rational exception—" Art thou also of Galilee?"

3. It is also the way of persecutors to bear down truth by making false and untrue grounds pass for current; for such are their reasonings here: "Search, and look: for out of Galilee ariseth no prophet;" where they lay down two false principles,—one was, that Christ came out of Galilee, whereas indeed he was born in Bethlehem; and the other was, that suppose it had been true that no prophet had hitherto arisen out of Galilee, yet it would not follow that none should ever arise out of it.

4. It is very great injustice to rub reproaches upon whole provinces of people within the visible church, and particularly to account of them as secluded from the participation of the gifts of God's grace, which are freely bestowed according to his pleasure; for herein they fail, not only that they reproach the whole province of Galilee, (a practice like to which did once breed great trouble, Judg. xii. 4,) but that they would seclude all of them from being ever capable of that gift of prophecy.

5. There is no council nor understanding against Christ but when he pleaseth he can dissipate all of it; for here, "every man went unto his own house," without doing anything. And albeit he take not always this mean of making their councils dissolve without conclusion, yet we may be certain that if they get permission to conclude, yet they shall never get their conclusions put in execution, or if they do execute them, yet they shall be far from the end which they propose to themselves to attain thereby, which is, the subversion of Christ, his kingdom, and truth.

6. When God hath the conspiracies of men against Christ to dissipate he needs not many probable means to effectuate it, but can cause the speaking of one word serve the turn to break the snare; for upon Nicodemus' word this followeth: " every man went unto his own house."

CHAPTER VIII.

In this chapter John continueth the narration of Christ's proceedings and doctrine at Jerusalem after the feast of tabernacles, and in it we have, 1. The history concerning the woman taken in adultery, and Christ's proceeding with those that brought her to him, and with herself, to verse 12. 2. Christ's preaching and offer to the Jews, ver. 12, with his justifying of his own testimony against them who contradicted it, ver. 13—20; his threatening of them with his departure, and that they shall be forced to see his glory, ver. 21—29 ; his preaching to them who believed on him, ver. 30—32 ; his refuting of the Jews, who boasted of their freedom and parentage, ver. 33—47, and railed at his person, opposing what he said of himself, ver. 48—58 ; and his escaping of their fury, ver. 59.

Ver. 1. Jesus went unto the mount of Olives.

2. And early in the morning he came again into the temple, and all the people came unto him; and he sat down, and taught them.

Unto this history of the adulterous woman somewhat is premitted [stated beforehand] in these verses, by way of introduction, which also points out the connexion of this purpose with the former. And, 1. Whereas his persecutors had houses of their own to go to, chap. vii. 53, he, after his preaching and debates, retires to the mount of Olives without the city that night, ver. 1. We find elsewhere that he went out and lodged by night in Bethany, (which was upon the side of that mount,) belike with Lazarus and his sisters, that so he might prevent any design they might have against him, to be acted in night uproars. (See Matt. xxi. 17.) But his early return, ver. 2, makes it probable that he rather went out to the mount itself, that he might pray in secret; and so it seems to be understood, Luke, xxi. 37, with chap. xxii. 39, 40; and this seems to have been his constant custom after this time, to leave the city by night. 2. Having spent the night there, he returns to the temple, and finding the people flock about him, he teaches them. Who these hearers were, whether the people that were now ready to depart on this day after the feast, (for whose cause Christ returns so early,) or the multitude of the inhabitants of Jerusalem, is not much material; only it seems that they were of the common sort, and few or none of the rulers. And as for his gesture in teaching, that " he sat down," it was their custom in these times, and a testimony of the respect that is due to them that carry the mind of God; and we find Christ sometimes preaches sitting, Luke, iv. 20, 21, sometimes standing, John, vii. 37, and at this time his weariness with night-watching might call for it. Nor is it much to be stood upon which of these gestures men use in preaching; but preachers ought in these things to accommodate themselves to seek the benefit of hearers, and that they be heard and seen by them.

DOCTRINES.

1. It is no strange thing to see Christ and his followers, for all their faithful services in an ingrate [ungrateful] world, yet wanting any comfortable accommodations in it; for after Christ hath spent the day-time in teaching, he wants a safe and convenient place to retire unto within the city, and must go out to " the mount of Olives." (See Luke, ix. 58.)

2. It is the duty of Christ's servants and people not to rest satisfied with any public and open performances in God's service, but they should also join therewith a conscientious observance of the duty of secret prayer; which is not only needful in ministers, that they may draw down blessings upon their endeavours, but in all the godly also; that it may be a witness of their sincerity, and a mean of keeping up communion with Christ, and of preventing much anxiety; therefore Christ, after his preaching all day, goes to prayer in " the mount of Olives."

3. As the sins of the elect deprived Christ of many a night's sleep, that so he might sanctify rest and sleep to his beloved, (whereof this passage is one instance,) so they who are fervent in following after communion with God will rather take their sleeping time than they should want an opportunity of secret prayer, as here Christ's practice doth teach.

4. As the general calling of Christianity is a very throng [constant] task, wherein a man needs never want an opportunity of doing service to God, yet without prejudice to his outward calling and occupation, so in particular a minister's task is very great, and preaching and prayer, and the duties of his calling following thereupon, may take up his whole time if he be faithful; as here Christ's practice doth teach, who having spent the night in prayer, early in the morning came again into the temple, and taught. (See Acts, vi. 4.)

5. As Christ can get hearers to himself when he pleaseth and purposeth to do good, even in despite of all his enemies, so affection to Christ and his doctrine will stand upon no impediment that would stop the way; therefore, albeit it was yet early, and the rulers were raging against Christ, yet " all the people came unto him."

6. Where affection is kindled, and draws men to frequent Christ's company, they will be sure of a meeting and to be taught by him; therefore, albeit he might justly have a great quarrel against that city, yet, since affection drew the people, he could not refuse them, but " sat down, and taught them."

Ver. 3. And the scribes and Pharisees brought unto him a woman taken in adultery; and when they had set her in the midst,

4. They say unto him, Master, this woman was taken in adultery, in the very act.

5. Now Moses in the law commanded us, that such should be stoned : but what sayest thou ?

6. This they said, tempting him, that they might have to accuse him.——

Followeth the history itself, wherein, first (in these verses), we have the case propounded to Christ by the scribes and Pharisees, who, while he is preaching, do present a woman taken in the act of adultery unto him, and, pointing out what was determined in Moses' law, do in an insinuating way ask his judgment, only that they might take some advantage of him by his answer; for if he should, according to his wonted offers of clemency, assoil her, they would condemn him as contrary to Moses; and if he condemned her to die, then they thought to make him odious to the people, as contradicting his own practice in eating with publicans and sinners, and his doctrine in offering mercy and grace so freely. We need not be inquisitive why they present only the woman, though it be probable that, however they were taken in the very act, yet the man had escaped from among their hands.

DOCTRINES.

1. Christ's servants ought not to think it strange when they get not through spiritual duties with ease, but do meet with many temptations and interruptions in them; for Christ himself was interrupted by these wicked men; they brought in " a woman taken in adultery," &c.

2. It gives just ground of suspicion when men who were violent enemies do on a sudden become flattering and insinuating friends; for it was for little good that they who even now were seeking to kill him do in a flattering way call him " Master," and do set this woman " in the midst," or in open judgment before him, and do seek resolution concerning her from him.

3. Such is the perversity of fallen man, that whatever God do testify of his displeasure, by word or judgments, against grossest sins, yet they are continued in and followed, yea, and committed in times when God calls them to solemn exercises of his worship; for albeit adultery be expressly prohibited as a gross iniquity, and albeit that and the like uncleanness had ofttimes drawn down very remarkable judgments, as on Sodom and the tribe of Benjamin, yet there is " a woman taken in adultery," and that in the time of their solemn feast.

4. Albeit men think to carry their sins very closely, and albeit uncleanness in particular be a work of darkness, yet the Lord, when he pleaseth, can easily bring it out to light; for she is taken " in the very act;" and albeit many may escape this, yet the Lord can make their sin find them out, and make their own consciences bring it out many years after it is committed.

5. Albeit the Lord may justly bring out hidden sin, that the sinner may be made a spectacle of his vengeance, yet ofttimes it proves a great mercy to the sinner when he gets not liberty to lurk in a sinful course, but is brought out to light with it; as here it proved in the issue: this woman, being discovered, is brought to Christ even by his very enemies, and (in appearance) gets good of him, which she had missed if she had not been found out.

6. The Lord doth so far detest the sin of adultery, violating the covenant of marriage,—and especially in women, who do corrupt a family by bringing in an illegitimate issue into it,—that it is his will that such a transgression be punished with death; for so do they repeat his law given by Moses, " that such should be stoned;" and being a punishment of a moral transgression, it should stand in force so long as the transgression is still the same. The law concerning the putting of adulterers to death is clear from Levit. xx. 10; Deut. xxii. 22; but for the particular way of it, by stoning, it seems to be gathered from that particular law concerning the betrothed virgin and him that lay with her, Deut. xxii. 23, 24.

7. It is the disposition of wicked men to make it their study to lay snares whereby they think to entrap God's people, and to seek advantages against them; partly by fair language, and partly by cunning tentations, that so they may make them and their way odious; for so do they deal with Christ—they flatter him, and ask, " but what sayest thou?" but they did it " tempting him, that they might have to accuse him." And albeit they gained nothing at Christ's hand in this, yet his followers have need to be cautious, and to beware of subtle insinuators; not that it is best to countermine subtlety with subtlety, but they should look on honesty as great safety and divine policy in such cases.

8. Christ doth easily discern the drift of his enemies, and doth know which are tempting, curious questions, and which are propounded out of necessity; therefore doth John, being taught of him, record what was their drift, " This they said, tempting him, that they might have to accuse him." And indeed, when any come to Christ with cases, he first looks into the questioner's heart, that he may know how it is affected with what he propounds before he answer it.

Ver. 6. —— But Jesus stooped down, and with his finger wrote on the ground, as though he heard them not.

7. So when they continued asking him, he lifted up himself, and said unto them, He that is without sin among you, let him first cast a stone at her.

8. And again he stooped down, and wrote on the ground.

9. And they which heard it, being convicted by their own conscience, went out one by one, beginning at the eldest, even unto the last: and Jesus was left alone, and the woman standing in the midst.

In the second place we have Christ's dealing with them who brought the woman, and propounded the case. And, 1. He writes upon the ground as if he heard them not, in testimony of his slighting them, ver. 6. 2. When his silence seemed to them to flow from some advantage they had of him in this matter, (and therefore they importune him the more,) he leaves the question, and turns to the questioners, bidding them search their own bosoms, and since they needed not witnesses, who were to cast the first stone, Deut. xvii. 7, he bids those among them who were without sin supply that office; and again writes upon the ground, in testimony of his dislike of them, ver. 7, 8. Upon this, 3. Followeth the effect of Christ's answer, which is, the conviction of these wicked men, who, being conscious to themselves what they were, and not willing to confess it, nor to debate with him who could bring them out to light before the people, take advantage of his stooping down to slip quietly away, leaving the woman and Christ alone, (not simply alone, for the multitude stayed, and the woman " in the midst," but all the accusers left them;) and this they did, " beginning at the eldest," who were most guilty, and most prudent to discern what was in this answer, ver. 9. For clearing this answer a little, consider—1. As for that phrase, " he that is without sin," which imports a complete purity, we need not here curiously distinguish it from that blamelessness and being irreprehensible which is elsewhere urged, 1 Tim. iii. 2, Titus, i. 6 ; seeing the law of God requires both, and it was their great presumption to insult so over the woman, and over Christ as an enemy to the law, when yet they were only not sinless, but not free of the like gross crimes, if not the same wherein the woman was taken. 2. Christ's requiring they should be without sin who executed this sentence doth not condemn magistrates who execute justice, though themselves be sinners, yea, though they be vicious themselves ; for he doth not speak as a magistrate, prescribing that none should be punished but by innocent and blameless men ; nor doth he condemn the doing of justice and punishing of sin in itself ; but as a teacher, he sheweth what God will find culpable in magistrates—to wit, if they make little conscience of their own sin when yet they punish sin in others. 3. Albeit Christ's discourse doth not answer directly to their question, yet it fully breaks their snare laid for him, and brings a snare upon themselves ; for it doth not strike against Moses' law, seeing he acknowledgeth the equity of the sentence of stoning, though he was not a judge to pronounce it, and as a minister, would have them look to their own consciences ; nor doth this rough dealing contradict his doctrine of free grace, seeing he is speaking to unhumbled Pharisees, that he may fit them for his mercy, and he deals sweetly with the woman afterward ; but as for them, his discourse doth indeed pinch them, while as they who boasted so much of respect to the law are found to regard it so little in their own practice that their consciences send them away confounded.

DOCTRINES.

1. As Christ knoweth who propound questions only to tempt him, and who desire to be taught, so he, who warmly entertains the one, doth justly slight the other as unworthy of an answer ; for " Jesus stooped down, and with his finger wrote on the ground, as though he heard them not." It is but curiosity to inquire what he wrote ; but his end in it was, not only to shew that it is fitter ministers do anything than employ themselves in civil affairs, but chiefly, to shew that their question was idle and deserved no answer.

2. Christ's enemies may get leave to think that they have some notable advantage of him and his followers, only that their own disappointment may be the more shameful and sad ; for before they are convinced, they think Christ is silent because he knew not what to say, and therefore " they continued asking him," as insulting over him in their own minds, if not also in their expressions.

3. Albeit Christ be tender and gracious towards humbled sinners, yet he will strictly press the law upon all such as conceit of their righteousness, and will not come to him ; therefore doth he deal so roughly with those men, and points out what the law required of them.

4. The perfect and spiritual law of God doth require of men, not only that they be without public and visible blemish, but that they be without sin or spot ; for so much doth Christ require of these unhumbled men, that they be " without sin."

5. It is the will of God that those who punish sin in others should be sensible of their own failings, and that the sense of their own sins make them tender towards others ; and it is a token of unsanctified spirits, when men who censure or punish others do not look upon their own ways, nor do abstain from all lewd practices themselves, nor look upon the worst of sinners as their own picture, if they were left to themselves ; for this is the scope of Christ's answer, as is before explained.

6. In our necessary meddling with wicked men it is our duty to take heed we do nothing that may seem to approve them in their wicked ways ; therefore, " again he stooped down, and wrote on the ground," to testify that as at first he liked not their discourse, so yet he approved it not (however he had answered it), nor would keep up conference with them.

7. As without Christ's power the most spiritual doctrine will do no good to the best of men, so when he pleaseth he can put an edge upon a very short sentence, to make it waken the most benumbed conscience, and cause it to imprint inward challenges upon the heart and outward shame upon the foreheads of men ; for so doth it here appear ; they are " convicted by their own conscience," and glad of an opportunity to steal away.

8. Awakened conscience will get other things to think upon than to be taken up with idle cavils about religion, or descanting upon the faults of others only ; for they quit both their tempting of Christ and accusing of the woman, and steal away.

9. A wakened conscience will tell a man that the longer he liveth his guilt is still increasing, and he hath daily the more cause to be ashamed of himself for it ; for so much is imported that " they went out, beginning at the eldest, even unto the last."

10. Every conviction of conscience is not saving, nor is every one in a state of grace whose conscience finds the edge of the word to make him ashamed of sin ; for these men are " convicted," and " went out," as being ashamed, who yet are but in the gall of bitterness.

11. It is a sure evidence of an unsound wakening of conscience when men's convictions make

them flee from Christ, and shun either his further convictions or comforts; whereas it is good not to go away from him when sin is discovered, and the truly humbled sinner is kept with him till he find favour; for so appears in them; being "convicted," they "went out" from Christ, and that "one by one," without noise, when he was now stooping down, that so he might not have occasion to say any more to them; whereas the poor woman, though let go, stands still "in the midst," in the place where she was sifted as a guilty person, till she hear what Christ will say to her.

12. All the plots of wicked men against Christ will at last tend to their own visible and open shame; for this was the issue of their enterprise. They came in with a resolution to entrap Christ, and they are sent out with much shame and confusion on their own faces.

Ver. 10. When Jesus had lifted up himself, and saw none but the woman, he said unto her, Woman, where are those thine accusers? hath no man condemned thee?

11. She said, No man, Lord. And Jesus said unto her, Neither do I condemn thee: go, and sin no more.

In the third place we have Christ's dealing with the woman herself, who being left by her accusers, and not condemned by them, he doth also dismiss her with a gentle warning to watch over her ways in time to come; in doing whereof he doth not make void the law of Moses, nor say that none ought to condemn her to death, but he declines to act the part of a civil magistrate in passing sentence upon her, and doth act the part of a minister of the gospel in absolving a humbled sinner.

DOCTRINES.

1. As they who run away from Christ when they are convinced do but go on in their sin and carry their shame with them, so they who attend upon Christ and betake themselves to the posture of condemned sinners, will at last get a gracious answer; as this woman's experience doth teach, who (when her accusers went out) did stay still, to her own great advantage.

2. It is necessary that such as are waiting on Christ for grace be serious observers of his dealing, that from thence they may learn to know what an one he is; for his questions, when he lifted up himself, "Where are those thine accusers? hath no man condemned thee?" did not flow from any ignorance in him, but served to excite her to consider the power of his word, and what effects it had produced, and to shew that his doings are not easily marked, even when they are acted before our eyes.

3. Such as are truly humbled with the sense of their sins will get little pleasure to meddle, save with those things which nearly concern themselves; for albeit Christ propounded two questions, yet she answers only to what concerns herself, and that no man had condemned her, not meddling with what concerned them.

4. Such as Christ hath a mind to do good unto are not to expect that so much will be intimated unto them at first, but they must be content to be exercised with attendance and speaking to Christ, till the complete deliverance come; for so much appears in his dealing with this woman; he speaks so in her cause to the Pharisees as encourageth her to stay still till she see what further he will say; then he leads her up to speak to him, and gives her a ground of an argument, that since no man had condemned h therefore he, the Saviour of sinners, would deal gently with her, and at last he brings out his sweet sentence.

5. The charge and office of the ministry is inconsistent in God's appointment with the exercise of the office of magistrate in one and the same person, and it is so weighty a calling that it is enough to take up the whole man; therefore doth Christ, the great messenger of the covenant and preacher of the gospel, refuse to take on that calling, "Neither do I condemn thee." (So also Luke, xii. 13, 14.)

6. It is the allowance of Christ that humble and cast-down sinners be gently dealt with by his ministers, and his rich grace will absolve such as do condemn themselves before him; for by this sentence he not only declines to exercise the office of magistrate, but doth absolve her whom he knew to be humbled in the court of conscience.

7. It ought to be no impediment to humble sinners to expect absolution from Christ that their sins are such as by the law of God and man deserve bodily death, or that they are to die a violent death for them; for though this sin deserved stoning by the law of God, yet that doth not hinder Christ to give her a pardon.

8. Grace is so absolute and free that it can make a very sudden change in sinners; it can take them, as it were, in the very height of their impiety, and convert and make pardoned saints of them; for so it appears in this woman, who being taken in the very act of adultery, goeth not away from Christ till she be absolved.

9. Such as have tasted of Christ's grace in pardoning their sin will retain so much sense of their own corrupt inclinations, and of their obligation to Christ for his mercy, that it will put them to a wary and circumspect walking for time to come; for so much is imported in the direction subjoined to her absolution, "Neither do I condemn thee; go, and sin no more." (See chap. v. 14.)

10. Albeit humble and pardoned sinners should have an eye especially upon the sins they have been formerly addicted unto, and upon gross and scandalous evils, that they break not out into them, yet they should also be sensible of their proneness to all sin, as having the seed of all sin within them, and should have an universal hatred against all sin, and be watchful over themselves that they fall not into any sin; therefore is the direction general, "sin no more," that she should not only be jealous of her own inclination to her former debordings, [crimes,] or oppose and strive against some sins, while she delighted in other sins, but that she should watch against all kind of sin.

Ver. 12. Then spake Jesus again unto them, saying, I am the light of the world: he that followeth me shall not walk in darkness, but shall have the light of life.

In the rest of the chapter we have Christ's preaching, conference, and debates with several sorts of hearers, which we will consider in order as they lie. As for the time wherein this was done, we need not determine that it was on another day than that wherein he absolved the adulteress, which some gather from this, that the Pharisees were then gone out, ver. 9, and are now come in again, ver. 13; for it may be conceived that those who now debate with him were some others than they who had brought in the woman, who remained among the multitude, to watch for all advantages; or it need not be thought strange that even they should have so much impudence as shortly to return back to oppose his ministry so much as they could.

In the first place, in this verse, we have Christ returning to his office of preaching, after that interruption made by the scribes and Pharisees, and making a rich offer of himself, which occasions all the subsequent debates and discourses; and in it, taking occasion, as would appear, of the sun's rising and bright shining in the morning, he holds out himself as the true Sun of Righteousness and light of the world, offering to all those who follow him that they shall not only have present light to order and sweeten their walking, but that this light shall bring life with it, and lead to eternal life. Whence learn—

1. Whatever interruptions wicked men lay in Christ's way, yet he will not be hindered from doing and offering good to sinners; for notwithstanding they hindered him in preaching, ver. 2, 3, yet now he returns to it again, "Then spake Jesus again unto them."

2. There is no better way to conciliate love to Christ than to study to know him well, in his natures, excellences, riches, and free offers to sinners; therefore doth he commend himself here, that they may follow him, " I am the light of the world," &c. (See Psalm ix. 10; Rev. xv. 3, 4.)

3. The whole world lies in darkness of itself, being ignorant of misery, and of the remedy thereof, following the works of darkness, and liable to affliction, wrath, and want of comfort, and to be cast into outer darkness, where there is weeping and gnashing of teeth; for so is imported in this doctrine, that without Christ mankind are as the world is without the sun, and the use of those lights which are enlightened thereby.

4. The remedy of this sad condition is only to be had in Christ, and he is able to cure all this darkness by enlightening the mind, and causing men to know themselves, by discovering and dispelling the works of darkness, removing of wrath and misery, giving clear and wholesome directions in duty, and cheering up and warming the hearts of his own with his comforts; for saith he, " I am the light of the world." (See chap. i. 4, 5, 9.) The Father is indeed a light to which no man can approach, and before whom angels do cover their faces; but this light being revealed in the Son, is brought near and made comfortable unto men. And his instruments and messengers are called lights, because they instrumentally convey this light which cometh originally from him.

5. Christ's grace and light are not confined to one place or sort of persons, but are patent to the world, and to men of all ranks and conditions in it; therefore is he called " the light of the world."

6. They who would participate of the riches that are in Christ ought to take him for their guide, and follow him, neither presuming to go before and prescribe unto him, nor yet loitering and lying by when he, in his example and directions, is going before; for the advantage of this offer is to him " that followeth me," saith he.

7. As it is the duty of men who would partake of Christ's riches to follow him, so they who follow him indeed will employ all the comfort they find in him to enable and encourage them to duty, and will account it sufficient if they be enabled to walk after him, whatever their lot be otherwise; therefore is the promise held out, containing what they may expect in walking.

8. They who follow Christ may expect that in his light they shall see light; they will not be left in darkness of ignorance, nor under the power of the ways of darkness, nor under the danger of outer darkness; and albeit sometimes they may be left under a dark condition, wanting comfort and feeling wrath, Isa. l. 10, yet neither is that their allowance, nor shall they constantly walk so, or be left altogether under such a condition, but in due time shall have light arising in darkness; for so is the promise, " he shall not walk in darkness, but shall have light."

9. The light that comes from Christ will have quickening life accompanying it, and doth in the issue tend to eternal life, whereas the false light of the wicked ends in sorrow, Isa. l. 11; therefore is it said, he " shall have the light of life," or that light which is accompanied with the present life of holiness, which in due time will end in eternal life.

Ver. 13. The Pharisees therefore said unto him, Thou bearest record of thyself; thy record is not true.

14. Jesus answered and said unto them, Though I bear record of myself, yet my record is true: for I know whence I came, and whither I go; but ye cannot tell whence I come, and whither I go.

In the next place we have Christ's first conference and debate with the Pharisees, who contradict his testimony, as worthy to be suspected, ver. 13; to which Christ replies, asserting the truth and certainty of his own testimony, ver. 14; challenging them for rash judgment of him, when yet he was not judging them, ver. 15; though, if he did it, his testimony were to be regarded, having not only himself but his Father to bear witness to him, which were a sufficient number of witnesses by the law, ver. 16—18; but they were ignorant of the Father, as they were of him, ver. 19; to which is subjoined that however he spake thus freely, and they had a great mind to take him, and had him among their hands, yet they were restrained, ver. 20.

In these verses we have their exception against his testimony, as obnoxious to be suspected, seeing he speaks so much in his own cause, ver. 13; and Christ, albeit, chap. v. 31, he did, by way of preterition, pass this, that he might bring in the many witnesses that pleaded for him, yet here he doth assert that his testimony concerning himself is true, which he confirms from this reason; that he came from God, and was to return to him again; and being certain of this, he might assert it, whereas they, being ignorant hereof, did carp at him. The force of this reason consists in these: partly, that he being God, who came from the Father in respect of his manifestation in the flesh, and was to return to him in regard of the manifestation of his glory in the human nature exalted, was a witness above all exception; partly, that being the great Angel of the covenant, and ambassador from the Father, to whom he was to return an account, he might lawfully publish his own instructions and commission, which were revealed only to himself, and ought to be credited; and partly, that he, perfectly knowing this, might boldly testify and stand to it.

DOCTRINES.

1. Christ's enemies are endless and restless in their oppositions unto the success of the gospel; for after their former interruption, ver. 3, he no sooner begins to preach again but they do again cavil.

2. Christ's rich offers will not prevail with malicious enemies, to make them quit their opposition and submit; for when he is not threatening, but graciously inviting sinners to partake of his fulness, they yet cavil.

3. Whatever just cause there be to suspect their testimony who are but sinful and mere men when they commend themselves, yet this derogates nothing from the glory of Christ's being true in his testimonies concerning himself; for albeit they think they have great advantage of Christ from this common principle, " Thou bearest record of thyself; thy record is not true," yet it hath no weight at all here. It is true, indeed, that the corrupt nature of man (which is prone to seek itself, and hunt after vainglory, which yet is as easily lost as obtained, and cannot bear our weight in a day of distress) may render such a testimony uncertain, but not necessarily prove it untrue, even in men,—for honest men may lawfully commend themselves in some cases, and yet not bear false witness, nor yet be guilty of self-seeking,—but it doth not at all hold true in Christ, who is separate from sinners, and not to be bound by the rules prescribed to men in such cases.

4. Enemies' opposing and interrupting of Christ will not make void his purposes, but he can make their opposition occasion much benefit to his people; for albeit they thought by cavils to hinder his preaching, yet his very defences and replies did bring forth most precious truths of the gospel, for the edification of his hearers then, and of his people to the end of the world.

5. Whatever be Christ's gracious condescendence for the conviction of sinners and confirmation of his own, yet he will not allow that any should deny him the glory of any of his prerogatives, and particularly of his truth; therefore, albeit he formerly condescended, chap. v. 31, to waive his testimony of himself, that so friends and foes might see how many witnesses he had for him, yet here, when they contradict it, he will not pass from it, " Though I bear record of myself, yet my record is true."

6. Christ being true God, that cannot lie, and who only can reveal himself and his will, and coming out of the bosom of the Father as ambassador into the world, is an authentic witness, above all exception, in what he reveals, and his naked testimony and assertion ought to be credited without seeking further proof or arguments; therefore doth he confirm the truth of his record from the consideration of whence he came.

7. As Christ and his followers came into the world for awhile, to do the service for which they are appointed, and then to go to God, so the exaltation of Christ doth put his divine original and authority, and consequently the truth of his testimony, out of all question; therefore doth he subjoin whither he goeth, not only as the comfortable issue of his toil, which he looked to, but as a clear proof that he came from God, and consequently that his record is true.

8. Such as are employed in commission from God to carry his mind, and do reckon that they have an account to make to God who sent them, will find a necessity to cleave to their commission, and to publish nothing but truth. So much also may be learned from Christ's argument, who, considering whence he came, and whither he goeth, doth therefore bear a true record.

9. Christ's knowledge of his own excellency and authority is sufficient to warrant the truth of his doctrine whoever else be ignorant of it; for he proves it true on this, " I know whence I came," &c., albeit, saith he, " ye cannot tell," &c.

10. They who would cleave to controverted and opposed truth, should not have it by guess only, but should certainly know and be persuaded of it, and then speak for it. So much also may be learned from Christ's confirming the truth of his record thus, that not only he was indeed from God, and his doctrine the truth, but " I know whence I came," &c.

11. It is men's ignorance (either simple or affected) of Christ's person and commission, that makes them so little regard, or lay so little weight on, his doctrine and testimony; therefore, in opposition to his knowledge, he subjoins, " but ye cannot tell whence I come, and whither I go," and therefore do carp at my testimony and doctrine concerning myself.

VER. 15. Ye judge after the flesh; I judge no man.

Before Christ produce any further proof of the truth of his record, he doth here challenge them for their censure of him; and as in the former verse he points out a difference betwixt himself and them in the point of knowing whence he came and whither he goeth, so here he points out another difference, and a defect in them, flowing from this mistake—to wit, that as they were ignorant of him so they judged carnally of him, and according to outward appearance, being led by their carnal principles, whereas he, on the contrary, judged no man; which is not to be understood, in opposition to their manner of judging, that he judged no man after the flesh,—for (though that be true, yet) then what is subjoined, ver. 16, would import that he might judge after the flesh,—nor is it to be understood that he judged no man in a political way, but only in an ecclesiastical way, as pointing out their faults; for neither in that respect will the opposition betwixt him and them stand, seeing they were not now judging him in any political way, but only censuring his doctrine and person,—nor yet is it Christ's meaning, in this place, to shew that he divests himself of that sovereign dominion and government that he hath over men and all creatures jointly with the Father, of which chapter v. 22, (for that he never quits;)—but his scope is, to shew that he forbore the exercise of it, in some respects, for a time; and particularly, 1. That his chief errand in this his first coming was not to judge men, but to purchase and offer salvation to lost sinners, chap. iii. 17, and if any were condemned, it was but an accidental event flowing from men's own corruptions. 2. More especially, now, when they were judging him, he was not judging, but teaching and making rich offers, and therefore their carriage was more blameworthy.

DOCTRINES.

1. Albeit malicious carpers, or other enemies, can do nothing to Christ's prejudice, yet will he not pass the wrong intended by them in their endeavours without a rebuke; therefore, albeit he hath shewed that their cavils could not make void his testimony, yet he will challenge them for their attempt.

2. Rash judging and censuring of Christ, his doctrine and way, is the ordinary fault of his enemies, and an injury which he will not endure at their hands; for this is their particular attempt, which he reproves, that they fell a judging.

3. Men by nature are so blind and fleshly that their judgment of Christ and his matters is to be suspected, and such as justly deserves a reproof from him; for this was, in part, their fault, "Ye judge after the flesh," or according to the dictates of your corrupt reason and hearts, which cannot perceive the things that are of God.

4. To judge of Christ according to visible and outward appearances of his person or kingdom, or according to our own prejudicate thoughts, is but a corrupt judgment, and such as doth provoke him to anger; for this further, and in particular, was their fault, in judging after the flesh, when their prejudices and blinded judgments let them see no more of Christ than his outside.

5. It is the will of God that his servants be found in meekness about their duty, when they are encountered with hard measure and unjust usage from their enemies; for so doth Christ's example teach, who, when they judged him, was judging no man, neither in the general exercise of his calling nor at this sermon in particular.

6. It speaks Christ's gracious condescendence unto lost man, that he first essays him with the sweet offer of salvation in the gospel, to see how that will work, before he proceed to a sentence of condemnation; for saith he, " I judge no man," in this my state of humiliation, and at this time in particular; and albeit he spake sometimes sharply unto them, yet it tended but to drive them to his mercy.

7. Christ's mild manner of dealing, even to his enemies, doth add to their ditty, [ignominy,] and aggravate their condemnation, who do not only slight but oppose him; therefore doth Christ mention this to shew how great their guilt was in malicious carping at him: " Ye judge after the flesh, I judge no man."

VER. 16. And yet if I judge, my judgment is true: for I am not alone, but I and the Father that sent me.

17. It is also written in your law, that the testimony of two men is true.

18. I am one that bear witness of myself, and the Father that sent me beareth witness of me.

Lest they should except that therefore he judged them not because he could not truly challenge anything, therefore he declares that he might judge them if he would, and if he did, his judgment were true. And thus he returns to assert the truth of his own record, and—1. He enlargeth the assertion, shewing that if he not only bare record of himself, but against them also, yet his record is true. 2. He adds a second reason, confirming this assertion, which is propounded, ver. 16, that he is not alone in what he doth, but the Father is with him, and it is confirmed, ver. 17, 18, that if the testimony of two men be sufficient in any matter, according to Moses' law, to prove it true, Deut. xvii. 6, how much more is his record true, being witnessed unto by himself who is God, and by the Father also, who by a voice from heaven, and by mighty signs and wonders, did declare and confirm who he was, and command he should be hearkened unto?

From verse 16, learn—1. Albeit Christ do condescend to offer salvation unto lost sinners, yet if he pleased, he might in place thereof judge and condemn them, and yet do no wrong; for he speaks here of his judging, as a thing he might well do, if he pleased.

2. Christ cannot err in judging of men; but as all his testimonies are true, so also he is true in judging, how cross soever it seem to us; for " yet if I judge, my judgment is true."

3. As all those who are employed by God in his service are never left alone by him in their difficulties, so in particular Christ and the Father are undivided in the work of judging of men, as in all other works; and the Father is still with him as being of the same essence, and as with his ambassador and servant, acting according to his instructions; therefore saith he, " I am not

alone, but I and the Father that sent me," where he proves the Father's conjunction with him from his being his Father by eternal generation, and from his sending of him.

4. Christ's union with the Father, in judging, is an infallible proof that he cannot err in that work, it being impossible that he who is God, one with the Father, and who in all things walks according to his Father's instructions, should err in any of his testimonies or records; therefore is it given as a reason why his "judgment is true: for I am not alone, but I and the Father that sent me."

From verses 17, 18, learn—1. The laws given by God do not serve for rules to direct or bind him, who is supreme and above all law, but to be a rule and direction to those to whom they are given; therefore it is called "your law," not that they were the penmen or prescribers of it, nor yet only because they gloried of it, albeit they did little regard it in practice, but because it was given for their use and direction.

2. It is the will of God that as men should not be rash in private judging, so in public controversies they should not proceed to judgment upon every report or single testimony, but at least the matter must be proven by two witnesses; for saith he, "It is written in your law, that the testimony of two men is true;" not that necessarily everything that is deponed by two witnesses is true,—for false witnesses may conspire to assert an untruth, 1 Kings, xxi. 13; Matt. xxvi. 60; Acts, vi. 11, 13,—but the meaning of the law is, that at least there shall be no fewer testimonies to prove anything; and as great care should be had in examining witnesses, to find out if there be any falsehood, (wherein, even in persecuting of Christ, the Pharisees were exact, Mark, xiv. 55, 56,) and for more security the Jews put the witnesses to confirm their testimony by being first in executing the sentence, Deut. xvii. 6, 7, so where two witnesses concur in one testimony, the matter is to be accounted legally true and proven, albeit the witnesses should lie.

3. Albeit Christ, as God, be above law, yet his ways are so just that the law can have no just exception against him; therefore doth he confirm his assertion from their own law; for if the testimony of two men (who are fallible, and may deceive) doth suffice to prove a matter to be true, how much more is he to be credited who is witnessed unto by the Father, and by himself as God witnessing of himself, as man and Mediator, seeing these witnesses are truth itself, who cannot lie nor be biassed?

4. The truth of Christ's offers unto lost sinners is so abundantly confirmed by unquestionable witnesses, that none can call them in question without egregious wrong done to God. So much also may be gathered from this double witness of himself, and the Father that sent him.

5. The Father and the Son, albeit one and undivided in essence and operation, yet are distinct persons, and did distinctly bear witness in this testimony concerning the man Christ and his offers as Mediator; for saith he, "I am one that bear witness of myself, and the Father that sent me beareth witness of me."

Ver. 19. Then said they unto him, Where is thy Father? Jesus answered, Ye neither know me, nor my Father: if ye had known me, ye should have known my Father also.

As before they carped at his testimony concerning himself, so now, little regarding what he said, they carp at his other witness, desiring to know who his Father was; for they, alleging he had none but Joseph, would look upon him to be as unfit a witness as they conceived himself to be; or if he should call God his Father, that would waken the old quarrel, chap. v. 18; but Christ doth not stand to answer their question, but declares they were both ignorant of the Father and him, and ignorant of the Father because they knew not him. Whence learn—

1. Let truth be never so clearly held forth, yet (without the power of grace) enemies will not be gained thereby, but they will still jangle and set their wit and parts on work to find out new cavils; for so do they here; all the fruit of Christ's doctrine on them is a new, taunting question, "Where is thy Father?"

2. Where there is greatest conceit of parts and abilities, there is ordinarily greatest real ignorance, especially of saving truths in a saving manner; for these great rabbis, who think themselves able enough to hold up the debate with Christ, get this sentence from him, "Ye neither know me, nor my Father."

3. Albeit the Father and the Son be two distinct persons, yet they are undivided in essence, so that the one cannot be known without the other; and particularly, albeit devils may believe there is a deity, and tremble, James, ii. 19, and albeit Jews and others may have some notions of him as creator of the world, yet there is no saving knowledge of God but in Christ, John, xvii. 3; therefore saith he, "Ye neither know me, nor my Father," and particularly, he asserts their ignorance of the Father because they knew not him.

4. The divine nature did so evidently shine in the Son that whosoever knew what a deity was might have seen it in him; and whosoever took up his deity were thereby forthwith led to know the deity of the Father; for saith he, "if ye had known me, ye should have known the Father also." And herein God's gracious condescendence is to be seen, who, since his divine nature could not be comprehended nor taken up by us, was pleased to reveal and manifest himself in his own Son, (the express image of his person,) clothed with our flesh, and to hold out this mirror unto us in that word which is near unto us, and which doth prevent our anxious thoughts about ascending up to heaven, or descending down unto the deep, Romans, x. 6—8.

Ver. 20. These words spake Jesus in the treasury, as he taught in the temple: and no man laid hands on him; for his hour was not yet come.

In this verse we have a conclusion subjoined to this first conference, wherein it is declared, that however he spake thus boldly, and that in a place of the temple where they had him as in a net, and however their rage was great against him, yet none of them meddled with him, God so ordering the matter because his time of suffering was not yet come. As for this place, the treasury, the Jews had a chest in Joash's time wherein they received the people's collections as they entered into the temple, 2 Chron. xxiv. 8, &c., and, it seems, they continued this practice afterward, Mark, xii. 41; Luke, xxi. 1; but this was a room, or chamber, belonging to the temple, wherein those treasures and other things belonging to the service of the temple were kept, of which see 1 Kings, vi. 5, &c.; 2 Chron. v. 1; xxxi. 11, 12; Neh. xiii. 5—9; x. 37, 38; Ezek. viii. 29. And as this was their custom then, so the Lord doth yet require that somewhat be laid up for religious uses, providing it be lawfully acquired and rightly employed.

DOCTRINES.

1. The many hazards wherein Christ and his servants may be, and the many advantages that enemies seem to have over them, should not cool their courage in doing duty; for "these words (which were so sharp) spake Jesus (even) in the treasury, as he taught in the temple."

2. As enemies are endless in their rage and attempts against Christ and his people, so the providence of God is as vigilant to preserve them so long as he seeth fit; for as before, so over again, "no man laid hands on him, for his hour was not yet come." The providence of God was as effectual for his preservation at one time as at another.

3. This frequent repetition of his preservation because his hour was not yet come serveth not only as an encouragement to his people in being faithful in their duty and trust, seeing they are guarded by him who can preserve so often, but further serves to teach—1. Many deliverances should never make us put thoughts of suffering in God's time out of our mind; for Christ's preservation so frequently is still seasoned with this, his hour was coming, though not yet. 2. Former preservation speaks so much of God's power and favour as may make his people resolute to endure suffering when his will is to expose them to it; for such use doth Christ make of this his frequent preservation when they take him, which is the meaning in part of Luke, xxii. 53. 3. Christ also makes use of it in that place, Luke, xxii. and Matt. xxvi. 55, to testify that as his bold and open carriage and his preservation in it did bear witness of his integrity, and of God's favour towards him, so their clandestine course did testify what confusion of conscience they had in it; and indeed, however enemies may carry themselves high when they are persecuting, yet their consciences within are a sufficient witness and torture to them, if they would suffer them to speak.

VER. 21. Then said Jesus again unto them, I go my way, and ye shall seek me, and shall die in your sins: whither I go, ye cannot come.

From this to the end of ver. 29 we have a new sermon and debate, wherein Christ threatening

them with his removal, and the sad separation that should be betwixt him and them, ver. 21, they, according to their custom, do tauntingly cavil at it, ver. 22; but Christ sheweth what their disposition was, contrary to his, ver. 23, and therefore they could not but perish, especially since they made no use of him, ver. 24, he having so often informed them what he was, so that they could not sin ignorantly, ver. 25; and further, Christ sheweth that though he had much to lay to their charge, yet he would forbear now, and content himself with this, that his Father, whom he obeyed, was true, and would call them to an account, ver. 26; and that (however they understood not this at present, ver. 27, yet) after his suffering, they should be convinced that he is the Messiah, obedient unto and approven of his Father, verse 28, 29.

In this verse we have the sum of this sermon, wherein, considering that they despised his rich offer, ver. 12, and not only so, but intended violence against him; therefore he threatens them with the removal of himself, and that however they seek him, yet they shall perish in their sins, and have no access to him. Of this see chap. vii. 34.

DOCTRINES.

1. The greatest of opposition will not drive Christ away where he hath a mind to stay, or till he please; for he would not be put away by their violence, but I go, saith he.

2. The wicked may at last get their will of Christ, so far as to be rid of him, but for a plague to them; for to them who would have taken him, ver. 20, he saith, "I go my way."

3. Where Christ's gracious offers are rejected, and himself persecuted, it is a presage that he will remove; for to such he saith again, as his next message after the former, ver. 12, "I go my way."

4. As Christ's removal is the saddest of judgments, so it is a judgment, the evil whereof is not easily laid to heart; therefore must it be so oft inculcated upon them as their saddest stroke.

5. Christ's removal from a people draws on such miseries as may make great despisers miss and need him, and make them glad to seek him, if so be they could find him; for "I go my way, and ye shall seek me."

6. Since reprobate men do sometimes seek Christ, whom they despised, not because they love him any better, nor because they purpose to give him any employment about their sin, but only to be rid of trouble by him; therefore such seekers do die impenitents for all their pains, and go to their graves before they be rid of their sins, and with their bones full of them; for to such he saith, "ye shall seek me, and shall die in your sins"—that is, die impenitent and pine away under the punishment of iniquity till they die, and that because they would not die to sin.

7. Such as do reject Christ here, and die impenitent and unreconciled with him, shall find his removal from them will end in eternal separation; therefore it is subjoined, "whither I go, ye cannot come."

Ver. 22. Then said the Jews, Will he kill himself? because he saith, Whither I go, ye cannot come.

In this verse we have their taunting reply to this sad threatening. They think there is no good place (nay, nor heaven) to which he can go, but they may well follow, if not go before him; and therefore they allege that he will take some black course of cutting himself off, and they will let him go to that without their company. Whence learn—

1. None are more ready to despise threatenings than they who most deserve them, and lie nearest the danger of them: for so appears in the answer given by these hearers.

2. Such as do once breed themselves to a despising of threatenings will grow still the longer the more hardened and insolent, till the execution of vengeance discover their folly; for now they are grown worse than in their former reply, chap. vii. 35. It is but cold matter of comfort that the more a man habituate himself in sin he grows the more bold and impudent, for that is a spiritual plague upon him.

3. Obdurate sinners may come to that height, that instead of trembling at threatenings they may mock at them and bitterly taunt the carriers of these sad tidings; for to such a height do these come, "Will he kill himself? because he saith, whither I go ye cannot come."

4. Lofty pride in mocking at the word, and taunting the messengers thereof, will not go away without exemplary punishment, and such scoffers may meet with that plague in reality which they in reproach cast upon the servants of God; for so befel these scoffers: they tauntingly suppose Christ will kill himself; but within few years, in the siege of Jerusalem, many of them were reduced to such despair in their extremities that they did indeed cut off themselves.

5. It is a great delusion among men, hindering the success of threatenings, and making them insolent and bitter when they are threatened, that they entertain a great conceit of their own worth, and will not be persuaded but it will be as well with them as any; for this was the cause of all this people's miscarriage. They conceived Christ could go to no good place from whence they would be secluded, and therefore they do so taunt him.

Ver. 23. And he said unto them, Ye are from beneath; I am from above: ye are of this world; I am not of this world.

24. I said therefore unto you, that ye shall die in your sins: for if ye believe not that I am he, ye shall die in your sins.

Christ in his answer doth not meddle with their perverse humours, but goeth on to confirm what he had said. And, 1. He pointeth out the reason and ground of his sad sentence—to wit, their original disposition, which is corrupt and earthly, and contrary to his, ver. 23, and this also is a cause of their ignorant mistake of their own danger. 2. From this he inferreth that he had justly said they should die in their sins, seeing they would not by faith embrace him, who only could apply a remedy to their evils, ver. 24. Whence learn—

1. It is not enough that wicked men be convinced of their evil deeds, unless they also study their original condition, and know that their evil practices do not flow only from a present tentation, or from evil breeding and education, but are the fruits of their natural corruption; therefore doth Christ point out this to these Jews.

2. Albeit man before the fall was raised up to enjoy a spiritual life and communion with God, yet by the fall he is cast down, and hath his original from beneath, and savours only of the world and of things therein; for so much doth he intimate to these Jews, "Ye are from beneath—ye are of this world."

3. Albeit Christ did take on our nature, yet he is altogether free of the sin and corruption thereof, being divine in his original and way of conception, and in his condition holy and separate from sinners; therefore saith he, "I am from above—I am not of this world;" where he doth not deny the truth of his human nature, but disclaims all communion with sin and the corruption of flesh and blood. And albeit it be said of his saints also that they are not of this world, John, xv. 19; xvii. 16; yet it is true of Christ in a singular manner, for he is absolutely unspotted by nature, they are so only by regeneration, and in part, and comparatively in respect of others.

4. As the study of Christ's divine original and condition is a glass wherein men may study the vileness of their own condition, so it is a sad evidence of separation from Christ's company, so long as men retain a total disconformity to him; for these ends doth he point out these two in their contrariety, "Ye are from beneath; I from above." (See Rom. viii. 29.)

5. Men continuing in their corrupt original without renovation from heaven cannot expect life eternal, but will perish in their sins; for he draws this from the former discourse, by way of conclusion, "I said therefore unto you, that ye shall die in your sins."

6. Albeit death be the desert of all sin, and God do daily threaten sinners with it, yet all this admits of the exception of faith in Christ; and as this only (and nothing else) can come betwixt the sinner and deserved wrath, so even the grossest of sinners shall not perish if they turn and fly to Christ; and when sinners do not this, their unbelief renders their case desperate and incurable; therefore is this threatening propounded with this exception, even to those malicious Jews, "If ye believe not that I am he, ye shall die in your sins."

7. It is not sufficient for preventing the due desert of sin, that men do pretend to faith in the Messiah unless they do acknowledge and embrace him as he reveals and offers himself; for this Christ requires as absolutely necessary, that "ye believe that I am he," where he meets with their fair pretences of believing in the true Messiah, and sheweth that unless they embraced him for the Messiah, how contemptible soever he

seemed to be, all these pretences would not avail them.

VER. 25. Then said they unto him, Who art thou? And Jesus saith unto them, Even the same that I said unto you from the beginning.

The Jews do captiously reply to his discourse, inquiring who he was that had laid so absolute a necessity upon them to believe on him. He answers, that he was even the same he had declared to them since the beginning that he began to preach—to wit, the Son of God and Saviour of the world; and by this he declares that their unbelief would be so much the more heinous, as it could not flow from ignorance, they being so often informed of the truth.

DOCTRINES.

1. As it is the lot of Christ and his servants to have their doctrine and threatenings in the name of the Lord entertained with reproach, so also will their persons be mistaken and set at nought; for such was Christ's lot; they scoff at his doctrine, ver. 22, and now they do in contempt inquire—"Who art thou?" their blind eyes not discerning his glory through the veil of his humiliation; and herein his people must resolve to share with him, 1 John, iii. 1.

2. As the truth of God is in all ages and times unchangeably the same, so it is the duty of the messengers thereof to be constant in preaching of it, and not to change their note, whatever contradiction and opposition they meet with; therefore doth he, notwithstanding all their malice, give this answer—"Even the same that I said unto you from the beginning," as not minding to change his note.

3. Albeit men may hear much which they slight and forget, yet the Lord will not forget to reckon with them according to what they have heard, whatever use they have made of it; therefore he doth not expressly answer to their question, but remits them to what he had said, to let them see that all of it would be laid on their account, to aggravate their obstinate unbelief.

VER. 26. I have many things to say and to judge of you: but he that sent me is true; and I speak to the world those things which I have heard of him.

Christ, meeting with so much obstinacy in these Jews, doth, in the rest of this discourse, give up with them, and declareth, that however he could not only discover, but convince them of much sin and maliciousness, yet, since they were so corrupt, he would rest satisfied in his Father's approbation, and would leave them upon God, who is true in his word, and particularly in his promises made to him, and who would certainly reckon with them for their despising of his doctrine, when he taught nothing but what he received from him. Whence learn—

1. As Christ hath still much more to say to the wicked than he will say to them in this world, so it is his sad judgment in particular on some that when he hath saddest quarrels against them, yet he gives over dealing with them; therefore saith he, "I have many things to say and to judge of you," when yet he gives them over, though they drew him to debate again. (See Ezek. iii. 26.)

2. When men do reject Christ and his doctrine, albeit they may be let alone for long enough, yet they have God's tribunal before which to answer for their contempt; therefore doth Christ leave them on God, who is true, and will avenge their contempt of him.

3. Though all the world should oppose Christ's doctrine, yet God will own and make it good, and will prove himself true in performing all the promises made to Christ and his servants, for taking order with such as oppose them and their message; therefore doth he acquiesce in this—"He that sent me is true;" to wit, generally in the doctrine which he delivered in his name, and particularly in the promises made to his Son, that he would own and support him in the work of redemption, and in the promises also made to his servants.

4. They who would be borne out against all the opposition of men, with the comfort of God's approbation, should make sure that they have his calling to what they undertake, and that they cleave faithfully to their commission; for hereby is Christ supported, He sent me, and I speak "those things which I have heard of him."

5. Such as are sure of God's calling and commission, and of the truth of what they receive, will be encouraged to preach it boldly, though all the world should not believe but oppose them; for saith Christ, "I speak (and that even) to the world (or openly) those things which I have heard of him." He was upon the Father's counsel, and knew the certainty of this doctrine, and therefore stands to it, and so others also, 2 Cor. iv. 13.

6. Christ's doctrine may safely be leaned to, as containing nothing else but what he hath heard and received from the Father; for so doth Christ call it, "those things which I have heard of him."

VER. 27. They understood not that he spake to them of the Father.

28. Then said Jesus unto them, When ye have lifted up the Son of man, then shall ye know that I am he, and that I do nothing of myself; but as my Father hath taught me, I speak these things.

29. And he that sent me is with me: the Father hath not left me alone; for I do always those things that please him.

This sad doctrine taking no effect by reason of their ignorance, who understood not that he spake of the Father when he mentioned him that sent him, Christ doth further certify them, that though now they were ignorant, yet after they had with wicked hands crucified him, then they should be made to know that he is the

Messiah, that he doth all things according to the Father's will, and that the Father is always with him, as being his obedient Son. Whence learn—

1. Were doctrine never so clear, yet Satan will keep men from understanding it, either by their ignorance or malice; for though he had ofttimes before spoken of him that sent him, yet "they understood not that he spake to them of the Father;" wherein there was not so much simple ignorance, as malice and prejudice, which transported them.

2. The ignorance of wicked and malicious men will be removed in due time, little to their advantage; therefore, Christ threatens that they who understood not shall know.

3. Such as do wickedly oppose Christ and his truth will readily run the length of bloody persecution before they cease; for so doth Christ forwarn them that they will "lift up the Son of man," by putting him to suffer on the cross. He calls himself here "the Son of man," to shew that he suffered only in that nature, and to point out his condescendence, that he became man that he might suffer.

4. Christ did so love his people that he willingly gave himself to redeem them, and would do nothing that might hinder his being put to that cursed death which might redeem them from the curse; therefore, albeit he warned them of it, yet he will not hinder it to take effect, nor so much as speak a word to stop it.

5. Wicked men are never further from their purpose than when they think they are nearest to it, and as this is true in their own prosperity, Psalm xcii. 6, 7, so also in their violent persecution of Christ and his followers; therefore doth Christ signify that by getting this advantage of him to put him to death they should gain nothing, but lose much. (See Micah, iv.11—13.)

6. The suffering of Christ and his followers, whatever enemies may account of it, or whatever it seem to be to flesh and blood, yet it is their real honour and exaltation; therefore doth he call their crucifying of him, a lifting up of the Son of man, not only because he was indeed lifted up upon the cross, but because it was an exaltation of him. (See chap. xii. 32.) It is an honour in saints to be employed to suffer, Acts, v. 41; it is accompanied with much of the Spirit of glory, 1 Pet. iv. 14, and is a step, and the way to glory, Luke, xxiv. 26, and therefore gets this name.

7. It is one peculiar advantage of suffering that Christ and his followers' true dignity and acceptance with God is never more clearly and convincingly seen than in the time of it, and after it; therefore it is subjoined, as a particular proof that it should be an exalting of him, that "then shall ye know that I am he," or the true Messiah, obedient unto and approven of God, as after followeth. And so we find accomplished in that, in his sufferings, Pilate and his wife give him a testimony; the centurion seeth his glory, Matt. xxvii. 54. The darkening of the sun, the rending of the rocks and the veil of the temple, the opening of graves, &c., did bear witness who he was; and afterwards the sad plagues that came on them, for rejecting of him, declared that he was the Son of God.

8. It is a sad judgment upon malicious, wicked men, that they are permitted to run the utmost length of their violence, and then, and not till then, their consciences and God's judgments are let loose upon them, to let them see and feel what a woeful course they have been upon; for so much also is imported here, that "when ye have lifted up the Son of man, then shall ye know that I am he," &c.

9. Christ in his works and doctrine, as he was taught them from the Father, as man, so they are altogether agreeable to the Father's will; for this is a truth, whereof he will have very enemies convinced—"I do nothing of myself; but as the Father hath taught me, I speak these things;" so that sinners are to come to and seek the Father in him, and ought to look on all he doth and saith as agreeable to the Father's will.

10. As the Father is inseparable from his Son Christ, in respect of the unity of the divine essence, so he is always with him as Mediator, being in him, as his ambassador, reconciling the world to himself, 2 Cor. v. 19, and with him, to support and uphold him as his servant, doing his work, according to the covenant of redemption, Isaiah, xlii. 1; therefore saith he, "He that sent me is with me: the Father hath not left me alone," though all the world should forsake me; wherein we may see how well pleased the Father is with the redemption of lost sinners, that he was still upholding the Son in it, and how richly they are made up who have him with them, be against them who will, as Christ here reckons.

11. Whosoever would have the comfort of God's presence and company in all conditions, ought to set themselves to please God, and observe his will in all things; for so did Christ find it; "for I do always those things that please him."

12. As Christ the Son did learn obedience, and submit himself to the will of the Father, so his obedience was full and complete, and in all things he did the Father was well pleased; for saith he, "I do always those things that please him."

Ver. 30. As he spake these words, many believed on him.

31. Then said Jesus to those Jews which believed on him, If ye continue in my word, then are ye my disciples indeed;

32. And ye shall know the truth, and the truth shall make you free.

In these verses John records that this his doctrine had success among many, and albeit it was but weak beginnings they had, (as appears by Christ's doctrine to them,) yet he exhorts them to perseverance, and encourages them in that study by promising—1. That so they shall prove themselves to be among the number of his real disciples. 2. That they shall increase in knowledge of the truth, and in feeling the power and efficacy thereof. 3. That they shall be made partakers of true Christian liberty. Whence learn—

1. Opposition made to Christ will not hinder the success of his gospel, but even the conten-

tions and debates occasioned by malicious men may do much good to many; for " as he spake these words, many believed on him." Even from amongst the crew of opposers he gathers followers.

2. As it is preaching which God hath appointed to be the mean of conversion, so in particular, when men consider either the danger of Christ's forsaking and giving up with them, or his own true excellency, as they are revealed in the word, it may be a mean to excite them to lay hold on him ; for this success followed upon his speaking these things, which may relate either generally to the whole preceding doctrine, wherein he leaves them to give an account to God of their despising of him, or particularly to the last words, wherein he points out his conjunction with and his being approven of the Father.

3. Christ is a tender cherisher of weak beginners, and will rather take pains to encourage them, than weaken their hands; for albeit they were weak, yet he calls it believing, and encourageth them to hold on.

4. Such as embrace Christ do stand in great need of confirmation, and should be seriously affected with that great undertaking wherein they engage; therefore doth Christ so much excite them, and labour to set their joints aright : albeit conversion be a very great work, yet confirmation of the converted is no small work, and a notable fruit of the ministry, Eph. iv. 8, 9, 12, 13.

5. It is not enough that men do embrace Christ for a fit only, but if they would reap the benefit of piety, they ought to persevere; and albeit such as do persevere may be kept a while without sensible feeling of the advantage of their course, yet in due time they shall find it; therefore doth he propound this condition to them, " If ye continue," and upon performance of that makes the promise.

6. They who would persevere indeed ought to cleave closely to the doctrine of Christ, not only renouncing false doctrine, and giving obedience to his truth, but as faith is begotten by the word, so it must be cherished and fed by it, and they must embrace and cleave to Christ as he reveals himself in the word, though otherwise they do not sensibly find his presence, yea, and their sense and fear and guilt may represent him otherwise than the word saith of him ; therefore saith he unto them, " Continue in my word."

7. It is the great privilege of lost sinners to be made disciples to Christ, taught of him, and admitted to follow him and be in his company, as a pledge of their being with him for ever; therefore it is held out as their encouragement and reward, " ye are my disciples."

8. As Christ hath some disciples who are so in reality, and others who are such but in show only, so whatever external privileges may follow on men's outward profession and show, yet there is no true ground of solid comfort but in being real disciples ; therefore doth he encourage them with this, which only could yield true comfort— ye are my disciples indeed, or truly, and in truth.

9. Albeit real converts be disciples unto Christ from the first moment of their conversion, yet that is ofttimes hid from them, till they give proof of their sincerity by perseverance, and then their fair advantages are intimated unto them; therefore saith he, " If ye continue in my word, then are ye my disciples indeed."   He saith not, then ye shall be my disciples, as if the reality of their state depended upon their perseverance, but, " then are ye my disciples"—that is, ye prove and make the truth of it manifest by your perseverance, and ye shall find the comfort of it yourselves.

10. As all natural men and counterfeit disciples are but ignorant of the truth of God, especially of the power and life that is in it, and accompanieth it, so even sound beginners may be for a time weak in these things; for so is here supposed, that however they had some beginnings, yet they were yet to " know the truth."

11. It is a very great advantage to get sound and saving knowledge of the truths of the gospel, that so faith may close with them, and men may be established in them, and kept on truth's side against all delusions, and be made partakers of the sweet refreshments that flow therefrom ; therefore it is held out as a rich encouragement, " ye shall know the truth."

12. Proficiency in knowledge, and the effects thereof, is not only believers' duty, which they should labour for, but it is God's promise to work it, who should be depended on for that effect; for it is his promise to true disciples, " ye shall know the truth."

13. Whatever be the weakness, ignorance, and wants, of weak beginners, and how little soever refreshment they find in the truths of the gospel, yet by perseverance and continuance all this will be helped, and they will still know more and more of the truth, and the consolations thereof; for " if ye continue, ye shall know the truth."

14. Since the fall of Adam there is no man but is born a spiritual slave without freedom, under the dominion and power of sin and Satan, and under the curse of the law ; for so is here imported, in that they need to be made free.

15. Such as do embrace Christ, and persevere in obedience to his word, albeit they be not loosed from that due subjection which in their several stations they owe to superiors, 1 Cor. xx. 21, 22, yet they are made partakers of true Christian liberty, and are delivered not only from the bondage wherein they were held by nature, when they were slaves to sin and Satan, and under the condemning and cursing power of the law, and from the external bondage of a yoke of ceremonies imposed upon the Jews, and of human precepts in things indifferent in God's worship, but also from that spirit of bondage which he lets out at first upon his own, in order to their future freedom, Rom. viii. 15 ; therefore saith Christ, " the truth shall make you free."   And albeit believers and they who continue in Christ's word do not always enjoy the possession and use of this liberty, but may be under bondage, terror, and fear, yet that is not their allowance, but flows from their own weakness, which apprehends all their bonds to be lying on, when really they are freed from them ; and therefore they should complain of themselves to God, and strive for the use of what is their right, by walking familiarly with God, and cheerfully and comfortably in his

service, and by making their liberty a law, to bind themselves more strictly to his obedience.

16. This making them free is here attributed to " the truth," whereas Christ only is the cause of our liberty, ver. 36 : but these are not inconsistent; for it is Christ indeed who purchaseth and applieth this liberty; Christ and this his purchase and offer are held out in the word, to be laid hold on there by faith, and so the believer comes to get the right and application of it, and he living by faith, the Spirit of adoption comes and seals up this liberty, Ephes. i. 13 ; Gal. iv. 6. So is this to be understood, " the truth shall make you free."

Ver. 33. They answered him, We be Abraham's seed, and were never in bondage to any man : how sayest thou, Ye shall be made free ?

The contentious Jews do here again interpose, and—1. They debate about their freedom and parentage, and Christ refutes their conceits, to ver. 48. 2. They fall a railing at his person, and contradict what he asserts of himself, and he doth vindicate himself and his doctrine, ver. 48—58. 3. They join violence with their railing, which he avoids, ver. 59. I shall take up the method and parts of the first branch of this debate in this order:—1. They excepting against the immediately preceding doctrine, and boasting of their own freedom, as being Abraham's children, ver. 33, Christ cleareth what is the great bondage of men, and how to be free from it, ver. 34—36, and sheweth that their being Abraham's seed after the flesh could not avail, since their malicious carriage and contempt of his divine word did evidence they had another original and father, ver. 37, 38. 2. They again laying claim to their descent from Abraham, he sheweth that in their carriage they were not like him, and so behoved to father themselves upon another in that respect, ver. 39—41. And, 3. When they (perceiving that he spake not of their carnal descent, but of their spiritual original) do assert that God is their Father, ver. 41, Christ evinceth the contrary from their want of love to him, ver. 42, and from their not understanding his preaching, ver. 43, and asserteth that they are of Satan, whom they imitate in being a murderer, ver. 44, 45 ; for he, being sinless, and a true teacher, ver. 26, their not hearkening nor believing in him did evince that they were not of God, ver. 47.

In this verse some Jews (not they who believed, but others) do except against his former doctrine, alleging that they being Abraham's children, and having never been in bondage to any man, it was needless to feed them with hopes of being made free. As for the grounds of their objection, it is nothing strange to see them deluded with a conceit of being Abraham's children, but it may seem strange they should say they were never in bondage, when yet they were bondmen in Egypt and in Babylon, and frequently, and at this time, were under the power of the Romans. But we are to conceive that either they stood not upon an impudent lie

to make good their point, or their meaning is, that however they were actually in bondage, yet by right, and according to the promise, they were free, and expected to be vindicated into outward liberty by the Messiah, and therefore they would not willingly take with being in a condition of bondage.

1. Such as would embrace Christ and a course of godliness may expect that beside tentations and discouragements from within, they will meet with oppositions and shakings without from those who cannot endure that any should be better than themselves ; for here these Jews fall a carping at Christ's offers that they may discourage these beginners. (See Matt. xxiii. 13.)

2. Men, in opposing of Christ's offers, are very subtle, and will be prompted by Satan to manage it so as may render them most invidious; for it appears in these men, who do not at all meddle with what he spake of " the truth," but only with the point of liberty, as knowing it was most invidious to insinuate to this people, who gloried so much in their liberty, that they were in bondage.

3. The most part of men are so carnal and blind, that they see no further than their outside and their outward condition, and so neglect their inward spiritual estate ; for this was the occasion of all their carping, that they understand Christ to speak only of bodily freedom and bondage, as knowing no other, as appears from the rest of their discourse.

4. Albeit spiritual bondage be in itself so sad and heavy that to be free of it might make all other bondage imaginable look like freedom, yet such is the blindness of men that it is but little or not at all known or discerned, and they live in their bonds with as much delight as fishes have in their own element ; for this in particular was the point they were ignorant of, as knowing and feeling no such bondage, and therefore carped at his doctrine.

5. Men's carnal apprehensions of their own condition, or of Christ's offer, or both, is a great cause wherefore they undervalue him and his offers as a thing they stand in no need of ; for so do these men carp at his offer to stumble these weak beginners, alleging that his offer of freedom was no great encouragement, since they needed it not.

6. Albeit Christ's offers be never so undeniably rich, yet the way of offering and conferring of his favours is ready to be a stumbling-block while men cannot endure to have them by free gift, or as bestowed on them who are miserable without them ; for so much also may be observed here : they do not carp simply at his offer of freedom in itself, liberty being so desirable, but that they should " be made free." They do not indeed desire to be servants or slaves, but free men, only they desire to have their freedom natural, and not adventitious ; they would be free-born, and not " made free." And this holds generally true in all his offers ; men can have nothing to except against the riches of God's favour, grace, and righteousness, only their natural pride cannot endure to have these things by free gift, to

have them in and by another, and not of themselves, &c. And this is it (however they palliate it) that makes self-condemned sinners stand out so long before they close with Christ's offers and submit to the righteousness of God.

7. Men's external privileges, in being born of religious parents and members of the church, do ofttimes prove a great stumbling-block to themselves, hindering them from seeing their need of Christ's offers, and from closing with them; for they lay this as a ground to all their exceptions and their despising of his offer: " We be Abraham's seed."

8. Such as do oppose Christ and his truth are ordinarily so void of conscience and awe of God that they will make no scruple of impudent lies, so they may thereby gain their point; and maintainers of truth should lay their account for such encounters and opposition; for so much doth their second exception,—" and were never ,in bondage to any man,"—according to the first interpretation, teach.

9. While men are puffed up with carnal dreams of their own privileges and worth, and with carnal expectations of great things to be done for them, they will not attain to the right use of any condition they are put under by God; for so much further do these words, as they are explained, teach. They were so much taken up with the imagination that they had right to be free men, and would be asserted into liberty, that albeit the Lord had sent all their captivities to teach them to understand these privileges spiritually, yet they would never be driven from their own conceits, nor would so much as hear of their own bondage; and therefore they made no right use of their afflictions, but all their care was how to get out of them, till the Lord made their attempting thereof prove their ruin at last.

Ver. 34. Jesus answered them, Verily, verily, I say unto you, Whosoever committeth sin is the servant of sin.

35. And the servant abideth not in the house for ever : but the Son abideth ever.

36. If the Son therefore shall make you free, ye shall be free indeed.

Followeth Christ's answer to this exception, consisting of two branches ; in the first whereof (in these verses) he cleareth what is the great bondage of men, from which freedom is to be desired, and is promised to the true children of Abraham. And albeit he might have reprehended them for their impudent lie, yet he chooseth rather to inform them meekly. And, 1. That the sad bondage whereof he spake was spiritual, wherein all they are held who give up themselves to a trade of sin, ver. 34. 2. That albeit such as were slaves in this respect might enjoy the external privileges of the church for a season, (as a servant abides in his master's house for a time,) yet they would be cast out at length, and separated from him who is the natural Son, and from all the adopted children, for ever; and therefore they ought to think seriously of the danger, that they may be excited to seek after freedom, ver. 35. 3. That the only way to attain to true freedom is by coming to him, ver. 36.

From verse 34, learn—1. Whatever advantage wicked men think to reap by opposing of the truth, yet Christ will disappoint them, and will take occasion thereby to make truth shine more clearly ; for whereas before he had spoken of their freedom but in a word, now, by reason of these debates, he explains that point of bondage and freedom more fully.

2. The matter of our spiritual bondage and freedom is a point of very great importance, and [it is] necessary that we should seriously study and be acquainted with it, and a point wherein we must submit to Christ's verdict, how contrary soever it be to our sense and apprehension of our own condition ; therefore doth he prefix his ordinary asseveration, " Verily, verily," to this doctrine.

3. Whatever be men's imaginations concerning their own condition, yet there is a more heavy bondage lying upon them than any outward slavery that can befal them, even to be under the slavery and bondage of sin; for so doth Christ assert that there are servants of sin, of whom he meant [to whom he referred] when he promised freedom.

4. Albeit all men by nature be born slaves to sin, yet, considering that there is freedom offered by Christ, and that they who embrace this remedy are not in this life fully freed from sin, therefore Christ will not reckon men slaves by their having sin in them, nor yet by their daily failings and infirmities, or by their falling now and then in foul faults through the violence of tentation, unless they make a constant trade of sin, and be under the dominion thereof, without controlment; for of these Christ speaks when he saith, " Whosoever committeth sin is the servant of sin." (See Rom. vi. 16 ; 2 Pet. ii. 19.) And this is the condition of natural men, who, being free from the yoke of righteousness, Rom. vi. 20, do voluntarily and without any opposition (unless it be some checks of a natural conscience, startling at some sin, or some thoughts of fear and shame) live in a trade of all sin, and under the slavish tyranny thereof, though this dominion appear more evidently in some sins than others ; and some of those who are unrenewed are judicially given up to be more visibly under the dominion of sin than others, not only as the just fruit of their voluntary living under that yoke, but that they may be beacons to the rest of their woeful slavery. As for renewed men, albeit they not only have sin in them, and do sin daily, but even have some particular evils that may be called predominants, in comparison of others, (which may easily be discerned by the great power and sway that they bear, even in commanding other evils to be committed or forborne, according as may contribute to advance them ; by violent and frequent relapses of saints into them ; by their unwillingness to admit of admonition and reproof for them ; and by their falling in them out of an inward propensity, when outward tentations are weak, or none at all, or very few,) yet since, as to the state of their person, they are set at freedom, and since the dominion is not universal as to all sins, nor is it perpetual or complete even as to these prevailing evils, therefore they can-

not be called servants of sin, as unrenewed men are; yea, albeit, in respect of degrees of mortification in saints, some sins are more predominant than others, some also are more strong in them, because they are the general evils of the time wherein they live, or because by natural inclination and constitution, or by education, (all which may be a bridle to some evils,) they are left more obnoxious and open to them, and some are left to be an exercise and daily matter of humiliation to them, yet I would not deny but all the sins of renewed men are their infirmities, not only in respect of God's pity, who will so account of them, but in respect of grace and the renewed parts suffering by them, which is greater under grosser evils against light than under sins of ignorance and mere infirmity. However, this is to be so understood, that godly men are to watch especially over these predominants, yet so as they take heed lest, in watching over one of these, many other evils that make less noise get liberty to grow up.

From verse 35, learn — 1. Such as will not be moved to consider the sinfulness of their spiritual bondage, that they may be rid of it, ought at least to consider of the danger that followeth upon it, to see how that will affect them; therefore doth Christ subjoin that consideration here, to excite them to employ him for their liberty.

2. The true difference betwixt spiritual slaves and those who are made free cannot be drawn from the enjoyment of external privileges of the church, which the one may partake of as well as the other; for it is imported that servants as well as sons may be " in the house." As a householder hath in his family not only children, but servants for several uses, so hath the Lord also in the church (which is his house, where he dwells and affords his special presence, and layeth up his special furniture) vessels of dishonour as well as vessels of honour, 2 Tim. ii. 20.

3. Whatever external privileges the slaves of sin enjoy, yet at last they will be cast out of all, and a separation will be made betwixt them and the children who are made free; for " the servant abideth not in the house for ever," as the Son doth. He insists in the metaphor of a family, wherein servants have term-days, and may be thrust away for faults, and are laid aside when the heritage cometh to be divided, as Ishmael, the son of the bond-woman was, after a long stay in Abraham's house, Gal. iv. 30.

4. It is the great advantage of those who flee to Christ to be freed from the slavery of sin, that not only do they get their liberty, but are made sons and children also; therefore is he who is not " the servant," called " the Son;" whereby we are not only, or so much, to understand Christ, (though he be indeed the natural and only begotten Son, through whom all the rest are made sons,) as the adopted children.

5. Such as are partakers of spiritual liberty, and of adoption, have not only the rich privilege of special and intimate fellowship with God, and of being under his special protection and care, and provided for by him, as children in their Father's house, but this happy estate is ensured to them; so that though they offend, and may be corrected, yet they will not be turned out of doors, as servants are; the doors are patent, to let them in when, like the prodigal, they have run away. And when they have been bred a while in the church, which is the lower room of this house, and have fed upon the hope and first-fruits of their inheritance, they will be carried up to the upper rooms of the church triumphant, there to get full possession and to enjoy God and his presence immediately and for ever; for the Son abideth in the house for ever.

From verse 36, learn — 1. Albeit spiritual bondage be such as we cannot shake it off, though we would, yet lost man hath this encouragement, that his freedom is not impossible; for here it is held out as a thing possible, upon some conditions, " ye shall be free."

2. Spiritual bondage is so great a misery, and deliverance from it so rich a mercy, that men would not delude themselves, either with a conceit of anything that may compense the want of it, or with an imagination that they are free, when they are not; therefore doth Christ excite them to use means that they may " be free indeed," or really, not contenting themselves with outward freedom, as if that were enough, nor with an imagination of spiritual freedom, while as yet they remain real slaves.

3. Christ is the heir of the family, having power to make free what servants he pleaseth, and none can ever partake of spiritual liberty but they who flee to him, and receive it from him; for " if the Son shall make you free, ye shall be free indeed," otherwise not. Albeit all the freed men be made sons, yet Christ here gets the name by way of excellency, as being the only Son by eternal generation, and he by whom all the rest are made sons.

VER. 37. I know that ye are Abraham's seed; but ye seek to kill me, because my word hath no place in you.

38. I speak that which I have seen with my Father: and ye do that which ye have seen with your father.

In these verses we have the second branch of Christ's answer; wherein he answers to the chief ground of their exception, taken from their descent from Abraham, from whence they concluded that (at least by right) they were freemen. In answer to this Christ maketh use of the distinction betwixt Abraham's seed after the flesh and after the Spirit, (of which Rom. ii. 28, 29; ix. 6, 7,) and declareth, that he would not deny but that they were Abraham's carnal seed, yet that could avail nothing since they did not follow his footsteps, but sought to kill him, as an evidence that his doctrine had no place nor respect in their hearts, which was not Abraham's way, ver. 37. And to inculcate this yet more, 1. He sheweth that the word which they despised was the doctrine committed to him from the Father, which Abraham would never have entertained as they did. 2. That their carriage proves that they have another original and father, whom they follow, than Abraham, and that this their father is contrary to him and his Father, whom Abraham worshipped and obeyed, ver. 38; and by this he indirectly points out that they were acted by Satan, whom he expressly names afterward, seeing they would not understand him when he spake thus.

From verse 37, learn—1. Christ, even in his dealing with wicked men, is most tender and meek, and rather willing to gain than deter them so long as there is any hope. So much appeareth in his way of reasoning here; for whereas in their other ground of exception (wherein they allege they were never in bondage, ver. 33,) he had them at a seen advantage of an impudent lie, at least of a vain imagination, yet after he hath cleared their mistake about spiritual bondage he doth not meddle at all with that exception, but only clears that wherein they seemed to have some advantage of truth on their side; and by this also he would teach all the maintainers of truth to make it their great study to clear and justify it in their debates, rather than to insult over adversaries, to embitter and estrange them yet more from the love of the truth.

2. Christ's knowledge of truth is infinite, and he doth propound it so infallibly and irrefragably that he knoweth beforehand all that can be said against it; for whereas they thought to surprise him with this objection, he tells them, "I know that ye are Abraham's seed." A finite, weak man might see his own shallowness by meeting with an objection he dreamt not of, but Christ's doctrine cannot be shaken by such means.

3. Albeit external privileges may be a snare to delude hypocrites, and make them conceit of freedom; and albeit Christ may make use of men's conceit of these privileges to convince them and agreeage [aggravate] their miscarriage, yet no privilege that men can boast of will make void Christ's truth concerning the spiritual bondage of men by nature, nor bring them into real liberty; for saith he, "I know that ye are Abraham's seed," that ye conceit of it, and expect much by it; but yet my doctrine stands true, and ye have the sadder account to make, who, enjoying that privilege, do not improve it better.

4. A little of men's practice is a surer rule to try them by than all their fair language or boasted privileges; therefore saith he, " I know that ye are Abraham's seed," but that will not avail to prove your point, since " ye seek to kill me." (See Matt. vii. 16.)

5. Men's cruel malice against Christ and his children proveth them to be yet in nature, and under the bondage of sin, whatever else they have to boast of; for by this he proves them servants of sin, though they were Abraham's seed, " Ye seek to kill me."

6. Whatever natural men and hypocrites pretend to, or seem to have, of estimation and respect to the doctrine of the gospel, yet really it hath no place with them. Either they have no room for Christ, or his directions or comforts, (as the word here imports,) as being sufficiently provided, as they think, without him; or they think his doctrine but cold comfort to wait upon and follow in a time of strait; or they cannot digest his spiritual instructions, as being so contrary to the dictates of flesh and blood, and laying a necessity on them to have so mean a conceit of themselves; or they affect it, not because

of his authority who speaks it, but because of novelty, fineness of expression, or the like external motives; or the affections they have do not make it sink down in their hearts, to take root there, and bring forth fruit, but it only fleets for awhile in their imagination; or if they be never so clearly convinced, yet out of pure malice they will reject and oppose it; therefore saith he, "my word hath no place in you." (See Jer. xxii. 21; Exod. vi. 9; 1 Cor. ii. 14; Acts, xvii. 19—21; Matt. xiii. 15, 20, 21.)

7. Where the word is barred out, and gets not room in men's hearts, there men are full of mischief and prone to all evil; and particularly, where the word preached is not received, men will readily turn persecutors; therefore saith he, " Ye seek to kill me, because my word hath no place in you;" for not only is this a just judgment of God upon such despisers, but the frequent inculcating of the word will irritate their corruption, and it will grow worse and worse. There is no member of the church, how civil or discreet soever, but if he receive not Christ's word into his heart is ready to turn a persecutor.

From verse 38, learn—1. Christ, as he is inseparable from the Father, so is he upon all his counsels, and knoweth his secrets; for saith he, I speak what I have seen with my Father—to wit, his eternal counsels concerning lost sinners, whereof I am made participant.

2. Christ also is the faithful interpreter and revealer of his Father's counsel for his people's good, and his doctrine is in all things agreeable to the counsel and will of God; for " I speak that which I have seen with my Father;" and this, as it sheweth the great privilege of the church, to whom these secrets are concredited, Rom. iii. 1, 2, so it doth highly aggravate their contempt who reject this messenger and his message, Heb. ii. 2, 3; xii. 25.

3. It is not enough that wicked men be shewed their evil way in itself, but they should be led up to see from what principle it flows, and what the dangerous consequents of it are; therefore doth Christ lead them up here to see what their malicious opposition unto him was, and whence it flowed.

4. It is one sad mark upon wicked men and adversaries to Christ, that as they are opposite unto him, so their opposition proveth that he and they are not children of one Father; therefore doth he point out himself and them as having different and contrary fathers: " I speak that which I have seen with my Father: and ye do that which ye have seen with your father;" whereas with his own children it is otherwise, John, xx. 17.

5. Let wicked men boast never so much of their parentage and privileges, yet their works and carriage do prove that Satan is their father, by whom they are acted and guided, and whose ways they do imitate; for saith he, " ye do that which ye have seen with your father;" where Satan is called their father, not in respect of the substance of their nature, which is neither created nor begotten by him, but in respect of the corruption of their nature and manners, into which he was a chief instrument to draw man in paradise, and doth yet foster and hold it on foot in his posterity. Likewise, while he saith, ye do

what ye have seen with him, it is not to be understood of any visible communion and intercourse betwixt Satan and every unrenewed man, but that they do according as he prompts and acts them, 2 Tim. ii. 26; Eph. ii. 2, and so do commit those evils wherein he fell before them, as is instanced, ver. 44.

6. It is a sad and humbling sight of natural men's condition to see them acted and led by Satan as effectually and really as ever their bodies were who were corporally possessed by him; therefore doth Christ by this point out the odiousness of their case unto them; and if this were well considered, it might not only discover how little wonder it is there be a great opposition betwixt them and the children of Christ, who are led by his Spirit; but it might humble them to think that they are under the conduct of such a guide, when they think they are only following some pleasant or profitable course; and it might let them who dream of a change of their manners when they please, see that it is not so easy a matter, but as hard as it was to dispossess the man that had the legion of devils in him.

VER. 39. They answered and said unto him, Abraham is our father. Jesus saith unto them, If ye were Abraham's children, ye would do the works of Abraham.

40. But now ye seek to kill me, a man that hath told you the truth, which I have heard of God: this did not Abraham.

41. Ye do the deeds of your father. ——

The Jews do except nothing against the first branch of Christ's doctrine concerning spiritual bondage, but finding that in his answer to their objection he had insinuated that they had some father of whom he had little good to say; and being either really ignorant, or wilfully seeming not to know that Christ spake of their spiritual parentage and pedigree, they again lay claim to Abraham as their father, of whom Christ durst say no ill, and so would render him odious as calumniating holy Abraham. Christ, in his reply, doth more clearly hold out that he is not speaking of their carnal descent according to the flesh, but of their original and parentage according to the Spirit. And, 1. He sheweth, in general, that if they were Abraham's children according to the Spirit they would imitate him in his works. 2. He sheweth, in particular, wherein their way was contrary to Abraham's, in that they persecuted him for telling the truth of God; and therefore, 3. They behoved to father themselves on another, in that respect, than Abraham.

DOCTRINES.

1. Conceit of privileges is a disease not easily cured, nor will men be easily taught or convinced of the evil of it; for after Christ hath sufficiently refuted this exception before, yet they will not be put from it, but repeat it again: "Abraham is our father."

2. It is an old trick of degenerate churches and churchmen to cry up the names of pious ancestors, to oppose them against the light of truth; for so do they hold up Abraham as their father, that anything Christ would say of their parentage might be repelled by that; and so do many, like them, cry up those from whom they have far degenerated; but if these saints departed knew how they were abused by these their degenerate sons, they would cry, Let them perish from under these heavens.

3. Whatever external privileges men may enjoy by being born of religious parents and members of the church, yet true grace is not an hereditary gift, nor doth carnal and outward succession make men partakers of spiritual privileges; therefore, albeit he had granted they were Abraham's seed, ver. 37, by carnal generation and succession, yet he makes a doubt of their being his spiritual seed till they prove it better: "If ye were Abraham's children," &c.

4. There is no just ground for any to boast of their religious progenitors, unless they follow their footsteps; for saith he, If ye were the children of Abraham, and would have that a privilege unto you indeed, "ye would do the works of Abraham." Such as do boast of religious parents, and yet will not imitate them, are but in effect reading a narrative to a sad sentence against themselves.

5. Albeit Abraham's carnal seed did enjoy many temporal, yea, and external church privileges, by virtue of the covenant made with him, yet none are his successors, as to participation of peculiar spiritual blessings and privileges, but only those who are followers of his faith and fruitfulness in piety; and they who do so may lay hold on all the spiritual promises made to him and his seed; therefore doth Christ require of these men, who were his carnal seed, that if they would partake of the promises made to him concerning spiritual freedom, they should prove their interest in him by another title, doing "the works of Abraham," and then their claim would be good. And this is a fair advantage and encouragement to gentiles. (See Rom. iv. 11, 12.)

6. As walking in any wicked course, so, in particular, the persecution of Christ and his followers is unbeseeming saints, and proves that the persecutors have no claim to the privileges of saints; therefore doth he instance this in particular, "Ye seek to kill me," who have told you the truth, to shew how unlike they were to Abraham, who did not this, and therefore could not claim to the privileges of his spiritual seed.

7. Albeit the Lord, in great mercy, will pass over the many violent fits of corruption in his people, which, through grace, and by fleeing to Christ, get smothered before they break forth, yet the Lord will judge of wicked men by their wicked endeavours and attempts, though they succeed not, seeing they are only withheld by some obstacle from without; therefore doth he charge it on them as sufficient to prove what they were, "Ye seek to kill me," though it had not taken effect. (See Psalm xxi. 11; xxviii. 4.)

8. Christ is a teacher who will not dissemble nor deceive or flatter his hearers, but will faithfully deliver the truth which he receives; for saith he, I have "told you the truth, which I have heard of God."

9. As a faithful declaration of the truth of God is the best service can be done to men, so

it is horrid wickedness and ingratitude in men, when they will not only persecute the innocent, but even those who are beneficial unto them, and do them best offices; for so doth Christ aggravate their cruelty : " Ye seek to kill me, a man that hath told you the truth." (See Ps. cix. 4 ; 2 Cor. xii. 15.)

10. Such is the perversity of the world, and their hatred to the truth of God pointing them out in their right colours, that the servants of Christ need expect no ease so long as they are faithful in their trust; for such was Christ's lot before them, " Ye seek to kill me, a man that hath told you the truth."

11. Wicked men can never attempt any violence against the servants of God because of their fidelity, but God will look upon the injury as reflecting on himself who entrusts them; for this cause doth Christ shew that the truth for which they did persecute him he heard of God, and so their quarrel was in effect against God, the author of that truth; and as this may deter men from such violent courses, so it may sweeten the bitter cup, when it is held to the head of any of God's servants.

12. Let wicked men cavil· never so much against Christ, or strive to clear themselves, yet he will not alter his verdict of them till they change their manners; therefore over again doth he conclude, " Ye do the deeds of your father"— that is, deeds like unto his, and deeds whereunto he driveth you.

13. Christ is so mild, even to his violent enemies, that when he reproves them, he rather desires that they should severely judge themselves than that he should deal too harshly with them; and when he reproves any it is their duty to set conscience on work to apply and enlarge the challenge against themselves; for these causes it is that he, now the second time, saith only, " Ye do the deeds of your father," not naming who that father is, but leaving that to their own consciences to gather when they should think seriously on the challenge.

VER. 41. —— Then said they to him, We be not born of fornication; we have one Father, even God.

The Jews are not yet silenced, but do bring forth a new objection in this verse, about their parentage and original; where, by " fornication," I do not understand bodily filthiness, but idolatry, which is frequently in the prophets called fornication, or adultery. And the scope of the verse is this : they perceiving now that Christ is not speaking of their carnal descent and pedigree, but of their spiritual original and descent, do assert that in this also they had enough to say for themselves, and that as Abraham was their father, in respect of carnal generation, so being considered in their spiritual state and being, they were the children of that one only true God; and this (without regarding his former reasons to the contrary) they labour to prove by this argument— that they were not born in an idolatrous state, but in the true church, nor were idolaters themselves, but worshipped God according to his

word, and therefore were his children. And though it may be objected that their progenitors were idolaters, as may be seen in Abraham, Josh. xxiv. 2, and frequently in their progenitors, throughout the history of the bible, yet that doth not render their ground untrue, (though it do not prove the conclusion, as will be seen afterward,) for even a church infected with idolatry may bring forth children to God, in respect of outward church state, so long as she hath not got a bill of divorce, Ezek. xvi. 20.

DOCTRINES.

1. Idolatry is indeed spiritual fornication, and a breach of that marriage covenant that is betwixt God and his church, and (whatever be God's indulgence for a time, yet) it doth deserve that the church should be rejected as not his wife, and that her children should be no more accounted his than bastards are allowed to succeed to an inheritance; for so much do they. acknowledge that it is " fornication," and that to be " born of fornication," and to " have one Father, even God," are not consistent. (See Hosea, i. 9 ; ii. 2.)

2. Desperate and malicious hypocrites may not only presume to glory that they are the successors of religious saints, but may be so impudent also as to boast of their adoption and communion with God; for so do they after their glorying of Abraham; they add, " we have one Father, even God." (See Matt. vii. 22 ; Hosea, viii. 2.)

3. Albeit it be a great mercy to be born members of a true church, and to worship God according to his own ordinances, yet that is not enough to prove any to be a true child of God; for albeit their argument be true, " We be not born of fornication, " yet it doth not hence follow that God is their Father, as Christ's reply doth teach us.

VER. 42. Jesus said unto them, If God were your Father, ye would love me : for I proceeded forth and came from God; neither came I of myself, but he sent me.

Unto the end of verse 47 we have Christ's reply to this exception, containing several particulars; and first, he evinceth that they are not God's children, which he proveth from this reason—that if they were so, certainly they would love him, seeing he is from the Father by eternal generation, and cometh into the world by his incarnation, not of his own head, but being sent of the Father. Whence learn—

1. Christ is a lovely object, and ought to be beloved of his church; for so is here required that they should love him; and whoso do not love the Lord Jesus Christ are excommunicated in the highest degree, 1 Cor. xvi. 22.

2. None can justly pretend any interest in God as his children but they that love Christ, who, in his divine nature, is the express image of his Father, and in his office is employed by him; for so much doth Christ's assertion and argument hold forth : " If God were your Father, ye would love me, for I proceeded forth (or came out, pointing at his eternal generation) and

came (in the present time, as it is in the original, to perform this office of Mediator) from God."

3. It is a point beyond all controversy that Christ was sent of the Father to be the Mediator and Messenger of the covenant to his church, and consequently that all his doctrine and works were according to his commission from the Father; therefore is it added for confirmation, " neither came I of myself, but he sent me."

4. These reasons, given by Christ, wherefore God's children should love him, taken from his eternal generation by the Father, and his being sent by him in commission, may further teach us in general—1. True lovers of God will give a room in their affections to others, according to the measure of their communion with, and interest in, God; for if the Father's children do love Christ, who is begotten of God, and is the express image of his person, then they will also love others who are begotten of him, and bear his image in part, 1 John, v. 1. 2. True lovers of God will love to have intercourse with him, and will love every messenger sent by him, and the messenger for the message sake; for that other ground, I came from God, and he sent me, holds out this general, that they could not be God's children unless they liked to hear from him, and liked those who bring the tidings. (See Gal. iv. 14, 15.)

Ver. 43. Why do ye not understand my speech? even because ye cannot hear my word.

This challenge may be understood generally, and so it contains a second proof that God was not their Father, taken from their not understanding of what he preacheth, which evidenceth that they were not only under a natural impotency to hear, but were so transported with malice that they could not hear with patience, and so were none of God's children. It may be also understood particularly as a challenge that they were so blinded with malice that they could not understand what he had spoken in general terms of their father, ver. 38, 41, and so it is a transition to the following verse, wherein he explains his mind. We need not stand on this difference, seeing this particular may come in well enough under the general challenge. And it teacheth—

1. It is a duty incumbent to all to understand what Christ speaks unto them, and where it is not so, Christ will make a quarrel of it; for he puts it home with a sharp question and challenge, " Why do ye not understand my speech?" not only to put them to consider from whence it flowed (of which afterward), but to testify his indignation against them for it.

2. Christ's wicked enemies are not only naturally impotent to hear the word of God aright, but are so blinded with malice that they cannot so much as with patience hear what he saith; for this doth Christ chiefly understand when he saith, " Ye cannot hear my word."

3. Men's own malice adds to their natural ignorance, and doth so blind them that they cannot understand never so plain truth; for ye understand not my speech because ye cannot hear my word. (See Matt. xiii. 9.)

4. Albeit God's children may have much ignorance, and may for a time be tainted with some error, yet as that is not good, so they who maliciously slight the means of knowledge, and do shut their own eyes, that they cannot and will not see, have nothing to evidence that they are the children of God; therefore doth Christ by this question put them to consider what their practice and condition flowed from, " Why do ye not understand my speech? even because ye cannot hear my word." For if men of one province and children of one family do understand the language and " dialect" (as some translate the word speech) of the country and family, and are discerned from others by their speaking of it, as Judges, xii. 6; Matt. xxvi. 73, then certainly they cannot be children of God's house who do not understand the language of it; and much more do they prove that they are not begotten by the seed of the word who cannot so much as endure to hear it.

Ver. 44. Ye are of your father the devil, and the lusts of your father ye will do. He was a murderer from the beginning, and abode not in the truth, because there is no truth in him. When he speaketh a lie, he speaketh of his own: for he is a liar, and the father of it.

Secondly. In this reply Christ doth clearly and positively shew unto them who is their spiritual father, of whom they are, which is even the devil, of which see what is said on verse 38. This he proves in general from their earnest following and endeavouring to execute those wicked lusts which reign in him, and their writing after his copy, and imitating of him, being acted by him. Then he instanceth this general in two particulars—of murder, and opposition to, and defection from, the truth; which as it appeared in Satan " from the beginning" of the creation, in deceiving our first parents, and opposing the truth God had delivered to them, and in drawing them under the stroke of temporal and eternal death, so it was to be seen in them also, in seeking to kill him, ver. 40, and opposing his truth, which he had hinted at, ver. 43, and doth more clearly prosecute in the following verses. Lastly, he clears God of all these lusts of Satan, shewing that they flowed from his own defection, and that all his lies are his own invention, and so they who followed these practices could not father themselves on God.

DOCTRINES.

1. It should be counted no absurdity, but the sound doctrine of Christ, to assert that not only they who boast much of privileges, but those who indeed are members of a true church, are nothing in reality, and in God's account, but limbs and children of Satan, so long as they are unconverted, and live in a wicked course; for saith Christ of these Jews, " Ye are of your father the devil."

2. Such as will not take with a reproof when it is mildly given by Christ, do provoke him to tell it out in sharper terms; for they would take

no notice of what Christ formerly spake in general of their spiritual parentage, and now he speaks it out, " Ye are of your father the devil."

3. Men's practices will prove that they are Satan's children, let them say what they will; and those do prove themselves to be eminently his children in whom he works the greatest conformity to himself; for Christ proves his own assertion, and refutes all they had to say against it with this: " the lusts of your father ye will do;" and according as they were eminent imitators of him, did they prove how eminent they were among his children.

4. Satan is full of raging wicked lusts, wherein his children, being acted by him, do imitate him; for there are " the lusts of your father," wherein they do resemble him.

5. Albeit Satan and his children do very often get many of their lusts fulfilled in the world, yet through the restraining power of God, and Christ's watchful providence over his own, many of their hot attempts are frustrated; for sometimes they prove but lusts, vexing chiefly themselves who have them, and ye will, or, desire to, do them, but can get no further.

6. God will not judge of Satan's children by their actings and success only, but by their desires and endeavours; and albeit they be ofttimes stopped in their course, yet he will account them Satan's children, because of their obstinate and wilful endeavours; for Christ proves the point by this as sufficient—ye will do, or, desire to do, " the lusts of your father;" for as yet they had gone no further than desires and endeavours in persecuting him.

7. As all unrenewed men are Satan's children, so, in particular, all liars, deceivers, doubleminded and bloody men, and especially despisers and opposers of Christ's truth, and bloody persecutors, are Satan's chief children; for these are the particular lusts whereby he proves them eminent children, even murder and lying, of both which they were guilty.

8. This doctrine delivered by Christ, concerning Satan's fall and practices, doth hold forth several useful instructions, which I shall point out in this order:—1. The most excellent and perfect of creatures, being left to themselves and the guidance of their best perfections, will not be able to stand or keep their integrity; for so much appears in this example of Satan, who being one of the most excellent creatures, yet being left to himself he " abode not in the truth," or in his original station and holiness, and in his cleaving to God, but turned aside to a vain, lying course, and to be a deceiver of others, as is afterward cleared. And he was in this defection " from the beginning"—to wit, of man's fall; so that however he was created perfect in one of the six days, yet before the fall of man he had left his first habitation. 2. The cause of Satan's fall was in himself, who of his own accord left his original holiness and station; for " he abode not in the truth," but forsook it. 3. As since Satan's fall there is no spark of goodness, holiness, or truth in him, (for " there is no truth in him;") so this depravation proves that he is fallen from that condition wherein he was created; therefore doth this come in by way of reason, that

since God made all his creatures good and perfect in their kind, therefore it must necessarily follow that " he abode not in the truth, because (now) there is no truth in him." And so the Lord is cleared of his fall. 4. Satan since his fall is a great enemy to man, and full of malice that man should fill that room from whence he fell. So much appears in his being " a murderer" and " liar," and that " from the beginning." He did begin soon, and continues long, so that God's people are to remember that they dwell in a world where Satan is going about full of rage. 5. Whatever mask Satan puts on in dealing with men, yet he is but seeking their destruction both of soul and body; for he is " a murderer." 6. Satan's attempt and success upon our first parents is a clear evidence of his designs against the children of men, and a sad document, shewing how far he may prevail with the best if they be left to their own free will; therefore is it peculiarly marked that " he was a murderer from the beginning," as a clear warning to all, from what he did to Adam and Eve, hazarding the destruction of their and all their posterity's souls, and bringing them all under the sentence of bodily death. 7. Satan's great engine for bringing about his bloody designs is lying and deceits; therefore is it subjoined, he is a liar; and by this he prevailed with our first parents, subtlely calling the truth of God in question; so that to give heed to his lies against the truth is, in effect, to give up our throat to the murderer. 8. As Satan is a very subtle and crafty adversary, full of cunning and sleight to entrap the simple, (see 2 Cor. ii. 10, 11; Eph. vi. 11,) so he is, in all he saith, a liar, and not to be trusted; for so saith Christ, there is no truth in him, he is a liar. Therefore though he transform himself into an angel of light, and busk up his projects, yet men are not to be taken therewith; and though he sometimes speak truth, (as sometimes he did commend Christ, Mark, i. 24; Luke, iv. 34; and his servants, Acts, xvi. 17; and may bear in true challenges upon believers,) yet he is still to be rejected as intending thereby to deceive; for by his commendation of Christ and his followers he intended either to make them be suspected, or to draw persecution on themselves by casting them out, as befel Paul. And when he pleads God's cause against his people, it is but to drive them from God; and when he chargeth upon them what they deserve, his scope is to deprive them of all hope of remedy, and persuade them that they shall be dealt with only according to deserving. 9. Satan's sin is of himself, and all the evil that is in the world, God is free of it; and only Satan as the enticer, and we as the consenters, are to blame for it; for " when he speaketh a lie, he speaketh of his own:" he is the father of it, or the inventor and beginner of it in himself and his followers.

Ver. 45. And because I tell you the truth, ye believe me not.

Here Christ doth confirm his assertion concerning their being of Satan; and as before he had proven they were of him, and imitators of him in murder, so here he proves the same in the matter of lying, shewing that they were like Satan in that also, because they will not believe him and his doctrine, even because it is truth. And upon this followeth the other, of their seeking to kill him because he told the truth, ver. 40.

DOCTRINES.

1. Rejecting of truth, and wilful and malicious contradiction thereunto, is the great trade of Satan the liar, and their practice who are his children and acted by him; for in this doth he instance Satan's lying, and their sinning like him.

2. As Satan since his fall hath cast off all awe of God, and neither fears his justice nor hopes for mercy, and doth maliciously oppose truth because it is truth, and crosseth him in his designs, so Christ's enemies, being acted by Satan, will oppose truth for no other reason but because it is truth. They will believe anything but truth, and the more true the doctrine be, the more will they oppose it; for " because I tell you the truth, ye believe me not."

3. Let wicked men oppose Christ's doctrine as they will, yet it is truth, and any doctrine they embrace beside is but a lie, which will disappoint them in the end; for however they believe not, yet saith he, " I tell you the truth."

VER. 46. Which of you convinceth me of sin? And if I say the truth, why do ye not believe me?

In the third place, Christ in this reply doth vindicate himself, and so prevents an objection and aggravates their infidelity; for whereas they might object against the former challenge, in ver. 45, wherefore should we believe thee, and leave our own religion for thy saying, whom we know not? Christ answers, that since none of them could convince him of any sin, and his doctrine was the very truth, therefore they could not but sin heinously in not giving him credit, whoever he were. Whence learn—

1. As Christ's public messengers are obliged to be irreprehensible and true in their doctrine, so this was eminently and singularly true of Christ, who was the spotless Lamb of God, and infallibly true in all his doctrine; for he was without sin, and said the truth.

2. It is not sufficient to condemn any that malicious men do calumniate and traduce them, unless they can also argue and make it out; for Christ requires of his accusers that they convince him of sin, or by arguing make it clear that what they assert is true.

3. Christ was so perfectly spotless and innocent, that albeit he lay buried under calumnies, yet none of his most malicious adversaries could ever make it good that he was guilty of one sin; for saith he, " Which of you convinceth me of sin?"

4. Albeit the blameless carriage of men doth serve much to make a way for their doctrine, and doth aggravate their sin who despise it, yet it should not be a snare to draw others to receive anything they say, unless it be made clear that it is truth; therefore, in grounding this challenge, Christ adds this to that of his sinlessness, " I say the truth."

5. As the doctrine of innocent and infallible Christ ought without controversy to be credited, so their consciences may look for a sad account and challenge who will not do so; for saith he, " If I say the truth, why do ye not believe me?" And it holds out also this general [doctrine], that no prejudice should hinder men from embracing that which is held out to be truth.

VER. 47. He that is of God heareth God's words : ye therefore hear them not, because ye are not of God.

In the last place, Christ concludes the discourse with a sad note upon them, and doth himself answer that question he had propounded ver. 46, shewing that the true cause why they did not believe nor hear his word was because they were not of God, which he illustrates from the contrary, and so leaves them again to consider of whom they were. This assertion, as it must necessarily be understood of grown-up persons, (for infants are still to be excepted in these ordinary rules,) so albeit to be of God be frequently understood of men's being elected from eternity, yet here it is chiefly to be understood of regeneration, because even the elect of God, so long as they are unregenerate, may be guilty of the same sins with the reprobate, and particularly in slighting the word; only, if we conjoin these two, to resist known truth, and to do so maliciously, (which was the sin of many of these Jews,) cannot befal any elect; for though Peter sinned wittingly, yet not maliciously, and though Paul sinned maliciously, yet he did it ignorantly and in unbelief, 1 Tim. i. 13.

DOCTRINES.

1. Men's respect to the word of God is a true touchstone, whereby they may try their own condition and state; for so doth Christ here teach us.

2. Men have nothing in them by nature that can entertain or receive the word of God with any due respect, but what they attain to of that kind is of God, and not of themselves; for he must be of God by election and regeneration who will hear God's words.

3. An elect child of God being renewed as he is begotten by the seed of God's word, so in his progress he will not resist the known light thereof, but will receive and feed upon it; and whatever may be his fits of tentation, yet he will never reject it maliciously; for " he that is of God heareth God's words." He heareth it with faith, submission, and fruitfulness; for so it is opposed to not believing, ver. 46. (See 1 Pet. i. 23; ii. 1—3.)

4. Whoever they be that do not regard the word of the Lord, but do maliciously reject it after conviction, prove themselves to be unregenerate, if not also reprobates; for " ye hear them not, because ye are not of God."

5. Consequences soundly and solidly deduced from scripture are scripture, and as valid a ground of faith as the ground from whence they are deduced; for so doth Christ here teach us by his own practice, deducing from that ground, " He that is

of God heareth God's words," this necessary and infallible consequence—"Ye herefore hear them not, because ye are not of God." And this penman is full of such deductions, warranting this way of arguing.

6. Whatever affront men think to put upon Christ by rejecting his doctrine, yet the real ignominy redounds to themselves; therefore, however they laid all the indignity of this opposition on Christ himself and on his doctrine, yet he tells them it flowed really from this—"Ye are not of God," but lying in a reprobate, unregenerate condition.

VER. 48. Then answered the Jews, and said unto him, Say we not well that thou art a Samaritan, and hast a devil?

From this to the end of the chapter these adversaries do change their way of proceeding with Christ. So long as they had any seeming ground or show of reason, they debate the matter; but now, being put from all that, they fall a railing at his person; and Christ defends and replies till they come to violence. It may be taken up in this order—1. They rail at him, ver. 48, and he vindicates himself as an honourer of his Father, and therefore they were in the wrong who reproached him, ver. 49, and behoved to make account to God for it, ver. 50; and he sheweth their loss who despise his word, which preserveth men from death, ver. 51. 2. They take occasion, from what he saith of his word, to carp again, objecting that Abraham and the prophets were dead, ver. 52, and that he should make himself greater than they, ver. 53; and he clears himself of ambition in this matter, charging it on them, ver. 54, 55, and sheweth that Abraham's joy depended on him, ver. 56, before whom he had a subsistence as God, though as man he was not old, ver. 57, 58; upon which assertion they betake themselves to violence, and he avoideth it, ver. 59.

In this verse we have their first attempt, wherein, taking advantage of his sharp censure of them, they charge him with being "a Samaritan," and possessed with an evil spirit. They do particularly charge him to be "a Samaritan," not only because they accounted the Samaritans the most impious of men, because of their apostasy from the church of Judah, and the true religion there, (whereof they account him also guilty by his doctrine,) but specially, because as the Samaritans were most bitter enemies unto and traducers of the Jews, (as may be seen in part, John, iv. 9,) so did they account of him who durst be so bold as to deny them to be children of God, and to say they were of the devil. As for the other charge, "thou hast a devil," it is true that elsewhere they do maliciously assert, against their light, that he was guided and assisted by Satan in his doctrine and miracles, Matt. xii. 24, but here, it seems, they only intend to retort his challenge, and do say he had a devil, which prompted him to say they were of the devil; and so the challenge is all one with the former of "a Samaritan," whom they looked on (as on all wicked men) as guided by an evil spirit; and

accordingly, Christ answers both in answering one of them.

DOCTRINES.

1. Albeit wicked enemies to truth may for a time enter the lists cf dispute, as if they minded to seek out and follow truth, yet conviction in debate will not gain ground upon them, as appears in these Jews, who when they are put to the worse in dispute, yet they come nothing the nearer to truth.

2. Unbelief and contempt of the truth will end in blasphemy, and impious men being convinced will turn railers and betake themselves to personal reflections against the persons of men who maintain the truth when they can do no better; for so do they deal with Christ.

3. Wicked men can vent no reproaches, calumny, nor blasphemies against Christ's servants and people, which Christ hath not sanctified in his own person, being called to his face the worst of men, a reproacher and enemy to the people of God, and one possessed with an evil spirit, as here we see.

4. There are none more ready to reproach Christ and his followers, as if they were possessed with an evil spirit, than those who are his real slaves themselves; for they who are of the devil, ver. 44, say of Christ, " thou hast a devil."

5. Such is the power of ignorance, prejudice, or malice, when men are possessed therewith, that they will draw bad conclusions, and put hard constructions upon best actions; for upon Christ's useful and true doctrine, they think they do well to draw these bad conclusions, " Say we not well (intimating they had a custom of it before) that thou art a Samaritan," &c., since thou speakest so.

VER. 49. Jesus answered, I have not a devil; but I honour my Father, and ye do dishonour me.

50. And I seek not mine own glory: there is one that seeketh and judgeth.

51. Verily, verily, I say unto you, If a man keep my saying, he shall never see death.

In these verses we have Christ's answer to this blasphemous calumny; and—1. He declareth that he had no devil, but was honouring his Father in what he did and said, and therefore it was their great sin thus to reproach him, ver. 49. 2. Lest they should think he took this ill, as an indignity done to him, he declareth that he was no selfseeker, nor hunter after vainglory, nor needed he avenge himself on them, since the Father will honour him, and take course with them who rub upon his glory, ver. 50. 3. To shew what his true glory is, and what their loss is who despise his word, he sheweth what blessed effects shall follow upon observing of his doctrine, ver. 51.

From verse 49, learn—Bitterest calumnies should be answered meekly by Christ's servants; and however men fail in duty to them, yet they should still cleave to duty; therefore doth Christ meekly deny the calumny, " I have not a devil," and refutes it with reason.

2. As it is the duty of all God's people to seek the honour of God as their chief end, so Christ did eminently honour his Father, both in his doctrine and obedience; for so saith he, "I honour my Father." (See John, xvii. 4.)

3. They who sincerely seek God's honour do prove that they are not guided and acted by Satan, whatever the world think or say of them; for so doth Christ prove his point, "I have not a devil; but I honour my Father."

4. Men's innocent lives and carriage is the best mean to refute unjust calumnies and reproaches; for so doth Christ refute their blasphemy, by his honouring of God in his carriage.

5. It is a commendable zeal for God's honour when his faithful servants will not suffer wicked men, who carry the devil's stamp and image, to father themselves on God as his beloved and dear people; for in this particularly did he honour his Father here, in telling them plainly what they were.

6. As men's honouring of God will not stop the mouths of malicious slanderers, so their sin is very great who reproach them who do honour God; and particularly, this holds true of Christ, who cannot be dishonoured but it rubs upon the Father also; therefore saith he, by way of sad challenge, "I honour my Father, and ye do dishonour me." (See John, v. 22, 23.)

From verse 50, learn—1. Such as unfeignedly seek God's honour will not hunt after vainglory, nor seek their own glory, save in so far as God's honour is stricken at by the reproaches cast on them; therefore doth Christ subjoin, "I seek not mine own glory."

2. Such as unfeignedly seek God's glory need not be anxious about the reproaches they meet with, seeing God undertakes to see to that; therefore also, lest they should think the want of honour from them grieved him, he saith, "I seek not mine own honour, there is one that seeketh and judgeth."

3. As Christ did honour the Father in going about the works of his calling, so the Father did undertake, and hath now honoured him, and will avenge all the blasphemies and reproaches that wicked men belch out against him; for saith he, "there is one that seeketh and judgeth."

From ver. 51, learn—1. Christ is never so angry with his foes as to forget his friends; yea, he delights to convey his threatenings against enemies, in promises to his children, if so be they will consider their loss, and yet take hold of his offer; therefore, instead of threatening, he makes a gracious promise, and that not only for the confirmation of any weak ones who were then hearing, but to try what such an offer might yet work upon these wicked men.

2. Albeit most part of men make but little account of the matter of their salvation, and those who have any thoughts about it are very averse from crediting Christ's naked word about the way to it, yet Christ would have it looked upon as a weighty business, and would have it out of all controversy that he will make good the word which he speaks concerning it; therefore doth he premit [introduce] his ordinary asseveration to this doctrine—"Verily, verily, I say unto you," that he may teach them that it is no light or trivial matter he is speaking of, and that he may remove all hesitation concerning the truth of his word.

3. Such as would receive any benefit by Christ's doctrine should not only hear it, but lay it up in their heart, and keep it in some measure of sincerity in their life; for it is required that they "keep my saying."

4. Albeit such as cleave to Christ, and make conscience of obedience to his word, may meet with very many troubles, and may ofttimes have very great fears about death and their eternal happiness, yet they shall be secured from eternal death and all their other troubles, and bodily death itself shall be swallowed up in victory; for "if a man keep my saying, he shall never see death"—to wit, eternal death, and consequently shall get a good account of all the steps betwixt him and eternal happiness.

Ver. 52. Then said the Jews unto him, Now we know that thou hast a devil. Abraham is dead, and the prophets; and thou sayest, If a man keep my saying, he shall never taste of death.

53. Art thou greater than our father Abraham, which is dead? and the prophets are dead: whom makest thou thyself?

In these verses they repeat their blasphemy, and think themselves confirmed in it, and that they have him at a seen advantage in what he last spake; for whereas he had said they should never see death who keep his sayings, they think that many ways absurd, and reflecting upon himself; for, 1. Then certainly Abraham and the prophets were none of his disciples, for they are all dead. Nay, 2. He behoved to be very arrogant who made himself greater than Abraham and the prophets, in that he ascribes a quickening virtue to his word, not only in respect of himself, but his hearers also; whereas they not only kept not others alive, but are dead themselves.

DOCTRINES.

1. Wicked men will be as little taken with Christ's promises as they are terrified with his threatenings; and they desire rather to have somewhat to carp at in them than to be drawn by the sweetness thereof to embrace them; for they rage as much here at his sweet promise as they did formerly at his sharp challenges.

2. As wicked men do reproach Christ out of malice, and all the arguments they pretend are but invented to cover their malice, so they will sometimes be forced to bewray themselves that it is so; for say they, "now we know that thou hast a devil;" and if but "now" they know it, why said they it before? Certainly all the arguments they bring forth were but invented to colour that resolution which they had laid down to reproach Christ.

3. Mistakes of Christ, and understanding of his doctrine in a carnal sense, give occasion to persecutors of many cavils; for upon these grounds doth their exception run, wherein they glory so much. They think it absurd enough if they can

infer from his discourse that he makes himself greater than Abraham and the prophets, which yet is the very truth; and they mistake him as if he were speaking of the first death, when he is speaking of the second death.

4. Christ's enemies do falsely pretend to be honourers of the saints, that they may bear him down; for so do they here cry up Abraham and the prophets, to make him odious.

5. Albeit saints be truly excellent, yet they have no privilege against bodily death, but must pay that debt, partly to be a testimony that they are by nature heirs to the first Adam, and do carry a body of corruption about with them while they are in the world, and partly that they may be translated to a better life; for even Abraham and the prophets, whom they cry up as singular, are dead.

6. Such as do in a carnal way overvalue the saints, prejudge Christ of his glory and due estimation; for so did they by their excessive commendation of them : " Art thou greater than our father Abraham," &c. And this disease is more frequent, not only in them who set them up in Christ's room to be sharers with him, in leaving merits to be made use of by the church, and in being mediators of intercession, but in them also who doat so much on saints as they forget to give Christ the glory of any excellency that is in them, and who implicitly follow them, not considering whether they be following Christ in that wherein they follow them or not.

7. Christ is truly singular and matchless, and if all the saints were put together, they are all nothing to him, and he can do that which they cannot all do; for this (together with the clearing of their mistake of what he spake concerning death) is the clear answer to all their cavil, that indeed he is greater than all of them put together.

VER. 54. Jesus answered, If I honour myself, my honour is nothing : it is my Father that honoureth me ; of whom ye say, that he is your God :

55. Yet ye have not known him ; but I know him : and if I should say, I know him not, I shall be a liar like unto you : but I know him, and keep his saying.

Followeth Christ's answer to this exception, and, 1. In general (in these verses) he clears himself of any ambition in this matter, and proves them guilty of it; whereas in their exception they thought it great ambition in him to prefer himself to Abraham and all the prophets; he answers (by way of concession) that if he himself, and of himself, did take this honour on him, it were of no worth; but he hath it of the Father, who doth allow and confer it on him. And whereas they might except that if this Father of whom he boasted so much be the true God, they had greater cause to lay claim to him than he had, he answers, that this proves them really guilty of that ambition wherewith they charge him, for they boast of him while as [yet] they have no saving knowledge of him; but he knows him,

and would be a liar, like unto them, if he should say that he knew him not, seeing he gives real proof of knowing him by keeping his word.

1. Such as hunt after vainglory, and seek after respect and estimation otherwise than God alloweth and approveth of, do hunt a shadow, and that which really is of no worth; for this is of general verity, " If I honour myself, my honour is nothing." (See 2 Cor. x. 18.)

2. Christ seeketh no glory but what the Father alloweth on him; and as he is God over all, blessed and honoured for ever, and as his human nature is honoured by being exalted to a personal union with the godhead, so whoever dishonour Christ, yet the Father alloweth and hath conferred honour on him as Mediator, to be a testimony how well he is pleased with the redemption of lost man performed by him, and to be matter of comfort to all them who seek to this exalted Prince, and matter of terror to all his and their enemies; for saith he, " If I honour myself, my honour is nothing; it is my Father that honoureth me."

3. What men have received from God with his approbation, and have his testimony for it, they may avow and maintain it against all opposition; therefore doth Christ not deny that honour they alleged he took to himself, but he avows it on this ground : " It is my Father that honoureth me."

4. Albeit Christ be in himself God all-sufficient, and so is not capable of any access of glory, yet it pleased him to condescend so far as to obscure his own glory under the veil of his flesh and state of humiliation, till he had perfected the work of redemption, and to account of his office of Mediator, and the dignity accompanying it, as great honour conferred upon him by the Father; therefore saith he, " my Father honoureth me" above Abraham and the prophets, that I can give life to them that keep my sayings.

5. Christ's greatest enemies may yet be so presumptuous and deluded as to soothe up themselves with a conceit of a special interest in God; for the Father is he " of whom ye say that he is your God."

6. Persecutors, pretending to interest in God, do but proclaim their own carnal ambition and self-seeking, and that they do but lie and deceive themselves; for he brings this as a proof of their ambition, and asserts that they were liars in so saying : " I shall be a liar like unto you."

7. As none are more ready to boast of an interest in God than they who know least of him, so none can prove an interest in him but they who know and acknowledge him as he is revealed in Christ by the gospel; for saith he, " Ye say that he is your God, but (to refute that) ye know him not"—to wit, savingly, in so far as they knew not him as Father to his Son whom he had sent, and acknowledged not the gospel to be his revealed will.

8. It is not sufficient for proving an interest in God that men do acknowledge God as he reveals himself, unless also obedience to his will be joined therewith; so much doth Christ teach by

his own evidence, that he is of God, contrary to theirs: "I know him, and keep his saying."

9. Such as are of God, and know him, should confidently avow their right and interest, and it is as great a wrong in a child of God to deny his right as it is in a profane man to claim an interest; therefore saith Christ, in opposition to them, " But I know him; and if I should say I know him not, I shall be a liar like unto you," who boast of an interest without ground.

10. Christ doth perfectly know the Father and his will, so that none can be deluded in resting on what he reveals of him; and he was perfectly obedient to the will of the Father in all things, so that nothing can be objected against them who flee to lay hold on his righteousness; for " I know him, and keep his saying."

VER. 56. Your father Abraham rejoiced to see my day: and he saw it, and was glad.

Secondly, Christ answers in particular to the ground of their exception; and, comparing himself with Abraham, (who was greatest, in their account, of any of the prophets they mentioned with him, and indeed was the father of the faithful,) he proves that he was greater than he; for Abraham knowing him, the true Messiah, to come of his seed, did earnestly desire to see that day, and did get a sight thereof by faith, to his joy and contentment. And by this he proves that Abraham's joy and comfort depended on him, and that he lived by faith in his words and the promises concerning him according to that, ver. 51; and, on the other hand, he proves by this that they were not Abraham's true children who rejoiced not in him and in the day of the gospel.

DOCTRINES.

1. Christ will make use of wicked men's boasted-of privileges to aggreage [aggravate] their faults; therefore doth he design him " your father Abraham"—to wit, according to the flesh, that they might see how far they were degenerated from him in manners.

2. The time of the gospel is not only a day, in respect of the dark ignorance in which the world lies without it, but it is Christ's day by way of excellency,—for albeit the gospel and Christ were known and embraced before, yet that treasure was but couched, for most part, under dark types, and seen at a great distance, and sin and the law and the curse did bear much sway; but now free grace doth eminently reign and shine,—and Christ in his own person did appear on earth in our nature, to publish these glad tidings more clearly; therefore doth he call it " my day."

3. Men were not saved before Christ's incarnation by anything beside Christ; but as Christ and the covenant of grace were known then, so men were made participant of him and his benefits by faith; for so is clear in the matter of Abraham, to whom it is supposed Christ was known, not only as God, but as Mediator, to be incarnate, otherwise he could not have desired a sight of him, and it is expressly asserted that he saw his day, " and was glad."

4. Such as indeed have heard tell of Christ, their knowledge will produce earnest desires after him; and such as prize Christ and salvation by him will look upon the time of the gospel and his incarnation as a very sweet sight; for Abraham hearing tell of it, he " rejoiced to see my day"—to wit, of my coming in the flesh, as Luke, x. 24; and this rejoicing presupposeth and includes an earnest desire.

5. Even the best of men stand in need of Christ, and according as they grow in real goodness their desires after him will grow; for so even Abraham, that eminent saint, " rejoiced to see my day."

6. The spiritual desires of God's people may be and (when they are well managed) are full of joy, begotten partly by the estimation of what they desire, seasoned with hope that they shall come speed in some measure, and partly by what they do really enjoy who are sincerely desiring and pursuing; their very hunger proves a blessedness, and that they do possess in part. Therefore it is said that Abraham rejoiced (or skipped for joy) to see my day. His heart was warmed with the thoughts of it even in desiring it.

7. The sincere desires of God's people will not be frustrated, nor will a sincere and cheerful pursuer be disappointed in God's way and measure; for he rejoiced to see, and he saw, not with bodily eyes, Luke, x. 24, but by faith, Heb. xi. 13.

8. The Lord, for wise reasons, may suspend the satisfying the desires of his people all their days in their way, and yet in effect be granting them in a way that is as good for them; for albeit Abraham saw not this day with bodily eyes in its full accomplishment, yet, for all that, " he saw it." The Lord indeed suspended the exhibition of Christ in the flesh till long after Abraham, because it would have crossed his purpose of reserving that to the fulness of time to have done otherwise (and saints must stoop to quit their will when it doth not consist with God's great purposes concerning his church); yet Abraham got that which was far better than a simple bodily sight; for albeit believers and the disciples in that time had a double advantage of getting both a bodily and spiritual sight, yet a spiritual sight of him, either in the word of promise before he came, or in the word of performance since his exhibition, is far beyond a bodily sight of him, which avails not without this, as was seen in the most part of them who saw and heard him.

9. The desires of the godly, which flow from faith, are well satisfied when they get more ground and encouragement yet to believe, and depend, and wait on; for Abraham behoved to believe before he could desire, and now his desires are satisfied with seeing more by faith.

10. Faith will see far off, and through many impediments, and will draw comfort from what is not only invisible at present, but not to come for a long time; for at that great distance, and through all these types, he saw my day and was glad.

11. A sight of Christ by faith, though at never so great a distance, and under many veils, will bring true peace and joy, and will satisfy a believer, however he desire often much more; for

"he saw it, and was glad." He was content of that, though his desire was after more, and it did indeed bring true joy unto him, and made him (with the rest of the patriarchs) confess they were strangers and pilgrims on the earth, Heb. xi. 13. I need not here curiously inquire why it is said that in desiring he " rejoiced," or skipped for joy, and in getting that sight he was only " glad." It may be conceived thus: that joy might be more solid, and make less noise, when men have greatest cause of joy, and particularly in enjoyment; or his " rejoicing" points at that more satisfactory measure of joy that he apprehended would be in seeing Christ incarnate, and with bodily eyes, as well as by faith, and his being " glad" points at the measure of joy he attained to in the sight he got, the other being reserved till he came to his rest.

VER. 57. Then said the Jews unto him, Thou art not yet fifty years old, and hast thou seen Abraham?

58. Jesus said unto them, Verily, verily, I say unto you, Before Abraham was, I am.

This last part of Christ's answer occasions a new exception against him, that he, who was so young a man, should presume to say he had seen Abraham, ver. 57. In answer to which, Christ asserts that however they take it, yet he is before Abraham—to wit, in respect of his godhead, though upon that also followeth that even then he exercised the office of Mediator according to the covenant of redemption in that nature, and so was the matter of the godlys' desire and joy, even from the beginning, as was said before of Abraham, ver. 56. While they say, " Thou art not yet fifty years old," though Christ was far younger, it may be conceived that Christ's condition and exercise, being a man of sorrows and acquainted with griefs, had altered him much, and made him seem older than he was, as, indeed, exercise of mind will waste men's bodies soon. Or it may be conceived to be spoken with a latitude, that it was very absurd that he, who had not lived so much as the half of an age, (reckoning a hundred years to an age,) should say he had seen Abraham, who was dead so many ages before. Likewise, they bewray their malice in their speech, obscuring what he had spoken of Abraham's seeing of his day, and putting in these words, " Hast thou seen Abraham?" as thinking it a disparagement that Abraham should take notice of him though he had lived since that time.

DOCTRINES.

1. The truth of God must not be the worse loved that it be sublime and above the reach of human reason, or that malicious men cannot, or will not, see and acknowledge it, but do account it absurd; for here a precious truth is rejected by them as absurd.

2. Such as look on Christ's outside only, and his state of humiliation, will never see his true excellency; and so many things are true of Christ as God, that flesh and blood, and they who look on him as mere man, will think them most absurd; for herein was their mistake, they look on him as man only, and therefore object, " Thou art not yet fifty years old, and hast thou seen Abraham?"

3. Let men oppose as they will, yet it is a truth beyond all controversy that Christ had a subsistence before his incarnation and becoming man, and consequently is true God; for saith he, " Verily, verily, I say unto you, Before Abraham was, I am." He followeth forth his subsistence no further than before Abraham, (though he be eternal,) because this was the matter now in controversy; and they who forge glosses to obscure this text, as speaking of no subsistence of Christ before his incarnation, do not only wrong Christ, as not answering distinctly to the Jews' question, ver. 57, but are in that respect more blind than the very Jews, who understood it so, and could not endure to hear it, ver. 59.

4. Christ's subsistence before his incarnation is immutable and unchangeable, not subject to the vicissitudes of time; therefore saith he, " Before Abraham was, I am," not, I was, to shew that this his subsistence is unchangeable, still present, and consequently eternal. This " I Am," is also a name of God, Exod. iii. 14, pointing out that he is, and hath an unchangeable being of himself, and that albeit there be that which may be known of God, Rom. i. 19, yet his nature is incomprehensible and unsearchable, and is most fitly expressed by this, " I am that I am," Exod. iii. 14. (See Judges, xiii. 18.)

VER. 59. Then took they up stones to cast at him: but Jesus hid himself, and went out of the temple, going through the midst of them, and so passed by.

Followeth now the issue of this long dispute, and particularly of this last contest. They look upon him as so absurd in what he had last spoken that they will reason no more, but seek to cut him off as a blasphemer; and he takes no more pains to convince them, but delivers himself miraculously from their fury. Whence learn—

1. Malicious persecutors will not hearken to truth, though never so clearly told them; but when all arguments fail them they will betake themselves to violence; for then they take up stones to cast at him, wherein they were injurious, in returning him the reward of a blasphemer who had told them the truth, and unjust, in their tumultuous procedure, and not taking a legal way. And this is it which may be expected of all contradictors of Christ's doctrine, if they get power, and be not bridled.

2. It is lawful for God's servants to withdraw from the fury of bloody persecutors when the persecution is personal, as Christ's example doth teach.

3. Our blessed Lord did condescend to sanctify all the weak means prescribed to his people in hard times in his own person; for he who could have destroyed them " hid himself," and made use of fleeing; " he went out," &c.

4. Christ can disappoint persecutors, and deliver his people, even in greatest extremity; for when they have him among their hands in the temple, he first " hid himself," and then

"went out of the temple, going through the midst of them," &c. Either he dazzled their eyes, and made himself invisible, both when he hid himself and went away; or having done so for awhile, while he hid himself, he did bind up their hands that they could not touch him when he went openly through them out of the temple; and so he evidenced his great power even in his infirmity, and so also doth he make his people prove strong while they are weak, and perfects his strength in their weakness.

CHAPTER IX.

In this chapter we have the history of Christ's curing of a blind man, with some consequents that followed thereupon. It hath an immediate connexion with the doctrine contained in the former chapter; and it seems that Christ coming out of the temple to avoid the Jews' fury, chap. viii. 58, did meet with the blind man begging on the sabbath in the way that led to the temple, ver. 8, 14, and therefore, in the original, ver. 1, the same word of " passing by," is repeated from chap. viii. 59, and Jesus is not named, but only it is said, " as he passed by," as being a continued discourse with that, chap. viii. 59, where he is named. The chapter may be taken up in these parts :—1. Christ's miraculous healing of a blind man, to ver. 8. 2. The conference of the neighbours about this matter, partly among themselves, and partly with the man himself, from ver. 8 to 13. 3. The proceeding of the Pharisees upon it among themselves, with the man, his parents, and again with the man himself, till they excommunicate him, from ver. 13 to 35. 4. Christ's comforting of the excommunicated man, by leading him up to the knowledge and faith of himself, ver. 35—38, and by shewing that he hath the administration of judgment in his hand, for the comfort of humble sinners and terror of proud Pharisees, ver. 39, which he maintains against the exceptions of some of them, ver. 40, 41.

Ver. 1. And as Jesus passed by, he saw a man which was blind from his birth.

The history of this miracle may be taken up in this order :—1. Christ the physician and the distressed man meet together, ver. 1. 2. Christ confers with his disciples about the Lord's end in afflicting him, ver. 2, 3, and about the necessity of his curing him, and that presently, ver. 4, 5. 3. He works the miraculous cure, ver. 6, 7.

In this verse it is recorded that Christ coming from the temple doth on the way perceive and take notice of this man, whose disease was naturally incurable. Whence learn—

1. Since the fall of Adam mankind is subject unto many miseries, and beside the spiritual plagues, and common miseries following thereupon, it pleaseth the Lord to leave some exemplary effects thereof, to be documents unto all; as here there is a man " blind from his birth," which flowed from sin as the fountain, cause, and

in-let, though Christ afterward denieth that God's end in this affliction is to punish sin.

2. Difficulties and diseases that are insuperable and incurable by the ordinary course of nature are yet not impossible for Christ to help, but a meet object for him to magnify his power on; therefore it is marked, that he " was blind from his birth," that so he may set out Christ's power, who cured that blindness that by natural means was incurable.

3. When Christ and his followers are driven by persecution from their station and employment, they are but driven to their thrift; and the Lord, ordinarily, doth let persecutors drive them away, because he hath other employment for them wherein they may do more good; therefore when Christ is driven out from preaching in the temple to malicious and violent enemies, an occasion of work and doing good is presently offered him, and he is thrust out, in God's providence, that he may come and heal this man, who also doth afterward make better use of his doctrine than they did.

4. No heat of persecution, or personal danger, and no throng whatsoever, will hinder Christ to give an affectionate look to one of his own in misery; for as he " passed by," fleeing the fury of the Pharisees, he saw the man, and looked so earnestly and tenderly on him that it occasioned the disciples' question, ver. 2; yea, it seems this man's misery (who afterward was converted to him) did so draw his eye to him that he saw him, and took notice of none else that were ou the way.

5. Albeit Christ's people in their distress may be blind, and cannot see him, yet he seeth them, and his seeing of them will move him to pity, so much the more as they see not; therefore is it marked that " he saw (and took special notice of) a man which was blind."

Ver. 2. And his disciples asked him, saying, Master, who did sin, this man, or his parents, that he was born blind?

3. Jesus answered, Neither hath this man sinned, nor his parents: but that the works of God should be made manifest in him.

Followeth a conference of Christ and his disciples before the working of the cure, consisting of two parts, in the first whereof, answering a question of the disciples, he shews what was the Lord's end in afflicting this man. Christ's taking so special notice of him, and (as would appear) his standing still beside him, leads the disciples also to take notice of him, and to move a question, whether it was his own or his parents' sins that had drawn on this stroke, ver. 2; and Christ declares that in this stroke God did not intend so much the punishment of the sin of either of them as the manifestation of his own glorious work, especially in curing of him, ver. 3. For clearing this question and answer, consider—1. The disciples' question is not concerning the principal efficient cause of this affliction, (for that was God,) but concerning the procuring and final cause of it—that is, whether he or his parents by some gross sin had procured this stroke, and God had sent it as a punishment for that sin. Consider—2. However there might be clear cause of conceiving him to be born blind for his parents' sins, (as it is to be cleared afterward,) yet it is more difficult to clear how that should be the punishment of his own sin, seeing he could not sin before he was born; but we need not, for clearing their meaning, recur to that conceit of transmigration of souls from one body into another, and consequently, that he should be punished for the sins of his soul committed while it was in another body; for albeit this was an opinion among pagan philosophers, and somewhat of it crept in among the Pharisees, as may be gathered in part from Matt. xiv. 2; xvi. 14, yet it is conceived that they only held the transmigration of righteous men's souls into other bodies, and not of the wicked's, such as the disciples supposed this man to be; nor yet need we understand them as conceiving that God, foreseeing what a sinner he would be, did thus punish him; for whatever reference a stroke may have to a future sin, either to prevent it or to cut short their power who would in process of time abuse it, yet affliction as a punishment is inflicted after the sin committed; nor yet need we assert that they looked on original sin as the Pharisees do, ver. 34, (of which in its own place,) never considering nor laying it to heart but where it is evidenced by such a stroke. But we are to conceive that they acknowledged original sin, and that this did deserve the greatest of afflictions and plagues, not only spiritual but bodily also, as is seen on some infants. Consider—3. Christ's answer is not to be understood—1, as if he denied them to have sin, whereof all are guilty since the fall, 1 Kings, viii. 46; Romans, v. 12; nor, 2, as if he denied that affliction entered into the world by reason of sin, Romans, v. 12, since if man had not sinned he had lived in a blessed estate according to the covenant of works; nor, 3, as if he or his parents had not sin enough to have deserved this punishment if God had pursued it; for the wages of the least sin is death, Rom. vi. 23; nor yet, 4, as if God did never send affliction as a punishment for sin, however he dealt in this particular; but the meaning is, that in afflicting this man the Lord did not so much purpose to punish their sins as to manifest his own glory; and so he would draw them from their curious questions to prepare themselves to be edified by his cure.

DOCTRINES.

1. Such as God hath a special purpose of love unto may yet be mistaken by his dear children, and get harder measure from them than Christ will give them, as here the disciples do to this man, upon whom Christ had mercy.

2. It is a great fault in Christ's disciples, being tenderly dealt with themselves, when they give out hard sentences against others, because of their afflictions, and do judge of their guilt according to the greatness of their afflictions, not considering that it is not dispensations, but the word, whereby men's estate and condition must be tried; for herein the disciples failed, who, being as yet the children of the bride-chamber, little acquainted with sorrows and griefs, and being little affected with the poor man's case, only desiring to hold up discourse when they see Christ so diligently observe him, would dive into his guilt and provocation, whereas no such thing was intended in the stroke; thus also did Job's friends deal with him.

3. Whatever be the Lord's forbearance towards sinners, yet all the posterity of Adam do bring as much guilt and sin into the world with them as deserves the saddest of afflictions; for their question imports this truth, that this man's sin did deserve that he should be " born blind." Original sin brings death even on infants, Rom. v. 12, 14, doth deserve eternal damnation, and consequently it needs not be thought strange if the Lord pursue it with temporal afflictions.

4. Albeit the Lord do not punish and condemn any eternally for the sin of any of their progenitors (except Adam, in whom all sinned) unless they do actually imitate them, yet he may justly afflict children in their bodies and estates, which they have from their parents, for the sins of their parents, and so punish their parents in them; for this truth is also imported in their question, that for his parents' sins he might be " born blind."

5. The sense of Christ's words is not always to be taken from what his speech at first view would seem to offer, but a special respect is to be had to all the occasions and circumstances thereof for finding out the truth; for so must we do here in finding out Christ's meaning in this speech, " Neither hath this man sinned, nor his parents," which being nakedly looked on in itself would seem to contain an untruth, contrary to the tenour of the scriptures, but being compared with the disciples' question, and what himself subjoins, the meaning is found to be that God by this affliction is not punishing their sin.

6. Albeit all men be sinners, and albeit every sin deserve both temporal and eternal judgments, yet the Lord doth not always intend the punishing and avenging of sin even when he is correcting such as are sinners, but may be intending a higher end; for this is the true doctrine and sense of these words, " Neither hath this man sinned, nor his parents, but that the works of God," &c. Beside the punishing of sin, and the end after-mentioned, we find in scripture that God doth afflict that he may exercise his sovereignty and dominion over men, and that he may try the faith of his own, as was seen in Job's case. And albeit in many cases it will be a great difficulty to attain to this comfort, that Christ is not eyeing or pursuing our guilt when we are under sad afflictions, yet we may safely follow this order:—1. In all afflictions we should remember that sin is the coal from whence these sparks do fly, and so (whatever be the Lord's end, yet) we are still to be humbled under the sense of sin as our duty when we are afflicted. 2. Albeit the Lord do not pursue any of his own with afflictions as enemies, yet there may be many failings and infirmities which the Lord requires they should be sensible of, especially when the rod is on, whatever be God's end in it; and in observing this Job came short, as Elihu teacheth, though he was a reconciled man wronged by his friends, Job, xxxvi. 8 — 10.

3. The Lord may be pointing at sin by afflictions when yet they are pardoned, and may send out rods on penitent and pardoned saints to vindicate his own glory, and make them more cautious in time coming. So did he deal with David, 2 Samuel, xii. 13, with ver. 10, 11, 14. 4. Albeit the Lord send some afflictions as punishments and corrections for sin, and some for trial of faith and other graces, yet it is not the Lord's mind that his children, being corrected for sin, should cast away their faith, but when they take with their guilt they ought to look on their affliction as a double trial of faith, having not only the affliction but guilt also to wrestle with ; and therefore they ought to take special heed to faith. 5. Whatever the children of God be commanded to look unto under affliction, either of guilt or trial, yet they ought still to lift up their eyes above that and to expect that somewhat of God is and will be manifested in their afflictions, and that this is his chief end in afflicting ; for so much doth the text expressly hold out; it is, that the works of God should be made manifest, and the expectation of this should be the chief exercise of saints.

7. Albeit the Lord hath created the world, yet his all-sufficiency is such as he can receive nothing from it nor be bettered by it, only it is a stage whereon he doth experimentally manifest and make known what he is; for this is his great end in all his works, and particularly in this, " that the works of God should be made manifest in him."

8. In God's dispensations towards men there are to be observed not one but many purposes and proofs of his attributes and workings ; for the works (not the work) of God are to be made manifest in him. His sovereignty appeared in afflicting, and his mercy and power in curing him ; yea, by this so much appeared as proved him to be the Messiah according to the scriptures, Isa. xxxv. 5.

9. Albeit the Lord do gloriously manifest himself daily in the ordinary works of his sovereignty, power, and mercy, yet such is the stupidity of men that this is but little observed unless he manifest himself in some extraordinary works also ; therefore must such an extraordinary disease and cure be that the works of God may be made manifest.

10. The Lord will not take advantage of the distresses of his people, but only that he may give them a proof of his love ; and he doth involve them in infirmities and distresses on purpose that he may let out his glory in doing them good ; for this man was born blind " that the works of God should be made manifest in him," and as thus he needeth our infirmities for him to work upon, so we may glory in them, 2 Cor. xii. 9, 10.

11. As the Lord hath divers ends in afflicting his people, so his ultimate and last scope will not be soon seen, but the afflicted may be kept long under a dark condition, supported by secret strength, and an unseen blessing, and little know the Lord's mind till he himself manifest it; for albeit sovereignty might still have been seen in this affliction, yet God had many other works to manifest which were little dreamt of by this man from his birth to that day, till now Christ bring them out by his word and work ; which may warn all to beware of rash judgment, and may encourage them who, lying long under affliction, do keep their eyes fixed upon Christ.

Ver. 4. I must work the works of him that sent me, while it is day : the night cometh, when no man can work.

5. As long as I am in the world, I am the light of the world.

In the second part of the conference, Christ, having answered their question, doth now prevent an objection by shewing reasons why he should cure him, and that presently, notwithstanding any hazard might redound to him for so doing. As for the objection which the disciples might have urged against his working this miracle, we have one propounded to the same purpose, chap. xi. 8, where Christ repeats this answer in part, ver. 9, 10. And here they might be ready to object that being but even now in peril of stoning by the Jews, chap. viii. 59, why would he irritate them again by this miracle, and not rather lurk? especially, why would he do it on the sabbath, as it is, ver. 14, seeing the like practice had bred him so much trouble before, as is marked, chap. v. and vii. 23, 25. Christ prevents all by shewing that he must manifest these works of God (of which ver. 3) by curing this man, and that presently ; for which he gives three reasons—1. That he is sent with a commission to do these works, ver. 4, and therefore must be diligently obedient. 2. That his affection to the service did bind the tie laid upon him the straiter, ver. 4 ; for when he considered that there was a time prefixed to him wherein to do these works in his own person, (to wit, the time of his life and ministry,) which being ended (as it was now shortly to expire) he could not have the like opportunity, therefore he would now be busy upon all hazards. 3. That he is " the light of the world," ver. 5, and therefore behoved to cure him. This imports, partly, that being the storehouse of lost man, in whom the remedy of all their miseries is hid up, he could not withhold from them what they needed ; and partly being to manifest himself the light of the world to cure their spiritual blindness, he would not omit to confirm it by this visible sign of curing a blind man. This reason is amplified from the consideration of the time wherein he exercised this office, " As long as I am in the world," which is but an enlargement of the second reason. And for clearing thereof, and of the whole second and third reasons, it is not needful to resume the doctrines concerning man's misery and lying in blindness and darkness, or that Christ is the only and true remedy of this evil,—for these truths in their full latitude have occurred, chap. i. 9, and viii. 12, and ought here to be considered only with reference to the present scope,—but whereas Christ speaks of his day, and of a night coming, and that he is the light of the world as long as he is in the world, the meaning is, not that ever he wants light, or an opportunity of doing good unto his people, or that he was not the light of the world, both before his incarnation and after his ascension, but Christ by this points out that during the time of his abode on earth he was this light in an eminent way; not only spiritually enlightening his people and doing great things for them, but personally and immediately, by his visible presence and external operation, doing them by his own hand, whereas this light shined formerly, and wrought in and by the ministry of the prophets, and after his ascension by the apostles. And so the force of the reason is, that Christ, considering that he was the light of the world, immediately and in his own person, only so long as he is in the world, and that he had a prefixed time for his going about and doing good in his own person, which was now near expired, therefore out of his great affection to his people, and to any service that might do them good, he would be busy and omit no time.

DOCTRINES.

1. Men are not to expect that they will get through with good and acceptable works without many discouragements, which may weaken the hands of flesh and blood; for so is here imported in that Christ obviates them.

2. Christ is so easy to be entreated and employed by his people that he will neither be discouraged nor forbidden to do them any good that they need; therefore will he not be hindered, but reasons against all delays.

3. Christ's works are all of them the works of God, being all approven of him, and God employing him to do good, that so he might manifest his love to miserable man through him, in a way most agreeable to his justice; therefore doth he call these things that he did in the days of his flesh, not only his own works, but "the works of him that sent me." (See 2 Cor. v. 19.)

4. Christ stood obliged to perform all those duties which he did in the days of his flesh, and being bound thereunto by a commission accepted from his Father, for which he was to give an account, therefore saith he, "I must work the works of him that sent me."

5. As Christ stands bound by obligation to perform all the duties required of a Mediator, so also he did affectionately undertake them, and employ himself therein; for so much doth that addition teach—I must work while it is day.

6. Opportunities of well doing in our station are not to be slighted, but taken hold of, for we should work "while it is day."

7. It may excite us to improve opportunities of well doing when we consider that, opportunity being lost, it is not easily, if at all, recovered, even albeit we should be willing to work; for when the day is past, "the night cometh when no man can work."

8. Christ our Lord was so willing to be employed for the good of his people that he studiously improved all opportunities, and did seriously lay to heart the short time he had to remain on earth, that so he might employ it thriftily, and go about doing good; for he applies to himself in this present case that general consideration—"I must work while it is day: the night cometh, when no man can work."

9. The fulness of Christ as Mediator, being given for the good of miserable sinners, is an argument with him, pleading that he should lay out himself for their help who are in need; for so is the force of his argument, "I am the light of the world;" and therefore I must let out of that furniture laid up in me for the help of this man.

10. Christ, by the miraculous cures wrought upon the bodies of the diseased, in the time of his being on earth, gave a visible document of what he was and would prove to needy souls who employ him. So much also is imported here, that he, being "the light of the world," would give a proof of it, and invite sinners to employ him as such by curing this blind man.

11. The Son of God's manifesting himself in our nature, and conversing with sinners on earth, preaching and working miracles among them, was a sweet and refreshful light of consolation to the world; for albeit he be the light of the world both before and after, yet this is true in a particular and eminent way, "As long as I am in the world, I am the light of the world." And this was that day of light so much desired and longed for, Luke, x. 23, 24; for this was the glorious manifestation of the love of God, when he became Immanuel, God with us, and when God not only dwelt with men, but in man's nature, and by his own preaching and miracles gave proof of that fulness of grace and truth that is in him.

12. Our Lord Jesus is so respective of lost sinners that he accounted it no small favour to get his bride in his own immediate guiding, and did so acquit himself in these days of his ministry as might witness what an one he was; for so much doth Christ's argument, drawn from this, import, "As long as I am in the world, I am the light of the world," which imports, by way of argument, these two—1. That in his esteem it was a great favour to be thus in his own person "the light of the world," and not to leave the ministration of his comforts to his servants, to be ministers thereof; and therefore he would be busy in this his time of it. And indeed it appears how much he delighted to be the immediate messenger and publisher of his love, in that before his incarnation he appeared in human shape, and spake himself with the patriarchs; and when his messengers do in his name speak a word in season to the weary, his love is such that, if it were fit, he would come and be the messenger himself. 2. That his bride being now, during this time of his ministry, left on his immediate hand, (the prophets being ceased, John after awhile laid by, and his disciples doing but little,) it was requisite he should be busy, and guide her so as she should miss no other, and he might let her find what a difference there is betwixt the bridegroom and his friends; and indeed he is matchless, singular, and like himself, in his guiding and dealing with his own.

VER. 6. When he had thus spoken, he spat on the ground, and made clay of the spittle, and he anointed the eyes of the blind man with the clay,

7. And said unto him, Go, wash in the pool of Siloam, (which is by interpretation, Sent.) He went his way therefore, and washed, and came seeing.

Christ having given these reasons why he behoved to cure this man, doth now fall about it, and having made clay with his spittle on the dust, and anointed the man's eyes therewith, he sends him to the pool of Siloam to wash, which he obeying doth recover his sight. As for this pool (of which also, Nehem. iii. 15,) it was a fountain springing out from Mount Zion, from whence flowed out the brook of Siloah, which watered a part of the city, of which Isaiah, viii. 6. And as divers allegories are invented by the wit of men on this miracle, (as if his making use of clay in this miracle did point out that he could cure the man who had made man at first of clay, and that his spittle making the clay did point out the efficacy and virtue that floweth from Christ's humanity, being now personally united to the godhead,) so, in particular, the signification of the name of this pool, which is "Sent," makes men conceive the name was given to it with an eye to the Messiah, who is Shiloh, Gen. xlix. 10; but as John's drift in interpreting the name is only (according to his custom) to make his meaning plain, so the name seemeth to have been given of old, only in testimony that they accounted it a special gift sent of God to have a fountain or brook among these hills, so commodious for their city ; or because it did flow out not constantly, but now and then, according as God was pleased to send it.

DOCTRINES.

1. Christ's affection to needy sinners, manifested in his word, is such as he will give real proof of it, according as it is needed ; therefore he contents not himself to have said so much of it, ver. 4, 5, but " when he had thus spoken," he works the miracle, and will give a present proof of what he had said.

2. Albeit it be our duty to pray when we are in distress, yet such is Christ's compassion as to give us what we need when we have little mind of it, and so cannot pray for it ; for when the man is not minding at all the cure of his disease, but is only sitting there to beg, then Christ conferreth this unexpected benefit upon him. And by this way of dealing, Christ gives ample encouragement to his own to pray in their distress, being confident that he who prevents prayer will undoubtedly hear them.

3. When Christ employeth any means for the help of the miserable, yet the power that doth them good is not in these means, but in and from Christ ; for neither could " clay" heal, nor " the pool" wash away blindness ; but that flowed from his omnipotency only ; and therefore, as we should rest on no means, so neither should we be discouraged in using means appointed by Christ, so long as we have his promise.

4. Christ can bring about wonderful deliverances and mercies to his people, even by means which seem improbable and contrary to nature ; for clay of itself is rather fit to put out seeing eyes than to open blind eyes.

5. Such as Christ takes in hand as his patients, he may make them sicker before he cure them, and put them in a worse condition to sense than they were before ; for so much also doth the application of " clay" teach. It addeth an external impediment to his natural blindness, and yet is all done in order to his cure. And thus it is also in spiritual conditions ; the strong man may make greatest trouble when he is to be put out, Luke, xi. 21, 22.

6. Where Christ doth good to any, he will first try their faith, by their subjection and obedience to his commanded means, before they find the comfortable issue ; for such is his method here : he first puts him to subject himself to have his eyes anointed with clay, and then to "go, wash in the pool of Siloam," before the cure be wrought. Whatever Christ may do in his sovereignty in grace, yet it is our duty to believe, as we would have his power and grace manifested on our behalf, Mark, ix. 22, 23 ; and faith's first work must be subjection and obedience to commanded duties, 2 Kings, v. 10—14.

7. Faith in Christ yields prompt obedience, and will repine at no command prescribing the means of help ; for " he went his way therefore, and washed. And this, no doubt, flowed from faith given him by Christ (who, it may be, hath said more to him than is here recorded,) which made him quit the opportunity of getting alms on the sabbath day, and essay so improbable like a mean.

8. As there is no difficulty too hard for Christ, so there are none who, trusting in him, shall obey and follow his prescribed means, but they shall obtain a good, and the promised issue, were it never so improbable ; for " he went—and washed, and came seeing."

9. If we compare Christ's method in this cure with that which he followeth in curing another blind man, Mark, viii. 22—25 ; wherein he opens a man's eyes by degrees, and here it is done at the first act ;—if, I say, we compare these, we shall not only find this difference, that whereas Christ abode with the one, therefore he did it by degrees ; but sending this man away, and leaving him, upon the first act of his faith and obedience he is cured ; as, indeed, Christ orders his dispensations according to the need of them he deals with. Such as he is to stay with in some visible and sensible way, he may give them more work about the curing of their diseases, that so they may employ him more ; whereas such as he is to withdraw from may get their business more easily done. But further, it will be found that this is common to both, that being to meet with so great a mercy as to be cured of blindness, it is not wrought at first on either, but the one with whom he stayeth is cured upon Christ's putting his hands twice upon his eyes, and this man hath a time of it, in going from before the temple to the pool, before he be cured ; not only that, many going with him and observing him, they might be witnesses of the miracle, but also that himself might have time to be prepared for such a wonderful and unexpected change. And so it teacheth, that great and unexpected mercies need much preparation to fit us for them as well as crosses, that so we may be armed with strength

to bear them, and with grace to improve them well.

Ver. 8. The neighbours therefore, and they which before had seen him that he was blind, said, Is not this he that sat and begged?

9. Some said, This is he: others said, He is like him: but he said, I am he.

10. Therefore said they unto him, How were thine eyes opened?

11. He answered and said, A man that is called Jesus made clay, and anointed mine eyes, and said unto me, Go to the pool of Siloam, and wash: and I went and washed, and I received sight.

12. Then said they unto him, Where is he? He said, I know not.

In the rest of the parts of the chapter we have the several effects and consequents that followed on this miracle, the first whereof (in this second part of the chapter) is among his neighbours and acquaintance, to whom it seems he returned with much joy when he found not Christ in the place where he left him, whereupon followeth their conference upon this matter, partly among themselves, and partly with the man himself. The conference contains the resolution of three questions—1. Whether such a cure had been wrought, and whether this man who now saw was the blind man who sat and begged? This the neighbours cannot clearly resolve; but some assert it, others allege that he is only like him, till he himself put it out of controversy, ver. 8, 9. 2. The second question is concerning the way of his cure, which they propound for further satisfaction in the matter, ver. 10, and he answereth, ver. 11, wherein he is able to give an account of Christ's name, which he had learned either from Christ himself or from some who had been witnesses of what Christ did, and had led him to the pool. 3. The third question is concerning Christ, the author of this cure; they desire to know where he is, and he cannot resolve them, ver. 12.

From verses 8, 9, learn—1. The glory of Christ's working for his people will not be gotten obscured, and it should be taken notice of by all, as they have occasion to see it; for this miracle shines forth among the neighbours, who, seeing the man, draw forth the knowledge of it by conferences and questions, and by their means it becomes more public.

2. The Lord may so order his dispensations, even towards them to whom he hath a purpose of good, as one cross may draw on another, and many miseries may tryst [meet] together; that so they may have much exercise, he may make their deliverance the more conspicuous, and may make many mercies concur in it; for this man had not only been blind, but his blindness had driven him to sit and beg, that law concerning the poor, Deut. xv. 4, not being carefully observed in these times of confusion and bondage, as appears also from Acts, iii. 2, and elsewhere.

3. Even the many disadvantages and miseries that trouble brings upon us may contribute, in due time, to make Christ's glory more conspicuous in our help; for that his blindness made him sit and beg, it contributed to make him more known than if he had been the son of a great man kept in a corner, and this made the glory of the miracle to spread the faster.

4. When Christ lets forth proofs of his power and love upon any in their miseries it will make so great and wonderful a change that they who knew them before may readily mistake and hardly know them, their condition being so different from what it was; for so appears in these neighbours, who differ in their judgments whether this was " he that sat and begged," or if " he is like him" only.

5. Such as have gotten proofs of Christ's favour in mercy will not be ashamed of their former miserable condition before they were helped; for they will seek Christ's glory, and not their own, in their deliverance; therefore, albeit this man, having now occasion to change his beggarly condition, seeing he could labour for his livelihood, might have let them continue in their uncertainties, yet he thinks no shame to profess, " I am he," and so puts them out of doubt that it is he who sat and begged.

From verses 10, 11, learn—1. It is not enough to take notice of any great work that is wrought unless we also take notice of Christ the author, and the way and manner of working it; therefore when they are assured that a great change is wrought on him, they inquire further, " How were thine eyes opened?" or, How was thy sight given to thee?

2. These difficulties and impossibilities which men apprehend in deliverance from trouble and which Satan makes use of to mar confidence, will but contribute to make Christ's power and glory the more conspicuous; for while they inquire, " How were thine eyes opened?" they do grant it was not an ordinary work, but worthy to be taken notice of, as being naturally impossible, that so Christ's doing of it might make their own eyes to be witnesses of his omnipotency.

3. Christ is the author of any good that is done to miserable sinners, and it needs never be inquired who makes the blind to see, the sick to be whole, &c., for it is Jesus who worketh all this. So much doth he clear in answering their question, " Jesus made clay, and anointed mine eyes," &c., and albeit it be but a particular instance, yet it is a point of general verity.

4. Such as have but small acquaintance with Christ should yet speak to his commendation upon the fruits they have found of it, that so it may prove an earnest and pledge of more; therefore, albeit Christ had made this miracle the first step of his acquaintance with the man, (as is not unusual with Christ to prevent his people, and begin acquaintance with especial favours,) and so he can speak of him but as a stranger little acquainted with him, but that he heard his name, " a man that is called Jesus;" yet he speaks what he knows to his advantage, and so is afterward brought to know him better.

5. It is not enough to set out the greatness of Christ's work unless also special notice be taken

of all the weak and improbable means he employeth to bring it about; therefore doth he so
punctually relate all the circumstances of the
miracle; he " made clay, and anointed mine eyes,"
&c., to set out his glory in it the more.

From verse 12, learn—1. A sight of Christ's
glorious working should learn men to inquire
after himself; for so do they on this information; " Where is he?" though in the issue they
proved not so sincere. But when men get notice of Christ's glory and working, they will
either be allured to inquire for him, that they
may seek him to enjoy him, as Cant. v. 9—16,
with vi. 1, or their malice will be irritated to seek
him, to do him an ill office.

2. Ignorance of Christ, and concerning him,
and where he is to be found, is no rarity even
among those who have got much good of him;
for the man who was healed, as he took him but
for a man, ver. 11, so he knoweth not where
he is.

3. Such as are truly humble will not be ashamed
to confess their ignorance; for so doth he, " They
said unto him, Where is he? He said, I know
not."

4. Christ by his withdrawing and not staying
for the man's return, would teach—1. That true
humility is an enemy to ostentation, and to hunting after vainglory; for to avoid this did he
withdraw. 2. That Christ is not so much taken
with the muddy affections and ravishing admira-
tions which a recent mercy may produce, as he
desires to have the sense of mercies solidly digested, to bring out solid and constant fruits;
therefore doth he avoid all the expressions of the
man's affections, which readily he would have
poured out when he came from the pool, and
doth not manifest himself to him till afterward
that he have more solidly digested it, and till he
have yet more need of him.

VER. 13. They brought to the Pharisees him
that aforetime was blind.

14. And it was the sabbath day when
Jesus made the clay, and opened his eyes.

15. Then again the Pharisees also asked
him how he had received his sight. He
said unto them, He put clay upon mine
eyes, and I washed, and do see.

In the third part of the chapter, to ver. 35, we
have the second effect or consequent that followed
on this miracle, and it contains the proceedings
of the Pharisees upon it when it is made known
to them; and it hath these particulars in it :—
1. Their debates and divisions among themselves
upon it, ver. 16. 2. Their conference with the
man about Christ, ver. 17. 3. Their conference
with his parents, ver. 18—23. 4. Their conference yet again with the man, which at last ends
in his excommunication, ver. 24—34.
In these verses somewhat is premitted [brought
forward] by way of introduction to all these proceedings; as, first, that the neighbours brought the
man to the Pharisees, ver. 13, not so much out of
their respect to Christ or the man, as to please
the Pharisees and council, who they knew were

vexed with the rising glory of Christ, and who
had made such a business of the miracle formerly
wrought by him on the sabbath. 2. The time
when this miracle was wrought, which had been
omitted in the history itself, is here recorded,
ver. 14, as being the ground why the neighbours
brought the man, and upon which the Pharisees
took occasion to inveigh against Christ. 3. They
examine the man concerning the circumstances
of the fact, that so they may know what to do;
and the neighbours (as would appear) having
given a short account that he had been born
blind, and that Jesus had cured him on the sabbath day, the man in his answer only adds to
what they had said, and relates the manner how
the miracle was wrought, ver. 15.

From ver. 13, learn—1. Whenever Christ begins to do a good turn to any, albeit they have
but little acquaintance of him, yet they may expect that their friends and neighbours, who before
pitied or respected them, will be ready to persecute them, and deliver them up into the hands of
the most cruel adversaries of Christ and his followers; for so befel this man, they brought him
to the Pharisees.

2. Ill instruments will never be wanting to
keep up contests betwixt Christ and his enemies;
for there are who brought him to the Pharisees,
to set them on edge against Christ.

3. Were churchmen never so vile and corrupt,
yet their titles and eminent places will still draw
carnal men rather to respect them, than Christ in
his state of humiliation; for this was it that made
these neighbours bring him to the Pharisees who
aforetime was blind; they are taken up with their
eminent places and titles, and therefore do take
their part.

4. When men are once engaged in a course of
persecution, and take delight in it, it is righteous
with God to give them up to many opportunities
of persecution till their cup be full; for it was
in God's judgment that they brought him to the
Pharisees; for they had been Christ's avowed
enemies, and had persecuted him formerly, and
now this poor man must not be persecuted but
by their hand, that so they may be made drunk
with blood and persecution, since they delighted
so much in it. (See Matt. xxiii. 31, 32.)

From verse 14, learn—1. Works of necessity
and charity to those in distress are very consistent with the due sanctification of the sabbath;
therefore doth Christ so often work these works
upon the sabbath to confirm this truth.

2. As no offence taken by men at the doing of
necessary and moral duties, whereby Christ is
honoured, should be regarded so as to drive us
from duty, so in particular the offence of wicked
persecutors is not to be regarded in doing of those
things that may set out the glory of God; therefore, albeit it was the old contest that he had
cured a man upon the sabbath, yet he will do it
over again, seeing the work is necessary, and the
doing of it then was an occasion to manifest the
glory of his work by their opposition, whereof
they had no occasion if he had done it another
time. It is true, we should give offence to none,
either Jew or gentile, 1 Cor. x. 32, but in doing
necessary duties no offence is given, it is taken
only; and albeit it should be matter of sorrow

when men do take offence unjustly, especially if they be godly, yet Christ will have no respect to the unjust stumbling of malicious persecutors, Matt. xv. 12—14.

3. Christ allows no composition with avowed and malicious enemies in matters of truth or duty; therefore also Christ will work these miracles on the sabbath day, that he might not seem to comply in the least with their superstitious opinions concerning the sabbath. (See Gal. ii. 3—5.)

From verse 15, learn—1. It is but in vain for men to think that their terror will drive a man from avowing what he hath found in Christ or received from him, unless he be under the strong power of a tentation; so much appeareth in this man. Albeit they were informed by the neighbours, (for the man needs not name Christ in his answer, of whom they had made mention,) yet again they also asked him, as thinking their authority and terror might cause him deny what he had said before his neighbours, that so there might be no more of the miracle; but all in vain, for he avows it clearly; and indeed it is a wonder how he is borne up in all this debate, seeing as yet he neither knew where Christ was, nor fully what he was; but as sense of this favour obliged him to Christ, so it may be thought admirable how much strength, courage, and ability men may be furnished with in defending Christ's cause.

2. They who would undertake to speak of Christ's working will but spill it in the telling, in comparison of those who have sensibly found it in themselves; therefore doth he, in this answer, add to their report, and lay it out fully, which (it seems) they had but thought worthy to be mentioned only in the general.

3. Such as are sensible of Christ's goodness in his working will look upon every circumstance in it as remarkable; therefore doth he so punctually relate the manner of the cure—" He put clay upon mine eyes, and I washed," &c.—not only that he might satisfy their question, "how he had received his sight," but to testify how much it affected him to dwell on every passage thereof.

4. Christ's favours are solid and permanent, and ought to be remarked that they are so; therefore doth he not only acknowledge that he saw, but yet still " I do see," as observing the continuance of the favour.

5. It is also required in men who receive favours from Christ that the continuance thereof do not render them tasteless, but that the sense of their former ill condition, and of Christ's mercy, be entertained, that so the favours may be still fresh; therefore also doth he say, " I do see," to testify the continuance of his affection and estimation of that mercy.

Ver. 16. Therefore said some of the Pharisees, This man is not of God, because he keepeth not the sabbath day. Others said, How can a man that is a sinner do such miracles? And there was a division among them.

Followeth the several proceedings of the Pharisees upon this matter; and first, They put the man aside a little, and enter into a debate among themselves about Christ; some do condemn Christ as not sent nor approven of God, because he did these things on the sabbath day; others plead that if he were such an one he could not work such miracles; and the debate grows to that height that it tended to a division, or schism. Whence learn—

1. Whatever boldness and resolution persecutors may seem to have in prosecuting their bloody courses, yet they have more vexations than every one knows, either among or within themselves; therefore, albeit the Pharisees appear very resolute in their dealing with others, yet here the Spirit draws the curtain, and lets us see what differences and debates there are among themselves.

2. Persecutors will be so malicious and impudent in their calumnies that no convincing arguments or apologies will satisfy them; for albeit Christ had fully refuted this calumny, chap. v., yet they maliciously urge it again: " This man is not of God, because he keepeth not the sabbath day."

3. The malice of persecutors is nothing the more approven that it is masked with a pretence of zeal, but is rather the more hateful that so corrupt dispositions should be covered with such a pretence; for this doth not excuse, but add to the fault, that they should let out all their malice under this cover: " he keepeth not the sabbath day."

4. Christ's enemies are so far from giving unto Christ his due glory, that they esteem him the worst of any; for they are so far from acknowledging him to be true God, that they will not so much as acknowledge him to be " of God" —that is, to be either a prophet or messenger sent of God, or a good man approven of him, which is all one as to account him a vile " sinner" and an impostor, as it followeth in the exception given in by others.

5. Some may be found, even in the cabin-councils of persecutors, who think not so harshly of Christ and his followers as others do, and who would do more for him if they had an opportunity; for here, even in their conclave, there are some to plead a word for him, either a Nicodemus or some who had convictions, but went no further.

6. Christ's miracles were such as even enemies were convinced they could not be wrought by notorious sinners and deceivers; for say they, " How can a man that is a sinner do such miracles?" where by " a sinner" we are not to understand him that only hath sin in him, but such a notorious sinner, and so eminent in a trade of it, as he may be better known by it than by his name, and particularly a notable impostor and deceiver in the matter of his calling and doctrine. And as we are not to conceive that all those who plead for him do believe him to be the spotless Lamb of God, so we need not dip into the strength of their argument, nor clear how it is consistent with what is elsewhere recorded in scripture, that Satan can work wonders, and that antichrist shall come with signs and wonders, which, though they be lying signs, in so far as they tend to the confirmation of a lie, yet some of them may be real in themselves, though not passing the reach

of natural causes, and so not real miracles. But we need not stand to justify all their sayings and apologies, whereof God makes use to mar the present designs of enemies; and it sufficeth us to know that Christ's miracles were so far above the reach of nature, and so evidently free of jugglery, that his very enemies, and they who had power to dignosce [decide] upon delusions, could not but be convinced. (See John, iii. 2.)

7. Albeit truth be the only best second to a man, and that which may make him stout, yet nature is impudent and bold in maintaining error, but if it be convinced of truth it doth assert it but timorously. So much may be gathered from their proceeding here. They who are against truth are bold, and speak first; but the other party come in last, and propound the matter only by way of question.

8. Christ, when he pleaseth, can divide the very conclaves and councils of his enemies, and raise a schism among them, that so he may put a stop to their violent proceedings; for " there was a division (or schism) among them," while none of the parties would cede to another.

Ver. 17. They say unto the blind man again, What sayest thou of him, that he hath opened thine eyes? He said, He is a prophet.

The second particular in their proceedings is their re-examination of the man concerning his thoughts of Christ; seeing they could not agree among themselves, they (whether the one or other party, or all of them, is not much matter) call the man again to know what his thoughts of Christ were, who had done this for him; and he, according to the weak measure of light received, freely declares him to be a prophet. Whence learn—

1. No rubs or stops and disappointments will break the malice of persecutors, but they will still to it again; for when their former examination had not produced unanimity among themselves, they try the man again, to see if they can draw anything out of him to carry their point. And it may be conceived that they would gladly have had somewhat out of the man, whereupon they might condemn Christ; for however persecutors have so much malice as to oppose Christ, yet they have so much terror as to wish others might have a prime hand in it.

2. Christ's friends must not expect to have done with their trials at one essay, but that enemies, by multiplied assaults, and many sifting questions, will labour to dash and confound them; for so do they with this man; after the former examination they put him again to it with a new question: " They say unto the blind man (who had been blind) again, What sayest thou of him?" &c.

3. When Christ hath done a good turn to any, it concerns them to consider what they think of him who hath done so for them; for this their question is in itself seasonable, whatever was their aim in it, " What sayest thou of him, that he hath opened thine eyes?"

4. When God draws forth weak professors to trial he can bear them up, though their know-ledge be but little, and can make them endure many as well as one assault; for he is as bold in this as in the former examination.

5. There may be, and is, more true knowledge of Christ in a poor man that hath tasted of his favour than in a whole conclave of persecuting doctors; for he saith more to his commendation, and more expressly, than even they who pleaded for him in the council.

6. When weak professors have said much of Christ, and more than persecutors can endure, yet they come far short in setting out his true worth; for he saith only, " he is a prophet," which though it was much, considering his small acquaintance with Christ, yet it is far short of what Christ is; for he doth not so much as ac-knowledge him to be that great prophet, Deut. xviii. 18, far less doth he see him to be the Son of God, till afterwards it be revealed to him, ver. 35—37.

Ver. 18. But the Jews did not believe concern-ing him, that he had been blind, and re-ceived his sight, until they called the parents of him that had received his sight.

19. And they asked them, saying, Is this your son, who ye say was born blind? how then doth he now see?

The third particular in their proceedings is their examination of the man's parents; when they can gain no ground of himself, they will not believe that he had been born blind, and there-fore try his parents if they own him for their son, and if he was born blind, and how he now recovered his sight; if so be they might possibly bring out somewhat to obscure the glory of this miracle. Whence learn—

1. It is the practice of corrupt churchmen to appropriate to themselves the privileges and titles of the people of God, as if none were worthy of these but themselves; therefore it seems the Pha-risees and council are called " the Jews," because they called themselves so, though it was a name common to all the nation; because not only were they of that nation, but they usurped it as only due to them, while they have a low esteem of the people, chap. vii. 49.

2. Persecutors are incessant in their malice and endeavours to smother the glory of Christ's clearest working; for so do they labour to get it denied that ever such a miracle was wrought, and do expect that possibly his parents, through fear, may deny that he was born blind.

3. When men are led by malice against Christ and his truth, they will be so impudent as not to give credit even to what they see; for they " did not believe concerning him, that he had been blind, and received his sight," though they were already convinced of it, and had condemned Christ for curing of him, ver. 16.

4. In a time of trial, not only they who are most eminently concerned and engaged, but even others, may be brought upon the stage; for not only the man, but his parents, are here brought out to give a confession—they did not believe until they called the parents, &c.

5. Persecutors are very subtle and politic, and

know how to make use of all advantages, and tempers, and interests of men, to bear down Christ and his truth ; for so doth appear here. They purpose to obscure and bear down the glory of this miracle, and finding the man so affected as they could not draw him to comply with them, they essay his parents, if possibly they, being less concerned and affected than the man, might be moved and tempted to deny somewhat of the truth.

6. It is the policy of persecutors to confound simple men with multiplicity of questions, and to dash them with their own prejudged thoughts upon the matter; therefore do they pose them with three questions at once, and do in their questions insinuate what they were inclined to believe,—ye say he was born blind, but we do not credit it.

VER. 20. His parents answered them and said, We know that this is our son, and that he was born blind :

21. But by what means he now seeth, we know not; or who hath opened his eyes, we know not: he is of age ; ask him: he shall speak for himself.

22. These words spake his parents, because they feared the Jews: for the Jews had agreed already, that if any man did confess that he was Christ, he should be put out of the synagogue.

23. Therefore said his parents, He is of age ; ask him.

In these verses we have, first, his parents' answer, wherein they expressly avow that he was their son, and that he was born blind, ver. 20, but for the way of his cure they waive it, and remit the narration of it to himself, as being of age sufficient to give an account of it, ver. 21. 2. We have a reason why they decline to answer this question, which was, the fear of excommunication, a decree being passed among the rulers that whoso confesseth Christ should be excommunicated, ver. 22, 23.

From verses 20, 21, learn—1. Natural affections may go very far in natural duties; and particularly, natural affection doth oblige, and will lead, parents not to deny their own children in their greatest miseries or dangers, or for any fear; for albeit their son had been blind, and is now in danger, and albeit they knew not but the Pharisees might be offended at this, yet they freely answer, " We know that this is our son, and that he was born blind."

2. Natural affection and resolution, how great soever it be, will not carry men to confess Christ and his truth when there is any danger in it; for how stoutly soever they own their son, yet for what concerned Christ they shift it : " By what means he now seeth we know not; or who hath opened his eyes, we know not;" wherein, whatever may be said in their behalf from what followeth, that they desire not the glory of the miracle to be obscured, but remit them to the fittest witness of it, yet they sin heinously by denying

their knowledge, and by their ingratitude in not avowing Christ, who had conferred so notable a benefit upon them in the person of their son.

3. Albeit men may hazard much for their friends in their private quarrels, yet such as are not stout for Christ will decline suffering in their own person, though they should hazard their dearest friends, and will let them suffer there alone ; and it is well if they prove not their greatest enemies ; for they by shifting trouble do expose their son to it : " He is of age, ask him ;" he shall speak for himself, as being from under their charge, and able to give an account of his own ways. And albeit it had not been lawful for them to obtrude themselves on suffering, yet when they are called to give a confession it was their fault to desert, not only the truth, but their son also.

From verses 22, 23, learn—1. Excommunication from the society of the people of God is an ancient and lawful ordinance in the house of God, however it be abused by men; for it was an ordinance, even in the church of the Jews, to put men " out of the synagogue." (See Ezra, x. 8.)

2. The best and most necessary ordinances of God may be abused by wicked men, and the authority of his judicatories, and the edge of his censures, ill employed, when church rulers are corrupt; for so it was here; in their council they had agreed to employ their authority, and the censures of the church, to bear down Christ. This should teach men not to reject everything which the corruptions of men do abuse.

3. Albeit the child of God may, for some miscarriages, fall under the censure of excommunication, yet it is an evidence of a corrupt time, when the edge of that censure is turned against the children of the house merely because of their adhering to Christ; for so was it here ; they " had agreed already, that if any man did confess that he was Christ, he should be put out of the synagogue." It is said, they " had agreed," albeit there was not only a Nicodemus and Joseph of Arimathea among them, but some others who thought more favourably of Christ, as would appear from ver. 16, and chap. xii. 42 ; and that because the corrupt part did agree, or those who were more honest being absent, others would not stand out against the common determination, however they had argued the cause ; or fear did make them agree that he should not be acknowledged for the Messiah, however they had accounted him a good man.

4. Excommunication is a censure not a little terrible when it is inflicted upon just grounds ; for whatever weakness was in their fear, (of which afterward,) yet it is an evidence that the members of the Jewish church did generally fear to undergo this censure.

5. Men, through long custom and formality, may be brought to stand in awe of church censures, who yet give no evidence that they stand in awe to sin against God, but rather of the contrary ; for however it be good in itself to be afraid of excommunication, yet (besides that this was an unjust decree) their shifting to confess the truth shews how they durst hazard on sin, and yet they fear excommunication. It may be,

indeed, that some outward inconveniences followed upon this censure, which made them so carefully avoid it, as is true in the case of rulers, John, xii. 42, 43; but as that is not the right cause wherefore church censures should be dreadful, so though there were no such thing, yet there are many who would not willingly be secluded from the privileges of church members, nor from the ordinances, who yet never long after God in them, nor do lay to heart that they may be judicially bound in heaven, though they be not bound on earth.

6. Albeit just excommunication be a sad sentence, yea, albeit when it is unjustly inflicted by a true visible church, it be so grievous as men should not willingly desire it, and should be affected with it, yet it is but a slavish and sinful fear when men are hindered to confess truth because men will excommunicate them; for herein did the man's parents fail, in that, for fear of this sentence, they declined their duty; and as carnal courage is but faint-hearted in Christ's matters, however it may be invincible in other difficulties, so slavish fear of this and the like inconveniences is base, and will prove an enemy to suffering unless it be well balanced with faith, Psalm lvi. 3.

7. They had decreed only, that " if any man did confess that he was Christ, he should be put out of the synagogue," and yet this makes them afraid so much as to confess that Christ had cured their son. The reason may be conceived, that the rulers were so malicious that a favourable word spoken of Christ was as much as if they had confessed him to be the Messiah,—as, indeed, in persecutors' account, it is sufficient to render men as bad as may be, if they be anything more charitable or not so malicious as themselves,— yet seeing they do not inflict this censure on those among themselves who pleaded for him, at least as not a sinner, ver. 16; nor do they excommunicate the man for all his free confession till (as they conceive) he carry himself unreverently towards them; therefore it may be conceived rather that their fear was so slavish as they durst not so much as confess that truth, which they might confess without hazard; and so it teacheth—that slavish fear is a very brutish passion, and will not only be moved at real hazards, but will multiply many imagined dangers; and when men are possessed and led by it they will not only do all that persecutors by their decrees require, but it will drive them even from duties which they might follow without hazard.

Ver. 24. Then again called they the man that was blind, and said unto him, Give God the praise: we know that this man is a sinner.

Followeth the fourth particular in their proceedings, to ver. 35, which is, their conferring of new [anew] with the man himself, wherein he endures several assaults from them, and doth answer them so as at last they excommunicate him. The first assault is in this verse; wherein, having called him in again, they deal with him in an insinuating way. And, 1. They exhort him to give God praise; whereby I do not understand so much that they, supposing the miracle was wrought, would exhort him to take no notice of Christ in it, whom they knew (as it is afterward) to be a sinner and wicked man, but to give God all the glory of it. But comparing this speech with Joshua's exhortation to Achan, Josh. vii. 19, we shall find this to be their meaning: they would have him to glorify God by a free confession of the truth, that either he was never blind, or that Christ cured him not, but he had been dissembling or colluding with Christ in the matter. 2. To press him to this they hold out their own thoughts of Christ, that they knew him to be a sinner, and would never believe that he could cure him, say what he listed. Whence learn—

1. Whatever be the malicious designs of enemies or the weakness of those who are called to make confession of the truth, yet the Lord can keep his own glory from suffering prejudice, and enemies from getting advantage; for so did it prove here. Albeit the rulers thought to have gained much by putting his parents to it, and they did indeed come short in their duty, yet the matter is so ordered as they gain no ground against Christ, and are put to essay other means.

2. Such as receive most eminent favours at Christ's hand must look to share in trials beyond others; for albeit his parents get one assault, as having shared in the favour conferred on their son, yet, his share being much more in the mercy, his trials are oftener renewed: " Then again called they the man that was blind." He behoved to get a trial according to the measure of mercy received; and withal, the Lord would breed him in this first school till he came to be fitted for a new proof of Christ, and till the persecutors get a greater dash by him; as the issue made clear.

3. Among other trials from persecutors, this is one—that they will smoothly insinuate with such as confess Christ if so be they may pervert them by that means; for here they lay aside all harshness, and speak him fair.

4. It is no strange thing to see men pretend to aim at nothing but the honour of God, when yet they are maliciously opposing Christ, his glory, and truth; and this is one of persecutors' policies, whereby they labour to ensnare the simple; therefore they pretend that in all this they aim at nothing but that he would " give God the praise."

5. The confession of the truth of anything whereof men are guilty is indeed an honouring of God, when they are called to it, not only in so far as it glorifieth his justice in what he shall inflict for it, but in so far also as it giveth him the glory of knowing what is secret, and of being a punisher of lying and dissimulation; therefore do they urge him to a confession in these terms, " Give God the praise."

6. Such is the perversity of Christ's enemies that they will not only load him with unjust calumnies, but will obtrude their judgment and opinion (if they be men in power) upon others, to prejudge them in their free confession; therefore, albeit they require a free confession, yet they pre-limit him, by obtruding their opinion as infallible upon him, " we know that this man is a sinner"—that is, albeit thou be deluded so

far as to think him a prophet, yet we, who have both authority and skill to judge, do certainly know he is a wicked sinner.

7. It is the malicious cruelty of persecutors that they impudently brand Christ and his followers with calumnies, and yet will never give them a fair hearing, nor make them out upon them; for albeit Christ had put them to it to convince him of sin, chap. viii. 46, yet they would never do that, and yet will not give over to traduce him; "we know that this man is a sinner."

VER. 25. He answered and said, Whether he be a sinner or no, I know not: one thing I know, that, whereas I was blind, now I see.

The man in his answer doth waive and pass what they had asserted concerning Christ's person, but as to the matter of fact, wherein they required a confession, he clearly asserts that he being blind was made to see by him. As for his answer concerning Christ's person, it may be conceived that it flowed from his weakness and dissimulation, in part, that he should say, "whether he be a sinner or no, I know not," seeing he knew well enough he was no sinner in their sense, as appears from verses 17, 31, 33. So hard is it to keep our feet in continuing trials; and because of this his shifting it may be conceived he is put to it to speak out his light more clearly afterward. But if we consider the manner of the expression more narrowly, "whether he be a sinner or no, I know not; one thing I know," &c., it would appear that he not only adheres to the confession of what Christ had done, but brings a most convincing argument to refute their calumny against his person; that let them judge of him as they would, yet he would not stand to debate it with words when he could refute them by Christ's deeds; for he or any one else could not in reason judge him to be a sinner who had done so notable a miracle, and he who had received a benefit could not but think well of him. Whence learn—

1. It is a great injustice to calumniate Christ and his followers when yet their practice and works do refute these calumnies; therefore doth he think their charge against Christ to be a sinner not worth the answering, when this miracle did clearly refute it.

2. Such as have received kindnesses from Christ will not have an ill thought of him, nor will the prejudices or opinions of any sway them in that matter; therefore doth he reject all their thoughts of Christ, upon the consideration of what he had done for him.

3. Such as have participated of Christ's goodness will not conceal his glory by denying the same, whatever hazard there be, or whoever shift to confess it; therefore, albeit his parents had declined to give a confession of this truth, and there was manifest hazard in confessing it, yet he will not deny it, "one thing I know, that, whereas I was blind, now I see."

4. No men can set such a price upon mercies, or on Christ the author of them, as they who have tasted of the bitterness of wanting them;

therefore, albeit the favour of eyesight be common generally to men, yet few are so affected with it as he, and that because it was given him after he had wanted it long, "whereas I was blind, now I see."

VER. 26. Then said they to him again, What did he to thee? how opened he thine eyes?

27. He answered them, I have told you already, and ye did not hear: wherefore would ye hear it again? will ye also be his disciples?

Seeing he will neither deny the miracle nor yet have evil thoughts of Christ, they give him a second assault, and pose him concerning the manner and way of his cure, if so be they might outweary him, or make him contradict, and so invalidate his own testimony, ver. 26; but he being encouraged by the Spirit, and perceiving their drift, doth answer them roundly, challenging them that he had told them before to little purpose, and, in derision, inquires for what end they were so careful to hear it? if they had a mind to become converts? which imports that he knew they would not give up their names to Christ, let him repeat it never so often. Whence learn—

1. Persecutors are importunate and incessant in their endeavours to pervert such as confess Christ, and to get advantage against them; for this repeated question doth import not only that this poor man put them to great puzzles, driving them to question him so passionately, but that they would not give over their endeavours to make him faint, or entrap him.

2. The obstinate continuance of persecutors in their incessant trying of weak professors is a sifting exercise which is apt to prevail with them who might endure one assault well enough; for they look on this course of holding him at it as a mean to prevail at last, and that, however they prevailed not at first, yet when he saw they were not wearied nor minded to give it over he might be broken.

3. The manner and way of working any good work is a special way to try whether the doer of it be approven or not; therefore do they so much insist on that, "What did he to thee? how opened he thine eyes?" if possible, they might gather some ground of challenging Christ as working the miracle in an unlawful way.

4. Albeit persecutors be politic, and confessors of truth ofttimes weak and simple, yet the Lord cannot only give them courage but wisdom also to discern the drift of persecutors; for so doth this man insinuate that he knew it was for little good they were so inquisitive.

5. It becomes the people of God well when they perceive men dallying with truth and Christ's working to put on a holy indignation and zeal; for so doth he here with these Pharisees, who are so inquisitive to know the way of the miracle, when they mind to make no right use of it.

6. It is the duty of friends to truth not to foster up enemies with answering their needless

questions, propounded only out of malice; for saith he, " I have told you already, and ye did not hear, (or believe, or liked not of it,) wherefore would you hear it again?" since it is just the same as it was.

7. They who were in esteem above others do by their malicious opposing of Christ become justly contemptible to the basest, and may lawfully be touched in the sore by the avowers of truth; for here they are so absurd that he who had been a blind beggar doth taunt them to their faces, and lets them know how he saw into their malicious disposition.

8. Albeit sinners be invited to hear what God saith, or what is reported of his doings, yet he will not be slighted by any; and such as, out of malice, will not give credit to what they hear, it is just they be denied further information, and that pearls be not cast before such swine; for so is imported here, " I have told you already, and ye did not hear; wherefore would ye hear it again?"

9. The right fruit of all we hear of Christ is to gain our consent to be disciples and followers unto him, and they who will not yield to that, it is just they get no more of his mind revealed unto them; for so is imported in this reasoning, " wherefore would ye hear it again? will ye also (among the rest) be his disciples?" For it implieth that since they had no purpose to become scholars unto Christ, there was no reason that his glorious works should be so much revealed to them.

Ver. 28. Then they reviled him, and said, Thou art his disciple; but we are Moses' disciples.

29. We know that God spake unto Moses: as for this fellow, we know not from whence he is.

Being angry at this boldness of the man, they give him a third assault, wherein—1. They declare that however he and such as he were so silly as to become disciples to him, (which was little matter,) yet they would cleave to Moses, from whom Christ and his followers made apostasy, ver. 28. 2. They give a reason of their resolution, which they think may render Christ suspected to him; they think they may lean to Moses, with whom they knew God spake, but as for Christ, they knew not whence he had his office and authority, as they allege, ver 29. Whence learn—

1. Corrupt men cannot endure to have their idols rubbed upon, and particularly corrupt churchmen take it ill when they are not in such estimation as they would; therefore do they rail on him because he did not give them reverence enough.

2. It is persecutors' policy to cast disgrace upon the course they persecute that so they may shame professors from it; therefore do they upbraid him with being Christ's disciple as a very odious course, which they would be very loath to join in, " Thou art his disciple."

3. Albeit it be the greatest honour of sinful men to be admitted disciples unto Christ, and their greatest ignominy who are not so, yet times may be so ill, even in a visible church, that it may be acounted the greatest of reproaches upon men that they give up their name to Christ; for they think it a reproach great enough when they may say, " Thou art his disciple."

4. The best of men may be mistaken and abused by their carnal successors; and particularly it is a great wrong when any instrument is cried up to Christ's prejudice, and when men do pretend to the doctrine of the scriptures when they are rejecting Christ; for say they, as a pretext, whereupon they do reject Christ, " But we are Moses' disciples." Moses did set forth Christ, and he pressed the law to lead them to Christ, and so none could be his disciples who were not Christ's disciples also; and yet they made use of Moses, and their adhering to his doctrine, to oppose and reject Christ.

5. Such as men do admit of as teachers to their souls should make sure that they are called of God, and have their doctrine from him; for this was sound, though ill applied by them, " we are Moses' disciples," for " we know that God spake unto Moses."

6. Such as are led by malice and prejudice against Christ will not only think basely of his person, but will not see the clear evidences of his authority and commission; for albeit this point had been often cleared before this, yet say they, " as for this fellow, we know not from whence he is," or who gave him commission.

Ver. 30. The man answered and said unto them, Why herein is a marvellous thing, that ye know not from whence he is, and yet he hath opened mine eyes.

31. Now we know that God heareth not sinners: but if any man be a worshipper of God, and doeth his will, him he heareth.

32. Since the world began was it not heard that any man opened the eyes of one that was born blind.

33. If this man were not of God, he could do nothing.

In these verses the man gives a solid answer to their frivolous cavil; he passes what they had spoken against himself, and doth not labour to diminish Moses' due esteem, but only replies to what they had excepted against Christ. And, 1. He propounds his reply by way of admiration, that Christ, having wrought such a miracle on him, yet they should be ignorant of his authority, ver. 30. 2. He proceeds, by solid argument, to evince that his working this miracle proved he was of God; wherein, 1. He layeth down a general proposition, that no gross sinners, but only such as did worship God and obey him, would be heard or obtain things at God's hand, ver. 31. 2. He subsumes [assumes], in particular, that Christ behoved to be heard of God, having wrought so great a miracle, and so singular, that none of the prophets, nay, nor Moses, of whom they boasted, did ever the like, ver. 32. 3. From this he concludes that certainly Christ was not a wicked sinner, but of God, seeing, if it were not so, he could not do anything of that kind, ver. 33. For clearing this argument, consider—1. We need not be curious to evince the truth of this assertion, that Christ's miracles proved his divine authority, however impostors and deceivers may also work wonders; for the greatness of his works and the way of doing them were so convincing that even enemies themselves could not deny it when they spake their real thoughts, ver. 16, John, iii. 2, nor could the greatest enemies contradict it, unless they maliciously sinned against the Holy Ghost, as Matt. xii. 24, 31. 2. While he supposeth that Christ prayed to God that he might work this miracle, we are not to conceive that he understood who Christ was, or that it was his way to pray to the Father in the state of humiliation, John, xi. 41, 42, but he only looks on him as mere man; and therefore he doth so commend the instrument as he exalts the power of God in what he did. 3. While he proves Christ to be heard because he wrought this miracle, the meaning is, not to prove that all that are not heard in an extraordinary way are sinners, but this holds only good in them who pretend to extraordinary callings, that they must prove it by some wonders, and doth also argue that none who are so heard are sinners. 4. Taking this assertion generally, " God heareth not sinners," it is not to be understood that even the grossest of sinners may not come to God to have their sins pardoned and removed, and expect to be accepted and heard through Christ, but the meaning is, that they cannot be heard in other things while they purpose to continue in their sins. 5. It is also to be considered, that in some respects God may hear even gross sinners so far as to give them many temporal favours, to their greater condemnation in the end; as witness his answer to Ahab's hypocritical repentance, 1 Kings, xxi. 27—29; yet this that is asserted here doth also hold good, not only because whatever God do for wicked men, yet he hates both their persons and their prayers, or because whatever God do for the wicked at some times, yet the perpetual assistance and favour of God accompanying Christ in all his life and actions did prove that he was none of these; but seeing the man (as appears) knew not so much of Christ, (nor doth he insist on any other proof but this one miracle,) therefore the very nature of this miracle, whereof the like was never done by any, did prove that he was of God; for however many miracles were wrought by prophets before him, yet some sort of miracles were reserved to be done by him, to evidence that he was the Messiah. The words being thus cleared in reference to the present scope, from ver. 30, learn—

1. Most learned men will grow blind and absurd when they oppose themselves against Christ and his truth; for so doth this man find these Pharisees to be.

2. Christ may give his weakest friends so much sound knowledge of him as will make them wonder at the blindness and absurdity of persecutors; for saith he, " herein is a marvellous thing, that ye know not from whence he is, and yet he hath opened mine eyes."

3. Such as are truly affected with Christ's dealing will wonder and be ill pleased that every one will not see as much in it as they do; for he wonders and takes it ill that they are not so affected with the miracle, and with Christ the author of it, as he was.

From verse 31, learn—1. Christ's weak followers will not want a mouth, and wisdom, and courage, to plead his cause and confound their adversaries in a day of trial; for this poor beggar is enabled solidly to reason against the rulers, to their confusion.

2. The generality of the visible church want not common and received principles, which, being well improven, might refute them in their many particular miscarriages; therefore doth he bring in a received principle to refute them in this particular: " we know that God heareth not sinners," &c., and therefore Christ cannot be a sinner.

3. Such as would be approven of God ought to be devoted unto him, to worship and call on him, and employ him in all things, that so they may come speed in particular exigents; for here it is required that a man be " a worshipper of God," and this makes way for his being heard in particular cases, such as this in debate was.

4. It is not enough to prove men religious or approven of God that they keep up a form of worshipping God, unless they walk tenderly in obedience to God's will, that so they may come speed in prayer, and do improve grace as it is received, to enable them yet to more obedience; for to be a worshipper of God and do his will must go together.

5. Albeit no mere man be free of sin in this life, yet such as sincerely worship God, and make conscience of obedience, do give evidence that they have fled to Christ for justification, and have attained to some victory over sin, and so are not sinners, or living in a state of sin, in Christ's account; for here, to be a sinner, and to worship God and do his will, are opposed each to other.

6. They only who thus worship God, and are not sinners, will find access to God in their prayers, and get answers to what they ask according to his will; for " God heareth not sinners; but if any man be a worshipper of God, and doeth his will, him he heareth"—that is, they who have extraordinary callings will come speed in extraordinary things, and others will come speed in their lawful desires, according to the tenour of God's promises to hear his people's prayers.

7. It is one special mean to clear men in the matter of their personal approbation and acceptance with God when they employ God much in prayer, and so come to find acceptance and audience from him; for by God's hearing a man, he cometh to gather that he is not a sinner, but a worshipper of God, and doer of his will.

From verse 32, 33, learn—1. Christ had many public evidences to witness for him that he was accepted and heard of God in the discharge of his office; for so doth he subsume [assume] that Christ by this miracle had proven it.

2. Christ is omnipotent to do that which never hath been done before; and when any come to him with a distress that never any had expe-

rience of the like, he can help them for all that, and make his dealing to them an experience to others, inviting them to employ him thereafter; for " since the world began was it not heard that any man opened the eyes of one that was born blind." I need not debate whether ever such a cure as that was wrought before, (whereof yet we read not in scripture,) nor whether other miracles formerly wrought may be paralleled with it, for (beside that Christ wrought it by his own proper power, not as the prophets wrought miracles, though the man knew not this) it was certainly a singular and great miracle, and whatever may be supposed of the man's mistake, yet the general truth holds good; and the man, in commending it thus, doth evidence that he looks on God's mercy in granting it to him as singular, which is far from their practice who undervalue the favours conferred upon themselves in comparison of what is done to others.

3. Whatever wonders Satan and his instruments may be permitted to work, to draw men from the truth, yet Christ's miracles were such as did clearly evidence he could never have wrought them unless he had been approven and sent of God; for " if this man were not of God, he could do nothing" — to wit, such as this work is.

VER. 34. They answered and said unto him, Thou wast altogether born in sins, and dost thou teach us? And they cast him out.

Followeth the conclusion of this contest, and the issue of all these assaults, wherein, being highly incensed, they upbraid him for his presumption, that, being such a base and vile man, he should presume to teach them; and not being content with this, they excommunicate him. Whence learn—

1. The putting of persecutors to silence by reason will not gain upon them, but rather drive them upon violent rage, as here we are taught.

2. It savours of pharisaical pride for men to account only themselves holy, and to look on others as vile; for so do they compare this man with themselves.

3. It is the woeful mistake of men that they do not take notice of sin unless they may grope it in some sad afflictions; for upon this ground it is that they say, " Thou wast altogether born in sins," as bearing the print of it, in being born blind. Albeit all have original sin, yet it seems they laid it little to heart, but where such fruits of it did appear.

4. Men's pride and conceit of their calling and gifts makes them look rather to the messenger that reproves them than to God, and makes them despise to learn anything from those who are baser than themselves; therefore say they, "dost thou teach us?"

5. It is also men's pride that when sound doctrine galls them it makes them break out upon the instruments that hold it out; as here was their practice.

6. It is also but an irrelevant objection flowing from men's pride, when the weakness or sinfulness of a messenger from God makes them reject the message; as here they will not be taught by him who was " altogether born in sins."

7. It is one part of suffering for Christ, which his followers are to resolve upon, to be unjustly excommunicated, in which case the sentence is null before God; for " they cast him out," but little to his prejudice, as will be seen in what followeth.

VER. 35. Jesus heard that they had cast him out; and when he had found him, he said unto him, Dost thou believe on the Son of God?

36. He answered and said, Who is he, Lord, that I might believe on him?

37. And Jesus said unto him, Thou hast both seen him, and it is he that talketh with thee.

38. And he said, Lord, I believe. And he worshipped him.

In the last part of the chapter we have Christ comforting the man after his excommunication by two grounds of comfort, the last whereof he maintains against the exceptions of some of the Pharisees. The first ground of comfort (in these verses) is, by leading him to knowledge of and faith in himself the Son of God, wherein is recorded—1. That Christ, hearing of his hard condition, doth find him out, and propound an overture to encourage him against that sentence, which is, to believe, ver. 35. 2. The man professing a willingness to believe, but desiring to be informed who was the Son of God, ver. 36, is resolved and cleared by Christ, ver. 37. 3. The man, being thus cleared, doth profess his embracing of him by faith, and in testimony thereof doth worship him, ver. 38.

From verse 35, learn—1. Men, by the persecution of enemies may be driven to their thrift, to need and get more proofs of Christ; for had they let this man alone, possibly this great mercy might have worn out of his mind; but by their tossing and excommunicating of him they put him to it, to need comfort, and so way is made for his receiving of it.

2. There are none of those who are dear to Christ, and have tasted of his mercy, but he hath an eye upon them, and doth know and take notice what lots they meet with in the world; for this is not hid from him, " Jesus heard that they had cast him out."

3. When Christ's people are crushed with troubles and ill usage, then it is his fit time to fall in and give them a tender visit; when they are deserted by all, they are left on him; for at this time he seeks and finds him. He takes advantage to do him good in this strait, as he had done formerly.

4. Christ will be at pains to seek and find his own in trouble, when they little know where to find him; for whereas the man knew him not, nor where to find him, yet he " found him."

5. Christ will draw near to them who are rejected of the world for his name's sake; and such as are unjustly excommunicated will be brought

the nearer to Christ; for he found him whom they had cast out.

6. Men may be put to trial with a lesser measure of knowledge, and a further measure be reserved for their encouragement when they are under it; for he had endured a sharp trial in Christ's defence before he knew him well, and now he is led up to know him to be "the Son of God," for his encouragement.

7. The main matter whereupon Christ trieth his own, and their great encouragement against suffering, is faith in Christ, whereby communion with him is entertained; for he propounds this as his only cordial, and the mean to reap benefit by him, and tries him about it—"Dost thou believe?"

8. Albeit faith must take up Christ in both his natures and all his offices, yet it never finds sure footing till it go through the veil of his humanity, and find him to be true God, and rest on him as such; therefore saith he, "Dost thou believe on the Son of God?"

From verse 36, learn—1. Christ may be present with his own, and speaking to them, and yet they not know him till he reveal himself; for saith he, when the Son of God is speaking to him, "Who is he, Lord?"

2. Weak and ignorant professors may yet have somewhat to witness their honesty; and namely, their sense and acknowledgment of their ignorance; some sparks of love to Christ, though they know him not well, and a strong desire to believe, and a desire after the knowledge of Christ that they may believe; which, in effect, is an evidence of begun faith desiring growth. All these appear in this question, proving the man's honesty, "Who is he, Lord, that I might believe on him?"

3. Whatever good desires there may be in the heart of one who is very ignorant, yet true faith is not content to go on implicit grounds, but seeks for clear knowledge of the ground it goeth upon; nor can there be solid faith without sound knowledge of that which we believe; therefore he doth not please himself with these beginnings, but desires to have his doubts cleared that he may believe indeed—"Who is he, Lord, that I might believe on him?"

4. The right end at which we should aim in our desires after the knowledge of Christ and heavenly things is, not barely to know and contemplate them, but that we may close with and embrace them by faith; for this man desires knowledge for that end, "Who is he, that I might believe on him?"

From verse 37, learn—1. Unto such as really miss Christ and desire after him, he is not so far off as they may conceive, but really present; for when he propounded the question, little thinking where he might be, he gets a speedy account that he whom he desires to know is present with him.

2. When Christ hath manifested himself to any of his people, it is his new gift to make them discern it; for saith he, "Thou hast seen him"— to wit, now, with bodily eyes, and before this thou hast seen his glory in the miracle, and yet he must be helped to discern this. (See 1 Cor. ii. 12.)

3. As Christ doth insinuate himself into the hearts and minds of his people by singular benefits which he conferreth on them; (as here he makes himself known to this man by his admitting him to see and hear him;) so it is his will that they carefully remember the favours he hath conferred on them; therefore doth he say, "Thou hast seen him," or, art seeing him, that he may keep him mindful of the mercy he had received in recovering his sight.

4. As it is of Christ's great condescendence that he stoops to speak to vile sinners, so the sure way of taking him up, even albeit he were bodily present, is by his word; therefore saith he, "Thou hast seen him," and not only so, but "it is he that talketh with thee;" whereby he not only commends his own love that did speak to him, but leads him not to look to his person only, but especially to his speech and doctrine.

5. The longer Christ keeps intercourse with a sinner, his manifestations of himself will be still the clearer and sweeter; for after he had made himself so known to this man, as he knew him to be a good man and a prophet, now he reveals himself to be the Son of God, for his further comfort.

From verse 38, learn—1. Whatever may be the power of unbelief when yet men have much notional knowledge of Christ, yet when Christ reveals himself to souls, it is accompanied with such power and life that they are drawn to believe and to confess him, as they have a calling; therefore upon this short information from Christ, "he said, Lord, I believe."

2. When one closeth with Christ by faith, it may and will put an end to all his perplexities and fears; for this cures him of all his distempers in his trials, "Lord, I believe."

3. True knowledge of the Son of God, and true faith in him, will beget much subjection, adoration and reverence, and will draw the heart to do homage to Christ; therefore is it subjoined, "and he worshipped him"—to wit, as God manifested in the flesh.

VER. 39. And Jesus said, For judgment I am come into this world, that they which see not might see; and that they which see might be made blind.

The second ground of comfort (which, it seems, Christ spake in the audience of all that were present) relates chiefly to the sentence of excommunication unjustly pronounced against this man; wherein, by "judgment" we are to understand his authority to administrate the affairs of his own church and people, as king and head thereof, leaving the judgment of complete recompence till the great day. And the effects of the administration of this authority are expressed in terms borrowed from the late miracle, in opening the eyes of the blind man, such whereof as are comfortable are the proper effects of his ministry, and those that are sad are but the accidental effects thereof, flowing from men's own corruption. So the meaning is—that he was come into the world to be the administrator and ruler of his own church, and the discerner of true members from the false, which (though he had not yet taken the external, ecclesiastical keys of the hands of the rulers of the Jewish church, yet) he did exercise in a spiritual way upon the spirits of men, by opening their eyes who, being ignorant, are humbled under the sense thereof, and by discovering their blindness, and giving them up judicially to be more blinded who are puffed up with a conceit of themselves. And by this Christ would shew that the man had no cause to be troubled at their excommunication, since it was not ratified in heaven ; but, on the contrary, his eyes had been opened to know more of Christ since his excommunication ; nor had the rulers cause to glory in their power and authority, since they were lying under so sad a sentence themselves, in their spiritual condition.

DOCTRINES.

1. Christ is supreme head and governor of his church, and doth administrate it justly, to the comfort of all those who are oppressed by unjust censures, and to the terror of those who do so oppress them ; therefore saith he, " for judgment I am come," to manage the government of my church justly, that those who are wronged, and bound on earth when they are not bound in heaven, may appeal to me, and that those who wrong them may expect a just recompence.

2. That which befel and followed upon the gospel in Judea, in the days of Christ's ministry, is the same which may be expected in all places of the world where it cometh ; for albeit it was a particular case to which Christ spake in the first place, yet saith he, " for judgment I am come into this world."

3. Men's natural blindness and brutishness in the matters of God, through a veil lying upon their hearts, is a great and chief part of their spiritual misery ; therefore doth he instance his administration, in the matter of making men " see," or be " blind ;" not only that he may allude to the late miracle, but that under that he may point out the great misery of spiritual blindness, and the mercy of illumination.

4. Men that are indeed ignorant in respect of others, and who are contemned by others as ignorant, do yet lie very near Christ's help if they be sensible of their want, and come to him with it ; for he hath a promise for them " which see not"—that is, such as this blind man, who was really ignorant and despised by the Pharisees as such, and yet sensible of it, and desiring to have it amended, as ver. 37.

5. Christ hath a remedy for all the grievances of sinners ; and particularly, he can open the eyes of the blind and make them know him, and those things which tend to their salvation ; " For judgment am I come, that they which see not might see."

6. It is a great plague on many that they are swelled with a conceit of their own abilities, and so are blasted to them, and do obstruct their own profiting by the gospel ; for there are who see—that is, who have a conceit they see, or, having some common abilities, do rest upon them.

7. As the gospel will discover much to be but

real darkness which before seemed otherwise, so they who conceit of their own light will, in God's judgment, be given up to reject the light of the gospel, and so grow more and more blind ; in both these respects it is true, they which see are made blind ; their light is discovered to be but real blindness, and they are given up to blind themselves more by opposing the light.

VER. 40. And some of the Pharisees which were with him heard these words, and said unto him, Are we blind also ?

41. Jesus said unto them, If ye were blind, ye should have no sin : but now ye say, We see ; therefore your sin remaineth.

Christ maintains this doctrine against the exceptions of some of the Pharisees, who following still upon him, and understanding him to speak of spiritual blindness, do carp that he should insinuate they were blind, verse 40 ; to which Christ answers that if they were sensible of their ignorance their case were more tolerable, and lay nearer help ; but their conceit that it was otherwise rendered it incurable.   Whence learn—

1. Christ and his followers will never want observers who lie in wait to take advantage against them and their doctrine ; for albeit he had left the Pharisees, chap. viii. 59, and the man was cast out by them while they are sitting in council, ver. 34, yet " some of the Pharisees which were with him heard these words."

2. Men may have abilities and judgment to understand Christ's doctrine, and to apply it pertinently, who yet want grace to make right use of it ; for that they do understand his speech to be spoken concerning spiritual blindness, and do apply it to themselves, is in itself right and imitable ; and yet it produceth but bad effects in them.

3. It is an evidence of men's blind conceit of themselves when they will not believe their misery when Christ tells them of it, nor can they endure to hear tell of it, or to take with misery, whatever advantage Christ holds out to them who do so ; for say they, in a rage, " Are we blind also ?" even we, who are teachers, as well as others ?

4. However conceited men please themselves in their own dreams, yet it were their great advantage to take with that they like so ill ; and their being sensible of misery were an evidence that they lay near mercy ; for albeit they could not endure to be accounted blind, yet Christ tells them, " If ye were blind" it were your greater advantage.

5. Let men's condition be never so bad, yet when they become sensible thereof they are in the way to have the sting taken out of it ; and an acknowledged evil condition is nothing in comparison of men's swelling with conceit under it, and in respect that Christ will really heal and pardon such ; for in these respects it holds true, " If ye were blind, (in your own esteem, and coming to me with it,) ye should have no sin"— to wit, in comparison of your guilt now, and I would really pardon and heal you, and it should not remain, as is after declared.

6. Men's conceit of their own condition as good enough is a sin against the very remedy, as hindering them from seeing their case, and consequently they labour not to cure it, but do go on in it, and as standing in the way of a pardon from Christ; for "now ye say, We see; therefore your sin remaineth"—that is, I do not pardon it, and ye go on to increase it daily.

7. There needs no more to make sinners miserable but to let them go on and lie over in their sin, and not be helped by Christ; for this is the sad sentence against them,—"therefore your sin remaineth."

CHAPTER X.

The doctrine contained in the first part of this chapter hath an immediate connexion with what was spoken in the close of the former, concerning Christ's authority to administrate the affairs of his church and people, as their true shepherd, and the Pharisees being but blind guides; and in this part of the chapter Christ propounds the parable concerning the true and false shepherd, ver. 1—5, which the Pharisees not understanding, ver. 6, he doth himself explain it, ver. 7—18, upon which a schism ariseth among the people concerning him, ver. 19—21. In the second part of the chapter we have a sharp contest betwixt Christ and some of his enemies; wherein, 1. They challenging him of want of freedom in his doctrine, and desiring him to declare freely what he was, he declares that both his doctrine and works had already cleared that case, ver. 22—25, and that their unbelief was an evidence of their reprobation, ver. 26, seeing they had not the properties of his sheep, ver. 27, and needed not expect those favours which he and his Father (with whom he was one) would confer upon his own, ver. 28—30. 2. They being about to stone him, pretending that they did it, not for any good work, but for alleged blasphemy, ver. 31—33, Christ doth prove, both by scripture and by his works, that it was no blasphemy to assert that he was the Son of God, and one with the Father, but it was their duty to believe it, ver. 34—38. 3. They being offended at this, do seek to apprehend him; but he withdraweth, and leaving the city, goeth to the place where John at first baptized, where his ministry is successful, ver. 39—42.

Ver. 1. Verily, verily, I say unto you, He that entereth not by the door into the sheepfold, but climbeth up some other way, the same is a thief and a robber.

2. But he that entereth in by the door is the shepherd of the sheep.

3. To him the porter openeth; and the sheep hear his voice: and he calleth his own sheep by name, and leadeth them out.

4. And when he putteth forth his own sheep, he goeth before them, and the sheep follow him: for they know his voice.

5. And a stranger will they not follow, but will flee from him: for they know not the voice of strangers.

This first part of the chapter containeth four particulars; whereof the first (in these verses) is the proposition of the parable (as it is called, ver. 6) concerning the true and false shepherd, who are described from their contrary marks and properties; the false shepherd, chiefly, ver. 1, and the true, ver. 2—5. In it several things occur to be cleared and observed. And,

First, the occasion and scope of the parable is briefly to be cleared; and for this end it is to be considered that the scribes and Pharisees took it in ill part that they were not looked on as the only teachers of the church, and they did disclaim that Christ had any authority to teach the people, chap. ix. 29; and in particular, they were grieved that Christ had not only asserted his own authority but had insinuated that they were blind guides, chap. ix. 39—41; therefore Christ, continuing his discourse to the same auditory that were present, doth by this parable point out himself as the true shepherd of his sheep, and consequently, that he was the true Messiah who had been promised under that name, Ezek. xxxiv. 23; and he doth, on the contrary, point out who were not the true shepherds; under which description are comprehended all those who either assumed to themselves the office of the Messiah; or who, in their entry to an ordinary calling, were intruders, and not of God's appointing, or were in their doctrine erroneous; or those who, albeit they had an external call, and preached sound doctrine, yet were but hirelings as to their fidelity in discharge of their trust. And as for the application of this to the present teachers of the church of the Jews, (which Christ doth in the first place intend here,) we are not to conceive that Christ doth contradict his own doctrine, Matt. xxiii. 2, 3, where he asserts their lawful calling, and men's obligation to hear what they taught according to the word; for albeit all that be true, yet they come in among false shepherds; partly, in so far as they were an order of Pharisees not instituted by God; partly, as they taught unsound doctrine, and, particularly, did corrupt the doctrine concerning the Messiah, and righteousness to be had by him; and partly, as they were but mercenary and unfaithful, either in the exercising of any lawful calling they had, or in dispensing the true doctrine which they acknowledged.

Secondly. Christ's grave asseveration, "Verily, verily, I say unto you," used both in the proposition of the parable, ver. 1, and the exposition of it, ver. 7, may teach—1. There is great need of frequent excitation and up-stirring to hear doctrine and lay it to heart; therefore doth he, in whose mouth no guile was ever found, 1 Pet. ii. 22, find it needful to stir them up by this grave introduction. 2. It is a matter of no small importance to people that they discern who are their true shepherds, and who are but intruders to deceive them; therefore doth Christ propound it thus, as a weighty point. 3. Christ by his doctrine hath not only gross or open vices, generally condemned by all, to reprove, but even those principles and courses that ordinarily pass current among all; therefore also is this asseveration premitted [placed before], to shew that it was a very weighty point, and hard to be received, as being contrary to the generally-received opinion that the Pharisees were the only true shepherds. 4. Such as are employed to carry truth should publish it in a reverent and grave manner, and so as their behaviour give no occasion to despise or reject it; therefore also doth Christ, by his own grave way of preaching, commend this doctrine to the hearers.

Thirdly. Christ's practice, both here and elsewhere, in making use of a parable in propounding spiritual truths, should be considered. And this way of speaking truth in borrowed terms, though taken from things known among men, did serve for these ends:—1. To make spiritual things plain and clear, being spoken of in terms borrowed from things wherewith we are best acquainted; (so John, iii. 12;) and as this doth commend plainness in the way of preaching, and sheweth Christ's great skill and happiness in expressing his mind to men's capacity, (which was a fruit of his perfect knowledge, seeing it is but men's darkness and confusedness that render them unable to express truth to the capacity of mean ones,) so also it puts us in mind that it is our duty, in observing these common things, whereof Christ makes use in preaching, to gather some spiritual instruction from them, as his practice doth teach. 2. Albeit the propounding of parables, being joined with the explications thereof, did tend to make truth more plain, yet, on the other hand, the naked propounding of parables without the explication did keep the matter dark, and that in God's righteous judgment upon malicious and wicked men, to whom the means of salvation do no good at all, Matt. xiii. 10—13. 3. This way of preaching did also tend to inculcate divine and necessary truths as being not only twice told, (once in the parable, and again in the exposition,) but use being made of such obvious things as might make the matter (being once understood) take deeper impression. And herein Christ's wisdom doth meet with an ordinary disease among men, which is, to receive but a slender impression of most material truths, which therefore they do easily let slip, Hebrews, ii. 1. 4. This way of preaching did also tend to beget and excite an appetite after divine truths, while as the hearers are held in suspense in hearing the parable, and excited to desire to know the explication, as was the disciples' frequent practice; and, indeed, where there is much wealth of spiritual doctrine, nothing is more difficult than to keep men in appetite after the word, and from loathing of it.

Lastly. Somewhat is here to be spoken of the whole structure and parts of this parable; for albeit it were very impertinent to explain here the properties of sheep, and their herds and folds, in themselves,—seeing that is not the doctrine intended here, but another thing is pointed at under that representation,—and albeit it be only required in a parable that the matter propounded be purpose-like in itself, having its own parts, all suitable and agreeing to the fabric of the parable, and that some of the chief parts, and the whole parable jointly considered, have some analogy to the purpose intended to be spoken of under that parable, so that to press every particular part thereof to point out some spiritual purpose is but to wrest the parable and the scope of him that useth it; yea, albeit Christ in the explication do chiefly insist upon that of the door, and the true and false shepherd, and do speak of the true shepherd chiefly with relation to himself; yet if we consider—1, that what is here explained is twice told, that we may be excited to consider it again and again; 2, that what is not expressly explained is yet touched in the by; 3, that this parable is not like to many others, wherein some purpose or thing is made use of for once, the scope whereof tends to illustrate the present purpose, but this, for most part, contains nothing but the very ordinary similitudes and borrowed expressions whereby the scriptures point out spiritual things and truths, and some of them are afterward repeated in this same chapter as familiar and plain doctrine; 4, that some things which are but hinted in the by in the exposition are more fully spoken to in the parable, so that we are remitted to it for the further consideration thereof;—if, I say, we consider these things, we may hold forth the structure and parts of this parable in these particulars, which are so many instructions:—

1. Albeit the Lord might justly have rejected all Adam's posterity upon the breach of the covenant of works, yet it pleaseth him, from among these lost ones, to select unto himself some to be vessels of mercy; for here he hath sheep, whereby (as is after cleared) are understood his elect and converted children, who are differenced from reprobate goats, as will be made visible at the last day. As for the reason of the name, and the resemblances betwixt them and sheep, sundry may be brought, from their harmless simplicity, their cleanliness and profitableness, their readiness to wander, their tractableness, &c., but those may suffice us which are recorded afterward in the parable.

2. Among other favours conferred upon Christ's people, he hath, in particular, appointed for them the privilege of a church society, wherein the elect are converted, and the converted live under his care and blessing, in the use of his ordinances, till they be fitted for glory; for the sheep have a sheepfold, which is expounded to be the church, as may be gathered from ver. 16. It is but a needless allegorizing to gather from hence the outward baseness of the church in this world, seeing the scope is only to shew that their church society is as suitable to them as a sheepfold is to sheep, and that however reprobates may be within the visible church, yet the good of the privileges thereof do redound only to the elect.

3. Albeit Christ's sheep are bound to watch over themselves, yet are they not altogether left to their own care of themselves, but he hath provided pastors for their better provision and security; for there is " the shepherd of the sheep," Christ himself and his sent servants; whereby is

intimated that they can no more safely want pastors than a weak flock can want a shepherd.

4. As God hath provided lawful ministers for the good of his people, so others are ready to obtrude themselves upon them under that name, who have no such warrant; for as there is the shepherd, so there are thieves and robbers, who yet will seek the sheep to follow them, and hear their voice, as if they were true shepherds, as is imported, ver. 5.

5. It is one clear evidence of a false shepherd that he doth not enter in a right way, or by the right door, but taketh some sinistrous course of his own; for so much may be gathered from this, that he entereth not by the door, but climbeth up some other way, of which more in the explication; and, on the contrary, the lawful shepherd entereth in by the door, and to him the porter openeth—that is, (without straining what Christ hath not explained,) he is admitted as a known man, and enters with God's approbation, and in his way, as a porter openeth to him whom the master of the house alloweth to be let in.

6. Such as do unwarrantably thrust themselves into the ministry are sent and do come for little good, but much hurt to the flock, let them pretend to what they will; for " the same is a thief and a robber," of which also afterward.

7. As faithful pastors have God's approbation in their entry, so they do acquit themselves faithfully in discharge of their trust; so is here held out in several particulars. His calling his sheep by name imports his particular inspection and care of every one of the Lord's flock, and his acquaintance with them and their conditions, which though it be eminently verified on Christ, yet it is the duty of every faithful pastor in his measure. His leading them out to their pasture must not be so strained as if the church, which is their fold, were not the place of their feeding also; but it imports that faithful pastors will make it their care not only to keep the Lord's people in some external church order, as sheep within a fold, but to feed them also with sound doctrine. His going before them when he putteth them forth, (which is the practice of shepherds in some countries,) imports not only his going before them by doctrine and good example, but also his vigilancy and care about them, and to protect and defend them.

8. The true sheep's carriage, in reference to these shepherds, doth hold forth several properties of Christ's true sheep. As—1. They are brought to be sensible of their need of direction from God; for they are guided by the voice of the shepherd. 2. They are gifted with discerning to know the voice and doctrine of Christ, and of his faithful servants; for they hear and "know his voice," as sheep in some countries do discern the voice of their own shepherds. 3. What directions they get, they do upon all hazards follow; for as sheep in some countries do follow their shepherd upon his call, so they "follow him." 4. They are so far enabled to discern false teachers and corrupt doctrine as they do approve of neither, and not only will not obey their doctrine, but will flee from them, that they be not infected nor ensnared with their allurements; for " a stranger will they not follow,"

(when he calls them to follow him in a wrong way,) " but will flee from him," (as one they will have nothing to do with at all,) and that because " they know not the voice of strangers"—that is, they do not approve them, though they have a knowledge of discerning, whereby they know them and their doctrine to be naught. This is asserted of Christ's sheep, not because they cannot at all err, nor yet only because it is their duty thus to do, (for that is common to them with reprobates,) but because—1. When any do either embrace false doctrine, or fall in liking with corrupt men, who run unsent, it is no sign of their grace, but of their corruption, so to do. 2. Whatever dangerous errors a child of God may be overtaken with, yet he will at length recover out of them. And, 3. Whatever may be said of a child of God's living and dying in some lesser errors in times of ignorance, yet such as persist in gross errors, and particularly in seeking another way of salvation beside Christ, (which is the first and chief thing Christ points at here in these Pharisees,) do prove that they are no sheep, whatever glorious shows they make.

VER. 6. This parable spake Jesus unto them: but they understood not what things they were which he spake unto them.

The second particular in this part of the chapter is the ignorance of the Pharisees, and their not understanding what Christ pointed at by this parable, which occasions the following explication. Whence learn—

1. Such as are most taken up with a conceit of their own knowledge and abilities are ordinarily most ignorant, especially of the doctrine of Christ; for these Pharisees (who could not endure to be accounted blind, chap. ix. 40) " understood not what things they were which he spake unto them."

2. It pleaseth the Lord sometimes to give unto conceited men many evidences of their own weakness, if so be they would make use thereof, to humble them; as here he gives a speedy proof that these conceited men were indeed blind.

3. It is a double mercy when Christ not only speaks unto a people, but doth make his mind plain thereby, and doth open their eyes to understand it; therefore is their ignorance marked, to shew the mercy of the following explication; and a particular sermon is made, to point out this privilege of getting knowledge of Christ's doctrine and parables, Matt. xiii. 10—12, &c.

VER. 7. Then said Jesus unto them again, Verily, verily, I say unto you, I am the door of the sheep.

The third particular in this part of the chapter is the explication of the parable, in so far as was needful or for Christ's present purpose, which we may take up thus:—1. Christ declares himself to be the door of the sheep, ver. 7, both in respect of pastors, ver. 8, and believers, ver. 9. 2. He declares himself to be the good shepherd, in opposition to tyrannous robbers, ver. 10, and to hirelings, ver. 11—13, and in respect of his fidelity and care of all his sheep, ver. 14—16. 3. He obviates the scandal that might be taken at that proof of his fidelity, of laying down his life, ver. 17, 18.

In this verse Christ doth gravely assert that he was in effect, to his elect and saints, what the door of the sheepfold is unto sheep. Whence learn—

1. Christ is a teacher who can make his own mind to be understood, and when he pleaseth he will so do, to the conversion, or at least the conviction, of the hearers; therefore, seeing they understood it not, he spake unto them again, that he might explain it.

2. Borrowed speeches and types are plain enough, if rightly understood, and the name of the type may be given to the thing typified without any transubstantiation of the substance of the one into the other, but only by reason of some similitude of properties and effects that is betwixt them; therefore saith Christ, " I am the door," because he is that unto his children which a door is unto sheep entering the fold.

3. Even Christ's elect are of themselves, and by nature, secluded from all access to God, and from all communion with him, in grace here or glory hereafter; for that they need a " door," it imports they are without.

4. It is by Christ only that lost sinners are admitted to partake of the privileges and benefits of grace here, or glory hereafter, and whoso come to him, and employ him on his own terms, will be admitted; for saith he, " I am the door of the sheep."

Ver. 8. All that ever came before me are thieves and robbers: but the sheep did not hear them.

In this verse Christ clears how he is the door in respect of other pastors; for clearing whereof we are not to understand that by those that came before him are meant the true prophets—for he speaks of them who came, and not of them who were sent,—but the speech relates, partly to them who before that time gave out themselves to be the Messiah, (as some, it seems, there were, Acts, v. 36;) and partly to them who did intrude themselves into a lawful office, not entering by him and his warrant who is the door, and who did not preach him up to be the only door by whom believers have access to God, or did establish any religious means and ways of reconciliation to God beside him. These, and such as these, whether they be before or after Christ in respect of time, yet come before him, in so far as they run without his commission and instructions; and though the context seem to refer it chiefly to them who were before him in time, yet these are sufficient characters whereby to try the like persons or courses in all ages. So the meaning is, that whosoever take upon themselves the person and office of the Messiah, and whosoever do usurp a lawful calling in the church without his call, and do not preach the sound doctrine of Christ, they are in effect, and ought to be accounted, but murderers and robbers; and whoever

do follow them and their doctrine, yet none of the elect will finally persist in such a course, as had been verified in the case of former seducers. Whence learn—

1. Such is the vanity and perversity of men's hearts, and so great, ofttimes, is the Lord's quarrel against the visible church, that there will not be wanting, in all ages, men of deluded and corrupt judgments to corrupt the doctrine and usurp the most eminent offices appointed for her good; for there is an all of them who come before him.

2. However men of old, and of late, have cried up themselves and their devised doctrines concerning the reconciliation and salvation of sinners, yet there is no Mediator but Christ, nor any access to the favour of God since the fall of man but by him; for all these came before him, as is explained, and so mistook the way.

3. As faithful teachers of Christ are a great blessing to the church, so they who run unsent, or corrupt the doctrine of reconciliation and salvation, which is only to be had by him, are a great judgment and plague, and ought to be looked on as such; therefore are they resembled to " thieves and robbers," of which ver. 10.

4. Albeit corrupt men will not want their own followers, who, for not receiving the love of the truth, are given up to strong delusions; and albeit not only the unconverted elect, but even regenerate saints, may for a time be overtaken, yet none of the elect will be suffered to persist finally in following these sect-masters, and their corrupt doctrines; for as it was before, " the sheep did not hear them," (to wit, so as is expressed in the doctrine,) so it will be still.

Ver. 9. I am the door: by me if any man enter in, he shall be saved, and shall go in and out, and find pasture.

In this verse he repeats the assertion that he is the door, and clears it with relation to the sheep, shewing that whoever entereth by him shall be put in a secure condition till they obtain eternal salvation, and shall be abundantly refreshed and fed. And by this he points out the necessity of pastors entering by him, and their pointing him out as the only way of salvation, which is the principal scope of the doctrine. To " go in and out" is not to be strained here as signifying that they who enter into the fold of the church may lawfully go out again, but as sheep are cared for by their shepherd, secured in their fold, brought out to pasture, and watched over there, so they should find in him protection and refreshment; and as men in times of peace go out and in securely about their affairs, so should they walk securely under his shadow. (See Psalm cxxi. 8.) Whence learn—

1. The absolute necessity of Christ is a doctrine never enough inculcated upon lost sinners, who either lie secure, dreaming of God's favour, or look to make their peace by other means without him. Therefore is it repeated, " I am the door."

2. It is not enough that men be convinced, and in their judgment do acknowledge the necessity

of Christ, and the great privilege of access through him, unless in their practice they improve and make use hereof; for he is " the door," that by him men may " enter in," and not stand afar off, commending the great privilege only.

3. Such as come to God through Christ, and do seek salvation only through him, shall be preserved in all hazards, till they attain to eternal salvation ; for " by me if any man enter in he shall be saved."

4. Such as come to God through Christ have allowance of much spiritual freedom, tranquillity, and security of mind in all their Christian course till they arrive at their complete rest; for he " shall go in and out," doth import this, that he shall not be shut up, but at freedom, that he may go about his lawful affairs, and may do it without anxiety or fear.

5. Such also as do thus come to God will find such satisfaction and spiritual refreshment for making them grow in grace as they shall not need to complain, or betake themselves to other comforts ; for he shall " find pasture."

VER. 10. The thief cometh not, but for to steal, and to kill, and to destroy : I am come that they might have life, and that they might have it more abundantly.

Christ proceeds to declare that as he is the door so he is the true shepherd; and that, first (in this verse), in opposition to those whom he called thieves and robbers—that is, they who give out themselves to be the Messiah, or who run unsent and bring corrupt doctrine. These he declares to be enemies, and not shepherds, as coming only to do the flock prejudice; but his errand is to give them life, and that in great abundance. Whence learn—

1. False teachers and seducers will have so many fair pretences and plausible shows and appearances that the evil of their way will not be soon seen; therefore must it be so much inculcated what it is the thief comes about.

2. Let seducers pretend never so fair, and people be never so much taken with them, yet they do really come for the hurt of the flock, and it will prove so, and be seen in the end ; for " the thief cometh not, but for to steal," &c.—that is the whole scope of their work. And this meets with the blind charity of any in the flock, who fear not so much hurt by their errors as they expect good by their fair shows of piety and parts.

3. Seducers are but thieves, in regard they do but make a prey of men, taking them away from Christ, stealing away their food that they may give them poison, and bereaving Christ of his glory and them of their happiness; and in regard they do all this in a clandestine and indirect way, therefore it is said, " The thief cometh not, but for to steal."

4. How happy soever blinded souls may think themselves in being made a prey to seducers, and in being deluded with their indirect insinuations, yet all this tends but to their destruction, and to their eternal ruin, if mercy prevent it not; for

as the thief cometh to steal, so also " to kill, and to destroy," and so they are robbers or murdering thieves, as ver. 8.

5. Christ is a shepherd who will be so far from destroying his flock that he will give life even to those of them who are dead ; for " I am come that they might have life."

6. Christ's great scope in coming to the world is to purchase and confer life upon his own elect ; and whatever his dealing towards them be, yet it all tends to this, and when they find it otherwise it is their own mistake; for saith he, " I am come that they might have life."

7. Christ by his coming not only intends life, but more abundant life to his flock—that is, 1. Albeit he gave life to his people before his coming, yet he hath let it out more abundantly since, to shew the difference betwixt the Sun of Righteousness now arisen, and the light that his people had (though from him) before. 2. He will not only give that life that may simply supply the necessity of his people, but such a superabounding measure as may testify his fulness, and may completely refresh them. 3. Having conferred this abundant life in conversion, he will make it grow more and more while they are within time, 1 Thess. iv. 1. 4. All this is but a drop in comparison of that abundance of life that is reserved for his people in glory. In these respects it is said, " I am come that they might have life, and that they might have it more abundantly."

VER. 11. I am the good shepherd : the good shepherd giveth his life for the sheep.

Secondly. Christ declareth himself to be the true shepherd, in opposition to hirelings, who, albeit they have a lawful calling, and do not come to kill with false doctrine, but do preach truth, yet are unfaithful in the discharge of their trust. In this verse Christ declareth what he is in opposition to these, asserting that he is that good shepherd, who layeth down his life for his sheep; for understanding whereof it should be considered that taking these properties of a shepherd strictly, they do properly and only belong to Christ, and by them he is distinguished, not only from hirelings or seducers, but from all true ministers also that are sent out in his name. But considering that he doth approve of lawful shepherds under himself, and doth only oppose himself here unto hirelings, we may (beside the consideration of what is peculiar to him, or requires a peculiar consideration in him) look to those properties as they are taken more largely ; and so some of them do belong also to his faithful servants in their measure and proportion, and by them they are distinguished from hirelings and false teachers.

DOCTRINES.

1. Whatever hirelings or seducers infest the church, yet the elect want not a shepherd ; and albeit Christ employ servants under him, yet he doth not give over the charge of his people, but remains still chief shepherd and overseer unto them, to care for them, and furnish food unto

them by his own appointed means; for in both these respects, I am the shepherd, saith he. (See 1 Pet. v. 4.)

2. Christ doth eminently deserve the title of a good shepherd, as being infinite in knowledge to discern all the necessities of his flock, and in pity and wisdom to deal tenderly with them, according to their necessities; for I am that good shepherd, saith he. (See Isa. xl. 11.)

3. Good and faithful shepherds do prefer the good of their flock even to their own life; and as Christ not only gives life to his sheep, but his own life for them, by way of ransom, so his faithful servants should not account their life dear so they may fulfil their ministry and bear testimony to the truth; for it is the character of a true shepherd, " the good shepherd giveth his life for the sheep." And Christ propounds it in general terms, to intimate that though this was eminently and singularly true of him as the Saviour of his people, yet his servants must be resolved to lay down their lives, not to expiate sin, but for the service of the church's faith.

VER. 12. But he that is an hireling, and not the shepherd, whose own the sheep are not, seeth the wolf coming, and leaveth the sheep, and fleeth: and the wolf catcheth them, and scattereth the sheep.

13. The hireling fleeth, because he is an hireling, and careth not for the sheep.

In opposition to these properties Christ declareth what the hirelings are who, minding only their gain, and having no interest in nor affection to the sheep, do, upon the sight of any danger from seducers or persecutors, desert their stations, and expose the flock to danger, ver. 12; and from this fleeing Christ concludes that such are hirelings, and care not for the flock, ver. 13. Whence learn—

1. It is not enough that men have an external lawful calling to the ministry, and that they be not erroneous, unless also they be faithful and single in the discharge of their trust; for beside thieves and robbers, there is also " the hireling," who is opposite unto and disapproven by Christ, as " not the shepherd."

2. Albeit it be the will of God that ministers and labourers get their wages, and be maintained, yet such as make it not the scope of their calling to honour God and seek the good of souls, but do mind only or chiefly their own gain and base ends, do prove themselves not to be honest ministers; for so is imported in his name, " an hireling, and not the shepherd."

3. As the sheep are all Christ's own by reason of his purchase of them and dominion over them, so every true pastor will account Christ's sheep as dear to him as if they were his own, and that because they are Christ's; and whoso do not thus respect them, they prove themselves to be but hirelings; for he is an hireling, " whose own the sheep are not," not only by way of possession, (for so they are Christ's only,) but in respect of affection; and so it is expounded, ver. 13, he " careth not for the sheep."

4. Albeit it be a sad enough stroke for the church to be under hirelings, yet Satan is not satisfied with that, but by God's permission may hound out erroneous teachers and persecutors to molest and vex her more; for beside the hireling, there is a wolf which troubles the sheepfold, whereby we are to understand both false teachers and persecutors, as readily corrupt doctrine is pressed with violence. (See Acts, xx. 29.)

5. Albeit ministers in some cases may lawfully flee, and particularly when the trial and danger is personal to themselves, yet when they look more to their own ease than to the flock's weal, and when, to avoid trouble, they desert the flock in times of error and common hazard, they prove themselves to be but hirelings; for he " seeth the wolf coming, and leaveth the sheep, and fleeth."

6. Men may have more light and foresee trials better than others, who yet want courage to abide them; and corrupt men will no longer follow Christ and duty than they think to compass their own ends by so doing; for " he seeth the wolf coming," and knoweth he is a wolf, and yet " he fleeth," as hoping to attain no more of his base ends in that way.

7. When Satan and his instruments are let loose upon a church, and pastors do prove unfaithful, there may be great havoc and desolation made in it; for in this case the wolf catcheth and scattereth all the sheep. Some he catcheth by error; he makes a prey of some by persecution, and whoso escape that trial may yet suffer scattering by divisions, or deprivation of mutual fellowship and solemn assemblies; and albeit all this be the wolf's fault, yet it is also put upon the hireling's account, who by his example in shifting trouble, and by his withholding the encouragement of doctrine, and his want of courage in maintaining truth, doth open a gap to the wolf, doth expose the sheep as a prey, and doth weaken their hands.

8. Whoever they be that prefer their own commodity and ease to the weal of the flock, and do desert their duty when the flock is in danger, do prove themselves to be but mercenary men and hirelings; therefore is it again repeated, " The hireling fleeth, because he is an hireling, and careth not for the sheep."

VER. 14. I am the good shepherd, and know my sheep, and am known of mine.

15. As the Father knoweth me, even so know I the Father: and I lay down my life for the sheep.

Christ proceedeth yet to clear that he is the good shepherd by other properties of a good shepherd, which also (with the former) do point out the differences betwixt him and false teachers and hirelings. In these verses he declareth himself to be the good shepherd, and proves it from that familiarity which is betwixt him and his people, he knowing and taking special notice of them, and they knowing and acknowledging him, ver. 14. This familiarity and relation is amplified, 1. From a similitude, or comparison, that it resembles, in part, that mutual knowledge and familiarity that is betwixt the Father and him. 2. From an effect on his part, that his respect and affection is such to his sheep that he will give his life for them, ver. 15.

DOCTRINES.

1. The tender relations in Christ towards his people are worthy to be often studied and meditated upon, and how he makes good these relations; therefore saith he over again, I am the shepherd, and " the good shepherd."

2. Christ hath particular and exact knowledge of all his elect, and who they are that shall be saved, wherein he will not be disappointed; for I know my sheep, doth import, in the first place, that he hath a knowledge of the individual persons, as 2 Tim. ii. 19; John, xiii. 18.

3. As Christ knoweth all his own, so he hath a special affection to them, and taketh special notice and care of them; so that he will not only have them converted, but being converted, his knowledge and affection will supply the defect of their prayers, and doth prove that his cures to their particular conditions cannot be misapplied. So much also doth this import, " I know my sheep"—that is, I affect and take special notice of them.

4. Whoever are beloved of Christ, as his sheep, he giveth unto them grace to know and acknowledge and love him; for it must be mutual, though it begin at him: " I know my sheep, and am known of mine."

5. There is a mutual knowledge, acquiescence, and affection betwixt the Father and the Son Christ, which tends much to the comfort of believers in him; for the Father knoweth me, and I know the Father. (See Prov. viii. 24—30.)

6. Albeit the acquiescence and affection betwixt the Father and the Son be matchless and incomprehensible, yet the relation and affection betwixt Christ and his sheep cometh nearest to resemble it of any other thing; for to this purpose is this brought in here, that, As the Father knoweth me, and I (as the words in the original will read) know the Father; so I " know my sheep, and am known of mine;" and albeit it hold good chiefly on Christ's part, yet their part is not to be wholly secluded who, though they come far short to make up the comparison, yet this is the pattern according to which he will carry them on, so far as they are capable. (See John, xvii. 21.)

7. Christ's affection is so real and great that he will give proof of it by the greatest effects his people can need, if it were to die that they may live; therefore doth he subjoin, " I know my sheep," as the Father knoweth me, &c., " and I lay down my life."

8. Christ came into the world and laid down his life only for his own elect, whom he knew, and whom he brings in to himself by actual conversion; for " I lay down my life for the sheep," and not the goats.

VER. 16. And other sheep I have, which are not of this fold: them also I must bring, and they shall hear my voice; and there shall be one fold, and one shepherd.

Christ proves himself to be the true shepherd from another property, which is, his care to enlarge his church by bringing in his own among the gentiles, who, albeit they did not belong to the church of the Jews, yet he would in due time convert and bring them in; and as he is that one shepherd, so he will make up one church of Jew and gentile, the partition wall being removed. Whence learn—

1. Whatever be the malice or opposition of wicked pastors against Christ, yet he will have his own elect and church in the midst of them; for here it is supposed that he had sheep in Judea, notwithstanding the malice of the rulers and Pharisees, with whom he will gather " other sheep" from among the gentiles.

2. Christ is a shepherd who not only hath a care of those that are brought in, but mindeth also the enlargement of his kingdom, as here we see; and herein honest pastors should imitate him.

3. Albeit Christ, in the days of his flesh, was minister of the circumcision only, Rom. xv. 8, and would neither go himself nor suffer his disciples to go into the way of the gentiles, yet the conversion of the gentiles, as it was fore-prophesied in the Old Testament, so it was approven by him, and he purposed to have it brought about in due time; so much doth this prediction teach us.

4. Christ's own, though as yet unconverted, are his sheep, in respect of his eternal purpose to bring them in, and his heart is upon them for that end; for he calls them " other sheep" which " I have," though they be not yet called, and he speaks of his purpose of love concerning them when they little knew him or it.

5. Christ's elect sheep may not only be living in nature for a time within the church, but they may be living without the pale of the church, to whom he will have the gospel sent, to convert them and bring them in: for those other sheep " are not of this fold," or, no Jews, nor of that church, which was the only church at that time; and yet were sheep.

6. Such as are Christ's sheep by election and purpose must not only be converted but brought in to the society of the visible church, to live under Christ's care and government; for they must be brought to the fold.

7. Christ himself is chief in bringing in his elect, whatever instruments be employed; and he is at pains to seek them and gain their consent, as being bound in the covenant of redemption to present all that are given him by charter blameless before the Father; therefore saith he, I bring them, and I must bring them, the matter not being left arbitrary, even in respect of his obligation.

8. God's purposes are so unchangeable, and Christ's grace, conferred and applied to the elect, so efficacious and invincible in operation, that he can undertake to prevail with them to whom he so applieth it; for he undertakes, " they shall hear my voice," which includes both faith and obedience.

9. All Christ's converts, in all times and places, will carry the same stamp, and have the same properties agreeable to the scriptures; for what was the mark of his sheep in Judea, ver. 3, the

same is the character of converted gentiles : " and they shall hear my voice."

10. As all true converts are brought in to the society of the church, so under the gospel the partition-wall betwixt Jew and gentile is broken down, and they make up but one catholic church; for " there shall be one fold."

11. Christ is the only one chief shepherd of the catholic church, dispersed through the world, of Jews and gentiles; for " there shall be one fold, and one shepherd."

Ver. 17. Therefore doth my Father love me, because I lay down my life, that I might take it again.

18. No man taketh it from me, but I lay it down of myself. I have power to lay it down, and I have power to take it again. This commandment have I received of my Father.

Because Christ had given that as one proof that he is the good shepherd, that he would lay down his life for the sheep, and the Jews could not endure to hear that their Messiah should suffer, yea, and his very friends stumbled at it, Matt. xvi. 22, therefore in these verses he closeth this discourse with obviating that scandal; and, 1. He declareth that the Father loveth him, because of this his suffering, which is not to be understood of that love wherewith he is loved as the eternal Son of God; but of love to him, and approbation of him, as Mediator, evidenced in his through-bearing [sustaining] of him in his duty, and his exaltation of him after his suffering. 2. He declareth that he was to lay down his life, not to continue death's prisoner, but that having paid the ransom, he might take it again with the Father's approbation. 3. (Which explains that expression of laying down his life) He declareth, that for the nature of his death it was not forced upon him, but he yielded to it by a voluntary dispensation, and would prove it was so by his recovering of himself again out of the bonds of death. 4. He declareth that he did all this in obedience to a command laid upon him by the Father, and this is the ground of the Father's love to him, and of his voluntary submission. All these, being put together, may take away all just ground of stumbling at his cross.

DOCTRINES.

1. Christ, held out with his ignominious cross, is the great stumbling-block of the world; for so is here imported.

2. Albeit shame and ignominy joined to the cross do add to the grievousness thereof, yet all that could not hinder Christ to undergo it for the good of sinners, Heb. xii. 2, and that he might cast a copy to his followers, 1 Pet. ii. 21, &c., yea, he not only bare the cross, but had so much courage under it as to commend it as lovely to them who were ready to stumble at it; therefore, whoever stumbled at it, yet not only saith he, " I lay down my life," but he propounds such considerations as may make it appear lovely.

3. Christ the Mediator is beloved of the Father, and is he in whom he is well pleased, that so all who come in under his shadow may be accepted in him; for saith he, my Father doth love me.

4. The Father is so well pleased with the reconciliation of lost sinners that he loveth Christ for the undertaking thereof, and is fully satisfied with his suffering for attaining that end; in both these respects it holds good, " Therefore doth my Father love me, because I lay down my life." The Father is pleased with him that he undertook that service, and is content with his death as a sufficient ransom.

5. Crosses that seem very gloomy, and have much displeasure in them, are yet consistent with the Father's love towards the sufferer, especially when they are well borne : so much may we learn from Christ's experience, who, albeit he drank of a very bitter cup, yet was beloved of the Father.

6. God's love manifested towards any, in their following of his way, is a sufficient cordial against all the bitterness of it; for albeit Christ's sufferings were bitter, and stumbled at by many, yet this sufficeth him, that " therefore doth my Father love me."

7. The backside and issue of Christ and his followers' cross being rightly considered, may sweeten all the rough way that leads to it; therefore doth he subjoin, as another encouragement, " I lay down my life, that I may take it again."

8. Christ having laid down his life for the redemption of lost man, did take it again, as a testimony that the Father was satisfied with his sufferings, and to be a ground of strong consolation to believers, and to remove the scandal of his ignominious death; for all these are to be found in his taking his life again.

9. Christ, in suffering death for sinners, was not forced to it, nor could enemies have reached him against his will; but he did it voluntarily, that so he might commend his love to sinners, and might teach us to act and suffer for him willingly, being confident that enemies can never reach us without our Father, Matt. x. 29; for " No man taketh it from me, but I lay it down of myself."

10. Christ, by his resurrection, gave a proof how voluntarily he rendered himself unto death; therefore saith he, " I have power" (not only an instruction from the Father, but a liberty at his own pleasure, as to anything men could do) " to lay it down, and I have power to take it again." And by this also he would prove that he can put a period to the sufferings of his own when he pleaseth, without any help of their crooked ways.

11. The way of accomplishment of our redemption was agreed upon betwixt the Father and the Son before the accomplishment thereof; therefore saith he, " This commandment have I received of my Father," which clears that he came into the world instructed how to go about this work. (See Ps. xl. 6, 7, with Heb. x. 6, 7.)

12. It pleased Christ to suffer death, not only voluntarily, but in a way of subjection to his Father's command, that so the merit thereof

might every way be full and acceptable to the Father; for " this commandment have I received." He was content to be a servant by paction, that so his suffering might be accepted for his people.

13. A command from God makes service, how ignominious like soever, become honourable; and it is our duty, in suffering times, to fix our eye on the command and will of God, and on his scope and purpose in them, and not on the cruelty or malice of instruments; for this is an argument to remove the scandal of his cross, that he did it in obedience to a command : " This commandment have I received of my Father."

VER. 19. There was a division therefore again among the Jews for these sayings.

   20. And many of them said, He hath a devil, and is mad ; why hear ye him ?

   21. Others said, These are not the words of him that hath a devil.   Can a devil open the eyes of the blind ?

The fourth and last particular in this part of the chapter is the effects or consequents of this sermon among the people, who are again divided in opinion about him, ver. 19 ; many of them do calumniate him as one possessed and mad, and therefore not to be heard, ver. 20, and others do maintain that his doctrine and the late miracle do sufficiently refute such a calamity, ver. 21. Whence learn—

1. Christ's doctrine will not want its own effect or operation among hearers, be what they will ; for here all of them are put to some exercise about " these sayings."

2. It is not to be expected that Christ's doctrine will have alike effects in all ; but as it gains ground on some, so others will harden themselves the more that they are dealt with ; as here we see in these different opinions about him and his doctrine.

3. Christ's doctrine, meeting with diversity of dispositions, is ordinarily an occasion of division or schism, by reason of the perverse obstinacy of some in opposing the truth, which others must maintain ; for " there was a division (or schism) therefore among the Jews for these sayings." This is neither to be imputed to the doctrine nor yet to the maintainers of truth ; for it is but men's corruptions which oppose true doctrine, and the friends of truth ought to reckon that division is better than agreement in evil.

4. As Christ's doctrine ordinarily finds wicked men as they were, if not worse, so he marks how often they relapse in the same opposition to him and his truth ; for these causes it is marked that " there was a division again," after the former debates of this kind, chap. vii. 43 ; ix. 16, to shew that they were still the same, and that he marked that it was so.

5. When divisions and schisms fall forth about Christ and his doctrine, it is no strange thing to see the most part join on the wrong side of the controversy ; for there are " many of them" who calumniate him, and but " others," or few only, who take his part.

6. Opposers of Christ and his truth are ordinarily so possessed with prejudice and malice that they will not so much as hear him, nor can they endure that others should hear him patiently ; for say they, " Why hear ye him ?"

7. The strongest arguments that prejudicate malice hath against Christ and his truth are calumnies against him and it, and the carriers thereof ; for this is their argument : " He hath a devil, and (which explains the former) is mad," and therefore ought not to be heard.

8. Malice is so prejudicate and blinded that no reason may be expected from those who are possessed with it ; but they will most unjustly and obstinately calumniate, if it were even Christ himself ; for albeit he came to destroy the works of Satan, and is the wisdom of the Father, yet say they, " He hath a devil, and is mad." And albeit they had often reproached him with this, chap. vii. 20 ; viii. 48, and Christ had refuted it, yet they still cast it up again.

9. Let malice be never so prejudged and violent, yet Christ will still get some to justify him and his doctrine ; for there are others who contradict this.

10. Christ's doctrine and works are sufficient to plead for him, and to refute adversaries, even to their face ; for they put it home against those malicious men, " These are not the words of him that hath a devil—Can a devil open the eyes of the blind ?"

11. Such as would own Christ, especially in a time of opposition, ought to study his doctrine and works, so as they esteem of his word in the first place ; therefore 'do they begin at that, " These are not the words of him that hath a devil," and then the commendation of his work followeth, " Can a devil open the eyes of the blind ?"

VER. 22. And it was at Jerusalem the feast of the dedication, and it was winter.

   23. And Jesus walked in the temple in Solomon's porch.

   24. Then came the Jews round about him, and said unto him, How long dost thou make us to doubt ? If thou be the Christ, tell us plainly.

Followeth the second part of the chapter, wherein is recorded a sharp contest betwixt Christ and some of the Jews his enemies. It seemeth to have followed not long after the former sermon, and that Christ had stayed in and about Jerusalem since he came up to the feast of tabernacles, chap. vii., till this time in winter ; and therefore, ver. 26, 27, he repeats the doctrine concerning his sheep as a thing they had lately heard. The first encounter betwixt them is contained, ver. 22—30, wherein they put him to it to speak out freely if he was the Christ, and he giveth them such an answer as was convenient.

In these verses we have recorded—1. The time of this debate, ver. 22. It was at a feast of dedication, or consecrating to God what they had built or repaired for his service. This feast was not kept in remembrance of the dedication of the tabernacle when it was set up in the wilderness, of which Num. vii. 1, &c.; for (beside that the tabernacle was now laid by) that dedication was in the first month, Exod. xl. 2, 17, which answereth in part to March and in part to April likewise; the dedication of the temple, when it was built by Solomon, was in the seventh month, 1 Kings, viii. 2, which answereth, in part, to September; and the dedication of the temple after the captivity was in the month Adar, Ezra, vi. 15—17, which answereth, in part, to February and March, for they kept the passover shortly after, Ezra, vi. 19; so that this dedication was that performed by the Jews in the time of the Maccabees, who, after they had repaired and cleansed the temple, and built an altar, did appoint a feast in memorial thereof, 1 Macc. iv. 59, and that in winter, or the month Chisleu, which answereth, in part, to December; and they did it in this season, because in the summer they were so infested with their enemies that they could not get the work attended. 2. We have recorded the place where this debate was—to wit, not only in Jerusalem, ver. 22, but in Solomon's porch of the temple, where Christ walked, ver. 23. It was the place where the people met, 1 Kings, vi. 3; and albeit that built by Solomon was destroyed by the Chaldeans, yet the other, that was built again, retained the ancient name, (so also, Acts, iii. 11.) 3. We have recorded their first question to Christ, upon which the controversy ariseth, ver. 24. While Christ is walking in Solomon's porch the malicious Jews encompass him, and challenge him that by reason of his want of freedom in doctrine they were kept in doubt and suspense, and therefore desire he would speak out plainly if he were the Christ. This they do, pretending to affect the knowledge of the truth, but in effect intending to ensnare him, and bring him upon the stage as affecting a kingdom, if he should declare himself to be the Messiah.

That this purpose may be yet more clear for grounding of doctrines, we are to consider, that much use is made of ver. 22, 23, as a warrant for consecration, or dedication of churches, and for observation of holy days enjoined by the church. And it is alleged that Christ's frequenting of the temple at that time is an evidence of his approbation thereof. But to refute this, consider—1. Whatever be said of this dedication in particular, yet it is certain that a dedication of the tabernacle and temple was practised with God's approbation under the law; and that the moral signification thereof (as also of dedicating their houses, and other things) doth stand still in force; but the ceremony itself is ceased with the ceasing of the typical holiness of places and things; and men may as well introduce the rest of the Jews' significant ceremonies as this. 2. This feast of dedication, or the yearly remembrance of it in an anniversary feast of eight days, (as the history hath it,) was but a human invention in these latter and declining times of the Jews; for, beside that they had no prophet to authorize this, (1 Macc. iv. 46,) as they had for their other sacred solemnities, it is remarkable, that in the dedication by Moses, Solomon, and those of the captivity, albeit they kept a festivity on that day, yet it is nowhere recorded that they appointed

so much as one day to be yearly observed in remembrance thereof; so that this latter practice, in memorial only of renewing the altar and some other decayed things, is rather to be looked on as an evidence of their declining than as a laudable pattern. 3. The apostles' naming of this feast, and Christ's frequenting the temple at that time, are no evidence of any approbation thereof; for John doth mention it in the history only to point out the circumstance of time so as was best known to the Jews, which doth no more import an approbation thereof than Luke's describing the time of Paul's travels by mentioning the Jewish feasts, Acts, xx. 6; xxvii. 9, doth import his approbation thereof among Christians. And Christ was present in the temple at that time, not to honour that feast or to countenance their human invention; nor doth it appear that he was there at this time, that he might take the opportunity of the concourse of people at that solemnity to publish more of his commission, as was his own and his followers' ordinary practice at other lawful solemnities and meetings of the people; for he was not now teaching in the temple, but only walking in Solomon's porch, when he was surrounded by the Jews; nor yet doth it appear that there was any great concourse at this feast in winter, or, at least, that the people frequented the temple much at it; but that they spent those days rather in carnal mirth than as holy convocations; (which is the ordinary best fruit that floweth from men's own traditions in religion;) and therefore Christ is said to walk in the porch, there being but few or none there till this crowd came about him. So that as the feast is named here only to point out the circumstance of the time of this debate, so Christ's walking in the porch is subjoined only to point out the circumstance of place, and to shew that while Christ is walking there (upon some occasion, into which we need not inquire) they enter upon this debate with him.

From the words thus cleared, we may learn—
1. When a church hath backslidden furthest in matter of doctrine and lively and spiritual worship, then she will be most forward to devise and observe ceremonies of her own wherewith to serve God; for it is in this church's declining time that they appoint and observe a " feast of the dedication."

2. As a church may, in God's justice, be put to such difficulties as outward troubles will interrupt their intentions of reformation, so one right use of such a dispensation is when it stirs up people to lay hold of all opportunities of any breathing time to set forward the work of God; for so much may be gathered from the time of this feast; " it was winter." Whatever fault was in their course, or appointing that feast, yet their repairing of the temple in winter (because of which they appointed and observed the feast at that time) intimates how they were molested with enemies in the summer, so that they could not attend the work; and how they take the opportunity of a time of breathing in winter to carry on the work.

3. Christ and his servants may on all occasions expect that Satan and his instruments will not be wanting to cast snares and tentations in

their way, and to seek advantage against them; for when he is walking in Solomon's porch he is assaulted with tempters, who came round about him. But he makes good use of this to bring out precious truths; and temptations were a part of Paul's library at Ephesus, to enable him to preach, Acts, xx. 19, 20.

4. Christ's enemies are full of subtle policies, and they can turn themselves into all shapes, to draw him (if it were possible) in a snare; for so doth their practice teach; they pretend great earnestness to be clear and settled in the point, but they had another design.

5. It is a very dangerous condition for men to live in suspense and uncertainty about the matters of religion; and especially not to be settled in knowing and resting upon Christ; therefore say they, in this particular, " How long dost thou make us to doubt? (or, hold us in suspense?) if thou be the Christ, tell us." Whether they had any real staggering in conscience, though overpowered with malice, or pretended to it only, is not much matter; but they propound it as a very dangerous condition (as it is indeed) to be so, and so much the worse the longer it continueth. The word imports to have the mind or soul hanging up, as a body in the air, and so to be fleeting, wanting a foundation to rest on, and this tends to the destruction thereof, as the word also signifieth.

6. Wicked men will not find the cause of their distempers within themselves so long as they can allege anything without them (if it were even Christ and his doctrine) to fasten it upon; for they lay it all to his charge, Thou makest us to doubt, alleging that he spake not plainly what he was; whereas (as Christ after cleareth) it was their own blindness and their darkness contracted through malice, that did hide all this from them.

7. It is a very malicious disposition in men when they seek advantage against Christ and his servants in their free doctrine, and when they desire them to speak freely, on purpose to bring them in a snare; for say they, " If thou be the Christ, tell us plainly," on purpose to entrap him.

VER. 25. Jesus answered them, I told you, and ye believed not: the works that I do in my Father's name, they bear witness of me.

Christ's answer to this question consisteth of four branches; in the first whereof (in this verse) he clears himself from being any cause of their unbelief or uncertainty in this matter, as having already cleared that case fully, both by his doctrine and miracles, and so the blame was all their own; whereas Christ saith, " I told you," albeit we will hardly find that expressly and in plain terms he had said to these persecutors that he was Christ, whatever he did to his disciples, and to some others, chap. iv. 25, 26; ix. 36, 37, yet we find that he had ofttimes said the equivalent, and spoken of himself in such terms as was only competent to the Messiah. (So chap. v. 25, 26; vi. 35, 48, 51, 53, 54, &c.; vii. 37, 38; viii. 12, 35, 56, 58; in this chap. ver. 9, 14—16, and elsewhere.)

DOCTRINES.

1. Whatever be the pretences of men for their unbelief, yet the true cause thereof is in themselves, and not in Christ or in his way of doctrine or dispensations; therefore doth he clear himself, and lay the blame on them.

2. Christ's word and his works are sufficient to ground our faith and confirm it concerning him, and what he is; therefore saith he, to clear himself, I have told you, and, " the works that I do in my Father's name, (as Mediator and ambassador,) they bear witness of me"—to wit, that I am the Messiah; for albeit the apostles were to do greater works, John, xiv. 12, yet they wrought them not in the same way, nor by their own power; but in his name, that they might testify and bear witness to his glory.

3. Such as do not acquiesce in Christ's word and working for confirmation of their faith will not profit by any other mean of their own devising; therefore doth Christ reject their desire concerning any further information, since they refused to profit by what he had said and done.

4. Whatever specious name men give to their own, not closing with Christ, yet in effect it is nothing else but infidelity, and the fruit of an evil heart of unbelief; therefore, whereas they said only, they were in doubt, or suspense, ver. 24, he tells them plainly, " ye believed not."

5. Where the Lord affords many means of knowledge and faith there unbelief will be the more heinous; for saith he, " I told you, and ye believed not; the works that I do in my Father's name, they bear witness of me;" and yet ye believe not, as is subjoined, ver. 26.

VER. 26. But ye believe not, because ye are not of my sheep, as I said unto you.

In the second branch of this answer, Christ points out the true cause of their infidelity; which is, not the obscurity of his doctrine, but their not being of his sheep—that is, not as yet converted, and not only so, but evidenced to be reprobates if they continue in that sin. And by this he prevents a great objection, and the scandal of their not embracing him who were eminent in that church; and sheweth that this contempt did not reflect on him, but on themselves. Whence learn—

1. Despisers of Christ will get no affront rubbed upon him, but all the prejudice and disgrace is their own; therefore doth he clear here, that their unbelief reflected on themselves.

2. Albeit Christ will not reveal unto men his eternal purposes concerning them till first they declare what is in their own hearts, yet as he knoweth who are elect, and who are reprobates, and as he hath recorded in his word the evidences of men that are reprobates, or, at least, in a reprobate condition, so he would have wicked men affected and affrighted by seeing such evidences in themselves; therefore, upon their unbelief, he leads them up to see, " ye are not of my sheep," that they might consider how deep their sin drew.

3. Men's unbelief under the means of faith

is a clear evidence of their being in a reprobate condition, and their continuance therein an evidence that they are reprobates; for " ye believe not, because ye are not of my sheep."

4. Christ's doctrine is not yea and nay, but still the same; and it is men's great fault, that being often warned of their danger, yet they mark it not, nor make use of it; therefore doth he subjoin, " As I said unto you"—to wit, in the foregoing parable, where it had been insinuated, and frequently elsewhere he had pointed out their dangerous condition. And by this he would tell them that his thoughts of them were still the same, and that it was their great stupidity not to take notice of what he had so often repeated.

Ver. 27. My sheep hear my voice, and I know them, and they follow me:

In the third branch of the answer Christ proves what he had said of them, by shewing the contrary properties of his sheep, which were wanting in them. These he repeats from the former parable and explication. Whence learn—

1. Whoever reject Christ, yet he will not want his own peculiar people, and their carriage will refute such as pretend to be God's people, and yet live wickedly; therefore doth he here again record that he hath " sheep," and what their carriage is.

2. It is an undeniable and special evidence of Christ's sheep, that they give up themselves to his teaching and direction, and do incline their heart and ear to take notice of what he saith; for it is repeated, as a special mark, " My sheep hear my voice."

3. As Christ's sheep hear him, so they meet with special care and providence from him, in that he not only knew them from eternity by special purpose, and draws them to him by special love, but hath an especial eye and care of them; for " I know them."

4. As it is the duty and property of Christ's sheep, not only to hear, but to follow his directions, so the consideration of his love and care should invite and encourage them so to do; therefore after that, " I know them," it is subjoined as their bound duty to so tender a Lord, "and they follow me." And this, with the other, of hearing his voice, doth complete their duty.

Ver. 28. And I give unto them eternal life; and they shall never perish, neither shall any man pluck them out of my hand.

29. My Father, which gave them me, is greater than all; and no man is able to pluck them out of my Father's hand.

30. I and my Father are one.

In the last branch of the answer, lest they should account it a small loss to be none of his sheep, Christ, to grieve them who would not embrace him, lets them see the fair privileges and allowance which he conferreth upon his sheep. And, 1. He assures them of eternal life, and of perseverance till they come to the full fruition

thereof, ver. 28. 2. He confirms this, from his own and his Father's power, which is employed about them for their preservation, and which is above all opposition, ver. 28, 29. 3. He confirms, further, wherefore he had joined his own power with the Father's in this work, by shewing that he and the Father are one in essence, and consequently have the same power and will; and therefore, as none can pluck them out of the Father's hand, so none can pluck them out of his hand, who is one with the Father, ver. 30.

From verse 28, learn—1. Such as come not to Christ are great losers, and the happy condition of those who would not follow them will be their eye-sore one day; therefore doth Christ preach to them the fair privileges of his people, to let them see how far they prejudged themselves, and to vex them. (See Psalm cxii. 10; Micah, vii. 10.)

2. All who come to Christ indeed get eternal life begun in them, in the bud of grace and in their right by faith; for " I give (saith he, in the present time) unto them eternal life." (See 1 John, iii. 9; 1 Pet. i. 5; Luke, xxii. 29, 30.)

3. This great privilege is Christ's gift, being both purchased and applied by him; for " I give unto them eternal life."

4. Albeit Christ's converted people may have many shakings and tossings in their condition, yet their final perseverance till they come into full possession of eternal life is certain; so that, whatever they lose by the way, yet they will not lose themselves eternally; therefore he who giveth eternal life doth also promise, " and they shall never perish."

5. When Christ confers his special favours and allowances on his sheep, he doth also take a charge of them and their allowances, and hath a special care of them; for so is imported here: the sheep, to whom eternal life is given, are in my hand, saith he. The form of speech—to be in his hand, imports not only that they are under his power, to do with them what he will, so that nothing is to be feared if he desert them not, but more especially it points out that they are still in his sight and under his care, whereby he testifieth his affection, and prevents any prejudice to them.

6. Such as are owned by Christ as his sheep, and so are put in a blessed condition, will not want adversaries to oppose them, and to endeavour to bring them down from their happiness; for it is supposed here that there will be somewhat (to wit, Satan, the world, and their own flesh) to endeavour to pluck them out of his hand.

7. Albeit the Lord do confer grace and faith upon his own, yet that is not sufficient to secure them, but these might decay of themselves, if it were not for the purpose of God in conferring thereof, and his power and everlasting arms preserving the same; therefore it is that, for securing of them, they need to be in his hand.

8. Christ is so unchangeable in his purposes of love, and so invincible in his power, that nothing shall be able to hinder their perseverance unto eternal life whom he takes in his custody and charge; therefore doth he confirm their perseverance thus: " Neither shall any pluck them out of my hand." As for those who grant that

indeed none can pluck them out unless they go out willingly of themselves, do clearly impugn Christ's reasoning, who upon this, that none shall pluck them out of his hand, doth infer that "they shall never perish," whereas, granting that distinction, it might be said, they may perish of their own accord, though they be not plucked out; but Christ, by this promise, doth give assurance of their certain perseverance.

From verse 29, learn—1. It is an argument of the saints' perseverance, and of Christ's employing his power for that end, that they are committed to him by the Father to be forthcoming for them; therefore doth he declare in this matter, My Father gave them me.

2. The Father doth so intrust Christ with his sheep, as yet he casts not off care of them; but as Christ is engaged for them, as the Father's servant and commissioner, so the Father is engaged to make them forthcoming to Christ, as the covenanted reward of his sufferings; and so the immutable Father and Son, and their invincible power, is employed for their preservation; therefore also they are in the " Father's hand," as well as Christ's.

3. The power of God is so invincible, and so far above all created opposition, and he doth so let out his power, in maintaining saints in the state of grace, as doth sufficiently assure them of the certainty of their perseverance; for so doth the argument run: " My Father is greater than all, and (therefore) no man is able to pluck them out of my Father's hand." And here they who except man's free will in this point, alleging they may go out of his hand, do wrong both the power of God, by implying that the idol of man's will must be exempt from his dominion, as if he could not command it, and his fidelity, who hath promised to subdue the will to his fear, that saints may persevere, Jer. xxxii. 40.

From verse 30, learn—1. Christ's working in behalf of his sheep doth demonstrate his greatness, and prove him to be God; therefore doth he here point out his preserving them with the Father, as flowing from and being an evidence of his eternal godhead.

2. Christ is so God as he is one in essence and nature with the Father; for saith he, " I and my Father are one."

3. Albeit Christ be one in essence with the Father, yet are they distinct persons one from another; for albeit they be " one," yet there is " I and my Father," and a plurality of persons, we ' are one."

4. Because the Son is one in essence with the Father, therefore are they equal in power, and with one consent and will are employed about the same work; for upon this ground, " I and my Father are one," it followeth that they are both about this work of preserving the sheep, and that his power is sufficient to preserve them, because the Father, with whom he is one, is greater than all.

VER. 31. Then the Jews took up stones again to stone him.

From this to verse 39 we have a second encounter betwixt Christ and the Jews, following upon the former; wherein, they going to stone him, ver. 31, he upbraids them for dealing so with him who had shewed them so many good works, ver. 32, and they alleging that it was not for his good works, but for blasphemy, ver. 33, he doth vindicate himself of that imputation, and sheweth that it was their duty to believe him, ver. 34—38.

In this verse we have the carriage of the Jews upon the former answer given to them: they, not finding that advantage they expected, whereupon they might have delated him to the Romans, do take hold (as they clear afterward) of a pretext of the law against blasphemy, Lev. xxiv. 14, 16, to condemn his doctrine, and thereupon do tumultuously take up stones to put him to death. Whence learn—

1. Whatever pretences persecutors have of a desire of plain doctrine, yet they will not get their malice hid, but will at last bewray that they cannot endure what they seem to desire; for they who were so earnest (ver. 24) to hear Christ speak out, are now enraged when he doth speak.

2. Violence and fury are the strongest weapons of persecutors, and it is that only that may be expected of them when Christ and his servants preach that which doth not please them; for upon hearing of the former doctrine they are so abrupt as presently they take up stones to stone him, and that without so much as telling the cause or pretence till afterward, ver. 33, that Christ draw it out of them; in all which we may see how far the fury of men in opposing truth doth outstrip the true zeal of the godly for truth.

3. As persecutors are incessant in their rage upon all new occasions, so the Lord marks that it is so, and how often men do let loose their fury against his Son and servants; therefore it is recorded that they " took up stones again," after they had done so before, chap. viii. 59, and at other occasions.

VER. 32. Jesus answered them, Many good works have I shewed you from my Father; for which of those works do ye stone me?

It seems that some stones were cast at Christ, and therefore he saith, " ye stone me." But in the heat of this fury he finds matter of encouragement to himself in what he had done to them; and therefore, that he may bridle their rage, he doth clear his own innocency, and upbraid them for this their proceeding, wherein they dealt so unjustly as to reward him evil for good, and most ingrately, both against him who sought their good in what he wrought, and against the Father, by whose authority, and in whose name, he had wrought. Whence learn—

1. Times of trial and persecution will put men to make inquiry, and to search what may be in them drawing on such a lot; for so much doth Christ's practice teach, who, by his commending all that he had done to them, doth insinuate a looking back to what it was he had done.

2. Let men never so oft pick a quarrel against Christ, yet as in the days of his flesh he suffered nothing for any fault he had done, so men shall never be able to instruct any evil he hath done,

wherefore he should be hated or persecuted; therefore saith he, For which works, shewed from my Father, do ye stone me? importing they could have no quarrel against him, unless they would quarrel a good turn.

3. It is Christ's way with his people and visible church to work gloriously for them, to multiply these his glorious works, and by his working, to set out his own and his Father's glory, and give evidence of their good will towards lost sinners; and all this he doth to gain upon their affections; for so much is imported in what he saith of himself, " Many good works have I shewed you from my Father," (manifesting his glorious power and rich good will by working these in his name,) because of which he reckons they should rather embrace than stone him.

4. Whatever be Christ's and his people's carriage in or towards the world, yet they may expect an ill meeting, and to be dealt with, not only unjustly, in being made to suffer for righteousness and well-doing, but ingrately, in being rewarded evil for good; for thus he hath paved the way, who though he had done thus to them, yet saith he, " ye stone me."

5. Albeit persecutors be unjust and furious, and may slander and cast iniquity upon sufferers, Psalm lv. 3, yet such as have a good conscience will have confidence towards God, and courage against enemies in the heat of trial; for Christ knowing his own innocency, it doth now bear him out, and leads him to gall them.

6. As sufferers ought to examine well what they suffer for, so persecutors should consider seriously of the cause of persecution, and wherefore they molest Christ and his followers; therefore doth he put them to consider, For what do ye stone me?

7. Such as will persecute Christ and his followers will never be able to acquit themselves of injustice and ingratitude, and of their contempt of God, and of his authority, whereby his Son and servants do act; for this question is a sharp challenge of their consciences, how they durst deal so towards him, and his Father, in whose name he wrought.

VER. 33. The Jews answered him, saying, For a good work we stone thee not; but for blasphemy; and because that thou, being a man, makest thyself God.

By this discourse of Christ it seems their hands were bound up for a time, but not their mouths. And in this verse, to avoid the dint [force] of his challenge, they lay aside the matter of his works (which ofttimes they carped at) without opposition or approbation, and take hold of a pretence of blasphemy, in that he, being a man, had made himself God, for which they would have stoned him.   Whence learn—

1. Persecutors, though they be most wicked, yet will be ashamed to avow the true cause of their persecuting Christ, and that they are dissatisfied with any good thing, or to let their course be seen in its own colours; therefore, albeit his works did clear this controversy, ver. 37, 38, and they did indeed hate him for them

more than for his alleged blasphemy, yet they are unwilling that that should appear, " For a good work we stone thee not."

2. It is the great policy of Satan and his instruments first to calumniate Christ and his followers, and then to persecute them because of those alleged calumnies; for say they, " we stone thee not; but for blasphemy."

3. Such is the perversity of men, even within the visible church, that, having occasion and a tentation [temptation], they may come to that height of impiety as to blaspheme God; and where men do so, they are guilty of death; for so much doth the law of Moses, which they pretend to obey here, import, both that some within Israel were ready to fall into that sin, and that such ought to be stoned, Lev. xxiv. 16.   Blasphemy properly signifies the hurting of one's fame, and being applied to God imports the wounding and depriving him of his honour and glory, which (omitting rash and idle swearing) is committed when men deny unto God what is due unto him; when they attribute unto him that which doth not beseem him; when they ascribe unto man that which is due only unto God; and when they curse and rail, or reproach God, his word, and works; and for preventing hereof, men should avoid unbelief and distrust, pride and self-love, and murmuring under dispensations.

4. Such corruption may creep into a visible church as even Christ may be accounted a blasphemer, and his most precious truths condemned as blasphemy; for so it was here, " we stone thee not; but for blasphemy, and (which explains and specifies what they accounted blasphemy) because that thou, being a man, makest thyself God;" where they do indeed understand Christ rightly, that he declared himself to be true God, equal with the Father; nor doth he contradict this, but confirm it in the following answer; only they wrong him in accounting it blasphemy. For albeit it be indeed blasphemy to assert that any mere man is God, in proper terms, (though in some respect some men do bear that name, ver. 34,) yet he had abundantly cleared before that as he was true man so he was true God also in the same person.

VER. 34. Jesus answered them, Is it not written in your law, I said, Ye are gods?

35. If he called them gods, unto whom the word of God came; and the scripture cannot be broken;

36. Say ye of him, whom the Father hath sanctified, and sent into the world, Thou blasphemest; because I said, I am the Son of God?

Christ by two arguments vindicates himself from the imputation of blasphemy in asserting himself to be God.   The first (in these verses) is founded on that scripture, Psalm lxxxii. 6, wherein—1. He doth in general prove that it is not blasphemy to call a man god in some respects, seeing magistrates get that name, Psalm lxxxii. 2. He argues upon this ground, not barely that he may call himself God, in the same sense that they get that name, but from the less to the more, thus: If they be called gods who are in that office, much more may I, who am separated to a higher employment, be called so, without blasphemy. But the scripture, which cannot be broken, hath called them so, therefore I may be called so. And this conclusion he propounds by way of question, to shew the absurdity of their assertion, his reason being considered, and that their consciences could not decline this consequence. For clearing the words, and this reasoning, consider—1. The ground on which magistrates are called gods ("unto whom the word of God came") may be understood of their calling to the office, as it is said of prophets, The word of the Lord came to them; and so several magistrates of the Jews got their office by the ministry of God's servants bringing that office and call to them; not that a call, ordinary or extraordinary, to every office, infers that title, but only a calling to that office of power and authority. It may as well be understood that the word came to them, not so much in respect of their calling as that, in that same scripture cited, God calls them so; and so it is an exposition of that word in the Psalm, I said, ye are gods—that is, the word came to them, and God, speaking in it, gave them that title. Thus the argument will run strong enough :—(1.) Since the word came to them, and spake to them under that name, it cannot be blasphemy to call men gods, as the Jews alleged. (2.) If they who, being on earth, are spoken to, and commanded, and reproved by the word, get that title, (as is clear from that Psalm,) much more is it due to him who, being from eternity with the Father in heaven, and not in the world, did stoop to come into it, to perfect the work of redemption. Consider—2. As for the ground whereon Christ argues that without blasphemy he may be called the Son of God, (that the Father hath sanctified him, and sent him into the world,) we need not understand this sanctification only, or so much of the sanctification and cleansing of his human nature from sin, as of the assumption of his human nature into the personal union, and of his consecration from eternity unto the office of Mediator, upon which followeth his actual sending into the world in the fulness of time. And albeit Christ, in this first argument, seems rather to refute the imputation of blasphemy than directly to prove how he is God, which he doth in the following argument, yet there is much insinuated here that evinceth it; as, 1. He sets himself so far above magistrates who get that style as doth necessarily infer he is God in a proper sense. 2. The office of Mediator, in which he is employed, is such as, albeit his sanctification and sending into the world about it do not make him God, yet it doth evidence and give us to know that he is God, seeing none but Jehovah could bear out in that office. Nor doth the Father's sending of him import any inequality, seeing an equal may send an equal with consent, yea, an inferior a superior. 3. He who is first sanctified before he be "sent into the world," did certainly subsist, and was, before his incarnation and coming into the world. 4. It was no small part of his sanctification and fitting for his office that his human nature was assumed

into a personal union with his godhead; and this seems to be imported in his sanctification by "the Father," and that he calls himself not God, as magistrates were, but "the Son of God," to shew, not only that he is not God as secluding the Father, but by eternal generation from the Father; but also that this sanctification by the Father, upon which he gathers this, doth relate to the elevation of the human nature into a personal union with the Son of God, as well as to his office.

From these verses, learn—1. The written word is the judge and rule whereby all controversies in religion must be decided; therefore doth Christ appeal to it: "Is it not written?"

2. Whoever be against Christ, or whatever skill or interest they pretend in scriptures, yet the scriptures will be still on his side; therefore doth he appeal to themselves if the scriptures, whereof they boasted, did not clear him of blasphemy? "Is it not written in your law?"

3. The scriptures are a great deep, and full of treasures, to be gathered by spiritual and sober observers; therefore doth Christ so solidly and profoundly reason from that text to his present purpose.

4. Whatever be the different subjects of holy scripture, yet all of it is a law, in so far as men are obliged to rule their conversation, affections, faith, hope, and fear, thereby; therefore, albeit elsewhere the Old Testament be distinguished into the law, prophets, and psalms, Luke, xxiv. 44, yet here the psalms, whence this text is cited, come under the name of law; and it may be also because the word in the Hebrew language (wherein, or in Syriac, a dialect of Hebrew, Christ spake) rendered "the law," signifies generally, "a doctrine."

5. As it is a peculiar privilege to have the word and oracles of God committed unto men, so it adds to men's guilt when they improve not this privilege, but continue ignorant of the truths therein contained; therefore doth he call it "your law," not by way of contempt, but to reprove them who enjoyed this privilege, and boasted of it, and yet were ignorant of it, and of what in it might refute their unjust aspersions.

6. It is an evidence of a malicious disposition in men when they do not put a favourable construction (in so far as it is consistent with truth) upon the words and actions of their neighbours; for so much doth Christ's reasoning in general charge upon them, that since the scripture calleth some men gods, they needed not, if malice had not blinded them, have charged blasphemy upon him, though he had been but a mere man.

7. Albeit magistrates be but men like their brethren, yet in respect of their office they have the glorious title of gods conferred upon them, as being his vicegerents, and as bearing some stamp of his authority and dominion; therefore saith the scripture, I said, ye are gods. This should both engage them to see to their qualifications and the exercise of their power; and others, to reverence and honour them.

8. Such as would have right to this glorious title, and the privileges contained therein, ought to have God's calling to the office they exercise; for "he called them gods, unto whom the word of God came," to call them to their employment.

9. Let magistrates be never so high, yet are they subject to God, and to the directions and injunctions of his word; for so also the word came to them as to servants, as appears in that psalm.

10. Things are in reality as the word of God calls them, whatever men imagine to the contrary; for if the word came to them, and he called them gods, that sentence must stand without impeachment of blasphemy.

11. Albeit men who do not reject the scripture will be very assiduous to wrest and throw it to countenance their opinions and ways, and to bring their light to it rather than seek light in it, yet its verdict doth stand unalterable; for " the scripture cannot be broken," or, loosed; that sentence, that they are gods, cannot be annulled, let men cavil or gloss it as they will.

12. Christ is so high above all principalities and powers as of necessity he must be true God; for so doth the force of his argument run, that if they were called gods, much more might he be called " the Son of God;" and therefore all the gods must worship him, even angels as well as magistrates, Ps. xcvii. 7, with Heb. i. 6.

13. Whosoever shall study Christ's glorious sanctification and separation from sinners, his glorious endowments, and high employment and office, must acknowledge that he is the eternal Son of God; for that the Father hath sanctified and sent him into the world doth infer that he is " the Son of God."

14. Christ's glory and godhead wants not a witness in the bosom of the greatest opposer, if Christ lay it at his door; therefore doth he put them to it: say ye, " Thou blasphemest; because I said, I am the Son of God?"

Ver. 37. If I do not the works of my Father, believe me not.

38. But if I do, though ye believe not me, believe the works: that ye may know, and believe, that the Father is in me, and I in him.

The second argument whereby Christ proves that it is no blasphemy to call himself God, and that he is God in very deed, is taken from his works; wherein he grants that if he did not divine works, flowing from that power common to him with the Father, they had some pretence of excuse for not believing him to be God, ver. 37; but since he did these works, they were bound to lay aside any prejudice against his person, and to be led by these works to acknowledge and believe him to be the true God, one with the Father, mutually existing the one in the other, ver. 38. And so in this argument Christ asserts and confirms the very thing they opposed, and what himself had said, ver. 30.

DOCTRINES.

1. Christ did so far condescend to cure the unbelief of men as to add glorious works to his word to declare who he is; for he hath the works of the Father pleading for him—that is, not only works done by the Father's authority, (for so his servants did work miracles,) but works done by that power which is common to him with the Father.

2. Albeit it be our duty to acknowledge and to believe in Christ, yet he requires no implicit and blind obedience in this point; but men should accurately try the grounds of their faith, and then on these grounds close with him; therefore doth he put them to this : " If I do not the works of my Father, believe me not," and afterwards, " that ye may know, and believe."

3. Christ's works were divine, even to the convincing of the greatest adversaries, and so clear, that Christ was content not to be believed if, after trial, their consciences did not find them to be so ; therefore he doth not decline them in this matter, but " If I do not the works of my Father, believe me not."

4. When Christ hath manifested never so much of himself, yet naturally men have prejudices against him and at believing in him; therefore he supposeth it as their fault: " ye believe not me."

5. Albeit Christ get much wrong by unjust prejudices of men, yet he doth not give over to mind and seek their good; therefore, albeit they believed not him, yet he followeth them with other means to draw them to believe, and warns them of their own sin if they did not: " Though ye believe not me, believe the works," &c.

6. Albeit it be our duty to rest content with God's word as the ground of our faith, not seeking any other proof; and albeit it be our great sin when it is not so; yet when he adds works to confirm his word, he may not only exact believing of us, but it is our sin undeniable if then we believe not; therefore saith he, " If I do, though ye believe not me, believe the works."

7. Christ is never rightly known and believed on but when he is taken up as one in essence with the Father; and that, however the person of the Son be distinct from the person of the Father, in respect of order of subsistence, properties, and order of working, yet the divine essence is undivided, and there is a mutual inexistence of one person in the other; for they must " know, and believe, that the Father is in me, and I in him."

Ver. 39. Therefore they sought again to take him : but he escaped out of their hand,

40. And went away again beyond Jordan into the place where John at first baptized; and there he abode.

Followeth the third encounter betwixt Christ and these Jews, and the event of this debate, wherein they let out more of their fury, and he departs from them to a place where he gets more comfortable employment; and so he leaves Jerusalem, after he had stayed in it since the feast of tabernacles, chap. vii.

In these verses we have the violent and continued fury of these Jews, who, being convinced, will not submit, but do run upon the light, and seek to take him; and his avoiding their fury, and withdrawing towards Bethabara, and abiding there. Whence learn—

1. Convictions of men's judgments will not

always gain upon them, nor will Christ's taking pains for that end do any good; for after all this clear reasoning, which they could not resist nor refute, they do not yield.

2. The more pains is taken upon malicious reprobates the greater will their malice grow, and their convictions, not being sanctified, will degenerate into violent opposition to the light and the messengers thereof; for without any yielding, " Therefore they sought to take him."

3. The many disappointments wherewith adversaries meet in their cruel designs will not mollify them nor hinder them to pursue the same designs on all occasions; for albeit they had essayed this course in vain before, yet " they sought again to take him."

4. Men cannot be so assiduous in prosecuting their cruel purposes but the Lord can as constantly disappoint them, and make one attempt prosper no better than another; for as of before so now again, " he escaped out of their hand."

5. Christ, in his own person, hath sanctified these means, whereof his people need to make use in their trials; therefore doth he make use of " escaping (or fleeing) out of their hand."

6. When men persist in their contempt and persecution of Christ he is provoked to leave them; for he " went away again (having been there before, chap. i. 28, 29) beyond Jordan, (or to Bethabara, chap. i. 28,) and there he abode."

7. When Christ is banished and persecuted from one place, he will not want another to which he may repair; for he hath a place " beyond Jordan" wherein to abide.

8. Where the Lord hath taken much pains on a people he will come to crave an account of the fruits thereof; therefore did Christ go to the place " where John at first baptized," to try what fruits his ministry had left behind it.

VER. 41. And many resorted unto him, and said, John did no miracle: but all things that John spake of this man were true.

42. And many believed on him there.

In these verses we have the success of Christ's ministry beyond Jordan, in that many resorted to him, and finding that Christ did surpass John, who never wrought any miracle among them, and that John's predictions concerning Christ were all verified, many of them do believe on him, not rejecting John, (as many of his followers did cleave to him in opposition to Christ,) but being led by his ministry to Christ. Whence learn—

1. When the Lord's servants are preserved in the midst of many dangers it is for very good purpose, and that they may yet do him more service in their generation; for Christ is preserved and sent away that he may get an abode and do good in this place.

2. When men do haunt and frequent public ordinances it is a presage that Christ hath some work to work there; for in this place, where many were converted, " many resorted unto him"—to wit, either of the inhabitants of the place, or of those who, by frequenting the passage there, had occasion to hear John often.

3. When Christ is well known he will be found far above the chief of his servants, and all their excellency nothing to his; for they said, " John did no miracle," as this man doth.

4. No man who speaks to the commendation of Christ according to his word will ever be found liars; and it is commendation enough to faithful servants that they are found true in what they say of him; for it is John's commendation, and an evidence of Christ's glory, " all things that John spake of this man were true."

5. The excellency of Christ is then only rightly studied when men do close with him and embrace him by faith; for this is the fruit of all their reasonings and observations, " and many believed on him there."

6. The pains taken by faithful ministers may lay long, like seed under the ground, and yet at last, by some new watering, break forth in fair fruit; for here John's ministry hath fruit upon Christ's coming long after he is dead.

CHAPTER XI.

THIS chapter contains the history of Christ's return into Judea, from which he had retired himself, chap. x. 39, 40, and a famous miracle —of raising Lazarus from the dead, wrought at his return, together with some effects and consequents that followed thereupon. The chapter may be taken up in three parts: 1. The antecedents of the miracle, some whereof are previous to his return to Judea, ver. 1—16, some of them fell forth after he came near to Bethany, and before he came to Larazus's grave, ver. 17—37, and some of them at the grave before the miracle was wrought, ver 38—42. 2. The miracle itself, ver. 43, 44. 3. The effects and consequents thereof, both in the spectators and in the chief rulers of the Jews, and in Christ himself, ver. 45—57.

VER. 1. Now a certain man was sick, named Lazarus, of Bethany, the town of Mary and her sister Martha.

2. (It was that Mary which anointed the Lord with ointment, and wiped his feet with her hair, whose brother Lazarus was sick.)

This being one of the greatest and most famous miracles, and being one of the last wrought by Christ, upon occasion whereof many passages of divine providence are manifested, and much precious doctrine published, therefore the antecedents thereof are so largely insisted on. And the antecedents previous to his return may be taken up in these :—1. A remote occasion of his return, and antecedent of the miracle, which is, Lazarus' sickness, ver. 1, 2. 2. A nearer occasion of his return, which was, a message sent to Christ in behalf of sick Lazarus, ver. 3.

3. Christ's present return to this message, both in word, ver. 4, and action, ver. 5, 6. 4. His preparation at last to return, with his conference with and trial of the disciples in that matter, ver. 7—16.

In these verses (which contain a remote occasion of his return and antecedent of the miracle) we have a description of the person on whom it was wrought—1. From his name, "Lazarus," the same as appears with Eleazar. 2. From his condition; he "was sick," or infirm, as the word imports. 3. From the place of his habitation and friends; he was of "Bethany," a village near to Jerusalem, ver. 18, and Mary and Martha (of whom Luke, x. 38, 39) were his sisters, as afterward appears. This village is called Mary and Martha's town, because they were born there, as John, i. 44, or because indeed it was Lazarus's and their property; and so they are afterward visited by them of Jerusalem as persons of respect, and the sisters get the name of it because they have been spoken of before, Luke, x. 38, and so are better known in this history than Lazarus yet was. Or the reason of this designation is rather because, whoever was master of this village, yet they are most eminent of any in it in Christ's account, they being godly, and he having been entertained there. 4. To make this description more clear, and because there are several Marys mentioned in the gospel, therefore John describes this Mary the sister of Lazarus, from a particular practice of hers, ver. 2, which doth not relate to that history, Luke, vii. 37, 38, which was done by another woman, but to that which is afterward mentioned, John, xii. 3, &c., and albeit that was done after Lazarus' sickness and restitution in order of time, yet John, who wrote the history long after, doth here record it by way of anticipation.

DOCTRINES.

1. As the Lord's children are not exempted from ordinary trials, and are never well but when they have some exercise or other, so their being under exercise is a mean to make both their honesty and God's love to them notour [notorious]; for Lazarus, a friend of Christ, "was sick;" and albeit he was a good man, yet there is no mention of him in the former history, Luke, x., but only of his sisters, till now that he is sick, and he is taken notice of, and Christ's love to him registrated [manifested].

2. Whatever bulk saints do bear in the world, yet they beautify the place where they dwell, and their house who entertain Christ is most eminent in his account were it never so mean otherwise; for this is the character Christ gives of Bethany—it is "the town of Mary and her sister Martha." It is needless to assert that Martha, who it seems was the eldest, Luke, x. 38, is named after Mary the youngest, because Mary was most eminent in piety, which Christ respects above all; for in the 5th verse we find this order inverted, and Martha placed first.

3. Christian friends, especially if they be also near in relation, are useful helps in a day of trial; therefore is mention made of Mary and Martha, upon occasion of Lazarus' sickness, because they were useful and eminent in the following passages, relating to their brother's recovery. (See Eccles. iv. 9—12.)

4. As for that practice of Mary recorded ver. 2, seeing it is only mentioned here to distinguish her from others, I shall remit it to the proper place, chap. xii., only we may gather from it—1. The Lord will not suffer men's actions to die with them, and particularly, a good turn done to Christ will not be forgotten of him; therefore, according to that promise, Matt. xxvi. 13, that this should be told of her, John doth here on this occasion record it. 2. Love to Christ is that which God takes especial notice of, and which doth commend them who have it; for it was an act of Mary's love which is so diligently recorded.

3. It is the will of God that posterity take notice of the eminent graces that have shined in saints, that they may imitate them; for this is recorded, not only to her commendation, but that Christ's commending it, and the savour thereof, may invite others to imitate her.

Ver. 3. Therefore his sisters sent unto him, saying, Lord, behold, he whom thou lovest is sick.

In this verse we have a second antecedent and a more near occasion of his return—to wit, the message of these sisters unto Christ, whose modesty and care of their sick brother not permitting them to go to him themselves, they send a messenger to acquaint him with the condition of their sick brother; and to prevail with him they describe their brother, neither from his name nor from any good in him, but from Christ's love to him. And albeit this their carriage in sending a messenger to acquaint Christ with their brother's sickness may seem to intimate their weakness in not knowing or not minding (by reason of their present grief) his omniscience, which might have taught them to acquiesce in their presenting the matter to him by prayer, yet as we find it not condemned that any came or sent to him while he was on earth, and their doing so contributed to make his glory conspicuous in his working, so their practice and the message they send do afford profitable instructions.

DOCTRINES.

1. Albeit Christ be looked on ofttimes as very troublesome company, and therefore men do drive him away, either from themselves by ill entertainment, or from the places they live in by persecution, yet it will be found that he may very ill be wanted in any place; for albeit Christ was driven away by the Jews' fury, chap. x. 39, 40, yet he is now missed and needed in Judea.

2. Albeit the bonds of nature will not always tie friends one to another, yet true piety will make the society of such comfortable, and make them truly useful one to another in straits; for here Lazarus and his sisters dwell together, and they bear a great weight in this his affliction, employing all means for his good, and being afterward heavily afflicted when they succeed not according to their desire.

3. As Christ hath taken on man's nature, so he hath also contracted a friendship betwixt himself and some lost sinners ; and as he respects all his creatures, as he is God, and all mankind, his parents, kindred, nation, friends, and acquaintance in their several relations as he is man, and loves all his elect as he is Mediator, so it hath pleased him also, as a good man, to bear especial love to some of his own elect as a man doth to his especial friends ; therefore is Lazarus described here to be, " he whom thou lovest," which doth not seclude his love to him in most of the former respects, but yet especially points at that especial love to him as a singularly good man ; so also did he love the beloved disciple, John, xiii. 23.

4. Whatever may be the expectations of men upon Christ's love to them, yet it will not exempt them from outward calamities ; for albeit they might think it strange that " he whom thou lovest is sick," yet both of these are consistent and may stand together.

5. Whatever men's straits be, bodily or spiritual, great or small, or whatever lawful means they employ when they are under them, yet then are difficulties rightly taken up when men look upon them as needing and calling for Christ ; and when, accordingly, the afflicted and their friends also do recommend the trial to him ; for such is their carriage ; they find a need of Christ for help under this bodily and outward trial, and accordingly " sent unto him."

6. In coming to Christ, and employing of him under difficulties, no impediment that may deter us ought to be regarded ; for albeit, in sending this message, it might be suggested that possibly he had more to do, and might do more good where he was ; that being far off he could not come in time, and that it was not safe to expose himself to the fury of the Jews ; yet they, being in need, pass over all these, and " sent unto him."

7. Albeit Christ may make use of a trial to beget friendship betwixt him and some of his elect, yet they have a great advantage who have it made up before ; for this is the ground of their confidence, that Christ loved Lazarus before : " He whom thou lovest is sick ;" and therefore, if ever men think they will stand in need of Christ, they should make acquaintance with him in time.

8. Whatever there may be on saints' part that would seem to commend them to Christ, yet true saints will renounce all that, and betake themselves only to his free love towards them ; for so much doth their practice teach. They do not describe Lazarus as their brother, as if they would boast of any credit with Christ by their worth ; nor do they mention any love in Lazarus's entertaining Christ's love ; but they betake themselves only to this : it is " he whom thou lovest."

9. Such as do believe Christ's love towards them ought also to believe that even their bodily infirmities are respected by him, and will be an acceptable errand to come to him withal ; for they do confidently employ him in this, " Behold, he is sick."

10. Where Christ's love is believed, it will be accounted enough to lay our case before him,

without prescribing the way of help to him ; therefore do they content themselves with this petition—" Behold, he whom thou lovest is sick," and they say no more. As saints can never have peace in any condition till they tell Christ of it, so they know there needs not much be said to a Father in limiting him to their desires ; but when they have laid their case before him to be considered, they may commit the answer to his wisdom and love.

VER. 4. *When Jesus heard that, he said, This sickness is not unto death, but for the glory of God, that the Son of God might be glorified thereby.*

Followeth a third antecedent of his return to Judea, containing Christ's present answer to this message, which consists of two branches : — 1. What he said, ver. 4. 2. What he did, ver. 5, 6. In this verse we have his speech, directed chiefly (as would appear) to the messenger, to carry back to Mary and Martha, for their encouragement ; wherein he declareth, that this sickness tended not to Lazarus's death, but to the manifestation of the glory of God in the glorifying of his Son, while he sets down the end of this sickness negatively, that it " is not unto death," albeit he did die. It is not sufficient to clear it thus, that it tended not to bring Lazarus to eternal death ; for albeit that be a great comfort, yet it is not chiefly intended here, as appears from what is after positively set down of God's purpose in this sickness ; but the meaning is, that albeit he should die, yet not irrevocably, and so as he should not be restored to life, even here again, as they understood his death, ver. 24. And thus also, Mark, v. 39, he denieth that a damsel is dead, but affirmeth that she sleepeth, because he was to raise her as out of a sleep.

DOCTRINES.

1. Whatever Christ doth to his own in affliction, yet he alloweth encouragement upon them ; therefore doth he dispatch away the messenger with comfortable news to the sisters ; and albeit his after dealing seem to contradict all this, (as there is never an encouraging word given, but a tentation will be let out after it, to try our faith about it,) yet he would have them stick by this, and would have them look on sweet looks and good words from Christ as more than half health in the midst of sorest trouble.

2. It is an encouragement to Christ's own in trouble that he is a skilful physician, who takes up their disease rightly, and what it tends to, so that they shall not perish through want of skill or wrong application of cures ; therefore, in the first place, he tells them that he knows the disease, what it is, and what it tends to : " This sickness is not unto death," &c.

3. It is Christ's allowance that his people, in looking on their troubles, do not judge of them by the first view, nor by their nearest end, (for so the end of this sickness was death,) nor yet by what of their own nature they portend and tend unto, (for in that respect also this sickness was unto death ;) but that they look to God's

furthest and most principal end in them, and to what God (who brings light out of darkness, meat out of the eater, and life out of death) can bring out of them; for it is in this respect that God would have them, for their encouragement, seeing that "this sickness is not unto death," as is before explained.

4. As God's own glory is his supreme end in all things, so in particular his scope in sending afflictions on his people is to make his glory conspicuous in their through-bearing [sustaining] under them, and in giving an issue from them; for saith he, "this sickness is for the glory of God," and albeit God do not manifest his glory in so extraordinary a way, when his people are in trouble, as he did on Lazarus's behalf, yet the general [doctrine] holds still true, that he will be glorified in all the exercises of his people.

5. The Lord's purpose to glorify himself on behalf of his people requires that they be exercised with sickness and other infirmities, that so he may magnify his power, wisdom, mercy, and love, towards and upon them; for there must be "sickness," that "the glory of God" may shine.

6. Were afflictions never so bitter and so grievous, yet this ought to sweeten them, if God take occasion thereby to honour himself; for this is an encouragement to sweeten the cup, and make them submit, that "this sickness is for the glory of God." (See John, xii. 27, 28; 2 Cor. xii. 9, 10.)

7. God is glorified, in that his Son Christ is glorified; and his glory in helping his people under trouble shines in proving Christ to be omnipotent and true God, equal with the Father in giving deliverance to them; for he clears that it is "for the glory of God," in this respect, "that the Son of God may be glorified thereby," so that, as none do honour the Father who do not honour the Son, John, v. 23, it may encourage saints that the Father accounts Christ's glorifying of himself on their behalf to be for his glory.

Ver. 5. Now Jesus loved Martha, and her sister, and Lazarus.

6. When he had heard therefore that he was sick, he abode two days still in the same place where he was.

In these verses we have Christ's present answer by deeds to this message—to wit, that however he loved not only Lazarus, as they propound it, ver. 3, but themselves also, ver. 5, yet when he heard of his sickness he stayed still two days before he motioned his return to Judea, ver. 6; this he did that, Lazarus being dead before he came, the two sisters might be the more fully tried, and his own glory might shine the brighter, for strengthening the faith of his people, as will be seen in the sequel of the history, particularly ver. 15.

DOCTRINES.

1. As God hath set his love on sinful dust, and Christ-man hath by his own practice sanctified holy friendship, so men's pretending and saying they are beloved of Christ is to little purpose unless Christ say so also; therefore is it confirmed here what they had expressed concerning Lazarus.

2. Such as, upon gospel terms and grounds, do lay claim to Christ's love, will not be repelled nor disappointed; for they say, it is "he whom thou lovest," and here, Amen is said to their claim; Jesus loved Lazarus.

3. It is a great mercy to be beloved of Christ, but it is a double mercy when the Lord lets out his love on a whole society and children of a family together; therefore it is added, "Jesus loved Martha, and her sister, and Lazarus," which might be a comfort to every one of them, in respect of the rest.

4. Saints' sobriety, in esteeming of themselves and in preferring others to themselves, will never lose them anything in Christ's estimation; therefore, albeit they mention only Lazarus as beloved of Christ, ver. 3, yet here themselves also are added. Unbelief is indeed no sobriety, nor yet is it sobriety in saints to shut out themselves from any part in Christ's love; yet when men have laid hold on him, it becomes them to prefer others, and make more noise of them than of themselves.

5. Albeit there may be much difference of growth among saints, and some may have more blemishes than others, yet Christ doth love true grace in any of his, how weak soever; therefore, albeit Martha was more worldly than Mary, Luke, x. 39—42, and it appears afterward she was not so broken-spirited as she, yet "Jesus loved Martha" as well as Mary.

6. Christ requires that his people's heart be guarded against any misconstruction of his dealing, by the faith of his love, and seeing love in all of it; therefore is this premitted of his love to them, to prevent any misconstruction of his stay till Lazarus should die.

7. There is no outward cross-dispensation, nor apparently harsh dealing, but it is consistent with love, and may flow from love to his own; and particularly, Christ may dearly love his own, and yet may delay to help them, even in their extremity, till a fit time come, wherein his glory may shine, and the mercy be more conspicuous; therefore upon this, that Jesus loved them, it followeth, "When he had heard therefore that he was sick, he abode two days still in the same place where he was."

Ver. 7. Then after that saith he to his disciples, Let us go into Judea again.

Followeth the last thing antecedent to his return, which is, his preparation to return, and his trial of the disciples about that matter. This is contained in several conferences with the disciples, to ver. 17, which shall be spoken to in order.

In this verse he excites and invites to go and return with him again, which draws on the following conference. Whence learn—

1. Such as seem to be but on-lookers in the trials of others may yet get a sharper trial by it than they expect; for so much may we learn from this conference in general, wherein the dis-

ciples get a trial about Lazarus' sickness, by reason of their own fear, and therefore he conferred with them, and said to his disciples, " Let us go," &c.

2. Christ will, in due time, satisfy the needy requests of his own, and will let it be seen that he doth not slight, however he delay them; therefore, " after that," when the two days are expired, he will " go into Judea again," to visit and restore Lazarus.

3. Christ may make the first view of a calling or duty appear more terrible to his followers for their trial than it will prove afterward; therefore doth Christ propound the invitation in these terms, " Let us go into Judea again," whereby he puts them in mind how they had been driven out of it, and yet will have them to it " again," though yet, for a time, they found no such hurt by going, as the sequel cleareth.

4. It may give ground of hope that a calling and duty will not be so hurtful as it appears dreadful, when Christ gives a call to it, and so puts us in his way, and when he offers to go with us and bear us company; for so is this sweetened, " Let us go," saith he, importing his call, and that he will go with them.

VER. 8. *His disciples say unto him, Master, the Jews of late sought to stone thee; and goest thou thither again.*

In this verse is recorded how they relished this invitation; they, being weak and unwilling to meet with suffering, are astonished at the call, and pretend great respect to him, and therefore oppose his motion as not proceeding from wisdom, wondering that he, who had been so lately in hazard, would cast himself in new difficulties. Whence learn—

1. As ofttimes spectators and on-lookers are more terrified with the cross than sufferers themselves, so in particular Christ did endure the cross, and make for it, with such resolution as astonished his followers; for he invites them to go into Judea, when they wonder he should go " thither again."

2. Such as are afraid to grapple with trouble will not readily let it be believed that they are so, but will bend their wits to seek some fair pretence whereupon they may decline it; therefore do they only hold out his danger, " The Jews of late sought to stone thee," &c., to hinder that journey; whereas, however it was true they did respect his safety, yet they were as much taken up with fear of their own danger, as may be gathered from ver. 16.

3. Men in following God's way may meet with enemies that are very near friends, and even disciples may cast impediments in their way who are on a good course; for even the disciples, who acknowledge him their Master, oppose him in his duty. (See Matt. xvi. 16, 17, &c., with 22.)

4. Men's wisdom, or their conceit of it, is a strong rebel against Christ; and it is the great presumption of disciples, when, instead of following Christ, they will offer him a counsel, as if they were wiser than he; for herein do they fail, when they vehemently urge him with a question,

" Goest thou thither again?" as if he had not considered the matter well enough.

5. The arguments of the wisdom of the flesh, and of carnal fear, are but invalid to satisfy the conscience. Hazards, either real or apparent, are strong motives to dissuade our carnal hearts from duty, but these are no sound arguments in divinity; for they think it a strong argument, " The Jews of late sought to stone thee; and (therefore) goest thou thither again?" But Christ counts not that sound that men should choose their way according to their apprehension of dangers or safety in it, but according as God clears a calling, whatever difficulty be in the way; as reckoning that many difficulties will tryst [meet] men with many proofs of love; and that as they but " sought to stone" Christ, and yet could not effectuate it, so the Lord can give safety, even in the midst of dangers, when he pleaseth.

6. It is the great sin of men possessed with the slavish fear of trouble, that not only they decline duty, but are selfish, so that they mind neither the honour of God nor the good of others, so they may keep themselves in safety; for so much appears in their declining Judea to be free of trouble, never.regarding Lazarus, or his sister's need, nor the glory of God, which was to shine in raising him up.

VER. 9. *Jesus answered, Are there not twelve hours in the day? If any man walk in the day, he stumbleth not, because he seeth the light of this world.*

10. But if a man walk in the night, he stumbleth, because there is no light in him.

Followeth Christ's answer to their objection against his resolution, consisting of two parts, the first whereof (in these verses) is general; concerning which they who understand this day, and the hours thereof, of man's lifetime, wherein he is to go about his business, do indeed speak this far truth, that the time of Christ's calling in that way was to be ended at his death, and that men could not reach him till the hours of his life were expired, and therefore he needed not fear; but neither doth that so fitly agree with what is subjoined, ver. 10, of men's stumbling in the night, nor yet with Christ's own practice, who, albeit he knew he should be in safety till his hour came, yet he did use lawful means, and follow the Father's call, in removing from place to place, as is manifest in his going lately out of Judea. Therefore, if we consider—1. The order that God hath established in nature, in appointing the day for men's labour, in all the hours thereof, and not the night, because men cannot but stumble in it, Psalm civ. 20—23; 2. Christ's particular answer, ver. 11, wherein he shews his calling for this journey,—if, I say, we consider these, we shall find the sense of this general answer to be this: that a calling from God is like daylight to a man, to prevent fear of stumbling, or inconveniency and danger; whereas he who neglects the opportunity thereof may fall in many inconveniences, like a man who neglects his journey till the evening or night, and therefore cannot choose but stumble, seeing he wants the light of day, and hath no light in him to supply that defect. And by this Christ leads them to understand that as he had a calling to leave Judea, so if he could clear a calling to return to it again, there was no danger, whereas to slight a calling would draw on real inconveniences.

DOCTRINES.

1. The great task and exercise of Christians ought to be to turn their eyes from studying inconveniences and hazards, to study their duty and calling, as their work and care, and then leave the care of events unto God; therefore doth Christ draw them, who were affected with fear of dangers, to consider seriously what calling there was for that undertaking.

2. As the Lord hath honoured the children of men by appointing unto them lawful callings, wherein they may serve him, whatever their calling be in itself, so he hath appointed times and opportunities of these callings, which are not to be neglected, for a calling is like the day, wherein a man may walk, and there are twelve hours in this day—that is, a prefixed time for going about this calling, as there is for daylight, which is not to be neglected more than a man would neglect the daytime to go about his business in it. The expression alludes to the custom of the Jews, who divided the day and the night each of them into twelve hours, and that both summer and winter, only they shortened the hours of the day in winter and lengthened them in summer; and so (contrariwise) the hours of the night.

3. A man that followeth a calling from God, and improveth all the opportunities thereof, is in a safe course, and so needs fear no danger; for as "If any man walk in the day, he stumbleth not, because he seeth the light of this world," or, the sun, so he that hath the light of his calling needs not stumble, but that may be to him as daylight is to passengers, (see 1 Pet. iii. 13;) for albeit following of God's call will not always keep men from trouble, but Christ himself, when his course was finished, and very shortly after this met with it, yet, 1. They will get their day finished, and shall not be interrupted, till they have finished their work, as Christ's experience teacheth. (See Luke, xiii. 31, 32.) 2. If they be not kept from difficulties, yet, following their calling, they are kept from the guilt of procuring them sinfully. 3. They may be sure they shall be blessed; and, 4. That God, who employs them, will make up all their losses to them. So that the clearness of God's call affords more peace than all the difficulties men can meet with in a calling can make void.

4. As man's life is but short, so the opportunities of following a calling from God are but short, and soon lost irredeemably; for it is but a day of twelve hours, after which a night cometh.

5. As men who run on danger without a calling may meet with many a snare, so they who neglect God's call for fear of trial may meet with sorer difficulties in their own way; for "if a man walk in the night, he stumbleth, because there is no light in him," to take up hazards which God hath appointed the sun to point out unto men. The meaning is, not only that he who runs without a call stumbleth, but that as a man, who having business to do in the daytime, yet doth not set out till night, doth exceedingly prejudge himself, so he who either rejects God's call, and takes him to follow his own counsels, or he who fits the opportunities of doing his calling, and comes too late, may meet with sharp trials.

Ver. 11. *These things said he: and after that he saith unto them, Our friend Lazarus sleepeth; but I go, that I may awake him out of sleep.*

Christ having in general cleared the usefulness and safety that is in following a calling, doth in this second part of the answer clear his own calling to this journey in particular—to wit, that he might raise Lazarus, who was now dead. Whence learn—

1. Christ hath an honourable relation unto and a near interest in them that believe; for he is the "friend Lazarus." (See Isa. xli. 8; Jam. ii. 23.)

2. The death of believers doth not break off Christ's relations or friendship to them, but he will remember them for good, even when they are dead; for he is "friend Lazarus," when dead, and I go to "awake him."

3. Such as are friends to Christ ought also to be looked on as friends by all Christ's followers; therefore doth he say, "Our friend Lazarus."

4. Albeit death be a common lot to the godly and the wicked, yet Christians ought to have Christian conceptions and Christian expressions of it, and indeed the nature thereof is changed to them; therefore saith he, "Lazarus sleepeth," which name is given to death, not only because he was shortly to raise him up, as easily as one awakes a sleeping man (and so afterward he saith, "I go, that I may awake him;" see also Luke, viii. 52, &c.,) but also because death is a sweet sleep to the godly, and a rest from their labours, till the morning of the resurrection, that he raise them up to inherit glory, Rev. xiv. 13; Psalm xvii. 15.

5. When Christ propounds difficulties to his people he hath also the remedy in his own hand, and when we are called to study difficulties, he warrants us also to study what he can do for us under them; therefore unto this, that "Lazarus sleepeth," he subjoins, "but I go, that I may awake him."

6. It is a calling to Christ to go where he may do good to any of his own, were it through never so many difficulties and dangers; therefore doth he subjoin this to the former general doctrine, as clearing his calling to this journey in particular, "These things said he: and after that he saith unto them, Our friend Lazarus sleepeth; but I go," &c.

7. Christ alone will have the glory of the good done to his people, and will not suffer any to share with him; for albeit he had invited them to go with him, as companions in the journey, ver. 7, yet he will acknowledge no companions in the miracle, "I go, that I may awake him."

8. Christ will choose that way of working for his people that may most manifest his own glory, albeit it should be a way full of hazard, of delays, and discoveries of his people's weakness; there-

fore, whereas they might object that he might more easily send his word of power, which might do the work more speedily, as John, iv. 49, 50, and with less hazard and cause of fainting fear to them, yet saith he, " I go," that the glory of the miracle might be more conspicuous, as the event testified.

Ver. 12. Then said his disciples, Lord, if he sleep, he shall do well.

13. Howbeit Jesus spake of his death : but they thought that he had spoken of taking rest in sleep.

Christ's manner of expression in clearing of his calling being mistaken by the apostles, though the phrase was very usual, they urge it against his going to Judea; for whereas Christ spake of Lazarus's death, they understand it of his resting by sleep in his sickness, and therefore propound that, this being a sign of health, he needed not to go heal him. Whence learn—

1. Even disciples are ready to mistake and misunderstand Christ's mind and words; for so they understand Christ's words otherwise than he meant them.

2. One great cause of our mistakes is the averseness of our mind from knowing anything but what we please; and that our corrupt affections do ofttimes guide our judgments; for the disciples, being averse from suffering, and glad of any excuse to keep out of Judea, do grip to Christ's expression of sleep to gather this fair pretence from it, " Lord, if he sleep, he shall do well;" whereas, if their passions and distempers had not blinded them, they might easily have perceived that Christ meant more by that expression, seeing he would not have undertaken such a journey merely to awake a sleeping friend out of a refreshful sleep.

3. It is no easy matter to bring even disciples to submit to God's will when it crosseth their own dispositions; for after all that Christ had said, they bewray that they continue still averse from going to Judea.

4. When Christ puts his people to it, they may expect to be tried both on the right hand and the left, 2 Cor. vi. 7, and to have both carnal fears of trouble and deluded hopes of exemption let loose upon them to bring forth what is in their heart; therefore, after they are tried with an affrighting sight of danger, ver. 7, 8, now, on the other hand, they are tried with hopes of being free of that journey, and by this they are sifted, as well as by the other, and the necessity of going was the more searching, after such a fancy.

Ver. 14. Then said Jesus unto them plainly, Lazarus is dead.

15. And I am glad for your sakes that I was not there, to the intent ye may believe ; nevertheless let us go unto him.

Christ having thus tried them, doth—1. Plainly, and without allegory or metaphor, tell them that Lazarus is dead. ver. 14; and so that his calling was clear. 2. Whereas it might be thought that he had by this delay neglected Lazarus, he declareth that it was to good purpose, and for the confirmation of their faith by the clearness of the miracle, that he was not there, but stayed away; and therefore he was glad of it. 3. Whatever might be objected, that it was now too late and out of time to go, yet he resolves to go for all that, ver. 15. Whence learn—

1. Christ doth not cast off his own, though they be both unwilling to suffer and ignorant, but meekly bears with them, and speaks again and again till they understand him ; for " Then said Jesus unto them plainly, Lazarus is dead."

2. It is an addition to the trial of the godly that ofttimes when their straits are at the greatest Christ is absent from them ; for " Lazarus is dead, and I was not there," saith he—to wit, in his humanity. And this Mary and Martha resent afterwards, ver. 21, 32.

3. Whatever may be the saints' thoughts of Christ's dealing under their distresses, yet his way of dealing is still the best; and he can give a good account that it is so, to satisfy their mistakes; as here he obviates all carping at his absence by shewing that if he had been there he could not have refused the supplications of the sisters to prevent Lazarus's death ; and so there had not been so glorious a miracle wrought for confirmation of faith ; whereas now, both his omniscience is evidenced in telling of Lazarus's death, and the miracle should produce profitable effects.

4. Christ can not only give an account of his seeming strange dispensations, but can produce matter of joy even out of the saddest of them ; for albeit Lazarus be dead, and his sisters drowned in sorrow, yet saith he, " I am glad that I was not there," to prevent it ; not that he wanted sympathy, but that he knew how to bring joy out of it.

5. As Christ minds his own glory in all his working, so he joins therewith the promoving of the true good of his people ; for this sickness and death of Lazarus is not only " for the glory of God," ver. 4, but " for your sakes" and good. So that saints will find his glory and their good still carried on together.

6. Christ, in afflicting any of his own, minds not only their own particular good, but the good of other saints also, by their observing the proofs of Christ manifested upon and to the afflicted; for not only Lazarus, but the disciples, (and sisters also,) get good and confirmation out of the trial and the issue of it.

7. Even such as live under the most eminent ministry for a long time, and are very eminent in Christ's house, and who have seen much of Christ, may yet be very weak in faith, and need confirmation thereof; for albeit these were called to be apostles, and had seen the most of all Christ's miracles, and lived under Christ's ministry till now that it is near an end, yet even at this time they need help to believe, or to be confirmed and strengthened in it, that " ye may believe." And it is still of general verity that whatever faith saints have, yet it needs daily confirmation and growth.

8. Confirmation and strengthening of faith is so needful and useful that it is not to be thought

strange if Christ send sharp trials on ourselves or others, to bring that about; yea, a saint is highly honoured when God afflicts him most sharply, if his afflictions and the issues of them be a mean to confirm others; therefore Christ thinks Lazarus's pain in his sickness and death, and the sharp sorrow of his sisters, but a small thing, and not to be stood upon, if it produce confirmation of faith, even in disciples: " I am glad I was not there, to the intent ye may believe."

9. As anything that may advance our good is matter of Christ's joy, so in particular there is nothing more pleasant unto him than to have his people believing and growing in faith: " I am glad, to the intent ye may believe."

10. Albeit Christ's absence from his people for a time may seem to discourage them much, yet very absence may tend to the strengthening of their faith afterwards; for " I was not there, to the intent ye may believe."

11. Whatever encouragement Christ allows upon his people, yet it is not to be expected that he will allow them their own desired ease by shifting their duty for any danger; for albeit he point out all these solid grounds of comfort, yet go to Judea they must: " Nevertheless let us go." And indeed, if they had gotten their own desired refreshment, they had missed of all these true comforts.

12. Inability and impotency in the needy will not hinder a meeting betwixt Christ and them, but he will go to them who cannot come to him; for such is his dealing to dead Lazarus: " Let us go unto him."

13. Christ's going unto or dealing even with the dead, is not useless, but to good purpose; for albeit it should seem it were too late to go now, " Nevertheless (saith he) let us go unto him."

VER. 16. Then said Thomas, which is called Didymus, unto his fellow disciples, Let us also go, that we may die with him.

This conference closeth with a particular discovery of Thomas Didymus, or the twin, as his name Thomas, in the Hebrew, also imports. He, seeing Christ so resolute, invites the rest to go and die with him, not with Lazarus, but with Christ; and the meaning is, that since Christ would not follow their counsel, but would run on his own death, there was nothing better for them than to run on the hazard with him, and so once be out of troubles and fears. In this resolution there doth indeed appear—1. Affection, in cleaving unto Christ; and, 2. Zeal in exciting others to the same; yet this resolution is but full of fear and diffidence, for had he believed what was spoken ver. 15, he would not have expected this issue of the journey.

DOCTRINES.

1. It is the duty of Christ's followers not to quit him, though it should cost them their lives; for so much doth this resolution teach.

2. It is their duty also to excite one another to duty in times of hazard: Let us go, saith he, and die.

3. Christ's followers have more fears and sad apprehensions than there is just cause; for let us go, and die, when Christ had told of another thing, imports so much. This produced an untimous exercise about suffering, wherein he proved not so resolute when he was called to it.

4. It breeds men much needless exercise that they will not believe nor expect the good that Christ promiseth them, but will judge of all things by their own apprehensions; for so was it with him, his eye was so on feared danger as he little regarded what Christ had promised.

5. The Lord doth not approve of that resolution in duty or suffering that doth not flow from faith, but from distrust; for herein did Thomas's resolution fail.

6. The Lord also dislikes men's willingness to suffer when it proceeds from a desperate wearing of their present lot, which makes them content to rid themselves of it by sharp sufferings; for this was also one of his faults, as hath been before explained.

VER. 17. Then when Jesus came, he found that he had lain in the grave four days already.

18. Now Bethany was nigh unto Jerusalem, about fifteen furlongs off:

19. And many of the Jews came to Martha and Mary, to comfort them concerning their brother.

Followeth to verse 38 some antecedents of the miracle after Christ came near to Bethany, and before he came to the grave, unto which, and those that follow, a preface and introduction is premitted [introduced] in these verses, which will give light to the following purpose. And namely, there is recorded—1. The length of time since Lazarus, who was to be raised, had been buried; Jesus finds that it was four days, ver. 17. 2. The nearness of Bethany to Jerusalem (namely, that it was a furlong less than two miles, eight furlongs making a mile) is marked, ver. 18. And that as for other reasons, so also to point out a reason why so many Jews came to bear Mary and Martha company, which is the third thing premitted [introduced], ver. 19.

DOCTRINES.

1. While as it is said Jesus found he had lain four days, we need not inquire how he found it, for we may conceive that as he knew of his death before, and had told of it, ver. 11, 14, so now he found, by report and information, that it was as he knew; as indeed his knowledge is infallible; though it may be also asserted, in general, that Christ as man (being freely acted by the godhead) was sinlessly ignorant of some things not incumbent to his calling, and did learn from experience, information, &c., Luke, ii. 52; Mark, xiii. 32; and by this he would curb the licentious wit of man, who would presume to know all things, and doth condescend to those who are ignorant of many things, providing they know what is incumbent to them in their stations.

2. Christ will have the difficulties of his own singular, and remarked to be so, that his glory

may be singular in ridding them out of these; therefore it is premitted [acknowledged] that " he had lain in the grave four days already," that his glory in raising him might be the greater, and it might be seen that however he delayed long, yet he came in time enough to raise him, as is after cleared; for this produced more fruit in his own than if he had not died, or had been but new dead; and it made his death to be divulged at Jerusalem, as appears by their coming to comfort the sisters, that so malice itself might not doubt of the miracle.

3. Such as have gotten good news from Christ concerning their difficulties may yet meet with many seeming sad disappointments before they find them accomplished; for they got news, ver. 4, " This sickness is not unto death," and yet he is not only dead, but " had lain in the grave four days."

4. Men's exercise of their calling may lie very near to hazards, that so they may exercise faith in God; for Bethany, the place where Christ's calling lay, " was nigh unto Jerusalem," where his cruel enemies were, and where he was to suffer, even " about fifteen furlongs off."

5. It is not inconsistent with Christianity to have moderate sorrow for the loss of friends, and to be so affected as to need comfort; for Martha and Mary need some " to comfort them concerning their brother." Only that they do come " to comfort," it shews that the sorrow should be moderate, and that the mourners should not reject consolation.

6. It is the duty of friends and neighbours to sympathize with and comfort others in distress; for so much were these Jews convinced of, who came (from Jerusalem, as is to be gathered from ver. 18) " to Martha and Mary, to comfort them concerning their brother."

7. It is a special advantage when God casts friends and comforters to be near people when they stand in need of them; therefore also it is marked that Jerusalem, whence they came, " was nigh to Bethany." Job had his friends further off.

8. Men may, upon some respects, love some who are truly godly, and yet not love Christ, nor yet love others who bear the same image; for as yet (as would appear from ver. 45) none of these believed in Christ, and so could not love him, and some of them were violent enemies, and yet they loved these godly women, and came " to comfort them." It may be because they were eminent women they are respected; and many who will not look on Christ will yet look to any who are in eminency; and therefore the good that is in such should be cherished, if so be it may gain others. It is also ordinary for natural men to like the parts of gracious persons when yet they do not love their graces; and whatever it be, certainly it is upon some by-respect that this love is founded.

Ver. 20. Then Martha, as soon as she heard that Jesus was coming, went and met him: but Mary sat still in the house.

The antecedents of the miracle, after that Christ came near to Bethany, and before he came to the grave, may be reduced to these two:—

1. Martha's meeting and conference with him, to ver. 28. 2. His meeting with Mary, and some consequents following thereupon, ver. 28—37.

Christ's meeting and conference with Martha contains several particulars, to be spoken in order, whereof the first (in this verse) is her meeting with him. She, though a good woman, and sensible of her loss also, yet being of a stronger mind than Mary, and consequently stirring most up and down, gets first word of Christ's approach, and goeth to meet him; whereas Mary, knowing nothing of this, stays still within. Whence learn—

1. As among the truly gracious some are more tender and spiritual than others, so the most godly are ordinarily more affected with griefs and more broken under them than others; for Martha is able to stir, and gets news of Christ, while as tender Mary sits still under her sorrows, and hears of no such thing. This may teach the godly, and especially weak and tenderhearted ones, not to measure every one by themselves; for those who have real good may have really different dispositions, and some come far short of others; and it may teach them whose minds are broken and made tender, as to guard lest every difficulty take too deep impression, so also to expect more liberal allowance from Christ, as Mary afterwards found.

2. Whatever comfort or sympathy men meet with from friends in their trouble, yet comfort from Christ also will be needed by all the godly; for albeit they had comforters, ver. 19, yet she " went and met him" when she heard of his coming, to welcome him as a needful guest; and it may be she met him without, as fearing hazard to him from the Jews that were in the house.

3. Martha had her own prejudice at Christ's carriage that he had not come sooner, as appears afterward, as well as she had faith; and yet faith prevails, that she stays not from him but goeth to him. It teacheth that unbelief is never deadly so long as a man is not kept from coming to Christ by it; and whatever complaints a man have of Christ's dealing, yet faith is still the conqueror, so long as all these complaints are poured out only in Christ's own bosom.

Ver. 21. Then said Martha unto Jesus, Lord, if thou hadst been here, my brother had not died.

22. But I know, that even now, whatsoever thou wilt ask of God, God will give it thee.

In the next place we have Martha's salutation and discourse to Christ at meeting; wherein, 1. Her passion breaks out in an indirect challenge, ver. 21, that his presence might have prevented her brother's death, and therefore regrets that he came not in time; and in this her weakness appears, not only in her indirect challenge, but partly in her presumption, believing that for which she had no ground,—for upon what ground could she know but Christ might have been there and yet her brother have died, seeing there was no promise to the contrary?— and partly in her limiting of Christ's power to his bodily presence, as if he could not have prevented his death if he had pleased, though he had not been there. 2. After her passion hath broken out she settles a little, and corrects it with a profession of her faith, that Christ, if he pleased, could yet amend all, ver. 22, though in this also her faith came short, in that she believes not Christ can do this by his own power, but only as an instrument employing God, or obtaining power of God, to do it, as was the way of men of God in former times.

From ver. 21, learn—1. The dear children of God have so much weakness and corruption as to flee out against Christ's way of dealing towards them when they are in trouble; for so much doth this indirect challenge teach.

2. Albeit saints may have much submission at their engaging in a trial, yet they may be ready to stagger, if Christ put them to it, to give a real proof of that submission; for albeit their message to Christ, ver. 3, spoke much submission and a referring of all to his will, yet here she declares that she cannot digest that it hath pleased him to let her brother die.

3. It is not easy for saints to take up Christ, and fasten their faith upon him aright; and in particular it is sometimes their fault that they give more credit to the presumptuous dreams of their own hearts, for which they have no warrant, than to what Christ reveals of himself; for she strongly asserts, " if thou hadst been here, my brother had not died," for which she had no ground at all. And generally it is the fault of men, that in the point of trust and diffidence they make a bible of their own thoughts, apprehensions, and fears, without regarding what the scripture saith.

4. It is also the fault of saints that in believing Christ's power and good will to do for them they yet limit him to their own conceived way of working, out of which they do not expect anything from him; and particularly, it is their great fault to limit his efficacy and power to his bodily presence; for herein also she failed, never expecting the preservation of her brother's life unless Christ " had been there," whereas he could have done it at never so great a distance.

From ver. 22, learn—1. Passion, when it is a tentation in saints, is hasty and first out, and takes the start of their better resolutions; for here it hath broken first out, whereas she hath better stuff within, here produced; and therefore as we are in straits to suspect that which posts first to the door to get out, Ps. cxvi. 11; xxxi. 22, so saints' passions, though they ought not to be justified, yet they ought not to be too narrowly examined and censured, as being but a violent tentation, treading upon grace for a season.

2. It is sinful in any, and particularly unseemly in a child of God, to persist in his passion when it hath burst forth; but he ought to revoke and correct it by faith; as here Martha subjoins a correction to the former expressions.

3. There is nothing can fall out, nor can the child of God's condition come to such a height, nor can the fruits of delays and disappointments be so desperate and deadly, but faith will see that it may all be yet amended and made

up again; therefore, albeit it was a sore dash that Christ came not up till he was dead, yet, saith she, " I know, that even now" all may be well enough.

4. It may exceedingly encourage saints to believe, when they consider that God's power is not limited, and that the Intercessor whom they employ will not be refused in anything he craves; for on this doth she build, " I know that whatsoever thou wilt ask of God, God will give it thee."

5. Faith, even when it goeth very far on in giving glory unto Christ, doth yet ordinarily come far short of what is his due; and when faith fleeth a very high pitch it may yet be full of weakness; for so was it in her faith, and her correcting of her former distemper. She believes only if he ask God will give; whereas, albeit indeed as Mediator and man he did employ the Father by prayer, of which we shall hear, ver. 41, 42, yet as God he wrought miracles by his own power, communicated with his essence from the Father by eternal generation.

VER. 23. *Jesus saith unto her, Thy brother shall rise again.*

In the third place we have Christ's meek answer to her discourse, wherein, passing over her infirmity, he comforts her with a promise that her brother shall rise again. Whence learn—

1. Great are the consolations which God hath laid up for his afflicted people, and he will do great things for them, in so far as he seeth good; for so much doth this wonderful promise, given for Martha's comfort, import.

2. It is a satisfactory and proper consolation against the death of those we love to believe a resurrection, wherein they shall be restored again; for by this doth Christ comfort her, " Thy brother shall rise again."

3. Christ doth propound this promise only in general terms, " He shall rise again," not mentioning the time when it should be; and this he doth partly to shew that however he was to raise her brother presently, yet the very general promise of a general resurrection is full of comfort, 1 Thess. iv. 13, 14, &c., and therefore he propounds her encouragement in these terms, lest any should stumble who have no warrant to expect such a particular favour; partly he doth it for the exercise of her faith, and to let see in her practice how far short our expectations may be of what Christ will do for his people, (she looks for resurrection at the last day; he is to raise her brother presently;) and partly that he may let in her consolation by degrees into her narrow-mouthed vessel; for as saints may be allowed to believe and expect a mercy when yet they cannot resolve every particular circumstance, how, or when, or by what means it shall come to pass, Esther, iv. 14, so they are so shallow as they can take in mercies but here a little and there a little.

VER. 24. *Martha saith unto him, I know that he shall rise again in the resurrection at the last day.*

In the fourth place we have Martha's exception upon this promise and offered comfort ; wherein, albeit she profess faith of a general resurrection and judgment, yet she seems to look on that as not sufficient for her encouragement, seeing it is common to all, and but far off. Whence learn—

1. It ought to be out of all controversy among Christians that there will be a day of judgment at the close of time, and a general resurrection of all the dead for that end ; for Martha believes this, though the pedagogy of the law was not yet expired, " I know that he shall rise again in the resurrection at the last day."

2. Such is the weakness of men, and their doting on their particular satisfaction, that they are ready to slight all the mercies and consolations of God unless they get that which they account a mercy ; therefore, albeit the general resurrection be no small comfort, and the resurrection of the just be far better than to be restored again to the toils of this life, yet she undervalues all that in comparison of her getting again her brother presently.

3. It is no strange thing to see men believing great things that are far off, and about which they have no present exercise, when yet their faith proves weak in the matter of their present trial, even albeit it be less difficult than that which they profess to believe ; for she can believe the resurrection of all men, and of him among the rest, at the last day, when yet she staggers at the matter of his being raised presently, and yet the one is as difficult as the other, and more difficult also.

Ver. 25. Jesus said unto her, I am the resurrection, and the life : he that believeth in me, though he were dead, yet shall he live :

26. And whosoever liveth and believeth in me shall never die. Believest thou this?

In the fifth place we have Christ's reply to her exception, for understanding whereof we are to consider that whatever faith Martha hath hitherto professed, yet—1. She hath not looked on Christ as able to do anything by his own power, but only by employing God in prayer. 2. She hath indeed professed her faith of a general resurrection, but doubted of her brother's being raised even now. 3. And in what she believes of a general resurrection she makes no mention of Christ's power to do it ; therefore Christ fits his answer to cure these evils in her, wherein, first, he layeth down a general assertion, " I am the resurrection, and the life"—that is, (if we take this truth in its full latitude, and with an eye to Christ's whole scope here,) he is the author of all resurrection and of all life, whether bodily or spiritual, as having absolute power and dominion over death, as God, and being life itself ; and therefore as he was to be eyed in her believing the general resurrection, so his power to raise and quicken the dead at that time was sufficient to prove he could even now raise her brother. And according to this interpretation, his being " the life," which is subjoined to his being " the resurrection," is not necessarily here to be understood only of that eternal life unto which the just are raised by Christ, and of which he gave a pledge by his raising up himself as Mediator, but it is to be taken generally, that he, as God, hath power to raise whom and when he will, as being the fountain of life, to give life to whom he will. But if we look to the purpose immediately subjoined we may take this assertion more strictly, and in a spiritual sense—that he is " the resurrection," in his first giving of spiritual life unto dead sinners, (which is further explained in the end of ver. 25,) and he is " the life," in continuing and preserving that spiritual life which he conferreth, which is further insisted on, ver. 26, as shall be cleared. This interpretation, as it is true in itself and agreeable to what followeth, so it needs not seclude the other, which is more general, and reacheth Christ's full scope, but may come in as a particular specially comprehended under it, as appears by his own commentary subjoined to it ; and therefore, secondly, he illustrates and confirms this general truth in a twofold particular assertion. One is, " He that believeth on me, though he were dead, yet shall he live ;" which, though it conclude well, if we understand it of a bodily resurrection, that they who close by him with faith, albeit they die bodily, yet he will raise them up to live again, and can do so when he pleaseth, yet comparing it with the following verse, which is conjoined with it by the copulative " and," as a further confirmation, and is undoubtedly to be understood spiritually, I incline rather to understand it spiritually, and that Christ is here proving himself to be the spiritual " resurrection" of a dead sinner, and that they who, being dead by nature, do lay hold on him by faith, shall partake of the first resurrection, and be made to live a life of grace ; and upon this doth the second assertion fitly follow, " Whosoever liveth and believeth in me shall never die," wherein he assures her that believers are delivered from spiritual and eternal death ; and so this adds to the former, for as in the former he proves himself chiefly to be " the resurrection," by raising up the dead to a state of life, so here he confirms further how he is " the life," by preserving and keeping in that life eternally which he had conferred upon believers, and stated them in it ; and this doctrine doth very well agree with Christ's scope in this place ; for hereby he not only leads Martha to eye him more than she did in what she believed, and to believe in him if she looked for a comfortable issue of her trial ; and to consider the mercy of spiritual resurrection when now she is taken up so much with raising up of her brother ; but this instance of spiritual resurrection and life is a very pregnant proof of that general truth that he is the resurrection and life, and sufficient to confirm that he can raise whom and when he will, no less power being required to the one than to the other, Ephes. i. 19, 20 ; Col. ii. 12. Thirdly, in this answer, Christ, having thus instructed her, doth pose her, if she believes this, and consequently will close with that promise, ver. 23, as to be presently performed.

From ver. 25, learn—1. Believers have need of daily instruction from Christ, that they may know and understand those things better which they believe in part; therefore albeit she believe a resurrection, ver. 24, yet Christ finds it needful to inform her better in many things about it.

2. It is not enough that we believe great benefits and mercies, unless we believe them to be in Christ, and seek them in him; for it is not enough she believe a resurrection, unless she believe that he is " the resurrection, and the life."

3. Christ is to be looked on, not as the instrument of life and resurrection to any, but as the author and principal worker thereof by his own power; for albeit many prophets and apostles have raised the dead, yet it can be said of none but he, " I am the resurrection, and the life."

4. Such as close with and enjoy Christ will find all things in him, and at their hand, which otherwise they may seek far off, and possibly not find; therefore, whereas she looked afar off to the latter day for the accomplishment of Christ's promise, he lets her see it in him at her hand, that he is " the resurrection, and the life," to raise up her brother even now.

5. As there is a spiritual resurrection of the soul in this life, so they who are acquainted with Christ's working therein, and in daily entertaining thereof, need find no difficulty to exalt Christ as the fountain of life and resurrection, and to believe that he is able to work wonderful outward deliverances, were it even to raise a dead body; therefore doth he bring in this instance, in the end of this and in the following verse, to prove that he is " the resurrection, and the life." and that he can raise her brother even presently. And indeed, all the wonders that God wrought of old upon the creatures for his people, a believer may find them all wrought within him, in his spiritual restoration.

6. By nature men are as estranged and far from grace as a dead man is from life; for so is here supposed that man is dead, and needs Christ to be " the resurrection."

7. The only fountain and cause of the recovery of this condition is in Christ, the author of both bodily and spiritual resurrection, as here we are taught.

8. The only mean to partake of this resurrection is by faith to lay hold on Christ; for he that believes in me shall live.

9. Christ being thus laid hold on, no bonds of spiritual death shall hinder his quickening virtue to raise them up; but he will make the very dead to live; for " he that believeth, though he were dead, yet shall he live." This is not to be understood as if any man that is dead by nature could in that estate lay hold on Christ by faith, —for he must first be prevented by passive regeneration, and the infusion of grace, — but the meaning is, that it is faith only that puts the sinner in a state of life, and is the saving exercise of infused grace, without which all antecedent exercises, of discovery and conviction of sin and misery, terror, &c., will not avail, as being common to saints and regenerate men with temporaries.

From ver. 26, learn—1. As the children of God are by regeneration put in a state of life, so they prove it by their after carriage, by exercising the functions of spiritual life, and being lively in

their way; for he to whom Christ is " the resurrection," to quicken him when he is dead, " he liveth."

2. As spiritual life flows only from Christ embraced by faith, so it must be entertained and preserved by the same mean of faith in Christ, for as the dead, by believing, do live, so he that liveth must believe in me, saith he. The keeping in of our spiritual life is a continued resurrection, as the preservation of the creatures is a continued creation; and as the same power is employed in begetting and entertaining this life, so the same mean of faith must still be kept in exercise, so that they are exceedingly in the wrong who, in their defections and distempers, and in their swoundings and faintings, do cast away their confidence.

3. The power of Christ will be forthcoming to preserve believers in him from an utter decay in their spiritual life, so that albeit they may be overtaken with some degrees of death, yet upon renewing of their faith they shall be recovered out of their swounds. He will also preserve them from eternal death, and bodily death itself shall not extinguish the life that is begotten and entertained by faith in Jesus Christ; for he that " liveth and believeth in me shall never die."

4. It is the will of God that when he reveals truth we embrace it by faith, and do not either reject it or give only a general assent to it in our judgments; therefore doth he pose her— " Believest thou this?" and thus should we daily pose our own hearts.

5. In particular, it is necessary that we be well grounded in the faith of getting life through Christ, and that we make special application of the general promise made by him concerning this, and that faith be not to seek in a pinch when Christ calls for it; for it is in these matters that he requires her to profess her faith— " Believest thou this?"

Ver. 27. She saith unto him, Yea, Lord: I believe that thou art the Christ, the Son of God, which should come into the world.

In the last place, we have Martha's answer to this question; wherein she assents unto what Christ had required her to believe, and adds a confession of her faith concerning his person and offices, which she professeth she hath believed before, as it is in the original. This she subjoins, not only as the ground of her faith in this particular, unto which she now assents, but her weak grip (as would appear) not being able expressly to apprehend all this which he hath spoken, though she assent unto it, therefore she passeth it in a word, and professeth her faith concerning his person and office, acknowledging him to be the promised Messiah, the Son of God, and consequently professeth she believeth all that may flow from this. Whence learn—

1. Weak faith may grow up to more clearness and assurance by conversing and conference with Christ, laying open our weaknesses to him, and receiving instructions from him; for her answer to Christ's question is, " Yea, Lord," affirming that she believed it, (though yet weakly,) and so

she is brought a further length than she had attained before, ver. 24.

2. In the matter of encouragements and promises the Lord hath so ordered it that some should be fundamentals, (such as the promise, I am thy God, the truths concerning Christ's person and offices, &c.,) which comprehend many promises in them; the rest being but a particular application of these generals to particular cases; as here her practice insinuates, recurring to this as a chief and comprehensive ground of comfort, that he is "the Christ," &c.

3. The consequences that flow *from* these fundamental encouragements and promises are so many and so full, that one who believeth the first may yet not see these consequences so clearly nor yet so firmly believe all that flows from it; for Martha (as would appear) cannot get all this so distinctly gripped [laid hold of], when yet she believes that he is "the Christ," &c., from which all of it necessarily flows. At least, this is clear, that she hath believed that he is "the Christ," &c., even when she doubted of this particular, which he calls her to believe. And this lets us see that they who believe these general encouragements have much more to be refreshed with than they have well considered, and that it is of God's rich love, condescending to our weakness, that he draws out these generals in particular promises, relating to our particular necessities.

4. When our faith staggers in any particular exigent, or proves weak in believing particular promises, it is our duty to recur to these general grounds of faith and encouragement, and hold them fast till we get more, and study the fulness that is in them, that we may be led on to more particular confidence; for such is her practice; whatever her former doubting or present weakness in believing were, yet she believes, and hath believed, that he is "the Christ," &c.

5. The studying of Christ's person and offices is a notable mean to confirm our faith in all the promises concerning all the benefits to be had in him; for this she layeth hold on for that end, "I believe that thou art the Christ, the Son of God, which should come into the world." The study of this will make us sure both of his good will, as Mediator, and power, as God, to do what he promiseth.

6. Christ is never rightly believed in, nor taken up, except he be acknowledged to be the Messiah promised unto the fathers, and the eternal Son of God; for so much doth her confession point out concerning him.

7. Christ was not unknown under the Old Testament, but was revealed and held forth in the promise; and accordingly the godly did close with him by faith, Acts, xv. 11; Heb. xiii. 8; Rev. xiii. 8; and as they saw him to be true God, so they did expect and wait for him to come into the world at the appointed time made of a woman, and so to be God and man in one person; for saith she, "Thou art the Christ, the Son of God, which should come into the world," intimating that he was revealed, and accordingly believed in, and expected by them before he came; and that they acknowledged him who was to "come into the world," by his being made flesh, to be God, "the Son of God."

8. All God's promises of and concerning the Messiah were fulfilled and accomplished in the person of Jesus Christ, the Son of Mary; for saith she of him now exhibited, "Thou art the Christ, the Son of God, which should come into the world," so that there is no other to be expected; and as this was true of his person, so all other predictions concerning the Messiah, in his life, death, resurrection, &c., were accomplished in him, as is frequently observed and recorded in the New Testament. And this may assure us that all God's promises shall be fulfilled in him to his people.

8. True faith in Christ will not judge of him by outward appearance, nor outward lots, but will pierce through all these clouds, and see his glory; for when he is in the form of a servant, and lately driven from Jerusalem, yet saith she, "I believe that thou art the Christ, the Son of God."

Ver. 28. And when she had so said, she went her way, and called Mary her sister secretly, saying, The Master is come, and calleth for thee.

Followeth the second antecedent of the miracle, after Christ was come near to Bethany, which is, his meeting and encounter with Mary, with some consequents that followed before he came to the grave, to ver. 38.

This may be taken up in six particulars, whereof the first (in this verse) is, the call given to Mary to come out to Christ. Martha, after the former conference, cometh to her sister (not of her own accord, but at Christ's command) to carry the news and message to her.

DOCTRINES.

1. Christ should be acknowledged, by all his own, to be their Master and Teacher, whose doctrine and direction they will follow; therefore is he designed by this common and acknowledged name among his followers, "The Master," or, Teacher.

2. Christ may be very near unto mourners and they not know of it, and they may be puzzled and perplexed for his absence when he is hard at hand; for while Mary is mourning at home, supposing that Christ is about Jordan, and grieving that he is not come, he is at her hand at Bethany: "The Master is come."

3. Albeit the tenderness and crushed condition of some may suspend their comfort from them, yet Christ will seek such at last, and not be at rest till he meet with them and comfort them; for it was by reason of Mary's crushed spirit that she is mourning still, and hears nothing of Christ, when Martha hath been comforted by him; yet Christ, knowing her distress, and that she is mourning, minds her, and will have her brought to him: He "calleth for thee."

4. Whoever they be that come to fetch a tender mourner to Christ, they come not of their own head, but have his allowance so to do; for so doth Martha tell this mourner, "The Master calleth for thee."

5. Such as have tasted of Christ's sweetness themselves are most fit messengers to invite others to him; for Martha is employed, after she hath met with Christ, and he hath fixed her faith on himself; "when she had so said, she went her way (being sent), and called her sister Mary," &c.

6. It may encourage mourners to come to Christ, that his respect to them is not suspended upon their coming, but he prevents them with warm invitations; for so will he have Mary encouraged: "The Master is come, and calleth for thee." (See Mark, x. 49.)

7. Such as have found Christ's tender kindness towards them will be tender of him and all that concerneth him; therefore doth she "call her sister secretly," lest these Jews who were with them, knowing of him, might bring him in some hazard. And albeit Christ himself was not afraid, yet it was very commendable that Christ's safety should lie near their heart whose necessity had brought him thither.

VER. 29. As soon as she heard that, she arose quickly, and came unto him.

30. Now Jesus was not yet come into the town, but was in that place where Martha met him.

In the second place is recorded Mary's obedience unto this call; she arose and went to him, where he yet stayed without the town.   Whence learn—

1. Whatever jealousy or prejudice mourners have at Christ's dealing, yet he will be still welcome news unto them, and they ought not to stay away from him; for though she was under the same tentation with Martha, yet she also arose and came to him.

2. News of Christ's approach will make fainting mourners revive, and be active to run and meet him; for she who sat drooping and faint in the house, as appears from ver. 20, 31, now, when "she heard that, she arose quickly, and came to him."

3. Such as have the opportunity of comfort from Christ will prefer him to all the comforts they can receive from friends; therefore "she arose quickly, and came to him," leaving all that were in the house comforting her.

4. In the days of Christ's flesh his calling went nearest his heart of anything, and he preferred the opportunities of doing good to all his own ease and accommodations; therefore it is marked as a reason why Mary went out unto him: "Jesus was not yet come into the town, but was in that place where Martha met him." He had not so much as entered the town to refresh himself, not for fear of the Jews, (for his hand and providence brings them out afterward, ver. 31,) but he chose this as a fit time and place to comfort Mary in, and his mind was upon working the miracle before he rested; and all this tends to shew what a faithful and merciful high priest he is, and how enlarged his heart is towards his people, when now he hath no particular necessity of his own to divert him.

VER. 31. The Jews then which were with her in the house, and comforted her, when they saw Mary, that she rose up hastily and went out, followed her, saying, She goeth unto the grave to weep there.

In the third place is recorded how the Jews who comforted her construed of her going out, as if she were going to weep at the grave, (as it seems this custom had crept in among them,) and therefore they follow her to interrupt her. Whence learn—

1. Such as are most tender, and most sensibly affected and burdened with trials, may expect not only greater sympathy from Christ, but also that (in so far as it is good for them) he will stir up other instruments, to take a more hearty lift at their condition; for so much appears in the practice of these Jews, who, perceiving Mary's greater need, sat with her in the house, and comforted her, and rose up hastily and followed her when she went out, whereas, it appears, they had taken little notice of Martha's going out or coming in.

2. It is a sinful practice of our nature to add to the burdens laid upon us by God, and feed our own sorrows by pensive thinking or looking upon that wherein God afflicts us; for their apprehension upon her going out intimates they had some such custom among them of going to graves "to weep there," that the sight of their loss might waken their sorrow.

3. It is no wonder to see the world and natural men mistake the ways of the godly, and to see even their natural comforters in trouble judge of them according to their own carnal principles and dispositions; for albeit there be no appearance that Mary had used this practice before, yet they misconstruct her going out: "She goeth unto the grave to weep there," not only because they knew not her calling to go to Christ, but this being nature's practice they could judge no better of her.

4. It is our duty to restrain carnal sorrow, if it were but by interrupting thereof, if we cannot be comforted under it; for so much doth their practice teach, they rose up hastily, and followed her, thinking to interrupt and scare her from her weeping, if she would not be recalled by them.

5. The Lord's providence doth ofttimes tryst [meet] men in following their ordinary duty with very unexpected favours; for while they are following Mary, to moderate her sorrows, providence leads them out to Christ, and to be witnesses of a glorious miracle.

6. There is much good to be gotten in the fellowship of the godly, and in studying to be steadable [useful] and comfortable to them in their distress; for it is in Mary's company, and while they are comforting her, they meet with this favour.

VER. 32. Then when Mary was come where Jesus was, and saw him, she fell down at his feet, saying unto him, Lord, if thou hadst been here, my brother had not died.

In the fourth place, Mary's discourse to Christ, when she met him, is recorded. It is the same regrate [reflection] which Martha had, ver. 21, only she expresseth it with great reverence and humility, and with much sorrow and many tears also, as appears from ver. 33, which it seems stopped the current of her speech, that she cannot declare anything concerning her faith, as Martha had done.

DOCTRINES.

1. The same tentation and groundless conceit that assaults one may also possess another; for Mary hath the same thoughts with Martha. It seems they conferred together about it, and so had strengthened one another in it, which is an usual fault among the godly; and as this was a tentation, so it is no wonder if Mary's tenderness were as much surprised with it as any; for albeit it be a fault, yet such weeds usually grow in best ground.

2. The more eminent any be in grace and acquaintance with Christ, the more humble and reverent will they be before Christ; for in this Mary outstrips Martha: "she fell down at his feet."

3. An humble and reverent saint will not be misconstructed of Christ under his fits of distemper; for by this she corrects her passionate speech, in that no prejudice nor tentation takes away her humble reverence; "she fell down at his feet, saying, Lord, if thou hadst been here, my brother had not died."

Ver. 33. When Jesus therefore saw her weeping, and the Jews also weeping which came with her, he groaned in the spirit, and was troubled,

34. And said, Where have ye laid him? They said unto him, Lord, come and see.

35. Jesus wept.

In the fifth place is recorded Christ's tender sympathy with Mary and her afflicted company in this strait, which leads him to the doing of the miracle. The occasion hereof is his observing of Mary's sorrow, with the sorrow of those who were in her company to comfort her. His carriage, or the expression of his sympathy upon this, consists in these:—1. "He groaned in the spirit, and was troubled," or, troubled himself, ver. 33. The word rendered groaning doth properly signify to have indignation, and consequently, strictly to charge under pain of displeasure; and so it may point out his indignation, not only at their weakness, evidenced in the way of their expressions to him, but chiefly against sin and Satan, that brought on all this misery; but certainly the root of all this was his tender respect to Lazarus, and to Mary's trouble and affliction. 2. Being thus affected he inquires for the grave, that he may give a proof of his sympathy, and being desired to come and see, he goeth on towards it, as appears from the following purpose, ver. 34. 3. Being in the way to the grave, the exercise of his spirit burst out in weeping, ver. 35.

From ver. 33, learn—1. Whatever be the expressions of any to Christ, yet the chief thing he looks to is what they express of an affected and sensible heart in that wherein they employ him; therefore, without heeding her language, it is remarked, he "saw her weeping."

2. It is commendable in men to be compassionate, and to join with friends in their sorrows; for the Jews are "also weeping which came with her."

3. None will prove able comforters of friends in distress but those who take deep impression of their sorrows; for those who came to comfort her, ver. 31, are also weeping with her.

4. Albeit Christ will respect the sorrows of any one mourner, yet it is a good token when the sorrows of many concur to plead with him for pity; for it is when he "saw her weeping, and the Jews also weeping with her," that his compassion bursts forth.

5. Christ will have some respect, even to the grief of natural men, joining with his people to lament their or his church's sorrows; for albeit these Jews were as yet unconverted, yet their weeping with Mary hath its own weight with him; he who respects the cry of young ravens and lions, Job, xxxviii. 41; Ps. civ. 21, and the mourning of a desolate land, Jer. xii. 11, doth certainly respect the sorrows of men, as they are men, and particularly when their sorrow is for a right cause.

6. Christ hath not only divine power, as God, to relieve his own, but as man also he hath compassion and a tender heart, to take an impression of their difficulties when they are affected with them, for weeping Mary meets with a tender, compassionate Christ here. And this may give saints boldness to come to him, Heb. iv. 15, 16, especially considering that we cannot have sorrow but he hath an eye to observe it, that he may sympathize, as Mary here finds; and it may make trouble sweet to us, considering that we have such a sympathizer.

7. Albeit Christ do not at first cure the troubles of his own, yet he doth sympathize with them under them. He will first put the afflicted in his heart, and then cure their disease; for here he first sympathizes, and then raiseth Lazarus. And in this respect he bare all the sicknesses which he cured, Matt. viii. 16, 17.

8. The difficulties of the Lord's people do not only waken up his affection to sympathize with them, but this his sympathy will burst forth in indignation against all their enemies and causes of their troubles; for so much also doth his groaning in the spirit import, that his indignation was kindled against Satan and sin, that drew on death and all this sorrow.

9. The nature of his commotion, and that he troubled himself, as it is in the original, doth teach—1. Christ our Lord was not muddy [confused] in his affections, nor overpowered by them; but he had them at his command. His commotions of mind were not only like the shaking of pure water in a clear glass, which still remains clear, but they arose and were calmed at his pleasure. And albeit this was proper and peculiar to himself, who was true God, and the spotless Lamb of God, yet if we were

more near him and like him, we should find our affections to be more servants and less masters; and without this, our very good affections are ofttimes so muddy [confused] that they mar us; our earnest desires after good are poisoned with impatient haste, and our very joy may mar believing, Luke, xxiv. 41. 2. Our Lord hath not those affections which are needful for his people's help far to seek, but they are ready to burst forth at his call; for when Mary's condition needs sympathy, he troubled himself; and so we, who need suitable affections and a right frame of spirit when many times we cannot attain them; yea, ofttimes our diligence in seeking them puts us further from them, by reason of our not taking a right way; if we could employ faith in him who can command these affections in himself, he could also soon give them unto us.

From verse 34, learn—1. Christ's tender affection and sympathy with his people will not lie hid in his heart, nor express itself only in some affectionate expressions, but will at last produce glorious actings for them; for the fruit of his groaning and trouble is, his inquiry for the grave, that he may raise Lazarus.

2. Christ takes pleasure to answer his people's necessities by deeds as well as by words, and (so to say,) to do and act his love, as well as to say it; yea, in great necessities he will not delay his people's help so long as even to comfort them by words; therefore, albeit it be his ordinary way to comfort his people, first by promises, Zech. i. 13, and then by actings, (and albeit he dealt so with Martha,) yet seeing Mary's great need, and his heart being weighed, he says no more, but will go to the action.

3. Albeit Christ will speedily help his needy people, yet he will so order his working as his glory may be most conspicuous in it; therefore, albeit he could have raised Lazarus, and made him come to them where they stood, and albeit he knew well enough where the grave was, yet he will inquire for it, and have them to conduct him to it, that so he may free this miracle from any suspicion of illusion, and may have them to be witnesses of his glory in it.

From verse 35, learn—1. As the Son of God did take on man's nature, and dwelt in our flesh, that he might lay a foundation of reconciliation betwixt God and man in his own person, so also he did take on these sinless affections and infirmities, which might not only prove him to be true man, but that he is a kindly brother and kinsman to miserable men, and might be a fit conduit to convey those bowels of compassion that are in God towards lost man; for so much is evidenced by his "weeping."

2. Christ, in the days of his flesh, was a man of sorrows and acquainted with griefs, that therein men might read the bitter fruits of sin, and they who flee to him may have matter of joy for ever; therefore it is marked, that "Jesus wept," which also was his frequent practice. (See Heb. v. 7.)

3. Christ hath no light touch of the miseries of his own, but they do deeply afflict and affect him; for he groans and is troubled, till he wept again.

4. Christ allows not that his affection and sympathy be hid from his afflicted people, but he would have them knowing it, and convinced of it; for therefore doth his groaning and trouble burst forth in " weeping," to be discerned by the beholders, as ver. 36.

5. Christ's tenderness and affection to his afflicted people will not long be hid or concealed, but it will burst forth through never so many clouds; for when he is troubled he will at last weep also in view of them all. Thus when he is dealing most harshly with the woman of Canaan, yet at last his heart cannot hide itself, Matt. xv. 22, &c. And in this, Joseph, in his dealing with his brethren, was a type of him.

6. Christ's inward exercise bursting forth in weeping may serve also further to teach—1. That all who get their bitter and sad exercise and sorrows suppressed, that they break not out to the dishonour of God, or weakening of the hands of others, have him to acknowledge, who, by venting his sorrows, both here and elsewhere, especially on the cross, Matt. xxvii. 46, hath shut up theirs. 2. That, on the other hand, when griefs and sorrows will not smother, that lot may be sanctified in his person, and we may have him for a companion who knoweth the heart of such an one.

Ver. 36. Then said the Jews, Behold how he loved him!

37. And some of them said, Could not this man, which opened the eyes of the blind, have caused that even this man should not have died?

The sixth particular recorded is the construction the Jews had of Christ's expressed sympathy; they, observing his sorrow, do admire his love to dead Lazarus, and marvel that he who had wrought such wonders might not also have prevented his death. It is most probable that they who admire his love were those Jews who were best affected to Christ, though they have not yet believed on him till afterwards, ver. 45, and that they who wonder he had not prevented his dying are those malicious Jews who, after the miracle, went and informed the rulers, ver. 46, and therefore the first sort are indefinitely named " the Jews" here, who are called many, ver. 45, and the other sort are, both here and ver. 46, called only some of them; or it may be conceived, that all of them concurring in wondering at his love to Lazarus, as a thing they could not deny, the more malicious sort do add that cavil and exception.

From verse 36, learn—1. Christ's love to his people is a very captivating and ravishing meditation; for that which took hold on them, and strikes them with admiration, is, "he loved him!" which was indeed a truth, that Christ, as he pitied Mary and her sister, so he respected Lazarus especially, and therefore burst forth in sorrow, through affection to him and them, and through indignation at Satan and sin, which drew on these miseries.

2. The fountain of any compassion shewed by Christ to his own in misery is not any worth in

them, but his own free love; for his compassionate weeping leads them up to his love as, the cause thereof.

3. Christ thinks no shame of his love to his people, but will avow it, and have it known sometimes to beholders; for he doth here so let it out as they mark it. (See Rev. iii. 9.)

4. Christ's sympathy and compassion towards his people proves his love to them, although they get not visible outgates from their troubles; for upon his weeping they gather "he loved him;" his sympathy and tears prove love, albeit the man died. And indeed, they who get a sight of Christ's tender heart will believe his love, whatever his dispensations be.

5. Christ's love and compassion is a wonder to them who know him not well; yea, it is in itself admirable, and such as see it will rather admire it than know how to comprehend it: "Behold (say they) how he loved him!" (See Eph. iii. 18, 19.)

6. Christ's love to his own will follow them even to their graves, as here he gives evidence "how he loved him" when he is lying in his grave. And albeit every saint do not meet with that proof of love which Lazarus got, in being raised up again, yet that love rests upon them till the general resurrection.

From verse 37, learn—1. Christ's love is readily misconstructed when he is letting it out most convincingly, and it is liker an enemy than a friend so to do; for there are here who indirectly carp at his love and the expressions of it, since he suffered the man to die.

2. Corrupt men, and the corrupt dispositions of men, will not readily believe Christ's love, unless it appear in some evidences and effects desired by them; for this is their indirect exception, that he caused not that "this man should not have died." Misconstructors of Christ's love are ordinarily limiters of his love, to be evidenced in such and such particulars.

3. Men may have much knowledge, and yet much malice against Christ; yea, knowledge is very dangerous if it be not sanctified and seasoned with grace and love; for these men can tell that he "opened the eyes of the blind," chap. ix. 6, and, it seems, are better acquainted with his proceedings than the others, and yet they carp at his love.

4. Christ hath given such proofs of his power as may convince malice itself that he can do greatest things for his people if it be for their good; for their reasoning grants that he which opened the eyes of the blind could have caused that this man should not have died.

5. When malice and prejudice hath said its worst against Christ's dealing it will be found in the end that he is doing better than we could desire; for all they could have expected was, that he should have caused that this man should not have died, which might have been done, and yet little of Christ or his love have been seen in it; for it might have been looked on only as a recovery out of a dangerous disease; whereas he is about to do that for Lazarus which sets forth his own glory, and makes his love to him conspicuous indeed.

Ver. 38. Jesus therefore again groaning in himself cometh to the grave. It was a cave, and a stone lay upon it.

Followeth, to verse 43, the antecedents of the miracle after Christ was come to the grave, which are, his rebuke of Martha's unbelief, which burst forth when he commanded to take away the stone upon the grave, ver. 39, 40, and his public thanksgiving to the Father after the stone was taken away, ver. 41, 42.

Unto these is premitted [introduced] in this verse—1. A declaration of his exercise in coming to the grave: he again groaned in himself, partly out of indignation at their unbelieving cavils, ver. 37, which he digested without answering; but chiefly this flowed from his sympathy and affection, which still continues, and is renewed at the sight of the grave; and it seems also that his praying, of which he gives so comfortable an account, ver. 41, drove him to these groans; for his prayers were very ardent, and he had hard exercise in them, Heb. v. 7, that he might be a fellow-feeler with all who tread these steps. 2. There is premitted [introduced] a description of the grave, which seems to be marked chiefly as an introduction to the following command to take away the stone.

DOCTRINES.

1. Christ our Lord was very serious in the works of his calling, and could be very serious about them, even in the midst of outward distractions; for in the midst of all this company, and while he is walking on in the way, he is exercised till he groan again.

2. Christ's compassion and sympathy is not an evanishing, passing thing, but will continue towards the needy till they get their issue; for he ceaseth not his groaning, but groaned again, in sympathy and prayer, till the work was done.

3. The unbelief of men, when Christ is about to do great things, is a grievous burden to him; for this groaning again relates also to their unbelief who were to be witnesses of this miracle, as is before marked. (See Mark, vi. 5, 6.)

4. Whatever be the desert of unbelief, yet Christ will not always be hindered by it to do good to the needy; but he will bear it as a part of our misery, and yet go on to his work; for he groaned in himself for it, and so cometh to the grave.

5. As decent and ordinary burial is in itself a mercy, and it is a judgment upon the wicked to want it, Jer. xvi. 4; xxii. 18, 19, so in the way of burial there is no respect to be had to superstitious conceits, nor yet to pomp and vainglory, but only that the dead be removed out of the sight of the living, Gen. xxiii. 4, and that their bodies be secured against external violence and injury, as being closed in hope of a resurrection; therefore it is marked of Lazarus's burial-place that it was only "a cave, and a stone lay upon it," that his body might not be violated nor injured.

Ver. 39. Jesus said, Take ye away the stone. Martha, the sister of him that was dead, saith unto him, Lord, by this time he stinketh: for he hath been dead four days.

40. Jesus saith unto her, Said I not unto thee, that, if thou wouldest believe, thou shouldest see the glory of God?

In these verses we have the first thing which occurred at the grave—to wit, a reproof of Martha's fit of unbelief, when Christ begins to prepare for the miracle. He commanding to remove the stone, her unbelief objects that it was needless, seeing he was so long dead, and it would raise a noisome smell now to open his grave, ver. 39; and he reproves this her unbelief, as being very odious, since he had given her a promise that upon her believing she should see the glory of God manifested in this miracle, ver. 40. Albeit we find not these express words mentioned by Christ, yet if we compare his general encouragement, ver. 4, with the doctrine he required her to believe, ver. 23, 25, 26, we shall find the same in substance.

From verse 39, learn—1. Whatever haste Christ make to relieve his needy people, yet he will so order his working as to take leisure to decipher the hidden unbelief that is in the hearts of any of his; therefore, when he cometh to the grave, he doth not at first raise the dead man, but takes time to have the stone taken away, that so Martha, (who very probably expected a very sudden miracle, or none at all,) seeing him employ no divine power, but only the help of men, to take away the stone, that he may look on a stinking body, may discover the unbelief of her heart.

2. Christ's miracles were such, and so clear, as all beholders might be witnesses of the truth of them, and that there was no juggling in the matter; therefore he who could have put away the stone, commands them, " Take ye away the stone," to prevent all suspicion of collusion or fraud in this matter.

3. Albeit the Lord's people may expect wonderful proofs of his power and love in their need, in so far as is for their good, yet in any distress we are not to expect that, where ordinary means may avail, Christ will work wonders and miracles for us; therefore, albeit he who could raise the dead could have also removed the stone, yet saith he to some about, " Take ye away the stone;" for that was a work which men could do, and therefore he will not appear in it; whereas none could raise the dead but himself.

4. When Christ is about to do good unto and for his people, they are ready to obstruct their own mercy by unbelief; as Martha's example doth teach.

5. In times of great strait saints may expect to have frequent and sore tossings, and that after their faith is settled they may yet be shaken of new [anew]; for Martha, whom Christ had brought to believe after her doubtings, doth now begin to doubt again.

6. Saints who have had their confidence fixed, when impediments are at a distance, may yet be in hazard of staggering when it comes to the push, and faith is to grapple with these impediments; for Martha, who closed her debate with Christ by believing, doth now doubt again, when the miracle comes to be done, and the grave to be opened.

7. It is a great impediment unto faith, and the exercise thereof, when either new impediments, not foreseen, do come in, and make a new battle, or when carnal reason bears sway in the heart, and judgeth of all things according to its discerning; for both of these concur here in her doubting; she had not thought, in her former conference, of this impediment, and her reason suggests that it was to no purpose to meddle with a man who " stinketh" in the grave.

8. When the Lord is bringing the difficulties of his people nearest an end, he may then give unto them most humbling discoveries of their own unbelief and distrust ever to see an issue, that so he alone may have the glory of bringing it about; for immediately before the miracle is wrought, Martha's unbelief doubts if ever it shall be.

9. Such is the frailty and loathsomeness of men's bodies, that however they have beauty and vigour while the soul possesseth and acteth them, yet a few days' separation of the soul by death will alter them so that dearest friends cannot endure them; therefore saith she, " By this time he stinketh," and that albeit "he hath been dead (but) four days."

From ver. 40, learn—1. God doth so order the affairs and conditions of his people as his glory may be manifested in and about them, and this is his chief aim and end in all he doth; therefore doth he describe the miracle from this, as his chief end in it, that it is a manifestation of " the glory of God."

2. It is the duty of the Lord's people to be more affected with the glory of God shining in his works than with any particular advantage redounding to them thereby; therefore, also, doth he hold out " the glory of God," to be seen in this miracle, as rather to be taken notice of by her than the raising up of her brother.

3. It may encourage God's people to expect the performance of his promise, how impossible soever it seem, that by so doing he will not only do them good, but will get occasion of setting forth his own glory, and that his glory is engaged to do them good; for this, further, is imported in this designation of the miracle as a manifestation of " the glory of God," that since his glory is engaged, she needs not be so anxious.

4. The way prescribed by God, wherein saints may meet with experimental manifestations of his glory, for their good and comfort, is first to give him glory by believing him and his word, the want whereof doth justly provoke him not to let forth himself; for " if thou wouldest believe, thou shouldest see the glory of God." (See Mark, vi. 6; Matt. xiii. 58; Luke, i. 20, 45; John, i. 50.)

5. Albeit faith for present have many disadvantages to grapple with, yet the sweet fruits that will follow upon believing may invite us to believe that we may partake of them; for albeit now the stinking body of her brother do mar her faith, yet it pleads strongly for faith, that if in that case she will hazard to believe, her believing shall lead her to " see the glory of God."

6. Faith's ground, whereupon it may thus hazard and expect this fair fruit, is God's word,

and not carnal reason; for I said unto thee, and therefore thou shouldst believe, to see.

7. Where God hath passed his word, and it is not credited, there is just ground of sharp rebuke and challenge; therefore saith he, " Said not I unto thee, that, if thou wouldest believe, thou shouldest see?" (See Numb. xxiii. 19.)

8. Albeit unbelief go masked ofttimes under a fair show of humility, or the like commendable disposition, yet in Christ's account it is an evil not to be tolerated, but sharply reproved, and an evil that should be quickly removed, that it get not leave to take root; therefore doth he so sharply and so speedily rebuke it.

Ver. 41. Then they took away the stone from the place where the dead was laid. And Jesus lifted up his eyes, and said, Father, I thank thee that thou hast heard me.

42. And I knew that thou hearest me always: but because of the people which stand by I said it, that they may believe that thou hast sent me.

The second antecedent at the grave is his thanksgiving to the Father after the stone was taken away, and before he wrought the miracle. Those who were commanded, ver. 39, taking away the stone, which it seems they had intermitted, till Martha's unbelief, interrupting them, was reproved, he (who had been praying to the Father) doth now—1. Publicly give him thanks for hearing him in this matter, ver. 41. 2. He gives a reason why he published this thanksgiving, which was, not because it was unusual for him to be heard who was never refused in any suit, but that those who were present might be convinced that he is the Mediator sent and approved of the Father, ver. 42. Christ's making use of prayer in this miracle doth nothing cross what was marked on ver. 22, 25, of his doing these things by his own power; for as God, he is a principal efficient, as man, he is the instrument of the godhead, and as Mediator, he acts as the Father's servant. And albeit he had spoken before of his own power as God, yet he chooseth rather to take this way before the people, to manifest that he was owned and approved by God, and not contrary to him, as the Jews gave it out.

From verse 41, learn—1. Unbelief in any of the Lord's people is not only their own sin, but when it breaks forth it is also a stumbling-block to others in their going on in their duty; for Martha's exception had hindered the men, and, it seems, drawn them to doubt with her, " Then (to wit, when she is reproved and passeth from it, and not till then) they took away the stone from the place where the dead was laid."

2. It is an evidence that the people of God have quitted their unbelief, or are not mastered with it, when they silence their reasonings and exceptions, and do not suffer unbelief to impede obedience to commanded duties; for this is the evidence that Martha is satisfied, in that she reasons no more, and in that she puts no new impe-

diments to hinder the removing of the stone, as Christ had commanded.

3. Such things as we do earnestly desire we ought to pray seriously for them to God; as Christ's practice doth teach us, who had been praying about this miracle, as is here imported.

4. Honest and sincere prayer will afford matter of praise; and men need not make much show or noise of their seeking of God, for God will openly reward them by public testimonies of his favour, calling for praise; for herein also hath our surety led the way, who praying in secret among the crowd, gets matter of public praise, and hath the fruits of the prayer appearing in the subsequent miracle.

5. Sincere seekers of God may know that their prayers are heard, albeit the thing sought be not as yet performed; for Christ acknowledgeth he is " heard," although the miracle was not yet wrought. And albeit he knew this in a peculiar way, yet saints also have rules whereby to discern this, John, xvi. 23; 1 John, v. 14.

6. God's hearing of prayer obligeth us to praise; and all those who know their need, and the mercy of God respecting their cry in their need, will not fail to make conscience of praise; for so doth his practice teach us, " I thank thee that thou hast heard me." (See Psalm l. 15.)

7. As those who expect and desire their prayers to be heard in mercy should make sure an interest in God, and that they are his children, so God's hearing of his people's prayers is a sweet confirmation of that interest, and this should be fed upon with a warm and thankful acknowledgment of that relation; for so doth Christ's example teach, who in this thankful account of his Father's answer expresseth this sweet relation, " Father, I thank thee that thou hast heard me," as indeed he was his Father in a special manner, and did give signal proofs thereof, in hearing him as Mediator.

8. Christ's people are so dear to him, that not only do their necessities call him to prayer for them, but his being heard in their behalf doth affect and oblige him, as if it were for himself; for he doth here not only pray, but accounts it matter of praise when he is heard.

9. Such as are rightly employed in spiritual duties, their heart and affections will be towards God and heavenward; and these affections will carry the outward man with them in so far as is convenient; for in this thanksgiving, " Jesus lifted up his eyes" to testify where his heart was. And albeit in his prayer we find neither words nor any such signs used, because it was secret, yet now, in this public thanksgiving, he will edify the hearers by this very outward directing of the eye.

From ver. 42, learn—1. Christ is a Mediator who continueth constant in the exercise of intercession for his own; for if he be heard always, then he prayeth always.

2. Such is the conformity betwixt the Father and the Mediator's will, and so strictly hath the Father obliged himself to his Son undertaking that office, that all he prays for is granted; for " thou hearest me always."

3. It is a special favour not only to be heard of God, but to know and be satisfied that it is so,

that we be not crushed under mistakes; therefore Christ publisheth it as a part of that favour to him as Mediator, " I know that thou hearest me always." (See 1 Cor. ii. 12 ; 1 John, v. 15.)

4. It concerneth the children of men to understand well how great acceptance Christ hath with the Father, that so it may deter them from coming in opposition to him, and may invite them to employ him who cometh such speed in their affairs; for this was his end in publishing this his success, not only to lay before them a pattern of duty in the like cases, as is marked on ver. 41, but chiefly, that he may be known. " But because of the people which stand by, I said it, that they may believe."

5. We do then take up Christ comfortably when not only we see his own affection and respect to us, but when we see him one with the Father and his ambassador, and that the Father is well pleased and to be found in him; for this is it he would have gathered from his acceptance in prayer, " That they may believe that thou hast sent me," and for this cause he chooseth rather to take this way than only to manifest his own power in this.

Ver. 43. And when he thus had spoken, he cried with a loud voice, Lazarus, come forth.

44. And he that was dead came forth, bound hand and foot with graveclothes: and his face was bound about with a napkin. Jesus saith unto them, Loose him, and let him go.

In these verses we have the second part of the chapter, containing the miracle itself, which is shortly done; for Christ calling on the dead man, as if he were alive, to come forth, he cometh out in the same posture wherein he was laid in his grave, and Christ requires some to loose him, that so they might be further confirmed of the truth of the miracle. Whence learn—

1. The upshot and close of Christ's dealing will richly compense all his delays and seeming harsh dealing ; for the issue of all this procedure in the former part of the chapter is, that Lazarus is raised again.

2. Albeit Christ may, in his people's trouble, take much time to exercise and prepare them for mercy, and to let out proofs of his compassion and sympathy, yet when that is done he can give an issue and help them in a moment; for now, when all these are over here, the miracle is presently dispatched. " And when he had thus spoken," and tried disciples and friends, removed their unbelief, manifested his own affectionate heart, &c., " he cried," &c.

3. Christ's word of command, whereby the world was created and is upheld, is sufficient to effectuate greatest things, if it were even to raise the dead ; for he did no more in bringing about this miracle, but cried, &c.

4. His crying " with a loud voice," in the audience of all, was not only an evidence of his omnipotency, and that, as he employed the Father, so also he put forth his own power in this miracle ; but further, it points out—1. His affection and earnestness to have the thing done, and sheweth that Christ is not a coldriffe [pretended] friend, but takes a hearty lift in what concerns his people. 2. It points out his confidence in the matter, and therefore he publicly enterpriseth it in the hearing of all, to teach that whatever our unbelieving hearts say, yet Christ is not afraid of his work, that it shall miscarry in his hand.

5. Christ in employing his omnipotency doth not look on things as they are in themselves, or seem to be unto us, but he calleth those things that are not as though they were, and in speaking to and commanding the powerless and dead, he giveth them life and strength to obey, for he cried, " Lazarus, come forth." His omnipotency speaks to him as to one living, and ready to come forth on a call, because at this very word he put life in him to hear and obey. (See Rom. iv. 17.)

6. Christ hath our life in his hand, to take it away or restore it at his pleasure, and when he calls even for the dead they will obey him, for " he that was dead came forth."

7. Whatever enjoyments men have within time, yet it is but little of these things they can take away with them ; for it is marked that he came out bound with graveclothes, and his face bound about with a napkin; not so much to point out a new miracle in the bosom of the other that a dead man should not only come out, but come out so bound as might hinder one to walk,—for it may easily be conceived that the bonds were so loose as he might creep one way or other out, and he knew the place better than to go wrong, though his face was covered,—but the scope, in part, is to point out how little Lazarus had carried away with him, even "graveclothes." (See 1 Tim. vi. 7.)

8. As Christ our Lord will work no needless miracles, so he will have all convinced of the reality of those he worketh ; therefore also will he bring him out in his graveclothes, and bids them " loose him, and let him go," that he may walk at freedom, that so they might see him bound as they had laid him in, and themselves, in handling and loosing him, might be further confirmed that it was a true miracle ; as also (as was marked on ver. 39) he would not loose him by a miracle, since men's hands could do that.

Ver. 45. Then many of the Jews which came to Mary, and had seen the things which Jesus did, believed on him.

46. But some of them went their ways to the Pharisees, and told them what things Jesus had done.

Followeth the third and last part of the chapter, containing some consequents and effects of this miracle, which may be taken up in these :— 1. What effects it had on the Jews who were with Mary, ver. 45, 46. 2. The consultations and conclusions of the rulers of the Jews, when they are informed of it, ver. 47—53. 3. The course which Christ took on this their resolution, ver. 54.

4. The diligence used by the rulers to have their resolutions put in execution at the feast, ver. 55—57. As for what was the part and carriage of Lazarus and his sisters upon the receipt of this mercy, it pleaseth the Lord to mention no more of it than what may be gathered from their piety, that they were not unthankful, and from his passing it over in silence, not that he did vilipend [vilify] it, but that great mercies will affect his people more than can be well said or expressed.

In these verses we have the first consequent of the miracle, which is, the diverse impressions it takes upon the Jews who were present; many of them believing and others of them persisting in unbelief; and not being able to do unto Christ what they would themselves, they delate [report] the matter to the Pharisees. Whence learn—

1. Christ doth not spread his net by doctrine and working, but for some notable fruit and effect; for here by raising up of one dead body he raiseth up many dead souls.

2. Albeit, for the most part, the generality are naught, yet at some times and in some societies it pleaseth him to work upon and gain the far greater part; for " many of the Jews believed," whereas " some" only, ver. 48, do persist in their ill course.

3. Such as come to do good unto the godly in their need may readily meet with more good to themselves by the means; for they " came to Mary," who find Christ, and are drawn to believe. It is said they came to Mary only because they came out to the grave after her, ver. 31; or because, however they came out of Jerusalem to comfort both her and Martha, ver. 19, yet they did it chiefly for Mary's sake.

4. Such as do rightly consider of Christ's glorious workings and manifestations unto and for his people may be abundantly convinced that he is the true Messiah, and see convincing grounds wherefore they should embrace and close with him by faith; for when they " had seen the things which Jesus did," (not only the miracle, for that alone could not work solid faith, though it might prepare for it, but his groaning, weeping doctrine, thanksgiving, the way of the miracle, &c.,) they " believed on him."

5. When Christ is prevailing fastest, yet his doctrine and working will never be well taken at all hands; for " some of them" are of another temper.

6. Not only the prevalent example of many will not work upon the obstinate, but their (other ways) good and moral principles will not contribute to draw them to Christ; for not only stand they out, being a few, when many yield, but though they had compassion to let out for a godly Mary and Martha, yet they will not embrace Christ.

7. The most glorious actings of Christ will be so far from prevailing with the obstinate that they will rather become the worse of them; for what greater act could there be than what Christ did here? and yet they are enraged, and make it a dittay [an accusation] against him

8. Albeit wicked men may pretend many prejudices against Christ and his dealing, wherefore they cannot embrace him, yet when all these are removed they will be nothing the better; for it was their great exception against Christ's love to Lazarus that he had not prevented his death, ver. 37, yet when that is removed in a glorious way they are not gained.

9. Albeit many who malign Christ have but small power to hurt him, yet, were their horns never so short, they will have them out against him; for they cannot hurt Christ themselves, but they will set others on work to do it.

10. Such as are prime agents against Christ, he will plague them with much employment of that kind, to fill up their cup; for " the Pharisees" must be told, that they may appear in this business.

11. Such as do instigate and stir up others to persecute, or do debate the godly to their malicious enemies, are in effect cruel persecutors; for it is marked as the evidence of their malicious disposition, that they went " to the Pharisees, and told them what things Jesus had done."

12. Christ can make use even of the malice of his enemies to make them publishers of his glory and praise; for their malice led them to tell the Pharisees " what things Jesus had done," and so there was no need of his friends to publish and confirm the truth of this miracle at Jerusalem.

VER. 47. Then gathered the chief priests and the Pharisees a council, and said, What do we? for this man doeth many miracles.

48. If we let him thus alone, all men will believe on him: and the Romans shall come and take away both our place and nation.

The second consequent of the miracle is the carriage of the rulers, being exasperated upon this information. It contains four particulars, the first whereof (in these verses) is their convening in council, and consulting upon the matter; wherein they propound the case, that Christ did many miracles, and the danger that would ensue if they took no course with him; that Christ, being so popular by reason of his miracles, will draw the people after him, and hereby will incense the Romans, and make them destroy the temple and their nation, seeing the people will be ready to move sedition and to cry up Christ as a king of David's progeny; and therefore they wonder at one another that they do nothing in the matter, and inquire at one another what to do.

From ver. 47, learn—1. Christ's enemies are very ready to receive delations [accusations] against him, and the more they see or hear that his glory shines they grow the worse; for when this is delated they are in a rage.

2. It is no strange thing to see authority and power against Christ, and to see even churchmen in the judicatories appointed by him plotting the ruin of him and his kingdom; for " the chief priests and the Pharisees gathered a council," (the sanhedrin of old, appointed by God,) that they may devise means to destroy him. By this the Lord would discover that there is no infallibility in men or judicatories, and would teach that he can carry on his work, albeit au-

thority and judicatories be against him; and that he ofttimes doth so that he alone may have the glory, whereas, otherwise, too much would be given to men. Those who met, or at least gathered and convened the council, are called "the chief priests," not only the high priest and his deputy,—or possibly also those who by courses succeeded in the high priesthood in that time of corruption, wherein that office was exposed to sale, as histories do record,—but it comprehends also the heads of the twenty-four orders of priests instituted by David, 1 Chron. xxiv. To these are joined " the Pharisees," which was the name of a sect among them; and they are named, not because none of these priests were of that sect, but to shew that other Pharisees, who had place in the council, did most frequently convene, as being the most bitter enemies to Christ.

3. Wicked persecutors are ordinarily so far from repenting their cruelty that they are angry they are so slow and not more violent; for notwithstanding all their former violence against Christ, yet " What do we ?" say they, or, Are we sleeping ?

4. The Lord's power and wisdom are so eminently employed about Christ, his truth, and people, that when persecutors have done their utmost they will find they have made small progress as to gaining of their purpose; for this, " What do we ?" imports also, that however they had opposed him all along, had traduced him and his ministry, banished him, endeavoured to ensnare him, sought to take him, &c., yet in effect they had promoved nothing as to hindering of him in his ministry, or the success thereof; and it will be thus still, even when they go a further length. (See Exod. i. 12.)

5. Albeit the wits of men may justle one against another, yet all their wit shall have enough to do when they employ it against Christ, and persecution shall be a task to perplex them, were they never so wise; for " What do we ?" imports also an anxious perplexity and irresolution what to do for the future, as may appear from Caiaphas's taxing their ignorance, ver. 49, 50. (See 1 Cor. i. 25 ; Prov. xxi. 30.) And albeit the saints may be also perplexed in God's way, for their humiliation, and that they may depend on God, 2 Chron. xx. 12, yet it is a judgment on wicked men in evil courses.

6. Whatever the enemies of Christ and his people do say and give out to the world, yet many of them may be and are inwardly convinced in their consciences that those whom they persecute are innocent and doers of good; for notwithstanding their many cavillations in public against Christ and his miracles, yet here, in their cabin council, they are forced to acknowledge he " doeth many miracles," and they have no evil to say of him. (So also Acts, iv. 16.) Christ was indeed thus innocent, and all Christians ought to study it, as being a great advantage to have such a testimony in the bosom of enemies, whatever effect it take.

7. Whatever be the innocency of Christ and his followers, or the convictions of bloody persecutors, yet ordinarily they take little effect; they neither heighten their estimation of the in-

nocent nor abate their rage against them; for though they acknowledge this, yet he is but " this man," by way of contempt, and they go on in their bloody resolutions against him.

From verse 48, learn—1. When Christ's kingdom begins to flourish in any measure, it is to be expected that carnal men, and especially corrupt churchmen, will raise a fire of persecution as the only remedy they know to blast it; for say they, " If we let him thus alone" all will go to ruin; and therefore they must persecute.

2. When Christ's enemies are pleased to speak out their minds plainly, it will be found that their interests and worldly state is their great idol, and that which drives them to persecute Christ; for this is their fear in substance, that they will lose their reputation by the people's leaving them and following of him, and that if their nation ruin, their power will be gone.

3. Persecutors do look on Christ's success with an envious eye, and in a multiplying glass, that so it may whet their malice against him; for when some few have believed, they take them up as so many that if he continue awhile " all men will believe on him," in which experience proved there was but too little truth.

4. Whatever be the real idols and interests of persecutors, yet they will labour to cover them with pretences of public good and safety; for albeit their own reputation and places swayed most with them, yet they give out this for their colour, " The Romans shall take away both our place (the temple that is dear to us, as what is our own) and nation."

5. It is the usual policy of persecutors to decline, by all means, to oppose Christ in his kingdom as Christ, and truth as truth; but they labour to colour the quarrel with some specious pretences, that so they may hide the odiousness of their course from others, and blind their own eyes, that they may not see they are fighting against God ; for they will persecute Christ, not as the Messiah, but as one who would bring ruin upon them by the Romans,—as Christ was called a Samaritan, a blasphemer, and one that had a devil, and then they did persecute him as such an one; and as of old Christians were covered with the skins of wild beasts, that dogs and lions might tear them more greedily, so is it still with Christians and truth; they suffer under odious imputations that it may seem more just to persecute them; they are called hypocrites, and under that cloak piety is hated, truth is called error, treason, and what not, and then suppressed.

6. It is the unjust prejudice and erroneous principle of many (and especially of statesmen and rulers) against Christ and his kingdom, that it is inconsistent with the safety of the nation and state where it is admitted; and the pretence of a necessity and interest of state is an old engine for bearing down Christ and religion; for this in particular is their pretence of not letting Christ alone: " All men will believe on him, and the Romans shall come and take away both our place and nation."

7. It is hellish injustice against Christ and his kingdom to father any miseries on a nation where he is received, on him or it; or to cut and carve upon religion and his kingdom so as men think

may best contribute to the safety of their worldly interests; for in both these they injure him. His doctrine allowed of no sedition, nor did he lay claim to a worldly kingdom; the receiving of Him by whom kings reign is the way to uphold states and nations, and any calamities that follow upon the gospel are not the fruits of the gospel, but of men's own sins, who make not use of such a jewel. And, on the other hand, it is their injustice that they will not consult what is right or wrong, duty or sin, in this matter, but what is profitable or hurtful, and that they will not admit of Christ if he contribute not to their standing; whereas, though the Romans should have destroyed them upon that account, yet what was that, if it were their duty, and they were in the way of God?

8. Such as bend their wits to find out indirect and sinful courses, whereby they may avoid feared trouble and establish themselves, it is righteous with God to make these same courses bring their fear upon them; and particularly they who seek to establish their own estate and power by the overthrow of Christ's kingdom do take the compendious way to establish his kingdom and overthrow their own; for they know no way to suppress Christ and save themselves from the Romans but to persecute him; and in the issue this advanced Christ's interest, and, in God's righteousness, drew the Romans upon them some few years thereafter.

Ver. 49. And one of them, named Caiaphas, being the high priest that same year, said unto them, Ye know nothing at all,

50. Nor consider that it is expedient for us, that one man should die for the people, and that the whole nation perish not.

Secondly. In the carriage of these rulers we have recorded what was Caiaphas's overture for preventing this danger. He propounds, very imperiously, a common rule of policy, that in a case of danger it is expedient one should be cut off for the good of a nation rather than the whole nation perish; and that therefore Christ was to be cut off, that so the nation might be freed of that hazard. This counsel and principle (beside what God intended in it, of which afterward) may have its own truth in it; that in the case of danger to a nation or society one is bound to prefer the safety of the whole to his own particular safety, or that justice is to be executed on a particular malefactor lest the neglect thereof make his sin national and bring judgments on a land; but this doth not at all justify the putting of an innocent man to death for the safety of any, (for that were to sin to avoid trouble,) far less doth it justify it when men do hereby not only cut off the innocent, but do not avoid, but in effect draw on ruin on the nation. He who gave the counsel is described from his office, that he was high priest, of which use is to be made in the following purpose; only what is added (that he was " the high priest that same year") points at the corruption crept in among them (as is recorded in history) in these latter times, in that

the office—which by God's appointment was astricted to the family of Aaron, and to continue during life—was either usurped by those who had most power extending the possessors, and held so long as they could, or was purchased by favour or money of their conquerors for so long time as pleased them, or they did agree upon. Their own ambition begot these practices under the Grecians, and that, together with Herod's policies, and afterwards the avarice of the Romans did continue them. And he is said to have been only for " that same year," because it had been the custom of the Romans, immediately before his election, to change them yearly; and however some might continue longer, yet it seems the paction was but from year to year. As to what further may be said concerning his office, and Annas being joined with him before, Luke, iii. 2, it may be spoken to, if need be, on chap. xviii. 13.

DOCTRINES.

1. As the most pure ordinances of God are easily corrupted by lewd men, so in particular the ambition of men, taking advantage of times of public confusion and oppression, doth ofttimes overturn the precious government and order of his house, while either they do what they list and is in the power of their hand, or employ their power with oppressors to make merchandize of the things of God; for thus and upon these grounds was the ordinance of the priesthood corrupted, while men either usurped it, or did serve the interests of, or gave money to, their conquerors to obtain it.

2. As men's wisdom, or their conceit of it, doth ordinarily fill them with pride and contempt of others, so such wit will readily never do well, nor lead men on right courses; for he gives his opinion, insulting over the rest, as knowing nothing at all, nor considering, when yet his wit led him only to crucify Christ.

3. Such as corrupt the ordinances of God, and take sinful courses to put themselves in power in God's house, will prove but small friends to Christ and his kingdom, whatever they seem otherwise to be; for it was he who procured himself to be " the high priest that same year" that gave this pernicious counsel against Christ.

4. Albeit it be the duty of all to prefer the public welfare of a church or nation to their own safety or interests, yet it is unlawful to promote never so public a good by sinful means; for herein did his opinion prove unsound in seeking to prevent the perishing of the nation.

5. It is a sinful principle in worldly policy to study to preserve the peace of a nation by cutting off those who promote the kingdom of Christ; for this in particular was the sin of his counsel, that albeit they had nothing to say against Christ, yet better he perish, were he never so good or right, than things should be in hazard; whereas, albeit this might have indeed preserved them, yet it was not a lawful mean.

6. Men's wit will never lead them right so long as they separate profit and expedience from lawfulness and right, and do prefer the one before the other; for in all this he looks only to what " is expedient for us."

7. The rarest wits of men, when they are left of God, and do make no conscience of sin to compass their designs, will but miscarry, and run upon the dangers they labour most carefully to avoid; for though this seemed most "expedient," and a short cut to be rid of Christ and secure the nation, yet neither succeeded with them; Christ and his doctrine prevailed still among them, and their nation did perish.

Ver. 51. And this spake he not of himself: but being high priest that year, he prophesied that Jesus should die for that nation;

52. And not for that nation only, but that also he should gather together in one the children of God that were scattered abroad.

In the third place, before the acceptation of this overture be recorded, John doth interlace some remark upon this opinion, wherein, 1. He points forth the hand of God overruling him in bringing out such a discourse, ver. 51. It is said, he spake this not of himself, but he prophesied, &c. The meaning is, not that he knew not what he would have been at in this opinion, or that he intended that by Christ's death Israel should be indeed redeemed from sin, or intentionally prophesied of him,—it is clear enough that he purposed nothing else but to put Christ out of the way, that there might be no occasion for the Romans to fall upon the nation,—but the meaning is, that in giving his wicked counsel to procure the safety of his nation from the Romans by putting Christ to death, God overruled his tongue to bring out an oracle concerning his purpose to save his people by the death of Christ. 2. John enlargeth this prophesy which Caiaphas uttered unawares, ver. 52, shewing that, in God's purpose, the benefits of Christ's death were to be extended further than to the nation of the Jews only, even to all the elect scattered through the world. It is further to be considered, that John's saying, being high priest, he prophesied, &c., doth make nothing at all for their opinion who assert the infallibility and assistance of the Spirit with popes, even albeit they be wicked men, such as Caiaphas was, who yet, being high priest, did prophesy concerning the death of Christ; for— 1. They have not yet proven from scripture that their popes have that warrant for their office, nor any of those divers privileges which the high priest of the Jews had. 2. The high priests of the Jews, even when they observed God's order in coming to it, albeit sometimes some of them did prophesy, and for a time they had the extraordinary gift of Urim and Thummim, yet they fell in gross errors; Aaron made the golden calf, Urijah brought in an altar after the pattern of that in Damascus, 2 Kings, xvi. 10, 11. 3. Since this man came not in an orderly way to his office, if they will argue from this, it will follow that not only their popes, whom they account to be lawfully chosen, but even their antipopes, whom they condemn, must have the same privilege of infallibility. 4. Such a prophecy as this doth indeed very well beseem them who sit in the tem-

ple of God as gods, and yet are bitter enemies to Christ and his truth; for he did not intentionally bring forth anything for Christ's advantage, only God overruled his tongue, in venting his wicked malice, that he should propound this oracle. 5. His being high priest is added, not as a reason why he did prophesy, (though some of them of old might have had revelations, and God may, when he pleaseth, even employ a wicked man that way,) but to shew that, because of his authority and place, which would readily incline the rest to follow him, therefore God overruled his tongue, that he should bring forth no overture concerning Christ but what was agreeable to his purpose in sending his Son into the world.

From these verses, learn—1. God's overruling hand can secure that in the consultations of men nothing shall be concluded concerning Christ or his church but what he hath appointed to be done; for so did he overrule this consultation and Caiaphas's overture. (See Acts, iv. 27, 28.)

2. The more power and sway any wicked men have, the more we are bound to believe that the overruling hand and providence of God will set bound and limits to their consultures and conclusions for the good of his church; for whereas it might be little regarded what others might say whose opinions were of less weight, yet when the high priest begins to speak, God overrules it, that he shall prophesy and utter an oracle.

3. In believing God's providence watching for his people's good, we are not to look to the intentions of men, nor to their malicious projects, but we ought to believe that even in these God overrules them to do nothing but what is for good; for he knew not that he was prophesying, nor intended any such thing, but was letting out the bitterest of his malice against Christ, and yet even then "he prophesied;" God overruled his malicious counsel that his purpose should be carried on thereby, and his tongue in uttering thereof, that it should be, in effect, an oracle.

4. The nation of the Jews, as they had the first offer of the death of Christ, and of the benefits flowing therefrom, so they have a special interest therein, to be manifested in due time; for it is an oracle, "that Jesus should die for that nation"—that is, his own in it.

5. Whatever be the interest of the Jews in the Messiah and his sufferings, yet God's intentions in giving him to die, and the fruits of his death, do extend further than to that nation; for so doth John guard this, "and not for that nation only." And by his correcting of this he intimates how sweet the calling of the gentiles was to him, and therefore he will not have it omitted; and how sweet the death of Christ and benefits thereof were in his account, that he will not suffer that Caiaphas should speak thereof too disadvantageously without correcting of him.

6. Albeit Christ's death, and the benefits thereof, be extended to all nations, yet not to all and every one in these nations, but only to his own elect; for they are "the children of God" only for whom he dies.

7. Such as Christ hath died for are by nature and in themselves in as bad a condition as any, being scattered and separated from God and Christ, and from the church, and one from an-

other; for they are "scattered abroad," not so much in respect of place (though that was true also), for there is no gathering of them into one place, as in respect of their state and condition, whereof their being gentiles, scattered up and down the world, was a badge and evidence, Eph. ii. 11—13.

8. Whatever be the state and condition of God's elect before conversion, yet in respect of his decree and purpose they are his children; as here they are called "the children of God."

9. Such as are elected and redeemed by Christ will be converted and brought near into the society of the church, if they have been pagans by state, and gathered together with all the rest of his people in one head, that so they may make up one body; for he shall "gather together in one the children of God."

10. As Christ is the purchaser of redemption for his elect, so he is the applier of his own purchase, and he who actually converts and brings them to enjoy the benefits of his death; for it is he who shall gather them together in one.

VER. 53. Then from that day forth they took counsel together for to put him to death.

The last thing recorded concerning these rulers and their carriage is the issue and conclusion of their consultation and debates—to wit, that agreeing to Caiaphas's opinion, they plot and contrive how to get it executed. Whence learn—

1. Church judicatories may not only err, but conclude most cruel things against Christ and his kingdom, as here we see.

2. An evil counsel against Christ is best heard, and gets most general applause among wicked men; for Caiaphas's overture prevails, "to put him to death."

3. Wicked men are not only assaulted with violent tentations, as the godly may be, but they come to maturity in them; for they conclude on persecution.

4. Wicked men are so hot on mischief, that having once concluded it, they are restless till it be executed; for "from that day they took counsel together for to put him to death"—that is, they concluded it, and set themselves to find out all means to make their conclusion take effect. They had essayed it before in a tumultuous way, but they do now orderly conclude it, and vigorously prosecute it.

VER. 54. Jesus therefore walked no more openly among the Jews; but went thence unto a country near to the wilderness, into a city called Ephraim, and there continued with his disciples.

In the third consequent of this miracle is recorded what was Christ's carriage upon their conclusion—to wit, that he withdrew himself to a more solitary and barren place, where he continued with his disciples till the time came that he was called to yield himself. The city Ephraim is only mentioned here and 2 Sam. xiii. 23. It

is conceived to have stood on the borders betwixt the tribes of Ephraim and Benjamin, having that Baal-hazor, 2 Sam. xiii., towards the east, and Ai (of which Josh. vii.) towards the west of it. And this wilderness, or more desert ground, may be conceived to be that running from Ai towards Gilgal, (and so by Ephraim,) of which mention is made, Josh. viii. 15

DOCTRINES.

1. Christ's enemies, in their most secret consultations, will not get a stroke stolen on him, but he knows all their projects and conclusions, and how to order his affairs accordingly; for his fleeing on that ground evidenceth that he was not ignorant of it: "Jesus therefore walked no more openly."

2. Men's being in God's way, and having confidence in him, ought not to hinder them in wary and prudent walking, that so they may avoid presumption, or tempting of him, by casting themselves into hazards; for even our Lord would walk "no more openly among the Jews" when there was hazard, till his time came.

3. As it is lawful for Christ's servants to flee when their death is decreed by enemies, and the persecution is personal, so they are not to take it ill if they be often and many times put to hard shifts for their own preservation; for after that Christ hath been forced ofttimes to withdraw before, he is yet put to it again.

4. Christ will readily get better shelter and entertainment in obscure and barren places than places of wealth and ease will afford him; for he must go "unto a country near to the wilderness, into a city called Ephraim, and there continue."

5. Whatever be Christ's lot, it is still the duty of his followers to cleave to him; for there he "continued with his disciples." (See Luke, xxii. 28.)

VER. 55. And the Jews' passover was nigh at hand: and many went out of the country up to Jerusalem before the passover, to purify themselves.

56. Then sought they for Jesus, and spake among themselves, as they stood in the temple, What think ye, that he will not come to the feast?

57. Now both the chief priests and the Pharisees had given a commandment, that, if any man knew where he were, he should shew it, that they might take him.

In the last consequent of this miracle is recorded what was the diligence of the rulers to have their conclusions executed at the ensuing feast of the passover. The order of the purpose seems to be this: the rulers had given a charge to the people, especially the inhabitants of Jerusalem, to spy out if they could find where Christ were, that so they might take him, ver. 57; in obedience to which, when the people are flocking together for preparation to the feast, ver. 55, they begin to inquire for him, and to reason among themselves, doubting whether he would come or not, ver. 56. Or it comes all to one purpose to conceive the matter thus : that the rulers and their emissaries seeking him, and not finding him themselves, they give a charge to all the people that they should give notice whenever they knew where he were. Whence learn—

1. Whatever shelter Christ or his followers find, for a time, in the use of lawful means, yet in troublous days they are to submit if it do not continue long, but that at last they must be brought on the stage; therefore it is marked that "the Jews' passover was nigh at hand," to intimate that Christ got not leave to lurk long in that place he retired unto.

2. As for this going up to purify themselves before the passover, albeit the Jews in these times were very superstitious, yet it is not clear that this was a practice of their own devising; for we find that ordinary preparation was requisite for sacrifices, 1 Sam. xvi. 5, and particularly for the passover, especially in purging leaven out of their houses, to which the apostle alludes, 1 Cor. v. 7, 8 ; see also Num. ix. 6, &c. ; 2 Chron. xxx. 18, 19 ; and it appears those who went up did it because of some special pollution, because of which they behoved to offer sacrifices, (as appears from the law, Lev. iv., v., vi. ; and chap. xiv., xv. 1—16,) which could be offered only at the temple in Jerusalem ; and therefore it is said many, not all, went up. And it teacheth, that as preparation is required for all the solemn service of God, so in special for participation of the Lord's table, and more particularly when men are lying under some notable pollution.

3. The godly can be no more earnest for Christ and his company than the wicked are to have his blood ; for as the godly at such a solemnity would be ready to seek him, as thinking a feast a poor feast if he were not there ; and as their affection to have him would readily be solicitous, and doubtful whether he will come or not; so it is with these bloodthirsty men ; they sought for Jesus, and, not finding him, spake among themselves, " What think ye," &c.

4. Whatever success God permit eager and bloodthirsty persecutors to get, yet they shall not want their own anxieties and vexations in getting their will ; for say they, " What think ye, that he will not come to the feast ?" the root of which expression was their anxiety and doubtfulness if he would come at all. And albeit he did come, and they got him crucified, yet the Lord will plague them with this vexation for a time.

5. Persecutors are unwilling to have their anxieties known, but they will labour to palliate them with fairest shows, yea, and even to make use of a cloak of piety to carry on their wicked purposes ; for so much also doth this speech import. They are anxious [afraid] that he will not come, that they may take him ; but they vent it in terms of spite against him, who, pretending to so much piety, yet will not come to that solemn feast. They will traduce him if he come not, and yet all their end in desiring him is that they may shed his blood.

6. When rulers are corrupt they do much mischief, and set a people on work against Christ ; as here we see in their "commandment."

7. Christ's followers must resolve not only on open enemies and opposition in trying times, but on secret spies and inquisitors, to ensnare and betray them ; for here they are set on work to find him out and delate him, "that they might take him."

8. Men sinning against conscience in a course are very eager and violent lest it should miscarry, and they can never be sure enough of their plots ; for this, among others, was one cause of their vigilancy. They sinned maliciously against light, and they cannot do too much to prevent a disappointment. So when Judas turns a traitor, he fears nothing so much as that he should vent his malice, and yet Christ should escape, and therefore he chargeth the soldiers to hold him fast, Matt. xxvi. 48, and to lead him away safely, Mark, xiv. 44.

CHAPTER XII.

In this chapter we have a rehearsal of several things which occurred betwixt Christ's return from Ephraim (whither he had retired, chap. xi. 54) to Bethany, and his eating of the passover with his disciples. It may be taken up in these particulars :—1. His return to Bethany and entertainment there, with some consequents that followed thereupon, ver. 1—11. 2. His triumphant entry into Jerusalem, with some remarkable observations upon it, ver. 12—19. 3. The desire of some Greeks to see him, with his doctrine upon that occasion, seasoned with strange exercise, ver. 20—36. 4. An account of the fruits of his ministry among the most part of the Jews, some not believing at all, ver. 37—41, others being but hidden believers, ver. 42, 43, together with Christ's farewell sermon to them, wherein he points out himself and his doctrine, verse 44—50.

Ver. 1. Then Jesus six days before the passover came to Bethany, where Lazarus was which had been dead, whom he raised from the dead.

The first part of the chapter containeth these particulars :—1. His return to Bethany, ver. 1. 2. His entertainment there, ver. 2, particularly by Mary, ver. 3. 3. Judas's quarrelling at Mary's deed, with Christ's apology for her and it, ver. 4—8. 4. The resort of the Jews to him at Bethany, ver. 9, with the Pharisees' resolution thereupon, ver. 10, 11.

In this verse we have Christ's return to Bethany, together with—1. A designation of the time of his return; it was "six days before the passover." 2. A new designation of the place, taken from the late miracle wrought upon Lazarus. While it is said he came there " six days before the passover," and yet, Matt. xxvi. 2, it is said that after two days is the passover, when yet the supper here mentioned is after that recorded to be given, Matt. xxvi. 6. We must (for reconciling these) consider that Christ's warning of the disciples of Judas's treachery was indeed, in order of time, after that supper, and four days after his coming to Bethany; for Judas went not away till after the disappointment and affront he got about the box of ointment, Matt. xxvi. 14, compared with the preceding purpose. And as for Matthew, he doth not observe the order of time, in recording that supper, (for Christ's entry into Jerusalem, which was after it, ver. 12 of this chapter, is recorded by him long before, Matt. xxi. 8, 9, &c.,) but having told how Christ warned the disciples of this hazard, Matt. xxvi. 2, he doth, upon that occasion, resume things that had been done before, to clear how he was betrayed—namely, that the priests consulting upon some expedients how they might catch Christ, Matt. xxvi. 3—5, Judas, who had been disappointed of gain by that ointment poured on Christ, went and offered his service to them, ver. 6—14, 15.

DOCTRINES.

1. Albeit men are bound by all lawful means to preserve themselves from the unjust violence of persecutors, yet when God's time and calling cometh, and when men see it is the will of God they should suffer, they ought to set their faces to it cheerfully; for whereas before Christ withdrew, chap. xi. 54, now, when "the passover"—the time of his suffering—draweth nigh, he comes to view again, and draws towards Jerusalem. (See Mark, x. 32, 33; Luke, ix. 51.)

2. He came so long before the time to Bethany, where Lazarus and others were, not only that he might stay there, and give an occasion to Judas to go his way to the rulers; or to attend till the people, hearing he was there, might meet him in a solemn manner, and he might be conveyed in state to the place of his sufferings, of which afterward; but his end more especially in this was to refresh and confirm his friends there with his company before he should be taken from them, and to refresh himself also before he went to his trials. And so it teacheth — 1. Where Christ hath love and an interest he will not stay long away; for here, after his retirement, he returns to Bethany. 2. When storms are arising, Christ will not forget his own to give them a visit sooner or later, to fortify them against them; for " six days before the passover," at which he was to suffer, he comes to Bethany, to refresh and confirm his friends by his company, and by warning them of his suffering, as it is, ver. 7. 3. It is a very refreshful cordial under sufferings to have the company and society of godly friends, with whom we may converse at any time; for Christ also subjected himself to make use of this; and as he seeks it in the garden, Matt. xxvi. 38, 40, so here he seeks it in Bethany. See how Paul esteems of a visit in his bonds, 2 Tim. i. 16—18.

3. Where Christ converseth with his people he will make a place famous by eminent proofs of his power and love for them; for now the former description of Bethany, chap. xi. 1, is laid aside, and it is most famous that Lazarus was there, " which had been dead, whom he raised from the dead."

VER. 2. There they made him a supper; and Martha served: but Lazarus was one of them that sat at the table with him.

3. Then took Mary a pound of ointment of spikenard, very costly, and anointed the feet of Jesus, and wiped his feet with her hair: and the house was filled with the odour of the ointment.

In these verses we have Christ's entertainment at Bethany; a supper is made for him, at which Martha served, and Lazarus sat with him, but Mary anoints Christ with precious ointments. This supper was made for him in the house of one Simon, a leper, (who, it seems, had been cured by Christ,) as may be gathered from Matt. xxvi. 6, 7, where Mary's deed is recorded, but her name suppressed, and it seems Lazarus and his sisters have been invited also. As for this practice of Mary, I shall leave what was extraordinary in it till its own place, ver. 7. Only, it being the custom in these countries to anoint their guests, and wash their feet at feasts, Luke, vii. 44, 46, she out of her great love will do it with great charge and expense; and whereas here it is said, she anointed his feet, and the rest say it was his head, Matt. xxvi. 7, we are to understand that she did anoint both, though she only wiped his feet; and breaking the box, and pouring it on his head, Mark, xiv. 3, it seems the copiousness thereof made it run from his head to his feet.

DOCTRINES.

1. As temporal things are due unto Christ and his ministers who sow spiritual things, 2 Cor. ix. 11, so they who have participated of his bounty will make him very welcome; for " there they made him a supper."

2. Albeit it be the great sin of men to pamper their own bodies and make provision for the flesh, yet it is not unlawful at some times to enjoy the liberal use of the creatures in a sober manner; for Christ doth not decline this " supper." Sometimes he went to the feasts of Pharisees, Luke, vii. 36; sometimes with publicans, Matt. ix. 10, &c., and xi. 19; not for their fare, but that he might gain them, as love is a very gaining way; and here he feasts with his friends that they may be refreshed together.

3. As for Martha's serving, albeit she was reproved for this at another time, Luke, x. 38—42, not simply for her serving Christ that way, but comparatively, and when it crossed better duties, yet now, when it interrupts no better duty, her care was commendable that she would serve, though the house was not her own; and it teacheth that when Christ is dear to any they will not disdain to stoop to do meanest service to him or his for his sake, as Martha served here.

4. As Christ's miracles are true and real, and not lying wonders, so the memory of his wonderful works are not to be forgotten, nor ought to wear out with length of time; for both these ends it is marked that " Lazarus was one of them that sat at the table with him," both to confirm the truth of his resurrection, as Mark, v. 43;

Luke, xxiv. 41—43 ; Acts, x. 41, and to keep us in mind of that wonderful work, that he who was once in his grave should now be eating.

5. According as men abound in love to Christ they will bring forth evidences thereof in serving of him ; as here Mary outstrips them all.

6. Love to Christ is ingenious to find out a way to evidence itself; and when all are busy it will find some work that is undone to be done to him and for him ; for when some are preparing the supper, Martha is serving, and Lazarus entertaining him at table, Mary finds out this to anoint his feet.

7. Love is very prodigal, (so to say,) and will spare no expenses on Christ ; for she took a pound of very costly spikenard to do this, of the worth whereof see ver. 5.

8. True love is still accompanied with humility and reverence to Christ, and when it doth most to Christ it keeps a man still humble ; for when she had done all this, she " wiped his feet with her hair," either to make them clean before the ointment came upon them, or to wipe off the ointment after it had suppled his feet.

9. As the fruits of love will not hide, so they have a fragrant smell ; for so much may be gathered, by allusion, from this, that " the house was filled with the odour of the ointment," and so the matter came to be known, which occasioned the subsequent quarrelling.

Ver. 4. Then saith one of his disciples, Judas Iscariot, Simon's son, which should betray him,

5. Why was not this ointment sold for three hundred pence, and given to the poor ?

In these verses is recorded a consequent of this practice of Mary—namely, Judas's quarrelling of it, which also was an occasion of his going and betraying his Master, as the other evangelists mark. Albeit the other evangelists lay this upon all the disciples, because, in appearance, they consented to him, and seconded him in so plausible a cause, yet John declareth it was he who raised the debate, and, under a pretence of caring for the poor, condemned this practice as a needless waste. Whence learn—

1. Very gross hypocrites may be near to Christ in outward profession, and may be entrusted in eminent employments ; for " Judas Iscariot, Simon's son, which should betray him," is one of his disciples.

2. Such as follow Christ on unsound terms, and will forsake and betray him in a strait, will be now and then bewraying their unsoundness beforehand, if they be well observed ; for he " which should betray him" brings out his covetousness here beforehand.

3. It is the great and woeful art of hypocrites that they mask their corrupt intentions with fair pretences, and that they desire to lurk so long as they can ; for all his language is, " Why was not this ointment sold for three hundred pence, and given to the poor ?" This whole sum, after the English account, amounts (according to the opinion of some concerning the Roman penny) to nine pounds seven shillings and sixpence, or (according to others) to eight pounds six shillings and eightpence. And as this points out the great liberality of Mary in this her practice, so Judas, by his mentioning thereof, insinuates that it was altogether needless to bestow so much on such a piece of service to Christ ; as, indeed, men are ready to account it great waste (as the word is, Matt. xxvi. 8) when a little is bestowed on Christ and his service, when yet they can waste more needlessly in serving their lusts, without noise or grudging. But this wanted not a fair pretence that Christ cared for no such costly anointing, and that it did not beseem their low estate. And withal, his great covetousness is masked with a pretence of care for the poor. It is very dangerous to live in times when cloaks of faults are as rife as the faults themselves.

4. It is the will of God that the poor be taken notice of, and supplied by every one according to his ability ; for so much appears in Christ's practice, who in his deep poverty did lay up somewhat for them, as Judas's exception imports. (See John, xiii. 29.)

Ver. 6. This he said, not that he cared for the poor ; but because he was a thief, and had the bag, and bare what was put therein.

Before John sets down Christ's answer, he doth first take off Judas's mask, and sheweth that this did not proceed from his care of the poor, but that having the bag in his custody, wherein any money Christ had was kept, and being a thief, he was sorry he lost such a prize, whereupon he might have preyed. He is called " a thief," either because he had already interverted some of that money which was in his keeping to his private use, or because he had purposed so to do, being resolved to forsake his Master, since he heard of his sufferings, and that they were now approaching. Whence learn—

1. Let men pretend never so fair to cover the naughtiness of their hearts, yet Christ knoweth all the secret deceits of the heart, and how contrary their intentions are to their pretences ; for here by his light it is cleared that " he cared not for the poor."

2. As Christ knoweth the naughtiness of every heart, so he will, in due time, one way or other, discover what is within men ; for here the veil is taken off Judas : " This he said, not that he cared for the poor."

3. Whatever hypocrites pretend, yet it is but themselves, and some interest or advantage of their own, they drive at in all they do ; for Judas's aim in all this was to reap advantage to himself.

4. It is egregious theft before the Lord when men do carry on their avaricious designs under pretence of caring for the poor ; and when, in affection or practice, they are not faithful in what is committed to their trust, but do intervert that to their private use which is designed for public or pious uses ; for thus was Judas " a thief," in taking to himself what was to be employed for the use of Christ and his disciples, or for the poor.

5. Riches and the bag are not in such esteem with Christ but that the basest of his followers may have them in keeping and under their power; for of all the twelve, Judas "had the bag, and bare what was put therein."

6. When Christ suffers men's corrupt affections and suitable tentations and objects to meet, it is a sad judgment and snare upon them, and a presage that he will give them up to a neck-break; for it was a sad judgment upon Judas, that being a thief, he had the bag, and so wanted not an opportunity to satisfy his covetous disposition.

Ver. 7. Then said Jesus, Let her alone: against the day of my burying hath she kept this.

Followeth Christ's answer and apology for Mary, in the first part whereof he defends her practice, which Judas had quarrelled, by shewing she did it upon an extraordinary cause and occasion—to wit, that foreseeing his death by faith, she would testify her affection to him by doing this last duty now which she could not expect to get done afterward. Whence learn—

1. It is a great sin in any, especially if they be of any eminency, to discourage any of the saints, or interrupt them in their serving of Christ; for Christ finds it needful to bid, " Let her alone," as knowing it might weaken her hands that she was checked by one of his apostles.

2. Christ will take the maintenance and defence of those who serve him against all that would oppose and carp at them; for he lets her say nothing, but interposeth on her behalf: " Let her alone."

3. Whoever misconstruct the honest actions of saints, yet Christ doth judge aright of them, and alloweth them his approbation; for Judas accounted it a waste, but Christ approves of it, as kept for the day of his burying.

4. Christ, in his suffering, death, and burial, is very honourable in the estimation of saints who know him right; and he doth esteem highly of his own sufferings; for her keeping this ointment for the day of his burying intimates that she by faith saw him honourable in his death as well as in his life, and that his death not only should be acceptable and savoury to God, but fragrant to all the elect, and should fill the world with a sweet smell. And Christ himself, who was never sumptuous, yet allows costly ointment on his burial, to testify how highly he prized and loved to lay down his life for his people.

Ver. 8. For the poor always ye have with you; but me ye have not always.

In the next place, Christ, having defended Mary, doth now answer to his great objection and pretence of caring for the poor. The defence is taken from this, that this opportunity of honouring him would not always last, whereas they might always have occasion to be charitable to the poor. He speaks it in the plural number, ye have the poor, &c., either because he would press this as a common duty on all as well as Mary, or

rather, he speaks it to all the disciples, who had joined with Judas in this act, as the other evangelists observe.

DOCTRINES.

1. Christ is so meek, even to his cruel enemies, that he will not always tell them all he knoweth of them when he reproveth them, but will let them discover themselves; for he will not tell Judas of his false heart, but simply replies to any ground of objection he alleged. And this he doth, partly, because more were engaged than Judas, whom therefore he will satisfy; partly, that he may warn men not to seek to carry their cause by reflections upon the persons of their opposites, while as they want solid reasons for their cause; partly, that he may teach all to beware of judging men's hearts when yet they have not discovered themselves; for he will not deal so with Judas; and partly, that from this his meek dealing towards a Judas, we may gather how much more meek he will be to his own.

2. The Lord hath so ordered that when diverse duties which cannot be performed together, tryst [meet] together in one juncture of time, the one of them may give way to the other for that time without sin; and particularly, duties which occur rarely, and cannot be got done afterward, should be gone about in the opportunity thereof, albeit other important duties be laid aside for that time, which may be overtaken at another time; as here he cleareth in the matter of putting this external honour upon him, when it trysts [meets] with the command of having a care of the poor; and for this reason he preferreth this duty to himself now, the poor ye have always, but me ye have not always.

3. Albeit it be a sin to defraud parents, the poor, or others, of what they may expect in duty, justice, or mercy, under a pretext of laying out what men have, for God, Matt. xv. 4—6, yet when Christ calls for anything we have, no other thing should come in competition with him; for when he calls for it he takes place of the poor here.

4. Men may sometimes have an opportunity of employing themselves, or their substance, in honouring of Christ or doing him service, which they will not so readily meet with again if they let it slip; for so much is imported here, " me ye have not always." Mary could not always have opportunity to testify her respect thus to Christ, nay, not when he was dead and buried, and therefore she takes this present opportunity.

5. The Lord will have his people never to weary of mercy to the poor, and therefore doth continue constant objects of pity among them; for " The poor always ye have with you." (See Deut. xv. 11.)

Ver. 9. Much people of the Jews therefore knew that he was there: and they came not for Jesus' sake only, but that they might see Lazarus also, whom he had raised from the dead.

10. But the chief priests consulted that they might put Lazarus also to death;

11. Because that by reason of him many of the Jews went away, and believed on Jesus.

In these verses is recorded a consequent of Christ's coming to Bethany when it came to be known he was there—to wit, that many Jews resorted thither, not only for his sake, but out of curiosity also, to see and speak with Lazarus, ver. 9, which is amplified from the rulers' reso lution thereupon to put Lazarus also out of the way, seeing his resurrection was a mean to draw many to Christ, ver. 10, 11. It is not needful to determine whether these Jews were some dwelling in Jerusalem and about it, or some of those who came up beforehand to the feast, chap. xi. 55, who also came out the next day to meet him in triumph, seeing, whoever they were, their coming contributed to set forth Christ's honour, and to irritate his enemies.

From ver. 9, learn—1. Where Christ pleaseth to make himself known he will get respect and followers, were there never so much hazard and opposition in the way; for albeit the rulers had concluded to put him to death, and he had withdrawn upon that, and they had given charge to spy him out, chap. xi. 53, 54, 57, yet "much people of the Jews knew that he was there: and they came." So soon as they heard of him they flocked to him.

2. Christ gives so glorious proofs of his power and love as may invite men to flock unto him; for he hath with him Lazarus, "whom he had raised from the dead," to make them flock unto him.

3. It is an argument to persuade Christ to help his people in their difficulties, that by so doing he not only doth them good, but doth also bring about the manifestation of his glory, and an increase of followers; for by raising Lazarus he draws them out to wait upon him. (See Psalm vii. 6, 7.)

4. Albeit Christ will get glory, even by the unsound actings and appearings of men for him, Philip. i. 16, 18; Psalm lxvi. 3; yet it is the sin of many that they flock to him rather out of curiosity than in sincerity, and that they choose rather to gaze upon his works than fall in love with the worker; for such was their fault here: "They came not for Jesus' sake only, but that they might see Lazarus also." They were curious to see such a rare sight, and possibly, also, to inquire somewhat of him concerning the state of the dead.

From verses 10, 11, learn—1. Such as betake themselves to bear down Christ do engage themselves in an endless vexing life, and a harder task than they are able to undergo; for they who would kill Jesus would "put Lazarus also to death," yea, they would kill many who would kill all whom Christ made objects of his mercy for inviting others to come to him. (See Exod. i. 12.)

2. Men once engaged in opposition to Christ will not readily be reclaimed by insuperable difficulties, nor the convincing beams of his glory shining in their eyes; for albeit this was a glorious work prevailing on others, and albeit they see more and more impediments in their way, yet they will go on.

3. None are so malicious and bitter enemies to Christ as corrupt churchmen when they once decline; for it is "the chief priests" who are so cruel as to kill a man for being the harmless occasion of drawing men to Christ, and whom God had newly delivered from death, and testified he would have him live.

4. It is the greatest preferment and most special mercy that can be conferred on any when they are made means and instruments of advancing Christ's honour and kingdom; for this was Lazarus's dignity, that because "many of the Jews went away, and believed on Jesus." It is not needful to assert that the faith of the most of them was sound, but the least degree of it in the worst of them was enough to irritate the rulers.

5. Such as have received special mercies from Christ, or are made instruments of his glory, may expect that they shall meet with a rub, and be made the butt of the malice of enemies; for there is a resolution against Lazarus's life, who was thus highly honoured.

6. How mad soever enemies be, or their projects cruel, yet they would be far enough from their point if Christ pleased, though they got their will; for suppose they had put Lazarus to death, could not Christ raise him up again as he had done even lately to their knowledge, and so make his glory shine yet more brightly?

VER. 12. On the next day much people that were come to the feast, when they heard that Jesus was coming to Jerusalem,

13. Took branches of palm trees, and went forth to meet him, and cried, Hosanna: Blessed is the King of Israel that cometh in the name of the Lord.

Followeth to ver. 20, the second part of the chapter, wherein is recorded Christ's triumphant entry into Jerusalem, according as was fore-prophesied; wherein, being now about to die, he will first be publicly honoured (after the manner of receiving kings into cities) and proclaimed King of Israel, and David's successor, in such a manner as became his spiritual kingdom, and that in despite of all his enemies. This triumph, as it is recorded by this evangelist, may be taken up in these:—1. The multitude's part in it, ver. 12, 13. 2. Christ's own part and action in it, ver. 14, 15. 3. The disciples not understanding of all this at present, ver. 16. 4. The seen cause moving the multitude to act thus, ver. 17. 18. 5. The Pharisees' part in all this solemnity, ver. 19. As for what is further and more amply recorded of this by the other evangelists I remit to its proper place.

In these verses is recorded the carriage of the multitude who are come to the feast, who (the next day after that many had been with Christ at Bethany) hearing that he was coming to the city, do solemnly meet him, carrying branches of palm trees, and with loud acclamations do proclaim him King of Israel, who is blessed, and cometh in the name of the Lord. As for their action of carrying "branches of palm trees," (with some whereof they strewed the way, Matt. xxi. 8, and others, it would seem, they carried in their hands,) we find, indeed, use made thereof at the feast of tabernacles, Leviticus, xxiii. 40; Neh. viii. 15. Now they carry them before him at this feast of the passover, to testify that he is the substance of all the feasts; and by this act, besides what was signified by the feast of tabernacles, is pointed out that he is a triumphant and victorious King, which is elsewhere signified by carrying of palms, Rev. vii. 9. As for their acclamations, they do thereby acknowledge that they see him to be the blessed Messiah and King of Israel, authorized and sent by the Father to perform this glorious work; and as for their Hosanna, (borrowed from Psalm cxviii. 25, as appeareth from the following words, " Blessed is he who cometh in the name of the Lord," taken from ver. 26 of that Psalm,) it signifieth Save now, we beseech thee, as it is rendered in that Psalm. And albeit, if we take it as directed to Christ, by way of prayer that he would save them, it doth import that it is a special way of honouring Christ in his kingdom when we seek and expect salvation from him, and in him only; yet that seems not to be their scope here, for, Matt. xxi. 9, it is, Hosanna to the son of David, or, Make safe now, or, Bring safety now to the son of David; and so it imports their hearty wish that his kingdom may prosper.

DOCTRINES.

1. If Christ saw it meet he could get himself glory, not only among spiritual observers, but even in the view of the world; for by this solemn triumph he discovers how easily he could open the eyes of men to discern what he is, and incline their hearts to flock unto him, and proclaim his glory; so that it is not for want of power that Christ doth so often obscure his glory under a veil.

2. As Christ can let out his glory when he pleaseth, so in particular he delights to appear most glorious in and about his sufferings; for here he who oftentimes entered Jerusalem privately, will now, at this last time, when he is going to the cross, enter in state. He will go triumphing to it, as well as he triumphs on it, Col. ii. 15, and after it, Psalm lxviii. 18.

3. When Christ's enemies are raging at him and his success he can vex them yet more by spreading his glory more and more; for when they are vexed with hearing of the confluence at Bethany, ver. 20, 21, even " the next day," they see him more glorified " coming to Jerusalem."

4. When men of great eminency in the church do slight Christ he can raise up others, even the meanest, to honour him and set out his praise; for it is not the rulers, nay, nor inhabitants of Jerusalem who do this, but " much people that were come to the feast." (See Matt. xxi. 15, 16; 1 Cor. i. 27.)

5. As it is the duty of the Lord's people to attend all the ordinances appointed by him, so their chief care should be to meet with Christ, and to be most taken up with him in them; for albeit they were come to the feast, yet when they heard that Jesus was coming to Jerusalem they went forth to meet him.

6. In Christ is to be found the substance of all the festivities and solemnities that were among the Jews; for before him they carry palms at the passover, which were used at another feast to testify that the stance [stations] of all trysted [met] in him.

7. Christ is a triumphant and victorious conqueror, who triumphs over all his enemies, and makes his people always to triumph in him, 2 Cor. ii. 14; therefore also is he met with " branches of palm trees."

8. It is the duty and commendation of the members of the visible church that they be well acquainted with scripture; for here the multitude do not only know but can apply passages in the Psalms, and concerning David's offspring, very fitly to Christ; and if they understood so much in these declining times, how much will this aggravate their guilt who are grossly ignorant in a time of clear light?

9. Christ is the true King of Israel and of his church, to rule, subdue, protect, and defend them, and they who get open eyes will see this, and embrace him as such; for they acknowledge him " the King of Israel." This he will have proclaimed in the world, oppose who will, Psalm ii. 7; compare chap. i. 49.

10. It doth commend Christ unto his people that he comes with his Father's power and authority, being approved and upheld by him in his kingdom, so that all who embrace him will find the Father well pleased in him; for this addeth to the joy and acclamation—he is " the King of Israel, that cometh in the name of the Lord," and upon this followeth, peace in heaven, or betwixt God in heaven and us, Luke, xix. 38.

11. Christ is a King perfectly blessed in himself, and a fountain of blessing to all his subjects, and is to be proclaimed and commended as such; for " blessed is the King of Israel," &c. (So Psalm lxxii. 14; cxviii. 26.) It is he in whom all families of the earth are blessed, Gen. xii. 3, and in whom they should bless themselves, Gen. xxii. 18, as it is in the original.

12. It is the duty of all such as love Christ heartily to wish and pray for the prosperity of his kingdom; for they cried Hosanna, as wishing safety and success to him and his kingdom.

Ver. 14. And Jesus, when he had found a young ass, sat thereon; as it is written,

15. Fear not, daughter of Sion: behold, thy King cometh, sitting on an ass's colt.

In these verses we have Christ's part and action in this triumph—to wit, that an ass being provided for him, he rode thereupon, to accomplish that prediction, Zech. ix. 9, of which I have spoken in its proper place. Albeit this be recorded here after the other of the people's acclamations, and it is probable the people were come to him on the way to the mount of Olives, or at least were coming on the way, before he sent for the ass, Matt. xxi. 1, 2, yet it is certain that he was riding before these acclamations were.

DOCTRINES.

1. When Christ manifests most of his glory in the world he will have it seen that his kingdom is not of this world; for in all this pomp he rides but on "a young ass," and that a borrowed one, without any furniture save his disciples' clothes, and accompanied but with a train of base people and children; all which might appear but very ignominious to a carnal eye.

2. We are not to carve out the glory of Christ's kingdom by our carnal conceptions and imaginations, but by his own word; for whatever ignominy appear here, yet it is glorious and greater glory than any we could devise, in so far as it agreeth with scripture and foregoing prophecies.

3. Christ's kingdom is so great a stranger to carnal glory and pomp that any mean splendour is very much unlike it; for this also takes off the ignominy that this was much glory and state to him who never used to ride before.

4. Albeit Christ became poor for us, yet he wanted not anything as he needed it, that so he might teach his people what care he will have of them; for albeit he possessed not so much as an ass, yet when he needed he "found a young ass," &c., or obtained the use of it from the owner.

5. Christ is a faithful observer of all that is written to see it duly performed, for he did all this to accomplish what is written.

6. The encouragements of the gospel are not held out unto men to cherish security, but to be an antidote against all their fears and discouragements; for the scope of the allowance, Zech. vi., to rejoice, shout, is here summed up in this, "Fear not."

7. Albeit men do not reach the height of consolation and joy allowed in Christ, yet they are to bless him in so far as they are kept from crushing fear; for so much also may be gathered from these two places compared; they rejoice in so far as they "fear not."

8. Christ is Sion's King, who will respect her and see her comforted, though all the world beside should sink; for it is to the "daughter of Sion," this encouragement is given from her King.

9. Whatever be Sion's perplexities, yet in Christ there is a remedy against all she can feel or fear; "Fear not, daughter of Sion, thy King cometh."

10. It is the church's comfort that Christ is a King to her, that he cometh to her and seeks her to do her good, and that, after long expectation, he will at last come to give her actual enjoyment; all these are imported in this encouragement, "Thy King cometh;" he leaves heaven to seek her on earth, and is now not held out in the promise as coming, but is actually come unto her.

11. Christ in his kingdom and glory is adorned with meekness and lowliness; and this is the comfort of his subjects, that they have to do with such an one; for this addeth to the comfort, "Thy King cometh, sitting on an ass's colt."

12. As Christ's love and condescendence is admirable in itself, and to be admired by all who see it, so even the church hath need to be stirred up to take notice of this as becometh; therefore a "behold" is prefixed to this to point out how admirable this is in itself, and yet how dull Sion is in remarking it, till she be stirred up and excited to it.

Ver. 16. *These things understood not his disciples at the first: but when Jesus was glorified, then remembered they that these things were written of him, and that they had done these things unto him.*

In this verse, John, omitting what is recorded of the disciples' part in this triumph by the other evangelists, doth only record their not understanding at present that which themselves or others were doing, till, after the glorification of Christ, that the Spirit was poured out, and then it was brought to their remembrance that this had been fore-prophesied, and accordingly had been performed. Whence learn—

1. Men may be in the midst of great mercies and actings, and may not only be witnesses of the Lord's working and the works of others, but even actors themselves in that which for the time they do little or nothing understand; for "these things understood not his disciples at the first." Men have much brutish ignorance fed with inadvertency, and may be little expecting the things that God is doing in such a time or case, Gen. xvi. 13; xxviii. 16, and therefore do not discern them.

2. When the Lord's people are ignorant and under a cloud, he useth not to take advantage of them, but can guide them as right as may be, so that a back look thereunto, when they get light, will be sweet unto them; for in all this they act as rightly as if they had understood, and afterwards they find that what was written of him they had done unto him. (See Psalm lxxiii. 22—24.)

3. However the Lord for a time suffer his people to lie under clouds, and ignorant of what he or they are doing, yet in due time he will clear them in so far as is needful; for afterwards they remembered, &c. (See John, xiii. 7.)

4. The treasures of knowledge hid up in Christ were not fully opened up till Christ was glorified; for "when Jesus was glorified, then remembered they," &c. Hereby is kept a due proportion betwixt the Head and his members, that he shall be first exalted before they get their full allowance; and hereby, also, Christ being exalted giveth evidence that he remembers his people. (See John, vii. 39; Acts, ii. 33; Eph. iv. 8.)

5. Confession of infirmity and ignorance is a sweet fruit of the Spirit poured out; and the more any have received they will be the more sensible of and ready to acknowledge their frailties; for John, the beloved disciple, being now enlightened, is most forward to record that they understood not these things at the first.

6. When the Spirit of God is most amply poured out he will still lead men to the scriptures to discern of Christ, and compare their own actings by it; for so was it in the disciples' best days: "they remembered that these things were

written of him, and that they had done these things to him."

.7. It is an evidence of Christ's being exalted at the right hand of the Father for the good of his people when he brings scriptures to their mind, makes them clear to them, and clears their practice thereby; for " when Jesus was glorified" this was a comfortable evidence of it, " they remembered these things."

VER. 17. The people therefore that was with him when he called Lazarus out of his grave, and raised him from the dead, bare record.

18. For this cause the people also met him, for that they heard that he had done this miracle.

In these verses is recorded what was the seen cause (for the unseen was the overruling hand of God) moving the multitude to come out and convey him in state—to wit, some of the people's (of whom, see chap. xi. 45) testimony concerning the miracle wrought on Lazarus, which, as they had published before, and so drew many other people out, so over again they proclaim it on that day, that they may contribute to the solemnity of the triumph. Whence learn—

1. It is the part of all such as have been witnesses to Christ's working, on themselves or others, to publish the same to his praise; for " the people that was with him when he called Lazarus, &c., bare record."

2. As it is at all times a sin to smother the praises of Christ, so, in particular, in days of solemnity it is our sin not to join and bring in what we know to make up the song; for they bring in that particular to make up the triumph.

3. In a day of Christ's power, and when he is to get glory to himself, he can furnish means, and make them effectual, to bring it to pass; for he makes that miracle an occasion to bring about this triumph.

4. It may encourage men to publish the praise of Christ's working, as they know of it, that God may make their weak endeavours effectual to work upon very many; for the testimony of some drew out this great confluence to Christ.

5. It is the duty of them who hear anything of Christ's commendation to go and seek him, and do homage to him; " For this cause the people also met him, for that they heard that he had done this miracle."

VER. 19. The Pharisees therefore said among themselves, Perceive ye how ye prevail nothing? behold, the world is gone after him.

In the last place John records what was the Pharisees' part in the time of this triumph, and seeing it. They are galled at the heart that they have had so little success of their endeavours, and that now all are flocking to him. We find some of them carping in the midst of the triumph, Luke, xix. 39, as having gone out with the rest to seek some advantage; but this seems to have been their language one to another, when they saw the people crowding out of the city.

1. In the day of Christ's greatest solemnity there will not be wanting some sore hearts at it, some Michal to despise David while he is dancing; and that is a part of the glory of the triumph, Ps. cxii. 10; Mic. vii. 10; for the Pharisees are here galled.

2. It is an evidence of a malicious disposition when men will neither serve Christ themselves, nor can endure that others should do it; for such is their humour here.

3. Greatest enemies will be convinced at last that, do what they will, their opposition against Christ and his installing in his kingdom will be to no purpose; for say they, " Perceive ye how ye prevail nothing? the world (that is, all sort of people) is gone after him," whereas we thought to have prevented that none at all should have gone.

4. It is a great plague upon persecutors that when they want success they will not observe God's mercy impeding them in an evil course, nor his hand resisting them, that so they might stop; but all their disappointments tend only to kindle their fury and heighten their rage; for under this disappointment all they breathe out is fury and envy.

5. As it is Christ's way to make his glory spread the more it is opposed and envied, (for the world goeth after him when they oppose,) so the envy of persecutors looks on Christ's success in a multiplying glass, to augment their own sorrow; for when they say, " Behold, the world is gone after him," albeit the world be taken for a multitude of all sorts of people in it, as now strangers and others are flocking out, yet their liberal way of expression intimates how much they resent it, and look on it as more than indeed it was.

VER. 20. And there were certain Greeks among them that came up to worship at the feast:

21. The same came therefore to Philip, which was of Bethsaida of Galilee, and desired him, saying, Sir, we would see Jesus.

22. Philip cometh and telleth Andrew: and again Andrew and Philip tell Jesus.

Followeth to verse 37, the third part of the chapter, wherein is contained Christ's doctrine and exercise upon occasion of some Greeks desiring to see him, who was now become so famous by reason of this triumph. It may be taken up in these:—1. Their desire, and way of propounding it, ver. 20—22. 2. Christ's answer, wherein, waiving their respects tendered to him, he preaches of the glory and fruit following upon his suffering, ver. 23, 24, and of their duty who would seek to make acquaintance with him, ver. 25, 26. 3. Lest this doctrine of his death and suffering should stumble them, he first, by sore exercise, ver. 27, and then by consolation sent from heaven, ver. 28—30, doth make it evident it was the mind of God he should suffer, and yet not sink under it. 4. Being calmed in his exercise, and cheered up with the late sensible consolation, he preaches more fully concerning the glorious fruits of his death, ver. 31—33. 5. An objection being moved against his doctrine concerning His suffering who gave out himself to be the Messiah, ver. 34, Christ doth press upon them to improve the present opportunity of his presence, and then closeth the conference by departing from them, ver. 35, 36.

In these verses we have the first particular in this part of the chapter, and an occasion of the ensuing purpose, which is, the desire of some strangers to see Christ; wherein we may consider—1. The persons who propound this desire. They are, certain Greeks that came up to worship. We find indeed that the Jews who were born and bred among the Greeks are called Grecians, or Grecists, Acts, vi. 7; ix. 29, because they lived among them, and used the Greek language, yea, and made most use of the Greek translation of the Old Testament. But these seem not to have been of that sort, for the designation is different in the original from that which is used Acts vi. and ix., and therefore it appears rather that these were devout gentiles who, embracing the true religion, did come up at solemn times to worship at Jerusalem. And albeit the natural Greeks, or posterity of Javan, were but a small part of the heathen nations, and possibly these were none of them, yet it is not unusual in the New Testament to comprehend all (or the most part of) nations that were not Jews under the name of Greeks, Rom. i. 16; x. 12; Gal. iii. 28; and that because the Grecian empire had before that time extended itself far, and so gave a name to the subjects of their dominion; and withal, the Greek language being generally in use in these countries, and some Greeks being incorporated with them, it is nothing strange they be so designed. Consider—2. Their desire, which is, that they may "see Jesus." It is not needful to determine whether they had already seen him in the throng, and now would be more familiarly acquainted with him, but it is clear, from Christ's answer and entertaining of this motion, that their desire did flow from curiosity, and as they came not to Jerusalem for this cause, so they mind no more but to see him. Consider—3. The way of propounding their desire, and how it comes to be propounded unto Christ. They do very respectfully propound the matter unto Philip, and he doth consult with Andrew, and then both of them present it unto Christ. Whatever may be commendable in this procedure, as that they make acquaintance with Christ by means of his apostles, and that Philip makes a stand in the matter till he get further advice, because these were gentiles who had been excluded in their first commission, Matt. x. 5, yet Christ's strange doctrine, on this proposition, intimateth that he did not relish it well. I shall not determine that they used this mean to get a meeting with Christ in private as not desiring to be seen owning him against whom the rulers had such indignation, chap. xi. 57, but this is clear enough, that they in propounding, and the disciples in entertaining it, keep too great a state in it, as if access unto Christ were not easy.

1. Albeit it pleased the Lord, till the fulness of time, to give up all nations, and did only choose the nation of Israel to be his peculiar people, yet it pleased him even then to bring in some strangers as the first fruits, till the fulness of the gentiles should be brought in, and the partition wall be taken away; for there were certain Greeks among them at the feast; and in dedicating of the temple a room was left for these, 1 Kings, viii. 41—43.

2. Whatever the Lord confer upon his people in their private and secret worship, yet it is their duty not to be content therewith, nor can they prove that it is sound and sincere unless they do also frequent public ordinances where they may be had, were it at a great distance; for these Greeks "came up to worship at the feast," though possibly they lived far off, some of them. Though there was somewhat typical in these feasts, yet they were also solemn parts of the Jewish worship; and their frequenting thereof at the Lord's command will condemn them who are not put to such pains, and yet prove negligent.

3. Christ, when he is known in any measure, will be thought a desirable sight; therefore they " would see Jesus."

4. Such as would make acquaintance with Christ ought not to neglect the ordinary means, or to make use of his servants; for in so far they were right, in that they came to Philip, " and desired him, saying, Sir, we would see Jesus." We need not conceive that they came to Philip upon any particular acquaintance because he was of Bethsaida of Galilee, which lay nearer the confines of the land, but because they met first with him. And they call him " Sir," though a fisherman, as being the civil compellation of these times given even to mean persons, John, xx. 15.

5. Many, even of them who make much noise of desiring to see Christ, may yet be driven so to do out of mere curiosity and for carnal respects; for such was their desire here, to " see Jesus," and but to see and gaze on him who had been made so famous in the late triumph.

6. It is the duty of disciples to make men's acquaintance with Christ; for whatever was their fault in not taxing what was amiss, or in their own way, yet it was no fault, but their duty, to make up the acquaintance.

7. It is a great mistake, and an injury done to Christ, to think that he will keep a state and distance from sinners who sincerely seek him, and his servants do but an ill office when they foment such apprehensions; for whatever they deserved, yet they mistake Christ when they thought he was like a king, who could not be come unto but by some of his courtiers and favourites; whereas many needy sinners did come to him immediately; and Philip finding strangers take notice of him, doth sin in making such a business of state of it as might confirm them in this opinion.

8. Christ's court would be but ill guided if any (though even disciples) did guide it but himself; men would readily befriend them who are not so welcome, and would neglect the needy, and might

point out Christ as more strange than indeed he is; for here the disciples, who slighted little children and the woman of Canaan, now, when they think their Master is like to be esteemed of among strangers, are foot and hand for them, though they were nothing so sincere, and they do, by consulting one with another, bear these strangers in hand, that it was not easy to find access to him, that so they may admire him the more.

VER. 23. And Jesus answered them, saying, The hour is come, that the Son of man should be glorified.

Followeth to verse 27, the second particular in this part of the chapter, containing Christ's answer to this proposition; wherein, 1. (in this verse) Slighting their curious desire, and tacitly reprehending the disciples' carnal way of managing it, he sheweth that he had other true glory to look to, which made him vilipend [despise] this carnal respect tendered unto him by strangers —to wit, the glory of, and following upon, his sufferings, which were near approaching. And withal, by this doctrine he points out that they ought to seek acquaintance with him, not as a man lately cried up by popular applause, but as a glorified Christ on the triumphant chariot of his cross, and exalted at the Father's right hand. Whence learn—

1. Christ takes no pleasure to satisfy the curiosity of men, nor in worldly glory, nor will he foster his followers in an estimation of it; therefore doth he slight this motion, and preaches what was of more importance. He will not call them into his presence, but by his doctrine doth testify he did not relish the respects they offered to him.

2. As sad sufferings may be following close after some sun-blink of glory and triumph, so it concerns the Lord's people to meditate and resolve thereupon, even in their best days; for after Christ's triumph, " the hour (of his suffering) is come," or near approaching; and he is meditating thereupon.

3. Divine Providence is so particular about all things, particularly about the sufferings of Christ and his followers, that not so much as the hour when the sufferings shall begin but it is determined; therefore saith he so particularly, " the hour is come," &c.

4. Such as would take a right look of the sufferings of Christ and his followers ought to look through all the pain, bitterness, or ignominy that is in them, and fix their eye upon the glory that is in that lot and followeth thereupon; for thus doth Christ leave us an example, who, in speaking of the approaching time of his suffering, declareth that he looks upon it as an hour wherein the Son of man is to be glorified. This was true, even of his very sufferings, that he was glorified in being called to exercise the office of a priest for his people, Heb. v. 4, 5. And so also saints have looked on their sufferings for him as a high honour conferred upon them, Acts, v. 41, but it was more visibly verified in the issue of his sufferings, 1 Pet. i. 11, when in his own per-

son he was exalted unto glory, Luke, xxiv. 26, and by the virtue of his death became great in the world, as ver. 32 of this chapter.

5. Such as get open eyes to discern the glory of the cross and the glory that abides Christ and his followers after their suffering, will not care for nor relish worldly pomp and glory, or carnal respect from men; therefore Christ slights this offer, because his eye was fixed elsewhere : " The hour is come that the Son of man should be glorified." (See Heb. xi. 24, 27 ; xii. 2.)

6. Christ will entertain no acquaintance with any unless his cross be beautiful unto them, and unless they lay aside doting on his bodily presence, and study communion with him in his sufferings and exaltation ; for while as they sought to converse with him bodily, and see his imagined outward glory, he in his answer remits them to his suffering and exaltation shortly approaching, to study acquaintance with him there.

VER. 24. Verily, verily, I say unto you, Except a corn of wheat fall into the ground and die, it abideth alone: but if it die, it bringeth forth much fruit.

In the next place, because Christ's suffering as the way to his glory did stumble many of those who had carnal imaginations concerning the Messiah, therefore (in this verse) he clears the necessity of his dying by a similitude taken from grain, which, unless it be sown and die in the ground, can produce no increase, but being sown, it bringeth forth much fruit ; even so, unless he died, there would be no conversion of lost men unto God. Whence learn—

1. The necessity and usefulness of the cross is not easily believed by the sons of men ; and it is a point to be received on Christ's word, who will not deceive; therefore doth he begin this doctrine concerning his sufferings with so grave an asseveration—" Verily, verily, I say unto you."

2. If Christ had not died, and continued for awhile under the power of death, we could reap no profit by him, nor would any have gone to heaven with him ; for " Except a corn of wheat fall into the ground and die, it abideth alone," and so had been here. It had been no prejudice to him, only his love could not be without us, nor had it been manifested unless he had brought many sons unto glory, but all the loss had been ours.

3. Christ's death hath produced a fair harvest of fruit on the earth, many being drawn unto him, and many sweet fruits flowing from his death to them ; for " if it die, it bringeth forth much fruit," and so is it here. And thus also doth the Lord bless the afflictions even of saints, to bring out much good.

4. The profit that flows from the cross of Christ and his followers ought to prevent any stumbling thereat ; for by this argument Christ obviates the scandal here. And indeed, if the fruit of the cross be an argument to move him to embrace it, much more should it take away our stumbling.

Ver. 25. He that loveth his life shall lose it ; and he that hateth his life in this world shall keep it unto life eternal.

26. If any man serve me, let him follow me ; and where I am, there shall also my servant be : if any man serve me, him will my Father honour.

In the last place, Christ having acquainted them with what was his true glory, and the way to it, doth now point out the way how to come and have communion with him therein—to wit, by taking up the cross, and following him. And for this end—1. He sets forth the danger of irresolution and the good of resolution in this point, ver. 25. A man that is sparing, if it were even of his life when Christ calls for it, doth take the ready way to lose it, and he who doth hazard it for him at his call is sure to live eternally. 2. He points out their obligation to this duty, that if any will be his servants, it is reason they follow him in the paths he hath trodden, ver. 26. 3. He subjoins, for the encouragement of such, that if they follow him as servants they shall enjoy his company, and if they honour him, the Father will honour them, ver. 26.

From verse 25, learn—1. It is not enough that Christ's followers leave off to stumble at his sufferings, or at the afflictions of others, unless they be content also to submit to the cross, without stumbling, in their own persons ; therefore doth he subjoin this doctrine to the former concerning his death, to breed them with the cross in their own persons.

2. Albeit Christ may let some easily slip through, and others get away with some small loss, yet he approves of no followers who are not resolved on the loss of what is dearest to them, yea, even of life, for his sake ; therefore doth he mention our life to be hated, not secluding other things, as parents, wife, children, houses, lands, &c., but including them all in this, as being the most precious enjoyment. And since some are put to that, all must resolve on it.

3. It is not enough that men quit anything for Christ, unless it be done with cheerfulness, zeal, and a holy indignation that anything, how precious soever, should come in competition with obedience to him ; therefore is it required that they hate their life ; which is not to be understood absolutely, as if it were a sin to love life, as it is the gift of God, or that they should weary of it ; but comparatively, that they should not love it more than Christ, Matt. x. 37, and should abhor that it should come in competition with duty to him.

4. Whatever be our obligations to Christ, yet men's inordinate affection to their temporal life is a great impediment to our duty, when it comes to that push ; for it is supposed that too many will love their life, (to wit, in this world, or their temporal life,) so as to prefer the preservation of it to obedience and a good conscience.

5. Whoever are careful to preserve their temporal life upon any terms, take the short cut to lose it and eternal life also ; for " he that loveth his life shall lose it." He both provokes Christ to plague that life, and cut it off, which he will not employ in a good cause, and however it fare with his temporal life, yet he loseth eternal life.

6. As the loose grip of things temporal is the surest and best grip, so when a man prefers service to Christ to his own life, it is the sure way to preserve both body and soul unto life eternal ; for " he that hateth his life in this world shall keep it unto life eternal." Sometimes the Lord may continue and preserve a man's life after he hath submitted to lose it for his sake ; but however that succeed, yet the other encouragement stands firm.

7. They who have the lively hope of eternal life will easily digest any temporal loss, especially when that hope cannot be attained without that loss ; for preservation " unto eternal life" is sufficient to persuade a man, when he is called to it, to hate " his life in this world."

8. Such as live by faith must renounce the principles of carnal sense and reason, and be content to walk on grounds contrary to these, especially in times of trial ; for they must learn that love and keeping of life is loss, and hatred and losing of it is keeping of it.

From verse 26, learn—1. Christ will not be content of glorious-like outside acquaintance with men unless they engage themselves in humble service to him ; therefore, in opposition to their desire of seeing him, ver. 21, he desires that men should serve him.

2. Such as give up themselves to serve Christ must not in their duties prescribe unto him, but must be content to follow his directions ; and in their lots they must not think it ill to be no better used than he was, but should account the worst condition sweet and easy, in that he essayed it and paved the way before them ; for saith he, " If any man serve me, let him follow me."

3. Such as serve Christ by following him shall be sure not only to see him, but to enjoy his company ; he will be with them in trouble, and not let them be alone, and they shall be brought at last to partake of the sweet issue that followed on his sufferings ; for " where I am, there shall also my servant be." (See Luke, xxii. 28, 29 ; John, xvii. 24 ; Rom. viii. 17.)

4. It is a sweet encouragement to sincere followers of Christ that in glory they shall have constant and near fellowship with him, which they are so much thirsting after in their pilgrimage ; for this is the encouragement of servants, " where I am, there shall also my servant be."

5. Whatever disgrace Christ's servants may meet with, yet to serve him is their true honour, and will be rewarded at last with visible honour ; for " If any man serve me, him will my Father honour." (See 1 Sam. ii. 30.)

6. He saith here, my Father will honour him, not only to point out that it is true honour only which is conferred by God, John, v. 44, but to teach that Christ as Mediator is so accepted of the Father that he will put marks of favour and honour upon all his servants.

Ver. 27. Now is my soul troubled ; and what shall I say ? Father, save me from this hour : but for this cause came I unto this hour.

Followeth to verse 31, the third particular in this part of the chapter, wherein (to prevent stumbling at his death) it is made evident, first by sore exercise, and then by consolation sent from heaven, that it was the will of God he should suffer, and yet not sink under it. His exercise is recorded, ver. 27, his outgate and consolation, ver. 28, unto which is subjoined an exposition of God's purpose in this way of comforting of him, upon occasion of the several thoughts of the people about it, ver. 29, 30.

In this verse his exercise is pointed out in these particulars :—1. That while he is preaching of his own death and suffering trouble doth seize upon his soul in the midst of his doctrine, and he is so overwhelmed that he cannot get it hid, but must tell it out before all his hearers. 2. That he is so perplexed that he knows not what to say. 3. That getting a vent in prayer, there is a conflict betwixt his averseness from this lot and exercise, and his submission to endure what his office called him unto. Now for clearing this soul-trouble of Christ (which we find very familiar to him, chap. xi. 33 ; xiii. 21 ; Matt. xxvi. 38 ; xxvii. 46,) we would consider— 1. The rise and cause of it was thus: the godhead hiding itself from the humanity's sense, and the Father letting out, not only an apprehension of his sufferings to come, but a present taste of the horror of his wrath due to man for sin, he is amazed, overwhelmed, and perplexed with it in his humanity ; and no wonder, since he had the sins of all the elect laid upon him by imputation to suffer for. And so this wrath is not let out against his person, but against their sins, which were laid on him. 2. Albeit Christ's soul was here troubled, (or jumbled and puzzled, as the word imports,) yet we are not to conceive there was any sin in this exercise of his, though the like may be muddy [impure] in us ; for we are like foul water, which being stirred becomes like a puddle, but he was like clean water in a clean vessel, which being never so often stirred and shaken yet keeps still clean and clear. 3. We are not to think it strange that the Son of God should be put to such perplexities in this trouble as not to know what to say ; for considering him as man, encompassed with our sinless infirmities, and that this heavy weight of wrath did light upon him on a sudden, it is no wonder it did confound all his thoughts as man. 4. These contrary desires and debates of Christ in his voluntary exinanition were without all sinful infirmity ; for in his desiring the trouble to be removed, he testified that his holy and sinless nature did abhor to lie under wrath ; and in his being willing to suffer he clears that in respect of his office and being our surety he denieth himself, and submits to what his office required of him, and what his Father had appointed him to suffer, how much soever he abhorred it.

From this whole purpose in general we may learn—1. The sad agonies of Christ's soul being under the burden of sin imputed to him is a mirror wherein we may read the bitter desert of sin, what bitter wrath follows upon it, and how abominable it is that produceth such fruits.

2. We may herein, also, read how impartial a judge God is, and how impartial in craving and taking satisfaction for sin, so that if his own beloved Son come betwixt sinners and the stroke, he will not spare him, but let out such sad soul-trouble upon him. And this may make the sins of the elect bitter to them that they did pierce Christ, and did make him a man of sorrows and acquainted with griefs.

3. This may also discover unto us what difficulty there was in the work of our redemption, that it put the Son of God to such pressures and perplexities to carry through it.

4. Herein also shines forth the love of the Father in giving his Son, and the Son's love in undertaking this hard task and drinking this bitter cup, for their sake who were living in enmity against him, and who cannot be profitable unto him.

5. Such as in the sense of sin and deserved wrath do flee to Christ, will find him a tender Saviour, who is experimentally acquainted with all their sinless infirmities, and with all those tentations they are vexed with, though without sin ; for he hath drunk of that bitter cup.

6. Christ, in his own person, hath sanctified trouble and distress of mind to all his followers, as here is left upon record.

7. In this exercise we may read to whom it is we owe any true peace of conscience we enjoy, even to him upon whom the chastisement of our peace was, and who endured this trouble that we might rest safely under his shadow.

8. The godly may also learn hence a good use of any trouble of mind that comes upon them ; even to learn hereby somewhat of his bitter sufferings for them, that so he may be more precious in their eyes.

9. We may read in this exercise and experience of Christ how soon a good condition may be clouded, and how any may be well and have help near them, and yet not see it ; for Christ while he is thus troubled is still the Son of God and beloved of him, and his outgate is very near, yet for the present he is overclouded and taken up with nothing but perplexity and horror.

10. Finally, this sad trouble and exercise of Christ may point out what will be the sad lot of all the wicked who have not Christ to satisfy for them ; for if this be done in the green tree, what shall be done in the dry ? Luke, xxiii. 31.

More particularly from the words and context learn—1. As sin hath infected both soul and body of the elect, and chiefly the soul, where it hath its chief seat, so Christ, to expiate this sin, did suffer unspeakable sorrows and trouble in his soul, as well as torture in his body ; for " my soul is troubled," saith he. (See Isa. liii. 10.)

2. Albeit some sufferings of the body be very exquisite and painful, and Christ's, in particular, was such, yet sad trouble of mind is far more grievous than any bodily distress, as Christ also found, who silently bare all his outward troubles, but must cry out of the other, " Now is my soul troubled."

3. Sad trouble of mind is very hard to conceal and smother from the knowledge of others, nor have they cause to complain of extremity who get it hid ; and they who get their exercise hid ought to acknowledge Christ, who was put to proclaim his trouble before a multitude, that

theirs might be more easy; and on the other hand, when any are driven to that extremity that they must cry out of soul trouble, they may find this exercise sanctified in Christ's person, who, in the midst of a multitude, must interrupt preaching and cry out, " Now is my soul troubled."

4. Albeit Christ be God over all, blessed for ever, yet it pleased him, in going through his sufferings, so to abase himself as to wrestle with horror, fears, and perplexities under them; and to fight with the weapons he hath left for saints in like cases, that so he may be a faithful and merciful high priest, and may assure them of success who, in the like case, make use of the like means; for whereas upon Christ's former doctrine, of his sufferings, and the duty of his followers to suffer, any might be ready to think that it was easy for him to speak of trouble and bear it in respect of others, therefore he lets them see that he had the same exercise, trouble, perplexities, and fears about it (though without sin) that saints have, and that he used the same weapons of prayer, wrestling, and submission that are left unto them.

5. A special mean for raising trouble in a tender mind is their thinking much upon it, which doth beget and waken it; for so was it with Christ; while he is thinking and preaching of his sufferings, trouble ariseth: " Now is my soul troubled," saith he. And albeit Christ was sinless in so doing, yet it is our sin ofttimes to beget trouble by our musing upon it.

6. There is a vast difference betwixt the most exact comprehension of trouble in the judgment and the experimental feeling thereof in the senses; the one may be without so much vexation and trouble as the other will produce. This also appears in Christ's exercise, who, though he understood perfectly what his sufferings should be, and had resolved upon them, yet when he came to feel trouble it raiseth all this perplexity. And however Christ went beyond us in this, that he met with all he resolved upon, which made it thus heavy, whereas we are ofttimes disappointed in our apprehensions, and get less than we look for; and so the trouble itself is ofttimes easier than the exercise and apprehension of it; yet this experience of Christ's may learn all never to trust their own resolutions for trouble, but to make ready for it if God send it on, as another thing to present sense and feeling than anything they could imagine.

7. How stout soever the hearts of men be, yet when the Lord lets out trouble for sin it will damp them, and put them to a nonplus in all their resolutions, that they shall not know what to do or say; for if the great teacher of his church, who hath much to say for our counsel and comfort in such cases,—if he, I say, under this cloud, be so puzzled as he is put to " what shall I say?" what may others expect?

8. As Christ, by his perplexity till he had nothing to say, hath purchased an open mouth to his people in their addresses to God, so when any of them are perplexed they ought not to be discouraged at it, but should look to him who hath tasted of that cup for their comfort and behoof. Therefore is it left on record that he was put to " what shall I say?" not asking counsel at any by this question, but testifying his real perplexity.

9. Prayer is the special mean of relieving troubled and perplexed souls, which will find out a vent and outgate to perplexity, if there be any to be found under or in heaven; therefore Christ betaketh himself to this remedy, and whosoever do neglect it and betake themselves to carnal shifts will prove physicians of no value and will heal their own wounds slightly, or prove miserable comforters, and add to their own sorrows.

10. As God doth not break off his relations to his people when he plungeth them under sad exercises and perplexities, but continueth still a Father, so it is the duty of saints to hold fast this interest, and to make use of it in prayer, and it may be cleaved unto in the midst of great perplexities; for in this Christ hath cast us a copy, who in all this agony pleads with God as his Father, and teacheth saints that they have warrant to do the like.

11. Albeit Christ's wrestling betwixt the inclination of his holy nature and his obligation by his office was free of sin, as hath been cleared, yet his experience of this exercise may teach saints that he will be very tender of their ravings in their fevers, and that he will pity them when they are tossed betwixt inclination and conscience of duty, betwixt a willing spirit and weak flesh, and when the flesh's word is first out and the Spirit's word followeth after it to correct it; for here he hath come as near us in this exercise as might be without sin, that he might sympathize with us in it.

12. Were our distress and perplexities never so great yet it is our duty to believe the power of God, that he is able to deliver us out of them all, if he please; for Christ's prayer, " Save me from this hour," or this sad fit of trouble, doth import that he believeth God could do it if he would.

13. The sense of wrath is insupportable to human flesh, and sinless nature will abhor to be under the wrath of God above any other sad lot; for both these are imported in this prayer of Christ, " Save me from this hour," as is before explained.

14. Saints ought not to be discouraged when the strength of exercise and tentation doth overturn their resolutions for a time, but they are to expect that after they are laid by they may yet recover and acquit themselves as becometh; for herein Christ hath paved a way, though without sin, who after his holy inclination would have declined his work, yet continues resolute to undertake it.

15. It is the duty of saints not to lean much to their own inclinations, especially under exercise, how innocent soever they seem to be, but they ought to reckon that usually their inclinations and choice are different from what is their duty, and the will of God concerning them; for so much doth Christ's exercise teach us, who though he without sin desired to decline wrath, yet he quits that desire because the thing desired was inconsistent with that to which God had called him.

16. The conscience of our duty and of our

obligation to God not to neglect it, ought to moderate our desires concerning our own safeties; for so doth Christ recal his former desire with this, " But for this cause came I unto this hour" —that is, this calling to suffer—this was laid upon me, and I have undertaken it, and therefore will not now decline it.

17. Christ commends his love unto his people, in that he would decline nothing that his office and calling required should be done for them, how much soever he abhorred it in his sinless nature; therefore after he had testified his abhorring this cup, yet for our sake he submits to drink it.

VER. 28. Father, glorify thy name. Then came there a voice from heaven, saying, I have both glorified it, and will glorify it again.

In this verse is recorded Christ's outgate and consolation; it begins at submission in his prayer, that God would so dispose of him as might glorify his own name without respect to his ease or inclination. And as this evidenceth the calm temper of his mind, so his consolation is perfected by a voice from heaven, testifying that as the Father had glorified his name already in Christ's life, so he would glorify it yet more in his death.

From Christ's submission, learn—1. It is the duty of God's children not to expect always, or at the first, an outgate by a change of God's dispensations towards them, but rather to seek it by a change of their own disposition within them, making them fit to undergo such dispensations; for herein Christ hath cast us a copy, in laying aside the inclination of his nature to be rid of trouble, and submitting to it.

2. It is the duty of saints under trouble to prefer the honour of God, and to seek how it may be advanced, before their own ease; for Christ ends all his debates with this—" Father, glorify thy name," though by my trouble and suffering.

3. Submission unto the will of God is a real outgate from trouble, and a special victory over it; for hereby Christ gets an issue of his agony and perplexities, " Father, glorify thy name." (See Matt. xxvi. 39; Acts, xxi. 14.)

4. The way to attain submission is to be tender of God's glory, and to account that dearer unto us than anything else; for this leads Christ to submit unto this bitter cup, that hereby the Father glorifieth his name; whereas, on the contrary, men's selfishness and want of zeal is a great enemy to their submission.

From the Lord's comfortable answer, learn— 1. Sorest exercises are not sent on God's children to destroy them, but when in their perplexities they seek to God and submit to him there will be a comfortable issue; for immediately " there came a voice from heaven," &c., and so not only is he delivered, but the sorer his exercise had been, it is the shorter.

2. There is no true comfort against soul-trouble but what comes from God, and is spoken by him from heaven; for this comforts Christ— " There came a voice from heaven." And albeit we are not to expect such extraordinary manifes-

tations, (nor did Christ simply need them in such a way, ver. 30,) yet it must be spoken from the word by God to the heart before we get ease.

3. Such as are truly exercised in conscience will find ease in comfortable promises, clearing their condition, from the word, albeit the trouble lie on; for thus Christ is comforted by " a voice from heaven" clearing his case.

4. Christ is a supplicant, whose voice is acknowledged by the Father, as the voice of his Son, in that for which he seeks to him; for here his supplication is answered by " a voice from heaven."

5. The Father is glorified in the life and sufferings of Christ, and not only doth the Son glorify him herein, but he undertakes to glorify himself; as here his answer doth shew, " I have both glorified it, and I will glorify it again."

6. The Lord's answers to troubled souls are very full, clearing all they do or can propound, and all they feel or is lying upon them; for he not only undertakes to glorify his name in that wherewith Christ is now troubled, but clears further what he had done.

7. God's speaking to a troubled soul brings not only comfort under their present pressures, but is a Pisgah from whence they may take a comfortable view of their by-past lots, and may see fair ground of hope for time to come; for in this comfort God clears both by-gones and the time to come: " I have both glorified it, and will glorify it again."

VER. 29. The people therefore, that stood by, and heard it, said that it thundered: others said, An angel spake to him.

30. Jesus answered and said, This voice came not because of me, but for your sakes.

In these verses, upon occasion of the several conjectures of the people concerning this audible voice, ver. 29, Christ doth expound God's purpose in this public way of comforting him; that he did it, not so much because Christ needed it, as to testify unto them that he was accepted of God, owned of him in his sufferings, and would be victorious over them through him. Whence learn—

1. God is very glorious and full of majesty, and appears so when he reveals himself; his voice, even in consolations, is glorious; for his voice here was such as the people " said that it thundered" when they heard it.

2. As natural men are ignorant of spiritual soul-trouble, so do they as little understand the consolations which God alloweth on those who are so exercised; for they understand nothing of this matter, but some (it seems) who were more remote, " said it thundered: others (more near) said, An angel spake to him."

3. It is the great fault of men that they delight rather to talk curiously of the extraordinary manifestations of God than study to know the use to be made of them; therefore they are curiously debating what this should mean, when Christ tells them they should study for whose sake it came.

4. Consolations are then double consolations when men are not only refreshed thereby, but

are led to know how they ought to be improven. Thus Christ is led to look on this voice for whose sake it comes, and knows what use should be made thereof.

5. All the glorious testimonies given unto Christ from heaven tended to point him out unto sinners as the true Messiah approven of God; and that for the conviction of the malicious, and for the encouragement and confirmation of their faith who flee to him; therefore saith he, " This voice came not because of me, but for your sakes." He needed, indeed, the consolation, and it might have been imparted to him in a private way; but this public way of declaring the consolation was for their behoof.

VER. 31. Now is the judgment of this world: now shall the prince of this world be cast out.

32. And I, if I be lifted up from the earth, will draw all men unto me.

33. This he said, signifying what death he should die.

In these verses is recorded the fourth particular in this part of the chapter—namely, that Christ being now calmed in his exercise, and refreshed with the late consolation, doth resume the point he had been upon, ver. 23, 24, and publisheth more fully the glorious fruits and effects of his death. The fruits of his death, here mentioned, are—1. The judgment of this world. 2. The casting out of Satan, the prince of this world, ver. 31. 3. The drawing of all men to him when he is lifted up from the earth, ver. 32, which lifting up he expounds to signify the manner of his death, ver. 33. Now for right understanding this purpose, the great difficulty is to take up rightly the first fruit of his death concerning " the judgment of this world," which may be diversely taken, according to the different acceptations of the words " judgment," and " world," which may be diverse ways expounded; for, first, taking the world for the world of the elect, (as 2 Cor. v. 19, and John, iii. 16, where the reasons of this denomination are given,) the meaning will be, that they are judged in Christ their head—that is, partly, they are condemned in him who in his sufferings represented and stood surety for them all, and was accused, sentenced, and put to an accursed death for them, and so God for sin condemned their sin in Christ's flesh, Rom. viii. 2; and partly, that by this judgment of Christ in their name there ariseth a judgment of absolution to them, in their own persons, through him. This in itself is a clear and useful truth, and doth well agree also with the casting out of Satan, after mentioned; yet it doth not exhaust the full scope of this place. And albeit the elect, considered by themselves, be sometimes called the world, yet it is not so clear in scripture that they should be called so emphatically, " this world," (which is usually taken in another sense,) especially when in the next words, and 2 Cor. iv. 4, " this world" are they of whom Satan is prince and god; for albeit he reign in the elect while they are children of disobedience and of wrath,

as well as others, Ephes. ii. 2, 3, yet it is not in respect of them that he is " prince of this world," and therefore the name is not so proper to them. Secondly. Understanding this purpose of the reprobate world over whom Satan is prince, the meaning is, that they are judged, or condemned, in the sufferings of Christ, which holds true in these respects—1. It seals up the condemnation of all those unto whom this purchase is revealed, and yet do reject the offer. 2. The sufferings of Christ are a pattern and exemplary, making manifest what is the judgment abiding the wicked, for whom this purchase is not made; for if this be done in the green tree, what shall be done in the dry? 3. They are condemned in Satan, their head and prince, who was foiled and cast out by the death of Christ on the cross, even as the elect are judged and absolved in the suffering and victory of Christ their head. These are indeed truths which do agree well with what followeth of the casting out of Satan; yet do not exhaust the scope either; for there is more that followeth on this ejection of him than all that. And therefore, thirdly, that I may fall upon a more full interpretation, it should be considered that the term, " this world," or, the world, as it is sometimes taken for this present life and the enjoyments thereof, in opposition to eternity, Luke, xx. 34; John, xiii. 1; 1 Cor. vii. 31, and elsewhere; so it is used sometimes to point out the state of this inferior world, and all persons therein, as they are corrupted and out of frame by the fall of man. Thus to be " of this world" is to be in a corrupt estate, John, viii. 23; we are not to be conformed to it, Rom. xii. 2; ought to keep ourselves unspotted from it, James, i. 27; the wisdom thereof is condemned, 1 Cor. iii. 19, and its courses, Ephes. ii. 2; and the world, and things thereof, are to be disclaimed as not being of God, 1 John, ii. 15, 16. Again: the word " judgment," in the Hebrew phrase, (usual to the New Testament,) doth signify the exercise of power and authority for reformation of abuses, and restoration of things that are out of frame to their right and primitive order, yet so as including a condemnation of all that bred this disturbance, or is worthy to be condemned, and an absolution and asserting into liberty all those who were wronged under that disorder. According to these significations of the terms, the sense of the words will be this, (agreeable to Daniel's prediction of Christ's making an end of sins, and bringing in everlasting righteousness, by his death, Dan. ix. 24,)—that whereas, by the fall of Adam, the world hath fallen into confusion and disorder, man hath fallen from integrity and happiness, Satan and sin have reigned and raged in the world, Rom. v. 21; Ephes. ii. 2; the children of this world have blessed themselves in their bad condition, and the elect have lien under slavery and bondage. Now Christ, by his death, hath taken away this disorder, by dethroning and condemning the disturbers, sin and Satan; by bringing in everlasting righteousness; by manifesting the condemnation of the wicked, and by restoring the elect to that happiness they were deprived of by sin. This I take to be the most satisfactory interpretation, partly, because it is most comprehensive; for albeit sin and Satan be condemned and cast out only in respect of the elect world, and the restoration be only purchased to them, yet the interpretation also includes all the other interpretations of condemning sin and Satan, and of the reprobates, as is before explained, and the absolution of the elect through him who was condemned as their surety; and partly, because it runs well with the rest of the fruits of his death here mentioned; for this "judgment of this world" is put first, as a comprehensive and general fruit, that hereby he reforms those things that were out of frame by the fall of man. The next, of Satan's casting out, is subjoined, to point out the mean and way of this restoration—namely, by dethroning the usurper and disturber. And the third, of drawing all men to him, is added as an effect and further explication of this restoration of the elect world; that he will draw them to himself, the fountain and channel of that happiness which they lost in Adam. It is further to be considered, for clearing the words, that while Christ saith, " Now," in his sufferings, " is the judgment of this world," and Satan, " cast out," we must avoid two rocks in understanding of them:—1. That we conceive not of this as if this judgment and casting out had not been in the world before the time of Christ's death,—for the elect were made partakers of the benefit hereof in all ages before the incarnation of Christ,—but the meaning is, partly, that this world was never judged, nor Satan cast out at any time, but by virtue of his death which he was now to suffer, and that now he was to pay the price, and fight the good fight, by virtue whereof it is that, in any age, Satan is foiled and the world judged; and partly, that now he was to have more visible and copious fruits of this judgment than formerly, especially throughout the world, and not among the Jews only. 2. We are not to conceive as if this judgment of restoration and the casting out of Satan were completed and perfected at the death of Christ; for albeit the purchase be then completely made, yet the application doth but follow in due time to the elect, and that is carried on by degrees, till, in the great day, there be a complete restitution of all things, Acts, iii. 21, and a solid victory and triumph over all our enemies. And therefore it is spoken of by way of promise for the future, the prince of this world shall be cast out, and, I will draw all men.

Not to repeat the several instructions which have been pointed at in the several interpretations of the first phrase, (all which are included in this interpretation,) we may further, from verse 31, learn—

1. Whatever be the sharp exercises of saints under the sense of wrath, yet it is to be expected they will have an end, if not also pass shortly over; for this encouragement is given us in the experience of our head, who is now in a short time calmed. (See Isa. liv. 7, 8.) And albeit Heman had a long time of it, Ps. lxxxviii. 15, yet he saw an end of it.

2. When the Lord seeth it fit to exercise his children with much and sore exercise, whereof they will not so soon see an end, yet such is his mercy as not to overdrive them, but to afford them a breathing time betwixt one pang and an-

other, which they should highly esteem of; for so is also verified in Christ, who, although he was a man of sorrows, and acquainted with grief, and another sad storm was abiding him after this, yet he gets this calm, and a clear sun-blink among hands.

3. How much soever exercise do perplex and confound the thoughts of saints, so that they will be tempted with strange thoughts and misconstructions of their lot, and of God's dealing towards them, yet, when the cloud is over, they will recal these thoughts, and look as comfortably on the saddest of their lots as ever. So much also doth Christ's experience teach, who in his exercise abhorred his suffering of the accursed death and the wrath of God; yet now, when he is calmed, he hath as sweet thoughts of that lot as formerly he had, ver. 23.

4. Such as would have their issues from trouble, and their exercise, blessed unto them, ought to make use thereof, and to improve them to the best advantage in their place and station; for herein Christ hath cast us a copy, who, being comforted, and getting a breathing time, doth fall a preaching again, and communicates his consolations to his hearers.

5. The best way of looking on our sad exercises and straits is to ponder the fruits that God will bring out of them, which may swallow up the bitterness and grief they put us unto, and which we do pore too much upon. So Christ is comforted over the bitterness of the cup of his sufferings, whereof he had a late taste, by looking upon the fruit thereof.

6. By the fall of Adam, this inferior world is out of frame and in disorder; not only is the whole creation groaning and travailing in pain, Rom. viii. 22, but all mankind by nature are lying in wickedness, with their backs upon God, after whose image they were created; and sin and Satan are raging in them at their pleasure, and making them fight against God, with whom they were entered in a covenant of friendship; for so is here imported, that there is need of a " judgment," or restoration, in " this world."

7. No mean that could be devised, beside the death of Christ, was able to reform this disorder, nor can put in frame those things that are out of course; for saith he, " Now (and by no other mean) is the judgment of this world."

8. Christ, by his death, hath restored the collapsed estate of this world. Albeit he permit the generality of men to lie over in their lost estate, as being debtor to none, yet even they are judged, in so far as they are inseparable from sin, which he destroyeth, and as their condemnation is made manifest. But in reference to the elect world, he hath destroyed and subdued sin (in the guilt, power, and effects thereof) and Satan, which disturb the world, and hath brought in righteousness, absolved them, and asserted them into liberty in himself; for " Now (saith he) is the judgment of this world."

9. Albeit it be said that " now," at Christ's death, this judgment is passed, yet it is not to be mistaken, when even the converted elect find sin in its guilt and power, and Satan (of whom in the next part of this verse) so prevalent and raging; for, (to clear what is already said in the explica-

tion,) 1. Though the purchase be then made, and the application be begun at their conversion, yet the full possession and victory is not attained till the end, 1 Cor. xv. 54, 55.　2. Whatever exercise it please the Lord to put them unto, yet the victory at last is sure, this purchase being made. 3. The raging of sin and Satan, which the elect feel and groan under, is an evidence they are cast out, whereas otherwise they would be at quiet, Luke, xi. 21, 22; Rom. vii. 9.　4. The reason why the converted elect find so little present fruit of this purchase is because they make so little use of an interest in Christ by faith and of the conquest we have in him our head, as Rom. vi. 11.　Thus are we to understand this purpose, " Now is the judgment of this world."

10. It makes up the great disorder of this world in respect of the elect, that not only they are under the power of corruption, but Satan also is daily blowing at the bellows of it, and himself also immediately suggesting wicked tentations; for here it is added, as a great cause of this disorder, that Satan is a " prince of this world," who must be "cast out," that this "judgment" may be.

11. Satan is a prince and ruler of those who live in sin, not by any right, but by tyrannical usurpation, who doth furiously drive them on in the service of sin; for he is " the prince of this world." (See 2 Cor. iv. 4; Eph. ii. 2; 2 Tim. ii. 26.)

12. Satan is an usurper who will not quit his possession with good will, unless he be cast out; for he must be " cast out ;" where it is otherwise, and he but goeth out, he doth but deceive, Matt. xii. 43—45.

13. Christ's death is Satan's overthrow; then did he spoil principalities and powers, Col. ii. 15, and the merit and efficacy of his death will cast him out of the elect by degrees; for " Now shall the prince of this world be cast out"—namely, out of his tyrannical usurpation in the world, in relation to the elect, and out of them.

From verses 32, 33, learn—1. The elect, who are made partakers of Christ's death, are in themselves a great number, gathered out of all nations and sexes of people, and are Christ's all, whom he careth for; therefore are they called "all men."

2. Whatever be Christ's purpose of love towards the elect, and his purchase for them, yet in themselves they are at a great distance from their happiness, till they be brought unto it; for they are drawn to him, which imports a distance.

3. The elect are not only far from Christ, but so averse from their own happiness, and have so many impediments in their way, that they must be drawn to it before they come; for " I will draw all men," saith he. (Comp. John, vi. 44.)

4. Christ will not want his purchase notwithstanding all these impediments; his death doth purchase life to them, and his efficacious power will bring them to participate thereof; for " I will draw all men," saith he.

5. They to whom Christ applies the efficacy of his death will find no place of rest till they be brought to communion with him, and abide with him; and he will not give over perfecting their happiness and drawing them till he bring them where he is; for " I will draw all men unto me"— that is, to communion with me through my death, and to be where I am.

6. Christ's cross will be glorious in their eyes who see the rich fruits thereof; therefore doth he describe it: " If I be lifted up from the earth"— to wit, on the cross, alluding to the brazen serpent as a glorious exaltation of him, when so many should flow to a crucified Saviour.

7. Christ knew his own death and the manner of it before he embraced it, and so he was not surprised with it, but made it his voluntary choice; for he spake this beforehand, " signifying what death he should die."

8. Christ's victories over sin and Satan are glorious and remarkable, not only in themselves, but also in the way and manner of them, that he should overcome by ignominy, weakness, suffering, and death; therefore is the exposition of this lifting up given, that we may ponder much this way of his success.

9. Christ's words ought not only to be reverently heard, but should be marked and pondered till they be understood; therefore John thinks it needful not to leave this one word uncleared.

Ver. 34. The people answered him, We have heard out of the law that Christ abideth for ever: and how sayest thou, The Son of man must be lifted up? who is this Son of man?

Followeth to verse 37, the last particular in this part of the chapter, containing an objection of the people against Christ's former doctrine concerning his sufferings, together with Christ's answer thereunto, and the close of this purpose.

In this verse is their objection; wherein, understanding well that title of " the Son of man" to be understood by Christ of himself, and that his lifting up was meant of his death who gave out himself to be the Messiah, they do object that the scripture (Psalm cx. 4, and elsewhere) speaks of the perpetual endurance of the Messiah, and therefore do disdainfully inquire who this Son of man is? seeing by his own concessions he could not be the Messiah, since he was to be lifted up and die.　The error and mistake in all this objection is their not considering and distinguishing of two natures in Christ's person, of both which the scripture speaks, Isaiah, liii. 7; 8, seeing he might be lifted up in the one, and yet abide for ever in respect of the other; likewise, their confounding his state of humiliation unto death with his state of exaltation after his sufferings, in which respect he abideth for ever.

DOCTRINES.

1. Christ's sweetest doctrine will not gain on wicked unbelievers, but they will carp and stumble, yea, they will rather voluntarily seek occasion of quarrelling than embrace and believe it; for notwithstanding Christ hath even now been owned from heaven, and his doctrine hath been most sweet, yet " the people answered him," and objected against his doctrine.

2. It is a necessary and commendable duty in the members of the visible church to be well acquainted with scriptures, and to improve all means for that end; for albeit they be " the people," (or multitude, as the word signifies,) yet

they can give an account what they have " heard out of the law," where, albeit the scripture pointed at be found in other places in the Old Testament rather than in the books of Moses, yet they call it " the law," for reasons mentioned in chap. x. 34; and they mention only what they have " heard" out of it, either because, being unlearned, they had no means of instruction but their hearing the word read in their synagogues, and yet they understand so much, or because, whatever other means of instruction they had by their own reading, meditation, or conference, yet they neglected not that special mean of edification by the public ordinances.

3. It is from the scriptures only that controversies in religion ought to be determined; for they object nothing to determine this controversy but what they " heard out of the law."

4. Men's knowledge and good parts will not lead them to believe in Christ unless they be sanctified, but will rather furnish them with weapons wherewith to oppose him and his truth; for these are men who understand Christ's language of lifting up, which John thinks needful to explain, ver. 32, 33, and who are well versed in the scriptures; and yet all the use they make hereof is to carp and quarrel.

5. It is the great comfort of believers that the Messiah endureth for ever, to apply his own purchase, and intercede for them, and to make them eternally happy with himself, who is the eternal and all-sufficient God; therefore was this sweet doctrine registrated in " the law that Christ abideth for ever." (See Heb. vii. 25.)

6. Christ's lifting up by death and his abiding for ever do very well consist together if rightly understood; for both these are true of him, when the law saith, " that Christ abideth for ever," and when himself (who is truth itself) saith, " the Son of man must be lifted up." And indeed, concerning Christ there are many seeming contradictions in scripture, as Isa. liii. 7, with 8; Isa. liii. 2, with Psa. xlv. 2; Isa. ix. 6, with John, xii. 27; (see also Matt. xxii. 42, 43, and elsewhere;) which, as they may be easily reconciled by considering that he is true God and true man in one person; by distinguishing betwixt his state of humiliation and of glory, and betwixt the carnal look that wicked men take of him and the spiritual look of right discerners; so they are very comfortable to study: for hereby is held out how low he stooped to reach sinners, and yet how high he is, that he may exalt them. Thus also do the scriptures speak of his church and her conditions in different and seeming contrary terms, as Cant. i. 5; 2 Cor. vi. 9, 10, and elsewhere; which also are easily reconciled by distinguishing betwixt the world's thoughts (and sometimes her own also) of her and God's thoughts of her; betwixt what she is in herself and what she is in her head; and betwixt what her conditions are and do portend in themselves, and what Christ brings out of them.

7. As all erroneous persons do seek patrociny [support] for their errors in scripture, (as here they do,) so a special mean of deluding souls and breeding error is when they look on one parcel of scripture without searching into it, John, v. 39, or comparing it with other scriptures which might illustrate and clear it, 1 Cor. ii. 13; for so do they run upon error, by fixing only on such scriptures as spake of the Messiah's abiding for ever, never looking to those which spake as clearly of his sufferings, as Isaiah, liii. throughout; Daniel, ix. 26; Psalm xxii. 16—18, and frequently.

8. Such members of the visible church as are not acquainted with soul misery, and are prepossessed with carnal delusions and fancies concerning Christ and his kingdom, will easily fall into errors concerning him were the contrary truths never so clear in scripture; for this was another occasion of their error. Albeit other scriptures might have cleared this objection, and these people generally knew the scriptures exactly, yet because not only they were not exercised under the sense of misery, needing a suffering Saviour, (which is an usual companion of delusion,) but their heads were filled with a dream of the carnal glory of his kingdom, therefore this blinded their eyes that they saw not, or considered not, those other scriptures. This also for a time blinded the disciples' eyes, that they little pondered the doctrine of Christ's sufferings, Matt. xx. 18—20, yea, and understood it not, Luke, xviii. 31—34.

9. It is an evidence of an impenitent, unhumbled, and wicked disposition in men when they think basely of a suffering Christ, and of his humiliation and death; for such is their temper here in inquiring so disdainfully, " who is this Son of man?" and that because he " must be lifted up."

10. Ignorance, error, and delusion are ordinarily accompanied with much pride and conceit; for so was it with these here. They think they have reasoned so strongly out of the law against his doctrine of the Son of man's suffering, that they insultingly conclude, " Who is this Son of man?" As if they said, We have undeniably argued that thou, the Son of man, cannot be the Messiah, be what thou wilt; for by thy own confession thou must die, and by the law Christ abides for ever. Thus, 1 Tim. vi. 3, 4, pride is joined with error and knowing nothing, and with doting about idle questions, which is an usual mark of delusion.

VER. 35. Then Jesus said unto them, Yet a little while is the light with you. Walk while ye have the light, lest darkness come upon you: for he that walketh in darkness knoweth not whither he goeth.

36. While ye have light, believe in the light, that ye may be the children of light. These things spake Jesus, and departed, and did hide himself from them.

In these verses we have Christ's answer unto and carriage upon this objection, so closing this whole purpose. And first, he will not answer any more directly to their cavilling objection, nor will he insist to clear how his suffering and abiding for ever are consistent, having already abundantly cleared all doubts by his former doctrine and miracles; only he indirectly points at what his former doctrine and miracles had proven

—to wit, that he is the Messiah and light of the world, (of which we heard, chap. viii. 12,) and that by his doctrine and ministry they had the true means of grace to direct them to heaven; and presseth upon them to walk in that light rather than to bark against it; which afterward, ver. 36, he expounds to be their believing in him, and answerable walking. Secondly, he subjoins reasons to enforce this exhortation. As, 1. They were to have but a little while of this light, his person first, and then the gospel holding him out, being to be removed from them; and therefore they had need to improve the opportunity better than to carp and dispute themselves from their happiness. 2. Upon the removal of this light, darkness of ignorance and misery would follow, and then they should wander like men in the dark. 3. If they believe and walk in the light, they shall be the children of light, and his true followers; and by these subjoined to the exhortation he clears also that, however it be a truth that he is to abide for ever, yet not as they understood it, for he was not to abide for ever with the Jews in person, far less was it his errand among them to set up a worldly kingdom; but he came for awhile to purchase eternal redemption that sinners might believe in him, and so become children of the light, and heirs of a heavenly kingdom. Thirdly, Christ having said this, leaves off his preaching and gets away from them. This he did partly to avoid danger, because he saw them begin to heat against him, and knew that his enemies were waiting for his life, and partly to begin the verification of that threatening of the light's departing from them. And however Christ preached and debated much in public at this his last entry into Jerusalem, which is noted by the other evangelists; yet not much after this. And however it was, yet John mentions no more of his public preaching after this, save only a little in the close of this chapter, all the rest which followeth being only spoken unto and with the disciples.

From ver. 35, learn—1. Albeit Christ be very tender of weak ones, who wander, and hath commanded that they be instructed in meekness who oppose, 2 Tim. ii. 25, yet when he hath clearly confirmed his truth, he looks upon the continued carpings of men as a testimony of their malicious disposition, which is neither to be dallied nor debated with; therefore will he not insist to answer to their cavil and objection, but puts them to their duty upon their peril.

2. As cavillations and disputes against the truth are an evidence that men's hearts are dead, and that they are idle in point of practice, so the best way of dealing with such, after the truth is cleared, is to press the practice of godliness upon them, and to let them see the danger of opposing that truth upon which they should be feeding; therefore doth he, instead of answering, press them to walk while they have the light, and points out the hazard of their ill improving of their time.

3. As Christ is the true light of the world, however he be despised by unbelievers, so men's slighting of him doth not diminish his estimation of his own worth, nor should believers think the less of him; for whatever their ca-

villations were, he proposeth himself to be esteemed of as "the light."

4. So long as men enjoy Christ and the means of grace they enjoy light and a sweet estate, if it be well improven, be their outward condition never so sad; for it may still be said in such a case, the light is with you.

5. It is a short while, for most part, that men enjoy the occasion of the means of grace; either they are taken away from the means, or the means are taken from them by persecution, or because of their abuse thereof; for saith he, "Yet a little while is the light with you."

6. Albeit Christ will not at first give up with despisers, yet when men who enjoy the means instead of improving thereof do fall a wearying of and carping at truth, it is a token that they will enjoy them but short while unless they repent; for unto these carpers it is said, "Yet a little while is the light with you," intimating his mercy that it was not yet away, and the danger of a sad and speedy change if they persisted. And however the Lord continue them with such for a time, yet they may be so hardened as not to profit thereby.

7. It may stir up men to improve the opportunity of the means of grace when they consider how short while they may enjoy them, and that their neglecting of the opportunity may shorten it; for it clearly followeth, "Yet a little while is the light with you," therefore "walk while ye have the light."

8. Such as do rightly improve an offer of Christ and the means of grace will be so far from carping thereat that they will not rest satisfied with any notional estimation thereof unless they reduce their knowledge into practice, and in the use of means be advanced in their way to heaven; for it is required that they walk while they have the light, as men make use of the daylight to do their business or travel in.

9. Such as neglect opportunity and abuse the means of grace are justly deprived of that light, and punished with darkness of ignorance and wandering in sinful courses, and of affliction and judgments; for that is the certification, "lest darkness come upon you" when the light is removed; and that is sadder than if they had never enjoyed the light.

10. When Christ is provoked to desert profane despisers of him, yet he will not want some to shine upon in the world; for the threatening is particular darkness upon you. For when he removed his bodily presence from them, and the gospel also, yet he took not this light from the world.

11. As it is the great mercy of those who enjoy and improve the gospel that they know what they are doing, and what to do in every condition, (for they are as men in daylight who see their way,) so it is a sad judgment on despisers, who provoke God to take away the means that they wander in darkness, stumbling on sinful courses, and walking by guess in every step, and that in affliction they know not whither to turn them; for so much is imported in this reason, "for he that walketh in darkness knoweth not whither he goeth."

From verse 36, learn—1. Sinners can never

enough be admonished of or ponder the danger of their neglecting an opportunity of the means of grace, and their duty to make use of it; therefore doth Christ again repeat the exhortation, insinuating the short time they were like to have the opportunity, " While ye have light, believe in the light."

2. Before there can be any answerable walking to an offer of Christ, or any use made of truth, use must be made of faith to close with the truth, and with Christ offered in it; therefore is their walking expounded here, " believe in the light," or the truth of the gospel, and in Christ shining in it.

3. Such as make use of the means of grace do reap fair advantage thereby, in getting and evidencing a good condition; for they are to do this " that ye may be the children of light"—a name given to saints, Luke, xvi. 8; Eph. v. 8; 1 Thess. v. 8; and elsewhere; and the meaning of this encouragement is, that by improving this opportunity they shall be translated out of the power of darkness into the kingdom of Christ, which is a kingdom of light; they shall become the sons of God, who is the Father of lights, James, i. 17, and participate of the sweet effects of Christ's being the light of the world; and by so doing they shall also evidence themselves to be children of light, illuminated by divine light to discern right and wrong, what is their true happiness and real misery, to be men who come to the light with their actions, and who are thirsting after that eternal light of glory.

4. Christ is not only terrible but even meek also to his opposers, if they would submit to him; and all his scope in shewing himself terrible is to drive them to his mercy, and to partake of the fruits of his meekness; for all his threatenings are sweetened with this, that his scope in them is to drive them to duty that they " may be the children of light."

5. There is hope even concerning those who wickedly oppose Christ and his truth that they may partake of his mercy if they will cast away their weapons and submit; for even to such it is offered here, that if they will do duty they may be the children of light."

6. It is needful not only to deal freely with wicked opposers but to discountenance them also, to see what that may work; for " these things spake Jesus, and departed"—that is, he went away at night to Bethany, as the other evangelists observe, and by this means also he did avoid their fury and plots within the city.

7. Convictions and offers do ofttimes so little prevail with wicked men that they do but heighten their malice; for Christ behoved to " hide himself" after this doctrine.

8. In cases of hazard from malicious men it is lawful to preserve our own lives by ordinary and lawful means; for Jesus hid himself from them.

9. Christ's servants must not weary of frequency of trials in discharge of their duty, and to be put to it again and again, even to save themselves from extreme violence; for Christ hath sanctified this lot in his own person, who was often put to hide himself.

Ver. 37. But though he had done so many miracles before them, yet they believed not on him:

38. That the saying of Esaias the prophet might be fulfilled, which he spake, Lord, who hath believed our report? and to whom hath the arm of the Lord been revealed?.

Followeth the fourth and last part of the chapter, wherein John, being about to close the narration of Christ's doctrine and miracles among the Jews, doth give an account of his success among the most part of them, (secluding the small number who believed in him,) who were either wicked misbelievers, and were nothing moved with his doctrine and miracles, but rather hardened, as had been fore-prophesied, to ver. 42, or hidden and timorous friends, who for carnal respects durst not avow or confess him, ver. 42, 43; and unto this he subjoins Christ's farewell sermon to them, ver. 44, &c.

In these verses is recorded—1. The open incredulity of the most part of his hearers. 2. An aggravation of this fault from the great diligence used to draw them to him, not only by doctrine, but by miracles, which they so much sought after. 3. This is illustrated by comparing this event with a foregoing prophecy, Isa. liii. 1. For clearing whereof, and the citation of it in this place, consider—1. This prophecy is applied to Christ's ministry, not as if it had no accomplishment in others,—for Isaiah makes mention of our report, which includes both himself and his fellow-prophets, who did publish and fore-prophesy of the gospel; and Christ's apostles and ministers also, Rom. x. 15, 16,—but the meaning is, that as Isaiah, in his time, preaching of Christ, had cause to complain of bad success, so his complaint is also a prediction of the like success of Christ, his apostles and ministers, in the days of the gospel. Consider—2. This their carriage is compared with the prediction, and they are said not to believe, " that the saying of Esaias might be fulfilled," not to free them from the sin and guilt of their unbelief, nor doth it hold out that this prediction was a cause thereof, or that God, by foretelling thereof, had any sinful influence in producing their unbelief, but it tends to shew that the event came to pass according to the prediction; and by comparing the prediction with the event he would partly point out the absolute and holy providence of God, without which nothing comes to pass, either acting or permitting it, and therefore he can foretel it so long beforehand; and partly he would prevent the stumbling of others at Christ and the gospel, by occasion of the Jews' rejecting him; seeing this was rather a proof that he was the Messiah, of whom it was fore-prophesied that he should be rejected by them. Consider—3. As for the citation itself, it contains a proposition of their fault, in a sad complaint that few or none gave credit to the report of the gospel, and an explication and amplification hereof, wherein, 1. This report is called " the arm of the Lord," because of its power and efficacy unto salvation, and chiefly because of Christ in it, of whom Isaiah speaks in the rest of that chapter, and who is the power of God, 1 Cor. i. 24. 2. Their unbelief is illustrated from a negative cause thereof—to wit, that this "arm of the Lord" is not revealed to them, namely, inwardly and effectually, for otherwise they did hear it. And this is spoken without all imputation unto [reflection upon] God, who is not a debtor unto any, to reveal Christ and his gospel to them, but may justly leave them in their natural estate.

From verse 37, learn—1. Where Christ doth sow and take pains among a people he will also reap and take notice what fruits they produce; as here he records by his penman the fruits of his ministry and pains.

2. The fruit of the gospel which Christ requires is, that men take him up who is offered there, what he is, and by faith close with him and make use of him accordingly; for this is the fruit he misseth : "they believed not on him."

3. It is the judgment of the Lord upon the world that the offer of Christ in his gospel doth not work upon the most part of hearers, and most faithful labourers do miss the fruits of their labours among them; for notwithstanding Christ's pains, "yet they (generally) believed not on him." (See Matt. xi. 16, 17; Isa. xlix. 4, 5.)

4. The great pains taken upon men contributes to aggravate the sin of their obstinate infidelity; for so is their sin agreeaged [aggravated] here: "Though he had done so many miracles before them, yet they believed not." These miracles were many in number, great in their nature, (as the word will also bear,) and clear, as being done "before them," to their conviction, and yet they prevailed not.

5. Such as are not bettered by the word, nor will believe it for itself, no other help they can crave will work upon them, nor cause them believe it; therefore doth he aggravate their fault from the "many miracles" that had been done, not to seclude the clear light of his doctrine from being an aggravation, but to shew that these despisers of the word were nothing the better for all the signs and miracles they so much sought after.

From verse 38, learn—1. The mean whereby sinners are brought to faith in Christ is their receiving and closing with the report of the word concerning themselves and him in the mouth of sent messengers; for herein consisted their not believing on him, that they believed not our report.

2. Whatever be unbelievers' carriage, yet it brings no discredit to the gospel, but to themselves; for in this complaint it gets still its honourable titles.

3. The gospel is the power of God to salvation, and Christ offered in it is the power of God to effectuate that for lost sinners which their own weakness (Rom. v. 6) or the law (Rom. viii. 3) could not bring to pass; for this is the honourable title of Christ and the gospel, "the arm of the Lord." (See Rom. i. 16.)

4. The gospel, and Christ offered in it, are only effectual in those to whom the offer is inwardly revealed by God; for they only believe our report " to whom the arm of the Lord hath been revealed." (See Matt. xi. 25.)

5. The gospel, in all ages, is met with unbelief in the most part of men, who are left to their own darkness and wickedness to reject it; for Isaiah said this of old, as true in his own time, and in Christ and his apostles' days, "who hath believed our report? and to whom hath the arm of the Lord been revealed?" The question imports that few or none did it, or were partakers of this mercy.

6. The obstinacy of men against the gospel is matter of wonder and of sad complaint to God from his faithful servants; therefore is it propounded so here, "Lord, who hath believed our report?" where John, following the Greek interpreters, adds the word Lord, which is not expressed in the Hebrew, though it be virtually included in this, that faithful ministers know not where to pour out their complaints but in their Master's bosom.

7. As even they who lived under Christ's ministry did, for most part, profit as little as those whom his servants labour among, so he will join in this sad complaint with his faithful servants against such; for he had cause to say, and did say with the rest, "who hath believed our report?" And this is very sad when the Saviour and Intercessor is put to complain of us.

8. In dark and misty cases it is useful to look to what the scriptures say of them, that we may direct and compose our thoughts accordingly; therefore are the foregoing prophecies looked unto in this matter as a ground of many useful thoughts.

9. Whatever other duties be required of ministers who are sensible of the unfruitfulness of their ministry, it is also required that they comfort themselves in this, that the holy and sovereign good pleasure of God is still accomplished by the ministry of the word; therefore is this prediction pointed at as a special mean to comfort ministers, when they see that things are according as God foretold they should be. (See Matt. xi. 25, 26; Acts, xiii. 48; Rom. xi. 7.)

10. However unbelievers may think to affront Christ by their rejecting of him, yet he will be disappointed by none of them, and he will improve their opposition to special advantages; therefore also is this prophecy cited, to shew that he knew well enough what they would prove, even long before they were, and that their not believing in him was an evidence he was the true Messiah, as hath been cleared.

11. God hath a holy providence, even about things that come to pass by contingent second causes, and depend upon men's free will; for he can foretel them here before they come to pass.

12. God's providence is so infallible that he will not be frustrated of his purposes; and an argument from the prediction of his word concerning anything is sufficient to conclude that it will come to pass; for here the event answereth exactly to the prediction.

13. Whatever be the providence of God about sinful men and their miscarriages, yet God and his providence are wholly free of blame, (he being the sovereign Lord, above the laws given to his creatures, bound to none, and not concurrent in

the wickedness of their actions,) and the guilt is wholly the sinner's, as being under the law, and voluntarily choosing the wicked course which he followeth. Therefore, albeit it be declared here that God's providence had a hand in this business, yet both in the prediction it is propounded by way of complaint, and here, by way of challenge against such sinners.

VER. 39. Therefore they could not believe, because that Esaias said again,

40. He hath blinded their eyes, and hardened their heart; that they should not see with their eyes, nor understand with their heart, and be converted, and I should heal them.

In these verses this their unbelief is further amplified, that not only they did not, but could not believe; and that not only the means wrought not upon them to draw them to Christ, but they were more hardened in their obstinacy thereby, according to another prediction of Isaiah, chap. vi. 10, the pertinent citation whereof is cleared, ver. 41. Now for clearing this purpose, and the text cited, consider—1. As for this impotency, that they could not believe, albeit it be true that all men naturally are unable for it, yet this place speaks principally of a further degree of impossibility, through contracted obstinacy and judicial obduration, of which the following text speaks. Consider—2. As for this inference from the prediction, and the comparing of the event with it—" they could not believe, because that Esaias said"—if we look to the simple prediction, it tends to the same purpose with the former, and to shew that the event was according to the prediction, for the ends mentioned on ver. 37, 38, but if we look to the matter of the prediction, the obduration and blinding mentioned have a further hand in the matter of their unbelief, as may be cleared. Consider—3. As for the matter of this citation, albeit if we compare this place with Isa. vi. 10; Matt. xiii. 15; Acts, xxviii. 27, we shall find some diversity in words, yet the purpose is the same; for the grossness and fatness of the heart is the same with the hardness thereof. And albeit the other places add the making their ears heavy, or dull of hearing, to the other two here mentioned, yet the scope of these places and this is the same, to shew that all passages were obstructed whereby the word might enter to work conversion, which brings salvation and healing with it. And for the words here in particular, albeit their not understanding with "their heart" may seem to import that their "heart" is to be understood of their mind and understanding, and the same with "their eyes," not bodily, but inward, and so the plague of blinding their eyes and hardening their heart shall be the same; yet it is more full and clear to understand the words of distinct plagues on the several faculties of their soul, that the eyes of their mind were blinded, and their will (signified by their "heart") hardened. And so their not understanding, added to their not seeing, is to be understood, not of a simple act of knowledge, but such an understand-

ing as produceth suitable effects upon the will and affections to work conversion, which is subjoined to it; and so to "understand" signifieth frequently so to know a thing as to approve and esteem of it, to be affected with it, or drawn to the enjoyment of it. Consider—4. As for the author and efficient of these plagues, if we compare the places before cited, we shall find divers named; in Matt. xiii. and Acts, xxviii., the closing of the eyes (and consequently the rest) is ascribed unto the sinners themselves. In Isaiah vi. the prophet is sent out to make their heart fat, &c., and here it is ascribed to Christ, even to him whose glory Isaiah saw, ver. 41, who in the beginning of this verse is spoken of in the third person, and in the end thereof speaks of himself in the first person, as is usual in the scripture. These are easily reconciled; for as men do sinfully harden themselves, so the Lord by a judicial stroke gives them up thereunto as a punishment, and the messengers of Christ do not only carry and intimate this sad sentence, but their doctrine is an occasion of men's stumbling and hardening of themselves, as it is of hewing and slaying, Hos. vi. 5. Consider—5. As for this judicial act of God, in blinding and hardening sinners, that we may understand it rightly, 1. As we must not conceive that God doth approve this sinful hardness and blindness in men, though, as a just judge, he inflict the punishment, so we are not to conceive of it as if he made them blind who did see, or hardened them who were soft and tender, but that by withholding of his grace (which he is bound to give to none) he leaves them to their own blindness and hardness, or gives them up to augment it, which is most properly a punishment. 2. This judicial blinding and hardening of sinners here mentioned may be called God's act, partly in so far as he sent to them the preaching of the gospel, which was an occasion they took hold of to harden and blind themselves, through the irritation of their corruptions thereby, and partly in that, to punish this their abuse, he withholds his efficacious grace, gives them to a reprobate mind and to the power of Satan, to harden and blind them more and more; and this exhausts the meaning in this place, that as they were hardened and blinded by Christ's doctrine and miracles, so he gave them up to be punished with more and more of it.

From this purpose thus explained, learn— 1. Men by nature are lying in a woeful and miserable deadly condition, full of deadly wounds and sores; for they need to be healed.

2. Whatever course men take to rid themselves of their miseries, yet there is no curing of their sores till God put to his hand; for it is he that must "heal them."

3. However men flatter themselves, yet none are indeed cured of these diseases by God but they who find grace to turn to him by true regeneration and repentance, which is the only way to cure their soul diseases, to sanctify and sweeten their other miseries, and to ensure eternal salvation to them; for this, and this only, is the way, that they "be converted, and I should heal them."

4. Let men have never so many flourishes, yet

none are truly converted but they who get open eyes to discern their own condition and the true remedy thereof, and whose hearts, will, and affections are touched with what they see to draw them to answerable practice; for they must see with their eyes and understand with their hearts who are converted.

5. Whatever convictions, practices, or other changes are wrought in men by the word, yet they must also flee to Christ, and close with him by faith, before they can prove they are truly converted; for to "believe," ver. 39, is explained by this in the testimony cited, ver. 40, to "be converted."

6. As all men are naturally unable to believe or turn to God, so this impotency is still the greater the more we are dealt with by the word and do not hearken to it; for so was it here, "they could not believe," and they had blinded eyes and hard hearts, opposite to the seeing eye and understanding heart.

7. As men's increase of blindness and hardness, under the means of grace, is their great sin, so it is also God's judgment upon them, who, as a righteous Judge, punishes sin with sin, and giveth them a surfeit of what they so much affect; for "he hath blinded their eyes, and hardened their heart." Thus saints are justly put to groan under in their partial obduration, when their bands lie on to humble them, after they are sensible of them, as Isa. lxiii. 15.

8. As Christ is free to convert and save whom he pleaseth, so when wicked men are most afraid of anything lest the word should be effectual to their conversion, and therefore do obstruct all passages whereby it might enter, it is just with him to reject them, and to give them up to multiply such impediments; for when they shut their eyes lest they be converted, Matt. xiii. 15, he justly blindeth their eyes, &c., that they should not be converted.

9. The scriptures are a complete storehouse for all cases, and for clearing all events that may occur; for as before their not believing, so here, that "they could not believe," hath a scripture to clear it, "because that Esaias said again," &c.

VER. 41. These things said Esaias, when he saw his glory, and spake of him.

In this verse the pertinent citation of these prophecies (chiefly the last) is cleared. And lest any should think these testimonies belonged only to Isaiah's days, and spake of the Father, John clears his citation was pertinent, and that however these passages had their own accomplishment in Isaiah's time, yet they belong also to these days of the gospel, and to the times of Christ, whose glory was seen and spoken of by Isaiah, Isa. vi. 1, 2, &c., and who spake of Christ in that and the other passage, Isa. liii. 1, 2; and therefore they were predictions of these times. Whence learn—

1. It is not enough to justify men's assertions in religion that they can bring many scriptures which seem to favour their opinions, unless they can clear they are pertinently cited, and that in their true meaning they hold out what they as-sert; therefore John not only cites scripture, but proves the pertinency of his citation.

2. This passage doth clearly demonstrate that Christ is true God, and that there are three persons in the blessed godhead; for Jehovah, who appeared and spake to Isaiah, is granted by all to be Father, and here the same glorious appearance is said to be the glory of Christ, and Acts, xxviii. 25, 26. The commission then given is ascribed to the Holy Ghost, as Jehovah, equal with the Father and the Son.

3. It pleased Christ our Lord to manifest himself to his people under the Old Testament sometimes in the likeness of a man, as a prelude to his incarnation, (as to Abraham and others,) and sometimes in resplendent glory, to give evidence of his godhead; as here Esaias "saw his glory," which gives us to understand that the glory of other visions shewed to the prophets were the glory of Christ also. (See 1 Cor. x. 9.)

4. The more of Christ's glory be seen, and the more means men have, the greater will the obduration of wicked men be; for "these things (of men's being blinded and hardened) said Esaias, when he saw his glory, and spake of him," intimating that as in his time there was never greater hardness than when most of Christ was seen and spoken of, so in the days of the gospel, when the Sun of Righteousness should shine most brightly, the hardness would be greatest of all.

VER. 42. Nevertheless among the chief rulers also many believed on him; but because of the Pharisees they did not confess him, lest they should be put out of the synagogue.

43. For they loved the praise of men more than the praise of God.

In these verses is recorded Christ's success among another sort of hearers, even hid and timorous friends, and those of chief rank. Of these it is said—1. That though they did indeed believe, yet they durst not confess nor avow Christ. 2. That the impediment hindering them was fear of excommunication from the Pharisees. 3. That the reason why this was an impediment was their love of credit and applause among men, which they, in this particular, preferred to the approbation of God, which albeit, where it beareth full sway, is an invincible impediment to grace, chap. v. 44, yet prevailing here but in part, and being only in one particular of not confession, it doth not annul the reality of their grace, though it prove the great weakness thereof.

From verse 42, learn—1. Even in times of greatest obstinacy, and where the word comes worst speed, the ministry will still have some success, and not be in vain; therefore is it declared, that in this time Christ had some hidden ones (beside his own flock that followed and avowed him) who "believed on him," when the generality were hardened. (See 1 Kings, xix. 18; Rom. xi. 4.)

2. Christ is so powerful in the ministry of his word that he will (when he pleaseth) work upon them who have many impediments in their way,

and who are amongst the most bitter enemies to him; for "among the chief rulers also (who were bitter enemies to Christ) many believed on him;" and albeit they were under so many tentations that they durst not confess him, yet they are made to believe.

3. Albeit the conversion of any be a work of omnipotency, yet the conversion of the greater sort of men, who have so many tentations and impediments in their way, is more to be admired than the bringing in of the meaner sort, especially in corrupt times of the church; therefore is it especially marked, that "among the chief rulers also many believed on him."

4. There may be true faith and grace where yet there is much infirmity to smother and bear it down; for they " believed on him," though they durst not avow it. This ought not to make men flatter themselves in their weakness, but should teach others to be charitable, and to encourage and stir up such to be more strong, having such a seed in them as will prevail, and not to weaken their hands from duty by thinking they are graceless because they are weak.

5. Faith is in a very weak condition when confession is not joined with it, and when men do not profess Christ and the true religion, nor avow him in troublous times, and by their conversation lift not up a banner, professing that they are his followers; for this was the infirmity of their faith, although they " believed on him, (yet) they did not confess him." Albeit a bare outside profession be to be condemned, yet if it be well grounded it is commendable and as necessary in its own kind as believing is in its kind, Rom. x. 10.

6. Carnal fear of men, and danger from them, is a great impediment to the avowing of Christ; for " because of the Pharisees they did not confess him." Albeit they were not so powerful against Christ as to hinder their heart from believing, yet they deterred them from confessing with their mouths. This is an impediment to be removed by trust in God, Prov. xxix. 25, and by the fear of his dreadfulness, Matt. x. 28.

7. It is a great judgment, and an evidence of great wickedness in men, when not only men will not come to Christ themselves, but are a terror to all those who would embrace and avow him; for such were " the Pharisees" here, because of whom " they did not confess him." (See Matt. xxiii. 13.)

8. Albeit all men are naturally afraid to hazard anything for Christ, yet, ordinarily, fear prevails most with them who are eminent, and have most to lose; for it was " the chief rulers, (who) because of the Pharisees, did not confess him," lest they should lose their place and reputation; but it was otherwise with the blind man, chap. ix. 30—34.

9. Excommunication is a divine ordinance in the house of God, and which was in force in the most corrupt times of the Jewish church; as here they kept it in use, to put men " out of the synagogue," of which we have spoken formerly.

10. Not only mean persons, but professors of greatest rank and place in the church are subject to the censure of excommunication, and it may justly be inflicted upon their miscarriage;

for herein also they followed the rule, that even " the chief rulers" were kept under hazard of being " put out of the synagogue."

11. In corrupt times of the church, Christ's ordinances are all abused, and the edge of censures turned against him and his followers; for so was it here; they who did confess Christ were in hazard to " be put out of the synagogue."

12. Excommunication is in itself a dreadful censure, and ought to be esteemed so by all church members, albeit the inflicting thereof unjustly ought not to terrify men from duty; for it was their carnal fear that made them shrink from duty, lest the Pharisees should unjustly inflict it, yet their fearing of it, though chief rulers, testifies how much that censure in itself was feared in that church.

From verse 43, learn—1. It is not enough to see the evils into which men break out and fall, unless also the causes drawing on this evil be seen and discovered; therefore doth John search into the fountain-cause driving them on this snare.

2. Shame and disrespect for Christ's cause is true glory and honour in God's account; for it is supposed that if they had lost " the praise of men," it had been their praise from God.

3. There is no greater snare to draw a man from duty than inordinate affection to his credit and reputation; for if all other losses they might have sustained, this entangled them most, that they would lose " the praise of men."

4. Self-love, and self-seeking, and hunting after credit and applause, are evils so dear to men, and so deeply rooted in them, that even believers may be overpowered by strong remainders thereof, even sometimes to the neglecting of God's testimony and approbation; for even they who " believed on him," ver. 42, yet " loved the praise of men more than the praise of God."

5. So long as men let thoughts of earthly credit and reputation swallow up the thoughts of divine approbation and praise, they will never clearly avow Christ and his truth in a time of trial; for " they did not confess him, (ver. 42,) for they loved the praise of men more than the praise of God," whereas the more men study to approve themselves to God, and rest in his approbation, the more vile will this world's praise grow in their eyes, and it will stumble them the less to want it.

6. Such as are taken up with their credit, and with applause from men, neglecting God's approbation, do make a very poor choice, and lose more than they can gain; for it is insinuated as their fault and disadvantage every way, that " they loved the praise of men (which is of no worth) more than the praise of God," wherein men's happiness consisteth.

Ver. 44. Jesus cried and said, He that believeth on me, believeth not on me, but on him that sent me.

Followeth Christ's farewell sermon to the Jews concerning his person, office, and doctrine, pointing out the advantages that men reap by believing in him, and the danger of rejecting him and his doctrine. And albeit the Greek particles which answer to each other, ver. 42, 44, do import that this doctrine had a special relation to the faintheartedness of those believers formerly spoken of, yet the subject-matter extends both to the open unbelievers and them; and the whole purpose may be taken up in several arguments, pleading against the unbelief of many, and the faintheartedness of believers who did not confess him. The first argument is insinuated in Christ's practice of crying, whereby he insinuates the importance of this subject, that they should believe in him, however they slighted it, and avows his zeal in this matter when others hid themselves. The second argument (in this verse also) points out the advantage of faith from the object thereof, who is God. They who believe on him, believe not on him, but on him who sent him, which is not to be understood, simply, that Christ is not the object of faith, but with relation to their conceptions of Christ as a mere man, and opposite to God, and so the meaning is; that which he calls them unto is not a faith in him as man, but a faith in God, and not a faith in him only, but a faith in the Father also, who is in Christ, and one and the same God with him, as the following verse cleareth. And so the encouragement is, that he being true God, equal and one in essence with the Father, their faith in believing on him should be in God, and they should find the Father in him, which might both stir up the unbeliever to believe, and the fainthearted believer to avow him. Whence learn—

1. Whatever be men's thoughts concerning Christ, and faith in him for attaining salvation, yet it is in itself a matter of greatest consequence and importance; therefore Jesus "cried, and said," when he spake of it as being necessary to be inculcated.

2. Whatever be men's carriage in maliciously rejecting or not avowing of Christ, yet true zeal in others ought not to be blunted, but rather set on edge thereby; for herein Christ is a pattern, who "cried," in commending his person and doctrine in the midst of that corrupt and fainthearted generation.

3. Christ's diligence and earnestness in persuading sinners to come to him is such as will leave all despisers inexcusable; for not only doth he come again in public, after he had lately departed from them, but when he came he zealously and affectionately "cried," to persuade them.

4. The reason why faith in Christ is so little endeavoured after by men, and why believers are so little bold in avowing of it, is because the worth and consequence thereof is so little seen; therefore Christ points out the excellency thereof as a special mean to convince and persuade them.

5. The worth of faith is then taken up when men study the object thereof well, and that they are not called to make flesh their arm, or to trust in dumb idols, but in the living and true God; therefore doth he commend faith here, that by believing on him they believe also "on him that sent him,' and consequently on him as true God, one with the Father. (See John, xiv. 1; 2 Tim. i. 12.)

6. It may encourage also to faith that believers do not only fasten upon an infinite Deity, but do ascend up to God through Christ the Mediator, and tryst [agree] with the Father in him, who is true God, one in essence with him; for this is the order here: by believing on me they believe "on him that sent me," saith he. (See 2 Cor. v. 19; iii. 4; 1 Pet. i. 21.)

7. For taking up the right meaning of scripture men must not always look to what the outward sound of words at first view would seem to say, but all circumstances and the speaker's scope must be seriously pondered; for unless we take these words as spoken with an eye to the Jews' apprehensions of Christ, we shall fall in a foul error, that believers do not believe on Christ, which is contrary to the very scope of the place, and to other scriptures, John, xiv. 1.

8. Albeit it pleased the Father to send Christ as his ambassador into' the world, and he came in obedience to that call, yet this diminisheth not the glory of the sender, nor of the person sent; for both Christ and he that sent him is true God, the object of saving faith.

VER. 45. And he that seeth me seeth him that sent me.

In this verse we have a confirmation of the second argument, that believers in Christ believe on the Father also, shewing that, Christ being one, not in person, but in essence, with the Father, none can see him spiritually and by faith but they must see the Father also, not only with him but in him, and one with him, as being the brightness of his glory, and express image of his person, Heb. i. 3; Col. i. 15. Whence learn—

1. True faith is accompanied with knowledge, and faith must contemplate Christ to feed on his fulness, and fix its eye on him for help and relief, as of old they did on the brazen serpent; for "he that believeth on me," ver. 44, is expounded to be, "he that seeth me."

2. Such as get an eye of faith to see Christ will see him true God, and one with the Father; for "he that seeth me seeth him that sent me." Unto a believer and a discerning eye the glory of his divinity will shine through his greatest abasement, as Matt. xvi. 16; xxvii. 54.

3. The Father is not to be seen but in the Son, nor can believers know what he is but by seeing what the Son is, and what they see the Son to be that the Father is in him; for "he that seeth me seeth him that sent me."

VER. 46. I am come a light into the world, that whosoever believeth on me should not abide in darkness.

The third argument pleading against these evils is taken from the fruit and utility following on faith in him—to wit, that he coming to be the light of the world, believers in him will partake thereof and not abide in darkness, of which we have had occasion to speak before. Whence learn—

1. The world without Christ is lying under the

power of darkness, both of ignorance and wickedness, and all miseries following thereupon, for the world needs light.

2. Christ is the discoverer of men's misery, and of the remedy thereof, and is the true cordial and comfort of sinners against all their miseries ; for saith he, " I am come a light into the world."

3. As Christ is the true light of the world, so it pleased him to be at pains to manifest himself unto the world, to make men partakers of the fruits and benefits thereof; for " I am come a light into the world, that whosoever believeth on me should not abide in darkness."

4. The way to partake of the benefits that are in Christ is to embrace his person by faith, and so to draw out that fulness of consolation that is in him; for the promise is made to whosoever believeth on him.

5. Believers in Christ, as they ought to shine as lights, being illuminated by him who is the light of the world, Phil. ii. 15, and as children of light, Eph. v. 8, so they shall by faith be translated out of the kingdom of darkness, as to the state of their person, Col. i. 13, and shall daily partake of that light of direction, refreshment, and consolation that is in him ; for " whosoever believeth on me shall not abide in darkness." And if men would in the first place cherish faith, their light and consolation would grow more.

VER. 47. And if any man hear my words, and believe not, I judge him not: for I came not to judge the world, but to save the world.

48. He that rejecteth me, and receiveth not my words, hath one that judgeth him : the word that I have spoken, the same shall judge him in the last day.

The fourth argument is taken from the sad judgment abiding all unbelievers and rejecters of him and his doctrine ; for which end he appealeth them to the judgment of the last day ; declaring that however in his first coming his errand was not to judge but to offer salvation and mercy to the world, yet they should be judged in the last day ; and though there were no other witness, yet his word preached should be a sufficient testimony against them at that time.   For further clearing of what is said of the end of Christ's coming, compare chap. iii. 17.   Only it is to be marked, that this argument strikes mainly against the wicked unbelievers, and not the other sort, save in so far as, by continuing in not confessing of him, when he inculcates that duty upon them, they prove themselves never to have been sound believers.

From verse 47, learn—1. Not only rich promises and gracious offers, but even sharp threatenings, are a mean appointed of God to stir up men to embrace the gospel ; therefore is the argument subjoined to the rest here.

2. Albeit the gospel be glad tidings of joy, and contain cordials and remedies against all the curses and threatenings of the law, yet it contains also threatenings against despisers, as terrible as any threatening of the law, as here we see.

3. Whatever be the judgments to come on those who hear not the gospel, yet their danger is by far the greatest who hear and obey not ; for this threatening is against them who hear Christ s words.   (See chap. xv. 22.)

4. Not only are they guilty of sin and liable to judgment who, having the opportunity, yet will not hear, or who hearing, do persecute, but even they also who, hearing, will not believe nor give credit to what hath been said, and close with it accordingly ; for the threatening goeth out against them who hear and believe not.

5. Such is Christ's mercy and long-suffering, that when men do not believe on him, yet he will essay them with mercy and leave them room for repentance and faith ; for saith he, " I judge him not"—to wit, as yet, and I came "to save the world."   Albeit the unbeliever be already condemned by the sentence of the law, John, iii. 18, and doth carry his dittay [condemnation] in his bosom with him, yet the full sentence and execution is not passed at first, but he is yet waited on.

6. Albeit Christ be always judge of the world, yet in his first coming he laid aside the person of a judge, and took on the office of a Mediator and Saviour to offer and purchase mercy ; for " I judge him not; for I came not to judge the world, but to save the world."

7. In Christ's first coming his proper errand was, and the nature of his work tended, to save sinners ; so that if it be an occasion of condemnation to any, they have themselves and their own corruptions to blame, in that they stumble at and do abuse their own mercy ; for it is held out here as Christ's proper errand, " not to judge the world, but to save the world."

From verse 48, learn—1. Christ and his doctrine are inseparable, and as the one is entertained so is the other ; for rejecting him is joined with not receiving his words, so that where the word hath no place he is rejected.

2. Whatever use men may seem to make of Christ's word, yet none are believers thereof but they who so hear as to receive and admit it into their hearts, and Christ in it ; for so not to believe, ver. 47, is expounded, " he rejecteth me, and receiveth not my words."

3. It is not their sin who are studying to believe and yet are kept wrestling under the power of unbelief, that Christ will bring into judgment, but the sin of those who care not to believe ; for such are to be judged here who reject me, &c.

4. It is a sad plague on wicked unbelievers who hear the gospel, that their unbelief is joined with disdain to Christ, and contempt of his gospel and grace, and that Christ will so judge of it ; for so Christ calls it here, " he that rejecteth me," (with contempt and disdain, choosing other things before me, as the word imports) " and receiveth, not my words," not accounting them worthy to have any place with him.

5. Albeit sin be not soon punished, yea, albeit Christ be the Mediator of sinners, yet such as despise him he will not keep them from judgment ; for such a man " hath one that judgeth him," whereby is meant, not so much that the Father doth judge them, though the Son at his

first coming do not, as that certainly they will not escape a judge and judgment, as is after cleared. (See Prov. xi. 2; Eccles. viii. 11, 12.)

6. However the Lord deal with men here, and however in his forbearance they may escape judgment, yet they will not escape the judgment of the last day, which will sadly enough compense all delays; for he shall be judged in the last day.

7. Albeit, in the day of judgment, wicked men will be called to an account for all their sins against the law, yet the contempt of the gospel will be their saddest dittay [condemnation]; for "he that rejecteth me, the word that I have spoken shall judge him"—that is, the word of the gospel delivered by Christ, in whose mouth soever it be, though it will have its own peculiar weight against those who heard him, that he came and spake it himself.

8. Though all other witnesses against a wicked man were gone, yet the word preached will stand up against him as a witness and dittay [accuser] in the great day; for "the word shall judge him in the last day." It shall be a witness of what was offered, and make up a dittay [accusation] against him for his contempt, upon which Christ shall pronounce sentence.

9. The word of God is so sure and infallible, that Christ's sentence in the great day (when heaven and earth shall pass away) shall proceed according to the verdict and testimony thereof; for "the word that I have spoken shall judge him in the last day." Christ will pronounce then according to what it sayeth now, and that as well in favour of believers as against unbelievers.

VER. 49. For I have not spoken of myself; but the Father which sent me, he gave me a commandment, what I should say, and what I should speak.

50. And I know that his commandment is life everlasting: whatsoever I speak therefore, even as the Father said unto me, so I speak.

The last argument serves to confirm and clear the former, and is taken from the authority of his doctrine; for whereas they might except that they were not afraid of his words, as being only his own, he answers, that he spake not of himself, but what was the Father's word also. And to confirm this :—1. He declareth that he had received a commission from the Father who sent him, concerning his doctrine, and what to say and speak. 2. That he was persuaded this doctrine delivered to him by the Father points out the true way to eternal life. 3. That he had exactly followed this commission in preaching, both for matter and manner. Hence the argument concludes strongly two ways :—1. That his word and doctrine being divine, and the Father's as well as his, it was sufficient to judge and condemn all despisers. 2. That his doctrine only pointing out the true way to life, and means of attaining it, they could not miss condemnation who would not hearken unto it. Whence learn—

1. Albeit Christ's doctrine be his own, as he is true God and the wisdom of the Father, yet it is not his own, as mere man, nor as secluding the Father, who is one God with him, and who gave him a commission and instructions as Mediator; for "I have not spoken of myself, but the Father which sent me, he gave me a commandment," &c.

2. The Father is the author and approver of Christ's doctrine, no less than Christ himself; "for I have not spoken of myself," &c.

3. No word but God's word is sufficient to condemn men for disobedience; and if men cannot prove their doctrine to be divine, it is neither to be obeyed nor are terrors for the neglect thereof to be regarded; therefore Christ takes this as the proof that his word shall judge men, ver. 48, "for I have not spoken of myself, but the Father which sent me, he gave me a commandment, what I should say, and what I should speak." And this he exactly followed, as ver. 50. The two words of saying and speaking, may be taken comprehensively, as pointing out all the ways of delivering his commission, by set and solemn preaching, or occasional conferences, and the whole subject-matter of his preaching, in precepts, promises, and threatenings. And so it will import, that his commission from the Father was full, both for matter and manner, and his discharge thereof answerable. Yet this variety of expression is not to be insisted on, seeing in the following verse Christ useth one of the words in place of both.

4. When men speak by commission from another, and according thereunto, the refuser of the message must be accountable to the author and sender thereof; for so doth Christ prove his word should judge them, seeing God is the author thereof, who will call them to an account.

5. The sum of Christ's doctrine, which he delivered from the Father, is to point out eternal life to lost sinners, and the way and means leading thereunto; for "his commandment (or the doctrine which I, at his command, have preached) is life everlasting." (See John, xvii. 3.)

6. Whatever esteem sinners have of the gospel, yet it is sure in itself that there is no salvation by any other way or doctrine, but by embracing thereof; and as Christ is, so every preacher ought to be persuaded of the excellency thereof; therefore saith Christ, in opposition to all their misconstructions, "I know that his commandment is life everlasting."

7. Christ is a true prophet, who spake neither more nor less in the doctrine of the gospel than what was the Father's will should be delivered to us; for "whatsoever I speak, even as the Father said unto me, so I speak."

8. It is the duty of the messengers of the gospel to cleave close to their commission, without adding or diminishing; for herein Christ's practice is a pattern of their duty.

9. Such as are persuaded of the excellency and absolute necessity of the gospel will cleave to it, and publish it in their stations, were their discouragements never so many, or the opposition made to them never so great; for upon this, "I know that his commandment is life everlasting; (Christ inferreth this by way of conclusion) whatsoever I speak therefore, even as the Father

said unto me, so I speak." Intimating that upon this knowledge of the worth of his doctrine he cleaves to it, and speaks it- however they contemned him and it.

CHAPTER XIII.

HITHERTO John hath recorded Christ's proceedings in his ministry with all sorts of people, and especially those things in his doctrine and miracles which had been omitted by the other evangelists. Now in this and the following chapters, to chap. xviii., he records Christ's carriage towards his disciples, in taking his farewell at the last passover, omitting (for most part) what the rest have set down, and recording what they had omitted. And in this, Christ having warned them of a traitor among themselves, of his removal from them by his death, and his resurrection and ascension following thereupon, and of their own trials and exercises they were to meet with, he doth largely let forth his heart unto them, in sweet cordials against his death and departure from them, in notable directions and encouragements unto them as preachers of the gospel, and in delivering his full testament to them, and to all saints in them; closing all with a solemn and public prayer to the Father.

In this chapter is recorded—1. Christ's washing of the disciples' feet, with the interpretation thereof, ver. 1—17. 2. His discovering of Judas the traitor, ver. 18—30. 3. Christ's doctrine to the disciples, upon Judas's removal, ver. 31—35. 4. His repression of Peter's rash presumption, ver. 36—38.

VER. 1. *Now before the feast of the passover, when Jesus knew that his hour was come that he should depart out of this world unto the Father, having loved his own which were in the world, he loved them unto the end.*

This first part of the chapter, containing Christ's washing of his disciples' feet, may be taken up in this order :—1. The circumstance of time is noted, wherein this and what followeth was done, together with some causes and considerations moving Christ so to do at such a time, ver. 1—3. 2. The fact itself is recorded, ver. 4, 5. 3. The interpretation thereof is subjoined, partly upon occasion of Peter's refusal, wherein, chiefly, this washing their feet is expounded, as it is a sign of inward washing, ver. 6—11; and partly, after he had done with washing, wherein he expounds what he meant by his doing of that servile employment of washing their feet himself at that time, ver. 12—17.

In this verse we have recorded a more general designation of the time, that it was before the feast of the passover; together with the first and chief cause and consideration leading Christ to this practice, and what followed—namely, that he did constantly and unchangeably love his own,

and therefore, knowing that now his time to depart from them was approaching at this feast, he was resolving beforehand to give them some ample proof of his love, as accordingly he did in washing their feet, preaching sweetly unto them, and praying for them. For clearing the words, consider — 1. While John saith that this was "before the feast of the passover," it is not so to be understood as if this were done before the feast, for that supper, ver. 2, (after which he washed their feet,) was the passover; but the meaning is, that he was thinking and resolving on this practice before he sat down, either that same day, or possibly some days before; and that, albeit it was done at the supper of the passover, yet it was done before the feast of unleavened bread at the passover, which began the day following, Lev. xxiii. 5—7, yea, and before the day which the Jews observed for eating the passover, as we shall hear on ver. 2. Consider—2. Whereas this love of Christ towards his own breaks forth in these sweet effects towards the disciples only, yet in this they are not to be looked on as so many individual men, nor as apostles, nor yet as representing ministers only, but also as representing all Christ's true children, who are edified and comforted by what he did to them, and whose allowance and legacy Christ did here commit to his apostles in their name, as to the general teachers of his church, to be by them and their successors published to his own throughout the world, and therefore the denomination is general, "his own," that every one who make sure an interest in him may put in their own name.

DOCTRINES.

1. As Christ came into this world to work the work of redemption, so there was a set time wherein he departed out of it, in respect of his bodily presence ; for there is an " hour," wherein " he should depart out of this world."

2. Christ chose the time of the Jewish passover to suffer in, that he might prove himself to be the substance of that type whose blood it is that delivers us from the destroying angel, and by whose obedience unto death we are delivered from the bondage of sin, the tyranny of Satan, and the leaven of corruption and unsoundness answerable to the temporal delivery of Israel from Egypt and Pharaoh, and their observation of the feast with unleavened bread ; therefore it is marked that at the feast of the passover his hour was come wherein he should depart out of this world. (See 1 Cor. v. 7.)

3. Christ was not surprised with his sufferings, nor were they carved out according to the will of enemies ; but the time thereof was determined, and he knew of it beforehand; for " Jesus knew that his hour was come."

4. Christ may be trusted by his people, and they may commit all their lots to him who is on all his Father's counsels, and knows all the machinations of his enemies; therefore is he pointed out here, as knowing all that was coming, even the treachery of Judas also, that he may be trusted in as an omniscient Lord.

5. It is not enough to foresee what troubles will come, or may come, unless we spend our time profitably in preparing and making ready for

them; therefore is Christ's knowing "that his hour was come" marked as a reason why he was so busy, in the following purpose—namely, that as his enemies were making ready, so he was making ready also; and having nothing to do for himself, he spends his time in preparing the disciples for the storm.

6. Christ not only lets out proofs of his love to his own, when they need them, but he is thinking thoughts of peace, and resolving to let them out, when they little dream of such a thing, till it appear; therefore it is. marked that, "before the feast of the passover," Christ was foreseeing the storm, and resolving to let out proofs of love to his disciples, which yet appeared not till after supper, ver. 2.

7. There is no difficulty so sad but Christ and his followers may get a comfortable look of it, were it even of death itself; for herein Christ hath cast a copy, who looked on his sad and bitter death, with what followed in his resurrection and ascension, as a departing out of this world unto the Father.

8. It is a comfortable sight of death unto saints that hereby they are translated from the miseries, toils, and vexations of this world, to go rest with and enjoy God; for herein hath Christ led the way, who "departed out of this world unto the Father," and did so look on his death.

9. It adds to the comfortable sight of death that saints do hereby not only go to God, but do go to him as their Father through Christ; so did Christ; for so did Christ depart "unto the Father," and made way for our going to him as a Father in him, as chap. xx. 17.

10. It adds also to the consolation, that as the time of our change is determined by God, so it is measured by hours, which will at last come to an end, and the prisoners be set free; for now, after some time and hours in serving his generation, the determined hour was come wherein he should depart out of this world.

11. Albeit Christ conversed but a short while in the world in respect of his bodily presence, yet he did make and daily makes a fair purchase in it by drawing sinners to himself; for he hath "his own" in it.

12. As Christ's people ought to resign themselves to him, and be wholly for him, so he hath a peculiar interest in them, is specially concerned in all their conditions, and allows special favours, privileges, and care upon them; for they are "his own," or his property, and peculiar ones.

13. Love, even the infinite love of tenderhearted Christ, is the allowance and portion of all his peculiar ones; for he "loved his own."

14. Albeit Christ leave his children in this tempestuous world to be humbled with the relics of sin, and tossed with the tempests of time, yet that doth neither take away their interest in him nor his love towards them; for he loved his own in the world.

15. The disadvantages of saints, and particularly their being left in the world when Christ went out of it, is so far from hindering his love towards them, that it is rather an argument why he should love them, and let out more of it; for it is not only not an hindrance of his love, but an argument also, he "loved his own," because they

"were in the world." And especially now, in his farewell, he would give a proof of it, considering the dangers unto which they were left exposed.

16. It is not enough to see Christ's love towards his saints in some particular passages, but they must labour to see an uninterrupted course thereof from the time of their closing with him; therefore now, at his farewell, he cleareth all bygones, that he had hitherto loved them, as well as he was now to give a proof of it, "having loved his own," &c.

17. Christ's love is not to be measured by kind outlettings to the satisfaction of sense, but the sum of all his dealing towards his own is love, which ought to be read in every condition and dispensation, were it even in keeping up his tender heart for a time; for albeit there had been many several passages betwixt him and his disciples, and some of them very cross to their humours, yet all is summed up in this: he had loved his own.

18. Christ's special love towards his own is unchangeable and incessant, till they be perfected and enjoy the full effects thereof; for having loved his own, he loved them to the end; he continued his love from the beginning till now he is to die for them and depart from them, and continueth it even then, and will do so till they be brought to the end of their journey.

19. Christ's love is not a decaying love, but a love that continually grows in effects; nor is it a love that consists only in good affection and wishes, but breaks forth in notable expressions, as he hath witnessed by his dying for his own; for "he loved them to the end," even to the death he suffered for them, and in so doing he loved them perfectly, as the word also will signify, proving that his love was a growing love, in letting out such abundant effects at the last.

20. When Christ's followers are in any danger, then unchangeable love will be on foot to cover their infirmities under tentation, and to provide cordials for them, and testify his special care of them; for this his love is marked as a cause why now (when he is to remove they are to be scattered and shaken with tentation, and left desolate) he will let out so much of his heart in the following purpose, and give them such sweet instructions in the following sign and explication thereof; and indeed his love suffers much in his disciples' need, and if there were no more, his love is enough to move him to see them well.

VER. 2. And supper being ended, the devil having now put into the heart of Judas Iscariot, Simon's son, to betray him;

3. Jesus knowing that the Father had given all things into his hands, and that he was come from God, and went to God;

4. He riseth from supper,——

In the first of these verses the circumstance of time wherein Christ did those things that follow is more exactly noted, that it was after supper; unto which is subjoined a second consideration leading him to the following practice—namely, that Satan had now prevailed with Judas to betray his Master, which, as it holds out a ground why our mild Lord, who hitherto had borne with Judas's naughtiness, and pointed at it only in general, is now pressed to discover him more particularly, ver. 21, since it concerned him in his glory to foretel it beforehand; so, more especially, it is a ground of his washing their feet, and of his following sweet and useful doctrine; for knowing his time to be now short, and that this night Judas would betray him, he doth busily bestir himself to pour out his heart in his disciples' bosom, and will let no minute of time slip, but in that one night did fully discover his heart unto them, and give an ample proof of that love mentioned ver. 1. In the other verse is subjoined a third consideration moving him to this practice—namely, that notwithstanding Judas's treachery, and his approaching sufferings, yet he knew his own excellency and greatness, that all power and authority is committed to him, and that as he came from God by his incarnation, so he was but returning to God by the chariot of his sufferings; which as it points out his admirable condescendence, that in the midst of such thoughts he will stoop to so base an employment, so it contains a sweet ground of his following practice, in that, however his hazard was near, yet seeing through all these clouds, he is at leisure to mind and promove his disciples' good, who would be in greater need through his suffering and removal from them.

For further clearing of verse 2, consider—1. Whereas it is said that "supper being ended," he did this, and yet, ver. 12, he sat down again after washing, and, ver. 26, meat is before him, of which he distributes to Judas, we are to consider that the words may very well be rendered, not only "supper being ended," but, while the supper was, or, while it was supper, intimating that he did what followeth in the time of the supper, and did interrupt it for a time for that end. However, it sufficeth us to know that the passover was eaten before he arose, and that which he sat down to again was a second service, or common supper subjoined to it, during which he instituted the sacrament of the supper. Consider—2. It is a greater difficulty to clear how Christ should eat the passover this night, and yet it should seem the Jews did not eat it till the night following, John, xviii. 28. They who assert that Christ did anticipate the time, and eat it a day sooner than was appointed, that so he, who was our true passover, might suffer on that day whereon God appointed the passover to be killed and eaten,—they, I say, seem not to remember that Christ was a fulfiller of all righteousness; nor was there any such prediction of Christ's suffering on that day as should necessitate him to transgress a positive precept; nor do they sufficiently clear the difficulty who assert that the Jews did eat the passover the same night with Christ, being the fourteenth day of the month; and that what is said, John, xviii. 28, of the Jews keeping themselves undefiled, that they might eat the passover, is not to be understood of the paschal lamb, but of the peace-offerings on the first day of the feast of unleavened bread, whereof the sacrificers had a share to feast on; for it will

not be cleared from scripture that to eat the passover is spoken of any other thing than of the very paschal lamb. Beside, John, xix. 14, the day whereon Christ suffered is called the preparation of the passover, and, ver. 31, the sabbath day thereafter is called an high day, which importeth more, as we shall hear. 1. Therefore, for clearing the difficulty, it is to be conceived that the Jews, by an ancient tradition, (received, as is supposed, in Babel,) whenever any extraordinary solemnity fell on the day immediately preceding an ordinary sabbath, used to translate the festivity to the sabbath following, lest there should be two days concurring wherein they might not work; and so here the first day of the feast of the passover, or unleavened bread, (which, with the last of the seven days of the feast, was a holy convocation, Num. xxviii. 16—18, 25,) falling, according to the appointment of the law, upon the day immediately preceding the sabbath, they deferred not only the following feast, but even the eating of the passover, till the evening of the fifteenth day of the month, which should have been the first day of the feast, (as seemeth to be clear from John, xviii. 28; xix. 14,) and the feast itself they conjoined with the ordinary sabbath following, for which cause it is called an high day, John, xix. 31, because of the conjunction of two festivities; for the mid-days of the feast of unleavened bread, betwixt the first and the last, were not so solemnly observed as to give such a denomination to this sabbath. Now Christ, not heeding their traditions, did punctually observe the day instituted by God, not so much out of necessity, because he had no longer time to live (for he might have prorogated his sufferings), as to shew how closely we ought to cleave to a rule in the matter of instituted worship, and how dangerous it is to deviate, let the alteration have never so many fair pretences for it. And whereas it may be objected that this differing from the common practice would have been full of hazard to Christ, and matter of accusation against him, which yet they never produce, it is to be conceived, for answer, not only that Christ did not stand on hazard who was now going to lay down his life, but further, also, that this matter, being private amongst his disciples and the master of the house, (who it seems was a secret friend,) could not so easily come to their knowledge; or, rather, (seeing Judas, when he went to the high priests, might easily have told it, if he had not been restrained,) that the Jews did so observe this tradition as yet, in these troublous times, any who pleased to submit to the instituted rule did follow it. Consider—3. While it is said that the devil had now put into the heart of Judas to betray him, the meaning is, not that either Satan only now began to tempt him to it, or that the matter was now perfected; for it is clear, from Matt. xxvi. 6—16, that upon occasion of the loss of the ointment, of which we heard, chap. xii. 3, 4, &c., he had made a bargain with the chief priests about this matter, and from ver. 27, 30, of this chapter it is clear that after this he was wholly given up to Satan, not only to project and capitulate about this business, but to put it speedily in execution; so the meaning is, that Christ took notice at this time that Judas was lately prompted by Satan to go and capitulate about the betraying of him, as a reason why he would now be busy with his disciples; and so the words will read, that already (before this supper) the devil had put it into his heart. To which may be added, further, that through his abuse of the sacrament of the passover, the devil got more footing to confirm him in this wicked resolution.

From verse 2, thus cleared, learn—1. Such as do seriously mind their duty, and consider the short time they may have for it, will diligently improve every moment of opportunity; for "supper being ended," (or, in the time of the supper,) Christ falls to work, and will not let that moment of time betwixt the paschal supper and the rest of that meal, and his instituting of the sacrament, pass away without some useful instruction to his disciples.

2. Such as conscientiously employ their time may, in a short minute thereof, (which being idly spent would seem nothing,) do much good in their station; for in a part of that night, after supper was ended, Christ not only taught his disciples by washing of their feet, but did deliver the sweet doctrine, and put up the solemn prayer that follows.

3. As at all times, so especially before and after the participation of the sacrament, men ought to study purity, and their obligation thereunto, that they may employ Christ to work it in them; for so much doth this circumstance of time, wherein he washed the disciples' feet, import. It was, "supper being ended," after their eating the paschal lamb, to teach them their obligation to purity who were made partakers of such a mercy; and before the sacrament of the supper, to teach them preparation.

4. Albeit Christ seem not always to take notice of men's plots against him, yet he hath still an eye upon them, and will give proof that he knows them, when either he is to discover, or prevent, or improve them; therefore, albeit John record nothing of Christ's taking notice of Judas's treachery when he was disappointed of the ointment, yet here it is remarked, that in due time use is made hereof, to move Christ to be diligent in dealing with the disciples, and to decipher him.

5. As the right use of sacraments is a special mean of much good to the godly, so Satan never gets greater advantage of wicked men than after their profane abuse of such precious ordinances; therefore also is it marked, that supper being ended, the devil hath now put it into his heart to betray him, or, confirmed him yet more in this wicked resolution.

6. Albeit men's corruptions be prone to all evil, and Satan have some hand in every evil, yet there are some sins that are singularly diabolical, and wherein Satan hath a chief hand, as being such as could not be acted by a man in an ordinary course of sinning, unless he were possessed and acted by Satan in an extraordinary manner; for this sin is not simply attributed to Judas, but the devil put into the heart of Judas Iscariot, Simon's son, to betray him. It was not a sin of human infirmity, but a devilish sin so to do. Such diabolical suggestions may be darted into the bosom of believers, and therefore they are warned to quench them, Eph. vi. 16; but the wicked do give way to them.

7. The way whereby Satan prevails with wicked men, is first to haunt and pester their hearts with his suggestions, till they be gained, and then he will easily carry them in their practice to act for him; for thus did he begin here, he put it into the heart of Judas Iscariot, &c.

8. Albeit the tentation and suggestion unto evil be from Satan, yet men's corruptions furnish him matter to work upon, and their dwelling upon wicked thoughts doth furnish occasion to him to tempt, and bloweth up the spark of his tentation into a flame; for thus it appears Satan got into his heart by reason of his covetousness, for being disappointed of the price of the ointment, chap. xii. 5, 6, he is grieved and vexed at it, and while he is thinking how to make it up some other way, Satan darts in this, that he should essay the trade of treachery, which presently kindled, as when fire is put to powder.

9. Whatever be Satan's design against the man whom he tempts, or against the saints, when he stirreth up persecutors, yet his great design is against Christ himself; for here he put into the heart of Judas to betray him, not so much regarding the disciples, so long as he was in the world to be the butt of his malice.

10. Satan doth oppose himself against Christ and his followers, not only by more immediate tentations (whereof Christ also had proof, Matt. iv.) or by stirring up open persecutors, but one of his special engines is to employ treacherous friends to betray him and them; for this was Satan's great work, to get a domestic, Judas, to betray him.

11. Satan getting way may not only prevail with most eminent visible professors, or ordinary teachers, but even with some among the very apostles, to do a piece of the worst service that ever was done to Christ; for here he puts into the heart of an apostle, Judas Iscariot, Simon's son, (so described, to distinguish him from another apostle of the same name, as chap. vi. 71,) to betray him.

12. No apprehension or thoughts of trouble did alter Christ's heart towards his people, but the more violent and near the storm was to him, the more diligent was he to lay out himself for their good; therefore is this treachery of Judas marked here, to shew that Christ's thoughts thereof did but stir him up to be more sedulous in instructing them. And if the thoughts of distracting trouble could not take him off from his care of them, we have the less cause to fear his forgetfulness of us, now when he is above all storms in his own blessed person.

From verse 3, learn—1. Whatever were the attempts of Satan and his instruments against Christ, and whatever his condescendence was to give way unto them, yet he was truly excellent and great in the midst of all his condescendence and sufferings; for even when Judas is consulting to betray him, it held true that the Father had given all things into his hands, &c.

2. Whatever it pleased Christ to condescend unto in his voluntary exinanition, yet he needed to be little discouraged at the attempts of enemies,

or his sufferings, as knowing his own excellency, even in his greatest abasement; for when Judas is seeking to betray him, Jesus knew, even then, that the Father had given all things into his hands, &c.

3. It is the duty of saints, in the time of their abasement and trials, not to dwell always on the thoughts of these, but to raise up their hearts in the consideration of their esteem with God through Christ, however the world account of them, and of the issue of their trials, however the world think to cut them off thereby as the offscouring of the earth; for herein Christ hath cast them a copy, who, while Judas is projecting his ruin, hath his heart fraught with thoughts of his own dominion and glory, and that as he came from God, so he went to God, by his sufferings.

4. Christ, as Mediator, hath a sovereignty and power over all things committed to him for his church's good; for the Father hath given all things into his hands, &c., (see chap. iii. 35,) wherein, as we may read his glory, so also—1. That saints may sleep soundly, having such a friend at the helm of providence. 2. That however wicked enemies seem to rage at their pleasure against Christ and his followers, yet they are given also into his hands; and that as he, in the midst of traitors and enemies, was yet in the hands (if not of friends, yet) of servants and slaves, so the most pernicious of them are given through him to the church for her good. 3. That men are but great fools when, notwithstanding all their covetousness, they must be content with a few things, and yet all things might be theirs, in a right sense and due order, through him, 1 Tim. iv. 8; Matt. vi. 33; Rom. viii. 32; for all things are his, and theirs in him. 4. That they are no less fools who make themselves slaves to anything, whereas in Christ they might be masters of all things. (See 1 Cor. iii. 21—23.)

5. Whatever were men's thoughts of Christ, yet he came from God in respect of the divine way of his conception, and his godhead's stooping to converse with us in the shape of a servant; and he was his ambassador, sent to deal with lost man in his name; for " he was come from God," yet so as he did not leave him.

6. However Christ and his sufferings were looked on by carnal man, yet thereby he returned to God, to be glorified with him as Mediator, yet so as he hath not left his people; for he " went to God."

7. Christ's thoughts of his excellency will not hinder his condescendence to his own, but in his thoughts of greatest glory he will evidence greatest humility, and his knowing of his own excellency makes him fit to mind his people in the midst of his greatest sufferings; for this purpose is premitted [introduced] his washing their feet, to shew how consistent his thoughts of this are with his lowly stooping, (knowing all this, " he riseth from supper," &c.) And it is subjoined to Judas's treachery, to shew how little that could hinder him, who was so high, from thinking upon his poor followers. Hereby also we are assured, that as his thoughts of his glory did not, so his possession of it doth not, hinder him from condescending to the necessities of his own.

VER. 4. ——And laid aside his garments; and took a towel, and girded himself.

5. After that he poureth water into a bason, and began to wash the disciples' feet, and to wipe them with the towel wherewith he was girded.

In these verses, the fact itself, of Christ washing his disciples' feet, is recorded, wherein appeareth his admirable humility and self-denial in that he layeth aside his state and his own refreshment, and riseth from supper while his servants sat still; he layeth aside his upper garments, (which were loose,) as servants used to do when they went to work, or to serve their masters; he girded himself with a towel, both to fasten his other garments upon him, that he might be more fit for the work, and to have it in readiness to wipe their feet with it; and having provided and brought the bason with water, he began to wash and wipe their feet, which lay out behind them, as they leaned at table, and which was a most servile employment, 1 Sam. xxv. 41. I shall not need here to inquire whether the Jews had such a custom as this, to wash their feet after their eating of the paschal lamb, which Christ here imitates in so singular a way, and improves to so notable spiritual advantage; nor shall I need here to insist on this practice, which is so fully explained afterward; only, for present, learn—

1. As Christ is infinitely glorious and exalted in himself, so is he admirably humble and condescending to his people; for our high Lord riseth from supper, &c., and began to wash his disciples' feet.

2. Christ's humility will stoop to do meanest things for his people, were it even to become a servant to them; for he acts all the parts of a mean servant here; and he did this, being on earth, to give proof what mean necessities of ours he will stoop to take notice of, though he be absent in body.

3. True humility is the compendious way to true honour, and to be least in Christ's house is the way to become greatest; for so doth he teach us, in that when he is about to go to God, verse 3, he most eminently kithes [looks at] his humility.

4. It is a special proof of Christ's love, and of his care of his people in the midst of his sufferings and glory, when he teacheth humility and promoves it in them by his word, example, or dispensations; for herein all the former considerations of his love to them, and his care of them, when he thinks of his sufferings and glory, did appear, in that he took this pains, not only to stoop to them, but to cast them a copy, and give them a lesson of humility.

VER. 6. Then cometh he to Simon Peter: and Peter saith unto him, Lord, dost thou wash my feet?

7. Jesus answered and said unto him, What I do thou knowest not now; but thou shalt know hereafter.

s

Followeth to ver. 12, an exposition of this fact, upon occasion of an interruption made by Peter; wherein chiefly this fact, and his doing of it, is explained, as it is a sign of another inward washing. This exposition may be drawn out in three branches, contained in his threefold answer to Peter's proposals and resolutions. In the first branch of the exposition, upon occasion of Peter's question, testifying his admiration, and shunning of such condescendence, he gives notice, in general, that there was somewhat more in it than the bare act, or than he saw for present, whereof he should be informed in due time. And this relates to his doing this act, both as it was a sign and as it was a servile employment in itself. We need not curiously determine whether he had washen any before he came to Peter, who had made no such scruple of it; but shall hold to what John here records, that coming to Peter, he meets with this stop flowing from Peter's forwardness, and gives an answer to it.

From verse 6, learn—1. Our Lord's humility yet further shineth, in that not only doth he stoop to do meanest services to his people, but will be at all the pains himself to do them good; for he cometh to Simon Peter to wash him, while he is sitting still at table.

2. There is no interruption or impediment laid in the way of Christ and his working but he can and doth improve it to precious ends and advantages; for out of Peter's refusal and interruption he brings out these precious instructions, which he would inculcate by his washing of their feet.

3. Christ's abasing of himself and condescending to his people ought not to obscure his majesty nor make them forget it; for in the midst of this his stooping he is to Peter, Lord.

4. Christ's abasement and condescendence for his people's good is truly admirable, and will be so in the eyes of the truly godly; for saith he, by way of admiration, "Lord, dost thou wash my feet?"

5. The admirableness of Christ's condescendence will appear, if, we consider, either how glorious he is who stoops, even the Lord, or how low he doth stoop, even to wash feet; or to whom he stoops, even to them who are unworthy of what he doth, and whom it beseems not to be so dealt with, though it beseem him well so to deal. "Dost thou wash my feet?" saith humble Peter.

6. As it is commendable to fear, even at Christ's manifested goodness, Hos. iii. 5, so saints ordinarily run to an extremity in that case, and do so fear and tremble at it as they are ready to decline and not to embrace it; for Peter's question imports not only his admiration at, but his desire to shun this condescendence, and doth put a stop to Christ's washing and conferring this favour on him. (See Luke, v. 8.)

7. Albeit Christ's stooping to us be a great abasement of himself, yet it is the great error of saints to think that he will not account it his great glory to serve them; for herein also Peter failed, in thinking Christ had forgot himself in this condescendence.

From verse 7, learn—1. Christ is very tender of the weaknesses of his own so long as they discover no obstinacy therein; for he gives a mild answer to Peter at first, till afterward his weakness bursts forth.

2. Every work of Christ towards his people, beside the work itself, carrieth some precious thing of him in the bosom of it, and is laden with lessons and great things of his wisdom, power, goodness, &c., for so is supposed here, that Christ is doing somewhat which Peter knows not, which is not to be understood of the simple washing their feet, (for Peter knew well enough that he was about to wash his feet,) but that this washing carried somewhat in the bosom of it.

3. That which the Lord is doing by his works is not often seen, in the meantime, by them to whom it is done; for " What I do thou knowest not now," yea, wherein do not we proclaim our ignorance and mistakes of what he is about? And no wonder we be in the dark here, if we consider—1. That the worker of these works is wonderful in counsel, and excellent in working, Isaiah, xxviii. 29, infinitely beyond politicians, whose projects and purposes are ofttimes hid from us, and therefore much more his. 2. That the way of his working and bringing about of his purposes is very strange and unperceivable; for he brings things out of nothing, Rom. iv. 17, one contrary out of another, as light out of darkness, 2 Cor. iv. 6; he brings meat out of the eater, and takes enemies in their own snares. 3. That his end in working is not to satisfy our sense and curiosity, but he chooseth such a way as may leave enemies to harden their hearts, and may try and humble his people.

4. Albeit we cannot dive into the depth of Christ's counsel in his working, yet we ought to reverence and adore him therein, and not to contest with him; and to yield implicit obedience to his will, revealing our duty in such a case; for albeit Peter know not now what he doth, yet he would have him so far crediting that he did it not in vain, as to submit to have his feet washed.

5. Christ will have us first yielding obedience to his will, because it is his will, and to wait his leisure till we know the reason of it; otherwise we do not obey because it is his will, but because of the reason of his command; for he will absolutely have him stoop to be washed by him, and then wait till hereafter, to know what it means, and for what end he doth it.

6. Such as in dark cases do absolutely submit to God's will, in the matter of duty or dispensations, shall, in due time, see a reason of his will, and know so much of his counsel and purpose in his working as is needful for them; for upon Peter's obedience is promised, that though what I do thou knowest not now, yet thou shalt know hereafter; as accordingly was made good in the following explication of all this; and when the Spirit was poured out, he, with the rest, understood more fully this and other things.

Ver. 8. Peter saith unto him, Thou shalt never wash my feet. Jesus answered him, If I wash thee not, thou hast no part with me.

In the second branch of this exposition, upon occasion of Peter's more peremptory refusal, there is a further exposition of the meaning of this washing, and of the necessity of what he intended to point at thereby; for Peter not acquiescing in what Christ had told him, but proceeding from admiration to a wilful refusal that Christ should wash his feet, as conceiving it his duty, in modesty, to refuse, however Christ should press it; Christ taking hardly with this, renounces all communion with him, and disclaims that Peter had any interest in him, unless he did wash him, which doth not import only that his wilful refusing to stoop to Christ's will in this external washing would, if he persisted in it, prove him to be in a bad condition, though that be true in itself, but chiefly, (as the following exposition of washing their feet in particular makes clear,) it points out that Christ, by washing their feet, would (not institute a sacrament, but) put them in mind of soul-washing, which as it can only be done by him, so without it men can prove no interest in him; and so the meaning of this washing in general is to point out the necessity of washing sinners by regeneration, justification, and begun sanctification, which was also the signification of their several washings under the law, Ps. li.

From Peter's refusal, learn—1. Men may have much seeming humility in the matters of God, which yet is but preposterous and sinful, and learned from carnal reason; for such was Peter's humility, condemned by Christ here. (See Col. ii. 18, 23.)

2. It doth not justify men's tentations and sinful humility that it seems to rise from much good, but we are to distinguish betwixt what is really good and what tentations Satan fastens on it; for this condemned humility did begin at admiration at Christ's condescendence, ver. 6, and grounded itself upon his respect to Christ and disesteem of himself.

3. It is an evidence men are under a tentation when they are stiff, and do pertinaciously stand out against Christ's verdict; and in particular it is but sinful humility when men will not submit to Christ's verdict and will; for this was the fault in Peter's humility, that he would not take satisfaction from Christ concerning what he was doing.

4. It is but sinful and preposterous humility which refuseth Christ's offer, whatever it be, or how unworthy soever we be of it; for this also was Peter's fault, "Thou shalt never wash my feet;" he thought himself unworthy of this condescendence, and therefore utterly refuseth to admit of his offer. See the contrary of this in the church's admitting of Christ's commendation, seeing he was pleased to have a desire towards her, Cant. vii. 1, 2, &c., with ver. 10.

From Christ's answer to Peter, learn—1. Saints, by what they do out of a pretext of humility, may be running on a snare, and deserving sad threatenings from him; for Peter's humility meets with this entertainment.

2. It is Christ's method ofttimes with his people to break their obstinacy with sad threatenings, and to boast them to their mercy, and from their preposterous humility, when fair dealing will not persuade them; for thus doth he deal with Peter.

3. It is the saddest of threatenings and judgments to be secluded from an interest in and communion with Christ; therefore is it held out to Peter as a very sad case, "Thou hast no part in me"—that is, no interest in him, and consequently no communion with him, nor share in that inheritance purchased by him, and so is no co-heir with him.

4. The contempt of an ordinance or command of Christ, how mean-like soever, deserves the saddest of threatenings, and that the contemner should be secluded from Christ; for this holds true, even of the outward washing, and his resisting thereof, when Christ required it, "If I wash thee not, thou hast no part with me;" by which sad threatening Christ drives Peter to submit.

5. Soul-purging from sin is so necessary that without it men can have no evidence of interest in or communion with Christ; for it holds chiefly true of the thing pointed at, "If I wash thee not, thou hast no part with me."

6. It is neither the goodness of our nature, nor legal purifications, or our own endeavours, that can either prove or make us clean; but it is Christ alone who must wash us, that we may participate with him, and who must apply the merit and efficacy of his blood for that end; for "If I wash thee not, (saith he,) thou hast no part with me."

VER. 9. Simon Peter saith unto him, Lord, not my feet only, but also my hands and my head.

In the third branch of this exposition, upon occasion of Peter's running to another extremity, Christ declares what he meant by washing their feet only. In this verse we have Peter's proposal, occasioning the explication; he being affrighted with the former threatening, and (belike) now understanding what Christ meant by this external washing, is so far from refusing that Christ should wash his feet, that he offers hands, and head, and all, to be washed. Whence learn—

1. It is so terrible a thing to be threatened with separation from Christ that the thoughts thereof will cause a child of God to draw nearer to him, and make him condescend to anything rather than admit of that; for this brake Peter's obstinacy, and made him say, "Lord, not my feet only, but also my hands and my head," before that be.

2. Saints, being sensible of sin, are ready to forget their renewed and justified estate, and to look on themselves as altogether polluted and corrupt; for this may also be understood as Peter's language, when he understood the signification of this washing; in which case he seeth not only foul feet, but head, and hands, and all, to be washed, and therefore upon that account he offers them all to Christ; which, though Christ clear it to be his mistake, yet it is ofttimes the sad exercise of saints.

3. It is the great infirmity of saints that they

run, for most part, upon extremes; and when they leave one extremity they return not to the right way, but fall on the contrary extremity; for whether we look to the external action or signification thereof, Peter did thus err, first in declining to be washed at all, and then in offering more to be washed than Christ required.

VER. 10. *Jesus saith to him, He that is washed needeth not save to wash his feet, but is clean every whit: and ye are clean, but not all.*

In this verse we have Christ's answer to this offer of Peter, wherein he clears what he meant by washing their feet only—namely, not only to testify his humility by stooping so low, but further, to point out somewhat concerning them. And—

1. He propounds his mind in general doctrine, wherein the similitude runs thus: that as a man going home from a bath needs not wash his whole body again, but only his feet, which contract filth by walking, (as they used in these hot countries to travel barefooted,) so saints, who are already washed by begun renovation and the justification of their persons, need not over again wash, as if every spot did alter their state, but ought only to be purging their affections and actions from the relics of sin by getting daily renewed remission, and studying sanctification daily. In saying, he that is washed is clean every whit, he doth not assert an absolute purity in any within time, nor yet is it only his meaning that he is clean by begun renovation, which is perfect in parts, though not in degrees; but the sense chiefly is, that by justification his person is clean, and that the man who, being renewed and justified, doth make daily use of his privilege of having access to the fountain opened up, for daily renewed remission, and washing of his foul feet, is clean every whit in God's account, nor is there any spot in him for which God will condemn him. 2. Christ makes particular application of this doctrine to the disciples, pronouncing that society clean, though with exception of some, (for which a reason is after given,) and that therefore they needed to wash no more but their feet.

DOCTRINES.

1. It is the will of Christ that saints in their exercises do put a difference betwixt the state of their persons and the several conditions into which they may fall; for here is a washed and clean man, who yet hath feet to be washed.

2. No man can be in an acceptable state but he to whom it is gifted by Christ, and communicated through his blood and spirit; for he is washed who is clean. (See 1 Cor. vi. 11.)

3. Saints whose persons are clean have yet, while they are within time, some pollution and relics of sin left, for their exercise and humiliation, and in their affections and actions are daily contracting filth; for he that is washed needeth to wash his feet. (See Psalm cxxx. 3; cxliii. 2.)

4. The infirmities of washed saints are not universal, nor like the voluntary wallowing of swine in the puddle, 2 Pet. ii. 22, but are only defilements of their feet, or of their affections and conversation in going through this polluted world; for so much is imported, that they need but to wash their feet, where the similitude imports, that this pollution reaches not their best parts, at least reigns not there; that it breaks forth rather in their practice than utterly poisons their heart; and that, however it have a fountain within, yet it is much helped on, by reason of pollution and entanglements without them, as men's feet are fouled by the ground they tread upon.

5. It is the duty, and ought to be the care of saints, not to please themselves in this, that their defilements are but infirmities, but they must be washed from them; for he that is washed needeth yet to wash his feet. So did Paul pursue the least relic of sin, Rom. vii.

6. Not only the justification of our persons, but even the washing of our infirmities must be Christ's work; for the external action Christ is about teacheth that he also must wash the feet.

7. Albeit a justified sinner can never be separated from Christ, yet as a man who never employs Christ for pardon and purging of his daily infirmities doth evidence that he is not justified, so a justified man will pursue these relics of sin, that so he may thereby be more and more confirmed in the assurance of his interest in Christ; for unto this washing of the feet Christ applieth that, ver. 8, "If I wash thee not, thou hast no part with me."

8. It is not Christ's will that saints, upon every new outbreaking, should cast loose their state, as if their regeneration and justification and reconciliation were made void thereby, but they are to hold that fast as a thing not to be renewed, (though when the discharge is dim they may seek a new extract,) and so go on to get that washed which is foul; for "he that is washed needeth not save to wash his feet."

9. Albeit saints be weak in faith and imperfect in sanctification, yet there is a gospel-reckoning, according to which they are every whit clean—namely, when they are justified and their sins pardoned, and when they are daily studying sanctification, and making use of daily remission and cleansing; for such an one is washed and clean every whit.

10. General doctrine is then only useful when particular application is made thereof; therefore Christ applies this to them, "And ye are clean."

11. It is not they who justify themselves that are clean, but those whom Christ accounts to be so; and his absolving word is sufficient to secure a saint, who is humbled with his own spots, that he is clean in his account; for here he gives this for their security, "Ye are clean."

12. Hypocrisy and uncleanness are so universal that it is rare to see the choicest or smallest society free from some infected therewith; for even among this select company there is an exception, "Ye are clean, but not all," or, all the persons in this society, as the word in the original clears. And no wonder it be so; for hereby the Lord would refute the conceit of the godly, that they can be fully separated from the wicked within time; hereby also are they exercised; and these unclean persons are made use of in the society as vessels of dishonour in a house, to carry forth

the filth from the rest; as heretics do take the tentations of saints to be their opinions; and hereby the Lord leads saints to abhor them, who otherwise gave too much way to them.

13. Christ never lets out his approbation unto any, but ordinarily he subjoins so much with it as may make them very circumspect and jealous of themselves; therefore, after that sentence, " Ye are clean," he subjoins so general an exception, " but not all," neither declaring whom or how many he excepted, that so every one might try himself.

VER. 11. For he knew who should betray him; therefore said he, Ye are not all clean.

John subjoins a reason why Christ made this exception, and points out who it was that he meant by this exception, even Judas, the traitor. Whence learn—

1. Christ knows a reason for everything he saith or doth, whether we know it or not, as here we see.

2. Albeit neither can men discern, nor ought they to judge hardly of others, who have not discovered themselves, yet Christ can distinguish betwixt true professors and latent hypocrites, and may let forth what he knoweth when he pleaseth; " for he knew who should betray him," and therefore said this.

3. Were hypocrites and traitors in never so excellent a society, and never so like saints in outward appearance, yet are they not clean in Christ's account; for Judas is excepted from among the clean by Christ, though he was among the apostles, and nothing yet had visibly appeared.

4. Doctrine delivered in mixed societies ought to be well guarded, that the unclean (if there were but one of them) do not put out their hands to the allowance of the clean; for Christ upon this ground makes the exception; " for he knew who should betray him; therefore said he, Ye are not all clean."

VER. 12. So after he had washed their feet, and had taken his garments, and was set down again, he said unto them, Know ye what I have done to you?

Followeth to verse 18, an exposition of this washing after Christ had done with it, wherein he explains it, as it was a servile employment performed by him to them, that hereby he might teach them humility. In this exposition we may observe six particulars, whereof the first (in this verse) contains somewhat antecedent to the exposition—namely, that before he perform his promise to Peter, ver. 7, he goeth on to wash all their feet, and having taken his garments, and sitten down, he inquireth at themselves if they understood what he meant by all this. Whence learn—

1. Whatever be the strugglings of saints against Christ's dealing, yet he will have his will, and carry through his purpose; for notwithstanding Peter's opposition, (wherein others, as humble as he, might have been ready to imitate him,) yet he washed their feet.

2. Christ's favours are not tendered compliments, but really conferred mercies, and he will come over much opposition to make them effectual; for he not only offered but really did wash their feet.

3. Albeit Christ's servants and people have a promise that he will make known his mind in things that concern them, which he will perform in due season, yet he will exercise their submission and obedience at leisure, before he perform it; for he washeth all their feet, takes his garments, and sate down again, and propounds this question before he make good that promise given to Peter, ver. 7.

4. Where Christ is about to teach his people he will first humble them under the sense of their own ignorance, and then will teach them; for this question " Know ye what I have done to you?" tends to discover their ignorance of the matter, to humble them.

5. It is the duty of Christ's scholars to be serious in attending what he is doing about them and to them, and to rouse up themselves to attend what he will teach thereby; for this question is also put to stir them up to attend to the former action and following explication.

VER. 13. Ye call me Master and Lord: and ye say well; for so I am.

In the second place, Christ layeth down a ground whereon to press the following doctrine and explication of this action, which is taken from the titles due to him, and given to him by the disciples. Whence learn—

1. Christ requires acknowledgments and due titles from his people, and they who know him will not deny them; for so was their use; " Ye call me Master (or Teacher) and Lord."

2. Many titles and all sovereignty over us is due unto Christ; he will not be content to be a Master to teach, as the Pharisees sometimes pretended to acknowledge, unless he be taken also for a Lord, who must be obeyed, and to govern and rule us; nor will he be pleased with glorious titles of Lord, Lord, when men will not stoop to hearken to his doctrine; therefore are they conjoined, " Master and Lord."

3. We can give no glorious titles to Christ, but they are due to him, and as he will accept of them, so he will be answerable to them; he is a faithful Teacher, and a Ruler who will protect and defend them who come under his protection; for saith he, " ye say well; for so I am."

4. Christ will not be content of titles or fair professions, unless men do improve them in practice, and do not give their own tongues the lie; therefore Christ takes hold of their acknowledgment to urge the following doctrine upon them, as being obliged thereunto by their own professions.

VER. 14. If I then, your Lord and Master, have washed your feet; ye also ought to wash one another's feet.

In the third place, we have Christ's doctrine inferred upon this ground, and the exposition of his carriage in washing their feet—namely, that by his doing thereof, who was their Lord and Master, to them his servants, he would teach them their duty, to condescend so low as to wash one another's feet, whereby we are not to understand only this particular service to be mutually done, (as some do formally and superstitiously imitate him herein,) but under this one abject peace of service all duties of love and condescendence, how base soever, are required; neither yet are outward actions of love to be understood as only comprehended under this, but it includes also all the internal ingredients thereof in the heart, such as humility towards God, a low esteem of ourselves, a high esteem of others, &c.; and by this direction, enforced from his own example, he would obviate the great emulation among his apostles, which (if not cured) might do so much hurt after his departure. From this purpose, (leaving the force of his example till the following verses,) learn—

1. Humility, love, and condescendence, are most necessary among the members of Christ; therefore doth he so seriously press these here. (See 1 Pet. v. 5.)

2. True humility doth not consist in external shows, but will stoop to the meanest service wherein one may be steadable [useful] to another, were it even "to wash one another's feet." (See 1 Cor. ix. 19, 20, &c.; Gal. v. 13.)

3. Albeit it bring rich advantage to the man himself who is humble and condescending, though none other should join with him in it, yet it is necessary for the general good of the church that mutual subjection to perform basest duties be the bond to bind saints one to another; for they should "wash one another's feet." The church doth then live in true peace when every one of her members becometh a servant to another.

4. Albeit men be ready to look on this humility and mutual condescendence as a free-will offering, for omitting whereof they are not convinced, and in performing of it they are much puffed up, yet it is a commanded duty, not to be omitted without sin, and in the performance whereof we are still unprofitable servants; for ye "ought to wash one another's feet."

5. Humility and mutual condescendence are especially necessary in ministers, that their pride and emulation do not mar the work of the gospel; therefore Christ stooped so low as, by his own example, to bind this upon his apostles. I have washed your feet, that ye may wash one another's feet.

6. The Lord alloweth of no superiority in any of his ministers over the rest, and requireth also that they lay aside any personal pre-eminence or prerogative, and by love serve one another; for they are all " to wash one another's feet."

VER. 15. For I have given you an example, that ye should do as I have done to you.

In the fourth place, this duty is more distinctly enforced from Christ's former practice in washing their feet; wherein he sheweth that he did it as an example to them, which therefore they are bound to imitate. Whence learn—

1. It is a commendable duty in the Lord's children to study to be good examples in their carriage one to another; for herein Christ hath led the way in giving good example.

2. Albeit Christ, as God and Mediator, hath done works of omnipotency, and by way of satisfaction for sinners, which are or can be imitated by none, yet in the matter of obedience to the law he hath done works expressly for imitation and example, which are to be marked; for saith he, " I have given you an example."

3. As in all duties of obedience, so especially in the matter of humility, Christ hath cast an excellent copy to his followers, both to encourage poor sinners to come to him, and excite them to follow him; for this is the particular, wherein saith he, " I have given you an example." (See Matt. xi. 29.)

4. Such as acknowledge Christ to be precious, as they will subject themselves to all his commands, so they will count it a strong obligation to any duty that Christ hath gone about it in his own practice and thereby commended it to them; for they ought " to wash one another's feet," ver. 14; " for I have given you an example," &c.

5. It stands as a general rule that what Christ hath done to us in love we stand bound in our stations, and to our power, to do the same to others; for " ye should do as I have done to you." Our imitation comes always short; but we must follow him in so far as we can attain. (See Matt. vi. 14, 15; 1 John, iii. 16.)

VER. 16. Verily, verily, I say unto you, The servant is not greater than his lord; neither he that is sent greater than he that sent him.

In the fifth place, this practice and example of Christ is further urged to press this duty, from the consideration of his excellency, which he had laid down as a ground, ver. 13, and summarily urged, ver. 14. As Christ's greatness above his servants is urged elsewhere to make them content with the lots he was exercised with, John, xv. 20; Matt. x. 24, 25; so here it is made use of to press them to that humility one towards another which he had shewed towards them. And this makes the argument from his example conclude more strongly that they who were so far inferior to him should not disdain to practice that condescendence he had used. Whence learn—

1. Whatever dignity Christ confer upon his servants and officers, yet he is the authorizer of them all, and Lord above them all, and over all his church; and it is the greatest dignity of any to be his servants and represent him in a commission; for so is here imported.

2. Christ's greatness and excellency contributes to set forth and commend his humility to us; therefore, in this action, he is so oft spoken of as Lord and sender of his servants. (See Phil. ii. 5—7.)

3. It becomes Christ's followers to affect no greater eminency in this world than Christ had, and not to disdain to stoop so low as he did; for if the servant be not made less than his Lord it is no reason he should look to be greater.

4. The consideration of our baseness should keep our minds lowly, and free of affecting superiority over our brethren ; for Christ presseth the duty on this ground, that they are but servants, and sent.

5. Whosoever doth refuse to walk humbly towards his fellow-disciples doth in effect deny his inferiority to Christ; for either he must deny that the servant is not greater than his Lord, or he that is sent than he that sent him, or else he must stoop to wash the feet of others.

6. Albeit our baseness be very visible in itself, especially when we are compared with Christ, yet it is not usually pondered by us as it ought, nor so studied as the fruits thereof may appear in practice; for it must be borne upon them with Christ's ordinary asseveration, " Verily, verily, I say unto you," to drive them to this condescendence.

7. Whatever be the shiftings of our ambitious hearts, yet Christ will not on any terms dispense with the want of humility and condescendence in his followers, but he will either have them stoop or else he will abase them ; therefore also doth he urge this with a " verily, verily," to press it as a grave and necessary matter; and in the rest of the words he so speaks as may import both their duty to imitate their Lord and Master, and his will (especially if they did not so) that they should meet with such humbling lots as he did.

VER. 17. If ye know these things, happy are ye if ye do them.

In the last place, Christ not being content with a bare speculation in this matter, and having sufficiently informed them of their duty in it, he comes very earnestly to press the practice thereof, and to encourage them thereunto by an annexed promise of blessedness. Whence learn—

1. Christ doth not approve of blind ignorance in his people, whatever their practice or conversation be, but requires that their practice be founded on sound and solid knowledge of his will ; for he requires that they " know these things," and then " do them."

2. When much pains is taken to inculcate duties, yet men may remain very ignorant, partly through their natural impotency, and chiefly through their inadvertency, and being transported with lusts and carnal imaginations; for " If ye know these things," is not only a supposition that knowledge must go before practice, but may import a doubt also if yet they were made capable of this doctrine ; for they were so transported with a carnal dream of the Messiah's kingdom that they could not understand his clear predictions of his sufferings, Luke, xviii. 31—34. And what wonder if their carnal emulation did hide this doctrine from them also?

3. The doctrine of humility and mutual condescendence is very comprehensive, and contains many duties in the bosom of it, which are called for in variety of cases and exigents ; therefore doth he speak of what is understood by " washing one another's feet," ver. 14, in the plural number, " Know these things," and " do them."

4. The Lord approves not, in the matters of religion, that men content themselves with knowledge and speculations, but it is his will that men, having known their duty, do put it in practice, and do prove the sincerity and soundness of their knowledge by their practice ; for so doth this connexion import, " If ye know these things, do them," and so prove that ye know indeed. (See James, i. 22—25.)

5. In particular, the Lord requireth the practice of humility, and it is the touchstone of men's sincerity, not what knowledge they have of it, the contemplation and notion whereof may be sweet, but what they do in practice on particular exigents which will be more bitter and trying than contemplation was ; for this in particular is the duty wherein he requires that practice follow knowledge.

6. Albeit our obedience and practice deserve nothing, yet it hath such a blessing in the bosom of it, and is the way to such rich blessedness as doth compense all loss and disadvantage; for this is the encouragement, " happy are ye if ye do them."

7. Albeit the condescending and humble man seem to lose much thereby in the world, yet blessedness is allowed to make it up ; and to attain the practice of humility is a blessedness in itself, in so far as it hides a man from many storms and discontentments wherewith others are blown over ; for of this in particular it is said, " happy are ye if ye do them."

8. Ambitious, proud men are so far from blessedness that they lie under a curse, especially if they know their duty and will not do it; for it followeth, on the contrary, if ye know these things, cursed are ye if ye do them not. (See James, iv. 17 ; Psalm cxix. 21.)

VER. 18. I speak not of you all : I know whom I have chosen : but that the scripture may be fulfilled, He that eateth bread with me hath lifted up his heel against me.

Followeth to ver. 31, the second part of the chapter, wherein Christ discovereth Judas's treachery, and that he was the traitor. The words may be taken up in four steps of progress in this discovery :—1. Christ in general intimateth that there were some unsound among them, and guardeth this business and the intimation thereof with necessary cautions and instructions, ver. 18—20. 2. Being pressed to it, and they not laying hold on the former intimation, he intimates more distinctly that there was one among them so rotten-hearted as to betray him ; whereat they are amazed, ver. 21, 22. 3. John being set on work by Peter to inquire concerning this traitor, Christ by a sign doth discover Judas to him, ver. 23—26. 4. This discovery producing woeful effects in Judas, Christ discovers more of his mind concerning his treachery to himself when he is going out to effectuate it, ver. 27—30.

In this verse—1. Christ proceeds to this general discovery, (whereof some hint had been given before, ver. 10,) by way of exception to the former doctrine. As he had formerly made an exception in pronouncing them clean, ver. 10, so here he declares that he expected not from all of them that they should be blessed in practising humility and mutual condescendence, ver. 17 ; but some one or other of them would be so far from serving his fellow-disciples that he would rise against his Master. 2. He gives the ground of this exception, and why he did thus pronounce of any of them—namely, that he knew whom he had chosen, the meaning whereof is, not so much that he knew what every one whom he had chosen to the apostleship would prove, and Judas among the rest, (though that be also true,) but he knew who they were whom, beside election to the apostleship, (wherein Judas shared also, chap. vi. 70,) he had chosen to eternal life, and whom not, and consequently knew who would prove faithful or false to him. 3. If any should inquire wherefore did he choose such a man to be an apostle, whom he knew would prove a traitor? he answers, that hereby was fulfilled a prediction in Psalm xli. 9, that one of his familiars and domestics should ingrately recompense his kindness, as if a beast fed by his master should kick against him. And this is the first caution and instruction subjoined to this intimation that they should not stumble at the business. As for this connexion of the prediction with the event compare what is said on chap. xii. 38 ; only here it should be considered that this is not a simple prediction, relating only to Christ and Judas, but was in part accomplished in Ahithophel's treachery against David, who in his sufferings of this kind was a type of Christ's sufferings from Judas, in whom that was chiefly accomplished. And albeit so much only be cited as is clearly applicable to Christ, that of a "friend, in whom I trusted," being more proper to David, seeing Christ never hoped for any good of Judas, (and so we ought to be wary in expounding scripture-types,) yet even that may in some sense be true of Christ, who entrusted Judas not only with the bag but with the ministry and apostleship itself, as well as the rest.

DOCTRINES.

1. Christ is very tender of his weak followers and loath to grieve them by bringing forth what may displease or stumble them; therefore doth he at first prepare their minds for these sad news, with such general intimations and cautions.

2. It is not sufficient that men hear truths, unless they make application thereof to themselves in particular ; for Christ's exception supposeth an application of what he said on their parts.

3. When truths are spoken in a general auditory men are very ready to misapply them, for therefore is a guard and exception needful. In this case, (to say nothing of the state of men's persons, whereby they may know much what they have right unto,) we should consider—
1. Want of fear in application of what is comfortable is a sad evidence of wrong application.
2. Whatever men's right be to what is comfortable, yet they cannot comfortably apply it unless they stand in real and sensible need of what is offered for their encouragement and furtherance in good, or do in sincerity lay hold on the offer to quicken them in their sense of need. 3. Albeit they may have right to apply comforts who sometimes will fall asleep upon them, yet the application is never comfortable but when some fruits thereof appear. So also threatenings are not savingly applied but when they stir up to diligence. 4. Ordinarily the hearts of good and bad are so froward that they are best at applying what they have least right unto; saints, when they are humbled, can lay hold on threatenings but cannot hear of promises; the wicked make no doubt of promises, but take no notice of threatenings ; and saints are most apt to grasp at promises when they are most secure.

4. So general is the corruption of men and their societies that comfortable things can hardly be spoken to the choicest and fewest number of them but there will be some to be excepted against as having no right thereunto ; for when Christ is propounding to his very twelve apostles a promise of happiness upon the practice of humility, there needs an exception, " I speak not of you all."

5. Ministers are not faithful, nor do they declare the whole counsel of God, unless with general promises they publish also needful cautions that none do stumble upon or abuse them ; for so much doth Christ's practice in excepting Judas teach. And albeit they cannot do as Christ did in pointing at the man, yet they must set down scripture cautions and limits to the promises, and the scripture qualifications of those who have right thereunto.

6. Whatever may be the excellences of men, and especially of Christ's servants, in respect of their gifts and success, yet true happiness belongs to none but to the chosen and elect ones ; for albeit the apostleship had very eminent effects, yet they are only happy in obedience whom he hath chosen. (See Luke, x. 17—20.)

7. Men may be chosen to very eminent employments who yet are not chosen to eternal life ; for by this exception Judas is secluded from among those whom he hath chosen ; so that we have need not to dote so much on what is adorning, but to seek what is saving.

8. Whatever be the means whereby men are kept faithful and carried on to happiness, yet the fountain of all this flows from the Lord's electing them to these means, and to the end following thereupon ; therefore the apostles' walking in the ways of happiness is attributed not so much to their grace as to his election, the fountain of their grace : " I know whom I have chosen," and who therefore will be happy in doing these things. And this is held out, partly, that all the good we have we may trace up to this fountain, and partly, that having made our calling and election sure, we may be comforted under the sense of great inward weakness. Hence it is that glorification is subjoined to election and justification, Rom. viii. 28, 29, and election is laid as a ground of security against final defection in trying times, Matt. xxiv. 24 ; 2 Tim. ii. 18, 19.

9. Christ is the author of election, as God equal with the Father, and he knoweth the number of his chosen ones, and who they are ; for " I know whom I have chosen." (See 2 Tim. ii. 19.)

10. Christ is not ignorant what any of his followers will prove, and that from the beginning; for Judas did not deceive him : " I know whom I have chosen."

11. There is much of Christ to be seen in the Old Testament by a discerning eye; and much acted in types which hath its full accomplishment in him; for the scriptures, speaking of David's suffering in the type from Ahithophel, is fulfilled in Judas's treachery against Christ.

12. In all the lots that befal Christ and his followers we are to guard against stumbling at them, by considering a sovereign providence of God in all of them; for Christ here guards the disciples' minds in this matter by letting them see that God foresaw it long before, and did foretel that which was now fulfilled.

13. Christ is most tender of fulfilling all scriptures, that so we may be encouraged to rest our confidence on what he saith in them; therefore doth he admit of a Judas into his fellowship, and permits him to betray him, that the scripture might be fulfilled, and there might be no cause of questioning the truth thereof. So, John x. 16, albeit he had affection to the gentiles, yet for the truth of God he confined himself to the ministry of the circumcision, Rom. xv. 8.

14. Christ and his followers do suffer not only from open enemies, which were in many respects an ease, but they are also persecuted by false bosom friends and familiars; for so found David the type, and Christ the substance : he that eateth bread with me hath lifted up his heel against me. (See Ps. lv. 12—14.)

15. It is the great treachery and horrid ingratitude of enemies that no favours nor familiarity will draw them from their enmity, but rather emboldens them thereunto; for albeit he eat bread with him, and his bread too, (as it is Ps. xli. 9,) yet, wantonly and ingrately, he hath lifted up his heel against me.

16. Whatever be the carriage of enemies, yet it is the duty of Christ's followers to heap coals on their heads by doing them all the good they can in their stations; for herein Christ hath left an example, who, albeit he knew what Judas was, yet let him eat bread with him. (See Ps. xxxv. 12—15; Rom. xii. 20.)

VER. 19. Now I tell you before it come, that, when it is come to pass, ye may believe that I am he.

In this verse a second caution and instruction is joined with this intimation, wherein (as in the former he gave a reason why he permitted such a thing to be so) he gives a reason why he now foretels of this treachery beforehand—namely, that when they should compare his prediction with the event when it came to pass, they might be so far from stumbling at it, that, on the contrary, it might afford them an encouragement to believe on him who, by the prediction, did prove himself God omniscient, and by his suffering these things did prove himself to be the true Messiah, of whom these things were fore-prophesied. Whence learn—

1. Christ is omniscient as God, and knoweth and can foretel things before they come to pass; for now I tell you before it come. (See Isaiah, xlviii. 5.)

2. Christ doth so order his own and his people's afflictions as, instead of bitterness and stumbling, a right observer may find many confirmations and advantages by them; for he so orders Judas's treachery (which would seem to have ruined all) as it may contribute to confirm them that he is God and the true Messiah. It is he indeed who brings meat out of the eater.

3. It is a notable fruit and advantage by saddest storms to be helped to know and believe more of Christ's excellency and sufficiency; for this is the fruit here, that " ye may believe that I am he."

4. Whatever degree of knowledge and faith in Christ saints attain to, yet they need more increase and confirmation, and to attain this is a difficult task; for albeit the disciples knew and believed what he was, yet he finds these pains needful, that they may be helped to believe more.

5. Christ, rightly taken up, will be believed to be matchless, singular, and inexpressible in his fulness and excellency; for this he aims at, that " ye may believe that I am he," or, that I am— to wit, that singular and inexpressible one.

6. A special mean to confirm faith by saddest dispensations is to compare these events with predictions concerning them, wherein we may read God's omniscience and providence, knowing and setting bounds to all these storms; for " I tell you before it come, that, when it is come to pass, ye may believe."

VER. 20. Verily, verily, I say unto you, He that receiveth whomsoever I send receiveth me; and he that receiveth me receiveth him that sent me.

In this verse we have a third caution and instruction subjoined to this intimation, wherein Christ holds forth this encouragement to all his faithful messengers, and all who receive them and their message, that these his servants are so dear to him and his Father, and his Father and he are so nearly interested in them and their message, that the respect shewed to them and it redounds both to him and his Father. His scope in this doctrine is, partly, to remove another exception that might be propounded upon occasion of Judas's treachery; for whereas upon his deserting and betraying of his Master men might be ready to think that he was but a bad Master, and that the office of apostleship was of little worth, since he had so lightly deserted it, Christ declares that this office was honourable in itself, and (however Judas had played the traitor, yet) he would get men to exercise it and to entertain them who did so to their own rich advantage; and therefore his treachery did no way reflect on him or his service, but did aggravate the traitor's guiltiness, who had deserted so honourable an office, owned not only by Christ but by his Father also. Partly, also, his scope is hereby to encourage the rest of the apostles, (as it is made use of, Matt. x. 40,) who being to be left by their Master, and sent out on service, wherein they might expect great difficulties (as is declared, Matt. x.), and being also pressed with the necessity of humility and condescendence, might be ready to think this a very hard and disadvantageous service. Withal, Judas's treachery, who was one of their number, might give them occasion to suspect that Christ would abhor their society for his sake; therefore he declares, that notwithstanding all that had come, if they would go about the employment as he required, he should own them in it, and whosoever received them should receive him and the Father also.

DOCTRINES.

1. Men's deserting of Christ and his service doth no way reflect on him or it, but upon the deserters themselves; nor will he want servants and those who will entertain them, desert him who will; for so much doth this doctrine, as it is a caution against Judas's treachery, teach, that he will have some to send and some to receive them, when Judas is gone.

2. Our Lord Jesus hath large understanding and capacity to take many things into his mind, and meet with all necessary cases at once; for by this doctrine he not only obviates Judas's treachery, but meets with the discouragements of the rest of his disciples, as hath been explained.

3. Albeit Christ's doctrine concerning the excellency of his service get but little credit in times of defection, and albeit his encouragements have but little place with those of weak hands, yet what he saith to the one or the other case is most grave and undoubted truth; therefore is his doctrine, which guardeth against the scandal of Judas's defection, and encourageth his disciples, confirmed by his ordinary asseveration, " Verily, verily, I say unto you."

4. In times of defection, such as continue faithful shall be the more precious in Christ's sight, and be allowed special encouragements by him; therefore doth he hold out such a cordial to his honest disciples, now, when Judas is to forsake him.

5. Whatever be the difficulties attending Christ's service, yet the service itself hath encouragement sufficient in its bosom against all of them; therefore is this encouragement held forth against their difficulties in the exercise of their office.

6. The humble, condescending man is so dear to Christ that he shares in all his lots, is respected in all the respects put upon him, and accounts himself slighted in all the affronts offered to him; for this doctrine also tends to encourage them to the humility he had pressed upon them, by shewing that he will do all for the humble, and will share with them in their entertainment in the world.

7. Whatever be the want of outward splendour or the ignominy and contempt of Christ's servants in the world, yet it is sufficient dignity and authority to bear them out, that they are clothed with a message and commission from him; for it is here supposed as their dignity, and sufficient to bear them out in the exercise of their office in the world, that he sends them.

8. It is the duty of people, in relation to Christ's messengers, to receive and embrace their doctrine, and their persons for their doctrine's sake, and to guard against prejudices at their persons, lest they stumble at their message; for so is here imported, They should receive whom I send. (See 1 Thess. v. 12, 13 ; Heb. xiii. 17.)

9. Christ's faithful servants are so taken up with zeal to their Master, and love to the welfare of souls, that their great encouragement within time is when their message, and themselves for its sake, are received and get place amongst men ; for this is their encouragement, that encouragement is given to men to receive them, as being their great scope. (See 2 Cor. vii. 2 ; 1 Thess. ii. 19, 20.)

10. Such as would approve themselves to be Christ's scholars ought not to hearken unto nor receive those who run without a calling, but only those whom he sends, 2 John, x. ; nor ought they to respect them who are sent, upon any carnal respect, Jude, ver. 16, but as they are sent and faithful in their trust, Matt. x. 41 ; nor are they to disrespect any who are sent and authorized by Christ, but whatever different measure of gifts there be, they must respect, and reverence, and hearken to all of them, as they are called to it ;— all these are included in this, that they are to receive whomsoever I send.

11. Whatever be the opposition unto or contempt of Christ's messengers, yet there will still be some to receive them when he sends them out ; for so is imported, that there will be some to receive whomsoever I send.

12. It is a comfortable encouragement to ministers in the discharge of their trust, and to people to receive them and their doctrine, that as God is inseparable from his Son Christ, in his person and office, so is Christ and his Father in him inseparable from his servants; the respect that is paid to them first is paid in them to Christ and his Father ; and so, on the contrary, doth the contempt of them reflect on him ; for " He that receiveth whomsoever I send receiveth me ; and he that receiveth me receiveth him that sent me," where, in the first place, their interest in Christ is asserted, and in the Father through him, and for further confirmation the Father's interest in Christ is asserted, who is not received nor known but in the receiving of Christ.

VER. 21. When Jesus had thus said, he was troubled in spirit, and testified, and said, Verily, verily, I say unto you, that one of you shall betray me.

Followeth the second step of this discovery of Judas, wherein he more distinctly clears his treachery, shewing that the lifting up of the heel, ver. 18, was in effect a betraying of him, and instead of that general [truth], that they were not all clean, ver. 10, nor had all of them an interest in that promise of happiness, ver. 18, he determines upon the number, that it was one of them who should betray him. The reason of this repeated and more particular discovery may partly be gathered from the following purpose: that they did not understand nor were affected as became with the former intimation, and therefore he repeats and presseth it till they be roused up by it; and partly, it is expressed in this verse to be Christ's trouble in spirit while his thoughts are upon Judas's treachery; a taste of his own sad sufferings following thereupon is let out upon his soul; and withal, his sorrow and indignation at the odious and ingrate treason, and the sad judgments to follow upon it, (as it is deduced, Matt. xxvi. 24,) did so take hold on him, that he must reveal it with serious testifications and asseverations. Whence learn—

1. Soul-pressures and troubles were no strangers to our blessed Lord, and he would have it well studied that he is acquainted with such conditions; therefore is his trouble in spirit here again marked.

2. Saints ought not to think it strange if, after deliverance from soul-trouble, they be again plunged into it, but must see that case sanctified unto them in Christ's person, who, after that sad fit, chap. xii. 27, is again "troubled in spirit."

3. Treacherous hypocrites in the church are a great trouble and matter of much vexation to the godly, either through their grief at their carriage, or by reason of the troubles which they raise to others; for upon Christ's speaking of Judas's treachery he is troubled at it in both these respects, as hath been cleared: "When Jesus had thus said, he was troubled in spirit."

4. Treacherous hypocrites, who are the instruments of Christ or his followers' sufferings, are in a horrible and woeful condition, both in respect of guilt and the judgments abiding them; for Christ could not think of Judas's treachery and end without trouble; and so will it be with all right discerners, whatever these hypocrites think of themselves.

5. Albeit soul-trouble be bitter, yet it is useful (especially in ministers) to draw forth truth with more clearness and edge to others; for herein Christ hath given a proof, the fruit of whose soul-trouble is, that he speaks out more distinctly what they understood not before, and brings it out solemnly, testifying it.

6. When Christ is about to exercise his people, and they will not be put to it by some means, he will still put them to it, till he rouse them up; for they making no use of the former intimation, he inculcates it again, till it become an exercise to all of them.

7. Christ perfectly knows all men, and particularly those who are more near to him in relations and fellowship; for he can give a distinct account that one of them is a traitor.

8. As great naughtiness may be in those who are very eminent, so their eminency renders their guilt more odious and horrible; that one of you should betray me.

9. It is hard to believe, if not almost incredible, what naughtiness there may be in eminent professors and ministers, which yet Christ knoweth well enough; therefore he must confirm it with, "Verily, verily, I say unto you, that one of you shall betray me."

10. Such as are really affected with the sin of treacherous hypocrites will not bluntly speak of it, in discovering or reproving it, but will evidence much zeal and indignation; for Jesus being troubled in spirit, testified, and gravely, and with much seriousness, intimates it.

11. In times wherein we may discern Satan to be employing eminent professors in an ill turn, it concerns every one to be upon his guard; therefore is this intimation yet more general, "one of you," not determining who, that all might be set on edge to try and search, as afterwards it followeth, and more fully in the other evangelists. (See Matt. xxvi. 21, 22.)

VER. 22. Then the disciples looked one on another, doubting of whom he spake.

In this verse we have an effect of this discovery among the disciples, that as men amazed they look one upon another, being ignorant of whom he spake. Their looking one upon another may be supposed partly to flow from their general amazement, and partly from their desire (who were conscious to themselves of no such intentions) to know by one another's countenances who was the guilty man. And it is like that at first they gazed one upon another through amazement, not knowing who might be the man, from which followed their particular inquiry at Christ, Matt. xxvi. 21, 22, and that afterward, being somewhat more confirmed, they looked if they could discover it by any symptoms in others, which not succeeding, Peter takes another course in the following purpose.

DOCTRINES.

1. There may such things fall forth in the church, and be acted by members thereof, as will surprise true professors with astonishment and amazement, who could never have believed such naughtiness to be in their societies; for so doth the disciples' carriage, upon this intimation, evidence.

2. When the Lord makes any intimation of a defection to be in the church, sincere professors will be jealous, and put to search themselves whether they be guilty or not; for upon this intimation of but one among twelve, all of them "looked one on another, doubting of whom he spake;" and albeit they were not conscious to themselves of any such wicked purpose, yet since he had spoken, all of them are jealous, and inquire concerning themselves, as the other evangelists observe. As for Judas, it is only marked that he inquired last of all, rather to hide himself from the rest than for any other end.

3. It is an evidence of sincere professors that they truly abhor all treachery against their Master, and will desire to know who are guilty of it, that they may abhor it in them; for their looking one on another, (together with their inquiry concerning themselves,) doubting of whom he spake, intimates also their abhorrency of that crime, with their desire to know who was guilty of it.

4. Albeit Christ sometimes give very clear intimation of some defection to be among his followers, yet he useth not to discover who the treacherous hypocrites are till they decipher themselves; for albeit he had warned them of the treachery of one of their number, yet they doubted of whom in particular he spake, as not being particularly named.

5. Treacherous hypocrites may lurk so close,

and carry matters so fair, as none can spy them out before they discover themselves, unless Christ extraordinarily reveal and point them out; for Judas in this business put on such a countenance as when they looked about yet they still doubted of whom he spake, and Peter and John are put to another shift to find him out.

Ver. 23. Now there was leaning on Jesus' bosom one of his disciples, whom Jesus loved.

24. Simon Peter therefore beckoned to him, that he should ask who it should be of whom he spake.

25. He then lying on Jesus' breast saith unto him, Lord, who is it?

26. Jesus answered, He it is, to whom I shall give a sop, when I have dipped it. And when he had dipped the sop, he gave it to Judas Iscariot, the son of Simon.

Followeth a further effect of the former discovery in Peter, occasioning the third step of the discovery, and a particular designation of the traitor unto John.   The sum of this purpose is the intimation that there was a traitor in their society; and the impossibility to know who he was, either by that intimation or by his countenance, kindles in Peter an earnest desire to know him; and being neither willing to propound his desire openly, seeing Christ had hitherto forborne to name him, nor being able to propound it secretly to Christ, by reason of his distance, he makes a secret sign to John, the beloved disciple, who sat nearest Christ, that he should inquire, who accepting of the employment, and propounding the matter to Christ, Judas is discovered to him by a sign secretly agreed upon betwixt Christ and him.   For clearing this a little, consider—1. Whereas John is said to lean on Jesus' bosom, it points at their custom in sitting at table, that they did lie upon beds, or couches, with their feet outward and their heads inward, leaning themselves on their elbows, and so the head of one lay near to the bosom of another, as John did here to Christ; yet not so near but there was some distance, for John, ver. 25. must lie on Jesus' breast, or raise up himself a little and fall upon it (as the original is) before he can propound the matter secretly.   Consider—2. Christ chooseth this way to discover Judas unto John, by giving a sop when he had dipped it, (which was some part of that supper before the sacrament was instituted,) partly, because this was a more secret way of designing him, seeing it was usual for Christ to distribute meat amongst them, and so none could know the matter but John, who understood his purpose in it, and (belike) Judas himself; and partly, because this sign was most agreeable to the prediction, Psa. xli. 9, and might put Judas in mind of his ingratitude.

From verse 23, learn—1. Albeit Christ love all his disciples and followers, yet as man he had degrees of love and familiarity with some beyond others; and as God also he may let out sensible evidences of love to some beyond others; for albeit he loved all his own, ver. 1, yet here there is one disciple " whom Jesus loved" in a singular way—to wit, as he was man, and in respect of kind manifestations of himself.

2. Such as are indeed beloved of Christ will esteem highly of this as their chief dignity, and far above any love they can have to him; for this is the character of the beloved disciple. Albeit he loved Christ, yet there is no word of that, but of Christ's love to him; and he gives himself no other name or title, as accounting it his chiefest glory to be called " one of his disciples, whom Jesus loved." (So also chap. xix. 26; xxi. 20.)

3. Such as are beloved of Christ, albeit they account it their great glory, yet they will entertain it with much modesty and sobriety; for John, in writing the history, when he speaks of these his privileges, yet never names himself who he was, till chap. xxi. 20, 24; that closing the history, he must declare who was the penman of it.

4. Such as are beloved of Christ will delight much in intimate familiarity with him, and will be admitted thereto; for it is John's choice and Christ's allowance that he leaned on Jesus' bosom.

From verse 24, learn—1. An honest heart is not satisfied with its own testimony unless also it get Christ's approbation; for Peter would know " who it should be of whom he spake," not only that he might know him, but that himself also might be assoiled by Christ.

2. It is necessary for those whose infirmities do frequently burst forth, that they do witness their integrity, by zeal and forwardness for Christ, and by being as eminent in duty as sometimes they are in their failings; for here Peter, who was ofttimes further wrong than the rest, manifests more zeal than all the rest, and is as eminent in his indignation against treachery. And indeed his failings were (for most part) not in the extreme of lukewarmness, but of rash zeal and respect to Christ.

3. It is commendable when the fruit of many reproofs appears in taking with faults, and reforming them in practice; for this is also to be observed in his carriage, who, being often reproved for his rash forwardness, doth now modestly beckon to John, that he should ask, though shortly after he returned to his old rashness.

4. It may be easily discerned by any, that such as are most beloved of Christ will get most of his mind; therefore Peter beckoned to him, that he should ask, not only because he was nearest Christ, but because, being beloved of him, he hoped he would tell him as soon as any.

From verses 25, 26, learn—1. Such as love Christ and are beloved of him may be very bold with him without misconstruction; for lying on Christ's breast he propounds the question.

2. Love's boldness doth not seclude reverence, but takes it along with it; for in the midst of this boldness he calls him Lord, and lieth on Jesus' breast, to inquire secretly, till he should know his pleasure whether he would reveal it or not.

3. As latent hypocrites are known only to

Christ, so they must be left to him to discover them, and we must not sit down on his throne of judgment; for John goeth to Christ to know this traitor, " Lord, who is it?"

4. They are not mistaken who expect that much of Christ's mind will be revealed to such as are beloved of him, and that in their familiar and reverent addresses they will be made welcome; for John gets a good answer, as Peter expected. " Jesus answered, He it is to whom I shall give a sop," &c.

5. Christ may be doing good to them who are but traitors to him, and by his outward favours be discovering to right discerners how disapproven they are of him; for he gives a sop to Judas Iscariot, the traitor, and by this discovers to John that he is a traitor.

6. Saints to whom Christ reveals not such things as they desire must reverence his dispensation; and when he doth not clear their doubts fully to them they are to rest satisfied in the testimony of a good conscience; for Peter, having done his duty to know the traitor, must rest satisfied that he is designed only to John, and when Christ doth not clear him expressly that it was not himself, he is left to look to the conscience of his own integrity.

Ver. 27. And after the sop Satan entered into him. Then said Jesus unto him, That thou doest, do quickly.

28. Now no man at the table knew for what intent he spake this unto him.

29. For some of them thought, because Judas had the bag, that Jesus had said unto him, Buy those things that we have need of against the feast; or, that he should give something to the poor.

30. He then having received the sop went immediately out: and it was night.

In these verses we have the consequents of this designation in Judas himself, occasioning a fourth step of this discovery, wherein Christ declares more of his mind to Judas himself concerning his treason. The sum of this purpose is to be conceived thus: Judas's guilty conscience making him suspect all things, he could not but observe the whisperings betwixt Christ and John, and that Christ after that had given him a sop, which (it is like) drew John, who knew the scope of that sign, to eye him in an odd way; therefore, perceiving or fearing that he was discovered, he is so embittered and vexed at it that he gives himself wholly up to Satan, and resolves to prosecute his treason speedily and effectually; upon which (and possibly he was now on his feet to go out to the chief priests) Christ lets him know that he knew his design, and bids him do his worst, ver. 27, which as the rest understood not, but some of them supposed that, as purse-master, he was sent out to provide somewhat against the solemnity of the next day, or ordained to give somewhat unto the poor, ver. 28, 29, so he is more hardened thereby to go on in his wicked course, and accordingly goeth out to effectuate it, though it was dark night, ver. 30.

From verse 27, learn—1. As Satan gets possession by degrees of wicked men, so it is hard, when once he gets footing, to prevent a more full possession; for Satan, who before trysted [agreed] with him, by casting tentations into his heart, now gets full possession, and " entered into him."

2. Traitors and hypocrites are so far from being reclaimed by the discovery of their naughtiness that they are rather more irritated thereby; for upon his perceiving that Christ had discovered him to John, by giving the sop, " Satan entered into him."

3. Christ, in his holy providence and righteous judgment, may do to hypocrites that whereupon they may take occasion to harden themselves unto perdition and to forsake him, yet without all imputation to [reflection upon] him; for upon this discovery he is set on edge by Satan against Christ, as if he had affronted him.

4. Satan gets ready entry in a man, nor can he long stand when he is given over of God; for Judas is given up by Christ to himself to do quickly what he did, when Satan possessed him to do this mischief.

5. As Christ knows all the naughtiness of traitors, so he is the permitter of the same, without any approbation of their sin; for " That thou doest, do quickly," is not a command, but a declaration of his prescience and permission.

6. When Christ hath long struggled with corrupt men to restrain and curb their naughtiness he may at last let loose the reins to them to do their worst; for having a traitor so long restrained in his company, he at last gives him up to himself. (See Psalm lxxxi. 11, 12; Prov. xiv. 14.)

7. Christ's willingness to suffer for his people made all attempts against him to be nothing terrible; for this permission imports also that he was willing to suffer, and therefore cared not how soon he would put him to it; and thus our willing resolutions should take off much of the terror of our sufferings.

8. Christ needs never restrain any of his enemies for any fear he hath of them, but can carry on his purpose, and triumph over their most violent oppositions; for this upgiving is also a defying of Judas to do his worst, and when he had so done, yet Christ should redeem his people and triumph over all the sufferings he brought him into by his treachery.

9. Men given over by God unto Satan will be very restless to execute mischief, and may speed well at it for a time; for " do quickly" is also a prediction of his activity and success as to the outward suffering.

From verses 28, 29, learn—1. It is no fault in sincere professors to be charitable even of hypocrites so long as they keep close; for it flowed in part from their charity that " no man at the table knew for what intent he spake this unto him," and some supposed some other thing. And it seems that John himself, to whom he was particularly discovered, did not suspect he would presently go about his treason, and therefore understood not this discourse, though possibly he joined not in the opinion some others had of him and it. And as for the rest, albeit it seems they should have known his treachery from Christ's answer to his question, Matt. xxvi. 25, yet it seems that Christ gave him that answer secretly, or he propounded that question but immediately before he went out.

2. Christ did so willingly suffer for his people, that by his own overruling hand he kept back all things that might hinder instruments to act therein; for this ignorance also flowed from the hand of God, lest they should have hindered him, and so should have marred the work Christ came about. (See Matt. xvi. 20; xxvi. 52—54.)

3. It is the will of Christ, that were men's portion but mean, yet they should not only provide for their own necessities thereby, and so live in an honest way, but should also be beneficial to the poor and indigent; for this construction, which some of them put upon Christ's words, teacheth that it was his custom, as at other times so now, out of his small stock, to " buy those things that we have need of against the feast," (or the solemnity of the first day of unleavened bread, being the morrow after the passover, Lev. xxiii. 5, 6; Num. xxviii. 16, 17,) and to " give something to the poor," and his practice in this is our rule.

From verse 30, learn—1. Checks given by Christ to enemies, which might reclaim them, do but irritate and render them worse; for after all this, he having received the sop went out.

2. Men given over by God, and possessed by Satan, are so impudent that they will not only attempt highest wickedness even against Christ, but will commit it even in Christ's presence, and when they know that he knoweth and seeth them; for albeit Christ had intimated that he knew what he was doing, yet he went out to act it.

3. Satan is violent in driving those acted by him very hastily and over all impediments to commit mischief; for "having received the sop he went immediately out," and that though " it was night," as being too good for works of darkness.

Ver. 31. Therefore, when he was gone out, Jesus said, Now is the Son of man glorified, and God is glorified in him.

Followeth to verse 36, the third part of the chapter, containing Christ's sweet doctrine to his disciples upon Judas's removal, wherein he speaks comfortably concerning Judas's errand, and doth direct his disciples concerning their carriage. It contains three points of doctrine, in the first whereof (in this verse) he points out how he looked upon what was to come upon him by Judas's treachery—namely, that he was to be glorified in and after his sufferings, and God to be glorified in him. Concerning this doctrine we may compare what is said on chap. xii. 23. Here we may learn—

1. Albeit hypocrites cannot pollute an ordinance of God to any but themselves, yet they are ofttimes such a burden and impediment to the societies of God's people as the company will fare the better when they are out of it; therefore Christ, who was speaking sad things while Judas was with them, and weighted and troubled,

ver. 21, now, when he is gone out, his mind is elevated, and he speaks comfortably and familiarly to the rest.

2. As there is no condition so hard but a child of God, through him, will get through it, Phil. iv. 13; and as there is no humbling pressure under their lot, but they may expect a blenk [supply] of comfort and ease after it; so ofttimes the Lord makes their sad lots easiest when they are nearest to come upon them, by his giving at that time the spirit of that employment; for Christ, who before was troubled, ver. 21, now when Judas goeth out to act his mischievous treachery is elevated in mind, and comforted. (See Heb. iii. 16.) And by this his comfort and rejoicing at this time he learns us how to rejoice when our dissolution is near, though we were to go through a red sea of blood and suffering unto that promised land.

3. Such as would rightly bear a cross ought to take a look of their condition quite contrary to the verdict of sense and reason; for so doth Christ look on his sufferings as a glorifying of him, both in themselves and in the effects thereof, which is a point flesh and blood would never reveal.

4. How ignominious soever Christ's sufferings were in themselves, yet they were not only the way to his glory, chap. xvii. 5; Luke, xxiv. 26; 1 Peter, i. 11; and the fruits thereof glorious, and such as exalted him in the world; but they were also glorious in themselves, and he glorified thereby in respect of his obedience to his Father, even to the death, his love that shined therein, the testimony of innocency he received from enemies, the glorious miracles in the time of his sufferings, and in respect that hereby he redeemed his elect, trampled upon and spoiled Satan, and triumphed over sin, and blotted out the handwriting of ordinances against us; for saith he, the Son of man is glorified, and that now, not only certainly, but instantly. And if he counted seeming ignominy to be his glory in respect of the service done thereby to his people, how much more should we account that our glory which may honour him.

5. Such as are truly zealous of God's honour will count no condition honourable unless God be glorified thereby, and where he gets honour a very ignominious condition will be honourable in their eyes; for this glorifies the Son, that " God is glorified in him."

6. As Christ was glorified by his own sufferings, so also the Father was glorified in him; not only in that he, being in the Son, all the glory of the Son is his also; but that Christ in suffering did glorify him in giving obedience to his will; the truth of his threatenings and his justice did shine in what he inflicted on his Son, and his wisdom and goodness did shine in the redemption of lost man by such a mean; for saith he, " and God is glorified in him." And albeit none can so glorify God in suffering as Christ did, yet through him he takes glory to himself in the sufferings of his servants, as they are a testimony to his truth and a commendation of his excellency, that they will not love their lives unto the death for his sake. (See chap. xxi. 19.)

VER. 32. If God be glorified in him, God shall also glorify him in himself, and shall straightway glorify him.

In this verse he confirms the one branch of the former doctrine by the other, and sheweth that if God be glorified in him and in his sufferings, then certainly he would glorify him in himself; and again inculcates that this should be straightway done in his approaching sufferings, and the glory hastening upon the back of that. Whence learn—

1. Albeit God be glorious, and to be glorified in all his working, yet his special glory, wherein he delights most, is that which is offered to him, and shines in his Son; for this is the glory of God which Christ insists so much on, that he is "glorified in him." (See 2 Cor. iv. 6.)

2. God's being honoured in any condition, or by any under such a condition, is a sufficient evidence that the condition is honourable, be it what it will, and that they themselves are and shall be honoured therein; for so doth Christ argue, "If God be glorified in him, God shall also glorify him in himself." (See 1 Sam. ii. 30.) It is honour abundance to get leave to honour God, and it portends much dignity to them who so do.

3. It is a sure evidence of future glory when men make it their chief study to honour God here; for so much also doth Christ's arguing teach. (See 2 Tim. iv. 7, 8.)

4. Whatever our discouragements may object to weaken our own hands from doing or suffering in a hard time, yet it is our duty to reason against unbelief, for our own encouragement; for so doth Christ's debating and reasoning the certainty of his approaching glory teach.

5. God will not only give fair promises to them who glorify him, but will at last give performance; and as we may always in some respect look on this, not as far off, but near at hand, so, after a while's exercise, our expectation will at last come to an issue; therefore doth he add, he "shall straightway glorify him."

6. Christ and his followers' true glory may be so little delayed by clouds of sufferings, that it may be very near when they are engaging in the throng of afflictions; for at that time, saith Christ, he "shall straightway glorify him."

VER. 33. Little children, yet a little while I am with you. Ye shall seek me: and as I said unto the Jews, Whither I go, ye cannot come; so now I say to you.

The second point propounded here to his disciples is a sweet and warm way of intimating his departure unto them; wherein, letting out his affection in a warm title and compellation, he intimates that he was shortly to depart from them, in respect of his bodily presence, and that (as he had said unto the Jews, ch. vii. 34, and viii. 21) though they should seek him, yet they were not able to come whither he went and was. Whereby we are to understand, partly, that while they entertained any carnal conceits of the Mes-

siah, as the Jews did, they should not find satisfaction in them, nor should they (as they were wont when they missed him) be able to follow him, and enjoy his bodily presence; and so when they sought him at the grave, they could not find him; but chiefly we are to understand that as the unbelieving Jews were secluded from coming to him in heaven, so was their coming to him there delayed, and a thing above their power, till he should come and fetch them; and particularly their following him to heaven, through the valley of suffering, was delayed for a time to as many of them as were to be called thereunto, as is cleared, ver. 36. Whence learn—

1. Albeit Christ's presence be the sweet cordial of his followers, yet he seeth it meet for wise ends, and for their exercise, to withdraw it from them sometimes, as here he did from his disciples.

2. Christ having fulfilled his ministry on earth, did withdraw, in respect of his bodily presence, not only from his foes, but even from his followers; for even to the disciples it is now, " a little while I am with you."

3. It is Christ's kindness to his followers that he advertiseth them of what is to come upon them, that so they may be armed against it and prepared for it; as here he beforehand intimateth his removal to his disciples.

4. It is our duty to consider for how small a moment we may have the occasion and opportunity of mercies, that we may be very busy, and improve it well; for therefore doth he advertise his disciples, " a little while I am with you," that they might not trifle away that moment of time wherein he was so busy with them in the following chapters.

5. When Christ doth anything that his followers think hard to digest, they are bound to believe that he doth it, not for want of care and respect, but in the abundance of his love to them; and that they have so much more room in his heart, that his dealing is sad; and that he leaveth his heart with them when otherwise he withdraweth; therefore doth he sweeten this sad intimation with a sweet title, not so usual before, " Little children."

6. A sweet word importing Christ's love is sufficient to bear up saints under saddest dispensations; for this is a sufficient cordial here to make up his removal, that he calls them " little children."

7. Such as do not undervalue the sweet consolations of Christ's word, and his speaking to them, will find him speak more sweetly in trouble than ever before; therefore doth he reserve such a title for such a time.

8. Whatever be Christ's dealing, in removing and withdrawing from his followers, yet he still retains the relation of a Father to them, and will have such a care of them as parents have of their young and tender children, who cannot care for themselves, and who used to be most dandled and tenderly dealt with; for so much doth this compellation, not only of " children," but " little children," import.

9. It is not inconsistent with Christ's love to his own that he deal and speak as sharply against their corruptions as against the corruptions of

the wicked; for in so far as the disciples were carnal he saith unto them as he said unto the Jews, as hath been explained.

10. Christ, by removing his bodily presence, hath cut off all grounds of hope of any carnal way of intercourse or communion with him, and laid on a necessity of studying a spiritual way of coming to him on all those who would enjoy him; for so much also doth this intimation, common to them with the Jews, import.

11. The wicked and the godly, even in their best frame, may be under the same outward dispensation, but in as far different a way as is betwixt their states and conditions; for even in respect of their coming to him in heaven he saith, " As I said unto the Jews, &c., so now I say unto you," but in a far different sense; for to the one he intimates his departure in judgment, by way of rejection of them; to the other, it is full of mercy, and accompanied with sweet affection; to the one, coming to him is absolutely denied; to the other, only delayed; to the one is intimated that as they cannot, so they shall not come where he is; to the other, it only intimates what they cannot do of themselves, but doth not seclude what he can do or will do for them.

12. Whatever men esteem of an enjoyed Christ, yet when he is gone he will be missed by his own; for when he is gone, " Ye shall seek me," saith he.

13. Christ's withdrawings tend to kindle desires after him, and to be at him, in the hearts of his own, together with earnest pursuing after him; for so much also is imported in this, " Ye shall seek me."

14. Christ, by removing his bodily presence from earth, hath taught his disciples to spend their lives in a sober desire, and hastening to be with him in heaven; for when he is gone, " Ye shall seek me, to come whither I go," saith he.

15. Saints must not expect always to get satisfaction, at first, in their most honest desires and endeavours, but to be exercised with further desiring and seeking; and particularly they must not expect to get up to rest with Christ in heaven till first they have wrestled awhile, and served their generation; for in this respect, though they seek him, yet " whither I go, ye cannot come."

16. Christ's own, by all their endeavours, are not able to get up to him in heaven unless he come and fetch them; for in this respect also it holds true, " ye cannot come"—to wit, not only presently, but of yourselves, even no more than the Jews can do.

VER. 34. A new commandment I give unto you, That ye love one another; as I have loved you, that ye also love one another.

The third point propounded by Christ containeth a direction concerning their behaviour in his absence, that they should love one another; which he presseth upon several grounds, whereof the first is, that the command enjoining it is a new commandment given by him; and the se-

cond (in this verse also) is taken from his own example, which might both persuade them unto and regulate them in the performance of that duty. While he calleth this commandment " new," the meaning is not that it was not enjoined before; for we find it enjoined in the law itself; and this same apostle doth recommend the whole doctrine of following Christ as being so " new " as yet it was old, 1 John, ii. 6—8; and particularly he recommendeth love as an old commandment, and not new only, 2 John, v.; nor doth it fully exhaust the meaning, that he made it " new " by renewing of that commandment and vindicating it from the corrupt glosses of the time, as he did also the rest of the law; nor yet sufficeth it to say that as it is a commandment which can only be performed by the new man, so it is enjoined in a new way by Christ, in conferring power and grace with the command, and writing it on our heart, that it may be obeyed, which no man had under the law by the law itself; for this is true also of other commands, and believers also under the law had it, though by another covenant than that of the law, as it was a covenant of works; therefore I conceive that by calling this commandment in special " new," is pointed out, (beside the former considerations,) partly, that the thing commanded is excellent; and so a new song seemeth to be understood for an excellent song, Psalm xxxiii. 3; and therefore Christ pitcheth on it as a chief and singular duty above many, to be recommended to his disciples; and so, if we look to this command, it is not only new, or renewed, in the enjoining thereof; Christ's recommending it anew adding a new obligation to what was lying on by the authority of the law; but the very matter of the command is " new," and declared excellent, in that Christ doth so much and so specially recommend it above others, and adds his authority and credit with his disciples to the former injunction of the law, to make it to be studied; and partly, hereby is pointed out that it is " new," in respect that it is urged upon a new ground, and after a new pattern and example; our love to others not being now to be regulated only according to our love to ourselves, as the tenour of the law runs, but a new ground and pattern being laid in Christ's loving of us, which makes the whole complex commandment be " a new commandment." And upon all these considerations it followeth that this commandment should still be " new " to us, our obligation to such a commander still sweetly binding, the subject matter so recommended by him still new and fresh, and sweetly alluring to obedience, and such a pattern still drawing our hearts to imitate it.

DOCTRINES.

1. The doctrine of the gospel contains not only sweet comforts but necessary commands and directions also for our attaining, improving, and clearing our right in these comforts; for here is a commandment given, and pressed by Christ in his sweet farewell sermon.

2. Christ is true God, and sovereign Lord over and Lawgiver unto his people, having authority to give a law unto them, binding their

conscience ; for a commandment I give unto you, saith he.

3. Sad lots may be made up and compensed, not only by sweet comforts from Christ, but may be made easy and much sweetened also by our cleaving to duty in such a lot ; for here mutual love is recommended as a mean to sweeten that sad lot of his removal ; so our love to him is left us to make up his being not seen, 1 Pet. 1—8 ; and, indeed, they are never sadly deserted (however they want comfort) who are not driven from duty ; nor is comfort allowed on any but those who cleave to duty.

4. While saints are absent from Christ, in respect of his bodily presence, it is especially required of them that they entertain mutual love, that so they may be mutually useful and comfortable one to another in such a languishing time, and while they are hated in the world ; that they may not fall in emulation and quarrels during their Master's absence, and so mar his work and their own peace, and expose his ways to reproach and obloquy ; and that they may be fitted to partake of the sweetness, blessing, and consolations which God hath commanded upon his people in their being united, Psalm cxxxiii. 1—3. For these causes (among others) doth Christ in his absence enjoin that they " love one another," and so may partake of the consolations left in his testament.

5. Albeit ofttimes we look on love as an indifferent and arbitrary thing, which we may practice or forbear at our pleasure, and according as we judge ourselves obliged or disobliged, yet Christ hath not left it arbitrary to us, but enjoined it as a debt and duty by his command ; for saith he, A commandment I give you, that ye love one another. (See Rom. xiii. 8.)

6. Whatever Christ commands, his enjoining of it puts a new obligation upon his children, and commends the thing enjoined as excellent for his sake, which therefore should not be entertained with formal and dead dispositions ; for it is " a new commandment," as hath been cleared.

7. Christ hath loved his disciples and followers, and so loved them as may well be a copy and pattern of all love ; for saith he, " I have loved you," and so loved, that he makes it their copy to " love one another, as I have loved you." As Jonathan's love surpassed the love of women, 2 Sam. i. 26, so doth his love infinitely surpass Jonathan's. And this is the reason why he presseth love so much, even because it was so much in his own heart.

8. Christ's love to us is a new obligation, pressing on us to love one another ; whosoever believe his love cannot but love him again, and will account themselves obliged to obey what he commands and recommends by his own example ; and particularly, to love them who have obtained like mercy with themselves, and do bear his image, and are begotten of him who hath loved them ; and they will be sensible of so much tenderness in him towards them as will oblige them to be tender and condescending towards their brethren ; for this is an argument, and makes it " a new commandment," in a special manner, " that ye love one another ; as I have loved you," and that so much the rather, as the one is the evidence of the other.   (See Matthew, xviii. 23—35.)

9. Christ's love is not only an argument obliging, but a pattern directing saints in their mutual love ; and albeit none can imitate him in the nature and kind of some acts evidencing his love, (as being acts peculiar to his office of Mediator,) nor yet can any come up to his measure in what is imitable, yet his love to us is a copy after which we should strive to write in this matter ; by being willing, ingenuous, and free in our love, as he was ; by loving sincerely, and not for byends ; by loving the saints as such, and because of their interest in him, as he " loved his own," John, xiii. 1, (and so love them all as he did, John, xiii. 1, not as James, ii. 2—4, and specially them that are most gracious, as John, xiii. 1, with John, xxi. 20 ;) by loving them, however they may hate us, as he loved them when enemies ; by loving them, not in word or tongue only, but in deed and real truth, as he gave his life for them he loved, by bearing their infirmities, and not pleasing ourselves but them for their good to edification, as he also did, Rom. xv. 1—3 ; and by loving them constantly as he loveth his own, John, xiii. 1. So much is imported in this : A commandment I give you, that as I have loved you, ye also love one another.

Ver. 35. By this shall all men know that ye are my disciples, if ye have love one to another.

This verse contains a third argument pressing this duty of mutual love, taken from the necessity thereof as the badge of their profession ; for as all sects and societies have their badges and observations, whereby they are known and distinguished from others, so Christ hath appointed this mutual love to be the badge whereby his followers may be discerned. Whence learn—

1. As Christ hath disciples in this world, so they serve a Master of whom they need not be ashamed ; but they may and ought to avow him in weal and woe, and look profanity and trouble out of countenance ; for it is supposed here as great honour, that " all men know that ye are my disciples."

2. Albeit true saints should not be ostentative, nor self-seekers, yet as they ought to assure their own hearts of their good condition before God, so they ought, in their station, to shine and appear such as they are ; for it is their duty, by lawful means and right walking, to make all men know that they are Christ's disciples.

3. As true mutual love of the brethren is an infallible evidence of regeneration, 1 John, iii. 10, 14, and iv. 7, so this love is the Christians' badge, whereby they are known to the world, and without which Christ and men may look upon them as runaways from their colours, be what they will otherwise ; for " By this shall all men know that ye are my disciples, if ye love one another." (See 1 Cor. xii. 31, with chap. xiii. 1—3, &c.)

Ver. 36. Simon Peter said unto him, Lord, whither goest thou? Jesus answered him, Whither I go, thou canst not follow me now; but thou shalt follow me afterwards.

Followeth the last part of the chapter, wherein Christ reprehends and represseth Peter's rash presumption in conceiting of his own ability to suffer with and for him, by foretelling his denying of him. And by this the wound is made yet wider, in that they were not only to want their Master, and one of them to betray him, but another to deny him under tentation, and all of them to forsake him, as this intimation was further enlarged at another time, Matt. xxvi. 31—35. The purpose contains two conferences or discourses that passed betwixt Christ and Peter; in the first whereof, (in this verse,) Peter, reflecting on what Christ had said, ver. 33, propounds a question to Christ, whither he went, which he did, not so much out of ignorance, as wondering that he should go anywhere from them where he could not follow, as the following discourse makes clear. Christ gives a mild answer to this proposition, assuring him that for the present he could not follow him, but should get the honour to follow afterward, whereby is not meant only that he was not yet ripe to come to glory with Christ, till he had finished his course, but chiefly, that he was not yet strong enough to suffer with and for him, and so follow him in that path to glory, as he should do afterward. Hence learn—

1. It is an evidence of our great weakness that in hearing one point may put us by the hearing of many other points, and the hearing of our danger impedes our hearing of our directions and encouragements under it; for by Peter's insisting on this point only, it appears he had not so well hearkened to what Christ said after that, ver. 34, 35, but that point had so vexed him that he could not rest till he thus burst out.

2. Such as have tasted of the sweet of Christ's society will be very loath to part with him, but would follow him wherever he goeth; for albeit Peter erred in limiting the comforts of Christ to his bodily presence, and in trusting too much to his own strength, yet it is commendable that he cannot digest Christ should go—to wit, where he and the rest might not follow.

3. Saints are ofttimes little acquainted with their own weakness and the deceitfulness of their heart, especially when their affection and willing spirit is looked unto, without considering that they have weak flesh also; for it flowed from Peter's ignorance of himself in this heat of affection, that he propounds this question, "Lord, whither goest thou?"—to wit, to be separate from us, or that anything should hinder us to follow. Not only may presumption think such a proposition of Christ's hard, but even love may sometimes dream of greater abilities than indeed it hath.

4. Christ deals tenderly with saints at first in the buddings of their infirmity, before they come to a height, as considering, not only what they are in their state, but what honesty there may be under their infirmities; therefore at first he gently informs Peter, as knowing what love to him lurked under his rash expression of his resolution.

5. Christ knows his own followers and their weakness better than they do themselves, and his verdict of them will prove true, whatever they think of themselves; for he repeats that doctrine which Peter questioned as still true, " Whither I go, thou canst not follow me."

6. As no man is able of himself to follow Christ or suffer for him, so they may be true saints who yet are so weak for a time as they are not able to suffer; for Peter is a disciple, and yet cannot follow Christ now.

7. Christ is so tender of his grace in his own that he will spare them, and not put them to it above their strength; for as Peter is not able " now," so his hard work is delayed till " afterwards," till he be better trained and more strengthened. (See Isa. xxviii. 27, and xlii. 3.)

8. The refreshments of saints, in services or comforts, are only delayed and not denied when they are withheld from them; for to follow Christ by suffering, and so to come to him in glory, is only denied " now," but not " afterwards."

9. Unto such as love Christ, and are sensible of their own weakness, it will be matter of encouragement to get a promise that they shall be able to serve Christ, and come to enjoy him, were it in a fiery chariot of martyrdom; for it is a promise and encouragement unto Peter, now grieved, " thou shalt follow me afterwards"—to wit, by suffering, into glory. And so was it afterwards, when Christ received him into favour after his denial, chap. xxi. 18.

10. Such as the Lord keeps for a time under much weakness, yea, and corrects their presumption with a fall, may yet be raised up and strengthened to suffer eminently for Christ; for Peter, weak at present, and afterwards slipping through his presumption, gets a promise, " thou shalt follow me afterwards."

Ver. 37. Peter said unto him, Lord, why cannot I follow thee now? I will lay down my life for thy sake.

38. Jesus answered him, Wilt thou lay down thy life for my sake? Verily, verily, I say unto thee, The cock shall not crow, till thou hast denied me thrice.

In these verses we have the second discourse betwixt Christ and Peter, wherein, Peter not digesting that he could not now follow, and looking on a violent death as the greatest impediment, he conceives it not impossible to hazard on that, and therefore rashly offers to follow him, though he should lay down his life for his sake, ver. 37, which presumption being detested by Christ, he represseth it by a prediction that he should deny him thrice that very same night, before the cock should crow, ver. 38.

From verse 37, learn—1. Men are not easily convinced of their presumption till experience discover it, nor do they always see reason to doubt of their own strength, even albeit Christ should warn them of it; therefore replieth he against Christ's warning, " Why cannot I follow thee now ?"

2. The greatest external impediment to hinder a man from following Christ is a violent death for his sake; for so doth Peter suppose here.

3. Albeit it be a very great difficulty in itself to suffer death for Christ and his truth, yet it is not a thing to be stood upon when we are called to it; and love to Christ should make it easy, and us willing to undergo it; for this is in itself commendable, that he was so willing to die : " I will lay down my life for thy sake."

4. As it is commendable to be valiant, courageous, and resolved for troubles for Christ's sake, so ofttimes, instead of this, saints may be pestered with presumptuous resting on their own strength to endure sufferings for Christ; for this offer flowed not from true magnanimity, but rash presumption in Peter, who vilipends [despises] death, and yet trembled at a damsel's voice.

5. The evidences of this presumption (as it is distinguished from true courage and resolution in God) may be gathered from Peter here. As, 1. Men are presumptuous when they heed not the word's verdict concerning their weakness, nor are humbled by what it discovers; for he heeds not, but contradicts Christ's verdict. 2. Men's condition looks like presumption when they lean to their present disposition and affections, and are not sent out of themselves to deny all these and trust in God only; for Peter here builds too much on his present fit of affection and resolution. 3. If men would avoid presumption, they ought not to boast of their courage before they have a do [trial], and be called to it, and get the promise of fortitude; for Peter is now stout when it is not his work, and he hath not the promise till afterward. 4. It is a great token of presumption when men look only on outward impediments, and do not seriously consider their own inward fainting dispositions; for he speaks only of death as an impediment, but considers not his own disposition, and how much is requisite within a man for such an undertaking, without which lesser sufferings will be formidable. 5. Presumption is always attended with the want of sobriety whereof true courage is free; for in all this he boasts without any fear or trembling. (See 1 Cor. x. 12 ; Rom. xi. 20.)

From verse 38, learn—1. Presumption is detestable and abominable to Christ, were it even in his own followers; for so much doth this question, by way of indignation, import, " Wilt thou lay down thy life for my sake ?"

2. Christ knoweth all his followers well, and what they will prove, even when he chooseth them, and letteth out his love upon them, as being God over all, and having diligently pondered all predictions concerning him as man ; for he can tell Peter what he will prove, and so all the disciples, from the predictions of the prophets, Matt. xxvi. 31.

3. Presumption and carnal confidence will never do service to Christ, but, on the contrary, men may be very presumptuous and confident of themselves when they are very near a fall; for presumptuous Peter is to " deny" his Master, and that " before the cock crow," which was the

sign whereof Christ made use afterward to reclaim him.

4. It is incredible how contrary men's carriage, in a time of tentation, may be to their presumptuous resolutions ; therefore Christ must confirm it with a " verily, verily."

5. When no other thing will convince men of their presumption and carnal confidence, Christ will refute them by letting them feel their own weight; for when Peter will not believe Christ, ver. 36, he gets this to shew him his folly ? yea, it seems from Matt. xxvi. 34, 35, that he vented the same presumption again in the way to the garden, and would not give credit to it, when Christ over again warned him of his danger, and therefore he must be humbled with such a fall.

6. When men once give way and yield to tentation, they would make no end of defection if mercy did not stop their course; for Peter is warned that he shall deny Christ thrice, and would have gone on if Christ had not reclaimed him.

CHAPTER XIV.

In the former chapter, Christ, as a faithful friend, not willing to delude his disciples with false comforts, hath ripped up all their wounds by telling them what they were to meet with. Now, in this and the two following chapters, he, by comfortable doctrine, proves himself to be the sympathizing high priest, and kithes [discovers] his skill in curing these wounds. And for this end, as he points out his sense of their case in themselves, through his absence, and that they would be troubled, orphans, hated and persecuted, so he holds forth rich consolations unto them and antidotes against these evils, together with directions concerning their duty for attaining and entertaining those consolations which should tend to their peace and joy.

In this chapter Christ's chief scope is to guard and encourage their hearts against that fear and trouble which seized upon them when they heard of his death and departure, and the treachery and faintheartedness that was among themselves, as may be gathered from ver. 1 and 27, where he dissuades them from these passions and distempers ; for which end he propounds several antidotes and grounds of consolation and encouragement, which may be reduced to these heads :— 1. Faith in him, as true God, equal with the Father, ver. 1. 2. The consideration of his errand in going, and that there was a necessity of his departure to heaven for their good, ver. 2. 3. That he would come again (having done his work) to fetch them, ver. 3. 4. That, in the meantime, they know whither he went, and what was the way thither; both which are propounded, ver. 4, and further cleared in answer to Thomas's objection, ver. 5—7, and the first of them yet further insisted on, upon occasion of Philip's proposition, ver. 8, 14. 5. That if they would prove their love to him by obedience, and not by heartless dejection for his absence, ver. 15, he would send the Spirit unto them, the excellency of which gift, and the advantages to be had by him, are recorded, ver. 16—26. 6. That he leaves his peace in legacy to them, upon which he repeats the exhortation, ver. 27. And (being to conclude this part of his discourse) he reproves them for not entertaining this intimation of his departure and return with joy, seeing it tended to his glory and their advantage, ver. 28, and the prediction of it would do them good afterward, ver. 29 ; and declareth, that he was not to speak much more unto them, but was shortly to be assaulted by Satan, and to suffer, not for anything in himself, but in obedience to his Father's will, ver. 30, 31, and therefore they ought to heed better what he said.

VER. 1. *Let not your heart be troubled: ye believe in God, believe also in me.*

This verse contains—1. Christ's scope in this doctrine, which is, to guard against and dissuade from that heart-trouble and perplexity which his former doctrine had raised in them. 2. The first antidote or argument of consolation to cure this distemper, which is double; for herein he supposeth that however he was to die as man, yet he is God, equal with the Father, and the object of faith. Next, he proposeth faith in himself with the Father, as a cordial to uphold their fainting and perplexed hearts. Whence learn—

1. Christ's dearest disciples and true followers are subject to much trouble of heart and to have their spirits so crushed as only God can support and uphold them ; for so was it with the disciples, their hearts were troubled, perplexed, and confounded, so that whole-minded men have need to look about them.

2. The Lord makes use of heart-trouble and exercise to fit his own for the consolations and proofs of his tender heart which he allows upon them, whereof otherwise they are not capable; for their heart-trouble draws out this sweet, comfortable doctrine.

3. Albeit heart-trouble be needful for saints as a mean of much good, yet they do ordinarily so exceed in it and debord [grieve] under it, as it becomes a fault in them ; therefore doth he dissuade from it : " Let not your heart be troubled." And herein they failed, both through excess and being immoderate in their sorrow, and in being troubled at that which might afford joy, ver. 28.

4. Albeit saints do ofttimes give over themselves to heartless dejection and discouragement, as conceiving they have no other cause or allowance, yet, be their case what it will, it is not the will of Christ they should entertain such a disposition, but that they should strive against it ; therefore doth he exhort them to oppose this distemper : " Let not your heart be troubled." Albeit nothing could seem sadder to them than the removal of his bodily presence, yet he counts it their fault that they were so addicted to sense as they could not expect to be comforted another way against it ; and therefore exhorts them to oppose their sorrow. (See 1 Sam. ii. 6 ; Ps. xlii. 5—11.) And upon the same ground ought saints

to oppose all discouragements (how just cause soever it seem to have) under which they would lie down and rest, without expecting an issue, or that the matter of their discouragement may prove a mean leading to a higher end, and which would drive them from Christ and mar his allowed consolations ; and for this end they should beware of passion, which desires do quarrel with, and be jealous of Christ, of ignorance, and mistaking his mind in trouble, and of carnal expectations, the disappointment whereof may crush them.

5. Whatever be saints' duty, to oppose discouragement and trouble, yet it is Christ only who is the physician of troubled souls, and who must speak the word and set them on work ; for he it is who gives this comfortable counsel and direction.

6. Christ is so tender of his grieved and troubled people that whatever weakness they kithe [discover], yet he will make it his chief work to see to their encouragement ; therefore, albeit he had his own bitter trouble, chap. xiii. 21, and was, that night and the day following, to grapple with wrath and hell and death, yet he forgets all that, and spendeth his time in comforting and easing them, " Let not your heart be troubled."

7. Such as take up Christ rightly will not be much dismayed at what befals him or his ; therefore doth he point out himself as God, that they might not stumble at his suffering nor their own scattering.

8. Christ, notwithstanding his abasement and suffering as man, is true God, the object of saving faith equally with the Father ; therefore doth he urge believing in him as they did believe in God.

9. The faith of humbled and troubled souls can bottom or fasten on nothing that is inferior to God, nor can any other thing bear their weight ; for it is a proof of his deity that he is the object of faith.

10. Albeit Christ do not remove from troubled saints the afflictions which raise their trouble, yet they have comfort sufficient if they believe ; for this is their encouragement who had Christ himself to comfort them—" believe."

11. It is the will of God that Christ's bodily absence be supplied and made up with faith, which will make an absent Christ present to a believer ; for it is to cure this disease that this remedy is applied—" believe."

12. Whatever other ground of consolation Christ allow upon his followers within time, yet the first encouragement must begin at believing, and faith must grip him, and hold him fast, till other encouragements spring up in its hand ; for this is the first encouragement, that must go before all the rest here subjoined, and make way for them.

13. Faith in God and Christ is so acceptable and well-pleasing unto Christ that troubled souls are commanded and invited to it, so that they sin if they believe not ; for saith he, " Ye believe in God, (or, Believe in God,) believe also in me."

14. While he conjoins himself with the Father, and presseth to faith in both, it serveth to teach—1. Faith, in laying hold on Christ, must ascend up through the veil of his flesh and office of Mediator, and fasten on him as true God, one

in essence and equal with the Father; for so doth this exhortation import. 2. Faith in God the Father must be joined with faith in Christ, in whom the Father is to be taken up in the matter of reconciliation, 2 Cor. v. 19, and through whom we must believe in God, 2 Cor. iii. 4 ; 1 Peter, i. 21 ; therefore it is required that with their believing in God they believe also in him. 3. It is a notable encouragement, inviting troubled souls to believe, when they consider the infinite latitude of the object of faith, as it closeth both with the Father and the Son, not secluding the Holy Ghost; for in the Son they will find eternal redemption, everlasting righteousness, and satisfaction ; in the Father, infinite love, and free grace accepting the elect in Christ; in the Holy Ghost, infinite virtue and power applying Christ's purchase; and in both Father and Son, (not secluding the Holy Ghost,) infinite power upholding and preserving the elect till they come to full fruition. So much also may be gathered from the distinct naming of the Father and Son as the object of their faith.

VER. 2. In my Father's house are many mansions: if it were not so, I would have told you. I go to prepare a place for you.

In this verse is contained the second argument of consolation, which (as Christ's consolations are all rich) contains a double encouragement in the bosom of it. For—1. He presupposeth it as a ground of the following consolation, that heaven, to which he went, was his Father's house, and was designed not for him alone to ascend unto, but for many more through him, (for whom there is room enough,) for their perpetual rest and abode. 2. He confirms this supposition from his fidelity and good will to them, assuring them he would never delude them with vain hopes. 3. He subjoins the principal consolation ; that his going to heaven was for their good, to prepare a place for them. Whence learn—

1. Such as study encouragement by faith ought to lift up their hearts to the hope of future glory, that so their consolation may be strong; therefore is this encouragement from the hope of glory subjoined to the former, of living by faith for the present, ver. 1.

2. Whatever be the tossed life of saints here, which the Lord in deep wisdom carves out for them, that they may indeed be strangers and pilgrims, yet it may encourage them that there is a solid and quiet resting-place prepared for them in heaven; for this cause doth he give it the name of a mansion. (See Heb. xiii. 14 ; Rev. xiv. 13.)

3. There is abundance of room in heaven and in God's love to receive sinners ; and albeit it hath not seemed good to him to save all, nor the most part, yet there are many to be saved and admitted into that blessed rest; therefore it is designed " many mansions ;" which is not to be carnally conceived of as if heaven were divided into so many cells ; nor yet as pointing at several degrees in glory ; but the expression is to be understood in opposition to [in connexion with] Christ's ascending at this time alone ; and by it he would in-

timate that there was room in heaven, not for him alone, but for many through him, in whose name he was a forerunner, as is after cleared ; so that none need to be deterred from coming to Christ by reason of the paucity of the elect.

4. It may sweeten the hope of glory unto saints when they consider that heaven is the house of God, wherein he will familiarly converse with his domestics ; wherein they will get a clear and full sight of him, shall enjoy full glory, as being in the King's palace, shall get a secure and quiet habitation, beyond the reach of enemies, enjoying the treasures which they laid up there before, and wherein all the children shall at last be gathered together ; therefore it is here described to be the " Father's house."

5. It adds to the consolation of saints, that however the glory and riches of heaven might crush their hopes that ever such unworthy ones as they should be so dignified, yet Christ as their head is lord and heir thereof, and he will come speed there for their behoof; therefore doth he so comfortably describe it, " my Father's house."

6. Christ is no false prophet or deceiver of his people ; he reveals all that is necessary for them to know, nor will he hide anything that is for their good; for in this he bids them credit his fidelity and love, " If it were not so, I would have told you."

7. Christ's deed and performance will never give his word the lie, nor will there be anything less found in heaven than he hath promised. So much also is imported in this here—" If it were not so, I would have told you."

8. There is no trial so bitter and sad but Christ can draw precious consolations out of it to his own, and bring it about for their good ; for what more sad to the disciples than to be separated from their Master? and yet he draws ground of comfort out of it, " I go (saith he, speaking of his voluntariness in dying) to prepare a place for you."

9. No man by nature hath any right to heaven until it be acquired and prepared for him ; for so is here imported, that a place must be prepared, even for disciples.

10. Albeit in God's decree heaven was prepared for the elect from the foundation of the world, Matt. xxv. 34, yet it is through Christ only that they come to get actual right to it ; for " I prepare a place for you," saith he.

11. As Christ by his death did purchase a right and title to heaven for saints, so by his ascension into heaven he prosecutes and applies that right ; for in his ascension he is declared acquitted and righteous in our name ; he led captive all those who might hinder us from it, Eph. iv. 8. As harbingers go before to prepare rooms for those who are to follow after, so he ascended as a common person to take possession in our name, Heb. vi. 20 ; Eph. ii. 6. As the high priest entered into the most holy place, with the names of the children of Israel on his breast, and with the blood of the sacrifices, Heb. ix. 7, so he hath entered heaven with our names on his heart, to present the merit of his blood continually, to pour out his Spirit to fit us for glory, and by his intercession to promove our going thither. (See Heb. ix. 11, 12.) Therefore saith

he, "I go (not only to die, but to my Father's house,) to prepare a place for you." So that his ascension proves the way is patent, is a pledge of our ascension, and assures us that the inheritance will be kept till we be ripe for it; which yet is not to be understood as if heaven had not been prepared for any before his ascension, but that without his miret [permission], either as ascended or to ascend, none hath access to heaven; so that he ascended first, in priority of nature, as the cause of the ascension of all his followers, though not first in priority of time.

12. Whatever be Christ's condition, it is still for the believers' good, and wherever he be, he is about their affairs; for as he descended from heaven, when our affairs required it, so also he ascended again on our affairs.

13. It is an undoubted pledge that Christ, exalted in glory, will not forget his followers on earth, that their affairs was a great part of his errand thither; for if he "go to prepare a place," we may be sure he will not forget his errand.

Ver. 3. And if I go and prepare a place for you, I will come again, and receive you unto myself; that where I am, there ye may be also.

The third argument of consolation is, that having done his work in heaven in their name, he will return and fetch them to glory and the full fruition of the promises; which is not only to be understood of his fetching particular believers at death, but chiefly of his coming at the great day, when he shall make one errand of all, and take up all his followers, to perfect them both in soul and body. This consolation is confirmed—1. From his errand in departing; if he go away on their affairs, he will stay no longer than their affairs require, but when he hath done his work, he will return. 2. (Which is also a description of that blessed estate, to the possession whereof he will take them.) From his love to their society, and therefore he will have them to be with himself, and where he is. Whence learn—

1. The faith of the second coming of Christ ought to uphold the hearts of believers during his absence; for this is another consolation—" I will come again, and receive you." (See Acts, i. 11; Titus, ii. 12. 13.)

2. It is the great consolation of believers that their living by faith shall at last end in fruition; and albeit this be only believed for the present, yet it may make all other exercises of faith comfortable, that this is one among the rest, even that their faith, having carried them through many a tempest and dark cloud, will at last resolve in sight and enjoyment; therefore is this consolation, of his receiving them, subjoined to the former of faith and hope, ver. 1, 2, as that which will perfect them all, being the day of full redemption, Luke, xxi. 28. (See 1 Cor. xv. 19, 54, 55.)

3. It is ample matter of encouragement to believers that not only shall they be eternally glorified, but that Christ doth condescend to do all the duties, for perfecting their happiness, that can be expected by reason of his relations; for as bridegrooms used to fetch their brides, so he will not decline to do that duty to his bride, how naughty soever she be, "I will come again and receive you." He not only knows she could never come to him otherwise, but his great love to her, and his purpose to make her glorious, doth endear her to him so that he will stoop to such duties.

4. It doth commend the love of Christ to believers, and augment their comfort, that he is so eminently active in promoving their eternal happiness, in all the steps thereof, and taketh the whole burden of it upon himself, leaving them little or nothing to do; for as it is he who descended for their behoof, and came to seek them when they had no mind of him, so it is he who goeth up again for them, who prepareth a place for them there, ver. 2, and who, after all that, cometh again and receiveth them. It is true, he hath enjoined believers their duty, which they must not slight through presumptuous leaning on him; yet not only doth not that merit anything, but he layeth on a yoke of duty on us, that we may employ him to work all our works in us, and for us, and so he will work in us both to will and to do.

5. A right study of Christ's errand to heaven may assure us that he is engaged to come again and perfect us, and that he will return when he hath done our employment there; for so doth he confirm this consolation, "If I go and prepare a place for you, (or, When I go and shall have prepared a place for you, as the one particle is often put for the other,) I will come again and receive you." This doth most clearly follow, because his love having taken on that employment will not put it off again, nor will he be unanswerable to his trust, nor lose all the pains he hath taken to purchase and prepare a place, by not coming again to perfect his own.

6. Albeit Christ removed his bodily presence from his followers, yet his love to them and their fellowship did not cease; nor will he rest satisfied till he and they meet to enjoy his company; for he who delighted among the sons of men before the world was, Prov. viii. 31, who delighted to converse with his people in human shape before his incarnation, and who took pleasure to spend his time busily among them, while he was with them in the days of his flesh, John, ix. 4, 5, even he is so tender in his love that he hath mind of returning before he go away, and before he want their company; he will yet leave heaven for their sakes, and "come again (saith he) and receive you unto myself, (and that for this end,) that where I am, there ye may be also."

7. As Christ's followers are in this life called to be conformed to his image, and to partake with him in sufferings, so his love will have them at last advanced to communion in glory with himself, in that measure which they, as his members, are capable of; for this is his purpose concerning them, "that where I am, there ye may be also."

8. It makes the hope of heaven sweet to saints when they consider that there they will meet

with and fully enjoy Christ, whom they have so often delighted to look upon through a veil, and whose company hath ofttimes offered them much of heaven upon earth, and in their saddest lots, and that they shall never again be separated from him ; therefore doth he propound this as their sweet encouragement, " I will receive you unto myself, that where I am, there ye may be also." (See 1 Thess. iv. 17.)

Ver. 4. And whither I go ye know, and the way ye know.

The fourth argument of consolation (propounded in this verse) is, that however he was to leave them, yet they knew whither he went, and which was the way thither. For clearing whereof, consider—1. As the place to which he went was to his Father, and his house, (as is cleared, ver. 2, and in the following purpose,) so by the way here he points out not only the way wherein he was to walk to glory, but the way also wherein they were to follow, as the following enlargement of this consolation maketh clear. 2. The way to heaven is (so to say) twofold; first, the way of dispensations and lots, wherewith saints are essayed in going through ; and thus, as Christ went to his Father by sad sufferings, so believers enter into the kingdom through much tribulation, Acts, xiv. 22. Secondly, the way of their duty, and the means whereby they may come to God, and walk through these difficulties, till they come to him in heaven ; and thus, as Christ paved a way for himself, so is he the way to all others, as we shall hear, ver. 6. Now albeit the first of these be not to be excluded here ; for we are to follow him in that way, 1 Pet. ii. 21 ; yet the last is chiefly insisted on in the explication. 3. As for the disciples' knowing of these, (which is contradicted by Thomas,) his assertion imports not only that they had been sufficiently furnished with means to have known, but that they did also know them, in part, and in some respect. So the meaning is, that it might sufficiently encourage them that they knew heaven and the Father to whom he went, and they were to follow, and were instructed that suffering and tribulation was the highway to heaven, both for him and them ; and that albeit he withdrew his bodily presence, yet they knew the way of corresponding with the Father in heaven, and had a sure way to guide them home.

DOCTRINES.

1. Believers, who do seriously study to know heaven, and what the resting-place of pilgrims is, will find rich consolation in it ; for this is one branch of the encouragement, ye know whither I go.

2. It contributes exceedingly to believers' encouragement by knowing heaven, to know that Christ is gone there and glorified with his Father for their good ; for this is the particular consideration, rendering this knowledge of heaven comfortable, " whither I go ye know"—namely, that I succumb not under my sufferings, but ascend to heaven to my Father.

3. It contributes much to the comfort of believers, and is their peculiar privilege in their absence from the Lord, as to know God and heaven, so to know the way that leads thither to be the way indeed, and to be armed against all misconstructions of the way, being compared with the end of it, to which it ofttimes looks so unsuitable ; for so much is held out in this encouragement, as it relates to the way of dispensation, wherein Christ went to heaven, and believers follow him. It is an encouragement, " the way ye know," and need not mistake sad sufferings, as if they were not leading to a crown, as too many do little believe that to lose is to gain, and to die the way to life.

4. It is not sufficient for the encouragement of believers that they have a contemplative knowledge of heaven, and the difficulties that lie in the way to it, unless also Christ's removal out of the world do estrange their affections from it, and make them become pilgrims, and set them on work to know the way and means how they may hasten after him, to come where he is ; and in the meantime may keep intercourse and correspondence with him, and through him with the Father. For this is the great encouragement, " ye know the way"—namely, that he is the way to the Father, to whom he goeth, as is after cleared.

5. Christ hath not left his followers without sufficient means of information concerning heaven and the way to it, and without such a measure of knowledge of these things as might be ample matter of encouragement if they knew how to discern and improve it ; for he asserts for their comfort, not only in respect of means, but as to their actual knowledge also, " whither I go ye know, and the way ye know."

6. Christ knoweth his people, and what they are, better than they do themselves, and his verdict of them is to be preferred before their own ; for notwithstanding their doubts, afterwards mentioned, he asserts, " whither I go ye know," &c.

Ver. 5. Thomas saith unto him, Lord, we know not whither thou goest; and how can we know the way?

Followeth to verse 8, a further clearing of this argument of consolation, in answer to Thomas's objection. His doubt is propounded in this verse, wherein, being rash, incredulous, and timorous, as was usual to him, (see chap. xi. 16 ; xx. 25,) and supposing that Christ would retire some whither and leave them, he objects, in name of all the rest, that they knew not whither he went, and consequently could not know the way ; this being a contradiction to Christ's assertion, ver. 4. The reconciliation thereof is not to be taken from this : that Christ only speaks of sufficient information given whereby they might have known ; and that Thomas objects that for all this they did not actually know ; for Christ afterward asserts that they actually knew in some measure ; but the true rise of the difference betwixt Christ and Thomas is—1. Christ asserts they did know, which holds true, though they did but know confusedly and in some measure; Thomas, finding no such distinct knowledge as he desired, objects that he knew not at all. 2. Christ knew that in this matter his disciples did know more than Thomas understood that he and they did know, and therefore he thus objects; for they know Christ in some measure, which was in substance the knowledge of the Father to whom he went, and of the way to him, as is after cleared, yet he knew not these things under the notions and terms of place and way, and therefore objects his ignorance. Whence learn—

1. The knowledge that saints attain unto is very little in respect of what they might have in the use of means afforded them, for in respect of measure, it is true which Thomas said, and yet contradicts not Christ's assertion: "we know not."

2. None will ever study to know, nor can they rightly know the way to heaven till first they attain to some knowledge of heaven itself to set them on work to inquire after the way; for upon this, "we know not whither thou goest," Thomas inferreth strongly "how then can we know the way?"

3. Such as are convinced and humbled under the sense of their ignorance will not stand to acknowledge it, that they may abase themselves before the Lord; for so doth Thomas acknowledge it here.

4. Such as are convinced of their own ignorance and infirmities will thereby become more sensible of the weakness of others also; for upon this ground it is that he speaks in all their names, "Lord, we know not."

5. It is an usual weakness in believers that their conviction of shortcoming doth drive them to think they have no good at all; for in this respect Thomas's confession comes short and contradicts Christ in saying simply "we know not."

6. Saints may have true good and knowledge of Christ, which he knoweth and alloweth them to be encouraged in, whereof yet they may be ignorant, and will not take with it; for Christ hath told them, "ye know," ver. 4, and yet saith he, "we know not." Sometimes saints are under tentation and in a fever, and so cannot discern their grace; sometimes they do so conceive of grace in its highest perfection that they cannot discern the small beginnings they have; and sometimes they know truths in substance, yet they cannot give a name to what they know, nor understand it under the notions and terms by which it may be expressed, as Thomas knew Christ, but not distinctly under the notion of the way, or as he in whom the Father is to be known. This may teach men condescendence in their expressions to others, and to beware of making their own conceptions of grace and truth a rule whereby to judge of all others; but they must vary expressions and notions till it be seen whether they know the thing itself or not.

VER. 6. *Jesus saith unto him, I am the way, the truth, and the life: no man cometh unto the Father, but by me.*

Followeth Christ's answer to this objection, wherein he cleareth those grounds of consolation propounded, ver. 4. And first, (in this verse,) as to the way to that place, he forbears to speak of the way of difficulties he and they were to go through, and clears only the way whereby they might come to heaven through these difficulties—to wit, by himself, who, as he made a way to himself by his own proper power and authority, so he is the way to all others, by whom alone men can come to the Father, as is inferred in the end of the verse. Unto this is subjoined, by way of amplification, that he is "the truth, and the life," which as it holds true in many respects that he is truth in his doctrine, the truth of all the types, and the quickener and preserver of spiritual life in his people, so it here points out, partly, the properties of this way, that he is that true and living way, and partly, the order of walking in and making use of that way, that first we must close with him by faith as truth, and doing so shall find him to be life in our walking, which is to be perfected as our prize at the end of the journey. Whence learn—

1. Christ is very tender of the acknowledged ignorance of his own, and will take pains to help it; for here he instructeth Thomas, who confessed his ignorance.

2. However saints may look upon their infirmities, ignorance, and doubts as very burdensome and useless, yet Christ can bring much good out of them to clear and confirm themselves and others the more; for Christ makes use of Thomas's doubt to clear up this argument of consolation more fully for the good of believers in all ages.

3. Such as rightly know heaven, and the way and means to wrestle through unto it, may easily digest difficulties in the way; for this cause it is that Christ insists no more on the rough path of trouble which leads towards heaven, because the knowledge of heaven, and of the Father there, and of Christ as the way thither, is enough to swallow it up, and therefore he insists only on that.

4. Man by nature is subject to many necessities and spiritual miseries, as being subject to go astray from the womb, and wanting a path wherein to walk towards happiness, being subject to error and seduction, and wanting light to discern the way of his happiness and to guide him in it, and being dead in sin legally and spiritually, unable to walk in the way, though it were pointed out, and needing no less than eternal life to prevent his eternal misery; for all these necessities are supposed in this, that he must be "the way, the truth, and the life."

5. Christ is an all-sufficient remedy for all our wants; he is the way for wanderers, and the path wherein exiles may return towards lost happiness; he is the truth, to lead them surely and to point out their path unto them; and he is the quickener of his people; for "I am the way, the truth, and the life," saith he.

6. Christ is the way to heaven and to the Father, not only as it is through him we must ascend up to the knowledge of the Father, or as he points out the way to happiness as a prophet, but as having, by his merit and satisfaction as priest, made a patent door whereby sinners may enter and approach to God, and being their ef-

fectual leader in that way as King; in these respects he is called "the way," (see Heb. x. 19, 20,) so that through him sinners may come forward.

7. Christ also is the truth, not only essentially in himself, and he from whom all truth is, but more especially he is the truth as a way to his people, and a true way; partly, in opposition to types and legal ceremonies, which were but shadows of this true way; John, i. 17; Col. ii. 17; partly, in opposition to all delusions and vanities of the world, whereby men think to attain happiness, all which, as they draw from Christ, the true way, so they will prove a lie and not the truth; partly, in respect of the promises, whereby we are encouraged in our way; all which in him are yea, and Amen, 2 Cor. i. 20; and partly, in respect of his directing us in the way, he is not only a way wherein to walk, but a way that will direct the passengers in walking, by the infallible directions of his word, by the inward direction and illumination of his Spirit accompanying the same, and by his gracious providence hedging them in from many debordings [difficulties]. In all these considerations it is Christ's prerogative that he is "the way and the truth," so that saints may trust his guiding and lean on their beloved.

8. It is Christ's prerogative above all other ways that not only he is the truth, but the life also; for other ways cannot furnish passengers, but they may faint and die in them, nor can they lead to a blessed rest; but he is a way who quickeneth the dead when they are brought to it, who furnisheth the passengers that walk in him, so that they will walk and not be weary, and who is the author of eternal life, who living by himself, and having merited life by his death, doth confer eternal life upon walkers at the end of their journey; therefore is it subjoined, " I am the life." (See chap. xvii. 2.)

9. The right method of making use of Christ as a way is first to close with him as truth and in his word of truth, and to walk on believing, upon which life will follow, both for present and everlastingly; for this way is, first " the truth," and then " the life."

10. It is man's chief misery to be separated from God, and his happiness to have access to him and enjoy him; for that is the advantage to be had in this way, even to come to the Father.

11. Christ is so the way to God as there is no other beside unto which a man can lean but it will deceive him; no saving knowledge of God can be had but by him; our reconciliation, vocation, access to God in prayer, and glorification, must be through him and by him; for " No man cometh unto the Father but by me."

12. Albeit there be no way unto God beside Christ; yea, albeit all things beside would discourage poor sinners; yet such as have fled to Christ may draw near with boldness; for albeit " No man cometh unto the Father but by me," and all doors beside be shut, yet saith he, " I am the way, the truth, and the life."

VER. 7. If ye had known me, ye should have known my Father also: and from henceforth ye know him, and have seen him.

In this verse the other ground of consolation propounded, ver. 4, is cleared, in answer to the second branch of Thomas's doubt, concerning the place whither Christ went, or the Father to whom he went in that place. Christ sheweth that this might be known by knowing of him, he being one in essence with the Father, the express image of his person, Heb. i. 3; Col. i. 15, and he in whom the fulness of the godhead dwelleth bodily. Hence Christ inferreth, in answer to Thomas's objection, that from henceforth they know and have seen him, not only in respect of sufficient means, but having known him, chap. vi. 69, they might henceforth know that they knew the Father in him, and had seen him formerly in seeing of him. Whence learn—

1. The Father is savingly known in the Son and in him only; to know or see him with mortal bodily eyes is impossible; the knowledge of him in the creation, and in external representations and manifestations of his glory is but imperfect, nor can it suffice to salvation; to know him in the law or covenant of works doth but work wrath; but in Christ he is held out to be known perfectly, and to salvation; for " if ye had known me, ye should have known my Father also." And this further clears that to know him is life eternal.

2. To know Christ rightly is the sum of all saving knowledge, both of God and of the way to him and happiness with him; therefore doth he solve all Thomas's doubts by pointing out himself as both the way and he in whom the Father may be known.

3. Christ's followers do need a new gift to discern what they have or know savingly, and to have it borne upon them by him for their encouragement; therefore, albeit the disciples had saving knowledge of the Father in some measure, yet they knew not so much till Christ bear it upon them, " ye know him."

4. It is the duty of believers to improve the means of encouragement which Christ affords them, and it is their fault not to see what he discovers to them of their enjoyment and condition; therefore saith he, " from henceforth ye know him;" not that upon the matter they knew him not before, in knowing the Son; but that now, after this information and discovery, they were bound no more to doubt, but to know that they knew him for their own encouragement.

5. It is the duty of those to whom Christ reveals their good condition, not only to improve it for the future, but to look back to the times of their mistake and ignorance, and make use of that which they then had and observed not, both for humiliation for their shortcoming, and for encouragement in him who was better to them than they were aware, therefore doth he not only allege, " ye know him" for present, but " have seen him" for the time past, that they might observe and improve that.

VER. 8. Philip saith unto him, Lord, shew us the Father, and it sufficeth us.

From this to verse 15, this branch of the consolation of knowing the Father in the Son is further insisted on by occasion of a new proposition of Philip, another disciple; and by this means also he clears up that argument of consolation insinuated ver. 1, that he was God, one and equal with the Father. This verse contains Philip's proposition, wherein he expresseth a great desire to have the Father shewed unto them, promising great satisfaction to himself and the rest thereby; but he fails, in that he is not satisfied with the right way of seeing the Father; but, declining to be led so far about to know the Father as he conceived the seeing of him in Christ to be, he desires, for their satisfaction, an immediate and clear sight of the Father, his glory and majesty. Whence learn—

1. The doctrine of Christ is not taken off his hand, even by disciples, except with much difficulty; for after Thomas's objection, Philip starts a new difficulty, when Christ is clearing them most sweetly.

2. It is the duty of disciples who are convinced of their ignorance not to rest in such a condition, but to labour after knowledge; for Philip, not knowing the Father as he desired, would have him shewed to them; and this is commendable in him.

3. Such as would have saving knowledge of God and divine mysteries must expect and seek it only from Christ; for this is commendable also, that he takes this course, "Lord, shew us the Father." (See Matt. xi. 27.)

4. Such as expect to be taught by Christ must employ him by prayer, with much humility and reverence; for "Lord, (saith he,) shew us the Father."

5. It is not sufficient we desire after knowledge of spiritual things, unless our desires be chiefly carried after the best things, and particularly to know God himself: "Lord, shew us the Father," saith he.

6. The sight and knowledge of God is full of satisfaction and refreshment, and believers will rest content therewith, whatever be their case beside: "Shew us (saith he) the Father, and it sufficeth us." (See Ps. xvi. 11.)

7. Saints, even in their best and spiritual desires, are subject to infirmities, and ready to be unsatisfied with Christ's way and manner of satisfying them; for Philip, not being satisfied with what Christ said, of knowing the Father in him, would know him in a way of his own, and have a nearer cut of it, as he thought: "Lord, shew us the Father."

8. The way of seeing and knowing God by faith, as he is revealed in his Son, is a way not satisfactory to a carnal heart; and believers themselves have a jealousy of it, in so far as they are carnal; for this is the sight of God which Philip declineth, and would have another before it suffice him.

9. When we are unsatisfied with Christ's way, and would have a way of our own, we shall find, upon trial, that the way we would be at is either impossible or unfit, or cometh far short of what we enjoy; for whereas he desireth Christ to shew them the Father, if he desire an immediate sight of him, that is impossible, and would consume mortal men; and if he mean only such a sight as Moses and others got, it cometh far short of what they had already.

Ver. 9. Jesus saith unto him, Have I been so long time with you, and yet hast thou not known me, Philip? he that hath seen me hath seen the Father; and how sayest thou then, Shew us the Father?

Followeth Christ's answer to this proposition, clearing the encouragement and his unity with the Father. It may be taken up in three branches; whereof the first (in this verse) is a reprehension of Philip's ignorance, and a complaint that, notwithstanding his long converse with them, yet he knew him so ill as not to see the Father in seeing of him, but taking no notice of that, did still call for a sight of the Father. Whence learn—

1. Even Christ's disciples may, for a long time, be but ill scholars and slow of conception, as here Christ finds them.

2. Ignorance in disciples is rebuke worthy, and Christ will not spare it in them; as here he reproves Philip.

3. Christ takes notice of the means of knowledge his people enjoy, and the continuance thereof with them, that he may aggravate their continued ignorance; for "Have I been so long time with you, and yet hast thou not known me?"

4. Christ may be very long with his people, and they be studying to know him, and yet not know him fully; for "hast thou not known me, Philip?" Not that he was simply ignorant of Christ, but that he knew him not so as to know the Father in him.

5. Christ doth reprove the ignorance of his followers with much tenderness, and so as may witness his affection to them and their welfare; therefore doth he propound the challenge by way of regrate, [reproof,] "Hast thou not known me?"

6. As the Father can only be savingly known in Christ, so none do know Christ rightly, and as they ought, unless they know the Father in him, who is the express image of his person, and he in whom the fulness of the undivided essence of the godhead dwells bodily; for Philip hath not known Christ aright, since he saith, "Shew us the Father," and that because, "he that hath seen me hath seen the Father;" so that if he had known him as he ought, he had not been ignorant of the Father.

7. The knowledge of God which is to be had in Christ is a most clear and distinct knowledge; for it is a sight; "he that hath seen me hath seen the Father."

8. The excellency and preciousness of things desired by saints will not bear weight before God if they be not put up in a right way, and if the desire be joined with inadvertency and not improving of means received; for albeit "shew us the Father" be a commendable desire, yet in so far as he propounds it in these terms, to know him without the Son, and as if they had not seen him already in the Son, Christ rejects it: "He that hath seen me hath seen the Father; and how sayest thou then, Shew us the Father?"

VER. 10. Believest thou not that I am in the Father, and the Father in me? the words that I speak unto you I speak not of myself: but the Father that dwelleth in me, he doeth the works.

The second branch of Christ's answer contains an information of the ground of this assertion, that they who know him know the Father—namely, that he is one in essence with the Father. This he presseth upon Philip's conscience, if he would not assent to it by faith ; and confirmeth it from his word, which is the Father's with him, and from his works, which were wrought not only by him, but by the Father with and in him, these being external works, which are common to the whole Trinity, by reason of the unity of essence, though they be distinct persons. Whence learn—

1. Christ, when he reproves his people, doth mind their good, and is willing to inform them, and direct them how to amend ; therefore doth he subjoin an information to his reproof, clearing the ground of their knowing the Father in him. And by this he teacheth all ministers to join doctrine with reproof, 2 Tim. iv. 2.

2. The true ground of our knowing the Father in the Son is his unity in essence with the Father, so that though their personal properties be distinct, yet the essence is the same in both, and the one is in the other ; for by this he cleareth his former doctrine, " I am in the Father and the Father in me."

3. It is faith only, and not our sense or corrupt reason, that must be employed to take up the mysteries of religion, and particularly that Christ is God co-essential with the Father ; for it is faith that is put to it in this matter, " Believest thou not that I am in the Father," &c.

4. It is our duty to put our hearts to it, to see what they believe in the mysteries of God, that so we may not take the naked assent of the mind for faith, and may be ashamed to harbour that secret unbelief in our hearts which we dare not avow nor own ; therefore doth Christ so put him to it, " Believest thou not that I am in the Father, and the Father in me?" to shame him from thinking otherwise.

5. The word preached by Christ, and transmitted to us in scripture, is the very word of God, the Father and the Son ; for " the words that I speak unto you, I speak not of myself," not only not of his own head, as he was an ambassador, but not of himself without the Father, as is further cleared, ver. 24, so that the word was his and the Father's who is in him.

6. Christ's works, both miraculous and those wrought in believers, being done by his own power, do prove him to be true God, one in essence with the Father, and the Father's also with him, by reason of that unity ; for " the Father that dwelleth in me (being the same in essence), he doeth the works"—to wit, with the Son.

7. It is our duty to make use of Christ's word and works, to confirm our faith in him as true God, one with the Father ; for these are not only arguments proving the point, but serving to excite Philip and the rest so to study them as to find proofs of a deity in them.

8. They who would profit by Christ's word and works in the knowledge of him should first begin and bottom themselves on his word, and find him God there, and then look out to his works for further confirmation ; therefore doth he first urge the argument of his word, and then subjoins that of his works.

VER. 11. Believe me that I am in the Father, and the Father in me : or else believe me for the very works' sake.

The third branch of Christ's answer contains an exhortation to all the disciples that they should believe this truth of his unity in essence with the Father ; which he presseth and confirmeth from three reasons ; whereof the first (in this verse) is the same in substance with that ver. 10, that he who is the truth speaks it, and hath confirmed it by his works. Whence learn—

1. The deity of Christ, and his unity in essence with the Father, is the main article of the Christian religion, to be studied and believed ; therefore doth he press it : " Believe that I am in the Father, and the Father in me."

2. This point of saving truth ought to be seriously and distinctly inculcated and studied and learned ; otherwise our consolation arising from the knowledge of our Mediator will not be so solid and so full as is allowed ; therefore, notwithstanding any imperfect knowledge they had of him, and what he had pressed on Philip, he doth again urge that they believe this : " Believe that I am in the Father," &c.

3. Christ doth so take care of one of his followers, whose infirmities become visible, as he will not forget others who may be in the like need ; for as he pressed Philip, ver. 10, so he presseth here all the rest to believe, whom he knew to be ignorant as well as Philip, though they had not expressed it. " Believe ye," saith he, to all of them, in the plural number.

4. The knowledge of Christ to be true God, under the veil of his manhood and state of humiliation, is as difficult as it is necessary, and a study wherein believers will find much matter of humiliation for their shortcoming ; for so much also doth this insisting on it teach us.

5. Christ takes pleasure in the soul-prosperity of his servants, and that for this end they study him well who is their fountain and storehouse, and do close with him by faith as true God ; therefore doth he exhort and entreat them to " believe."

6. Christ is a witness who will not lie ; and as it is only on his testimony we must fasten in matters of faith, so his testimony is worthy of all credit and acceptation by faith in our hearts ; for the exhortation is a reason to itself, " believe me," saith he, since I have said it.

7. Christ, by his condescending to add works to the testimony of his word, for confirmation of our faith, and that albeit he be God, who cannot lie, doth teach his people not to try men by their words, but their power, 1 Cor. iv. 19, and to examine all the fair professions of men by their

fruits; for this other branch of the argument, taken from his works, is added, not because his word needs such a witness in itself, but, in part, to teach us caution in the like case.

8. Christ's works, joined with his word, do so clearly point him out, that they may extort an acknowledgment of his godhead from men, and will exceedingly heighten the sin of them who will not trust in him as God; therefore saith he, "or else believe me for the very works' sake;" whereby he doth not allow them not to believe himself speaking in his word, nor yet approves of that faith as saving which is begotten by his works without the word, but declareth that his works were so clear proofs of a Deity as none without impudence could deny it, nor without great sin misbelieve a truth so confirmed.

VER. 12. *Verily, verily, I say unto you, He that believeth on me, the works that I do shall he do also; and greater works than these shall he do; because I go unto my Father.*

The second reason confirming this truth, and pressing the exhortation, (which also is an argument of consolation against his removal,) is contained in a promise that believers in him shall do the works that he did, and greater also, through faith in him, who after his ascension shall let out proofs of his deity with them in a more ample manner than he manifested himself in the state of his humiliation. For clearing of this purpose, and the scope thereof, consider—1. The works of Christ, which here he parallels with those to be done by believers, are not his works of redemption as Mediator, nor his works of creation and providence as God, which are incommunicable with any, but his miraculous works, and works wrought on the hearts of men by giving success to his ministry. 2. As for those believers who are to do these and greater works, whatever may be said, in a sound sense, of every believer's doing great things, and overcoming the world through faith in him, yet the parallel holds clearer to restrict it to the apostles and others in the primitive times, who were endued with extraordinary power, and sent abroad to preach the gospel. 3. As for the parallel itself, that it is promised they shall do these, and greater than these, and that albeit Christ did raise the dead, open the eyes of the blind, &c., and cure every disease, it may be thus cleared: partly, they were greater in respect of number, they working many miracles for number beyond what he did, and many for kind which he did not, as speaking with new tongues, and the like, (see Mark, xvi. 17, 18, and elsewhere;) partly, albeit his miracles in themselves were as great as any of theirs, yet, in the way and manner of them, the power did shine more conspicuously than in some of his; for he did cure men by his word, and by the touch of his garment, but they did cure many by their shadow passing by, Acts, v. 15, and by napkins carried from them, Acts, xix. 12; and partly, and chiefly, this is to be understood of the effects of these their miraculous works, and of their ministry which these works did accompany; for Christ was the minister of the circumcision only,

and by his doctrine and miracles did prevail but with few of them, as himself often complaineth; but the apostles did bring in thousands by one sermon at Jerusalem, and by their doctrine and miracles did bring down idols, and set up the kingdom of Christ throughout the world. 4. Whereas Christ by his works proveth himself equal with the Father, ver. 11, and yet promiseth they shall do greater things, we should be far from conceiving that this doth anything weaken the argument whereby he proveth his deity, far less doth it exalt them to aspire to any equality with him; for whatever difference there be betwixt the works wrought by him and them, yet herein is the infinite difference betwixt him and them, that he wrought them by his own power as God, but all they did was by faith in him, who put forth his power to do the works, and accordingly they did them in his name; so that albeit the doing of these works tended to their encouragement, yet the glory thereof redounded only to him. 5. This reason why they shall do greater works, "because I go unto my Father," doth not infer there should be any addition to his power then, as God, but that at that time his godhead (which in the days of his flesh was hid under the veil of a servant's shape) should more gloriously manifest itself. 6. This encouragement of their doing greater works tends not only to prove him exalted as Mediator after his sufferings, as Acts, ii. 33, but also to prove that assertion, ver. 11, that he is one with the Father; because it is an evidence of his absolute and divine power that he can confer this dignity upon others (not as the apostles did, ministerially, by laying on of hands, but) through faith in his name; and withal, it is he who doth these works by them, as is after cleared, ver. 13, 14.

DOCTRINES.

1. We have need to be often excited, to consider seriously the weight and gravity of that which Christ speaketh; therefore is so frequent use made of this asseveration, "Verily, verily, I say unto you."

2. Christ will bring that unto saints, out of their worst and saddest conditions, which they could neither apprehend nor believe unless he had said it; therefore doth this promise of the great things for which his removal maketh way need to be confirmed with a "verily, verily," that the disciples might give credit unto it.

3. As it is by faith in Christ only that saints are enabled to do great things, (and therefore the promise is made to him "that believeth on me," it will make Peter walk on the sea, and only unbelief will make him sink,) so the want of Christ's bodily presence needs be no hindrance to faith to close with him and draw virtue out of him, for enabling to do greatest things; for the promise is made to him "that believeth on me," that he shall do the works that I do, and greater than these, after he is ascended.

4. Albeit Christ only, of all the sons of men, was true God and man in one person, yet the power and virtue of his godhead is not astricted to his own person, but is communicable in the effects thereof to his members; so that he will

do that in them and by them which only God can do; and they shall not want divine power for carrying them through in what they have to do; for " He that believeth on me, the works that I do shall he do also," &c.

5. Christ can and ofttimes doth work that by weak and contemptible means which he doth not by stronger and more probable causes; and he did more in the world by his weak servants than he was pleased to do himself; for albeit believers be but weak creatures, yet greater works shall he do (saith he, of every one here intended) than these done by himself, who is God over all.

6. Men's lawful and spiritual employments, and Christ's presence with them therein, are notable encouragements to believers during Christ's absence; for their work and great success in it is one great encouragement to the disciples here. And as Christ alloweth encouragement upon none who are not about their employment, so it is a great comfort that the saddest of conditions afford matter of comfortable employment about them, and that work may keep saints in their pilgrimage from thinking too much long [too much thinking].

7. Christ is a wise dispenser of his allowances, who ofttimes reserveth greatest manifestations of himself for saddest times, wherein as they are least expected, so they are most needed; therefore is this more ample manifestation reserved for that sad time wherein the disciples were saddened with his departure, and might be ready to think that all that power whereby he wrought was quite removed with his own bodily presence.

8. Christ's exaltation hath neither diminished his power nor his tender care of his own, but, on the contrary, he doth make his exaltation, his unity as God, and acceptance as Mediator, with the Father, conspicuous in the world, by his liberality and bounty towards them; for this is the reason why believers shall do greater works, " because I go to my Father." (See Eph. iv. 8.)

VER. 13. And whatsoever ye shall ask in my name, that will I do, that the Father may be glorified in the Son.

14. If ye shall ask any thing in my name, I will do it.

The third reason confirming this truth, and pressing the exhortation, (which also is not only another argument of consolation against his removal, but doth further clear the former promise, ver. 12, by shewing the way how faith employeth Christ for doing these great things,) is contained in a promise that he will do for them whatsoever they ask in his name; which he twice inculcates, for further confirmation, and amplifieth the promise from his end in it, which is, that the Father may be glorified in and through him, in what he doth in answer to their prayer. For further clearing of the purpose—1. This general truth, " whatsoever ye shall ask," &c., doth not open a door to vent all our desires to God, be what they will, in hope of audience, (for we must ask according to his will,) but the meaning is, that what things are agreeable to his will, and fit for them to receive in their station, and for advancing his glory

and kingdom therein, they shall be done for them, being sought in faith, were they never so difficult, never so many for number, and never so frequently needed. And it is comprised in this general truth, that it may take in not only that particular of power to do these great works, but all other things also which believers may need. 2. This promise contains not only a proof of his Mediatorship and his success therein in obtaining what is sought in his name, and a proof of his love to them in his absence, by giving them occasion to believe their own eyes in his answers, but a proof of his godhead also; partly, in that none can be Mediator betwixt God and man but he who is true God as well as man; and partly, because he promiseth to be not only a Mediator to procure but a God to act and work these things, and that hereby God shall be glorified in him, as working in and with him, by reason of the unity of essence.

DOCTRINES.

1. As they who are sensible of Christ's bodily absence in heaven will send many messengers of prayer thither where he is gone, so prayer is a special mean whereby we may know much of Christ's deity, and of his love in his absence; for here he recommends asking as that which they will be put unto, and that whereby they may know what he is. So that it is no wonder that those who neglect prayer do fall into many mistakes of Christ.

2. True faith and prayer are inseparable companions, as being begotten together, so that faith begins its life in crying to God, and as growing up together, mutually straightening and setting one another on work, till at last they end together, faith resolving in sight, and prayer in uninterrupted praise; therefore are they conjoined here, to believe on him, and, to ask in his name.

3. True prayer is conjoined with and floweth from a sense of indigency setting the supplicant on work to his duty with earnestness and humility as a needy beggar; for so much doth the word rendered to ask import in the original; and where this is not in some measure, men do but what they can to mock God in prayer.

4. Prayer must be offered up to God in the name of the Mediator Christ; it is through him we must go to God, and our encouragement in pleading and our hope of acceptance must be grounded on his merit and intercession, and on the Father's love to him and to sinners in him; for this is the description of true prayer, what ye ask in my name.

5. The Lord alloweth and requireth frequency and multiplicity of employments to be put upon him by prayer; and let us put him to it never so often and for never so many things, he will never weary of it, but rather will suspend us in what we ask because we ask not enough; for so much is imported in this general truth, " whatsoever ye shall ask," even all that we would have Christ doing for us, as is after cleared.

6. It is the will of Christ that supplicants who come to the Father through him be not discouraged with the difficulty or seeming impossibility of what they need and ask according to his will, but that they expect to obtain that by prayer

which they cannot effectuate any other way; for so much also is imported in this, " whatsoever (how difficult soever it be) ye shall ask."

7. As the answer of what we ask in Christ's name is most certain, so it is Christ who is the doer thereof, and who delighteth to manifest his godhead much in dispatching the affairs of his people; for saith he, " whatsover ye shall ask in my name, that will I do."

8. Christ's end in answering the desires of his people is the setting forth of his own and his Father's glory, which as it may encourage us to expect he will do that which will thus glorify his Father and him, so it should teach us to glorify him in observing his power and good?will in answering, and to improve what we receive to his glory; for saith he, " that will I do, that the Father may be glorified in the Son."

9. As Christ is glorified in his doing for his people, so is the Father glorified in him, as being true in his testimony concerning him, and as being in him working these things; for " the Father is glorified in the Son."

10. Albeit believers have many jealousies concerning the answer of their prayers, yet they are all without ground, and it is most certain their desires will be granted; therefore doth he again repeat the promise, ver. 14, intimating that they need such confirmations, and that this is a word he will not recal.

11. It is not enough to be sure of the answer of our prayers, or that we do receive them, unless we see much of Christ's heart and activity therein; for this cause it is again repeated, " I will do it."

Ver. 15. *If ye love me, keep my commandments.*

Followeth the first argument of consolation against their heart-trouble, contained in a promise of sending the Comforter, even the Holy Spirit, unto them; and because of the riches thereof, and because the other consolations are improven by receiving of the Spirit, therefore this purpose is largely insisted on, to ver. 27, in this order :—1. He presseth upon them their duty towards him in his absence, especially that they may attain this promised Comforter, ver. 15. 2. He subjoins the promise of the Comforter, ver. 16, 17. 3. He insists upon several benefits which they shall reap by enjoying of this Comforter, ver. 18—26.

In this verse, he enjoins them their duty in his absence; that they should love him, and evidence the same by observation of his commandments. And by this direction, partly, he corrects their fond way of expressing love to him, by doting on his bodily presence, and sorrowing immoderately for his absence; partly, he prescribes a remedy and antidote against their heart-trouble, by diversion or revulsion, in turning the stream of their affection, which bred this heart-trouble, into the channel of diligence about duty; and partly, he sets them on the right way of attaining the promised Comforter, as the connexion with the following verse imports : " Keep my commandments. And I will pray," &c. Whence learn—

1. It is the character of every true disciple of Christ that they do love their Lord and Master; for so is supposed here as their duty and practice, " Ye love me." (See 1 Cor. xvi. 22.)

2. The love of disciples to Christ must not and will not be obstructed by his seeming hard dispensations, nor quenched by his absence; for though he be now to remove, yet he supposeth they have and will have love to him, " Ye love me."

3. Love to Christ must not be said only, nor will it lie lurking in the heart, but must and will break forth in proofs and evidences of itself; therefore Christ requires a proof of their love, " If ye love me, keep my commandments."

4. True love to Christ may sometimes be so overpowered with unbelief, haste, and our impetuous passions, as the proofs thereof, how vehement soever, yet are not so right as becomes; therefore is there need of direction how to evidence their love, in opposition to the proofs they gave thereof.

5. Obedience to the commandments is the true touchstone and evidence of love to Christ; and in Christ's absence they do not evidence such pure love to him who are ready to lie down and die through discouragement, as they who are most at their work, and are most busy about his errands; for by this doth he try them, and this doth he recommend as an evidence of love in his absence, " If ye love me, keep my commandments."

6. True obedience must flow not only from the fear of God but from love and sense of our obligation to Christ also, and disciples will look on commandments and give them obedience as very sweet for his sake; therefore also doth he presuppose love to him as a principle of obedience, and recommends the commandments to be observed as his, " keep my commandments."

7. To be much about duty and service in obedience to Christ's commandments is a very present diversion and cure of heart-trouble, which is but fed with idle discouragement; and it is the way to a more perfect cure, which cannot be expected by lazy droopers; for this direction is both a cure in itself, and fits them for obtaining the following promise, as hath been said in opening up of the words.

Ver. 16. *And I will pray the Father, and he shall give you another Comforter, that he may abide with you for ever;*

17. *Even the Spirit of truth; whom the world cannot receive, because it seeth him not, neither knoweth him: but ye know him; for he dwelleth with you, and shall be in you.*

In these verses is contained the argument of consolation itself and the promise of the Spirit, which is subjoined to the former direction as a fruit following thereupon, and as an encouragement against the difficulties they would meet with in doing their duty; not that formerly they were wholly destitute of the Spirit, but that now they were to receive him in more ample

measure. The gift promised is here described :—
1. From the way of his coming: Christ intercedes with the Father, and he sends him, not secluding the Son as God, from whom he proceeds, and who also sends him from the Father, chap. xv. 26 ; xvi. 7 ; though here he speak only of himself as Mediator. 2. From his titles, taken from his office and work in believers ; he is a " Comforter," and " Advocate," as the word also is rendered, 1 John, ii. 1, and " another Comforter," as being a distinct person from the Father and the Son, and working comfort in believers in a distinct way of applying Christ's purchase to them, and sealing and bearing witness to it in them ; he is likewise called " the Spirit of truth," ver. 17, not only in his own essence but in his operation in believers, leading them in all truth ; of which afterward, ver. 26, and chap. xvi. 13. 3. From his permanency in believers, that he will abide with them for ever, and not depart from them, as Christ took away his bodily presence. 4. From the singularity of the gift, as being peculiar to believers ; for the world cannot receive him because of their ignorance ; but they having knowledge of him by his begun presence, their knowledge and communion shall be continued and augmented. By " the world," here we are not to understand only those who are eminent in it, or all without the church, but all who are of the world, in the state of nature, and addicted to the world and under the power of sin. And while it is said, the world cannot receive him, it holds true of reprobates whom the Lord hath determined to leave in their woeful natural condition, that they can never receive the Spirit of regeneration, nor any comfort flowing therefrom, though they be partakers of the common and even extraordinary gifts of the Spirit. But if we take " the world" more generally, for men in the state of nature (whereof there may be many elect), the meaning is, that they cannot receive him—to wit, so long as they continue in that state, and till he translate them ; far less are they capable of such a gift in the increase thereof, (which is the thing here promised,) more than a dead man is capable of nourishment. Though in this place he seemeth chiefly to point at the reprobate world, who are of the world, and continue so ; and albeit the promise be made particularly to the apostles, and they had the accomplishment thereof in a singular way, yet the encouragement is to be extended to all believers who find the Spirit a " Comforter" and "Spirit of truth" to them, though not in so extraordinary a manner.

From verse 16, learn—1. None can expect the consolations of Christ by his Spirit unless they testify their love to him by obedience ; and they who do so have his word, whereupon they may expect needful comfort ; for upon these terms mentioned, ver. 15, " I (saith he) will pray the Father, and he will give you another Comforter."

2. Christ's bodily presence was a great comfort to his disciples, and during the time of his converse with them he was so tender of them, so kind to them, and took such burthen and care of them, as did much refresh and ease them ; for while he promiseth " another Comforter," instead of himself, it intimates he had been a " Comforter" himself. Hence it was that he would not let them fast, nor did put hard burthens on them, but let them see his glory preached sweetly unto them, and went betwixt them and all difficulties.

3. Christ doth not remove one Comforter from his people but he will give another and make up their loss ; for when he is to remove " another Comforter" is promised.

4. As disciples can have no true comfort but by the Spirit, so a large measure thereof is allowed them to supply the want of Christ's bodily presence ; for he is the " Comforter" during Christ's absence—namely, in a larger measure than they had before.

5. Whatever be the operations of the Spirit of Christ in believers, yet the scope of all his employments and his exercising of them tend in the end to comfort them ; therefore gets he this style of a " Comforter" in relation to them.

6. The Spirit of God in believers is not only a Comforter to plead, apply, and bear in the consolations of God, purchased by Christ, upon their hearts ; but is their Advocate also, who pleads their cause with God, by furnishing them with prayers and groans that cannot be uttered, to be put up in the hands of Christ, the Mediator of intercession ; for the " Comforter" is the " Advocate" also, as the word imports. (See Rom. viii. 26, 27.)

7. The Holy Ghost is a person in the godhead distinct from and equal with the Father and the Son ; for he is "another Comforter," distinct from the Son, and equal with him, in that he is a " Comforter" also, as he is ; and he is given by the Father, and so distinct from him ; and his giving or sending him is no note of superiority, nor being sent, of inferiority, (for equals may send one another,) but it only points at the order of the persons in their substance and operation ; and so, as the Holy Spirit proceeds from the Father and the Son, so he is given by both in their order of subsistence to believers.

8. In expecting this great promise of the " Comforter," believers ought not to look to their own merits or the worth of their obedience, which can promise no such thing, but their eye must be fixed on the free grace of God, who doth freely gift his Spirit to his own ; for albeit a duty be required of them who expect this mercy, ver. 15, yet saith he, " the Father shall give you another Comforter."

9. As it is Christ's work in heaven to intercede for his people and to procure their comforts, notwithstanding the sinfulness and shortcoming of their prayers, and the difficulty of things desired ; and therefore he should be acknowledged in all the comforts they receive, as minding them in heaven ; so in particular the Spirit, who is the great Comforter, is conferred upon them through his mediation, which is the channel through which free grace runs out towards sinners ; for " I will pray the Father, and he shall give you another Comforter."

10. Albeit many, yea, all the outward comforts of believers are movable, yet the Holy Spirit is given unto them without reversion, and is an abiding consolation and Comforter for all times and all cases ; for he is given, " that he may

abide (and abide a Comforter, answerable to his name) with you for ever."

From verse 17, learn—1. As the Spirit of God is true, yea, truth itself in his essence and person, so is he true in his office of Comforter to believers, all his consolations being solid and real, and free of delusion ; for the Comforter is " the Spirit of truth."

2. As the Holy Ghost is the revealer of truth, so he comforts by the word of truth, and by leading believers to rely thereupon ; for thus is he the " Spirit of truth" leading men to the word of truth, and making it effectual for their comfort, so that without the word there is no enjoying of the Spirit of Christ.

3. As the gift of the Spirit in his special dispensations is very rare, so it will add to the commendation of this encouragement if we study the singularity thereof, and what a difference the Lord puts therein betwixt his own and the world; therefore is he commended from this, the world cannot receive him, but ye know him. So also are other mercies commended and to be studied, Psalm cxlvii. 19, 20 ; Deut. iv. 7, 8.

4. The world and natural men are great strangers to the Spirit of Christ ; they are not capable of such a gift, nor do they desire after it, but believers live on hid manna to them ; for he is " the Spirit of truth ; whom the world cannot receive."

5. As the Spirit of Christ, where he is received, bringeth light and knowledge along with him, so the reason why he is so little desired is because he is so little known, and what sweetness is to be had in enjoying of him. And so it rubs no indignity on him that the world desireth him not ; for that which is subjoined, " because it seeth him not, neither knoweth him," is both a cause of their not receiving him, as 1 Cor. ii. 14, and a proof that they have not received him, since they do not know him, as, on the contrary, in the end of the verse, disciples know him because he dwells with them ; their knowledge is a fruit of inhabitation. As for the two words here used of seeing and knowing, we need not be curious to put a difference betwixt them, as if the first pointed out that as they saw him not with bodily eyes so they took as little notice of his visible operations ; and the second charged upon them that they did as little understand with their hearts as they did see with their eyes ; or that the first points out their simple ignorance and not seeing of him, and the second, that since they have not seen him they do not esteem nor desire him, since knowledge must draw out affections. It sufficeth to know that by these expressions is pointed out their utter ignorance of him, and Christ prevents all curious criticisms by comprehending the contrary case of disciples in this one for both, " ye know him."

6. A cause of men's ignorance and not desiring of the Spirit is, that they are of the world, and so transformed into a conformity with those things they lust after, as they become brutish, and can neither discern nor desire what is their true excellency and happiness ; for they are " the world," and therefore cannot receive him, nor see or know him.

7. The brutish stupidity of the world will not hinder God's kindness to his own, in communicating and revealing his Spirit unto them ; nor should it hinder disciples to study to know and desire after him ; for saith he, " but ye know him ;' ye both know and desire after him.

8. No light will discover the Spirit but himself, nor can any know him but they who enjoy him ; for " ye know him ; for he dwelleth with you."

9. The Spirit's presence in believers is very intimate and familiar ; for he not only " dwelleth with you," to be assisting in what they need, but " shall be in you," as in his temple, 1 Cor. iii. 16 ; vi. 19.

10. Where the Spirit is given he will not change his dwelling ; but believers' enjoyment of him shall be blessed with constant and increasing enjoyment ; for as " he dwelleth with you," so he " shall be in you," in a more large measure and constant abode.

Ver. 18. I will not leave you comfortless : I will come to you.

Followeth, to verse 27, the third particular in this argument of consolation, wherein Christ propounds (for their encouragement) and, where need is, amplifieth several benefits which they shall reap by enjoying his Spirit. They may be reduced to six, which I shall name as I go through ; and some of them may be conceived as the Spirit's more proper work, as he is a " Comforter," as most of the first five, and the last as more peculiar to him as " the Spirit of truth," though we need not so curiously distinguish, seeing in every one of them he is both a " Comforter" and " Spirit of truth."

The first benefit (in this verse) is, that he will not leave them in their uncomfortable and orphan condition, but will come again unto them, not only in his bodily presence after his resurrection, and at the great day, but by his Spirit, as an assured pledge of his presence, till at last he return to complete their redemption. Whence learn—

1. Such is ofttimes the weakness of believers' faith, and the abundance and greatness of their discouragements, that promises must be often repeated before they can admit of them, or be comforted in them ; therefore, after the former promise of " another Comforter," he must and doth over again tell them, " I will not leave you comfortless."

2. Believers, in Christ's absence, and without him, will stand in need of great comfort, being, like orphans, exposed to deceits and injuries, unable to do for themselves, and having none to do for them, but desolate and despised, and exposed as a prey to every one ; for so is supposed here, that they are " comfortless," or orphans, as the word is.

3. Albeit believers may be such orphans in themselves, yet they have Christ's word for it that they shall not be left so, but taken up and cared for by him ; for saith he, " I will not leave you comfortless," or orphans.

4. Let believers have what they will, yet they are still orphans, and want comfort, unless it

come by the Spirit of Christ; for it is by the Spirit this is made good, " I will not leave you comfortless."

5. The Spirit, in comforting, taketh the patronage of believers as a tutor of orphans, guiding and defending them, and managing their affairs; so that they who expect his comfort must give up themselves to be led by him; for it is by his presence that they are not left orphans, but have him for a tutor.

6. Christ loves so well to be present with his people that he never withdraws his presence one way but he cometh to them another way; therefore saith he, when removing in respect to his bodily presence, " I will come to you."

7. When the Spirit cometh unto believers, Christ cometh unto them, not only because they are one in essence, but partly, because it is equivalent to his bodily presence, yea, and richly compenseth all that ever any had thereby; so that they who have the Spirit ought not to complain of his absence in that way he was present with the disciples, nor of anything the church can expect within time; and partly, because the coming of the Spirit is not to obscure Christ, or cause him to be forgotten, but to keep his memorial fresh, as if he were come again in person, of which more on chap. xvi. 14. For these causes it is, that by sending of the Spirit " I will come to you," saith he.

VER. 19. Yet a little while, and the world seeth me no more; but ye see me : because I live, ye shall live also.

The second benefit they reap by enjoying of the Spirit is a sight of Christ, while the world are to be deprived of the sight they had and abused. This was performed, not only, or so much, in their seeing him bodily after his resurrection, as in a sight of his spiritual presence coming by his Spirit, whereby he will confirm his coming to them, ver. 18, and which they shall enjoy in the present time (as the words read, " ye see me,") till they come to that everlasting and full sight in glory. The third benefit is life, whereby they are enabled to see and enjoy him, whereof he gives his own life, after his resurrection, as a pledge. Whence learn—

1. It will not suffice believers that Christ do come unto them, unless it be gifted them also to discern and see him when he is come; otherwise he may be present, and yet they want the comfort thereof, because they see him not; therefore to the former promise of his coming, ver. 18, this is added, " ye see me."

2. It is the deplorable and woeful estate of the world that when Christ is most earnest in comforting his own, they are thrust by as having nothing to do with these consolations; therefore is the encouragement guarded and amplified from the contrary state of the world: " The world seeth me no more; but ye see me."

3. Whatever manifestation of Christ contemners of him enjoy, they will be deprived of it; for they are to be deprived of what they had of his bodily presence: " The world seeth me no more."

4. Contempt of Christ doth ripen fast for a stroke; for " yet a little while, and the world seeth me no more."

5. Such as do not acknowledge Christ's coming in the flesh shall never see his coming in the Spirit; and such as despised Christ in his humiliation deserve that they should never get another sight of him to their comfort; for this also is imported in this, " the world seeth me no more," not only that they should not enjoy his bodily presence, but that they should see him no other way, as the contrary promise to the believer maketh clear.

6. It is the great misery of the wicked that they are eternally debarred from a sight of Christ in favour and mercy, though they will see him one day in terror; for so much also is imported in this general truth, " The world seeth me no more."

7. As a sight of Christ is the sweet life and happiness of believers, so it is their advantage that in saddest times, when Christ is, to outward appearance, dead and gone, and the world secluded from seeing him, yet by his Spirit they shall enjoy a sight of him, till they come to see him in glory; for, in opposition to the world, it is subjoined as their comfort, " but ye see me."

8. The Spirit of Christ is an enlivening Spirit, making believers capable of his presence; he is their present life, and a pledge of their living eternally; for it is added, as another benefit by the Spirit's coming, " ye shall live."

9. Albeit our Lord Jesus died for believers, yet it was not possible that he should be holden of death, but he rose again and liveth for ever; for it is held out as a truth after his departure through the valley of the shadow of death, " I live." (See Rev. i. 18.)

10. The life of believers is derived from Christ's life, who is our Head, communicating quickening virtue by his Spirit to all his members; and their life stands in a continual dependence upon his life, without which it cannot subsist; for " because I live, ye shall live also."

11. Christ hath made the life of believers in him as certain as it is certain he liveth, seeing by his living after his death they are absolved, and life is purchased to them, and in his exaltation he hath taken possession in their name, and stands engaged to make his members partake of his life and fulness; for so much also is imported in this, " Because I live, ye shall live also."

VER. 20. At that day ye shall know that I am in my Father, and ye in me, and I in you.

The fourth benefit redounding to them by the Comforter's coming is, that whereas they had lately bewrayed much ignorance of him, and of his unity with the Father, then they should understand the great mysteries of God's kingdom, that he is in the Father, and consequently the Father in him, and that there is a communion betwixt believers and him, and consequently the Father and them in him. This was accomplished to the apostles when the Spirit was poured out, and is, in its own measure, made good to every believer in due time. And under this is comprehended the substance of the mystery of redemption, that there is an essential union betwixt the Father and him as God, and that as Mediator he is in the Father by dependence, and the Father in him by sustentation of his human nature under his sufferings, and by approbation, and that there is a mystical union betwixt him (who is in the Father) as Head, and all believers as members. Whence learn—

1. Albeit Christ be ofttimes little known, yea, and much misconstructed, yet it is most necessary to know him, and what his interest in the Father is; therefore it is held out as a singular fruit of the Spirit to understand this.

2. Albeit true believers may be clouded with much ignorance, yet Christ hath his time and way to make them understand the mysteries of God, to their comfort and salvation; for " at that day (when he sends the Comforter) ye shall know," though now ignorant.

3. Christ, rightly known, will be seen to be one in essence with the Father, and consequently approven of him, and he in whom the Father is to be found; and to know this is the great encouragement of believers; for it is held out as their encouragement, " Ye shall know that I am in the Father."

4. It exceedingly adds to the comfort of believers to know that Christ, who is one with the Father, hath also a mystical union and communion with them, so that God and sinners tryst [meet] together in Christ, who is in both, though in a different manner; for this completes the encouragement, " Ye shall know that I am in the Father, and ye in me, and I in you.'

5. The communion betwixt Christ and believers is mutual, they being in him by faith and needy dependence, and he in them by his Spirit, as the root of their spiritual being, and to make all his fulness forthcoming for them; for it is " ye in me, and I in you."

6. The communion betwixt Christ and believers is very near and intimate, so that there can be no separation, and the fruits and comfort of it must be very real; therefore is it called a being " in" one another.

7. Believers may have an intimate communion with Christ, who yet stand in need to be made to know that it is so; for this communion is true for the present, " I am in the Father, and ye in me," &c., and yet the knowledge of it is but to come, Ye shall know in that day; so that it is a great privilege to know our privileges already received.

VER. 21. He that hath my commandments, and keepeth them, he it is that loveth me : and he that loveth me shall be loved of my Father, and I will love him, and will manifest myself to him.

The fifth benefit (the same in substance with some of the former) is, that they shall be beloved of the Father and him, and in testimony thereof he will manifest himself to them. This he illustrates and amplifies from their duty, and the qualification required in Christ's disciples—namely, that they evidence love to him by their respect to his commandments, which, as he had formerly

inculcated, ver. 15, as the way to obtain the Comforter, so he presseth it over again as the mean to attain to those benefits which they were to reap by the Spirit's presence. Whence learn—

1. When Christ is most sweetly comforting his people it is not his mind they should be emboldened to cast off duty thereby, but rather that they be encouraged to duty, as the way to clear their right to these comforts, and to assure them that what they receive is not a delusion, nor are they abusing it; therefore doth he again, in the midst of these consolations, put them in mind of duty and of the evidences of true love to him.

2. Christ is a Lawgiver to give commandments to his people, and who renders them sweet by coming from him who hath evidenced so much love to sinners, and by so imposing them evidenceth that he knoweth their burthen and is ready to take employment to enable them to obedience; for he owneth the rule of believers' duty as his law, " my commandments."

3. As variety of duties are imposed upon believers, so it is the will of Christ that none of them be slighted, and that none please themselves in observing one or more, when yet they lay others aside; for he requires a duty in reference to his commandments, even all of them. (See Ps. cxix. 6.)

4. Christ's commandments are not entertained as they ought, except when there is an endeavour of actual obedience thereunto; for he requireth it of the approven man, that he " keep my commandments."

5. None can make conscience of obedience as becometh unless they first know their duty, and unless they have a high estimation of the authority of the law and excellency of the thing commanded; for it is required, that first they have the commandments, by knowing them in their judgment, and by keeping them in their heart as a precious jewel, and then they will keep them, and testify their respect thereto by having them still in their eye, and regulating all their practice thereby. (See Ps. cxix. 11.)

5. Albeit many loose professors pretend love to Christ who yet neglect their duty, yet, in Christ's account, none do truly love him but those who make conscience of obedience; therefore, to refute all such delusions, he saith again, " He (and he only) that hath my commandments, and keepeth them, he it is that loveth me."

7. Albeit we be unprofitable servants, when we have done all, Luke, xvii. 10, yet, of free grace through Christ, obedience will not want a reward; as here he promiseth.

8. To get more confirmation and evidences of the love of God in Christ is a rich reward and encouragement unto duty, and this every tender walker is sure of; for this is the promise here.

9. As the love of God in Christ doth prevent our love and obedience, so it is his will that the sensible manifestations and refreshful proofs thereof be drawn out by us in the way of obedience and diligent use of means; for this is the order here : " He that loveth me shall be loved of my Father ;" not as if our love begun first, 1 John, iv. 10, but that his love setting them on work to obedience, and begetting love in them,

as it did prevent them, so it will give them a rich meeting.

10. As the love of God in Christ is the rich allowance of obedient believers, whatever they get beside, so his conferring of his Spirit upon them is a rich evidence of his love ; for that the Father and Son loveth them is evidenced by the sending of the Spirit unto them, as the scope of this whole purpose teacheth. So doth it also prove sonship, Gal. iv. 6.

11. Christ is so acceptable to the Father, that whoever respect him are beloved of the Father, and his love and the Father's do still concur, so that who is beloved of the one is beloved of the other; therefore saith he, " He that loveth me shall be loved of my Father, and I will love him."

12. Christ's love to his people consists not in empty compliments, but in real manifestations of good will ; for " I will love him, and will manifest myself to him."

13. As Christ alloweth special manifestations of himself upon his own, by lifting up the light of his countenance upon them, by intimating his good will unto them, his fulness and righteousness for them, so this unto a believer is above any evidence of his love beside ; therefore is this given as the proof of his love to them, " I will manifest myself unto him." (See Ps. iv. 6, 7 ; xxvii. 4.)

14. As only believers and tender walkers are capable of special manifestations of Christ, so their tender walking is so far from obscuring of Christ that the more tender they are they will need more of Christ, his good will and righteousness, to be manifested to them, to cover them and the defects which they will discover in their walking; for even a keeper of the commandments needs this encouragement, " I will manifest myself to him."

15. Christ can be known only by his own light, and until he manifest himself believers will remain ignorant of him, and be ready to mistake him; for this cause, saith he, " I will manifest myself."

Ver. 22. Judas saith unto him, not Iscariot, Lord, how is it that thou wilt manifest thyself unto us, and not unto the world?

In this and the two following verses this their duty and encouragement is further insisted on, by occasion of Judas's question, who is declared not to be the traitor, but a good man, the brother of James the son of Alphæus, and the penman of that epistle of Jude, as appears from the first verse thereof, and who also is called Lebbæus, Matt. x. 3, with Luke, vi. 16. He, in this verse, hearing of the former promise, desireth to be informed how Christ would manifest himself to them and not to the world ; which is to be understood not only of this manifestation, and the way of it, in itself, and that Judas, being acquainted only with bodily manifestation, wondereth how Christ should shew himself to his own and the world not see him; but chiefly, he desireth hereby to be informed of the cause and reason why the Lord makes that difference in his special mani-

festations. And we are to conceive that his desire in this floweth not so much from any undervaluing thoughts of grace, as if it were not rich enough for all the world, nor yet from any low esteem of himself and the rest, making him wonder why they are admitted to this favour, when others, no worse than they in themselves, are secluded, as from some pride and conceit of somewhat in themselves, differencing them from others, to which he desireth Christ's assent ; as may be gathered from Christ's neglecting to answer directly to his question. Whence learn—

1. It is the will of God that neither the wicked be honoured nor the godly disgraced, but that honest men should be known and reputed such, and that traitors be accounted what they are; therefore, mentioning Judas, he guards that it was not Iscariot, that none should brand this honest man because he was of the same name.

2. Christ's disciples may find many difficulties in his doctrine which will put them to many questions; as here we see, comparing it with the practice of some of the rest, even in this same chapter.

3. All doubts and difficulties, wherewith disciples are puzzled, ought to be put up to Christ for resolution, as here Judas's practice doth teach.

4. Ignorance and carnal conceptions of the things of God breed many difficulties in things that otherwise are very clear ; for so " how is it that thou wilt manifest?" &c., may relate to his conceit of a bodily manifestation, which makes it a difficulty to him how a difference can be made ; though the other interpretation seem to reach the scope better.

5. There is a real difference put by Christ betwixt the world and his own in the matter of special manifestations ; for so is here imported.

6. Albeit there be no cause in the creature why Christ should make this difference, yet even good men, when privileges and mercies are heaped upon them, are ready to dream of some inherent worth in themselves preferring them above others; for so much doth this question teach, " How is it that thou wilt manifest thyself unto us, and not unto the world?"—that is, not only, What way wilt thou take that the one shall see thee and not the other? but, What moveth thee to make the difference? wherein he desireth somewhat from Christ, to confirm him in a conceit of some worth in them.

Ver. 23. Jesus answered and said unto him, If a man love me, he will keep my words : and my Father will love him, and we will come unto him, and make our abode with him.

24. He that loveth me not keepeth not my sayings : and the word which ye hear is not mine, but the Father's which sent me.

In these verses we have Christ's answer upon this question ; wherein—1. He repeats his doctrine concerning their duty, asserting again that love to him will draw men to keep his words and obey them. 2. He repeats and enlargeth the former encouragement, assuring them that the

Father and he will love such, and that his manifestation of himself shall be by his Father's and his coming to make abode with them. 3. He amplifieth this their duty from the contrary, ver. 24, that disobedience to the word argueth that there is no love to him, and that this is a heinous sin, and will obstruct these comfortable promises, seeing the word, which they observe not, is the Father's as well as his. Now for the scope of this answer, in relation to Judas's question, we find not that Christ doth directly answer to his question, either as to the way of this manifestation, or cause of this difference in it; only, as by his propounding the matter in general, he curbs him for appropriating that privilege to themselves only, so by repeating and amplifying the former doctrine he leads them from inquiring about others to see to themselves, and from studying the secret counsel of God, and causes of his dispensations, to study the means that God hath appointed for attaining communion with himself, and to abhor the contrary evils, because of the sinfulness thereof, and because they would deprive them of so great a mercy.

From verse 23, learn—1. Albeit Christ be very tender of his people yet he will not cherish them in their folly and humours, nor satisfy their curiosity or conceit; therefore doth he so much waive his question in this answer.

2. It is a great fault when disciples become curious priers into the case of others, and the secret counsel of God and causes thereof, neglecting what is commanded, and turning idle in the point of duty; for this is the fault Christ finds in his question, that it imports so much idleness as needs the enforcing of duty, and terrifying from disobedience; as, indeed, much idleness in the point of real duty makes but too much work about what we have nothing to do withal.

3. Whatever be Christ's tender condescendence to his people, yet he will not lay aside his sovereignty over them, nor exempt them from duty; for notwithstanding all his encouragements, yet he still insists upon the necessity of love and obedience if they would partake of his comforts.

4. A true lover of Christ is faithful to him and his interests, and what he commits to him in his word he will carefully observe, in his understanding, affection, and practice; for "If a man love me, he will keep my words."

5. Christ will never recal nor make void what he hath promised for the encouragement of his own, and whosoever love him shall find themselves richly recompensed in his and the Father's free love; therefore saith he again, "And my Father will love him"—to wit, in, and with, and through me.

6. Where God loveth any, both the Father and Son will keep a sweet and intimate fellowship with them, and will be at pains to make up the distance; for "we will come unto him," &c.

7. God and Christ's fellowship with believers is constant, for all times and all difficulties, till they be taken up to be with him for ever; for we will "make our abode with him."

From verse 24, learn—1. It may stir up believers to their duty when they consider the great sin and loss of disobeyers; therefore is this illustrated, by propounding the contrary sin, which imports the contrary hazard of being deprived of fellowship with God.

2. Disobedience to Christ, and want of love to him, are inseparably conjoined, let men pretend what they will; for "He that loveth me not keepeth not my sayings."

3. It aggravates the sin of disobedience that the gospel is the very word of God, both the Father's and the Son's; therefore doth he set out their sin from this: "The word which you hear is not mine, (to wit, as he is man, or his alone as he is God,) but the Father's which sent me."

4. Obedience to the commandments of God is not required as a simple act of love and courtesy, but as a testimony of subjection to divine authority; and those who will not study love to Christ that they may obey him, ought to look to the authority of God, which will not be vilipended [despised]; therefore is the authority of the word thus held out to despisers, as also to guard believers that they be not driven from their duty by the fear of men; "The word which ye hear is not mine, but the Father's which sent me."

Ver. 25. These things have I spoken unto you, being yet present with you.

26. But the Comforter, which is the Holy Ghost, whom the Father will send in my name, he shall teach you all things, and bring all things to your remembrance, whatsoever I have said unto you.

The sixth benefit which they shall reap by the Spirit is instruction and teaching, as he is the Spirit of truth; and that, however Christ had taught them all things necessary, and yet they continued rude and incapable, and his doctrine was very dark to them, as appeareth by the many questions they had lately started, ver. 5, 8, 22, yet the Holy Ghost should effectually and clearly teach them all things, and bring to remembrance what he had spoken, but they, through ignorance, negligence, or sorrow, had forgotten. It is not needful for us to determine whether these " all things" to be taught by the Spirit be the same with those " all things," which Christ had said, which the Spirit not only brings to remembrance, but doth make them plain unto them, or whether, beside what Christ had said, and the Spirit brings to remembrance, some particulars were remitted to the Spirit's immediate and extraordinary teaching of the apostles, as chap. xvi. 12, 13; for in this it sufficeth us to know that these " all things," be what they will, were revealed to the apostles for the good of the church, and by them to the church in writing; so that there is no room left for traditions, or extraordinary and immediate revelations; nor is it to be expected that the Spirit, which brings Christ's doctrine to remembrance as true and excellent, will reveal and teach any new thing contrary to what Christ said, which were to make the Spirit contradict himself. Yet if we consider the matter narrowly, we shall find that the scripture warrants us rather to assert that these "all things" which the Spirit taught them were the same which Christ had said; for, chap. xv. 15, Christ made known to them all that he had heard of his Father—namely, which is necessary for the church to know, and Acts, i. 3, Christ, after his resurrection, continued with them forty days, instructing them, and " speaking of the things pertaining to the kingdom of God," and that so fully, as their commission is limited to whatsoever he had already commanded them, Matt. xxviii. 20. It is true, the apostle, 1 Cor. vii. 12, 25, 40, mentions somewhat wherein he gave direction, being guided by the Spirit, to which the Lord had not so expressly spoken; but in that he relates especially to things that had not been determined in the law of Moses, not to what Christ had said; and however it be, these particulars are not sufficient to make so general a distinction betwixt the expressions. And so here is held forth a twofold work of the Spirit in reference to Christ's doctrine:—1. Whereas Christ had revealed to them the sum of all Christian religion, and yet they were not capable thereof, therefore the Spirit was sent to enlighten their understanding, and to explain those things more fully and distinctly which Christ had spoken summarily, as they were able to hear them; and of this is that to be understood, chap. xvi. 2, not of any new doctrine or articles of faith, but of the more distinct explication of what he had delivered. '2. The Spirit by this teaching did bring to the apostles' remembrance, for their further confirmation, that these things had been spoken by Christ, though then they did not understand them, and afterwards forgat them, as chap. ii. 22; xii. 16.

DOCTRINES.

1. The seed of the word may be sown, whereof yet no visible fruit may appear for a time; as here is to be seen in Christ's speaking to the disciples, who for a time were not much (if at all) bettered by it.

2. The word of the Lord may not be operative and fruitful, even in the godly, for a time, and when they first hear it, which yet afterward may do much good; for Christ soweth the seed among the disciples, which yet took not effect till the Spirit was poured out, and then it did good.

3. The efficacy of the word doth not always accompany the outward ministry, nor doth it depend upon the ability and liveliness of the teacher, unless the Spirit do accompany it in the hearts of hearers; for albeit even Christ (considered as an outward teacher) spake these things, being present with them, yet the " Comforter" is needed to make them effectual.

4. It is the Holy Spirit only who makes the ministry and outward teaching effectual, and who, where he cometh, doth freely, fully, and effectually make the word plain and lively to believers; for albeit Christ's ministry took not effect in them at first, yet here is the remedy—the Comforter shall teach you. He is a remedy against gross ignorance and error, against our not making progress in knowledge, against our ignorance and inadvertence through astonishment in trouble, and against our perplexities through the multitude of dark steps in our path.

All which should stir us up to seek after and entertain such a teacher.

5. As the Spirit is the great Comforter of his church, particularly by his teaching, which all tends to their comfort, so he is a Comforter to none to whom he is not also a Sanctifier; for the Comforter is the Holy Ghost, in respect of his sanctifying operation.

6. The special benefits (and particularly the Spirit) bestowed upon believers are given through the mediation of Christ, and serve to be tokens of his love and remembering them in his kingdom; for saith he, the Father will send him in my name.

7. The apostles were fully instructed by the Spirit in all things pertaining to the kingdom of God, so that in the matter of religion nothing is to be hearkened unto beside or contrary to that which God revealed to them, and by them to the church; for " he shall teach you all things."

8. The true Spirit of Christ taught the apostles no other thing but what Christ had said unto them; nor doth he teach believers anything but what Christ hath taught by his prophets, himself, and his apostles; for these " all things" which he shall teach, are " all things whatsoever I have said unto you," as hath been cleared.

9. Christ's disciples are frequently subject to forgetfulness of what Christ saith unto them; occasioned partly by their ignorance, chap. xii. 16; partly, by the little interest and felt need they have of what the word saith; partly, by their slothful negligence, being taken up with other things; and partly, by their trusting to their own understanding and memory; therefore need they to have all things brought to remembrance.

10. The ignorance, dulness, and forgetfulness of disciples doth lose them many a fair opportunity, and would irrecoverably deprive them of fair advantages, if mercy prevented it not; for Christ, their wealth, is away before they knew what it meant, and they are left ignorant and forgetful of what he had taught.

11. Such as are humbled under the sense of their ignorance, and do seek after and entertain the presence of the Spirit, will find him a remembrancer of saving truths, which they have heard, as they need them; for he shall " bring all things to your remembrance, whatsoever I have said unto you."

VER. 27. Peace I leave with you, my peace I give unto you : not as the world giveth, give I unto you. Let not your heart be troubled, neither let it be afraid.

Christ being now about to close this exhortation and part of his farewell sermon, doth in this verse point out the sixth argument of consolation —namely, his peace, as a result of all the rest, which, both in its own nature and donation, differeth far from the world's peace. And upon this he repeats the exhortation propounded ver. 1, and so goeth on to the conclusion of this part of his discourse. Whence learn—

1. Christ's disciples are allowed true peace in all dispensations, to uphold their hearts, so that whatever their outward trouble be, yet they may

have peace with God, Rom. v. 1, quiet under all dispensations, and an ordering of outward afflictions, so as they need not mar their peace; for peace is his allowance here.

2. True peace is Christ's peace, as being the purchaser thereof, the object in whom they have it, chap. xvi. 33, and he who gifts it; therefore calls he it, "my peace."

3. Christ's peace doth not depend upon his bodily presence, but may be continued when he is gone, and is an antidote to supply that want and loss; for when he is to remove, " Peace, I leave with you," saith he.

4. Whatever be the believers' unworthiness, or not deserving of peace, yet it may answer all objections that it is Christ's legacy and free gift; for " peace I leave with you, my peace I give unto you."

5. The excellency of Christ's legacies, and the privileges enjoyed by his people, ought to be studied as far transcending what they enjoy at their best who do not come to him; therefore doth he make the comparison betwixt the world's peace and his.

6. Christ's peace is far different from the peace which is given or enjoyed by the world, for that is ofttimes in sin, or is but a lethargy of security portending sad trouble, or but (at best) a freedom from outward trouble when yet they are at enmity with God; but his peace is solid and true peace; therefore saith he, " not as the world giveth, give I unto you."

7. Christ's peace doth also differ from the world's peace in the way of giving it; they ofttimes give words of peace without reality, but he is real in what he saith; they may wish peace when they cannot give it, but his peace is real and effectual, Job, xxxiv. 29; they cannot perpetuate any peace they afford or wish, but his peace is firm, and he preserveth his people in it. This also is imported in these words, " not as the world giveth, give I unto you."

8. The heart-trouble wherewith saints are ofttimes exercised is ready to beget many heart-terrors and fears for the future; for here heart-trouble and being afraid go together.

9. Christ may be dealing very comfortably with his people when yet their perplexities and fears do continue and lie on; for as at the beginning, ver. 1, so here, after all his sweet discourse, their distemper continueth; their heart is troubled, and it is afraid.

10. As there is no true cure of heart-troubles and fears but in Christ, so his consolations and peace are sufficient to guard the heart against them all; so that saints, having this allowance, cannot without sin continue in their perplexities; therefore, after all these consolations, and particularly that of his peace, he repeats the exhortation, as a duty which they cannot decline, " Let not your heart be troubled, neither let it be afraid."

Ver. 28. Ye have heard how I said unto you, I go away, and come again unto you. If ye loved me, ye would rejoice, because I said, I go unto the Father: for my Father is greater than I.

From this to the end of the chapter we have a conclusion of this part of the discourse, in prosecution of that exhortation, ver. 27, which may be reduced to two heads:—1. A reproof that they entertained not his doctrine, and particularly the news of his departure, with joy, for which he giveth two reasons, ver. 28, 29. 2. A declaration that this was his farewell sermon, and therefore to be better hearkened unto, ver. 30, 31.

In this verse is contained—1. The sum of what he is now teaching them, to wit, concerning his departure and return again to them. 2. The use they should have made even of the saddest part of this doctrine concerning his departure—namely, not to be grieved and troubled, as they were, but rather to rejoice. 3. What the want of this evidenced in them, even the want of such love to him as became them, which would have made them rejoice. 4. The first reason why they would rejoice if they had loved him—namely, because he went to the Father, who is greater than he, (not as God, but as man and Mediator, and in his present state of humiliation,) and therefore his exaltation out of his estate of humiliation into glory with the Father should have made them rejoice, especially considering that this his exaltation tended to their advantage.

DOCTRINES.

1. It is needful that disciples consider seriously what they hear, and that for this end needful doctrines be frequently repeated and inculcated upon them; therefore doth Christ put them in mind what they had heard; " Ye have heard how I said unto you," &c.

2. Saints are not to pore only on what is sad in Christ's doctrine or dealing, but to study also what lenitives he allows to sweeten the other; therefore, with his going, which is bitter, he mentions his return, which is as sweet, " Ye have heard how I said unto you, I go away, and come again unto you."

3. Albeit there were no other encouragement by the way, during Christ's absence, yet the hope of his coming again might allay the grief of his departure; therefore it is subjoined, as a sufficient lenitive, " I go away, and come again unto you."

4. Not only Christ's sweet dispensations, but even the hardest trials of saints, and his most sharp dispensations to them, afford matter of joy if rightly studied; therefore doth he pitch upon the saddest of it, and urge it as matter of joy: " ye would rejoice, because I said, I go unto the Father." (See James, i. 2.)

5. Christ by departing out of the world is exalted unto a more glorious estate than that in which he was during his abode on earth; for so is imported in that he goeth unto the Father, who is greater than he; whereby, as man and Mediator, he is advanced to be next in glory to the Father, and as God he layeth aside that veil under which he appeared in his state of humiliation, and lets out that glory which he had with the Father before the world was, John, xvii. 5.

6. The exaltation of Christ is a ground of much joy to believers, as being, not only his advancement, but an evidence that he hath accomplished all things for which he came into the world, and a pledge that he will execute his offices in a more

glorious way for their good; for this is matter of joy, "I go unto the Father: for my Father is greater than I."

7. It is the great fault of believers that they choose rather to carp at Christ's dealing than to study matter of encouragement in it, and that their self-love (desiring to be much humoured and pleased) doth mar all right use of his dispensations; therefore doth he give them a mild challenge, that their desire to enjoy his bodily presence had marred the joy they might have gathered at his departure.

8. Saints may seem to have much fond love to Christ, and they love to make a great stir, when yet it is not love to him, but self-love, that aileth them; therefore, albeit they thought it was love to him that so disquieted them, yet saith he, " If ye loved me, ye would rejoice," &c.

9. True love to Christ will make men submit to what honours him, how much soever it cross them; for albeit this separation might be very sad to them, yet " If ye loved me, ye would rejoice, because I said, I go unto the Father," to be exalted.

10. Albeit self-love make saints think they are upon the only way of their own good, yet, upon serious search, it will be found that in opposing Christ's will they oppose their own real good also; for his exaltation being for their advantage, they who rejoiced not at it did forsake their own mercy.

VER. 29. And now I have told you before it come to pass, that, when it is come to pass, ye might believe.

This verse contains a second reason why they ought to rejoice at this intimation of his departure to the Father—namely, that this prediction, compared with future events proving his exaltation for their good, would confirm their faith, and therefore they were bound to rejoice in whatsoever would advance faith. Whence learn—

1. It should be the great study of saints, in this vale of their pilgrimage, to acquaint themselves with believing, as that whereby Christ's bodily absence is mainly supplied, and that which will bring them the peace and joy which is allowed upon them, Rom. xv. 13; therefore doth Christ take so much pains to train and breed them, that they " might believe."

2. The scope of Christ's word to his people is to lead them to believe in him; for " now I have told you, that ye might believe."

3. Such as would rightly improve Christ's word, for feeding of faith, ought to compare his dealing with his word, and to see somewhat of him and the accomplishment of his word in everything that comes to pass; therefore he requireth that they not only hearken to what he told now " before it come to pass," but observe also what he doth " when it is come to pass."

4. The comparing of Christ's predictions with events according to the same contributes much to the confirmation of faith, as pointing out Christ's foreknowledge and providence, and the certainty of the word, which he faileth not to accomplish; therefore saith he, " Now I have told you before

it come to pass, that, when it is come to pass, ye might believe." (Compare chap. xiii. 19.)

5. Our Lord may make disciples' hard condition contribute more for their good and the strengthening of their faith than if they had not met with these conditions; therefore doth he so order it, that his departure and the consequents thereof shall contribute so much to their further confirmation.

6. True disciples ought to rejoice in whatsoever may contribute to confirm their faith, how much soever it vex them otherwise; for this is a reason why they ought to rejoice, that this intimation contributed that they " might believe."

7. Whatever be Christ's dispensations towards his people, yet he is not deficient in whatsoever is needful to encourage them to believe, and to confirm them in it; for in all these sad dispensations he was still doing what might help them to faith, that " ye might believe."

8. As there is no faith but it needs that we should grow in it, (as here the disciples, who believed, need to believe more,) so the Lord, when he gives many encouragements to believe, requires more faith of his people; for now, when he gives this new help of a prediction, and the accomplishment thereof, he requireth an answerable measure of faith, that " ye might believe" yet more.

9. Albeit we are ready to think that Christ's bodily presence were a notable help to faith, yet Christ, by his exaltation unto glory, gives such proofs of his deity and fulness, and of his minding of his people, as layeth on a stricter obligation to believe in him than any beside; so that not to believe much now is a more heinous fault than at any other time; for " when it is come to pass," and evidenced by effects, that he is gone to the Father, it is specially required then that " ye believe."

VER. 30. Hereafter I will not talk much with you: for the prince of this world cometh, and hath nothing in me.

31. But that the world may know that I love the Father; and as the Father gave me commandment, even so I do. Arise, let us go hence.

These verses contain a second branch of the conclusion of this part of his discourse; wherein he intimates that this was his farewell sermon, and that he was not to speak much after this with them, being to enter the lists with Satan at the Father's commandment. And therefore it is to be inferred (for nothing of his scope, or the use they were to make of this, is expressed here) that they were to hearken better to this discourse of their Lord and Master in taking his leave, which could not but contain matter profitable to them, (as being his last words,) and not suffer themselves to be distracted with fear and trouble. In the words there is—1. An intimation that he was shortly to break off discourse with them, being to engage in his sufferings against Satan, the prime instrumental cause therein. 2. To prevent any scandal that might arise upon his being exposed to Satan's malice, and his dying in that conflict, he declareth that he went to die, not because Satan had any power over him, or ground of challenge against him in himself, but merely that he might testify his love and obedience to the Father who laid that duty upon him. 3. To testify how willingly he obeyed this command, he declareth himself willing to go meet his enemy, and warns them to make ready to go out with him, to see his obedience acted, and withal that they might have better opportunity to shift for themselves. Now concerning this, that Christ bids them " Arise," &c., it should seem that Christ at this word arose from the communion table, and that the rest of his sermon, and the prayer, in the three following chapters, were spoken either on their feet in the same room, or in the way to the garden. But it is clear from chap. xviii. 1, that after all that, and not till then, he went forth ; and withal, it is not very probable that this his solemn sermon and prayer were delivered in a confused posture, or that Christ, continuing still in the same room, would quit the grave and composed posture wherein he. and they were sitting, and put them all to their feet to hear it out ; and therefore it seems that by this exhortation he only puts them in mind to make ready to go away when he had done ; and so goeth on with his sermon.

DOCTRINES.

1. When difficulties, to which we are called, draw near, we should make ready to go and meet them ; therefore Christ is making ready to meet with his sufferings, and intimateth that he would close his preaching for that end.

2. It should stir up believers to improve opportunities of grace, and of Christ's company, when they consider how soon they may be deprived thereof ; therefore he stirs them up to attention, by putting them in mind that they would not have opportunity to hear him much after this : " Hereafter I will not talk much with you."

3. Christ will never be so throng [occupied] but he will take leisure to speak what is needful for his needy people ; therefore, albeit he knew the Jews were making fast ready, yet he saith not, he will talk no more, but " not much," and for all the haste he goeth on to speak out his mind ; so in the midst of his sufferings he hath a look to reclaim sliding Peter, Luke, xxii 61, and a word for his mother and John, when he is on the cross, John, xix. 26, 27.

4. It is a point to be frequently studied, that Satan, through God's permission, exerciseth a tyrannical dominion among the sinful children of men, that so it may be lamented that Christ wants so much of his due ; for this cause is he so often pointed out to be " the prince of this world."

5. Christ in his sufferings for the elects' sin had to do not only with the malice and cruelty of men, but with Satan and the powers of hell, who also have chief hand in all the persecutions of the saints ; therefore doth he describe his sufferings from this cause : " The prince of this world cometh"—to wit, in and with his instruments, to use his utmost endeavours against him.

6. It may add much to the comfort of saints, that Satan and all his forces did bend and essay their strength against Christ their surety, so that if they prevailed not against him, saints may, in him, look upon them as conquered enemies ; therefore hath he recorded for our comfort that " the prince of this world cometh" against him.

7. Albeit the best of men have much within them of corruption and naughtiness, upon which Satan may fasten his tentations and suggestions, and inflame them with his fiery darts, and much guilt upon which he may accuse and foil them, if left to themselves, yet Christ being without sin, Satan had no power over him in any of these respects ; for he " hath nothing in me"—that is, his power over men came in only by sin in them, but Christ being free of sin, Satan had nothing of his own in him, either of guilt, for which to accuse him, or of corruptions, upon which to fasten his tentations and make them prevail.

8. It is believers' great advantage, that what Christ did undergo was for nothing in himself, but all for them ; therefore doth he hold out, for their comfort, he " hath nothing in me."

9. All the power, malice, and policy of Satan cannot prevail over Christ, and his followers in him, save in so far as God permitteth ; for so much also is imported in this, he " hath nothing in me," and consequently could not prevail or have power over him, unless he voluntarily yielded himself to suffer, as is after subjoined.

10. Satan is so malicious a tempter and assaulter that he will not spare even those in whom he hath no right, and against even whom he knoweth he will not succeed ; for he " cometh" against Christ, though he " hath nothing in him." And therefore they who take all his tentations for current do far mistake ; for he durst offer to call in question unto Christ himself, if he was the Son of God, Matt. iv. 6.

11. All that Christ suffered for the redemption of sinners was by the order and at the command of the Father, who did covenant with him concerning this work ; for " as the Father gave me commandment, even so I do."

12. In our going about duty and enduring of hard lots, it is good to eye the will and appointment of God, not only that we propound not wrong ends, but that we may look more to God and his mind in these lots than to men's malice and projects ; therefore doth Christ so much fasten his eye, not on Satan, but on the Father's " commandment."

13. As love to God ought to be the rise of all our obedience, so true love to him will draw men to obedience in hardest services ; for herein Christ hath cast a copy, the motive of whose suffering was love to the Father's glory : " I love the Father ; and as the Father gave me commandment, even so I do."

14. It is of singular importance and use that men do study Christ's love and obedience to the Father in his sufferings, both for admiration and delighting in it, and for imitation ; for he doth this, " that the world may know that I love the Father ; and that as the Father gave me commandment, even so I do."

15. Christ alloweth not that men say much of their love and obedience unless they prove it by practice ; therefore, after he hath professed so much of his love and obedience : " Arise,

(saith he,) let us go hence," that I may give proof thereof.

16. Christ did enter the lists, in his sufferings, with much willingness and alacrity, with much courage and resolution, that so he might commend his love to us, and encourage us to do the like through him; therefore saith he, "Arise, let us go hence," that I may grapple with the difficulty.

17. Christ was so real in his resolute undergoing of sufferings and death that he did not decline any witnesses and triers thereof; therefore saith he to them, "Arise, let us go hence," taking them out with him, not only that he being taken in the garden they might have better opportunity to flee than if he were taken in that room, but that, being with him, they might, as much as they durst, be witnesses of his willingness and courage.

CHAPTER XV.

In this chapter Christ continueth his farewell sermon to the disciples, pressing upon them that they would study communion with him by faith, whereby they might not only enjoy his presence (which they so much desired) in a spiritual manner, but also might be made fruitful, which is so acceptable to him; and more particularly insisting that they should love one another, as he had loved them; and that so much the rather, as they should meet with much hatred in the world.

So the chapter may be taken up in three parts. The first part contains an exhortation to communion with him and fruitfulness in obedience. For which end — 1. In borrowed expressions, from a vine, husbandman, and branches, he premits a general doctrine, pointing out the order of divine dispensation of spiritual things, for enabling professors to fructify, and God's answerable dealing with them, according as they declare themselves, ver. 1, 2. 2. He makes application of this to the disciples, declaring what sort of branches they were, ver. 3, and exhorting them, partly, to perseverance in communion with him, as the root and cause, from the consideration of their barrenness without him, and their fruitfulness being in him, ver. 4, 5; from their danger, if they neglect it, ver. 6, and from the advantage of access to God, if they be in him, ver. 7; and partly, unto fruitfulness as the effect, (the exhortation to which is only implied) as honouring God, and evidencing their good condition, ver. 8, and as a mean to keep them in Christ's love, ver. 9, 10. 3. By way of conclusion to this part of the chapter, he shews that his scope in all this doctrine was, not to discourage them, but to promove their constant and full joy, ver. 11.

In the second part of the chapter, having pressed fruitfulness in general, he singles out one peculiar fruit of mutual love as most necessary for them in his absence; and presseth it from his own example, ver. 12. And to enforce this— 1. He giveth evidences of his love to them, in his dying for them, ver. 13, (which is a friendship, in which they should assure themselves of an interest, ver. 14,) in communicating secrets with them, ver. 15, and in preventing them by his grace, and furnishing them with ability, in their persons and callings, to glorify him, and giving them access unto God for anything they wanted, ver. 16. 2. Upon this he repeats and enforceth the exhortation by way of conclusion, ver. 17. In the third part of the chapter he forewarns them of the hatred and persecution they were to meet with in the world, and armeth them against the same, by several arguments of consolation and encouragement, some whereof do guard them against stumbling at their own afflicted condition, and are taken from his own example and lot, ver. 18; from their good condition, which their trouble from the world evidenceth, and the inevitableness of trouble, considering they are not of the world, ver. 19; from the equity that was in exercising them with that lot, and the inevitableness thereof, considering their relation to Christ, ver. 20; and from the goodness of their cause, ver. 21. Some of them do yet further vindicate the former arguments from any exception that might be made against them; for whereas in them it is supposed that Christ was unknown and hated in the world, and they would be hated for his sake, at which his weak followers might stumble, therefore Christ propounds arguments, not only to encourage them under their sad lot, but to obviate all scandal and offence at his being hated in the world, and his followers for so good a cause—namely, that this hatred of him did evidence the miserable condition of persecutors, as being inexcusable, and haters of the Father also, ver. 22—24; that this their unjust hatred was foretold in scripture, ver. 25, and that all these unjust aspersions against him should be wiped off by the testimony of the Holy Ghost concurring with and assisting them in their ministerial testimony concerning him, ver. 26, 27.

Ver. 1. *I am the true vine, and my Father is the husbandman.*

Christ being, in the first part of this chapter, to recommend communion with himself, and fruitfulness, to his disciples, he doth (in this and the next verse) premit [introduce] a general doctrine thereunto, in borrowed terms, consisting of two branches; whereof the first (in this verse) points out the order of divine dispensation for enabling professors to fructify; that himself resembles a vine, being the vine-stock into which the branches are engrafted, and he and his members a vine with many branches; that the Father resembleth a husbandman, in his care about this vine; and that professors are as branches engrafted into him the vine, that so they may fructify, as is here supposed, and is further intimated in the next verse. Now we need not insist on the occasion or rise of this discourse, whether it was upon seeing a vine from the window of the room, or because this metaphor is very frequent in scripture, or was fit for his present purpose; nor is it convenient to insist on these borrowed expressions and comparisons further than may set out Christ's present scope, which is, that Christ is the root and fountain of his people's spiritual subsistence and fruitfulness, and that the Father hath a special hand and care about him and them for that end.

DOCTRINES.

1. Figurative expressions are neither unusual nor obscure in scripture language, whereby one thing is said to be another, though distinct in their nature and kind, and that without any transmutation of the one into the other, or annihilation of either, but because of some mystical representation and signification, or because of similitude of properties and effects; therefore doth Christ say here, " I am the vine," accounting that expression nothing obscure to his rude disciples, although he and a vine were very different things, only because it did resemble him in some respects.

2. Spiritual minds may and ought to profit much by the observation of common things, and by improving of them to spiritual use and advantage; therefore doth Christ use these borrowed terms, to teach them, whenever they observed vines, (which were plentiful in that country,) to be put in mind thereby of somewhat in Christ. And to this scope do his other parables, taken from common things, tend.

3. Christ, in his offices and relations to his people, doth most fitly resemble a vine, as being but small and weak in outward appearance in the state of his humiliation, as vines are, especially in winter; as being planted in the fat soil of the love, life, and favour of the Father, the fulness of the godhead, and the Spirit without measure, that he may have influence in abundance for all his members, as vines are planted in a fruitful soil, Isaiah, v. 2; as spending himself in fruitfulness to his people, as vines are only useful for fruit-bearing; as yielding refreshful and sweet fruit to cheer up the hearts of his people, as the vine doth for the use of man, Ps. civ. 15; as submitting to be trod in the wine-press of God's anger, that thereby fruit might redound to his people, as the fruit of the vine is pressed, that it may be drink unto men; and as being the root in which all his members must subsist, and the fountain of all their spiritual life and furniture, as the vine is to all its branches. For these, among other causes, doth Christ resemble himself unto a vine in scripture; and here, especially for the last cause, " I am the vine."

4. What Christ is unto his people that he truly and really is; whatever they look to beside for spiritual support and influence will but deceive them; and whatever excellency there be in good and necessary things, for the use of man, it is all but a shadow of that perfection which is in him for the good of his people, and what they are in their kind weakly, that he is in a more excellent way in his kind; therefore saith he, " I am the true vine;" not that he really is a vine, or that a vine is not true in its own kind, but that he, and he only, is that fountain of grace and life unto his people which is pointed at under this similitude; and that in his fulness in this kind he far outstrips the excellency of the vine in its kind.

5. As Christ, in his relations to his people, resembles the vine, so the Father in this matter resembleth a husbandman, as being the planter of this vine, and appointer of Christ to be the Head of the elect, and endowing him with sufficiency and fulness for that effect; as being also the engrafter of the branches in the stock, by bringing the elect to Christ, and giving them faith whereby they are united to him; and as testifying his love and delight in this new plantation, by caring for it, visiting, supporting, protecting, pruning, and purging it, that it may be fruitful; for these causes saith he also, " My Father is the husbandman." By which we are taught that both the Father and the Son do concur in procuring and promoving the prosperity of believers.

VER. 2. Every branch in me that beareth not fruit he taketh away : and every branch that beareth fruit, he purgeth it, that it may bring forth more fruit.

The second branch of this general doctrine points out the Father's various and answerable dispensations, as husbandman, towards professors and branches of this vine, according as, by their fruitfulness or unfruitfulness, they declare themselves to be true or counterfeit branches, and to be really, or in show only, engrafted in Christ; taking away such as are unfruitful, and purging the fruitful that they may abound in fruit. Whence learn—

1. The condition of professors is most fitly resembled to branches of a vine; as having no subsistence nor sap of themselves, but in Christ, more than branches have without a vine-stock; and as being obliged to have as strict and near conjunction with him as branches have with the tree; which they will have, if they be really engrafted in him; for these causes doth he call them branches here.

2. Professors are not all of one sort, nor are they all in Christ after one way and manner, some being only in him by external and visible communion, as being in the visible church, and externally covenanting and professing relation to him; others being also in him by faith, as having spiritual inward communion with his person; for so is here expressed, that there are branches in him which bear not fruit, and branches that bear fruit.

3. The true touchstone whereby to discern one sort of branches from another is, not their leaves or profession, but their fruit; for here the character of the one is, " Every branch in me that beareth not fruit," and of the other, " every branch that beareth fruit." And in this they fitly resemble vine-branches, which are useless if they be not fruitful. Ezek. xv. 2, &c.

4. External and fruitless branches will at last be taken away by the discovery of their hypocrisy and unsoundness, and that they have no interest in him; sometimes also by their just seclusion from church-society, and at last by their final separation from Christ; for " every branch in me that beareth not fruit he taketh

away," as the husbandman taketh away useless branches from the vine. (See ver. 6.)

5. There is no branch so fruitful but it hath many imperfections and wants; for even "every branch that beareth fruit" needeth to be purged and to "bring forth more fruit."

6. One particular imperfection in fruitful branches is, that they have many luxuriant superfluities growing up with their fruit, which hinder the increase thereof; not only a remainder of corruption, but much corruption growing up with their grace, especially when they are in a flourishing condition without exercise; therefore do they need to be purged, as vine-dressers do with luxuriant branches in vines, which grow up with their fruit.

7. Whatever be the imperfections of those who hold inward communion with Christ, yet they shall not be taken away nor separated from him, but their imperfections and frailties shall endear them to the Lord's care; for such branches shall not be taken away, but purged.

8. It is a rich blessing and reward of fruitfulness, in the godly's account, to be blessed with more fruitfulness; for this is a promise to them, it shall "bring forth more fruit."

9. However the Lord's dealing with his people may cross their humours and cut off many superfluities which are dear to them, yet he minds their real good and fruitfulness thereby; for "he purgeth it, that it may bring forth more fruit."

10. Men are then assured that the operations of the Lord's word and Spirit upon them, and the afflictions and crosses they meet with are blessed to purge them from their dross, when they abound in solid and real fruits; for when he purgeth it, it bringeth forth more fruit.

Ver. 3. Now ye are clean through the word which I have spoken unto you.

Followeth the second thing in this part of the chapter, wherein application is made of this general doctrine to the disciples' case, in a declaration and an exhortation. In this verse is contained a declaration what sort of branches they were—namely, not fruitless, but "clean" ones, that is, who, by being purged and cleansed from their superfluities, (as is promised, ver. 2,) are assured that they are fruitful branches, really and internally engrafted in Christ; and so were they regenerated, justified, and sanctified in part. This their purity is amplified from the instrumental cause or mean thereof, which is the word he had spoken to them. Whereby we are to understand, partly, that the word preached by him was believed by them, and the mean which wrought on them to come to him to be cleansed; and partly, and more particularly, because, by the general sentences already pronounced by him concerning believers in him, (such as that, John, iii. 36,) and more especially by that sentence passed in their favours, applying that general truth to them, chap. xiii. 10, they might be confirmed and assured that they were already clean and justified. Hence learn—

1. It is the duty of all professors to make sure what interest they have in Christ, and for that end to find some difference betwixt them and formal and external professors; therefore Christ, speaking of divers sorts of branches, finds it needful to assure them that they were not of the worst, but best sort, "Now ye are clean," to learn them and all others to make that sure.

2. Albeit it be the duty of professors who are doubtful of their state to study after fruitfulness in God's way, whereby at last they will come to have their interest cleared, yet it is a notable encouragement to fruitfulness if first they be assured of an interest, and they are to make much use of faith for that end; therefore doth Christ premit [introduce] this, "Ye are clean," that hereby he may make way for the following exhortation to fruitfulness.

3. Such as are indeed ingrafted in Christ are also indeed clean, not only by imputation of his righteousness, hiding all their impurity, but by sanctification also, whereby they are clean, in part, in respect of what they were, and others still in nature are, and a purification of them is begun, which will constantly be carried on till it be perfected in the day of Christ; therefore is a branch in him, verse 2, declared here to be a clean branch, "Ye are clean." And thus doth he graciously account of them, notwithstanding their many spots, whereas he would look otherwise upon a painted Pharisee.

4. As it is the work of the Spirit and of faith to apply Christ's merit and efficacy for cleansing of sinners, so his word is also instrumental therein, as being the glass wherein to see our corruption; that which sets us on work to seek purging, which discovers our remedy, and which, being hid in the heart by faith, will keep us from sin; for "Ye are clean through the word which I have spoken unto you." So that where the word is not operative on men, it is no evidence they are purged, or that what they seem to be is real.

5. Such as by faith have fled to Christ for righteousness, and are set on work by the word to study sanctification, are (by virtue of Christ's sentence pronounced in the gospel, that believers shall not be condemned, but have eternal life) actually justified and absolved from sin in God's sight, albeit as yet they have not attained to reflect upon themselves, and to know that they have believed, nor yet to partake sensibly of the seal of the Holy Spirit of promise which useth to follow after believing; for so much also is imported in this, "Ye are clean through the word which I have spoken unto you," or, the general sentences passed in favour of believers, in his doctrine to them, are theirs, and do absolve them, albeit both before and now they need to have it told to them by him.

Ver. 4. Abide in me, and I in you. As the branch cannot bear fruit of itself, except it abide in the vine; no more can ye, except ye abide in me.

5. I am the vine, ye are the branches: He that abideth in me, and I in him, the same bringeth forth much fruit: for without me ye can do nothing.

Christ by this declaration having assured them of their good estate, doth now subjoin his exhortation, wherein he doth press them to communion with him, from several arguments and considerations, to ver. 8. And because fruitfulness is the necessary effect thereof, which he aims at in the exhortation, therefore he presseth and commendeth it also, ver. 8—10.

In these verses is contained—1. The exhortation to perseverance in close communion with himself, as the root and cause of that fruitfulness which he requireth of his members. 2. This is not only pressed by an argument, couched in the very bosom of the exhortation, that their abiding in him is the way to have him abiding in them, and so the communion should be mutual, but further, there is the first express reason and argument pressing the exhortation subjoined; and it is taken from the inseparable connexion that is betwixt communion with him and fruitfulness, so that the latter cannot be without the former. This he declareth—1. Negatively; that without him and communion with him they can no more be fruitful than a branch that abideth not in the vine. 2. Positively; that abiding in him they shall abound in fruit, which again is confirmed and amplified by their impotency to do anything without him. Whence learn—

1. When believers are assured of their good condition it is their duty to cherish it and persevere in it; therefore doth he subjoin this exhortation to the former declaration.

2. It is the duty and will be the practice of lively believers, who are in Christ, to entertain the sense of their own impotency and emptiness, and to love to be kept in a dependence on Christ, that so they may study an intimate and constant conjunction with him, and dependence on him; for so much is imported in this exhortation, "Abide," which imports constancy, and that "in me," which imports intimacy.

3. Such is our dulness and laziness, and our averseness from self-denial and the way of dependence, that even when we have tasted the good of communion with Christ we have need to be exhorted and encouraged to continue in it; for so much do these exhortations, and the pressing thereof with so many arguments, import.

4. As the conjunction and inhabitation must be mutual betwixt Christ and believers, so the union shall not break on his side, but if they abide in him by faith and needy dependence, he will not fail to abide in them by his gracious presence and furniture; for saith he, "Abide in me, and I in you;" the latter part whereof is not an exhortation, (save in so far as he exhorts them, by abiding in him, to continue his presence with them,) but a promise.

5. Holiness and fruitfulness ought and will be so lovely and desirable in the esteem of true believers that the hope of progress therein will persuade them to submit to the use of all appointed means, and particularly to make much use of Christ; therefore it is urged as a pressing argument to abide in Christ, that unless they do so they cannot be fruitful; and the urging of this as an argument is in effect the exhortation to fruitfulness, which afterwards is further pressed and urged.

6. It is as certain that a person not abiding in Christ, for securing the state of his person, and for continual influence and furniture, cannot do good works, as it is certain a withered branch, cut off from a tree, cannot bring forth fruit; for " as the branch cannot bear fruit of itself, except it abide in the vine; no more can ye, except ye abide in me."

7. As believers are to study their own emptiness, so ought they to study the fulness of Christ, as able and willing to supply all their wants, if they abide in him; for these two are held out together, that he is " the vine," as they are the " branches."

8. The more we study faith in Christ, and close and constant adherence to him, the more shall we not only be fruitful, but abound in fruit; for " he that abideth in me, and I in him, the same bringeth forth much fruit."

9. It is no easy matter to convince believers of their own insufficiency without Christ, but again and again self-conceit will lift up its head, unless it be frequently hammered down; therefore it is again needful to assert, " without me ye can do nothing."

10. Whatever moral commendable actions men may do upon moral principles, yet unless a man's person be in Christ he is utterly impotent to do a good and acceptable work; and whatever a regenerate man may do by the power of gifts, or habits of grace received, yet he cannot do it in a lively and acceptable way without a constant dependence and entertaining of communion with Christ; for it is an argument why they should be, and abide in him, " without me," or being separate from me, " ye can do nothing."

11. It is not sufficient that men see their impotency to do greater or more difficult things without Christ, unless also they be convinced of inability to do the least thing; for the assertion is, " without me ye can do nothing." (See 2 Cor. iii. 5.)

12. The sense of our inability is never rightly studied when either we lie secure or discouraged under it, unless it be an argument inviting and persuading us to draw near unto Christ; therefore it cometh in here by way of argument, pressing that they would abide in him, that they may have much fruit, " for without me ye can do nothing."

Ver. 6. If a man abide not in me, he is cast forth as a branch, and is withered; and men gather them, and cast them into the fire, and they are burned.

The second argument pressing the exhortation is an enlargement of what is said, ver. 2, and taken from the danger of apostasy, and which those professors will incur who being outwardly, by visible communion, in Christ, do not evidence the reality of their inward fellowship by constant adherence to him, and drawing virtue from him for fruitfulness, but do fall off and decline. This is held forth under the usual similitude, that as branches which do not incorporate with the tree, but do hang by it, or fall off, are by the vine-dresser cast away, and having withered awhile, are gathered to be fuel for the fire, so rotten members who make apostasy are cut off from Christ, and in due time sent unto the pit. Whence learn—

1. As the case of those who are altogether without Christ is dreadful, so their case is much sadder who have been in Christ by visible profession, and study not reality, that they may abide. Saddest of wrath will look them in the face when they look out of Christ and go from him; for such is the threatening here against them that abide not in him.

2. Albeit no real saints can totally and finally fall away and perish, yet the elect have need that the danger of apostasy, and the dreadful wrath following upon it, be laid before them, to make them afraid of defection; therefore is this threatening laid before the disciples, to press them to their duty, albeit it will be only verified in the outward fruitless branches, who are to be cut off, ver. 2. And the propounding thereof to the disciples doth not import they were of that sort, or that they could make total defection from Christ and grace, but only that there is an inseparable connexion betwixt such apostasy and wrath. And this intimation of the danger of apostasy is one of Christ's means whereby he makes the elect to persevere.

3. As apostates do voluntarily fall off, and choose to depart from Christ, so he doth cast them forth as fruitless branches, by giving them judicially up to their apostate courses, (whereby Christ will disown them, as having no interest in him, his love and favour, according as they renounced him,) if not also by their excommunication from the society of the church; and all this as but an earnest of his rejecting of them for ever; for "If a man abide not in me, he is cast forth as a branch."

4. Apostates who are fallen off from Christ, and given up by him, will not only dry up, in all their gifts and seeming graces, their performances and fair blossoms of professions, but shall grow worse and worse, and ripen in profanity by degrees, till the day come wherein all their false hopes and peace, their carnal joy and sensual comforts shall quite dry up and forsake them; for as a branch cast out of the vineyard so shall they wither.

5. Whatever apostates may think they reap for the present, yet the issue of apostasy will be eternal wrath and hell, which is only suspended till their cup be full; and in the last day all apostates shall be sent thither together; for they shall be as withered branches, which " men gather, and cast them into the fire, and they are burned."

VER. 7. If ye abide in me, and my words abide in you, ye shall ask what ye will, and it shall be done unto you.

The third argument pressing the exhortation (wherewith also the exhortation is repeated and further explained) is taken from the great advantage of access to God, and success in prayer, if they be and abide in him. Whence learn—

1. As the communion betwixt Christ and be-lievers is very intimate, so they who have attained to it need frequent up-stirring to persevere in it, not only to prove the reality of what they have thereby, and that by continuance they may reap the fruits of communion, which they will not find at first, John, viii. 31, 32, but also because, for the most part, men are so ignorant of the way of constant employing of Christ in all things, so unwilling to deny themselves and depend, so ready to swell with conceit if they have anything for the present, and so hotly assaulted with tentations if their faces be towards Christ, and kept so poor and empty in themselves, in Christ's deep wisdom, that they get not leave to run away from him, that they are every day ready to weary of this duty; therefore it must be again recommended that " ye abide in me."

2. Albeit when a man hath fled to Christ he may exercise him sharply, and permit him to be buffeted very sore, yet nothing doth warrant him to give over abiding in him, or to think that Christ will cast him off; for whatever his dealing be we are allowed to credit nothing to the prejudice of his word, which still saith to such, " Abide in me."

3. Such as do entertain communion with Christ will not only be much conversant with his word, but will study to have it deeply rooted and constantly settled in their heart by faith, meditation, and prayer; for of such as abide in him it is verified, " my words abide in you." (See Col. iii. 16.)

4. The way how such as have fled to Christ to find communion with him ought to take him up and find communion mutual, is in and by the word; for on our part, when we are driven out of ourselves to be found in him, our only recourse is not to seek to climb up to heaven or descend to the deep, but to lay hold on him in a word of promise, and to trust to it, whatever be the verdict of tentation, or sense, or dispensations. And on his part, he is to be found in his word, hid in our heart by faith, and being sought without his word he is sought without himself; and it is by his breathings on his word laid up by faith in our hearts that he sensibly evidenceth how near he is to us; therefore, in place of his abiding in us as the other branch of mutual communion, he puts the word abiding to shew that he is to be found only in his word, and that they who have the word abiding in them by faith have him abiding in it, " If ye abide in me, and my words abide in you." (See Rom. x. 6—8.)

5. As it is sense of need which driveth believers to Christ, so by their coming to him their sense of need is not taken away but rather augmented, their clearer light making greater discoveries, and enjoyments begetting much work and many errands; for here it is supposed if they abide in him they will have yet more work for prayer. And indeed, it is by this means that he keeps them abiding in him, whereas otherwise they would be ready to run away; so that to grow in sense of need is not a mark of one wanting communion, but of the contrary.

6. Whatever be the wants and necessities of them who keep communion with Christ, yet abiding in Christ will breed [supply] them, that they can see no outgate [escape] but by prayer,

nor can they essay any other mean till first they go to God ; for abiders in Christ are put to " ask," and see the necessity and excellency of prayer.

7. As prayer is the only outgate [outlet] for abiders in Christ, so they are actual supplicants, and their keeping of communion promoveth prayer, the Spirit being a Spirit of prayer in them, and their keeping communion with him making them delight to have many errands to him, that so they may be much in his company ; for of them it is said " ye shall ask."

8. Such as keep communion with Christ will thereby find a conformity promoved betwixt God and their will in the matter of their desires ; so that, in so far as they are renewed and hold communion with him, their unruly lusts will be subdued, and their unlawful desires, whether for matter, manner, or end, will be laid aside, and they will acquiesce in the good pleasure of God, and seek the most excellent things ; therefore it is offered here, " Ask what ye will ;" not that men are warranted to pray for what they will, or to expect an answer in whatsoever they desire, but that, in so far as they abide in him, and his words abide in them, their wills will be limited in asking by his word and will, and the Spirit in them will make intercession according to the will of God, Rom. viii. 26, 27 ; though otherwise their unrenewed part will be debording [sorrowing], and when they interrupt their communion, lusts will make their prayers muddy [confused].

9. Such as keep communion with Christ will not only see their wants and be put to prayer, but they will have a high estimation of the answer of their prayers, as a thing they cannot want ; for it is an encouragement to them that it shall be done unto them.

10. A right sense of need in supplicants and a due estimation of the hope of audience is an argument to move them to entertain communion with Christ, and not to go far from him lest they miss their help when they have most need ; for it is an argument strongly pressing them to abide in him, that what they ask shall be done to them. (See Micah, vii. 7.)

11. Such as, entertaining communion with Christ, do conform their desires to his will, and present and prosecute them by prayer, though they were never so many or difficult to compass, yet they shall get a good answer, and they, dwelling constantly in Christ's bosom, shall find it but a short step to go to God through him, and get audience in every particular need ; for " ye shall ask (even) what ye will, and it shall be done unto you." And albeit he may exercise supplicants for a time for their good, yet they shall succeed at last, according to the tenour of the promise, (see 1 John, v. 13, 14 ;) whereas the ill entertainment of communion makes us speed worse in our particular suits, even albeit the things desired be lawful.

Ver. 8. Herein is my Father glorified, that ye bear much fruit ; so shall ye be my disciples.

In this and the two following verses Christ doth press fruitfulness upon his disciples, which formerly he had recommended as the effect of keeping communion, and as a strong motive to it ; so that by these arguments he doth not only press fruitfulness in itself, but also doth more strongly urge them to keep communion with him, since fruitfulness (which is so commendable) cannot be attained without it. The arguments pressing fruitfulness are three ; whereof the first is, that it honoureth God, and the second (also in this verse), that it evidenceth unto them, and confirmeth them in their good estate and high privilege of being his disciples. Whence learn—

1. Christ abhorreth all pretences of keeping communion with him which doth not appear in effects ; for this end it is that he is not content to press abiding in him unless he press fruitfulness also, as the true evidence thereof.

2. Such as would prove themselves to hold communion with Christ ought not to rest satisfied with flowers and leaves of a profession and external shows, but must study for solid fruit and good works ; for he requireth " fruit."

3. True members of Christ ought to abound with fruit, even all the fruits of the Spirit, Gal. v. 22—24, (not pleasing themselves with some few that they would cull out, neglecting others, 2 Cor. viii. 7, nor seeking most after what may please or adorn themselves, neglecting the really best things, 1 Cor. xii. 31,) and studying chiefly to abound in those fruits which the dispensations of the time and their own stations, in their several relations, call for, Rom. xii. 15 ; 1 Pet. iii. 1—5 ; therefore it is required that there be "much fruit." And albeit truly fruitful souls, as sometimes they find no fruits of God's dispensations towards them, so they find not themselves abounding in fruits of duty, yet if they be sensible of their barrenness, and it be matter of lamentation and humility that they are so, and that they do not keep communion with Christ to make it otherwise ; if they seriously desire fruitfulness in duty and under dispensations, and do not rest on any measure they have, Christ will look on them as having much fruit, and they are bound to believe fruit when they do not see it.

4. As Christ sought his Father's glory in all he did, so true believers, who keep communion with him, will be tender of and dearly affected with God's honour, and what may promove it, and will be ashamed of self-seeking or want of zeal for God, who by many favours hath proven himself a Father, and purchased them that they may be for his glory ; for as this prevailed with Christ, so he propounds it as a strong argument to move his followers to study fruitfulness, " Herein is my Father glorified."

5. Fruitfulness, especially when we abound in it, (otherwise men may get through who do not honour him as they ought,) doth indeed honour God, as evidencing his fulness and fidelity to his own, Psalm xcii. 13—15 ; as begetting high thoughts of him in their hearts who participate of this his bounty, John, xvi. 14 ; and as drawing in others to glorify him, Matt. v. 16 ; 1 Pet. ii. 12 ; for however some think they glorify him by a naked profession, and others are so presumptuous as to pretend to glorify him by persecuting his servants, Isaiah, lxvi. 5, yet saith

Christ, " Herein is my Father glorified, that ye bear much fruit ;" so that they have need to look to it who by their barrenness would reproach him as if he were a wilderness, Jer. ii. 31.

6. How contemptibly soever men think of a relation to Christ, John, ix. 27, 28, yet it is the high dignity of sinful men to be disciples to him ; therefore it is held out as a sweet encouragement to be " my disciples."

7. Such as are disciples indeed will need daily confirmations that they are so, and will look on it as a privilege whereof they ought daily to assure themselves, and make evident to others that they have right to it by submitting to be taught by him, and following his directions daily ; for this is the force also of the argument pressing them to their duty, " ye shall be my disciples"— that is, not made disciples, for that goeth before fruitfulness, but confirmed that they are such indeed, John, viii. 31, and the world convinced of it, John, xiii. 35 ; which is in its own kind as needful as to be a disciple; for they who are admitted to that privilege cannot but daily feed upon it, and need daily confirmations of it, their good condition not permitting them to sleep, but cherishing tenderness in them.

8. Albeit our fruitfulness do not merit heaven, nor be any cause of our good condition, yet it is the way to happiness, and the infallible evidence of our good condition and estate ; for " so (by bearing fruit) shall ye be my disciples."

VER. 9. As the Father hath loved me, so have I loved you: continue ye in my love.

10. If ye keep my commandments, ye shall abide in my love ; even as I have kept my Father's commandments, and abide in his love.

The third argument pressing fruitfulness is, that hereby they continue in his love. For understanding whereof, albeit his love, wherein we are to continue, may be understood of our love to him as a special effect of communion with him, and of his love to us, which he so much commends, ver. 9, and as a root of fruitfulness and obedience, which is enjoined ver. 10 ; and it is true indeed that love to Christ is one of the fairest fruits of faith and communion with him ; that love must be the root of well-doing, and is never idle, but must be about obedience, John, xiv. 15 ; that the faith of his love to us cannot but beget love to him ; that Christ delights to be loved by us, and therefore exhorts unto it ; and that he requireth constancy and continuance in this love, as, if it be sincere, it will be constant ;—it is true, I say, these points are sound, and arise from this exhortation and purpose annexed to it, so understood, (and it is not fit to restrict the interpretation of scripture, where it may be taken largely,) yet the purpose and scope in this place seems chiefly, if not only, to lead us to understand it of his love towards us in the assurance and sense whereof we are to continue, and which we are to entertain by tender walking. And so in the words—1. He propounds the greatness and matchlessness of his love to them, ver. 9. 2. Upon this he inferreth that it was their duty by all means to entertain the sense of that his love constantly, and not to forfeit the right or lose the sight of such a jewel, ver. 9. 3. (To press the point of fruitfulness,) he assureth them there was no way to abide in this love, but by tender walking, which he further confirms from his own example, who, by obedience, did continue in his Father's love. ver. 10.

From verse 9, learn—1. It tends to the advantage and comfort of those who have fled to Christ to know that he is dearly beloved of the Father, and therefore the Father cannot but be well pleased with them in him ; therefore doth he tell them, " the Father hath loved me."

2. Christ, being beloved of the Father, is a storehouse to receive, and a conduit to convey, that love to his people through him, as his assigns and members, and he doth himself love them; for " the Father hath loved me, and I have loved you."

3. The love of Christ towards his own is matchless, and can be resembled by no love on earth, but is like the Father's love to him, as being eternal, sincere, and intimate, incomprehensible, infinite, and unchangeable, as the other is ; for " as the Father hath loved me, so have I loved you." (Compare chap. x. 15.)

4. It is not enough, in Christ's account, that he hath matchless love towards his own, unless they also know of it, and he persuade and assure their hearts thereof, notwithstanding the sense of their own unworthiness ; and their mistakes in measuring his love by themselves, who are but shallow creatures ; therefore doth he take pains to assure them, that " so have I loved you."

5. Such as are assured of the love of Christ, and are sensible of the matchlessness thereof, will be most tender of entertaining the sense of it, and for a world would not provoke him to withdraw it ; therefore, from the former intimation of his love, he inferreth, not only as their duty, but what will be their practice if they study it rightly, " continue ye in my love." And this he premits [introduces] as a forcible motive to press them to fruitfulness. (See Cant. ii. 7 ; iii. 5.)

From verse 10, learn—1. Christ's matchless love to his people ought not to turn them idle, nor doth disengage them from duty ; but he hath imposed a yoke upon them, which should be sweet because imposed by him ; therefore, with his love, he intimates that he hath service for them, " my commandments."

2. The sense of Christ's love begets a love to him, which will not be idle, but very laborious ; for to be beloved and to keep his commandments go together. (See 1 Thess. i. 3.)

3. As obedience is an evidence of our love to Christ, so it is the mean of keeping us in the sense and assurance of his love to us, without which we are but deluded ; for " If ye keep my commandments, ye shall abide in my love." (See 1 John, ii. 5.)

4. True fruitfulness and tender walking in the sense of Christ's love to us, must appear, not in service of our own devising, but what he prescribes ; and in obeying the commands, not out of fear only, but out of love to Christ ; for to " bear much fruit," ver. 8, is here explained, to

keep the commandments, and, "my commandments."

5. Christ hath fully performed all that was enjoined him to do and suffer as the surety of believers; for in this he is a wonderful pattern and mirror of obedience; "I have kept my Father's commandments." (See chap. xvii. 4.)

6. Christ, by his obedience to the Father, doth continue in his love, and is not out of court, but in a capacity to make sinners welcome through him; for saith he, I "abide in his love."

7. Christ, in his great love to his people, hath essayed those duties and means of entertaining the love of God which he prescribes unto them; that so he may make their way easy by his going before them; may sympathize with them in their hard services; may engage them not to decline to follow such a leader, or the way he took for attaining special favours; and may, by his perfection, cover their infirmities, so that through him they may have that success which he himself had; for these ends doth he urge their duty from his own example, "even as I have kept my Father's commandments, and abide in his love," and particularly, that they may not seek another way of entertaining the Father's love than he walked in, and that he may assure them their weak endeavours through him should keep them in the Father's love, as he by his perfect obedience did abide in it.

8. Such as would entertain the love of God ought to look on Christ's example, not only as an engagement to obedience in general, but as a pattern to be imitated, particularly in what is imitable; and namely, in his humility and self-denial, his submission to the Father's will, his meekness in suffering, his cheerfulness and delight to do the will of God, his universal and constant obedience, &c.; for so much also is imported, that they should keep the commandments, even as I kept, &c., that the practice was not only an engagement, but a pattern to them.

VER. 11. These things have I spoken unto you, that my joy might remain in you, and that your joy might be full.

This verse contains the last particular in this part of the chapter, wherein (by way of conclusion) Christ points out his scope in all this doctrine, (which also holds true of the whole word of God as it is spoken to believers, John, xx. 31, with 1 Pet. i. 8;) for whereas by these many and pressing exhortations they might readily be discouraged and mistake him, therefore he declareth that his aim in all this was to have his joy abiding in them, in a full and constant manner, and that therefore he had pressed communion with himself, and fruitfulness flowing therefrom, as the way to attain and entertain such a mercy; and so it is a new argument to fruitfulness, that so they may promove and secure their own true joy. Whence learn—

1. Christ's dealing and speaking to his people may seem ofttimes so contrary and cross to his great scope as they will readily mistake him unless himself expound what he aims at; therefore must he declare for what end he hath said this, "These things have I spoken unto you, that my joy might remain," &c., as being a thing they could not well discern of themselves.

2. Christ doth allow on his people joy and rejoicing, on his own terms, and in his order; for this is his scope here, "that my joy might remain in you."

3. Believers, in laying hold on their privilege of rejoicing, ought not to look on their worth or deserving, but on his allowance, and what he hath purchased and will confer upon them; for so much doth he intimate (as a part of the meaning) when he calls it "my joy" by way of purchase, allowance, and gift, and therefore "your joy" by right.

4. Whatever believers may apprehend in Christ's sharp dealing and doctrine, or whatever be Christ's nearest end in it, yet ultimately it tends to testify his care of their welfare, and to further and advance their true joy; for "these things" (even pressing exhortations to difficult duties, and sharp threatenings, which could not but humble and exercise sensible souls; even these things) "have I spoken unto you, that my joy might remain in you." (See chap. xiv. 28.)

5. Albeit the joy of believers be Christ's purchase and free gift, yet it is allowed upon none but those who walk in the ways of fruitfulness and obedience, as an evidence of their good estate and interest in him; for "these things," concerning fruitfulness, tend to their joy; so that the joy of wilfully fruitless souls is but delusion, (albeit they who are humbled in the sense of unfruitfulness may rejoice in free grace offered in the covenant, 2 Sam. xxiii. 5,) and our laziness is a great obstructer of our joy.

6. As believers will disdain to rejoice in anything beneath Christ, so, albeit they do evidence their interest in joy by fruitfulness, yet they will be far from rejoicing therein; only it leads them up to rejoice in him who is the Author of all, and with whom they are assured they hold communion by their fruitfulness; therefore also, unto fruitful disciples, it is called "my joy"—namely, a joy in him, and not in their own fruitfulness, far less in other carnal things.

7. Christ doth allow unto believers not only flashes and fits of joy, but a constant, solid, uninterrupted joy; for his will is, that "my joy remain in you," whereas the wicked's will wither. (See Phil. iv. 4; 1 Thess. v. 16.)

8. If believers would make more conscience of tender walking, and of constancy in fruitfulness, their joy would be more constant and less interrupted; for fruitfulness, which he hath been pressing, is the mean to attain this end, "that my joy remain in you," whereas by barrenness they overcloud their own good condition.

9. The joy of believers in Christ is in itself a full joy, needing no other carnal joy to be added with it to fill the heart; being a joy that will bear out under all discouragements, and a joy far different from the worldling's joy, which is full of heaviness, Prov. xiv. 13; for so it is here called, a full joy.

10. Believers, within time, do never taste so much of spiritual joy but more is allowed, and more is to be expected in the way of tender and

fruitful walking; for his scope in exhorting to fruitfulness is, " that your joy might be full," yet fuller, not in regard of the object, but in their sensible enjoyment thereof.

11. Whatever be the small measure of joy believers do enjoy by reason of their fruitlessness, diffidence, discouragement, and straitening in their own bowels, and how oft soever that they have been interrupted, yet it is Christ's purpose and aim to have their joy constant and full, and he will not give over till it be so; for his ultimate scope, in his dealing with them, and his doctrine to them, is, " that your joy might be full," as it will be at last, Psalm xvi. 11; Matt. xxv. 23; and herein it differs from the joy of the wicked, which ends in heaviness, Prov. xiv. 13.

VER. 12. This is my commandment, That ye love one another, as I have loved you.

Followeth, to verse 18, the second part of the chapter, wherein Christ singleth out one particular fruit of mutual love, which in this verse he enjoineth, and presseth from his own example. (Compare chap. xiii. 34.)

DOCTRINES.

1. Albeit Christ require that we study an universal obedience and fruitfulness in all that he hath commanded, yet it is his will we be carried most towards those fruits which are most excellent and necessary; for this cause it is that, having formerly pressed fruitfulness in general, he now descends to press this one particular fruit. (See 1 Cor. xii. 31.)

2. The true touchstone of our communion with Christ, and of fruitfulness in the duties of his service, is the conscientious performance of duties of the second table; therefore doth he insist so particularly on this duty of mutual love, as a mean to evidence the reality of their fruitfulness.

3. Of all duties to our neighbour, and particularly of one saint to another, love is the most excellent, as being the sum of the law, the fountain of all other duties, and the mean of making believers useful each to other; therefore doth he require this in particular, " that ye love one another." (See 1 Cor. xii. 31, with chap. xiii. 1, 2, &c.; Rom. xiii. 8.)

4. It is a sufficient obligation to mutual love that Christ hath commanded and enjoined, who must be obeyed, whatever our inclinations be; for saith he, " This is my commandment, that ye love one another."

5. Christ's love to believers is both an obligation unto mutual love and a pattern of it; and whoever would be sure of his love to them ought to study mutual love, as a fruit thereof; therefore saith he, " Love one another, as I have loved you." This will persuade us to love even them who are base, unprofitable, who have wronged us, &c., as he did.

VER. 13. Greater love hath no man than this, that a man lay down his life for his friends.

That Christ may enforce this duty from his example, he doth commend his love to them,

(which they are to imitate) from several evidences thereof; whereof the first (in this verse) is his laying down his life for them; which being the greatest evidence of friendship among men, Rom. v. 7, doth set out the greatness of his love to them; and that so much the more, as though they were friends in his purpose when he died for them, and were to be reconciled and brought into friendship by his death, yet they were then in themselves enemies, Rom. v. 8, 10. Whence learn—

1. Christ will let no opportunity slip whereby he may unfold his heart and manifest somewhat of his love to his people; therefore, in pressing this duty of mutual love, he insists on such arguments as may not only press it, but may also agree with his principal drift in this sermon, which is, to let out his tender heart unto them.

2. Such as would make right use of Christ's love ought to be much in the study thereof, and to know distinctly what it is; therefore doth he insist to commend his love, that the example may be more binding.

3. Christ's love to believers is so large that we cannot comprehend or take it up but in resemblances and comparisons; therefore must he set it out here by the shadow of the love of friends.

4. Christ did really lay down his life for and in place of his people, they standing guilty before the tribunal of divine justice, he, as their surety by the covenant of redemption, was surrogate in their room, their sins being charged on him, and they set free; for " he laid down his life for his friends." (See Isa. liii. 5.)

5. The benefit of Christ's death is intended only for his friends, who are chosen of God, and given to him to be reconciled and made friends; for he laid down his life " for his friends," and them only.

6. Christ's laying down his life for his people is the clearest mirror wherein to read his love; for he proveth that he had loved them, in that he " laid down his life."

7. Christ's love in dying for his people doth shine in this, that although they were enemies in themselves, yet he had a friendly respect to them, and did follow them, till he drew them into a covenant of friendship; for this doth commend his love, that he laid down his life for them as friends, though they were enemies.

8. Christ's love to his people is the most matchless of loves, and essay whom we will none will bid so much for us or our love as he; therefore doth he commend it as singular: " greater love hath no man than this, that a man lay down his life for his friends;" yet he had done this, and more also, in that he had done it before they were brought into actual friendship with him.

VER. 14. Ye are my friends, if ye do whatsoever I command you.

Before Christ proceed to another evidence of his love and friendship, he takes occasion to apply this privilege of his dying for his friends to them, upon condition of their obedience; hereby commending this his friendship as worthy that they should assure themselves of an interest in it, by friendly carriage and obedience on their part; which makes way for the exhortation to mutual love in particular, which he afterwards resumes. Whence learn—

1. Christ's offers of friendship are never esteemed of as they ought unless we be stirred up thereby to make sure an interest therein on right terms; therefore doth he take occasion to urge them to make sure of such a privilege. And indeed, even disciples are not rashly to lay hold on it, but upon sure grounds.

2. There is a real friendship made up betwixt Christ and believers, consisting in an intimate conjunction and unity, harmony and agreement in mind and will, sympathy and fellow-feeling, mutual delight in the fellowship of one another, communion in estates and conditions, &c.; therefore saith he, "Ye are my friends." (See 2 Chron. xx. 7; Isa. xli. 8; James, ii. 23.)

3. Friendship with Christ doth not disengage his friends from duty, nor will they so far miscarry as to neglect obedience as bond-servants; for these two will go together, to be "my friends," and to "do what I command you."

4. As friendship obligeth to obedience, so only friends to Christ can obey rightly; friendship will carry them through the hardest of duties, and will make them cordial, cheerful, zealous, universal, and constant in their obedience; for in this respect also do these go together.

5. Albeit Christ will not overdrive his friends in his service, yet his dominion over them is unlimited, and he will have them to decline nothing which he shall be pleased to enjoin; for they must do "whatsoever" he commandeth.

6. Obedience unto God is a true evidence of friendship with him; and they who, having fled to Christ, do yet keep themselves in the posture of servants, and are willing to do service to him, he will esteem of them as friends; for "ye are my friends, if ye do whatsoever I command you." (See James, ii. 23.)

Ver. 15. Henceforth I call you not servants; for the servant knoweth not what his lord doeth: but I have called you friends; for all things that I have heard of my Father I have made known unto you.

A second evidence of Christ's love (and a reason why he changeth their style from that of servants, usual to him before, Matt. x. 24; John, xiii. 16, into that of friends) is, his communication of secrets and of his counsel with them, unto which no mere servant is admitted by his master. For understanding of this, consider—1. While he refuseth to call them servants any more, but friends, it is not to be understood as if they were henceforth to be exempted from obedience, or from being servants indeed; for in the former verse, and ver. 20, we have both name and thing of "servants" continued; but the meaning is, they were not to be mere servants, but friends also, and used like friends. 2. This also cleareth what is said, that a "servant knoweth not what his lord doeth"—namely, that common and ordinary servants in the world, though they know so far of their lord's mind as to understand their duty, yet they are not admitted into their master's secrets, nor to know his purposes in what he employs them about; but the disciples were privileged servants, who were admitted to know the counsel of God revealed to Christ. 3. While it is said that "henceforth" he changeth their title, it is not to be understood as if they were not friends before, yea, he calls them so with an eye to their after sufferings, Luke, xii. 4; but that now, being to remove, he lets out his heart and good will more fully. 4. As for Christ's revealing to them all that he had heard of the Father, compare what is said, chap. xiv. 25, 26, only it is not to be understood of that infinite treasure of knowledge communicated from the Father to the Son, as God; but he speaks here as the prophet of the church, sent out to reveal all things necessary to salvation, whereof he kept nothing back.

DOCTRINES.

1. Albeit Christ's followers ought to be his servants, as being created, and especially as being redeemed by him, and because of the many benefits conferred on them daily, yet by being servants they are friends also, in regard of intimate communion and tender usage; for "I call you not servants; but I have called you friends."

2. The dignity of believers is a growing dignity, so that the longer they follow Christ they will know more of the high privileges allowed by him upon them; for this cause saith he, "Henceforth I call you not servants, but I have called you friends;" and so after his resurrection he goeth higher, and calleth them "brethren," John, xx. 17.

3. Christ hath many sweet encouragements and proofs of his love abiding his people in a time of trial which they will not get at another time; therefore he reserveth this sweet style till the time of their sad trial by reason of his departure; and therefore it is given them before, when he speaks of their sufferings, Luke, xii. 4.

4. Christ's love to his people is not diminished by his bodily departure from them, but rather he thereby takes occasion to let out more of it; therefore also doth he choose to call them "friends," now when he is to remove.

5. In so far as believers list themselves to be servants to Christ, they must stoop to be ignorant of what he pleaseth not to reveal, and must bless him that they know their duty, and should go about it, not inquiring into the reasons of it; for this is the lot of servants, (though disciples be advanced to get more, when their Master pleaseth,) "A servant knoweth not what his lord doeth."

6. All the Father's counsel, and what is needful for us to know, is faithfully revealed by Christ to his apostles, and by them to the church; for "all things that I have heard of my Father I have made known unto you."

7. As the apostles were admitted into great friendship in being taught the mind of Christ, so it is an evidence of Christ's friendship to his people that they understand the counsel of God in his word, and that the secret of the Lord is with them, to clear their election unto them, to make them know and esteem the mysteries of the kingdom of God; to make them discern the

secret of his favour and good will, notwithstanding their unworthiness and many thick clouds; to clear his purposes in his strange working in the world; and to clear their way in dark steps and cases; and all this by his word, made clear and lively to them by the Spirit; for this is the reason why he calls them "friends," which is true of all believers in their measure, as of the apostles in theirs; for "all things that I have heard of the Father I have made known unto you."

VER. 16. Ye have not chosen me, but I have chosen you, and ordained you, that ye should go and bring forth fruit, and that your fruit should remain: that whatsoever ye shall ask of the Father in my name, he may give it you.

A third evidence of Christ's love is held out in three particulars, each of them following upon another—1. That his mercy had prevented them in their election, both eternal unto salvation, and their effectual calling as the effect thereof, as also unto the office of apostleship. 2. That being chosen, he had appointed them to bring forth much and remaining fruit, in their private stations and public callings. 3. That for anything they needed to enable them to be fruitful, they should have access to the Father through him for obtaining thereof. Whence learn—

1. Such as are true believers and have indeed given up themselves to Christ, to do him service, ought and will have a singular estimation of Christ, preferring and exalting him in their hearts above all other things; for "ye have not chosen me" is not an absolute denial, but, on the contrary, imports he had done so, only in respect of order he had chosen them before. (See Phil. iii. 12.)

2. It is naturally incident to all men to dispute in their minds against the freedom of God's grace, and to be ambitious to have matter of boasting in themselves, and to see somewhat moving God to let out his love upon them; therefore must Christ not only assert his choosing of them, but remove any conceit of their choosing him first: "Ye have not chosen me," &c.

3. Whatever debate there be in this matter, yet our Lord is the preventer of all good in us, both by his eternal election and by effectual vocation, as also by predeterminating concurrence and influence to every good work in particular; for "ye have not chosen me, but I have chosen you." (See 1 John, iv. 10.)

4. As no man may take any office to himself in Christ's church, unless both the office be appointed by him, and they appointed and called to it, so the reason why he calls any to do him service in a particular office in his church is not any worth in them, but his own free grace, who furnisheth them and setteth them to work; for this holds true also of their office: "Ye have not chosen me, but I have chosen you."

5. Such as God hath chosen to eternal life, and effectually called, are likewise ordained to serve Christ and bring forth fruit to him, in their private stations and public employments;

therefore it is subjoined, "and ordained you, that ye should bring forth fruit."

6. Such as Christ hath honoured with a ministerial charge in his house ought not to loiter in it, nor to please themselves with a high conceit of their own dignity and advancement; but it should be their care to spend themselves in gaining souls and bringing in fruit to Christ; for this holds true of the apostles in their calling in particular, "I have chosen you, and ordained you, that ye should go and bring forth fruit." (See Matt. xxviii. 19.)

7. Albeit believers and Christ's servants be bound to their duty in their stations and offices, yet their fruitfulness depends not on their diligence, but on Christ's commanded and appointed blessing; for this "I have ordained (or put and appointed) you, to go and bring forth fruit," imports not only that he had appointed them to endeavour fruitfulness in the use of means, but that he had appointed fruitfulness to follow upon their endeavours. (See Eph. ii. 10; Acts, xiii. 48.)

8. The fruits of a man's carriage and calling, which Christ approveth of, must be real and solid, not empty and evanishing; for it is fruit that may remain.

9. The solid fruits which believers and ministers bring forth shall not be lost, but they will remain to God's glory and their own good, nourishing and confirming their faith and hope, and confirming ministers in their calling, that they are approven of God in it; for thus also their fruit remaineth in its use and effect.

10. Whosoever are faithfully studying to be fruitful in their calling, and particularly honest ministers, will find many humbling wants in themselves for carrying through in it as becometh; therefore it is subjoined to the former, that they will be put to need prayer.

11. Such as truly discern their own inabilities and wants will find no help for them but by prayer to God, nor any access to God in prayer, but through Christ; for they will be put to "ask the Father," and that "in my name," saith he.

12. It commends Christ's love to his people that when he emptieth them, that they may be sent to God through him, they shall not be disappointed, but get a good answer, were their difficulties never so many or so great; for this is an evidence of his love: "Whatsoever ye shall ask of the Father in my name, he shall give it you."

13. Albeit it be only of free love, and through Christ's merit, that the prayers of believers do find access, yet their fruitfulness is the way wherein to come speed, as evidencing their persons to be reconciled, their condition to be good, and that they seek not things from God, to consume on their lusts, James, iv. 3, but to enable them to more fruitfulness; for this depends on the former, "that your fruit should remain: that whatsoever ye shall ask, &c., he may give it;" where fruitfulness is commended as the way to come speed, and yet no merit to be placed in it, but the supplication put up in Christ's name.

VER. 17. These things I command you, that ye love one another.

Christ having thus commended his love to them as the pattern and motive of their duty, he doth repeat and resume the former exhortation, ver. 12, and presseth it over again by way of conclusion from the former grounds. Whence learn—

1. Mutual love is a duty of great importance, and very excellent in the sight of God; therefore doth Christ so oft repeat and inculcate it.

2. Our hearts by nature are very dull in taking up our duty, and very untoward and averse from the duty of mutual love; for so much also doth the inculcating of this exhortation teach us.

3. Such as take a full and serious view of Christ's love to them cannot but see themselves engaged to mutual love, and to be without excuse if they neglect it; for upon the former grounds he here repeateth it, as a duty that cannot be declined.

4. The duty of mutual love is very comprehensive, and containeth many duties in the bosom of it, to which love will stoop and condescend; therefore Christ exhorts to it as to many duties: " These things I command you, that ye love one another." (See Rom. xiii. 8; 1 Cor. xiii. 4—7.)

VER. 18. If the world hate you, ye know that it hated me before it hated you.

Followeth the third and last part of the chapter, wherein Christ, that he may yet more excite them to mutual love, doth forewarn them of the hatred and persecution they were to meet with in the world; and armeth them against the same by several arguments of consolation and encouragement, to ver. 22; which in the following purpose he further confirmeth, and vindicates them against all stumbling-blocks and exceptions.

In this verse their case is intimated that the world would hate them; unto which is subjoined the first argument of encouragement, taken from his own example and lot, so assuring them that in their sufferings they had fellowship with him who was hated of the world before them. Whence learn—

1. As believers may look for love from Christ and saints, so they must expect trouble and hatred from the world; for unto the former doctrine concerning Christ's love, and their duty to love one another, it is subjoined, that the world will hate you.

2. The world's hatred of believers is a strong argument to persuade them to love one another; for this is also subjoined as an argument to press mutual love, that they are sure to meet with hatred from others. And indeed, when love decayeth, God useth to kindle it up by storms of persecution, which cause saints to draw together.

3. Christ is a faithful Master, who will hide from his servants nothing of their danger and difficulties; and it may assure us of the reality of his encouragements, that he giveth so free warning of dangers; therefore doth he faithfully warn them here.

4. Persecution ariseth from men's worldly dispositions, and their being of the world; and all who are so are fair to be cruel persecutors, as they have opportunity; for the world hates you, saith he.

5. As the persecution of saints floweth from implacable malice in the world against them, so whoever do hate godliness, and the godly for its sake, they are already engaged in a course of persecution, and will go a further length as they have permission and opportunity; for this cause doth he comprehend all their persecutions and sufferings under the name of hatred, as being a persecution in God's account, and the rise of all the world's cruelty.

6. Hatred and persecution from the world is a very hard and difficult lot to saints, unless Christ do encourage them against and under it; therefore doth he not only forewarn, but arm them also.

7. Such as would bear out under sad lots ought to be well acquainted and study seriously the condition of Christ and his church in all ages; and what they know, Christ will put them to it, to improve it; therefore doth he appeal to their knowledge in this matter of their encouragement, " ye know," &c.

8. Christ is the prime object of the world's hatred, and they who hate his members do hate himself first, and them because of somewhat of him in them; for saith he, " it hated me before it hated you."

9. As it is a great encouragement in suffering times to know that believers before us have met with the like lots, Matt. v. 12, so, in particular, Christ's going before us in enduring the world's hatred may exceedingly encourage sufferers, Heb. xii. 1—3; for hereby, not only is his great love commended, who would offer himself to an ingrate [ungrateful] world, Luke, xxiii. 34, but it serves further to guard our hearts against the calumnies cast upon us in our sufferings, since he who was innocent, and the Lord of glory, was persecuted under the notion of a Samaritan, and what not? to point out our dignity, that we should be made conform to our Head, were it but in suffering, and that we should be served heirs to that enmity that began at him, and which lights on us for his sake; to assure us of his sympathy in whose quarrel we are embarked, and who drank of that cup himself; to assure us how easy this suffering will be, he having essayed it before us, (as nothing will prove hard to a believer which Christ hath once tasted of,) so that we need no more but to follow him to the spoil; and to assure us of the victory, since he hath already triumphed over the world's hatred in our name. So much is held forth for the comfort of sufferers in this argument, " If the world hate you, ye know that it hated me before it hated you."

VER. 19. If ye were of the world, the world would love his own: but because ye are not of the world, but I have chosen you out of the world, therefore the world hateth you.

The second argument of consolation is taken from what their suffering from the world may evidence unto them—namely, that they are not of the world, but chosen out of it, and therefore the world hates them; whereas if it were otherwise with them the world would love his own.

So the force of the argument is, partly, that they behoved to make for trouble as being inevitable, considering they are not of the world ; and partly, their suffering from the world was so clear an evidence of their good condition that they ought not to be discouraged at it. What Christ saith, that "the world would love his own," doth not contradict the frequent experiences of wars, contentions, and emulations among men of the world; for, 1. If we compare the hatred they carry towards their own with what they have against the godly, it is nothing so violent and extreme. 2. They differ not in contrary general principles and ends, but only in contrary lusts, and when the interest of one interferes with another, and crosseth it. 3. They do easily agree in hating the godly, as Herod and Pontius Pilate did. 4. Albeit some wicked men hate some wickedness, yet it is not a pure hatred, but for their own corrupt ends.

DOCTRINES.

1. There are in this world two seeds who stand in opposition one to another, and betwixt whom there is a conspicuous difference ; for there are some " of the world," and some "not of the world."

2. The difference betwixt the godly and the world is not of the godly's making, but doth flow from God's free grace ; for " ye are not of the world, but I have chosen you out of the world," by eternal election and actual vocation, whereby they are made not to be conformed to this world, in judgment, affections, and practice.

3. Christ by his free grace can make a great change in men, and make excellent vessels out of the vilest matter ; for saith he, " I have chosen you" to all this dignity and excellent condition, " out of the world."

4. Saints, being separate from the world and their courses, must expect to be hated by the world upon that very account; and that because the world hates God and his image in them, and they cannot endure to be condemned by the light that shineth in the godly ; for " because I have chosen you out of the world, therefore doth the world hate you."

5. As the world do keep up their love from the godly, so their love will be little worth to a right discerner, when he considereth that to be beloved of the world is but an ill token, and evidenceth that either the person beloved is of their own stamp, or, at least, complieth too much with their evil fashions ; therefore doth he illustrate this from the contrary : " If ye were of the world, the world would love his own."

6. As evidences of our regeneration are worthy to be sought after at any rate, so in particular it may sweeten the world's hatred to saints, when they consider that the world cannot sincerely love what is good ; and therefore their hating of them for good is a real confirmation of their good estate ; for this is the encouragement, that the world hateth you, because " I have chosen you out of the world."

Ver. 20. Remember the word that I said unto you, The servant is not greater than his lord.

If they have persecuted me, they will also persecute you ; if they have kept my saying, they will keep your's also.

The third argument of consolation (amplifying and enlarging the first, and wherein he expounds that hatred, ver. 18, to comprehend both persecution of their person and contempt of their doctrine) is taken from the inevitableness of trouble, considering their relation to Christ as servants to their master ; and the equity that is in this, that they should be no better entreated than he was, both in their person and ministry. Whence learn—

1. Christ's words are not spoken at random, but to good purpose, and may, long after they are heard, serve us in much stead ; therefore doth he remit them to the word that he said unto them, Matt. x. 24 ; John, xiii. 16.

2. The word of God, rightly improven, is a special mean of patience and encouragement under sufferings ; therefore doth he send them to it.

3. As we ought not to slight the word, but lay it up as we hear it, so in an hour of tentation and trouble we ought to remember on what we have heard, as being spoken for our use in such cases ; therefore saith he, " Remember the word that I said unto you," when they are to resolve on troubles.

4. Of all that we hear, nothing is so effectual to arm us with patience, and encourage us under troubles, as to be much acquainted with Christ, his usage in the world, and his deportment under it ; therefore doth he, in particular, call to remembrance what he had said concerning his suffering who was their Master.

5. Christ's servants cannot in reason expect better entertainment than he found in the world ; for he mentions his sufferings that they may close with that truth, " The servant is not greater than his lord," which, as before it preached humility, chap. xiii. 16, so here, patience and submission.

6. Such as have a low esteem of themselves and a high esteem of Christ, who yet stooped to suffer more than they are put to, will easily be brought to stoop and be patient in trouble ; therefore doth he propound the comparison under the terms of servant and Lord, that thoughts of the one and the other may persuade them to submit, and not think it strange that " if they have persecuted me, they also persecute you," &c.

7. Hatred against Christ and his servants will resolve in cruelty against their persons as there is opportunity ; for so doth he explain it, they persecuted me and will persecute you.

8. As contemners of doctrine in the mouth of faithful messengers are upon their way to persecute their persons, so also their very contempt is a most cruel persecution in Christ's account, and in the account of godly ministers, who cannot but be sadly afflicted with the ill success of their ministry ; for both these causes it is added to the persecuting of their persons, " If they have kept my saying, they will keep yours also"— that is, they will keep the one no better than they did the other.

9. Whatever pretence of respect men may have to the word, yet they are but real despisers thereof

so long as they do not lay it up as a treasure in their heart, and observe it in their practice; for this is it he requireth, that they keep his saying.

10. It is the great advantage of believers that Christ and they have the same common friends and enemies, and are embarked together in sufferings; therefore doth he parallel their case with his, "If they have persecuted me, they will also persecute you; if they have kept my saying, they will keep yours also."

Ver. 21. But all these things will they do unto you for my name's sake, because they know not him that sent me.

The fourth argument of consolation is taken from the goodness of the cause of their sufferings, as being for his name's sake; which is further amplified from the cause of the world's violence on that quarrel—to wit, their ignorance of God who sent him, and consequently of the wise contrivance of the mystery of redemption. Whence learn—

1. The godly, and particularly faithful ministers, ought to expect trial from the world in great multiplicity and variety; therefore saith he, "All these things will they do unto you," pointing chiefly to that opposition both against their persons and doctrine, ver. 20.

2. It is the duty of believers, and particularly of faithful ministers, to own and avow the name of Christ, his truth and glory, whatever befal them; for their suffering "for his name's sake," importeth that they stand for it.

3. The great quarrel of the world against believers is for the name of Christ; and as when the world was heathenish this quarrel was avowed, so however now some other thing be pretended, yet it is the quarrel still; for "all these things will they do unto you for my name's sake."

4. A good cause may make suffering for it easy, when we consider our mercy to be honoured to be for Christ; and that we have so much sin and guilt as might draw on more uncomfortable exercise; for it is an encouragement here that they will do these things unto you for my name's sake. (See Acts, v. 41.)

5. None do oppose the doctrine of the gospel in the mouths of Christ's servants, or do persecute them for its sake, but they bewray their gross ignorance thereof, and of God and Christ, and what relation he hath to the Father; for they will do these things, "because they know not him that sent me."

Ver. 22. If I had not come and spoken unto them, they had not had sin: but now they have no cloke for their sin.

Because the former arguments of consolation contain somewhat at which his weak followers might readily offend; as namely, that Christ should be unknown and hated in the world, yea, and so hated as they his followers should be hated for his sake; therefore Christ subjoins other arguments to encourage them, by obviating all scandal which might be taken at the cause of their suffering, and his being hated in the world. The first argument is taken from the miserable condition of persecutors, which their hating of him did evidence. This is prosecuted in three particular aggravations of their sin who did so; in the first whereof (in this verse) is declared, that however their ignorance, ver. 21, might seem to plead for them, yet his presence and doctrine did take away all excuses and pretexts, did prove them to hate him out of inexcusable malice, and did so aggravate their guilt that it had otherwise been nothing, in respect of what it is now. Whence learn—

1. The consideration of the great sin of persecutors may encourage the godly, and guard their heart under suffering, as being an evidence that God approveth of them and their quarrel when he is so displeased with those who oppose them, and that they cannot take them to the other side, but they must make God their party; for this is an argument of consolation taken from the aggravation of the sin of persecutors.

2. As the presence and doctrine of Christ in the world is the greatest of mercies offered unto it, so it is a sad case when that mercy is by men turned into a plague, and matter of dittay [reproach] against themselves; as here, his coming and speaking unto them was an occasion to render them inexcusable.

3. Albeit all men, even those who live without the written word, be guilty of sin, both original and actual, yet sins against the gospel and of those who hear it are of so deep a dye that the sins of the world besides are no sins in comparison thereof; and that because these sins are against the greatest of mercies, yea, and the remedy of sin, and against great means, therefore saith he, "If I had not come and spoken unto them, they had not had sin."

4. It is a great snare upon sinners that when they do greatest wrongs they may have many clokes of hypocrisy, or pretexts of ignorance, necessity, infirmity, &c., to hide from themselves and others the odiousness thereof; for so is imported that they had some "cloke" or pretext of excuse "for their sin."

5. Albeit the Lord will graciously consider and pity his own, who plead ignorance, infirmity, or tentation in particular failings, providing they be sincere and flee to the blood of Christ, even for purging away of these failings, yet the doctrine of the gospel doth take away all pretence and excuse from wicked sinners, as holding out convincing light that they cannot pretend ignorance, and letting them see a remedy if they will come to Christ; for "now they have no cloke for their sin."

6. It doth highly aggravate sin when men persist in it after all pretexts are taken from them; for this made other sins to be no sin in comparison of theirs, that "now they have no cloke for their sin," and yet do sin on.

Ver. 23. He that hateth me hateth my Father also.

The second aggravation of their sin is that their hatred of him is joined with hatred of the Father also. Whence learn—

1. Whatever wicked men do pretend, yet na-

turally they are haters of God, in so far as they love him not with all their heart, or do hate that he should cross their lusts by his commands, providences, and corrections; for there are, saith he, who hate my Father.

2. The great opposition and hatred against God in the world appears chiefly in opposition against Christ, who is the great butt of contradiction in the world; therefore are they conjoined here, and the one as clearing the other.

3. Let men pretend never so much holiness or respect to God, yet if they hate Christ or his gospel they are but haters of God, who is one in essence with his Son, who sent him into the world as his ambassador, and who is in him reconciling the world by the word of the gospel; therefore, whereas Christ's being hated by the Pharisees, who gave out themselves to be so eminent for God, might seem to rub on himself, he removes and retorts this saying, " He that hateth me hateth my Father also."

VER. 24. If I had not done among them the works which none other man did, they had not had sin: but now have they both seen and hated both me and my Father.

The third aggravation of their sin is taken from his great miracles; that having done so great and singular works among them which they had seen, yet they did both hate him and his Father, and so came to a height of sin in comparison of which other sins were as nothing; while he saith, he had done works which none other man did, to omit what is said of his promise to his disciples, chap. xiv. 12, whose works are not here to be secluded, but are a part of his works, rendering them inexcusable, it is only to be marked that however many miracles were done by many before him, yet his did surpass them all for number, variety, kind, (as not being terrible, as many of Moses's miracles were,) and manner of doing them, in his own name, and not as others, who obtained the doing thereof only by prayer from God. Beside, this was sufficient for their conviction, that no wicked man, such as they supposed him to be, could do what he did.

DOCTRINES.

1. Christ did work such miraculous works as were singular, and evidently cleared what he was; for they were " works which none other man did."

2. Christ's condescending to prove what he was, and to confirm his doctrine by unparalleled miracles, doth aggravate the sin of despisers far above what it would be without them ; for as he said before of his doctrine, ver. 22, so here also of his miracles confirming the same, " If I had not done among them the works which none other man did, they had not had sin." And this doth also teach us, who have the same doctrine confirmed by the same miracles.

3. Clearest light and conviction of God's singular power in or with any of his will not gain enemies; but the more God manifests of himself to or in his people they may look for the more opposition; for they have seen (not only with their eyes, but many of them convinced in their minds) and yet hated.

4. The clearness of conviction and light, when it doth not gain men, will contribute much to heighten their malice against what they see, and will not embrace; therefore is hatred subjoined as following seeing; " they have both seen and hated both me and my Father."

VER. 25. But this cometh to pass, that the word might be fulfilled that is written in their law, They hated me without a cause.

The second argument of consolation, obviating the scandal of his being hated in the world, is taken from the prediction thereof in scripture. For this end he citeth a passage from Psalm xxxv. 19, which though it had its own accomplishment in David as a type, yet it relateth also unto Christ as the substance. For this connexion of the prediction with the event compare what is said on chap. xii. 37—40. Only hence learn—

1. The eyeing of God and his decree and providence about hard lots is a mean to make them more easy and less stumbled at; for hereby we are encouraged to believe that there is more in them than we can see, and that nothing cometh to pass without him; therefore doth he guard against their stumbling at his lot by pointing out a decree and providence in it intimated long ago.

2. The comfortable sight of God's purpose and providences about his people is only to be found in scripture, and when it is found agreeable to a scripture way; therefore doth he remit them to see this in what was " written in their law."

3. It is a sad case when men's greatest dignities contribute to aggravate their iniquity, as it will be with the abusers thereof; therefore doth he call the scripture " their law," (of which title, see further on chap. viii. 17; x. 34,) to point out their great sin whose privilege it was to enjoy the word, Rom. ix. 4, and yet were persecutors, rather accomplishing what was foretold of persecutors than obeying the directions thereof.

4. The scriptures are of infallible verity, and may be learned to [relied on] in what they declare, promise, or foretel; for " this cometh to pass, that the word might be fulfilled that is written in their law." He will see nothing of it unaccomplished.

5. Christ hath been a very sweet subject to the church of the Old Testament, to think, speak, and sing of him; for by many citations applied to him it is apparent he hath been much in their mind.

6. Christ's sufferings are a very sweet meditation to saints in their troubles, as assuring them of a sympathizer, and that the sting is taken out of their sufferings; therefore David, in the Psalms, speaking of his own sufferings, doth so often look out to the sufferings of Christ, as this and other citations make manifest.

7. It evidenceth the world's malice against Christ and his followers, that their innocency cannot shelter them from their cruelty; and it is

Christ and his people's encouragement that their malice and cruelty is causeless; for so much is imported in the scripture cited, as it relates to David and Christ both, "They hated me without a cause." (See Psalm cix. 4.)

VER. 26. But when the Comforter is come, whom I will send unto you from the Father, even the Spirit of truth, which proceedeth from the Father, he shall testify of me:

27. And ye also shall bear witness, because ye have been with me from the beginning.

The third and last argument of consolation, obviating this scandal, is, that however he had suffered unjustly, and lien under many aspersions cast upon him by the world, and much hatred of his person and doctrine from them, yet all these should be wiped off by the coming of the Spirit, who should testify of him, and make his person and doctrine to be acknowledged in the world. And they themselves should be enabled to bear witness concerning him, having been with him from the beginning. As for the conjunction of the Spirit's witnessing and theirs, it is thus to be understood: that the Spirit, being poured out on them, should enable them to bear witness of him, and should be assisting to them therein, partly by his extraordinary work upon themselves, and the miraculous works accompanying their doctrine, and partly by accompanying their testimony with conviction upon many, and with his inward seal upon the hearts of believers.

From ver. 26, (omitting what hath been said of this Comforter, and Spirit of truth, in chapter xiv. 16, 17,) learn—1. As the Father and Son are two distinct persons in the godhead, so the Holy Ghost is the third person, who proceedeth from the Father and the Son, for he is sent, and cometh and testifieth, which are things proper to a person; and he "proceedeth from the Father," and the Son sendeth him from the Father, which necessarily supposeth his proceeding from him; because this order of operation and sending by the Son from the Father followeth upon the order of his subsistence.

2. The great doctrine of the gospel is to hold out Christ what he is, that men do not mistake or calumniate him, but may embrace and believe in him; for in this all these witnesses must concur to "testify of me."

3. The doctrine of the gospel concerning Christ is so great a mystery that it is very hardly believed and received in the world; for so much is imported in that there must be so many witnesses. (So 1 Tim. iii. 16; it is a mystery that he is "believed on in the world.")

4. Neither the hearing of Christ himself preach, nor the sight of his glorious miracles, will work on a people without the concurrence of the Spirit poured out; therefore, albeit Christ had these witnesses, ver. 22, 24, yet it is needed further that the Spirit testify of him.

5. The Spirit of the Lord did sufficiently vindicate Christ's glory, and confirm the truth of the gospel, by his miraculous operations in the primitive times; for by this mean was Christ testified of, and to this doth Christ remit his disciples for their encouragement.

6. Not only did the Spirit afford sufficient matter of confirmation and conviction in these his extraordinary operations, but where he pleaseth to carry these on in hearts, he will either make men savingly acknowledge the excellency of a despised Christ, or at least convince them thereof; for this prediction, "He shall testify of me," imports, not only that he shall afford sufficient matter of testimony, but that eventually also it should be, one way or other, effectual on many.

From ver. 27, learn—1. The Spirit beareth no testimony unto Christ but with and according to the testimony given by the apostles in their doctrine and writings, for they are conjoined here, "He shall testify, and ye also shall bear witness." (See Acts, v. 32.)

2. It is the great work and high honour of apostles and ministers to commend Christ, and to bear witness of his excellency, against all calumnies, prejudices, and misconstructions, of one or other; for it is their work to "bear witness."

3. Such as would be faithful witness-bearers of Christ have need of much of the Spirit to enable, assist, and accompany them; therefore the one must go before and with the other; "he shall testify, and ye shall bear witness."

4. It may confirm our faith in embracing the apostle's testimony of Christ, that what they delivered concerning him they were eye and ear witnesses thereof, and intended not to deceive us; as may appear from the nature of their doctrine, so cross to our humours; by their not seeking their own ease or interest in preaching it; by not going into corners with their testimony, but avowing openly what was openly done, none daring refute them; and by their harmony among themselves; for they are fit witnesses, "because ye have been with me from the beginning." (See 1 John, i. 1.) Hence it was that only such an one was chosen to supply Judas's room, Acts, i. 21, 22.

5. As God admits any of us to know anything of Christ, we are bound to witness the same, in our places and stations; for so much may this general truth teach us, "Ye shall bear witness, because ye have been with me," &c.

CHAPTER XVI.

IN this chapter (wherewith this farewell sermon is closed) Christ goeth on to let out more of his heart unto his disciples, and doth resume many of the most necessary points formerly spoken of, and sweetly enlargeth the same. The chapter may be taken up in four principal parts: in the first whereof, Christ further prosecutes that purpose begun in the former chapter concerning their sufferings; wherein he intimateth his scope in foretelling thereof, ver. 1, expresseth more particularly what sufferings they were to meet with, ver. 2, propoundeth grounds of encouragement under such a lot, ver. 3, 4, and giveth a reason why he did no sooner give them this distinct warning, ver. 4. In the second part of the chapter he again intimateth his departure, reprehending their abuse of this warning, ver. 5, 6; and encourageth them against the bitterness of this lot—1. By the promise of the Holy Spirit, who would not come but on his departure, ver. 7, and who, being come, would convince the world, ver. 8—11, instruct them, ver. 12, 13, and glorify him, by what he should communicate of and from him who is one and equal with the Father, ver. 14, 15. 2. By a promise that, however he was shortly to be removed, yet they should shortly after that see him again; which is propounded, ver. 16, and (by occasion of the disciples' doubtfulness, ver. 17, 18,) is more fully explained, ver. 19—22. 3. By a promise of their increase in knowledge, and (4) of success in their prayers put up in his name; both which are propounded, ver. 23, and further amplified and enlarged, ver. 24—28. In the third part of the chapter, the disciples making a fair profession of their proficiency by his former doctrine, ver. 29, 30, their presumption herein is checked, and they forewarned of their scattering and deserting of him, ver. 31, 32. The last part of the chapter containeth the conclusion of the whole sermon, pointing out his scope in all of it, ver. 33.

Ver. 1. These things have I spoken unto you, that ye should not be offended.

In the first part of the chapter, Christ prosecutes his former doctrine concerning his disciples' sufferings, in four particulars; in the first whereof (in this verse) he points out what he aimed at in intimating and foretelling this their hard lot—namely, that by this warning they might be so armed and so fortified by the encouragements subjoined as not to stumble at it when it came to pass. Whence learn—

1. Christ speaks nothing to his people at random, but what he hath well digested as needful for them, and which they should accordingly ponder and esteem of; therefore doth he shortly resume what he had spoken, as being of much importance, and seriously to be thought upon by them. "These things have I spoken unto you."

2. It is not enough to consider what Christ saith, unless also we take notice of his scope in speaking of it; which ofttimes we are ready to mistake unless he reveal it. Therefore, whereas they might be ready to sink in sorrow upon this intimation, he must tell them he hath another scope in it, "These things have I spoken unto you, that ye should not be offended."

3. It is no strange thing to see many things concerning Christ's person, doctrine, way of dealing, &c., occur as stumbling-blocks in the way of professors, to make them fall and turn out of the way; and particularly, afflictions and persecutions accompanying Christ and the gospel are grievous stumbling-blocks, and do prove a neck-break to many; for it is here supposed that by reason of this lot they will be ready to " be offended," or stumbled and scandalized, to divert them from good, and tempt them to make apostasy.

4. Afflictions and persecutions are so searching and trying that even the best have need to be guarded against the scandal thereof; for even disciples have need to be spoken unto, that they be not offended.

5. How strongly soever tentations and prejudices may seem to plead for stumbling at Christ in a day of trial, yet it is most necessary that professors do not stumble, seeing there is no safe retreat without a neck-break; therefore doth he propound it as a necessary duty, that however matters go, they be not offended.

6. Whatever stumbling-blocks be laid in the way of professors, and how many soever do stumble and fall upon them, yet there are sufficient means to prevent their stumbling, and to convince them that there is no just cause why they should offend; for here he intimateth that he had taken sufficient course " that they should not be offended."

7. The word of Christ (and particularly his intimation of the cross, and encouragements against the same) is a sufficient guard against offences and scandals at the cross; for—1. His intimation warneth men of their danger, so that they have themselves to blame if they be not armed with resolution, but still promise great things to themselves; and it doth assure believers that he hath an eternal purpose and effectual providence about these things, which he can foretel before they come to pass. 2. He guardeth this intimation with so many encouragements and antidotes in the word, as it cannot prove deadly to them that improve the same. 3. The word rightly improven doth purge out idols and lusts, which tempt men to stumble, doth direct their way in dark cases, that they may not stumble, and doth afford such confirmations of faith as may support their hearts under trouble, and such intimations of the severity of God as may deter them from apostasy. Therefore saith he, " These things (both of intimation and encouragement, mentioned in the former chapter) have I spoken unto you, that ye should not be offended." Not only was this the scope of his doctrine and intimation, but these were a sufficient mean to prevent their stumbling, however they, not improving the same, were offended for a time, Matt. xxvi. 31.

Ver. 2. They shall put you out of the synagogues: yea, the time cometh, that whosoever killeth you will think that he doeth God service.

In the second place, he more particularly expresseth what sufferings they were to meet with, not naming every particular kind of suffering, but instancing in two of the saddest kinds thereof, which may comprehend all the rest as inferior thereunto; one, of spiritual censures of the church, of which excommunication is the saddest; the other, of bodily sufferings, whereof a violent death is the sharpest. Both these he warns them of, foretelling that they may look for excommunication from the Jews as a church, (of which see chap. ix. 34; xii. 42,) and for violent deaths from them or others, in a tumultuous way, or from civil authority abusing their powers; yea, and that they may look, in their saddest sufferings, to be laden with reproach, their persecutors, through blind zeal, thinking it acceptable service, and a sweet-smelling sacrifice to God, to put them to death. In speaking of excommunication and death, he subjoins death to the former as sadder than it; not because it is simply sadder to die than to be cut off from the society and privileges of God's people, (if their excommunication had been such,) but because in this case their excommunication was unjust, and therefore the less to be regarded. And albeit they did suffer death also unjustly, yet it was more sharp, in respect that death is naturally bitter to men, and because that by death they were cut off from doing service to their Master, whereas they might go on in their work, notwithstanding the sentence of excommunication. For it is further to be considered, that (beside that this sentence was eminently unjust, in regard of the cause, being for preaching in the name of Christ) the Jews, after their rejecting of the offer of Christ, that was first to be made unto them, Acts, xiii. 46, did become no church, and so had no power of church-censures, and consequently any they inflicted were null in themselves. And however they had continued a church, yet the apostles, being general officers, were above the reach of any particular church power; and consequently, however such a sentence might now affright them to think of it when they were rude and ignorant, and afterward it might be some trial, in so far as it did render them odious and suspected to them who could not discern aright, and so put some stop to the success of their ministry, yet the sentence being null, they might warrantably go on; yet not at all leading a preparative to any particular ministers to contemn the sentences of a true church, upon their own alleagance [judgment] of the corruption thereof, and of the injustice of the cause of the sentence, as may be cleared from what is said.

DOCTRINES.

1. As persecution and the cross do usually accompany Christ and his followers, so general resolutions for afflictions are not of any worth unless men also lay their account, and resolve on what in particular they may meet with; therefore doth he warn them particularly what they may expect, that they may accordingly be resolved.

2. Such followers of Christ as would be armed, indeed, ought to resolve that they will meet with, not one, but many trials of all sorts, and that they may be essayed with the utmost violence that men's malice can invent, or their power in church or state can reach, either in an orderly or a tumultuous way; therefore doth he forewarn them of a variety of particular trials, and that in the greatest extremity.

3. A fixed resolution, through the power of Christ's grace, may carry a saint through the greatest difficulties he can meet with; for all these are propounded as things they may get digested in their resolutions. (See Acts, xx. 23, 24.)

4. Followers of Christ may lay their account, not only to be persecuted by pagans, or openly profane men, but even by church-members, yea, and church-guides, or they who pretend to be so; for whereas he had foretold them of the world's hatred, chap. xv. 18, now he explains it, that even they who have power to put out of synagogues would be against them.

5. Albeit a church censure, unjustly inflicted, and by them who are no church, or have no such power, be of no weight before God, yet it is an affliction, requiring much resolution in the sufferers, that persecutors account themselves not only a church, but the only true church, yea, and are very eminent in power in it, and do account Christ's suffering followers not worthy to have room in it, but that they ought to be excommunicated; for in this respect he propounds it as a trial to be digested by them, " They shall put you out of the synagogues."

6. When followers of Christ have tasted of lesser sufferings, they are not to sit down there, but to lay their account that they may meet yet with sadder, and by bearing lesser troubles they are to prepare themselves for greater; therefore doth he subjoin a violent death as a trial to be expected after they are excommunicated.

7. The consideration of sadder sufferings which saints have endured, and ourselves may meet with, ought to sweeten lesser trials, and make us digest them with the greater moderation, and will do so, if we be preparing, as we ought, for these sad things; therefore doth he teach them to swallow up the thoughts of excommunication with apprehending what sadder things they should make ready for; " They shall put you out of the synagogues; yea, (or but,) the time cometh that they shall kill you."

8. As no extremity of torment can justify men in denying Christ and his truth, nor will prevail with them who love and cleave to him to do so, so followers of Christ ought to prescribe no measure of sufferings for themselves to endure, less than a violent death itself, for Christ's cause; therefore doth he require that they have a resolution even to be killed in this quarrel; " whosoever killeth you."

9. Death itself were easy to be digested by saints, if so be the quarrel and their integrity were clearly owned; but they must resolve to have shame and ignominy accompanying their cross, to be buried under ignominy and calumnies, as if they were malefactors, and their cause to be traduced as unjust, odious, seditious, &c.; for this is the bitter sting of their suffering, that persecutors pretend they are for God, even in persecuting them; " whosoever killeth you will think that he doeth God service." (See Heb. xii. 2.)

10. Corrupt and erroneous men may have much blind zeal in their false way, which is very furious and violent, and the cause of much cruelty and bloodshed against true professors; for from this zeal doth their cruelty flow, " whosoever killeth you will think that he doeth God service."

11. It will never justify men's actions that they have good intentions in them, or do follow their

blinded conscience and zeal; but they may grossly err under these pretexts, unless what they do be warranted by the word; for they had all these pretences who killed the apostles; " whosoever killeth you will think that he doeth God service."

Ver. 3. And these things will they do unto you, because they have not known the Father, nor me.

In the third place, he subjoineth two lenitives and encouragements to sweeten this hard lot, and make them digest it; the first (in this verse) is taken from the original and cause of persecutors' malice, which is, their ignorance of the Father and him; of which chap. xv. 21.

DOCTRINES.

1. Persecutors of God's children, as taking no notice who they are, do bewray their ignorance of God and Christ, at least in so far as they persecute, were they never so good otherwise; for " these things will they do unto you, because they have not known the Father, nor me."

2. Men who are and continue ignorant of God and Christ are in hazard to turn persecutors if they have the tentation; for this being the cause of persecution, it is no wonder the effect follow upon it.

3. Albeit it be in itself a sad case that so many men pretending to be for God should yet be ignorant of him and his Son, yet it should sweeten the sad cup of sufferers that they know their persecutors are so ignorant; for the quarrel may comfort them, they need not fear them who are not approven of God; and if he be not known, they should not take it ill if they be not acknowledged for what they are, 1 John, iii. 1; therefore doth he comfort them, by letting them see this ignorance of persecutors.

Ver. 4. But these things have I told you, that when the time shall come, ye may remember that I told you of them. And these things I said not unto you at the beginning, because I was with you.

The next lenitive and encouragement (in the beginning of this verse) is, that this prediction should be useful and comfortable to remember it, when it came to be accomplished. Whence learn—

1. As much is heard by God's people, whereof they reap little profit, till affliction bring them to remember it, so, in particular, afflictions will bring the doctrine of the cross to remembrance; for " when the time shall come, ye may remember that I told you."

2. It is most necessary that God's people be forewarned, in peaceable times, of approaching trouble; if not for any present use they get of it, yet because of what it may produce afterward; for " these things have I told you, that when the time shall come, ye may remember."

3. However predictions of trouble by Christ may be ready to sadden the hearts of saints, yet the prediction, being compared with the event, and the remembrance thereof, when it comes to pass, is very comfortable; the prediction thereof beforehand serving to acquaint us therewith before it come, that we may be disposed for it, by a voluntary resolution, and patience; serving also to prove him to be the omniscient God, and that he hath a providence in our troubles, and is not an idle spectator thereof; and the certainty of his predictions, being verified in the matter of trials, may assure us of the certainty of what he foretels concerning our deliverance, Zech. viii. 14, 15. Therefore is this given them as an encouragement: " But these things have I told you, that when the time shall come, ye may remember that I told you of them."

In the fourth and last place (in the end of the verse) Christ having told the usefulness of foretelling this now, doth obviate an objection, and give a reason why he gave warning no sooner—namely, because he was with them; and so as they were tender and weak, needing his bodily presence, so he was the great butt of men's malice in that time, and they lurked safely under his shadow. Albeit Christ had formerly inculcated that disciples behoved to take up their cross, and had told them much of their hard lots, when he gave them their first commission, Matt. x., yet he saith, " These things I said not unto you at the beginning," not only because they were awhile with him, even before he had said so much to them, and before they were called to the apostleship; nor yet only because he gave them now, ver. 2, a more distinct and particular intimation of the kind and degrees of their suffering than at any time formerly; but chiefly, what he formerly foretold at a distance, he now foretels as things they were shortly after his removal to be essayed with.

DOCTRINES.

1. Christ is a prudent and tender guider of his followers, and knoweth the fit seasons of tender usage, of general intimations of troubles at distance, of putting them in mind to make for approaching trouble, and of laying the cross actually on; for so much is imported in his not telling his disciples at the first what he now tells them, and they afterward met with.

2. His not telling his disciples these things at the beginning, because he was with them, may serve to teach us, in all ages—1. Christ is so tender of his followers' weakness, that he will not put them to hard essays till they be confirmed, and trained, and fitted for them; therefore did he at first stay with them as a tutor and safeguard, and trained them up with seeing sufferings endured in his person, till they themselves were confirmed, (see Matt. ix. 16, 17,) so that when Christ puts saints to trials, they may reckon they are fitted for them, unless they have neglected the opportunity, or do for present cast away their confidence. 2. Christ's presence is the only sweet shelter and safeguard against troubles and storms; for as he gave them an easy life while he was with them, Matt. ix. 15, so, in all cases, his spiritual presence will arm sufficiently against trouble, if not to prevent it, yet to take the sting out of it. 3. It may encourage

saints in their sufferings, that Christ is the great object of the persecutors' malice, and they for his sake, so that if they could reach him, they would not care for them ; for so much appeareth, in that while he was with them they had no present use for the doctrine of sufferings, as any way like to fall on them.

3. When Christ hath trained his people till their strength grow up, they may expect that after his sweet presence and sensible consolations they will meet with a storm ; for now he tells them of that as near approaching, which he said not at the beginning.

4. Saints, after long sparing, may expect their trials will come thick and threefold upon them, and that their being under one trial will not be a shelter to hide them from another ; for now he is not to be with them, which was a trial sad enough, and they are to make for other sad sufferings at the same time.

5. The Lord may so order as to send afflictions on his people when they seem to be worse provided for them, and yet they shall be better borne through than if it had been otherwise ; for it might seem very unseasonable to them to tryst [appoint] their trials with the time when they should want his bodily presence, and yet he made them in a better condition, when deprived of his bodily presence, and having trials, than when enjoying it, and wanting trials ; as the event did prove.

Ver. 5. But now I go my way to him that sent me ; and none of you asketh me, Whither goest thou ?

6. But because I have said these things unto you, sorrow hath filled your heart.

Followeth, to ver. 29, the second part of the chapter, wherein Christ, by several encouragements, comforts them against his departure, unto which, in these verses, he premits [introduces], 1. The repeated intimation of his departure to him that sent him. 2. A reprehension of their not making use of, but rather abusing this intimation, in that they did so give up themselves to sorrow at the news as they neglected the opportunity of informing themselves concerning his departure, and whither he went, which might have been of special use to them.

From verse 5, learn—1. The sensible and sweet enjoyments of saints are not permanent, but subject to changes while they are within time ; for " I was with you," ver. 4, " But now I go my way."

2. Whatever violence was used towards Christ in his removal out of the world, yet his departure was voluntary in his own due time, after he had done his work, and not till then ; for saith he, " I go my way," and that " now," having done my work, and not till now.

3. Christ and his followers never want sufficient considerations to beautify and sweeten their saddest lots, and to swallow up the bitterness thereof ; therefore doth he point out his sufferings in lovely colours : " I go my way to him that sent me," which takes in the whole passages of his removal, in his death, burial, resurrection, ascension, and glorification ; and this was a most

comfortable sight of it, both to himself, who, after his toil, was to triumph with his Father, and to them, who were hereby taught that he had finished his work, and was to be exalted for their good and behoof.

4. As men ought not to undertake employments unless they be sent of God to do them, so they who are entrusted by him must again appear before him to give an account of their trust, and to be rewarded by him if they have been faithful ; for herein Christ is our pattern, who being sent of the Father doth now go his way to him that sent him, to give an account of his commission, and to be glorified with him.

5. It is a sweet consideration to those who are exercised about the absence of Christ, to know where he is and whither he is gone, that so they may know where to find him, what to do in his absence, and what advantage they may reap by his exaltation ; for he propounds this as the great and needful case to be resolved, " Whither goest thou ?"

6. It is our great fault that we can reckon our loss by God's exercising of us, but are not careful to see the advantages therein ; for they studied enough upon his going away, but nothing upon this, wherein the advantage lay, " Whither goest thou ?"

7. It is not enough to look upon our sufferings in their present bitterness, unless we look also upon the issue of them ; for so much doth Christ teach us in his own case, that they should not only consider that he did go, but whither he did go.

8. The issue of Christ and his followers' troubles is not easily discerned by us, nor can we understand it without his teaching ; for it is he who must resolve that question, " Whither goest thou ?" and it must be asked at him.

9. Christ is most willing to teach his people what may be for their instruction and comfort, and will quarrel when they do not put him to it ; for he quarrelleth that " none of you asketh me, Whither goest thou ?"

10. It is the great sin of saints to trifle away their time, and particularly not to improve short opportunities of enjoying Christ, and before a storm, that they may get somewhat to fit them for it ; for it is his challenge [charge], that knowing he was to depart shortly, they passed away that moment in sorrow and stupidity, not improving the present opportunity of his company to resolve cases which might be comfortable to them when he was gone : " Now I go my way, and none of you asketh me, Whither goest thou ?" Where he insinuateth that it was their duty to be throng [assembled] and busy during that moment.

11. Men may seem to be somewhat busy about important cases, and in seeking resolution of great difficulties, who yet, in Christ's account, are but really idle ; for albeit Peter did propound this very question to him, chap. xiii. 36, yet he challengeth, " none of you asketh," &c., because he did not so ask as seeking the right use of the resolution, to be confirmed in the exercise of believing, or informed concerning the effects of his departure for that end ; but only in a way of carping, and presumptuous boasting of his own strength.

From verse 6, learn—1. As it is no wonder saints be ofttimes exercised with sorrow under the apprehension of trouble, so it is most usual for them to keep no moderation in their sorrow, but to let loose the reins to themselves in it; for sorrow filled their heart.

2. Christ approveth not of immoderate sorrow in his followers, did the cause and rise thereof seem never so lawful, as being an imputation on him, as if he were a cruel master, and a mean to deter others from his service; therefore doth he challenge them for this : " sorrow hath filled your heart."

3. It is the great weakness of saints that in their distempers they turn even the good word of God, which is spoken for their encouragement, into matter of grief and sorrow ; for saith he, " because I have said these things unto you, sorrow hath filled your heart." This intimation tended to guard their hearts, and the news contained what was useful and comfortable for them, ver. 7, and chap. xiv. 28, and yet they filled them with sorrow.

4. A great cause of saints' excessive distempers under the dispensations wherewith they are exercised, is because they are too much addicted to sense, so that if it be not satisfied with the outward or inward sensible comforts which sometimes accompany profession and religion, or if they be deprived of what is sensible, sweet, and pleasant to them, they account all to be gone; whereas believing is more comfortable and useful; and because they look for great things in the world, and therefore are confounded with disappointments of their expectations ; for it was upon these grounds these news did so afflict them: they were exceedingly taken up with his sensible bodily presence, and hoped to be advanced in the world by him, when he should come to that temporal kingdom which they dreamed of; and therefore could not endure to hear of his removal, which deprived them of their present enjoyments and future carnal hopes.

5. Immoderate and excessive sorrow is exceeding sinful, (as for other reasons, so) because it stupifieth men, and layeth them by from needful duty, to which they are called in their difficulties ; for he reprehends their sorrow, not only in itself, but as it caused that sinful negligence which he reprehends, ver. 4, " None of you asketh me, Whither goest thou? But because I have said these things unto you, sorrow hath filled your heart."

VER. 7. Nevertheless I tell you the truth; It is expedient for you that I go away: for if I go not away, the Comforter will not come unto you; but if I depart, I will send him unto you.

From this to ver. 16 we have the first encouragement, whereby Christ sweetens these sad tidings, and labours to mitigate their excessive sorrow. The encouragement is taken from the promise of sending the Holy Spirit to compense the want of his bodily presence; concerning whom, 1. He asserts in this verse that they could not partake of that mercy but upon his removal.

2. In the following purpose he propounds the benefits to be expected by the Spirit's coming, beyond what they enjoyed by his bodily presence, that so they might be induced to submit to his departure, as making way for the Comforter's coming.

In this verse Christ asserts that however they relished the news of his departure, yet it was expedient, and for their behoof, that he should remove; which he cleareth by shewing the necessary connexion betwixt his departure and the Spirit's coming, who is so excellent a gift. This he instructs, both negatively, that if he did not go away the Spirit would not come; and positively, that upon his removal he would send him unto them; which is not to be understood as if they or others could not, or had not received the Spirit before his ascension, but that the Spirit was not to be poured out so largely upon the members till after his exaltation and glorification who is their Head, as chap. vii. 39.

DOCTRINES.

1. Christ's dealing may be very expedient and useful when yet it is very unsatisfactory to sense; for what filled their heart with sorrow is nevertheless expedient for you, saith he; so that he is to be judge of what is good for us, and not we ourselves.

2. We are ordinarily so addicted to our corrupt sense that the usefulness of an afflicted and humbling condition is hardly believed, even out of Christ's own mouth; therefore must he so strongly assert it, " I tell you the truth; it is expedient."

3. As all Christ's word is of infallible verity, so we are to look on it as such, that it may comfort us under afflictions, and uphold us against the testimony and apprehension of our sense; therefore doth he lead them to lean on this, as their support under all tentations to the contrary, " I tell you the truth; it is expedient for you that I go away."

4. As Christ doth nothing for or to his people but what is useful and profitable for them, so he is so tender as not to withhold what is useful because it satisfieth not their sense, but is grievous to their flesh, as knowing well that what is profitable will be pleasant in the end, however they look on it for present; for it was of his mercy that since it was expedient he went away, therefore he did go, let them resent it for present never so sadly.

5. Christ's people and their welfare are so dear to him, that in all that he did and that befel him, and in all the changes of his condition, he was still doing and minding that which was for their profit ; for as it was because it was expedient for them that he came to earth and stayed in it, so he went away again, not because he was weary of them and their company, nor yet only because he was to be glorified himself, but " because it is expedient for you that I go away," and be exalted into glory.

6. The Spirit of God, as he is largely communicated under the gospel, is so sweet an Advocate and Comforter, that his presence may compense the saddest of losses, were it even of the bodily presence of Christ; for here it is insinuated that

he is such a gift as it is a great favour to want Christ's bodily presence to make way for his coming; and that, because he is that " Comforter," by way of excellency, above that comfort they had by his bodily presence, and who can comfort believers in all places at once, whereas his bodily presence was confined to one place; therefore saith he, " If I go not away, the Comforter will not come; but if I go, I will send him."

7. As Christ's bodily presence is not the most powerful and refreshing way of comfort, however it was needful in its time and refreshful in its measure, so believers are not capable of the full consolations of the Spirit but by the removal of his bodily presence out of the world; for not only did he, by his death and going out of the world, merit it, and he must be glorified and enter into his kingdom before his members participate so largely of his fulness, but they were so dull while he was with them that they could not be capable of these comforts till they were weaned from a bodily presence, and exercised with trouble; therefore saith he, " If I go not away, the Comforter will not come." So that they who dote still on a corporal presence of Christ, do thereby stop the way of the comforts of a spiritual presence.

8. Christ, by sending of the Spirit after his ascension, doth not only prove himself true God, the second person of the blessed Trinity, from whom (as from the Father) the Holy Ghost proceedeth and is sent; but also, that as Mediator, justice is satisfied by his death; that he, as the Head of believers, is glorified, chap. vii. 39, and entered in possession of his dignity, Acts, ii. 33, and that being thus exalted, he is still mindful of his brethren. So much is imported in this, " If I depart, I will send him unto you."

9. Christ being now exalted, there is free access to partake of the Spirit by all those who do employ him for that effect; for being departed, he will send him to them who ask him.

Ver. 8. And when he is come, he will reprove the world of sin, and of righteousness, and of judgment:

The benefits to be reaped by the Spirit's coming (which would richly compense his departure) are three; the first relates to the world, whom the Spirit will convince of three great points—sin, righteousness, and judgment, which being here named only, are distinctly insisted upon in the three following verses, and the grounds upon which they shall be convinced of every one of them, and the evidences thereof, produced.

For clearing of this purpose a little, consider— First, As for the act here ascribed to the Spirit, of reproving, or rather, convincing, I take it to import, not only his offering and affording sufficient means which might convince men, but also the success of these means, and his effectual and actual convincing of them thereby; and that not only by illuminating them with knowledge, which may be without conviction, nor yet by bearing in challenges and reproofs only, for there may be challenges and reproofs without thorough convic-

tion, but further, by arguing them out of their principles and grounds to a contrary opinion, (as the word imports,) and bearing in of truth so as they are put to silence, and cannot in reason gainsay it.

Secondly. As for the object of this work of the Spirit, by " the world," who shall be convinced, I understand men in the world, and particularly men in the state of nature and yet unconverted, whether they be elect or reprobate, and that not a few, but many of them; all which are frequently expressed in scripture by the name of " the world."

Thirdly. As for the nature, scope, and tendency of this work of conviction, what it shall produce or tend to, there is some difficulty in determining thereof; for some, however they speak of this conviction of the world in general as a common work, yet, in explication of the particulars whereof they are to be convinced, they restrict it to the world of the elect, whom the Spirit convinceth of these things in order unto and in working of their conversion, as shall be after cleared. Others again do restrict all of it to the reprobates, who get no more but conviction, or at least, do understand it of a work of conviction of these particulars, common to both elect and reprobates, whereby the Spirit beareth witness unto Christ, and the truth of the Christian religion among men; whether the Lord carry them on a further length, or let the work sist [stop] only there. I do conceive it most suitable to understand it as comprehending both of these— both what is common to elect and reprobates, and what the Spirit further works upon the elect in the work of their conversion. And for clearing hereof, and the scope of the whole purpose, I shall speak a little to a few things. 1. It should be considered, that however the purpose here mentioned do relate to what the Spirit will work upon the world, yet Christ's scope in speaking of it is to encourage his disciples, as appears from ver. 7, " It is expedient for you that I go away, for I will send the Comforter to you, and he shall convince the world." They were much saddened with the apprehension of his removal, and that in his absence they were to be engaged in a difficult service of the ministry, and of standing for him, wherein they might probably expect much hazard and difficulty, and little success, they being but weak men; their Master, for whom they stood, but despised as a seducer and mock king, even among the Jews; their message very unpleasant, as being so contrary to flesh and blood, and the principles universally received and carnal interests of men; and consequently, the opposition to be made unto them very strong, violent, and universal. Now to guard against all these, Christ giveth this encouragement, among others, that they should receive the Spirit, by whom this raging world should be convinced, and so their opposition taken off, or blunted and made easy. 2. This being Christ's scope in this encouragement, it is most safe to extend this promised conviction to all the effects of their ministry, and of the Spirit's work accompanying the same, both on the elect and reprobate; and that we so take in his common work upon them who are reprobates, and continue still in the state of nature, notwithstanding that work, as we seclude not his saving work in gathering and drawing in the elect; for as it was to be a comfort to them to see the Spirit so owning them as even the world should be convinced, so it would be much more comfortable to them when the Spirit should make that conviction saving on any, and so not only take off or blunt their opposition, but make them real friends. 3. It should be considered, (for clearing the purpose,) what were the means of working this conviction, or the operations of the Spirit in bringing about the same, for the encouragement of the disciples. These were many, without and extrinsical unto the persons convinced, if taken one by one; as namely, the extraordinary endowments conferred in large measure upon the apostles, whereby they, who were known to be unlearned, mean men, were enabled to speak with many tongues, and to preach learnedly, powerfully, and boldly; their daily preachings (being thus endowed) of the sweet doctrine of the gospel, and the law in subordination thereunto; and that notwithstanding all their sufferings and ill usage, which they went through with invincible courage and fortitude; the many miracles and cures wrought by their hands; the casting out of devils; the gifts of the Spirit conferred by the laying on of their hands; the silencing of Satan's oracles through the world by the sound of their ministry; and the glorious effects of their doctrine where it was received, by destroying the kingdom and power of Satan, and bringing in of light, holiness, and consolation. Unto these (and divers others) without them, several operations are to be added which were wrought in or upon the persons convinced; as namely, extraordinary cures wrought upon some of themselves, both elect and reprobate; common and clear illumination, and temporary gifts, conferred upon both of them, and some of them in an extraordinary measure; strong impressions to take notice of these operations of the Spirit without them; together with saving operations accompanying all these upon the hearts of the elect. 4. The effects of these means and operations, or the conviction itself wrought thereby, to the encouragement of the apostles, come next to be considered. And as these means were extraordinary, so the effects were to be answerable; for if we look upon the history of the Acts, which containeth a signal accomplishment of this prediction, we shall find strange effects following upon the pouring out of the Spirit, even in those who were not converted, at least not as yet. Some were pricked at the heart, who had not yet attained to evangelical repentance, Acts, ii. 37, with 38; some, in the gall of bitterness, did desire to share with the apostles in their great privileges, Acts, viii. 18, 19; some upon their thrones were almost persuaded to be Christians by a prisoner in a chain, Acts, xxvi. 28; some had strange changes, illuminations, and flushes for a time, who yet were not converted, as is to be supposed of many who were drawn in by the apostles' preaching, and of others who afterwards did, and daily do embrace the gospel; some were forced to magnify them, who did not join with them, Acts, v. 13; some would have worshipped them, who were yet pagans, Acts, xiv. 10, 11; some were astonished with what was

done by the apostles, Acts, viii. 14, and with their fortitude and abilities, Acts, iv. 13, and were nonplussed in their resolutions what to do with them when they were in their power, Acts, iv. 16, 17, yea, and so bridled, that they were afraid to meddle with them, Acts, v. 34, 35; unto all which, and many more wonderful effects of these operations, may be added, that the elect did not only share in these common operations, but were in due time (by these means, and particularly by the word) savingly convinced and brought to Christ and fixed upon him;—all which conviction, though it be attributed to " the world," and was indeed very general in process of time, yet it is to be understood with this necessary limitation, that some, yea, many, remained still in their stupidity, and were not effectually convinced for all this; yea, some who were convinced were yet not bridled, but given up to contradict and blaspheme against the Holy Ghost, for the trial and exercise of the apostles and other professors, and that the Spirit might magnify his power in them, and convince the world, by their invincible courage and patience, and God's preserving of them many times, and making the work prosper in their hands in the midst of their sufferings, more than if these malicious men had never opposed them.

Fourthly. As for the particulars whereof they are to be convinced—" sin, righteousness, and judgment"—they come to be more distinctly spoken to in the following verses, where the grounds of this conviction are spoken of. Here, in general, it sufficeth us to know, 1. If we look upon this work of conviction as it is common to elect and reprobate, and as the Spirit's testimony about them relates to Christ and the Christian religion, these were the points of controversy betwixt the apostles in preaching of the gospel, and the world; for Christ, being the subject of the gospel, the great opposition related unto him, whether he was the Son of God and true Messiah, and therefore, whether they were guilty of great sin who did not believe him and receive his testimony, and continued still in a state of sin so long as they embraced not him; whether he was righteous in himself, and the only giver of righteousness to sinners, or a seducer and Samaritan, and one without whom they were righteous, as the world alleged; and whether he was an exalted Prince, above Satan and all powers and idols, able to absolve his friends and subjects, and condemn his enemies; or only a mock king and a base person, as he was traduced to be;— all which he promiseth shall be determined to their advantage. 2. If we look on this, as it is proper to the elect, in the work of their conversion, the words contain a sweet method of bringing about this work; first, to convince them of sin, by letting them see the hazard of their natural condition, through continuance in unbelief; next, to convince them of righteousness to be had in Christ only, as a remedy to this condition; and then to convince them of judgment and dominion, and of deliverance from spiritual slavery, and the pulling down of Satan's kingdom by being in him;—of all which, albeit the reprobate may get a common conviction, as it is hinted in the former consideration, yet these things are further and more effectually and savingly carried on in the hearts of the elect, to their conversion and settling upon Christ.

This purpose, thus explained by parts, may be taken up in this brief sum; that whereas the apostles, after Christ's departure, were to be engaged in hard service, with much disadvantage and difficulty, Christ comforts them by shewing that he would pour such a measure of the Spirit upon them, and by his Spirit so accompany them in their ministry as should make it successful in the world, to the conviction even of enemies and reprobates, and to the further gaining upon others; so that the work should go on, his kingdom be established in the world, and his glory shine, and they be comforted and carried through, notwithstanding all the opposition they should meet with.

From the words so cleared, learn—1. The service of the ministers of Christ in carrying through the work of the gospel is not only difficult, but impossible, unless they be singularly assisted by Christ therein; for so is here imported, that they need the Spirit for carrying on this work.

2. The Spirit of Christ accompanying weak means and instruments can bring about great things to the advancement of his kingdom in the world, without any visible force, and with mere spiritual weapons, in despite of all opposition that can be made thereunto; for so is here promised, that the Spirit, in them and with them, shall effectuate this work, how weak soever they were.

3. It is the great consolation of Christ's faithful servants and followers to enjoy his presence and blessing upon their calling and employment, and particularly of faithful ministers, to have his kingdom prosper and men wrought upon by their ministry; for this is the apostles' encouragement, and in this the Spirit is a Comforter to them, that he shall " convince the world," to make their labours successful.

4. The men of the world are very corrupt and ill-principled in reference to the doctrine of the gospel, and have very many mountains standing in the way thereof; for they need to be convinced of all these points here mentioned, and have opinions and principles opposite thereunto to be rooted out, as the word imports.

5. These corrupt principles of the world are not easy to be rooted out, but will require great light and strong conviction before they be put from them; for they must be convinced and argued out of them to the contrary opinion before they quit them.

6. For conviction of the world it will not be sufficient that never so sharp reproofs be given them, nor yet only that they have clear light and evidence of what they are to assent unto, unless also the Spirit come to bear in these things upon them and effectually convince thereof; for it is he who must " convince the world," not only by sufficient external means and operations without them, but by inward working making that effectual.

7. The Spirit of the Lord is an effectual convincer where he pleaseth to work; where clear illumination and strong reasoning will not avail, he can irresistibly convince and batter down strong holds; and where he will not convert yet he can so put to silence and bridle opposition that it shall be ineffectual; for he shall " convince the world," saith he.

8. As Christ's saving work on his people must begin with and be carried on by the convictions of the Spirit, so they may get convictions, and that by the Spirit, who never get more, and are never converted; for, on the one hand, conviction is so far from saving grace that they who have it in a deep measure have yet need, not only of faith, but also of repentance, Acts, i. 37, 38, and, on the other hand, it concerneth God, in his honour, sometimes to go thus far on with the world, for the promoving of his kingdom, and that they may not go on with a high hand; therefore it is promised that he shall convince even the world; so that they who were never convinced are yet in a worse condition, and do not know how soon the Lord may kindle that fire in their bosoms though they sleep secure for the present. And men would not rest upon convictions when the Lord lets them see " sin," and yet never removeth it, " righteousness," and yet never conferreth it, and " judgment," of authority to absolve the righteous and condemn the wicked, and yet never giveth them to flee to Christ to obtain the one or to be freed from the other.

9. The Spirit's manifestations and operations in the primitive days of the gospel do abundantly assert the truth of the Christian religion, and refute all the corrupt principles of men concerning Christ, so that all who then saw or felt them, or since do hear thereof by the sound of the gospel, (still accompanied with the ordinary operations of the Spirit where it is received,) are without excuse if they continue ignorant of or averse and opposite unto the true religion, and Christ offered in the gospel; for by these means the Spirit hath convinced " the world of sin, and of righteousness, and of judgment," as the great points in controversy concerning Christ and the Christian religion, as hath been cleared. So that however all in all ages be not actually convinced, yet (beside that generally it is so, in some measure, where the gospel cometh) it is a standing testimony, leaving all those without excuse who hear the gospel and yet continue in atheism, infidelity, scepticism, and irreligion; and the effectual conviction of others leaves them yet more without excuse.

10. As there are many steps and degrees of operation in converting souls to Christ, so the Spirit of the Lord, where he undertaketh this work in his own, will effectually carry them through them all, in their due order; for so much also doth this work of convincing " of sin, righteousness," &c., as it is proper to the elect, import; that he will not only give them a light touch and ineffectual impression of those things which reprobates may have, but will effectually carry them from step to step till they be convinced of the truth of these things and of their need of the two last, and made to close therewith to their comfort. And herein the order of the Spirit is to be observed, so that if we miss the comfortable conviction of righteousness, we should see if we do not stop it by want of conviction of sin; and if we want comfortable conviction of free-

dom from slavery, and absolution through Christ, we may find it obstructed by our not closing with righteousness when we are convinced of sin.

VER. 9. *Of sin, because they believe not on me;*

The particulars generally named in the former verse are now more particularly insisted on and cleared, from the grounds upon which the world shall be convinced of them. And first, for sin; they shall be convinced thereof, because they believe not in him; which being taken more generally in reference to the conviction of the world, both elect and reprobate, holds out, that the operations of the Spirit, communicated by and from Christ now ascended, shall prove him to be the Son of God, the great Prophet, and true Messiah, and so shall convince them of their great sin in rejecting and not believing him and his testimony. Being taken more particularly in reference to the elect, it holds out that the Spirit shall begin at convincing them of sin, and shall withal convince that the wretchedness and desperateness of their condition lieth not so much in their other sins as in their unbelief and not closing with Christ; whereof the world also may get a taste in being convinced of their miserable condition by reason of sin, since they do not embrace him, the remedy, though they do never amend it, whereas the elect are convinced till they make use of the remedy. Whence learn—

1. The world without Christ is lying in a miserable condition and state of sin; for so is here imported.

2. The world is so blind and stubborn in their course of sinning, that neither natural light nor judgments and afflictions, yea, nor the doctrine of the word, without the assistance of the Spirit, will discover sin, nor let them see the sinfulness thereof; and that because men are blind by nature, that they see not their own case, and they have so many subterfuges of fathering their sins on others, (as Adam, Evah, and Aaron did, Gen. iii. 12, 13; Exod. xxxii. 22—24,) of pretence of custom, of giving fair names to foul sins, &c., that they see not the sinfulness of what they acknowledge; therefore it must be the Spirit who convinceth of sin. So that when men have the word, it must be made searching by the Spirit of God, before it discover them to themselves, Rom. vii. 9, 13, 14; yea, and loving-kindness must be applied and believed before sin be abominable as it ought. Ezra, ix. 13, 14.

3. The Spirit is able to convince men who otherwise will not be convinced of sin, and doth so to many whom he will never convert; for he shall convince the world of sin.

4. Conviction of sin is the first work that the Spirit works upon a soul which he is to draw in to himself; for this conviction, in reference to the elect, beginneth here.

5. Unbelief is the great sin whereof men are to be convinced, and do need the Spirit for that end. This holds true in divers respects:—
1. If we look on this sin in itself, it is the great sin against the gospel, and their great guilt who opposed and rejected him—a sin greater than any against the law, and very injurious to Christ, and a sin, that (however men by nature's light may see other sins) we shall never see the ill of but by the Spirit. 2. If we look on it in reference to other sins, it is the sin that defiles all our actions, how morally good soever they be; the sin that binds all our other sins upon us, seeing it is only by faith in Christ we draw virtue for subduing thereof, and the sin which renders all our other sins incurable and unpardonable, as being a sin against the remedy and holding us back from it; therefore is this conviction of sin thus instructed, "because they believe not on me." Not only as it is a prime and great sin in itself, but as it hath influence on other sins and serveth to convince men of the woeful ill of their sinful condition so long as they continue to reject the remedy.

6. It is not enough men see a general view of their sinful state unless they take it up distinctly, and the root and cause thereof, without which they will never know how to set about the cure of it; therefore, in convincing "of sin" he convinceth of unbelief as the root from whence the misery, or at least the desperateness of that condition floweth.

7. All conviction of sin is ineffectual unless men also see their unbelief and the sinfulness thereof, to be convinced of it and humbled for it; for so much doth this working of the Spirit import; he convinceth "of sin, because they believe not on me."

8. Faith in Jesus Christ is a duty so spiritual, and above the reach of nature, and a duty which souls convinced of sin are so averse from, that the neglect hereof and the sin of unbelief will not be seen without the working of the Spirit; for this is a conviction of sin requiring the operation of the Spirit, that men see themselves guilty of sin because they believe not on him.

9. When self-condemned sinners are led to find faith, and the necessity thereof pressed upon them, and are made to see the ill of unbelief, and to endeavour to be rid of it and to essay faith, they ought not to look on this as a tentation or presumption in them, but as the very work of the Spirit of God; for he is sent forth for this end, to convince men "of sin, because they believe not on me."

VER. 10. *Of righteousness, because I go to my Father, and ye see me no more;*

The next thing whereof the Spirit convinceth the world is "righteousness," not their own, but Christ's; and that both the righteousness of his person, and his righteousness as Mediator, imputed to his people to their justification. Both these are strongly grounded and concluded from this, that he goeth to the Father, and continueth with him, so that even his disciples see him no more after his ascension. For—1. When the Spirit, sent from Christ, by his extraordinary operations doth make it manifest that Christ remained not dead, but rose again and ascendeth and liveth with the Father in glory and majesty, (as these gifts and operations sent down by him do evidence,) it will necessarily follow that he was not a seducer and Samaritan, but that righteous One, who, however he was rejected of men, yet is approven of God. 2. As Christ laid down his life to purchase righteousness for us, which otherwise was unattainable by the works of the law, Gal. ii. 21, so by his resurrection and ascension, and pouring out of the Spirit in large measure, he makes it evident that he is accepted by the Father in our name, and liveth for ever to apply his righteousness unto us, Rom. iv. 25. So the scope of this is, that however the world did traduce Christ, and, leaning to their own righteousness, did reject him and his righteousness, yet the Spirit's coming, as a fruit of his ascension, shall convince them that he was just and righteous, and that righteousness is to be had only in and through him; and further, this same Spirit making use of these means, and particularly of the word, shall convince self-condemned sinners that they ought and may rely on him for righteousness. Whence learn—

1. Even Christ himself was not free from the horrid imputations of the foul mouths of traducers more than his followers; for his "righteousness" was in debate among them.

2. Whatever be the imputations cast upon Christ and his followers in their sufferings, yet God will make the issue thereof at last clear them; for whatever thoughts they had of him while suffering, or whatever pretence they might seem to have while he was on earth, subject to our sinless infirmities, yet his going to his Father after that did serve sufficiently to convince them.

3. Christ's exaltation with the Father, and the evidences thereof communicated to the church by the Spirit, do abundantly proclaim him to be that holy and righteous One, of whom it is blasphemy to harbour any prejudice and misconstruction; for he shall "convince the world of righteousness, because I go to my Father."

4. It is not sufficient that men be convinced of sin, unless they also be driven to seek righteousness to cover the same; for this conviction of righteousness must follow upon the former, of conviction of sin. And without this neither a sight of sin nor acknowledgment of Christ as righteous in his own person will avail.

5. It is a point which the Spirit hath put beyond all controversy that the righteousness of fallen man is only in and through Christ, so that all who seek another way of righteousness do go against a clear conviction; for he shall "convince the world of righteousness."

6. Imputed righteousness is a point whereof the Spirit only can convince men, and make them submit to it. Men are not only naturally ignorant thereof, as not being according to the covenant of works, Rom. iii. 21, but their proud hearts are averse from such a way of it, Rom. x. 13, and self-condemned sinners, finding nothing in themselves, are afraid to lean to that which is without them till the Spirit bear it in upon them and cause them to close with it; therefore they must be convinced of the righteousness, and that by the Spirit.

7. Christ's acceptation with the Father after his suffering, evidenced by the pouring out of the Spirit, doth evidence his righteousness to be so perfect and acceptable to the Father, and himself in such a capacity to apply his righteousness, and to own them who flee unto him, that self-condemned sinners may with confidence rest under the shadow of his righteousness; for so much is imported in that he will convince "of righteousness, because I go to my Father," and there live for ever to make intercession. (See Rom. viii. 33, 34.)

8. Such as would have the comfortable use of Christ's righteousness must not lean to sense or sight, but betake themselves to faith; for so much may be imported in that, "ye see me no more," which not only confirms his going unto and continuing with the Father, because they see him no more, but find rich gifts come from him; but sheweth, that in participation of his righteousness they must not expect to have sense satisfied with a bodily sight of him. He saith, "Ye see me no more"—to wit, after his ascension to the Father, till the day of judgment, and though they saw him after his resurrection, yet not in his former state, and but in a transient way.

Ver. 11. Of judgment, because the prince of this world is judged.

The last thing whereof the Spirit convinceth the world is "judgment," in the understanding whereof we shall be much helped by what is said on chap. xii. 31; for "judgment," in scripture, in relation to the object or things about which it is employed, doth ofttimes signify the exercise of power and authority to dispose of them, and put and keep them in order; and in relation to the subject and person in whom it is, it signifieth the having of authority so to order these things. Here the interpretation may be fetched from Acts, ii. 36, that Jesus in his exaltation is made both Lord and Christ, and here the Spirit convinceth the world that he is both; that he is Christ, by convincing them of his righteousness, ver. 10, and that he is Lord, by convincing them of "judgment," and that all power and judgment is committed to him; which is evidenced and proven by his judging Satan, the prince of this world, over whom he triumphed in the cross, Col. ii. 15, and made his purchase and conquest evident by his casting out of Satan from those possessed by him, his silencing Satan's oracles in the world, and casting him out of those who receive the gospel and are converted, destroying the kingdom of wickedness and darkness, and translating them into his own kingdom, and into a state of holiness and light. This is the general scope of this purpose, that the world shall be convinced of Christ's dominion by his seen power over Satan, under which (among many other things) is to be comprehended a judgment of condemnation of all the wicked in Satan, their prince and head, and a judgment of absolution, and vindication into liberty and freedom from Satan's slavery, in favour of those who flee to him, and in whom the work and kingdom of Satan is destroyed.

DOCTRINES.

1. Satan is a prince who, by his tyrannical usurpation, and by a voluntary consent of deluded

souls, doth get and exercise a tyrannical government over the children of men, so long as they are without Christ; for he is "the prince of this world."

2. Christ by his death did condemn and overcome Satan, and hath made his conquest evident to the conviction of men by the effects and operations of his Spirit, in doctrine condemning Satan and his work in men, casting him out miraculously, and destroying his work in believers; for he supposeth it as a clear and undeniable truth that "the prince of this world is judged."

3. By this judging of Satan the Spirit hath made it undeniably evident that Christ hath all authority and power to preserve his church, triumph over his enemies, and order all the confusions that Satan and sin have occasioned in the world; for whatever were their thoughts of Christ, yet when it shall be evident that Christ took Satan, the great disturber, to task, and foiled him, it cannot in reason be denied, but he is sovereign Judge and Lord, having all power in his hand, and all his adversaries under his feet; he shall convince the world " of judgment, because the prince of this world is judged."

4. By the power of Christ, evidenced in condemning and triumphing over Satan, it is made apparent to all the wicked that their condemnation is already passed, in the judgment and condemnation of Satan, their head and prince, and to all the godly who flee to Christ, that they are absolved and freed from the tyranny and kingdom of Satan, in Christ the conqueror; for thus this "judgment" may be branched out on both hands, as proving the condemnation of the wicked and absolution of the believer, " because the prince of this world is judged."

5. Such as are savingly convinced of Christ's righteousness ought also to be convinced of their absolution and deliverance from Satan thereby, and to feel the effects of Christ's dominion, in his daily subduing of Satan within them, and it will be their comfort to find this; for so much is imported in reference to the elect, as this is subjoined to the former particulars, that not only, having fled to Christ for righteousness, who hath given visible evidences of his dominion over Satan, they may be comforted in their deliverance from such a tyrant, but that having found righteousness in Christ to cover their guilt, ver. 10, the next work of the Spirit will be to convince them of Christ's authority to rule, and that not so much by any outward or common effects without them, as by his destroying of Satan and his kingdom within them. For upon the justification of believers the Spirit evidenceth Christ's getting a throne in their heart, to vindicate them from the slavery of corruption, by casting down Satan from his dominion and power over them, and convinceth them " of judgment," and freedom from slavery thereby, " because the prince of this world is judged." And where conviction in this particular is not, it brings conviction of righteousness in question.

Ver. 12. I have yet many things to say unto you, but ye cannot bear them now.

13. Howbeit when he, the Spirit of truth, is come, he will guide you into all truth: for he shall not speak of himself; but whatsoever he shall hear, that shall he speak: and he will shew you things to come.

Hitherto Christ hath insisted upon the first benefit to be expected by the coming of the Spirit, for their encouragement; the second followeth, in these verses, relating more immediately to the apostles themselves, wherein is promised, that however, for present, they were not capable of the many things he had to say unto them, ver. 12, yet the Spirit should, by his coming, supply that defect; and, 1. Should guide them into all truth, as being the Spirit of truth, and speaking what is common to him with the Father and Son. 2. Should shew them things to come, by being a Spirit of prophecy to them, as extraordinarily gifted men, and by revealing the great things abiding them and others, as believers, ver. 13. How this purpose, ver. 12, compared with ver. 13, ought to be understood, is already cleared on chap. xiv. 25, 26. (Compare also chap. xv. 15.) In sum it imports, that whereas Christ had spoken many things summarily which he was ready to enlarge, but that their incapacity hindered him, he here undertaketh that the Spirit should make up this, by enlightening their understanding to take up what he had said, and by explaining and enlarging the same more distinctly. They who (to favour unwritten traditions) do assert from this that the Spirit did teach somewhat which Christ had not taught them, do nothing at all promove their own cause; for whatever was taught them by Christ himself, or by the Spirit afterward, was by them faithfully communicated to the church, and committed to writing. And for those things which men urge as unwritten traditions, beside the scripture, they are such toys as Christ needed not say, " Ye cannot bear them," seeing they might easily be borne by them who have less than the apostles then had, and are more common and trivial than many things he had taught them.

From verse 12, learn—1. Many are the precious truths of the gospel to be learned by believers, and which are needful and comfortable for them to know; for there are "many things to say."

2. Christ's heart is so large and so tender towards his followers, that he hath never said enough when he hath said most, for their instruction and encouragement; for after all the former sweet doctrine, " I have yet many things to say unto you," saith he.

3. Our hearing and learning much of divine truth ought to tend mainly to let us know that there is more to be learned, that so we may be humbled in what we know, and our desires may be kindled after the knowledge of more; therefore also doth he break off the former sweet instructions with this—" I have yet many things to say unto you."

4. As men by nature are incapable of divine truths till they be taught them by the Spirit, so even they who have received the Spirit in some measure may yet remain very incapable, so long as they want a further measure of the Spirit, and

do continue under weakness and errors of mind prepossessing them, or do give up themselves to excessive sorrow ; for so it was even with the disciples, notwithstanding the measure of the Spirit they had received. They continued still so carnal and weak, were so prepossessed with errors concerning Christ's kingdom, and so taken up with sorrow, ver. 6, that he must say, ye cannot bear these many things now.

5. Men are never sufficiently capable of divine truths unless their understandings do comprehend them, and their hearts and affections do digest them as not to be stumbled or quarrelled at, that so they may reap the fruit of them ; for so much doth the expression, " ye cannot bear them," import. It may allude to burden-bearers, who do shrink under too heavy burdens, as their weak understandings and pre-occupied affections were ready to do under these high and spiritual truths, or to weak stomachs, which cast up the strong meat they cannot digest.

6. The most choice of outward means and advantages will not profit men, nor cause them to make progress, unless the Spirit concur therewith ; for they had even Christ to teach them, and yet they " cannot bear" his words, to profit thereby.

7. Our own infirmity, dulness, and incapacity, do obstruct our mercies, and hinder the revelation of many precious truths unto us ; for Christ saith not these " many things," because they " cannot bear them."

8. As Christ takes particular notice of the state of his disciples, so he tenderly deals with them according to their strength, and condescends to their weakness and incapacity ; for he spares at this time to let out these things unto them, because they " cannot bear them now." (See Mark, iv. 33.)

From verse 13, learn—1. There are no infirmities of saints, wherein they do not approve themselves, for which Christ hath not a remedy ; nor do they lose any opportunity which he cannot make up ; therefore, whereas they lost many advantages they might have reaped in his company, by their own greatness, he subjoins this as a comfort, that it should be made up by the Spirit's coming.

2. It is by the Spirit only that men who do not profit under outward means will be enabled to profit, who, when he cometh, doth reveal truths clearly, and bear them in with life and power upon the heart, and doth renew men's spirits to embrace and submit unto them ; for it is by this means that the disciples' losses are made up, " Howbeit when the Spirit is come, he will guide you."

3. As it is the duty of believers to know all revealed truths necessary for them in order to salvation, or in their places and stations, so they will need the Spirit's teaching and guiding for taking up all and every divine truth, even the least and smallest point of it ; for it is needful " he guide into all truth."

4. The doctrine revealed by the Spirit unto the apostles containeth all necessary truths, and so is a most perfect rule of faith and manners ; for it is promised unto them, that " he will guide you into all truth."

5. It doth set forth both the truth and divine authority of the doctrine of the apostles, that it is taught by the Spirit, who is a Spirit of truth, and that the doctrine is not his only, but communicated by him from the Father and Son also ; therefore is he here called " the Spirit of truth." And it is given as a reason why he will " guide into all truth ; for he shall not speak of himself (only) ; but whatsoever he shall hear, (with and from the Father and the Son,) that shall he speak."

6. It contributes to the encouragement of believers that the Spirit of God, which taketh charge of them, knoweth things to come, and so can reveal them that they may be encouraged or warned, and hath a sovereign providence over and about them ; for this his knowledge is imported, in that he will " shew things to come."

7. The Spirit of Christ did communicate unto the apostles, and by them unto the church, such infallible predictions of things to come as were needful to be known, and are useful to the church in all ages ; for " he will shew you things to come," saith he.

8. The Spirit of Christ by the doctrine of the apostles did bring life and immortality, and the future glory of believers, to light, 2 Tim. i. 10 ; and where he cometh, doth so clearly and fully persuade believers thereof, as may bear them out under all present pressures and discouragements ; thus also doth he " shew things to come," by their doctrine, and to them and all succeeding believers.

VER. 14. He shall glorify me : for he shall receive of mine, and shall shew it unto you.

The third benefit to be expected by the Spirit's coming (and an enlargement of the former) is, that he shall glorify Christ by communicating and shewing unto them what he receives of him ; which is to be understood, not only of that truth that he communicates from Christ unto them, of which, ver. 13, but also of all those extraordinary gifts, and that power to work miracles ; of that efficacy, accompanying and bearing in the doctrine of Christ ; of his bringing all that to a glorious effect which Christ had done for his people in his state of humiliation, which otherwise seemed very ignominious ; and of his communicating the influences of the fulness of Christ in heaven to believers on earth ; by all which, communicated from Christ, he shall make it evident that Christ is glorious, and to be acknowledged as such by his people. Whence learn—

1. It is not only the particular satisfaction of believers, but Christ's honour also, that they should look to in their spiritual enjoyments ; so that it is not enough they be refreshed and satisfied unless he also appear glorious and become great in their hearts thereby ; for this tends to their encouragement, that by what they shall receive from the Spirit, " he shall glorify me," saith Christ.

2. Albeit Christ's person, doctrine, actions, and sufferings, in the state of his humiliation, were clouded under obscurity and ignominy, yet as he is still glorious in himself, so **the Spirit**

after his ascension did, and in all ages doth, proclaim his glory and excellency, in his person, doctrine, and operations, to the conviction and satisfaction of believers; for " he shall glorify me."

3. It is the work of the Spirit, where he is communicated, not to extol or teach men to cry up themselves who do receive him, nor yet to glorify and exalt any other thing in the church but Christ alone; exalting his person, making his word singularly effectual, pointing out his ignominious sufferings as the only mean of life, and himself as the storehouse of his people; for the true Spirit " shall glorify me," saith Christ.

4. As all the fulness communicated by the Spirit to the church in the primitive times and after ages is communicated from Christ, (for it is " mine," saith he, " he shall shew it unto you,") so the way to have Christ high in our hearts is to have the Spirit keeping intercourse betwixt him and us, and conveying daily of his fulness, and the warm thoughts of his heart and good will to us; for this is the Spirit's employment, and by this he glorifieth Christ; for " he shall receive of mine, and shew it unto you."

Ver. 15. All things that the Father hath are mine: therefore said I, that he shall take of mine, and shall shew it unto you.

Lest by the former expression, of the Spirit's receiving and communicating of what is Christ's, the Father should seem to be secluded from this great work, therefore he subjoins for explication, that, by reason of the unity of essence, all things are so the Father's as they are his also, and therefore he might call those things his which the Spirit should shew, as being communicated by the Spirit from the Father and him. Whence learn—

1. The way to understand aright what Christ saith is to compare one passage with another; therefore doth he, by this following passage, explain what seemed harsh in the former, that " he shall take of mine, and shew it unto you."

2. Christ is to be so eyed in the large allowances communicated unto his church, as we forget not the Father, but rather we ought to see the fulness and rich good will of the Father in what Christ communicateth, and Christ's own excellency, who hath all fulness that is in the Father, to communicate; therefore he asserteth that " all things that the Father hath are mine," as the reason of that expression, " He shall take of mine," &c.

3. Such is the strict union of the persons of the blessed Trinity, that there is among them a perfect communion in all things; for " all things that the Father hath are mine," and so the Spirit's also.

4. As there is an union in essence, and communion among the persons of the Trinity, so their order of subsistence and operation is distinct, the Son being and working from the Father, and the Holy Ghost from the Father and the Son; for saith he, " All things that the Father hath are mine" from him, and the Spirit " shall take of mine, and shew it unto you."

Ver. 16. A little while, and ye shall not see me: and again, a little while, and ye shall see me, because I go to the Father.

From this to ver. 23 is contained the second encouragement, whereby Christ comforts his disciples, and mitigates their excessive sorrow for his departure. In this verse the encouragement is more briefly propounded; that however he was shortly to be removed from them in respect of his bodily presence, being now to suffer death, and leave the world, yet they should shortly after that see him again, and he should find a way to be indeed present with them. For understanding whereof, albeit that reason of his going " to the Father," may lead us to understand it of his appearing again to them bodily, after his resurrection, and that since he was not to abide under the power of death, but to rise again and ascend to his Father, they should get a sight of him by the way, yet I take not this sight to be understood here further than as it was a forerunner of greater things. For this is to be done " in that day" wherein they were to be endowed with much knowledge, and to come much speed in their prayers put up in his name, ver. 23, which is not to be restricted to that time betwixt his death and ascension, but was rather verified after his ascension. And upon the same ground, albeit the enjoyment and sight of Christ in heaven (which every believer may expect after a short while) do indeed complete that joy which is propounded, ver. 20, as the fruit of their seeing of him, yet it is not to be restricted to that either; for in that day they will need no prayer, as, ver. 23, it is said they shall in the day they shall see him. Therefore it is most clear to understand the encouragement thus: that however he was shortly to die and remove from them, yet seeing he was not to abide under the power of death, but to ascend and be exalted with the Father, he would therefore give proof of his exaltation and good will towards them by pouring out of his Spirit, whereby they should enjoy a spiritual sight of him, as chap. xiv. 19, and by this their sad hours should be sweetened (as also all believers') till they come to full sight and full joy in heaven. Now, albeit this encouragement, thus explained, together with the rest that follow, do all depend upon the pouring out of the Spirit, as fruits and benefits to be reaped thereby, as well as those that are formerly mentioned in this chapter,—and so may all be reduced to that general encouragement, of the coming of the Holy Ghost, —yet seeing Christ doth not here (as in the former) name this as a fruit of the Spirit's coming, therefore I have made it a distinct encouragement.

DOCTRINES.

1. The life of believers within time is made up and consists of great variety of lots, having and wanting sweets and sours mixed together, and succeeding one to another; for so it is here declared, they are now seeing, shortly not to see, and after that to see again.

2. The great exercise of believers is about the enjoying or wanting a sight of Christ; and this

sight of Christ is so precious to them that it moves all the wheels of their affections, and makes fair weather or foul, according as they want or enjoy it; it being still winter when he is absent, and whenever he returns, he brings the spring with him; therefore is all their exercise summed up in this, " ye shall not see me," and " ye shall see me," and this is it which begets the joy and sorrow after mentioned.

3. Whatever be Christ's tender condescendence, at some times, to his people, yet they are to expect that within time they will get satisfaction to their sense but for a short time; for so did the disciples find in the matter of his bodily presence, and so will believers find in the matter of sensible enjoyments; " A little while," (being all put together,) or, but now a little while, in respect of what they had enjoyed, chap. xiv. 9, " and ye shall not see me." The word imports a serious and intent seeing and contemplating, and is attributed ofttimes to a sight of the mind, and it may insinuate that now they should not get him seen so distinctly as formerly, or that his removal should so confound them for a time as they should not so much as get him contemplated with the eyes of their mind till the Spirit come upon them.

4. It is the will of Christ that believers be not surprised with the withdrawing of Christ's sensible presence, but that, in the midst of enjoyments, they resolve and be armed for it; therefore, while they enjoy his company, he doth warn them, " A little while, and ye shall not see me."

5. Christ when he doth withdraw his sensible and bodily presence is yet not absent from believers, but hath a way of presence, wherein spiritual minds may discern and see him; for notwithstanding his removal, " ye shall see me," saith he. The word imports a full and clear sight, as if he were before their eyes.

6. As the sensible enjoyments of believers are but short while they are within time, so their desertions and clouds are but short also; they may think the time long because of their affection, and they may prolong their own affliction by taking in an idol in the room of an absent Christ, and by not making use of desertion as they ought; but he alloweth that their sad hours be short, and however it be, they are so in respect of eternity; for " again a little while, and ye shall see me."

7. Christ's suffering for and departing from his people hath neither changed his affection to them nor deprived him of ability to do for them; but they are the rather so much the dearer to him as the price of his sufferings, and by his exaltation he is able to be powerfully present with them, by the pouring out of his Spirit; for it is a reason of their seeing him, " because I go to the Father," having laid down the price of their redemption.

VER. 17. Then said some of his disciples among themselves, What is this that he saith unto us, A little while, and ye shall not see me: and again, a little while, and ye shall see me: and, Because I go to the Father?

18. They said therefore, What is this that he saith, A little while? we cannot tell what he saith.

In these verses is recorded the occasion of Christ's further enlarging and explaining of this encouragement, taken from the ignorance and stumbling of some of his disciples, who, repeating this doctrine, and making inquiry among themselves about the meaning thereof, do still remain ignorant of his true sense therein, not understanding any part of the words, and least of all, that they should see him, because he goeth to the Father, seeing thereby, it would seem, he would rather be removed out of their sight. Whence learn —

1. It is commendable in disciples that they hear Christ's doctrine with such attention as to receive and retain it, though they do not understand it; for so do they repeat all he said, testifying how attentive they were, however their understanding was darkened.

2. Let doctrine be never so plain and never so frequently repeated, and let means be never so many, and hearers most attentive, yet they will continue ignorant till Christ enlighten their minds; for albeit this plain doctrine had been inculcated before, and almost in the same terms, chap. xiii. 33, yet say they, once and again, " What is this that he saith unto us ?" &c.

3. When Christ's followers are ignorant of any truth, it concerns them to be inquisitive about the same, and to make use one of another for that end; for they said among themselves, " What is this that he saith unto us, A little while," &c.

4. Using of means will not avail, nor can believers help one another to understand truth, unless Christ shine in with light; for after their repeating of the words, and an inquiry among themselves once and again, the result is, " we cannot tell what he saith."

5. When believers are in trouble, and essaying to rid themselves out of difficulties without employing of Christ, ordinarily such a condition and exercise are attended with fits of bitterness; for they, being much grieved this night, and labouring among themselves to clear this matter, but to no purpose, do repeat his words, and once and again inquire, " What is this that he saith ?" and in the end resolve, " we cannot tell what he saith ;" whereby they not only express their own ignorance, but some bitterness also, indirectly carping at his expressions, and challenging that he should so speak unto them.

VER. 19. Now Jesus knew that they were desirous to ask him, and said unto them, Do ye enquire among yourselves of that I said, A little while, and ye shall not see me: and again, a little while, and ye shall see me?

In this verse is contained Christ's preface to the explication of this encouragement, wherein, by making known that he understood their perplexity and their desire to be resolved, he testifieth his willingness to clear their doubt, and makes way for it, preventing their inquiry. Whence learn—

1. Whatever be the perplexities of saints, and their weakness under them, yet they know Christ to be the only resolver of their difficulties, and cannot be at rest till they get light; for their inquiry among themselves not succeeding, it is subjoined, notwithstanding their indirect carping, that "they were desirous to ask him," that so they might attain to light in the matter.

2. Albeit believers stand ofttimes in sensible need of Christ's help, and be desirous thereof, yet they are kept back from employing of him, partly by their unwillingness to bewray their own indigence, and partly, by reason of their ill-ordered respect to him, which keeps them at a needless distance with him; for albeit "they were desirous to ask him," yet they proceeded no further than a desire, as being unwilling to bewray their ignorance, and respecting their Master so as they were afraid to ask him.

3. Christ is so infinitely omniscient, and hath so vigilant an eye over the condition of his people, as he knoweth and taketh notice of their secret doubts and perplexities before they be propounded to him; for "Jesus knew that they were desirous to ask him," and by that question, "Do ye inquire among yourselves?" &c., he lets them see he knew their secret reasonings and debates.

4. Christ will not cast off his dull and weak followers, but their necessity hath a mouth of its own to his omniscience and infinite love, whereof he will give proof by preventing their inquiry; as here, however they were ignorant, and stood off from asking him, yet he prevents them with a resolution of their doubt.

5. When disciples are about the use of some means for resolving of their doubts, Christ will in due time come and clear them; for so much is imported in that he takes notice that they were inquiring among themselves of that he said; and while they were about that mean he cometh and resolveth them.

6. Albeit Christ do prevent his perplexed people, and do approve of their use of any lawful means, yet he accounts it still a fault that they should not employ him in doubtful cases; for this question, "Do ye inquire among yourselves?" &c., doth not only import his notice-taking of their exercise, and an approbation thereof, in so far as they were not resting in ignorance, but making use of that mean; but also an indirect challenge that they should inquire "among themselves," and not employ him.

Ver. 20. Verily, verily, I say unto you, That ye shall weep and lament, but the world shall rejoice: and ye shall be sorrowful, but your sorrow shall be turned into joy.

In this verse is subjoined Christ's exposition of this encouragement, wherein (explaining the causes by the effects) he declareth, that however, by his absence, they should have sad sorrow, while the world should be rejoicing, yet their sorrow should end in joy; which, as it was verified to the disciples in their joy after their sad hours for his suffering and removal, so it is also made good to believers in all ages, who have their joys and sorrows succeeding each other, but still their joys last.

DOCTRINES.

1. Christ's doctrine to his followers, especially concerning their allowed comfort under and after sorrow, is not empty and vain promises, but serious and solid truth; therefore is it conformed here, and ver. 23, with a double asseveration, "Verily, verily, I say unto you."

2. It is the great fault of discouraged believers that they are slow of heart to believe Christ's allowed encouragements; and yet it is most acceptable to him that they give credit to them, and rest upon them; for this asseveration imports not only the gravity of the matter, but further, also, that we are averse and unwilling to believe it, and that Christ is earnest we should give credit thereto.

3. It is very suitable that answerable affections go along with our conditions, and that our conditions be evidenced thereby; therefore doth he here explain his being not seen, or seen, by them, ver. 16, by their sorrow and joy, as evidencing how they were affected with these dispensations.

4. As it is the lot of believers to meet with sorrow in the world, so Christ's absence and removal will be the chief cause of most bitter sorrow to them; not that they are allowed to mourn without hope, but by their sorrow for this they testify their estimation of him, that nothing can be comfortable to them without him, and that they do keep his room in their heart till he come again; and withal, when he is absent, and their sun down, they will meet with many dark clouds and sharp showers to fill them with grief; for when they see not him, "ye shall weep and lament," saith he.

5. The world are so opposite to Christ and his people, that it is the time of their joy when Christ is removed, and the godly set down in sorrow thereby; for these two go together, "ye shall weep and lament, but the world shall rejoice." (See Rev. xi. 10.)

6. As it is the wretched disposition of the world to rejoice in the want of Christ out of the world, and in the godly's affliction, so the Lord, in his holy providence, may sometimes permit them this advantage of rejoicing, partly, that it may add to the exercise of his afflicted people; partly, that the disposition of some wicked men may be discovered who otherwise would carry smoothly, Luke, ii. 34, 35; partly, to let them see that when they have got their will for a time, yet it will not avail them; and partly, to embitter their future sorrow by these fits of joy, Rev. xviii. 7: for these causes it is that the Lord permits that "the world shall rejoice." So that such advantages might be matter of terror to them, if they looked rightly upon them.

7. Christ would not have his people pleasing themselves with the dream of a constant calm, but seriously laying their account to meet with sorrow and grief for their exercise and trial, and to fit them for his joy; therefore doth he again tell them, "ye shall be sorrowful."

8. As the wicked's joy is but for a moment, and goeth before a sad storm of sorrow, which will be their last and final portion, so the sorrows

of the godly will end in joy, and joy will be the upshot of all their griefs; yea, their present sorrow shall afterward afford matter of joy; for "your sorrow shall (not only end in, but) be turned into joy," as he turned water into wine. (See Ps. cxxvi. 5, 6.)

VER. 21. *A woman when she is in travail hath sorrow, because her hour is come: but as soon as she is delivered of the child, she remembereth no more the anguish, for joy that a man is born into the world.*

22. And ye now therefore have sorrow: but I will see you again, and your heart shall rejoice, and your joy no man taketh from you.

This explained encouragement is (in these verses) illustrated from a similitude taken from a woman in travail, which is propounded, ver. 21, and applied, ver. 22, to this purpose; that as a woman in travail hath bitter pangs and sorrows, and yet all that is shortly swallowed up in the joy she hath for the birth of a man-child, so however they were in sorrow, yet his seeing them again shall afford them cordial and permanent joy.

From verse 21, learn—1. The Lord, in the ordinary course of his providence in the world, hath given ample proof of his power and good will, and that he is able to bring bitter lots to a sweet issue, whereof the godly should make use, for their own encouragement in sad lots; therefore doth he lead them to comfort themselves by the example of a woman in travail, and elsewhere he remits them to the consideration of other his works in the world.

2. The godly may expect that their hours of sorrow will be very sharp and bitter, that so their trial may be complete and searching; therefore it is compared to the sorrow of a woman in travail, as being very bitter, and nearer the birth the sharper, and such as God only can open the womb and give an issue from it.

3. Their sorrows also do resemble that of a woman in travail, in respect that as this pain is the fruit of Evah's transgression, so whatever be the Lord's love or scope in exercising his own, yet the original and rise of all their troubles is sin, and they are sent to put them in mind what they are, to chasten and humble them for bypast failings, or to mortify the roots of sin, and prevent it for the future.

4. It may contribute to sweeten the bitter sorrows of saints that they are as necessary to make way for the consolations of Christ as pangs are to make way for child-bearing; for in this also the comparison holds.

5. The sorrows of saints may be more easy to them when they consider that they are but for a set time, and by their violence and extremities are hasting to an issue; for so a woman's sorrow is when "her hour is come," and but an hour, which will pass over.

6. It is ample matter of hope and encouragement to sorrowful saints that their afflictions and sorrows will not only have an issue, but are bringing forth somewhat that will be as a man-child brought forth by a travailing woman; for so is here imported, that their afflictions are as a travailing in birth, bringing forth some fruit, and that they shall not miscarry, but a man-child be born.

7. The fruit of saints' afflictions and sorrows will be so full as may swallow down all the bitterness of their former trouble; for in this also they resemble a woman "delivered of the child," who "remembereth no more the anguish, (that is, thinks nothing of it, though otherwise it be good to remember it for instruction,) for joy that a man is born into the world." (See Heb. xii. 11; 2 Cor. iv. 17.)

From verse 22, learn—1. Believers' sorrow for the absence of Christ is so great that the very apprehension and intimation of his removal begets sorrow; for "now therefore (saith he) ye have sorrow," even before I be gone.

2. Christ doth take special notice of the sorrow of his own when it is for his sake, and because of his removal; for he intimateth so much to them, "ye now therefore have sorrow."

3. The sorrow of saints for Christ's absence will not be perpetual, but ought to be measured by the present, "now," as not knowing how soon he may put a period to it; for so much also is imported in this, "now ye have sorrow, but I will see you again."

4. Kindly sorrow of saints can only be removed by Christ's coming to them, and their enjoying the light of his countenance; and he will not stay away, but be at pains himself to comfort such; for "I will see you again," to remove your sorrow.

5. It completes the joy of mourning saints that not only they see Christ, but do know that he seeth them, and hath an eye of kindness towards them, and an eye of providence and care about them; therefore, in place of "ye shall see me," ver. 16, it is here, "I will see you again."

6. Albeit the joy of the godly may be interrupted for a time, yet it will never totally be extinguished, but will revive after sorrow; for here is rejoicing after sorrow.

7. It is Christ's work, not only to afford matter of joy unto his people, but effectually to bear it in, for their encouragement; for here he undertakes, "Ye shall rejoice."

8. The joy of the godly doth far outstrip the carnal delight and mirth of the wicked, whose heart is sorrowful in the midst of laughter, Prov. xiv. 13, whereas this is a solid joy, which upholds and refreshes the heart; for "your heart shall rejoice," saith he.

9. The joy of believers is a permanent joy, whereof they shall never be totally deprived till they enter into the ocean of eternal joy, Matt. xxv. 21, 23, for "your joy no man taketh from you." It cannot be denied but sometimes it is interrupted by their peevish refusing of it, and by tentations taking it from them; but yet, 1. They want not still some measure of joy, in so far as they are not totally discouraged. 2. They want not matter of joy, when themselves do put it from them. 3. Tentations prevail to take away their joy when they put not themselves and it in Christ's custody, who here undertakes to make them rejoice. 4. Whatever their

wrestlings and faintings be, yet they shall be carried through till they come to obtain everlasting joy, where sighing and sorrow shall flee away, and not be found, though they were sought, whereas now we both seek and find them too often.

Ver. 23. And in that day ye shall ask me nothing. Verily, verily, I say unto you, Whatsoever ye shall ask the Father in my name, he will give it you.

In this verse we have propounded the third and fourth encouragement, whereby Christ mitigates the excessive sorrow of his disciples because of his departure from them. The first of them is, that in that day, when the Comforter shall come, they shall see him again, they shall ask him nothing; which is not to be understood of prayer, as if he would have them exempted from prayer, or that they should not pray to him alone, but to the Father with him and through him. For the first of these is blasphemous, and the second not to the purpose, seeing it is not to be supposed they had neglected the Father in their prayers formerly, and betaken themselves only to him. Withal, the grave asseveration prefixed to the latter part of the verse, which speaks of prayer, evidenceth that there he beginneth a new purpose, different from this, here spoken of; and the word here rendered " to ask," albeit it sometimes signifies to desire or seek by prayer, and be so used by Christ speaking of his own praying to the Father, ver. 26, and often in chap. xvii., yet, 1. In the latter part of the verse, where he speaks of their praying, he useth another word, which properly signifieth to seek by prayer, that so by the different words he might point out that the purposes are different. 2. The word here doth properly signify to ask questions, or to propound doubtful things, whereof we are ignorant, that we may get resolution in them; and so it is used in this same chapter, verses 5, 19, 30, in relation to which passages, and to what is said by way of explication, ver. 25, compared with ver. 29, 30, I take this encouragement to contain a promise of their illumination and growth in knowledge of the mysteries of the gospel, propounded by way of opposition to their present necessity of asking many questions at him, in regard of their dulness and ignorance. But now he promiseth that in that day they shall have more illumination than to make a doubt of everything, and should ask him nothing; which yet is not so to be understood as if, after the Comforter were come, there should be no doubts, or that he would exempt them from a necessity of depending upon and employing of him for resolution thereof; but it is to be understood comparatively in reference to their present condition, that they should not, as now they did, stick at every scruple, and be puzzled and perplexed about every purpose of divine truth, but should be more familiarly acquainted with his doctrine. Whence learn—

1. Ignorance of divine mysteries is so great an affliction to disciples, and illumination and knowledge thereof so great a mercy, as it may sweeten sad dispensations, and deserveth a special remark in their account; for it is here an encouragement against his departure, and it is a day of remark ("that day"), to be delivered from their ignorance.

2. It is by the Spirit only that men are enabled to understand divine mysteries, and this is more fully and clearly communicated by him in the days of the gospel than formerly; for it is " in that day," when the Comforter cometh, that they shall " ask nothing."

3. As Christ is very gracious to his people in granting them sense of necessities, and in supplying thereof when they come unto him, so he also tenders their weakness by preventing them in many needs, and so prevents their many perplexities and anxieties, which otherwise they might be put to; therefore is this promise thus propounded, " ye shall ask me nothing," because, albeit it was enough to have him ready to resolve their questions, when they put him to it, yet this was very hard to them, and therefore he prevents them with a gift of knowledge. So, albeit he will never have his people freed from dependence on him, yet, out of his respects to their weakness, he gives sense many visible props, where faith is put to an exercise. He could feed the world immediately from heaven, as he did Israel, but since our weakness would be ready to faint under such a dispensation, therefore he hath established another course.

The other encouragement here propounded is, that they shall have success in their prayers put up in his name, concerning which compare chap. xiv. 13, 14, and xv. 7.

DOCTRINES.

1. The matter of hearing the prayers of believers is of great importance in Christ's account; and whatever our fears and tentations be about it, yet the verdict of his word is to be trusted to in that matter; therefore doth he begin this encouragement with his usual asseveration, " Verily, verily, I say unto you."

2. There is no measure of enjoyment which believers have within time which should take them off from prayer and seeking; for when the former promises are accomplished, it is yet imported they must " ask."

3. Times of much light have need of much prayer to sanctify that light, and make it effectual for answerable ordering of our practice; for " in that day," when they shall get knowledge, and " ask nothing," they must still " ask" by prayer.

4. As the necessities of believers, and the good things they expect, are many, so all their comfortable enjoyments must come by prayer; for " whatsoever ye shall ask," imports that their prayers must be universal, reaching to all their felt needs and expected mercies.

5. Prayer must be offered up through Christ and in his name, as testifying the sense of our own unworthiness to come before God with our services; our high estimation of Christ's worth, merit, and credit with the Father, who can make our services acceptable; and our confidence that he will own us and our services, and that the Father will be well pleased therewith in him; for they must ask the Father in his name.

6. Prayer put up in Christ's name for things lawful will get a good answer; and albeit the Lord will exercise our faith, to believe this when we see it not; our patience, to wait for it; and our discerning, to take up his wise contrivance of answering, when he suspends the particular we desire; and albeit he may also suspend and deny answers for a time to particular suits, when either we are lying under unrepented guilt, or have neglected prayer till we come to a strait, or have not sense as we ought of what we seek; and also that he may try what men's deportment will be when their prayers are not answered; yet this is a truth of eternal verity, " Whatsoever ye shall ask the Father in my name, he will give it you."

7. Such as are given to prayer, and do receive answers thereunto from heaven, need not be discouraged for the want of Christ's bodily presence, seeing, by the acceptance of their prayers in heaven, they will get constant proofs of his good will; for this is an encouragement here against his removal, that they shall have intercourse with him, by their praying and his answering. And indeed, to be frequent in prayer is the way to entertain the sense of his love, and the want thereof begets jealousies and coldrifeness [coldness].

Ver. 24. Hitherto have ye asked nothing in my name: ask, and ye shall receive, that your joy may be full.

In this and the following purpose, to ver. 29, both these encouragements are amplified and enlarged, though not in the order they are first propounded. The purpose may be reduced to four heads; in the first whereof (in this verse) he amplifieth the last of these encouragements concerning prayer, declaring that hitherto they had not asked anything in his name, and exciting them to amend this, that so by receiving good answers they might have full joy to guard and refresh their hearts, which were so grieved at the news of his departure. As for that he saith, " Hitherto have ye asked nothing in my name," it is not so to be understood as if the disciples and other godly persons had not prayed only before that time, or had not directed their prayers to God through the Mediator; but the meaning is, partly, more generally to point out the difference betwixt the way under the law and under the gospel; in the one, their use-making of a Mediator in prayer was involved under many types and shadows, particularly that of the mercy-seat, and though they directed their prayers to God through a Mediator, and by virtue of the covenant, yet it was without any particular application of that office of Mediator unto the person of Jesus, the son of Mary, as not being yet manifested; and it is not unlikely that the disciples and others, whatever thoughts they had of Christ, yet hitherto they had not so distinctly made use of him, in his office of Mediator, in the matter of prayer. But under the gospel, especially after the pouring out of the Spirit, veils are taken away, and the Mediator exhibited in person, to be distinctly and clearly made use of in prayer; partly, the meaning is, more particularly to point out the shortcoming of the disciples, who, whatever use they made of Christ in prayer, yet had asked and received nothing in comparison of what they were allowed to ask and should afterward receive. Whence learn—

1. We are so unwilling, upon the one hand, to pray, and Christ so willing to be employed, that he can never enough press us to that duty; therefore doth he insist in pressing them to "ask," and is so forward in it that he enlargeth it before the other encouragement mentioned before it, in the former verse.

2. It is a notable encouragement unto prayer, that now, under the gospel, the person of the Mediator is exhibited in our flesh, acquainted with all our infirmities, though without sin, and the way of employing him more distinctly and clearly held out than under the law; for by this he excites them to ask, that hitherto they had asked nothing in his name, but now might ask, as hath been explained.

3. It may also encourage saints to prayer, that let them seek never so much in his name, yet he will be so far from reproaching them with his bounty that he counts they have sought nothing in respect of what his love alloweth, and what he will do for them if they ask; for so much also (as hath been explained) is imported in this, " Hitherto have ye asked nothing in my name," and therefore ask yet more, saith he.

4. It doth yet more encourage men to pray to God through Jesus Christ, when they consider that his fair offers of audience are not empty promises, but will be seconded with real performances; for " ask, and ye shall receive," saith he, appealing to their own experience concerning the reality of his offers, if they will employ him.

5. Christ alloweth joy unto his people to sweeten and cry down the noise of all their discouragements and sorrows; for he alloweth they should have "joy" to assuage their grief, because of his departure.

6. The joy allowed by Christ upon his people is a full and complete joy, and groweth up by degrees, till they find it so, according as they make use of the means wherein it is to be found; therefore doth he call it a full joy, or, a joy fulfilled to their satisfaction, by their praying and his answering.

7. As the joy of believers cometh to them by the mean of prayer, so they are allowed joy even in their address-making to God through Christ, considering what hope there is in such an undertaking, and what a dignity and mercy it is that such as they should be drawn to such an employment, and admitted to serve in it; for if joy be fulfilled when they get an answer, then, certainly, it should be begun while they are praying.

8. Such as pursue prayer in Christ's name till they get an answer will find their joy thereby completed; as evidencing how glorious their head and surety, Christ, is, and how acceptable naughty persons and performances are in heaven through him, and as putting a lustre and double beauty upon every mercy, when it cometh that way out of the hand of God; for " ask (saith he), and ye shall receive, that your joy may be full," or fulfilled.

VER. 25. These things have I spoken unto you in proverbs: but the time cometh, when I shall no more speak unto you in proverbs, but I shall shew you plainly of the Father.

In the second place, Christ insists upon and amplifieth that encouragement which was first propounded, ver. 23, concerning increase of knowledge. And as there he propounded the promise in opposition to their present necessity of asking questions, so here it is propounded in opposition to his present way of teaching, and that he would not speak to them in proverbs or parables, as formerly, but would fully and plainly reveal the Father to them. As for " these things," which Christ saith he spake in proverbs, they are not to be restricted to the immediately preceding purpose in this chapter, but should be more generally extended to the most part of his doctrine hitherto, particularly in this last sermon, much whereof they did not understand, as appeared in their frequent objections, reasonings, and questions. He saith he hath spoken these things " in proverbs," or parables; whereby we are not to understand any dark or enigmatic speeches, as if his doctrine had been obscure in itself,—for his doctrine was plain in itself, and what he spake darkly to the multitude he explained to them,—but the meaning is, partly, that much of that he spake, however it was clear in itself, yet to them it seemed as obscure as if it had been all parables,—and so appears from ver. 16, 17, &c.,—but after the Spirit's coming he was to speak plainly and fully, even in respect of their conception and understanding; partly, that Christ, in regard of their weakness and incapacity, had but briefly touched many things which would be but dark to them till the Spirit should come, as ver. 12, 13, and had often made use of similitudes and parables, in this sermon and at other times, whereby, albeit he condescended to their capacity, yet (as he saith, chap. iii. 12) he spake but earthly things and not heavenly—that is, pointed out heavenly things by earthly resemblances, which did eclipse much of the lustre these truths should have when he should teach them plainly by his Spirit. Whence learn—

1. As clearest truths will be but dark mysteries, even to disciples, till the Spirit enlighten them, so Christ lets out light by degrees, and teacheth according to his people's capacity; for both these are held out in this acknowledgment, " These things have I spoken to you in proverbs."

2. It is the comfort of saints that what measure of light and instruction they need and yet want at one time, it is but reserved for another; for it sweetens their case to whom he had spoken in proverbs, that " the time cometh, when I shall no more speak to you (saith he) in proverbs."

3. The clear and full manifestation of saving truth was communicated by the Spirit to the apostles, and by them to the church; for it is at that time " I shall shew you plainly (saith he) of the Father."

4. The great and fundamental doctrine of the gospel revealed by the Spirit is the knowledge of God as the Father of Christ, and our Father in him; and consequently of the mystery of redemption; for this is the doctrine he will teach, " I shall shew you plainly of the Father."

VER. 26. At that day ye shall ask in my name: and I say not unto you, that I will pray the Father for you:

27. For the Father himself loveth you, because ye have loved me, and have believed that I came out from God.

In the third place, Christ resumeth and yet further amplifieth that purpose concerning prayer in his name, promising that when the Spirit shall come they shall get alacrity and willingness to the duty of prayer, and shall find easy access in their suits, having Christ's intercession to make way for them, and the Father's love (as it were) preventing that; and that because they have loved him and believed him to be the Mediator and Ambassador come out from God. For clearing of the words, consider—1. While Christ saith, " I say not that I will pray the Father for you," the meaning is, not that he will lay aside his office of intercession for believers, which as they will still need it so it is a strong pillar of their confidence, Rom. viii. 33, 34; Heb. iv. 15, 16; vii. 25; neither is it only the meaning that by this sort of speech he would most certainly assure them of it, it being a privilege so sure as he needed not to say more to assure them of it; as indeed his love is a real love, which hath more substance than show; but conjoining it with what followeth in the beginning of the next verse, we shall find the meaning to be, that they had not only his intercession, but the Father's love, upon which to ground their hope of audience; and that he was not to intercede for them with the Father as with an enemy or one unwilling to accept of them, being now reconciled, but that the Father did love them, and out of his love to them had appointed him Mediator. 2. While Christ fetcheth the reason of the Father's love from their love to him, the meaning is, not that their love to Christ did prevent the Father's love to them, but that the Father having loved them and brought them to love Christ, doth reward this their love with more proofs of his love in hearing their prayers.

DOCTRINES.

1. Not only is the answering of prayer Christ's work, but it is he also who undertakes to make his people pray, and giveth them his Spirit for that effect; for saith he, by way of promise, " At that day (when the Spirit shall come) ye shall ask in my name."

2. The prayers of saints put up in Christ's name are so many ways welcome in heaven as they cannot but be accepted; therefore he assureth them of access by shewing them how many things concur to obtain access and an answer.

3. We ought so to eye Christ's intercession as we forget not also to ascend up to the Father's love as rendering our persons and prayers ac-

ceptable, that double encouragements may make our consolation strong, and that we may not have wrong thoughts of the Father; for this cause saith he, " I say not unto you, that I will pray the Father for you: for the Father himself loveth you."

4. Such as are beloved of God do get grace to flee to Christ, and to love him; for " ye (whom the Father loveth) have loved me."

5. As God's love doth beget love in his people, so he is graciously pleased to reward and foster this love with more of his love; for " the Father (whose love prevents his people) loveth you, because ye have loved me."

6. Love to Christ cannot be without faith, and where love is it proves faith; for " ye have loved me and believed."

7. True faith ought to close with Christ as the great Ambassador of the Father, God and man, coming out from the Father by his incarnation, and coming into the world to work the work of our redemption; for ye " believed that I came out from God;" which includes the Father's good will in sending of him, and proves his godhead, in that he " came from God," as well as the truth of his manhood was confirmed by his appearing on earth, and his office to be the only Mediator, as coming out from God for that effect.

8. Faith in Christ is so acceptable that God will reward it with proofs of his free love; for " the Father loveth you, because ye believed that I came out from God."

Ver. 28. I came forth from the Father, and am come into the world: again, I leave the world, and go to the Father.

In the last place, Christ, to confirm them in what they had believed concerning him, ver. 27, and explain that which they understood not, ver. 16, doth set forth himself more fully as the object of saving faith, both in his state of humiliation in his coming into the world, which they had already comprehended, and in his state of exaltation in going out of the world, which they should after understand more fully. Whence learn—

1. Christ craves nothing to be believed by his people but what is the real truth; for as he commends them for believing that he "came out from God," ver. 27, so this is the very truth, " I came forth from the Father," &c.

2. Jesus Christ, as he is the Ambassador of the Father, so he is true God, equal with him; for being with the Father before his incarnation, " he came forth from the Father," and was not sent only.

3. It pleased Christ Jesus, out of love to his people, to leave the Father and come into the world; not by being separate from the Father, but by obscuring his deity and glory under the veil of our flesh and sinless infirmities, and conversing with us for working our redemption; for so is this to be understood, " I came forth from the Father, and am come into the world."

4. Christ, having perfected his work on earth, did leave the world by ascending up to heaven to perfect the work of our redemption and salvation, where he manifests his glory, having put off the veil of our infirmities; for " again, I leave the world, and go to the Father." And by this he clears the matter of his removal to them and lets them have a sweet sight of it.

5. As Christ's coming into the world was voluntary, and flowed from his love, so was his departure also voluntary, and he was not compelled thereunto by men; for " I am come (saith he) into the world," and " I leave it," and " go."

6. The way of Christ's coming into the world may serve to clear controversies. concerning the matter of his removal; for the one is here paralleled with the other; and therefore as his coming was sensible and in a bodily way, so also is his removal sensible and takes away his bodily presence. And as his humanity and body were not in heaven while he was in the world, so it is not here now after that he is gone to the Father.

Ver. 29. His disciples said unto him, Lo, now speakest thou plainly, and speakest no proverb.

30. Now are we sure that thou knowest all things, and needest not that any man should ask thee: by this we believe that thou camest forth from God.

In these and the two following verses is contained the third part of the chapter, wherein Christ doth give a meet entertainment to their fair profession of proficiency and faith concerning him. These verses contain their profession, wherein—1. Being satisfied with his former way of doctrine, they profess that he spake plainly and without proverbs, and consequently that they had made proficiency and understood him. 2. They deduce two inferences from this, testifying their further proficiency, beside the understanding of what he said—1. That by his preventing their question, ver. 19, they were persuaded of his omniscience, and that none needed to inform him of their case by questions, as if he were ignorant thereof. 2. That the knowledge and experience of this his omniscience did further confirm them in the faith of his deity. Now concerning this profession, as it cannot be denied but there is some good in it, and they had sound faith, which Christ acknowledgeth, ver. 27, and they had already professed it, chap. vi. 69, so when we consider Christ's entertainment thereof we shall find some excess of presumption in it; for albeit Christ did indeed speak plainly, yet the time was not come wherein he had promised they should ask him nothing, ver. 23; and therefore they presumed more of their knowledge than they had cause; and albeit they believed that truth, that he came forth from God, and that upon solid ground, yet their faith was not full enough, since they had not employed their faith about the matter of his removal, which he had pressed upon them, ver. 28.

DOCTRINES.

1. Whatever divine truth Christ seems to speak more obscurely in one place, it will be

found fully cleared and explained elsewhere; for " now (say they) speakest thou plainly, and speakest no proverb."

2. It is a great comfort to Christ's followers to understand his word, and it is the property of divine truths that when they are apprehended in any measure they do wonderfully affect and refresh the heart; for say they, by way of admiration, " Lo, now speakest thou plainly," &c., being wonderfully refreshed with the light they received.

3. Christ will be found omniscient by all them who know him rightly; for " we are sure that thou knowest all things," &c.

4. Preventing means give his people but little to do, and are very affecting when they are found; for it held in their pains, and did very much affect them, that he gave proof he needed not any man should ask him.

5. Christ doth then become very precious to hearts when he by his word meets with what is in their hearts; for this did ravish them, that he needed not be asked, but lighted upon what was in their thoughts, ver. 19.

6. Christ is then rightly taken up in his properties when he is acknowledged to be God, and when faith closeth with him as such; for it followeth on the former, " By this we believe thou camest forth from God."

7. When weak beginners get any measure of knowledge or faith they are in peril to run upon the extremities of rashness and presumptuous conceit; for with this was their profession here hinted, wherein they speak as if they had attained to a full measure, and needed not depend on the promise of the Spirit.

8. When we try the solidity of our faith we should look especially to its ground, whether it be the solid word of God, or some extraordinary work only, which may affect for a time, but not prove constant enough; for in this their professed faith was faulty, that it was begotten rather by the act of his proving his omniscience than by the word.

9. We may have very low thoughts of our own faith, at its best, when we consider the many defects thereof, and how far short it cometh; for in this their faith was faulty, that however they believed he " came forth from God," yet their faith fell short in what was their present exercise concerning his return to the Father.

Ver. 31. Jesus answered them, Do ye now believe?

32. Behold, the hour cometh, yea, is now come, that ye shall be scattered, every man to his own, and shall leave me alone: and yet I am not alone, because the Father is with me.

These verses contain Christ's entertainment of this profession, wherein, taking hold of their profession of faith in so far as it was real, and checking their presumption and carnal confidence therein, (for both these are imported in that question, ver. 31,) he warneth them, that their faith should get a trial, and their presumption a sad

shake very shortly, when at his trial they should be scattered, and put to shift for themselves, leaving him alone, who yet should not be alone, having the Father with him. Whence learn—

1. Christ takes notice of no effect his doctrine produceth unless faith be one and a chief effect, for of all they said he takes notice of that as of greatest importance, if it had been such as they thought it was, " Do ye believe?"

2. When men have attained to some measure of faith they may have yet cause to be humbled that they have been so long in learning that lesson; for " Do ye now (and not till now) believe?"

3. Christ takes notice of men's attaining to any measure of faith, that he may put them to work; for " Do ye now believe?" is a taking hold of what they grant, that now he may put them to that exercise mentioned afterward, which before could not so conveniently be done.

4. Christ doth hate presumption and carnal confidence, were it even in his dearest people; for this question doth also import his disdaining of their presumption, and that he would shortly give them a proof how far they were mistaken.

5. As when men are enabled to believe they ought to look for work, so presumption, mixed with faith, doth portend a winnowing storm, and that near at hand; for " Do ye now believe? The hour cometh, yea, is now come, (even that same night,) that ye shall be scattered," &c.

6. Presumption is a disease not easily cured by any caution and warning from the word, till the presumptuous find his own weight in trial; for this must refute it—an hour of scattering.

7. Though Christ be most tender of the broken spirits of his people, and of their sad condition, yet he will not spare to humble them when presumption is aloft, were their condition otherwise never so sad; for when he is comforting them against his departure, he hath yet a sad word to check their presumption.

8. The doctrine of trials is ofttimes but carelessly heard by presumptuous men, and they may meet with that which they little ponder; therefore a " behold" is prefixed to this doctrine.

9. The trials of Christ and his followers, as they are violent, so are they determined by God, and short; for it is an hour, a bitter hour indeed, but a determined and short hour; and therefore we should take heed an hour produce not that which may shame us for ever.

10. Continued presumption and carnal confidence will undoubtedly cause men to fall when trial cometh, were they even Christ's own dear children; for here the ensuing storm is described, from the sad effect it should produce in them, of scattering and leaving him. And if we consider their true grace, their special and intimate acquaintance with Christ, the many proofs of favour conferred on them, the many proofs they got and saw of his divine power, their singular engagements to Christ, and their being forewarned of their danger;—if, I say, we consider these things, and that yet they fall, it may let us see that nothing will bear out men, if deserted, or given up to the power of presumption.

11. Scattering, and the dissipation of the societies of God's people, is one of the sad fruits of

persecution; for " ye shall be scattered, every man."

12. Scattering is then not only our affliction, but our sin and weakness, when trouble and hazard makes us selfish, and seek to shift for ourselves, little considering the hazard of the interest of Christ; for this follows on their presumption, " ye shall be scattered, every man to his own"— that is, not only going to their own home, as afterward they did, but their shifting for themselves, when they " leave" their Master " alone" in the garden.

13. It is a part of the trial of honest sufferers that in their sharpest conflicts they may be deserted even of them who not only make fair professions, but have real honesty, and may be left in the gap there alone; for herein Christ hath paved the way, who was left alone; and albeit none could join with him in enduring those sufferings whereby he redeemed his people, yea, albeit his care was to have them exempted, chap. xviii. 8, yet it was a trial and exercise unto him to be thus left alone.

14. Let never so many desert Christ and his truth, yet he will own and stand to it; for he is left alone, and yet stands alone in that conflict.

15. The condition of sufferers is not so desolate and solitary as spectators or sense at first view would judge; for though they leave him alone, " yet I am not alone," saith he.

16. God may be pursuing his own dear children in great displeasure, with whom he is yet graciously present, upholding them with the one hand as he smites with the other; for " the Father is with me," saith Christ, when yet the Father is pursuing him hotly for the sins of the elect, and deserting him, Matt. xxvii. 46.

17. The presence of God alone is sufficient to sustain a soul, when deserted of all, under saddest difficulties; for though ye " leave me alone, yet I am not alone, because the Father is with me."

VER. 33. These things I have spoken unto you, that in me ye might have peace. In the world ye shall have tribulation: but be of good cheer; I have overcome the world.

In this verse is contained a conclusion, not only of the immediately preceding purpose, or chapter, but of the whole farewell sermon, wherein, having spoken many and divers things to them, wherewith they were variously affected, he sheweth that his scope in all of it was to promove their peace in him; the necessity whereof appeareth from the troubles they shall meet with in the world; and the efficacy of his peace to counterbalance the bitterness of worldly trouble is held out, partly, in the effect thereof, that having peace they may be of good cheer, or bold; and partly, in the ground of this courage, that Christ hath overcome the world. Whence learn—

1. As peace is Christ's allowance to his people, so the drift of all he speaks to them tends to promove their good and peace; his very brangling of their presumption and warning them of dangers tends not to take away their confidence in his good will, nor to brangle their peace, but to excite them to make it surer; for " these things (in this sermon and in the immediately preceding warning) have I spoken unto you, that ye might have peace."

2. It is Christ only who can give and speak peace to his people; for " I have spoken, that ye might have peace." (See Psalm lxxxv. 8; Job, xxxiv. 29.)

3. The peace of believers is begotten by the word, as faith is, and it takes root there; so that while the word is for them, they need not be dismayed; for upon this, " I have spoken," doth this follow, " that ye might have peace."

4. The peace of God conferred upon believers is a most excellent gift, and sufficient, though they have no more, as being the fruit of justification and reconciliation; as being that which gives a deliverance in the midst of troubles, which will guard hearts in the midst of violent blasts, Phil. iv. 7; which will make men keep from sinful courses, which would disturb their peace more effectually than the apprehension of wrath and hell; and which stays the mind on God in the midst of inward shakings, Isa. xxvi. 3. For these reasons is all their allowance from Christ comprehended under the name of " peace."

5. It is in Christ alone that we have right or access to any true peace, and in him we must entertain it; for saith he, " that in me ye might have peace."

6. Peace with God through Christ will not keep men from blasts of outward trouble, but the one is consistent with the other; yea, the world's hatred will readily follow on Christ's friendship; for when in me ye have peace, " in the world ye shall have tribulation."

7. Saints may not only expect trouble from the world, but that their trouble shall be very pressing and searching; for " ye shall have tribulation," or, a pressing distress, as the words import.

8. Even the dearest of saints are obnoxious to tentations, of fainting, fear, and diffidence, when sharp trouble assaults them; for they will need a word of encouragement—Be of good courage.

9. No outward trouble ought to disturb saints' peace, but their peace with God ought to appear in courageous and confident encountering with trouble; for after his allowed peace, " in the world ye shall have tribulation, but be of good cheer," or bold, saith he.

10. The world and all things therein that might disquiet saints are vanquished and overcome by Christ upon the cross, so that they may well terrify, but cannot hurt them; for " I have overcome the world."

11. Christ's victory over the world is ground of encouragement to all his suffering people against the power and policy of the world; considering that however Christ will not exempt them from a battle and exercise, yet they are partakers of his victory by faith, 1 John, v. 4, and shall (abiding in him) find, in the end, that they have to do with enemies already vanquished; for saith he, " Be of good cheer, I have overcome the world."

CHAPTER XVII.

This chapter contains Christ's solemn prayer to the Father after the farewell sermon, wherein, by supplicating for himself, his disciples, and all his members, he sanctifieth the use of prayer to all his followers, by making use thereof in his own person for obtaining what he needed; he maketh his latter will and testament, leaving his legacies to his followers, and leaveth us a pattern of his perpetual intercession in heaven, as our great High Priest, for upholding the ministry and church, shewing what his heart will be in his absence, and what he liveth for ever to accomplish. And he speaks all this openly, in his disciples' audience, that he may confirm them in the faith of his love, may assure them of what he prays for, and may teach them, by his example, what to ask for themselves.

The chapter may be taken up in three parts: in the first, he prayeth for himself, that the Father would glorify him, pressing the same by arguments, taken not only from the sweet relation betwixt the Father and him, but more expressly from the time wherein he asketh this, from his glorifying the Father, being glorified by him, ver. 1, from his calling and charge to give eternal life to the elect, ver. 2, 3, and from his fidelity in his charge and commission, ver. 4, upon which he repeats and explains his petition, by way of conclusion, ver. 5. In the second part of the chapter is contained his prayer for his eleven apostles expressly, wherein — 1. He describes them for whom he is to pray, giving an account of his diligence and success with them, ver. 6—8. 2. He appropriates his prayer and intercession to them, in opposition to the world, for several reasons, ver. 9, 10. 3. He propounds his first petition for their preservation, that so they may be kept in unity, ver. 11, pressing it upon several grounds, ver. 12—14, and repeating and explaining the same, ver. 15, reinforcing one of the former reasons to persuade it, ver. 16. 4. He propounds a second suit for their sanctification, ver. 17, pressing it by two arguments, ver. 18, 19. In the third part of the chapter, he prayeth for the apostles and the whole church expressly, ver. 20, wherein he prays for spiritual unity to them, as being notably advantageous, ver. 21, (for attaining whereof he allows excellent privileges upon them, ver. 22, particularly union with God through him, as the way to union among themselves, ver. 23,) and for union in place with himself in heaven at last, ver. 24; in the meantime recommending them, (and particularly the apostles,) on weighty grounds, to the Father's love and his inhabitation, ver. 25, 26.

Ver. 1. These words spake Jesus, and lifted up his eyes to heaven, and said, Father, the hour is come; glorify thy Son, that thy Son also may glorify thee:

In this verse (after a short transition, intimating a connexion betwixt the former doctrine and this prayer, and a declaration of his posture in prayer, with his eyes lift up to heaven) is contained—1. A proposition of his petition for himself, that the Father would glorify him, of which more on ver. 5, only in sum it imports his desire that God would glorify him, by sustaining him in his approaching agony, that in it he might triumph over all his and his people's enemies, by proving him to be the Son of God, even in his sufferings, as he did by many miracles at his death, Matt. xxvii. 45, 46, 51—53; and all this but as a prelude to his being glorified in his resurrection, ascension, and exaltation at the Father's right hand, of which ver. 5, and which was to be manifested in the world by the propagation of his spiritual kingdom. 2. Some of the reasons pressing this petition: one is couched in that sweet relation betwixt the Father and him, implied in the titles of Father and Son. But there are more expressly subjoined—1. A reason taken from the time wherein he asketh this, that " the hour is come"—namely, the hour of his agony, wherein he expected support, and to be glorified, according as he would need and was promised to him in the covenant of redemption, Psa. lxxxix. 21, 22; Isa. xlix. 8; l. 8, 9; Psa. xvi. 10, with Acts, ii. 31. As also upon the back of that, the hour of his promised exaltation, having waited his time, and done the will of the Father in the form of a servant. 2. Another reason, taken from a consequent of granting his desire, and his end in propounding of it—namely, that the Father glorifying him he might also glorify the Father, whose glory shines in the glory of his Son, and in his obedience, sufferings, and success. From all which, learn—

1. Prayer to God is a special mean to make believers lively in all duties, and to make the word and all our endeavours effectual for that end; for " these words spake Jesus," in preaching, and then subjoins prayer for a blessing upon what he said, wherein he asks those things of the Father which he had pressed upon them.

2. Christ is so real in his love to his people that he will say nothing to them for their encouragement but what he will say of them and for them in his compeering [appearing as an equal] before the Father on their behalf; therefore, having spoken these things to them, wherein he had let out much of his heart and love to them, he doth now confirm the same by speaking as much of them to God, hereby assuring them that he would be the same in absence that he was when present.

3. As it is the duty of the Lord's people to study always spiritual-mindedness, to set their affections upon things above, and to visit their fair inheritance by sending their affections thither, till themselves follow after, so in particular it is their duty in prayer to rouse up their affections, and set them to God and heavenward, and to testify their want hereaway, and that all their confidence and expectation depends on God, and on his help and consolations sent from heaven; for so much doth Christ's example teach, who in prayer " lifted up his eyes to heaven, or to God, in that place where his glory is specially manifested, and his followers made completely happy with him; and by this posture did testify the heavenly and depending frame of his spirit.

4. Albeit the Lord know the most secret de-

sires of the heart, and do respect and hear the very thoughts of his people, yet it is their duty, as they have opportunity, to make use of their tongue in prayer, that so they may do him homage with the whole man; nay, by that means (among others) excite their own affections in prayer, and may edify others in their place and station; for some (at least) of these causes it is that Christ in prayer spake in the audience of his disciples, he " lifted up his eyes, and said," and by his practice and example would teach us our duty.

5. Prayer is a notable mean for carrying men through in trials; and Christ hath sanctified it, and encouraged his followers to make use thereof, by employing it as his weapon in his greatest extremity and need, and that upon grounds of common interest, that so in all things he might be like his brethren; for here, in the apprehension of his approaching agony, he betakes himself to prayer on his own behalf, using arguments of interest common to him with his brethren in him, " Father, glorify thy Son."

6. So rich is the Lord's allowance to his people that in the midst and throng of their saddest pressures they may have hearts filled with thoughts and expectations of great glory to be conferred upon them in and after their sad sufferings; for his thoughts, when he looks upon his approaching sufferings, are, "Glorify thy Son."

7. Christ, in his saddest sufferings, was still glorious in himself, and appeared so to the conviction of others, and all his sufferings are now crowned and shut up in great glory; for now, and shortly after, was the Son glorified.

8. God hath it absolutely in his hand to confer glory and honour upon his suffering children, and to glorify himself in them, so that none can impede him in it; for saith he, " Father, glorify thy Son."

9. Albeit saints need not persuade God to grant what they ask agreeable to his will, yet it is necessary they use arguments in prayer, that they may assure their own hearts, may evidence their confidence to his glory, and may testify their instancy in urging of their suits; therefore doth Christ press his petition with so many reasons.

10. Interest in God and familiarity with him are of great use in a day of strait, and are the wheels upon which prayer to God will move sweetly; therefore doth Christ couch this encouragement in the bosom of his prayer, that God is his Father, and he his Son, to teach us to make that interest sure which may beget so much confidence in prayer in a day of need, seeing a father can deny nothing that is good to a child, nor will many words be needed to a father when the child is in distress.

11. Christ hath a sweet fellowship with and special interest in the Father; and his approaches to him, for himself or his people, are full of souly confidence, and such as cannot be ineffectual; for to him it belongs in a special manner (and to all others only through him) to plead these relations of Father and Son, and to expect audience because he stands in so near relation to God.

12. Whatever be the excuses of saints in ordinary, yet they may still expect that needful and promised proofs of love will not be withheld in the hour of their distress, and that honest prayers will avail much when distress is great, and nothing left but prayer; for now, when " the hour (or the set time appointed for his suffering) is come," he betakes himself to prayer, confidently expecting that then the Father will glorify his Son. (See Heb. iv. 16.)

13. The only way to come speed at God's hands in obtaining promised mercies is patiently to wait his time, submitting to be exercised in our faith, audience, patience, and subjection to him, till the hour of deliverance come; for Christ, having a promise of being glorified, not only in but after his sufferings, doth quietly continue under the form of a servant, till now " the hour is come," wherein God had promised to glorify him. (See Heb. x. 36.)

14. As God's being a Father gives sweet ground of encouragement in prayer to his children, so it is an evidence of sonship when they have cleanly aims in their prayers, and are led to make sweet use of the sweet answer of prayer; for so Christ clears his sonship from his aim in this suit, and the use he purposed to make of it, " that thy Son also may glorify thee."

15. To be cleanly in our aim in prayer, and make honest use of the answer thereof, is the way to come much speed in prayer; for this is an argument pressing audience, that the Son, being heard, will glorify him. (See James, iv. 3.)

16. It is a true evidence of sonship when men's chief aim, in all they ask and obtain, is the glory of God, and that they may be enabled actively to concur in glorifying of him; for this is Christ's first and chief aim, premitted to [preceding] all the rest, " That thy Son also may glorify thee."

17. The glory of the Son is the glory of the Father also; and he is glorified in the glorification of his Son, and by his Son so glorified: in the suffering of his Son he is glorified in his obedience; his justice against sin, his wisdom in finding out a way of redemption, and his love to lost man, shine in that matter; in his exaltation he is glorified, in his fidelity and power, and consummating the work of redemption by his Son. And Christ thus exalted glorifieth him by the preaching of the gospel and subduing the world to his obedience; for these two go together, " Glorify thy Son, that thy Son also may glorify thee."

18. It may assure believers that their wellbeing will bear much sway in heaven when they consider that both the Father and Son are glorified therein; that the Son is glorified in being carried through in suffering for them, and in perfecting their redemption, and in triumphing over all their enemies, and that the Father is glorified in thus glorifying of his Son; therefore is this spoken in the audience of his disciples, to encourage them, by hearing the Father and Son's glory so much concerned in this business.

VER. 2. As thou hast given him power over all flesh, that he should give eternal life to as many as thou hast given him.

In this verse is contained a third express argument pressing his petition; it is taken from the trust committed to him, and that the Father had given him authority over all persons, to order and dispose of them so as he might bring about the salvation of the elect. And therefore he desires to be glorified, that he may be answerable to that trust; that the Father would bear him through in suffering, that so he may purchase eternal life to them, and would glorify him after his sufferings, in his exaltation in heaven, that he might perfect his work, and exercise that power and authority, and apply his purchase, for the actual salvation of the elect. So the argument contains a second subordinate end, which he propounds in his prayer—namely, the glorification of the elect, which also is a mean of his glorifying of the Father, who delights to be glorified in their salvation. Whence learn—

1. It is Christ's great care, next unto his Father's glory, to discharge his trust faithfully, in order to the eternal welfare of his own; therefore doth he make it an argument why the Father should glorify him, that he may discharge this trust.

2. Such as are entrusted and employed by God may expect that he will not desert them in the discharge of their trust, when they come and employ him by humble, confident prayer; for Christ, in prayer, expects that the Father, as he hath given him this power, &c., will glorify him, that he may do what is committed to him.

3. Christ, even as Mediator, hath sovereign power and authority over all things, so that they are but frail flesh before him, and he may dispose of them as he will; for there is power, or authority, over all flesh, given to him by the Father, or a donative power and kingdom as Mediator. He restricts this power to " all flesh," not secluding all other things which are under his power, Matt. xi. 27 ; xxviii. 18 ; John, iii. 35 ; but comprehending them under those, as being the great visible obstructors of his people's happiness.

4. Beside the power given unto Christ over all creatures, there are a certain number of men given by the Father unto Christ in the covenant of redemption, that he may redeem, take charge of, and be forthcoming for them ; for there are here some thus given him, of which more, ver. 6. (See John, vi. 37, 38, &c.)

5. Life eternal is that which Christ intends for his people, and he will never rest satisfied till he crown his other mercies to them with putting them in possession thereof; for it is his aim here to " give eternal life to as many as thou hast given him."*

6. Life eternal is a gift peculiar only to the elect, who are given to Christ, and is conferred only upon them, and upon all of them; for he gives " eternal life to as many as (or to all) thou hast given him," and to none else.

7. Whatever be the gracious endowments conferred upon the elect within time, yet eternal life is a free gift unto them : for he gives " eternal life to as many as thou hast given him."

8. It may confirm the elect, who are drawn to Christ in the certain expectation of eternal life, that the dispensation thereof is committed unto Christ, their head and surety ; for thou hast given him authority " that he should give eternal life."

9. It doth yet further confirm their faith, that it is by the consent and appointment of the Father that Christ hath this dispensation, and doth let forth all those proofs of love which they feel ; for saith he, " thou hast given him power, that he should give eternal life."

10. The accomplishment of the elects' society, in bringing them to heaven, is a work of no small difficulty ; for it requires a Mediator so eminently qualified, with " power over all flesh," to bring it about.

11. There is in Christ sufficient ground of confidence that he will save his own, whatever difficulties be in the way. He hath not only sufficient merit to purchase it, and wisdom, fidelity, love, and care, to guide them in the way to it, but power also to draw them in and hold them in, and power over all things that might impede or promove their salvation to dispose of them so as they may be subservient to that great work ; for " thou hast given him power over all flesh, that he should give eternal life to as many as thou hast given him."

VER. 3. And this is life eternal, that they might know thee the only true God, and Jesus Christ, whom thou hast sent.

The former argument is further explained, by clearing what life eternal is—namely, a saving knowledge of God as the only true God, in his essence and attributes, in opposition to idols, and a knowledge of him as he is manifested in Christ, the Father's Ambassador ; which is both the way and mean of attaining eternal life, and the beginning of it, while it is known by faith here, and eternal life hereafter shall consist in the full sight and fruition thereof. For further clearing of this purpose, consider—1. Christ's scope in inserting this explication in his prayer is, not to inform the Father, but partly, to inform the disciples, for whose edification he thus prayed in their audience ; partly, to press the argument strongly ; for the glorifying of Christ to give eternal life should glorify the Father, by his being known and acknowledged by believers ; and it was needful Christ should be supported in his agony, and afterward exalted to give eternal life, seeing eternal life consisted only in knowing God in his Christ. Consider—2. While Christ propounds the Father to be "the only true God," the meaning is, not to seclude himself and the Holy Spirit from being the true God also, one in essence and equal in power and glory with the Father,—for that is a truth fully asserted throughout the scripture, John, xx. 28 ; Acts, xx. 28 ; and elsewhere ; and in the same prayer, ver. 5, Christ is said to have had glory with the Father before the world was ; now before the world was, there was nothing subsisting, to have glory or any other thing, but only the true God ; and so Christ, with the Holy Ghost, must be true God also,—but for clearing of the words we should consider that this exclusive " only " is not joined with the word Father, as if it ran thus : Only the Father is the true God ; but it runs with the words that follow, " the only true God." And so when it is said the Father is "the only true God," the meaning is, that God, or the deity which subsists in the person of the Father, is the only true God, or godhead, in opposition to all idols and supposed deities, not secluding the other persons in whom that true godhead subsists also, seeing the essence is one in all the three, and every one of them are that only true God. Withal, for confirmation of this it should be considered that in scripture there are such words of restriction made use of, in things ascribed to one or other person of the godhead, which yet are not to be taken absolutely, as secluding the rest of the persons, but only in relation to the creatures ; as Matt. xi. 27, it is said, " None (as it is in the original) knoweth the Son, but the Father, or the Father, but the Son," &c., in both which assertions it is not to be supposed that the Son or Father are secluded from knowing themselves, though the knowledge of the one be ascribed only to the other ; but it is to be understood that no creatures know the one or the other until the Son reveal them. Nor is the Spirit either secluded from knowing the Father and Son, by these expressions, seeing he searcheth even the deep things of God, 1 Cor. ii. 10, but only the creatures. So here, take this restriction as we will, and it secludes not the Son and Spirit from being that true God, but only sheweth that idols are not that true Deity.

DOCTRINES.

1. The happiness of believers would be much studied by them, wherein it consists, and what is the way to it ; and for this end there is need of Christ's own teaching ; therefore doth he take occasion, for their edification, to insert this description of life eternal.

2. It may sweeten believers' condition unto them when they consider how much the Father and Son do interest themselves in their happiness ; therefore doth he propound their eternal happiness as a thing wherein both of them are so much concerned, as hath been explained.

3. The estate unto which believers are and will be advanced by Christ is a state of life, and only worthy of that name, any other estate beside being but a state of death ; therefore doth he call it life, and "life eternal," even as it is begun here. (See Acts, v. 20, where it is called "this life" by way of excellency.) And for our assurance of an interest in this state we should be sensible of our being dead without it, and sensible of what annoyeth this life, when we have received it ; we should seek after food suitable for entertaining of our life, and be active in such motions and duties as do flow from the principle of such a life.

4. Whatever other life men live, yet it is but fading, their best days vanity, and few, and evil ; but it is the happiness of believers that their begun life is everlasting, and will be perfected in glory ; for it is "life eternal."

5. Eternal life, as it is begun here, and the way to attain to the full enjoyment thereof in heaven, consists in the knowledge of God, as it includes faith in him, and suitable affections and practice ; for " this is life eternal, that they might know thee," as knowledge consists not in a bare act of the understanding, but takes the will and affections along with it.

6. It is necessary to the saving knowledge of God that he be taken up as God, in his nature and attributes, as he hath revealed himself, and that he be known to be really and truly that which he reveals himself to be ; for they must know him God, and " the true God."

7. Albeit there be many things cried up as god in the world, and in men's estimation, yet they are but vanities and lies, and only Jehovah is the true God ; and they who know him savingly will acknowledge him as such, renouncing and crying down all idols, all delights and confidences beside ; for he is "the only true God ;" and they must know and acknowledge him as such.

8. Whatever knowledge of God men attain unto as the true God, in opposition unto idols, yet that will not be sufficient unto salvation unless Christ the Mediator be known also, and God in him, and in his dispensation of grace in sending him into the world ; therefore are these conjoined here, to " know thee the only true God, and Jesus Christ, whom thou hast sent."

9. To know Christ savingly, or to salvation, is to know him, as in his person and natures, so in his offices and the trust committed to him ; and to know that he is sent and approven of the Father in going about his work ; and what are the terms upon which he engaged, and did come into the world to perform this work ; what the Father promised unto him, and he again unto the Father ; for so is the knowledge of Christ, in order to salvation, qualified, to " know Jesus Christ, whom thou hast sent."

Ver. 4. I have glorified thee on the earth : I have finished the work which thou gavest me to do.

A fourth argument pressing the petition is taken from his fidelity in discharging the trust committed to him, in that he had glorified the Father by accomplishing the work which was laid upon him to do ; upon which, in the next verse, he repeats his suit. He saith, " I have finished the work ;" for albeit in heaven he be still working for us, and working that which was given him by the Father to do—namely, in so far as concerns the application of his merit for the actual salvation of the elect ; yet the work of reconciliation (as the distinction is, Rom. v. 10), or of purchasing redemption, was given him to be done on earth, and he finished it there ; and albeit he had not as yet, when he prayed this, finished all that was given him, yet he might well say this, because he had finished all that was hitherto requisite to be done, and had in his will and resolution gone through all that was yet before him, and was shortly to perform all things till he might say, " It is finished," chap. xix. 30 ; in reference to which he makes this profession.

DOCTRINES.

1. None are sent into the world to be idle, but have a task and service laid upon them, of their general calling and particular station ; for Jesus Christ himself had work on earth.

2. We cannot acceptably serve our generation, nor will God accept any work we do, unless his glory be our chief aim in it; for "I have glorified thee," saith he, in this work.

3. To glorify God is so much the more remarkable as it is not suspended till we come to heaven, where we may do it without interruption; but is set about on earth, where so few mind that work, and where there are so many difficulties and tentations to divert us; for it contributes to commend his service, that "I have glorified thee on the earth," saith he.

4. Christ, by his preaching, miracles, sufferings, and obedience to the death, and his whole conversation, and frequent ascribing of the great things he did to his Father, did glorify him, and demonstrate his power, truth, wisdom, justice, mercy, and other attributes; for saith he, I have glorified thee on the earth," which may encourage believers, that their surety hath served God so acceptably.

5. Such as have been sincerely aiming at God's glory will still be endeavouring to glorify him more and more; for he who had glorified him on earth, propounds it, verse 1, as his aim still, "that thy Son may glorify thee."

6. As God is glorified by men's work and actings, and not by bare professions only, so God is the imposer of men's tasks upon them, and will be glorified by no works of men, but what are by himself assigned to them in their stations; for "I have glorified thee (in) the work which thou gavest me to do."

7. Men must not only begin, but perfect also their work unto the end, before they receive a full reward; for so much doth his example teach, "I have finished the work."

8. Christ did nothing on earth in working out our redemption but what was the will of the Father, and by him committed unto him; for his work was the work which he gave him to do. (See John, vi. 39.) So that, Christ working it, and it being the will of the Father, it must be acceptable.

9. There was nothing committed to Christ by the Father, to be done on earth, for the purchasing of our redemption, but he did finish it; so that the debt is paid, justice satisfied, and sin, Satan, and death spoiled, so that nothing remains now but the application of his purchase, and communication of that to his people which they already have in him their Head; for the doing whereof he is now exalted and glorified; for " I have finished the work which thou gavest me."

10. Such as expect a comfortable issue of their life, and desire to make a comfortable testament, ought to make it their chief care to glorify God, in going incessantly about his service in their station, till they finish their course; for herein Christ hath left us a pattern, who, being to seek to be glorified with the Father after his death, ver. 5, hath here this sweet testimony, " I have glorified thee on the earth: I have finished the work," &c. (See 2 Tim. iv. 7, 8; Isa. xxxviii. 1—3.)

VER. 5. And now, O Father, glorify thou me with thine own self with the glory which I had with thee before the world was.

In this verse Christ repeats and explains his petition, by way of conclusion following upon the former argument, wherein he restricts the former general petition to be glorified, ver. 1, to the enjoyment of that glory he had before the world was, as presupposing his being glorified in being borne through in his sufferings, and including, by way of consequence, the manifestation of his glory in his spiritual kingdom in the world. The sum of the petition is, that since he had finished his work on earth, therefore the Father would advance him to the possession of that glory he enjoyed from all eternity. For clearing whereof we are to consider, that as Christ was from all eternity the glorious God, so we are not to conceive of any real change in this glory of his godhead, as if by his estate of humiliation he had suffered any diminution, or by his estate of exaltation, any real accession were made to his glory as God; but the meaning is, that Christ, having (according to the paction passed betwixt the Father and him) obscured the glory of his godhead for a time, under the veil of the form of a servant and our sinless infirmities, Phil. ii. 5—8, doth now expect, (according to the tenour of the same paction,) after he hath done his work, to be exalted, and openly declared to be the Son of God, Rom. i. 4, the veil of his estate of humiliation, though not of our nature, being taken away. It is further to be considered, that however this eternal glory be proper to him as God, yet he prays to be glorified in his whole person, " Glorify me," because not only was his human nature to be exalted to what glory finite nature is capable of, but the glory of his godhead was to shine in the person of Christ, god-man, and in the man Christ, though without confusion of his natures and properties

DOCTRINES.

1. It is the property and prerogative of the true God to be glorious and excellent, and consequently to be delighted in as such, and reverenced; for this is the evidence of his godhead, that he hath glory proper to him.

2. The glory of God is not borrowed from the creatures, but is essential, immutable, and eternal before any creature was; for it is a glory " before the world was."

3. Jesus Christ is true God, and was infinitely glorious from all eternity; for he who now appears in the form of a servant had glory " before the world was."

4. As all solid glory is only in heaven with God, so Christ's divine glory is with the Father, communicating with him in the divine essence and glory; therefore is this glory expected " with thine own self, (and) the glory which I had with thee;" whereby is not only to be understood, that he is to be glorified in heaven with the Father, and exalted there in his person as god-man, before he spread his glory as Mediator in the world; but that in his glory, as God, he communicates with the Father, being in and with the Father, and rejoicing alway before him, as the Son of his bosom, John, i. 1, 18; Prov. viii. 30.

5. It pleased the glorious Son of God, in obedience to the Father, to humble himself, and obscure the glory of his godhead, that he might be

like his brethren, and a fit Mediator for sympathy and suffering; and that he might engage his life and glory for redeeming of the elect, and lay by his robes of Majesty, not to be reassumed till he gave a good account of that work; for here he humbles himself to have his glory to seek from the Father (in respect of his person, god-man) upon the performance of what was entrusted to him, " I have finished the work," &c., ver. 4, " And now glorify me," saith he.

6. Christ did so faithfully discharge his trust, and perfect the work of our redemption, as the Father was engaged by paction to glorify him; and accordingly, Christ, God incarnate, is exalted with the Father in glory and majesty; for now he hath so finished the work as he may seek to be " glorified," as he is; so that believers may be as sure that all things necessary for their redemption are done, as it is sure that Christ is glorified; and as by the incarnation of the Son of God his godhead is brought near unto us, and he fitted with those human affections and sinless passions suitable to what we needed of him, and to a surety and high priest, so by the uniting of his humanity to his godhead in one person, and the exaltation thereof unto that height of glory, he is elevated above all such weaknesses of mutability and emptiness which do accompany and usually corrupt these affections and passions, and render them useless and uncomfortable in those who are but mere men.

Ver. 6. I have manifested thy name unto the men which thou gavest me out of the world: thine they were, and thou gavest them me; and they have kept thy word.

7. Now they have known that all things whatsoever thou hast given me are of thee.

Followeth, to ver. 20, the second part of the chapter, wherein Christ prayeth for his eleven disciples, wherein, albeit some things be peculiar to them, yet several grounds of the petitions, and the petitions themselves, are common to them, not only with ministers, but with all the elect, to be converted by the apostles' ministry, either mediately or immediately; and so they may, in this part of the prayer, be looked on as representing the whole ministry and church, and the purpose as much one in substance with the following part of the chapter. Only Christ, for the full encouragement of his followers of all sorts, would first pray somewhat for the apostles expressly, lest they should think they were lost among the bulk of professors; and would have somewhat expressly for all believers in all ages, that they might not think they were forgotten by him, and only his disciples cared for in this his solemn prayer to the Father.

In the first branch of this part of the chapter, Christ describes those whom he prayeth for, and giveth an account of his diligence about them, and success with them; whereby he not only giveth a notable instance of his fidelity, which he had asserted, ver. 4, but doth also recommend them to the Father's care and love, and that the petitions put up for them may be answered. This description and account is propounded in these verses, which may be taken up in this order; that, for interest, those for whom he prayeth were the Father's by eternal election, and committed to his care and trust, to purchase, apply, and promove their happiness; and for the matter of diligence and success, he had, in discharge of his trust, taken them in teaching, and revealed the Father unto them; which (being done in subserviency to his eternal purpose of election) had so succeeded, as they had kept the Father's word, and acknowledged Christ to have received his authority, commission, furniture, and doctrine, from the Father. And so Christ gives a fair account of his bringing in of the elect, in that he had converted the apostles, who were to be his instruments in converting of the rest throughout the world, and layeth a ground of confidence to be heard in their behalf taken from God's eternal interest in them and their converted estate. Whence learn—

1. It doth commend the love of God towards fallen men, that fallen angels, being cast off without hope of recovery, are admitted to the hope of redemption and restitution after their fall; for this great trust of Christ is discharged towards men. (See Heb. ii. 16.)

2. Christ's commission extends not to all the world, but to some in it only; for he gives an account of " the men which thou gavest me (saith he) out of the world," even the apostles and other elect.

3. Whatever difference there be in God's eternal purpose, or wrought by Christ's grace, in those committed to him, yet God's love and Christ's grace finds them in the same condition with others till the difference be made; for they are given " out of the world."

4. All those of whom Christ takes special care are the Father's by a peculiar interest, as being appropriated for him in his eternal purpose of election; for " thine they were," saith he, not as all other things are, but elected by him to be his peculiar people.

5. The elect, being the Father's property, are not entrusted with that happiness intended and to be conferred upon them, but are given over to Christ, and committed to him in the covenant of redemption, that he may die to satisfy justice and obtain eternal redemption for them, and may apply his purchase, in converting them, and preserving them and their furniture till they come to obtain everlasting life; for " thine they were, and thou gavest them me," not only to the apostleship, of which, ver. 12, but entrusted to him, with all the elect, in that paction betwixt the Father and the Son, of which chap. vi. 37, 39. So that they who are under his charge may be sure, considering his infinite sufficiency for it, and his fidelity to the Father who hath entrusted him.

6. The first visible evidence of election, and of men's being committed to Christ's trust, breaks forth in the work of conversion; for upon these two it followeth, " and they have kept thy word." This is not only Christ's charge to see it done, but the Father's also, who engageth to draw Christ's purchase unto him, John, vi. 44, so that conversion is a fruit of God's eternal love, and of

Christ's taking charge of us, both which we may look back and read, when we find that change wrought. (See Acts, xiii. 48.)

7. True and effectual conversion is wrought by the word of God, as the instrument, so that any change wrought by another mean will not avail, nor is there any hope of them who contemn the word, let them have what other means they will; for "I have manifested thy name, and they have kept thy word." (See 1 Pet. i. 23; Luke, xvi. 31.)

8. It is not the naked proposition of the word that will avail to conversion unless the heart be opened, and the word borne in with such efficacy as to reveal God in his nature and attributes, of justice, mercy in his Christ, power, holiness, &c., as the fragrant smell thereof may invite sinners to draw near; for "I have manifested thy name," saith he, in order to their conversion.

9. Whoever be the instrument administering the word, yet it is Christ that must reveal the Father in and by it, and make it effectual; for "I have manifested thy name," saith he; not only by his preaching in person, but by his powerful operation and illumination, which must be his work in all ages, though ministers be his instruments.

10. However reprobates do live obstinate under the word, to their own perdition, and however the elect may lie long unconverted, yet the word, being administered to them as a subservient mean of executing the decree of election, will in due time prevail in Christ's hand to their conversion; for I have manifested thy name unto the men which thou gavest me, who were thine, and they have kept thy word.

11. Such as have found the word effectual to their conversion will be sure to lay it up in their heart as their daily food, and to observe it in their practice, and to do so because of the authority of God shining in it; for this is an evidence of their conversion, "they have kept thy word," that so they may be nourished by the same mean by which they are begotten.

12. It is also a special evidence of true conversion to know Christ savingly and the mystery of redemption, to know Christ's union with the Father, his commission and authority from him as Mediator, and to see God in Christ; for this is another evidence of his success, they looked not on Christ as the malicious Jews did, but "now they have known that all things whatsoever thou hast given me (the office of Mediator, and furniture for it) are of thee," and not usurped by me, or of myself, nor any invention of man, but all divine and heavenly; which commendation, with what follows, ver. 8, seems to be grounded on their profession, chap. xvi. 30.

13. Whatever may be the weakness and ignorance of true converts for a time, yet being in Christ's hand, and through his blessing on the means, they will at last come up to a more full measure; for saith he, "Now they have known, &c.—to wit, in respect of degrees of knowledge, and fixedness in it.

14. Jesus Christ, the great Advocate of his people, doth cover their defects, esteem of their small beginnings, considering what he purposeth to make them; and however he point out their faults to themselves, to humble them, yet he will present and commend their weak beginnings to his Father; therefore, albeit he chide their presumption in their professing after his commending of them, chap. xvi. 27, 30—32, yet here, and in the following verse, he doth notably commend them to the Father.

15. Albeit it be our duty to embrace Christ offering himself, and to be converted, and it is our great happiness when it is so, yet it is put on Christ that he should not only give an account of his diligence, but of his success also, and that he not only offer salvation to the elect, but present them also converted to his Father; as here, and in the following verse he doth.

16. Such as have embraced Christ's offer have sweet ground of confidence to be respected of the Father, and heard in prayer; considering both his eternal love and interest, and the grace of God in them, needing his preservation and upholding; therefore doth Christ present them as those who were the Father's, and are now converted, that so he may be accepted in his prayers for them; for albeit he intercede and prevail for the conversion of the elect, as knowing who are given him, yet they can have no comfort of it unless they be converted.

Ver. 8. For I have given unto them the words which thou gavest me; and they have received them, and have known surely that I came out from thee, and they have believed that thou didst send me.

In this verse Christ insists to enlarge and amplify this his account of diligence and success about them; shewing that he had delivered them no word but what the Father had given him, and that they had received it, and certainly believed the truth concerning his person and office, that he came out and was sent Ambassador from the Father. Whence learn—

1. Christ is not a slighter of his trust, nor will he content himself superficially to discharge it, but will so go about it as he may abide the strictest inquest concerning his fidelity in it; therefore doth he over again, by way of confirmation, insist to give his account, "for I have given," &c., as not declining to be tried and better tried concerning it.

2. Conversion unto God is a business of so great importance as men ought not easily to satisfy themselves about it; therefore also doth he again give an account of the way of their conversion, that we may learn to try and try again if we be converted indeed. (See 2 Peter, i. 10.)

3. In the trial of conversion it is not enough to see what change is wrought, but what the word is that wrought it; that it be not a word of error, but the sound word of truth coming from Christ; for saith he, "I have given unto them the words which thou gavest me; and they have received them."

4. Whatever word be held out for the conviction and conversion of sinners, yet the divine original and authority thereof must be studied and acknowledged before it be effectual or received and obeyed; for in order to their conver-

sion he saith, " I have given unto them the words which thou gavest unto me," even divine truth; which they acknowledged to be of God, ver. 7.

5. The word of divine truth concerning the conversion and salvation of lost man is delivered by the Father to Christ, the great Prophet of his church, that he may communicate the same to his people, and see to the preservation thereof in the world; for these words are " the words which thou (saith he) gavest me." So that the doctrine of the gospel proceeds from the Father, and Christ is entrusted with the preservation thereof in this corrupt world.

6. Christ is faithful in his prophetical office, and hath concealed no truth necessary to salvation, but delivered all that was entrusted to him by the Father; for " I have given them the words which thou gavest me."

7. As the elect do all of them, in due time, welcome and entertain God and Christ's word, and all of it, whatever it say, so they who do receive the word so as to open their hearts to it as a word of truth, admitting the convictions, consolations, and directions thereof, do give true evidence of their conversion thereby; for this was an evidence thereof in the apostles, " they have received them," which includes that knowledge and believing after mentioned. And where the word is not thus received and welcomed, there it will pursue and overtake sinners, Zech. v. 6.

8. The word of Christ is never savingly received but when Christ is known and embraced, as offering himself therein; for this was the sum and scope of his doctrine, and the evidence of their conversion, that they have known " that I came out from thee," &c. (See chap. xx. 31.)

9. Christ is to be taken up by lost sinners, not as their fancy or fear would point him out, but as he hath revealed himself in his saving word; for they have received the words, and thereby have known, &c.

10. Christ is then savingly known when he is known in his person and offices, and that the Father is in him, and he his Ambassador, reconciling the world; for " they have known that I came out from thee, and that thou didst send me," of which chap. xvi. 27.

11. Believers ought to be well rooted in their knowledge of Christ, his person, and offices, considering the many tentations and assaults they will meet with to shake them in this particular; for they have surely (or truly) known, &c.

12. For settling of believers in the point of knowing Christ, they must not expect such evidences as are usual in natural things, but must submit, and be content with the evidence of faith, which, how obscure soever it seem, is a sure knowledge in its own kind; for they have surely known, is expounded, " they have believed that thou didst send me."

Ver. 9. I pray for them : I pray not for the world, but for them which thou hast given me ; for they are thine.

10. And all mine are thine, and thine are mine ; and I am glorified in them.

In these verses is contained the second branch of this part of the chapter, wherein Christ appropriates his prayer to his apostles, and his elect in them, in opposition to the world. For which he giveth several reasons: as—1. That they are his charge given him by the Father. 2. That they are the Father's also by eternal election; unto which he subjoins an illustration, clearing how they are the Father's, being given to him —namely, that both as God he hath a communion with the Father in all things, and as Mediator also; as the elect were given to him by the Father, and all things for their behoof, so they continued still the Father's in respect of election, and it was his work to make them the Father's again, by converting and dedicating them to him. 3. That he was glorified in them, and therefore would intercede for them. All which makes it clear that he doth not restrict this intercession to the persons of the apostles only, but to all those who are not of the world, but have the same interest in the Father and him, for whom also he prayeth expressly, ver. 20.

DOCTRINES.

1. Jesus Christ is the great High Priest, not only to offer up himself a sacrifice for sin, but by his prayer and intercession to complete his work and apply his purchase; for " I pray," saith he, as giving in this action a pattern of his perpetual intercession in heaven.

2. It is no small privilege to have interest in Christ's intercession, who hath perfect knowledge of all the necessities of his people, and of the true remedy and supply thereof; who hath fidelity and tenderness not to slight those whom he undertakes; who is not refused of any suit he puts up for them, chap. xi. 42, and whose merit and intercession is sufficient to render naughty persons and services acceptable; therefore it is held out as a special privilege, " I pray for them," &c. (See Heb. vii. 25.)

3. Christ did not go about the exercise of his mediatory office at adventure, not knowing whether many or few, all or none, would reap benefit thereby; but he knew distinctly for whom he appeared, and for whom not; for saith he, " I pray for them : I pray not for the world."

4. Christ was so far from laying down his life for all in the world, that all in and of the world are secluded from any part in his intercession, except only the elect; for whatsoever some do say of Christ's praying as a man under the law, wherein he looks not so much to the event as his duty, and so may pray for them in whose behalf he is not heard; to which they refer that prayer, Luke, xxiii. 34,—whatever, I say, they assert of this kind, (wherein I shall not be positive, though that petition, Luke, xxiii., for his ignorant persecutors, got a large answer in the conversion of so many of them, Acts, ii., and afterwards,) yet the world is here secluded from his intercession as Mediator, and only the elect taken in : " I pray for them : I pray not for the world," which yet doth no way militate against our duty of praying for all manner of men who have not sinned unto death; for his praying is grounded upon the distinct knowledge of the will of God, and whom he will save, and therefore he prays distinctly;

whereas we, wanting this knowledge, ought to pray for all men, with submission to the will of God.

5. Whatever the elect be in themselves, even after they are converted, yet the charge and trust of them being committed to Christ, it doth engage him to intercede for them ; so that all his wounds bleed, and his credit in heaven is employed when they have to do; for " I pray for them which thou hast given me," saith he.

6. The elect are so given to Christ as they are still the Father's, in respect of his eternal election and good will towards them ; for " them which thou hast given me, they are thine."

7. It is a notable encouragement to employ God on behalf of the elect, that he hath such an interest in them, and being chosen by him, they are cast upon him and left upon his help ; for upon this consideration doth he commend his given ones to the Father in prayer : " for they are thine," and that he commends none to him but those whom he first gave him.

8. Christ's people have room in his heart and affection, not only because of his interest in them, and charge of them, but because of the interest the Father hath also in them, whose beloved Son he is; for this is not only a reason why the Father should respect his prayers for them, but also why he so heartily undertakes to pray for them : " for they are thine ;" which should teach all, in their stations, heartily to respect and care for those persons or things wherein God hath an interest.

9. There is a communion and reciprocal interest in all things betwixt the Father and his Son, who is heir of all things, Heb. i. 2, and betwixt the Father and Christ as Mediator, in the elect ; for " all mine are thine, and thine are mine."

10. This communion and interest tends much to the advantage of God's people, as having interest both in the Father and the Son; so that Christ will not neglect those who are not only his own peculiar property, entrusted to him, but his Father's also, and will have a care to make them forthcoming to the Father; and the Father will respect those, and his Son in interceding for them, who are not only his beloved Son's charge, but his own also. Therefore are both the former arguments conjoined in this : " And all mine are thine, and thine are mine," to assure us how careful Christ will be of them, and how acceptable these endeavours will be to the Father.

11. Christ, who is the Lord of glory, and needs nothing from the creature, doth yet stoop to take glory from his people, in so far as he glorifieth himself in them ; for " I am glorified in them."

12. How unworthy soever Christ's people be, yet it is a sufficient argument moving him to do for them, and to prevail in what he doth, that he doth manifest his own glory in so doing, and by the fruits thereof in them ; for this is another argument why he intercedes for them, " and I am glorified in them"—namely, by doing good to them, and by their behaviour, being so dealt with ; and particularly, as they were apostles, by their preaching to the world his triumphs were proclaimed, and the world subjected to his obedience. And this may assure us that the more our endeavour and aim be to glorify God and Christ, we have the clearer ground to expect the acceptation of our prayers.

VER. 11. And now I am no more in the world, but these are in the world, and I come to thee. Holy Father, keep through thine own name those whom thou hast given me, that they may be one, as we are.

Followeth to verse 17, the third branch of this part of the chapter, wherein his first petition for his apostles is propounded, pressed, and explained. In this verse the petition is propounded, that the Father would preserve those whom he had given him, in an ill world, that they may be kept in unity. The petition is ushered in with a proposition of their case, that they are to be left in the world, deprived of their Master's company who had a care of them, and therefore he must leave them upon Divine protection, not secluding his own spiritual, but only bodily presence. Which purpose is more fully expressed in the following verse.

DOCTRINES.

1. Christ after his ascension is no more in the world in respect of his bodily presence, though he continue still in it as God, and by his governing and assisting Spirit; for saith he, being now shortly to die and ascend to heaven : " Now I am no more in the world."

2. Christ when he removed out of the world did ascend to his Father, and enjoy full fellowship with him, as having done his work on earth, and being to appear constantly in heaven, in name of his children; for saith he, " I come to thee."

3. Albeit Christ's people be all dear to him, yet he doth leave them behind him on earth for a time, that they may glorify him by serving their generation ; may have occasion to draw out many proofs of his love, and be trained and fitted for their eternal inheritance ; for " Now I am no more in the world, but these are in the world."

4. Albeit Christ's followers will get tender usage while they are weak and infirm, yet they must not expect always to lurk and be dandled, but must come out and meet with blasts, wherein they may give proofs of their proficiency by such tender usage ; for the disciples, who were sheltered so long under their Master's protection, are now left alone, deprived of his bodily presence ; " I am no more in the world, but these are in the world." (See Matt. ix. 14, 15.)

5. The world is so barren a soil to grace, saints' corruptions lay them so open to the tentations thereof, and those of the world are so bad company to those who are gracious, that they would be very miserable unless they had somewhat beside the world and the consolations thereof to sweeten their lots unto them and uphold them ; therefore doth he recommend them to the Father's care and pity upon this consideration : " These are in the world." (See 1 Cor. xv. 19.)

6. None of Christ's given ones are obnoxious to miseries and hazards, but only those who are yet in the world, all the rest who are gone hence

being in a condition of complete and immutable happiness; therefore he is only solicitous and prayeth for those that " are in the world."

7. Christ, by removing his bodily presence, took not away his heart from his people on earth, nor did cast off his care of them; for in his farewell he discovers much sense of their need; " These are in the world."

8. As Christ's removal did not, so neither doth his exaltation into glory change his heart from respecting his people, but he looks on his exaltation as calling for some fruits to descend to his followers on earth from him their exalted Lord; and his tender heart will never be free of cares and desires about them so long as he and they are not in one condition, but he exalted at the Father's right hand, and they left wrestling on earth; for upon these considerations doth he recommend their case; " These are in the world, and I come to thee."

9. Christ's tender heart, and care of his people in his absence, appeareth in that he is very sensible of their difficulties on earth, (" These are in the world,") in that his keeping them in the world to honour him and do him service, doth endear them to him, and engage him to see to all that may befal them, (as here he doth take notice of them before the Father, since he left them in the world,) and in that, in his bodily absence, he is careful to supply all wants by his intercession; as here his practice doth teach.

10. Saints on earth (though truly gracious, yet) do need constant preservation, as having many trials and tentations of Satan, and much laziness and inward lusts, to deprive them of their good condition, and ruin them; for this is a necessary suit—keep them.

11. As saints ought to be content with preservation, so they will get it, (for what he prayeth for is granted,) and when Christ withdraws one mean of preservation, he will still afford another; and what his followers want of outward or sensible encouragement shall be supplied in a spiritual way. All these are imported in this, that when Christ, who had kept them, (as it is, ver. 12,) is to be removed, he finds out a way of their preservation; I am no more in the world; Father, keep them.

12. The want of Christ's bodily presence on earth, to oversee and preserve his flock, is richly supplied by his intercession as Mediator, and the divine protection of the Father to whom they are committed; for " I am no more in the world," and to supply that, he prayeth, Father, keep them, making up that loss by his intercession and the Father's power.

13. It is the duty of all such as have souls committed to their charge to put them on God's hand, and to be earnest with him for his care over them; as Christ's example doth teach, " Father, keep those whom thou hast given me."

14. As the elect are committed to Christ's charge, to give an account of them, so also is the Father engaged for their conversion, (John, vi. 37; Isa. liii. 11,) and for their preservation, being converted, as being not only his own, given to Christ out of his love to them, but as being engaged to Christ, that he shall not be frustrated of the reward of his sufferings, but have a seed to

glorify him eternally; therefore doth Christ not only constantly preserve them by his Spirit, but doth leave that burden also on the Father; " Father, keep those whom thou hast given me." (See John, x. 28, 29.)

15. It gives great ground of confidence in Christ's intercession for his people, that he prayeth to his Father, and their Father in him; and believers, in their addresses to God through Christ, ought to take him up as Christ's Father, and theirs in him; for by this warm title, " Father," Christ would not only intimate his own familiarity, but would give us a fair ground of hope that he shall be heard for us, and direct us how to pray for ourselves.

16. Confidence of interest in God should be seasoned with much reverence in prayer, and we should close with such attributes in God as are suitable to our conditions and petitions, and may help our confidence; for both these causes doth Christ add that epithet, " Holy Father," to teach us that as he is a Father, so he is holy and reverend, and that none who draw near to him should entertain motions or desires contrary to his holiness; and to assure us that a petition for preservation from the evil of the world cannot but be acceptable to a holy God; and that he who is the holy God is able to preserve and continue them holy, and will not make void his promise to his Son concerning his given ones. Thus is his holiness engaged in every promise, Psalm lx. 6; lxxxix. 35.

17. God, who hath undertaken the preservation of his people, doth hold out in himself sufficient ground of confidence that he is both able and willing to do it, and can find reasons in himself for it; for so is imported in this, keep them in, or " through thine own name;" which imports both that God's name, or what he hath revealed of himself, is a strong tower to which they may flee, there being sufficiency of power, wisdom, mercy, immutability, &c., in him to keep them safe on all hands; as also that he will preserve them because his name is called upon them, and for his name's sake, and because his glory is engaged, and will shine in so doing, whatever they be in themselves; and because he can reveal his name, and make his name known unto them, that they may cleave to him and be preserved.

18. Only those who are given to Christ have assurance of Divine protection and preservation; and all of these have warrant to expect it, even the smallest and weakest, as well as the greatest apostle; therefore is the prayer conceived generally, without restriction to the apostles only, " keep those whom thou hast given me," all of them, and only them.

19. Union among the children of God, in judgment, Rom. xii. 16, affection, Gal. v. 14, 15, and practice, (evidenced by entertaining society, Mal. iii. 16, condescendence, Rom. xii. 16, and mutual admonition, Col. iii. 16,) is a special blessing and fruit of Christ's intercession; the great fruit of their preservation by the Father from the evils and snares of the world; and the condition and state wherein they may expect all other promised and needful blessings, Psa. cxxxiii. 1, 3; therefore doth he comprehend all the good things intended

for them in this one, " that (as they have many bonds of union, Eph. iv. 4—6, so) they may be one," and in being one, participate of the blessings purchased by him, and evidence their preservation from the snares of the world, and their being kept near God; " keep them, that they may be one." And as this is a singular mercy among professors of all sorts, so especially among ministers, such as the apostles were.

20. Albeit this union among the people of God cannot any way equal that incomprehensible union betwixt the Father and Son, yet it ought and will in some measure resemble it, and look heaven-like; and that, partly, in respect of the strictness of the union, they being in their own measure one in nature, judgment, will, and operation, as the Father and Son are; and partly, in respect of the sweet exercises of holiness, truth, and righteousness, wherein they are united, as the Father and Son do eternally delight each in other. For this cause doth he pray " that they may be one, as we are."

21. Whatever be the bonds tying Christians together, Eph. iv. 4—6, and whatever prudential considerations and motives they have to induce them to obey the command of God in keeping together in unity, (as Gal. v. 15, and elsewhere,) yet it is only the power of God that can keep the bond of unity inviolable; and unless he keep them near him, and free from the evils of the world, their union will break, and their being overpowered with flesh will break out in the bitter fruits of strife and division. Therefore saith he, " Holy Father, keep them, that they may be one, as we are."

VER. 12. *While I was with them in the world, I kept them in thy name: those that thou gavest me I have kept, and none of them is lost, but the son of perdition; that the scripture might be fulfilled.*

This petition Christ presseth by three arguments; the first whereof (in this verse) is taken from his care of those given him while he was bodily present with them. He had such a care of them as he can make a fair account that none of them are lost; only Judas was gone, who, though he were chosen to the apostleship, chap. vi. 70, yet was never given to be redeemed or saved by him, but was one destined to perdition, of whose defection and ruin the scriptures, speaking of him under the type of Ahithophel and other of David's enemies, (Acts, i. 20, with Psa. lxix. 25, and cix. 8,) had foretold. From which Christ would infer, that he being (not to quit his charge, which he exerciseth with the Father still, but) to remove from them in respect of his bodily presence, as ver. 11 and 14, therefore the Father must keep them, that his pains be not lost. Whence learn—

1. Christ the Son of God did for a time condescend to be present with his people in human shape, as for other ends, so to testify his tenderness and respect to their infirmity, Matthew, ix. 15, 16, and to give a proof that he will still be tender of his people; for " I was with them in the world."

2. There is no time wherein disciples, while they are in the world, will not need care and oversight without themselves for their preservation; for as now they were to need, so then they did need to be kept.

3. Albeit Christ, while he was in the world, had his own throng of sharp exercise and sufferings, yet all that did not hinder him to lay out himself in caring for his people, and to make his bodily presence comfortable to them; for " while I was with them in the world, I kept them."

4. Christ did exercise this charge of keeping his people in the Father's name—that is, not only out of love to the Father, whose name is called upon them, (as true ministers care for them, because of their relation to Christ, John, xxi. 15,) but also by the power of God, and his attributes, communicated to him from the Father as God, and concurring with him in carrying on his work as Mediator; whereby, as he leaves us a pattern of self-denial in the enjoyment of all our gifted excellences, so he teacheth all believers to ascribe the glory of their perseverance to God only; for these causes, and in these respects, he saith, " I kept them in thy name."

5. Christ is so faithful in caring for those committed to him, that he can make a fair account of one and all of them, and of his dealing and dispensations towards them, that none of them are missing, but all well and safely kept and guided; for " those that thou gavest me I have kept, and none of them is lost." And this is some shadow of the great account he will make of all his flock in the last day.

6. When Christ hath taken pains upon his people, as they will still need more, so he takes an argument, from what he hath done, to do more for them, because he will not lose the pains he hath taken; therefore doth Christ plead, that since he had taken so much pains, and kept them, therefore the Father would keep them still, as he hath desired.

7. As there are in the world given ones, of whom Christ will have a care, so there are sons of perdition and men appointed to destruction for their sin; for so saith Christ, there is " but the son of perdition," which cannot come in here by way of exception, as if the meaning were, I have lost none of them whom thou hast given me, except Judas; for it is clear, from John, vi. 37, 39, 40, that none of all those the Father gave him shall perish; and Judas was never given to Christ to be redeemed, but only to the office of apostleship; but it comes in by way of opposition (as the original particle is frequently used) to this sense, I have lost none of them thou hast given me; but Judas is lost, or, though Judas be lost. And the expression used for designation of Judas doth serve to obviate an exception; for whereas it might be objected how had he lost none, since Judas was gone, he answers that he was therefore lost because he was never so given to him, but from the beginning was a son of perdition, or, a man appointed to destruction, as the Hebrew phrase imports.

8. Sons of perdition may be not only in the world, and in the visible church, but even very high in Christ's court as to external employment

and service; for so was Judas given to be an apostle, whose defection necessitates Christ to vindicate himself that he was not the less faithful in his trust, though such an eminent man did perish.

9. Sons of perdition are such as will not be the better of any means or care, but will perish were they even in Christ's own company, and his hands (as to outward dispensations) about them; for so Judas, in Christ's own court, is " the son of perdition," and will and doth perish.

10. The defection and destruction of reprobates, were they never so eminent, doth not any way rub on Christ's fidelity in his account, they never being given to him to save them; for he gives a faithful account to his Father, though " the son of perdition" be lost.

11. God is not deceived by the defection and perishing of any, how eminent soever, but as he had his eternal purpose about them, so he could give an account what would become of them, if it were needful, long before they had a being; as he gives proof in his foretelling of Judas, and his defection and ruin, so long before, in " the scripture."

12. The scriptures of God are o infallible verity, in threatenings, promises, or predictions, for " the scripture must be fulfilled."

13. The best way to read strange and cross dispensations is to see a hand and providence of God in them, which may quiet our hearts till we get a more full and distinct account of his mind in them; therefore, in mentioning " the son of perdition," he leads us to " the scripture," wherein God, by foretelling thereof, testified his providence about it, and to the fulfilling thereof by his defection, that we may see nothing in it but that wherein he had a holy hand.

Ver. 13. And now come I to thee; and these things I speak in the world, that they might have my joy fulfilled in themselves.

The second argument, pressing the petition, is taken from Christ's end in putting up the petition in the disciples' audience, and the event that should follow upon the Father's granting the same —namely, the fulfilling and completing of their joy who were much discouraged with the removal of his bodily presence. The sum of the argument is, that he being to remove and take away his bodily presence, which had been so comfortable to his disciples, albeit his intercession in heaven might have sufficed for obtaining what they needed; yet he would recommend them to the Father, and pray for preservation to them, in their own audience, that so they might be encouraged, seeing his care of them, and having hope of audience to such a suit put up by such a petitioner. And therefore he would infer that the Father will not disappoint their hope, but fulfil their joy, by granting the request. Whence learn—

1. Christ's removal out of the world looked very sweet upon him, as being a coming to his Father, with whom he is so familiar; and in him death is sanctified and sweetened to all his followers, as being a departing to him, that they may be with him for ever, Phil. i. 23, 1 Thess. iv. 17. So doth he describe his removal, " Now come I to thee."

2. Christ is very condescending in his dealing with and for his people, and doth not only what is simply needful, but what in reason may abundantly satisfy them, notwithstanding their tentations and infirmities; for albeit his intercession, being exalted at the right hand of the Father, was sufficient to bring about needful benefits, yet for their satisfaction he will even pray in their audience, " These things I speak in the world." And this should gain our consent to say he doth all things well, and by what we see of his condescendence in any particular to trust him in others more dark.

3. Joy is allowed by Christ upon all his followers; it is his scope in his dealing towards them, and he hath done and daily doth what may breed them joy ; for this is his scope here, that they may have joy. (See Phil. iv. 4 ; 1 Thess. v. 16.)

4. The faith and knowledge of Christ's intercession for his people, that they may be preserved and made to persevere, is such a pledge of their sure estate and of his good will towards them, as may afford abundant matter of joy in their saddest case; for " these things I speak in the world, that they might have joy."

5. The joy of believers is of Christ's allowing, is his work in them, and a joy in him over all that they find in themselves; therefore doth he call it " my joy."

6. Christ's joy, allowed on his people, is a complete joy, far beyond the empty joy of the world, in midst whereof the heart is sorrowful; and albeit the full degrees of their joy will meet them in heaven, yet their joy here is full in parts, as satisfying the mind, calming their storms, and staying their foot against all essays, if they improve it right. Therefore is this joy, in that he prays for them, and their joy in obtaining their answer, called a fulfilled joy.

7. Christ doth not only take care to give his people cause of joy, but to make them rejoice in it also, and that with an inexpressible joy, whereof others are ignorant; therefore will he have it " fulfilled in themselves,"—that is, their hearts filled with it, and feeding on that hid manna whereof strangers are not partakers, as Prov. xiv. 10.

8. The Father doth allow that which Christ doth for the encouragement of his people, and will not let it be ineffectual; for this is Christ's argument for obtaining his suit, which certainly hath weight with the Father, " These things I speak in the world, that they might have my joy fulfilled in themselves.

Ver. 14. I have given them thy word; and the world hath hated them, because they are not of the world, even as I am not of the world.

The third argument, pressing the petition, is taken from the world's opposition to them, being converted. The word which Christ gave them, ver. 8, had so far wrought upon them as to regenerate them, and make them dissent from the world in judgment, affection, and conversation, so rendering them conformed in some measure to him their Head. And this change made them incur the world's hatred, which doth call for divine preservation. Whence learn—

1. As it is Christ's great favour and kindness to give his word unto his people, so where it is given with a blessing and rightly received, it draws the receiver to a disconformity with the world, and not to be of it, though he be in it; for "I have given them thy word," and "they are not of the world."

2. It doth exceedingly commend the grace of God in saints, that albeit they be kept in the world, and forced to walk among the many snares thereof, yet they are separated from it, and not conformed unto it; for though they are "in the world," ver. 11, yet "they are not of the world."

3. Whatever civility men of the world may have, yet all of them are so opposite to grace and godliness that they will not only oppose it in themselves, but hate and persecute it in others, one way or other, if it were but by traducing piety, that they may persecute it under some odious name; for "the world hath hated them, because they are not of the world." So that when it seems to be otherwise, we may reckon either that professors of religion are but too much like the world, and little like Christ, or that the world's malice is but overpowered and bridled till they get an opportunity.

4. It may encourage saints to endure opposition from the world for religion's sake, that the quarrel wherein they suffer is most glorious, and what the world hates in them is their greatest ornament before God; for he points out to them that the quarrel is "because they are not of the world."

5. It may encourage them also in this conflict, that in their state and suffering they have a conformity with Christ their Head, conformity with whom is a great dignity; for by this also doth he encourage them, "they are not of the world, even as I am not of the world." He or his kingdom are not of this world more than they are, and their suffering on this account redounds to him, who is first hated, and for whose sake, and because of conformity with him, they are hated.

6. The world's opposition to saints, because of their separation from it, doth engage God to see the more carefully to their preservation; for it is an argument why the Father should keep them, "The world hath hated them, because they are not of the world."

VER. 15. I pray not that thou shouldest take them out of the world, but that thou shouldest keep them from the evil.

16. They are not of the world, even as I am not of the world.

In these verses—1. Christ repeats and explains the former petition, shewing, for their instruction, that he desired not as yet they should be freed from all danger and trouble, by taking them away out of the world by death, but that he would preserve them in the midst of troubles from the tentations and snares of their troubles, ver. 15.

2. He presseth and enforceth the petition, thus explained, upon the reason propounded, ver. 14, taken from their condition opposite to the world, and conformed to him their Master, verse 16. Whence learn—

1. Christ's followers have need to guard against mistakes of what he saith, that they do not delude themselves, nor let their own lusts put a commentary upon his doctrine; therefore doth he explain his own meaning, not to inform his Father, but to prevent their mistakes.

2. Such as are employed to speak in public for the edification of others ought to make it their study to accommodate their speech to the capacity of their hearers; as Christ here doth so speak, as may clearly explain his meaning unto them.

3. Christ hath more ways than one whereby to secure his people against all they can meet with; as here he hath one way of preservation, which he layeth by for a time, and another, which he pitcheth upon.

4. There is one fair outgate from all troubles abiding saints, when by death they shall be translated out of the world, and above the reach of all their difficulties; for this is one outgate, though he will not make use of it at this time, to "take them out of the world." (See John, iii. 17—19; Rev. xiv. 13.)

5. Albeit death be very often desired by saints in their perplexities, yet Christ seeth it meet rather to exercise them for a time, and fit them for proofs of his love, than to grant that desire; and however we ought still to have our eye upon our rest, and make ready for it, yet we are not anxiously to long after it, till his time come, nor to weary of life, especially because of any trouble, persecution, or inconvenience we meet with in his service; therefore Christ, who loves his people better than they do love themselves, will not pray for this, "I pray not that thou shouldest take them out of the world."

6. Believers, while they are thus left by Christ in the world, are exposed to manifold hazards, having not only outward troubles, but Satan and sin taking advantage of their troubles, to drive them wrong; for they are in this world, in the midst of "the evil," not so much of outward trouble, from which he will not always preserve them, but Satan, the wicked one (as the word will read), and "the evil" and wickedness to which they are exposed in an evil world, and by the many pressures they meet with.

7. Albeit Christ will not remove his people from these hazards, yet they are no way able to guard themselves against them, but must resolve to have much to do, and very little, or rather nothing, in themselves wherewith to do it; for they must be kept, or else they are undone.

8. When Christ seeth it not fit to remove his own out of the world, he will see to their preservation in it, so as though they get now and then the foil, yet his intercession is a sure pledge that they shall recover again; for these two go together, "I pray not that thou shouldest take them

out of the world, but that thou shouldest keep them."

9. Christ doth abundantly testify his care and diligence about his people when, albeit he doth not exempt them from troubles, and these may be very sharp, yet he keeps them from the evil thereof, or from spiritual hurt thereby; and when, albeit he doth not deliver them even from assaults and tentations from that evil, yet he upholds them by sufficient grace, 2 Cor. xii. 7—10; for herein doth his care appear, in praying that the Father should "keep them from the evil."

10. Albeit many, when they look upon Christ's promises and allowances, and his intercession for his people, be ready to delude themselves with vain hopes of that which Christ never allowed upon them, yet they who are content with being preserved from evil, however they be tempted and exercised, are no way deluded when they expect this from Christ; for it is his express will, when he explains himself, that they should be kept from the evil.

11. It is frequently to be studied by believers that their separation from the world is an evidence of their conformity with Christ, and consequently that they are like to him, in enduring opposition from the world because thereof; therefore is it again held out, "They are not of the world, even as I am not of the world."

12. Believers' disconformity with the world and conformity with Christ is a sure pledge that the Father will keep them from the evil of the world, and will not lose those good things which grace hath begun in them; for this is an argument why he should "keep them from the evil," ver. 15, "They are not of the world," &c.

Ver. 17. Sanctify them through thy truth: thy word is truth.

Followeth the fourth and last branch of this part of the chapter, containing Christ's second petition for his apostles, which is propounded in this verse, and pressed by two arguments, ver. 18, 19. The petition is, that the Father would "sanctify them," which, albeit it sometimes signify the consecrating of a man and setting him apart to an office, as the apostles also were, ver. 18, yet here it imports somewhat beside and subservient to that—namely, that the Lord would confer upon them the grace of sanctification, and so consecrate them unto himself as believers, and so also fit them for that employment to which he had devoted and consecrated them. Unto this is subjoined the instrumental cause of their sanctification, "through thy truth," whereby is not only signified that he would have them sanctified in truth, or truly, of which we may hear, ver. 19, but that the word of truth is the mean and instrument of sanctification; and to prevent all mistakes he declares that this truth is in the word, against all them who seek truth beside it. Whence learn—

1. Such as are Christ's followers indeed, and may make comfortable application of other benefits of his intercession, must be men sanctified by habitual graces of holiness infused into them, which will not only break forth in some few acts of religion and righteousness, but must so devote and consecrate them to God as they may not withdraw themselves to another use; for so much is imported in this that Christ prays for, unto his apostles, "Sanctify them," intimating that where he intercedes for any, he also prayeth for and in due time works this in them.

2. It is not enough that men have a begun work of sanctification in them unless they grow up in it daily more and more; for he prayeth for those who were already converted and sanctified, as he maketh his account, ver. 6—8, that the Father would "sanctify them," and carry them on in sanctification till it be perfected in glory. Such will be invited to grow who entertain the sense of what they have received, 1 Pet. ii. 2, 3, who are sensible of their shortcoming in what they have, Phil. iii. 12, 13, and who fear backsliding, and consider that not to grow is the way to decay; and they will study to evidence this growth by persevering in their first principles, not loving again what once through grace they loathed, nor building up what they once destroyed, and by growing in grace, especially in sense of their pollution, humility, love, painfulness, &c.

3. Whatever principles or obligations men have to keep them from the evils of the world, and from Satan in it, yet all these will not avail unless they be not only truly sanctified but be growing therein; therefore is this petition—"Sanctify them," subjoined to the former, ver. 15, of keeping them, as being the effectual mean of their preservation.

4. As sanctification is the duty of believers, laid upon them by God, so it is also his work in them who principleth them for it, and works it in them, when they in the sense of their own inability do put it upon him; for Christ, by prayer, seeketh it of the Father, "Sanctify them."

5. As the truth of God is the rule of true sanctification, nothing being holiness in God's account, how specious soever it be, unless it be according to that truth, so the truth of God, which is the instrument of regeneration, hath also a special influence in the matter of daily sanctification, 1 Pet. ii. 2; the word of command being made effectual to press the duty, the word of promise to encourage it, 2 Cor. vii. 1; 2 Pet. i. 4, and the word and doctrine of the cross of Christ holding out virtue enabling to duty, 1 Cor. i. 18, and exciting faith, which purifieth the heart, Acts, xv. 9. In both these respects he prayeth, "Sanctify them through (or in) thy truth," both as the rule and touchstone of sanctification, and as a mean and instrument of it.

6. It is not safe for men to cry up their own or others' sanctification to the countenancing of the errors which they maintain, but they must prove the truth of their holiness by the truth which hath been instrumental in it, and must reckon that the holiness they have is either counterfeit or else hath been wrought, not by their errors, but by the power of some real truths which they have or do still hold, and that therefore, by embracing error, they do exceedingly wrong their piety, by depriving themselves of the mean which doth beget and cherish it; for these causes

doth Christ so expressly pray, not only, " Sanc-tify them," by what mean soever, but, " Sanctify them through thy truth," as the only mean of true holiness.

7. Whatever efficacy truth hath in the matter of sanctification, it doth all come from God, who must be employed by prayer to make the word successful for that end ; for so much doth Christ's example teach, who prayeth to the Father, " Sanctify them through thy truth." (See 2 Thess. iii. 1.)

8. Whatever ways men do dream of for find-ing the truth of God, yet it is only to be found in the word of God, and all other ways beside will but produce delusion and lies ; therefore doth he subjoin, to prevent all mistakes, " Thy word is truth."

9. Whatever may be the hesitations of men concerning the word of God, yet it is his infal-lible verity, and will not deceive them who be-take themselves to it for direction and encou-ragement; for " Thy word is truth." (See Ps. xii. 6 ; 2 Pet. i. 19.)

Ver. 18. As thou hast sent me into the world, even so have I also sent them into the world.

The first argument pressing this petition is taken from their employment and calling to be his ambassadors in the world, which presseth the necessity of their sanctification. This their call-ing and commission is amplified from its simili-tude and likeness unto the Father's sending of him, which (as all similitudes have their own dis-similitudes, and are not to be strictly pressed in every thing) is not to be extended to all the ends of Christ's coming into the world,—for he alone came to die for and redeem his people,—but only to his ministerial office of preaching the gospel ; in which, albeit there was some resemblance be-twixt Christ and the apostles, as to the matter of extraordinary calling and assistance, immediate direction, and great difficulties, yet there was also as great difference, both in respect of their persons and authority, he being the Lord and true God, they but mere men and servants ; in respect of the manner of their furniture, he being fur-nished inwardly by the substantial in-dwelling of the godhead, they by extrinsical revelation and assistance ; and in respect of the measure of assistance, he being furnished without mea-sure and constantly, and they only but in part, and when it pleased the Spirit to breathe.

DOCTRINES.

1. Christ is the great apostle of our profession, sent to us by the Father ; so that we need not think shame of a profession which is owned by such an one as he is ; for " thou hast sent me into the world." (See Heb. iii. 1.)

2. Christ hath employed the apostles, and their successors in their own room, to be his ambassadors, and to supply his place, as he was a preacher of reconciliation ; so that as they ought to study an imitation of him, 1 Cor. xi. 1, so they ought to be received in their ministry, as coming in Christ's stead, 2 Cor. v. 20 ; Gal.

iv. 14 ; therefore saith he, " As thou hast sent me into the world, so have I also sent them," as is before explained.

3. It doth commend the love of God that he hath employed the ministry of his Son and ser-vants even in this corrupt world, that out of such base materials he may build up an excellent church and habitation to himself ; and that he may encourage the most desperate to come to him, who out of such gathereth his precious jewels, 1 Cor. vi. 9—11 ; Titus, iii. 2—4 ; there-fore it is said that both he and they are sent " into the world."

4. Beside the obligations and necessity which lie upon ministers with all saints to be holy, Heb. xii. 14, their calling doth particularly call for sanctification and separation from the world as necessary by divine precept and for the well-being of the ministry, that so they may stand in their Master's counsel, and be kept near him, that their face may shine and they may be more suc-cessful in their ministry ; for this is a condition calling for the granting that suit, that they may be sanctified, even that they are " sent into the world." It is true, men may be lawful ministers, yea, and successful also in their ministry, who are not sanctified themselves ; for even Judas was an apostle. And Christ is here more ex-pressly praying for his eleven apostles, who, be-side that they were apostles, were given to him also by the Father, in opposition to the world and the son of perdition, who yet was an apostle, ver. 9, 12, yet his reasoning in prayer doth lay before all ministers how needful it is they be sanctified, not only in order to their own salva-tion, but even that their labour may be more successful ; and this his reasoning doth plead for holiness to all ministers, (who employ him for that end,) in their own measure, however the extraordinary employment of the apostles did plead for an extraordinary measure of this sanc-tification, that they might be kept from error, being sanctified through the truth, and made fruitful in their great work.

5. When God doth call his servants to any employment his calling may assure them of fur-niture, and what they need for discharge of that calling ; and particularly, Christ will have a spe-cial care to furnish church officers sent out by himself ; for this is the face of Christ's pleading in prayer, which prevails with the Father, that since they are sent into the world, therefore they may get sanctification ; " Sanctify them," ver. 17, for " I have sent them into the world." (See John, xx. 21, 22.)

Ver. 19. And for their sakes I sanctify myself, that they also might be sanctified through the truth.

As the former reason pressing this petition is taken from their need of sanctification in respect of their calling, so this second is taken from the cause and purchase of their sanctification, by his sanctifying himself that they may be sanc-tified ; for clearing whereof, consider—1. Christ's sanctifying of himself is not to be understood of any personal cleansing now in doing, or to be done by him, for he was without spot from his first conception, nor yet of that purity of his nature only, but with relation to some further sanctification ; but as, in the language of the Old Testament, things are said to be sanctified when they are set apart, fitted, and prepared for some special service and employment,—and particularly priests are said to be sanctified to their office, and sacrifices to be offered up,—so Christ's sanctification imports that as the Father did sanctify, or consecrate, and send him into the world, John, x. 36, so he did consecrate himself unto the Lord on the elects' behalf, a priest and sacrifice without spot ; and did consecrate himself to the whole work of his mediatory office, and particularly did offer himself a sacrifice for sin, that they might be sanctified.   Consider—2. The effect of his sanctifying of himself is that they may be sanctified through the truth, or in truth, whereby may be understood, as formerly, ver. 17, that the virtue of his death accompanying the word of truth is that which sanctifieth ; and further also it may import that by his sanctifying of himself they are sanctified in truth, or truly, and that not only in opposition to counterfeit sanctification, but in opposition also to legal purifications by the use of the ceremonies of the law, which were but a shadow of true holiness, whereas the virtue of Christ's death, being the truth of these shadows, doth truly and in truth sanctify.

DOCTRINES.

1. Christ, in going about the office of Mediator, and offering up himself a sacrifice, did wholly consecrate and set himself apart for his people's behoof, that he might be theirs and seek their weal and not his own ; for their sakes he sanctified, or consecrated, and set apart himself to that work ; which may engage them not to be their own, but wholly his.

2. As the Father did consecrate and sanctify his Son to the office of Mediator, John, x. 36, so he also did consecrate himself as having inherent worth, and not needing external consecrations, and as being a most willing agent in this work ; for " I sanctify myself," saith he.

3. Albeit the elect be in themselves polluted, and have no worth to merit any purification from God, yet there is enough in Christ and his consecrating himself a sacrifice to the Father to supply all their worthlessness, and obtain what they need ; " for their sakes I sanctify myself, that they may be sanctified."

4. True sanctification of the elect flows from Christ's sanctifying and consecrating himself to the Father for them. Not only doth the merit of his suffering, being imputed, make them appear without spot and wrinkle in him, but the virtue of his death and sacrifice must be applied, to sanctify them inherently ; for " I sanctify myself, that they may be sanctified."

5. Christ did sanctify and consecrate himself a sacrifice in the Father, not for those who die in their pollution, but for those only whom he in time sanctifies thereby ; for " I sanctify myself, that they may be sanctified ;" the one followeth upon the other, not in the apostles only, but all the elect.

6. Christ doth approve of no sanctification but that which is truly such, and abhors all counterfeits of it, and such as rest on outside sanctification, or shadows of true holiness only ; for that is his aim, that they may be sanctified in truth.

7. Whatever effects good inclinations and education, moral principles or example, or church discipline and ordinances, or afflictions on men, may produce, yet true sanctification flows only from the application of Christ's sacrifice, and it is that which makes the word of truth effectual for sanctifying of them truly ; for upon his sanctifying himself it followeth that they are sanctified in truth, and " through the truth."

Ver. 20. Neither pray I for these alone, but for them also which shall believe on me through their word ;

21. That they all may be one ; as thou, Father, art in me, and I in thee, that they also may be one in us : that the world may believe that thou hast sent me.

Followeth the third part of the chapter, wherein Christ prayeth for the apostles and whole church of believers expressly, seeking several benefits unto them. In these verses—1. He describes those for whom he prays—namely, not the apostles only, but all those who to the end of the world should, by the word preached by them, either immediately, or mediately in the mouth of other messengers, be converted and drawn to believe on him, ver. 20. 2. He propounds his first suit for them, the same in substance with what he had sought unto the disciples, ver. 11—namely, that they may be preserved in unity, and be one in the Father and him, as he and the Father are one, and the Father in him, and he in the Father. This suit he amplifieth and presseth from the final cause thereof—namely, that by their union the world may be convinced and made to believe the truth of the Christian religion, and that Christ is an Ambassador sent by the Father into the world, ver. 21. This unity prayed for doth indeed include and presuppose their unity in relation to Christ and God in him, in which they are stated by believing, and which is the root of the other unity ; but that which it most expressly holds out is, unity in love flowing from the other, and which is visible to the conviction of the world.

From verse 20, learn—1. Albeit Christ, when he departed out of this world, left but a few followers, and his weak disciples, being entrusted with the word of reconciliation, were to meet with persecution and opposition, yet he knew certainly his kingdom was to spread, as accordingly he hath accomplished in the world ; for here he supposeth for certain that there will be them who shall believe.

2. Christ's love and heart are enlarged to take in all his people throughout the world, and to employ himself in his mediatory office and intercession for them ; therefore, after his prayer for himself and for his apostles, he doth now shew how large his affection is. " Neither pray I for these alone, but for them also which shall believe."

3. Christ's love towards his people is a preventing love, even before they have a being, and before they come to him; and whoever do in any age embrace him shall find that they were in his heart, and were as tenderly regarded and minded of him, in his suffering and solemn intercession on earth, as any of his followers then present with him; for here, before they are or do believe, they are remembered, and he hath left a blank that all believers in all ages may put in their own name, as prayed for by him, when he prayeth for his apostles. "Neither pray I for these alone, but for them also which shall believe."

4. The character whereby Christ's followers, and those whom he prays for, are discerned, is their faith in him, whereby they are driven out of themselves to embrace and rely upon him, and to have all their subsistence by him; for "I pray for them which shall believe on me," where, albeit he pray for them before they believe, and that the means may be kept to them till they be brought to believe, yet the thing here prayed for supposeth them in a state of believing, and him interceding for what is needful to them in that state. And albeit his intercession have influence also upon their believing, and is a mean to draw them to it, yet Christ doth not mention that in the apostles' audience, because none can make comfortable application of Christ's intercession to themselves, till first they be drawn to believe.

5. True faith is begotten by and grounds itself upon the word of God delivered by the apostles, without doting on signs and wonders, or expecting any other revelation of the mind of God; for "they believe on me through their word;" which also imports, that that word will be continued, and a ministry to preach it, so long as there is a church, or any to be converted.

6. Such as are taught to discern the divine authority of the word will not stumble at the despicableness or meanness of instruments carrying the same, but will close with it by faith to salvation; for albeit it be "their word," as the instruments, who were but mean and despised men in the world, yet they "believe on me through their word."

From verse 21, learn—1. The whole bulk of believers and the catholic church, though of different nations and conditions, are but one body in Christ their Head, having one spirit, one faith, one baptism, &c., Eph. iv. 4—6; for this is Christ's aim, wherein he succeeds, that they which shall believe "may be one."

2. Whatever diversity there be among believers in administrations, gifts, and operations, yet this doth not, nor ought hinder their being one in him; and all of them have a like interest in him and his love; for when he mentions the apostles, who were extraordinarily gifted, and all believers of all sorts, he prayeth "that they all may be one."

3. As it is the great dignity and privilege of believers to be one, so their improving of this privilege and living in unity is the sum and compend [substance] of their happiness, and the mean of obtaining all other blessings; therefore doth Christ so often pray for this, and for this

only, in place of all, "that they may be one." (See Psalm cxxxiii. 1—3; James, iii. 16.)

4. Whatever be the bonds of unity among believers, or their obligations to it, yet the improvement thereof, to the uniting of them, must be sought and given of God, and Christ's intercession made use of for that end; for so much doth Christ teach us, while he prayeth, "that they all may be one."

5. The union of believers, prayed for by Christ, is not every combination or consent, even of saints, nor a conjunction in any sinful course, but it is an union in God, and in the ways of God; for this doth Christ pray for, "that they may be one in us."

6. The way to keep up true union among saints is, that they keep close communion with God in Christ, lest otherwise, if they be carnal, this breed strife, 1 Cor. iii. 3; for so much also is imported in this prayer, "that they may be one in us," or, by being in us, and keeping communion with us.

7. The true union of believers among themselves doth resemble that union betwixt the Father and Son, partly, in respect of the strictness of the union, that this union cometh nearest to that inexpressible union, (though indeed it be infinitely short of it,) and doth far surpass any other conjunction; and partly, that as the Father being in the Son, and the Son in the Father, they do mutually delight each in other, as a consequent of their union, Prov. viii. 30, so this union of believers is testified and entertained by spiritual exercise of mutual edification; to which also may be added, that from this union betwixt the Father and the Son who is our Mediator, this union of believers doth flow, that they are made one in them; therefore again doth Christ pray, "That as thou, Father, art in me, and I in thee, they may be one in us."

8. The true union of believers will not consist in contemplative notions or outward professions, but ought to express itself in visible fruits; as here is subjoined, "that the world may believe," &c.

9. In expressing the fruits of union, believers ought not only to respect the honour of God and their own edification, but they ought to study such a conversation as may either convince or convert others, and bring them to the acknowledgment of Christ and his truth; for this is the end propounded here, "that the world may believe that thou hast sent me." (See 1 Pet. iii. 1, 2.)

10. The people of God walking in an united way is a special mean to convince the world of the excellency of Christ, and of the truth of the Christian religion, and so either leave them inexcusable or convert them; whereas schisms and rents among them is a ready mean to beget and cherish atheism in the world; for when "they are one in us, the world shall believe that thou hast sent me."

VER. 22. And the glory which thou gavest me I have given them; that they may be one, even as we are one:

In this verse, Christ (to press this suit before the Father, and convince his apostles and all believers of the necessity of this union) holds forth what excellent privileges he had conferred and allowed upon them to advance their union, even a communication of that glory given to him by the Father; which is not to be understood as if the essential glory and attributes of Christ as God, or the glory of the personal union of the manhood of Christ to his godhead, or of the office of Mediator, were communicable to any other, or that any glory given to him is communicated to any in the same measure with him; nor yet only of the glory of the apostleship or ministry committed to him,—for that was given only to the apostles and their successors, this to all believers,—but the meaning is, that as his incommunicable glory is made forthcoming for them, so the glory of sonship, of his sanctification without measure, of being in God's secrets and dwelling in his bosom, and of his union with the Father, is communicated to them in its own kind and measure, and they are made sons, sanctified in part, admitted to the knowledge of the Father's secrets, and to be one with the Father in him; and all this in order to their union, which also is a resemblance of that glory of his unity with the Father communicated unto them.   Whence learn—

1. Christ is truly glorious, having not only essential glory, the same and equal with the Father's glory, and which was declared to be in him, by his exaltation, but our nature being exalted in him to the glory of the personal union, and of the offices and dignities following thereupon; for there is " the glory which thou gavest me."

2. Christ is communicative of his fulness to his people, all his excellences being either communicated to them to partake of, or daily forthcoming for them; for " the glory which thou gavest me, I have given them."

3. All that is in Christ for believers, or communicated to them from him, cometh by free gift, without any deserving on their part, and should be esteemed of as an excellent gift; for " I have given them the glory."

4. What believers have in and from Christ doth advance them to a glorious estate, and is their begun glory and salvation, so that none but they have any true glory, nor is anything enjoyed by men truly glorious but the grace and other privileges they enjoy in and from him; for it is " the glory which I have given them."

5. It is not enough we know what we have in Christ and from him, unless we also take up the end for which it is allowed, and improve it accordingly; therefore doth he subjoin, " I have given them that glory, that they may be one."

6. All Christ's communication of himself to believers doth tend to advance their union; their union among themselves, in some sort of resemblance with that union betwixt the Father and him, and their union with God through him for that end, is in itself a part of that glory which he giveth them; and all their participation, of the fruits of that incommunicable glory which is in Christ, and all that is communicated by Christ to them, should fit them the more for union, and make them grow in humility and mutual condescendence for that effect, and not puff them up; for " the glory which thou gavest me, I have

given them; that they may be one, even as we are one."

7. Christ would have the excellency of union studied, in the gloriousness thereof, in his large communications for the advancement thereof, and in the resemblance it hath with the union betwixt the Father and him; therefore doth he so point it out here, to the conviction of all, " I have given them the glory," even " to be one," and " that they may be one, even as we are one."

8. Such as would promove the welfare of God's people ought not only to wish or pray for it, but must also be active in their station for promoving thereof; for so much doth Christ's practice teach, who, as he prayed for this union, so he " gave them the glory, that they may be one."

9. It may, upon the one hand, shame believers from division and dissension, that hereby they do what they can to deprive themselves of that glory gifted by Christ, to be one as the Father and he are, and to make void the fruit of all his glorious communications; and, on the other hand, it may assure them who long for union, that Christ, whose desire and allowance it is, and who hath laid out so much for it, and is daily interceding with the Father for that effect, will, in due time, bring it about among his people; therefore, both to shame his people from their contentions and neglect of union, and to press his suit before the Father, how averse soever they be, he useth this argument, " The glory which thou gavest me, I have given them, that they may be one," &c.

VER. 23. I in them, and thou in me, that they may be made perfect in one; and that the world may know that thou hast sent me, and hast loved them, as thou hast loved me.

In this verse Christ yet insists to clear and press his suit for obtaining union of believers among themselves.   And for this end—1. He propounds the way of their union among themselves, instancing one particular branch of that glory given them, ver. 22, for that end, even union with himself, and with the Father through him, which, as it is a great dignity in itself, so it tends to the perfecting of their union among themselves. 2. He again amplifieth and presseth the suit from the final causes thereof; where unto that end formerly mentioned, ver. 21, of the conviction of the world of his authority and commission, another also is added, that hereby the world shall be convinced of the Father's love to his followers according as he loved him. Whence learn—

1. Christ takes up an inhabitation in his people by his Spirit, so that they become one with him; for it is their allowance, " I in them."

2. The Father dwells in Christ, not only as he is one God with him, but also as he is man, in whom the fulness of the godhead dwells bodily; so highly is our nature dignified in his person; for thou art in me, saith he.

3. Albeit there can be no union betwixt God and fallen man immediately, yet through Christ this union is made up; and Christ being in us,

and we united to him, the Father also, in him, is in us, and we in him ; for thus is our union here with God made up, " I in them, and thou in me."

4. It is by our union with Christ, and with God through him, that our union among ourselves is perfected ; for by this mean they are " made perfect in one."

5. Whatever excellency the Lord confer upon every particular believer, yet their perfection consists in their union among themselves, and with Christ their Head and Storehouse, and with the Father in his fulness through him ; for no one member hath the perfection of the whole body, but of a part only, nor hath it that perfection separate from the body, but in it, and being united with it, to supply its own proper function ; and the whole body, thus united, hath its perfection in and from Christ and the Father ; for so doth Christ's conjoining of all these teach us : " I in them, and thou in me, that they may be made perfect in one."

6. It is never enough studied how necessary union is to convince the world of the excellency of Christ and his doctrine ; therefore it is again repeated, as a forcible argument pressing this union, " that the world may know that thou hast sent me." And as the apostles' union and consent in doctrine did contribute to this end, so also doth the union of the people of God in every age, in its own measure.

7. It tends to the great encouragement of believers, that Christ their Surety is beloved and accepted of the Father ; for " thou hast loved me," saith he.

8. Every believer also is really beloved of the Father, so that whatever he do unto them there is still love in it, and they keep a room in his affection ; for " thou hast loved them," saith he.

9. The Father's love to believers doth resemble his love to his Son Christ ; for though his love to his eternal and only Son be matchless and necessary, not voluntary, as his love to us is ; nor are we loved for our own sakes as he is ; nor is he capable of some effects of love we receive ; yet this love doth most resemble it of any ; and albeit, considering him as Mediator, there is a great difference betwixt us who are beloved, and Him for whose sake we are beloved, yet the resemblance doth also here hold ; and the Father loveth Christ and all his as one mystical body, and loveth them eternally, immutably, and freely, as he loved the Mediator ; yea, that same love that is let out on Christ as Mediator is conveyed through him to us ; for " thou hast loved them, as thou hast loved me," not in respect of equality, but by way of similitude and resemblance.

10. The love of God towards some of fallen mankind is such as ought not to be concealed, but Christ would have it published, to the conviction or conversion of others ; therefore he would have " the world know that thou hast loved them."

11. Union among believers is so great a work of God, evidencing so much of his care and love, and is the condition upon which he rains so many showers of blessings and mercies, that it serves exceedingly to convince the world of God's love to them when they are thus united, and are reaping the fruits thereof ; for hereby " the world

shall know that thou hast loved them as thou hast loved me."

Ver. 24. Father, I will that they also, whom thou hast given me, be with me where I am ; that they may behold my glory, which thou hast given me : for thou lovedst me before the foundation of the world.

In this verse is contained another suit put up by Christ in behalf of all his people ; wherein, having prayed for their spiritual union among themselves, and for union with him and with the Father through him, he now prayeth for their union in place with himself in heaven at last, and describeth the blessed estate of believers in heaven. 1. From their company, that they shall be with him where he is. 2. From their exercise, which shall be, to behold that glory given unto him, which is further commended from the fountain cause thereof, even the Father's eternal love to him. Of this glory of Christ compare ver. 1, 5.

DOCTRINES.

1. It is a sweet way to keep our hearts fresh and lively in prayer when we have many thoughts of that tender relation betwixt God, to whom we pray, and us ; therefore Christ, who began his prayer with the sweet style of " Father," ver. 1, doth so often repeat the same, ver. 11, here, and ver. 25, that the thoughts of that relation might sweeten his heart, and renew his ardour and affection.

2. The thoughts and hope of eternal life ought and will warm believers' hearts towards God, and excite much alacrity and affection in them ; for so much also doth Christ's practice teach, who, beginning to speak of his glory flowing from the Father's love, and of heaven and eternal life to be conferred upon all his followers, his heart warmeth, and he breaketh out with that sweet compellation, " Father."

3. While Christ expresseth his petition in these terms, " I will," it doth not import any imperious, commanding way, repugnant to his former way of humble supplication ; but it only imports that in this his supplication he was making his latter will and testament, and leaving his legacies, which he was sure would be effectual, being purchased by his effectual merits, and prosecuted by his affectionate and earnest requests and intercession, all which are imported in this expression. And so it teacheth us, that as all these things sought in this prayer are believers' duty to study after them, so are they Christ's legacies, purchased and earnestly prayed for by him, which will certainly be forthcoming to them ; for saith he, concerning them, " I will" that they be.

4. Christ is very desirous and much taken up with his people's fellowship and company, so that before he remove his bodily presence from them his heart is upon meeting and fellowship again ; as here we see in his prayer before his departure. And this he maketh evident from day to day, in that, until that time of meeting come, two or three are not gathered in his name, but he is in the midst of them.

5. Spiritual communion with Christ will at last

end in glory, and in communion with him in place in heaven : Christ will never rest satisfied till their begun communion be thus perfected; and however the world and our hearts do oft-times look on spiritual communion but as a fancy, yet heaven shall confirm the reality thereof, and that it was to good purpose to believe and wait on ; and what difficulties we find in entertaining communion here, shall then be removed, and we shall get Christ conversed with without an impediment; therefore, unto the former way of union among themselves, and with him, ver. 21, 23, this union in place is subjoined.

6. Such as have attained to spiritual communion with Christ, and are growing therein, will long after the completing thereof in heaven, and after union in place with him ; as here Christ's practice and method doth teach, who, after praying for the former, doth ascend higher to pray for this also.

7. As it is only the elect who are given to Christ that do attain salvation, and all they do certainly attain it, so whatever preparations Christ work in them in order to their salvation, yet as free love is the fountain, so it is also the perfecter of their salvation, and grace will be as free in a saved man's account the last hour as the first; therefore, in this suit, Christ doth only design them, " they whom thou hast given me," to intimate, not only that only such and all such do attain salvation, but also that this is to be looked to as the great cause and fountain of their salvation, as well as of their conversion, chap. vi. 37. So much also doth he intimate by his praying for their salvation as well as for their conversion.

8. The glory and happiness of heaven to the elect will consist much in being in Christ's company, in whom they delight so much on earth, to follow the Lamb whithersoever he goeth, and to enjoy him fully, without separation any more ; for so is heaven here described in Christ's prayer, " that they may be with me where I am," though not secluding the Father in this nor in what followeth, with whom we are through the Son.

9. Christ, the Head of believers, is now truly glorious and highly exalted in heaven; his glory being openly declared as God, and he put in possession of glory as man ; for saith he, there is " my glory, which thou hast given me."

10. Whatever rays of Christ's glory be made manifest to believers on earth, in his church, and his manifestations to them, yet it cannot be fully seen on this side of time, so transcendent and infinite is it; for it is not till " they be with me where I am," that they shall " behold my glory."

11. The day is coming wherein believers shall be completely happy in a sight of Christ's glory, when he shall be conspicuously glorified and admired in his saints, 2 Thess. i. 10, and glorified by them ; and when, all veils being laid aside, and they fitted for a more full fruition, shall visibly and immediately behold and enjoy him ; therefore is their condition in heaven described as consisting in this, " that they may behold my glory, which thou hast given me."

12. Spiritual and heavenly mercies are then rightly seen and acknowledged when God's love, as the fountain thereof, affects the heart; for so much doth Christ's practice teach us, who, speaking of the glory given him, doth fall out in a commendation of that love whence it flowed, " for thou lovedst me."

13. Christ the Mediator is beloved of the Father with an everlasting love, evidenced in his exalting of him in glory, that so sinners may expect to be accepted in him ; for saith he, " Thou lovedst me before the foundation of the world."

VER. 25. O righteous Father, the world hath not known thee: but I have known thee, and these have known that thou hast sent me.

26. And I have declared unto them thy name, and will declare it : that the love wherewith thou hast loved me may be in them, and I in them.

In the close of this solemn prayer, Christ, having prayed that his people may be glorified with him, doth (in the meantime, till they come to that blessed state) recommend them to the participation of that love wherewith himself was loved, and to his own inhabitation ; which desire he grounds upon their condition opposite to the world, and that they were separated from the world's fashions; for whereas the world doth not know God, nor acknowledge him as they ought, yet it was not so with them. However (as is imported) they knew not the Father fully, yet he knew him, and they knew Christ to be the Father's ambassador; and he had revealed the Father to them in some measure, and would reveal him yet more, that so they might partake of those mercies desired. This desire is not so much propounded prayerwise as by way of confident assurance that he should obtain from his righteous Father what he desired to them, considering what they were, and what he would make them ; hereby yet further assuring us of his success with the Father in the work of intercession. It is also to be marked, that however this suit have place for all believers when they are brought to that condition here mentioned, yet, considering that here Christ speaks expressly of those to whom he had already revealed the Father, ver. 26, we are to conceive that, in the first place, he points at his apostles already converted, and that he would close his prayer with a word yet again more expressly in their behalf, for their encouragement.

DOCTRINES.

1. Christ hath so large a heart and so distinct an eye upon his people, that at once, without any distraction, he can be taken up with his whole church, and yet not forget any particular member or society of his people ; and he hath such a care of every one, as if he had no more to care for but that one ; for here, in praying for all believers, he brings out a word more expressly for the apostles, to let them see how one thought and care doth not justle out another with him.

2. In our prayers we ought to ground ourselves well upon the knowledge of God in his attributes, that as we may be ashamed to seek such things as beseem not such a God to give, so we may be

encouraged in what we are allowed to seek; therefore doth Christ give this title to God—"righteous Father," it being a righteous and approven petition, and God, who is righteous, engaged to Christ, and to believers in him, by his promise to grant it.

3. Christ is a supplicant, who, according to the tenour of the paction betwixt the Father and him, can face the bar of righteousness and justice on our behalf, and be sure to come speed; therefore also doth he design him "righteous Father," expecting that in righteousness he could not be refused.

4. Albeit the complete happiness of believers be laid up in heaven, yet Christ allows enough for their through-bearing till they come there; as here we see in this large allowance till that suit, ver. 24, be granted.

5. The love of God in Christ, and the enjoyment of an interest and communion with him, is sufficient for believers' encouragement, till they arrive at full fruition in heaven; for that, in particular, is their allowance here.

6. As Christ the Mediator is dearly beloved of the Father, so he is a storehouse thereof and a conduit to convey that love to his people; for so is his desire here, "that the love wherewith thou hast loved me may be in them." (See ver. 23.)

7. It is Christ's allowance and desire that not only his people be beloved of the Father, but that they have the faith and lively feeling thereof, to refresh their hearts and drive away clouds and jealousies; for it is his desire that his love may be " in them," and they possess it, and feel it, and dwell in it, and feed upon it.

8. It is by being and abiding in Christ that believers come to partake and possess the love of the Father; and when they wander away from him it is no wonder if a cloud come over their good condition; therefore are these conjoined, " That the love &c. may be in them, and I in them."

9. Christ is so tender and liberal towards his people that he communicateth himself with all he giveth them; his love (so to say) being given over again with his love, and his heart communicated with all he bestoweth; for this cause also are they conjoined, " The love in them, and I in them," to shew that he giveth himself with that love which is laid up in him, to be derived through him to them.

10. As Christ knoweth to whom he prayeth, so he knoweth well who and what they are for whom he prayeth, and on whose behalf the Father will hear him; and he would have all his people, who expect the benefit of his intercession, to make sure their acquaintance with God, and their separation from the evil manners of the world; therefore, as he takes up a " righteous Father" in this suit, so he recommends those he prayeth for as not like the world, who " have not known the Father," to teach us that however he intercede for the elect, who know him not, that they may know him, yet none but such as this change is wrought upon can make comfortable application of the benefit of his intercession.

11. It is the great sin of the world and men unconverted, that they do not know God, what-ever they pretend; what they seem to know is but by hearsay; they have no solid impression of it; they do not know God in Christ practically and savingly, and therefore all they know beside is nothing; they do not affect and love God; and true knowledge, in scripture language, imports also affection; and they do not practise what they know, and so are but really ignorant. For these causes, and in these respects, it is said, " The world hath not known thee."

12. As God's sovereignty doth shine in withholding the knowledge of himself from whom he pleaseth, Matt. xi. 25, 26, so also his righteousness is conspicuous in it; for the world doth not love to know God, and therefore justly are they filled with their own ways, Psa. lxxxi. 11, 12; they will not be at pains to know him, Psa. x. 4; and what wonder they suffer hunger because of their idleness? and they abuse what light they have, and therefore it is justly taken from them, Rom. i. 21—24, &c. Therefore, as in other respects before mentioned, so in this respect also, he is called " righteous Father," in that " the world hath not known him."

13. Albeit the world do not know nor acknowledge God, yet he is content with the acknowledgment he gets among his people; and it is their commendation that they do know him when so many are ignorant of him; in both these respects is their condition here held out and commended to the Father, in opposition to the world.

14. The best of saints within time will find no perfect opposition betwixt the world and them in themselves, but only in Christ, and what he is for them and for their behoof; therefore, to supply their defect in knowledge, (which is here supposed,) the opposition begins with this, " but I have known thee."

15. Christ doth perfectly know the Father, that he may cover and rectify all our ignorance, in our uptaking of him and addresses to him, and that we may be assured he will give no false character of him; for it is recorded, for the disciples' behoof and advantage, " I have known thee."

16. Whatever degrees of ignorance saints lie under, yet it doth commend them to God if they know Christ as Mediator and Ambassador of the Father, and so know God in Christ, and in order to salvation; for in this Christ commends his rude disciples, " these have known that thou hast sent me." (See 1 Cor. ii. 2.)

17. Whatever measure of knowledge of God believers have attained unto, it cometh all from Christ, who is the fountain of all the light the church receives, and who only can manifest him truly and savingly unto sinners; for so doth he commend their weak knowledge from the cause of it, " I have declared unto them thy name."

18. As what Christ hath been, or is, that he will still be to his people, (for " I have declared, and will declare," saith he,) so he is an undertaker to his Father for his people, and engageth himself to be forthcoming for what is wanting in them, that so their imperfections may not deprive them of his allowance; therefore, that they may not be deprived of what here he desireth to them, he undertakes for what they want: " I have declared, and will declare it."

19. Albeit the knowledge and grace of believers be but small, yet if it be growing it will not want the reward of a larger measure; therefore doth he undertake for the increase of their knowledge: "I will declare thy name," that upon this consideration they may be admitted to partake of this prayed-for mercy.

20. Christ hath so absolute power over the hearts and understandings of his people that he can, when he pleaseth, break in with light upon them, and cause their hearts take with it; for he undertakes, "I will declare thy name," which is not only a promise that he will afford sufficient means, but also that he will effectually make them know the Father, and so put them in a condition for receiving this desired mercy, which the offer and having opportunity of means could not do.

21. As the true knowledge of God in Christ is an evidence that men are converted, and so have access to the possession of the Father's love, and communion with Christ, so, in particular, the true knowledge of him will beget faith in him and love to him, whereby the sense and assurance of his love is made clear to their hearts; in both these respects doth Christ, on these grounds, recommend them to the Father's love, "I have declared thy name, &c., that the love may be in them," &c., because this knowledge did evidence them to be converted, and so to have right to this love, and because it did put them in a near capacity and fitness to partake of the sense and fruits thereof. And so their possession of this love depends and followeth upon this knowledge.

CHAPTER XVIII.

HITHERTO John hath recorded Christ's life and doctrine, with some miracles confirming the same, insisting chiefly on what the rest of the evangelists had omitted. Now he proceeds to record his exercise and sufferings, chap. xviii. and xix., and his begun victory over them, in his resurrection, which was confirmed by several apparitions, chap. xx. and xxi.

Christ's sufferings may be taken up in this order:—1. His sufferings in the garden, where he was taken. 2. His sufferings in the high priest's hall. 3. His sufferings in Pilate's judgment-hall. 4. His sufferings on Mount Calvary, the place where he was crucified. 5. His burial, which was the capestone [completion] of his sufferings. In handling of all which, albeit a harmony of all the evangelists would take in all circumstances, yet I shall keep by what John saith, (who, no doubt, hath a sufficient, as all of them together, an abundant narration,) clearing what is spoken here, and, so far as is necessary, from the rest. And however every particular and circumstance of his sufferings be full of rich mysteries, which can hardly be dipped into, yet we cannot go wrong if, in interpreting thereof, we follow these general rules:—1. That Christ really suffered and died for his people and in their stead, satisfying Divine justice for them, and bearing that curse

which was due to man for sin, 1 Pet. iii. 18, and elsewhere. 2. That Christ did suffer all this meekly and willingly, not by compulsion or constraint, Isa. liii. 7; John, x. 17, 18. 3. That by what he suffered is pointed out what we deserved, and that by his suffering of it we are delivered from it, and a contrary good purchased unto us. He was condemned by a high priest, that we, who deserved condemnation, might be absolved by our High Priest; he wore a crown of thorns that we might wear a crown of glory, &c. 4. That in his way of suffering he is a pattern to his people, how they ought to bear the afflictions he sends upon them, 1 Pet. ii. 20—23. 5. That by his drinking the cup of sufferings he hath sanctified those afflictions to his members and followers, who fill up what is behind of his sufferings, Col. i. 24—namely, in so far as they are a testimony to the truth. (See John, xv. 18.)

In this chapter, first, John records Christ's sufferings in the garden, (whither he went after his former doctrine and prayer, ver. 1,) and to which Judas (as knowing the place, ver. 2) brought a band of men to take him, (ver. 3,) where, after a conference with those who came to take him, wherein he gives a proof of his deity, though he be going to suffer, ver. 4—6, and exempts his disciples from the trial, ver. 7—9; and after a reprehension of Peter's rash behaviour, ver. 10, 11, he is taken and bound, and carried away to the high priests, ver. 12—14. Secondly. He records Christ's sufferings in the high priest's hall, together with Peter's threefold slip there. And, 1. He declares how Peter, with some difficulty, getting in after his Master, ver. 15, 16, doth at the voice of a damsel deny him, ver. 17, and yet stayeth still in a place so full of snares, ver. 18. 2. He giveth an account of Christ's conflict with the high priest, ver. 19—21, and with one of his servants, ver. 22—24. 3. He declareth that Peter, staying still there, did yet twice deny his Master, ver. 25—27. Thirdly. He recordeth a part of Christ's trial in Pilate's judgment-hall, to which the Jews brought him, ver. 28, wherein, after some debates betwixt Pilate and the Jews, about entering of the process, ver. 29—32, Pilate examines him concerning his kingdom, and gets a meet answer, ver. 33—37, which Pilate, little heeding, goeth out to the Jews, and absolveth Christ, ver. 38, and endeavours (but in vain) to release him, by occasion of their custom at the feast, ver. 39, 40.

VER. 1. When Jesus had spoken these words, he went forth with his disciples over the brook Cedron, where was a garden, into the which he entered, and his disciples.

2. And Judas also, which betrayed him, knew the place: for Jesus ofttimes resorted thither with his disciples.

3. Judas then, having received a band of men and officers from the chief priests and Pharisees, cometh thither with lanterns and torches and weapons.

John, omitting Christ's agony in the garden, as having been largely spoken to by the rest, and contenting himself to record (in this part of the chapter) how he was taken and bound there, and carried away from thence, he doth premit [introduce] three necessary particulars to that narration; the first whereof (in these verses) is the convening of all parties in this place. He first records how Jesus, after the former sweet exercise, goeth out of the city to this garden beyond the brook Cedron, with his disciples, ver. 1; next, he declareth that, this being a place frequently haunted by Christ and his disciples, and so known to Judas, ver. 2, he came there well guarded, to take him, ver. 3. I need not here insist to describe this garden, nor yet to shew that, as Adam sinned in a garden, so Christ would suffer in a garden, to expiate the guilt of this sin in all his people. But we may from verse 1, learn—

1. It is the duty of Christ's followers not to expect always so sweet a life as preaching, hearing, communicating, and prayer, but to lay their account that after such exercises they may be called to suffer, and after fair blenks [sunshine] may meet with black storms; for so much doth Christ's example teach, who, when he " had spoken these words," (in preaching and prayer, and had instituted and celebrated the supper,) " went forth" &c. to his trial.

2. Such as have committed themselves to God and left any of whom they have charge on him, may very safely leave them in the midst of hazards, and themselves hazard to look trouble in the face; for more particularly, " When Jesus had spoken these words, (in the former prayer, wherein he had prayed to the Father for himself, and left his disciples upon him,) he went forth" to encounter death, and is not afraid to be taken from his disciples and leave them in the world, since he had put them in so sure a hand.

3. It is the duty of the Lord's people to be resolute in undergoing suffering, and to offer themselves voluntarily to God, to underlie it, in so far as they have a calling; and herein Christ is an eminent pattern, who " went forth over the brook Cedron," (a little brook running betwixt Jerusalem and the mount of Olives, of which see 2 Kings, xxiii. 6, and elsewhere,) and entered into the garden, where he was to meet with several conflicts.

4. His taking his disciples with him and their following of him may serve to teach, partly, how affectionately Christ is to be followed when he is foretelling of his departure; for on their part it imports their hanging on him, Luke, xxii. 39, as Elisha did on Elijah, till the fiery chariot parted them; partly, that we should be thrifty in spending every moment of our time, whatever incumbrances we have; for Christ in all this throng [confusion] took them with him, that by the way he might inform them of their scattering, and appoint the meeting-place after his resurrection, as it is recorded, Matt. xxvi. 31, 32; partly, that Christ hath sanctified in his own person the desolate and low condition of his people, wherein they would be glad of the meanest encouragement, even from the company of weak Christians, and yet cannot have it; for he also took them with him that they might watch with him in his

agony, wherein yet they disappointed him, as is recorded Matt. xxvi. 38, 40; and partly, that as naturally we are averse from trouble, especially from suffering for Christ, so it is his people's duty to train and breed themselves for such lots, both by the observation of the courage of others, Heb. vi. 12; xii. 1, (which, no doubt, made many in the primitive times so stout,) and by the observation of their own weakness in lesser assays, that being humbled thereby they may put themselves in Christ's hand, who may make notable instruments of those who at first are very weak; therefore, also, did he take them with him, not that they might suffer at this time, but that they might be bred for their after sufferings by beholding his courage and power, and by getting a taste of their own weakness, to make them more self-denied, and eager to recover themselves at another time.

5. Such as would bear out under trial and persecution ought not to be found sleeping, but in the first place should make all sure with God that trial do not surprise them while they have not entreated the face of the Lord, 1 Sam. xiii. 12. Therefore also doth he enter into the garden, that there he may endure his agony, and wrestle with his Father before Judas came, as is cleared by the rest.

From verses 2, 3, learn—1. As it is our duty to be very diligent with God when troubles are eminent or incumbent, so we ought not to leave all to the pinch of extremity, but should be making ready beforehand; for " Jesus ofttimes resorted thither with his disciples," (see Luke, xxi. 37; xxii. 39;) and this he did, not only to sanctify unto his followers ill entertainment, notwithstanding the services they do to the world, as he preached all day and yet lay in the fields all night, Luke, xxi. 37; or to sanctify essays of hazards and trials, whereby they are fitted for greater trouble when it cometh; as he was long before so pursued as he could not conveniently lodge by night in Jerusalem; but further he did this, that in the night-time he might give himself there to prayer, as was his custom, (Matt. xiv. 23,) and that before his agony came.

2. As believers ought not to rush upon trials without a calling, so they ought not timorously to decline them, but should set their face towards them, Luke, ix. 51; Mark, x. 32; for he went where Judas knew the place, to shew that as he would not run to Judas, so he would not go out of his usual way, though he knew his knowing of it would afford him an advantage.

3. Christ may be persecuted by men who have been very eminent in his service, even by one of his twelve apostles, as Judas was, and by them who in their office were types of himself, such as the chief priests were. And this should prevent our stumbling at the defection of such; and by this all are warned that were they never so eminent, or had stood never so long, yet they ought to take heed of an entertained idol lest that draw them in the snare, as these priests were by their credit, and Judas by his love to the world.

4. Wicked apostates and persecutors are not asleep in their designs and actings, but are very vigilant and active when, it may be, Christ's fol-

lowers are asleep and careless; for in the dark night Judas cometh with his crew, and that at the time when Christ could not get his disciples kept awake, as it is recorded, Matt. xxvi. 45—47.

5. Christ will not stand to let persecutors have all outward advantages of him, that so his victory over them may be more conspicuous; for therefore is there a Judas, who knew his retiring places, to lead out " a band of men (of those Romans who kept the tower next the temple, whether with Pilate's consent or not it is not needful to determine) and officers (or servants) from the chief priests and Pharisees, (and that) with lanterns and torches and weapons." And all this against Christ alone.   They made use of lanterns and torches, although it was full moon at the time of the feast, that so they might be sure to find him out.

6. Persecutors want not their own fears and tossings in the violent courses they undertake against Christ and his people, but may have ofttimes more perplexity than the sufferers have in bearing what they are permitted to inflict; for therefore also was it that Judas came, and they sent him thus attended and provided, even out of fear lest the matter should miscarry.

Ver. 4. Jesus therefore, knowing all things that should come upon him, went forth, and said unto them, Whom seek ye?

5. They answered him, Jesus of Nazareth. Jesus saith unto them, I am he. And Judas also, which betrayed him, stood with them.

6. As soon then as he had said unto them, I am he, they went backward, and fell to the ground.

The second thing premitted to [preceding] Christ's taking in the garden is a conference betwixt him and them who came to take him.   The conference is twofold, or the same conference twice repeated in order to his twofold scope in it.   His scope in the first conference (in these verses) is to give a proof of his deity, even in this his low condition, as may be gathered from the progress.   In it we may consider—1. The posture wherein Christ was at their coming, ver. 4, which was the cause of his so courageous going out to them, and his conferring so mildly with them; where it is to be conceived, as is recorded by the rest, that he is now a little eased of his agony, Luke, xxii. 43, and that (as is here recorded) he saw clearly through all the sufferings he was to meet with, and so is composed in his mind.   2. The conference itself, ver. 4, 5, wherein, inquiring and getting an account that they were seeking Jesus, he meekly informs them that it was he.   3. The effect that followed upon this declaration, ver. 6; his meek word is accompanied with so much divine power that upon the hearing thereof they fall backward to the ground.

From verses 4, 5, learn—1. Peace with God in a trial will make all the rest of the trial, in so far as it is outward, very easy; for this stout and meek going forth to encounter trouble followeth upon his ease of his agony.

2. The Lord can so order the exercises of his people, as, however they may have heavy pressures upon their mind, yet he can intermit the extremity thereof when they need strength for outward difficulties, and let it return again when the strait is over; for so it seemeth did he deal with his Son, who though he had an inward agony all the while of his passion, yet the violence thereof is intermitted in the garden, when they came to him, and we hear no more of it till they leave him on the cross, where again he is made to cry out of it.

3. The consideration of the inevitableness of trouble, in God's providence, ought to make us willingly stoop thereunto; especially, when we have tasted of former gracious deliverances and preservation, we ought to stoop when his hour cometh, and not seek always to be free; for " Jesus therefore, knowing all things that should come upon him, went forth"—that is, knowing that this was the time of his suffering, and that now he was not to be preserved and hid as formerly, he went forth to them, and not away, as at other times he had done.

4. There is nothing makes us more readily to be dashed with trouble than our not knowing or considering what trouble is; when we misrepresent trouble, it terrifieth, but when we look not only on the necessity and inevitableness, but on the usefulness, measure, and event of it, it will appear much more tolerable, and rather a friend than an enemy; for so much also is imported in this, " Jesus, knowing all things, &c., went forth."   He saw through his sufferings, what they should be and what they would tend to, and therefore was not afraid, but went forth.

5. Such as are at peace with God, and have seen through their sufferings, will be in a very composed frame, and at themselves in the height thereof; for this conference and inquiry, " Whom seek ye?" imports, not any ignorance or curiosity, but that, on his part, he was meek and composed, his agony being somewhat settled, and he seeing through his trouble.

6. It concerns persecutors to take good heed what they are doing, and especially to consider with whom they have to do, and against whom their attempts are; for this question, " Whom seek ye?" as to them, imports that they should have considered whom they were seeking, which if they had well considered they had not done as they did, 1 Cor. ii. 8.

7. The Lord, when he pleaseth, can hide and preserve his people, not only among lions and in fires, but even in the midst of their foes; for their answer importeth, that at first, albeit Judas stood with them, yet they knew him not, otherwise they had not so spoken—we seek " Jesus of Nazareth," but, we seek thee. (See Genesis, xix. 11; 2 Kings, xvi. 18, 19, &c.; Jeremiah, xxxvi. 26.)

8. It is the usual trade of Satan and his instruments to load Christ and his followers with reproachful titles, that under these they may persecute them more securely; for so much doth the name given to Christ by them, " Jesus of Nazareth," import—a contemptible and false designation, invented by the Pharisees, and instilled into the multitude's head, that so they might the more

safely persecute him, without fearing to wrong their Messiah, who was to come out of Bethlehem. And this may warn us, that where Christ and his ordinances are traduced, contemned, and reproached, there he may be crucified.

9. Christ our Lord did not shift trouble, but voluntarily offered himself, when he was sought, in his people's stead, that so enemies might blame themselves if they were not satisfied; therefore saith he, " I am he," and shifts it not.

10. It is subjoined to this answer, that " Judas, which betrayed him, stood with them," not only to point out Christ's meekness, who gives this answer, though provoked by his presence, and to point out the providence of God, who hid him, that he could not be known, though Judas was with them,—but further, it points out, that apostles will grow very impudent, and that this is taken notice of by Christ; therefore it is marked, that in this black course Judas impudently " stood with them."

From verse 6, learn—1. It was not the power of men prevailing over Christ, but his own willingness, that brought him to suffer; nor would Christ have anything to outshine his affection in his sufferings; therefore, before he is taken, he causeth them to go backward and fall to the ground, to testify that they could not have taken him unless he had consented to it.

2. It is a very dreadful and terrible thing to be in opposition to Christ, how contemptible soever he and his followers seem to be; for so much doth this shake upon them who came to take him teach us.

3. Believers may expect that much of divine power will be manifested upon and about them in their sufferings; for so did Christ their forerunner find in his sufferings.

4. Proofs of God's power are to be expected by sufferers, not so much to exempt them from suffering and trouble, as (beside their being inwardly supported thereby) to convince enemies, if possible, and to let them see what he can do if it were needful; for such was the proof Christ got here, in that " they went backward, and fell to the ground," whereby he convinced them of the evil of their way, and how ineffectual he could make it, if he pleased, though he let the trial go on.

5. The word of Christ, how contemptible soever it seem to be, is full of majesty, and accompanied with divine power, and terror to his enemies, when he pleaseth to let it out; for " As soon as he said to them, I am he, they went backward," &c. And if his lamb's voice was so terrible, how dreadful will he be when he roars as a lion? and if that sweet word, " I am he," which comforted the disciples, John, vi. 20, be their terror, how terrible will it be when he speaks to them as they deserve?

Ver. 7. Then asked he them again, Whom seek ye? And they said, Jesus of Nazareth.

8. Jesus answered, I have told you that I am he: if therefore ye seek me, let these go their way:

9. That the saying might be fulfilled,

which he spake, Of them which thou gavest me have I lost none.

In these verses is contained Christ's second conference with these men, his scope in which is to exempt his disciples from the trial. In order to which, they (as appears) rising and coming forward again, he propounds the former question; and getting the same answer that formerly they gave, ver. 7, he binds them to their commission, offering himself, and will have his disciples exempted, ver. 8, which is amplified from a commendation of his fidelity, in that he would perform that word so lately spoken, chap. xvii. 12, ver. 9. Whence learn—

1. Some of the sons of Adam, and especially persecutors, may be so far given up to obduration, a seared conscience, and desperate wickedness, as even wonders wrought upon them and against them in their evil course will not avail to reclaim them, but they will either be insensible of the Lord's hand, or seeing it, will harden themselves the more to go on; for albeit, by their former fall, they might have been convinced of his power and godhead, yet they will not quit their wicked course, but come again, avowing that they seek him.

2. Christ himself is the great butt of persecutors' malice; so long as he was in the world the stream of their malice ran against him, and when they assault his followers, it is because they cannot reach him. He is first hated of the world, and they for his sake, and could the world reach him in heaven, they would not much trouble themselves with his followers; for so much may be gathered from their profession, we seek " Jesus of Nazareth," being compared with what Christ makes out of it, ver. 8, that the disciples must be free, as not minded by them, nor put in their commission by those who sent them.

3. Christ, in the throng of his own trials, is yet mindful of his followers, to preserve and care for them; for when he is to enter the lists himself, he is solicitous for his disciples; " I am he; let these go away."

4. Christ, in his lowest and suffering condition, doth set bounds to persecutors which they cannot transgress; for his reasoning, " If therefore ye seek me, let these go their way," had been of small force with these absurd men for the exempting of his disciples if there had not been a commanding power with it to bound them, as it did.

5. Christ's offering of himself to undergo his bitter sufferings doth indeed exempt his people from the like; and he goeth betwixt them and all storms in so far as they are destroying; for so much may be gathered from his reasoning in this particular, " If ye seek me, let these go their way." Albeit he do not exempt his followers from outward troubles, as he did the disciples at that time, yet his offering himself unto and underlying that cursed death did exempt them and all his own from that punishment due to sin, and satisfaction required by justice for it; so that when justice challengeth them, they may send it to Christ, who was taken for them all. And as for outward afflictions, all that they meet with are but some few drops, sanctified and sweetened to them, by his essaying of that lot before them.

6. Christ is so tender of his followers that he will not put them to any trial till they be ripe and fitted for it; so that when he sends a trial we are to reckon that we shall be enabled for it, if it were but because he sends it, provided we do not cast away our strength, nor sin it away from us; for therefore would he have them " let these go their way" for this time, because they were but yet weak, till after his resurrection, that the Spirit was poured out upon them.

7. Christ is a faithful keeper and performer of his word, and they are not ill provided who have but his naked word to uphold and assure their hearts in greatest extremities; for this was also a reason why he would exempt them at this time, " That the saying might be fulfilled which he spake, Of them which thou gavest me have I lost none."

8. What Christ hath done for his people may be looked on as a pledge of what he will still do, according as they need; for that account which Christ makes of his by-past diligence, chap. xvii. 12, is here looked on as a promise to " be fulfilled" in their preservation at this time also; and that, not only because in that passage he gave an account of his whole care till his removal from them, and so of this also, though not yet manifested, but also, that we may be assured that he will never change his way with his people so long as they need it.

9. That sweet word, chap. xvii. 12, is here applied to bodily preservation from an outward trouble, though it chiefly point at their soul's preservation from the evil, as he explains it, chap. xvii. 15, when he prays for the continuance of that preservation from the Father; because that not only during the time of his being with them he did indeed hide them from outward troubles, as here was verified, but further, in sparing them outwardly at this time he had also a respect to their souls, which might have been crushed had they been engaged in trial, as Peter's experience makes evident. And so it teacheth that as to tender the body and outward man with prejudice to the soul is great cruelty, so where Christ undertakes the charge of men's souls he will also have a care of their body and outward condition, in subserviency to their souls' welfare. He will respect their very bodies and outward man, and will not expose them to hazards, save when it is for their souls' good, and when he is to get service thereby. And he will make it evident at last, that he is not prodigal of their bodies, nor casts them away when he exposeth them to suffering.

Ver. 10. Then Simon Peter having a sword drew it, and smote the high priest's servant, and cut off his right ear. The servant's name was Malchus.

11. Then said Jesus unto Peter, Put up thy sword into the sheath: the cup which my Father hath given me, shall I not drink it?

The third thing premitted to [preceding] Christ's taking and binding is his reprehension of Peter's rash behaviour. Christ being a taking (as it is, Mark, xiv. 46, 47,) the disciples inquire if they should fight, and before Christ return an answer, Peter, in his furious zeal, breaks forth (Luke, xxii. 49, 50) and cuts off the right ear of one of the servants of the high priest, whose name is here recorded for further confirmation of the truth of the history. This carriage Christ reproves, bidding Peter put up his sword, not to be reserved for a fitter time, to be employed in any churchman's hands, but to teach him that these were not his weapons. And whereas the other evangelists record several reasons of this reproof and command—(namely, that this fact was without the bounds of his calling; that he needed not such poor shifts, having other help enough, if it were needful; that he would not have the scripture made a liar; and that he ought to suffer thus far, being not yet hardly handled, or suffer them to go so far as God hath permitted them; all which are held out, Matt. xxvi. 52—54; Luke, xxii. 51,) the beloved disciple takes most notice of that reason, wherein love shined so conspicuously, that he would drink that cup of affliction which the Father had given him to drink for the good of his people.

From ver. 10, learn—1. Men may do things which seem to speak much zeal and affection to Christ, which yet are full of dross, and reprovable before him; for albeit it was great stoutness in the disciples to offer their service to Christ against the whole band, with their two rusty blades, and in Peter, to hazard his life among them, yet Christ's entertainment of this offered service sheweth how unsavoury it was.

2. It is a great fault in men to run upon a service to which they have no calling, did the service seem to speak never so much zeal; for it was Peter's fault, being a private man, to run to a sword to fight for his Master.

3. It is a great blemish in men not to be solid, but full of flashes, and sudden violent resolutions and actings, which, as they ordinarily drive men to debord [hurry] in going about that which is right, so they ofttimes end in as great an extremity of turning their back on what is right; for this was also Peter's fault; others of them, no doubt, had as much love to Christ, and as much valour as he, had they been called to shew it; but he was a rash and forward man, soon set on foot to what seemed good, but with much of his own spirit and wrath, which worketh not the righteousness of God, and as soon driven to an extremity of fear and fainting, as afterward we shall find.

4. Men cannot go right (whatever their way or zeal in it seem to be) who wait not upon direction, but either neglect to seek it, or, having sought it, do neglect to wait for his light, and run the way unto which their own spirits incline; for so also did Peter here; all of them having inquired at Christ, he prevents an answer by following his own inclination, Luke, xxii.

5. It is a great evidence of men's distempers [impatience] when they will not learn to overcome by suffering, but would repel one injury with another; when all the outgate of [release from] trials they look for is how to bear them down, or fall upon the inflicters of them, but know not that to suffer and stoop is an outgate

[release], Rom. xii. 19—21; for this also was Peter's fault, that he could fight but not suffer.

From ver. 11, learn—1. It is a great sign of Christ's love that he reproves his people for their faults; for he reproves not Judas and the band so sharply (though he give them a check, Luke, xxii. 53) as he doth Peter, "Then said Jesus unto Peter, Put up thy sword into the sheath," &c.

2. Afflictions are measured by God to his people, both for quantity and quality; therefore are they called a "cup," which, as it is a comfort to the godly that their lot is in a friend's hand, so it may terrify the wicked whose lot is also carved out, and who will not get so much affliction as they please, but so much as the justice of God seeth meet to measure out unto them, Psalm lxxv. 8.

3. It may sweeten the lot of Christ and his followers that even the bitterest potions come not from God as a Judge, but as a Father; for even all that Christ drank (and it was very bitter) was "the cup which my Father hath given me."

4. Subjection unto God doth well become his people, and to see them endure that willingly which he calls them unto; for by this means the cross is made sweet, whereas rebellion and want of subjection is the very curse of crosses; therefore doth Christ appear so eminent in subjection; "The cup which my Father hath given me, shall I not drink it?" (See Matt. xxvi. 39, 45.)

5. Love to God, and faith in his love, will make any condition carved out by him sweet to us, and us submissive to undergo it, considering that nothing but good can be expected from him who is goodness and love itself; for so doth Christ argue, "The cup which my Father hath given me, shall I not drink it?" His love to his Father, and his seeing him a Father in it, made him stoop to it.

6. Christ did so love his Father, and to suffer for his people, as he would not be hindered to suffer, but drank that cup heartily, as minding to be often refreshed with his people's love to Him again who had so loved them; for when Peter did what he could to impede his sufferings, he saith, Should I not drink that cup?

7. Such as would entertain submission in bearing hard lots ought to repel all thoughts of outgate [release] and ease, and hold their eye still upon their trial, lest squint-looks towards a possibility or probability of deliverance do blunt their resolutions; therefore doth Christ repel anything that Peter by his carriage might suggest of escaping that danger; Should I not drink the cup? (See also Matt. xvi. 23.)

VER. 12. Then the band and the captain and officers of the Jews took Jesus, and bound him,

13. And led him away to Annas first; for he was father in law to Caiaphas, which was the high priest that same year.

14. Now Caiaphas was he, which gave counsel to the Jews, that it was expedient that one man should die for the people.

In these verses is recorded how Christ was taken and bound in the garden, and carried away to the high priests, Annas and Caiaphas, the last of which is described from that counsel which he gave before this time concerning Christ, chapter xi. 50, to shew that he was Christ's inveterate enemy, and would be very earnest to have his own project take effect. For clearing this purpose, consider—1. As for that corruption, that this priesthood is reckoned by years, see what is said on chap. xi. 49, 50. But the greater difficulty is, which of the two, Annas or Caiaphas, was the high priest that year. The parenthesis in our translation (which hath no ground in the original, and is contrary to the way of placing it in our old translation) would seem to imply that Annas was he, who indeed before this time had this office, and was before Caiaphas in dignity, Luke, iii. 2; and afterward we find him in office, Acts, iv. 6; but for clearing of it, in general, it need not stumble us that we find in scripture both of them called high priests at once; for in the Jewish church the high priest (called also the chief priest) had his sagan, or deputy, who, in case of his infirmity or pollution, did minister for him, and is called the second priest, 2 Kings, xxv. 18; Jer. lii. 24; and so both of them might be in place at once. Now, in particular, not only the Jewish history, but the scripture itself, makes it apparent that Caiaphas was the high or chief priest at that time; for so he is called, chap. xi. 49, and here also, the parenthesis being laid aside; therefore also it is that Christ is sent by Annas to him, ver. 24, as to the high priest, and it is before him, and the council convened in his house, (as the other evangelists record,) that Christ is examined and condemned, whereas the council might have been convened at Annas's house, had he been in the chief office. So the meaning of ver. 13 is only this: That Christ being taken is brought first to Annas's house, partly, as being nearest to them, and partly, out of respect to him, as having been sometime high priest, and now father-in-law to the high priest, and to refresh him with a spectacle so grateful to him, seeing (as may be gathered from ver. 24) he went not to the council himself, but sent Christ thither. Consider—2. As for the place wherein Peter denied his Master, and Christ was examined before the high priest, albeit John do insert Peter's first fall, and part of Christ's examination, before he mention that he was sent to Caiaphas, ver. 24, and so should seem to pass over anything he endured in the hall of Caiaphas; and albeit it be all one, as to the truth of the doctrine in itself, whether these things fell out in Annas or Caiaphas's hall; yet the other evangelists make it clear (see Matt. xxvi. 57, 58, &c.) that these things were done before Caiaphas and in his hall. And we are to conceive that, Christ being brought to Annas, he sent him immediately to Caiaphas's house, where the council was convened, where Peter denied him, and he was examined; and so that, ver. 24, is immediately to be subjoined to ver. 13, it being subjoined there to his examination, not as done after that, but only that John may clear how Christ came to be examined before the high priest, even because Annas had sent him thither, though he had not mentioned it before; and for this cause also it is that, ver. 14, Caiaphas is described, from his inveterate malice, as supposing that Christ was now brought before him, as is also set down in the margin of our Bibles, out of some original copies.

From this purpose, learn—1. Albeit the Lord seem not to regard who wrong his children and people, yet he doth take notice of all of them, in due time to requite it; for here he takes notice who took Christ, both of " the band," and their "captain," and of " the officers of the Jews." (See Isa. xlvii. 6.)

2. Christ being taken and bound doth serve to teach, partly, that every one of Adam's posterity is by nature a bondservant and slave to sin, and liable to justice; for he behoved to be bound, to expiate this slavery of his own; partly, that by Christ's being bound, such as are given to him have a right purchased to be free from this slavery and bondage, whereof they are made partakers by coming to him; for by his being bound his own are freed. And they ought to be so much the more strictly tied in the bonds of love to him, and should endeavour to enjoy their privilege, and freedom from the slavery of sin and terrors of the law, and from a spirit of bondage.

3. As it is a sad judgment on men when they delight to see the bonds of Christ and his followers, so it may be their lot to be made a grateful spectacle to their enemies, and this Christ hath sanctified in his own person; for they " led him away to Annas first," &c., which was an evidence of his wicked disposition, that he longed for such a sight, and is an instruction to saints, informing them what their lot may be, since their Head and Lord was carried from place to place, (even to Herod, as is marked by the rest,) to be a spectacle to his enemies. (See 1 Cor. iv. 9.)

4. Let churches or persons glory never so much in their privileges, yet all men are but liars, and the most eminent of them may degenerate so far as to corrupt the ordinances of God, and become most bitter enemies unto Jesus Christ and his truth; for albeit the church of the Jews had as fair promises as any particular church, yet even there the ordinance of the priesthood is degenerated from the first institution, and become an annual, or yearly office; and the high priest and his father-in-law are they who take most pleasure in beholding the sufferings of Christ, yea, who have greatest hand in them.

5. Christ in his suffering met with all extremities and disadvantages, that so he might sanctify such lots unto his people, and might purchase to them (when he saw it good for them) more tender usage in their sufferings; for therefore it is marked, ver. 14, who this Caiaphas was, not only to shew that the malicious designs and projects of persecutors are not forgotten by God, however he spare them for a time, but that we might know Christ had to do with an inveterate and bitter enemy. And from this it floweth that sometimes his followers find bitter usage and extreme violence very easy and sweet, and (on the other hand) that sometimes they find even enemies and persecutors more mild and compassionate. (See Psalm cvi. 46; Jer. xv. 11.)

Ver. 15. And Simon Peter followed Jesus, and so did another disciple: that disciple was known unto the high priest, and went in with Jesus into the palace of the high priest.

16. But Peter stood at the door without. Then went out that other disciple, which was known unto the high priest, and spake unto her that kept the door, and brought in Peter.

Followeth the second part of the chapter, containing an account of what occurred in the high priest's hall. It consisteth of three branches, in the first whereof (to ver. 19) Peter's first slip and denial of his Master is recorded. In these verses is declared how Peter cometh to get into the place of trial—namely, that (with another disciple known to the high priest) following his Master afar off, he is stopped at the door, when the other got in, till that other disciple, making use of his acquaintance in the house, removeth that stop. For clearing whereof, consider— 1. As for that " other disciple, known to the high priest," (and, as appears by his dealing with the maid, to his family also,) albeit it may seem to have been John, the beloved disciple, who useth thus to speak of himself in the third person, as chap. xx. 2—4, and elsewhere, yet there is no sufficient ground to think that it was either he or any other of the eleven; for it is not very probable that obscure men, who for three years and a half had been disciples to Christ, should yet (any of them) be so familiar in the high priest's house, who was so cruel an enemy to Jesus; and therefore it should seem he was one of Christ's hidden disciples, (of whom, chapter xii. 42,) who, hearing of the business, followed on with Peter, (whom it seemeth he met by the way,) and got easy access by reason of his acquaintance there. Consider—2. As for this practice of Peter, (or of John either, if so be that other was he,) albeit it was not unmeet Christ should have some witnesses there, to mark all that was done, and a hidden disciple might act that part well enough, yet seeing all the eleven disciples were dismissed at that time, ver. 8, and warned of their hazard, and the trysting [meeting] place assigned after his resurrection, Matt. xxvi. 31, 32, and particularly, Peter being forewarned of his fall, Matt. xxvi. 33, 34, and that he could not follow his Master now, John, xiii. 36, it may be concluded that he did rashly (however it seem affectionately) thus to hazard in such a place of trial; especially, having no other errand (as is marked, Matt. xxvi. 58) but only to see the end, to applaud and congratulate his Master, if he escaped, and to shift for himself if it fell out otherwise.

DOCTRINES.

1. The Lord's people may draw themselves under many self-created crosses and trials, not only in so far as by sin they procure they should be inflicted, Jer. ii. 19, or by their bitterness and unbelief do render their own condition grievous unto them, as Jonah did, but more especially

when they run without a calling, and cast themselves upon tentations, in ensnaring places and company; for thus did Peter here, when he "followed Jesus" into the high priest's hall; whatever zeal or affection seem to be in it.

2. We are bound to have charity, that even many who have much acquaintance with greatest persecutors may yet in their hearts be friends to Christ, though their faintness and reservedness cannot be approved; for there is "another disciple, known unto the high priest," who "went in (without interruption) with Jesus into the palace of the high priest." So was there an Obadiah in Ahab's court, and a Rahab in Jericho.

3. Albeit Christ in his suffering seem to be deserted of all, and his enemies may think they have driven his followers from him, and now he is in the power of them and their complices, yet he wants not, even in such societies, some who are friends, and witnesses of their injustice; for here, one "known unto the high priest," who "went in with Jesus," was a "disciple," and was a witness to all their procedure.

4. When the Lord's people are running upon snares, it may please him to lay an impediment by his providence in their way, whereof they ought to make use, to examine their way better; for so much did the Lord call Peter unto, when in his providence the other got in, but he "stood at the door without," the gate, it seems, being strictly kept, so that no strangers got in, possibly out of fear lest Christ should be rescued. It is of general verity that impediments laid in our way call us to examine it, though it prove not always ill, because impeded, but the Lord thereby would only exercise our dependence and other graces.

5. As when the voice of conscience is often slighted, it may be stricken dumb, that it molest not the sinner, so when providential dispensations crossing our way are not regarded, the Lord may take away these impediments, and let men go on without difficulty, though little to their profit; for he standing without still, the other disciple interposeth and obtaineth access for him to the place where he fell in the snare.

6. It is the duty of friends to take heed lest, in seeking too much to pleasure their friends, they prove instruments of their destruction, at least of their real hurt; for so this disciple, by his kindness and care of Peter, helped him into the snare.

Ver. 17. Then saith the damsel that kept the door unto Peter, Art not thou also one of this man's disciples? He saith, I am not.

In this verse is recorded Peter's trial and fall when he is got in, where at the voice of a damsel, who kept the door, he denieth his Master, or that he was one of his disciples. Whence learn—

1. In an hour of trial, Christ and his followers may expect to be so contemptible that even the weakest and basest will insult over them; for here a weak damsel (either knowing Peter, by the other disciples' information who brought him in, or suspecting what he was by his trembling or feared-like carriage) doth fall a cavilling with Peter as one of Christ's disciples.

2. As the Lord ordinarily giveth a dash to presumption by letting it succumb under weakest trials, so we ought to look on every trial as above us without his strength; for here stout Peter, meeting with a weak damsel, and being encountered with soft words, "Art thou not also one of this man's (not this seducer's) disciples?" yet he succumbs. Though it be here propounded by way of question, and elsewhere absolutely asserted, Thou wast with Jesus, Matt. xxvi. 69, all cometh to one purpose; for this question is not propounded by way of doubt, but as strongly asserting it.

3. In this miscarriage of Peter we may read how the Lord will have conceit punished, even in his own; how carnal resolutions to cleave to Christ will fail men in an extremity; and how small a great sin will seem to be, and how easily digested, in an hour of fear and tentation; for so much appears in Peter, who, notwithstanding his esteem of his Master, and his strong resolutions, doth now speak out that foul word—I am not one of his disciples.

Ver. 18. And the servants and officers stood there, who had made a fire of coals; for it was cold: and they warmed themselves: and Peter stood with them, and warmed himself.

This branch of the first part of this chapter is here closed with an account of Peter's carriage after this his slip—namely, that he continued still warming himself among the rest in a place so full of snares, which also did occasion his repeated denials of his Master. He had been standing there at his first denial, Mark, xiv. 67, but having withdrawn a little into the porch, where he heard the cock crow the first time, Mark, xiv. 68, he returns back again and continueth with them till he is assaulted of new [anew], as we find here, ver. 25.

DOCTRINES.

1. Such as are cruel persecutors of Christ may yet be furnished with store of outward accommodations, that so saints may not dote upon those things which are so frequently cast to dogs; for "the servants and officers (who had taken Christ) had a fire of coals to warm themselves, for it was cold."

2. One given up to a tentation of fear may have large more vexation and tossing with shifting of trouble than a resolute sufferer with enduring it; for so appears in Peter's carriage, who sometimes shifts himself from among the crowd (as is marked by the rest); and again, fearing lest that might render him suspected, he cometh among them, and stands with them, either that he might be hid in the throng, or might bear out his denial with his confident carriage.

3. The conscience of a child of God may be strangely deadened and laid by for a time, by a sin against light, and not become soon tender again; for though he had denied his Master, and the cock had crowed once (as is elsewhere recorded), to give him warning, yet he "stood with them," and went not out to mourn. Thus was it with David in the matter of Bathsheba and Uriah; and in Peter it is especially to be observed

that his care and tossing about his own preservation hindered his conscience to do its duty, which
testifieth that that care was a snare unto him.

4. The children of the Lord's refreshments
and accommodations are many times so dear
bought, that it were far better to want them than
to go out of God's way to find them ; for " Peter
stood and warmed himself;" but the high priest's
fire was a snare to a disciple, and he was forced
to vomit up that morsel when he left the fire, and
went out, and wept bitterly.

VER. 19. The high priest then asked Jesus of
his disciples, and of his doctrine.

In the second branch of this part of the chapter
John gives an account of a conflict betwixt
Christ and the high priest, (omitting several
other passages recorded by the rest,) ver. 19—21,
and with one of his servants, ver. 22 —24.   In
this verse is recorded the high priest's examination of Christ, and putting him to give an account
of his disciples and doctrine, as supposing him
guilty of sedition and schism in gathering disciples, and of heresy in his doctrine, whereby he
gathered them.   Whence learn—

1. Christ and his followers may expect no fair
procedure of law from persecutors, even when
they seem to observe some form of it ; for though
it was the high priest's office to examine such
cases, yet there is much informality here ; not
only in that they had taken him before, and
would have him now to answer before an armed
guard, and in that their mind was pre-occupied
not to let him go on any terms, Luke, xxii. 67, 68,
but in that they have taken and arraigned him
before they have any articles of accusation to lay
to his charge, and to prove by witnesses, (as is
also clear from the rest,) putting it upon himself
to give an account and accuse himself.

2. It is not unusual for the best of doctrines
and practices to pass up and down in the world
under the most odious names and imputations,
so that we should not take notice of things according to the names usually given them ; for so
is Christ here in his practice supposed guilty of
sedition and schism, in gathering disciples and
followers, and his doctrine insinuated to be unsound, and such as could not abide the light, and
therefore had been taught in corners, as Christ
in his answer understands his question.   Thus
also was the gospel and preachers thereof esteemed of, Acts, xvii. 6 ; xxiv. 14 ; xxviii. 22 ;
though yet, upon clear information, these imputations did easily evanish, Acts, xxvi. 28, 31, 32.

3. It pleased Christ to underlie the imputation of sedition, schism, and heresy, as a per-
turber both of church and state, that so he might
not only sanctify such a lot to his followers, but
might expiate our seditious revoltings and rentings from God, and one from another, and that
false doctrine and those corrupt principles which
our first parents hearkened unto, and all of us by
nature do entertain ; for so much may be gathered from his being accused in the matter " of
his disciples, and of his doctrine."

4. Whatever zeal to religion and sound doctrine persecutors of Christ and his followers do

pretend, yet it is some other thing that pincheth
them ; and particularly, corrupt churchmen do
ofttimes make a great noise about religion as
wronged, when yet the thing that troubleth them
most is the decay of their own reputation among
people ; for therefore doth he inquire, first, " of
his disciples," and then, " of his doctrine," as being indeed not so much troubled with the matter
of his doctrine (had it been never so unsound, as
it was indeed the truth of God proceeding from
truth itself) as that thereby disciples were made,
and so the reputation of him and his complices
lessened among the people.

VER. 20. Jesus answered him, I spake openly
to the world ; I ever taught in the synagogue, and in the temple, whither the Jews
always resort ; and in secret have I said nothing.

21. Why askest thou me? ask them which
heard me, what I have said unto them : behold, they know what I said.

Christ, in his defence and answer, waiveth the
matter of his disciples, and answereth concerning
his doctrine.   And—1. He gives a brief account
of his way and manner of preaching, ver. 20 ;
that he had not (as the accusation indirectly implied) gone into corners with it, but had taught
openly to the world, and particularly in the temple and synagogues, where the Jews were his
ordinary hearers, and so had not carried himself
as if he durst not avow his doctrine.   2. From
this he gathereth an inference, ver. 21, wherein
he accuseth their illegal procedure who would have
him to accuse himself, and would not proceed legally in examining witnesses in so public a matter,
to whom he appeals.   For clearing this purpose,
consider—1. While Christ saith, " I spake openly,"
and declines to have spoken anything " in secret," his meaning is, not to condemn men's
preaching of truth secretly in a time of violent
persecution, yea, and that private teaching and
exhortation be joined with public preaching,
Acts, xx. 20 ; but his scope is only, in matter of
fact, to shew what his practice had been, that so
he may condemn the high priest's proceeding ;
and withal, by this he would shew that however
men may preach in secret in some cases, for the
preservation of their persons, yet they ought not
so to do, as desiring to have truth concealed, as
if it were not justifiable, nor might be avowed in
itself.   Consider—2. This profession of Christ
doth nothing contradict his practice elsewhere,
in teaching the disciples secretly, Mark, iv. 34,
for he taught his disciples no other thing, for
kind of doctrine, but what he taught publicly,
only he expounded it to them ; and withal, he
did so, not that it might be concealed, but that
they might proclaim it, Matt. x. 27.   Consider—
3. Christ's refusing to give an account of his
doctrine is no way a denying or disavowing of his
doctrine, but only a legal defence ; for albeit a
man, after he is legally convicted of a crime, may
be dealt with to confess it, as Joshua dealt with
Achan, yet there is no reason why men should
expose themselves, when they are under trial, to

the fury of those who are lying in wait to ensnare and ruin them.

From verse 20, learn—1. That Christ doth not answer concerning his disciples, which was the first part of the high priest's interrogatory; we may conceive the reason to be, not so much because, possibly, he intended it after he had answered first to the matter of his doctrine, but was impeded by the uncivil carriage of the high priest's servant, ver. 22; nor yet only because he would not ensnare and betray them by giving an account of them; but chiefly, to shew that his doctrine, being well considered, that other question needed not be answered, nor would he be found seditious in gathering disciples thereby; for not only had he in his doctrine taught those whom he healed to go unto the priests according to the law, and those who conversed with him to give Cæsar his due, but his doctrine being the doctrine of the Messiah, there could be no sedition or schism, though all Israel should embrace him and it. And so it teacheth, that a man's doctrine and grounds should be first considered before any effects or consequents following thereupon be judged. For albeit sometimes a man may have truth on his side, which yet is not of that importance nor so relevant a ground as to make an open schism and rent upon it, yet where weighty matters of truth are held out by a man in his station, his cause is sufficient to ward off all imputations arising from odious-like consequents following upon the publishing thereof.

2. Saints in their sufferings ought to account of truth and their cause as the precious treasure, carefully to be owned and defended, that it suffer nothing by them; therefore, albeit Christ sometimes would not answer their calumnies and accusations, partly, as being frivolous, and partly, to testify that, being considered as our Surety, he had nothing to say, there being nothing charged on him but bis people were guilty of it, or their sins deserved it; yet here (as at other times also) he answered, to testify that however he yielded his person, yet he would not yield his cause as unworthy to be owned; and hereby giveth his followers an example what to do in their sufferings. (See Eph. vi. 19, 20.)

3. Such as have truth on their side may speak it boldly and freely, as that which may be avowed and will bear them out who own it; and men ought thus to speak it as they have a calling; for saith Christ, "I speak openly," or confidently, both "to the world" in general, and particularly "in the synagogue and temple, whither the Jews always resort." (See Acts, iv. 29.)

4. Whatever care should be had that pearls be not cast before swine, yet the truth of God ought to be published by his servants indifferently to the world, in their stations, as being debtors to all, and not knowing upon whom the Lord may make their ministry successful; and however it succeed, a testimony is to be left against the incorrigible;- therefore saith Christ, "I spake openly to the world," or to all indifferently and freely to whom he had a commission.

5. It is a commendable practice of members of the visible church to frequent the public ordinances and places appointed for that end; and herein the diligence of men who live in a dege-

nerate and corrupt church may condemn the negligence of others; for it is here supposed that in this time "the Jews did always resort in the synagogue for their ordinary sabbath services, and in the temple, where their more solemn and ceremonial worship was performed.

6. Christ's preaching not only openly to the world, but more especially "in the synagogue and in the temple," where there were Jews of several tempers, and many of them set to ensnare him and jangle with him, may serve to teach, not that his love was great who sought them so earnestly, who yet were about to crucify him, Matt. xxiii. 37, and that the power accompanying his doctrine is such as there may be hopes of prevailing thereby, even among the most corrupt societies of men; as he publisheth his doctrine among his most cruel enemies, where, no doubt, he prevailed with some, John, xii. 42; but further, it teacheth that truth must be preached as men have a calling, where there are many disadvantages and strange humours of people to encounter; and that faithful ministers must not always expect such auditories as they would desire for tractableness and subjection; for Christ, the Prince of teachers, "taught in the synagogue and in the temple."

7. Ministers of the gospel, in their preaching thereof, ought to renounce the hidden things of dishonesty, either in conveying lawful duties in a clandestine, base way, which is apt to render them suspected, or by their so ordering their way as they may decline contempt or hatred, or may compass some base by-ends; for so much doth Christ's example teach, who "in secret said nothing," as is before explained. (See 2 Cor. iv. 2; 1 Thess. v. 22; 2 Tim. iii. 6.)

From verse 21, learn—1. A man's public carriage (especially if he be one whose carriage is, for most part, notour [notorious] and known) being examined and found right, it is full of hazard, and evidenceth great want of charity to suspect his integrity or his carriage in other things, unless there be good ground for it; therefore Christ, carrying himself openly in his doctrine, counts it very informal to judge him as a heretic or seditious person, unless it could be instructed by his hearers. And herein men fail exceedingly by their envy and secret whisperings, of which see Prov. xxvii. 4; 2 Cor. xii. 20.

2. A man being by the law of nature obliged to self-defence, and against self-murder, ought therefore not to accuse himself before a judge; therefore Christ declineth so to do, "Why askest thou me?"

3. Whatever liberty men have to decline such witnesses as do profess their malicious and partial disposition, and that they will not make conscience of lying, so they may condemn the innocent, yet the carriage of Christ's followers should be such as they need not decline any witnesses who will declare the truth; therefore Christ appeals indifferently to his hearers, be they who they will, if they would tell what he said, "Ask them which heard me what I have said unto them."

4. It is the duty of hearers to be able to give an account of what they hear, as they are called

to it; for Christ supposeth this of them, " Behold, they know what I said," though few of many hearers attain to so much.

> VER. 22. And when he had thus spoken, one of the officers which stood by struck Jesus with the palm of his hand, saying, Answerest thou the high priest so?
>
> 23. Jesus answered him, If I have spoken evil, bear witness of the evil: but if well, why smitest thou me?

In these verses is recorded Christ's conflict with one of the high priest's officers, who smites Christ ignominiously, and challengeth him for speaking in such a manner to the high priest, ver. 22. The reason whereof is not to be taken from this, that Christ, appealing to his hearers, ver. 21, (of which sort these officers also had been, chap. vii. 32, 46,) he, by this practice, will clear himself of any respect to his doctrine; but the cause of it was his respect to the high priest, his master; and he thus dealeth with Christ because he answered not reverently, as he conceived, and because he carried himself so confidently. Christ, in his answer, ver. 23, doth tax this way of procedure, urging, that if he had spoken wrong the court was now sitting legally to examine him, and he might orderly accuse and bear witness, and not abuse him; and if he had spoken right, it was a great injury so to use him, especially before a judicatory.

From verse 22, learn—1. Corrupt masters have ordinarily corrupt servants; and as sometimes servants may corrupt their masters, so it is as frequent that servants are corrupted by their masters, Prov. xxix. 12; for here the officers are such as their master was.

2. Men's greatness (though accompanied with no goodness) doth ordinarily so dazzle the eyes of others that they think it intolerable any should not dote on them, as themselves do, were their courses never so evil; for that he was " the high priest" is enough to make this officer take it ill that Christ did not (as he thought) give more reverence to him. and that although he was unworthy, and nothing like that office, and was even now persecuting Christ.

3. Great ones, and their adherents, do think their authority contemned if they be not absolutely humoured, and get all their will, though to the prejudice and quitting of truth; for albeit Christ, in his answer, do only tax their illegal proceeding, and adhereth to truth and the defence thereof in a legal way, yet this officer cannot endure he should thus stand to his point, and not yield to the high priest, and therefore with a buffet inquireth, " Answerest thou the high priest so?"

4. Christ did endure buffeting and contemptible usage, even from inferior servants, giving his cheek to the nippers, to testify that shame and reproachful usage was our due, yea, even to be buffeted with Satan's messengers; and that such as flee to him have the curse of such a lot removed, and it sanctified unto them; for to teach and purchase this was our Surety stricken with the palm of this officer's hand.

From ver. 23, learn—1. However men may think to drive Christ and his followers from truth and duty by buffeting, yet that will not prevail, so long as they cannot be convinced that God is against them; which would prevail with a conscience that otherwise will not be beaten from truth; therefore Christ, being thus abused, insists mainly on this, if he had spoken evil or well, as the thing to be discussed, before he could alter his way.

2. Albeit Christ require that his people resist not evil, yet his meaning is only to bind up their hands from private revenge, and not to shut their mouths from complaining to authority; for here his own practice expounds that precept, Matt. v. 39, in that, though he will not avenge himself, yet he complains of the injury before their judicatory, and warrants the man not to strike him illegally, but to " bear witness of the evil."

3. There is no cause that cometh before men, but (for the most part) it is like to have fairer justice than Christ's cause, all men being unreasonable and absurd here, who have not faith, 2 Thess. iii. 2; for so much doth Christ's arguing import, where, by an argument, pinching on all hands, he intimates he got foul play, whether he had spoken evil or well.

4. Christ in his own person hath underlien [undergone] unreasonable usage, that he might expiate our desert hereof, and our absurd walking contrary to God, and might sanctify such a lot to his followers, and assure them that he, having drunk this cup for them, will see them righted and get fair play, one way or other; for so much may we gather for our use, from this usage whereof he complains.

> VER. 24. Now Annas had sent him bound unto Caiaphas the high priest.

Before that John proceed to the last branch of this part of the chapter, he doth here subjoin how Annas (to whom Christ was sent, ver. 13) had sent him bound to Caiaphas; not (as hath been cleared on ver. 12—14) as if the things formerly recorded had been acted upon him before he was brought thither, but only, by way of conclusion to the former purpose, and by way of transition to what followeth, he declareth that Christ before this had been brought to the high priest's hall, where he was examined and injured by the high priest's servant, and where Peter denied him, though he had not mentioned his bringing thither before. From the purpose in this verse, learn—

1. It pleased the Father to expose his Son Christ to the malice of his enemies, who shewed him no mercy, but the uttermost of their rage, that so he might purchase a better lot for his people; for therefore it is marked, that as he came bound to Annas, ver. 12, 13, so he doth not release him, but " sent him bound unto Caiaphas," his mortal enemy.

2. God will not only mark what cruelty people exercise against Christ and his followers themselves, but how they contribute to and are instrumental in their ill usage from others; therefore it is marked, to the perpetual infamy of Annas, that when he had insulted awhile over Christ

he " sent him bound unto Caiaphas," where he might be yet more cruelly handled.

3. It pleased our Lord in his sufferings to condescend to come bound as a delinquent before a high priest, that so he might teach his people what delinquents they were before the tribunal of God, and might purchase for them a more comfortable and free access to himself, their high priest, and to the Father through him; for so much may be gathered from his being " sent bound unto Caiaphas the high priest." (See Heb. iv. 14—16.)

VER. 25. And Simon Peter stood and warmed himself. They said therefore unto him, Art not thou also one of his disciples? He denied it, and said, I am not.

26. One of the servants of the high priest, being his kinsman whose ear Peter cut off, saith, Did not I see thee in the garden with him?

27. Peter then denied again: and immediately the cock crew.

Followeth in these verses, the third branch of this part of the chapter, wherein Peter's second and third denial of his Master are recorded. John doth in brief declare that Peter, after his first denial, staying still in the crowd, and warming himself, (as is also formerly marked, ver. 18,) was the second time assaulted and challenged as one of Christ's disciples, and doth again deny it; and that after awhile (as is marked, Luke, xxii. 59) he is the third time assaulted by one who had interest in the man whom Peter had hurt, and who had seen him in the garden with Christ. But he persists in his denial, till the cock crew the second time, which being accompanied with Christ's looking on him, and his remembering what Christ had foretold, is a mean to draw him to repentance, as is marked by the rest. For clearing this purpose, consider—1. Whereas in his second assault it is here said, in general, that " they (to wit, who were present) said unto him," &c., and yet two of the rest assert this assault to have been by a maid, Mark, xiv. 69; Matt. xxvi. 71; and another, that it was by a servant, Luke, xxii. 58. This difficulty may be thus reconciled: that a maid and a servant assaulting him, and he seeming to neglect them, the whole company, or many of them, do charge him with it, which puts him on the snare of an open denial. 2. As for the third assault, the differences betwixt the evangelists may be thus reconciled: that being challenged to be one of Christ's followers, as being a Galilean, whose speech bewrayed him, Matt. xxvi. 73; Mark, xiv. 70; Luke, xxii. 59; this servant which saw him in the garden (and belike saw him also cut off his kinsman's ear) confirmeth the challenge; all which importunity, and possibly some intimation that it was known what he had done in the garden, precipitates him upon a third denial. 3. As for the manner of his denial, there is no great difficulty, for it is the same thing in substance that he is said to deny by all of them—to wit, that he was Christ's disciple, or with him. Only while the rest observe

that he denied to have known Christ, or to understand of what they spake when they challenged him, it points out to what an absurdity his fears drave him, in that he professeth his ignorance of Him of whose fame and report almost none in the land were ignorant. And his swearing and cursing, recorded by them to have accompanied his denial, doth further point out what the violence of the tentation was, and what stuff may lurk in the bosoms of saints, ready to break out when there is a tentation.

From verse 25, learn—1. The Lord takes strict and constant notice of men's deportment and walking upon snares, however they little heed it themselves; and the longer they do so he is the more offended; therefore it is yet again remarked, that all this while " Simon Peter (yet) stood and warmed himself" in that place, among such company.

2. Such as do cast themselves in unwarrantable company, and continue among them, partaking of their accommodations, do not readily escape without a soul trial and slip, and that more than one, for Peter standing and warming himself, his carriage casts him upon the snare of a new denial.

3. Men are so much the nearer a fall as they continue among snares and tentations, when the Lord is eminently calling them to their duty, and to mourn for their former failings, and so their carriage is nothing answerable to what their condition or the Lord's dispensation calls them aloud unto; for this addeth to his guilt, and ripens him for a new assault and fall, that he " stood and warmed himself," when he should have been mourning his former denial.

4. As Satan is always tempting believers, as he hath opportunity, so especially, when he hath gained any ground upon them, he is an eager pursuer of them by his fitted means and instruments, and their falling in any degree is but a prelude to greater tentations; for Satan, having prevailed by the voice of a weak damsel, doth now the second time assault him, by a maid, a servant, and many together; " They said therefore unto him, Art thou not also one of his disciples?"

5. As Satan is ready to tempt and assault sliding disciples, so they, being once entered in a course of defection, are ready to persist and go yet further wrong, especially when they are not sensible of their former failings; for he again " denied it, and said, I am not," and that with an oath, as is recorded by the rest.

6. It is the great sin of Christ's disciples to deny their Master, or themselves to be his disciples and followers; for this was Peter's fault, He said, I am not one of his disciples. And albeit it was his eminent slip to renounce his Master by an avowed denial, yet others have need to look to it, who, though they profess him, yet their practice doth refute their profession, Tit. i. 14; 2 Tim. iii. 5; and namely, when they practise not such duties as are required of disciples, such as hearing and abiding in his word, John, x. 27; viii. 31; self-denial, and bearing of his cross, Matt. xvi. 24; mortification, Gal. v. 24; walking after his Spirit, Rom. viii. 1; meekness, Matt. xi. 29; mutual love, John, xiii. 35; and several other duties recorded in scripture.

From verses 26, 27, learn—1. As Satan is incessant in pursuing, so he knoweth how to fit tentations to every man's humour, that they may take; therefore Peter, being all this while possessed with fear, hounds out " his kinsman, whose ear Peter cut off," (whereof, belike he had some intimation,) and one who saw him in the garden, that these considerations working yet more upon his fear, might drive him to a new and more gross denial.

2. As it is Satan's element to sin and draw others to multiply sin after sin, so saints especially may expect that when they slip they will be most of any incessantly pursued, to add sin after sin; it being Satan's delight to engage them especially in sin against God, and by the throng of tentations to keep them from recovering their feet; therefore doth he thus pursue Peter the third time.

3. It is the duty of the Lord's people, when they are tempted, to consider what impediments the Lord layeth in the course of their sinning, that so they may be ashamed to go on ; and it is their great sin when they do otherwise; for whatever was Satan's aim in choosing this instrument to assault him the third time, yet the Lord thereby would shame him from his denial by bringing in so clear evidences against him that he was a disciple, which he could not shift without much impudence, and without open wronging of his Master as not worthy to be owned, and that before them who certainly knew he had been one of his followers ; all which did contribute to make his sin of denial the more odious.

4. Saints' weakness is such as, being assaulted, they may fall again and again in the same sin ; as here Peter's threefold denial teacheth us, " Peter then denied again." It is, indeed, more grievous, when men fall often again into the same sin, even after they have repented for their former falling into it, (though the scripture declareth not that to be inconsistent with the state of grace in a person,) but it may be more frequently incident to saints to relapse often while they are still kept going under the power of tentations, without getting liberty to draw their breath, or recollect themselves, which was Peter's case here, and pleads for more pity.

5. A gap being once made in the conscience by sin, it will easily grow wider, and one sin will prove a needle to draw in the thread of another sin ; as here Peter's experience doth witness, who by one denial is drawn to another, and who from simple denial proceeds to denial with an oath, and then with cursing, as the rest observe.

6. When saints begin to slip, and do not make conscience of repentance for it, God may let their defection rise to a very great height, till they see cause to abhor themselves indeed ; for so much also doth this experience teach. He not heeding, nor being affected with his first denial, the Lord gives him up to more denials, and that with swearing and cursing, that so his conscience may be alarmed with the grossness of his way. And indeed, solid repentance in a backsliding way is seldom attained till the defection come to some height of grossness.

7. Whatever be men's conceit of themselves, yet the event will clear that Christ's verdict concerning man's frailty is true, and that their presumption is a liar; for here " immediately the cock crew," to witness that before this time, prefixed by Christ, Peter had denied him thrice, according to his prediction, John, xiii. 38.

8. Albeit the Lord suffer his own to slip through tentation, that he may correct their proud conceit of themselves and teach them to abide more in him, yet he will not utterly lose, but will recover them ; for " the cock crew," to put Peter in mind of what passed betwixt Christ and him ; which, being accompanied with other means, draws him to repentance, as is marked by the rest.

9. The same means which men have had, and yet have profited nothing by them, may yet be much useful when God commands a blessing ; for albeit Peter was alarmed by the cock's crowing first, after his first fall, Mark, xiv. 68, yet he never remembereth Christ's words, but goeth on, and the same mean, with Christ's look, is blessed.

10. The Lord is ofttimes in mercy pleased to recover his people by very speedy repentance, after their trial for discovering of their weakness is over ; and particularly, such as, through violence of tentations, are driven upon sin, do readily sooner recover by repentance than they who, upon resolution and with deliberation, engage in a course of sin ; for Peter being under a violent tentation in this his sinning, " immediately the cock crew," to give him warning to repent, which accordingly succeeds.

Ver. 28. Then led they Jesus from Caiaphas unto the hall of judgment : and it was early ; and they themselves went not into the judgment hall, lest they should be defiled ; but that they might eat the passover.

Followeth the third and last part of the chapter, containing a part of Christ's trial, and the procedure about him, in Pilate's judgment hall. It may be taken up in four branches, in the first whereof (in this verse) is recorded how they led Jesus unto " the hall of judgment," (or the place where the Roman governors used to sit in judgment,) to have him sentenced and condemned by Pilate, and executed accordingly; before all which we are to conceive (as is marked by the rest) that the chief priests and their council had (beside their examination of himself, ver. 19) examined false witnesses against him, and adjured himself to declare what he was, and upon his confession condemned him of blasphemy, and adjudged him to be worthy of death. And then, with all speed, they bring him to the Roman governor, as is here marked. Unto which John subjoineth that they themselves would not enter into the judgment hall, lest, being defiled, they should be kept from the passover, which they did not eat till this day, as hath been cleared on chap. xiii. 2.

DOCTRINES.

1 It may shame the Lord's people, in their negligence in going about his service, to see the activity of wicked men in their ill courses, particularly in their opposition to Christ; for here,

having been at it all night, they do not yet weary, but led him away, " and it was early," and they go themselves, and do not send officers only.

2. It pleased the Lord so to order as Christ should be brought before a pagan judge, and be by him condemned; one reason whereof is given, ver. 31, 32, which I remit to its proper place, and do add—1. Christ would not be slain tumultuously, as the Jews cut off Stephen, Acts, vii., but would be judicially condemned, that so sin might be condemned in the flesh, Rom. viii. 3, and he might fully satisfy for his people, and abide a full process in law. 2. By this lot he would expiate our being under the dominion of foreign powers, of sin, Satan, and the kingdom of darkness. 3. Christ, by getting his innocency asserted by Pilate, (which the Jews would never grant,) and yet being by him condemned, would have it cleared, that he suffered not for himself, but for others. 4. By this means both Jews and Gentiles had a hand in his death, that both might have an occasion to look to him whom they had pierced, to excite them to repentance and mourning. 5. Hereby also he hath sanctified unto his people their being brought before judgment seats (even of unfriends or strangers to religion) for his sake;—all these considerations may be read in this, that " they led Jesus from Caiaphas unto the hall of judgment."

3. Men may pretend to very much zeal in external performances of religion who yet are but naughty, yea, and cruel, bloody persecutors; for so appears in these here; " They themselves went not into the judgment hall, lest they should be defiled; but that they might eat the passover." It is not needful to determine whether it was a tradition of their own or a determination by God, that entering into the judgment hall should defile them, that they might not eat the passover; or whether they apprehended pollution from somewhat they might meet with there, rather than from entering simply to the place; but this is clear in it, that they pretend to respect the passover, and are careful to avoid pollution, when yet they are seeking the life of the Lord of glory. (See Matt. xxiii. 23.)

Ver. 29. Pilate then went out unto them, and said, What accusation bring ye against this man?

30. They answered and said unto him, If he were not a malefactor, we would not have delivered him up unto thee.

Followeth to ver. 33, the second branch of this part of the chapter, containing some debates betwixt Pilate and the Jews about the entering of Christ's process. It may be taken up in a twofold proposition of Pilate, and their answer thereunto; in the first whereof (in these verses) Pilate will not stand on terms with them, but goeth out unto them, and desireth they would produce an accusation against Christ, upon which he might formally and legally proceed, ver. 29. The Jews, in answering, suspecting that probation might succeed but ill, as it had before with themselves, Mark, xiv. 55—59, do interpose their own credit and reputation with Pilate, instead of an accusation,

indirectly taking it as an affront that he should require an accusation from them, or think that such men as they would bring any before him to be condemned but an evil-doer, ver. 30.

From ver. 29, learn—1. It is the duty of rulers, not only to do justice, but to be ready to do it timously, and with as great expedition as may be; for this is commendable in Pilate, that though it was early when they came, ver. 28, yet he is ready to hear them. (See Exodus, xviii. 13.)

2. It is also commendable in men of power and eminency not to stand on terms with their inferiors, nor carp at their scruples and weaknesses, but to pass over all these, and do them justice; for this is also commendable in him, that when they scruple to enter into " the judgment hall," ver. 28, he stands not on that, but " went out unto them," far contrary to the practice of many great ones, who, if their inferiors cross any of their humours, will be sure to give them a meeting when they come into their hands. (See Job, xxxi. 13, 14.)

3. It is agreeable to justice that no man be condemned without an accusation produced and proven against him, and that men in power do not gratify a man to death, (as the words will read, Acts, xxv. 16,) nor make use of their authority to pleasure friends, or satisfy their own lusts, seeing judgment is not theirs, but the Lord's; therefore Pilate, a heathen, is clear to follow this order, " What accusation bring you against this man?"

From verse 30, learn—1. Albeit the Jews could lay nothing to Christ's charge before Pilate, but either that he was against Cæsar, which was a lie, or that he called himself the Son of God, which was indeed a truth; yet here he is presented as " a malefactor," or a notorious and noxious evil-doer, whereby he would, partly, teach what we indeed were in whose room he stood, even such notorious delinquents, unworthy to live on the earth; and partly, he would sanctify unto his people their lying under unjust imputations and calumnies, which he essayed, being traduced as an enemy to Cæsar; and would sanctify unto them their living in times wherein clearest truths are persecuted under odious names; as his calling himself the Son of God was accounted blasphemy.

2. Men may be very lavish in blasting the reputation of others who yet would be loath to be so dealt with by others; but ordinarily, they who make an idol of their own credit do regard least the credit of others; for they stand not to traduce Christ as " a malefactor," who yet take it ill that Pilate should seem to rub on them by calling for an accusation.

3. It is an old trick of corrupt churchmen and persecutors to abuse civil powers, and to make use of any respect they have from them to give them bad impressions of the godly, and set them on edge against them; as here these corrupt rulers do make use of any respect Pilate had to them, to condemn Christ on their word; " If he were not a malefactor, we would not have delivered him up unto thee."

4. Men ought to take heed how they employ any credit God hath given them with men, as

being a talent for the use whereof they will be called to an account, and it is an evidence that men's credit, authority, or parts, are plagued to them when they hang at their wrong side, and they labour to turn men against Christ and his truth, because such as they are against him; as here, notice is taken that they employed their credit in this wicked way. (See John, vii. 48, 49.)

VER. 31. Then said Pilate unto them, Take ye him, and judge him according to your law. The Jews therefore said unto him, It is not lawful for us to put any man to death:

32. That the saying of Jesus might be fulfilled, which he spake, signifying what death he should die.

Pilate, in his second proposition, remits the trial and censure of Christ to themselves, to be gone about according to their law; but they, in their answer, decline that they had power to put any man to death, ver. 31, in which a special providence is remarked, ver. 32. For clearing of this proposition and answer, and the whole purpose, consider—That it is asserted by many that the Jews, being now under the power of the Romans, though they had not power to inflict capital punishments for crimes condemned also by the Roman laws, yet they had power, not only to judge of lesser faults, and to inflict punishments which were not unto death, but might also put men to death for blasphemy against God and their own law, whereof they judge Christ to be guilty; therefore they understand this speech of the Jews, " It is not lawful for us to put any man to death," as importing, not that they might not do it at all, nor yet only that they would gratify Pilate, by renouncing their power that they might engage him for them, but that they might not do it at that time, in regard of the holiness of the feast; for which cause also it seems that Herod delayed the intended execution of Peter till after Easter, Acts, xii. 4. And they strengthen this assertion from this consideration: that suppose this power had been taken from them, yet in this case they could not object want of power or liberty, unless it had been because of the holiness of the time, seeing Pilate had granted them liberty to judge him. But whatever be asserted to this purpose, yet upon accurate search of the Jewish records, and other passages, it will be found that they had indeed power of lesser censures, or punishments, as may be gathered from Matt. x. 17; 2 Cor. xi. 24; that they had also power in capital crimes against their own religion to examine the nature and quality of the offence, and to determine what it deserved, as they did in Christ's case, John, xix. 7; Matt. xxvi. 65, 66; and in doing whereof in the case of Paul they complain that they were interrupted by Lysias, Acts, xxiv. 5—7. Neither is it to be denied also that in their practice they somewhat went further, and in a tumultuous way did cut off capital offenders (as they conceived them to be) in the matter of their religion, without any legal process, or owning of the Roman governor. But as

for matter of right or liberty granted them by the Romans, they had no power at all to put any to death till he were brought before the governor, who was to take cognition of the cause, and to give out sentence, and see it executed. This appeareth all along here, in their bringing Christ unto Pilate, after they had condemned him, in their very clear profession of the want of power in this place, and in their prosecuting Christ incessantly before Pilate's judgment seat, till he pronounced sentence against him. We do not find Pilate, in the first entering of this process, give any hint of any such power; nor is it to be doubted, but if they had any such power, or had they looked upon Pilate's speech as giving them liberty to put him to death themselves, they would greedily have embraced it, rather than put the matter in hazard wherein they think themselves so much concerned, especially now, when they find Pilate like to stand so much on points with them; to say nothing that they were very tender in the matter of their liberty and power, and therefore would not willingly quit any right they had, or slight any liberty granted them. And if they who did persecute Christ to death in the time of the feast could not sentence him at that time, yet, no doubt, on the former considerations, they would have kept him till the feast was over, for which they might have a guard of Roman soldiers, as well as they had one for apprehending him.

These things being considered, I take the scope and meaning of these verses to be this: That Pilate, partly, having no will to meddle with Christ, whom he knew to be delivered to him for envy, and partly, being irritated by their presumptuous and illegal answer to his proposition, ver. 29, 30, doth remit the matter back to themselves, that if they judged him worthy only of some lesser punishment, they might inflict the same according to the liberty yet continued with them; or if they meant that he deserved more, even death, when they called him " a malefactor," he, in a bitter taunt, declares that if that were their way, according to their laws and religion, to condemn a man upon trust, and put him to death without an accusation and formal process, he would let them do on; but as for him, if he knew not the crime, to cognosce upon [recognise] it, he would never be their executioner to pronounce sentence and execute it, such procedure being no ways agreeable to the Roman custom, Acts, xxv. 16; and so his speech is rather a sharp reflection upon them and their laws than any permission to them to execute any such power. The Jews, in their reply, declare that they had no power at all to put any man to death, and therefore had brought him to him; whereby they both intimate that they thought that he deserved more than they had power to inflict, and withal, they would pacify Pilate, by acknowledging his power, and declaring how they were content he should exercise it among them. But in all this John observeth a providence of God, not that the Jews employed not the power which they had, or was now permitted to them, to put him to death, nor yet only that they did it not tumultuously, but that they had no such power at all, that so he might (according to his own prediction, Matthew, xx. 19 ; John, xii. 32,) die under a pagan ruler, and might die a Roman death, and be crucified, which was more significant than stoning, the ordinary death inflicted by the Jews for blasphemy, Lev. xxiv. 16, which was the crime they falsely charged on Christ, John, ix. 7 ; Matthew, xxvi. 65, 66 ; and would have stoned him for it before, John, x. 33.

From these verses, thus cleared, learn—1. Even pagans may be more clear and just in their proceedings with Christ and his followers than corrupt men in the church, who have abused the offer of much grace ; for so doth appear here in Pilate and these rulers of the Jews ; he doth not suppose Christ to be guilty of so much as they intend, nor is he so forward and informal as they are.

2. It is the great sin of many men, that having no true piety they will yet pretend to much of it, whereby, and by their unanswerable walking, they expose religion to reproach, and render it detestable, even to pagans ; for their presumptuous commending of themselves, to commend an unjust procedure against Christ, verse 30, draweth out from Pilate this tart reflection upon their law and religion, " Take ye him, and judge him according to your law."

3. It is also ordinary with God to expose those justly to reproach who hunt after the idol of their own credit in a sinful way ; for this also reflects upon themselves as well as upon their law.

4. It is no strange thing to see many idols of men stoop and give place to greater idols, coming in competition therewith ; and, particularly, malice against Christ, his truth and followers, is ordinarily so violent in persecutors that they will renounce their credit and pack up injuries very grievous to them, to get that satisfied ; for this speech, " It is not lawful for us to put any man to death," is not only an ingenuous acknowledgment that they had no power to deal with Christ as they thought he deserved, but points out also how they startle not at this check given them, but insinuate with him as acquiescing in their want of power, (which yet was the thing they most affected,) that so they might get him on their side to condemn Christ.

5. The Lord hath a supreme hand and providence in the least things which concern Christ and his followers, and especially in their sufferings ; for that they want power, and he is left in Pilate's hand, there was a providence in it, " that the saying of Jesus might be fulfilled," &c.

6. In this way of Christ's dying under a stranger, and by crucifying, (omitting what hath been said on ver. 28, and may be further spoken of his being crucified, in its proper place,) these passages of providence come to be observed :—1. That Christ is a faithful keeper of his word, and will not fail to see that performed which he speaks therein ; for so appeareth in the first place ; all these things were, " that the saying of Jesus might be fulfilled," and he might be found true in his predictions. 2. That Christ is the true Messiah, as being sent into the world, when now the sceptre was departed from Judah, according to the prophecy, Gen. xlix. 10 ; for he foretold this death, and his delivering to the gentiles to

be crucified, when the Jews wanted power, as here they confess, that this might contribute to the confirmation of this great truth. 3. Christ would be put to a most cursed, ignominious, and painful death, that he might testify his love to his own, and fully satisfy for them, and might lead them to inherit a blessing ; for all these concurred in this death ; a more easy way of it being long ago pronounced accursed, Deut. xxi. 23, he would choose the most accursed kind of it, which withal was most ignominious and painful. 4. Christ also, by his posture in this death, being lifted up with his arms stretched out upon the cross, would invite all his people to look and come to him, who stands with open arms ready to receive them, and make them partakers of his purchase.

Ver. 33. Then Pilate entered into the judgment hall again, and called Jesus, and said unto him, Art thou the King of the Jews?

34. Jesus answered him, Sayest thou this thing of thyself, or did others tell it thee of me?

Followeth, to verse 38, the third branch of this part of the chapter, containing Pilate's examination of Christ, and his answers to his questions ; concerning which, we are to conceive that Pilate, following his own way, will have some accusation against him before he proceed ; and they, to satisfy him, do accuse Christ of affecting a kingdom, as is recorded, Luke, xxiii. 2 ; upon which Pilate proceeds to the examination. It may be taken up in three discourses betwixt him and Christ ; in the first whereof (in these verses) Pilate inquireth if he was the King of the Jews, and would grant that crime whereof they accused him ; Christ desires, in the first place, before he answer, to know whence that accusation might flow, whether from his own apprehension or from the Jews ; whereby he would put Pilate to it, to consider either his own simplicity, if he himself did suspect him to be a king, such an one as he dreamt of, when yet he saw nothing in him like such a state ; or his levity and credulity, if he did receive such an improbable report and delation from others ; or his injustice, if, to please malicious delators and accusers, he intended that process against him. Whence learn—

1. It is a plague upon the children of men that all of them by nature have still somewhat to make them jealous of Christ, and afraid of him and his company ; for as the Pharisees feared the blasting of their reputation by him, and others are afraid that he will not give liberty to their lusts, so Pilate hath his own prejudice, in that he is accused to be " the King of the Jews." Happy are they who are delivered from prejudices at him.

2. It is, in particular, the great prejudice of rulers and great men against Christ, that they apprehend that his kingdom and power in his church is prejudicial to their authority and power in the earth ; for that is the thing Pilate fears, when he inquires, " Art thou the King of the Jews?"

3. It is exceedingly reproachful either lightly

to take up or lightly to receive and hearken unto calumnies and reproaches cast upon men, or yet to gratify those who are known to pursue the innocent maliciously; for so much doth Christ's questions to Pilate point at.

4. Men ought not to be borne with in their dallying with conscience and justice, especially in matters which concern God and his truth, but should be put to it, either altogether to disclaim conscience and equity, or else to walk according to the rules thereof; for so much also do Christ's questions drive Pilate unto, that he would not dally in this process if in his conscience he knew it but frivolous and invented by malice.

VER. 35. Pilate answered, Am I a Jew? Thine own nation and the chief priests have delivered thee unto me: what hast thou done?

36. Jesus answered, My kingdom is not of this world: if my kingdom were of this world, then would my servants fight, that I should not be delivered to the Jews: but now is my kingdom not from hence.

In the second discourse, Pilate, being a little commoved, declines being the author of this accusation, as being no Jew, nor acquainted with their controversies, nor caring for their religion, or the king they expected, and fathers this whole business on the Jews, Christ's own countrymen, and their church-rulers withal, desiring to know what he had done which might so incense them against him, ver. 35; Christ, having reasoned with the man, doth now come expressly to answer to the accusation concerning his kingdom, and speaks so much of it, negatively, as might satisfy Pilate, that it might well enough consist with the safety of the Roman state; therefore he sheweth that his kingdom was not a worldly kingdom, and for proof thereof he instanceth how far he was from aspiring to a kingdom by force of arms, in that he would not so much as permit his servants to fight in his defence, as they offered to do when the Jews came to take him. Whence learn—

1. Pilate's commotion, evidenced in his reply, " Am I a Jew?" did not only flow from his respect to his credit, which he could not suffer that Christ should touch upon, how justly soever; but also that his natural conscience was touched, and that he is not willing Christ should put his conscience to it, seeing he could not follow it, and yet keep his politic, smooth way. It teacheth, that they who not only are sinfully tender of their credit, but they to whom a conscience (what they have of it) is a vexation and a cross to their designs, will readily meet with many vexations by reason thereof, and in the end make shipwreck of it; as it fared with Pilate, who is here irritated, knowing that Christ touched him in the quick, and afterward giveth up himself to go over the belly of his conscience.

2. Even moral civility in men will account it as great a reproach as may be, and a matter of shame, to be the author and inventor of calumnies and reproaches against others; for Pilate declines this, and fastens it upon the Jews, " thine own nation and the chief priests have delivered thee unto me."

3. Such is the iniquity and corruption of time, that hardly shall the most unjust aspersion be cast on any but it will leave some impression of guilt, at least with some; therefore, albeit Pilate knew the Jews' accusation to be frivolous, and of envy, yet it gives him occasion to suspect some quarrel, which causeth to inquire, " What hast thou done?"

4. Not only hath Christ, as God, an universal kingdom of power and providence, even over the highest of men, Dan. ii. 21; 1 Tim. vi. 15; Prov. viii. 15, 16; but, as Mediator, he hath a donative kingdom in and over his church, to the preservation and propagation whereof his kingdom of power is subservient, Matthew, xxviii. 18, 19; for so is here imported, that even in his state of exinanition he hath a kingdom—" my kingdom."

5. It is no strange thing to see truth so misrepresented as may stumble many, which yet, being heard and cleared, will offend none; for whereas this truth, that he is a king, was so represented as might offend Pilate, Christ lets him see that this needed not at all stumble him.

6. Albeit Christ's kingdom be in the world, yet it is not of the world; not only in respect of the subjects, who ought not to be of the world, but chiefly in opposition to worldly kingdoms; the benefits thereof not being earthly, Romans, xiv. 17, it being managed in a spiritual way, and with spiritual weapons, 2 Cor. x. 4, and coming without external pomp and observation, like unto the kingdoms of the world, Luke, xvii. 20, 21; for so much is imported in this assertion, " My kingdom is not of this world," whereby he removeth all cause of fear in Pilate.

7. It is the property of Christ's subjects and servants to be affectionate to their Lord and Master, and to be ready to do whatsoever is lawful for the good of his kingdom; for so is imported in that his servants would fight if it had been warrantable. And hereof all made offer, and Peter gave a rash proof, as we heard on ver. 10.

8. It is an evidence that Christ's kingdom is spiritual, that it is carried on, not by force of arms, as worldly kingdoms are, but by spiritual means; therefore doth Christ confirm his assertion (not by scripture, which Pilate knew not, but) by that known instance, " If my kingdom were of this world, then would my servants fight, that I should not be delivered to the Jews." Whereas private men, aspiring to a worldly kingdom, do use violence and force of arms, he had prohibited his disciples to fight in his defence in the garden. This is not to be understood as if Christ disallowed that they to whom he hath given the sword should defend his kingdom therewith; for if magistrates, even as magistrates, should be nursing parents to the church, and ought to kiss the Son, as the scriptures do record, then certainly they may and should employ their power as magistrates for removing of idolatry and setting up the true worship of God, and for defending thereof against violence. But Christ's purpose and scope in this may be fully taken up in these :—1. Christ, in his present state of humiliation, came into the world, not to get visible powers on his side, but

to abase himself and suffer, Matt. xx. 28; and to this the words in the text relate, while it is said, they did not fight, " that I should not be delivered to the Jews;" but in his state of exaltation he hath given, and will give, more ample proofs of his power, even in crushing kings and potentates, who oppose him and his kingdom, Ps. ii. 9, 10, 12; cx. 5, 6, (which is sometimes brought to pass by war,) and in employing the kings of the earth to hate the whore and burn her with fire, Rev. xvii. 16. 2. Christ, by hindering his servants to fight, who were but private men as to any civil power, and officers in his church, hath taught, that private men are not warranted to draw the sword, were it even in defence of religion, but they ought to maintain it by suffering when called to that extremity; and that the sword is not the weapon put in churchmen's hands for the defence of religion. 3. By this inhibition also, as it relates to Pilate's apprehensions, we are taught, that it is not lawful for professors of religion to take up arms for this end, that they may, under pretext of religion, set up any such kingdom as Pilate might apprehend, to the prejudice of the lawful magistrate; but it is the will of Christ that they enjoy their power and dignity, (they allowing Christ the exercise of his spiritual kingdom;) that religion commend itself by loyalty to authority, and by avoiding of sedition; and that religion or saintship be no sufficient ground to warrant men to entitle themselves to any power in the state to which they have no lawful calling; but rather, that it teach them to keep and adorn their stations. 4. Whatever case may warrant fighting in defence of religion, yet the influence thereof is but very accidental, as to this great end of promoting the spiritual kingdom of Christ; for not only did the gospel overspread much of the world by the preaching and sufferings of professors, before magistrates did befriend it, but even their power, when it is employed, can but reach to set up the outward exercise of religion, and to the repelling of external force, but can, itself alone, do nothing to the conscience, or to the keeping out of Satan, which is effectuated only by Christ's spirit accompanying and blessing his own spiritual weapons.

9. Men's practice is the clearest proof of their way and inclinations, whereby men ought in charity to judge of them, unless they have strong evidences to the contrary; therefore upon this, that his servants did not fight, Christ clearly inferreth, " But now is my kingdom not from hence."

VER. 37. Pilate therefore said unto him, Art thou a king then? Jesus answered, Thou sayest that I am a king. To this end was I born, and for this cause came I into the world, that I should bear witness unto the truth. Every one that is of the truth heareth my voice.

In the third discourse, Pilate, gathering from what Christ had said of his kingdom, that he held himself to be a king, desires a clear confession thereof; and Christ giveth him that good confession mentioned, 1 Tim. vi. 13, adding—

1. That he came into the world to bear witness unto the truth, where, without distinguishing curiously betwixt his being born, as being spoken in relation to his person, or human nature subsisting in it, and his coming into the world, in relation to his office, (seeing both may be looked on as one and the same,) we may look upon this, either generally, that his office at this time was, in part, to preach truth and avow it, and to prove himself a king by making it successful, and to confirm it by his suffering; or, more particularly, that he came into the world to bear witness to this truth, that he was a king, and so to publish that decree, Psalm ii. 6, 7, and avow it to the death. 2. He addeth, that every one that is of the truth heareth his voice; whereby he prevents an objection that might be moved against the truth of his doctrine and witness, as being so ill entertained; and cleareth, that however few do receive it, either his doctrine in general or this in particular, that he is a king, yet this doth not make void the truth thereof, seeing all who are of the truth, or born of God, and begotten by the word of truth, and who love the truth, and do not delight in lies, will hear him, and embrace his doctrine and testimony.

DOCTRINES.

1. Sufferers may expect they will have to do with politic and quick-sighted men, who will sift all their discourses, and draw out their mind concerning those things wherein they think they may have most advantage of them; for so doth Pilate, upon Christ's former discourse, urge him to speak it out, " Art thou a king then?" yet not so much (as appears from the sequel, in that he troubled him not for it) because of any fear he had of his kingdom, as to try if he would adhere to such a ridiculous-like profession, which in his judgment might expose him to mockery and contempt.

2. Truth ought to be stoutly maintained and avowed when we are called to it, how absurd soever it seem to be in itself, and how unpleasant soever it seem to be unto men; for so doth Christ here answer, " Thou sayest that I am a king," or, it is so, as thou sayest, and thou rightly gatherest it from my words—a stout confession, as to the matter of it, and yet modest, as to the manner, in that he doth it not vauntingly, but simply, " Thou sayest it," and after cleareth that he did it out of conscience and duty; to shew that courage and modesty must go together in owning of truth.

3. Christ is indeed King of his church; and where he gathereth his church there he sets up his kingdom, wherein his laws are to be obeyed and acknowledged by his subjects, and which he will protect and defend, in despite of all his enemies; for this truth is clearly held out here, for the church's comfort, " Thou sayest that I am a king."

4. By persecution the Lord giveth occasion to his servants to publish truth, and make it known to the greatest of men, who possibly otherwise would never hear so much of it as is then spoken in their own audience; for by Christ's suffering Pilate cometh to hear his doctrine, and that concerning his kingdom. And beside this also, their very sufferings invite men to inquire after their

doctrine for which they suffer, which probably otherwise they had not taken notice of, Phil. i. 12, 13.

5. Every man is sent into the world, and employed by God for some end and service, which they should much mind, and labour to be faithful in their employment and trust, upon all hazards; therefore doth Christ, as man and Mediator, look to the end for which he was born, and the cause for which he " came into the world;" which being to " bear witness unto the truth," therefore he will here avow it on all hazards, even before Pilate.

6. As it is the eminent employment put upon all professors of religion that they bear witness to the truth, or give a testimony to the worth thereof; partly, by their open avowing of it and suffering for it, when they are called to it in times of hazard; and partly, in their ordinary carriage, by publishing truth in their stations, by subjecting their walking, thoughts, and reasonings to it, and by magnifying the truth thereof, in opposition to their tentations and discouragements, which, when men neglect, they will never prove stout in suffering for it; and particularly they are bound to bear witness unto the kingdom of Christ; so Christ himself is the great Captain of these witnesses; he is the great preacher of truth, whose powerful sceptre, as a King, is the word of truth; who stands for the maintenance of truth, and particularly of this truth, that he is a King over his own church, to order the affairs thereof; and who did seal this and the whole truths of God by his blood; for he declareth this to be one of his great ends and works in the world, to " bear witness unto the truth," as a pattern to all others in their stations, and an encouragement to all who follow his pattern that they have such a champion of truth, who yet doth maintain it, though be come no more into the world in person, nor suffer any more.

7. Albeit the most part of the world do little regard Christ's doctrine, yet it is the very truth, and all the lovers and friends of truth will own it, and whoso do otherwise, bewray their own estrangement from truth, and are indeed delighters in lies; for "every one that is of the truth heareth my voice."

Ver. 38. Pilate saith unto him, What is truth? And when he had said this, he went out again unto the Jews, and saith unto them, I find in him no fault at all.

In the last branch of this part of the chapter is recorded Pilate's carriage and dealing with Christ's accusers, after his examination of him, and that in two particulars; the first whereof is, that Pilate, abruptly breaking off the conference with Christ, disdainfully inquiring what truth is, goeth forth to the Jews, and absolveth Christ, declaring that he judged him innocent. Whence learn—

1. Christ and his followers may seem ofttimes great fools in their sufferings, as suffering for things of no moment in the esteem of men, who, as the Lord ofttimes draweth the controversy for which the godly suffer to a very small hair and

point of truth, so they account it great folly for men to suffer for any divine truth; for so much doth Pilate's question, " What is truth?" import.

He propounds it, not so much for satisfaction, seeing he went out, not waiting for an answer, as testifying that he looked on truth, and particularly that which Christ now avowed, as a very trivial thing for him to hazard so much upon.

2. Men's own wit and knowledge is so great an idol to them that they can hardly endure to be reputed ignorant, or to esteem of any truth as excellent wherewith they are not acquainted; for this also occasioned Pilate's disdainful question, to which he will not stay for an answer. He could not endure to hear that truth commended, the knowledge whereof (as he might gather from Christ's last words) was wanting in him, and the Romans, who were reputed so wise a people.

3. Christ was cleared, even by his enemies and persecutors, to be innocent in his own person, that believers may be confirmed in the faith of his suffering for them, and his standing in their room, and of his fitness for that work, being a spotless sacrifice; therefore it is recorded that " he went out again unto the Jews, (who would not enter to him, ver. 29,) and saith unto them, I find in him no fault at all."

4. Men's passions and particular prejudices and resentments against persons ought not to blind their judgments, nor bias them in cognoscing upon causes; for this is commendable in Pilate, that though he had been somewhat commoved, ver. 35, and not much taken with what Christ said of truth, yet when he cometh out, he saith, " I find in him no fault at all."

5. The Lord can make use, not only of men's natural conscience, but even of their atheistical disposition and contempt of truth and religion, to bring about the good of sufferers, when he pleaseth, in the vindication of their innocency; whereby he teacheth them to eye him much who can make what use he pleaseth of everything; for it was Pilate's contempt of what Christ preached of his kingdom and truth, in the beginning of the verse, which concurreth with his natural conscience to make him think nothing of the accusation, and absolve him. So also was Paul released, Acts, xviii. 12, 16.

Ver. 39. But ye have a custom, that I should release unto you one at the passover: will ye therefore that I release unto you the King of the Jews?

40. Then cried they all again, saying, Not this man, but Barabbas. Now Barabbas was a robber.

In the next place, Pilate, having absolved Christ, endeavours also to release him, with the Jews' good liking; and taking occasion of their custom of having some one prisoner released to them at the feast of the passover, he propounds (as is marked, Matt. xxvii. 17,) Barabbas, a murderer, and Christ, to them, insinuating his desire that they should choose Christ; but they generally (both rulers, and the people persuaded by them, Matt. xxvii. 20) do refuse him and seek Barabbas to be set at liberty. As for this custom of the Jews, it appears not to have been devised by the Roman governors, for gratifying of the Jews, but a custom of their own, invented in their declining times to honour their feast of the passover, and to be some memorial of their redemption from Egypt, and of their so much desired liberty. And now, having no power themselves to release whom they would, they have recourse to the governor, who was necessitated to yield to their custom, Luke, xxiii. 17, belike to prevent tumults. And as for the nature of this custom, as it was sinful of themselves to devise anything relating to their sacred solemnities, and to dispense with the law of God, requiring that justice should be executed against malefactors, so in this particular they manage it most wickedly, in preferring a notorious malefactor to innocent Christ.

DOCTRINES.

1. Long, inveterate customs do ordinarily prevail much among people, were they never so sinful and abominable, and so much the more, as they have any specious pretext; as here, there continues a wicked custom of releasing one at the passover, gilded over with a pretext of respect to that feast, which yet indeed made it the more abominable before God, that such a course should pretend any relation to his ordinance.

2. If we look on Pilate's part in this procedure, it may teach, partly, that human policy and carnal friends and their interposing will readily do Christ and his followers little successful service in a strait; for he doth but deal for Christ in a politic way, which did not avail; partly, that whatever men have of a conscience of duty, yet that doth not avail before God, so long as they put not forth themselves to the utmost, in their stations, to see that done which is right; for albeit Pilate's endeavours serve indeed to clear Christ's innocency, and that Pilate in conscience judged him so, yet all that is not enough in him, seeing he did not employ his authority and power to rescue and defend the innocent, but doth only essay oratory and policy; and, partly, that such as would faithfully follow conscience and light had need to hold a loose grip of all other enjoyments and interests, and particularly to avoid affectation of popularity; for this was Pilate's snare, that though he judged Christ innocent, and that he ought to be delivered, yet not being willing to lose the people, he only useth insinuations and policies, "Will ye that I release unto you the King of the Jews."

3. If we look on the Jews' proceeding in this business, it may teach, partly, that men, obdured and hardened by God's judicial stroke, will neither regard civility, reason, nor common sense; light will not convince them, nor equity persuade them to what is right; for so appeared in these obstinate Jews, albeit Pilate's procedure was very effectual in its kind; for he propounds to their choice with Christ a man whom common civility might make them ashamed to own, or seek to exempt from punishment, and prefer him to Christ; he insinuates his own inclination, and that it would be a courtesy to him if they would seek Jesus to be released, "Will ye that I

release him unto you?" withal, he names him "the King of the Jews," insinuating that his death would tend to the discredit of their nation, being one bearing such a name, (which they afterward resent, chap. xix. 21,) and accusing the multitude of levity who not-long since had proclaimed him their king, and now would have him crucified; and yet all this prevails not with them, "they cried all again"—that is, in answer to him, or "again," after that former cry, that he would observe their custom in releasing some one, of which, Mark, xv. 8,—"saying, Not this man, but Barabbas. Now Barabbas was a robber;" partly, it teacheth that no persons, how vile soever, are so odious in the eyes of the enemies of God as Christ and his followers and friends; for so much did Christ find in his own person, Barabbas, a robber, being preferred to him.

4. If we look to the hand of God and Christ in all this, (without which nothing was done in this business, Acts, iv. 27, 28,) it may teach— 1. Christ would have it evidently seen by us that he suffered by the appointment of God, and that he loved to do so, in that he would not suffer any endeavour for his releasement to succeed. 2. He would also not be released, but crucified, at the passover, that he might prove himself the true passover sacrificed for us, and dying at such a time the smell of his death might spread far and near, by reason of the great concourse at this time. 3. Christ hath sanctified unto his people disappointments in the matter of deliverance, when otherwise it might seem probable, hereby also encouraging them to suffer when by these disappointments it is clear they should suffer; for he in his own person is not released, albeit the governor endeavoured it. 4. While Barabbas, a robber, is preferred to Christ, it may serve to put us in mind, that however in himself, and as to them who sought his life, he was most innocent, yet considering him in his suretyship he had more to suffer for than ever Barabbas committed, and therefore is arrested by Divine justice, while the other is permitted to escape; and this should invite every one who claimeth interest in his death to lay to heart his share in those provocations and crimes which were then charged upon Christ. 5. Christ hath sanctified unto the godly their being worse esteemed of in the world than the worst of men, and their being held unworthy to live on the earth, where many wicked men are tolerated, (see 1 Cor. iv. 9—13; Acts, xxii. 22,) and that even by corrupt churchmen; for they preferred Barabbas, a robber, to himself.

CHAPTER XIX.

IN this chapter John prosecutes the narration of the rest of Christ's sufferings before Pilate, and in the place where he was crucified, together with his death and burial. It may be taken up in three parts. In the first part is recorded some further sufferings of Christ, and Pilate further dealing with him, and about him with the Jews, before he proceed to the sentence of death, to ver. 13; and namely, that Pilate, having scourged and otherwise abused Christ, ver. 1—3, doth yet declare him innocent before the Jews, and labours to move them to pity and to cease their further rage by looking upon him in such a case, ver. 4, 5; but this not prevailing with them, and Pilate yet asserting his innocency, and refusing to hearken to them, ver. 6, they bring in a new accusation of blasphemy against Christ, ver. 7, which, together with a new conference with Christ upon that subject, and the matter of his power over Christ, ver. 8—11, makes him yet more desirous to release him, till they bring an accusation against himself as no friend to Cæsar in this business, ver. 12.

In the second part of the chapter is contained the sentence of death pronounced against Christ, with the answerable execution, and what occurred till he gave up the ghost, to ver. 31, wherein these particulars are recorded:—1. That Pilate, being terrified with their accusation, after some formalities in procedure, (whereby he thought to transfer the guilt upon them,) passeth sentence that he should be crucified, ver. 13—16. 2. The execution of this sentence, with an account who they were that suffered with him, ver. 16—18. 3. The title put upon his cross, with some debates about it, ver. 19—22. 4. His sufferings from the soldiers, being now upon the cross, and that according to the scriptures, ver. 23, 24. 5. His company who stayed beside the cross, and his care of his mother, being then present, ver. 25—27. His thirst immediately before his death, and their giving him vinegar to drink, according to the scriptures, ver. 28, 29. 7. His testament and death, ver. 30.

In the third part of the chapter some consequents following upon his death are recorded; and namely—1. A confirmation of this truth, that he was really dead, wherein is recorded the Jews' desires to Pilate that the death of those who suffered might be hastened by the breaking of their legs, that so they might be removed, because of their solemnity, ver. 31, and that the soldiers did execute this upon the other two, ver. 32; but finding Christ already dead, they do not break his legs, ver. 33, but make his death sure by a new wound, ver. 34, the certainty whereof John confirms as being an eye-witness, ver. 35; and doth clear these passages by comparing them with the scriptures, ver. 36, 37. 2. His honourable burial by Joseph, who begged his body of Pilate, ver. 38, and Nicodemus, who provided ointment and spices, ver. 39, and both together do decently bury him in a new grave, ver. 40—42.

Ver. 1. Then Pilate therefore took Jesus, and scourged him.

2. And the soldiers platted a crown of thorns, and put it on his head, and they put on him a purple robe.

3. And said, Hail, King of the Jews! And they smote him with their hands.

The first part of this chapter may be summed up in these four branches: the first whereof (in these verses) contains Pilate's cruel usage of Christ, by scourging of him, ver. 1, by causing to crown him with thorns, and clothe him with purple, ver. 2, hereby punishing his affecting of a ridiculous kingdom, as he supposed, and affronting him with salutations as a mock king, and by injurious smiting, ver. 3. If we look on Pilate's scope in all this, it was mainly to gratify the Jews by some lesser punishment, and to induce them to pity Christ thus grievously afflicted for their pleasure, as will appear in the following purpose; hence it is subjoined to the preceding purpose with a "therefore," ver. 1, intimating that since Pilate's design succeeded not, to get him released instead of Barabbas, he essayed this as another mean, thinking to spare his life by scourging of him; and albeit some of the other evangelists mention this scourging after his condemnation, yet John doth set it down in its own order, which they only recapitulate as a thing done before that. But if we look upon this usage in itself it was a part of Christ's suffering for us, both painful and loading him with contempt and ignominy. Whence learn—

1. Great men in God's account are guilty of the faults of their inferiors when they connive at them, and do not reprove and repress them, much more when they command and enjoin them; therefore it is said, "Pilate took Jesus, and scourged him," because the soldiers did it (as it is ver. 2, and in the rest of the evangelists) at his command, and he, being present, (as is implied ver. 4,) gave way to all their cruelty in it. (See 2 Sam. xii. 9.)

2. As this scourging and painful crowning of Christ doth not warrant any to think basely of him, as if he were without any desirable form or beauty, (as it is, Isaiah, liii. 2,) but doth rather point him out to his people as white and ruddy, white in his innocency, and ruddy in his sufferings, and therefore should be accounted the chief among ten thousand, Cant. v. 10, and fairer than the children of men, Psalm xlv. 2, so in particular, his scourging (which was a reproachful usage of any ingenuous and free man, Acts, xvi. 37; xxii. 25, and was no doubt painful, and so much the more painful and violent, as Pilate thereby intended to move the Jews to pity) may point out—1. The peace of rebel man was not to be purchased at an easy rate, nor could his wounds be healed but by sharp stripes and sore wounds on his Surety; for so much did his scourging for our sakes point out; Isaiah, liii. 5; 1 Peter, ii. 24. 2. Sin in fallen man hath universally spread itself through the whole man; so that, as no faculty of the soul, so no member of the body is free of it. So much may be gathered from this, that all the parts of Christ's body (many whereof smarted in this scourging, and the rest by other means) behoved to suffer for expiating thereof. 3. Christ in his own person hath sanctified that method of proceeding with his followers, that every one of them who are received by the Father be also scourged by outward trials and other exercises; for he, their Head and Lord, was "scourged."

3. His being crowned with thorns, beside what may be gathered from it with the following particulars, serveth to teach—1. That he is the truth and substance of that type of the ram caught in

a thicket by the horns, or head, who was offered up instead of Isaac, Gen. xxii. 13, as he is instead of his people. 2. That his sufferings, however sharp, are indeed his crown and his glory, and he accounted so of them that we might learn to glory in his cross, Gal. vi. 14. 3. That his kingdom on earth is but contemptible in outward appearance, and managed and promoved by much thorny trouble. (See Matt. xx. 21, 22.) 4. Thorns being a curse following upon man's sin, Gen. iii. 18, his bearing thereof in a crown would teach, that by his sufferings he turneth all the curses of his people into crowns and blessings. 5. That as the rose groweth out of the thorn, so out of this thorny crown hath sprung unto him a crown of glory and honour, Heb. ii. 9, and many crowns, Rev. xix. 12, and crowns unto his followers also, Rev. ii. 10; 2 Tim. iv. 8.

4. This thorny crown, being conjoined with the " purple robe," (used only by kings and great men,) together also with the sceptre of a reed mentioned by the rest, and their saluting him as "King of the Jews," all which was done in derision and contempt of his affected royalty, as they alleged; and in testimony that they did deride him, they in the meantime smite him with their hands;— all these, I say, being conjoined together, may teach—1. The kingdom of Christ being spiritual is accounted but folly and matter of derision to the world; for so much doth their carriage towards him as a king teach. 2. Christ in his person hath sanctified unto his people their being made spectacles and a matter of derision to the world, 1 Cor. iv. 9, 13; Psalm cxxiii. 4; for he, in his own person, did endure this bitter scorn. 3. Christ, by suffering for alleged affecting of royalty and a kingdom, hath expiated the high presumption of his people in affecting to be like God, Genesis, iii. 5. 4. His enduring of this mockage [mockery] for his people points out what contempt and everlasting confusion abides them who are not in him; for if this be done in the green tree, what shall be done in the dry?

Ver. 4. Pilate therefore went forth again, and saith unto them, Behold, I bring him forth to you, that ye may know that I find no fault in him.

5. Then came Jesus forth, wearing the crown of thorns, and the purple robe. And Pilate saith unto them, Behold the man!

In the second branch of this part of the chapter is recorded what was Pilate's scope in all this— to wit, not that he might revenge or punish any real fault in Christ, but that having gratified them thus far, by afflicting the innocent lest they should be accounted unjust in accusing him, they would now in pity be content, and crave no more to be done to him; for which end, having thus dealt with Christ in the judgment hall, he goeth forth again (after the former time, chap. xviii. 28, 29,) to the Jews, who stayed without, declaring how he had found Christ innocent and therefore could not condemn him, but would present him to them, to see if they would be persuaded to let him go; and withal he would let them see what he had done to him, to gratify them and to move them to pity. And accordingly he is brought forth in that sad posture, and presented as an object of pity and compassion. Whence learn—

1. The tenderness of men's conscience cannot be known or tried so much by their propounding of a good end as by their choosing of cleanly and warrantable means for attaining their end; for Pilate's end was good in seeking to have Christ delivered, but he chose wrong means, in that he dealt so cruelly with the innocent, and cared not to send him away with ignominy and great affliction, so he got him delivered.

2. It is no new trial for innocents to meet with many affronts and injuries in their trials, if it were but to gratify their accusers and salve their credit; for Christ is here found innocent, and yet he must not come off, nor be brought out to be delivered by them, but when he is all pained and bloody, and wearing " the crown of thorns, and the purple robe," lest they should be rubbed upon as accusing him unjustly.

3. Christ in his sufferings was innocent of any personal crime, even in the consciences of his persecutors, whereby the Lord made it clear that his sufferings were for others; for saith Pilate, not only here, but often, " I find no fault in him;" and he brought him forth that they might know this, evidencing, by bringing him forth, that he could not condemn him, and that he desired they would rest satisfied with what he had done.

4. Whatever men may have of a natural conscience, yet well-doing is above the power thereof; it will only tend to further their own condemnation; for Pilate acquits him, " I find no fault in him," and yet he abuseth him, and bringeth him out, wearing " the crown of thorns, and purple robe," &c.

5. Carnal policy in God's ways will never do any good, but rather tend to greater trouble; for Pilate's policy in scourging and abusing of Christ, and bringing him out with " the crown of thorns, and purple robe," is so far from delivering him, that it augments his trouble, and he is both scourged and crucified, whereas he might otherwise have been crucified only.

6. It is an evidence of monstrous cruelty in men, when not only the innocency of sufferers, but their bitter sufferings, though innocent, will not mollify their hearts and assuage their fury; for Pilate propounds Christ, thus abused, as an object pleading for pity, " Behold the man!" And whatever use they made of this sight, yet we should behold the Son of God in that his deep exinanition, not carnally to pity him, but, in his example and lot, to learn condescendence and stooping, and obedience and subjection to the will of God, Phil. xxv. 6—8; Matt. xxvi. 39, to study the desert of sin, that we may abhor it, and to read his love towards his people, Rom. v. 8.

Ver. 6. When the chief priests therefore and officers saw him, they cried out, saying, Crucify him, crucify him. Pilate saith unto them, Take ye him, and crucify him : for I find no fault in him.

7. The Jews answered him, We have a law, and by our law he ought to die, because he made himself the Son of God.

In the third branch of this part of the chapter is recorded the success and fruit of this policy of Pilate—to wit, that this sight of Christ did not move them to pity, but awaked their cruelty, and made them importunately to cry out that he might be put to death; and that, Pilate declining to be their butcher in executing of an innocent man, they bring a new accusation against Christ, that he was a blasphemer, and therefore by their law ought to be put to death, wherein, finding Pilate not much moved with the accusation concerning his kingdom, as seeing little hazard to the state in tolerating Christ, they bring in this accusation from their law, wherein he behoved to credit them, as not being able to judge it of himself. Whence learn—

1. Persecutors will not be satisfied with any measure of affliction so long as Christ, or his truth or cause, have any life in them; for " when the chief priests and officers saw him, they cried out, saying, Crucify him, crucify him," as thirsting for his death, though he was already sore afflicted; and what they cannot obtain with reason, they will endeavour to prevail in it by impudent importunity and tumultuous outcries.

2. Christ submitted to be denied all pity in his sufferings, and to have men's face hid from him, not only that he might sanctify such a lot to his followers, but that they might find bowels of pity under their troubles, in so far as shall be for their good, Jer. xv. 11; xxxi. 20; for so much may be gathered from this part of his suffering, that he found no compassion, but was cruelly pursued.

3. Divine justice pursuing sin could not be satisfied but only by the death of the Surety of sinners, nor could that burning fire be quenched but by his blood; for there was an overruling hand of God craving for complete satisfaction to justice in his being crucified.

4. A natural conscience may cleave long to truth and duty against much opposition, and yet at last quit it; for so much appears in Pilate, who, notwithstanding all this vehemency, yet stands by his point : " Take ye him, (saith he,) and crucify him (of the meaning whereof, see chap. xviii. 31): for I find no fault in him." He declines for their pleasure to crucify an innocent man, and will rather let them do it than put his hand to it. Only it is to be marked, that however this permission points out chiefly a sad reflection on their cruelty and injustice, yet it insinuates also that his chief scope was to be rid of this process, since he could not get his will; but that succeeds not, since he employed not his power to rescue the innocent. And indeed, when men have any light or conscience in trying times and cases, they will not get leave to lurk, but must either closely follow their light, and act by it in their stations, or else they will be given up to go over the belly of light and act against it, as Pilate did.

5. Persecutors are incessant and endless in their machinations, plots, and calumnies against Christ and his followers; and when one plot or accusation miscarrieth they will be sure to find another, for so do they here; when the former challenge, that he made himself a king, avails not, they bring another, and do not claim to any power upon Pilate's concession, but do take upon them only to point out the law.

6. Where religion keeps not the first place, it is an argument of no zeal, whatever men do pretend; for in this they bewray their unsoundness, that this accusation of blasphemy cometh in the second place, after that of his being an enemy to Cæsar, which they first propounded, as was cleared on chap. xviii. 33.

7. Such as are indeed blasphemers, and do arrogate to themselves what is proper to God only, by the law of God they ought to be put to death; for it was indeed agreeable to the law, and may be taken in as a branch of that law against blasphemy, Lev. xxiv. 16, that he ought to die who maketh himself the Son of God. But Christ was not guilty, who did not make himself, but was indeed the Son of God.

8. It is no strange thing to see corrupt and bloody men cry down most necessary and saving truths as blasphemous errors, and to abuse and misapply scriptures for that end, and to deceive others; for they reckon that saving truth of Christ's godhead to be blasphemy, and wrest the scriptures to draw Pilate to be of their mind : " We have a law, and by our law he ought to die," &c.

Ver. 8. When Pilate therefore heard that saying, he was the more afraid;

9. And went again into the judgment hall, and saith unto Jesus, Whence art thou? But Jesus gave him no answer.

In the last branch of this part of the chapter we have recorded some consequents and effects following upon this last accusation, before Pilate is persuaded to condemn him. And in the first place (in these verses) is declared, that Pilate, hearing this, is so far from condescending to their desire that he is the more afraid, hearing tell of the divinity of him whom he judged to be innocent, and of whose fame he, no doubt, heard much, ver. 8; and that, studying to inform himself concerning this matter, by conference with Christ himself, he gets no answer, ver. 9. Whence learn—

1. It is evident to right discerners that all the designs and well-contrived plots of persecutors would little avail, but rather turn to their prejudice and disappointment, if the Lord see it fit to exempt his people from trial; for albeit God would not have Christ delivered, yet this new accusation doth not make Pilate more forward to persecute Christ, but " more afraid" to meddle with him. (See Prov. xxi. 30.)

2. Such as do but halt in following their duty will have more fear and trouble than even sufferers who walk straightly; for it is insinuated that Pilate, who did not closely follow his light, had fear before, and now " he was more afraid"

upon this information, as having walked upon so unsafe grounds.

3. Serious thoughts of a Deity will strike terror even in a natural heart and conscience, especially when they are following a course which their own conscience cannot approve; for when he heard that saying of his making himself the Son of God, " he was the more afraid," considering what he had done to him, and that contrary to his light. And albeit it be not sufficient that men have a fear or horror only upon the thoughts of a godhead, unless it be seasoned with love, yet they come far short of Pilate who have not so much.

4. Impartial observers, and even the natural consciences of men, might have had strong apprehensions of the divinity of Christ, notwithstanding the abject-like condition of his person; for albeit Christ was in the form of a servant, and now in a low condition before Pilate, yet " when he heard that saying, he was the more afraid," as suspecting it might be true that he was the Son of God. And this he might conjecture, not so much because pagans did fancy that their idol-gods did descend in human shape, Acts, xiv. 11, as that his mind was illuminated to consider what they said, and compare it with the fame that went of Christ's miracles.

5. Such as have any small beam of light concerning Christ ought to help and increase it by inquiry and search; for so doth Pilate inquire, " Whence art thou?" or, what is thy original and parentage?

6. The best way to know Christ is to learn it from himself, who only can reveal himself, and declare what he is; for so much may be gathered from Pilate's practice, though he saw not so far into it himself: he " went again into the judgment hall, and saith unto Jesus, Whence art thou?"

7. That Jesus gave him no answer, may hold ont—1. On Christ's part, he stood not there now to defend himself or impede his sufferings, and therefore he will not discover that which might deter him, so willing was he to pay that ransom for his people. 2. For believers' cause, he was content to answer many questions and accusations with silence, that he might purchase unto them the answer of a good conscience, and liberty and boldness to speak unto God. 3. On Pilate's part, it may not only be conceived that Pilate was incapable of such a mystery, but further—1. His seeking of light in this particular flowed not from love, and such seeking hath no promise to come speed. 2. He had slighted truth when it had been revealed to him before, chap. xviii. 38, and such as do so are justly deprived of further information. 3. By this refusal of an answer Christ would discover some naughtiness in his heart, as appeareth from the following verse. And this is Christ's usual way with those that converse with him, to try and cause them discover what is in their bosom; and he doth this very often by suspending the satisfaction of their desires, at least for a time.

Ver. 10. Then saith Pilate unto him, Speakest thou not unto me? knowest thou not that I have power to crucify thee, and have power to release thee?

11. Jesus answered, Thou couldest have no power at all against me, except it were given thee from above: therefore he that delivered me unto thee hath the greater sin.

In the next place, Pilate being offended at Christ's silence, and that, as he judged, he considered not whom he misregarded, and that he had power to dispose of him at his pleasure, Christ, out of zeal to his Father's honour, and in opposition to Pilate's pride, answers—1. Concerning his power, that he had no power against him unless it were given him of God; whereby we are to understand, in general, that he had no absolute power or authority (as no man else) over him or any other, but he was subordinate to God in it, from whom it was given. Hence, in particular, it followeth, partly, that he had no right or authority over him who was an innocent, to do him wrong, since no such authority was given him from above; nor had he power to judge of him or his cause, who was God also, without especial dispensation of God, but he might have escaped their hands, as ofttimes formerly he had done; and partly, that however, notwithstanding he had no right, he would be at it, to act against him, yet it was not in his power to execute any such purpose without the permission of God; and so, in sum, Christ refutes his proud boasting of his power, by letting him see that there was a power above him, to whom his power and authority was subordinate and subject, that it was by a particular dispensation he had any power over him, and that he had no right to do wrong as he pleased to any, (though he boasted of it,) nor could he execute any such purpose without the permission of God. 2. Christ answers concerning Judas and the Jews who had delivered him into his hands, and declareth that however he should sin in employing his power to crucify him, yet they had greater sin who put him in his power, and had treacherously betrayed and given him up. This is subjoined to the former, by way of inference and conclusion, " Therefore he hath the greater sin," and it concludes, not only thus, upon Pilate's proud boast, that the greater his power was, as he alleged, ver. 10, the greater was their sin who put him under the hazard of such a power; but more clearly, upon Christ's former speech, thus: if his power was of God, they sinned the more who would have him abuse that power by crucifying of him, and especially they who knew more from the scriptures of the subordination of human powers to God, and what Christ was, than Pilate did.

DOCTRINES.

1. Superficial tinctures of good in unrenewed men will soon appear what they are, if they get a tentation; for albeit Pilate had even now been afraid of what he had heard spoken of Christ, ver. 8, yet now, when he is irritated with his silence, he appears in his own colours, " Speakest thou not unto me?" &c.

2. Men's pride and conceit of their own greatness and power, if they be in any authority, will

readily cause them miscarry upon the least appearance of provocation; for this did mislead Pilate here, " Speakest thou not unto me? Knowest thou not that I have power?" &c.

3. It is the great sin and snare of men in power that they think they may employ their power as they please, and may dispose of those who are under them according to their own humour and will, without controlment or opposition; for this was Pilate's reckoning here. Albeit in his conscience he had absolved Christ as innocent, and therefore would have had him released as one whom he might not wrong, yet when his pride is aloft, he thinks he may do what he pleaseth, " Knowest thou not that I have power to crucify thee, and have power to release thee?"

4. Men in their proud fits care not what snare they run upon, nor what inconvenience they follow, so their pride get a vent, and they get leave to insult and boast; for Pilate, in this proud boasting, doth not consider nor regard that his own confession, that he " had power to release Christ," did condemn him if he did not release him, but he must speak out his proud thoughts, whatever be the consequents.

5. Proud and insolent boasting of men will not find Christ silent, but whatever else it be that he seem to take no notice of, he will be sure to appear against pride, especially when it reflects upon God, and the privileges and protection his suffering people enjoy in him; for Christ, who even now would not answer anything, doth in this case answer, and is not silent.

6. Whatever men on earth boast of their power and authority, yet in their highest state they are subordinate and subject to God, and must be accountable to him and are overruled by him; for so much is held out here, " Thou couldest have no power at all, except it were given thee from above."

7. As no man can have any lawful authority but what is warranted by God, so no authority or power which men have doth warrant them to do anything against innocent men or justice; nor should they reckon that they can do anything but what they may warrantably and lawfully do; for so much also is imported in this: Men have no power, (or authority, or right,) except what is given from above, and so as they may not usurp power, so they may not employ it as they please, (Micah, ii. 1,) but as God approveth.

8. That Christ was under the power of any man, how eminent soever, did flow from the peculiar dispensation of God, who ordered it to be so for the redemption of his people, and not because he was obnoxious to their power, being the true God, and innocent in his own person as man; for this holds true of him in a peculiar way, " Thou couldest have no power at all against me, except it were given thee from above."

9. When Christ or his followers are in the hands of men they should so look on themselves in their hands, as being first and chiefly in the hand of God, without whose permission they can neither conclude nor execute anything; but either he will overrule and disappoint them, or what they do his people ought to see his hand in it; for so much further may be gathered from this, for the comfort of believers, that however great men, ofttimes, will not respect what is right or wrong, yet it may still be said, " Thou couldest have no power at all against me, except it were given thee from above."

10. Albeit all be guilty of sin who have hand in persecuting of Christ, yet the same sin may be more heinous in one than another, and is capable of many aggravations, considering the persons who act it, and other circumstances; for here, Judas and the Jews have the greater sin; albeit Pilate had sin in it, yet they had greater sin, and their sin was the more odious, considering who they were, and what they did.

11. Such as treacherously betray Christ and his followers, and do instigate civil powers against them, may be more guilty, in God's account, than they who deal with open violence against them; for this was a part of the aggravation of their sin, that they betrayed and gave him up to the civil power: " He (Judas, or the Jews, who are spoken of indefinitely, and in the singular number) that delivered me unto thee hath the greater sin."

12. It is a very great aggravation of the sin of persecutors when they will not content themselves to satisfy their rage by violence upon any terms, but will have men's authority, which is the ordinance of God, prostituted and abused to satisfy their cruelty, and will have oppression and persecution acted under the specious pretext of justice; " therefore (because thou hast no power, except it be given thee) he that delivered me unto thee, (that thou mayest abuse that power in crucifying me,) hath the greater sin."

13. As the greatest height of impiety is readily to be found within the visible church, so all the aggravations of sin are yet further heightened when it is committed by such, and by men who, having knowledge of what is right, do yet out of malice go wrong, and seek to draw others with them; for " therefore (also) he that delivered me unto thee hath the greater sin," because they were members of the visible church, and knew better whence men have their authority, and how far Christ was above his reach, (except by particular dispensation,) than Pilate did; and yet out of malice they persecuted him, and stirred up Pilate against him.

Ver. 12. And from thenceforth Pilate sought to release him: but the Jews cried out, saying, If thou let this man go, thou art not Cæsar's friend: whosoever maketh himself a king speaketh against Cæsar.

In the last place, Pilate, retaining still some of that former impression of fear, ver. 8, and being now calmed and further instructed by Christ's answer to his proud boasting, endeavours yet more to have Christ released, but is assaulted and opposed by the Jews, who, renewing their former challenge concerning Christ's kingdom, do accuse Pilate of treason against Cæsar's authority; and this did at last crush all his resolutions, as the sequel cleareth.

DOCTRINES.

1. Men's moral principles and natural conscience may lead them for a long time to cleave to

what is good, notwithstanding any opposition or irritations from without, or stirrings of corruption from within; for albeit Pilate, in this endeavour, had been not only often opposed by the Jews before, but his corruption had been stirred by Christ's carriage towards him, yet he overcometh all that, and " from thenceforth sought to release him," though the means he essayed be not expressed.

2. Natural men's moral principles will lead them to own Christ but very ineffectually, and so as they may wrong no other important interest; for albeit he yet stood for Christ's releasement, yet he who boasted of his power to release Christ at his pleasure, ver. 10, will not employ his power for that end, but only " sought to release him," if it might be with their good liking.

3. Such as befriend Christ, especially if they be but natural men, will not be so instant but his enemies will be as stubborn, and with unwearied obstinacy will prosecute their malicious designs till they be satisfied; for all these often renewed endeavours of Pilate do not outweary the Jews, but they " cried out," &c.

4. Christ's enemies are so malicious and cruel that they prefer his ruin to all interests and considerations whatsoever; for so much doth this renewed challenge hold out, " If thou let this man go, thou art not Cæsar's friend," &c. They regard not to be accounted negligent and careless in matters of their own law, but do pass from their accusation of blasphemy, ver. 7, and return to that of his kingdom, if so be it will carry their point better; and they appear mighty zealous for Cæsar, and enraged that his deputy did not regard his interest more, (though indeed they had no great liking to him,) and all that they may get Christ crucified, and Pilate excited to it.

5. It is no strange thing to see Christ and his followers persecuted as enemies unto authority, though unjustly; for he is not to be let go upon this account, " If thou let this man go, thou art not Cæsar's friend; for whosoever maketh himself a king speaketh against Cæsar."

6. Such is the malice of Christ's enemies that they do not only pursue himself and his followers, but they do hate and malign and (as they have opportunity) accuse all those who are not so cruel as themselves, but would shew any favour to him or his people; for so do they here accuse Pilate, " If thou let this man go, thou art not Cæsar's friend."

Ver. 13. When Pilate therefore heard that saying, he brought Jesus forth, and sat down in the judgment seat in a place that is called the Pavement, but in the Hebrew, Gabbatha.

14. And it was the preparation of the passover, and about the sixth hour: and he saith unto the Jews, Behold your King!

15. But they cried out, Away with him, away with him, crucify him. Pilate saith unto them, Shall I crucify your King? The chief priests answered, We have no king but Cæsar.

16. Then delivered he him therefore unto them to be crucified.——

Followeth the second part of the chapter, the first branch whereof (in these verses) contains the sentence passed by Pilate against Christ; wherein we have to consider—1. What it was that drew Pilate, after so much reluctancy and opposition, to condescend at last unto it—to wit, that being affrighted with that accusation against himself, ver. 12, he dare stand it out no longer, but brings forth Christ to the open view, and sits down as judge to cognosce upon [take cognizance of] the cause, in the judgment seat—a place getting its name from its being paved, and that somewhat high above the place where spectators were, as the Hebrew or Syriac name signifieth, ver. 13. 2. The time is marked wherein Pilate is persuaded to proceed in the process, ver. 14. In general, it is recorded that it was on the day of the preparation, wherein the Jews were to eat the passover, as is cleared on John, xiii. 2; and in particular, that it was about " the sixth hour" of the day; yet, Mark, xv. 25, it is called " the third hour" when they crucified him, and, Matt. xxvii. 45, it was " the sixth hour" when the darkness came on, after he was crucified; for understanding and reconciling whereof it is to be remembered that the Jews did reckon twelve hours in every day, from sun-rising to sun-setting, John, xi. 9; and accordingly, so many also in the night. And albeit these hours were, for the most part, unequal, the hours of the day being shortened in winter and lengthened in summer, and contrariwise those of the night, yet at the time of Christ's passion (being near or at the equinox) they were equal, the sun rising about six o'clock, according to our account. Again, as they divided the hours of the night in four watches, reckoning three hours to a watch, (of which see Lam. ii. 19; Luke, xii. 38; Exod. xiv. 24; Matt. xiv. 25,) so they also divided the hours of the day in four quadrants, or great hours, for ordering the time of their sacrifices, and ordinary prayer, which they went about thrice a day, Psa. lv. 17; Dan. vi. 10. The first was called " the third hour," answering to our ninth, Matt. xx. 3, and was the time of morning-prayer and sacrifice in the temple; the second was called " the sixth hour, Matt. xx. 5, answering to our twelfth; and this also was an hour of prayer, Psa. lv. 17; Acts, x. 9; the third was called " the ninth hour," Matt. xx. 5, answering to our three, afternoon, and this was the time of evening-prayer and sacrifice, Acts, iii. 1; x. 3; and the last, answering to our sixth at night, was called the twelfth, being the time of their retirement from labour and beginning of the first night-watch, and so they who wrought but one hour are said to be hired at the eleventh hour, Matt. xx. 6, 12. Now these differences among the evangelists may easily be reconciled thus: that the time of his crucifying was when the third (or ninth) hour was passed; and the time intervening betwixt that and the sixth (or twelfth) hour was begun, or possibly much of it spent; and that this time intervening is sometimes named from the third hour already passed, and sometimes from the sixth or twelfth current, which is the cause of the seeming difference; so Christ was condemned and nailed to the cross some time after the ninth hour, according to our account, and before the twelfth, after which the darkness followed at or about the sixth hour, or some short time after it. The difference also may be reconciled by taking in the Roman way of reckoning the hours with that of the Jews. They reckoned (as we do) from midnight to midday, and again from midday to midnight, assigning to each of them twelve equal hours. And so we may conceive that John reckons the time of Pilate's sitting down in the judgment seat to sentence Christ, according to the Roman account, that it was about our six in the morning, and the Jewish first hour of the day, and that Matthew and Mark reckon the time after the manner of the Jews. And as it needs not seem strange that John, speaking of the action of a Roman, doth design the time thereof according to the Roman account, so this reckoning leaveth sufficient time for all that is related by any of the evangelists to have been done betwixt Pilate's sitting down in the judgment seat and their crucifying of Christ. 3. We have to consider some previous proceedings of Pilate, after he is set in judgment, before he gives out the sentence, ver. 14, 15, wherein he presents Christ to the Jews as their King, and they refusing him, and crying out that he should be crucified, he again urgeth how unmeet it was they should desire him to crucify their King; but they rejecting him, and acknowledging Cæsar only, he proceeds to judgment. In all which we are to conceive, that Pilate, being resolved not to incur Cæsar's displeasure, wherewith they threatened him, is but seeking some shift to satisfy or quiet his own conscience; and therefore he will offer him unto them as their King, being willing to deliver him, if they will accept of him; but seeing they, who were more concerned than he, do reject him, he thinks he is not bound to insist any longer. To which, other considerations, blindfolding him, are to be added, as they are marked by the rest—namely, that he washed his hands in testimony of his innocency, and laid his blood upon them, and they took it on; and that he thought he could do no good by struggling, but rather occasion a tumult, Matt. xxvii. 24, and therefore (as natural men will not hazard on a duty unless they see some probability of success, far less will they hazard where difficulties occur) he thinks it better to let alone than to lose the people, and run the hazard of Cæsar's displeasure. 4. Unto all this the sentence itself is subjoined, ver. 16, that he delivered him to them to be crucified, or gave out sentence, and delivered him over that it might be executed. He delivered him to them, or to the Jews, not that they were the executioners, for the soldiers acted that part, but in all this he gratified them, and he committed it to them, to oversee and satisfy themselves in the execution, as it appeareth that they went along with the soldiers to see that nothing was omitted.

From this purpose, thus cleared, learn—1. Men who seem to act for Christ, and yet entertain an idol, may expect that it will be touched, ere all be done, to try whether they respect Christ or it most; for Pilate meets with a saying that touched the very idol of his interest and credit with Cæsar.

2. Men are never throughly tried till their duty come in competition with their idol and interest, and they who stand out very stoutly before may then succumb and give over, as all men who want saving grace will do; for " when Pilate therefore heard that saying, he brought Jesus forth, and sat down in the judgment seat," &c. He could stand it out no longer, when avowing of Christ came in competition with Cæsar's favour; so that they lay snares for themselves who entertain idols.

3. Albeit natural men may ofttimes wish well to Christ and his interest, yet they will not part with anything for him if the matter be in their choice; and particularly, they will not incur the displeasure of great ones for his sake; for albeit he desired Christ might be released, yet he will sit down in the judgment seat, and condemn Christ, before he hazard the loss of Cæsar's favour and what might follow upon that. Natural men may indeed be involved in the common calamities of a war with others in defence of religion, and may lie under the necessity of losing much that way, but they will not freely undergo anything in a way of suffering of personal and particular persecution.

4. Albeit the hazard of men's interests and idols withdraw them from duty to Christ, as thinking thereby to preserve them, yet ordinarily such projects succeed not, but whatever it be that tempts men to forsake and relinquish their duty to Christ, it doth justly disappoint and ruin them; for the keeping of Cæsar's favour, and to please the Jews also, Mark, xv. 15, made Pilate condemn Christ, and yet, as histories record, he lost that people's affections, and they by their complaints made him to lose Cæsar's favour, so that he cut off himself.

5. Malicious enemies of Christ are most obstinate in their pursuit and violence against him, and this is to be expected from them; therefore is the time marked, that " it was the preparation of the passover, and about the sixth hour," to point out the Jews' obstinacy, that albeit they had been at it all night, and now the day of their preparation is come, yet they endure all this, and lay aside all other things till they be satisfied in this.

6. Christ stooped to be kept long in pain and bonds, and to have his sufferings lengthened by all the endeavours that were used for his release, that so he might expiate our guilt, which deserveth indeed eternal sufferings if it were laid on us; that he might, by his example, warn us to prepare for trials of long continuance, and by his going before us sanctify them unto us; that he might be a meet High Priest for them who are ready to weary and sink under the continuance of their trials; and that he might sanctify unto his people the lengthening of their afflictions by any means used for their deliverance; for these causes also it is marked that after all his toil in the preceding night he is kept in bonds, wearied and pained with scourging, crowning with thorns, and smiting, till " the sixth hour," and that before he come to the extremity of his suffering.

7. The consciences, even of natural men, after they have begun to point out duty, will not soon be satisfied nor silenced, no, not when they meet with strong tentations; for albeit Pilate be so dashed with the fear of Cæsar that he sits down on the judgment seat, yet his conscience will not let him proceed to sentence till he follows such a course as he thinks may satisfy it, as hath been cleared; so that men who have made defection from a good course have certainly more disquiet from their consciences than every one knoweth. And if conscience as a counsellor and informer be so difficult to satisfy, it will be much more so when it turns a tormentor and executioner.

8. When men are once broken, and resolved to go contrary to conscience, they will find strange shifts, and devise principles of light to heal the wound of conscience, and that they may not seem to cross it; for so much do Pilate's propositions to them point at, as hath been explained. It is dangerous when men are once engaged in their wicked resolutions, for then their wits are set on work, not to find out what is right, but what may make their way plausible to themselves or others, and may stop the mouth of conscience.

9. It is but a poor shift for men to think to satisfy their consciences with their good wishes and weak endeavours about their duty, when yet they suffer themselves to be carried away with the importunity of others, and do not effectually set about what is right; for herein Pilate satisfieth himself that he offers their King to them, " Behold your King!" and evidenceth an averseness from proceeding, " Shall I crucify your King?" but is crossed with their importunity, " Away with him," &c.

10. It will not satisfy conscience that men have others more concerned and knowing than themselves, (upon whom they think they may lay the blame of any evil,) so long as they suffer anything to be done contrary to their trust and power; for this is another shift of Pilate, that since the Jews, who were more concerned in their king, and understood these things better than he, will have Christ crucified, he thinks they should bear the blame. But it was his duty to have employed his authority and power to hinder injustice.

11. When men begin to faint in their duty, and to seek shifts, it is righteous with God they find many, and that Satan and his instruments be let out to importune them, till they be quite broken in all their resolutions; for Pilate, being in this temper, justly meets with their importunate cries, " Away with him, away with him, crucify him; we have no king but Cæsar," to drive him on into the snare.

12. It is the great and crying sin of the visible church that they contemn and neglect the offer of salvation and the messengers thereof; and particularly that they reject Christ from reigning over them; for this was the great sin of the Jews here, that they cried " Away with him, away with him, crucify him," and in contempt of him profess, " we have no king but Cæsar." And this sin is repeated by all those in the visible church who reject and despise his offer of himself in the gospel, and who crucify him afresh unto themselves, Heb. vi. 6.

13. Malicious persecutors will not be mollified in their rage by any consideration; nor will their political interests or discontents (though otherwise weighty in their eyes) engage them to Christ or his cause, but they will rather sacrifice all their interests and digest all their other discontents than not have Christ crucified; for albeit they were exceedingly averse from Cæsar's power over them, and did affect liberty and a king of their own, yet that they may get Christ crucified they digest all this, and profess, " we have no king but Cæsar." And albeit their being under the foreign power of Cæsar was a clear proof that Shiloh, or the Messiah, was come, yet they are so violent as they regard not that.

14. No less was sufficient to satisfy Divine justice for the sins of the elect than the death of their Surety; and Christ having undertaken this work, justice did pursue him to the death; therefore was it so overruled, that they cried, " crucify him," and accordingly he is sentenced and delivered to be crucified, after all his former sufferings.

15. Christ's followers should resolve, after they have suffered much, to suffer yet more; and they should not decline to have all their other sufferings crowned with a violent death at last, if called to it; for so much also doth the example of Christ their Head teach them.

16. When a man's conscience, who seemed to befriend Christ, is once lulled asleep, he will be ready to run as great a length in cruelty as any other; and he who hath once made shipwreck of any kind of a good conscience will come behind with no enemy, if he turn not worse; for Pilate, now overcome, satisfieth all their desire in this particular—he delivered him to be crucified.

17. It may be the lot of Christ's followers, and an addition to their trial, to be given up to the power of their most inveterate enemies, to execute all their spite upon them; for so fared it with Christ in his own person; he was delivered to them (or to the Jews) to be crucified.

Ver. 16. —— And they took Jesus, and led him away.

17. And he bearing his cross went forth into a place called the place of a skull, which is called in the Hebrew, Golgotha:

18. Where they crucified him, and two other with him, on either side one, and Jesus in the midst.

In the second branch of this part of the chapter is contained the execution of the sentence; that he being condemned they led him away to Mount Calvary, bearing his own cross, and there crucified him with two other with him, one on either hand. Not to repeat what hath been said of this way of Christ's suffering, on chapter xviii. 28, and on ver. 31, 32, where a providence is observed in it, we may, from this purpose, learn—

1. Sufferers may expect not only to have cruel resolutions taken, and cruel sentences given out

against them, but to have them cruelly executed; for so was it with Christ; he being condemned, " they took him, and led him away ;" and he met with this, not only to shew that our sins deserved not only threatened, but real inflicted punishment, or to purchase to his followers many a sweet disappointment in their sufferings; but that he might sanctify such a lot to them when sufferings are permitted to come to an extremity.

2. As the Lord marks the activity of persecutors against Christ, and propounds it to be marked by his people, to shame them when they are negligent for him; (for therefore doth he record that after his condemnation " they" immediately " took Jesus, and led him away,") so his eye is most upon them who are most malicious against him; for albeit the soldiers were actors in this business, yet for this cause he marks specially that " they (or the Jews to whom Pilate delivered him) took him, and led him away."

3. Christ submitted to be accounted an execrable person, and in an execrable condition, and one whom none would own, that so we might inherit a blessing in him; therefore went he forth " bearing his cross," as one accursed, whom none in all the company would help to bear his cross, till one was compelled to help him, as the rest observe.

4. It may please the Lord to let trial and great weakness tryst [meet] together, and to lay on crosses when we seem very unmeet for bearing of them; for Christ, after he is wearied all night, and spent with former sufferings, is made to bear his cross, till he faint again.

5. Sufferers may get few sympathizers, even of dearest friends; and Christ endured this lot that he might be a tender friend to us; for he bare his cross without any of his followers to help him, but another must be compelled when he needs it.

6. Whatever be our weakness and discouragement under trial, yet it is our great victory voluntarily to submit and bear it; for notwithstanding this his low condition, yet he, " bearing his cross, went forth," and was not drawn, but bears on till he faint again.

7. The place to which he is carried to be crucified is called " the place of a skull," (which is the signification also of the Hebrew or Syriac name, Golgotha, to which also the name Calvary, Luke, xxiii. 33, agreeth ;) and it gets this name, not so much because the form of that mountain resembled a skull, as because there were many skulls of executed malefactors lying or buried there. He was brought to this place to suffer, not only to shew how loathsome we and our sins are before God, in that our Surety must suffer in so loathsome a place; but further it teacheth— 1. Our Lord is the true substance of that sacrifice slain without the camp, whose blood was brought into the sanctuary, Heb. xiii. 11, 12. And however he was esteemed of among men, in suffering here, yet his blood hath made way, and opened an entry into heaven. 2. By this he hath sanctified the contempt of his people in the world, and taught them to go out unto him, bearing his reproach, who suffered without the gate,

Heb. xiii. 12—14. 3. By this he hath shewed how by his death he will be death's death, in that he suffered and triumphed over death in " the place of a skull," where there were many monuments of death's triumph over others.

8. Christ, by his suffering this death of being crucified, hath taught us—1. We by nature are under the curse, and he hath undergone that curse that all who flee to him may be freed from it, and that all their conditions may be blessed, and their very crosses turned into blessings; therefore did he undergo this cursed death, Gal. iii. 13. 2. By his pouring out of his blood, even unto death, which flowed abundantly (as from other places, both before his being crucified and after his death, so also) from his hands and feet, he hath pointed out to us that as there is no remission of sins without the shedding of blood, Heb. ix. 22, so he hath opened up that fountain for all who come to him. 3. By this way of shedding his blood, by piercing of his hands and feet, which were sensible parts, and his being hanged up, nailed to the cross, to continue in pain for a long time, and his wounds continually widening by the weight of his body till he died, we are taught what the bitter fruit of sin is, how great his love was that did submit to endure this sharp and long-continuing pain, and how we are bound to look on him whom we have pierced, till our hearts be pierced and bleed again. 4. His being fastened, and continuing there upon the cross for a space before he died, may teach how resolute he was to endure that assault till justice were satisfied; that he kept and stood in the field there, to endure the uttermost that enemies could do against the work of redemption, and to grapple with all of them till they had no more to say against his people; and that he would give a proof how certainly he is to be found at his cross, with stretched-out arms, ready to receive all them who seek for life in him, and through his death. 5. His being lifted up thus nailed to the cross, may teach, partly, that we deserved no room, neither in heaven nor earth, and therefore our Surety was lifted up betwixt both, and hence also was the sun darkened, (as for other causes, so) to shew that we deserve not so much as that the sun should shine upon us; and partly, that his suffering was indeed his exaltation; he was lifted up in it by triumphing over his enemies there, and he is exalted in the world as crucified.

9. Albeit Christ in his own person was the spotless Lamb of God, yet so heinous and so many were the sins of the elect charged upon him, that in Divine providence he is not only reckoned among transgressors, Isa. liii. 12, but as the chief of them; therefore it is so ordered, that he is crucified, and other two with him, and Jesus in the midst, as the most notable of them. And this may teach the elect not to mince or extenuate their own sins, which were charged on Christ as so odious.

10. Christ was content to be accounted and undergo the lot of a malefactor, not only that he might free us, who were indeed evil doers, but that he might sanctify unto his people their being looked upon and entreated as evil doers; therefore also was he crucified in such company.

Ver. 19. And Pilate wrote a title, and put it on the cross. And the writing was, JESUS OF NAZARETH THE KING OF THE JEWS.

20. This title then read many of the Jews: for the place where Jesus was crucified was nigh to the city: and it was written in Hebrew, and Greek, and Latin.

21. Then said the chief priests of the Jews to Pilate, Write not, The King of the Jews; but that he said, I am King of the Jews.

22. Pilate answered, What I have written I have written.

The third branch of this part of the chapter contains the title put by Pilate upon Christ's cross, and his declining to alter it at the Jews' desire; in all which we are not only to look upon Pilate, as following the Roman custom, in publishing the faults of condemned and executed malefactors, and as affronting the Jews who had so impudently urged him to crucify Christ; but we are to look to God also, who by this title would have him proclaimed the true King of Israel. Whence learn—

1. It is a good use to be made of the cutting off of delinquents, that justice be cleared and the guilty ashamed, and that others be warned to fear; for upon these grounds it was a commendable practice in itself, that a title was put upon the cross of malefactors, containing their crime, and the cause of their death, and that "it was written in Hebrew, and Greek, and Latin," that all present, of different nations and languages, might read and understand it.

2. Christ hath sanctified his people's being unjustly condemned as traitors, by suffering upon that account, and by having this title written over his head, "The King of the Jews."

3. Christ's intended shame doth tend to the real manifestation of his glory; for Pilate set up this title to brand him as an affecter of a worldly kingdom; but hereby God would have it proclaimed that he is "Jesus of Nazareth, the King of the Jews;" that he is a King in the midst of his sufferings; that he did indeed triumph in them, spoiling Satan, and converting one of them that was crucified with him; and that the glory of this suffering King should be conspicuous and acknowledged in all nations, of all languages, as this title was written in the three principal languages.

4. Inveterate and violent enemies against Christ shall meet with perpetual reproach, never to be wiped off; for therefore doth Pilate write him "the King of the Jews," and that in three languages, that they reading it (as it is ver. 20) might read their own reproach, in having one who was called King of their nation crucified, and that, in God's holy providence, it might be their perpetual reproach to have crucified him who was indeed their King.

5. The Lord leaveth cruel persecutors to be ambitious and tender of their own credit, when he is to affront them; that as they have served themselves of their lusts and idols, so he also may serve himself of them, to make them the more sensible of their affronts; therefore it is marked, that when they read this title, the cross being near the city, ver. 20, their ambition renders the affront of this more grievous to them, and they desire to have it altered; "Then said the chief priests of the Jews to Pilate, Write not, The King of the Jews; but that he said, I am King of the Jews."

6. Such as are not tender of God's honour, and of Christ and his interest in the world, God in his justice will be little tender of them, their idols and interests, when they come to be rubbed upon; for in this answer of Pilate, "What I have written I have written;" we are not only to look to Pilate, as cleaving to their Roman customs, which did not admit that their public programmes or tables should be altered after they were published; nor yet only as requiting them with inexorableness who had been so inexorable to his desire of releasing Christ; but we are chiefly to look to the hand of God, who will not have their ambition satisfied, nor allow any tenderness in the matter of their supposed credit, who had so cruelly pursued Christ to death.

7. God's decree concerning the kingdom of Christ is immutable, nor will he have the glory of it obscured or borne down by any opposition; for so much also doth this answer of Pilate point out, that as Christ was the King of the Jews, however they fretted, so the Lord in his providence would not have the publication thereof on the cross hindered by any entreaty of theirs, and therefore Pilate is overruled to answer, "What I have written I have written."

Ver. 23. Then the soldiers, when they had crucified Jesus, took his garments, and made four parts, to every soldier a part; and also his coat: now the coat was without seam, woven from the top throughout.

24. They said therefore among themselves, Let us not rend it, but cast lots for it, whose it shall be; that the scripture might be fulfilled, which saith, They parted my raiment among them, and for my vesture they did cast lots. These things therefore the soldiers did.

In the fourth branch of this part of the chapter, Christ's suffering from the soldiers is recorded; that having stripped him of his garments when they fastened him to the cross, they do divide those garments which could be parted among them, and cast lots for his woven coat, which could not be divided; all which was done according to that foregoing prophecy, Ps. xxii. 18, which whatever accomplishment it had in David the type, yet it pointed ultimately at Christ's sufferings. Not to seek any allegory, we may from this purpose learn—

1. Instruments will not be wanting to crucify Christ, if it were but for his old clothes, and those but little worth; for these soldiers crucify him, though they got but his garments for their reward.

2. Christ did submit, not only to be crucified, but to suffer naked, the soldiers dividing his garments and coat among them, hereby to teach us—1. That all flesh are really naked before God by reason of sin, Exod. xxxii. 25; 2 Chron. xxviii. 19, and therefore our Surety behoved to suffer naked. 2. That he offered himself a real captive in his sufferings, that so he might fully satisfy justice by being under the power of his enemies, till he redeemed himself by the strong hand, having fully paid the price; for therefore did he submit to be stripped naked, as conquerors used to do with prisoners. 3. That by this suffering naked he would expiate our abuse of apparel, and purchase to us a liberty to make use of suitable raiment, and such as becometh us in our station. 4. That by this suffering naked he would purchase unto them who flee to him, to be covered with righteousness and glory, and to walk with him in white for ever, and would point out the nakedness of those who not being found clothed with his righteousness shall not be clothed upon with immortality and glory, 2 Cor. v. 2, 3. 5. He would also, by this, teach all his followers to resolve on nakedness in their following of him, as a part of their conformity with their Head, John, i. 21; Rom. viii. 35; Heb. xi. 37, and that therefore they should not dote much on their apparel when they have it.

3. A sight of God and his will, in the trials of Christ and his followers, will make them very sweet unto them, and should be a mean to prevent stumbling; for this cause is it subjoined, that it was done " that the scripture might be fulfilled," &c.

4. God hath a providence about the smallest circumstances of the suffering of Christ and his followers; for scripture had foretold, even concerning the parting of Christ's garments, and casting lots for his vesture, to shew there was a providence in these things, though they were but very common.

5. When Christ and his people are very low, yet the scripture stands firm, and will not be broken, if it were but about the matter of an old coat; and however Christ and his followers be put in the hands of wicked men, led by their wicked principles, yet the least circumstance of their sufferings are overruled by God, and men shall not transgress the bounds set by him; for this being foretold, " These things therefore (and no more than had been foretold) the soldiers did." And albeit they did this, and no more, freely, yet it was necessary, in regard of the prediction, that they did it, and went no further.

Ver. 25. Now there stood by the cross of Jesus his mother, and his mother's sister, Mary the wife of Cleophas, and Mary Magdalene.

26. When Jesus therefore saw his mother, and the disciple standing by, whom he loved, he saith unto his mother, Woman, behold thy son!

27. Then saith he to the disciple, Behold thy mother! And from that hour that disciple took her unto his own home.

In the fifth branch of this part of the chapter we have recorded what was Christ's care of his mother, who, with two other women, and John, the beloved disciple, (as is gathered from ver. 26, with chap. xxi. 20, 24,) did stand beside his cross. Christ in the midst of his suffering taking notice of her sorrowful and desolate condition, (he being to die and depart from her, and Joseph being dead, as would appear,) recommends her to John as a mother to her son, who accordingly takes her home with him and careth for her. It is said, Mark, xv. 40, 41, that these two women, with many others, were looking afar off; but it seems here that they, with Christ's mother, had drawn nearer than the rest; and that after his death (which is the time wherein Mark observes that to have been) they retired to the rest.

DOCTRINES.

1. This their standing by the cross of Jesus was not to be any ways assisting or helpful to him in that great work he was now about; nor yet did it flow only from natural affection, no, not in his mother, but from their faith seeing through his sufferings, and unto what they did tend; nor yet doth it only serve as a pattern of Christian practice, teaching us to stand beside his cross, and feed upon his sufferings and our interest in them; but further, it may teach—1. Christ's followers may have many sad days about Christ and his interests, both for their own trial, and that the thoughts of many hearts may be discovered; for in this sight Mary found that accomplished which Christ had foretold, Luke, ii. 35, and so the rest also, every particular of his suffering being a wound to their hearts. 2. Christians are bound not to forsake nor desert such as suffer for truth, but they should be comfortable to them by their sympathy and countenance when they can do no more; for albeit they could not join with Christ in that great work, yet they look upon him as a suffering man, and their standing by the cross, and their tender looks upon him, were, in their own measure, sweet to him who had cruel enemies round about him, and many a piercing and insolent look upon him in that day, Ps. xxii. 17; and their practice towards him is a pattern of our duty towards sufferers. (See 2 Tim. i. 15—17; iv. 16, 17.)

2. Albeit the generality, even of professors, may turn their back upon sufferers, and they are to expect that as a part of their trial, yet they will not want some to countenance them when God seeth it meet; for here of all his followers a very few did stand by the cross of Jesus; and yet a few stood by it, " his mother, and his mother's sister, (or kinswoman who was,) Mary of Cleophas, and Mary Magdalene, with the disciple whom he loved."

3. Such as seem but weak in respect of others may yet prove stronger than they in a trial, and those of the weaker sex may be enabled to outstrip others; for all those (except John) who stood by him when the rest were gone are weak women. And albeit we are not to ascribe this courage to anything in themselves, even of what they had received, yet it may be considered, that as all of these were eminently gracious, and as grace did excite " his mother, and his mother's

sister," to testify their natural affection to him, so also, in particular, John was much beloved of Christ, and Mary Magdalene had seven devils cast out of her by him; and it may be expected that such as enjoy the sense of Christ's love, and do entertain the sense of his special kindness, will cleave to him as long as any.

4. Christ takes notice of all who sincerely testify their affection towards him, and doth indeed respect them, though possibly they get not all alike expressions of his respect; for here all are recorded who " stood by the cross of Jesus," as a testimony that he took notice of their affection, though he speak to none but to his mother and John, and doth take particular care of her only; and because of this it is recorded that he saw them.

5. That Christ, in the midst of this his extreme pain and agony, is at leisure to take notice of his mother and John, and to express his care of her; it may teach, partly, how wisely the Lord doth order the trials of his own, and that he will give them such intermissions of the extremity of exercise as may be needful for them or their affairs; for hereof hath he given proof in the suffering of his Son, who though he still continued in bodily pain, yet got some intermissions and ease of that overwhelming cloud of soul-trouble which pursued him because of our sins, so that he can think of something beside; partly, it may teach that Christ, even in his extreme suffering, began his triumph over it in part, and testified himself a conqueror; for so much appears, not only in that he was always free of any sinful perturbation which might confuse his thoughts, but in that his sinless perplexities also are at his command as God, to moderate them when his thoughts were otherwise to be employed; and partly, it may teach, that Christ's heart is at all times upon his people, to perform all the duties towards them to which he is bound, either as a man under the law, or as Mediator; for in the extremity of his pain his free thoughts are upon his mother, to care for her, and upon a beloved disciple, to give him a proof of his love in this honourable employment. And if his thoughts were at this time thus employed, how much more are they so in glory, when he hath no exercise or suffering of his own to take him off?

6. By Christ's care of his mother at this time, recommending her to John, as a mother to a son, to be cared for, he would teach—1. That it is the will of Christ that children honour their parents, and have a care of them in their decayed and desolate condition; for so much doth he teach in his own person, who was not only subject to his mother and his supposed father in his life, but hath a care of his mother at his death. (See Matt. xv. 4—6.) 2. No personal trouble or trial upon ourselves doth exempt us from the performance of duties towards others, in our relations, nor warrant us to lay thoughts thereof aside; for Christ, in his extreme suffering, accounts it his duty to provide for his mother at his death. 3. Christ is so tender as he will not fail to have a care of them who are little minding their own condition and trials, but are chiefly taken up with what concerns him; for while his mother stands by his cross, afflicted and affected with his

sufferings, he is finding out a way how she may be provided and cared for. 4. The Lord never removeth one comfort or mean of subsistence from his people, but he will provide some other to put in the room thereof, in so far as is for their good; for now he is to be removed who was not only her Redeemer, but comfortable to her as her son; and albeit none could fill his room, even in that respect, yet he provides one who, by taking her home, might supply her want in some measure as a son to her : " Behold thy son! Behold thy mother!"

7. Christ calls her "woman," and not "mother," in this his care, not because he would reprehend any fault in her, as chap. ii. 4, nor yet only because he would not discover her to the soldiers, who were standing by, to be his mother; but that he might teach, that it is the duty of all, especially in their suffering, to have the moderation of their affections towards their relations mixed with the conscientious discharge of duty towards them, that so their affections may not blunt them in their great service, and yet they may not neglect any needful or possible duty, which might bring scandal and reproach upon what they suffer for, or their suffering for it; therefore doth he call her " woman," to testify how far he was above these relations in his suffering, which testified his obedience to the Father, and his love to his people, and yet he neglects not to provide for her.

8. That John gets this trust put upon him, and he takes it on, it may teach—1. Such as are beloved of Christ, and do dwell in the faith thereof, may expect that peculiar advantages shall be cast in their way daily by Christ; for it is to the disciple whom he loved that he saith, " Behold thy mother!" and puts him on this honourable service. 2. Such as do possess and feed upon the love of Christ will desire no greater benefit and advantage than to be honoured to do service to any of his; for this is John's advantage, that Christ will say to him, " Behold thy mother!" and it so affects him, that " from that hour that disciple took her unto his own home," or looked upon her, and took care of her, as his mother and one of his family.

VER. 28. After this, Jesus knowing that all things were now accomplished, that the scripture might be fulfilled, saith, I thirst.

29. Now there was set a vessel full of vinegar : and they filled a spunge with vinegar, and put it upon hyssop, and put it to his mouth.

The sixth branch of this part of the chapter contains the accomplishment of a scripture prophecy, in Christ's thirsting, and their giving him vinegar to drink immediately before his death; in recording whereof, it is insinuated that his thoughts in his suffering ran upon his work, and what was appointed him to accomplish; and that, finding all was accomplished which he was to do before his death, but only that passage, Psalm lxix. 21, he, for the accomplishment thereof, intimates to them that he thirsted, and gets but vinegar to drink, according to the prediction. It appears here, that it was their custom to have vinegar at the place of execution, though it be not needful to determine for what use they had it, whether to sprinkle it in the air, or for men to make use of it to prevent infection or any evil smell by reason of the dead bodies; or whether to apply it to the wounds of the condemned, either to hasten the effusion of blood and their death, or (as some will) contrariwise, to prolong their pain, and keep them from fainting. It sufficeth us to know, that it was not so made use of here, but given him for drink in their cruelty. It appears also, from Mark, xv. 23, that before he was crucified they offered him wine mingled with myrrh, whereof it seems they made use to stupify the senses of the sufferers, that they might feel no pain; and that they mixed this with vinegar and gall when they offered it to Christ, Matt. xxvii. 34. But he refused it, and having tasted it would not drink of it; yet now he received so much of it as may be an accomplishment of the prediction.

DOCTRINES.

1. All that Christ was to endure and suffer came not at random, nor at the pleasure of men, but was foredetermined by God, and accordingly recorded in scripture; for so is imported in that he was about the accomplishing of all things which were recorded in the scripture, and to be fulfilled. (See Acts, iv. 27, 28.)

2. Christ in his suffering did not respect his own ease, but his great care was to fulfil all things that were enjoined and appointed for redemption of his people; that so he might testify his love to them, which was not asleep in his trouble, and might by his example teach us to make it our great care in suffering rather to do our duty than how to get ease and deliverance, Acts, xx. 24; therefore, upon the cross, his study was to see that he did all things requisite, till he might know "that all things were now accomplished."

3. Christ is most faithful in fulfilling and making good whatever he hath spoken in his word, and will not have that made void on any terms; for "knowing that all things were now accomplished" which were to be suffered before his death, only this one prediction remains, and therefore "that the scripture might be fulfilled, he saith, I thirst." He did not express his need to them, as hoping or expecting to be refreshed by them, but only that he might fulfil the scriptures which foretold of this part of his suffering. And when all other things are accomplished, he will continue in pain upon the cross, and endure this cruel usage, "that the scripture might be fulfilled."

4. Christ's extreme thirst may serve, partly, to point out unto us the extreme violence of his suffering, that he was so heated with inward agony, and exhausted with watching, pain, and effusion of blood, as drew on a burning thirst; in all which we should read his love and condescendence, and acknowledge that it is from him we have the case of our suffering and exercise; partly, to point out that as Christ suffered in all his members, to expiate our sin, so particularly he endured thirst, which was a stroke on his tongue, Psalm, xxii. 15, that he might suffer for and expiate the sins of our tongue; and partly, to point out that for expiating our sin in eating and drinking and pleasing our palate and taste, and to purchase unto us the use of the creatures with a blessing, he would suffer this thirst, which will be the eternal punishment of gluttons, Luke, xvi. 24, 25, and gets no refreshment, as after followeth.

5. Sufferers for righteousness may expect to meet with all the cruelty, despite, and mockery, in their extremity, that malicious enemies can invent; for so much doth Christ's lot teach us; when he said, I thirst, "they filled a spunge with vinegar, and put it upon hyssop, and put it to his mouth," that he might suck out the vinegar instead of drink. We need not curiously determine whether that reed (upon which it is said the spunge was put, Matt. xxvii. 48, that so the spunge might reach his mouth on the cross) was of hyssop, (which was not the herb commonly so called, but in that country a sort of tree,) or whether both the hyssop and reed were joined together; but this is certain, that they did this out of cruelty and spite, and that the Lord so ordered it, not only that he might expiate our abuse of refreshments (as hath been said), but that we might expect the like lot.

6. It pleased Christ to undergo this sad lot for our sakes, that when he expressed his need of drink he gets not so much as a drink of water, but only vinegar, that so he might teach his people that their sins deserved they should be deprived of the least and most common comforts, and that he hath drunk all the bitter of what they do deserve; and that, by his being insulted over when he expresseth his need, he hath purchased unto them a right construction of and a meet and comfortable answer unto their prayers; for so much also may we gather from this, that when he said I thirst, they put vinegar to his mouth.

7. It is the sweet way of reading the cruel usage of enemies to see them overruled by God in all they do, and that they will not get their malice vented further than he hath appointed, and that in all they do they are but fulfilling his counsel, though they little mind this; therefore it is said of this their inhuman carriage in particular, that they did it "that the scripture might be fulfilled."

VER. 30. When Jesus therefore had received the vinegar, he said, It is finished: and he bowed his head, and gave up the ghost.

In the last branch of this part of the chapter we have Christ's testament and death recorded. After he hath received of the vinegar he publicly proclaimeth that by what he had suffered and was even now to undergo he had finished all that was committed to him, and so voluntarily and submissively yielded up the ghost. Whence learn—

1. Albeit Christ refused the wine mingled with myrrh, (as was marked on the former verses,) because he would not be stupified in suffering, but would be active and voluntary in it, that so he might commend his love, and teach us to

avoid unsensibleness under trials; yet now he receives the vinegar, and at least tastes of it, in testimony of his subjection to God who had fore-prophesied of this lot, and to teach us subjection to what God appoints for us in all things.

2. Christ closed not his sufferings till all was finished he had to do; he not only endured the utmost extremities of enemies' malice, and bare them all, but he fulfilled all scripture prophecies, and the substance of all the types were accomplished in him; he fulfilled all that God determined to be paid for expiating of sin, so that no more ransom is to be paid; and so did finish the work of our redemption, and purchased that whereby we are perfected for ever; for saith he, " It is finished," whereby he not only gives an account that he had finished what was hitherto required or foreprophesied, but by this testament he gives a comfortable account of his immediately ensuing death also. (See John, xvii. 2.)

3. Death, and no less than death, is the wages of sin; therefore, after the former sufferings, our Surety behoved also to give up the ghost, to finish his work.

4. Christ, by undergoing bodily death for his people, hath hereby purchased that however they must die, yet death is no punishment of sin to them; for his suffering of death hath taken that sting out of it.

5. Christ did not die by constraint, but voluntarily, and of his own accord yielded himself death's prisoner; for whereas the bowing of the head is naturally a sign of death, Christ, before he died, " bowed his head," in testimony that he died voluntarily, and went to meet death, and " gave up the ghost," by a real separation of soul and body, which could not have been if his body had been everywhere.

6. Whatever desertions Christ endured as our Surety, yet it tends to our great comfort that he died at peace and reconciled to his Father. So much is imported in that he " gave up," or rendered, the ghost, or his spirit, into the hands of his Father, as is further cleared from his last prayer, Luke, xxiii. 46.

VER. 31. The Jews therefore, because it was the preparation, that the bodies should not remain upon the cross on the sabbath day, (for that sabbath day was an high day,) besought Pilate that their legs might be broken, and that they might be taken away.

Followeth the third part of the chapter, containing two consequents following upon his death; the first whereof, to ver. 38, contains some passages tending to the confirmation of this truth, that he was really dead, and to clear the accomplishment of some further prophecies concerning him; in which the Jews, the soldiers, and John, do each of them act their part.

In this verse we have the Jews' part in clearing up this truth, and making way for the accomplishment of these predictions. They desire Pilate (who had power of the bodies of condemned men) to have the bodies of those now crucified taken away from the cross and buried; and lest by this desire they should seem to incline to the sparing of their lives, they propound that their legs may be broken to hasten their death, that so they might be removed; the reason of which desire was, that seeing, according to the law, the land was defiled with those who were hanged, (especially if not timously buried,) Deut. xxi. 22, 23; they judged, more especially, that their continuance on the cross on that high sabbath (when the ordinary sabbath and the first day of the feast of unleavened bread did concur together, as is marked on John, xiii. 2) might pollute them and their feast; and therefore, and because of their preparations and eating the pass-over that night, they would have it speedily done. And this desire, and the granting thereof by Pilate, did make way for that which followeth. Whence learn—

1. Christ our Lord was content to be made a curse for us, Gal. iii. 13, and to bear the curse, that it might not be ours. He was looked upon as one who would defile all things, that he might expiate our pestiferous and infectious dispositions; and he submitted to be accounted a polluter of their solemn feasts in his suffering, that so he might expiate our being spots in the feasts of charity, Jude, ver. 12. So much may we gather from his condition here, and the Jews' esteem of him, that his body (among the rest) might " not remain upon the cross on the sabbath day."

2. It is a commendable care in all the members of the visible church to endeavour that curses or accursed things abide not upon their land, or that it be not defiled by others; for so much doth the common equity of this law, upon which they found their desire, point out in the general; and though the ceremony be ceased, yet the substance remaineth, providing it be rightly applied in particular cases. (See 1 Cor. v. 2, 6, 7.)

3. The Lord can make use even of bloody enemies to do service to his suffering people as they need, whatever their intentions and designs be; for Christ now hanging on the cross with ignominy, and as a curse, his very enemies are consulting and careful to have him taken out of that condition, and that " the bodies should not remain upon the cross," though they intend him no courtesy in so doing, but do it only upon other grounds; yea, they devise to put him to further pain, and that his " legs might be broken."

4. God ordereth so by his providence as he will prevent any cruel purposes of his enemies which might make void his purposes concerning his own; therefore it is said, " the Jews besought Pilate," &c., which doth not import any connexion with the former purpose concerning his death, as if they had known of it, but that God kept them off from any such purpose till the time that he was dead, and so prevented the breaking of his bones, which would have made void a prediction.

5. Men, through formality and custom, may be strictly bound to perform the duties of ceremonial or external worship, whose consciences, notwithstanding, never scruple to violate the most weighty precepts of the law; for they observe the ceremonial precept, " that the bodies should not remain upon the cross," and therefore " besought Pilate that they might be taken away,"

and yet scruple not to crucify the Son of God, yea, and to use him with all rigour, and " besought that their legs might be broken." (See Prov. vii. 14, 18.)

6. It is agreeable to the will of God that special respect be had to the observation of the sabbath, and that it be remembered and thought of aforehand, that we may prepare for it; for this in general and in itself was commendable, that they so respect the ceremonial precept concerning those who were hanged, as they account it a special pollution " that the bodies should remain upon the cross on the sabbath;" and their ceremonial observance of the preparation (not only to the feast of the passover, but to the ordinary sabbath) may put us in mind that we ought to remember the sabbath day, that we may keep it holy.

7. The more solemnities or considerations exciting us to serve God do, in his providence, concur at one time, the greater should our care be to improve that time, and to observe it according to the rule; for so much may we learn from their care of the sabbath, upon this consideration, that " that sabbath day was an high day," for the reason formerly given. And albeit it was but from a tradition of their own (as hath been observed on John, xv. 2) that two solemnities concurred at this time, yet whenever, in following God's institution, the sabbath and some extraordinary feast fell to be on one day, they did observe it the more solemnly, as their practice in this case maketh evident; and this should point out our duty unto us.

Ver. 32. Then came the soldiers, and brake the legs of the first, and of the other which was crucified with him.

33. But when they came to Jesus, and saw that he was dead already, they brake not his legs:

34. But one of the soldiers with a spear pierced his side, and forthwith came thereout blood and water.

In these verses we have the soldiers' part contributing to clear this truth and accomplish prophecies; they (upon Pilate's granting this desire and commanding of them, both which are to be supposed here) do execute what the Jews desired upon the other two, ver. 32; but finding Christ already dead, they do not break his bones, ver. 33, but one of them will make all sure by thrusting a spear into his side, and searching for life at the well-head thereof, and accordingly there came out blood out of his heart, and water from about it, proving that he was really dead, ver. 34; in all which the Lord had an overruling hand, to see to the accomplishment of prophecies, as is after cleared. Whence learn—

1. All things outward may come alike to all, and however men may be in different conditions before God, yet he may let their outward lot be equal; for here, albeit (as the rest observe) there was great difference betwixt these two, the one being penitent and the other not, yet they are alike handled; they came, " and brake the legs of the first, and of the other which was crucified with him."

2. Albeit where the Lord pardons sin there remains no satisfactory punishment to be paid by the sinner to justice, yet the Lord may see it fit to pursue pardoned men with rods, for their own exercise, and the instruction of others; for albeit the one was pardoned, yet he not only suffered death, but his legs were broken.

3. Christ our Lord was not only nailed to the cross but did really die and give up the ghost to satisfy Divine justice; for of this the soldiers were witnesses, who " when they came to Jesus, (they) saw that he was dead already." And that he was so soon dead before the other two doth not only evidence that he, having death at his command, might die when he listed and when he had done his work; but also, that he had more upon him than any of them, and therefore was the sooner dispatched by death, and taken away as a prisoner.

4. No opposition will make void the purposes of God, but opposition and difficulties in the way of what he hath purposed are let forth for this very end, that he may manifest the immutability of his counsel; for albeit the Jews' desire, Pilate's command, and the soldiers' intentions, concurred to break his bones; and albeit there was great hazard they would execute it, having broken the legs of those on every side of him; nor was there any ground to expect that these bloody soldiers would exercise their cruelty upon him, though dead, (as they did in piercing of his side,) yet seeing God had determined the contrary, they are impeded; " they brake not his legs."

5. The Lord needs not miraculous ways and actings whereby to fulfil his purposes, but he may bring about his especial providences and purposes in a very common way, and in the ordinary actions of men; for this purpose of God is fulfilled of their own free accord, upon a clear and rational ground; " when they saw that he was dead already, they brake not his legs."

6. Albeit Christ overruled his enemies, that they should not make void his purposes, yet no cruelty was omitted towards Christ, dead or alive, which might testify the great desert of our sins; nor was there any needful evidence wanting which might make clear the truth of his death; for " one of the soldiers with a spear pierced his side," &c. Albeit they were overruled that they should not break his legs, yet they cease not to exercise cruelty upon his dead body, and put the truth of his death out of controversy.

7. That Christ's side was thus pierced may point out unto us how deeply he was wounded for our sins, and that, as his side was pierced and a passage opened to his heart, so by his suffering we may look into his heart wounded with love to us, and pouring out itself for us; and that as a hole was made in Adam's side to take out a wife, so a hole was made in his side to take in his beloved bride to his heart. All this may we gather from this, that " one of the soldiers with a spear pierced his side."

8. That water and blood came out at this wound serveth not only to confirm that he was

really dead, the spear piercing his heart and drawing out the blood thereof and the water that was about his heart to refresh it; but it may further point out that it is he who came by water and blood, 1 John, v. 6, and that from the merit and efficacy of his death there floweth out water to regenerate and wash us from our uncleanness, and blood, for obtaining remission, and for sprinkling and quieting of the conscience.

VER. 35. And he that saw it bare record, and his record is true: and he knoweth that he saith true, that ye might believe.

36. For these things were done, that the scripture should be fulfilled, A bone of him shall not be broken.

37. And again another scripture saith, They shall look on him whom they pierced.

In these verses we have John's part in this business, who, 1. Bears witness of the certainty of his death, and of the truth of those proceedings confirming the same, for confirmation of the faith of others, ver. 35. 2. He clears these proceedings of the soldiers by comparing the same with scripture, shewing how they were accomplished thereby; and particularly, that their not breaking his bones was an accomplishment of the truth of that type of the passover, Exod. xii. 46; Num. ix. 12, and that the promise made to all the godly, Psalm xxxiv. 20, was eminently accomplished in him; and that their piercing of his side was agreeable to that prediction, Zech. xii. 10, wherein it is foretold that the Messiah was to be pierced, which is all that John points at here, though there it be further intimated that they (or the Jews of whom the prophet is speaking) pierced him, their malice and cruelty being the chief wheel that moved in this matter, and set Pilate and the soldiers on work; and therefore the Jews are said to crucify him by the soldiers' hands, as Acts, ii. 36. There is also further intimated in that prediction a promise of the conversion of those who thus pierced him, the full accomplishment whereof is yet to come; and this imports, further, that he was not only pierced by their cruel persecuting of him, but by and for their sins also, as hath been cleared in its proper place.

From verse 35, learn—1. John is so careful to add his testimony concerning these things, and particularly his death, not only to stop the mouths of cavillers, who might be ready to allege that he was taken away before he was dead; but further, yet again to teach us that it is a point about which faith ought to be much employed, that Christ truly died for our sins, 1 Cor. xv. 3, that so we may see that Divine justice is truly satisfied for sin, and may employ faith to get sin truly slain and subdued by the virtue of his death.

2. It is also firmly to be believed that Christ and his followers are not in the hands of enemies, to be disposed of as they please, but that God overruleth all of them to bring about his purposes by them; for this also was a part of John's remark and testimony, not only that Christ died, but that the soldiers did omit or exercise cruelty towards him (in not breaking his legs and yet piercing his side), according as had been purposed by God, and foretold in scripture, as is after cleared.

3. The doctrine of the gospel concerning Christ is a doctrine of faith, and it is to be assented to by faith, whoever there be to say to the contrary; for his scope in publishing of this, as of other gospel truths, is, "that ye might believe."

4. As faith loveth not to walk on slippery and unsure grounds, so the word affordeth sufficient ground of certainty for faith to fasten upon; for John here declareth the certainty of this truth, "that ye might believe."

5. It is a great confirmation of the certainty of the doctrine of the gospel, that the penmen thereof were eye and ear witnesses of what they publish; for "he that saw bare record," &c. (See 1 John, i. 1—4.)

6. Such as are made witnesses of anything concerning Christ, it is their duty and will be their care (if they be affected therewith) to publish the same in their stations, to the edification of others; for so did John in his station, "And he that saw it bare record, that ye might believe."

7. Whatever exceptions unbelievers have against the doctrine of the gospel, yet it is sufficient to condemn them, and to encourage believers, that the doctrine is true in itself, that the publishers were assured of the truth thereof, both by sight and by faith, and that they were so guided by God as they would have been loath to publish anything for a ground of faith which was not a truth; all these are imported here, "His record is true (in itself): and he knoweth that he saith true," not only in respect of his seeing what he saith, but by the spirit of faith comparing what he saw with the scriptures (as after followeth),—" and he knoweth that he saith true, (and publisheth only such things as he is so persuaded of,) that ye might believe."

From verse 36, learn—1. The only best way of reading and being edified by the passages of providences about Christ and his followers is to compare the same with scripture; for so doth John clear these passages; "for these things were done that the scripture should be fulfilled."

2. Such is our weakness and inadvertency that we need help to take up those scriptures which point out Christ in the Old Testament, and which serve to expound the lots he met with, and to confirm our faith in him and his sufferings; therefore doth John help the church in all ages by pointing at the scripture which should be fulfilled.

3. Christ is the truth and substance of that type of the paschal lamb, and the true passover sacrificed for us, 1 Cor. v. 7, in whom and in his sufferings all that is really to be found which is pointed out and typified by that shadow; therefore what was ordained concerning the paschal lamb is applied here to him as the substance of that type, "A bone of him shall not be broken."

4. Christ was not crushed by or under his suffering, but did subsist under all of it till he triumphed over it; for whatever was the reason of not breaking the bones of the lamb, (as their great haste in going out of Egypt, that they might not stay to break the bones and eat the marrow,) yet in the substance it pointed at this, that he was not broken under his suffering, but his bones were kept whole, as being shortly to rise again and triumph over it. And to this also may that passage, Psalm xxxiv. 20, be applied, which proveth true of believers under their trials, that they are not quite crushed by them, because it was true of him first.

5. Christ and his followers are in the hand of God in their sufferings, who carveth out the measure, weight, and every circumstance of their trouble, and leaveth it not to the will of adversaries; for so much also doth that passage, Psalm xxxiv., hold out, that God so keeps them as not so much as a bone is broken when he will have it otherwise; and this is true of Christ first, and of others through him.

6. Albeit Christ endured so much from men as might put him to death, yet he would have it seen that he died voluntarily, and that he was not violently compelled to die; for so much further doth the truth and substance of that type point out, " A bone of him shall not be broken ;" he voluntarily prevented their cruelty by yielding up the ghost, so that they needed not violent [force] him, nor hasten his death, as they did with the rest.

From verse 37 learn—1. Christ is pointed out, not in one only, but in many of the writings of the Old Testament; and they need to study much in all the writings thereof who would understand what is foretold of him, and compare the same with the accomplishment, for their own edification; therefore doth John make use yet of more scripture to clear these proceedings, " And again another scripture saith."

2. All the scriptures are divine and of alike infallible verity, so that one of them will prove true and be accomplished no less than another; for in these proceedings, as one, so " another scripture" is fulfilled, and gets accomplishment.

3. God in his providence hath determined and appointed the least circumstance and manner of the sufferings of his people; for so appears particularly in the sufferings of Christ, concerning whom it was foreprophesied that he should be pierced, as the soldiers did.

4. The scripture is the true and infallible determiner who are most guilty of persecution in God's account; and according to this rule it will be found that malicious upstirrers unto cruelty are more guilty than the ignorant executors thereof; therefore doth the scripture ascribe this act to the Jews; they pierced him, by the hand of the soldiers; as either giving a particular command for this deed, or being generally guilty of all that followed upon their malicious persecuting of him, and by their interposing with Pilate, ver. 31, occasioning this cruelty.

5. The Lord may be so gracious to persecutors as to give them a sight of their cruelty in mercy, and a sight of mercy together with it; for so is this prediction held out in a promise of their conversion, as is cleared in Zech. xii.—They shall look on him whom they have pierced.

Ver. 38. And after this Joseph of Arimathæa, being a disciple of Jesus, but secretly for fear of the Jews, besought Pilate that he might take away the body of Jesus: and Pilate gave him leave. He came therefore, and took the body of Jesus.

39. And there came also Nicodemus, which at the first came to Jesus by night, and brought a mixture of myrrh and aloes, about an hundred pound weight.

40. Then took they the body of Jesus, and wound it in linen clothes with the spices, as the manner of the Jews is to bury.

41. Now in the place where he was crucified there was a garden; and in the garden a new sepulchre, wherein was never man yet laid.

42. There laid they Jesus therefore because of the Jews' preparation day; for the sepulchre was nigh at hand.

The second consequent following upon Christ's death is his honourable burial, performed by Joseph of Arimathæa (who belonged to that place Arimathæa, the same with Ramah, or Ramathaim, but dwelt at Jerusalem, as appears by his garden and grave in it, Matt. xxvii. 59, 60) and Nicodemus; the first whereof begged his body of Pilate, and (as the other evangelists mark) provided fine linen, and the second brought fine spices; and they jointly wound and embalmed his body after the Jewish manner, and do bury him in a new grave near the city, where they lay him with some haste, because of the Jews' preparation.

In all this procedure we may consider—First, That it behoved Christ, not only to die, but to be buried, and lie awhile in the grave, as the lowest state of his humiliation; whereby—1. He would have all yet further confirmed of the truth and certainty of his death, which is so necessary to be believed; therefore is all this solemnity used, and Pilate's doubting of his death, Mark, xv. 44, with other circumstances, are so narrowly marked. 2. He would teach us that sin doth not only deserve death, but that the sinner also should remain death's prisoner, as he continued under the power thereof for a season. 3. He would accomplish what was foretold in the type of Jonah, Matt. xii. 39, 40, and would point out that by his death and burial he hath appeased the wrath of God which was burning against his people, as upon Jonah's casting into the sea it was calmed, and ceased from raging against others. 4. He would publish his entire conquest over death, in that he pursued it into its place, and there triumphed over it by his resurrection, Acts, ii. 24, and would assure us that the grave can retain none of his followers longer than he pleaseth, seeing he hath loosed and broken the bands thereof. (See 1 Cor. xv. 55.) 5. He would sanctify and perfume believers' graves, and make that cold bed sweet unto them by his lying down there. 6. As his lowest step of his humiliation was his passage towards his glorious resurrection, so he hath purchased unto his people that their low abasements should tend to their higher exaltation. 7. He would also by this point out that virtue and efficacy which is in his death, extending to the very burial of sin, as he himself was not only dead, but buried. (See Rom. vi. 4; Col. ii. 12.)

Secondly. We are to consider the persons employed in this action, the one being described by the other evangelists to be a rich man and an honourable counsellor, and (as here also) a secret disciple, or one of these, John, xii. 42; and the other being a master and teacher of Israel, and described here rather from that timorous act, chap. iii. 2, than from his more bold, though not yet full, pleading on Christ's behalf, John, vii. 50, 51. This consideration, and their owning Christ in the general, may teach us—1. A suffering Christ is nothing the less precious in the eyes of a right discerner; for here he is thought worthy to be owned by these eminent men, and they run much hazard and bestow much cost upon his burial. 2. Such as are taught to live contentedly under want, and are ready to suffer and to be forsaken of all, when God calls them to it, may expect God's remarkable care of them when they need it, and to get needful proofs thereof after their trial is over; for so is verified in Christ's experience, who being content to become poor, and being now in his suffering left even by his disciples, yet wants not honourable persons, perfumed with the smell of his death, who bestow expense upon his burial. Those who resolve on these terms to follow God may expect all things to be theirs, as they need them. 3. The Lord may have special favours to bring about for his people, not only when they are asleep, (as Adam was when the Lord prepared him a wife,) but even when they are dead, and so altogether without them, as here also Christ's experience doth teach, who when he died had neither winding-sheet nor a place of burial provided, and yet both are provided for him in an honourable way. And though this was singular in Christ, that he lived still as God, to provide what was needful for him, yet in this also hath God's love kithed [been shewn] towards many of his people, in his care of their posterity after they were dead and gone. 4. There may be many friends to Christ who, for a long time, may lurk through fear and weakness, and yet they may, through God's mercy to them, become more bold afterward; for here Joseph of Arimathæa, being a disciple of Jesus, but secretly, for fear of the Jews, and Nicodemus, which at the first came to Jesus by night, do now at last openly avow and own him. 5. Such may be the Lord's mercy towards his own as they may become more courageous in a time of great trial than they have been in times of less hazard; for they who before were timorous and fearful to own Christ, do now in this great hazard openly appear for him, the one going to Pilate, (and that boldly, as it is, Mark, xv. 43,) and both of them openly concurring to bury him; such courage did then spring up out of the ashes of Christ's death. And indeed, when God looseth the bonds of fainthearted friends, how easy will it be for them to come over all their former fears!

Thirdly. We are to consider the particulars of their preparation before his burial, here mentioned—namely, that Joseph craves liberty of Pilate to take away his body, and obtains it, and takes down his body; that Nicodemus brought abundance of fine spices; and that both together wound his body in linen cloth, applying the spices after the Jewish custom, which was, not to unbowel the dead and then to embalm them, but only to apply the spices outwardly, and it is like that, being in haste here, they took not such leisure as otherwise was usual. These particulars may teach us—1. It is the will of God that zeal and affection run in a right channel, and keep his way, being (as pure, so) peaceable and orderly; for Joseph goeth first and sought Pilate's leave, who had power of the dead bodies, ver. 31, and obtains it before he do anything. 2. It is the will of God, and very commendable, that the living do perform due honour to the dead bodies of saints; and such as have received mercy from Christ will think no expense too much, were it even bestowed on his dead body; for " a mixture of myrrh and aloes, about an hundred pound weight," is employed this way, together also with fine linen, as it is, Mark, xv. 46. (See 2 Chron. xvi. 14; Jer. xxii. 18, 19; Psa. lxxix. 2.) 3. It was believed, even in the church of the Jews, that there should be a resurrection of the same bodies which were dead; for so much also did this practice of embalming among the Jews point at, (though the heathen also borrowed it from the patriarchs, albeit they were ignorant of the resurrection;) they wound his body with linen clothes, with the spices, in expectation of the resurrection thereof, though, it may be, not believing that he should rise on the third day. Only, seeing Christ hath now given a clear pledge of our resurrection by his own rising from the dead, there is no cause why that custom should be continued for that end.

Fourthly. Their burying of him in a new grave in a garden (which was Joseph's own, Matt. xxvii. 60) may teach, not only that he would be buried in a garden, to expiate Adam's sin in the garden, and that he was buried in another man's grave who suffered for the sins of others, but further—1. It is men's duty to acquaint themselves with the thoughts of mortality in time, that so they may be the more ready when death comes; therefore had Joseph his sepulchre ready in the garden, daily before his eyes. 2. Self-denying affection unto Christ will quit anything to him that he calls for or needs; for Joseph quits his grave to Christ. 3. All suspicion of any other's rising instead of Christ, or of his rising by the virtue of any other, was prevented by his being buried in " a new sepulchre, wherein was never yet man laid;" and so none could rise out of it but he, nor could he be raised by any virtue from any other buried there before him, as a man was raised at the touch of Elisha's bones, 2 Kings, xiii. 21.

Fifthly. A reason is given why he was buried there—namely, that being the preparation day, wherein they could not attend long, therefore they hastily laid him there, as being near at hand, and belike also they did not, by reason of this, attend upon all the particular circumstances required in embalming of him. This may teach— 1. Albeit ceremonial performances give place unto moral duties, and men may lawfully omit the one when they come in competition with the other, yet men ought so to follow the one as they strive (so far as is possible) to overtake all; therefore they so go about the burying of Christ as they make all the haste they can, to observe "the Jews' preparation day." 2. When the Lord doth not let things frame with his people as they would, it doth ofttimes prove to be so because they shall not need what he is not pleased to give; for they got not leisure to wait upon this business, but hastily laid him in that sepulchre, for it "was nigh at hand," because he was not to need a grave long, nor to need that way of embalming which they would have used towards him. 3. The Lord also did so order that every passage about Christ's burial, and even those which his friends would have had done otherwise, did contribute to his great scope of glorifying Christ; for therefore also was it ordered that they, being hastened, laid him in the sepulchre which was "nigh at hand," that so he might rise in the view of all his enemies, where they had the stone sealed, and a guard to keep him in; whereas, had he been carried further off, the matter had been more obscure, and might have seemed more doubtful. And thus also doth he bring about his glory by that wherein his people could little expect it should be so.

CHAPTER XX.

This and the following chapter contain Christ's exaltation and begun triumph over all his enemies, by his rising again from the dead; which being done without witnesses, all the evangelists do confirm the truth of it by recording the several steps and degrees of the manifestation thereof; and namely, by the empty grave, which did more obscurely put it out, as the dawning of that bright day, by the testimony of angels, which was yet a clearer light; and by his own apparitions, which were the full shining of that Sun of Righteousness in that morning of his resurrection.

In handling this begun exaltation of Christ, I shall (as formerly) speak only to what is recorded by John, save in so far as may be needful for clearing the greatest contrarieties which seem to be betwixt him and the rest. And in this chapter, first, Christ's resurrection is evidenced and confirmed by the empty grave. And that, first, unto Mary Magdalene, ver. 1; next, unto Peter and John, who being informed by Mary of what she had found, ver. 2, do run to the grave, ver. 3, 4, and find it empty, and do observe such circumstances as persuade John to believe, ver. 5—8, (though they had not considered or believed the scriptures before, which

spake of this matter, ver. 9,) and so they return back again, ver. 10.

Secondly, Christ's resurrection is further evidenced and confirmed by three apparitions and manifestations of himself. First, to Mary, who, staying weeping and looking into the grave, ver. 1, gets a vision of two angels, who confer with her, ver. 12, 13; then she meets and conferreth with Christ, as yet unknown to her, ver. 14, 15, who afterward maketh himself known unto her, ver. 16, and gives her directions and a commission, ver. 17, which she obeyeth, ver. 18. Secondly, to all the disciples, except Thomas, to whom he appeareth that night at their meeting, confirming them in the faith of his resurrection by his usual salutation, ver. 19. and by ocular demonstration to their comfort, ver. 20; and reneweth and confirmeth their calling to the ministry, ver. 21, endowing them with furniture for that office, ver. 22, and asserting their authority in the discharge thereof, ver. 23. Thirdly, to all the disciples, and Thomas with them, who being absent the former time, and refusing to believe upon their report unless he himself got sensible satisfaction of his own prescribing, ver. 24, 25, Christ, after a week, appears to them again, after the former manner, ver. 26, offering satisfaction to Thomas's doubtfulness, ver. 27, which drawing out a fair confession from him, ver. 28, it is entertained with a reproof and caution, ver. 29.

Thirdly, John being about to close his narration, professeth his passing over many other such passages, in regard those which are marked are sufficient to faith and salvation, ver. 30, 31.

Ver. 1. The first day of the week cometh Mary Magdalene early, when it was yet dark, unto the sepulchre, and seeth the stone taken away from the sepulchre.

In this verse is recorded how Mary Magdalene, coming early to the sepulchre, on the first day of the week, purposing to see the sepulchre and anoint the body of Jesus, (as is observed by the rest,) finds the stone rolled away, and (as appears from her report, ver. 2, and is recorded, Luke, xxiv. 2, 3,) finds also the grave empty. Albeit the other evangelists do declare that there were other women beside, who went to the grave, (whether in one or two companies I will not determine,) yet she is only named here, as being most famous in this history, for her affection, zeal, and activity, and one who acts an eminent part in the subsequent passages. And as for Christ's mother, who stayed so stoutly by the cross, chap. xix. 25, albeit John had taken charge of her, chap. xix. 27, we are not to suppose that she was yet retired from Jerusalem, but was still there, as well as John, ver. 2, with Acts, i. 14, and yet we do not find her stirring with this or any other company about his grave, I shall forbear to determine whether she came not to anoint him, as believing his resurrection, (as faith will hold in much needless anxiety and toil, though yet Christ made good use of their weakness,) or whether her great grief did so far surpass that of the rest as she could not be so active as they; as the greatness of grief or love will readily obstruct the expressions thereof; but it is greatest sobriety to leave the inquiry of those things which God hath concealed.

DOCTRINES.

1. Affection may shine very eminently in weak instruments, and greatest services are ordinarily done by weak things, or those things wherein we most abase ourselves; for here weak women, and Mary Magdalene among them, are on foot early, and ready to perform such service as they thought most suitable unto Christ, when the disciples have not yet appeared.

2. Great things received in mercy from Christ will shine forth in great activity for him in men's stations, and according to the measure of light they have received; for therefore is Mary Magdalene only named here, because of her activity and eminency, being eminently engaged to Christ, who had cast seven devils out of her; and albeit she was weak in her undertakings, yet that ought not to obscure her affection.

3. True affection towards Christ will not cool through length of time, nor will it be quenched by impediments cast in the way, but will wait on and burn the brighter when it gets opportunity; for her affection being kept up from shewing itself, by reason of the Jewish sabbath, Luke, xxiii. 56, it doth not extinguish, but on the third day appeareth, and that " early, when it was yet dark." They set out at that time, though it was towards sun-rising when they came to the sepulchre, Mark, xvi. 2.

4. As it is most agreeable to scripture-rules to begin the sabbath in the morning, so it doth begin early, and we ought to consider upon this, that we may begin early to the work of sanctifying thereof; for this time of their coming out is called, the end of the sabbath, as it begun to dawn towards the first day of the week, Matt. xxviii. 1, to intimate that then the Jewish sabbath ended, and the first day of the week, or Christian sabbath, begun; and albeit they set out " the first day of the week early, when it was yet dark," yet Christ (who rose upon that, being the third day) was risen before they came, and so the Christian sabbath was begun. To which, if we add the long continuance of sabbath-service, (as hath been the practice of affection at some times, Acts, xx. 7,) we may gather useful directions for our sanctifying thereof.

5. Christ is ofttimes sought where he is not to be found, even by those who have much affection to him; for she cometh to find him in his grave, and anoint him there, and she " seeth the stone taken away from the sepulchre," (the angel having rolled it away, Matt. xxviii. 2, not because Christ needed that help, but to testify angels' attendance upon our exalted Lord,) and findeth that he is not in the grave. Her unbelief, though joined with affection, did speak but poorly of Christ, in that she came to seek him in his grave who was among the living; and thus not only do they miss him who seek him in dead and unapproven ceremonies and ordinances, and in a dead, formal way, but even his own, when they seek him in a dead, discouraged way under difficulties, as if he were dead and would not do for them.

6. That this is in particular marked, that she " seeth the stone taken away," &c., which was the great difficulty they were thinking upon by the way, Mark, xvi. 3, 4; it may serve to teach, partly, that difficulties may appear very great which yet the Lord's providence may make very easy, as appeareth in the matter of removing this stone to their hand; and partly, that so long as we continue in unbelief, and in our mistakes of Christ, the change of our condition, or removal of apprehended difficulties, will not serve our turn, but will rather beget new sorrows and doubts; for their thought was, that if the stone were taken away they should find Christ, and now it is taken away to discover that they are further from finding him in their way.

7. Whatever disappointments affectionate saints meet with, by reason of their weakness, they will find in the end that all of these tend to their advantage; for such was the issue of her disappointment here; though it bred present solicitude, yet in the end she found that she was disappointed of a dead Christ that she might find him living.

8. In this narration this great article of our faith is here supposed, that Christ is risen from the dead; which believers ought to feed upon, as proving him to be true God, who rose again by his own power, Rom. i. 4; as proving the justification of all those who flee to him, (seeing as in his death he laid down the price, so in his resurrection he got a discharge in our name, Rom. iv. 25, and so will appear the second time as our discharged Surety, without sin, to our salvation, Heb. ix. 28;) as affording matter of glorification to saints against all the challenges of sin and the law, Rom. viii. 34; as confirming and assuring the renovation and sanctification of all those who seek to be partakers of his resurrection, as to be partakers of mortification by the efficacy of his death, Rom. vi. 4, 5; Eph. ii. 6; Phil. iii. 10; and as assuring believers of their resurrection and future glory, seeing our Head will draw all his members after him, 1 Pet. i. 3; 1 Cor. xv. 20, 55—57. This great truth is there preached unto Mary, by " the stone taken away from the sepulchre," though as yet she saw not so much in it.

9. As this great truth of the resurrection itself, so also the way and circumstances thereof are to be studied and pondered for our use; therefore here and elsewhere are these so narrowly marked; and in particular, we may remark here—1. That he rose without observation and witnesses; for albeit several felt that earthquake, and the watch and the women saw that angel which descended at his resurrection, Matt. xxviii. 2—5, yet it appears not that any of the watch saw him rise, and those women who came first find the sepulchre empty; nor afterward did he appear openly to all, whereby he might have prevented that report which was spread abroad, Matt. xxviii. 11—15, but only to his disciples and brethren, 1 Cor. xv. 5—7; and did leave this truth to be believed from the word, holding out these evidences and apparitions, 1 Cor. xv. 4, hereby teaching, that however Christ did undeniably witness the truth of his glory and exaltation, yet

he will rather have it the object of our faith than of our sense, while we are within time. 2. That he rose on the third day, and that very early, having lien only one whole day and night, (which was their sabbath,) and but a part of the first day, which was their preparation ; and now on the third, being "the first day of the week early, when it was yet dark," he riseth again. Hereby not only did he fulfil the type of Jonah, Matt. xii. 40, but did also prove both that he was really dead, and yet that he felt no corruption, (according to the scriptures, Psalm xvi. 10, with Acts, ii. 31, and xiii. 35—37,) having lien so short while in the grave ; and more particularly, he hasted through his sufferings to his glory, that he might make way for and give a pledge of our speedy outgates, as we need them, Hos. vi. 2. 3. That he rose on " the first day of the week," that he might perfect the work of redemption, and the new creation, on the day when the first creation began, and might sanctify and set apart that day to be the Christian sabbath, which therefore is called the Lord's day, Rev. 1. 10, and was the day of some of his solemn appearings to his disciples, ver. 19 and 26 of this chapter, and the day observed by the church for solemn meetings and worship, 1 Corinthians, xvi. 1, 2 ; Acts, xx. 7. 4. That the first evidences of his resurrection were more obscure, and such as at first did increase their fears and perplexities, or, at most, but beget astonishment; for all that Mary seeth is but the stone taken away, and the empty sepulchre, which augments her sorrow ; the disciples do not believe the women's report, Luke, xxiv. 11, and what Peter himself saw did produce only wondering at first, Luke, xxiv. 12 ; hereby not only did he prepare their weak spirits for the full comfort of this mercy, in his clear apparitions, by sending more dark evidences of it beforehand ; but we may also learn from it how much perplexity saints may have about their real mercies and comforts, even while they are amongst their hands, so long as they are in the dark, and cannot discern them.

Ver. 2. Then she runneth, and cometh to Simon Peter, and to the other disciple, whom Jesus loved, and saith unto them, They have taken away the Lord out of the sepulchre, and we know not where they have laid him.

Followeth the evidencing of Christ's resurrection, by the same proof of the empty grave, unto Peter and to John, who is here again described (as frequently before) by his Master's love to him. The narration of this manifestation may be taken up in four particulars ; the first whereof (in this verse) is the occasion of their going to seek this proof—namely, that Mary cometh unto them with a report of what she had found, representing the matter in such sad and disadvantageous terms as her unbelief and discouragement could invent. For clearing of this purpose, consider—1. Albeit all the disciples were present when Mary with the rest of the women made their report, Luke, xxiv. 9, 10, yet it is said here only that she ran to Peter and John, because

they only made any use of her report, for the rest accounted them but idle tales, and believed not, Luke, xxiv. 11; and albeit neither Peter nor John believed as yet, (as appeareth from ver. 8, 9, with Luke, xxiv. 12,) yet they will go and be further informed.   Consider—2. The greater difficulty here is, how Mary is said to report only that Christ was taken out of the grave, and yet it appeareth from Matt. xxviii. 5—7, and Luke, xxiv. 4—8, that angels had told them he was risen, and it is said expressly, Luke, xxiv. 9, 10, that Mary Magdalene was amongst those who told the angels' tidings.   This difficulty may be cleared two ways: 1. That Mary coming with the first to see the sepulchre, Matt. xxviii. 1, and finding it empty, she ran away with the sad news before the angels told these tidings to the rest; and where it is said, she with the rest told these things, Luke, xxiv. 10, it may be thus expounded: that every one of them told their own part; Mary told of the empty sepulchre, and the rest of the women (who came after her, and before Peter and John ran to the sepulchre) told that they had seen angels, and what they had heard from them. 2. It may, with as little violence to the text, be cleared thus : that indeed they told the angels' message, Luke, xxiv. 22, 23, but so as they did not believe it, and they told also what is here recorded as their own sense of the matter, whatever angels said to the contrary.

DOCTRINES.

1. It is a commendable duty of saints when they are in any distress, especially concerning Christ, to repair unto the society of his disciples, and communicate their case with them, whatever be the success; for whatever was Mary's weakness, yet it is commendable that she goeth and acquainteth the disciples with her sad case.

2. Affection unto Christ will make such as miss him very active in communicating their losses, though ofttimes such haste, joined with unbelief, doth cause them promove but little ; for therefore is it marked, that "she runneth, and cometh" to the disciples, out of her affection, though her unbelief made it be to little purpose.

3. Albeit all who get any tidings concerning Christ are bound to make use thereof, and it will be marked as their fault when they do not so, yet, in some respect, those only may be said to be present and spoken to who make use of any such tidings; and for others, what is spoken may be said to be in vain to them, Jer. viii. 8 ; for this cause it is said here only, that " she cometh to Simon Peter, and to the other disciple whom Jesus loved," because they made some use of her news, as hath been cleared. It is said, Luke, xxiv. 24, that certain of them which were with the disciples went to the sepulchre, not that they were sent by common consent, but went of their own accord.

4. Such as do slide in an hour of tentation ought not to lie still, but recover themselves by repentance, Jer. viii. 4, 5, and being recovered, they ought to return to the society of the Lord's people, to keep communion with them, and to run one hazard with them ; therefore we find Simon Peter, who had repented before, returned unto the disciples again.

5. As backsliders should be encouraged to return, considering that they have the church's affection ready to receive them again, and confirm their love towards them, 2 Cor. ii. 8, (as here Simon Peter is admitted amongst them,) so the more any have tasted themselves of the love of Christ, they will be the more ready, with tenderness, to welcome backsliders, and such as do come in; therefore it is specially marked that " Simon Peter, and the other disciple, whom Jesus loved," were together, and afterward they keep together. A man so qualified as John was a fit man to receive and welcome a penitent Peter. And thus also Barnabas, the son of consolation, did entertain Paul, Acts, ix. 26—28; xi. 25, 26. And thus will those who are indeed spiritual deal with such as have fallen, Gal. vi. 1.

6. Unbelief, though joined with affection, may mistake God's dealing so far as not only to look upon real mercies as trials, but to point out supposed trials in the blackest colours, (enough to discourage a whole meeting of disciples,) and as sadder than their real afflictions; yea, the more affection there be, unbelief may abuse it, to render their apprehensions yet sadder; for affectionate Mary represents this great mercy of Christ's resurrection as sadder than the death and burial of Christ; for then, though he was dead and buried, yet she knew where to find him, to tender her respects to his dead body; but now saith she, " They (either some friends, out of their respects, or his foes, or some others; see ver. 15,) have taken away the Lord out of the sepulchre, and we (I, nor any of the women who were with me) know not where they have laid him."

7. It is sad to affectionate souls when Christ is away from them, but much sadder when they know not where to seek or find him; and this doth usually follow on the other; for both these concurred in Mary's trial, in this particular way of finding Christ here: " They have taken away the Lord, &c., and we know not where they have laid him." And this also is the lot of deserted souls, John, xxiii. 3, 8, 9; Cant. iii. 1—3; v. 6, 8, which may teach them who enjoy Christ to entertain him well, lest they not only want him, but involve themselves in a perplexed labyrinth; and may point out their tolerable condition unto them, who though they want, yet they know what to do, and how to come speed.

8. Such is the power of unbelief and tentation that even real encouragements will beget and feed discouragement and fear; for the empty grave, which should have comforted her, occasions all this mistake and sorrow: " They have taken away the Lord out of the sepulchre."

9. Unbelief also is so powerful, and God's wonderful actings do ofttimes so overcome our weak faith, that even an angel from heaven will not prevail to persuade us of them till the Lord come; for albeit (as hath been cleared) angels had told her and the rest of Christ's resurrection, yet she insists on this as her real thought of the business, " They have taken away the Lord," &c. A lie is far more easily believed than truth in an hour of tentation, and she credits her own heart and sense better than an angel's testimony.

10. Whoever look upon God's dealing, and the passages they meet with, without the word, will readily mistake and feed their own tentations; for whereas the angels had remitted them to Christ's doctrine to clear this passage, Luke, xxiv. 6, 7, she looks only to the empty grave, and judgeth according to her sense: " They have taken away the Lord out of the sepulchre."

11. In all this regrate [sorrow] she calls him " the Lord," a title proper to him in a peculiar sense, and which she uttered in another sense here, than when she gave that title to him, when she supposed him to be the gardener, ver. 15. It doth not only point out her great respect to him, when dead and gone, as she supposed, and that indeed he was " the Lord" still, even when dead, as she supposeth him now to be; but further, this title, as it is proper to him in a peculiar sense, (and she intends it so,) doth contain a refutation of all her mistakes; for his being " the Lord," and that even when dead, in her account, doth evince that he was not to be detained a prisoner by death, but was now risen, the time prefixed by him for his continuance in the grave being expired; and so it may teach—1. Even in the greatest fits of saints' unbelief a right discerner may yet read some faith; as may be gathered to be in Mary, from this compellation. So in the church's complaint, Isa. xlix. 14, " my Lord," is not only the language of affection, regrating [regretting] that such a one had forgotten her, but the language of faith also, cleaving to an interest in him, though she discern it not, being overpowered with sense, which saith he had forgotten her. 2. What saints do sometimes believe in the midst of their tentations, if it were enlarged as it ought, would refute all their unbelief; for as her acknowledging him " the Lord," doth refute her present diffidence and mistake, so when saints believe an interest in God, and that he is theirs, when yet they are plunged in perplexities about many particulars, his being their God is sufficient to give them comfortable ground of hope in all these.

VER. 3. Peter therefore went forth, and that other disciple, and came to the sepulchre.

4. So they ran both together: and the other disciple did outrun Peter, and came first to the sepulchre.

The second particular in this narration is the use which Peter and John make of this information, and that they went to the sepulchre to see; which being generally propounded, ver. 3, is more particularly spoken of, ver. 4, that they both ran towards the sepulchre, and that John, being more young and vigorous than Peter, did outstrip him in running. Whence learn—

1. When saints find any intimation that Christ is missing, they should take with the alarm, and it is their duty to bestir themselves to seek a good account of that dispensation; for albeit there was much unbelief here, yet it was commendable that, when they heard the news, they " went forth, and came to the sepulchre," to see what news they could get.

2. Such as have fresh sense of their own frailty and of Christ's love will be most active to inquire

after an absent and missed Christ; for it is "Peter" new recovered, "and that other disciple," who "went forth," &c.

3. Such as have fallen foully ought not only to recover by repentance and join themselves with the society of saints, but ought to evidence their recovery by their activity, and being with the first in testimonies of affection; for so appeareth in Peter, who now, being recovered, is with the first of the disciples who go to search after Christ. And it may be that therefore Peter only is named in this undertaking, Luke, xxiv. 12, because the fallen man's diligence and recovery was specially remarkable.

4. Diligence is required, and is a commendable testimony of affection, in disciples' inquiry and making search after Christ; for "they ran both together."'

5. Albeit affection will put believers to all the diligence they can, yet every one is not to be tried by another's measure of expressing his affection; for one may be as affectionate as another, who yet may be retarded, and come short in expression of what that other attaineth unto; for so appeareth in Peter and John, "they ran both together," but "the other disciple did outrun Peter, and came first to the sepulchre." John being young, and of a nimble body, did outrun Peter, who yet loved Christ as well as he, and was running as fast as he could. And thus also may many be borne down in their activity in respect of others, by reason of their infirmity of body, tentations of mind, or other infirmities, whose affections, notwithstanding, are as fervent towards Christ.

Ver. 5. And he stooping down, and looking in, saw the linen clothes lying; yet went he not in.

6. Then cometh Simon Peter, following him, and went into the sepulchre, and seeth the linen clothes lie,

7. And the napkin, that was about his head, not lying with the linen clothes, but wrapped together in a place by itself.

8. Then went in also that other disciple, which came first to the sepulchre, and he saw, and believed.

9. For as yet they knew not the scripture, that he must rise again from the dead.

The third particular in this narration is their success and observation when they came to the sepulchre, ver. 5—8, with the effect it had upon John, ver. 8, and his remark and account thereupon, ver. 9. In general it is supposed here that they found the sepulchre empty, and Christ not in it; but more particularly, John records their progress and particular observations there; and namely, that he, coming first, contented himself to look in and see the linen clothes lying wherein they had wound Christ's body, but went not in, as contenting himself with the sight, or possibly being afraid to enter because he had heard that angels were there, ver. 5. That Peter, coming after, went into the grave, and observed more distinctly the order how these linens lay, ver. 6, 7, and that he, following Peter's example, went also in, and saw and observed the same more distinctly also, ver. 8. Unto this John subjoins an account of the effect this sight had upon him, that it persuaded him to believe, ver. 8, which he amplifieth from an acknowledgment of their common evil of not taking up and believing the scriptures, which spake of the resurrection of Christ. Concerning this believing of John, and his acknowledgment thereupon of their ignorance and unbelief of the scriptures, consider—1. Albeit by some it be conceived that he believed no more than what the women had told, that Christ's body was taken away, and that because they knew not the scriptures as yet, therefore he could believe no more; and albeit so much only be recorded as the general account of their diligence when they returned from the grave, or at least the hearers understood it so, Luke, xxiv. 24, yet this being recorded particularly of John, it seems more probable that upon this sight he did believe his resurrection, and that it was true which the angels had said to the women, though it was but in some weak measure, and it may be he was as easily shaken again. Nor is it needful to debate whether their not believing upon Mary's report—that she had seen Christ, Mark, xvi. 9—11, (which was after this, as appears, ver. 18)—was true only of the body of them, John being excepted, or whether he staggered again. Only this is beyond all controversy, that both Peter and Mary (who went also with them, as appears, ver. 11) did believe so much as that his body was taken away, and therefore it needed not be remarked as anything singular in him that he believed so much. And withal, this interpretation helps us to put a difference among all these three who were now at the sepulchre: Mary believes no more than she did, and therefore stayeth still about the grave till she got a sight of Christ to comfort her, ver. 11, 12, &c.; Peter, though it seems he goeth a further length, yet doth not believe, but only wondereth, and is astonished at these things, Luke, xxiv. 12, and gets a sight of Christ before the rest of the disciples, to clear and confirm him, Luke, xxiv. 34; 1 Cor. xv. 5; but John doth here believe, and therefore needs no such particular confirmation till afterward that he getteth it with the rest. Consider—2. This amplification and reason subjoined, ver. 9, albeit being applied generally to all, or the most part of them who were there, (as it is generally expressed,) it is true they did not believe his resurrection, but only that he was taken away, or did wonder and were confounded with what they saw, and that because they did not even then consider nor believe the scriptures. But applying it particularly to John, it holds thus true of him, that he did believe only when he saw, and not before, because he had not heeded nor believed the scripture speaking of Christ's resurrection till he saw this accomplishment; whereas, had he believed the scripture, he might have been assured of this before he saw these things. And so John, when he gets faith, acknowledgeth his fault, recording it in this narration, and acknowledgeth it was a common fault among them.

DOCTRINES.

1. There were such clear evidences to be seen about Christ's grave as made it apparent that he was indeed risen from the dead, and was not conveyed away either by friends or foes, or any other for their own ends; for the lying of " the linen clothes," observed by both of them, did clearly witness this. Beside that it would have been a terror to have handled a naked, dead man, what could be the end of any party to carry away his body and leave these? It is not to be supposed that any friends (could they have had access to him through the guards) would have so handled his blessed body as to carry it away naked, nor could it have agreed with their design to carry him away by stealth to take leisure to strip him; and as for his foes or others, it is to be supposed they would rather have had the fine linen and the spices than his body, and so would never have left these behind when they carried it away; yea, the orderly lying of the linens, and that not so much as a napkin was away, but orderly wrapped and laid up, (as is remarked by Peter, ver. 7,) doth evidence that this was not done in haste or confusion.

2. That Christ, rising from the dead, left his grave-clothes behind him, (which yet were all the clothes he had, the soldiers having parted his garments,) whereas Lazarus came out with his grave-clothes, John, xi. 44. It may serve to teach us, not only what he hath purchased to us by his death and resurrection, even a restitution to that blessed estate through him wherein Adam was in innocency, (when he needed no garments,) though the complete enjoyment thereof be suspended till eternity, wherein we shall be perfected, and shall not only need nothing to cover our outward nakedness, but shall leave that infirmity and corruption which accompanieth us to the grave behind us, as he left his grave-clothes; but further, it teacheth that Christ rose again, not to live any more in this world nor to die any more, but to live and reign for ever, and therefore he left his grave-clothes, whereas with Lazarus it was otherwise, he being to live in the world for a space, and then to die again.

3. A little stand in any good course may put a man behind even those who otherwise were behind him; for John outran Peter in coming to the grave, ver. 4, and yet, standing a little at the grave, Peter, who was behind, doth get before him and get a more distinct sight.

4. A sincere and constant follower of his duty, though slow, may at last attain to cast a copy to those who are more forward; for Peter, though slow, yet holding on, attains to cast John a copy, who came before him.

5. A sincerely forward man is so humble as to be content to learn a lesson even from one who hath sometimes fallen foully, and who even now was behind him; for John learns this lesson from Peter's example, and went in also and saw.

6. The Lord's way of working with his own is diverse, and he may gift faith to one of his own, when yet another, having the same means, is left under the power of unbelief for a time; for " he saw, and believed," which Peter and Mary as yet did not.

7. Faith is so far above the reach of nature that it is hard to induce even saints to believe when they want satisfaction to their sense; for " he saw, and believed," and not till he saw.

8. It is our great fault and the fruit of much ignorance, peevishness, and averseness from the way of faith, that plain scriptures, which might comfort us, lie beside us unobserved, or not believed and trusted; for so much doth John's acknowledgment import, when " he saw, and believed," and so got insight in and gave credit to the scriptures; he acknowledgeth that as yet, or before this, he had not known the scripture; not that he could be simply ignorant of what Christ had so often told, and the angel had even now sent them word of by the woman, but that he had not heeded or pondered and believed it.

9. When the Lord condescends to give us sensible satisfaction for the help of our faith, it is our duty not to rest upon such a way, and always to suspend our believing till we get the like again; but we ought rather to look on it as a reproof for our not studying or heeding and not believing naked truth, and accordingly should humble ourselves and acknowledge our fault; therefore John, getting this sight, acknowledgeth his fault, that he did not before believe, " for as yet they knew not the scripture, that he must rise again from the dead." They did not heed and ponder those things which were revealed in the word so as to feed upon them by faith.

10. Any evil, and particularly the evil of ignorance or not believing the scripture, is the more odious and grievous to a godly man the more it be common and frequent; therefore doth John bring out this reason and acknowledgment in general, " they knew not the scripture," not so much to give a reason why the other two believed not as yet, far less to extenuate the matter, but to aggravate this fault, which he found in himself when he perceiveth it so common, and so sad fruits of it yet in the rest.

11. The children of God may be much in the dark, and much overpowered with unbelief by reason of their ignorance, and in an hour of tentation, who yet are not to be cast off, nor is it to be despaired but they will recover themselves; therefore John only saith, " as yet they knew not the scripture," which yet afterward they did, and it seems he himself now attained to know it in part.

Ver. 10. Then the disciples went away again unto their own home.

The last particular in this narration is the return of these two disciples after their sight and observation. It is not here determined whether they returned together, or rather (as may be gathered from Luke, xxiv. 12.) each of them there alone, and that Peter got a sight of Christ by the way, Luke, xxiv. 34. This is certain, that (partly through fear lest they might be surprised by any who should be stirring thereabout, and partly through irresolution what to do next) they return " unto their own home," not to the places of their abode and habitation, (for they stay yet at Jerusalem, as is recorded, ver. 19, and elsewhere,) but to the rest of the company from whence they came. Whence learn—

1. It may be the lot of Christ's disciples at some times to run much hazard in their inquiries after Christ, which should teach us to esteem highly of liberty and freedom; for therefore is it marked here, that " the disciples went away again," as not daring to stay about the grave.

2. When disciples have got some clearing in dark cases they may yet be kept under great irresolution and uncertainty by reason of their ignorance, and for their trial and exercise, till Christ do clear and confirm them yet more; as here, John believing in some measure upon what he saw, and Peter wondering in himself, they know not what to do next, but " went away again unto their own home."

VER. 11. But Mary stood without at the sepulchre weeping: and as she wept, she stooped down, and looked into the sepulchre.

Followeth to verse 19, Christ's evidencing of the truth of his resurrection by his appearing unto Mary, who was the first that got a sight of him, as appeareth from Mark, xvi. 9. This narration may be taken up in six particulars, the first whereof (in this verse) is her carriage and exercise about the sepulchre; and that after the disciples were gone she continued there weeping and looking into it. Whence learn—

1. Albeit there are ofttimes many errors in the way of affectionate saints, yet those whom Christ is to manifest himself most and first unto are such as cannot want him, but must incessantly wait on till they get him; for in opposition to the disciples' practice, verse 10, it is subjoined, " But Mary stood without at the sepulchre." Not only might she stay there with less hazard than the men, but when their irresolution and fear sent them away, her affection (though overpowered with more unbelief than any of them had) keeps her still waiting on, and so, though her failings were many, she gets the first sight of Christ.

2. Albeit affectionate saints may have much causeless sorrow about Christ, yet want (whether real, or apprehended only, which yet is real to the apprehender) should be evidenced by some expressions of affection witnessing their respect to what they want; for it was in itself commendable that she " stood weeping" for a supposed dead and lost Christ, though it was her mistake to think so.

3. There may be much affection expressed towards Christ and a sight of him when yet we look the wrong way to find him; for " as she wept, she stooped down, and looked into the sepulchre," not only to feed her eyes and sorrow with the sight of the empty sepulchre, but also to try if possibly he might be found there, though it was found empty before; and it may be, some stir made by the two angels (of whom ver. 12)

drew her to look what she might yet find there. However, as it was commendable that her excessive sorrow did not drive her from the use of such means as she thought most probable, so it is certain she sought him where he was not to be found.

VER. 12. And seeth two angels in white sitting, the one at the head, and the other at the feet, where the body of Jesus had lain.

13. And they say unto her, Woman, why weepest thou? She saith unto them, Because they have taken away my Lord, and I know not where they have laid him.

The second particular in this narration is her seeing of two angels in the sepulchre, and their conference with her. These appearing in splendent white raiment, do question her concerning the cause of her sorrow, and she returns an account of her case in the same terms as she had done to the disciples, ver. 2. Whence learn—

1. Such is the Lord's respect towards affectionate mourners after Christ, as they shall not want needful comfort, albeit angels should be sent with the message; for distressed Mary " seeth two angels" sent with an useful message to her.

2. Their appearing in " white" served to point out their spotless purity who are God's constant attenders, and to hold out what they should aim at who look to dwell with God for ever, Heb. xii. 14, and what in the end they will be, Rev. vii. 13.

3. Their posture, " sitting, the one at the head, and the other at the feet, where the body of Jesus had lain," served not only to confirm that he was not taken away, but had indeed risen, seeing they appear in and at his grave, and so he could not be still dead whom they serve; but further, it pointed out, that it is through Christ alone, and by virtue of his death and sufferings, that God is reconciled to sinners, and they have access unto him upon a mercy seat; for therefore do they " sit at the head and feet, where the body of Jesus had lain," as the cherubims sate upon either end of the mercy seat, to evidence what his death and burial had procured unto sinners.

4. The case of such as are indeed seeking Christ is so sweet and sure that their heartless and dejected sorrow is causeless (even themselves, when they are in their right wits, being judges) and worthy of reprehension and challenge; therefore are they sent with this commission unto her, " Woman, why weepest thou?" which is a speech full of comfort, intimating that she had no cause to weep, yet seasoned with a reproof that she should weep so heartlessly; and herself is put to judge (when she is in a right frame) of the truth and justness of this challenge. And indeed, it is but our low stature, who cannot see afar off, which is the great cause of our anxiety; whereas their question imports that were she elevated as they were, to see the truth of the matter, she would not be diffidently anxious.

5. The want of Christ is matter of sorrow indeed to a lover of him. The sorrow and joy of an affectionate saint are chiefly taken up about the enjoying or wanting of Christ; and when he is

away, (either really, or to their sense,) they will not easily be convinced of any excess in sorrow and anxiety; for she justifieth her challenged weeping from this, " Because they have taken away my Lord," as pleading that she could not sorrow enough, or too much, because of this.

6. Unbelief and mistakes once taking place in an affectionate heart are not easily rooted out, and do prove real obstructions, hindering the mind from adverting to anything which might cure them; for albeit, since she first vented this her mistake to Peter and John, ver. 2, she had met with much which might have cleared her, (as her repeated sight of the empty grave with Peter and John, and her sight of angels there, and her reproof from them,) yet she heeds none of these, but persists in her apprehension, " They have taken away my Lord, and I know not where they have laid him."

7. Whatever be the mistakes of saints concerning Christ, through ignorance and unbelief, yet it is a blessed sense of absence of Christ, and of the continuance thereof, when it causes affection towards him to grow; as here it doth in Mary; before, he was " the Lord," now, " my Lord."

VER. 14. And when she had thus said, she turned herself back, and saw Jesus standing, and knew not that it was Jesus.

15. Jesus saith unto her, Woman, why weepest thou? whom seekest thou? She, supposing him to be the gardener, saith unto him, Sir, if thou have borne him hence, tell me where thou hast laid him, and I will take him away.

The third particular in this narration is Mary's meeting with Christ, and conferring with him, before she knew him; she, turning about from the angels, seeth Christ, but knew him not, ver. 24, and he inquiring concerning her sorrow, and whom she was seeking after, she, supposing him to be the gardener, makes offer, that if he had removed his body, and would shew her where he had laid it, she would carry him away, not to trouble him any more, ver. 15. Whence learn—

1. No company will satisfy or refresh such as love and are seeking Christ, when they find not him nor satisfactory news concerning him among them; therefore, albeit Mary enjoy the company of angels, yet since she saw not Christ there, and what they said (whatever it was in itself, yet) did not satisfy her, therefore, " when she had thus said, she turned herself back." It is not needful to determine whether she did this of her own proper motion, or whether some noise of one behind her, or some motion of the angels upon Christ's appearing, occasioned it, but this is certain, that not finding satisfaction there, she stays not with them, but takes hold of all other occasions of finding him. (See Cant. iii. 3, 4.)

2. When means do not afford present satisfaction to seekers of Christ, it is not because they shall not be satisfied, but because Christ will be more immediately (though never without the use, or in the neglect of means) seen in comforting them; for therefore is it that angels did not satisfy her to her sense, because Christ himself was to give her satisfaction; and Christ stops their further conference by his appearing and causing her turn back, as delighting to comfort her himself.

3. Christ is not so far off as readily affectionate saints do apprehend, but is near at hand, to manifest himself and be found when their hopes are lowest, and all probable means do fail; for now, when she knoweth not where they have laid Christ, and no mean had yet given her the comfort she desired, Christ is yet at her hand; " she turned herself back, and saw Jesus standing," and not dead, as she supposed.

4. Christ is so condescending to his affectionate people as when they fail exceedingly in their way of seeking him yet he will seek them in their way, and will give them, not what they desire, but what they need; for albeit she fail in seeking a dead Christ at or in his grave, yet, considering her affection and need, he cometh unto her; " she saw Jesus standing."

5. Christ may be very present and near unto his people when yet he is not discerned, by reason of their weakness and shortcoming in expectation; for " she saw Jesus standing, and knew not that it was Jesus," not because he took on a strange shape, but because she was not only withheld, for a time, from knowing him, as Luke, xxiv. 16, 31, but her weakness and not expecting a living Christ made her not to discern him.

6. When Christ appeareth, even to give sensible satisfaction to his own, he will own and approve what any sent from him have said in his name, as sufficient to encourage them, and as a ground of reproof that they made not use thereof accordingly; therefore doth he at first speak the same thing in substance which the angels had said, " Woman, why weepest thou," &c., that when she came to know him she might consider that that message had been sent by him for her encouragement, and that there was more in it than she saw.

7. Christ may, for a time, seem to carry himself strangely, even towards those whom he loveth dearly, that so he may bring out more of their affection, and more of their weakness also, both which are useful for them; therefore doth he at first speak like a stranger. " Woman, why weepest thou? whom seekest thou?" which though it import much, yet it is not so homely nor so clear, as he speaks afterward.

8. Whatever be saints' apprehensions concerning Christ, or their enjoying of him, yet he is in such a case, and their condition so good, as may justly condemn all excessive sorrow; for so much doth this question and challenge, " why weepest thou?" import; that however she mourned for him as dead, and for her own want of him, yet he was alive and near her, and therefore she had no cause so to weep.

9. People ought to take good heed how they set and employ their precious affections, and upon what, and for what, they pour them out liberally; for so much also do these questions, " why weepest thou? whom seekest thou?" import; that she should look whom she sought so affectionately; and we all ought to examine whether our affections be let out upon things, according as they are of worth in themselves.

10. As saints, considering whom they seek when they are seeking Christ, may help to beget affection in the pursuit, so also it may hinder affection from being heartless and dejected in making inquiry; for so much, further, do these questions import, that however her seeking Christ might kindle her affection towards so desirable an object, her very seeking of him portended so much as might drive away all excessive or desperate sorrow.

11. As our own false and weak conceptions breed our mistakes of Christ, (for she supposed him to be the gardener, because she thought none other could be there so early,) so our mistakes of him do lead us to improve opportunities of his presence but very poorly; for this mistake causeth the force and importance of his question sink nothing in her mind, and draweth out so poor and diffident, though affectionate, an answer.

12. Love to Christ will make us stoop low, even to the meanest, if thereby we may get a sight of him, or be furthered to do him service; therefore doth she, with so much respect, petition the supposed gardener in this matter, " Sir, (saith she,) if thou have borne him hence," &c.

13. Love to Christ will set him so high in saints' esteem as they will think he should be so also in everybody's eyes; therefore saith she only, " if thou have borne him hence," not naming him ; and this she did, not only because she might suppose he had heard what passed betwixt the angels and her, or might know whom she meant, if he had removed his body, but because Christ was the only one in her mind, therefore she thinks every one should know and esteem of him.   Thus also doth the spouse design him to others—Him whom my soul loveth, Cant. iii. 3.

14. Unbelief and mistakes are so prevalent with saints, in the hour of their tentation, that they are not soon removed, and they will sooner apprehend anything than the truth concerning Christ ; for after all her doubts concerning the empty grave, and the taking away of Christ, ver. 2, she now supposeth it might have been done by the gardener, " if thou hast borne him hence," not to bury him in a more fitting place, but as troubling the garden ; and that albeit Joseph had allowed him the grave.   And so she supposeth him to be dead still.

15. Affection towards Christ will not stand to consult with ability, but with itself and its desires, and accordingly will undertake and endeavour to do him service, though never so far above its strength ; therefore doth a weak woman, all alone, offer to bear away the body of Christ, to see it more conveniently buried, " Tell me where thou hast laid him, and I will take him away."

VER. 16. Jesus saith unto her, Mary.   She turned herself, and saith unto him, Rabboni; which is to say, Master.

The fourth particular in this narration is Christ's making himself known to Mary, which he doth with a word, to her satisfaction.   Whence learn—

1. Such is the power of mistake that saints may turn their back even upon a present Christ, while he is not discerned, as expecting no satisfaction nor comfort from him ; and saints may be brought very low in their disappointments on all hands, who yet will get satisfaction ; for that " she turned herself," when he spake again to her, imports she was looking away, even from him, towards the grave, as formerly she had turned from the angels, ver. 14.

2. Love in Christ cannot long conceal itself nor him from affectionate, needy saints, but will come over even their failings to afford them comfort ; for notwithstanding her failings, in her mistakes of his presence and concerning his resurrection, he speedily makes himself known.

3. A little thing, yea, even one word, when Christ blesseth it, will bring comfort to needy souls, and will open their eyes, and cure their distempers ; for Jesus but saith unto her, Mary, and she turneth herself, &c., as one now satisfied.

4. Christ hath a particular knowledge of his own, and there is a mutual knowledge betwixt Christ and his sheep, that they, when their senses are exercised, will discern and know his voice when he speaketh but a little, and that after they have mistaken him before in their distempers; for he " saith unto her, Mary," as knowing her particularly ; and though she heard him speak before and knew him not, yet now this word brings her to know him and discern his voice.

5. As a sight and the discerning of Christ is very ravishing to such as love him, (for so much is imported that she can say no more but Rabboni,) so whenever he appears to his own they will evidence their respect to him as to a Master and Teacher, who must guide and instruct them ; therefore doth she make use of this warm compellation, " Rabboni; which is to say, Master," as evidencing how sad it was to her to be left masterless, and how sweet it was to get a Master and Teacher again.

VER. 17. Jesus saith unto her, Touch me not; for I am not yet ascended to my Father: but go to my brethren, and say unto them, I ascend unto my Father, and your Father; and to my God, and your God.

The fifth particular in this narration is Christ's direction and commission to Mary, now when she knoweth him.   It doth appear that she was about to touch and embrace Christ, but he prohibits her, and sends her with a commission to acquaint his disciples with his begun exaltation ; and that having now risen from the dead, he was to ascend unto the Father for their comfort, and the further clearing of their interest in God through him.   As for this prohibition to touch him, the reason subjoined, and the matter given her in commission to the disciples concerning his ascension, may seem to import a reproof of her carnal disposition, who doted on his bodily presence, and delighted to be touching him, and to teach her that (now he being risen from the dead) he would not be trysted [met] with, nor enjoyed in a carnal, corporal manner, as formerly, but she is to expect and wait till his ascension, and then she and the rest might tryst [meet] with him and touch him, not bodily, but spiritually and by faith.   And it is indeed true, that even the most affectionate saints may be exceeding carnal in their way of and desires after enjoying of Christ, and that Christ, being now exalted, it requires much spiritual converse with him, and that we do not expect a carnal or bodily presence, it being the woeful fruit of carnal dispositions that because men cannot ascend up to Christ by faith, therefore they fancy a carnal and bodily presence of Christ on earth with them. Yet I take not this as the only nor chief scope of this speech; for however, after Christ's ascension, it is the gross mistake of men to fancy or dote upon his bodily presence, (as that interpretation beareth well, agreeably to the scriptures;) and it was Mary's fault, if she looked on this as the highest degree of his exaltation, and did not expect that he was to ascend into heaven, but to stay among them, as formerly; yet we find that many were admitted to touch him, in expression of their affection, and for confirmation of their own faith, Matt. xxviii. 9; and Christ invites them to it, Luke, xxiv. 39; and Thomas is reprehended, not simply for desiring of this, but because he would not otherwise believe. Therefore I take up Christ's scope to be, as in part, to put her in mind that he was to ascend, and therefore she was not to feed herself with any expectation of his bodily presence to be continued with them as formerly, so chiefly to excite her to make haste with the good news to his disciples, seeing there was yet time enough before his ascension, wherein she might converse with him and touch him, so far as was needful for the confirmation of her faith.

DOCTRINES.

1. Seldom do affectionate souls meet with Christ but they fall into some miscarriage, and do need caution or reproof; for Mary needs this prohibition, "Touch me not," being ready to miscarry through her carnal disposition running in affection's channel, or through selfishness, and forgetting the needy disciples.

2. Whatever Christ withhold from any of his, in their doing service to him, he knows how to make it up, in so far as is for their good; for so much doth this reason import, "for I am not yet ascended to my Father," and therefore Mary may get time enough, after this service is over, to satisfy herself with touching of him.

3. It is the will of Christ that such as have any good news of him do publish it in their station, to the edification of others, especially of those who are in distress and sorrow, and that they do not selfishly please themselves only; for saith he, "Touch me not," which might satisfy thyself; "but go to my brethren," &c., who are in deep sorrow, and know not so much as thou dost.

4. Whatever we may think of our conditions, yet in Christ's account it is more acceptable to be about service for Christ, and doing good to others in our station and generation, than to be enjoying and reaping our own particular content and satisfaction; for Christ propounds it as better to Mary to be the messenger of these good news than to stay with him satisfying her own senses.

5. Christ's glory and exaltation doth not dimi-

nish his affections towards his people, but rather the expressions thereof are enlarged; therefore, after his resurrection, his thoughts run earnestly upon the sorrow of the disciples, to have it eased, and that under the name of brethren, ("go to my brethren, and say unto them," &c.,) whereas before, servants, little children, and friends, were their usual designations. Yea, Peter, the fallen man, is not forgotten by name, Mark, xvi. 7.

6. Christ's most satisfactory manifestations within time are not fitted to our carnal desires and dispositions, but are usefully seasoned with such a degree of distance as may disappoint these, and teach us to be more spiritual, and may train us on to long after the full enjoyment of him in heaven; therefore doth Christ, both in his speech to Mary and in his commission to the disciples, put them in mind of his ascending to the Father, that their carnal hearts might not look on his resurrection as the highest pitch of his glory, and so dream that there was no more to do but enjoy him as formerly, but that they might be prepared shortly to want his bodily presence, that so they may seek to enjoy him by faith.

7. Christ doth very far exceed the weak desires of his people in affording them ground of comfort; for whereas she and the disciples would even now have been content of a dead Christ, much more of a Christ living and risen again, Christ allows them greater news of a Christ glorified in heaven, " I ascend," &c.

8. Whatever carnal hearts do think of a bodily presence of Christ, yet his removal and exaltation in heaven is believers' great advantage, and the ground of their comfort, as proving their Surety to stand in right terms with the Father after he hath paid the price to justice; that it is his Father and God with whom he is to deal on their behalf; and that he, being thus exalted, is able to do for them and save them to the utmost, Heb. vii. 25; for however the disciples doted on his bodily presence, yet he sends these as good news, " I ascend," and that " to my Father and to my God," and so he is accepted, having satisfied justice, and stands on good terms of acceptance because of these relations.

9. Christ's exaltation and interest in the Father as Mediator is also comfortable unto believers in this respect, that they share with him in his interests, and what he is he makes them to be through him, in their own proportion and measure; for so are the news sent, " I ascend to my Father and to your Father, and to my God and your God." He is his Father and God in a peculiar way, and ours through him, and because he is so to him.

10. God hath dignified believers with that near and warm relation of his being a Father to them in his Son, so that, as they ought to carry themselves as children to him by subjection, Heb. xii. 7, 9, and obedience, Mal. i. 6; 1 Pet. i. 14, 15; so they may expect that in all his dealing he will retain a fatherly affection towards them; will allow them humble confidence in prayer, Gal. iv. 6; will spare and pity them, Mal. iii. 17; Psa. ciii. 13; will provide for them, Matt. vi. 25, 32; will protect and preserve them, 1 Pet. i. 3, 5; and will give them a kingdom, Luke, xii. 32, as being sons and joint sons with Christ, and so joint

D D 2

heirs with him, Rom. viii. 17 ; and being begotten to that hope, 1 Pet. i. 3, 4. Therefore is this held out for their encouragement, that God is " my Father and your Father," and this is premitted to the other, because of the warmness of the relation, and that we may look upon his godhead through this perspective.

11. He who is the Father of believers is true God also, and doth gift himself unto them in that relation of being their God through his Son, that as they should make him their God indeed, and depend upon him only, so they may expect all the fulness that is in God to be theirs as they need it ; therefore also is it added, " my God and your God"—a privilege and interest whereof all the particular promises are but a commentary, and which contains in it more than we can ask, or think, or conceive, Eph. iii. 20 ; 1 Cor. ii. 9 ; and more than every believer can see at first, as Christ instanceth in the matter of the resurrection, Matt. xxii. 31, 32.

VER. 18. Mary Magdalene came and told the disciples that she had seen the Lord, and that he had spoken these things unto her.

The last particular of this narration is Mary's obedience to this command of Christ. Whence learn—

1. Obedience unto Christ's command will be sweet, and readily gone about by affectionate saints, and will be preferred to their own particular satisfaction, when they are in a right frame ; for whatever Mary thought of Christ's company, yet at his command she " came and told the disciples that she had seen the Lord."

2. Whatever saints do meet with in and from Christ, yet his word and speeches are not to be neglected, as being most sure and of constant use ; therefore she tells, in particular, " that he had spoken these things unto her."

VER. 19. Then the same day at evening, being the first day of the week, when the doors were shut where the disciples were assembled for fear of the Jews, came Jesus and stood in the midst, and saith unto them, Peace be unto you.

Followeth unto verse 24, Christ's appearing unto all his disciples, except Thomas, as is clear from ver. 24, &c. In this narration we have recorded the time and way of his appearing, and his scope in it. The time of it was that same day on which he arose, and that in the evening, when the disciples were met together and conferring upon what evidences they had formerly received of his resurrection, as may be gathered from Luke, xxiv. 33—35, with 36 ; and the manner of his appearing was, that when they are thus closely met, and had shut the doors for fear of the Jews, he on a sudden appears in the midst of them ; which is not to be understood as if he had come in through the door by penetrating thereof, and yet his body and the door retaining still their true quantities and dimensions ; nor yet as if his body were invisible everywhere, and

did but become visible when and where he pleased ; for Christ doth often argue the truth of his resurrection from his having the properties of a true body, amongst which properties the having of dimensions and extended quantity, and being circumscribed in one place at one time, are not the least considerable, but most essentially requisite to a body ; and it is expressly said, he " came and stood in the midst," and consequently he was not there before. Beside, it is here marked that " the doors were shut," not to point out his miraculous coming through the door, but the time when he came, that it was unexpected by them. And it is to be conceived that he did insensibly, as to them, open the doors, and so came in, and after that shut them, rather than that he came through the door ; for so we find the Lord hath done in other cases, Acts, v. 19 ; xii. 10. His scope in appearing is partly to confirm them in the faith of the resurrection, ver. 19, 20, and partly, to renew and confirm their calling to the ministry, ver. 21—23 ; for assuring them of the truth of his resurrection, he giveth two evidences that it was he who appeared to them ; whereof the first (in this verse) is his usual salutation and allowance of peace unto them. Whence learn—

1. Christ by his appearing " that same day at evening, being the first day of the week," did not only begin to honour and sanctify that day, by his appearing and presence, which he had appointed for the Christian sabbath, but doth further teach us, that he is not slack concerning his promise, but his love will come and will not tarry, and he will rather prevent than prorogate his terms ; and by this rule are we to correct our thoughts concerning his dealing ; for albeit he had set the tryst [meeting], after his resurrection, to be in Galilee, Matt. xxvi. 32, and the angels had repeated the same to the women, Mark, xvi. 7, yet his love will not stay so long, but he will come unto them " the same day at evening."

2. It is the duty of scattered saints to gather together in times of straits, and to make use of the fellowship one of another, as conveniently they may ; for now the scattered " disciples were assembled," and conferring one with another, and communicating what light any of them had received, as hath been cleared. (See Mal. iii. 16 ; Acts, i. 14.)

3. It hath been no strange thing in the church that saints have been put to frequent their assemblies with great fear, and have been forced to meet in the dark night, and with great caution, because of danger from persecutors ; for they were met " at evening, and the doors were shut where the disciples were assembled for fear of the Jews." And this may teach us to bless the Lord for our liberty.

4. The danger and hazard wherein disciples are will not hold Christ from their company ; and he can come, even when he is little expected, and many impediments are in his way ; for when they are in this case, and when the doors are shut, and they little expect him, " Jesus came and stood in the midst," which posture also points at the manner of his presence among his people, as Matt. xviii. 20—namely, that he is very near to

every one of them, and they all round about him, and that he takes not a weak lift, nor hath a remote influence upon their way and society.

5. Peace is Christ's company and allowance to his people where he cometh; and as it is he who can command and speak peace, so he alloweth it upon them, whatever his dealing be, or he speak unto them beside; for by this he evidenced his presence, that he " saith unto them, Peace be unto you," which was his allowance and legacy before his suffering, chap. xiv. 27 ; and this he alloweth upon them, however he upbraideth them at the same time, as it is Mark, xvi. 14, and in opposition also to any terror they might have by reason of his so sudden and unexpected appearing among them.

VER. 20. And when he had so said, he shewed unto them his hands and his side. Then were the disciples glad, when they saw the Lord.

The next (and a more clear) evidence of his resurrection is, by shewing them his pierced hands and side, and the scars and wounds which he yet retained after his resurrection, (though it be needless to determine whether he keep them to all eternity, or not,) which doth fully confirm, and affect them with much joy. Whence learn—

1. Christ after his resurrection had still the same body, for substance and essential properties, which he had before his suffering; for by shewing his hands and his side, as they had been pierced, he makes it evident to them that it was the same body, and consequently that it was truly he who appeared now to them.

2. Christ, even in his exaltation, looks upon his sufferings for his people as his crown and glory; therefore did he rise again with his pierced hands and side, (as is clear from this, compared with ver. 25, 27,) and retained these prints (at least for a time) in his state of exaltation.

3. Christ will not forget how dearly his people, though worthless, cost him, that so he may see the better to his purchase; therefore also did he retain the print of these wounds, at least for a time, in his begun exaltation.

4. It is the church's great comfort, not simply that Christ is alive, but that he had been dead, and was now alive, having overcome all their enemies; for this also may be gathered from his shewing them his hands and his side, whereby he would point out unto them that he was returned unto them a conqueror over death and all his sufferings. (See Rev. i. 8.)

5. Whatever sight believers get of Christ, yet it is still needful to look upon him as pierced by their sins, that this may season their other exercise with useful tenderness and sorrow ; for this further may be pointed at in his shewing them his hands and his side, that he would keep them in mind, even in his exaltation, how he had been pierced for their sakes.

6. Christ is the most joyful sight to disciples of any that ever they see ; and whatever their condition be, yet a sight of him will make them glad, especially after they have had sad apprehensions about the want of him ; for of this sad company it is said, " Then were the disciples glad, when they saw the Lord."

VER. 21. Then said Jesus to them again, Peace be unto you: as my Father hath sent me, even so send I you.

The second part of Christ's scope and errand in appearing is to confirm and renew their calling to the apostleship and work of the ministry, who had just cause to be much shaken with the remembrance of their faintheartedness in his late sufferings. It containeth three particulars ; in the first whereof, (in this verse,) after a preface, wherein he reneweth his allowance of peace unto them, he doth in general commissionate and send them to the work of the ministry, as the Father sent him. Whence learn—

1. Disciples are so often essayed and opposed in their enjoying of Christ's allowed peace, that they need to have the sense thereof, and their right thereunto, often renewed and repeated unto them by Christ ; therefore he said unto them again, (after that verse 19,) " Peace be unto you."

2. The sum of the employment of the ministers of the gospel is peace, as being sent to publish the glad tidings of the gospel of peace, and the scope of their work being to bring people to enjoy sound and solid peace in the due order ; therefore also doth he say, " Peace be unto you," in reference to their commission and employment.

3. Preachers of the gospel of peace have much need of Christ's peace, both to support them under the tribulation they will meet with, in discharge of their trust, and to enable them experimentally to preach that peace unto others ; therefore further doth he say, " Peace be unto you," to qualify and encourage them for this work, and that they, having received this peace, might be fit preachers of it.

4. It pleased the Father to send his own Son into the world, clothed with a commission, that hereby he might give a proof of his great love unto lost man ; for " My Father hath sent me," saith he.

5. Christ did not leave his church destitute when his own ministry was ended, but hath substituted a ministry in his name, till the end of the world ; for saith he, " I send you," which was true of them and their successors to the end of the world, Matt. xxviii. 19, 20.

6. Ministers are of Christ's sending and employing by his sovereign authority, as his courts and ministers do, ministerially in his name, send them out ; they must not run unsent ; they who want them, and would have them blessed to them, should seek them of him ; they who are lawfully called are to act in his name and authority, which is to be acknowledged by people in their discharge of their trust, and such messengers are to be looked on as a great and special gift bestowed on the church by her exalted Lord. All this is imported in this, " I send you," now when he is risen from the dead, in his begun exaltation. (See Eph. iv. 8—11.)

7. This proportion and comparison instituted betwixt Christ's sending and theirs, " As my Father hath sent me, even so send I you," is not to be understood universally, as to all the works and ends for which Christ was sent,—for he was sent to satisfy Divine justice, and to do the work of redemption, which they were not,—but it is to be understood of the work of the ministry and preaching of the gospel. Nor yet is there an equality to be urged here, but the proportion and distance is still to be observed and kept betwixt the Lord and his servants, and the Bridegroom and his friends. Nor is the resemblance only in this, that as Christ was immediately sent by the Father, so were they (as apostles) immediately sent by him. But Christ's being sent by his Father, and their being sent by him, do agree— 1. In the strictness of the commission, that as Christ did always the will of the Father, so they must not dispense with what is committed to their trust, nor be the servants of men. 2. They agree in having the same promise of success and blessing in their labours, as the apostles richly found. 3. They do agree in the matter of their authority, so far as, however he be the Lord and they servants, yet they come clothed with the same authority, being in Christ's stead to the people of God, 2 Cor. v. 20, and Christ, and God in Christ, being despised in the affronts put upon them in the exercise of their ministry, Matt. x. 42.

VER. 22. And when he had said this, he breathed on them, and saith unto them, Receive ye the Holy Ghost :

In the next place, Christ who sends them doth also furnish them with the gifts of the Spirit for that office, some fruits whereof, before that full measure was let out upon them, Acts, ii., doth appear in what is recorded of them, Acts, i. 15, &c. Whence learn—

1. Where Christ doth employ and send out any about his work, their call from him (being embraced and followed in obedience thereunto, and with dependence upon him who hath sent them) doth assure them of furniture for their calling also; for they are conjoined here, " I send you," ver. 21; " And when he had said this, he breathed on them," &c.

2. The furniture of ministers for discharge of their calling must be the Spirit of God communicated unto them by Christ, in his gifts and qualifications suitable and requisite to their work, and who must be daily sought for quickening and keeping fresh that furniture which floweth from him, and for making the exercise of these gifts effectual; for it is " the Holy Ghost," who furnisheth the apostles in their measure and station, and so also other ministers. They were indeed extraordinarily gifted, without any previous study and acquired abilities; and other ministers, albeit they ought to make conscience of ordinary means for enabling them to that work, 1 Tim. iv. 13, yet it is from the Spirit of God that they must be gifted with the spirit of that employment, and with common and ordinary gifts for it, and it is he who must accom-

pany them in that work, and make it lively and effectual.

3. The Holy Ghost cometh upon every professor, and particularly ministers, by free donation and gift from Christ; he is the acquirer of that furniture unto them, and their great work is to receive it of his liberality; for saith he, " Receive ye the Holy Ghost."

4. This breathing on them, when he communicated this furniture, being an extraordinary sign of his communicating this extraordinary furniture, is therefore not to be imitated by any in ordinary who have not the dispensing of these endowments; only, Christ's making use thereof may serve, partly, to point out some resemblance betwixt this sign of breathing and the inspirations and refreshful breathings of this Spirit upon them, and their gifts who receive it; and as the Spirit's descending at the sign of fiery cloven tongues, Acts, ii. 3, served to point out their being furnished to speak divers languages, so his being communicated by the sign of breathing holds out that where he cometh he quickens and puts life in men's spirits, (as by God's breathing the first man was made a living soul, Gen. ii. 7,) and doth refresh and make them fruitful, as Cant. iv. 16; partly, it serveth to point out Christ's godhead, who hath the gifting of the Spirit in his hand, and who can easily, as by a breathing, furnish the most rude and unlearned, and make them extraordinarily able; according as the soul of the first man was easily created.

VER. 23. Whose soever sins ye remit, they are remitted unto them; and whose soever sins ye retain, they are retained.

In the last place, Christ asserts their authority in the discharge of their commission, and in governing his house, and remitting or retaining of sins, whether by the key of knowledge or doctrine in preaching, or of order and discipline; and he declareth, that what they act this way ministerially, according to their commission, is ratified in heaven, as being but the declaration and intimation of the sentence already passed there. This power is elsewhere called "the keys of the kingdom of heaven," Matt. xvi. 19, and the power of binding and loosing, Matt. xviii. 18.

DOCTRINES.

1. Christ's house is not a den of confusion, but a house of order, wherein he hath a lamp of doctrine, whereby he doth doctrinally declare his mind concerning his subjects and their duty, and a rod of discipline, whereby he judicially deals with them as their case requireth; for so is here imported, that there is a power of remitting and retaining sins, both doctrinally and by judicial procedure.

2. This power in the house of God is committed to Christ's own officers and ministers sent by him unto his church; so that, however private persons may declare the mind of God concerning the sin of others; yea, and reprove, exhort, or comfort out of charity; yet his ministers are to do it by office, and with authority; for it is ye (whom I send, ver. 21) who are to remit and retain sins.

3. This power in the house of God is committed equally and in common to all ministers, so that one doth not share in it more than another; for here it is given to the apostles in common, " Whose soever sins ye remit," &c. And thus the keys of the kingdom are not given to Peter only, but here expressly to all.

4. All the members of the church are subject to the order established by Christ in his house, and none ought to free themselves from his yoke; all are bound to submit to his doctrine in the mouths of his servants, and all also are under his rod of government; for their authority is universal, over whosoever need the exercise thereof.

5. The exercise of this ministerial authority over church-members is committed unto Christ's servants, not in reference to the good which is in any to crush it, but in reference to their sin, to deal with them because of it, according as their condition requireth; their power in doctrine is exercised about all sin, as sin, were it never so secret and inward, and their power in discipline about sin only as it is scandalous and infectious; for their power here is about sins, and over persons because of this.

6. The exercise of ministerial authority about the sins of church members consists in the remitting and retaining thereof, according to the due order and rules of the word; and particularly, that such as are penitent, and feel the bonds of their sin, they do declaratively, and by authority from Christ, absolve and loose them, and do also take off any censure judicially inflicted for their scandalous behaviour; and such as are impenitent, that they do, by doctrine in Christ's name, declare their sins not to be remitted, but bound upon them, and that, as need requires, they do by a judicial sentence tie them straiter, that so they may feel the bonds, and seek to be loosed; for so is held out here, that they are ministerially to remit and retain sins.

7. This exercise of ministerial authority, however carnal hearts may contemn and slight it, either in doctrine or discipline, yet, being gone about according to the rules of the word, it is so effectual as it is ratified in heaven, and the penitent or obstinate sinner will find God's mind towards them to be according as is declared in his name on earth; for upon these terms is their authority asserted, " Whose soever sins ye remit, they are remitted unto them; and whose soever sins ye retain, they are retained." (See Matt. xviii. 18, 20.) And this may be matter of terror to the obstinate, and of encouragement to the penitent, who are meet objects of the comfortable exercise of ministerial authority.

VER. 24. But Thomas, one of the twelve, called Didymus, was not with them when Jesus came.

25. The other disciples therefore said unto him, We have seen the Lord. But he said unto them, Except I shall see in his hands the print of the nails, and put my finger into the print of the nails, and thrust my hand into his side, I will not believe.

Followeth unto verse 30, Christ's appearing to all the disciples, when Thomas was with them, occasioned chiefly, (as is clear from the sequel,) by Thomas's diffidence. The narration of this appearing may be taken up in five particulars; the first whereof (in these verses) is the occasion of his appearing at this time; and this is either more remote, that Thomas (of whom we have already heard, chap. xi. 16, and xiv. 5) was not with them at their last meeting with Christ, being not as yet returned from his lurking place, ver. 24, or more near, that when the rest of the disciples acquainted him (either having sought him out, or he coming unto them) that they had seen the Lord, he wilfully professeth he will not believe unless he get the sensible satisfaction prescribed by himself, ver. 25; for clearing whereof we are to consider that it was not his sin simply that he desired a sight of Christ, nor yet that he sought that evidence of his pierced hands, and of the hole of his side, (which it appeareth was now known to all the disciples, though John only records that he saw it, chap. xix. 34, 35,) seeing that was the same evidence which Christ himself had given, ver. 20, and his desire of this did evidence his affection unto a crucified Christ; but it was his fault not to believe the truth of Christ's resurrection till he not only saw this, but thrust his hand also into his side, for further satisfaction. Neither was it his sin that simply he would not hearken to their report, as men, in this matter, seeing that is no sure ground of faith; but it was his sin that he did not believe the scriptures, which spake of Christ's resurrection, and so did not believe them as God's witnesses unless he got sensible satisfaction.

DOCTRINES.

1. They may be truly gracious who yet are very timorous in a trial, and will not recover from their fears so soon as others; for Thomas, a godly man, " was not with them," nor had returned to the society as yet, when the rest had recollected themselves.

2. Negligence in frequenting the society and assemblies of the people of God casts men far behind, and prejudgeth them much; for " Thomas, one of the twelve, called Didymus, (of the signification whereof, see on chap. xi. 16,) was not with them when Jesus came," and so he was deprived, not only of the good news which Mary and others brought them, but of that comfortable sight of him also which they got, and he is left in many snares and doubtings, from which they are delivered.

3. Disciples ought to be communicative in their station of what they have received; and when their hearts are refreshed with a sweet sight of Christ they cannot but make it known, as they have a calling and opportunity; for " The other disciples therefore said unto him, We have seen the Lord," which no doubt they told with all the circumstances of it, whereof this was the sum, and that which most affected them, and stuck with them.

4. Christ should be very great in his disciples' estimation, and their respects to him should be upon the growing hand; for now he is still the Lord, ver. 2, 13, 18, 20, 28, and chap. xxi. 7, 12,

15, 16, &c., which was a style more rarely given him before.

5. Unbelief is strangely rooted in the hearts of all men. yea, even of godly men and disciples, so that they may frequently fall into that sin, and be very pertinacious in it; for so much doth Thomas's example teach us, " I will not believe," saith he.

6. Our carnal hearts know no way, nor will admit of any cure of unbelief, unless they get all the objects of faith under the view of their senses; for so is it with Thomas here; he will see, and lest his sight should be deluded, he will touch also, and " thrust his hand into his side."

7. It is the great sin and weakness of men when they do not believe unless they get satisfaction to their senses, seeing faith is the evidence of things not seen, Heb. xi. 1. But it is yet a greater sin, and a height of presumption, to be wilful in unbelief, and to be so bold as to say they will not believe, upon grounds revealed and afforded by him, unless they get their will; which is a limiting of the Holy One of Israel; for this was Thomas's fault, " Except I shall see, &c., I will not believe."

> VER. 26. And after eight days again his disciples were within, and Thomas with them : then came Jesus, the doors being shut, and stood in the midst, and said, Peace be unto you.

The second particular in this narration is Christ's appearing to them again after a week, when Thomas is met with them, and that after the former manner, and with the former salutation. Whence learn—

1. This appearing of Christ among them is said to be " after eight days," not eight days after Thomas's professed unbelief, (though it is like the disciples had told him the good news speedily,) but after his former appearing, ver. 19, and upon the first day of the next week. And he did then appear unto them, not only because it was their usual meeting day, or to try the faith of the rest, by Thomas's continuing in doubting and unbelief, but chiefly, to teach us that however the Lord will help and cure the unbelief of his own, yet when they are wilful and peremptory in it, it is righteous with him to let them lie under it for a time, till they feel the evil and bitterness of it, and till they see their deserving to be given up to it, that so they may magnify his mercy who cometh over it; therefore doth Thomas meet with this correction, that he seeth not Christ till " after eight days," and so had a sad week of it.

2. The people of God ought not to forsake their mutual societies and assembling of themselves together, but they should continue therein, as they expect the renewed presence of Christ with them; for it is when " again his disciples were within," that Jesus came, " the doors being shut, and stood in the midst."

3. Whatever be the failings or unbelief of saints, yet it is commendable in them to be amending their other known faults and neglects; and there is still hope of their case, so long as they use the means whereby they may be cured

of their unbelief, and do not, with their unbelief, quit the use of means also; for it is here marked, that in this meeting Thomas was with them, though yet doubting; wherein appears that, being sensible of his former loss, he keeps the society and meetings of the disciples, to see what clearing he might find; and so not only amended his former fault, (which yet is most rare to see,) but waits on in the use of appointed means.

4. It is the duty of Christ's followers not to lose or cast off any, though weak and unbelieving, so long as they can get them along with them in any duty, and so long as there is any hope of their amendment, and being reclaimed; for so it was commendable on the disciples' part that Thomas was with them and they had not cast him off. Where this condescendence is wanting, many may be lost who otherwise would be recovered.

5. Christ will not be wanting to come over the infirmities of his own to do them good, and he can make good use of their worst things, and is so willing to manifest himself that he will let no opportunity of it slip; for he makes use, even of Thomas's doubting, as an occasion of appearing over again, as is clear from the whole tenour of this narration, both what precedes and what followeth.

6. Christ is not changeable in his love and allowance of peace to his people, but is yesterday, and to-day, the same for ever; therefore over again doth he repeat his salutation, "and said, Peace be unto you."

> VER. 27. Then saith he to Thomas, Reach hither thy finger, and behold my hands; and reach hither thy hand, and thrust it into my side : and be not faithless, but believing.

The third particular in this narration is his dealing with Thomas, indirectly reproving him for his faithlessness, and offering unto him the satisfaction he desired to cure this evil. Whence learn—

1. Christ perfectly knoweth and is acquainted with the cases and distempers of his people, and can tell them what aileth them, albeit they do not tell him; for his discourse with Thomas intimateth that, without any information, he knew Thomas's doubtings and unbelief.

2. Albeit Christ's followers do provoke him by their unbelief, yet he will not quit them, but will deal with them so much the more beyond others as their need and weakness is greater; therefore, when he appeareth here, he dealeth only with Thomas, though most faulty and weak, " Then saith he to Thomas," &c.

3. Christ hath a great quarrel at unbelief in his people, (either when they do not believe and ponder the truth of what he reveals, or make not due application thereof to themselves,) as being exceedingly injurious to him, and obscuring his glory, and as obstructing their own good; for this Christ reproves, and would have amended in Thomas, " be not faithless, but believing."

4. Such as have publicly sinned to the offending of others should be publicly dealt with, to

take with and amend their fault, that so their recovery may strengthen those whom their failings were ready to weaken; therefore doth Christ deal with and seek to reclaim Thomas, in presence of all the disciples, to whom he had professed his wilful unbelief.

5. Christ's offering this satisfaction to Thomas, prescribed by himself, is not a warrant to every unbeliever and tempter of him to seek and expect this or the like signs of their own prescribing, for helping of their faith; for Christ's reproof, insinuated with his offer, and expressed after Thomas's confession, ver. 29, doth point it out as a sin, and should teach all believers their duty, that they be warned by his example to be humbled that any such presumption should enter their hearts, and to reject the first motions of it. And indeed, such signs not being promised by God, it is a limiting of him, and a high presumption, to prescribe them unto him; and it speaks their proud despising and contemning of the means appointed by God so to do; and whatever effect this offer had upon Thomas, yet there is no promise that any of these signs prescribed should work faith, when we believe not the word, Luke, xvi. 29—31, and therefore it were to no purpose to grant them. Yet this procedure with Thomas may teach us—1. Unbelief is so hateful to Christ in his people, and he is so sensible of the prejudice they sustain thereby, that he is very careful and earnest to have it removed and cured; for so much doth his offering him, even his will, to amend his fault, teach us. 2. Christ is very condescending to his people in their infirmities, and doth ofttimes yield very much to their weakness and peevishness, which yet it is their fault to seek, and of others to imitate them in it; for so much also doth this instance of his condescendence to Thomas teach us. 3. Christ may deny that to a believer which he will grant to a weak believer; and yet the believer is more approven, though kept at a distance, than the unbeliever who is so dealt with; for believing Mary gets not so much as leave to touch him, ver. 17, when unbelieving Thomas gets an offer both to see and touch, but with a check. 4. Unbelievers can limit Christ to no proof of his love which implieth not a contradiction, but if he saw it fitting, he could give it; so that it is not for want of power that such tempters are not satisfied, but because he will not learn them to slight his word, on which they ought to build; for here, by offering unto Thomas all he desires, he gives proof how easy it were for him to satisfy the like unreasonable desires.

VER. 28. And Thomas answered and said unto him, My Lord and my God.

The fourth particular in this narration is the use which Thomas makes of this offer. It seems he did not presume to touch Christ, or thrust his hand into his side, but contented himself with seeing Christ, ver. 29, as abhorring his own folly in so prescribing. But upon what he saw, and upon the consideration of Christ's condescendence and his weakness, he gives a fair confession concerning Christ's deity, and closeth with him. Whence learn—

1. Great mountains of unbelief, which seem insuperable unto saints, will easily flow down and evanish at Christ's presence; for Thomas's wilfulness is now cured without making use (as appeareth) of all that he required.

2. It is the duty of such as have offended others by their failings, to be eminent and exemplary in their recovering of themselves; and God may ofttimes make the last to be first, in their outstripping others who were before them; for here Thomas, who had miscarried so far, giveth a fairer confession than any of the rest had done.

3. When Christ is well seen, and the way of his resurrection and his condescendence to his people are well considered, he will be undeniably seen to be God; for Thomas, now persuaded of his resurrection, and considering his dealing with him, crieth out that he is God, seeing no man could rise so as he did, but he who is God also, which his tender kindness to himself did further confirm.

4. Christ being looked upon in his glory, and as God, it may and should allure hearts to close with and embrace him; and they who indeed consider him to be such an one cannot but claim to an interest in him; therefore Thomas calls him, my God.

5. Such as find the sweetness of an interest in Christ as their God, it will persuade their hearts to allow unto him a dominion and lordship over them, to guide and dispose of them at his pleasure; for Thomas here conjoineth these, " My Lord and my God."

VER. 29. Jesus saith unto him, Thomas, because thou hast seen me, thou hast believed: blessed are they that have not seen, and yet have believed.

The last particular in this narration is Christ's reproving of Thomas, now when he is recovered, wherein he extenuates his believing now, and not till now, and commends and blesseth all those who shall believe, though they see not; as all they do who embrace and close with Christ crucified and risen again, as he is held out in the gospel; as all those also who believed before his incarnation, though they were not eye witnesses thereof.

DOCTRINES.

1. Though Christ be tender and condescending to cure the unbelief of his people, and though they may recover out of their fits, and give a fair profession of their faith, yet he would not have them forgetting the evil of their unbelief, to reprove and judge themselves for it; therefore now, when Thomas is believing, yet he will rebuke him for his weakness.

2. Christ is a skilful and tender physician, who allows not, nor intends that we should be put away, or our faith weakened by his reproofs; therefore he will not reprove, except in an indirect way, ver. 27, till first he believe and be strengthened.

3. To suspend our believing upon our sight is reproof-worthy, and in some sort extenuates that faith in Christ's account; and such as get satisfaction to their sense to cure their unbelief ought

yet to consider that Christ hath a quarrel at them, whereof they ought to be sensible and humbled for it; therefore saith Christ, by way of extenuation, " Thomas, because thou hast seen me, thou hast believed;" where he doth not condemn the rest of the disciples, who both believed and saw, but only his suspending his faith on his seeing.

4. It is a great blessedness and mercy to believe and get faith, as putting them who get it in a blessed and sweet estate of calmness and assurance, and furnishing them with a shield, whereby to ward off many fiery darts, and being a pledge and forerunner of sweet manifestations and performances from the Lord; for " blessed are they that have believed." (See Luke, i. 45.) And this holds true of all believers, even of Thomas's own faith, though some share more in it than others.

5. The less sensible evidence there be of the object of faith, (provided it be revealed in the word,) there is the greater blessedness in believing thereof; and such faith will be the more excellent and commendable in Christ's sight, as participating more of the nature of faith, and giving more glory to him; for " blessed are they that have not seen, and yet have believed." (See Rom. iv. 19, 20 ; Matt. xv. 22—28 ; 1 Pet. i. 8.)

Ver. 30. And many other signs truly did Jesus in the presence of his disciples, which are not written in this book :

31. But these are written, that ye might believe that Jesus is the Christ, the Son of God; and that believing ye might have life through his name.

In the last part of this chapter, John being about to close this evangel, and many other things coming into his mind which Christ had done after his resurrection, he (so to say) draweth pen from paper, confessing there were many such like, which he was not directed to write, (not only because some of them were recorded by the rest, but) in regard what he had written was sufficient to faith and salvation, and to clear what Christ was, and confirm that salvation is to be had through faith in him. For clearing of this purpose, consider—1. That those things which John confesseth to have omitted here are particularly such things as were done by Christ after his resurrection; for these were done " in the presence of his disciples," whereas those things he did before his death were done generally before all ; though it be also true of those his other acts, that they were not all recorded by him, nor by the rest, chap. xxi. 25. 2. What John propounds, ver. 31, as his end in writing these things, is indeed the scope of all this history of the gospel written by him, and so doth relate to all he hath formerly written ; but it doth particularly relate to those signs formerly mentioned, which in their own kind, and in the way of miracles' influence, were sufficient (without adding any more) to confirm the doctrine all along delivered concerning the person of the Messiah, and the way of obtaining salvation through him. 3. John doth omit the writing of these signs, and tells of it, not to give occasion of slandering the scriptures as imperfect, nor to curious men to inquire after them, and obtrude them upon the church ; for what he omits are not points of doctrine, but only particular signs of the same nature and kind with those recorded ; and what he records is sufficient to salvation, in so far as miracles are props to faith, as he cleareth, ver. 31. Beside, how shall any know infallibly that the miracles they allege to be Christ's are truly such, seeing the word doth not point them out particularly ? And if any think scripture is imperfect, because it hath not all these signs, how can they assert they have indeed marked all, seeing they are many and innumerable, chap. xxi. 25, and so, by their own principles, the church shall be at a loss still. 4. Albeit those recorded by John be sufficient for the ends recorded by him, yet we are not to think that Christ's doing of those he omitted was useless, though it was not needful he should write them ; for not only was it necessary for the time that they should be multiplied, to confirm the doubting disciples in the faith of his resurrection, but it is needful for us to know he did so many, though we know not in particular what they were.

DOCTRINES.

1. It speaks out Christ's great praise and glory that beside the many glorious acts recorded to be done by him, particularly after his resurrection, we may be persuaded that he did many more, and that he is one whose glorious acts it were an endless task to publish ; for this end, and that we may have high thoughts of Christ, doth John record that " many other signs truly did Jesus in presence of his disciples, which are not written in this book." And this speaks his praise more than if John had recorded many more particulars.

2. The Lord would have his people not doting too much on signs and miracles, which are only extraordinary and remote props of faith, but would have them acquiescing in what he works or records of these; therefore doth John omit the narration of many particulars, which the disciples saw, to the church in after ages, that they might learn, not to rest much on these, but to fasten upon the word, which is sufficiently confirmed by what is recorded.

3. The scriptures are not intended mainly for recording multitudes of signs and miracles for the satisfaction of curiosity, or which might induce idle men to read them for recreation or putting off time, but the great scope of the scriptures is to direct men how to know Christ and save their own souls ; therefore John doth omit these signs, enough being recorded in subserviency to the great end of the scriptures, " that ye might believe," &c. And this should be the trial, how we read scriptures, and how we profit thereby.

4. No imperfection can be fastened upon scripture in matters of faith, or necessary to salvation, nay, nor in affording sufficient signs for confirming the doctrine held out therein, even albeit it be clear that particular things done by Christ are not recorded therein; for John grants this, and yet asserts the perfection of the scriptures, " But these are written, that ye might believe," &c. (See 2 Tim. iii. 16, 17.)

5. The great scope of the scriptures is, in the

first place, to direct us to know and take up Christ rightly, who is the kernel and marrow of all the scriptures, to whom the law and all the prophets bear witness, and who is the great subject of the gospel; for so is here held out, " These things are written, that ye might believe that Jesus is the Christ," &c.

6. Christ is only savingly known and taken up by faith; there is no coming to the treasures of the scriptures, nor to study him in them, but by faith, and no perspective beside will be transparent; for " these things are written, that ye might believe," &c.

7. The great point concerning Christ, to be known and believed from the scriptures, is, that Jesus, the son of Mary, is the only promised Messiah, and anointed of the Father, he in whom all the law types and shadows are accomplished, and in whom the promises are yea, and Amen; and that the same Jesus is also, in unity of person, the Son of God by eternal generation, one in essence, and equal in power and glory with the Father; for this is the great point to be believed, " that Jesus is the Christ, the Son of God," which is a large and needful study.

8. The scriptures are also written to point out that there is an eternal life, only worthy of the name of life, and which otherwise is hid from the world, 2 Tim. i. 10, and to point out how this life may be attained; for so is held out in the next place as his end of writing, " that ye might have life."

9. The scriptures do point out no way of attaining salvation but only through faith in Christ, and that " in his name," or as he hath revealed himself; and it doth hold out the way and due order wherein sinners ought to flee to him, and how they ought to abide in him, and doth promise eternal life to all who do so; for the subject and doctrine of the scriptures is, " that believing ye might have life through his name." (See Acts, iv. 12.)

10. As it is a part of our way to heaven to be sound in the faith and knowledge of Christ, so a right knowledge of him as he is revealed in the scriptures, and hath confirmed and evidenced the same by his miracles, is a special mean to excite men to seek after him, and salvation through him, and to encourage them to rely on him for attaining of salvation; therefore is the one subjoined as following on the other, that believing Jesus to be " Christ, the Son of God," as the word holdeth out, and he hath made good by these signs, they will seek life with him and through him, and will be encouraged to " believe" that they shall " have life through his name."

CHAPTER XXI.

This chapter contains (beside the conclusion of the whole book) a narration of a new appearing and manifestation of Christ unto seven disciples, with what followed thereupon, which being summarily propounded, ver. 1, is prosecuted at large in the rest of the chapter; and namely, that they going a fishing, but without success, ver. 2, 3, Christ appears to them in the morning and conferreth with them unknown, ver. 4, 5; that he afterward makes himself known by a miraculous draught of fishes afforded them, ver. 6, 7, upon which they come to land to him, ver. 7, 8, where they see his preparation for their dinner, ver. 9, are led to take notice of the greatness of the miracle wrought for them, ver. 10, 11, and dine with him, exceedingly reverencing him, ver. 12, 13, (and this is marked to be the third time he had appeared to them, ver. 14;) and that he conferreth with Peter particularly, whom he restoreth to his former dignity, upon the profession of his love to him, ver. 15—17, and warneth him concerning his future sufferings, commanding him to follow him, ver. 18, 19; and checks his curious inquiry concerning John, ver. 20—22, in a speech which occasioned a mistake among the disciples, but causelessly, as John cleareth, ver. 23, who here takes occasion to close this history, asserting that he was the penman thereof, and was persuaded of the certainty of it, ver. 24, and acknowledgeth that many things done by Christ are omitted in his narration, it being impossible to record them all, ver. 25.

Ver. 1. *After these things Jesus shewed himself again to the disciples at the sea of Tiberias; and on this wise shewed he himself.*

John, in the close of the former chapter, having shewed that Christ, after his resurrection, did many signs in presence of his disciples which he had not written, doth in this chapter give a notable proof thereof, by recording one notable appearing of Christ, wherein many signs concurred. This he propoundeth generally in this verse, undertaking to describe it in its circumstances, and mentioning the place where it was done—namely, at and beside some part of the lake of Gennesareth, which here gets the name from the city Tiberias, (which was built upon the side of that lake,) and is elsewhere called the sea of Galilee, John, vi. 1. Christ had wrought some miracles before in this lake, and in the towns of Galilee about it he had preached and wrought many miracles; and now he doth appear there after his resurrection, (as his solemn meeting with the disciples was in Galilee also, Matt. xxviii. 16, 17,) that he may bring to their remembrance what had passed there formerly.

DOCTRINES.

1. It is needful we be much confirmed in the faith of the resurrection of Jesus Christ, as being a truth not easily believed indeed, and being believed is full of rich comfort, and a sure pledge that all Christ's and his people's sufferings, though even unto death, will end in glory; therefore, " after these things," (and Christ's shewing himself so often in the former chapter,) " Jesus shewed himself again," to confirm their faith who had yet some scruples, as may be gathered from ver. 12.

2. Such as are to publish the truths of Christ

unto others ought to be solidly persuaded of them themselves, and do need much from Christ for that effect, that so they may publish them from a sure persuasion, 2 Cor. iv. 13; therefore did he " shew himself again to the disciples," who were, most part, if not all, of them to publish these glad tidings throughout the world.

3. Christ's presence and manifestations of himself are not restricted to any one place, but wherever his people are there he will manifest himself as they need; for " Jesus shewed himself to the disciples at the sea of Tiberias," as well as at Jerusalem, from whence they were now returned, for reasons to be after mentioned.

4. The particular passages and circumstances of Christ's manifesting of himself to his people ought to be narrowly observed and taken notice of, as being full of rich use and instruction; therefore doth John, who was an eye-witness, undertake here to describe them, " and on this wise shewed he himself."

Ver. 2. There were together Simon Peter, and Thomas called Didymus, and Nathanael of Cana in Galilee, and the sons of Zebedee, and two other of his disciples.

3. Simon Peter saith unto them, I go a fishing. They say unto him, We also go with thee. They went forth, and entered into a ship immediately; and that night they caught nothing.

The particular narration of this appearing and manifestation may be branched out in these heads:—1. The antecedents thereof, ver. 2, 3. 2. His appearing unto them, though unknown, and his conference with them, ver. 4, 5. 3. The way how he manifests and makes himself known unto them, ver. 6, 7. 4. Some particular effects and consequents of this manifestation, before his conference with Peter, ver. 7—14. 5. His conference with Peter, ver. 15—23.

In these verses the antecedents of his shewing himself are recorded, that these seven disciples being together, they do, upon Peter's motion, go a fishing, wherein they labour all night without any success. As for these seven, four of them were called to be apostles, and so, it may be, were the two who are not named. As for Nathanael, (of whom chap. i. 45, &c., we do not find him to be one of them, unless under another name, (as some suppose he was called Bartholomew,) but only a disciple and follower of Christ. And as for their society and being together at this time, rather than others of the apostles, we need not curiously inquire concerning it. It is sufficient to know that those named were countrymen of Galilee, and so may we judge of the other two, and so they had occasion to be more frequently together, and are now met at this time, and that, as would appear, at Peter's house, who makes the motion of following his trade. It is also to be marked, that this overture, propounded by Peter, and embraced by the rest, of returning to their former calling, did not proceed from their distrust and quitting of their ministerial calling,—for we are not so

to conceive of them who were already endowed with the Holy Ghost in some measure, chap. xx. 22,—but the true cause was, that being only designed, not yet actually employed nor fully endowed for that calling till the Spirit was more fully poured forth upon them, and those forty days after the resurrection of Christ being set apart for their confirmation in the faith of his resurrection by his frequent appearing unto them, and for their further instruction by Christ, in the matters of the kingdom of God, which they were afterward to publish, Acts, i. 3; and they, at this time, being returned from Jerusalem to Galilee, to keep that meeting which Christ had appointed in Galilee, of which Matt. xxviii. 7, 16, 17, they did lawfully go about their ordinary employment till the day of the meeting came. However, Christ took occasion of this to manifest himself.

DOCTRINES.

1. The most special and remarkable manifestations of Christ to his people are given them when they are together; for " There were together Simon Peter," &c. And albeit Peter made a motion for himself, " I go a fishing," which might have separated them, yet providence keeps and sends them along together till this manifestation come.

2. It is a commendable duty in those who are made sensible of their loss by being absent from the societies of saints to attend them more constantly afterwards; for here we find Thomas constantly continuing in the company of the rest of the disciples.

3. Christ doth not esteem of men nor deal with them according as they are of note among others, providing they be honest, and disciples indeed; for it is marked, to the commendation of " two other of his disciples," that they " were together" with the rest, and Christ sheweth himself to them as to the rest, though their names be not expressed, as the rest's [others] are.

4. It is the will of Christ that his followers do not neglect their lawful calling (though never so base) as they may overtake it; and in going about their lawful callings they may expect special manifestations of Christ; for it is commendable in them that they cast not off their mean calling, but " Peter saith, I go a fishing," and " they say unto him, We also go with thee," and " they went forth, and entered into a ship immediately." And it is while they are about this employment that Christ sheweth himself to them.

5. The children of the Lord are subject to the same difficulties of earning their daily bread, and of hazard, toil, and difficulties in their calling with others, that so they may know they are by nature of Adam's stock as well as others, and may not expect singular lots in outward things; for his disciples are put to earn their bread by fishing, and they are put to work at it all night, not for fear, but because it was the fittest season; and they work so hard as they must strip themselves almost naked (as appeareth ver. 7) through heat; and all this for their livelihood, and ofttimes with little profit, as after followeth.

6. It may please the Lord ofttimes to deny his

people success in their lawful employments; and that, either when their hearts are too eager and keen upon the world he doth justly cross them, to teach them mortification and sobriety; or because, if success were constant, God would not be so clearly seen in his bounty, and therefore he crosseth that we may acknowledge him more; or because, he is to appear eminently for his people, therefore he makes way for his appearing, by denying success upon their endeavours; as here, skilled fishers, well acquainted with this lake, and the way of speeding in it, do that night catch nothing. And this maketh way for his after prospering of them in a miraculous manner.

VER. 4. But when the morning was now come, Jesus stood on the shore: but the disciples knew not that it was Jesus.

5. Then Jesus saith unto them, Children, have ye any meat? They answered him, No.

The second branch of this narration contains Christ's shewing himself unto them upon the shore in the morning, though they do not know him, ver. 4, together with his conference with them before they knew him, wherein, dealing with them as a stranger and one coming to buy fishes, he draweth out a confession of their bad success, ver. 5; and as this his appearing, though unknown, made way for his manifesting of himself, so this conference makes way for the miracle whereby he discovered himself.

DOCTRINES.

1. It is usual for Christ to make use of his people's difficulties as a preparation to some special manifestations of himself; for so find they here, " that night they caught nothing," ver. 3; " But when the morning was now come, Jesus stood on the shore."

2. As for not knowing of him, I will not determine whether it was because of the darkness, (it being but yet morning,) together with their distance from Christ, being about two hundred cubits, ver. 8, or by reason of some extraordinary restraining of their sight and discerning for a time, but it may teach us, that Christ is not always discerned when he is present, and it is one mercy to enjoy his company, and another to know indeed that it is he; for " Jesus stood on the shore; but the disciples knew not that it was Jesus;" and they after confer with him as with a stranger.

3. When Christ is about to manifest himself for his people, he will not only have them empty, but will have the sense of it renewed; for saith he, " Children, have ye any meat?" The word signifieth what is eaten with bread, as fish, flesh, &c., and here it is taken for fishes; and here he propounds this question, not inquiring as one caring for their eating, but he deals as a stranger coming to buy, that so he may draw out a sensible confession of their want, to make way for the following miracle; " They answered him, No."

4. It is commendable in neighbours, or those who have occasion to converse and traffic toge-

ther, that they entertain a good correspondence, by courteous, familiar, and discreet expressions one to another; therefore saith Christ, " Children, have ye any meat?" And he useth this compellation here, not as one made known to them, to point out his familiar respects unto and care of them, as a father hath of his little children, but as the courteous and familiar expressions of neighbours in these places.

VER. 6. And he said unto them, Cast the net on the right side of the ship, and ye shall find. They cast therefore, and now they were not able to draw it for the multitude of fishes.

7. Therefore that disciple whom Jesus loved saith unto Peter, It is the Lord.——

The third branch of this narration contains the way how he came to make himself known unto them. He, having drawn out a confession of their want and ill success, adviseth them where to cast out the net, promising them success; which they obey, (not because they knew him as yet, but because they are not willing to neglect any opportunity or counsel, or possibly because they have supposed him to have skill,) and get a great draught, ver. 6. And by this he is first discerned by John, and by him Peter is informed, ver. 7; which is not to be understood as secluding the rest, (for they come also, ver. 8,) but he speaks it, in audience of all, to Peter, as being nearest him, or Peter is only marked to be spoken to, because of his singular conduct upon this information.

DOCTRINES.

1. Christ our Mediator is true God, and hath a providence over all the creatures; even the fish of the sea are under his feet, and he knoweth where they swim, and can command and bring them to his people's hands when he pleaseth; for he knoweth where the fishes are to be found, as having brought them (as appears) from some other part of the lake to the place where they so long sought and found none. " Cast the net on the right side of the ship, and ye shall find."

2. When Christ is about to do great things for his people, yet he will not have them neglecting means and endeavours; for though he bring the fish to their hand, yet he will not cast them into the ship, but commands them to " cast the net."

3. Those to whom the bad success of their toil is blessed, they will become tractable thereby, and will be ready to hearken to counsel; for the disciples, toiled with labour and bad success all night, do hearken to the counsel of a supposed stranger, " They cast therefore."

4. Christ suffered no decay of his power by his sufferings and death, but is as able to work wonders and do for his people as ever; for as before he had wrought such a wonder as this, Luke, v. 5, 6, so here again, after his resurrection, " and now they were not able to draw it for the multitude of fishes."

5. Christ is not only a God near hand, but a God afar off also, and can do as much for his people at a distance as when he is nearer hand

to them; for, Luke v., he wrought the like miracle when he was with them, now he works this when he is upon the shore, and they in the ship.

6. Christ did afford this miraculous success, beyond anything they not only met with, but could expect in their ordinary diligence, not to give his people any ground of expecting constantly such allowances in outward things, but as to confirm by this (as by other proofs) that he is true God, and to persuade them that his allowances and workings are liberal, like himself, so also to teach his people, by this and the like instances, that he could wonderfully provide outward things for them, if it were for their good; as here the disciples find " they were not able to draw it for the multitude of fishes." And this should teach believers to rest contented with the ordinary allowances which their wise and all-sufficient Lord carveth out unto them.

7. As Christ will not always keep himself as a stranger, but will be known to his people, so he takes pleasure to make himself known unto his people by a good turn done for them; for at last he makes himself known, and it is by this miraculous allowance, compared with the like miracle, Luke v., that John knew him.

8. Christ's working will speak for itself, and a right discerner will know him by his working, though he should never speak one word to tell what he is; for therefore that disciple said, " It is the Lord," though he had not told so much.

9. Love to Christ, and feeding on the sense of his love, will help a disciple to discern and know him as soon as any; for it is " that disciple whom Jesus loved" who first knew " it is the Lord."

10. Whatever singular excellency there be in any disciples, it floweth not from anything in themselves, but from Christ's love to them; for it was because he was " that disciple whom Jesus loved" that it is given him to love and know the Lord.

11. Such as are dignified with any ability to discern Christ ought to be communicative thereof for the good of others; for " that disciple saith unto Peter, It is the Lord."

VER. 7. —— Now when Simon Peter heard that it was the Lord, he girt his fisher's coat unto him, (for he was naked,) and did cast himself into the sea.

8. And the other disciples came in a little ship; (for they were not far from land, but as it were two hundred cubits,) dragging the net with fishes.

In the fourth branch of this narration some particular effects and consequents following upon this manifestation of Christ, before his conference with Peter, are recorded, to ver. 14, together with John's account of the number and order of this manifestation, ver. 14. The first effect of Christ's manifestation is their coming to land to him, after they knew it was he; Peter, waiting for nothing but that he come not naked, doth cast himself into the sea to come to Christ, ver. 7. The rest come so fast as they can, without neglecting the benefit conferred upon them by Christ; therefore they make haste to come in a little ship, (which it seems stood beside the other,) seeing it would come sooner than the greater vessel, and do drag the net with fishes after them, ver. 8. As for Peter's coming, we are not to conceive that he came walking miraculously on the sea,—for we are not to multiply miracles needlessly,—nor yet that he could wade, seeing they were at some distance from the shore, and the sea so deep as to carry a ship with all those men and their fishing instruments; but that he cast himself into the sea, to come swimming.

DOCTRINES.

1. A sight of Christ is inviting and alluring, and will make those who know him come to him; as here they all come when they know him.

2. In the church of Christ, and even among disciples and apostles, there is great variety of tempers, and dispositions, and endowments; every one hath not alike perfection in the same degree, nor is it to be expected that all will be alike, though all may be sincere and approved; for here John is most eminent in discerning Christ, Peter is most forward in zeal, and yet all do willingly come to Christ.

3. One disciple may outstrip another in expressions of forwardness and zeal, who yet cometh not behind him, either in knowledge or solid love; for here John is eminent in knowledge, and was a true lover of Christ, and yet Peter outstrips him in this expression of affection, which flowed, partly, from his natural disposition, and partly from the sense of his late fall.

4. The shortest cut will seem far about, if a nearer could be had, to a soul filled with zeal and desire to be at Christ; for so did appear in Peter, who could not stay in a ship, though he could come but little sooner by swimming.

5. Zeal will make a man, when he seeth Christ, forget and quit all to be at him; for Peter waits not upon the draught of fishes, but when he " heard that it was the Lord, he girt his fisher's coat unto him, (for he was naked,) and did cast himself into the sea." He only stayed that he might not come naked, and girt his coat to him, that it might not hinder him, nor he lose it, in swimming.

6. To swim through deep seas (if it were of blood) to be at Christ is a sweet way to a zealous man, if it should bring him a moment sooner than another mean; for therefore did Peter willingly " cast himself into the sea."

7. Affection unto Christ doth not warrant men needlessly to cast away his benefits, or neglect his bountiful providence in outward things, providing they omit no diligence to come to Christ; for so much doth the practice of the rest of the disciples teach, who indeed came, but " dragging the net with fishes." And this their carriage is justified both by Christ's command, ver. 10, and Peter's own practice, ver. 11; and albeit both he be commendable in his way and they in theirs, and yet in some circumstances they are contrary to other, yet these may be very consistent, if we mark these particulars:—1. Christ doth approve of all who sincerely endeavour to come to him, and who lay no impediments in their own way,

nor follow their lawful employments for a bye-end, albeit all be not alike speedy and forward; for both are approved that they come, and they also, though they come not so soon as Peter, because they make no wilful delay, but take "a little ship," that they might come the sooner, seeing they might hazard in it, being "not far from land," &c. And their aim in bringing the net with them was not so much to enrich themselves as that they might not lose what Providence had brought unto them. 2. The sincerity and desire of saints to be at Christ is not to be measured by what at some time themselves or others attain unto; for this was an extraordinary gale of affection in Peter, not at all times attained by himself, and therefore it doth not defame them who follow the ordinary way of expressing affection unto Christ in such cases. 3. Some may the more warrantably express their affection to Christ by neglecting at some time all other affairs, that they have others to do them for them, and so they do not miscarry through their laying them by; for Peter might the more safely leave all and come to Christ, that there were others sufficient to bring the draught to land; otherwise it had not been commendable in him to leave them, and it had been their sin if all had done as Peter did. Though this also must be added, that however men have others to do affairs for them, yet that will not warrant them always to neglect a worldly calling, (if that be their station,) though at some times it may. 4. It were safe for us to conjoin both these practices, as pointing out our duty in relation to several times, and to make Peter's practice of leaving all our rule in extraordinary cases and times, and when we are called to forsake all; as Peter had some reason to be forward now above the rest, because of his foul fall. And to make their practice our rule in ordinary cases, and so to follow duty and have a care of worldly affairs, as they do not sinfully retard us from coming unto Christ. 5. In our ordinary walking also the conjoining of these practices would make complete Christians; to be like Peter in our affections above, (as no doubt they also were,) and undervaluing these temporary things, about which we must, notwithstanding, be necessarily taken up, and being ready to abandon and forsake them when called so to do, as he did; and to be like them in our outward carriage, conscientiously following duty in obedience to a command.

Ver. 9. As soon then as they were come to land, they saw a fire of coals there, and fish laid thereon, and bread.

The next consequent recorded here is his preparation for their dining with him, which they observed when they came to land, and which it seems he did by miracle. Whence learn—

1. Christ can afford wonders on all hands, where he is, to his people; and it is no strange thing, where he cometh, to see wonders and mercies heaped one upon another; for here, after a miracle at sea, they meet another mercy miraculously provided at land: "As soon then as they were come to land, they saw a fire of coals there, and fish laid thereon, and bread."

2. Christ delights to prove and manifest his godhead and power in shewing kindness, and letting out needful favours upon his people; for being to prove his godhead, he chooseth to give a proof of it by giving them food, which now they needed, rather than by any other extraordinary work.

3. Christ hath a very tender respect to the meanest necessities of his people, to see to the supply thereof; therefore hath he fish and bread ready for them who had been at hard labour all night.

4. Albeit Christ bind us to the use of lawful means, yet he hath given abundant proof that he needs none of our diligence to provide for us, but can do it without us; that so we may not cease to trust him when either we are debarred from the use of means or they do not succeed with us; therefore, albeit he tied them to fishing, yet when they came to land, he lets them see he can feed them without any of their provision: "They saw a fire of coals there, and fish laid thereon, and bread."

Ver. 10. Jesus saith unto them, Bring of the fish which ye have now caught.

11. Simon Peter went up, and drew the net to land full of great fishes, an hundred and fifty and three: and for all there were so many, yet was not the net broken.

The third consequent recorded is the discovery of the reality and greatness of the miracle wrought for them; Christ, before he dine with them, will have the disciples (who had come to him, and left net and all so soon as they got it so near the shore as the sea could not take it away) to bring of the fishes they had caught, which they obeying, do find there were a great many fishes, and yet the net not broken, as formerly it had been in the like case, Luke, v. 6. Christ's end in bidding bring of the fishes was not chiefly for their present eating, (seeing he had already provided for them, ver. 9,) though it may be, also, he allowed this, that their taste of the fish, as well as the sight of the multitude thereof, might confirm and assure them it was a real miracle,—and the original word, here rendered "fish," is not against that sense,—but his chief end was to feed their minds with a sight of the greatness and reality of the miracle, before he fed their bodies; for so much doth their observation, ver. 11, point out to us. And while this going up, (to wit, into the ship, that he might come at the net,) and drawing the net to land, is ascribed unto Peter only, it is not to be understood as if he alone did it, but he only is mentioned, because of his forwardness to give obedience, as he had been formerly forward to come to Christ.

DOCTRINES.

1. Christ will not be wanting to give evidence how well he approves of his people's following of a lawful calling, and that they have a care of their outward enjoyments in their own place; for here his command justifieth them who brought

the net along with them, ver. 8, in that, when all have left it, as well as Peter, he bids them "bring of the fish," and Peter, by his obedience to the command, doth also clear that he accounted it no cause of reproach that they left it out formerly, as he did.

2. Christ is a great esteemer of people's diligence and using of means, and of his goodness will ascribe all that he doth for them to their diligence, that so they may be encouraged (not to conceit of it, but) to continue in it; for albeit he gave them these fish by miracle, yet in regard of their casting out the net, and dragging it to land, he ascribes it all to them : "Bring of the fish which ye have now caught."

3. When disciples have seen much of Christ in his working, they need yet a more particular observation thereof, that they may see and consider his glory more distinctly, and they may be affected of new [anew] with it, and it may take more deep impression in their minds; therefore, albeit they had seen and known Christ already by this miracle, ver. 6, 7, yet for these causes will he have them "bring of the fish," that they may look again, and more distinctly and narrowly, upon the miracle.

4. To be taken up with the serious and distinct observation of Christ's working is more useful and refreshful to right discerners than to enjoy his bodily presence, and than bodily refreshment to hungry men; therefore, now, when they are in Christ's company, and are going to dine, who, it seems, had fasted long, yet Christ sent them away for a time, from himself and from their meat, to go observe the miracle : "Bring of the fish which ye have now caught."

5. True love, which draws disciples to hasten to be at Christ, will also make them prompt and nimble in obeying his commands; for as Peter was eminent in his haste to be at Christ, so now he is noted as eminent in going about what is enjoined, and therefore he is only named, "Simon Peter went up, and drew the net to land."

6. As affection to Christ will elevate disciples' minds above the world and the things of it, so in their following of a calling the chief and greatest beauty that they will see in it is, that Christ hath commanded it, and therefore they will follow it, but with their heart above it; for so much may we learn from this practice of Peter, conjoined with his former practice, ver. 7. In the first, he gave proof how far his heart was above these things, and here he gives proof how beautiful that service is when commanded by Christ.

7. Most strict observation and inquiry about Christ's working will never diminish his glory, but will contribute to set out more distinctly the greatness of his power and liberality; for before, they only found the net full, so that they could not draw it, ver. 6, now, they find distinctly that it was " full of great fishes," and not of other trash, which might have fallen into the net; and particularly, that there were " an hundred and fifty and three."

8. The more distinctly men do consider Christ's works, they will not only find them the more wonderful, but will find a wonder in a wonder in them; for beside the great number of fish, it is marked as a new wonder, "and for all there were so many, yet was not the net broken," as it had been in the like case formerly, Luke, v. 6, though the original word, being the same here and there, doth evidence that it was a net of the same kind. Only it is to be marked, that as there the greatness of the miracle is pointed out by the breaking of the net, so here it is amplified from this new wonder, that the net brake not; to teach us that Christ manifests his power sometimes one way and sometimes another, as he pleaseth, and that he will not be limited by us in the way of his working.

VER. 12. Jesus saith unto them, Come and dine. And none of the disciples durst ask him, Who art thou? knowing that it was the Lord.

13. Jesus then cometh, and taketh bread, and giveth them, and fish likewise.

The fourth consequent recorded is his inviting them to dine, with their going about it; betwixt which there is interlaced the disciples' reverencing of him, who, albeit they had yet some scruples concerning all this his shewing of himself, which his speaking to them and assuring them that it was he would easily have removed, yet, being persuaded they were but groundless scruples, and that indeed it was the Lord, they do so reverence him as they are ashamed to trouble him with such questions. Whence learn—

1. Christ is very tender even of the bodies of his people; and alloweth (not pampering, but) that they should have a sober and moderate care of them, as being the tabernacles of his own Spirit; therefore is he the first motioner of their refreshing their bodies, "Jesus saith unto them, Come and dine;" and albeit he suspended their dinner till they had secured their purchase, and had observed their miracle, ver. 11, 14, yet now he will confer none with them till they had dined, ver. 15.

2. Albeit it be not expressly said here that Christ did eat with them, as it is Luke, xxiv. 42, 43, yet it is implied in this invitation, not go, but " Come and dine;" not that he needed meat now, but thereby he would confirm the truth of his resurrection; and as by the former miracle he proved himself true God, so by this he would prove that he was true man still, and so doth teach us, that our exalted High Priest continueth our kinsman, and bone of our bone, and flesh of our flesh, still; and that he was going in our nature to take possession for us in heaven.

3. Albeit also it be not expressed that he blessed the meat, or gave thanks, yet it is to be understood as his ordinary practice, not only before, chap. vi. 11, but even since his resurrection, Luke, xxiv. 30, 35. Only it is clear here that he giveth it still, to teach us that our daily bread and the blessing thereof cometh from him, and is to be sought from him continually.

4. Weak believers will not get their doubts and scruples soon overcome, even when they know they are wrong; for they " knew it was the Lord," and yet they had some doubts which would have put them to inquire, "Who art thou?"

5. Christ is so condescending as to judge of

his people by their better part, and to account them knowers and believers who yet have some ignorance and doubtings, providing they approve not thereof; for so doth John record them as "knowing that it was the Lord," though they had these doubts.

6. Albeit the best way to refute and remove the meanest doubt be to lay it before Christ, yet it is a commendable duty, and a testimony of reverence to Christ, when those who get many proofs of his love are ashamed to own their unbelief, or to bring it out as a real doubt when it assaults them, but do either suppress it or complain of it as unreasonable; for "knowing that it was the Lord, none of the disciples durst ask him, Who art thou?" They are ashamed to own it as a real doubt, but do suppress it; and indeed, however they might have complained of it, as their weakness, unto Christ, yet it had been their sin to have given any consent or way unto it, as this question would import they had.

VER. 14. This is now the third time that Jesus shewed himself to his disciples, after that he was risen from the dead.

Unto this breach of the narration John subjoins a remark of the number and order of this appearing of Christ unto them, and that it was the third in order since his resurrection, the other two being recorded, chap. xix. 20, 26. Only it is to be understood that John is here speaking of his more public appearings to all or many of his disciples together. Otherwise, before this he had appeared oftener, to Mary, to Peter, the disciples going to Emmaus, and the women.

DOCTRINES.

1. Christ hath abundantly proven the truth of his resurrection, his shewing himself frequently to his disciples, being as so many witnesses confirming the same; for here is "the third time," or witness, proving this; after which he confirmed it further, on the Mount of Galilee, Matt. xxviii. 18, and at Jerusalem, in the time of his ascension, Acts, i.

2. Christ's tender condescendence again and again to remove and cure his people's unbelief is much and seriously to be studied and taken notice of; therefore also is it marked, that "now the third time he shewed himself to his disciples," &c., to cure their unbelief in this matter.

3. Christ's present favours should be a mean to bring his former mercies to remembrance, that use may be made of all together; therefore also doth John upon this occasion thankfully remember the former, and record that "this is now the third time that Jesus shewed himself to his disciples, after that he was risen from the dead."

VER. 15. So when they had dined, Jesus saith to Simon Peter, Simon, son of Jonas, lovest thou me more than these? He saith unto him, Yea, Lord; thou knowest that I love thee. He saith unto him, Feed my lambs.

16. He saith to him again the second time, Simon, son of Jonas, lovest thou me? He saith unto him, Yea, Lord; thou knowest that I love thee. He saith unto him, Feed my sheep.

17. He saith unto him the third time, Simon, son of Jonas, lovest thou me? Peter was grieved because he said unto him the third time, Lovest thou me? And he said unto him, Lord, thou knowest all things; thou knowest that I love thee. Jesus saith unto him, Feed my sheep.

In the fifth branch of this narration, Christ's conference with Peter is recorded, and that both concerning himself, to ver. 20, and concerning John, ver. 20—23. That which concerns Peter himself seems to have been his special end in shewing himself at this time, (as his general end was to confirm the truth of his resurrection,) but that which concerneth John was only occasionally drawn out by Peter's curiosity. Christ's conference concerning Peter consists of two parts; in the first whereof, (in these verses,) Peter, upon profession of his love unto Christ, is restored unto and confirmed in his apostolic office and former dignity, which he had forfeited by his foul and gross fall. Christ's threefold question concerning Peter's love tends only to draw out a threefold answer from Peter, and that his professed repentance might be as frequent as his denial; and, consequently, we are not to look upon Christ's threefold injunction to Peter to feed his lambs and sheep as three distinct commands, enjoining divers things, but only as one command thrice repeated upon occasion of his threefold answer; and therefore I shall take them together in drawing observations from them.

And first, this whole purpose, with the dependence thereof upon what precedes, may teach in general—

1. Apostasy and denial of Christ, though even out of weakness in a time of strait, is a matter full of hazard, and brings disciples to a loss not easily recovered; for Peter, by reason of his fall, needs a kind of restitution, and a confirmation of new [anew] in his office and dignity. And albeit not only he had wept bitterly immediately after his fall, but Christ, after his resurrection, and before this time, had remembered him in particular in that message to the disciples, Mark, xvi. 7, and had appeared to him alone, Luke, xxiv. 34, yea, and had confirmed him in his office with the rest, when he appeared to all of them, John, xx. 21, 22, yet here again he is brought publicly on a stage to testify his repentance before them all.

2. When Christ doth put his people on service, and calls for evidences of their love to him, he first prevents them with proofs of himself, his power, love, and care to engage them to their duty; for this inquiry after Peter's love, and his engaging him to service, was not till after he had given proof of himself by the miracle, and "when they had dined," and after their bodies were refreshed by him.

Secondly, Christ's question unto Peter, and the thrice repeating and way of propounding it, may teach—

1. Love to Christ is the Christian's badge, and he is a runaway who deserts that standard; for by this Christ trieth Peter, "Simon, son of Jonas, lovest thou me?"

2. Ministers who are called to take charge of Christ's children and flock had need of much love to him, no service about them being approven if it flow not from this, but be undertaken for by respects, and there being no possibility, without this love, to endure the many blasts they will meet with from without in their calling, nor the much toil they will have, even with and from the flock themselves; therefore is the inquiry concerning this premitted, "Lovest thou me?" as a needful qualification for discharge of the trust committed to him.

3. Whatever love men may warrantably profess they have unto Christ, yet it doth not allow them to swell in their own eyes because of it, or because of any dignity conferred upon them as lovers of Christ; and saints, in their repenting for their failings, should look back to the low estate from whence Christ raised them, that they may see their ingratitude the more in backsliding or forsaking him; therefore doth he guard all these questions with this designation—Simon, not Peter, which was the name he gave him, chap. i. 42, and "son of Jonas," a poor fisherman, that now he might, in professing his repentance and renewed love, affect his heart with thoughts of his low estate, from whence he was exalted, and to which Christ might justly debase him again, and leave him as he found him, "Simon, son of Jonas;" and that, in professing his love and embracing this charge, he might still remember his original.

4. The sense of the Lord's people's backslidings should be a whetstone to sharpen their love to Christ, and to make them not content to return to a formal way of profession after their foul slips, unless there be a new edge upon them to recover their losses, and prevent the like failing in time to come; therefore doth he inquire particularly at Peter, "Lovest thou me?" as one who, if he were truly recovered, ought to be eminent in love, and have it more deeply rooted in his heart, that he slide not again, and in testimony of his sense of Christ's kindness, who looked upon him after his fall.

5. True repentance ought and will not only be sincere and real, but as eminent in the effects thereof as sinner's fall hath been; therefore doth he pose him thrice concerning his love, to try if he was real in his profession, and might indeed stand to it, and that his threefold profession of love might be answerable to his threefold denial.

6. Such as have fallen grossly in an hour of tentation, and have through mercy recovered again, ought yet still to be jealous and suspicious of themselves, as having grossly given the lie to their former professions; for so much also doth the repetition of these questions teach, that he would have Peter not easily trust himself in the like profession, considering how well he had said before when yet he had done so ill. And so Peter takes it, being grieved that it is the third time propounded, ver. 17, and that he was now become a suspected man.

7. Christ at last propounds this question with a comparative qualification, "Lovest thou me more than these?" (that is, more than any of the rest do love me;) not so much pointing out that a fallen and restored man (as also every saint) should strive to outstrip another in this grace, as reflecting upon his former conceit of himself and his singular undertaking, Matt. xxvi. 33, and it may be, also, reflecting upon his late forwardness in coming out of the ship, ver. 7, and trying if, because of that, he would boast of any singular love to him. And so, with the offer of accepting his sincere love and his calling for it, he rips up his former conceit of himself; and so it teacheth, partly, that the evil of saints' apostasies and defections will never be throughly cured by any returning out of some particular evil course, unless the fountain, cause, and root of their evils be cured, and continually abhorred and watched over; therefore Christ presents that to him which had occasioned his former fall, to see what he thinks of it, and if it did continue with him; and partly, that Christ alloweth his people to season their bitter thoughts of their own evils with the offer of his love and acceptance of what is good and sincere in them; for he so propounds this indirect challenge, as he guards it with an offer of his present acceptance of his love, which is implied in the question.

8. In the second and third questions, Peter, having in his answer modestly declined to make any comparisons, Christ omits this qualification, and propounds the question simply, "Lovest thou me?" to teach, that he covereth and passeth by infirmities when he seeth us convinced of them.

Thirdly, as for Peter's threefold answer to these questions, we need not curiously distinguish betwixt the word in the question whereby Christ expresseth love to himself, as signifying a greater degree of love, and the word used by Peter in his answer, as signifying a lesser degree, and that as he would not compare with others, so he would not boast of the measure of his own love, but professeth sincere love, though weak. For Christ in his third question useth that same word wherein Peter answers. And if any distinction ought to be made betwixt the expressions, Christ by using both in his inquiries would teach us that he takes notice of and is willing to accept of lesser degrees of sincere love, as well as of greater; for he interrogates concerning both, implying his acceptance of either; and that even such as are sober and dare not profess an eminent measure of love to Christ, but only some weak degree of it, had yet need to examine if they be sincere and real even in that they profess; and therefore Christ, after Peter hath changed the word he had used into another, in the two former answers, will the third time pose him, if he dare avow the sincerity and reality of what he professeth. And upon this, it seems, Peter was grieved, ver. 17, that not only he had inquired "the third time," but had also called in question that weak measure of love he had professed. However it be, as to the force and signification of these words, yet we may from his answers learn—

1. It is very possible for fallen saints to recover their feet, and attain to love again, as here Peter's experience doth testify.

2. A lover of Christ indeed may humbly avow his love before him, as often as he inquireth concerning it; as here Peter doth thrice, " Yea, Lord, I love thee."

3. A sincere lover of Christ will, by his falling, be taught sobriety, and not to boast of himself above others; for Peter makes no comparisons in answer to Christ's first question, but simply ranks himself among lovers of him, " Lord, I love thee."

4. They who would prove themselves lovers of Christ indeed, must not only satisfy and please themselves in the matter, but should appeal to his knowledge, and be sure that he knows and approves of them as such; for saith he, " Lord, thou knowest that I love thee."

5. Such as would approve themselves unto Christ ought to look upon him as knowing all things, and that therefore he will not be deceived with any shows; for so much doth Peter express in his third answer, " Thou knowest all things, thou knowest that I love thee."

6. Our sight of the grace of God in us, after our backslidings, should be joined with the sense of our falling; for the third time, " Peter was grieved," whereby (not to speak of any failing in him, by grieving at what Christ did) Christ would put him in mind how his former sliding had justly rendered him suspected, that his profession of love might be joined with sensible thoughts thereof.

Fourthly, Christ's charge put upon Peter, and thrice repeated, may teach—

1. Christ may make good use of saints who fall foully in an hour of tentation, and may raise them up again, to do him eminent service in their generation; for fallen Peter is again entrusted with the charge of his " sheep and lambs."

2. Saints' love to Christ cannot extend to him, but he assigns it all to his people, that whoso love him may shew kindness to them in their station; for upon Peter's profession of love to him, he enjoins him, " Feed my lambs," as the notable proof of it, and as reckoning that it should be a great evidence of love to him to have a care of them.

3. Ministers ought to look upon Christ's people as very seriously recommended to them, and therefore should very seriously mind their work about them; for therefore is this charge thrice laid on Peter, that he may mind it much.

4. Such as would be faithful in a ministerial charge ought to look upon the people of their charge as Christ's in a near relation, loved of him, committed to their charge by him, and to be gained to him; therefore doth he in this commission call them, " my lambs, my sheep."

5. Ministers ought also to look upon the variety of tempers and degrees of strength which are in the people committed to their charge, that so they may deal with them, and have a care of them accordingly; therefore doth he design them by the name of weaker " lambs," and stronger " sheep." (See Isa. xl. 10.)

6. It is a great part of ministers' work to feed Christ's people with sound and wholesome doctrine; and so to dispense it as to condescend to the capacity of the weakest; for in the first command he is to " feed," or afford food, and that even to the " lambs."

7. It is not sufficient that ministers be able to feed unless they also govern and rule the people committed to their charge, and do every other duty of a good shepherd unto them; and even the strongest ought to subject themselves unto this government; for in the second repetition of the charge it is " feed," or govern, and play the shepherd, (for the word is different from the former,) and that even to the " sheep."

8. The strongest of professors will not, within time, attain that height of perfection and sanctity as to outgrow ordinances or a ministry, or not to need them, and ministers are bound to deal with them accordingly; therefore, in the third repetition of the charge, he useth the word first used, " feed," or provide and afford food, and that even to " my sheep," as well as to lambs.

Ver. 18. Verily, verily, I say unto thee, When thou wast young, thou girdedst thyself, and walkedst whither thou wouldest: but when thou shalt be old, thou shalt stretch forth thy hands, and another shall gird thee, and carry thee whither thou wouldest not.

19. This spake he, signifying by what death he should glorify God. And when he had spoken this, he saith unto him, Follow me.

In the next part of Christ's conference with Peter he warns him of his future sufferings, promising that he should prove more stout than in his former trial. This he propounds more darkly, ver. 18, and alluding to the custom of these eastern people, who, wearing long garments, did gird them up by binding their loins when they went a journey; and to the custom of binding malefactors when they were carried from place to place, or to the place of execution. He sheweth a great difference that should be betwixt his case in youth and in old age: in his youth he girded up his loins and walked at his own pleasure; but in his old age others should bind him, and carry him whither his natural inclination did not lead him. And in ver. 19 he explains this, shewing that he spake of his violent death, sweetening it with this consideration, that hereby he should glorify God, and commanding him presently to follow him. Whence learn—

1. Love to Christ must be evidenced, not only by active doing of duty, but by suffering also unto death, if we be called unto it; and ministers especially, when they undertake the charge of Christ's flock, ought to lay their account for such a lot; therefore is this prediction joined with the former injunction as another proof of Peter's love to Christ.

2. The matter of suffering would not be lightly thought upon, but we should have grave and serious thoughts of it, that afflictions in some measure abide us, that it is our duty to resolve for the worst, and that suffering will indeed try us, and therefore we should be laying

up for such a strait; for these causes doth he begin this doctrine with a grave asseveration, "Verily, verily, I say unto thee," &c.

3. There will be great difference betwixt a saint trusting in his own strength, and the same saint leaning upon and supported by God; he who before durst not look a damsel in the face will in the other case dare to look death in the face; for so appeared in Peter, of whom Christ foretels this, when he is minding him of his former failing.

4. As it is the duty of saints always to look on suffering for Christ as their great honour, (Acts, v. 41,) so in particular, when a saint is indeed penitent for his shifting of suffering and sliding in a time of trial, it will be his great comfort to know that he shall have the honour to suffer, and be borne through in it; that (so to say) he may be avenged on trial for his two eyes; for here it is held out for Peter's encouragement that Christ will employ him, who had proven so weak, yet to suffer unto death for his name; as a soldier who is shamefully beaten desires nothing so much as another day wherein he may shew his valour and repair his credit.

5. As nature hath an antipathy at death, and particularly a violent death, so saints have not an inclination to suffering ready to let out at their pleasure, till God give them victory and resolution; therefore is his suffering called another's girding him, and carrying him whither he would not; not only shewing that naturally he would be averse from it, or that he would have no hand in his own suffering and death, but that take him in his own resolutions and inclinations and he would decline such a lot, though grace made him submit and stretch out his hands, that they might gird him; and this sheweth how needful it is that the most resolute of men do seek willingness from Christ, lest their natural inclinations prevail; and that even where there is a natural antipathy and fear of death and suffering, yet Christ may make eminent and resolute martyrs of them, they depending on him, as many martyrs who have been long exercised with the fear of death have found in experience.

6. The thing which nature, especially while men are young and in vigour, would still be at, is to be their own masters, not subject to the law of God, nor to the tossing providences about the world; for this was Peter's way, and what he delighted in then, "When thou wast young, thou girdedst thyself, and walkedst whither thou wouldest." He was his own man, and delighted to walk as he pleased, and at random and liberty.

7. Men may expect strange changes in their lots and exercises in the several turns of their life before they go off the world; and particularly when men engage themselves in Christ's service they may expect a strange change to follow on it; not only will their consciences within them curb their extravagant and lawless walking, but whereas there were none before to trouble them, now there must be nothing but bonds and death for them. So much doth this opposition betwixt Peter's lot in his youth and old age teach us. "When thou wast young, thou girdedst thyself, &c.; but when thou shalt be old, thou shalt stretch forth thy hands," &c.

8. That Christ promiseth he shall not suffer till he be old, he teacheth, partly that the timing of his people's suffering is in his hand, and he can when he pleaseth give them a fair time wherein to serve him, before he call them to seal the truth by their sufferings,—for Peter is old before they gird him, &c., (see Luke, xiii. 31, 32,)—and partly, that Christ may call his people to suffer when their visible ability is least, that so the power carrying them through may be seen to be of him; therefore also doth he suffer when he is old, when albeit old age might quench many lusts in him, and experience and time might settle him, yet his natural vigour was decayed, and fears usually accompanying old age might retard him.

9. Christ would have his doctrine distinctly taken up and understood by hearers; therefore as Peter understood this well enough, so John explains it for our use, shewing that Christ spake of Peter's death in these terms.

10. The sufferings of saints do contribute to set out the glory of God; the glory of the truth of the word when they are ready to seal it with their blood, and to stand to the defence thereof unto death; the glory of the truth and riches of his promises and of eternal life held out therein when they hazard on the enmity and opposition of all, and on death itself, in the faith and hope thereof, and do look on eternal life as sufficient to compense all their losses; and the glory of his excellency and all-sufficiency, when they count all things but vanity and loss that they may please him, and so they proclaim their faith to be richly made up in him; therefore saith he, that by his "death he should glorify God."

11. The consideration that God is glorified by any lot should put a lovely face upon it, were it even suffering a violent death to saints; therefore is this propounded as the lovely sight of his suffering, that hereby "he should glorify God." (See John, xii. 28.)

12. Saints ought to give proof of their sincere resolutions for sufferings by their close following of Christ in their present service; therefore doth Christ subjoin, "And when he had spoken this, he saith unto him, Follow me;" where it appears, from ver. 20, that Christ rose from the rest of the company, and went away when he gave this command. And this he did, not so much for any present journey, as by calling him to obey this present command, to leave all his enjoyments and company, and follow him wherever he goeth, he takes proof of his sincerity, and whether he is resolved indeed to follow Christ in suffering, when he shall be called to it, and would have him begin to practise that lesson in time, that he might be the more fit for it when it came to a push; and so we will find it made use of, ver. 20.

13. It is the duty of such as would either serve or suffer for Christ to make him their pattern and copy in what is imitable; and it is their encouragement and may sweeten their way that he hath gone before them; therefore also bids he him "follow me," to point out not so much his duty of present going after him, as thereby to signify his duty to imitate Christ in all his actions, particularly in his care of his sheep

and resolution for suffering; and to hold out this encouragement, and how it might be sweet to follow him.

Ver. 20. Then Peter, turning about, seeth the disciple whom Jesus loved following; which also leaned on his breast at supper, and said, Lord, which is he that betrayeth thee?

21. Peter seeing him saith to Jesus, Lord, and what shall this man do?

22. Jesus saith unto him, If I will that he tarry till I come, what is that to thee? Follow thou me.

In these verses we have Christ's conference with Peter concerning John the beloved disciple; wherein is recorded that after Christ and Peter had left the rest of the company, John of his own accord did follow on, which Peter turning back and observing, he inquires at Christ (who had foretold of his own sufferings) what should become of John. For which he is checked by Christ as meddling with that which concerned him not, and he sheweth him that although it should please him not only to exempt John from suffering death, but to continue him alive till his own second coming, it ought not at all to retard him in his resolutions, and therefore he commands him to follow him and cleave to his duty, which by this means he had neglected. Whence learn—

1. Much love to Christ, and much of the sense of his love, will make a man an earnest pursuer after Christ, and to cleave to him, even when Christ seems to take no notice of him; therefore John followed, when Christ had bidden only Peter follow him, and when it seems the rest did not stir; and in this he is described to be " the disciple whom Jesus loved," one who had been very familiar with Christ, and " leaned on his breast at supper," and very inquisitive concerning Christ's safety, " and said, Lord, which is he that betrayeth thee?" (of all which see chap. xiii. 23,) and therefore he could not stay behind.

2. The children of the Lord are subject to many distractions and interruptions in following their Christian course, and do often look or turn aside, and intermit their earnest eyeing of their mark and prize; for when Peter is bidden to follow Christ at this time, hereby to teach him closely to follow his calling, and set his heart and eye upon it, and what he was to meet with, (as the check and repetition of that command in this verse doth teach us,) he turned about to look to somewhat behind him, and that either merely of his own accord, or because he had heard some noise of one following. (See Luke, ix. 62.)

3. Albeit the intermissions of the children of God in their duty may seem very little and small, yet ofttimes it casts them upon snares and tentations, which are ready to catch and detain them more, and so draw out reproofs from Christ; for Peter, but " turning about, seeth the disciple whom Jesus loved following," and this occasions his curious question, and draweth out a reproof, not only for his looking back, but for his curiosity.

4. Christ abhorreth curiosity in his people, and that when they have so much needful exercise among their hands, yet they should meddle more with what concerneth them not so much; for when Peter propounds this question, " and what shall this man do?" or, and what this man? —that is, what shall become of him? (as Christ's answer makes it clear,)—he gets this answer, " what is that to thee? follow thou me;" not that Christ condemns solicitude for our brethren which floweth from charity, but that he is ill pleased with his idle curiosity when now he had received a strict command to follow him.

5. It is a sin to be anxious or too much careful about what Christ will do with his beloved people; for so much also doth Christ's reproof of his inquiry concerning the beloved disciple import that it was weakness in Peter to be any way troubled concerning him.

6. Christ hath sovereign authority to dispose of his own, and to keep them longer or shorter time in the world, and give them ease or trouble, as he pleaseth, without giving an account of his dealing to any; for saith he, " If I will that he tarry till I come, what is that to thee?" Wherein there is no hint given that John should not suffer, and that he should live long, and till Christ should come by his judgments against the nation of the Jews (though these proved true in the event); but it is only an absolute supposition that if Christ pleased to preserve him alive, even till his second coming, or otherwise disposed of him at his pleasure, neither Peter nor any other had anything to say to it.

7. As Christ will come again, so the sweet notion under which saints should take up the last and dreadful day is that Christ will then come again unto them; for so doth Christ here point out that day, " I come." (See 1 Thess. iv. 16, 17.)

8. It is the duty of saints not to compare the Lord's dealing with themselves and others, so as to be thereby withdrawn from, or discouraged in, their own duty and lot; for whereas Peter might think it strange if he only were called to suffering, Christ takes him off looking to his dealing with John, and bids him mind his own work, " If I will that he tarry till I come, what is that to thee? follow thou me." Such comparisons (however sometimes they may sharpen us, and afford matter of praise, yet) do ofttimes breed many inconveniences; for we are naturally inclined to be discontent with our own condition, and to think that best which we want, and so will more readily be grieved if we got a harder lot than others; whereas Christ hath variety of services, and may lay them on as he pleaseth; and beside, such comparisons may ofttimes tempt men to sit up from duty when they see the security of others.

9. Such as would avoid curiosity, and much needless and vain exercise, ought closely to follow their own work and calling; therefore doth Christ withdraw him from all these inquiries by bidding him again, " follow thou me."

Ver. 23. Then went this saying abroad among the brethren, that that disciple should not die: yet Jesus said not unto him, He shall not die; but, If I will that he tarry till I come, what is that to thee?

In this verse John clears a mistake that continued in the church, occasioned by their misunderstanding of Christ's speech. They imagined, upon Christ's speech, that John should not die, (and it is like they were confirmed in their mistake by John's living so long after the rest of the apostles,) whereas Christ said no such thing, but only, by way of supposition, asserted that suppose he should keep him never so long alive, Peter had nothing to do with it. Whence learn—

1. The people of God are brethren, and ought to entertain and cherish mutual affection, and live in concord as brethren; therefore had they this designation in the primitive times, " The brethren."

2. Even Christ's own speeches were mistaken by the saints in purest times, much more may others be mistaken, and their words wrested contrary to their sense and meaning; for here a mistake ariseth upon what he said.

3. It may commend unto us the wisdom of God, in leaving with us, and astricting us unto the written word, when we see erroneous traditions so soon on foot in the church concerning Christ's words which were not written, and the mistake growing by going from hand to hand, till the writers of scripture refute it ; for here we see an unwritten and erroneous tradition going " abroad among the brethren," till John clear the mistake and refute it when he wrote this gospel.

4. Such as would rightly understand Christ's speeches must take good heed to every word and particle in his expression; to the form of speech, whether it be absolute, or by way of supposition; and to Christ's scope in it, according to which we must take up his meaning; for hence arose their mistake; they took Christ's way of speech as absolute, " that that disciple should not die," whereas he spake only by way of supposition; for " Jesus said not, He shall not die; but, If I will that he tarry till I come," &c. And they look upon his speech as tending to give a promise concerning John's life, whereas Christ's scope was only to shew Peter that he had nothing to do with the matter, albeit he should continue him, " If I will that he tarry till I come, what is that to thee ?"

Ver. 24. This is the disciple which testifieth of these things, and wrote these things: and we know that his testimony is true.

25. And there are also many other things which Jesus did, the which, if they should be written every one, I suppose that even the world itself could not contain the books that should be written. Amen.

John takes occasion of this mistake and the clearing thereof to close this evangel. And, 1. He asserts that he was the penman thereof, and sets his seal to the truth and certainty thereof, ver. 24. 2. Lest any should think that his love to Christ, being the beloved disciple, should move him to forge anything in this narration; and lest they might wonder how he got so much to write, especially after the other three had written; therefore, as chap. xx. 30, he subjoined a parti-

cular conclusion to the signs done by Christ after his resurrection; so here (ver. 25) he subjoins a general conclusion to this gospel, professing that he gave not over for want of matter, it being impossible to write all fully and particularly that Jesus did, but because it pleased the Lord not to overcharge the church with an infinite narration, which he expresseth in an hyperbolic term, which imports this much, that the books which might be written of this subject would burthen and overcharge the world, and men's judgments and memories could not overtake or retain the narration of all particular passages. This acknowledgment of John, that " there are many other things which Jesus did," and yet are not written, being extended generally to passages in his whole ministry, is to be understood with the rules, and according to the caveats, mentioned on chap. xx. 30, 31, and as nothing derogatory to the perfection of scriptures in the matters of faith and manners which is there asserted, notwithstanding these things are omitted. For albeit a great many of Christ's miracles in the course of his ministry (which properly are to be understood by " things which Jesus did") be not recorded, yet neither will that argue that any point of doctrine is omitted, nor yet that the doctrine is not sufficiently confirmed to us by the miracles that are recorded, and by their declaring that there were yet many more. Yea, suppose it be granted that many particular conferences and sermons which Christ had in the course of his ministry are not written, yet it will not follow that the sum of these, and of all his doctrine, is not recorded in what is written ; but, on the contrary, the wisdom of God chose to comprehend all that was needful in a brief sum, (even of the sermons that are recorded,) for the ease and benefit of the church. And as for them who, upon these expressions, would gather that many things needful to salvation are not to be found in scriptures, but to be sought out of unwritten traditions, I would have them, before they assert such a thing, resolve these questions for the satisfaction of the church, in this great article so nearly concerning her,—1. If the penmen of the spirit of God have taken pen from paper, accounting that sufficient which they have written, how dare they undertake that task which those have given over? 2. If those things not written be alike necessary with what is written, what reason can be given to any unbiassed person why the Lord should cause write the one, and yet leave the other to uncertain tradition, and the frail and corrupt memories of men ? 3. If the Lord was not pleased to write them, but transmit them by tradition, (as they do not only assert, but pretend grave and weighty reasons why the Lord did so,) upon what ground do they presume at all to stuff their writings with them, and do not leave them as he left them ? 4. If all these be necessary to salvation, and yet " the world could not contain the books that should be written" of them were they written, how shall they instruct that they have marked them all? and how will they satisfy the church that she hath yet a perfect rule of scripture and all the traditions they have recorded being put together? 5. With what face can they, upon this pretext, obtrude traditions upon the church which are not only be-side, but clearly contrary unto the written word of God, as if the Spirit of God did contradict himself? The truth is, John closeth with this, because what he had written was sufficient, and the rest not possible to be overtaken, nor yet necessary to be recorded for the use of the church in all ages, though they were necessary for the time, and it be useful for us to know there were many such things, though they be not particularly recorded ; as is marked on chap. xx. 31, 32.

From this purpose, learn—This gospel was written by John the beloved disciple, who being employed by Christ as a meet penman of such sublime doctrine, did out of love and duty write so sweetly of Christ; and hereby gives us occa-sion to try what love such a message by such a penman doth produce; for " This is the disciple which testifieth of these things."

2. All this narration is of divine truth, what-ever we think of it, and whatever many do esteem of it and other scriptures, yet it wants not witnesses who were eye and ear witnesses, and fully persuaded, to assert the truth of it ; for saith he, " we know (speaking of himself in the plural number, or of himself with the rest of the apostles) that his testimony is true.

3. It is the duty of ministers to assert the truth of their doctrine, and to set to (as it were) their messengers' seal to Christ's truth which they publish for their own exoneration, and for the encouragement of believers, and as a witness against all who receive it not ; therefore doth John call all his doctrine, " his testimony," and asserts that " we know that his testimony is true."

4. It is impossible to get all said which might be said of Christ, and to his commendation ; for so doth John assert, that " if the things which Jesus did should be written every one, even the world itself could not contain the books which should be written." And this may not only point out his excellency and the weakness of our judgments and memories, but whereas our curiosity is still desirous to hear and know more, this breaking off may call us back rather to see how we practise what it hath pleased him to re-cord.

5. The Lord, in writing scripture, hath been pleased only to give us a short sum of the doc-trine preached by Christ and his servants, and an account of a part only of the miracles wrought by Christ, that so he might shew his respect to our infirmity and weakness, and might take away all excuse from the lazy and negligent, by comprising his mind and will in so little bulk ; for therefore is John directed only to record this much, and to omit the rest which could not be overtaken.

6. This whole gospel is divine truth, worthy to be embraced and received by faith, and that we set our seal to the truth of it, and feed upon it accordingly ; therefore doth John close all, set-ting his Amen to this doctrine. " Unto him that loved us, and washed us from our sins in his own blood, and hath made us kings and priests unto God and his Father; to him be glory and do-minion for ever and ever. Amen." (Rev. i. 5, 6.)